MOON H███KS®

PACIFIC MEXICO

Puerto Vallarta basks on the inner edge of the Bay of Banderas.

PACIFIC MEXICO

To Nogales, AZ   To Hidalgo de Parral and U.S.   To Chihuahua and U.S.   To Monterrey and U.S.

Piaxtla R.

SINALOA

Presidio River

Durango

Mazatlán

Acaponeta River

Sierra Madre Occidental

Altiplano

Fresnillo

Zacatecas

NAYARIT

San Luis Potosi

San Blas

Tepic

Santiago Lerma River

Aquas-calientes

Dolores Hidalgo

Rincón de Guayabitos

Leon

Guanajuato

Puerto Vallarta

GUADALAJARA

Irapuato

Bajio Valley

JALISCO

Lake Chapala

Volcanic

Nevado de Colima

Lake Pátzcuaro

Morelia

TZINTZUNTZÁN

Uruapan

Pátzcuaro

LAS CAMPANAS

Tancitaro

Central

Barra de Navidad

COLIMA

Colima

TINGANIO

Manzanillo

MICHOACAN

Tecomán

Balsas River

Playa Azul

Lázaro Cárdenas

Ixtapa-Zihuatanejo

GUERRERO

PACIFIC

OCEAN

0   50 mi

0   50 km

To Monterrey and U.S.

To Matamoros and U.S.

Ciudad Victoria

85

80

UNITED STATES OF AMERICA

MEXICO

STATES OF PACIFIC MEXICO

MEXICO CITY

SINALOA
NAYARIT
JALISCO
COLIMA
MICHOACAN
GUERRERO
OAXACA

CENTRAL AMERICA

Queretaro

85

55

57 D

TULA

90 D

TEOTIHUACÁN

15

Toluca

MEXICO CITY

Highlands

190

Malinche

Popocatepetl

Citlaltepetl

Veracruz

Gulf Of Mexico

Ixtapan

XOCHICALCO

Puebla

150 D

150 D

Bay of Campeche

Taxco

160

Izúcar de Matamoros

180 D

180

Cuerna-vaca

190

Tehuacan

Coatzacoalcos

180

51

95 D

Tuxtepec

145

95

131 D

175

To Yucatan

Chilpancingo

Huajúapan de León

Nochixtlán

Sierra Madre de Oaxaca

Sierra

Tlaxiaco

Oaxaca

185

Madre

125

MONTE ALBÁN

MITLA

190

OAXACA

del

175

Juchitán

Isthmus Of Tehuantepec

200

Acapulco

Ometepec

Sur

Tehuantepec

Pinotepa Nacional

200

Huatulco

Salina Cruz

Gulf of Tehuantepec

To Central America

Puerto Escondido

Puerto Ángel

© AVALON TRAVEL PUBLISHING, INC.

Guadalajara cathedral

MOON HANDBOOKS®

PACIFIC MEXICO

INCLUDING PUERTO VALLARTA, ACAPULCO, MAZATLÁN, GUADALAJARA, AND OAXACA

SIXTH EDITION

BRUCE WHIPPERMAN

AVALON
TRAVEL

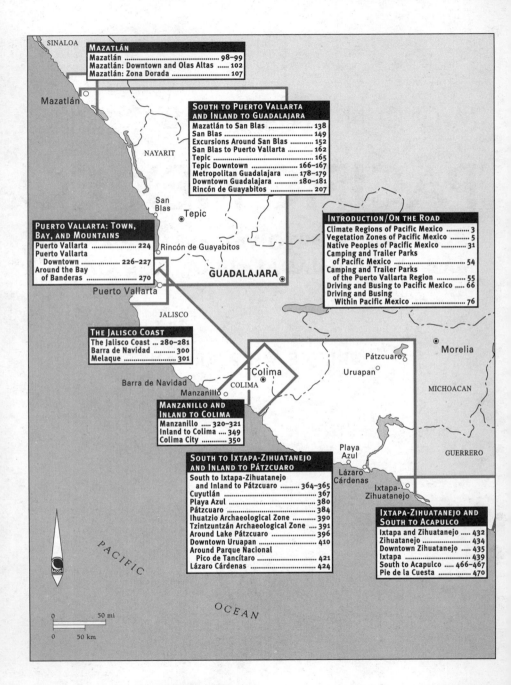

SINALOA

Mazatlán

NAYARIT

San
Blas

● Tepic

Rincón de Guayabitos

Rincón de Guayabitos

GUADALAJARA ●

Puerto Vallarta

JALISCO

● Morelia

Pátzcuaro ○

Uruapan ○

○ Colima

Barra de Navidad
COLIMA
Manzanillo ○

MICHOACAN

Playa
Azul
○

GUERRERO

Lázaro ○
Cárdenas

Ixtapa-
Zihuatanejo ○

PACIFIC

OCEAN

0   50 mi

0   50 km

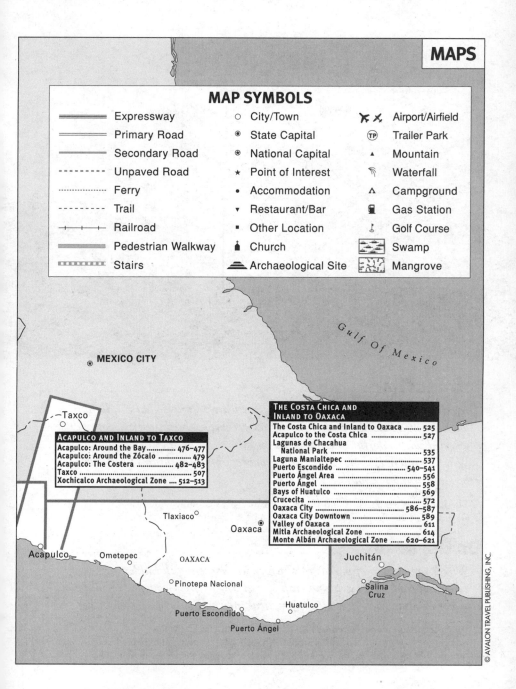

MAPS

MAP SYMBOLS

═══ Expressway	○ City/Town	✈ ✕ Airport/Airfield
── Primary Road	◉ State Capital	ⓉⓅ Trailer Park
── Secondary Road	⊛ National Capital	▲ Mountain
--------- Unpaved Road	★ Point of Interest	⟋ Waterfall
·············· Ferry	• Accommodation	∆ Campground
-------- Trail	▼ Restaurant/Bar	Gas Station
┼─┼─┼ Railroad	■ Other Location	Golf Course
Pedestrian Walkway	⛪ Church	Swamp
Stairs	⚑ Archaeological Site	Mangrove

Gulf Of Mexico

⊛ **MEXICO CITY**

Taxco

Tlaxiaco ○

Oaxaca ◉

Acapulco ○   Ometepec ○   OAXACA   Juchitán

○ Pinotepa Nacional   Salina Cruz ○

Huatulco ○

Puerto Escondido ○

Puerto Ángel ○

© AVALON TRAVEL PUBLISHING, INC.

Contents

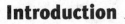

Introduction

Mexico's Pacific coast beckons with balmy waters, jungle-clad headlands, palm-fringed beaches, and glittering resorts. From the shore rise cool highlands studded with colorful colonial cities and the ruins of ancient kingdoms. Whether you're looking for luxury or backcountry adventure, Pacific Mexico has something for you.

What's your vision of paradise? Whether it's snorkeling in hidden coves, exploring traditional arts and crafts, or dining on fresh-caught fish under a shady palapa, *you'll find all the practical information you need right here.*

Mazatlán

Known as the "Pearl of the Pacific," Mazatlán is a land of perpetual summer, its coast sprinkled with rugged islands and crystalline beaches. Here you can watch fishermen peddle their daily catch in the morning, relax at a shady sidewalk café in the afternoon, and then dance the night away.

South to Puerto Vallarta and Inland to Guadalajara

An eden of flowering forests, verdant valleys, and orchard-covered plains, the Nayarit Coast is known for its sleepy beach hideaways. Head inland to stroll the sunny streets of Guadalajara, the most Mexican of cities, and drink in its grand architecture, soulful mariachi music, and colorful markets.

Puerto Vallarta: Town, Bay, and Mountains

Perched on the sparkling Bay of Banderas, Puerto Vallarta is really two cities in one: the shiny new hotel zone and the stucco-and-tile old town nestled beneath jungle hillsides. In the rustic retreats ringing the bay, you'll find respite from the bustle of resort life.

The Jalisco Coast 279

Head to the homey country resorts lining Jalisco's Costa Alegre and savor what the locals have enjoyed for years: all the sun, sand, and seafood you could ever want. They don't call it the Happy Coast for nothing.

Manzanillo and Inland to Colima 319

Legends say that Chinese traders, dreaming of riches, visited Manzanillo Bay centuries before the Spanish conquest; modern travelers come for the balmy winters and splendid fishing. Surrounded by the mountain thrones of ancient gods, the refined city of Colima invites coastal visitors to its more temperate heights.

South to Ixtapa-Zihuatanejo and Inland to Pátzcuaro 362

Follow the highway as it hugs the shorelines of Colima, wild, little-traveled Michoacán, and Guerrero. Or take the high road to Pátzcuaro, where you can wander through narrow colonial lanes and gaze at mystery-shrouded monuments of long-ago emperors.

Tecuanillo, Boca de Apiza; Tecomán; Northern Michoacán Beaches: San Juan de Alima, Playa La Brisa, La Placita, Playa La Ticla, Faro de Bucerías. Playa Maruata, Playa Arena Blanca, Playa Carecitos, Playa Picnilinguillo, Barra de Nexpa, Caleta de Campos

Ixtapa-Zihuatanejo and South to Acapulco 431

Ixtapa and Zihuatanejo offer two distinct worlds only five miles apart. Zihuatanejo still resembles the easygoing seaside town visitors have enjoyed for years, while Ixtapa serves up luxury with high-rise hotels and stunning sunset vistas. Along the road to Acapulco, stop to savor idyllic fishing villages and wildlife-rich esteros, waiting to be explored.

Acapulco and Inland to Taxco 475

Its name long synonymous with palm-shaded beaches, good food, and merrymaking, lively Acapulco lives up to its reputation. As Acapulco thrives on what's new, charming Taxco luxuriates in what's old, with its cobbled hillside lanes and a venerable silver-crafting tradition.

The Costa Chica and Inland to Oaxaca

The Little Coast offers outdoor adventure, from touring lagoons teeming with birds to riding the pipeline at Playa Zicatela, Mexico's best surfing beach. In the Valley of Oaxaca, you can climb amid spectacular ruins, visit villages famed for handicrafts such as woodcarving and weaving, and meet the native artisans themselves.

Resources

ABOUT THE AUTHOR
Bruce Whipperman

In the early 1980s, the lure of travel drew Bruce Whipperman away from a 20-year career of teaching physics. The occasion was a trip to Kenya that included a total solar eclipse and a safari. He hasn't stopped traveling since.

With his family grown, he has been free to let the world's wild, beautiful corners draw him on: to the ice-clawed Karakoram, the Gobi Desert's trellised oases, the pink palaces of Rajasthan, Japan's green wine country, Bali's emerald terraces, and now, Pacific Mexico's palm-shaded beaches, colorful towns, and pine-scented highland valleys.

Bruce has always pursued his travel career for the fun of it. He started with slide shows and photo gifts for friends. Others wanted his photos, so he began selling them. Once, stranded in Ethiopia, he began to write. A dozen years later, after scores of magazine and newspaper feature stories, *Moon Handbooks Pacific Mexico* became his first book. Later, a second book, *Moon Handbooks Puerto Vallarta,* then a third, *Moon Handbooks Oaxaca,* and now a fourth, *Moon Handbooks Guadalajara,* have brightened still more pathways for Mexico travelers.

Travel, after all, is for returning home, and that coziest of journeys always brings a tired but happy Bruce back to his friends, son, daughter, and wife, Linda, in Oakland, California.

For him, travel writing heightens his awareness and focuses his own travel experiences. He always remembers what a Nepali Sherpa once said: "Many people come, looking, looking; few people come, see."

Bruce invites readers of *Moon Handbooks Pacific Mexico* likewise to "come see"—and discover and enjoy—Pacific Mexico's delights with a fresh eye and renewed compassion.

Introduction

Scarcely a generation ago, Mexico's tropical Pacific coast was dotted with a few sleepy, isolated towns and fishing villages, reachable only by sea or tortuous mountain roads from the interior. That gradually began to change until, in 1984, the last link of Mexico's Pacific Coast Highway 200 was completed, a palmy thousand-mile path for exploring Mexico and the new tourist region of Pacific Mexico.

The choices seem endless. You can enjoy numerous resorts, some glittering and luxurious and others quiet and homey. In between the resorts stretch jungle-clad headlands, interspersed with palm-shaded, pearly strands where the fishing is good and the living easy.

When weary of lazing in the sun, visitors can enjoy a trove of ocean sports. Pacific Mexico's water is always balmy and fine to fish, swim, surf, sailboard, kayak, water-ski, snorkel, and scuba dive. For nature enthusiasts, dozens of lush jungle-fringed coastal lagoons are ripe for wildlife viewing and photography.

The coastal strip would be enough but Pacific Mexico offers more: within a hour's flight or a day's drive of the tropical shore rise the cool oak- and pine-tufted highland valleys. Here, colonial cities—Guadalajara, Tepic, Colima, Pátzcuaro, Uruapan, Taxco, Oaxaca—offer fine crafts, colorful festivals, baroque monuments, traditional peoples, and the barely explored ruins of long-forgotten kingdoms. In short, Pacific Mexico is an exotic, tropical land, easy to visit, enjoy, and appreciate, whether you prefer glamorous luxury, backcountry adventure, or a little bit of both. This book will show you the way.

Boca de Tomatlán on Puerto Vallarta's Bay of Banderas

The Land and Sea

On the map of North America, Mexico appears as a grand horn of plenty, spreading and spilling to its northern border with the United States. Mexico encompasses a vast landscape, sprawling over an area as large as France, Germany, England, and Italy combined. Besides its size, Mexico is high country, where most people live in mountain valleys within sight of towering, snowcapped peaks.

Travelers heading south of the Río Grande do not realize the rise in elevation, however. Instead, brushy, cactus-pocked plains spread to mountain ranges on the far blue horizon. Northern

Mexico is nevertheless a tableland—the altiplano—that rises gradually from the Río Grande to its climax at the very heart of the country: the mile-high Bajio (BAH-heeoh) Valley around Guadalajara and the even loftier Valley of Mexico.

Here, in these fertile vales, untold generations of Mexicans have gazed southward at an awesome rampart of smoking mountains, a grand volcanic seam stretching westward from the Gulf of Mexico to the Pacific. In a continuous line along the 19th parallel, more than a dozen volcanoes have puffed sulfurous gas and spewed red-hot rock for an eon,

WHEN TO GO

Although temperatures and rainfall are crucial in deciding when to go to Pacific Mexico, they don't tell the whole story. Crowds, high-priced high seasons and low-priced low seasons are also factors. The first thing to consider is that Pacific Mexico has two sharply defined seasons: wet summer-fall and dry winter-spring. For folks arriving from the U.S. west coast the summer contrast is sharp. The change from dust-dry California in August to tropical-moist Pacific Mexico can be exotically refreshing.

But Pacific Mexico is too hot in the summer, people say. This, however, isn't always the case. In fact, increased summer cloud cover and showers can actually push average daily July, August, and September temperatures lower than bright and clear May and June. And being near the coast, Pacific Mexico nights never get warmer than balmy, even during the summer.

The other summer plus is the vegetation. If you like lush, green landscapes, the summer-fall may be your season. This is true everywhere, but especially in the highlands, when myriads of multicolored wildflowers decorate the roadsides and the clouds seem to billow into a thousand-mile-high blue sky.

By contrast, during the admittedly sunnier and more temperate winter, by late January it hasn't rained for months. In natural areas trees are bare of leaves, grass is brown, and cactuses seem to be the only green plants. The landscape continues dry and dusty Feb.–April, turning hot in May, until

the cooling rains arrive and green breaks out again by late June.

Crowding and high prices are also another factor. If you want to avoid both, don't go to Pacific Mexico resorts during the high Christmas–New Year's rush (Dec. 20–Jan. 3) and Semana Santa pre-Easter week up through and including Easter Sunday. For similar reasons it may be best to avoid the Day of the Dead holiday (Oct. 30.–Nov. 3), when tourists flock in, especially in Michoacán and Oaxaca.

Well, then when should you go? If you shun crowds, but like the sunny, temperate winter, January, a low occupancy miniseason, is a good bet, especially on the beach. The landscape still retains some green and hotels often offer discounts.

September through mid-December are also good months to go. Hotel prices are cheapest, the landscape is lush and green, it's cooler and isn't so rainy as July and August. However, in September, some Pacific Mexico beach resorts, especially Ixtapa-Zihuatanejo-Troncones, and Manzanillo, and to a lesser extent, Acapulco and Puerto Vallarta, are too empty for folks who enjoy lots of company. Although beaches are beautifully uncrowded, your favorite restaurants and entertainments may be closed down until mid-October. The pace picks up, however, from November through mid-December, when moderate temperatures, blue skies, low prices, and enough company create the best of all possible Pacific Mexico worlds.

building themselves into some of the mightiest peaks in the Americas. Most easterly and grandest of them all is Orizaba (Citlaltépetl, the Mountain of the Star), rising 18,856 feet (5,747 meters) directly above the Gulf. Then, in proud succession, the giants march westward: Malinche, 14,640 feet (4,462 meters); Popocatépetl, 17,888 feet (5,452 meters); Nevado de Toluca, 15,016 feet (4,577 meters); until finally the most active of all—the 13,087-foot (3,989-meter) Volcán de Fuego (Volcano of Fire)—fumes next to its serene twin, the Nevado de Colima (14,220 feet, 4,334 meters) above the long, plumy shoreline of Pacific Mexico.

PACIFIC MEXICO

This sun-drenched western coastland stretches along 1,000 miles of sandy beaches, palm-strewn headlands, and blue lagoons, from Mazatlán in the north and curving to the south-east past Acapulco to the new vacation land of Bahías de Huatulco in Oaxaca.

Pacific Mexico is a land washed by the ocean and sheltered by the western mountains: Sierra Madre Occidental and its southern extension, the Sierra Madre del Sur. Everywhere, except in the north where the coastal plain is broad, these green jungle-clad sierras rise quickly, sometimes precipitously, above a narrow coastal strip. Few rivers and roads breach these ramparts, and where roads do, they wind through deep *barrancas,* over lofty passes to temperate, oak-studded highland valleys.

Climate

Elevation rules the climate of Pacific Mexico. The entire coastal strip (including the mountain slopes and plateaus up to 4,000 or 5,000 feet) basks in the tropics, never feeling the bite of frost. The seashore is truly a land of perpetual

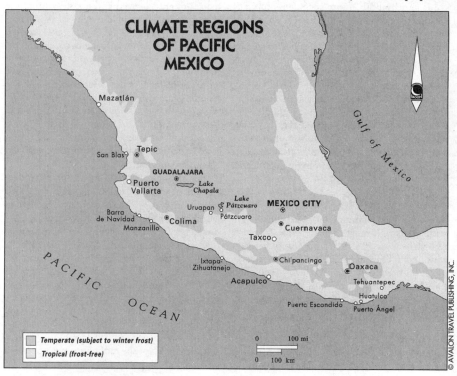

summer. Winter days are typically warm and rainless, peaking at 80–85°F (26–28°C) and dropping to 60–70°F (16–21°C) by midnight. The north-to-south variation on this theme is typically small: Mazatlán will be a few degrees cooler; Acapulco, a few degrees warmer.

Summers on the Pacific Mexico beaches are warmer and wetter. July, August, and September forenoons are typically bright and warm, heating to the high 80s (around 30°C) with afternoon clouding and short, sometimes heavy, showers. By late afternoon, clouds part, the sun dries the pavements, and the breeze is often balmy and just right to enjoy a sparkling Pacific Mexico sunset.

The highlands around Guadalajara, Pátzcuaro, Taxco, and Oaxaca experience similar, but more temperate seasons. Midwinter days are mild, typically peaking around 70°F (21°C). Expect cool, but frost-free, winter nights between 40° and 50°F (9–14°C). Highland summers are delightful, with afternoons in the 80s (27–32°C) and pleasant evenings in the mid-70s (21–26°C), perfect for strolling. May, before the rains, is often the warmest, with June, July, and August highs being moderated by afternoon showers. Many Guadalajara, Pátzcuaro, Taxco, and Oaxaca residents enjoy the best of all possible worlds: balmy summers at home and similarly balmy winters in vacation homes along the Pacific Mexico coast.

Flora and Fauna

Fascinating hothouse verdure—from delicate orchids and bulbous, fuzzy succulents to giant hanging philodendrons—luxuriates at some roadside spots of Pacific Mexico, as if beckoning admirers. Now and then visitors stop, attracted by something remarkable, such as a riot of flowers blooming from apparently dead branches or what looks like grapefruit sprouting from the trunk of a roadside tree. More often, travelers pass long stretches of thorny thickets, viny jungles, and broad, mangrove-edged marshes. A little knowledge of what to expect can blossom into recognition and discovery, transforming the humdrum into something quite extraordinary, even exotic.

VEGETATION ZONES

Mexico's diverse landscape and fickle rainfall have sculpted its wide range of plant forms. Botanists recognize at least 14 major Mexican vegetation zones, eight of which occur in Pacific Mexico.

Directly along the coastal highway, you often pass long sections of three of these zones: savanna, thorn forest, and tropical deciduous forest. The other five are less accessible.

Savanna

Great swaths of pasturelike savanna stretch along the roadside south of Mazatlán to Tepic. In its natural state, savanna often appears as a palm-dotted sea of grass—green and marshy during the rainy summer, dry and brown by late winter.

Although grass rules the savanna, palms give it character. Most familiar is the **coconut**, the *cocotero (Cocos nucifera)*—the world's most useful tree—used for everything from lumber to candy. Coconut palms line the beaches and climb the hillsides—drooping, slanting, rustling, and swaying in the breeze like troupes of hula dancers. Less familiar, but with as much personality, is the Mexican **fan palm**, or *palma real (Sabal mexicana)*, festooned with black fruit and spread flat like a señorita's fan.

The savanna's list goes on: the grapefruitlike fruit on the trunk and branches identify the **gourd tree,** or *calabaza (Crescentia alata)*. The mature gourds, brown and hard, have been carved into *jícaros* (cups for drinking chocolate) for millennia.

Orange-sized, pumpkinlike gourds mark the **sand box tree,** or *jabillo (Hura polyandra)*, so-named because they once served as desktop boxes full of sand for drying ink. The Aztecs, however, called it the exploding tree, because the ripe gourds burst their seeds forth with a bang like a firecracker.

The waterlogged seaward edge of the savanna nurtures forests of the **red mangrove,** or *mangle colorado (Rhizophora mangle)*, short trees that

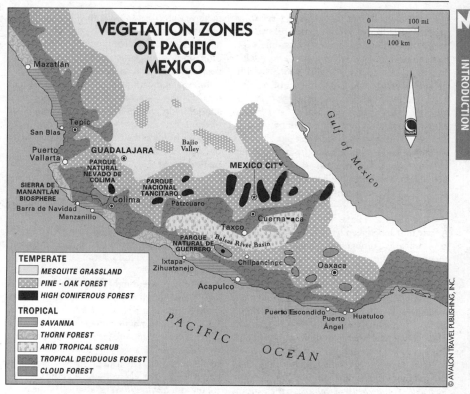

VEGETATION ZONES OF PACIFIC MEXICO

Mazatlán

Tepic
San Blas
Puerto Vallarta
GUADALAJARA
Bajío Valley
PARQUE NATURAL NEVADO DE COLIMA
SIERRA DE MANANTLÁN BIOSPHERE
Barra de Navidad
Manzanillo
Colima
PARQUE NACIONAL TANCITARO
Pátzcuaro
MEXICO CITY
Taxco
Cuernavaca
PARQUE NATURAL DE GUERRERO
Balsas River Basin
Ixtapa-Zihuatanejo
Chilpancingo
Oaxaca
Acapulco
Puerto Escondido
Puerto Ángel
Huatulco

Gulf of Mexico

PACIFIC OCEAN

0   100 mi
0   100 km

TEMPERATE
- *MESQUITE GRASSLAND*
- *PINE - OAK FOREST*
- *HIGH CONIFEROUS FOREST*

TROPICAL
- *SAVANNA*
- *THORN FOREST*
- *ARID TROPICAL SCRUB*
- *TROPICAL DECIDUOUS FOREST*
- *CLOUD FOREST*

© AVALON TRAVEL PUBLISHING, INC.

seem to stand in the water on stilts. Their new roots grow downward from above; a time-lapse photo would show them marching, as if on stilts, into the lagoon.

Thorn Forest

Lower rainfall leads to the hardier growth of the thorn forest, the domain of the pea family—the **acacias** and their cousins, the **mimosas.** Among the most common is the **long spine acacia,** with fluffy, yellow flower balls, ferny leaves, and long, narrow pods; less common, but more useful, is the **fishfuddle,** with pink pea-flowers and long pods, a source of fish-stunning poison. Take care around the acacias; some of the long-thorned varieties harbor nectar-feeding, biting ants.

Perhaps the most spectacular and famous member of the thorn forest community is the **morning glory tree,** which announces the win-

ter dry season's end by blooming a festoon of white trumpets atop its crown of seemingly dead branches. Its gruesome Mexican name, *palo del muerto* (tree of the dead), is exceeded only around Taxco, where folks call it *palo bobo* (fool tree), because they believe if you take a drink from a stream near its foot, you will go crazy.

The cactuses are among the thorn forest's sturdiest and most spectacular inhabitants. In the dry Río Balsas basin (along Highway 95 inland from Acapulco) the spectacular **candelabra cactus** *(cordón espinosa)* spreads as much as 60 feet tall and wide.

Tropical Deciduous Forest

In rainier areas, the thorn forest grades into tropical deciduous forest. This is the "friendly" or "short-tree" forest, blanketed by a tangle of summer-green leaves that fall in the dry winter to reveal thickets of branches. Some trees show bright fall reds and yellows, later blossoming with brilliant flowers—spider lily, cardinal sage, pink trumpet, poppylike yellowsilk *(pomposhuti),* and mouse-killer *(mata ratón),* which swirl in the spring wind like cherry-blossom blizzards.

The tropical deciduous forest is the lush jungle coat that swathes much of coastal Pacific Mexico. And often, where the mountains rush directly down to the sea, the forest likewise spills right over the headland into the ocean. Vine-strewn thickets often overhang the highway, like the edge of some lost prehistoric world, where you might expect a remnant dinosaur to rear up at any moment.

The biological realities here are nearly as exotic. A four-foot-long green iguana, looking every bit as primitive as a dinosaur, slithers across the pavement. Beside the road, a spreading, solitary **strangler fig** *(Ficus padifolia)* stands, draped with hairy, hanging air roots (which, in time, plant themselves in the ground and support the branches). Its Mexican name, *matapalo* (killer tree), is gruesomely accurate, for strangler figs often entwine themselves in death embraces with less aggressive tree-victims.

Much more benign is my favorite in the tropical deciduous forest: the **Colima palm** *(Orbygna guacuyule), guaycoyul,* or *cohune,* which means magnificent. Capped by a proud cock-plume, it presides over the forest singly or in great, graceful swaying groves atop seacliffs. Its nuts, harvested like small coconuts, yield oil and animal fodder.

Excursions by jeep or foot along shaded, off-highway tracks through the tropical deciduous forest can bestow delightful jungle scenes; however, unwary travelers must watch out for the poison-oaklike *mala mujer* (evil woman) tree. The oil on its large five-fingered leaves can cause an itchy rash.

Pine-Oak Forest

A couple of hours' drive inland (especially on the mountain roads from the coast to Guadalajara, Taxco, and Oaxaca), the tropics give way to the temperate pine-oak forest, Pacific Mexico's most extensive vegetation zone. Here, most of Mexico's 112 oak and 39 pine species thrive. At

the lower elevations, bushy, nut-yielding piñon pines sometimes cover the slope; then come the tall pines, often Chihuahua pine and Montezuma pine, both yellow varieties, similar to the ponderosa pine of the western United States.

Interspersed with them are oaks, in two broad classifications—*encino* (evergreen, small-leafed) and *roble* (deciduous, large-leafed)—both much like the oaks that dot California hills and valleys. Clustered on their branches and scattered in the shade are the *bellota* (acorns) that distinctly mark them as oaks.

Mesquite Grassland

Although much of Pacific Mexico's mesquite grassland has been tamed for agriculture, outlying districts, notably in the highlands northeast of Guadalajara, still exhibit its typical landscape, similar to the semiarid plateau land of the U.S. Southwest.

Despite its seemingly monotonous roadside aspect, the mesquite grassland nurtures surprisingly exotic and unusual plants. Among the most intriguing is the **maguey** (mah-GAY), or century plant, so-called because it's said to bloom once, then die, after 100 years of growth, although its lifetime is usually closer to 50 years. The maguey and its cactuslike relatives—such as the very useful **mescal, lechuguilla,** and **sisal,** all of the genus *Agave*—each grow as a roselike cluster of leathery, long, pointed gray-green leaves, from which a single flower stalk eventually blooms.

Century plants themselves, which can grow several feet tall and equally wide, thrive either wild or in cultivated fields in ranks and files like a botanical army on parade. These fields, prominently visible from National Highway 15 west of Guadalajara, are eventually harvested, the leaves crushed, fermented, and distilled into fiery 80-proof tequila, the most renowned of which comes from the town of Tequila near Highway 15.

Watch for the mesquite grassland's *candelilla (Euphorbia antisyphillitica),* an odd cousin of the poinsettia, also a Mexico native. In contrast to the poinsettia, the *candelilla* resembles a tall (two-to three-foot) candle, decorated with small white flowers scattered upward along its single vertical stem. Abundant wax on the many pencil-sized stalks that curve upward from the base is useful for anything from polishing your shoes to lubricating your car's distributor.

Equally exotic is the *Japtropha dioica,* called the **sangre de dragón** (dragon blood), which also grows in a single meaty stem producing two-inch-long lobed leaves with small white flowers. Break off a leaf and out oozes a clear sap, which soon turns blood-red.

High Coniferous Forest

Pacific Mexico's least accessible vegetation zone is the high coniferous forest, above about 9,000 feet, which swathes the slopes of the area's tallest peaks, notably the Nevado de Colima, elev. 14,220 feet (4,334 meters), and Tancitaro, elev. 12,665 feet (3,860 meters), in Michoacán. These pristine green alpine islands, accessible only on horseback or by foot, nurture stands of magnificent pines and spruce and grassy meadows, similar to the higher Rocky Mountain slopes in the United States and Canada. Reigning over the lesser species is the regal **Montezuma pine** *(Pinus montezumae),* distinguished by its long, pendulous cones and rough, ruddy bark, reminiscent of the sugar pine of the western United States.

Arid Tropical Scrub and Cloud Forest

Pacific Mexico's two rarest and most exotic vegetation zones are far from the coastal tourist centers. You can conveniently see the great cactus forests of the arid tropical scrub habitat (which occupies the wild, dry canyonland of the Río Balsas intermountain basin) either along Highway 95 inland from Acapulco, or along Highway 37 or the toll *autopista* between Playa Azul and Pátzcuaro. Finally, travelers who drive to high, dewy mountainsides, beginning around 7,000 feet, can explore the plant and wildlife community of the cloud forest. Oaxaca's northern Sierra (two hours' drive north of Oaxaca city, about 15 miles north of Ixtlán de Juárez) and the Sierra de Manatlán (in the roadless de facto wilderness 40 miles northeast of Manzanillo, near Minatitlán) preserve such habitats. There, abundant cool fog nourishes forests of tree ferns, lichen-draped pines, and oaks above a mossy carpet of orchids, bromeliads, and begonias. For more details, consult M. Walter Pesman's delightful *Meet Flora Mexicana* (which is out of print, but major libraries often have a copy). Also informative is the popular paperback *Handbook of Mexican Roadside Flora,* by Charles T. Mason Jr. and Patricia B. Mason. (See Suggested Reading.)

WILDLIFE

Despite continued habitat destruction—forests are logged, wetlands filled, and savannas plowed—Pacific Mexico still abounds with wildlife. In the temperate pine-oak forest zone of Pacific Mexico live most of the familiar birds and mammals—mountain lion, coyote, jackrabbit, dove, quail—of the American Southwest.

The tropical coastal forests and savannas, however, are home to species seen only in zoos north of the border. The reality of this often dawns on travelers when they glimpse something exotic, such as raucous, screeching swarms of small green parrots rising from the roadside, or a coati nosing in the sand just a few feet away at the forested edge of some isolated Pacific Mexico beach.

Armadillos, Coatis, Spider Monkeys, and Tapirs

Armadillos are cat-sized mammals that act and look like opossums but carry reptilianlike shells. If you see one, remain still, and it may walk right up and sniff your foot before it recognizes you and scuttles back into the woods.

A common inhabitant of the tropics is the raccoonlike coati *(tejon, pisote).* In the wild, coatis like shady stream banks, often congregating in large troops. They are identified by their short brown or tan fur, small round ears, long nose, and straight, vertically held tail. With their endearing and inquisitive nature, coatis are often kept as pets; the first coati you see may be one on a string offered for sale at a local market.

If you are lucky, you may glimpse a band of now-rare brownish-black spider monkeys *(monos)* raiding a forest-edge orchard. And deep in the jungle fastness of southeast Oaxaca, you may find a tracker who can lead you to a view of the endangered tapir. On such an excursion, if you

© BRUCE WHIPPERMAN

The savanna, often marshy during the wet summer, is home to cattle and their egret companions.

are really fortunate, you may even hear the chesty cry of—or even see—a jaguar, the fabled *tigre*.

El Tigre

"Each hill has its own *tigre*," a Mexican proverb says. With black spots spread over a tan coat, stretching five feet (1.5 meters) and weighing about 200 pounds (90 kilograms), the typical jaguar resembles a muscular spotted leopard. Although hunted since prehistory, and now endangered, the jaguar still lives throughout Pacific Mexico, where it hunts along thickly forested stream bottoms and foothills. Unlike the mountain lion *(puma)*, the jaguar will eat any game. Jaguars have even been known to wait patiently for fish in rivers and to stalk beaches for turtle and egg dinners. If they have a favorite food, it is probably the piglike wild peccary *(jabalí)*. Experienced hunters agree that no two jaguars will, when examined, have the same prey in their stomachs.

Although humans have died of wounds inflicted by cornered jaguars, there is little or no hard evidence they eat humans, despite legends to the contrary.

BIRDS

The coastal lagoons of Pacific Mexico lie astride the Pacific flyway, one of the Americas' major north-south paths for migrating waterfowl. Many of the familiar American and Canadian species, including pintail, gadwall, baldpate, shoveler, redhead, and scaup, arrive Oct.–Jan., when their numbers will swell into the millions. They settle near food and cover—sometimes to the frustration of farmers—even at the borders of cornfields. Among the best places to see their spectacle is the **Marismas Nacionales** marsh complex around the Sinaloa-Nayarit border, west of coast Highway 15 between Mazatlán and Acaponeta.

Besides the migrants, swarms of resident species—herons, egrets, cormorants, anhingas, lily-walkers, and hundreds more—stalk, nest, and preen in the same lagoons.

Few spots are better for observing seabirds than the beaches of Pacific Mexico. Brown pelicans and huge black-and-white frigate birds are among the prime actors. When a flock of pelicans spots a school of their favorite fish, they go about their routine deliberately: singly or in pairs they circle and plummet into the waves and come up, more often than not, with fish in their gullets. Each bird then bobs and floats over the swells for a minute or two, seemingly waiting for its dozen or so fellow pelicans to take their turns. This continues until they've bagged a big dinner of 10 to 15 fish apiece.

Frigate birds, the scavengers par excellence of Pacific Mexico, often profit by the labor of the teams of fisherfolk who haul in fish right on village beaches by the netful. After the fishermen auction off the choice morsels—perch, tuna, red snapper, octopus, shrimp—to merchants, and the villagers have scavenged everything else edible, the motley residue of small fish, sea snakes, skates, squids, slugs, and sharks is often thrown to a screeching flock of frigate birds.

(For more details on Mexico's mammals and birds in general, check out Starker Leopold's very readable classic, *Wildlife of Mexico,* and other works in the Suggested Reading section.)

> *Unlike the mountain lion, the jaguar will eat any game. Jaguars have even been known to wait patiently for fish in rivers and to stalk beaches for turtle and egg dinners.*

REPTILES AND AMPHIBIANS
Snakes and Gila Monsters
Mexico has 460-odd snake species, the vast majority shy and nonpoisonous; they will generally get out of your way if you give plenty of warning. In Mexico, as everywhere, poisonous snakes have been largely eradicated in city and tourist areas. In brush or jungle areas, carry a stick or a machete and beat the bushes ahead of you, while watching where you put your feet. When hiking or rock-climbing in the country, don't put your hand in niches you can't see.

You might even see a snake underwater while swimming offshore at an isolated Puerto Vallarta region beach. The **yellow-bellied sea snake** *Pelamis platurus* (to about two feet), although shy, can inflict fatal bites. If you see a yellow and black snake underwater, get away, pronto.

Some eels, which resemble snakes but have gills like fish and inhabit rocky crevices, can inflict nonpoisonous bites and should also be avoided.

The Mexican land counterpart of the *Pelamis platurus* is the **coral snake** *(coralillo),* which occurs as about two dozen species, all with multicolored bright bands that always include red. Although relatively rare, small, and shy, coral snakes occasionally inflict serious, sometimes fatal, bites.

More aggressive and generally more dangerous is the Mexican **rattlesnake** *(cascabel)* and its viper relative, the **fer-de-lance** *(Bothrops atrox).* About the same in size (to six feet) and general appearance as the rattlesnake, the fer-de-lance is known by various local names, such as *nauyaca, cuatro narices, palanca,* and *barba amarilla.* It is potentially more hazardous than the rattlesnake because it lacks a warning rattle.

The Gila monster (confined in Mexico to northern Sonora) and its southern tropical relative, the yellow-spotted, black *escorpión (Heloderma horridum),* are the world's only poisonous lizards. Despite its beaded skin and menacing, fleshy appearance, the *escorpión* bites only when severely provoked; even then, its venom is rarely, if ever, fatal.

Crocodiles
The crocodile, *cocodrilo* or *caimán,* once prized for its meat and hide, came close to vanishing in Mexican Pacific lagoons until the government took steps to ensure its survival. Now officially protected, crocodiles live in the wild in a few isolated breeding populations, while government and private hatcheries are breeding more for the eventual repopulation of lagoons where they once were common. Hatcheries open for touring are in San Blas, Nayarit, and Lagunas de Chacagua, Oaxaca.

Two crocodile species occur in the region. The true crocodile *Crocodilus acutus* has a narrower snout than its local cousin, *Caiman crocodilus fuscus,* a type of alligator *(lagarto).* Although past individuals have been recorded at up to 15 feet long (see the stuffed specimen at the Tepic anthropology and history museum or the live ones at the Mazatlán aquarium), wild native crocodiles are usually young and two feet or less in length.

Turtles

The story of Mexican sea turtles is similar: they once swarmed ashore on Pacific Mexico beaches to lay their eggs. Prized for their meat, eggs, hide, and shell, the turtle population was severely devastated. Now officially protected, sea turtles come ashore in numbers at a few isolated locations. Of the three locally occurring species, the green turtle *tortuga verde* is among the most common. From tour boats, it can often be seen grazing on sea grass offshore in the Bay of Banderas. (For more sea turtle details, see the special topic "Saving Turtles" in the Coast of Jalisco chapter.)

FISH AND MARINE MAMMALS

Shoals of fish abound in Pacific Mexico waters. Four billfish species are found in deep-sea grounds several miles offshore: **swordfish, sailfish,** and **blue** and **black marlin.** All are spirited fighters, though the sailfish and marlin are generally the toughest to bring in. The blue marlin is the biggest of the four; in the past, 10-foot specimens weighing more than 1,000 pounds were brought in at Pacific-coast marinas. Lately, four feet and 200 pounds for a marlin, and 100 pounds for a sailfish, are more typical. Progressive captains now encourage victorious anglers to return these magnificent "tigers of the sea" (especially the sinewy sailfish and blue marlin, which make for poor eating) to the deep after they've won the battle.

Billfish are not the only prizes of the sea, however. Serious fish lovers also seek varieties of tuna-like **jack,** such as **yellowtail, Pacific amberjack, pompano, jack crevalle,** and the tenacious **roosterfish,** named for the "comb" atop its head. These, and the **yellowfin tuna, mackerel,** and *dorado,* which Hawaiians call mahimahi, are among the delicacies sought in Pacific Mexican waters.

Accessible from small boats offshore and by casting from shoreline rocks are varieties of **snapper** *(huachinango, pargo)* and **sea bass** *(cabrilla).* Closer to shore, **croaker, mullet,** and **jewfish** can be found foraging along sandy bottoms and in rocky crevices.

Sharks and **rays** inhabit nearly all depths, with smaller fry venturing into beach shallows and lagoons. Huge **Pacific manta rays** sometimes appear to be frolicking, their great wings flapping like birds, not far off Pacific Mexico shores. Just beyond the waves, local fisherfolk bring in **hammerhead, thresher,** and **leopard sharks.**

Also common is the **stingray,** which can inflict a painful wound with its barbed tail. Experienced swimmers and waders avoid injury by both shuffling (rather than stepping) and watching their feet in shallow waters with sandy bottoms. (For more on fishing and a chart of species encountered in Pacific Mexico waters, turn to Sports and Recreation in the On the Road chapter.)

Seals, Sea Lions, Porpoises, and Whales

Although seen in much greater numbers in Baja California's colder waters, fur-bearing species, such as seals and sea lions, do occasionally hunt in the tropical waters and bask on the sands of island beaches off the Pacific Mexico coast. With the rigid government protections that have been in force for a generation, their numbers appear to be increasing.

The **California Gulf porpoise**—*delfín* or *vaquita* (little cow)—is much more numerous. The smallest member of the whale family, it rarely exceeds five feet. Its playful diving and jumping antics can occasionally be observed from Puerto Vallarta–based tour and fishing boats, and even sometimes right from Bay of Banderas beaches.

Although the **California gray whale** has a migration pattern extending only to the southern tip of Baja California, occasional pods stray farther south, where deep-sea fishermen and cruise and tour boat passengers see them in deep waters offshore.

Larger whale *(ballena)* species, such as the **humpback** and **blue** whale, appear to enjoy tropical waters even more, ranging the north Pacific tropics from Puerto Vallarta west to Hawaii and beyond.

Offshore islands, such as the nearby Marietas and María Isabel (accessible from San Blas), and the Revillagigedo (ray-vee-yah-hee-HAY-doh) Islands 300 miles due west of Puerto Vallarta, offer prime viewing grounds for Mexico's aquatic fauna.

History

Once upon a time, perhaps as early as 50,000 years ago, the first bands of hunters, following great game herds, crossed from Siberia to the American continent. For thousands of years they drifted southward, many of them eventually settling in the rich valleys and plains of North and South America.

Many thousands of years later, perhaps around 10,000 B.C., and in what would later be called Mexico, people began gathering and grinding the seeds of a hardy grass that required only the summer rains to thrive. They selected and planted the larger seeds, and their grain eventually yielded tall plants with long ears and many large kernels. This grain, which they eventually called *teocentli* (sacred seed, which we call maize or corn), led to prosperity.

EARLY MEXICAN CIVILIZATIONS

Plentiful food gave rise to leisure classes—artists, architects, warriors, and ruler-priests—who had time to think and create. With a calendar, they harnessed the constant wheel of the firmament to life on earth, defining the days to plant, to harvest, to feast, to travel, and to trade. Eventually, grand cities arose.

Teotihuacán

Teotihuacán, with a population of perhaps 250,000 around the time of Christ, was one of the world's great metropolises, on a par with Rome, Babylon, and Chang'an. Its epic monuments still stand not far north of Mexico City: the towering Pyramid of the Sun at the terminal of a grand, 150-foot-wide ceremonial avenue faces a great Pyramid of the Moon. Along the avenue sprawls a monumental temple-court surrounded by scowling, ruby-eyed effigies of Quetzalcoatl, the feathered serpent god of gods.

Teotihuacán crumbled mysteriously around A.D. 650, leaving a host of former vassal states from what would be the Yucatán to Pacific Mexico free to tussle among themselves. These included

Xochicalco, not far from present-day Taxco, and the great Zapotec center of Monte Albán farther southwest in Oaxaca. From its regal hilltop complex of stone pyramids, palaces, and ceremonial ball courts, Monte Albán reigned all-powerful until it, too, was abandoned around A.D. 1000.

The Living Quetzalcoatl

Xochicalco, however, was flourishing; its wise men tutored a young noble who was to become a living legend. In A.D. 947, Topiltzín (literally, Our Prince) was born. Records recite Topiltzín's achievements He advanced astronomy, agriculture, and architecture and founded the city-state of Tula in A.D. 968, north of old Teotihuacán.

Contrary to the times, Topiltzín opposed human sacrifice; he taught that tortillas and butterflies, not human hearts, were the food of Quetzalcoatl. After ruling benignly for a generation, Topiltzín's name became so revered that the people began to know him as the living Quetzalcoatl, the plumed serpent-god incarnate.

Quetzalcoatl was not universally loved, however. Bloodthirsty local priests, desperate for human victims, tricked him with alcohol; he awoke groggily one morning in bed with his sister. Devastated by shame, Quetzalcoatl banished himself from Tula with a band of retainers. In A.D. 987, they headed east, toward Yucatán, leaving arrows shot through saplings, appearing like crosses, along their trail.

Although Quetzalcoatl sent word he would reclaim his kingdom during the 52-year cyclical calendar year of his birth, Ce Acatl, he never returned. Legends say that he sailed east and rose to heaven as the morning star.

The Aztecs

The civilization that Topiltzín founded, known to historians as the Toltec (People of Tula), was eventually eclipsed by others. These included the Aztecs, a collection of seven aggressive immigrant subtribes. Migrating from a mysterious western land of Aztlán (Place of the Herons; see the special topic "Aztlán" in the South to Puerto

Vallarta and Inland to Guadalajara chapter) into the lake-filled valley that Mexico City now occupies, around A.D. 1300, the Aztecs survived by being forced to fight for every piece of ground they occupied. Within a century, the Aztecs' dominant tribe, whose members called themselves the Mexica, had clawed its way to dominion over the Valley of Mexico. With the tribute labor that their emperors extracted from local vassal tribes, the Mexica founded a magnificent capital, Tenochtitlán, on an island in the middle of the valley-lake. From there, Aztec armies, not unlike Roman legions, marched out and subdued kingdoms for hundreds of miles in all directions. They returned with the spoils of conquest: gold, brilliant feathers, precious jewels, and captives, whom they sacrificed by the thousands as food for their gods.

Among those gods they feared was Quetzal-coatl, who, legends said, was bearded and fair-skinned. It was a remarkable coincidence, therefore, that the bearded, fair-skinned Castilian Hernán Cortés landed on Mexico's eastern coast on April 22, 1519, during the year of Ce Acatl, exactly when Topiltzín, the Living Quetzalcoatl, had vowed he would return.

THE CONQUEST

Although a generation had elapsed since Columbus founded Spain's West Indian colonies, returns had been meager. Scarcity of gold and of native workers, most of whom had fallen victim to European diseases, turned adventurous Spanish eyes westward once again, toward rumored riches beyond the setting sun. Cortés, then only 34, had left his base in Cuba in February 1519, with an expedition of 11 small ships, 550 men, 16 horses, and a few small cannon. By the time he landed in Mexico, he was burdened by a mutinous crew. His men, mostly soldiers of fortune hearing stories of the great Aztec empire west beyond the mountains, had realized the impossible odds they faced and became restive.

Cortés, however, cut short any thoughts of mutiny by burning his ships. As he led his grumbling but resigned band of adventurers toward the Aztec capital of Tenochtitlán, Cortés played

Quetzalcoatl to the hilt, awing local chiefs. Coaxed by Doña Marina, Cortés's native translator, mistress, and confidante, local chiefs began to add their armies to Cortés's march against their Aztec overlords.

Moctezuma

While Cortés looked down upon the shimmering Valley of Mexico from the great divide between the volcanoes, Moctezuma, the emperor of the Aztecs, fretted about the returned "Quetzalcoatl." It is no wonder that the Spanish, approaching on horseback in their glittering, clanking armor, seemed divine to people who had never known steel, draft animals, or the wheel.

Inside the gates of the Venicelike island-city it was the Spaniards' turn to be dazzled: by gardens full of animals, gold, and palaces, and a great pyramid-enclosed square where tens of thousands of people bartered goods gathered from all over the empire. Tenochtitlán, with perhaps a quarter of a million people, was the great capital of an empire as large and as rich as any in Europe.

Moctezuma, the lord of that empire, was frozen

MALINCHE

I f it hadn't been for Doña Marina (whom he received as a gift from a local chief), Cortés may have become a mere historical footnote. Doña Marina, speaking both Spanish and native tongues, soon became Cortés's interpreter, go-between, and negotiator. She persuaded a number of important chiefs to ally themselves with Cortés against the Aztecs. Clever and opportunistic, Doña Marina was a crucial strategist in Cortés's deadly game of divide and conquer. She eventually bore Cortés a son and lived in honor and riches for many years, profiting greatly from the Spaniards' exploitation of the Mexicans.

Latter-day Mexicans do not honor her by the gentle title of Doña Marina, however. They call her Malinche, after the volcano—the ugly, treacherous scar on the Mexican landscape—and curse her as the female Judas who betrayed her country to the Spanish. *Malinchismo* has become known as the tendency to love things foreign and hate things Mexican.

by fear and foreboding, however. He quickly surrendered himself to Cortés's custody. After a few months, his subjects, enraged by Spanish brutality and Moctezuma's timidity, rioted and mortally wounded the emperor with a stone. With Moctezuma dead, the riot turned into a counterattack against the Spanish. On July 1, 1520, Cortés and his men, forced by the sheer numbers of rebellious Aztecs, retreated along a lake causeway from Tenochtitlán while carrying Moctezuma's treasure with them. Many of them drowned beneath their burdens of stolen Aztec gold, while others hacked a bloody path through thousands of screaming Aztec warriors to safety on the lakeshore.

That infamous night is now known as Noche Triste (Sad Night). Cortés, with half of his men dead, collapsed and wept beneath a great *ahuehuete* cypress tree (which still stands) in Mexico City.

A year later, reinforced by fresh soldiers, horses, a small fleet of armed sailboats, and 100,000 Indian allies, Cortés retook Tenochtitlán. The stubborn defenders, led by Cuauhtémoc, Moctezuma's nephew, fell by the tens of thousands beneath a smoking hail of Spanish grapeshot. The Aztecs, although weakened by smallpox, refused to surrender. Cortés found, to his dismay, that he had to destroy the city to take it.

The triumphant conquistador soon rebuilt it in the Spanish image: Cortés's cathedral and main public buildings—the present *zócalo*, central square of Mexico City—still rest upon the foundations of Moctezuma's pyramids.

NEW SPAIN

With the Valley of Mexico firmly in his grip, Cortés sent his lieutenants south, north, and west to extend the limits of a domain that eventually expanded to more than a dozenfold the size of old Spain. He wrote his king, Charles V, ". . . the most suitable name for it would be New Spain of the Ocean Sea, and thus in the name of your Majesty I have christened it."

The Missionaries

While the conquistadores subjugated the local people, missionaries began arriving to teach, heal, and baptize them. A dozen Franciscan brothers impressed native Mexicans and conquistadores alike by trekking the entire 300-mile stony path from Veracruz to Mexico City in 1523.

The missionaries were a more humane counterbalance to the brutal conquistadores. Missionary authorities generally enjoyed a sympathetic ear from Charles V and his successors, who earnestly pursued Spain's Christian mission, especially when it dovetailed with their political and economic goals.

The King Takes Control

After 1525, the crown, through the Council of the Indies, began to wrest power away from Cortés and his conquistador lieutenants. Many of them had been granted rights of *encomienda:* taxes and labor of an Indian district. In exchange, the *encomendero,* who often enjoyed the status of feudal lord, pledged to look after the welfare and souls of his native Mexican charges.

From the king's point of view, though, tribute pesos collected by *encomenderos* translated into losses to the crown. Moreover, many *encomenderos* callously exploited their native wards for quick profit, sometimes selling them as slave labor in mines and on plantations. Such abuses, coupled with European-introduced diseases, began to reduce the indigenous population at an alarming rate.

After 1530, the king and his councillors began to realize that the native Mexicans were in peril, and without their labor, New Spain would vanish. They acted decisively: new laws would be instituted by a powerful new viceroy.

Don Antonio de Mendoza, the Count of Tendilla, arrived in 1535. He set the precedent for an unbroken line of more than 60 viceroys who, with few exceptions, served with distinction until independence in 1821. Village after village along Mendoza's winding route to Mexico City tried to outdo each other with flowers, music, bullfights, and feasts in his honor.

Mendoza wasted no time. He first got rid of the renegade opportunist (and Cortés's enemy) Nuño de Guzmán, whose private army, under the banner of colonization, had been laying waste to a broad western belt of Pacific Mexico, now

Jalisco, Michoacán, Nayarit, and Sinaloa. (Guzmán, during his rapacious five years in Pacific Mexico, did, however, manage to found several towns: Guadalajara, Tepic, and Culiacán, among others.)

Hernán Cortés, the Marqués del Valle de Oaxaca

Cortés, meanwhile, had done very well for himself. He was one of Spain's richest men, with the title of Marqués del Valle de Oaxaca. He received 80,000 gold pesos a year from hundreds of thousands of native subjects on 25,000 square miles from the Valley of Mexico through the present states of Morelos, Guerrero, and Oaxaca.

Cortés continued tirelessly on a dozen projects: an expedition to Honduras, a young wife whom he brought back from Spain, a palace (which still stands) in Cuernavaca, sugar mills, and dozens of churches, city halls, and presidios. He supervised the exploits of his lieutenants in Pacific Mexico: Francisco Orozco subdued the Zapotecs in Oaxaca, while Pedro de Alvarado accomplished the same with the Mixtecs, then continued south to conquer Guatemala. Meanwhile, Cristóbal de Olid subjugated the Purépecha in Michoacán, then moved down the Pacific coast to Zacatula on the mouth of the Río Balsas. There (and at Acapulco and Tehuantepec), Cortés built ships to explore the Pacific. In 1535, he led an expedition to the Gulf of California (hence the Sea of Cortez) in a dreary six-month search for treasure along the Baja California coast.

Cortés's Monument

Disgusted with Mendoza's meddling and discouraged by his failures, Cortés returned to Spain, where he got mired in lawsuits, a minor war, and his daughter's marital troubles, all of which led to his illness and death in 1547. Cortés's remains, according to his will, were eventually laid to rest in a vault at the Hospital de Jesús, which he founded in Mexico City.

Since latter-day Mexican politics preclude memorials to the Spanish conquest, no monument nor statue anywhere in Mexico marks his achievements. Cortés's monument, historians note, is Mexico itself.

COLONIAL MEXICO

In 1542, the Council of the Indies, through Viceroy Mendoza, promulgated its liberal New Laws of the Indies. The New Laws rested on high moral ground: the only Christian justification for New Spain was the souls and welfare of the indigenous people. Colonists had no right to exploit the natives. Slavery, therefore, was outlawed and *encomienda* rights were to revert to the crown at the death of the original grantees.

Despite uproar and near-rebellion by the colonists, Mendoza (and his successor in 1550, Don Luis Velasco) kept the lid on New Spain. Although some *encomenderos* held on to their rights into the 18th century, chattel slavery was abolished in Mexico—300 years before Abraham Lincoln's Emancipation Proclamation.

Peace reigned in Mexico for 10 generations. Viceroys came and conscientiously served, new settlers arrived and put down roots, friars preached and built country churches, and the conquistadores' rich sons and daughters played while the native Mexicans worked.

The Role of the Church

The church somewhat moderated the natives' toil. On feast days, they would dress up and parade their patron saint through the streets and later eat their fill, drink *pulque,* and ooh and aah at the fireworks.

The church profited from the status quo, however. The biblical tithe—one-tenth of everything, from crops and livestock to rents and mining profits—filled church coffers. By 1800, the church owned half of Mexico. Moreover, the clergy (including lay church officers) and the military were doubly privileged. They enjoyed right of *fuero* (exemption from civil law) and could be prosecuted by ecclesiastical or military courts only.

Trade and Commerce

In trade and commerce, New Spain existed for the benefit of the mother country. Spaniards enjoyed absolute monopolies by virtue of the complete prohibition of foreign traders and goods. Colonists, as a result, paid dearly for oft-shoddy

POPULATION CHANGES IN NEW SPAIN

	Early Colonial (1570)	Late Colonial (1810)
peninsulares	6,600	15,000
criollos	11,000	1,100,000
mestizos	2,400	704,000
indígenas	3,340,000	3,700,000
negros	22,000	630,000

Spanish manufactures. The Casa de Contratación, the royal trade regulators, always ensured the colony's yearly balance of payments would result in deficit, which would be made up by bullion shipments from New Spain mines (from which the crown raked 10 percent off the top.)

Despite its faults, New Spain lasted three times longer than the Aztec empire. By most contemporary measures, New Spain was prospering in 1800. The native labor force was completely subjugated and increasing, and the galleon fleets were carrying home growing tonnages of silver and gold worth millions. The authorities, however, failed to recognize that Mexico had changed in 300 years.

Criollos—The New Mexicans

Nearly three centuries of colonial rule gave rise to a burgeoning population of more than a million criollos—Mexican-born European descendants of Spanish colonists, many rich and educated—to whom power was denied.

High government, church, and military office had always been the preserve of a tiny but powerful minority of *peninsulares*—whites born in Spain. Criollos could only watch in disgust as unlettered, unskilled *peninsulares* (derisively called *gachupines*—wearers of spurs) were boosted to authority over them.

Although the criollos stood high above the *mestizo*, native Mexican, and *negro* underclasses,

that seemed little compensation for the false smiles, the deep bows, and the costly bribes that *gachupines* demanded.

Mestizos, Indígenas, and African Mexicans

Upper-class luxury existed by virtue of the sweat of Mexico's mestizo, *indígena* (native, or indigenous), and *negro* laborers and servants. African slaves were imported in large numbers during the 17th century after typhus, smallpox, and measles epidemics had wiped out most of the native population. Although the African Mexicans contributed significantly (crafts, healing arts, dance, music, drums, and marimba), they had arrived last and experienced discrimination from everyone.

INDEPENDENCE

The chance for change came during the aftermath of the French invasion of Spain in 1808, when Napoléon Bonaparte replaced King Ferdinand VII with his brother Joseph on the Spanish throne. Most *peninsulares* backed the king; most criollos, however, inspired by the example of the recent American and French revolutions, talked and dreamed of independence. One such group, urged on by a firebrand parish priest, acted.

El Grito de Dolores

"¡Viva México! Death to the gachupines!" **Father Miguel Hidalgo,** shouting his impassioned *grito* from the church balcony in the Guanajuato town of Dolores on September 16, 1810, ignited action. A mostly *indígena*, machete-wielding army of 20,000 coalesced around Hidalgo and his compatriots, Ignacio Allende and Juan Aldama. Their ragtag mob raged out of control through the Bajío, massacring hated *gachupines* and pillaging their homes.

Hidalgo advanced on Mexico City but, unnerved by stiff royalist resistance, retreated and regrouped around Guadalajara. His rebels, whose numbers had swollen to 80,000, were no match for a disciplined, 6,000-strong royalist force. Hidalgo (now "Generalisimo") fled north but was soon apprehended, defrocked, and executed. His head and those of his comrades—Aldama, Allende, and Mariano Jiménez—were hung from the walls of the Guanajuato granary (site of the slaughter of 138 *gachupines* by Hidalgo's army) for 10 years as grim reminders of the consequences of rebellion.

The 10-Year Struggle

Others carried on, however. A mestizo former student of Hidalgo, **José María Morelos,** led a revolutionary shadow government in the present states of Guerrero and Oaxaca for four years until he was apprehended and executed in December 1815.

Morelos's compatriot **Vicente Guerrero** continued the fight, joining forces with criollo royalist **Brigadier Agustín de Iturbide.** Their Plan de Iguala promised "Three Guarantees"— the renowned Trigarantes: Independence, Catholicism, and Equality—which their army (commanded by Iturbide, of course) would enforce. On September 21, 1821, Iturbide rode triumphantly into Mexico City at the head of his army of Trigarantes. Mexico was independent at last.

Independence, however, solved little except to expel the *peninsulares*. With an illiterate populace and no experience in self-government, Mexicans began a tragic 40-year love affair with a fantasy: the general on the white horse, the gold-braided hero who could save them from themselves.

The Rise and Fall of Agustín I

Iturbide—crowned Agustín I by the bishop of Guadalajara on July 21, 1822—soon lost his charisma. In a pattern that became sadly predictable for generations of topsy-turvy Mexican politics, an ambitious garrison commander issued a *pronunciamiento,* a declaration against the government. Supporting *pronunciamientos* followed, and old revolutionary heroes Guerrero, Guadalupe Victoria, and Nicolás Bravo endorsed a "plan"— the Plan de Casa Mata (not unlike Iturbide's pre-

> *Benito Juárez's similarity to his contemporary, Abraham Lincoln, is legend: Juárez had risen from humble Zapotec origins to become a lawyer, a champion of justice, and the president who held his country together during a terrible civil war.*

vious Plan de Iguala)—dethroning Iturbide in favor of a republic. Iturbide, his braid tattered and brass tarnished, abdicated in February 1823.

Antonio López de Santa Anna, the eager 28-year-old military commander of Veracruz, whose *pronunciamiento* had pushed Iturbide from his white horse, maneuvered to gradually replace him. Throughout the late 1820s the government teetered on the edge of disaster as the presidency bounced between liberal and conservative hands six times in three years. During the last of these upheavals, Santa Anna jumped to prominence by defeating an abortive Spanish attempt at counterrevolution at Tampico in 1829. "The Victor of Tampico," people called Santa Anna.

The Disastrous Era of Santa Anna

In 1833, the government was bankrupt; mobs demanded the ouster of conservative President Anastasio Bustamante, who had executed the rebellious old revolutionary hero, Vicente Guerrero. Santa Anna issued a *pronunciamiento* against Bustamante; Congress obliged, elevating Santa Anna to "Liberator of the Republic" and "Conqueror of the Spaniards," and naming him president in March 1833.

Santa Anna would pop in and out of the presidency like a jack-in-the-box 10 more times before 1855. First, he foolishly lost Texas to rebellious Anglo settlers in 1836. He later lost his leg (which was buried with full military honors) fighting the emperor of France.

Santa Anna's greatest debacle, however, was to declare war on the United States with just 1,839 pesos in the treasury. With his forces poised to defend Mexico City against a relatively small 10,000-man American invasion force, Santa Anna inexplicably withdrew. United States Marines surged into the "Halls of Montezuma," Chapultepec Castle, where Mexico's six beloved Niños Héroes cadets fell in the losing cause on September 13, 1847.

In the subsequent treaty of Guadalupe Hidalgo, Mexico lost nearly half of its territory—the present states of New Mexico, Arizona, California, Nevada, Utah, and Colorado—to the United States. Mexicans have never forgotten; they have looked upon gringos with a combination of awe, envy, admiration, and disgust ever since.

For Santa Anna, however, enough was not enough. Called back as president for the last and 11th time in 1853, Santa Anna, now "His Most Serene Highness," financed his final extravagances by selling off a part of southern New Mexico and Arizona, in what was known as the Gadsden Purchase, for $10 million.

REFORM, CIVIL WAR, AND INTERVENTION

Mexican leaders finally saw the light and exiled Santa Anna forever. While conservatives searched for a king to replace Santa Anna, liberals (whom Santa Anna had kept in jail) plunged ahead with three controversial reform laws: the Ley Juárez, Ley Lerdo, and Ley Iglesias. These *reformas,* augmented by a new Constitution of 1857, directly attacked the privilege and power of Mexico's landlords, clergy, and generals: Ley Juárez abolished *fueros,* the separate military and church courts; Ley Lerdo forbade excess corporate (read: church) landholdings; and Ley Iglesias reduced or transferred most church power to the state.

Conservative generals, priests, and *hacendados* (landholders), along with their mestizo and *indígena* followers, revolted. The resulting War of the Reform (not unlike the U.S. Civil War) ravaged the countryside for three long years until the victorious liberal army paraded triumphantly in Mexico City on New Year's Day 1861.

Juárez and Maximilian

Benito Juárez, the leading *reformista,* had won the day. Juárez's similarity to his contemporary, Abraham Lincoln, is legend: Juárez had risen from humble Zapotec origins to become a lawyer, a champion of justice, and the president who held his country together during a terrible civil war. Like Lincoln's, Juárez's triumph didn't last long.

Imperial France invaded Mexico in January 1862, initiating a bloody five-year imperialist struggle, infamously known as the **French Intervention.** After two costly years, the French forces pushed Juárez's liberal army into the hills and installed the king whom Mexican conservatives thought the country needed. Austrian Archduke Maximilian and his wife, Carlota, the very models of modern Catholic monarchs, were crowned emperor and empress of Mexico in June 1864.

The naive Emperor Maximilian I was surprised that some of his subjects resented his presence. Meanwhile, Juárez refused to yield, stubbornly performing his constitutional duties in a somber black carriage one jump ahead of the French occupying army. The climax came in May 1867, when liberal forces besieged and defeated Maximilian's army at Querétaro. Juárez, giving no quarter, sternly ordered Maximilian's execution by firing squad on June 19, 1867.

RECONSTRUCTION AND THE PORFIRIANA

Juárez worked day and night at the double task of reconstruction and reform. He won reelection but died, exhausted, in 1871. The death of Juárez, the stoic partisan of reform, signaled hope to Mexico's conservatives. They soon got their wish: **General Don Porfirio Díaz,** the "Coming Man," was elected president in 1876.

Pax Porfiriana

Don Porfirio is often remembered wistfully, as old Italians remember Mussolini: "He was a bit rough, but, dammit, at least he made the trains run on time."

Although Porfirio Díaz's humble Oaxaca mestizo origins were not unlike Juárez's, Díaz was not a democrat: when he was a general, his officers often took no captives; when he was president, his country police, the *rurales,* shot prisoners in the act of "trying to escape."

Order and progress, in that sequence, ruled Mexico for 34 years. Foreign investment flowed into the country; new railroads brought the products of shiny factories, mines, and farms to modernized Gulf and Pacific ports. Mexico balanced its budget, repaid foreign debt, and became a respected member of the family of nations.

The human price was high. Don Porfirio allowed more than 100 million acres—one-fifth of Mexico's land area (including most of the arable land)—to be acquired by wealthy Mexicans and foreigners. Poor Mexicans suffered the most. By 1910, 90 percent of the *indígenas* had lost their traditional communal land. In the spring of 1910, a smug, now-cultured, and elderly Don Porfirio anticipated with relish the centennial of Hidalgo's Grito de Dolores.

REVOLUTION AND STABILIZATION

¡No Reelección!

Porfirio Díaz himself had first campaigned on the slogan. It expressed the idea that the president should step down after one term. Although Díaz had stepped down once in 1880, he had gotten himself reelected for 26 consecutive years. In 1910, **Francisco I. Madero,** a short, squeaky-voiced son of rich landowners, opposed Díaz under the same banner.

Although Díaz had jailed him before the election, Madero refused to quit campaign-

EMILIANO ZAPATA

Although the multitude of streets, towns, *ejidos,* and monuments named after Emiliano Zapata (1879–1919) mark him as a true national hero, his name is not free of controversy. Although his Zapatista guerrillas (1910–1919), often crude and cruel, committed their share of atrocities, all the warring factions of the 1910 Revolution share the same guilt.

Emiliano Zapata's legacy nevertheless remains, embedded in both Mexican law and the hearts and minds of all Mexicans who have benefited from his selfless struggle to realize his broad social vision.

For Emiliano Zapata, achievement didn't come easy. He was born of poor mestizo parents, in Anenecuilco, Morelos, on August 8, 1879. The modest thatched-roof home of his birth still stands, restored as a museum, three miles south of the main market town of Cuautla. Young Emiliano, orphaned when he was still a child, grew up in the care of relatives. As a youth he experienced firsthand the results of then-president Porfirio Díaz's land policies, which resulted in ancestral village fields' being gobbled up, both legally and illegally, by rich hacendados. Consequently, by 1900, thousands of Zapata's campesino neighbors were toiling as virtual serfs on the very land that had been stolen from them.

When he was a young man, Emiliano's intelligence, forthright honesty, and natural leadership qualities earned him considerable community standing. Although determined to correct local in-

justices, he started out by working within the established order, accepting the presidency of the Anenecuilco municipal government. When conciliatory measures to address the local campesinos' grievances against the landholders failed, Zapata took justice into his own hands and organized posses to forcibly eject the offending hacendados. This earned Zapata the ire of the Díaz government, which sent Zapata fleeing for his life, into the mountains with his guerrilla band of followers.

At the same time, in late 1910, Francisco Madero had been agitating for revolution from Texas. Zapata sent messengers north and liked what they told him about Madero. When, in early 1911, Madero crossed the Rio Grande and joined Pancho Villa's forces to capture Ciudad Juárez, Zapata's growing guerrilla regiment moved quickly, seizing Cuernavaca, the Morelos state capital, by mid-May.

Pressed on all sides, Díaz's army and government quickly fell apart, and on May 25, 1911, Díaz resigned. As Madero, Pancho Villa, and (now General) Zapata rode in triumph into Mexico City, Díaz fled into exile to France.

Immediately, however, Zapata began quarreling with Madero's cautious legalistic approach toward the problem of land and justice for Zapata's poor followers. "The land belongs to only those who work with their hands," Zapata asserted. Exasperated with Madero and his elite advisers (Zapata could barely read), Zapata stormed out of

ing. From a safe platform in the United States, he called for a revolution to begin on November 20.

Villa and Zapata

Not much happened, but soon the millions of poor Mexicans who had been going to bed hungry began to stir. In Chihuahua, followers of Francisco (Pancho) Villa, an erstwhile ranch hand, miner, peddler, and cattle rustler, began attacking the *rurales,* dynamiting railroads, and raiding towns. Meanwhile, in the south, horse trader, farmer, and minor official Emiliano Zapata and his *indígena* guerrillas were

terrorizing rich *hacendados* and forcibly recovering stolen ancestral village lands. Zapata's movement gained steam and by May had taken the Morelos state capital, Cuernavaca. Meanwhile, Madero crossed the Río Grande and joined with Villa's forces, who took Ciudad Juárez.

The *federales,* government army troops, began deserting in droves, and on May 25, 1911, Díaz submitted his resignation.

As Madero's deputy, **General Victoriano Huerta,** put Díaz on his ship of exile in Veracruz, Díaz confided, "Madero has unleashed a tiger. Now let's see if he can control it."

Mexico City in front of his Zapatista cavalry, openly breaking with with Madero, in November 1911.

In an honest attempt at conciliation, Madero came to Morelos to persuade Zapata to lay down his arms. Before the proceedings were over, however, federal troops, under orders from Madero's treacherous military commander, Victoriano Huerta, invaded Morelos. Fed up, Zapata rearmed his troops, and despite recommendations that he execute Madero on the spot, sent him packing back to Mexico City.

So for seven bloody years, Zapata's guerrillas, which by 1914 had grown to a formidable "Liberating Army of the South," battled government forces in Morelos, Guerrero, Puebla, and Oaxaca.

Emiliano Zapata

Despite the continued killing, chaos, and personal exhaustion, Zapata remained incorruptibly dedicated to his credo, codified as the famous Plan de Ayala, that declared *"¡Tierra y Libertad!"* ("Land and Liberty!") for all must be the overriding goal of any just Mexican government.

Finally, by 1919, "Constitutionalist" forces, under the leadership of "First Chief" Venustiano Carranza and General Alvaro Obregón, had promulgated a constitution and, from Mexico City, controlled most of Mexico. Zapata, who never trusted the Constitutionalists, despite their liberal Constitution of 1917, remained a thorn in Carranza's side. Carranza got one of his officers, Colonel Jesús Guajardo, to feign surrender of his entire well-equipped regiment to Zapata, at Chinameca Hacienda, south of Cuautla. Zapata, desperate for supplies and reinforcements, fell for the bait, and was gunned down by a platoon of snipers inside the Hacienda on April 10, 1919.

Although Constitutionalist soldiers displayed a badly shot-up body on the Cuatla plaza that they claimed to be Zapata, some witnesses believed otherwise. Rumors persisted for years that somewhere, Emiliano Zapata lived on; and that when the people needed him again, he would return.

The Fighting Continues

Emiliano Zapata, it turned out, was the tiger Madero had unleashed. Meeting with Madero in Mexico City, Zapata fumed over Madero's go-slow approach to the "agrarian problem," as Madero termed it. By November, Zapata had denounced Madero. *";Tierra y Libertad!"* ("Land and Liberty!") the Zapatistas cried, as Madero's support faded. Federal troops in Mexico City rebelled; Huerta forced Madero to resign on February 18, 1913, put him under house arrest, and then had him murdered four days later.

The rum-swilling Huerta ruled like a Chicago mobster; general rebellion, led by the "Big Four"—Villa, Alvaro Obregón, and Venustiano Carranza in the north, and Zapata in the south—soon broke out. Pressed by the rebels and re-fused U.S. recognition, Huerta fled into exile in July 1914.

The Constitution of 1917

Fighting sputtered on for three years as authority see-sawed between revolutionary factions. Finally, Carranza, who controlled most of the country by 1917, got a convention together in Querétaro to formulate political and social goals. The resulting Constitution of 1917, while restating most ideas of the *reformistas'* 1857 constitution, additionally prescribed a single four-year presidential term, labor reform, and subordinated private owner-ship to public interest. Every village had a right to communal *ejido* land, and subsoil wealth could never be sold away to the highest bidder.

The Constitution of 1917 was a revolutionary expression of national aspirations, and, in retro-spect, represented a social and political agenda for the entire 20th century. In modified form, it has lasted to the present day.

Obregón Stabilizes Mexico

On December 1, 1920, General Alvaro Obregón legally assumed the presidency of a Mexico still bleeding from 10 years of civil war. Although a seasoned revolutionary, Obregón was also a prag-matist who recognized peace was necessary to implement the goals of the revolution. In four years, his government pacified local uprisings, disarmed a swarm of warlords, executed hun-dreds of *bandidos,* obtained U.S. diplomatic recognition, assuaged the worst fears of the clergy and landowners, and began land reform.

All this set the stage for the work of **Plutarco Elías Calles,** Obregón's Minister of Gobernación (Interior) and handpicked successor, who won the 1924 election. Aided by peace, Mexico returned to a semblance of prosperity. Calles brought the army under civilian control, balanced the budget, and shifted Mexico's social revolution into high gear. New clinics vaccinated millions against smallpox, new dams irrigated thousands of pre-viously dry acres, and campesinos received mil-lions of acres of redistributed land.

By single-mindedly enforcing the pro-agrarian, pro-labor, and anti-clerical articles of the 1917 constitution, Calles made many influential ene-mies. Infuriated by the government's confisca-tion of church property, closing of monasteries, and deportation of hundreds of foreign priests and nuns, the clergy refused to perform mar-riages, baptisms, and last rites. As members of the Cristero movement, militant Catholics crying *";Viva Cristo Rey!"* armed themselves, torching public schools and government property and murdering hundreds of innocent bystanders.

Simultaneously, Calles threatened foreign oil companies, demanding they exchange their ti-tles for 50-year leases. A moderate Mexican supreme court decision over the oil issue and the skillful arbitration of U.S. Ambassador Dwight Morrow smoothed over both the oil and church troubles by the end of Calles's term.

Calles, who started out brimming with revo-lutionary fervor and populist zeal, became in-creasingly conservative and dictatorial. Although he bowed out peaceably in favor of Obregón (the constitution had been amended to allow one six-year nonsuccessive term), Obregón was assassi-nated two weeks after his election in 1928. Calles continued to rule for six more years through three puppet-presidents: Emilio Portes Gil (1928–1930), Pascual Ortíz Rubio (1930–1932), and Abelardo Rodríguez (1932–1934).

For the 14 years since 1920, the revolution had first waxed, then waned. With a cash sur-plus in 1930, Mexico skidded into debt as the Great Depression deepened and Calles and his cronies lined their pockets. In blessing his minister of war, General Lázaro Cárdenas, for the 1934 presidential election, Calles expected more of the same.

Lázaro Cárdenas, President of the People

The 40-year-old former governor of Michoacán immediately set his own agenda, however. Cárdenas worked tirelessly to fulfill the social prescriptions of the revolution. As morning-coated diplomats and cabinet ministers fretted in his outer office, Cárdenas ushered in delegations of campesinos and factory workers and sympathetically listened to their problems.

In his six years of rule, Cárdenas moved public education and health forward on a broad front, supported strong labor unions, and redistributed 49 million acres of farmland, more than any president before or since.

Cárdenas's resolute enforcement of the constitution's Artículo 123 brought him the most renown. Under this pro-labor law, the government turned over a host of private companies to employee ownership and, on March 18, 1938, expropriated all foreign oil corporations.

In retrospect the oil corporations, most of which were British, were not blameless. They had sorely neglected the wages, health, and welfare of their workers while ruthlessly taking the law into their own hands with private police forces. Although Standard Oil cried foul, U.S. President Franklin Roosevelt did not intervene. Through negotiation and due process, the U.S. companies eventually were compensated with $24 million plus 3 percent interest. In the wake of the expropriation, President Cárdenas created Petróleos Mexicanos (Pemex), the national oil corporation that continues to run all Mexican oil and gas operations.

Manuel Ávila Camacho

Manuel Ávila Camacho, elected in 1940, was the last general to be president of Mexico. His administration ushered in a gradual shift of Mexican politics, government, and foreign policy as Mexico allied itself with the U.S. cause during World War II. Foreign tourism, initially promoted by

the Cárdenas administration, ballooned. Good feelings surged as Franklin Roosevelt became the first U.S. president to officially cross the Río Grande when he met with Camacho in Monterrey in April 1943.

In both word and deed, moderation and evolution guided President Camacho's policies. *"Soy creente"* ("I am a believer"), he declared to the Catholics of Mexico as he worked earnestly to bridge Mexico's serious church-state schism. Land-policy emphasis shifted from redistribution to utilization as new dams and canals irrigated hundreds of thousands of previously arid acres. On one hand, Camacho established IMSS (Instituto Mexicano de Seguro Social), and on the other trimmed the power of labor unions.

As World War II moved toward its 1945 conclusion, both the United States and Mexico were enjoying the benefits of four years of governmental and military cooperation and mutual trade in the form of a mountain of strategic minerals that had moved north in exchange for a similar mountain of U.S. manufactures that moved south.

CONTEMPORARY MEXICO
The Mature Revolution

During the decades after World War II, beginning with moderate President **Miguel Alemán** (1946–1952), Mexican politicians gradually honed their skills of consensus and compromise as their middle-aged revolution bubbled along under liberal presidents and sputtered haltingly under conservatives. Doctrine required of all politicians, regardless of stripe, that they be "revolutionary" enough to be included beneath the banner of the PRI (Partido Revolucionario Institucional—the Institutional Revolutionary Party), Mexico's dominant political party.

Mexico's revolution hasn't been very revolutionary about women's rights, however. The PRI didn't get around to giving Mexican women, millions of whom fought and died alongside their men during the revolution, the right to vote until 1953.

Adolfo Ruíz Cortínes, Alemán's secretary of the interior, was elected overwhelmingly in 1952.

He fought the corruption that had crept into government under his predecessor, continued land reform, increased agricultural production, built new ports, eradicated malaria, and opened several automobile assembly plants.

Women, voting for the first time in a national election, kept the PRI in power by electing liberal **Adolfo López Mateos** in 1958. Resembling Lázaro Cárdenas in social policy, López Mateos redistributed 40 million acres of farmland, forced automakers to use 60 percent domestic components, built thousands of new schools, and distributed hundreds of millions of new textbooks. *"La electricidad es nuestra"* ("Electricity is ours"), Mateos declared as he nationalized foreign power companies in 1962.

Despite his left-leaning social agenda, unions were restive under López Mateos. Protesting inflation, workers struck; the government retaliated, arresting Demetrios Vallejo, the railway union head, and renowned muralist David Siqueiros, former communist party secretary.

Despite the troubles, López Mateos climaxed his presidency gracefully in 1964 as he opened the celebrated National Museum of Anthropology, appropriately located in Chapultepec Park, where the Aztecs had first settled 20 generations earlier.

In 1964, as several times before, the outgoing president's interior secretary succeeded his former chief. Dour, conservative **Gustavo Díaz Ordaz** immediately clashed with liberals, labor, and students. The pot boiled over just before the 1968 Mexico City Olympics. Reacting to a student rebellion, the army occupied the National University; shortly afterward, on October 2, government forces opened fire with machine guns on a downtown protest, killing and wounding hundreds of demonstrators.

Maquiladoras

Despite its serious internal troubles, Mexico's relations with the United States were cordial. President Lyndon Johnson visited and unveiled a statue of Abraham Lincoln in Mexico City. Later, Díaz Ordaz met with President Richard Nixon in Puerto Vallarta.

Meanwhile, bilateral negotiations produced the **Border Industrialization Program.** Within

a 12-mile strip south of the U.S.-Mexico border, foreign companies could assemble duty-free parts into finished goods and export them without any duties on either side. Within a dozen years, a swarm of such plants, called maquiladoras, were humming as hundreds of thousands of Mexican workers assembled and exported billions of dollars worth of shiny consumer goods—electronics, clothes, furniture, pharmaceuticals, and toys—worldwide.

Concurrently, in Mexico's interior, Díaz Ordaz pushed Mexico's industrialization ahead full steam. Foreign money financed hundreds of new plants and factories. Primary among these was the giant Las Truchas steel plant at the new industrial port and town of Lázaro Cárdenas at the Pacific mouth of the Río Balsas.

Discovery, in 1974, of gigantic new oil and gas reserves along Mexico's Gulf coast added fuel to Mexico's already rapid industrial expansion. During the late 1970s and early 1980s billions in foreign investment, lured by Mexico's oil earnings, financed other major developments—factories, hotels, power plants, roads, airports—all over the country.

Economic Trouble of the 1980s

The negative side to these expensive projects was the huge dollar debt required to finance them. President **Luis Echeverría Alvarez** (1970–1976), diverted by his interest in international affairs, passed Mexico's burgeoning financial deficit to his successor, **José López Portillo.** As feared by some experts, a world petroleum glut during the early 1980s burst Mexico's ballooning oil bubble and plunged the country into financial crisis. When the 1982 interest came due on its foreign debt, Mexico's largest holding company couldn't pay the $2.3 billion owed. The peso plummeted more than fivefold, to 150 per U.S. dollar. At the same time, prices doubled every year.

But by the mid-1980s, President **Miguel de la Madrid** (1982–1988) was straining to get Mexico's economic house in order. He sliced government and raised taxes, asking rich and poor alike to tighten their belts. Despite getting foreign bankers to reschedule Mexico's debt, de la Madrid couldn't stop inflation. Prices skyrocketed as the peso deflated to 2,500 per U.S. dollar, becoming one of the world's most devalued currencies by 1988.

Salinas de Gortari and NAFTA

Public disgust led to significant opposition during the 1988 presidential election. Billionaire PAN candidate Michael Clothier and liberal National Democratic Front candidate Cuauhtémoc Cárdenas ran against the PRI's Harvard-educated technocrat Carlos Salinas de Gortari. The vote was split so evenly that all three candidates claimed victory. Although Salinas eventually won the election, his showing, barely half of the vote, was the worst ever for a PRI president.

Salinas, however, became Mexico's "Coming Man" of the 1990s. He seemed serious about democracy, sympathetic to the *indígenas* and the poor, and sensitive to women's issues. His major achievement, despite significant national opposition, was the North American Free Trade Agreement (NAFTA), which he, U.S. President George Bush, and Canadian Prime Minister Brian Mulrooney negotiated in 1992.

Incoming U.S. President Bill Clinton continued the drama by pushing NAFTA through the U.S. Congress in November 1993, and the Mexican legislature followed suit two weeks later. However, on the very day in January 1994 that NAFTA took effect, rebellion broke out in the poor, remote state of Chiapas. A small but well-disciplined campesino force, calling itself **Ejército Zapatista Liberación Nacional** (Zapatista National Liberation Army—EZLN), or "Zapatistas," captured a number of provincial towns and held the former governor of Chiapas hostage.

To further complicate matters, Mexico's already tense drama veered toward tragedy. While Salinas de Gortari's chief negotiator, Manuel Camacho Solís, was attempting to iron out a settlement with the Zapatista rebels, Luis Donaldo Colosio, Salinas's handpicked successor, was gunned down just months before the August balloting. However, instead of disintegrating, the nation united in grief; opposition candidates eulogized their fallen former opponent and later earnestly endorsed his replacement, stolid technocrat **Ernesto Zedillo,** in Mexico's first presidential election debate.

In a closely watched election relatively unmarred by irregularities, Zedillo piled up a solid plurality against his PAN and PRD opponents. By perpetuating the PRI's 65-year hold on the presidency, the electorate had again opted for the PRI's familiar although imperfect middle-aged revolution.

New Crises, New Recovery

Zedillo, however, had little time to savor his victory. Right away he had to face the consequences of his predecessor's shabby fiscal policies. The peso, after having been pumped up a thousand-fold to a value of three per dollar as the "new" peso in 1993, continued to be artificially propped up for a year, until it crashed, losing a third of its value just before Christmas 1994. A month later, the new peso was trading at about six per dollar, and Mexican financial institutions, their dollar debt having nearly doubled in a month, were in danger of defaulting on their obligations to international investors. To stave off a worldwide financial panic, U.S. President Clinton, in February 1995, secured an unprecedented multibillion-dollar loan package for Mexico, guaranteed by U.S. and international institutions.

Although disaster was temporarily averted and Mexico became an overnight bargain for dollar-spending travelers, the cure for the country's ills required another painful round of inflation and belt-tightening for poor Mexicans. During 1995, inflation soared by 52 percent, pushing already-meager wages down an additional 20 percent. More and more families became unable to buy staple foods and basic medicines. Malnutrition soared sixfold, and Third-World diseases, such as cholera and dengue fever, resurged in the countryside.

At the same time, Mexico's equally serious political ills seemed to defy cure. Raul Salinas de Gortari, an important PRI party official and the former president's brother, was arrested for money laundering and political assassination. As popular sentiment began to implicate Carlos Salinas de Gortari himself, the former president fled Mexico to an undisclosed location.

Meanwhile, as negotiations with the rebel Zapatistas sputtered on and off in Chiapas, popular discontent erupted in Guerrero, leading to the massacre of 17 unarmed campesinos at Aguas Blancas, in the hills west of Acapulco, by state police in June 1995. One year later, at a demonstration protesting the massacre, a new, well-armed revolutionary group, **Ejército Popular Revolucionario** (People's Revolutionary Army, or EPR), appeared. A few months later, EPR guerrillas killed two dozen police and soldiers at several locations, mostly in southwestern Mexico. Although President Zedillo's immediate reaction was moderate, platoons of soldiers were soon scouring rural Guerrero, Oaxaca, Michoacán, and other states, searching homes and arresting suspected dissidents. Public response was mostly negative, though some locals felt that they were far better off in the hands of the army rather than those of state or federal police.

Mexican democracy, however, got a boost when notorious Guerrero governor Ruben Figueroa, who had tried to cover up the Aguas Blancas massacre with a bogus videotape, was forced from office. At the same time, the Zedillo government gained momentum in addressing the Zapatistas' grievances in Chiapas, even as it decreased federal military presence, built new rural electrification networks, and refurbished health clinics.

The Political Cauldron Bubbles On

Nevertheless, continued federal military presence, especially in Guerrero, Oaxaca, and Chiapas, seemed to trigger violent incidents. Worst was the massacre of 45 indigenous campesinos, including women and children, at Acteal, Chiapas, in late December 1997 by paramilitary gunmen. Federal investigators later linked the perpetrators to local PRI officials. In mid-1998, the EPR appeared in Ayutla, Guerrero, passing out leaflets to villagers and giving impromptu speeches. Government soldiers responded with repression, violent searches, and torture. Finally, federal troops cornered and killed 11 suspected EPR members in a schoolhouse 50 miles east of Acapulco.

The rough federal army and police searches, arrests, and jailings energized a flurry of political action. Local human rights groups protested unpunished violence, including dozens of homicides over land disputes and bitter local political, economic, and ecological conflicts, especially in rural areas of southern Pacific Mexico.

Fortunately, foreign visitors have been unaffected by such disputes. Along well-traveled highways, in resorts, towns, and sites of tourist interest, foreign visitors to Pacific Mexico are generally much safer than in their home cities in the United States, Canada, or Europe.

Economic Recovery and Political Reforms

The best news for which the Zedillo administration could justly claim credit was the dramatically improving national economy. By 1999, annual inflation had dropped below 15 percent, investment dollars were flowing back into Mexico, the peso had stabilized at about eight to the U.S. dollar, and Mexico had paid back every penny of its borrowed U.S. bailout money.

Moreover, in the political arena, although the justice system left much to be desired, a pair of unprecedented events signaled an increasingly open political system. In the 1997 congressional elections, voters elected a host of opposition candidates, depriving the PRI of an absolute congressional majority for the first time since 1929. A year later, in early 1998, Mexicans had participated in their country's first primary elections—in which voters, instead of politicians, chose party candidates.

Although Zedillo's presidential ride had been rough, he entered the twilight of his 1994–2000 term able to take credit for an improved economy, some genuine political reforms, and relative peace in the countryside. The election of 2000 revealed, however, that the Mexican people were not satisfied.

End of an Era: Vicente Fox Unseats the PRI

During 1998 and 1999 the focal point of opposition to the PRI's three-generation rule had been shifting from lackluster left-of-center Cuauhtémoc Cárdenas of the PRD to relative newcomer Vicente Fox, former President of Coca-Cola Mexico and clean former PAN governor of Guanajuato.

Fox, who had announced his candidacy for president two years before the election, seemed an unlikely challenger. After all, the minority PAN had always been the party of wealthy businessmen and the conservative Catholic right. But blunt-talking, six-foot-five Fox, who sometimes campaigned in *vaquero* boots and a ten-gallon cowboy hat, preached populist themes of coalition building and "inclusion." He backed up his talk by carrying his campaign to hardscrabble city *barrios,* dirt-poor country villages, and traditional outsider groups, such as Jews.

In an orderly, closely monitored election, on July 2, 2000, Fox decisively defeated the PRI candidate Francisco Labastida, 42 percent to 38 percent, while Cárdenas polled a feeble 17 percent. Fox's win also swept a PAN plurality (223/209/57) into the 500-seat Chamber of Deputies lower house (although the Senate remained PRI-dominated).

Nevertheless, in pushing the PRI from the all-powerful presidency after 71 consecutive years of domination, Fox had ushered Mexico into a new, more democratic era.

Despite stinging criticism from his own ranks, President Zedillo, whom historians were already praising as the real hero behind Mexico's new democracy, made an unprecedented early appeal for all Mexicans to unite behind Fox.

On the eve of his December 1, 2000, inauguration, Mexicans awaited Fox's speech with hopeful anticipation. He did not disappoint them. Although acknowledging that he couldn't completely reverse 71 years of PRI entrenchment in his one six-year term, he vowed to ride the crest of reform, revamp the tax system, and reduce poverty by 30 percent by creating a million new jobs a year through new private investment in electricity and oil production and by forming a new common market with Latin America, the United States, and Canada.

He promised, moreover, to secure justice for all by a much-needed reform of police, the federal attorney general, and the army. Potentially most difficult of all, Fox called for the formation of an unprecedented congressional "Transparency Commission" to investigate a generation of past grievances, including the 1968 massacre of stu-

dent demonstrators, and assassinations of, among others, a Roman Catholic cardinal in 1993 and a popular presidential candidate in 1994.

Vicente Fox, President of Mexico

Wasting little time getting started, President Fox first headed to Chiapas to confer with indigenous community leaders. Along the way, he shut down Chiapas army bases and removed dozens of military roadblocks. Back in Mexico City, he sent the long-delayed peace plan, including the indigenous bill of rights, to Congress. Zapatista rebels responded by journeying en masse from Chiapas to Mexico City, where, in their black masks, they addressed Congress, arguing for indigenous rights. Although within a few months, in mid-2001, Congress had passed a modified version of the negotiated settlement, and the majority of states soon ratified the required constitutional amendment, indigenous leaders condemned the legislation as watered down and unacceptable, while proponents claimed it was the best possible compromise between the Zapatistas demands and the existing Mexican constitution.

Meanwhile, Mexico's economy, reflecting the U.S. economic slowdown, soured in 2001, losing half a million jobs and cutting annual growth to a feeble 2.5 percent, down from the 4.5 percent that the government had predicted. Furthermore, a so-called "Towelgate" furor (in which aides had bought dozens of $400 towels for the presidential mansion) weakened Fox's squeaky-clean image.

On the positive side, by mid-2002, Vicente Fox could claim credit for cracking down on corruption and putting drug lords in jail, negotiating a key immigration agreement with the United States, keeping the peso stable, clamping down on inflation, and attracting a record pile of foreign investment dollars.

Furthermore, Fox continued to pry open the door to democracy in Mexico. In May 2002, he signed Mexico's first freedom of information act, entitling citizens to timely copies of all public documents from federal agencies. Moreover, Fox's long-promised "Transparency Commission" was taking shape. In July 2002, federal attorneys were taking unprecedented action. They were questioning a list of 74 former government officials,

© BRUCE WHIPPERMAN

The election of opposition leader President Vicente Fox has led to renewed Mexican political ferment.

including ex-President Luís Echeverría, about their roles in government transgressions, notably political murders and the University of Mexico massacres during the 1960s and 1970s.

On balance, in mid-2002, critics were writing that "Fox still has time" to accomplish what he promised. More significantly, Mexican voters, who eventually will judge Fox's success or failure in the voting booth, are by and large still cheering for Fox. Furthermore, it's important not to forget the prime fact of July 2, 2000: that, in pushing out the PRI after 71 years and cleanly electing an opposition president, Mexicans have taken a crucial, irreversible step in their long journey toward democracy and justice for all.

Economy and Government

THE MEXICAN ECONOMY

Post-Revolutionary Gains

By many measures, Mexico's 20th-century revolution appears to have succeeded. Since 1910, illiteracy has plunged from 80 percent to 10 percent, life expectancy has risen from 30 years to nearly 70, infant mortality has dropped from a whopping 40 percent to about 2 percent, and, in terms of caloric intake, Mexicans are on average eating about twice as much as their forebears at the turn of the 20th century.

Decades of near-continuous economic growth account for rising Mexican living standards. The Mexican economy has rebounded from its last two recessions because of plentiful natural resources, notably oil and metals; diversified manufacturing, such as cars, steel, and petrochemicals; steadily increasing tourism; exports of fruits, vegetables, and cattle; and its large, willing, low-wage workforce.

Recent Mexican governments, moreover, have skillfully exploited Mexico's economic strengths. The Border Industrialization Program has led to millions of jobs in thousands of border maquiladora factories, from Tijuana to the mouth of the Rio Grande. Dependency on oil exports, which led to the 1980s peso collapse, has been sharply reduced. Foreign trade, a strong source for new Mexican jobs, has burgeoned since the 1980s because of liberalized tariffs as Mexico joined General Agreement on Tariffs and Trade (GATT) in 1986 and NAFTA in 1994. As a result, Mexico has become a net exporter of goods and services to the United States, its largest trading partner. Although Mexico suffered a peso collapse of about 50 percent (in relation to the U.S. dollar) in 1995, the Zedillo administration acted quickly. Belt-tightening measures brought inflation, which had initially surged, down to 20 percent per year, and foreign investment flowed back into Mexico by mid-1996. Although some factory and business closures led to increased unemployment in 1995, benefits from the devalued peso, such as increased tourism and burgeoning exports, contributed to a generally improving economy during the 1990s.

In 2001, however, the U.S. economic slowdown decreased demand for Mexican products; consequently, Mexico lost more than half a million jobs, forcing economic growth down to a weak 2.5 percent for 2001. But, fortunately, the slower growth resulted in neither significant inflation nor weakening of the peso.

Long-Term Economic Challenges

Despite huge gains, Mexico's Revolution of 1910 is nevertheless incomplete. Improved public health, education, income, and opportunity have barely outdistanced Mexico's population, which has increased nearly sevenfold—from 15 million to 100 million—between 1910 and 2000. For example, although the illiteracy rate has decreased, the actual number of Mexican people who can't read, about 10 million, has remained about constant since 1910.

Moreover, the land reform program, once thought to be a Mexican cure-all, has long been a disappointment. The *ejidos* of which Emiliano Zapata dreamed have become mostly symbolic. The communal fields are typically small and unirrigated. *Ejido* land, formerly constitutionally prohibited from being sold, has not traditionally served as collateral for bank loans. Capital for irrigation networks, fertilizers, and harvesting machines is consequently lacking. Communal

farms are typically inefficient; the average Mexican field produces about *one-quarter* as much corn per acre as a U.S. farm. Mexico must accordingly use its precious oil dollar surplus to import millions of tons of corn—originally indigenous to Mexico—annually.

The triple scourge of overpopulation, lack of arable land, and low farm income has driven millions of campesino families to seek better lives in Mexico's cities. Since 1910, Mexico has evolved from a largely rural country, where 70 percent of the population lived on farms, to an urban nation where 70 percent of the population lives in cities. Fully one-fifth of Mexico's people now live in Mexico City.

Nevertheless, the future appears bright for many privately owned and managed Mexican farms, concentrated largely in the northern border states. Exceptionally productive, they typically work hundreds or thousands of irrigated acres of crops, such as tomatoes, lettuce, *chiles,* wheat, corn, tobacco, cotton, fruits, alfalfa, chickens, and cattle, just like

© BRUCE WHIPPERMAN

Stonemasonry is still a common trade in Mexico.

their counterparts across the border in California, New Mexico, Arizona, and Texas.

Staples—wheat for bread, corn for tortillas, milk, and cooking oil—are all imported and consequently expensive for the typical working-class Mexican family, which must spend half or more of its income (typically $500 per month) for food. Recent inflation has compounded the problem, particularly for the millions of families on the bottom half of Mexico's economic ladder.

Although average gross domestic product figures for Mexico—about $8,000 per capita compared to more than $30,000 for the United States—place it above nearly all other Third-World countries, averages, when applied to Mexico, mean little. A primary socioeconomic reality of Mexican history remains: the richest one-fifth of Mexican families earns about 10 times the income of the poorest one-fifth. A relative handful of people own a large hunk of Mexico, and they don't seem inclined to share any of it with the less fortunate. As for the poor, the typical Mexican family in the bottom one-third income bracket often owns neither car nor refrigerator, and the children typically do not finish elementary school.

GOVERNMENT AND POLITICS

The Constitution of 1917

Mexico's governmental system is rooted in the Constitution of 1917, which incorporated many of the features of its reformist predecessor of 1857. The 1917 document, with amendments, remains in force. Although drafted at the behest of conservative revolutionary Venustiano Carranza by his handpicked Querétaro *"Constitucionalista"* congress, it was greatly influenced by Alvaro Obregón and generally ignored by Carranza during his subsequent three-year presidential term.

Although many articles resemble those of its United States model, the Constitution of 1917 contains provisions developed directly from Mexican experience. Article 27 addresses the question of land. Private property rights are qualified by societal need; subsoil rights are public property,

and foreigners and corporations are severely restricted in land ownership. Although the 1917 constitution declared *ejido* (communal) land inviolate, 1994 amendments allow, under certain circumstances, the sale or use of communal land as loan security.

Article 23 severely restricts church powers. In declaring that "places of worship are the property of the nation," it stripped churches of all title to real estate, without compensation. Article 5 and Article 130 banned religious orders, expelled foreign clergy, and denied priests and ministers all political rights, including voting, holding office, and even criticizing the government.

Article 123 establishes the rights of labor: to organize, bargain collectively, strike, work a maximum eight-hour day, and receive a minimum wage. Women are to receive equal pay for equal work and be given a month's paid leave for childbearing. Article 123 also establishes social security plans for sickness, unemployment, pensions, and death.

On paper, Mexico's constitutional government structures appear much like their U.S. prototypes: a federal presidency, a two-house Congress, and a Supreme Court, with their counterparts in each of the 32 states. Political parties field candidates, and all citizens vote by secret ballot.

Mexico's presidents, however, have traditionally enjoyed greater powers than their U.S. counterparts. They need not seek legislative approval for many cabinet appointments, can suspend constitutional rights under a state of siege, can initiate legislation, veto all or parts of bills, refuse to execute laws, and replace state officers. The federal government, moreover, retains nearly all taxing authority, relegating the states to a role of merely administering federal programs.

Although ideally providing for separation of powers, the Constitution of 1917 subordinates both the legislative and judicial branches, with the courts being the weakest of all. The Supreme Court, for example, can only, with repeated deliberation, decide upon the constitutionality of legislation. Five separate individuals must file successful petitions for writs *amparo* (protection) on a single point of law in order to affect constitutional precedent.

Democratizing Mexican Politics

Reforms in Mexico's stable but top-heavy "Institutional Revolution" came only gradually. Characteristically, street protests were brutally put down at first, with officials only later working to address grievances. Generations of dominance by the PRI led to widespread cynicism and citizen apathy. Regardless of who gets elected, the typical person on the street would tell you that the officeholder was bound to retire with his or her pockets full.

Nevertheless, by 1985, movement toward more justice and pluralism seemed be in store for Mexico. During the subsequent dozen years, minority parties increasingly elected candidates to state and federal office. Although none captured a majority of any state legislature, the strongest non-PRI parties, such as the conservative pro-Catholic Partido Acción Nacional (PAN) or National Action Party and the liberal-left Partido Revolucionario Democratico (PRD), elected governors. In 1986, minority parties were given federal legislative seats, up to a maximum of 20, for winning a minimum of 2.5 percent of the national presidential vote. In the 1994 election, minority parties received public campaign financing, depending upon their fraction of the vote.

After his 1994 inaugural address, in which he called loudly and clearly for more reforms, President Ernesto Zedillo quickly began to produce results. He immediately appointed a respected member of the PAN opposition party as attorney general—the first non-PRI cabinet appointment in Mexican history. Other Zedillo firsts were federal Senate confirmation of both Supreme Court nominees and the attorney general, multiparty participation in the Chiapas peace negotiations, and congressional approval of the 1995 financial assistance package received from the United States. Zedillo, moreover, organized a series of precedent-setting meetings with opposition leaders that led to a written pact for political reform and the establishment of permanent working groups to discuss political and economic questions.

Perhaps most important was Zedillo's campaign and inaugural vow to separate both his government and himself from PRI decision-making. He kept his promise, becoming the first Mexican president, in as long as anyone could remember, who did not choose his successor.

A New Mexican Revolution

Finally, in 2000, like a Mexican Gorbachev, Ernesto Zedillo, the man most responsible for Mexico's recent democratic reforms, watched as PAN opposition reformer Vicente Fox swept Zedillo's PRI from the presidency after a 71-year rule. Moreover, despite severe criticism from his own party, Zedillo quickly called for the country to close ranks behind Fox. Millions of Mexicans, still dazed but buoyed by Zedillo's statesmanship and Fox's epoch-making victory, eagerly awaited Fox's inauguration address on December 1, 2000.

He promised nothing less than a new revolution for Mexico and backed it up with concrete proposals: reduce poverty by 30 percent with a million new jobs a year from revitalized new electricity and oil production, a Mexican Silicon Valley, and free trade between Mexico, all of Latin America, and the United States and Canada. He promised justice for all, through a reformed police, army, and the judiciary. He promised conciliation and an agreement with the Zapatista rebel movement in the south, including a bill of rights for Mexico's native peoples. With all of Mexico listening, Fox brought his speech to a hopeful conclusion: "If I had to summarize my message today in one sentence, I would say: Today Mexico has a future, but we have lost much time and wasted many resources. Mexico has a future, and we must build that future starting today."

People

Let a broad wooden chopping block represent Mexico; imagine hacking it with a sharp cleaver until it is grooved and pocked. That fractured surface resembles Mexico's central highlands, where most Mexicans, divided from each other by high mountains and yawning *barrancas,* have lived since before history.

The Mexicans' deep divisions, in large measure, led to their downfall at the hands of the Spanish conquistadores. The Aztec empire that Hernán Cortés conquered was a vast but fragmented collection of tribes. Speaking more than 100 mutually alien languages, those original Mexicans viewed each other suspiciously, as barely human barbarians from strange lands beyond the mountains. And even today the lines Mexicans draw between themselves—of caste, class, race, wealth—are the result, to a significant degree, of the realities of their mutual isolation.

POPULATION

The Spanish colonial government and the Roman Catholic religion provided the glue that through 400 years has welded Mexico's fragmented people into a burgeoning nation-state. Mexico's population, more than 100 million by the year 2000, increased during the '90s, but at a rate diminished to about half that of previous decades. Increased birth control and emigration largely account for the slowdown.

Mexico's population has not always been increasing. Historians estimate that European diseases, largely measles and smallpox, wiped out as many as 25 million—perhaps 95 percent—of the *indígena* population within a few generations after Cortés stepped ashore in 1519. The Mexican population dwindled from an estimated 20 million at the eve of the conquest to a mere one million inhabitants by 1600. It wasn't until 1950, four centuries after Cortés, that Mexico's population recovered to its preconquest level of 20 million.

Mestizos, Indígenas, Criollos, and African Mexicans

Although by 1950 Mexico's population had recovered, it was completely transformed. The mestizo, a Spanish-speaking person of mixed blood, had replaced the pure Native American, the *indígena* (een-DEE-hay-nah), as the typical Mexican.

The trend continues. Perhaps three of four Mexicans would identify themselves as mestizo: that class whose part-European blood elevates them, in the Mexican mind, to the level of *gente de razón* (people of reason or right). And there's the rub. The *indígenas* (or, mistakenly but much more commonly, Indians), by the usual measurements of income, health, or education, squat at the bottom of the Mexican social ladder.

The typical *indígena* family lives in a small adobe house in a remote valley, subsisting on corn, beans, and vegetables from its small, unirrigated milpa (cornfield). They usually have chickens, a few pigs, and sometimes a cow, but no electricity; their few hundred dollars a year in cash income isn't enough to buy even a small refrigerator, much less a truck.

The usual mestizo family, on the other hand, enjoys most of the benefits of the 20th century. They typically own a modest concrete house in town. Their furnishings, simple by developed-world standards, will often include an electric refrigerator, washing machine, propane stove, television, and car or truck. The children go to school every day, and the eldest son sometimes looks forward to college.

Sizable *negro* communities, descendants of 18th-century African slaves, live in the Gulf states and along the Guerrero-Oaxaca Pacific coastline. Last to arrive, the *negros* experience discrimination at the hands of everyone else and are integrating very slowly into the mestizo mainstream.

Above the mestizos, a tiny criollo (Mexican-born white) minority, a few percent of the total population, inherits the privileges—wealth, education, and political power—of its colonial Spanish ancestors.

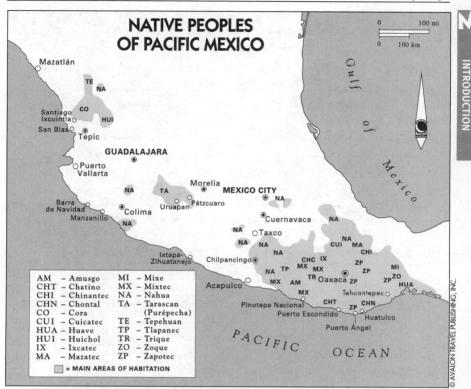

NATIVE PEOPLES OF PACIFIC MEXICO

AM	– Amusgo	MI	– Mixe
CHT	– Chatino	MX	– Mixtec
CHI	– Chinantec	NA	– Nahua
CHN	– Chontal	TA	– Tarascan
CO	– Cora		(Purépecha)
CUI	– Cuicatec	TE	– Tepehuan
HUA	– Huave	TP	– Tlapanec
HUI	– Huichol	TR	– Trique
IX	– Ixcatec	ZO	– Zoque
MA	– Mazatec	ZP	– Zapotec

= MAIN AREAS OF HABITATION

© AVALON TRAVEL PUBLISHING, INC.

THE INDÍGENAS

Although anthropologists and census takers classify them according to language groups (such as Náhuatl, Mixtec, and Zapotec), *indígenas* generally identify themselves as residents of a particular locality rather than by language or ethnic grouping. And although, as a group, they are referred to as *indígenas* (native, or aboriginal), individuals are generally uncomfortable at being labeled as such.

While the mestizos are the emergent self-conscious majority class, the *indígenas,* as during colonial times, remain the invisible people of Mexico. They are politically conservative, socially traditional, and tied to the land. On market day, the typical *indígena* family might make the trip into town. They bag tomatoes, squash, or peppers, and tie up a few chickens or a pig. The rickety country bus will often be full and the

mestizo driver may wave them away, giving preference to his friends, leaving them to trudge stoically along the road.

Their lot, nevertheless, has been slowly improving. *Indígena* families now almost always have access to a local school and a clinic. Improved health has led to a large increase in their population. Official census figures, however, are probably low. *Indígenas* are traditionally suspicious of government people, and census takers, however conscientious, seldom speak the local language.

Recent figures, however, indicate 8 percent of Mexicans are *indígenas*—that is, they speak one of Mexico's 50-odd native languages. Of these, a quarter speak no Spanish at all. These fractions are changing only slowly. Many *indígenas* prefer the old ways. If present trends continue, the year 2019, 500 years after the

INDIGENOUS POPULATIONS OF PACIFIC MEXICO

For the Pacific Mexico states (from north to south) the 2000 government census totals were:

State	Indigenous Population (over five years of age)	Total Population (over five years of age)	Percent of Total
Sinaloa	49,700	2,130,000	2.3
Nayarit	37,200	769,000	4.8
Jalisco	39,300	5,323,000	0.7
Colima	2,900	421,000	0.7
Michoacán	121,800	3,342,000	3.6
Guerrero	367,100	2,572,000	14.3
Oaxaca	1,120,300	2,924,000	38.3

The same government sources tabulate indigenous peoples by language groupings. Although such figures are probably low, the 2000 figures revealed significant populations in many local areas:

Language Group	Population	Important Centers
Tepuan	17,000	Sinaloa-Durango
Cora	15,600	Nayarit (Acaponeta)
Huichol	27,900	Nayarit-Jalisco (Santiago Ixcuintla, Huejuqilla)
Nahua	8,100	Jalisco (Ciudad Guzmán)
Tarasco	114,000	Michoacán (Pátzcuaro)
Nahua	160,000	Guerrero (Taxco and Chilpancingo)
Mixtec	363,000	Western Oaxaca (Huajuapan, Tlaxiaco, and Santiago Jamíltepec)
Tlapanec	93,000	Eastern Guerrero (Tlapa de Comonfort)
Amusgo	40,000	Oaxaca-Guerrero (San Pedro Amusgos and Xochistlahuaca)
Chinantec	107,000	Northern Oaxaca (Valle Nacional)
Chatino	40,000	Southern Oaxaca (Santos Reyes Nopala)
Zapotec	380,000	Central, Eastern, and Southern Oaxaca (Tlacolula, Ocotlán, Tehuántepec)
Chontal	5,000	Southeastern Oaxaca (Santiago Astata)
Trique	16,000	Western Oaxaca (Juxtlahuaca)
Chocho	1,000	Northwestern Oaxaca (Coixtlahuaca)
Cuicatec	12,000	Northern Oaxaca (Cuicatlán)
Huave	14,000	Southeastern Oaxaca (San Mateo del Mar)
Mazatec	175,000	Northern Oaxaca (Huatla de Jiménez)
Mixe	106,000	Northeastern Oaxaca (Ayutla)
Zoque	5,000	Southeastern Oaxaca (San Miguel Chimalapa)
Ixcatec	1,000	Northwestern Oaxaca (Ixcatlán)

Spanish arrival, will mark the return of the Mexican indigenous population to the pre-conquest level of 20 million.

Indígena Language Groups

The Maya speakers of Yucatán and the aggregate of the Náhuatl (Aztec language) speakers of the central plateau are Mexico's most numerous *indígena* groups, totaling roughly three million (one million Maya, two million Náhuatl).

Indigenous population centers, relatively scattered in the north of Pacific Mexico, concentrate in the southern states of Guerrero and Oaxaca. The groups are not evenly spread, however. The language map of Oaxaca, for example, looks like a crazy quilt, with important Zapotec, Mixtec, and other centers scattered along the coast and through the mountains surrounding Oaxaca city.

Dress

Maps and figures, however, cannot describe the color of a fiesta or market day. Many country people, especially in Oaxaca, still wear the traditional cottons that blend Spanish and native styles. Men usually wear the Spanish-origin straw sombrero (literally, shade-maker) on their heads, baggy white cotton shirt and pants, and leather huaraches on their feet. Women's dress is often more colorful. It can include a *huipil* (long, sleeveless dress), often embroidered in bright floral and animal motifs, and a handwoven *enredo* (wraparound skirt that identifies the wearer with a particular locality). A *faja* (waist sash) and, in the winter, a *quechquémitl* (shoulder cape) complete the ensemble.

RELIGION

"God and Gold" was the two-pronged mission of the conquistadores. Most of them concentrated on gold, while missionaries tried to shift the emphasis to God. They were famously successful; more than 90 percent of Mexicans profess to be Catholics.

Catholicism, spreading its doctrine of equality of all persons before God and incorporating native gods into the church rituals, eventually brought the *indígenas* into the fold. Within 100 years, nearly all native Mexicans had accepted

Mexicans honor their indigenous heritage by donning *traje* (ancestral tribal dress) for the festival of the Virgin of Guadalupe.

© BRUCE WHIPPERMAN

the new religion, which raised the universal God of humankind over local tribal deities.

The Virgin of Guadalupe

Conversion of the *indígenas* was sparked by the vision of Juan Diego, a humble farmer. On the hill of Tepayac north of Mexico City in 1531, Juan Diego saw a brown-skinned version of the Virgin Mary enclosed in a dazzling aura of light. She told him to build a shrine in her memory on that spot, where the Aztecs had long worshipped their "earth mother," Tonantzín. Juan Diego's brown virgin told him to go to the cathedral and relay her instruction to Archbishop Zumárraga.

The archbishop, as expected, turned his nose up at Juan Diego's story. The vision returned, however, and this time Juan Diego's brown virgin realized that a miracle was necessary. She ordered him to pick some roses at the spot where she had first appeared to him (a true miracle, since roses had been previously unknown in the vicinity) and take them to the archbishop. Juan Diego wrapped the roses in his rude fiber cape, returned to the cathedral, and placed the wrapped roses at the archbishop's feet. When he opened the offering, Zumárraga gasped: imprinted on the cape was an image of the brown virgin herself—proof positive of a genuine miracle.

In the centuries since Juan Diego, the brown virgin—La Virgen Morena, or Nuestra Señora La Virgen de Guadalupe—has blended native and Catholic elements into something uniquely Mexican. In doing so, she has become the virtual patroness of Mexico, the beloved symbol of Mexico for *indígenas*, mestizos, *negros,* and criollos alike.

In the summer of 2002, Pope John Paul journeyed to Mexico to perform a historically momentous gesture. Before millions of joyous faithful, on July 31, 2002, the frail aging pontiff elevated Juan Diego to sainthood, thus making him Latin America's first indigenous person to be so honored.

Every Mexican town and village celebrates the cherished memory of the Virgin of Guadalupe on December 12. This celebration, however joyful, is but one of the many fiestas that Mexicans, especially the *indígenas,* live for. Each village holds its local fiesta in honor of its patron saint, who is often a thinly veiled sit-in for a local preconquest deity. Themes appear Spanish—Christian vs. Moors, devils vs. priests—but the native element is strong, sometimes dominant. During Semana Santa (Holy Week) at Pinotepa Nacional in coastal Oaxaca, for example, Mixtec people, costumed as Jews, shoot arrows skyward, simultaneously reciting traditional Mixtec prayers.

On the Road

BEACHES

It's easy to understand why many Pacific Mexico vacationers stay right at the beach. And not just at the famous crystalline stretches of Mazatlán, Puerto Vallarta, Manzanillo, Ixtapa, Acapulco, and Puerto Escondido. Many flee the big resorts and spread out along the whole coast—gathering at small beach hideaways such as San Blas, Rincón de Guayabitos, Cuyutlán, Playa Azul, Troncones, Pie de la Cuesta, and Puerto Ángel—while others set up camp and enjoy the solitude and rich wildlife of hundreds of miles of even more pristine strands. Shorelines vary from mangrove-edged lagoons and algae-decorated tidepools to shoals of pebbles and sand of dozens of colors and consistencies.

Sand makes the beach—and Pacific Mexico has plenty—from warm, black mica dust to cool, velvety white coral. Some beaches drop steeply to turbulent, close-in surf, fine for fishing. Others are level, with gentle, rolling breakers, made for surfing and swimming.

Beaches are fascinating for the surprises they yield. Pacific Mexico's beaches, especially the hidden strands near resorts and the hundreds of

Drive on sand sparingly, and only with four-wheel drive.

© BRUCE WHIPPERMAN

miles of wilderness beaches and tidepools, yield troves of shells and treasures of flotsam and jetsam for those who enjoy looking for them. Beachcombing is more rewarding during the summer storm season, when big waves deposit acres of fresh shells—among them conch, scallop, clams, combs of Venus, whelks, limpets, olives, cowries, starfish, and sand dollars.

During the summer-fall rainy season, beaches near rivermouths are often fantastic outdoor galleries of wind- and water-sculpted snags and giant logs deposited by the downstream flood.

Viewing Wildlife

Wildlife watchers should keep quiet and always be on the alert. Animal survival depends on their seeing you first. Occasional spectacular offshore sights, such as whales, porpoises, and manta rays, or an onshore giant constrictor, beached squid or octopus, crocodile, or even a jaguar looking for turtle eggs are the reward of those prepared to recognize them. Don't forget your binoculars and Steve Howell's *Bird-Finding Guide to Mexico* (see Suggested Reading).

(For extensive notes on good hiking, tidepooling, wildlife-viewing, and shell-browsing spots, see the destination chapters.)

WATER SPORTS

Swimming, surfing, sailboarding, snorkeling, scuba diving, kayaking, sailing, and personal watercraft riding are Pacific Mexico's water sports of choice. (For details on local favorite spots, conditions, rental shops, and equipment, see the destination chapters.)

Safety First

Viewed from Pacific Mexico beaches, the Pacific Ocean usually lives up to its name. Many protected inlets, safe for child's play, dot the coastline. Unsheltered shorelines, on the other hand, can be deceiving. Smooth water in the calm forenoon often changes to choppy in the afternoon; calm ripples that lap the shore in March can grow to hurricane-driven walls of water in November. Such storms can wash away sand, temporarily changing a wide, gently sloping beach into a steep one plagued by turbulent waves and treacherous currents.

Undertow, whirlpools, cross-currents, and occasional oversized waves can make ocean swimming a fast-lane adventure. Getting unexpectedly swept out to sea or hammered onto the beach bottom by a surprise breaker are potential hazards.

Never attempt serious swimming when tipsy or full of food; never swim alone where someone can't see you. Always swim beyond big breakers (which come in sets of several, climaxed by a huge one, which breaks highest and farthest from the beach). If you happen to get caught in the path of such a wave, avoid it by *diving directly toward and under it*, letting it roll harmlessly over you. If you are unavoidably swept up in a whirling, crashing breaker, try to roll and tumble with it, as football players tumble, to avoid injury.

Look out for other irritations and hazards. Now and then swimmers get a nettlelike (but usually harmless) jellyfish sting. Be careful around coral reefs and beds of sea urchins; corals can sting (like jellyfish) and you can additionally get infections from coral cuts and sea-urchin spines. *Shuffle* along sandy bottoms to scare away stingrays before stepping on one. If you're unlucky, its venomous tail-spines may inflict a painful wound. (See Health Problems in the Health and Safety section for first-aid measures.)

Snorkeling and Scuba Diving

Many exciting clear-water sites, such as Puerto Vallarta's Los Arcos, Manzanillo's Bahía Santiago, Zihuatanejo's Playa Las Gatas, Isla Roqueta at Acapulco, and Playa Estacahuite at Puerto Ángel, await both beginner and expert scuba divers. Veteran Pacific Mexico divers usually arrive during the dry winter and early spring when river outflows are mere trickles, leaving offshore waters clear. In the major tourist centers, professional dive shops rent equipment, provide lessons and guides, and transport divers to choice sites.

While convenient, rented equipment is often less than satisfactory. To be sure, serious divers bring their own gear. This should probably include wetsuits in the winter, when many swimmers begin to feel cold after an unprotected half-hour in the water.

Surfing, Sailing, Sailboarding, and Kayaking

In addition to several well-known surfing beaches, such as Matanchén at San Blas, Puerto Vallarta's Punta Mita, and Barra de Nexpa south of Manzanillo, Pacific Mexico has the country's acknowledged best surfing beach—the Playa Zicatela "pipeline" at Puerto Escondido.

The surf everywhere is highest and best during the July–Nov. hurricane season, when big swells from storms far out at sea attract platoons of surfers to favored beaches (except at crowded Acapulco Bay, where surfing is off-limits).

Sailboarders, sailboaters, and kayakers—who, by contrast, require more tranquil waters—do best in the Pacific Mexico winter or early spring. Then they gather to enjoy the near-ideal conditions at many coves and inlets near the big resorts.

While beginners can have fun with the equipment available from rental shops, serious surfers, sailboarders, sailboaters, and kayakers should pack their own gear.

POWER SPORTS

Acapulco and other big resorts have long been centers for water-skiing, parasailing, and personal watercraft riding. In parasailing, a motorboat pulls while a parachute lifts you, like a soaring gull, high over the ocean. After 5 or 10 minutes it deposits you—usually gently—back on the sand.

Jet Ski boats ("wave-runners" or personal watercraft) are like snowmobiles except that they operate on water, where, with a little practice, beginners can quickly learn to whiz over the waves.

Although the luxury resort hotels generally provide experienced crews and equipment, crowded conditions increase the hazard to both participants and swimmers. You, as the patron, are paying plenty for the privilege; you have a right to expect that your providers and crew are well-equipped, sober, and cautious.

Beach Buggies and ATVs

Some visitors enjoy racing along the beach and rolling over dunes in beach buggies and ATVs (all-terrain vehicles—*motos* in Mexico), balloon-tired, three-wheeled motor scooters. While certain resort rental agencies cater to the growing use of

© BRUCE WHIPPERMAN

Surfing conditions are fine on many Pacific Mexico beaches, as this San Blas cartoon illustrates.

ON THE ROAD

such vehicles, limits are in order. Of all the pro-liferating high-horsepower beach pastimes, these are the most intrusive. Noise, exhaust, and gasoline pollution, injuries to operators and bystanders, and the scattering of wildlife and destruction of their habitats have led (and I hope will continue to lead) to the restriction of dune buggies and ATVs on beaches.

TENNIS AND GOLF

Most Mexicans are working too hard to be playing much tennis and golf. Although there are almost no public courses or courts, Pacific Mexico's resort centers enjoy excellent private facilities. If you are planning on a lot of golf and tennis, check into (or inquire about court rental at) one of the many hotels with these facilities. Use of hotel tennis courts is often, but not always, included in your hotel tariff. If not, fees will run about $10 per hour. Golf greens fees, which begin at about $50 for 18 holes, are always extra.

(See the destination chapters for plenty of golf and tennis listings.)

FISHING AND HUNTING

Experts agree Pacific Mexico is a world-class deep-sea and surf fishing ground. Sportspeople routinely bring in dozens of species from among the more than 600 that have been hooked in Pacific Mexico waters.

Surf Fishing

Most good fishing beaches away from the immediate resort areas will typically have only a few locals (mostly with nets) and fewer visitors. Mexicans typically do little sportfishing. Most either make their living from fishing, or they do none at all. Consequently, few shops sell sportfishing equipment in Mexico; plan to bring your own surf-fishing equipment, including hooks, lures, line, and weights.

Your best general information source before you leave home is a good local bait-and-tackle shop. Tell the folks there where you're going, and they'll often know the best lures and bait to use and what fish you can expect to catch with them.

In any case, the cleaner the water, the more in-

FISH

A bounty of fish darts, swarms, jumps, and wriggles in Pacific Mexico's surf, reefs, lagoons, and offshore depths. While many make delicious dinners (albacore, red snapper, pompano), others are tough (sailfish), bony (bonefish), and even poisonous (puffers). Some grow to half-ton giants (marlin, jewfish), while others are diminutive reef-grazers (parrot fish, damselfish, angelfish) whose bright colors delight snorkelers and divers. Here's a sampling of what you might find underwater or on your dinner plate.

albacore *(albacora, atún):* 2–4 feet in size; blue; found in deep waters; excellent taste

angelfish *(ángel):* one foot; yellow, orange, blue; reef fish*

barracuda *(barracuda, picuda):* two feet; brown; deep waters; good taste

black marlin *(marlin negro):* six feet; blue-black; deep waters; good taste

blue marlin *(marlin azul):* eight feet; blue; deep waters; poor taste

bobo *(barbudo):* one foot; blue, yellow; found in surf; fair taste

bonefish *(macabi):* one foot; blue or silver; found inshore; poor taste

bonito *(bonito):* two feet; black; deep waters; good taste

butterfly fish *(muñeca):* six inches; black, yellow; reef fish*

chub *(chopa):* one foot; gray; reef fish; good taste

croaker *(corvina):* two feet; brownish; found along inshore bottoms; rare and protected

damselfish *(castañeta):* four inches; brown, blue, orange; reef fish*

dolphinfish, mahimahi *(dorado):* three feet; green, gold; deep waters; good taste

grouper *(garropa):* three feet; brown, rust; found offshore and in reefs; good taste

grunt *(burro):* eight inches; black, gray; found in rocks, reefs*

jack *(toro):* 1–2 feet; bluish-gray; offshore; good taste

mackerel *(sierra):* two feet; gray with gold spots; offshore; good taste

teresting your catch. On a good day, your reward might be *sierras, cabrillas,* porgies, or pompanos pulled from the Pacific Mexico surf.

You can't have everything, however. Foreigners cannot legally take Mexican abalone, coral, lobster, clams, rock bass, sea fans, shrimp, turtles, or seashells. Neither are they supposed to buy them directly from fishermen.

Deep-Sea Fishing
Mazatlán and Manzanillo are renowned spots for the big prize marlin and sailfish, while Zihuatanejo and Acapulco run close behind.

A deep-sea boat charter generally includes the boat and crew for a full or half day, plus equipment and bait for 2–6 people, not including food or drinks. The full-day price depends upon the season. Around Christmas and New Year and before Easter (when reservations will be mandatory) a boat can run $400 and up at Mazatlán or Manzanillo. At lesser-known resorts, or even at the big resorts during low season, you might be able to bargain a captain down to as low as $200.

Renting an entire big boat is not the only choice. Winter business is sometimes so brisk at resorts that agencies can make reservations for individuals for about $60 per person per day.

Pangas, outboard launches seating 2–6 passengers, are available for as little as $50, depending on the season. Once in Barra de Navidad six of my friends hired a *panga* for $50, had a great time, and came back with a boatload of big tuna, jack, and mackerel. A restaurant cooked them as a banquet for a dozen of us in exchange for the extra fish, and I discovered for the first time how heavenly fresh *sierra veracruzana* can taste.

Bringing Your Own Boat
If you're going to do lots of fishing, your own boat may be your most flexible and economical option. One big advantage is you can go to the many excellent fishing grounds that the charter boats do not frequent. Keep your equipment simple, scout around, and keep your eyes peeled and ears open for local regulations and customs, plus tide, wind, and fish-edibility information.

mullet *(lisa):* two feet; gray; found in sandy bays; good taste

needlefish *(agujón):* three feet; blue-black; deep waters; good taste

Pacific porgy *(pez de pluma):* 1–2 feet; tan; found along sandy shores; good taste

parrot fish *(perico, pez loro):* one foot; green, pink, blue, orange; reef fish*

pompano *(pómpano):* one foot; gray; inshore bottoms; excellent taste

puffer *(botete):* eight inches; brown; inshore; poisonous

red snapper *(huachinango, pargo):* 1–2 feet; reddish pink; deep waters; excellent taste

roosterfish *(pez gallo):* three feet; black, blue; deep waters; excellent taste

sailfish *(pez vela):* five feet; blue-black; deep waters; poor taste

sardine *(sardina):* eight inches; blue-black; offshore; good taste

sea bass *(cabrilla):* 1–2 feet; brown, ruddy; reef and rock crevices; good taste

shark *(tiburón):* 2–10 feet; black to blue; in- and offshore; good taste

snook *(robalo):* 2–3 feet; black-brown; found in brackish lagoons; excellent taste

spadefish *(chambo):* one foot; black-silver; found along sandy bottoms; reef fish*

swordfish *(pez espada):* five feet; black to blue; deep waters; good taste

triggerfish *(pez puerco):* 1–2 feet; blue, rust, brown, black; reef fish; excellent taste

wahoo *(peto, guahu):* 2–5 feet; green to blue; deep waters; excellent taste

yellowfin tuna *(atún amarilla):* 2–5 feet; blue, yellow; deep waters; excellent taste

yellowtail *(jurel):* 2–4 feet; blue, yellow; offshore; excellent taste

*generally too small to be considered edible

Fishing Licenses and Boat Permits

Anyone 16 or older who is either fishing or riding in a fishing boat in Mexico is required to have a fishing license. Although Mexican fishing licenses are obtainable from certain travel and insurance agents or at government fishing offices everywhere along the coast, save yourself time and trouble by getting both your fishing licenses and boat permits by mail ahead of time from the Mexican Department of Fisheries (Oficina de Pesca). Call at least a month before departure (tel. 619/233-6956, fax 619/233-0344) and ask for applications and the fees (which are reasonable but depend upon the period of validity and the fluctuating exchange rate). On the application, fill in the names (exactly as they appear on passports) of the people requesting licenses. Include a cashier's check or a money order for the exact amount, along with a stamped, self-addressed envelope. Address the application to the Mexican Department of Fisheries (Oficina de Pesca), 2550 5th Ave., Suite 101, San Diego, CA 92103-6622.

Hunting and Freshwater Fishing

Much game, especially winter-season waterfowl and doves, is customarily hunted in freshwater reservoirs and coastal brackish marshes in Sinaloa, Pacific Mexico's northernmost state. Some of the most popular hunting and fishing reservoirs are **Dominguez** and **Hidalgo,** near colonial El Fuerte town (an hour northeast of Los Mochis). Farther south, just north of Culiacán, is reservoir **López Mateos,** while farther south is **Comedero,** a lake about two hours by car north of Mazatlán, or six hours north of Tepic.

Bag limits and seasons for game are carefully controlled by the government Secretary of Social Development (Secretaría de Desarrollo Social), SEDESOL. It and the Mexican consular service jointly issue the various required permits through a time-consuming and costly procedure, which, at minimum, runs months and hundreds of dollars. For more details on Mexican hunting regulations and permits, consult the AAA (American Automobile Association) *Mexico TravelBook* (see Suggested Reading).

Private fee agencies are a must to complete the mountain of required paperwork. Among the most experienced is the **Mexico Advisory Services,** P.O. Box 76132, Los Angeles, CA 90076, tel. 213/385-9311, fax 213/385-0782, www.mexicoadvisoryservices.com.

For additional help, including useful hunting and fishing details, many travel tips, sites, lodges, and RV parks throughout Mexico, get a copy of Sanborn's *Recreational Guide to Mexico,* published by Sanborn's insurance agency ($12 including postage and handling). Order with credit card by calling tel. 956/686-3601 or tel. 800/222-0158 or by writing P.O. Box 310, McAllen, TX 78502. For more information, see www.sanbornsinsurance.com.

BULLFIGHTING

It is said there are two occasions for which Mexicans arrive on time: funerals and bullfights.

Bullfighting is a recreation, not a sport. The bull is outnumbered seven to one and the outcome is never in doubt. Even if the matador (literally, killer) fails in his duty, his assistants will entice the bull away and slaughter it in private beneath the stands.

La Corrida de Toros

Moreover, Mexicans don't call it a "bullfight"; it's the *corrida de toros,* during which six bulls are customarily slaughtered, beginning at 5 P.M. (4 in the winter). After the beginning parade, featuring the matador and his helpers, the picadores and the banderilleros, the first bull rushes into the ring in a cloud of dust. Clockwork *tercios* (thirds) define the ritual: the first, the *puyazos,* or "stabs," requires that two picadores on horseback thrust lances into the bull's shoulders, weakening it. During the second *tercio,* the banderilleros dodge the bull's horns to stick three long, streamered darts into its shoulders.

Trumpets announce the third *tercio* and the appearance of the matador. The bull—weak, confused, and angry—is ready for the finish. The matador struts, holding the red cape, daring the bull to charge. Form now becomes everything. The expert matador takes complete control of the bull, which rushes at the cape, past its ramrod-erect opponent. For charge after charge, the matador works the bull to exactly the right spot in the ring—in front of the judges, a lovely señorita, or perhaps the governor—where the matador mercifully delivers the precision *estocada* (killing sword thrust) deep into the drooping neck of the defeated bull.

Benito Juárez, as governor during the 1850s, outlawed bullfights in Oaxaca. In his honor, they remain so, making Oaxaca unique among Mexican states.

Festivals and Events

Mexicans love a party. Urban families watch the calendar for midweek national holidays that create a *puente* or "bridge" to the weekend and allow them to squeeze in a three- to five-day minivacation. Visitors should likewise watch the calendar. Such holidays (especially Christmas and Semana Santa, pre-Easter week) mean packed buses, roads, and hotels, especially around Pacific Mexico's beach resorts.

Country people, on the other hand, await their local saint's or holy day. The name of the locality often provides the clue. For example, in Santa Cruz del Miramar near San Blas, expect a celebration on May 3, El Día de la Santa Cruz (Day of the Holy Cross). People dress up in their traditional best, sell their wares and produce in a street fair, join a procession, get tipsy, and dance in the plaza.

FIESTAS

The following calendar lists national and notable Pacific Mexico holidays and festivals. Dates may vary. If you want to attend a specific local fiesta, first contact a local travel agent or tourism bureau for information. (But, if you happen to be where one of these is going on, get out of your car or bus and join in!)

Jan. 1: **¡Feliz Año Nuevo!** (New Year's Day; national holiday).

Jan. 1–5: **Inauguration** of the Cora governor in Jesús María, Nayarit (Cora indigenous dances and ceremonies).

Jan. 6: **Día de los Reyes** (Day of the Kings; traditional gift exchange).

Jan. 12: **Día de Nuestra Señora de Guadalupe** in El Tuito, Jalisco, an hour's drive south of Puerto Vallarta (Festival of the Virgin of Guadalupe; parade, music, evening Mass, and carnival).

Jan. 13–17: **Fiesta of the Sweet Name of Jesus** (Dulce Nombre de Jesús), in Santa Ana del Valle, Tlacolula, and Zimatlán, Oaxaca. Troupes perform many traditional dances, including the Dance of the Feathers.

Jan. 20–21: **Fiesta de San Sebastián,** especially in San Sebastián del Oeste (near Puerto Vallarta), Jalisco, and Pedro y San Pablo Tequixtepec, Pinotepa Don Luis, and Jalapa de Díaz, Oaxaca.

Jan. 23–Feb. 2: **Fiesta de la Virgen de la Salud** in Colima, Colima; processions, food, dancing, and fireworks.

Feb. 1–3: **Festival of the Sea** in San Blas, Nayarit (dancing, horse races, and competitions).

Feb. 2: **Día de Candelaria** (blessing of plants, seeds, and candles; procession; and bullfights).

Feb. 7–23: **Fiesta de Villa Alvarez** (in Colima, Colima; bullfights, rodeos, and carnivals).

February: During the four days before Ash Wednesday, usually in late February, many towns and villages (most famously Mazatlán), stage **Carnaval**—Mardi Gras—extravaganzas.

Second Friday of Lent (nine days after Ash Wednesday): **Fiesta del Señor del Perdón** (Lord of Forgiveness); big pilgrimage festival in San Pedro and San Pablo Tequixtepec, Oaxaca.

March 10–17: **Fiesta de San Patricio** (St. Patrick's Day festival); processions, boat regatta, dances, food, and carnival at San Patricio-Melaque (Barra de Navidad), Jalisco.

March 11–19: Week before the **Day of St. Joseph** in Talpa, Jalisco (food, edible crafts made of colored *chicle,* or chewing gum,

Local *charreadas* are big events, especially in country towns and villages.

dancing, bands, and mariachi serenades to the Virgin of Talpa).

Fourth Friday before Easter Sunday: **Fiesta of Jesus the Nazarene** in Huaxpaltepec, Oaxaca; native Dance of the Conquest; big native country fair.

March 18–April 4: **Grand ceramics and handicrafts fair,** in Tonalá (Guadalajara), Jalisco.

March 19: **Día de San José** (Day of St. Joseph).

March 21: **Birthday of Benito Juárez,** the "Hero of the Americas" (national holiday); especially in Benito Juárez's birthplace, Guelatao, Oaxaca, with a whirl of traditional dances.

Late March or April (the Sunday preceding Easter Sunday): **Fiesta de Ramos** (Palm Sunday) in many towns and villages, but especially in Sayula, Jalisco (on Highway 54 south of Guadalajara; local area crafts fair, food, dancing, mariachis).

April (Good Friday, two days before Easter Sunday): **Fiesta de la Santa Cruz de Huatulco** (Holy Cross of Huatulco) in Santa María Huatulco, Oaxaca.

April: **Semana Santa** (pre-Easter Holy Week, culminating in Domingo Gloria, Easter Sunday national holiday).

May 1: **Labor Day** (national holiday).

May (first and third Wednesdays): **Fiesta of the Virgin of Ocotlán,** in Ocotlán, Jalisco (on Lake Chapala, religious processions, dancing, fireworks, regional food).

May 3: **Día de la Santa Cruz** (Holy Cross) in many places, especially Salina Cruz and Tehuantepec, Oaxaca, and Mascota, Jalisco.

May 3–15: **Fiesta of St. Isador the Farmer** in Tepic, Nayarit (blessing of seeds, animals, and water; agricultural displays, competitions, and dancing).

May 5: **Cinco de Mayo** (defeat of the French at Puebla in 1862; national holiday).

May 10: **Mothers' Day** (national holiday).

May 10–12: **Fiesta of the Coronation of the Virgin of the Rosary** in Talpa, Jalisco (processions, fireworks, regional food, crafts, and dances).

May 10–24: **Book fair** in Guadalajara (readings, concerts, and international book exposition).

May 15–30: **Velas (Fiestas) de San Vicente Ferrer** (in Juchitán, Oaxaca; Chontal and Huave dances and fair).

June 15–July 14: **National Ceramics Fair** in the Tlaquepaque district, Guadalajara (huge crafts fair; exhibits, competitions, and market of crafts from all over the country).

June 24: **Día de San Juan Bautista** (Day of St. John the Baptist); fairs and religious festivals, playful dunking of people in water).

June 28–29: **Regatta** in Mexcaltitán, Nayarit (friendly rivalry between boats carrying images of St. Peter and St. Paul to celebrate opening of the shrimp season).

June 29: **Día de San Pablo y San Pedro** (Day of St. Peter and St. Paul).

July 1–15: **Fiesta of the Precious Blood of Christ** in Teotitlán del Valle, Oaxaca, featuring the Danza de la Pluma (Dance of the Feather).

July: **Lunes del Cerro** (in Oaxaca city; a two-week extravaganza of native dances, events and fairs, beginning on the first Monday after July 16; among Mexico's most colorful).

July 20–30: **Fiesta de Santiago Apóstol** (St. James the Apostle) in many locations, but especially Santiago Laollaga, Suchilquitongo, Jamiltepec, Pinotepa Nacional, and Juxtlahuaca, Oaxaca.

August: **Copper Fair** in Santa Clara del Cobre, Michoacán.

Aug. 14: **Fiesta de la Virgen de la Asunción** (Virgin of the Assumption) in Tlaxiaco, Oaxaca; Aug. 15 in Nochixtlán, Oaxaca; and Aug. 13–16 in Huazolotitlán, Oaxaca.

Sept. 14: **Charro Day** (Cowboy Day all over Mexico; rodeos).

Sept. 15–16: **Independence Day** (national holiday; mayors everywhere reenact Father Hidalgo's 1810 Grito de Dolores from city hall balconies on the night of September 15).

Sept. 27–29: **Fiesta de San Miguel** in San Miguel Tequixtepec and Teotitlán del Camino, Oaxaca; dance of the "Cristianos y Moros" (Christians and Moors).

Oct. 1–2: **Fiesta de San Miguel Arcángel** in Puerto Ángel, Oaxaca.

Oct. 4: **Día de San Francisco** (Day of St. Francis); traditional dances, especially in Uruapan, Michoacán.

Oct. 12: **Día de la Raza** (Columbus Day, national holiday that commemorates the union of the races).

Oct. 12: **Fiesta of the Virgin of Zapopan** in Guadalajara (procession carries the Virgin home to Zapopan from the Guadalajara downtown cathedral; regional food, crafts fair, mariachis, and dancing).

October, second Sunday: **Fiesta del Santa Cristo de Tlacolula** (Holy Christ of Tlacolula) in Tlacolula, Oaxaca.

October (last Sunday): **Día de Cristo Rey** in Ixtlán del Río, Nayarit (Day of Christ the King, with "Quetzal y Azteca" and "La Pluma" *indígena* dances, horse races, processions, and food).

Nov. 1: **Día de Todos Santos** (All Souls' Day, in honor of the souls of children; the departed descend from heaven to eat sugar skeletons, skulls, and treats on family altars).

Nov. 2: **Día de los Muertos** (Day of the Dead, in honor of ancestors; families visit cemeteries and decorate graves with flowers and favorite food of the deceased). Especially colorful in and around Morelia and Pátzcuaro, Michoacán, and in Oaxaca.

Nov. 7–30: **Feria de la Nao de China** (in Acapulco; a fair celebrating the galleon trade which linked colonial Acapulco with Asia).

Nov. 20: **Revolution Day** (anniversary of the revolution of 1910–1917; national holiday).

Nov. 28–Dec. 5: **National Silver Fair** in Taxco, Guerrero. Mexico's most skilled silversmiths compete for prizes amid a whirl of concerts, dances, and fireworks.

Late Nov.–Dec. 8: **Fiesta de la Virgen de Juquila**, Oaxaca's biggest fiesta; national pilgrimage in Santa Catarina Juquila.

Dec. 1: **Inauguration Day** (National government changes hands every six years: 2000, 2006, 2012 . . .).

Dec. 8: **Día de la Purísima Concepción** (Day of the Immaculate Conception).

Dec. 12: **Día de Nuestra Señora de Guadalupe** (Festival of the Virgin of Guadalupe, patroness of Mexico; processions, music, and dancing nationwide, especially in downtown Manzanillo and Puerto Vallarta).

Dec. 16–18: **Fiesta de la Virgen de Soledad** in Oaxaca city.

Dec. 16–24: **Christmas Week** (week of *posadas* and piñatas; midnight Mass on Christmas Eve).

Dec. 23: **Fiesta de los Rábanos** (radish sculpture competition on the main plaza in Oaxaca city).

Dec. 25: **¡Feliz Navidad!** (Christmas Day; Christmas trees and gift exchange; national holiday).

Dec. 26: **Vela Tehuantepec** (in Tehunatepec, Oaxaca, everyone in town dances to the lovely melody of the *Sandunga*).

Dec. 31: **New Year's Eve.**

Arts and Crafts

Mexico is so stuffed with lovely, reasonably priced handicrafts (*artesanías,* ar-tay-sah-NEE-ahs) that many crafts devotees, if given the option, might choose Mexico over heaven. A sizable fraction of Mexican families still depend upon homespun items—clothing, utensils, furniture, native herbal remedies, religious offerings, adornments, toys, musical instruments—which either they or their neighbors craft at home. Many such traditions reach back thousands of years, to the beginnings of Mexican civilization. The accumulated knowledge of manifold generations of artisans has, in many instances, resulted in finery so prized that whole villages devote themselves to the manufacture of a certain class of goods.

> *Mexico is so stuffed with lovely, reasonably priced handicrafts that many crafts devotees, if given the option, might choose Mexico over heaven.*

In Pacific Mexico, handicrafts shoppers who venture away from the coastal resorts to the source towns and villages will most likely benefit from lower prices, wider choices, and, most important, the privilege of encountering the artisans themselves. There, perhaps in a patio-shop on a dusty Tonalá side street or above a breezy Pátzcuaro lakeshore, you might meet the people and view the painstaking process by which they fashion humble materials—clay, wool, cotton, wood, metal, straw, leaves, palm fronds, bark, paper, leather—into irresistible works of art.

BASKETRY AND WOVEN CRAFTS

Weaving straw, leaves, palm fronds, and reeds is among the oldest of Mexican crafts traditions. Mat and basketweaving methods and designs 5,000 years old survive to the present day. All over Mexico, people weave *petates* (straw mats) upon which vacationers stretch out on the beach and which local folks use for everything, from keeping tortillas warm to shielding babies from the sun. Around Acapulco and along the Oaxaca coast, you might see a woman or child waiting for a bus or even walking down the street while weaving creamy white palm leaf strands into a coiled basket. Later, you may see a similar basket, embellished with a bright animal—parrot, burro, or even Snoopy—for sale in the market.

Like the origami paper-folders of Japan, folks who live around Lake Pátzcuaro have taken basketweaving to its ultimate form by crafting virtually everything—from toy turtles and Christmas bells to butterfly mobiles and serving spoons—from the reeds they gather along the lakeshore.

Hatmaking has likewise attained high refinement in Mexico. Workers in Sahuayo, Michoacán (near the southeast shore of Lake Chapala), craft especially fine sombreros. Due east across Mexico, in Becal, Campeche, workers craft Panama hats, *jipis* (HEE-pees), so fine, soft, and flexible that you can stuff one into your pants pocket without damage.

Although Huichol men in the states of Nayarit and Jalisco do not actually manufacture their headwear, they do decorate them. They take ordinary sombreros and embellish them into Mexico's most flamboyant hats, flowing with bright ribbons, feathers, and fringes of colorful wool balls. (See the Tepic and Puerto Vallarta destination sections for many Huichol crafts sources.)

CLOTHING AND EMBROIDERY

Although *traje* (ancestral tribal dress) has nearly vanished in urban Mexico, significant numbers of Mexican women, especially in remote districts of Michoacán, Guerrero, Oaxaca, Chiapas, and Yucatán, make and wear *traje*. Most common is the *huipil*, a full, square-shouldered, short- to midsleeved dress, often hand-embroidered with animal and floral designs. *Huipiles* from Oaxaca include designs from San Pedro de Amusgos (Amusgo tribe: white cotton, embroidered with abstract colored animal and floral motifs); San Andrés Chicahuaxtla (Trique tribe: white cotton, richly embroidered red stripes, interwoven with green, blue, and yellow, and hung with colored ribbons); Yalalag (Zapotec tribe: white cotton, with bright flowers embroidered along two or four vertical seams and distinctive colored tassels hanging down the back). Beyond Oaxaca, Yucatán Maya *huipiles* are among the most prized. They are of white cotton, embellished with big, brilliant machine-embroidered flowers around the neck and shoulders.

Shoppers sometimes can buy other, less common types of *traje*, such as a **quechquémitl** (shoulder cape), often made of wool and worn as an overgarment in winter. The **enredo**, a full-length skirt, wraps around the waist and legs like a Hawaiian sarong. Mixtec women in Oaxaca's warm south coast region around Pinotepa Nacional commonly wear the *enredo*, known locally as the **pozahuanco** (poh-sah-oo-AHN-koh) below the waist, and when at home, go barebreasted. When wearing their *pozahuancos* in public, they usually tie a **mandil**, a wide calico apron, around their front side. Women weave the best *pozahuancos*, using cotton thread dyed a light purple with secretions of tidepool-harvested snails, *Purpura patula pansa*, and silk dyed deep red with cochineal, extracted from the dried bodies of a locally cultivated scale insect, *Dactylopius coccus*. On a typical day, two or three women will be selling handmade *pozahuancos* at the Pinotepa Nacional market.

Colonial-era Spanish styles have blended with native *traje*, producing a wider class of dress, known generally as **ropa típica.** Lovely embroidered blouses *(blusas)*, shawls *(rebozos)*, and dresses *(vestidos)* fill boutique racks and market stalls all over Pacific Mexico. Among the most popular is the so-called **Oaxaca wedding dress,** made of cotton with a crochet-trimmed riot of diminutive flowers hand-stitched about the neck and yoke. Some of the finest examples are made in San Antonino Castillo, just north of Ocotlán in the Valley of Oaxaca.

In contrast to women, only a small fraction of Mexican men—members of remote groups, such as Huichol, Cora, and Tarahumara in the northwest, and Maya and Lacandón in the southeast—wear *traje*. Nevertheless, shops offer some fine men's *ropa típica*, such as wool jackets and serapes for northern or highland winter wear, and *guayaberas*, hip-length, pleated tropical dress shirts.

Fine embroidery *(bordado)* embellishes much traditional Mexican clothing, tablecloths *(manteles)*, and napkins *(servilletas)*. As everywhere, women define the art of embroidery. Although some still work by hand at home, cheaper machine-made factory lace and needlework is more commonly available in shops.

Leather

Pacific Mexico shops offer an abundance of leather goods, which, if not manufactured locally, are shipped from the renowned leather centers. These include Guadalajara, Mazatlán, and Oaxaca (sandals and huaraches), and León (shoes, boots, and saddles). For unique and custom-designed articles you'll probably have to confine your shopping to the expensive tourist resort shops. For the more usual though still attractive leather items such as purses, wallets, belts, coats, and boots, veteran

ON THE ROAD

shoppers go to local city markets. Most notable among these is Guadalajara's suburban Zapopan and Tlaquepaque villages and downtown Libertad Market, where an acre of stalls offer the broadest leather selection at reasonable prices (after bargaining) in Pacific Mexico.

FURNITURE

Although furniture is usually too bulky to carry back home with your airline luggage, low Mexican prices allow you to ship your purchases home and enjoy beautiful, unusual pieces for a fraction of what you would pay—if you could find them—at home.

A number of classes of furniture (*muebles,* moo-AY-blays) are crafted in villages near the sources of raw materials—either wood, reeds, bamboo, or wrought iron.

Sometimes it seems as if every house in Mexico is furnished with wood **colonial-style furniture.** The basic design of much of it dates at least to the Middle Ages. Although variations exist, most colonial-style furniture is heavily built. Table and chair legs are massive, often lathe-turned; chair backs are usually straight and vertical. Although usually varnished, colonial-style tables, chairs, and chests sometimes shine with inlaid wood or tile, or animal and flower designs. Family shops turn out good furniture, usually in the highlands, where suitable wood is available. Products from shops in Guadalajara's Tonalá and Tlaquepaque villages, Lake Pátzcuaro (especially Tzintzuntzan), Taxco, and Olinalá, Guerrero, are among the best known.

A second, very distinctive class of Mexican furniture is *equipal,* usually roundish tables, chairs, and sofas, made of brown pigskin or cowhide stretched over wooden frames. Factories are mostly in Guadalajara and nearby Tlaquepaque and Tonalá villages.

It is intriguing that **lacquered furniture,** in both process and design, has much in common with lacquerware produced half a world away in China. Moreover, Mexican lacquerware tradition both predated the conquest and was originally practiced only on the Pacific, where legends persist of preconquest contact with Chinese traders.

Consequently, a number of experts believe that the Mexicans learned the craft of lacquerware from Chinese artists, centuries before Columbus.

Today, artisan families in and around Pátzcuaro, Michoacán, and Olinalá, Guerrero, carry on the tradition. The process, which at its finest resembles cloisonné manufacture, involves carving and painting intricate floral and animal designs, followed by repeated layerings of lacquer, clay, and sometimes gold and silver to produce satiny, jewel-like surfaces.

A few villages produce furniture made of plant fiber, such as reeds, raffia, and bamboo. In some cases, entire communities, such as Ihuatzio (near Pátzcuaro) and Villa Victoria (in Mexico state, west of Toluca), have long harvested the bounty of local lakes and marshes as the basis for their products.

Wrought iron, produced and worked according to Spanish tradition, is used to produce tables, chairs, and benches. Ruggedly fashioned in a riot of baroque scrollwork, pieces often decorate garden, patio, and park settings. Many colonial cities, notably San Miguel de Allende, Toluca, Guanajuato, Guadalajara, and Oaxaca are wrought-iron manufacturing centers.

GLASS AND STONEWORK

Glass manufacture, unknown in pre-Columbian times, was introduced by the Spanish. Today, factories scattered all over the country turn out mountains of *burbuja* (boor-BOO-hah)—bubbled glass tumblers, goblets, plates, and pitchers, usually in blue, green, or red. Finer glass is manufactured in Guadalajara; especially in suburban Tlaquepaque and Tonalá villages, you can watch artisans blow glass into a number of shapes, notably, paper-thin balls in red, green, or blue.

Artisans work stone, usually near sources of supply. Puebla, Mexico's main source of onyx (*onix,* OH-neeks), is the manufacturing center for the galaxy of mostly rough-hewn, cream-colored items, from animal charms and chess pieces to beads and desk sets, which crowd curio shop shelves throughout the country. *Cantera,* a volcanic tufa stone occurring in pastel shades from pink to green, quarried locally, especially near Pátzcuaro and Oaxaca, is used similarly.

For a keepsake from a truly ancient Mexican tradition, don't forget the hollowed-out stone *metate* (may-TAH-tay), a corn-grinding basin, and the three-legged *molcajete* (mohl-kah-HAY-tay), a mortar for grinding *chiles*.

HUICHOL ART

Growing demand, especially around Puerto Vallarta, has greatly stimulated the supply of Huichol art. Originally produced by shamans for ritual purposes, pieces such as **beaded masks,** *cuadras* (rectangular yarn paintings), **gourd rattles, arrows,** and yarn *cicuri* (God's eyes) have a ritual symbolism. Eerie beaded masks of wood often represent the Huichols' earth mother, Tatei Urianaka. The larger *cuadras,* of colored acrylic yarn painstakingly glued in intermeshing patterns to a plywood base, customarily depict the drama of life being played out between the main actors of the Huichol pantheon. For example, as Tayau (Father Sun) radiates over the land, alive with stylized cactus, flowers, peyote buds, snakes, and birds, antlered "Brother Deer" Kauyumari heroically battles the evil sorcerer Kieri, while nearby, Tatei Urianaka gives birth.

JEWELRY

Gold and silver were once the basis for Mexico's wealth. Her Spanish conquerors plundered a mountain of gold—religious offerings, necklaces, pendants, rings, bracelets—masterfully crafted by a legion of native metalsmiths and jewelers. Unfortunately, much of that indigenous tradition was lost because the Spanish denied access to precious metals to the Mexicans for generations while they introduced Spanish methods. Nevertheless, a small goldworking tradition survived the dislocations of the 1810–1821 War of Independence and the 1910–1917 revolution. Silver-crafting, moribund during the 1800s, was revived in Taxco, Guerrero, principally through the joint efforts of architect-artist William Spratling and the local community.

Today, spurred by the tourist boom, jewelry-making is thriving in Mexico. Taxco, where guilds, families, and cooperatives produce sparkling silver and gold adornments, is the acknowledged center. Scores of Taxco shops display the results—shimmering ornamental butterflies, birds, jaguars, serpents, turtles, and fish from ancient native tradition. Pieces, mostly in silver, vary from humble but attractive trinkets to glittering necklaces, silver candelabras, and place settings for a dozen, sometimes embellished with precious stones.

Other subsidiary jewelry-crafting centers include Guadalajara (gold and opals), Oaxaca (preconquest replicas and gold and silver filigree), Pátzcuaro (silver filigree and earrings), Puebla (sand-cast gold and silver), and Guanajuato (gold and silver, especially earrings.)

WOODCARVING AND MUSICAL INSTRUMENTS
Masks

Spanish and native Mexican traditions have blended to produce a multitude of masks—some strange, some lovely, some scary, some endearing, all interesting. The tradition flourishes in the strongly indigenous southern Pacific states of Michoacán, Guerrero, Oaxaca, and Chiapas, where campesinos gear up all year for the village festivals—especially Semana Santa (Easter week), early December (Virgin of Guadalupe), and the festival of the local patron, whether it be San José, San Pedro, San Pablo, Santa María, Santa Barbara, or one of a host of others. Every local fair has its favored dances, such as the Dance of the Conquest, the Christians and Moors, the Old Men, or the Tiger, in which masked villagers act out age-old allegories of fidelity, sacrifice, faith, struggle, sin, and redemption.

Although masks are made of many materials—from stone and ebony to coconut husks and paper—wood, where available, is the medium of choice. For the entire year, village master carvers cut, shave, sand, and paint to ensure that each participant will be properly disguised for the festival.

The popularity of masks has led to an entire

ON THE ROAD

made-for-tourist mask industry of mass-pro-duced duplicates, many cleverly antiqued. Ex-amine the goods carefully; if the price is high, don't buy unless you're convinced it's a real an-tique.

Alebrijes

Tourist demand has made zany wooden animals *(alebrijes),* or (ah-lay-BREE-hays), a Oaxaca growth industry. Virtually every family in certain Valley of Oaxaca villages—notably Arrazola and San Mar-tin Tilcajete—runs a factory studio. There, piles of *copal* wood, which men carve and women finish and intricately paint, become whimsical giraffes, dogs, cats, iguanas, gargoyles, dragons, and most of the possible permutations in between. The far-ther from the source you get, the higher the *alebrije* price becomes; in Arrazola, what costs $5 will probably run about $10 in Pacific Mexico and $30 in the United States or Canada.

Others commonly available are the charming colorfully painted wooden fish carved mainly in the Pacific coastal state of Guerrero, and the bur-nished, dark hardwood animal and fish sculp-tures of desert ironwood from the state of Sonora.

Musical Instruments

The great majority of Mexico's guitars and other stringed instruments are made in Paracho, Mi-choacán (southeast of Lake Chapala, 50 miles north of Uruapan). There, scores of cottage fac-tories turn out guitars, violins, mandolins, *viruelas,* ukuleles, and a dozen more variations every day. They vary widely in quality, so look carefully be-fore you buy. Make sure that the wood is well cured and dry; damp, unripe wood instruments are more susceptible to warping and cracking.

METALWORK

Bright copper, brass, and tinware; sturdy iron-work; and razor-sharp knives and machetes are made in a number of regional centers. **Copper-ware,** from jugs, cups, and plates to candle-sticks—and even the town lampposts and bandstand—all come from Santa Clara del Cobre, a few miles south of Pátzcuaro, Mi-choacán.

Although not the source of **brass** itself, Tonalá, in the Guadalajara eastern suburb, is the place where brass is most abundant and beautiful, ap-pearing as menageries of brilliant, fetching birds and animals, sometimes embellished with shiny nickel highlights.

A number of Oaxaca family factories turn out fine **cutlery**—swords, knives, machetes—scrolled **cast-iron grillwork,** and a swarm of bright **tinware,** or *(hojalata)* (oh-hah-LAH-tah), mirror frames, masks, and glittering Christ-mas decorations.

Be sure not to miss the miniature *milagros,* one of Mexico's most charming forms of metal-work. Usually of brass, they are of homely shapes—a horse, dog, or baby, or an arm, head, or foot—which, accompanied by a prayer, the faithful pin to the garment of their favorite saint whom they hope will intercede to cure an ail-ment or fulfill a wish.

PAPER AND PAPIER-MÂCHÉ

Papier-mâché has become a high art in Tonalá, Jalisco, where a swarm of birds, cats, frogs, gi-raffes, and other animal figurines are meticu-lously crafted by building up repeated layers of glued paper. The result—sanded, brilliantly var-nished, and polished—resembles fine sculpture rather than the humble newspaper from which it was fashioned.

Other paper goods you shouldn't overlook in-clude piñatas (durable, inexpensive, and as Mex-ican as you can get), available in every town market; colorful decorative cutout banners (string overhead at your home fiesta) from San Salvador Huixcolotla, Puebla; and *amate,* wild fig tree bark paintings in animal and flower motifs, from Xalitla and Ameyaltepec, Guerrero.

POTTERY AND CERAMICS

Although Mexican pottery tradition is as di-verse as the country itself, some varieties stand out. Among the most prized is the so-called Ta-lavera (or Majolica), the best of which is made by a few family-run shops in Puebla. The la-bels Talavera and Majolica derive from Talavera,

© BRUCE WHIPPERMAN

pottery from Atzompa, Oaxaca

ON THE ROAD

the Spanish town from which the tradition migrated to Mexico; before that it originated on the Spanish Mediterranean island of Mayorca (thus Majolica), from a combination of still older Arabic, Chinese, and African ceramic styles. Shapes include plates, bowls, jugs, and pitchers, hand-painted and hard-fired in intricate bright yellow, orange, blue, and green floral designs. So few shops make true Talavera these days that other, cheaper, lookalike grades, made around Guanajuato, are more common, selling for as little as one-tenth of the price of the genuine article.

More practical and nearly as prized is hand-painted, high-fired stoneware from Tonalá in Guadalajara's eastern suburbs. Although made in many shapes and sizes, such stoneware is often sold as complete dinner place settings. Decorations are usually in abstract floral and animal designs, hand-painted over a reddish clay base.

From the same tradition come the famous *bruñido* pottery animals of Tonalá. Round,

smooth, and cuddly as ceramic can be, the Tonalá animals—very commonly doves and ducks, but also cats and dogs and sometimes even armadillos, frogs, and snakes—each seems to embody the essence of its species.

Some of the most charming Mexican pottery, made from a ruddy low-fired clay and crafted following pre-Columbian traditions, comes from western Mexico, especially Colima. Charming figurines in timeless human poses—flute-playing musicians, dozing grandmothers, fidgeting babies, loving couples—and animals, especially Colima's famous playful dogs, decorate the shelves of a sprinkling of shops.

The southern state of Guerrero sustains a vibrant pottery tradition. Throughout Pacific Mexico, you'll find the humble but very attractive unglazed brightly painted animals—cats, ducks, fish, and many others—that folks bring to resort centers from their village family workshops.

Much more acclaimed are certain types of pottery from the valley surrounding the city of Oaxaca. The village of Atzompa is famous for its tan, green-glazed clay pots, dishes, and bowls. Nearby San Bártolo Coyotepec village has acquired equal renown for its black pottery, sold all over the world. Doña Rosa, now deceased, pioneered the crafting of big round pots without using a potter's wheel. Now made in many more shapes by Doña Rosa's descendants, the pottery's exquisite silvery black sheen is produced by the reduction (reduced air) method of firing, which removes oxygen from the clay's red (ferric) iron oxide, converting it to black ferrous oxide.

Although most latter-day Mexican potters have become aware of the health dangers of lead pigments, some for-sale pottery may still contain lead. The hazard comes from low-fired pottery in which the lead has not been firmly melted into the glaze. Acids in foods such as lemons, vinegar, and tomatoes dissolve the lead pigments, which, when ingested, eventually result in lead poisoning. In general, the hardest, shiniest pottery, which has been twice fired—such as the high-quality Tonalá stoneware used for dishes—is the safest.

WOOLEN WOVEN GOODS

Mexico's finest wool weavings come from Teotitlán del Valle, in the Valley of Oaxaca, less than an hour's drive east of Oaxaca city. The weaving tradition, carried on by Teotitlán's Zapotec-speaking families, dates back at least 2,000 years. Many families still carry on the arduous process, making everything from scratch. They gather the dyes from wild plants and the bodies of insects and sea snails. They hand-wash, card, spin, and dye the wool and even travel to remote mountain springs to gather water. The results, they say, *valen la pena,* (are worth the pain): intensely colored, tightly woven carpets, rugs, and wall-hangings that retain their brilliance for generations.

Rougher, more loosely woven, blankets, jackets, and serapes come from other parts, notably mountain regions, especially around San Cristóbal de las Casas, in Chiapas, and Lake Pátzcuaro in Michoacán.

Accommodations

Pacific Mexico has thousands of lodgings to suit every style and pocketbook: world-class resorts, small beachside hotels, homey *casas de huéspedes* (guesthouses), palm-shaded trailer parks, and hundreds of miles of pristine beaches, ripe for camping. The high seasons, when hotel reservations are generally recommended, are mid-December through March, during pre-Easter week, and the month of August.

The hundreds of accommodations described in this book are positive recommendations—checked out in detail—good choices, from which you can pick according to your taste and purse.

Hotel Rates

The rates listed in this book are U.S. dollar equivalents of peso prices, taxes included, as quoted by the hotel management at the time of writing. Low- and high-season rates are quoted whenever possible. They are intended as a general guide only. Since rates fluctuate sharply according to local demand, quoted figures will probably only approximate the asking rate when you arrive. Some readers, unfortunately, try to bargain by telling desk clerks that, for example, the rate should be $30 because they read it in this book. This is unwise, because it makes hotel managers and clerks reluctant to quote rates for fear readers might hold their hotel responsible for such quotes a few years later.

In Pacific Mexico, hotel rates depend strongly upon inflation and season. To cancel the effect of the relatively steep Mexican inflation, rates are reported in U.S. dollars. However, when settling your hotel bill, *you should always pay in pesos.*

Saving Money

The hotel prices quoted in this book are rack rates, the maximum tariff, exclusive of packages and promotions, that you would pay if you walked in and rented an unreserved room for one day. Savvy travelers seldom pay the maximum. Always inquire if there are any discounts or packages (*descuentos o paquetes*—des-koo-AYN-tohs OH pah-KAY-tays). At most times other than the super-high Christmas to New Year and Easter weeks, you can get at least one or two free days for a one-week stay. Promotional packages available during slack seasons may include free extras such as breakfast, a car rental, a boat tour, or a sports rental. A travel agent or travel website can be of great help in shopping around for such bargains.

You nearly always save additional money if you deal in pesos only. Insist on both booking your lodging for an agreed price in pesos and paying the resulting hotel bill in the same pesos, rather than dollars. The reason is that dollar rates quoted by hotels are often based on the hotel desk exchange rate, which is customarily about 5 percent, or even as much 15 percent, less than bank rates. For example, if the clerk tells you your hotel bill is $1,000, instead of handing over the dollars or having him mark $1,000 on your credit card slip, ask him how much it is in pesos. Using the desk conversion rate, he might say

© BRUCE WHIPPERMAN

A feast of accommodations, from luxury hotels to cozy mountain cabins, abound in Pacific Mexico.

one of these gateways, it may pay to contact the airlines for more information.

GUESTHOUSES AND LOCAL HOTELS

Most coastal resorts began with an old town, which expanded to a new *zona hotelera* (hotel strip) where big hostelries rise along a golden strand. In the old town, near the piquant smells, sights, and sounds of traditional Mexico, are the *casas de huéspedes* and smaller hotels where rooms are often arranged around a plant-decorated patio.

Such lodgings vary from scruffy to spic-and-span, and humble to luxurious. At minimum, you can expect a plain room, a shared toilet and hot-water shower, and plenty of atmosphere for your money. High-season rates, depending on the resort, average $15–40 for two, depending upon amenities. Discounts are often available for long-term stays. *Casas de huéspedes* will rarely be near the beach, unlike many local hotels.

Medium and Larger Older-Style Hotels

Locally owned and operated hotels make up most of the recommendations of this book. Many veteran travelers find it hard to understand why people come to Mexico and spend $200 a day for a hotel room when good alternatives run $35–80, high season, depending upon the resort.

Many locally run hostelries are right on the beach, sharing the same velvety sand and golden sunsets as their much more expensive international-class neighbors. Local hotels, which depend as much on Mexican tourists as foreigners, generally have clean, large rooms, often with private-view balconies, ceiling fans, and toilet and hot-water bath or shower. What they often lack are the plush extras—air-conditioning, cable TV, phones, tennis courts, exercise gyms, and golf courses—of the luxury resort hotels.

Booking these hotels is straightforward. All can be dialed direct (from the United States, dial 011-52, then the local area code and number) for

something like 9,000 pesos (considerably less than the 10,000 pesos that the bank might give for your $1,000). Pay the 9,000 pesos or have the clerk mark 9,000 pesos on your credit card slip, and save yourself $100.

For stays of more than two weeks, you'll most likely save money and add comfort with an apartment or condominium rental. Monthly rates range $500–1,500 (less than half the comparable hotel per diem rate) for comfortable one-bedroom furnished kitchenette units, often including resort amenities such as pool and sundeck, beach club, and private-view balcony.

Airlines regularly offer air/hotel packages, which, by combining your hotel and air fees, may save you lots of pesos. These deals customarily require that you depart for Pacific Mexico through certain gateway cities, which depend on the airline. Accommodations are usually, but not exclusively, in luxury resorts. If you live near

information and reservations; like the big resorts, many even have U.S. and Canada toll-free 800 information numbers. Always ask about money-saving packages (*paquetes*) and promotions (*promociones*) when reserving.

INTERNATIONAL-CLASS RESORTS

Pacific Mexico has many beautiful, well-managed international-class resort hotels. They spread along the pearly strands of Mazatlán, Puerto Vallarta, Manzanillo, Ixtapa, Acapulco, and Bahías de Huatulco. Their super-deluxe amenities, moreover, need not be overly expensive. During the right time of year you can vacation at many of the big-name spots—Sheraton, Westin, Camino Real, Fiesta Americana, Krystal—for surprisingly little. While high-season room tariffs ordinarily run $150–350, low-season (May–Nov., and to a lesser degree, Jan.–Feb.) packages and promotions can cut these prices to as low as $100. Shop around for savings via your Sunday newspaper

travel section, travel agents, and by contacting the hotels directly through their toll-free 800 numbers or websites.

APARTMENTS, BUNGALOWS, CONDOMINIUMS, AND VILLAS

For longer stays, many visitors prefer the convenience and economy of an apartment or condominium or the luxurious comfort of a villa vacation rental. Choices vary, from spartan studios to deluxe beachfront suites and rambling, view homes big enough for entire extended families. Prices depend strongly upon season and amenities, from $500 per month for the cheapest to at least 10 times that for the most luxurious.

A Mexican variation on the apartment style of accommodation is called a bungalow, although, in contrast to English-language usage, it does not usually imply a detached dwelling. Common in Mazatlán and Manzanillo and in smaller beach resorts, such as Bucerías, Rincón de Guayabitos, Barra de Navidad, and Zihuatanejo,

RESORT TOLL-FREE NUMBERS AND WEBSITES

These hotel chains have branches (** = outstanding, * = recommended) at Mazatlán (MZ), Puerto Vallarta (PV), Nuevo Vallarta (NV), Guadalajara (GD), Manzanillo (MN), Ixtapa-Zihuatanejo (IX), Acapulco (AC), Huatulco (HU), and other Pacific Mexico locations.

Barceló, formerly Sheraton (IX*, HU*); tel. 800/346-5454; www.barcelo.com, www.mexicotravelnet.com

Camino Real (PV**, GD**, AC, HU*, Oaxaca**); tel. 800/7CAMINO (800/722-6466); www.caminoreal.com

Club Maeva (MN**); tel. 866/275-8392; www.maevaresort.com

Club Med (IX**); tel. 800/CLUBMED (800/258-2633); www.clubmed.com

Fiesta Americana (GD*, PV**, AC**, Oaxaca); tel. 800/FIESTA1 (800/343-7821); www.fiestaamericana.com.mx

Holiday Inn (MZ, GD*, PV, IX, AC); tel. 800/HOLIDAY (800/465-4329); www.sixc.com

Hyatt (AC**); tel. 800/228-9000; www.hyatt.com

Las Brisas Hotels (MN*, IX**, AC); tel. 888/559-4329; www.lasbrisas.com

Marriott (PV); tel. 800/228-9290; www.marriot.com

Mexico Boutique Hotels (Punta Mita**, PV*, Majahuitas*, Las Alamandas**, Careyes**, Tamarindo*, Barra de Navidad*, IX**, AC**, HU); U.S. tel. 877/278-8018, Can. tel. 866/818-8342; www.mexicoboutiquehotels.com

NH Krystal (PV**, IX**); tel. 800/231-9860; www.nh-hoteles.com

Qualton Club (PV*, AC); tel. 399/327-1847

Sheraton (PV); tel. 800/325-3535; www.sheraton.com

Sierra Hotels (NV*, MN*); tel. 800/515-4321; www.misvacaciones.com

Sun Resorts (PV*, Los Angeles Locos*, Punta Serena*); tel. 800/713-3020

Westin (PV); tel. 800/228-3000; www.westin.com

a bungalow accommodation generally means a motel-type kitchenette-suite with less service, but with more space and beds. For families or for long stays by the beach, when you want to save money by cooking your own meals, such an accommodation might be ideal.

At the low end, you can expect a clean, furnished apartment within a block or two of the beach, with kitchen and regular maid service. More luxurious condos (which usually rent for $500 per week and up) are typically high-rise ocean-view suites with hotel-style desk services and resort amenities, such as a pool, hot tub, sundeck, and beach-level restaurant.

Higher up the scale, villas and houses vary from moderately luxurious homes to sky's-the-limit beach-view mansions, blooming with built-in designer luxuries, private pools and beaches, tennis courts, and gardeners, cooks, and maids.

Shopping Around

You'll generally find the most economical apartment, condo, and house rental deals through on-the-spot local contacts, such as the tourist newspaper want ad section, neighborhood "for rent" signs, or local listing agents.

If you prefer making rental arrangements before arrival, you can usually write, fax, email, or telephone managers—many of whom speak English—directly, using the numbers given in this book. Additional rentals are available through agents (see the Mazatlán, Puerto Vallarta, Bucerías, Barra de Navidad, and Ixtapa-Zihuatanejo sections) who will make long-distance rental agreements.

Additionally, a number of U.S.- and Canada-based agencies list some of the more expensive Pacific Mexico vacation rentals through toll-free information and reservations numbers and websites. For example, try Villa de Oro Vacation Rentals, 638 Scotland Dr., Santa Rosa, CA 95409, tel. 800/638-4552, www.villasdeoro.com; Villas of Mexico, P.O. Box 3730, Chico, CA 95927, tel. 800/456-3133, www.villasofmexico.com; and Condo and Villa World, 4230 Orchard Lake Rd., Suite 3, Orchard Lake, MI 48323, tel. 800/521-2980 from the United States or 800/453-8714 from Canada, www.villaworld.com.

Even more Pacific Mexico vacation rental homes and condos, many of them moderately priced, are accessible via websites. For starters, try www.choice1.com, www.mexicofile.com, and www.mexconnect.com. (For others, see Internet Resources and the destination chapters.)

Yet another fertile vacation rental source is the Sunday travel section of a major metropolitan daily, such as the *Los Angeles Times* or the *San Francisco Chronicle,* which routinely list Pacific Mexico vacation rentals. Also, local real estate agents, such as Century 21, who specialize in nationwide and foreign contacts, sometimes list (or know someone who does) Pacific Mexico vacation rentals.

Home Exchange

You may also want to consider using the services of a home exchange agency or website whereby you swap homes with someone in Pacific Mexico for an agreed-upon time period. (See the Internet Resources section for home-exchange websites and toll-free numbers.)

CAMPING AND PALAPAS

Beach camping is popular among middle-class Mexican families, especially during the Christmas-New Year week and during Semana Santa, the week before Easter.

Other times, tenters and RV campers usually find beaches uncrowded. The best spots (see the destination chapter maps and text for details) typically have a shady palm grove for camping and a *palapa* (palm-thatched) restaurant that serves drinks and fresh seafood. (Heads up for falling coconuts, especially in the wind.) Cost for parking and tenting is often minimal—typically only the price of food at the restaurant.

Days are often perfect for swimming, strolling, and fishing, and nights are balmy—too warm for a sleeping bag, but fine for a hammock (which allows the air circulation that a tent does not.) However, good tents keep out mosquitoes and other pesties, which may be further discouraged by a good bug repellent. Tents can get hot, requiring only a sheet or very light blanket for sleeping cover.

ON THE ROAD

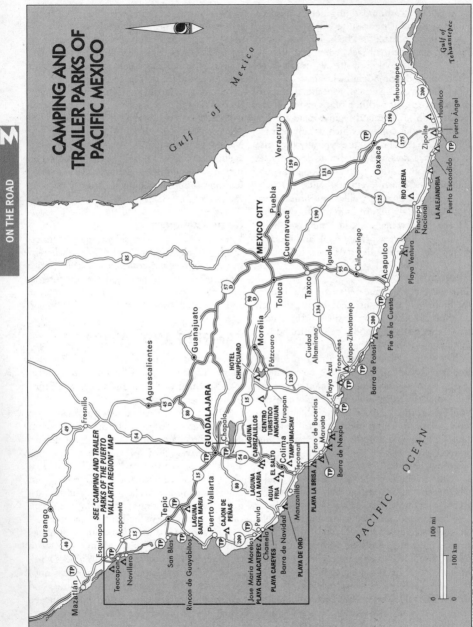

CAMPING AND
TRAILER PARKS OF
PACIFIC MEXICO

SEE "CAMPING AND TRAILER
PARKS OF THE PUERTO
VALLARTA REGION" MAP

© AVALON TRAVEL PUBLISHING, INC.

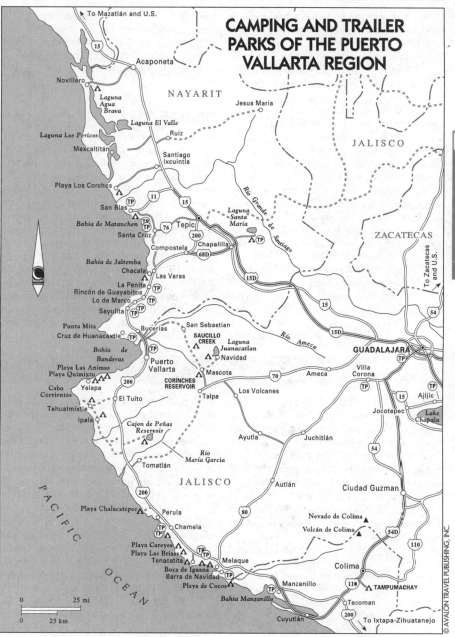

CAMPING AND TRAILER PARKS OF THE PUERTO VALLARTA REGION

To Mazatlán and U.S.

15

Acaponeta

Novillero

Laguna Agua Brava

NAYARIT

Jesus Maria

JALISCO

Laguna El Valle

Ruiz

Laguna Los Pericos

Mexcaltitán

Santiago Ixcuintla

Playa Los Corchos

San Blas

Bahía de Matanchen

Santa Cruz

11   15

76   Tepic

200

Laguna Santa María

Río Grande de Santiago

ZACATECAS

Compostela   Chapalilla

68D

Bahía de Jaltemba

Chacala

Las Varas

15D

To Zacatecas and U.S.

La Peñita

Rincón de Guayabitos

Lo de Marco

Sayulita

15

54

Punta Mita

Cruz de Huanacaxtle

Bucerías

San Sebastian

SAUCILLO CREEK

Laguna Juanacatlan

Navidad

Río Ameca

15D

GUADALAJARA

Bahía de Banderas

Puerto Vallarta

CORINCHES RESERVOIR

Mascota

70   Ameca

Villa Corona

Playa Las Animas

Playa Quimixto

Cabo Corrientes

Yelapa

200

El Tuito

Talpa

Los Volcanes

15   Ajijic

Tehualmixtle

Ipala

Cajon de Peñas Reservoir

Ayutla

Juchitlán

Jocotepec

Lake Chapala

Río María Garcia

Tomatlán

JALISCO

Autlán

54

Ciudad Guzman

200

Playa Chalacatepec

Perula

Chamela

80

Nevado de Colima

Volcán de Colima

54D

110

Playa Careyes

Playa Las Brisas

Tenacatita

Boca de Iguana

Barra de Navidad

Playa de Cocos

Melaque

Colima

Manzanillo

116   TAMPUMACHAY

Bahía Manzanillo

Tecoman

200   To Ixtapa-Zihuatanejo

Cuyutlán

PACIFIC OCEAN

0   25 mi

0   25 km

As for camping on isolated beaches, opinions vary, from dire warnings of *bandidos* to bland assurances that all is peaceful along the coast. The truth is somewhere in between. Trouble is most likely to occur in the vicinity of towns, where a few local thugs sometimes harass isolated campers.

When scouting out an isolated place to camp, a good rule is to arrive early enough in the day to get a feel for the place. Buy a soda at the *palapa* or store and take a stroll along the beach. Say *"Buenos días"* to the people along the way; ask if the fishing is good *("¿Pesca buena?")*. Above all, use your common sense and intuition. If the people seem friendly, ask if it's *seguro* (safe). If so, ask permission: *"¿Es bueno acampar acá?"* ("Is it okay to camp around here?"). You'll rarely be refused. For an informative and entertaining discussion of camping in Mexico, check out *The People's Guide to Mexico* (see Suggested Reading).

Some *palapas* (thatched beach houses) are still rented in small coastal resorts. Amenities typically include beds or hammocks, a shady thatched porch, cold running water, a kerosene stove, and shared toilets and showers. You usually walk right out your front door onto the sand, where surf, shells, and seabirds will be there to entertain you. *Palapa* rentals are available in Maruata and Barra de Nexpa (Michoacán coast, not far north of Playa Azul), Puerto Escondido, and Zipolite (near Puerto Ángel).

TRAILER PARKS

Campers who prefer company to isolation usually stay in trailer parks. Dozens of them dot Pacific Mexico's beaches and inland cities, towns, and scenic mountain spots. The most luxurious have electricity, water, sewer hookups, and many amenities, including restaurants, recreation rooms, and swimming pools; the humblest are simple palm-edged lots beside the beach. Virtually all of them have good swimming, fishing, and beachcombing. Prices run from a high of around $20 per night, including air-conditioning and power, to a few dollars for tent space only. Significant discounts are generally available for weekly and monthly rentals. (See the map "Camping and Trailer Parks of Pacific Mexico" and destination chapters for details.)

Food and Drink

Some travel to Pacific Mexico for the food. True Mexican food is old-fashioned, home-style fare requiring many hours of loving preparation. Such food is short on meat and long on corn, beans, rice, tomatoes, onions, eggs, and cheese.

Mexican food is the unique product of thousands of years of native tradition. It is based on corn—*teocentli*, the Aztec "holy food"—called *maíz* (mah-EES) by present-day Mexicans. In the past, a Mexican woman spent much of her time grinding and preparing corn: soaking the grain in lime water, which swells the kernels and removes the tough seed-coat, and grinding the bloated seeds into meal on a stone metate. Finally, she patted the meal into tortillas and cooked them on a hot, baked mud griddle, a *comal* (KOH-mahl).

Sages (men, no doubt) wistfully imagined that gentle pat-pat-pat of women all over Mexico to be the heartbeat of Mexico, which they feared would cease when women stopped making tortillas.

Fewer women these days make tortillas by hand. The gentle pat-pat-pat has been replaced by the whir and rattle of the automatic tortilla-making machine in myriad *tortillerías,* where women and girls line up for their family's daily kilo-stack of tortillas.

Tortillas are to the Mexicans as rice is to the Chinese and bread to the French. Mexican food is invariably some mixture of sauce, meat, beans, cheese, and vegetables wrapped in a tortilla, which becomes the culinary be-all: the food, the dish, and the utensil wrapped into one.

If a Mexican man has nothing to wrap in his lunchtime tortilla, he will content himself by rolling a thin filling of salsa (*chile* sauce) in it.

MEXICAN FOOD

On most Mexican-style menus, diners will find variations on a number of basic themes:

Chiles rellenos: Fresh roasted green chiles, stuffed usually with cheese but sometimes with fish or meat, coated with batter, and fried. They provide a piquant, tantalizing contrast to tortillas.

Enchiladas and **tostadas:** variations on the filled-tortilla theme. Enchiladas are stuffed with meat, cheese, olives, or beans and covered with sauce and baked, while tostadas consist of toppings served on crisp, open-faced tortillas.

Guacamole: This luscious avocado, onion, tomato, lime, and salsa mixture remains the delight it must have seemed to its Aztec inventors centuries ago. In non-tourist Mexico, it's served sparingly as a garnish, rather than in appetizer bowls as is common in the U.S. Southwest (and Mexican resorts catering to North Americans). (Similarly, in nontourist Mexico, burritos and fajitas, both stateside inventions, seldom, if ever appear on menus.)

Carnes (meats): *Carne asada* is grilled beef, usually chewy and well-done. Something similar you might see on a menu is *cecina* (say-SEE-nah), dried salted beef, grilled to a shoeleather-like consistency. Much more appetizing is *birria,* a Guadalajara specialty. Traditional *birrias* are of lamb or goat, often wrapped and pit-roasted in maguey leaves, with which it is served, for authenticity. In addition to *asada,* meat cooking styles are manifold, including *guisado* (stewed), *al pastor* (spit barbecue), and *barbacoa* (grill barbecued). Cuts include *lomo* (loin), *chuleta* (chop), *milanesa* (cutlet), and *albóndigas* (meatballs).

Moles (MOH-lays): uniquely Mexican specialties. *Mole poblano,* a spicy-sweet mixture of chocolate, *chiles,* and a dozen other ingredients, is cooked to a smooth sauce, then baked with chicken (or turkey, a combination called *mole de pavo*). So *típica* it's widely regarded as the national dish.

Quesadillas: made from soft flour tortillas, rather than corn, quesadillas resemble tostadas and always contain melted cheese.

Sopas: Soups consist of vegetables in a savory chicken broth, and are an important part of both *comida* (afternoon) and *cena* (evening) Mexican meals. *Pozole,* a rich steaming stew of hominy, vegetables, and pork or chicken, often constitutes the prime evening offering of small side street shops. *Sopa de taco,* an ever-popular country favorite, is a medium-spicy cheese-topped thick *chile* broth served with crisp corn tortillas.

Tacos or **taquitos:** tortillas served open or wrapped around any ingredient.

Tamales: as Mexican as apple pie is American. This savory mixture of meat and sauce imbedded in a shell of corn dough and baked in a wrapping of corn husks is rarely known by the singular, however. They're so yummy that one tamale invariably leads to more tamales.

Tortas: the Mexican sandwich, usually hot meat with fresh tomato and avocado, stuffed between two halves of a crisp *bolillo* (boh-LEE-yoh) or Mexican bun.

Tortillas y frijoles refritos: cooked brown or black beans, mashed and fried in pork fat, and rolled into tortillas with a dash of vitamin-C-rich salsa to form a near-complete combination of carbohydrate, fat, and balanced protein.

Beyond the Basics

Mexican food combinations seem endless. Mexican corn itself has more than 500 recognized culinary variations, all from indigenous tradition. This has led to a myriad of permutations on the taco, such as *sopes* (with small and thick tortillas), *garnacho* (flat taco), *chilaquile* (shredded taco), and *chalupa* (like a tostada).

Taking a lesson from California *nouveau* cuisine, avante-garde Mexican chefs are returning to traditional ingredients. They're beginning to use more and more *chiles*—habanero, *poblano,* jalapeño, and more—prepared with many variations, such as *chipotle, ancho, piquín,* and *mulato.* Squash flowers *(flor de calabaza)* and cactus (nopal) leaves are increasingly finding their way into soups and salads.

More often chefs are serving the wild game—*venado* (venison), *conejo* (rabbit), *guajalote* (turkey), *codorniz* (quail), *armadillo,* and *iguana*—that country Mexicans have always depended upon. As part of the same trend, *cuitlacoche* (corn mushroom fungus), *chapulines* (French-fried small grasshoppers), and *gusanos de maguey* (maguey worms) are being increasingly added as ingredients in fancy restaurants.

ON THE ROAD

Hot or Not?

Much food served in Mexico is not "Mexican." Eating habits, as most other customs, depend upon social class. Upwardly mobile Mexicans typically shun the corn-based *indígena* fare in favor of the European-style food of the Spanish colonial elite: chops, steaks, cutlets, fish, clams, omelettes, soups, pasta, rice, and potatoes.

Such fare is often as bland as Des Moines on a summer Sunday afternoon. *No picante*—not spicy—is how the Mexicans describe bland food. *Caliente,* the Spanish adjective for "hot" (as in hot water), does not, in contrast to English usage, imply spicy, or *picante.*

Vegetarian Fare

Strictly vegetarian cooking is the exception in Mexico, as are macrobiotic restaurants, health-food stores, and organic produce. Meat is such a delicacy for most Mexicans that they can't understand why people would give it up voluntarily. If vegetable-lovers can manage with corn, beans, cheese, eggs, *legumbres* (vegetables), and fruit, and not be bothered by a bit of pork fat *(manteca de cerdo),* Mexican cooking will suit them fine. On the other hand, if pork fat bothers you, ask for your food *sin manteca* (without lard).

Seafood

Early chroniclers wrote that Aztec Emperor Moctezuma employed a platoon of runners to bring fresh fish 300 miles every day from the sea to his court. In Pacific Mexico, fresh seafood is fortunately much more available from thousands of shoreline establishments, varying from thatched beach *palapas* to five-star hotel restaurants.

Pacific Mexico seafood is literally there for the taking. When strolling certain beaches, I have often seen well-fed, middle-class local vacationers breaking and eating oysters and mussels right off the rocks. In the summer on some Pacific Mexico beaches, fish and squid have been known to swarm so thickly in the surf that tourists can pull them out by hand. Villagers up and down the coast use small nets (or bare hands) to retrieve a few fish for supper, while communal teams haul in big netfuls of silvery, wriggling fry for sale right on the beach.

Despite the plenty, Pacific Mexico seafood prices reflect high worldwide demand, even at the humblest seaside *palapa*. The freshness and variety, however, make even the typical dishes seem bargains at any price.

Fruits and Juices

Squeezed vegetable and fruit juices, *jugos* (HOO-gohs), are among the widely available

---

CATCH OF THE DAY

Ceviche (say-VEE-chay): A chopped raw fish appetizer as popular on Puerto Vallarta beaches as sushi is on Tokyo sidestreets. Although it can contain anything from conch to octopus, the best ceviche consists of diced young shark *(tiburón)* or mackerel *(sierra)* fillet and plenty of fresh tomatoes, onions, garlic, and *chiles,* all doused with lime juice.

Filete de pescado (fish fillet): sautéed *al mojo* (ahl-MOH-hoh)—with butter and garlic.

Pescado frito (pays-KAH-doh FREE-toh): Fish, pan-fried whole; if you don't specify that it be cooked lightly *(a medio),* the fish may arrive well done, like a big, crunchy French fry.

Pescado veracruzana: A favorite everywhere. Best with red snapper *(huachinango),* smothered in a savory tomato, onion, *chile,* and garlic sauce. *Pargo* (snapper), *mero* (grouper), and *cabrilla* (sea bass) are also popularly used in this and other specialties.

Shellfish: These abound: *ostiones* (oysters) and *almejas* (clams) by the dozen; *langosta* (lobster) and *langostina* (crayfish) *asado* (broiled), *al vapor* (steamed), or fried. Pots of fresh-boiled *camarones* (shrimp) are sold on the street by the kilo; cafés will make them into *cóctel,* or prepare them *en gabardinas* (breaded) at your request.

delights of Pacific Mexico. Among the many establishments—restaurants, cafés, and *loncherías*—willing to supply you with your favorite *jugo,* the juice bars *(jugerías)* are often the most fun. Colorful fruit piles usually mark *jugerías.* If you don't immediately spot your favorite fruit, ask anyway; it might be hidden in the refrigerator.

Besides your choice of pure juice, *jugerías* will often serve *licuados.* Into the juice, they whip powdered milk, your favorite fruit, and sugar to taste for a creamy afternoon pick-me-up or evening dessert. One big favorite is a cool banana-chocolate *licuado,* which comes out tasting like a milk shake minus the calories.

Alcoholic Drinks

The Aztecs sacrificed anyone caught drinking alcohol without permission. The later, more lenient, Spanish attitude toward getting *borracho* (soused)

has led to a thriving Mexican renaissance of native alcoholic beverages: tequila, mescal, Kahlúa, pulque, and *aguardiente.* Tequila and mescal, distilled from the fermented juice of the maguey, originated in Oaxaca, where the best are still made. Quality tequila (named after the Guadalajara-area distillery town) and mescal come 76 proof (38 percent alcohol) and up. A small white worm, endemic to the maguey, is customarily added to each bottle of factory mescal for authenticity.

Pulque, although also made from the sap of the maguey, is locally brewed to a small alcohol content between that of beer and wine. The brewing houses are sacrosanct preserves, circumscribed by traditions that exclude women and outsiders. The brew, said to be rich in nutrients, is sold to local *pulquerías* and drunk immediately. If you are ever invited into a *pulquería,* it is an honor you cannot refuse.

Aguardiente, by contrast, is the notorious

ON THE ROAD

A TROVE OF FRUITS AND NUTS

Besides carrying the usual temperate fruits, *jugerías* and especially markets are seasonal sources of a number of exotic (followed by an *) varieties:

avocado *(aguacate*—ah-wah-KAH-tay): Aztec aphrodisiac

banana *(platano):* many kinds—big and small, red and yellow

chirimoya* *(chirimoya):* green scales, white pulp; sometimes called an anona

ciruela:* looks (but doesn't taste) like a small yellow-to-red plum

coconut *(coco):* coconut "milk" is called *agua de coco*

grapes *(uvas):* Aug.–Nov. season

guanabana:* looks, but doesn't taste, like a green mango

guava *(guava):* delicious juice, widely available canned

lemon *(limón*—lee-MOHN): uncommon and expensive; use lime instead

lime *(lima*—LEE-mah): douse salads with it

mamey* *(mamey*—mah-MAY): yellow, juicy fruit; excellent for jellies and preserves

mango *(mango):* king of fruit, in a hundred varieties June–November

orange *(naranja*—nah-RAHN-ha): greenish skin but sweet and juicy

papaya *(papaya):* said to aid digestion and healing

peach *(durazno*—doo-RAHS-noh): delicious and widely available as canned juice

peanut *(cacahuate*—kah-kah-WAH-tay): home roasted and cheap

pear *(pera):* fall season

pecan *(nuez):* for a treat, try freshly ground pecan butter

piña anona:* looks like a thin ear of corn without the husk; tastes like pineapple

pineapple *(piña):* huge, luscious, and cheap

strawberry *(fresa*—FRAY-sah): local favorite

tangerine *(mandarina):* common around Christmas

watermelon *(sandía*—sahn-DEE-ah): perfect on a hot day

zapote* (sah-POH-tay): yellow, fleshy fruit; said to induce sleep

zapote colorado:* brown skin, red, puckery fruit, like persimmon; incorrectly called *mamey*

fiery Mexican "white lightning," a locally distilled, dirt-cheap ticket to oblivion for poor Mexican men.

While pulque comes from age-old indigenous tradition, beer (introduced by 19th-century German brewers) is the beverage of modern mestizo Mexico. More full-bodied than "light" U.S. counterparts, Mexican beer enjoys an enviable reputation.

Those visitors who indulge usually know their favorite among the many brands, from light to dark: Superior, Corona, Pacífico, Tecate (served with lime), Carta Blanca, Modelo, Dos Equis, Bohemia, Tres Equis, and Negro Modelo. Nochebuena, a hearty dark brew, becomes available only around Christmas.

Mexicans have yet to develop much of a taste for *vino tinto* or *vino blanco* (red or white table wine), although some domestic wines (such as the Baja California labels Cetto and Domecq and the "boutique" Monte Xanic) are at least very drinkable and at best, excellent.

Bread and Pastries
Excellent locally baked bread is a delightful surprise to many first-time visitors to Pacific Mexico. Small bakeries everywhere put out trays of hot, crispy-crusted *bolillos* (rolls) and sweet *panes dulces* (pastries). The pastries vary from simple cakes, muffins, cookies, and doughnuts to fancy fruit-filled turnovers and puffs. Half the fun occurs before the eating: grab a tray and tongs, peruse the goodies, and pick out the most scrumptious. With your favorite dozen or so finally selected, you take your tray to the cashier, who deftly bags everything up and collects a few pesos (two or three dollars) for your entire mouthwatering selection.

Restaurant Price Key
In the destination chapters, restaurants that serve dinner are described as budget, moderate, expensive, or a combination thereof, at the end of each restaurant description. **Budget** means that the entrées cost under $7; **moderate,** $7–14; **expensive,** over $14.

A *restaurante* (rays-tah-oo-RAHN-tay) generally implies a fairly fancy joint, with prices to match. The food and atmosphere, however, may be more to your liking at other types of eateries (in approximate order of price): *comedor, café, fonda, lonchería, jugería, taquería.*

Shopping

What to Buy
Although bargains abound in Mexico, savvy shoppers are selective. Steep import and luxury taxes drive up the prices of foreign-made goods such as cameras, computers, sports equipment, and English-language books. Instead, concentrate your shopping on locally made items: leather, jewelry, cotton resort wear, Mexican-made designer clothes, and the galaxy of handicrafts for which Mexico is renowned.

Handicrafts
A number of Pacific Mexico regional centers are renowned sources of crafts. A multitude of family shops in Guadalajara and its suburban villages of Tlaquepaque and Tonalá, the Lake Pátzcuaro region, Taxco and its village hinterland, and the Valley of Oaxaca all nurture vibrant traditions with roots in the pre-Columbian past. This rich cornucopia spills over to the Pacific resort centers, where it merges with troves of local offerings to decorate sidewalks, stalls, and shops all over town.

Bargaining
Bargaining will stretch your money even further. It comes with the territory in Mexico and needn't be a hassle. On the contrary, if done with humor and moderation, bargaining can be an enjoyable way to meet Mexican people and gain their respect, even friendship.

The local crafts market is where bargaining is most intense. For starters, try offering half the asking price. From there on, it's all psychology: you have to content yourself with not having to have the item. Otherwise, you're sunk; the vendor will sense your need and stand fast. After a few minutes of good-humored bantering, ask for *el último precio* (the final price), in which, if it's close, may be just the bargain you've been looking for.

Buying Silver and Gold Jewelry

Silver and gold jewelry, the finest of which is crafted in Taxco, Guadalajara, and Guanajuato, fills a number of shops in Pacific Mexico. One hundred percent pure silver is rarely sold because it's too soft. Silver (sent from processing mills in the north of Mexico to be worked in Taxco shops) is nearly always alloyed with 7.5 percent copper to increase its durability. Such pieces, identical in composition to sterling silver, should have ".925," together with the initials of the manufacturer, stamped on their back sides. Other, less common grades, such as "800 fine" (80 percent silver), should also be stamped.

If silver is not stamped with the degree of purity, it probably contains no silver at all and is an alloy of copper, zinc, and nickel, known by the generic label "alpaca," or "German" silver. Once, after haggling over the purity and prices of his offerings, a street vendor handed me a shiny handful and said, "Go to a jeweler and have them tested. If they're not real, keep them." Calling his bluff, I took them to a jeweler, who applied a dab of hydrochloric acid (commonly available as "muriatic acid") to each piece. Tiny, tell-tale bubbles of hydrogen revealed the cheapness of the merchandise, which I returned the next day to the vendor.

Some shops price sterling silver jewelry simply by weighing, which typically translates to about $1 per gram. If you want to find out if the price is fair, ask the shopkeeper to weigh it for you.

People prize pure gold partly because, unlike silver, it does not tarnish. Gold, nevertheless, is rarely sold pure (24 karat); for durability, it is alloyed with copper. Typical purities, such as 18 karat (75 percent) or 14 karat (58 percent), should be stamped on the pieces. If not, chances are they contain no gold at all.

Getting There

BY AIR

From the United States and Canada

The vast majority of travelers reach Pacific Mexico by air. Flights are frequent and reasonably priced. Competition sometimes shaves prices to as low as $250 or less for a Mazatlán or Puerto Vallarta round-trip from Los Angeles, Denver, or Dallas.

Air travelers can save lots of money by shopping around. Don't be bashful about asking for the cheapest price. Make it clear to the airline or travel agent that you're interested in a bargain. Ask the right questions: Are there special-incentive, advance-payment, night, midweek, tour package, or charter fares? Peruse the ads in the Sunday newspaper travel section for bargain-oriented travel agencies. Check airline and travel websites, such as www.orbitz.com, www.expedia.com, and www.travelocity.com.

Although some agents charge booking fees and don't like discounted tickets because their fee depends on a percentage of ticket price, many will nevertheless work hard to get you a bargain, especially if you book an entire air-hotel package with them.

Although few airlines fly directly to Pacific Mexico from the northern United States and Canada, many charters do. In locales near Vancouver, Calgary, Ottawa, Toronto, Montreal, Minneapolis, Chicago, Detroit, Cleveland, and New York, consult a travel agent for charter flight options. Be aware that charter reservations, which often require fixed departure and return dates and provide minimal cancellation refunds, decrease your flexibility. If available charter choices are unsatisfactory, then you might choose to begin your vacation with a connecting flight to one of the Pacific Mexico gateways, such as San Francisco, Los Angeles, San Diego, Denver, Phoenix, Dallas, Houston, Atlanta, Chicago, San Jose, or Oakland.

You may be able to save money by booking an air/hotel package through one of the airlines that routinely offer them from their Pacific Mexico

AIRLINES

The air carriers with the greatest number of direct connections between Pacific Mexico and North American destinations are listed below in approximate descending order of activity. Destinations include Mazatlán (MZ), Puerto Vallarta (PV), Manzanillo-Barra de Navidad (MN), Guadalajara (GD), Ixtapa-Zihuatanejo (IX), Acapulco (AC), Mexico City (MX), Morelia (MO), Uruapan (UR), Colima (CO), Huatulco (HU), Tepic (TP), Los Cabos (LC), and La Paz (LP). Other popular Pacific Mexico destinations, such as Oaxaca and Puerto Escondido, are air-accessible via Mexico City.

Airline	Origin	Destinations
Mexicana	Los Angeles	MZ, GD, MX, LC, MO
tel. 800/531-7921	San Francisco	GD, MX, MO
www.mexicana.com	San Jose	GD, MX, MO
	Tijuana	GD, MX
	Denver	MX
	Chicago	PV, GD, MX, MO, AC
	Miami	MX
	San Antonio	MX
	Oakland	GD
	Toronto	MX
	Montreal	MX
Aeroméxico	Los Angeles	PV, GD, MX
tel. 800/237-6639	Tijuana	MZ, GD, AC, MO, TP, MX
www.aeromexico.com	New York	MX
	Miami	MX
	Houston	MX
	San Diego	MX, LC
	Atlanta	GD, MX
	Phoenix	GD, MX
	Dallas	MX
World of Vacations charter	Toronto	PV, MN, IX, AC
tel. 800/661-8881	Vancouver	PV, MN
www.worldofvacations.com	Calgary-Edmonton	PV, MN
	Winnipeg	PV
	Regina	PV
	Saskatoon	PV
Alaska Airlines	Seattle	MZ, PV, MN, IX, LC
tel. 800/426-0333	San Francisco	MZ, PV, IX, LC
www.alaskaair.com	Los Angeles	MZ, PV, MN, IX, LC

ON THE ROAD

	San Diego	PV
	Phoenix	PV, LC
American tel. 800/433-7300 www.aa.com	Dallas Los Angeles Chicago Miami	PV, GD, AC, MX GD, LC MX GD, MX
Delta tel. 800/221-1212 www.delta.com	Los Angeles Dallas Atlanta New York	PV, GD, MX MX GD, MX MX
Aerocalifornia tel. 800/237-6225 (no website)	Los Angeles Tijuana Tucson	MZ, GD, MN, TP, LC, LP, MX MZ, GD, CO, MX GD, LP
America West tel. 800/363-2597 www.americawest.com	Phoenix	MZ, PV, GD, MN, IX, AC, LC, MX
Continental tel. 800/231-0856 www.continental.com	Houston	MZ, PV, GD, AC, LC, MX
Allegro tel. 877/443-7585 (no website)	Oakland Las Vegas	GD, MX GD, MX
Azteca tel. 888/754-0066 (no website)	Laredo El Paso Tijuana	MX MX PV, GD, MO, UR
Air Canada tel. 888/247-2262 www.aircanada.com	Toronto	MX
Aviacsa tel. 800/758-2188 (no website)	Los Angeles	GD, MX, Leon, Guanajuato, Monterrey

gateway cities. (For gateway cities, see the special topic "Airlines.")

Mexicana: tel. 866/263-9732
Alaska: tel. 800/468-2248
America West: tel. 800/356-6611
American: tel. 800/321-2121
Aeroméxico: tel. 800/245-8585
Continental: tel. 800/634-5555
World of Vacations (Canada charter): tel. 800/661-8881
Delta: tel. 800/872-7786

From Europe, Latin America, and Australasia

A few airlines fly across the Atlantic directly to Mexico City. These include **Lufthansa,** which connects directly from Frankfurt; and **Aeroméxico,** which connects directly from Paris and Madrid. In Mexico City, connections to Pacific Mexico are available via Mexicana, Aeroméxico, and Aerocalifornia airlines.

From Latin America, **Aeroméxico** connects directly with Mexico City, from Sao Paulo, Brazil; Santiago, Chile; and Lima, Peru. A number of other Latin American flag carriers also fly directly to Mexico City.

Very few flights cross the Pacific directly to Mexico, except for **Japan Airlines,** which connects Tokyo to Mexico City, via Vancouver. More commonly, travelers from Australasia routinely transfer at New York, Chicago, Dallas, San Francisco, or Los Angeles for Pacific Mexico.

Baggage, Insurance, "Bumping," and In-Flight Meals

Tropical Pacific Mexico makes it easy to pack light. (See the "Packing Checklist" chart.) Veteran tropical travelers condense their luggage to carry-ons only. Airlines routinely allow a carry-on (not exceeding 45 inches in combined length, width, and girth), small book bag, and purse. Thus relieved of heavy burdens, your trip will become much simpler. You'll avoid possible luggage loss and long baggage-check-in lines by being able to check in directly at the boarding gate.

Even if you can't avoid checking luggage, loss of it needn't ruin your vacation. Always carry your irreplaceable items in the cabin with you. These should include all money, credit cards, traveler's checks, keys, tickets, cameras, passport, prescription drugs, and eyeglasses.

At the X-ray security check, insist that your film and cameras be hand-inspected. Regardless of what attendants claim, repeated X-ray scanning will fog any undeveloped film, especially the sensitive ASA 400 and 1,000 high-speed varieties.

Travelers packing lots of expensive baggage, or who (because of illness, for example) may have to cancel a nonrefundable flight or tour, might consider buying **travel insurance.** Travel agents routinely sell packages that include baggage, trip cancellation, and default insurance. **Baggage insurance** covers you beyond the (typically $1,000 domestic, $500 international baggage; check with your carrier) liability limits. **Trip cancellation insurance** pays if you must cancel your prepaid trip, while **default insurance** protects you if your carrier or tour agent does not perform as agreed. Travel insurance, however, can be expensive. Traveler's Insurance Company, for example, offers $1,000 of baggage insurance per person for two weeks for about $50. (For more information, see the travel websites in the Internet Resources section or call a travel agent.) Weigh your options and the cost against benefits carefully before putting your money down.

It's wise to reconfirm both departure and return flight reservations, especially during the busy Christmas and Easter seasons. This is a useful strategy, as is prompt arrival at check-in, against getting "bumped" (losing your seat) by the tendency of airlines to overbook the rush of high-season vacationers. For further protection, always get your seat assignment and boarding pass included with your ticket.

Airlines generally try hard to accommodate travelers with dietary or other special needs. When booking your flight, inform your travel agent or carrier of the necessity of a low-sodium, low-cholesterol, vegetarian, or lactose-reduced meal, or other requirements. (Seniors, travelers with disabilities, and parents traveling with children, see Specialty Travel under Information and Services.)

BY BUS

As air travel rules in the United States, bus travel rules in Mexico. Hundreds of sleek, first-class buses lines with names such as Elite, Turistar, Futura, Transportes Pacífico, and White Star (Estrella Blanca) depart the border daily, headed for Pacific Mexico.

Since North American bus lines ordinarily terminate just north of the Mexican border, you must usually disembark, walk to the Mexican immigration (*migración*) office just across the border. After having completed out the necessary but very simple paperwork, proceed to the nearby taxi stand (*sitio taxi*) and hire a taxi (agree upon the price before getting in) to take you the few miles to the *camionera central* (central bus station).

First-class bus service in Mexico is much cheaper and more frequent than in the United States. Tickets for comparable trips in Mexico cost a fraction (as little as $50 for a 1,000-mile trip, compared to $100 in the United States).

In Mexico, as on United States buses, you often have to take it as you find it. *Asientos reservados* (seat reservations), *boletos* (tickets), and information must generally be obtained in person at the bus station, and credit cards and traveler's checks are not often accepted. Neither are reserved bus tickets typically refundable, so don't miss the bus. On the other hand, plenty of buses roll south almost continually.

Bus Routes to Pacific Mexico

From California and the western United States, cross the border to Tijuana, Mexicali, or Nogales, where you can ride one of several bus lines along the Pacific coast route (National Highway 15) to points south: Estrella Blanca subsidiaries (Elite, Turistar, Transportes Norte de Sonora) or independent Transportes del Pacífico.

At Mazatlán or Tepic, depending on the line, you transfer or continue on the same bus, south to Puerto Vallarta and/or Manzanillo, or west to Guadalajara. Allow a full day and a bit more (about 30 hours), depending upon connections, for the trip. Carry liquids and food (which might be only minimally available en route) with you.

From the midwestern United States, cross the border from El Paso to Ciudad Juárez and ride independent line Omnibus de Mexico or Estrella Blanca subsidiaries (luxury-class Turistar or Transportes Chihuahuenses) via Chihuahua and Durango. Both Transportes Chihuahuenses and Turistar may offer one or two daily departures direct to Mazatlán. Otherwise, transfer at Durango to a Mazatlán-bound bus, and continue as above.

From the southeastern and eastern United States, cross the border at Laredo to Nuevo Laredo and ride Estrella Blanca subsidiaries Transportes del Norte, Turistar, or Futura direct to Durango. At Durango, transfer to a Mazatlán bus, where you can continue south, as described above.

From the central or eastern United States, it may be more convenient to ride a bus from the border direct to Guadalajara, where you can easily transfer to one of many buses bound for Pacific Mexico western and southern destinations of Puerto Vallarta, Barra de Navidad, Manzanillo, and Michoacán. (For bus connections in Guadalajara, see Getting There and Away in the the South to Puerto Vallarta and Inland to Guadalajara chapter.)

Travelers heading directly to Oaxaca city or the far southern coastal destinations of Acapulco, Ixtapa-Zihuatanejo, and the Oaxaca coast should ride from the border directly to Mexico City, Terminal Norte (North Terminal). At Terminal Norte, ride Autobúses del Oriente (ADO) or Cristóbal Colón directly to Oaxaca city. For the south coast from Terminal Norte, ride an Estrella Blanca subsidiary bus (Turistar or Futura) to Acapulco, where you can transfer to coast-route buses bound either northwest for Ixtapa-Zihuatanejo, or southeast for Puerto Escondido on the Oaxaca coast. If somehow the above connections are not available at Terminal Norte, share a taxi—don't try it by public transit—across town to either Terminal Tapo, the Mexico City east terminal, or Terminal Sur, the Mexico City south terminal. At Terminal Tapo, board a Oaxaca city–bound bus, probably Cristóbal Colón or ADO (Autobúses del Oriente)—via *corta*—the expressway "shortcut." At Terminal Sur, board an Acapulco-bound Estrella Blanca subsidiary (Turistar, or Futura) bus.

From the U.S. border east, allow two days'

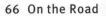

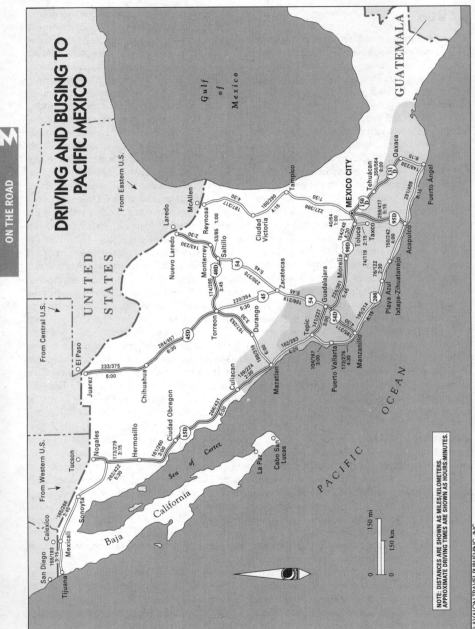

DRIVING AND BUSING TO PACIFIC MEXICO

NOTE: DISTANCES ARE SHOWN AS MILES/KILOMETERS.
APPROXIMATE DRIVING TIMES ARE SHOWN AS HOURS:MINUTES.

© AVALON TRAVEL PUBLISHING, INC.

travel for Acapulco, Ixtapa-Zihuatanejo, or Oaxaca city, and three days for Puerto Escondido-Puerto Ángel. From midwestern or western border points, add another day.

BY TRAIN

Privatization is rapidly putting an end to most passenger train service in Mexico, with the exception of the Copper Canyon tourist route.

One of the few remaining passenger train rides in Mexico begins with a bus trip or flight south to Chihuahua, where you board the Chihuahua-Pacific Railway train and ride west along the renowned Copper Canyon (Barranca del Cobre) route to the Pacific. Finished only during the early 1960s, this route traverses the spectacular canyonland home of the Tarahumara people. At times along the winding, 406-mile (654-km) route, your rail car seems to teeter at the very edge of the labyrinthine Barranca del Cobre, a canyon so deep that its climate varies from Canadian at the top to tropical jungle at the bottom. The railway-stop village of Creel, with a few stores and hotels and a Tarahumara mission, is the major jumping-off point for trips into the canyon. For a treat, reserve a stay en route to Pacific Mexico at the Copper Canyon Lodge in Creel. From there, the canyon beckons: explore the village, enjoy panoramic views, observe mountain wildlife, and breathe pine-scented mountain air. Farther afield, you can hike to a hot spring or spend a few days exploring the canyon bottom itself. For more information, call tel. 248/340-7230 or 800/776-3942; write Copper Canyon Hiking Lodges, 2741 Paldan St., Auburn Hills, MI 48326; or check www.coppercanyonlodges.com.

Copper Canyon Tours

Some agencies arrange unusually noteworthy Copper Canyon rail tours. Among the best is **Canyon Travel,** 900 Ridge Creek Ln., Bulverde, TX 78163-2872, tel. 830/885-2000, 800/843-1060, www.canyontravel.com, which employs its own resident, ecologically sensitive guides. Trips vary from small-group, rail-based sightseeing and birding–natural history tours to customized wilderness rail-jeep-backpacking adventures.

Elderhostel has long provided some of the best-buy Copper Canyon options, designed for seniors. Participants customarily fly to Los Mochis on the Pacific coast, then transfer to the first-class Mexican Chihuahua-Pacific train for a four-day canyonland adventure. Highlights include nature walks, visits to native missions, and cultural sites in Cerrocahui village and Creel, the frontier outpost in the Tarahumara heartland. The return includes a comfortable overnight at Posada Barranca, at the canyon's dizzying edge. For more information and reservations, contact 11 Ave. de Lafayette, Boston MA 02111-1746, tel. 877/426-8056, or www.elderhostel.org.

Another worthy tour provider is **American Orient Express,** which specializes in luxury Copper Canyon rail sightseeing tours. Operators employ restored vintage rail cars with class-act amenities, including gourmet cuisine, plush lounges, and deluxe sleeping compartments. Trips begin at Tucson, visiting Saguaro National Park, the Sea of Cortez (including a sealife-viewing excursion), colonial El Alamo town, river rafting at El Fuerte, and a Mayo indigenous folkloric dance at the village of Tehueco. The tour climaxes along the Chihuahua-Pacifico rail route at the dizzying mile-high rim of the Copper Canyon. From the Chihuahua endpoint terminal, continue by bus or air south to Pacific Mexico. Tariffs run about $3,200 per person; for more information, dial tel. 800/320-4206, and/or visit www.AmericanOrientExpress.com.

BY CAR OR RV

If you're adventurous, like going to out-of-the-way places, but still want to have all the comforts of home, you may enjoy driving your car or RV to Pacific Mexico. On the other hand, consideration of cost, risk, wear on both you and your vehicle, and the congestion hassles in towns may change your mind.

Mexican Car Insurance

Mexico does not recognize foreign insurance. When you drive into Mexico, Mexican auto insurance is at least as important as your passport. At the busier crossings, you can get it at insurance "drive-ins" just north of the border. The many Mexican auto insurance companies are government-regulated; their numbers keep prices and services competitive.

Sanborn's Mexico Insurance, one of the best-known agencies, certainly seems to be trying hardest. It offers a number of books and services, including the *Recreational Guide to Mexico* (see Suggested Reading), a good road map, "smile-by-mile" *Travelog* guide to "every highway in Mexico," hotel discounts, and more. Much of the above is available to members of Sanborn's "Sombrero" Club. Sign up for membership, buy insurance using your credit card, and order books through its toll-free number, tel. 800/222-0158. For other queries, call tel. 956/682-7433, write Sanborn's Mexico, P.O. Box 310, McAllen, TX 78502, or log on to www.sanbornsinsurance.com.

Alternatively, look into **Vagabundos del Mar,** an RV-oriented Mexico fishing and travel club that offers memberships that include a newsletter, caravaning opportunites, discounts, insurance and much more. Call tel. 800/474-2252 for a free information packet or look at www.vagabundos.com.

Mexican car insurance runs from a bare-bones rate of about $5 a day to a more typical $10 a day for more complete coverage ($50,000/$40,000/$80,000 public liability/property damage/medical payments) on a vehicle worth $10,000–15,000. On the same scale, insurance for a $50,000 RV and equipment runs about $30 a day. These daily rates decrease sharply for six-month or one-year policies, which run from about $200 for the minimum to $400–1,600 for complete coverage.

If you get broken glass, personal effects, and legal expenses coverage with these rates, you're lucky. Mexican policies don't usually cover them.

You should get something for your money, however. The deductibles should be no more than $300–500, the public liability/medical payments should be about double the ($25,000/$25,000/$50,000) legal minimum, and you should be able to get your car fixed in the United States and receive payment in U.S. dollars for losses. If not, shop around.

A Sinaloa Note of Caution

Although *bandidos* no longer menace Mexican roads (but loose burros, horses, and cattle still do), be cautious in the infamous marijuana- and opium-growing region of Sinaloa state north of Mazatlán. It's best not to stray from Highway 15 between Culiacán and Mazatlán or from Highway 40 between Mazatlán and Durango.

ROAD SAFETY

Hundreds of thousands of visitors enjoy safe Mexican auto vacations every year. Their success is due in large part to their frame of mind: drive defensively, anticipate and adjust to danger before it happens, and watch everything—side roads, shoulders, the car in front, and cars far down the road. The following tips will help ensure a safe and enjoyable trip:

- **Don't drive at night.** Range animals, unmarked sand piles, pedestrians, one-lane bridges, cars without lights, and drunken drivers are doubly hazardous at night.
- Although **speed limits** are rarely enforced, *don't break them.* Mexican country roads are often narrow and shoulderless. Poor markings and macho drivers who pass on curves are best faced at a speed of 40 mph (64 kph) rather than 75 (120).
- **Don't drive on sand.** Even with four-wheel-drive, you'll eventually get stuck if you drive often or casually on beaches. When the tide comes in, who'll pull your car out?
- **Slow down** at the *topes* (speed bumps) at the edges of towns and for *vados* (dips), which can be dangerously bumpy and full of water.
- Extending the **courtesy of the road** goes hand-in-hand with safe driving. Both courtesy and machismo are more infectious in Mexico; on the highway, it's much safer to spread the former than the latter.
- For maximum speed and safety, use Mexico's *cuota autopistas* (toll expressways) when convenient. (See the maps: color frontispiece, Driving and Busing to Pacific Mexico, and Driving and Busing Within Pacific Mexico.)

Curious tourists have been assaulted in the hinterlands adjacent to these roads.

The Green Angels
The Green Angels have answered many motoring tourists' prayers in Mexico. Bilingual teams of two, trained in auto repair and first aid, help distressed tourists along main highways. They patrol fixed stretches of road twice daily by truck. To make sure they stop to help, pull completely off the highway and raise your hood. You may want to hail a passing trucker to call them for you (toll-free Mex. tel. 800/903-9200 for the tourism hotline, which might alert the Green Angels for you).

If, for some reason, you have to leave your vehicle on the roadside, don't leave it unattended. Hire a local teenager or adult to watch it for you. Unattended vehicles on Mexican highways are quickly stricken by a mysterious disease, the symptoms of which are rapid loss of vital parts.

Mexican Gasoline
Pemex, short for Petróleos Mexicanos, the government oil monopoly, markets diesel fuel and two grades of unleaded gasoline: 92-octane premium and 89-octane Magna. Magna (MAHG-nah) is good gas, yielding performance similar to that of U.S.-style "regular or super-unleaded" gasoline. (My car, whose manufacturer recommended 91-octane, ran well on Magna.) It runs about $.55 per liter (or about $2 per gallon.)

On main highways, Pemex makes sure that major stations (spaced typically about 30 miles apart) stock Magna.

Gas Station Thievery
Although the problem has abated considerably in recent years (by the hiring of female attendants), boys who hang around gas stations to wash windows are notoriously light-fingered. When stopping at the *gasolinera,* make sure that your cameras, purses, and other movable items are out of reach. Also, make sure that your car has a lockable gas cap. If not, insist on pumping the gas yourself, or be super-watchful as you pull up to the gas pump. Make certain that the pump reads zero before the attendant pumps the gas.

DISASTER AND RESCUE ON A MEXICAN HIGHWAY

My litany of Mexican driving experiences came to a climax one night when, heading north from Tepic, I hit a cow at 50 mph head-on. The cow was knocked about 150 feet down the road, while I and my two friends endured a scary impromptu roller-coaster ride. When the dust settled, we, although in shock, were grateful that we hadn't suffered the fate of the poor cow, which had died instantly from the collision.

From that low point, our fortunes soon began to improve. Two buses stopped and about 40 men got out to move my severely wounded van to the shoulder. The cow's owner, a rancher, arrived to cart off the cow's remains in a jeep. Then the police—a man and his wife in a VW bug—pulled up. *"Pobrecita camioneta"* ("Poor little van"), the woman said, gazing at my vehicle, which now resembled an oversized, crumpled accordion. They gave us a ride to Mazatlán, found us a hotel room, and generally made sure we were okay.

If I hadn't had Mexican auto insurance I would have been in deep trouble. Mexican law—based on the Napoleonic Code—presumes guilt and does not bother with juries. It would have kept me in jail until all damages were settled. The insurance agent I saw in the morning took care of everything. He called the police station, where I was excused from paying damages when the cow's owner failed to show. He had my car towed to a repair shop, where the mechanics banged it into good enough shape so I could drive it home a week later. Forced to stay in one place, my friends and I enjoyed the most relaxed time of our entire three months in Mexico. The *pobrecita camioneta,* all fixed up a few months later, lasted 14 more years.

A Healthy Car
Preventive measures spell good health for both you and your car. Get that tune-up (or that long-delayed overhaul) *before,* rather than after, you leave.

Carry a stock of spare parts, which will be more difficult to get and more expensive in Mexico

ON THE ROAD

than at home. Carry an extra tire or two, a few cans of motor oil and octane enhancer, oil and gas filters, fan belts, spark plugs, tune-up kit, points, and fuses. Be prepared with basic tools and supplies, such as screwdrivers, pliers including Vice-Grip, lug wrench, jack, adjustable wrenches, tire pump and patches, tire pressure gauge, steel wire, and electrical tape. For breakdowns and emergencies, carry a folding shovel, a husky rope or chain, a gasoline can, and flares.

Car Repairs in Mexico

The American big three—General Motors, Ford, and Chrysler—as well as Nissan and Volkswagen are represented by extensive dealer networks in Mexico. Latecomers Toyota and Honda are represented, although to a much lesser extent. Getting your car or truck serviced at such agencies is straightforward. While parts will probably be higher in price, shop rates run about half U.S.

© BRUCE WHIPPERMAN

Mexican *llantera* (tire repair) service is generally expert, quick, and inexpensive.

prices, so repairs will generally come out cheaper than back home.

The same is not true for repairing other makes, however. Mexico has few, if any, other Japanese car or truck dealers; and other than Mercedes-Benz, which has some truck agencies, it is difficult to find officially certified mechanics for other Japanese, British, and European vehicles.

Many clever Mexican independent mechanics, however, can fix any car that comes their way. Their humble repair shops *talleres mecánicos* (tah-YER-ays may-KAH-nee-kohs) dot town and village roadsides everywhere.

Although most mechanics are honest, beware of unscrupulous operators who try to collect double or triple their original estimate. If you don't speak Spanish, find someone who can assist you in negotiations. *Always* get a written cost estimate, including needed parts and labor, even if you have to write it yourself. Make sure the mechanic understands, then ask him to sign it before he starts work. Although this may be a hassle, it might save you a much nastier hassle later. Shop labor at small, independent repair shops should run $10–20 per hour. For more information, and for entertaining anecdotes of car and RV travel in Mexico, consult Carl Franz's *The People's Guide to Mexico.*

Bribes (Mordidas)

The usual meeting ground of the visitor and Mexican police is in the visitor's car on a highway or downtown street. To the tourists, such an encounter may seem mild harassment by the police, accompanied by vague threats of going to the police station or impounding the car for such-and-such a violation. The tourist often goes on to say, "It was all right, though . . . We paid him $10 and he went away. . . . Mexican cops sure are crooked, aren't they?"

And, I suppose, if people want to go bribing their way through Mexico, that's their business. But calling Mexican cops crooked isn't exactly fair. Police, like most everyone else in Mexico, have to scratch for a living, and they have found that many tourists are willing to slip them a $10 bill for nothing. Rather than crooked, I would call them hungry and opportunistic.

Instead of paying a bribe, do what I've done a dozen times: remain cool, and if you're really guilty of an infraction, calmly say, "Ticket, please." *("Boleto, por favor.")* After a minute or two of stalling, and no cash appearing, the officer most likely will not bother with a ticket but will wave you on with only a warning. If, on the other hand, the officer does write you a ticket, he will probably keep your driver's license, which you will be able to retrieve at the *presidencia municipal* (city hall) the next day in exchange for paying your fine.

Crossing the Border

Squeezing through the border traffic bottlenecks during peak holidays and rush hours can be time-consuming. Avoid crossing 7–9 A.M. and 4:30–6:30 P.M.

Highway Routes from the United States

If you've decided to drive to northwestern Pacific Mexico, you have your choice of three general routes. At safe highway speeds, each of these routes requires a minimum of about 24 hours of driving time. Maximize comfort and safety by following the broad toll *(cuota)* expressways that often parallel the old narrow nontoll *(libre)* routes. Despite the increased cost (about $60 for a car, double or triple that for a motorhome) the *cuota* expressways will save you at least a day's driving time (including the extra food and hotel tariffs) and wear and tear on both your vehicle and your nerves. Most folks allow three full south-of-the-border driving days to Mazatlán-Guadalajara-Puerto Vallarta.

From the western and Pacific United States, follow National Highway 15 (called 15 D as the toll expressway) from the border at Nogales, Sonora, an hour's drive south of Tucson, Arizona. Highway 15 D continues southward smoothly, leading you through cactus-studded mountains and valleys, which turn into green to lush farmland and tropical coastal plain and forest by the time you arrive in Mazatlán. Watch for the peripheral bypasses *(periféricos)* and truck routes that guide you past the congested downtowns of Hermosillo, Guaymas, Ciudad

Obregón, Los Mochis, and Culiacán. Between these centers, you speed along, via *cuota* (toll) expressway all the way to Mazatlán. If you prefer not to pay the high tolls, stick to the old *libre* (free) highway. Hazards, bumps, and slow going might force you to reconsider, however.

From Mazatlán, continue along the narrow (but soon to be replaced) two-lane route to Tepic, where Highways 15 and 15 D fork left (east) to Guadalajara and Highway 200 heads south to Puerto Vallarta and beyond.

If, however, you're driving to western Pacific Mexico from the central United States, cross the border at El Paso to Ciudad Juárez, Chihuahua. There, National Highway 45 D, the new *cuota* multilane expressway, leads you southward through high dry plains past the cities of Chihuahua and Jiménez where you continue by expressway Highway 49, to Gómez Palacio-Torreón. There, proceed southwest toward Durango, via expressway Highway 40 D. At Durango, head west along the winding but spectacular two-lane trans-Sierra National Highway 40, which intersects National Highway 15 just south of Mazatlán. From there, continue south as described above.

Folks heading to western Pacific Mexico from the eastern and southeastern United States should cross the border from Laredo, Texas, to Nuevo Laredo. From there, you can follow either the National Highway 85 nontoll *(libre)* route or the new Highway 85 D toll *(cuota)* road, which continues, bypassing Monterrey, where you proceed via expressway Highway 40 D all the way to Saltillo. At Saltillo, keep going westward on Highway 40 or expressway 40 D, through Torreón to Durango. Continue, via the two-lane Highway 40 over the Pacific crest all the way to National Highway 15, just south of Mazatlán. Continue southward as described above.

Direct Routes to Pacific Mexico's Deep South

For folks heading from the United States directly for Pacific Mexico's southern destinations of Acapulco, Ixtapa-Zihuatanejo, or Oaxaca, three basic routes are available. From California or the west, the quickest way is to go via Nogales to Guadalajara, where you continue east toward Mexico

City via crosstown expressway Av. Lázaro Cárdenas to toll expressway 90 D. If headed for Acapulco and the south coast, bypass Mexico City at Toluca, by turning south via toll expressway 55 toward Ixtapan del Sal, after which signs direct your connection with toll expressway 95 D south to Acapulco. If headed directly for Oaxaca city, ride expressway 90 D to Mexico City, where you must make your way east through the sprawling metropolis (see special topic "Mexico City Driving Restrictions" in the Acapulco and Inland to Taxco chapter) and connect with eastside toll expressway 150 D through Puebla. Continue east to toll expressway 131 D, thence southeast, via Tehuacán to Oaxaca.

From the midwestern and eastern United States, cross the border from McAllen, Texas, to Reynosa. From there, head southward to Mexico City, where you continue, across town, either south where you connect with toll expressway 95 D to Acapulco; or east, where you connect with toll expressway 150 D (through Puebla) to toll expressway 131 D via Tehuacán to Oaxaca.

BY FERRY

The former trio of passenger and vehicle ferries *(transbordador)* that connected Baja California, across the Gulf of California, with mainland Mexico, have contracted to a single line that connects La Paz, Baja California Sur, with Topolobampo, near Los Mochis, in Sinaloa. Moreover, service is subject to change and cancellation. Keep up with the latest Baja ferry news by dialing toll-free Mex. tel. 800/696-9600, or by logging on to www.baja-web.com (click "destinations," then "La Paz," then "ferry schedule").

If you do go by ferry, you cannot stay in your vehicle during the approximately half-day trip. Options include *salón* (reclining coach seats), *turista* (shared cabin with bunks), *cabina* (private cabin with toilet), and *especial* (deluxe private cabin). Tariffs range about $20–80 per person. Additional vehicle fees run about $60 for a motorcycle, about $270 for an automobile or light RV, and more for a large motor home.

There is hope, however, for passengers without cars. At this writing, a new, fast hydrofoil passenger ferry was operating between La Paz and Topolobampo, fare about $50. For more information, log on to www.baja-web.com and/or contact the hydrofoil office in La Paz, 612/125-6303, fax 612/123-4223.

BY TOUR, CRUISE, AND SAILBOAT

For travelers on a tight time budget, prearranged tour packages can provide a hassle-free route for sampling the attractions of Pacific Mexico's coastal resorts and colonial cities. If, however, you prefer a self-paced vacation, or desire thrift over convenience, you should probably defer tour arrangements until after arrival. Many Pacific Mexico travel and tour agencies are as close as your hotel telephone or front lobby tour desk and can customize a tour for you. Options vary from city highlight tours and bay snorkeling adventures to inland colonial cities shopping and sightseeing overnights to boat adventures through wildlife-rich mangrove jungle hinterlands. (For local possibilities, see the destination chapters.)

Travel agents will typically have a stack of cruise brochures that include Pacific Mexico ports such as Mazatlán, Puerto Vallarta, Ixtapa-Zihuatanejo, and Acapulco on their itineraries. People who enjoy being pampered with lots of food and ready-made entertainment (and who don't mind paying for it) can have great fun on cruises. Accommodations on a typical 10-day winter cruise (which would include several days in port) can run as little as $100 per day per person, double occupancy, to as much as $1,000 or more.

If, however, you want to get to know Mexico and the local people, a cruise is not for you. Onboard food and entertainment is the main event of a cruise; shore sightseeing excursions, which generally cost extra, are a sideshow.

Sailboats, on the other hand, offer an entirely different kind of sea route to Pacific Mexico. Ocean Voyages, a California-based agency, arranges passage on a number of sail and motor vessels that regularly depart to Pacific Mexico ports such as San Diego, Los Angeles, San Francisco, Seattle, and Vancouver, British Columbia. It offers custom itineraries and flexible arrangements that can vary from complete round-trip voyages to weeklong coastal idylls between Pacific Mexico ports of call. Some captains allow passengers to save money by signing on as crew. For more information, contact Ocean Voyages, 1709 Bridgeway, Sausalito, CA 94965, tel. 415/332-4681 or 800/299-4444, fax 415/332-7460, sail@oceanvoyages.com, www.oceanvoyages.com.

SPECIAL TOURS AND STUDY OPTIONS

Some tour and work-study programs include in-depth activities centered around arts and crafts, language and culture, wildlife-viewing, ecology, people-to-people work-study, or off-the-beaten-track adventuring.

Copper Canyon Tours

The naturalist-guided **Betchart Expeditions** tour customarily begins at Los Mochis, the western terminus of the Copper Canyon railroad. Highlights include the colonial town of El Fuerte (1564), wildlife-viewing in the Sinaloan thorn forest, the Jesuit Tarahumara Indian mission at the Copper Canyon village of Cerrocahui, the Cusarare "Place of Eagles" waterfall, and folkloric dances in the colonial city of Chihuahua. For more information, contact Betchart Expeditions, 17050 Montebello Rd., Cupertino, CA 95014-5435, tel. 800/252-4910, fax 408/252-1444, bx@aol.com, www .betchartexpeditions.com.

The nine-day **Mexi-Mayan** Copper Canyon trip customarily includes visits to Chihuahua Mennonite colonies and the Tarahumara Indian mission in Creel, and climaxes with a Mayo Indian fiesta (or an Easter pageant) near Los Mochis. For details, contact Mexi-Mayan Academic Travel, at 12 S. 675 Knoebel Dr., Lemont, IL 60439, tel. 630/972-9090, 800/337-6394, fax 630/972-9393. (For Copper Canyon route details and more tours, see By Train in the Getting There section.)

Elderhostel

Elderhostel's rich offering includes several educational travel programs in a number of Pacific

Mexico locations, including the Copper Canyon, Mazatlán, Guadalajara, Pátzcuaro, Uruapan, and Oaxaca. The Mazatlán "Art and Language" program immerses participants both in basic Spanish conversation and beginning or advanced watercolor painting. One of the Guadalajara programs, "Art of Colonial Mexico," involves sketching and painting and exploration of Guadalara's rich trove of art, highlighted by a visit to the renowned Hospicio Cabañas museum for viewing and discussion of Diego Rivera's arresting murals. The program continues to the Michoacán highland towns of Uruapan and Pátzcuaro, providing a colorfully appropriate setting for participants to create their own art in the stimulating environment of crafts villages, preconquest ruined cities, and colorful markets. A separate Guadalajara program, "Language and History of Mexico," provides hostelers with opportunities to hone their language skills in practical encounters and appreciate history in context, while exploring the architectural, art, and craft treasures of Guadalajara and Zacatecas.

Elderhostel also offers festival programs, one of which centers around the November Day of the Dead in Michoacán. The 10-day tour (including four days in Pátzcuaro and its nearby island villages) includes ancient ruined cities, crafts villages, folkloric dance performances, and climaxes with the Day of the Dead observances which, although somber in most countries, are joyful and lively in Mexico.

Yet another pair of Elderhostel tours lead participants in explorations of Oaxaca's rich cultural and natural heritage. "Oaxaca: Spanish Language and Hispanic Culture" emphasizes practice in conversational Spanish, while "Exotic Mexican Birds and Their Habitat" centers on natural history in the countryside. Both programs include visits to archaeological sites of Monte Albán and Mitla and appreciation of indigenous tradition through visits to pottery, weaving, and woodcrafting villages and evening excursions to enjoy Oaxacan food and folkloric music and dance. Accommodations include both hotel rooms and homestays with Mexican middle-class families. For details, write or phone for the international catalog: Elderhostel, 11 Ave. de Lafayette, Boston,

MA 02111-1746, tel. 877/426-8056, TTY 877/426-2167, or visit www.elderhostel.org.

Holistic Retreats

Mar de Jade, a holistic-style living center at Playa Chacala, about 50 miles (80 km) north of Puerto Vallarta, offers unique people-to-people work-study opportunities. These include Spanish language study at Mar de Jade's rustic beach study-center and assisting at its health clinic in Las Varas town nearby. It also offers accommodations and macrobiotic meals for travelers who would want to do nothing more than stay a few days and soak in Mar de Jade's lovely tropical ambience. (For more details of the Mar de Jade area and accommodations and fees, see the Road to San Blas section in the Nayarit Coast chapter.) For additional information, contact Mar de Jade in Puerto Vallarta, tel./fax 322/222-1171 or 322/222-3524, info@mardejade.com, or www.mardejade.com.

Another similar, more deluxe (but simply spartan) spa option is **Rancho Río Caliente Spa,** nestled in the sylvan pine-oak forest hinterland about 20 miles west of Guadalajara. Accommodations are in a tranquil cluster of brick cottages beside and above the steaming Río Caliente, which gushes, steaming hot, from a nearby cliff-bottom. Inside, the approximately 50 comfortably austere accommodations, each with its own fireplace, are enclosed in attractively rustic brown brick walls, with shiny tile floors, comfortable beds, handmade wooden furniture, and immaculate shower baths.

Rates begin at about $160 per day per person, including taxes and all meals (macrobiotic, alcohol-free) and many activities, including sauna, hot pools, hiking, discussion groups, and wildlife-viewing (but no exercise machines.) Available spa treatments are extensive but extra. Contact its North American agent, Spa Vacations, P.O. Box 897, Millbrae, CA 94030, tel. 650/615-0601, riocal@aol.com, or visit www.riocaliente.com.

Ecoadventuring

Adventurous, physically fit travelers might enjoy the off-the-beaten-path biking, snorkeling, fishing, kayaking, hiking, and sightseeing tours of Seat-tle-based **Outland Adventures.** Its itineraries (typically about $100 per day) run 3–10 days and include lots of local color and food, accommodations in small hotels, and sightseeing in the Jalisco coast hinterland of beaches, forest trails, mangrove lagoons, and country roads. For more information, contact Outland's owner-operator Dan Clarke at P.O. Box 16343, Seattle, WA 98116, tel./fax 206/932-7012, outlandadventures@foxinternet.net, or log on to www.-outlandadventures.natureavenue.com. Dan's Mexico headquarters is Villa Montana, which he also rents, in the beach village of La Manzanilla, a few miles north of Barra de Navidad. For more information on Villa Montana rentals, log on to www.choice1.com/villamontana.htm, or the La Manzanilla website www.mexicomexico.info.

A Puerto Vallarta ranch, **Rancho El Charro,** Francisco Villa 895, Fracc. Las Gaviotas, Puerto Vallarta, Jalisco 48300, tel. 322/224-0114, aguirre@pvnet.com.mx, organizes naturalist-led **horseback treks** in the mountains near Puerto Vallarta. Tours run several days and include guided backcountry horseback riding, exploring antique colonial villages, camping out on the trail, swimming, hearty dinners, and cozy evenings at a rustic hacienda. Tariffs begin at about $1,000 per person. For more information, take a look at www.ranchoelcharro.com.

Grassroots Exploring

Travelers interested in an in-depth people-to-people exploration of vanishing indigenous traditions might enjoy following anthropologist-guide George Otis, founder of **Urraca Expeditions,** into the rugged indigenous Mayo and Huichol Sierra Madre heartland of Sinaloa and Nayarit. For more information, log on to George's website, www.urraca.com.

Alternatively, socially concerned travelers might consider a **Global Exchange** tour. Global Exchange is a non-profit research, education, and political action organization working for social justice worldwide. Recent programs have included "Teaching for Change in Guerrero," "Day of the Dead in Oaxaca," and "Coffee, Crafts, and Fair Trade" in Oaxaca and Chiapas. For upcoming itineraries, contact its Reality Tours department,

2017 Mission St., #303, San Francisco, CA 94110, tel. 415/255-7296, 800/497-1994, fax 415/255-7498, gx-info@globalexchange.org, www.globalexchange.org.

Wildlife-Viewing

Naturalists should consider the excellent **Field Guides** birding tours, one customarily centered in wildlife-rich Jalisco and Colima backcountry, and the other in Oaxaca's central valley and tropical south coast. For more information, call toll-free tel. 800/728-4953, fax 512/263-0117, email fieldguides@fieldguides.com, or visit www.fieldguides.com.

The **National Audubon Society** also offers Mexico birding tours. Itineraries have included the Copper Canyon, Baja, and Oaxaca (which includes four days in the Valley of Oaxaca and four days in the lush south coastal mountain jungle near Puerto Escondido.) Contact the National Audubon Society, 700 Broadway, New York, NY 10003-9562, tel. 212/979-3066, 800/967-7425. For updates, see www.audubon.org/market/no.

Additionally, Betchart Expeditions (see Copper Canyon Tours section) usually offers a Monarch Butterfly Safari, in the Michoacán mountain hinterland, half a day's drive east of Lake Pátzcuaro. The tour's three-day climax begins with an overnight in antique mining village Angangueo. Then, participants enjoy two days of on-foot woodland exploring, wondering and delighting at the miracle of the monarch butterflies who, having migrated thousands of miles to roost by the millions, carpet their remote high forest habitat in a fluttering riot of color.

The remote lagoons and islands of Baja California, about 200 miles (300 km) due west of Mazatlán, nurture a trove of marine and onshore wildlife. Such sanctuaries are ongoing destinations of winter **Oceanic Society** expedition-tours from La Paz, Baja California. Tours customarily include several islands and feature a week of marine mammal-watching, snorkeling, birding, and eco-exploring, both on- and offshore. For details, contact the Oceanic Society, Fort Mason Center, Bldg. E, San Francisco, CA 94123, tel. 415/441-1106, 800/326-7491, fax 415/474-3395, www.oceanic-society.org. This trip might make an exciting overture or finale to your Pacific Mexico vacation. You can connect with the Oceanic Society's Baja California (La Paz-Los Cabos) jumping-off points via Mexican Airlines' (Mexicana, Aéromexico, or Aerocalifornia) mainland (Mazatlán/Guadalajara/Puerto Vallarta) destinations.

Spanish Language Instruction and Homestays

Other options exist for travelers interested in small-group Spanish language instruction, including homestay options in several Pacific Mexico centers. Contact one of the experienced agencies, such as the **National Registration Center for Study Abroad,** at P.O. Box 1393, Milwaukee, WI 53201, tel. 414/278-0631, fax 414/278-8884, inquire@nrcsa.com, www.nrcsa.com; or **Amerispan Unlimited,** P.O. Box 40007, Philadelphia, PA 19106-0007, tel. 215/751-1100, 800/879-6640, fax 215/751-1986, info@amerispan.com, www.amerispan.com.

ON THE ROAD

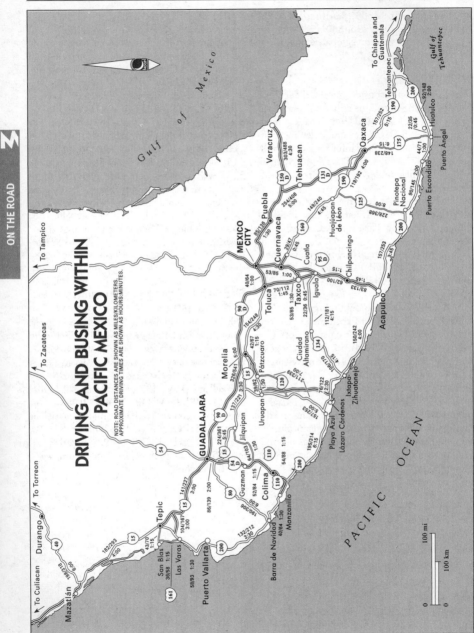

DRIVING AND BUSING WITHIN
PACIFIC MEXICO

NOTE: ROAD DISTANCES ARE SHOWN AS MILES/KILOMETERS.
APPROXIMATE DRIVING TIMES ARE SHOWN AS HOURS:MINUTES.

© AVALON TRAVEL PUBLISHING, INC.

ON THE ROAD

Getting Around

BY AIR

Mexicana, Aeroméxico, Aerocalifornia, and some smaller carriers, such as Aerocaribe, Aeromorelos, Aviacsa, and Azteca, and light-plane charters connect some of the main destinations of Pacific Mexico. In the north, a scheduled network connects Mazatlán, Puerto Vallarta, Guadalajara, Manzanillo-Barra de Navidad, Colima, Morelia. and other Mexican destinations. In the south, the same is true of Ixtapa-Zihuatanejo, Acapulco, Puerto Escondido, Puerto Ángel-Huatulco, and Oaxaca. Although much pricier than first-class bus tickets, domestic airfares are on a par with U.S. prices.

Travelers may book tickets by contacting agencies in the destination cities. (See destination chapters for airlines' local agency phone numbers.)

Local Flying Tips

If you're planning on lots of in-Mexico flying, upon arrival get the airlines' handy (although rapidly changeable) *itinerarios de vuelo* (flight schedules) at the airport.

Mexican airlines have operating peculiarities that result from their tight budgets. Don't miss a flight; you will likely lose half the ticket price. Adjusting your flight date may cost 25 percent of the ticket price. Get to the airport at least an hour ahead of time. Last-minute passengers are often "bumped" in favor of early-bird waiting-listers. Conversely, go to the airport and get in line if you must catch a flight that the airlines claim is full. You might get on anyway. Keep your luggage small so you can carry it on. Lost-luggage victims receive scant compensation in Mexico.

BY BUS

The bus is the king of the Mexican road. Dozens of lines connect virtually every town in Pacific Mexico. Three distinct levels of service—super-first-class (or luxury), first-class, and second-class—are generally available. **Luxury-class** (usually called something like "Primera Plus," depending upon the line) express coaches speed between major towns, seldom stopping en route. In exchange for relatively high fares (about $50 Puerto Vallarta-Guadalajara, or Oaxaca-Puerto Escondido, for example), passengers often enjoy rapid passage and airline-style amenities: plush reclining seats, air-conditioning, an on-board toilet, video, and aisle attendant.

Although less luxurious, but for about two-thirds the price, **first-class** service is frequent and always includes reserved seating. Additionally, passengers enjoy soft reclining seats and air-conditioning (if it is working). Besides their regular stops at or near most towns and villages en route, first-class bus drivers, if requested, will usually stop and let you off anywhere along the road. (For information on routes and bus station locations, refer to the destination chapters.)

Second-class bus seating is unreserved. In outlying parts of Pacific Mexico, there is even a class of bus beneath second-class, but given the condition of many second-class buses, it seems as if third-class buses wouldn't run at all. Such buses are the stuff of travelers' legends: the recycled old GMC, Ford, and Dodge schoolbuses that stop everywhere and carry everyone and everything to even the smallest villages tucked away in the far mountains. As long as there is any kind of a road, the bus will most likely go there.

Now and then you'll read a newspaper story of a country bus that went over a cliff somewhere in Mexico, killing the driver and a dozen unfortunate souls. The same newspapers, however, never bother to mention the half-million safe passengers for whom the same bus provided trips during its 15 years of service before the accident.

Second-class buses are not for travelers with weak knees or stomachs. Often, you will initially have to stand, cramped in the aisle, in a crowd of campesinos. They are warm-hearted but poor people, so don't tempt them with open, dangling purses or wallets bulging in

ON THE ROAD

WHICH BUSES GO WHERE

Destination	Bus Lines
Acapulco, Gro.	EL, FR, EO, FU, TUR, FA, GAC
Barra de Navidad-Melaque, Jal.	AC, ACP, EL, ETN, PP, TCN
Chapala, Jal.	AGC
Colima, Col.	AO, EL, ETN, OM, PP
Guadalajara, Jal. (new terminal)	ACP, ATM, AO, EL, ETN, FU, OM, PP, TC, TN, TP
Guadalajara, Jal. (old terminal)	AGC, AMT
Huatulco, Oax.	CC, EL, EV, OP
Las Varas, Nay.	EL, TNS, TP, TNN
Lazaro Cardenas, Mich.	ACU, EL, FU, AO, FA, GA, RP, AJ, PAR
Manzanillo, Col.	AC, AO, ACP, EL, ETN, FA, GA, PP, TNS
Mazatlán, Sin.	EL, TC, TN, TNS, TP
Oaxaca, Oax.	CC, ADO, AU, SUR, CUE, OP, EV, FP, ERS
Pátzcuaro, Mich.	EL, AO, FA, GA, RP, PAR, FA
Pinotepa Nacional, Oax.	EL, CC, FR, FP, OP, EV, ERS
Pochutla-Puerto Angel, Oax.	EL, CC, OP, FP, EV, ERS
Puerto Escondido, Oax.	EL, CC, OP, EV, ERS
Puerto Vallarta, Jal.	AC, EL, ETN, PP, TCN, TNS, TP
Rincón de Guayabitos-La Peñita, Nay.	EL, PP, TNS, TP
Salina Cruz, Oax.	EL, CC, OP, FP
San Blas, Nay.	TNS, TNN
Santiago Ixcuintla, Nay.	TNN
Taxco, Gro.	FR, EO, FU
Tepic, Nay.	EL, FU, OM, TC, TNS, TNN, TP
Uruapan, Mich.	EL, AO, FA, GA, RP, PAR
Zihuatanejo, Gro.	EL, AO, FA, GA, GAC, ACU, RP, PAR, FA

back pockets. Stow your money safely away. After a while, you will be able to sit down. Such privilege, however, comes with obligation, such as holding an old woman's bulging bag of carrots or a toddler on your lap. But if you accept your burden with humor and equanimity, who knows what favors and blessings may flow to you in return.

Tickets, Seating, and Baggage

Mexican bus lines do not usually publish schedules or fares. You have to ask someone who knows (such as your hotel desk clerk), or call the bus station. Few travel agents handle bus

tickets. If you don't want to spend the time to get a reserved ticket yourself, hire someone trustworthy to do it for you. Another option is to get to the bus station early enough on your traveling day to ensure that you'll get a bus to your destination.

Although some lines accept credit cards and issue computer-printed tickets at their major stations, most reserved bus tickets are sold for cash and handwritten, with a specific seat number, *número de asiento,* on the back. If you miss the bus, you lose your money. Furthermore, airlines-style automated reservations systems have not yet arrived at many Mexican

Bus Key

AC	Autobuses Costa Alegre (subsidiary of FA)
ACP	Autocamiones del Pacifico
ACU	Autotransportes Cuauhtemoc (subsidiary of EB)
ADO	Autobuses del Oriente
AGC	Autotransportes Guadalajara-Chapala
AJ	Autobuses de Jalisco
AMT	Autobuses Mascota Talpa Guadalajara (blue)
AO	Autovias del Occidente
ATM	Autotransportes Guadalajara-Talpa-Mascota (red)
AU	Autobuses Unidos
CC	Cristobál Colón
CUE	Cuenca
EB	Estrella Blanca
EL	Elite (subsidiary of EB)
EO	Estrella de Oro
ERS	Estrella Roja del Sureste
ETN	Enlaces Transportes Nacionales
EV	Estrella del Valle
FA	Flecha Amarilla
FP	Fletes y Pasajes
FR	Flecha Roja (subsidiary of EB)
FU	Futura (subsidiary of EB)
GA	Galeana (subsidiary of FA)
GAC	Gacela
OM	Omnibus de Mexico
OP	Oaxaca-Pacifico
PAR	Parhikuni
PP	Primera Plus (subsidiary of FA)
RP Ruta	Paraiso
SUR	Autotransportes del Sur
TC	Transportes Chihuahuenses (subsidiary of EB)
TCN	Transportes Cihuatlán
TN	Transportes del Norte (subsidiary of EB)
TNN	Transportes Noroeste de Nayarit
TNS	Transportes Norte de Sonora (subsidiary of EB)
TP	Transportes del Pacífico
TUR	Turistar

ON THE ROAD

bus stations. Consequently, you can generally buy reserved tickets only at the local departure (*salida local*) station. (An agent in Puerto Vallarta, for example, cannot ordinarily reserve you a ticket on a bus that originates in Tepic, 100 miles up the road.)

Request a reserved seat, if possible, with numbers 1–25 in the front (*delante*) to middle (*medio*) of the bus. The rear seats are often occupied by smokers, drunks, and rowdies. At night, you will sleep better on the right side (*lado derecho*) away from the glare of oncoming traffic lights.

Baggage is generally secure on Mexican buses. Label it, however. Overhead racks are generally too cramped to accommodate airline-sized carry-ons. Carry a small bag with your money and irreplaceables on your person; pack clothes and less-essentials in your checked luggage. For peace of mind, watch the handler put your checked baggage on the bus and watch to make sure it is not mistakenly taken off the bus at intermediate stops.

If your baggage gets misplaced, remain calm. Bus employees are generally competent and conscientious. If you are patient, recovering your luggage will become a matter of honor for many of them. Baggage handlers are at the bottom of the pay scale; a tip for their mostly thankless job is very much appreciated.

On long trips, carry food, beverages, and toilet paper. Station food may be dubious, and the sanitary facilities may be ill-maintained.

If you are waiting for a first-class bus at an intermediate *salida de paso* (passing station), you have to trust to luck that there will be an empty seat. If not, your best option may be to ride a more frequent second-class bus.

BY CAR OR RV

Driving your own car in Mexico may or may not be for you. (See By Car or RV under the Getting There section before deciding).

Rental Car

Car and jeep rentals are an increasingly pop-

CAR RENTAL AGENCIES

Alamo	tel. 800/522-9696
	www.alamo.com
Avis	tel. 800/831-2847
	www.avis.com
Budget	tel. 800/472-3325
	www.budget.com
Dollar	tel. 800/800-4000
	www.dollar.com
Hertz	tel. 800/654-3001
	www.hertz.com
National	tel. 800/227-3876
	www.nationalcar.com
Thrifty	tel. 800/367-2277
	www.thrifty.com

ular transportation option for Pacific Mexico travelers. They offer mobility and independence for local sightseeing and beach excursions. In the resorts, the gang's all there: Hertz, National, Dollar, Avis, Budget, Thrifty, and a host of local outfits. They generally require drivers to have a valid driver's license, passport, a major credit card, and may require a minimum age of 25. Some local companies do not accept credit cards, but offer lower rates in return.

Base prices of international agencies such as Hertz, National, and Avis are not cheap. With a 17 percent value-added tax and mandatory insurance, rentals run more than in the United States. The cheapest possible rental car, usually a used, stick-shift VW Beetle, runs $40–60 per day or $250–450 per week, depending on location and season. Prices are highest during Christmas and pre-Easter weeks. Before departure, use the international agencies' toll-free numbers and websites (see the special topic "Car Rental Agencies") for availability, prices, and reservations. During nonpeak seasons, you may save lots of pesos by waiting until arrival and renting a car through a local agency. Shop around, starting with the agent in your hotel lobby or with the local Yellow Pages (under *Automoviles, renta de*).

Car insurance that covers property damage, public liability, and medical payments is an absolute "must" with your rental car. If you get into an accident without insurance, you will be in deep trouble, probably jail. Narrow, rough roads and animals grazing at roadside make driving in Mexico more hazardous than back home. (For important car safety and insurance information, see By Car or RV under Getting There.)

BY TAXI, TOUR, HITCHHIKING, AND TRAIN

Taxis

The high prices of rental cars make taxis a useful option for local excursions. Cars are luxuries, not necessities, for most Mexican families. Travelers might profit from the Mexican money-saving practice of piling everyone in a taxi for a Sunday outing. You may find that an all-day taxi and driver, who, besides relieving you of driving, will become your impromptu guide, will cost less than a rental car.

The magic word for saving money by taxi is *colectivo:* a taxi you share with other travelers. The first place you'll practice getting a taxi will be at the airport, where *colectivo* tickets are routinely sold from booths at the terminal door.

If, however, you want a private taxi, ask for a *taxi especial,* which will cost about three or four times the individual tariff for a *colectivo.*

Your airport experience will prepare you for in-town taxis, which rarely have meters. *You must establish the price before getting in.* Bargaining comes with the territory in Mexico, so don't shrink from it, even though it seems a hassle. If you get into a taxi without an agreed-upon price, you are letting yourself in for a more serious and potentially nasty hassle later. If your driver's price is too high, he'll probably come to his senses as soon as you hail another taxi.

After a few days, getting taxis around town will be a cinch. You'll find that you don't have to take the more expensive taxis lined up in your hotel driveway. If the price isn't right, walk toward the street and hail a regular taxi.

In town, if you can't find a taxi, it may be because they are waiting for riders at the local stand, called a taxi *sitio.* Ask someone to direct you to it: *"Disculpe. ¿Dónde está el sitio taxi, por favor?"* ("Excuse me. Where is the taxi stand, please?")

Local Tours and Guides

For many Pacific Mexico visitors, locally arranged tours offer a hassle-free alternative to rental car or taxi sightseeing. Hotels and travel agencies, many of whom maintain front-lobby travel and tour desks, offer a bounty of sightseeing, water sports, bay cruise, fishing, and wildlife-viewing tour opportunities. (For details, see the destination chapters.)

Hitchhiking

Most everyone agrees hitchhiking is not the safest mode of transport. If you're unsure, don't do it. Hitchhiking doesn't make for a healthy steady travel diet, nor should you hitchhike at night.

The recipe for trouble-free hitchhiking requires equal measures of luck, savvy, and technique. The best places to catch rides are where people are arriving and leaving anyway, such as bus stops, highway intersections, gas stations, RV parks, and the highway out of town.

Male-female hitchhiking partnerships seem to net the most rides, although it is technically illegal for women to ride in commercial trucks. The more gear you and your partner have, the fewer rides you will get. Pickup and flatbed truck owners often pick up passengers for pay. Before hopping onto the truck bed, ask how much the ride will cost.

Train

Recent privatization has put an end to passenger train service in virtually all parts of Pacific Mexico. Drive or take a bus instead.

Information and Services

PASSPORTS, TOURIST CARDS, AND VISAS

Your Passport

Your passport (or birth or naturalization certificate) is your positive proof of national identity; without it, your status in any foreign country is in doubt. Don't leave home without one. United States citizens may obtain passports (allow four to six weeks) at local post offices. For-fee private passport agencies can speed this process and get you a passport within a week, maybe less.

Entry into Mexico

For U.S. and Canadian citizens, entry by air into Mexico for a few weeks could hardly be easier. Airline attendants hand out tourist cards *(tarjetas turísticas)* en route and officers make them official by glancing at passports and stamping the cards at the immigration gate. Business travel permits for 30 days or fewer are handled by the same simple procedures.

Entry is not entirely painless, however. The Mexican government charges an approximate $20 fee per person for a tourist card. For air and bus travelers, this is no problem, since the fee is automatically included in the fare. The entry fee can be a bit of a hassle for drivers, however. At this writing the government does not allow collection of the fee by border immigration officers. Instead, the officers issue a form that you must take to a bank, where you pay the fee. For multiple entries this can get complicated and time-consuming.

In addition to the entry fee, Mexican immigration officials require that all entering U.S. citizens 15 years old or over must present proper identification—either a valid U.S. passport, original (or notarized copy) of your birth certificate, military ID, or state driver's license, while naturalized citizens must show naturalization papers (or a laminated naturalization card) or valid U.S. passport.

Canadian citizens must show a valid passport or original birth certificate. Nationals of other countries (especially those such as Hong Kong, which issue more than one type of passport) may be subject to different or additional regulations. For advice, consult your regional Mexico Tourism Board office or consulate. For more Mexico-entry details, visit the Mexico Tourism Board's website at www.visitmexico.com or call toll-free tel. 800/44-MEXICO (800/446-3912).

More Options

For more complicated cases, get your tourist card early enough to allow you to consider the options. Tourist cards can be issued for multiple entries and a maximum validity of 180 days; photos are often required. If you don't request multiple entry or the maximum time, your card will probably be stamped single entry, valid for some shorter period, such as 90 days. If you are not sure how long you'll stay in Mexico, request the maximum (180 days is the absolute maximum for a tourist card; long-term foreign residents routinely make semiannual "border runs" for new tourist cards).

Student and Business Visas

A visa is a notation stamped and signed on your passport showing the number of days and entries allowable for your trip. Apply for a student visa at the consulate nearest your home well in advance of your departure; the same is true if you require a business visa of longer than 30 days. One-year renewable student visas are available (sometimes with considerable red tape). An ordinary 180-day tourist card may be the easiest option, if you can manage it.

Entry for Children

Children under 15 can be included on their parents' tourist cards, but complications occur if the children (by reason of illness, for example) cannot leave Mexico with both parents. Parents can avoid such red tape by getting a passport and a Mexican tourist card for each of their children.

In addition to passport or birth certificate,

MEXICO TOURISM BOARD OFFICES

More than a dozen Mexico Tourism Board (Consejo de Promoción Turístico de Mexico) offices and scores of Mexican government consulates operate in the United States, Canada, Europe, and South America. Consulates generally handle questions of Mexican nationals abroad, while Mexico Tourism Boards serve travelers heading for Mexico.

For straightforward questions and Mexico regional information brochures, call toll-free U.S./Can. tel. 800/44MEXICO (800/446-3942) or Europe tel. 800/11-2266, or visit the website www.visitmexico.com. Otherwise, contact one of the North American regional or European or South American Mexico Tourism Boards for guidance:

In North America
From Arizona, California, Colorado, Hawaii, Idaho, Montana, Nevada, New Mexico, and Utah, contact **Los Angeles:** 2401 W. 6th St., 5th Floor, Los Angeles, CA 90057, tel. 213/351-2069, fax 213/351-2074, losangeles@visitmexico.com.

From Alaska, Washington, Oregon, Idaho, Wyoming, and Montana and the Canadian provinces of British Columbia, Alberta, Yukon, Northwest Territories, and Saskatchewan, contact **Vancouver:** 999 W. Hastings St., Suite 1110, Vancouver, British Columbia V6C 2W2, tel. 604/669-2845, fax 604/669-3498, mgto@telus.net.

From Texas, Oklahoma, and Louisiana, contact **Houston:** 4507 San Jacinto, Suite 308, Houston TX 77004, tel. 713/772-2581, fax 713/772-6058, houston@visitmexico.com.

From Alabama, Arkansas, Florida, Georgia, Mississippi, Tennessee, North Carolina, and South Carolina, contact **Miami:** 5975 Sunset Dr. #305, Miami, FL 33143, tel. 786/621-2809, fax 786/621-2907, miami@visitmexico.com.

From Illinois, Indiana, Iowa, Kansas, Michigan, Minnesota, Missouri, Nebraska, North Dakota, Ohio, South Dakota, and Wisconsin, contact **Chicago:** 300 N. Michigan Ave., 4th Floor, Chicago, IL 60601, tel. 312/606-9252, fax 312/606-9012, chicago@visitmexico.com.

From Connecticut, Delaware, Kentucky, Maine, Maryland, Massachusetts, New Hampshire, New Jersey, New York, Pennsylvania, Rhode Island, Vermont, Virginia, Washington D.C., and West Virginia, contact **New York:** 21 E. 63rd Street, 3rd Floor, New York, NY 10021, tel. 212/821-0313 or 212/821-0314, fax 212/821-3067, newyork@visitmexico.com.

From Ontario and Manitoba, contact **Toronto:** 2 Bloor St. W, Suite 1502, Toronto, Ontario M4W 3E2, tel. 416/925-2753, fax 416/925-6061, toronto@visitmexico.com.

From New Brunswick, Newfoundland, Nova Scotia, Prince Edward Island, and Quebec, contact **Montreal:** 1 Place Ville Marie, Suite 1931, Montreal, Quebec H3B2C3, tel. 514/871-1052 or 514/871-1103, fax 514/871-3825, montreal@visitmexico.com.

In Europe
In Europe, travelers may use the tourism information number, all-Europe toll-free Mex. tel. 800/11-2266, visit the website www.visitmexico.com, or contact the local offices directly:

London: Wakefield House, 41 Trinity Square, London EC3N 4DT, England, UK, tel. 207/488-9392, fax 207/265-0704, uk@visitmexico.com.

Frankfurt: Taunusanlage 21, 60325 Frankfurt-am-Main, Deutschland, tel. 0/6925-3509, fax 0/6925-3755, germany@visitmexico.com.

Paris: 4, Rue Notre-Dame des Victoires, 75002 Paris, France, tel. 1/425-896122, 1/425-69213, fax 1/428-60580, france@visitmexico.com.

Madrid: Calle Velázquez 126, 28006 Madrid, España, tel. 91/561-3520, 91/561-1827, fax 91/411-0759, spain@visitmexico.com.

Rome: Via Barbarini 3-piso 7, 00187 Roma, Italia, tel. 06/487-4698, fax 06/487-3630, fax 06/420-4293, italy@visitmexico.com.

In South America
Contact the Mexico Tourism Board in either Argentina or Chile:

Buenos Aires: Av. Santa Fe 520, 1054 Buenos Aires, Argentina, tel. 1/4393-7070 or 1/4393-8235, fax 1/4393-6607, argentina@visitmexico.com.

Santiago: Bucarest 162, Providencia, Santiago, Chile, tel. 562/234-5899, fax 562/234-5898, chile@visitmexico.com.

ON THE ROAD

minors (under age 18) entering Mexico without parents or legal guardians must present a notarized letter of permission signed by both parents or legal guardians. Even if accompanied by one parent, a notarized letter from the other must be presented. Divorce or death certificates must also be presented, when applicable. Airlines will require the name, address, and telephone number of the person meeting unaccompanied minors upon arrival in Mexico.

Pacific Mexico travelers should hurdle all such possible delays far ahead of time in the cool calm of their local Mexican consulate rather than the hot, hurried atmosphere of a border or airport immigration station.

Entry for Pets

A pile of red tape can delay the entry of dogs, cats, and other pets into Mexico. Be prepared with veterinary-stamped health and rabies certificates for each animal. Contact your regional Mexico Tourism Board (see special topic "Mexico Tourism Board Offices"), call tel. 800/44-MEX-ICO (800/446-3942), or visit www.visitmex-ico.com for assistance.

Don't Lose Your Tourist Card

If you do, be prepared with a copy of the original, which you should present to the nearest federal Migración (Immigration) office (on duty long hours at Pacific Mexico international airports) and ask for a duplicate tourist permit. Lacking this, you might present some alternate proof of your date of arrival in Mexico, such as a stamped passport or airline ticket. Savvy travelers carry copies of their tourist cards while leaving the original safe in their hotel rooms.

Car Permits

If you drive to Mexico, you will need a permit for your car. Upon entry into Mexico, be ready with originals and copies of your proof-of-ownership or registration papers (state title certificate, registration, or notarized bill of sale), current license plates, and current driver's license. The auto permit fee runs about $25, payable only by non-Mexican bank MasterCard, Visa, or American Express credit cards. (The credit-card-

only requirement discourages those who sell or abandon U.S.-registered cars in Mexico without paying customs duties.) Credit cards must bear the same name as the vehicle proof-of-ownership papers.

The resulting car permit becomes part of the owner's tourist card and receives the same length of validity. Vehicles registered in the name of an organization or person other than the driver must be accompanied by a notarized affidavit authorizing the driver to use the car in Mexico for a specific time.

Border officials generally allow you to carry or tow additional motorized vehicles (motorcycle, another car, large boat) into Mexico but will probably require separate documentation and fee for each vehicle. If a Mexican official desires to inspect your trailer or RV, go through it with him.

Accessories, such as a small trailer, boat shorter than six feet, CB radio, or outboard motor, may be noted on the car permit and must leave Mexico with the car.

For updates and details on documentation required for taking your car into Mexico, call the toll-free Mexican government number in the United States, tel. 800/446-3942, or visit the website www.visitmexico.com. For more details on motor vehicle entry and what you may bring in your baggage to Mexico, consult the AAA (American Automobile Association) *Mexico TravelBook*.

Since Mexico does not recognize foreign automobile insurance, you must buy Mexican automobile insurance. (For more information on this and other details of driving in Mexico, see Getting There.)

Crossing the Border and Returning Home

Squeezing through border bottlenecks during peak holidays and rush hours can be time-consuming. Avoid crossing 7–9 A.M. and 4:30–6:30 P.M.

Just before returning across the border with your car, park and have a customs *(aduana)* official *remove and cancel the holographic identity sticker that you received on entry.* If possible, get a receipt *(recibo)* or some kind of verification that it's been canceled *(cancelado).* Tourists have been fined hundreds of dollars for inadvertently carrying uncanceled car entry stickers on their windshields.

At the same time, return all other Mexican permits, such as tourist cards and hunting and fishing licenses. Also, be prepared for Mexico exit inspection, especially for cultural artifacts and works of art, which may require exit permits. Certain religious and pre-Columbian artifacts, legally the property of the Mexican government, cannot be taken from the country.

If you entered Mexico with your car, you cannot legally leave without it except by permission from local customs authorities, usually the Aduana (Customs House) or the Oficina Federal de Hacienda (Federal Treasury Office). (For local details, see Information and Services in the destination chapters.)

All returnees are subject to U.S. immigration and customs inspection. These inspections have become generally more time-consuming since Sept. 11, 2001. The worst bottlenecks are at busy border crossings, especially Tijuana and to a lesser extent, Mexicali, Nogales, Juárez, Nuevo Laredo, and Matamoros, all of which should be avoided during peak hours.

United States law allows a fixed value ($400 at present) of duty-free goods per returnee. This may include no more than one liter of alcoholic spirits, 200 cigarettes, and 100 cigars. A flat 10 percent duty will be applied to the first $1,000 (fair retail value, save your receipts) in excess of your $400 exemption. You may, however, mail packages (up to $50 value each) of gifts duty-free to friends and relatives in the United States. Make sure to clearly write "unsolicited gift" and a list of the value and contents on the outside of the package. Perfumes (over $5), alcoholic beverages, and tobacco may not be included in such packages.

Improve the security of such mailed packages by sending them by Mexpost class, similar to U.S. Express Mail service. Even better (but much more expensive), send them by Federal Express or DHL international couriers, which maintain offices in Pacific Mexico resort centers.

For more information on U.S. customs regulations important to travelers abroad, write for a copy of the useful pamphlet *Know Before You Go,* from the U.S. Customs Service, 1300 Pennsylvania Ave., Washington, DC 20229. You may also order at tel. 202/354-1000. For more information, log on to www.customs.gov.

Additional U.S. rules prohibit importation of certain fruits, vegetables, and domestic animal and endangered wildlife products. Certain live animal species, such as parrots, may be brought into the United States, subject to 30-day agricultural quarantine upon arrival, at the owner's expense. For more details on agricultural product and live animal importation, write for the free booklet *Travelers' Tips,* by the U.S. Department of Agriculture, Washington, D.C. 20250, tel. 202/720-2791.

For more information on the importation of endangered wildlife products, contact the Fish and Wildlife Service, 1849 C. St. NW, Washington, DC 20240, tel. 202/208-4717.

MONEY
The Peso: Down and Up
Overnight in early 1993, the Mexican government shifted its monetary decimal point three places and created the "new" peso, which now trades at about 10 per U.S. dollar. Since the peso value sometimes changes rapidly, U.S. dollars have become a much more stable indicator of Mexican prices; for this reason they are used in this book to report prices. You should, nevertheless, always use pesos to pay for everything in Mexico.

Since the introduction of the new peso, the centavo (one-hundredth of a new peso) has reappeared, in coins of 10, 20, and 50 centavos. Incidentally, the dollar sign, "$," also marks Mexican pesos. Peso coins (*monedas*) in denominations of 1, 2, 5, 10 and 20 pesos, and bills, in denominations of 20, 50, 100, 200 and 500 pesos, are common. Since banks like to exchange your traveler's checks for a few crisp large bills rather than the often-tattered smaller denominations, ask for some of your change in 50- and 100-peso notes. A 500-peso note, while common at the bank, may look awfully big to a small shopkeeper, who might be hard-pressed to change it.

Banks, ATMs, and Money-Exchange Offices

Mexican banks, like their North American counterparts, have lengthened their business hours. Banco Internacional (Bital) maintains the longest hours: as long as Mon.–Sat. 8 A.M.–7 P.M. Banamex (Banco Nacional de Mexico), generally the most popular with local people, usually posts the best in-town dollar exchange rate in its lobbies; for example: *Tipo de cambio: venta 9.615, compra 9.720,* which means it will sell pesos to you at the rate of 9.615 per dollar and buy them back for 9.720 per dollar.

ATMs (automated teller machines), or *Cajeros Automáticos* (kah-HAY-rohs ahoo-toh-MAH-tee-kohs), are rapidly becoming the money source of choice in Mexico. Virtually every bank has a 24-hour ATM, accessible (with proper PIN identification code) by a swarm of U.S. and Canadian credit and ATM cards. *Note:* Some Mexican bank ATMs will "eat" your ATM card if you don't retrieve it within about 15 seconds of completing your transaction. Retrieve your card *immediately* after getting your cash.

Although one-time bank charges, typically about $2 per $100, for ATM cash remain small, the money you can usually get from a single card is limited to about $200 or less per day.

Even without an ATM card, you don't have to go to the trouble of waiting in long bank service lines. Opt for a less-crowded bank, such as Bancomer, Banco Serfín, Banco Internacional, or a private money-exchange office *(casa de cambio)*. Often most convenient, such offices often offer long hours and faster service than the banks for a fee (as little as $.50 or as much as $3 per $100).

Keeping Your Money Safe

Traveler's checks, the traditional prescription for safe money abroad, are widely accepted in Pacific Mexico. Even if you plan to use your ATM card, buy some U.S. dollar traveler's checks (a well-known brand such as American Express or Visa) as an emergency reserve. Canadian traveler's checks and currency are not as widely accepted as U.S. traveler's checks, and

European and Asian traveler's checks are even less so. Unless you like signing your name or paying lots of per-check commissions, buy denominations of $50 or more.

In Pacific Mexico, as everywhere, thieves circulate among the tourists. Keep valuables in your hotel *caja de seguridad* (security box). If you don't particularly trust the desk clerk, carry what you cannot afford to lose in a money belt. Pickpockets love crowded markets, buses, and airport terminals where they can slip a wallet out of a back pocket or dangling purse in a blink. Guard against this by carrying your wallet in your front pocket, and your purse, waist pouch, and daypack (which clever crooks can sometimes slit open) on your front side.

Don't attract thieves by displaying wads of money or flashy jewelry. Don't get sloppy drunk; if so, you may become a pushover for a determined thief.

Don't leave valuables unattended on the beach; share security duties with trustworthy-looking neighbors, or leave a bag with a shopkeeper nearby.

Tipping

Without their droves of visitors, Mexican people would be even poorer. Deflation of the peso, while it makes prices low for outsiders, makes it rough for Mexican families to get by. The help at your hotel typically get paid only a few dollars a day. They depend on tips to make the difference between dire and bearable poverty. Give the *camarista* (chambermaid) and floor attendant 20 pesos every day or two. And whenever uncertain of what to tip, it will probably mean a lot to someone—maybe a whole family—if you err on the generous side.

In restaurants and bars, Mexican tipping customs are similar to those in the United States: tip waiters, waitresses, and bartenders about 15 percent for satisfactory service.

Credit Cards

Credit cards, such as Visa, MasterCard, and to a lesser extent, American Express and Discover, are widely honored in the hotels, restaurants, craft shops, and boutiques that cater to foreign tourists. You will generally get better bargains, however, in shops that depend on local trade and do not so readily accept credit cards. Such shops sometimes offer discounts for cash sales.

Whatever the circumstance, your travel money will usually go much further in Pacific Mexico than back home. Despite the national 17 percent ("value added" IVA) sales tax, local lodging, food, and transportation prices will often seem like bargains compared to the developed world. Outside of the pricey high-rise beachfront strips, pleasant, palmy hotel room rates often run $40 or less.

COMMUNICATIONS

Using Mexican Telephones
Although Mexican phone service has improved in the last decade, it's still sometimes hit-or-miss. If a number doesn't get through, you may have to redial it more than once. When someone answers (usually *"Bueno"*) be especially courteous. If your Spanish is rusty, say, *"¿Por favor, habla inglés?"* (¿POR fah-VOR, AH-blah een-GLAYS?). If you want to speak to a particular person (such as María), ask, *"¿María se encuentra?"* (¿mah-REE-ah SAY ayn-koo-AYN-trah?).

Since November 2001, when telephone numbers were standardized, Mexican phones operate pretty much the same as in the United States and Canada. In Puerto Vallarta town, for example, a complete telephone number is generally written like this: 322/222-4709. As in the United States, the "322" denotes the telephone area code, or *(lada)* (LAH-dah), and the 222-4709 is the number that you dial locally. If you want to dial this number long distance *(larga distancia),* first dial "01" (like "1" in the United States), then 322/222-4709. All Mexican telephone numbers, with only three exceptions, begin with a three-digit *lada,* followed by a seven-digit local number. (The exceptions are Monterey, Guadalajara, and Mexico City, which have two-digit *ladas* and eight-digit local numbers. The Mexico City *lada* is 55; Guadalajara's is 33; Monterey's is 81. (For example, a complete Guadalajara phone number would read 33/6897-2253.)

In Pacific Mexico towns and cities, direct long-distance dialing is the rule—from hotels, public phone booths, and efficient private Computel telephone offices. The cheapest, often most convenient, way to call is by buying and using a public telephone Ladatel card. Buy them in 20-, 30-, 50-, and 100-peso denominations at the many outlets—minimarkets, pharmacies, liquor stores—that display the blue and yellow Ladatel sign.

Calling Mexico and Calling Home
To call Mexico direct from the United States, first dial 011 (for international access), then 52 (for Mexico), followed by the Mexican area code and local number.

For station-to-station calls to the United States from Mexico, dial 001 plus the area code and the local number. For calls to other countries, ask your hotel desk clerk or see the easy-to-follow directions in the local Mexican telephone directory.

Another convenient way (although a more expensive one) to call home is via your personal telephone credit card. Contact your U.S. long-distance operator by dialing tel. 001-800/462-4240 for AT&T; 001-800/674-6000 for MCI; or 001-800/877-8000 for Sprint.

Yet another (although expensive) way of calling home is collect. You can do this in one of two ways. Simply dial 09 for the local English-speaking international operator, or dial the AT&T, MCI, and Sprint numbers listed in the previous paragraph.

Beware of certain private "To Call Long Distance to the U.S.A. Collect and Credit Card" telephones installed prominently in airports, tourist hotels, and shops. Tariffs on these phones often run as high as $10 per minute (with a three-minute minimum), for a total of $30, whether you talk three minutes or not. Always ask the operator for the rate, and if it's too high, take your business elsewhere.

In smaller towns, you must often do your long-distance phoning in the *larga distancia* (local phone office). Typically staffed by a young woman and often connected to a café, the *larga distancia* becomes an informal community social center as people pass the time waiting for their phone connections.

Post, Telegraph, and Internet Access

Mexican *correos* (post offices) operate similarly, but more slowly and less securely, than their counterparts all over the world. Mail services usually include *lista de correo* (general delivery, address letters *"a/c lista de correo,"*), *servicios filatelicas* (philatelic services), *por avión* (airmail), *giros* (postal money orders), and Mexpost secure and fast delivery service, usually from separate Mexpost offices.

Mexican ordinary mail is sadly unreliable and pathetically slow. If, for mailings within Mexico, you must have security, use the efficient, reformed government Mexpost (like U.S. Express Mail) service. For international mailings, check the local Yellow Pages for widely available DHL or Federal Express courier service.

Telégrafos (telegraph offices), usually near the post office, send and receive *telegramas* (telegrams) and *giros* (money orders). *Telecomunicaciones* (Telecom), the new high-tech telegraph offices, add telephone and public fax to the available services.

© BRUCE WHIPPERMAN

While in Mexico, deposit your mail in a *buzón* (mailbox).

Internet service, including personal email access, has arrived in Pacific Mexico's cities and larger towns. Internet "cafés" are becoming increasingly common, especially in the resort centers. Online rates average about $3 per hour.

Electricity and Time

Mexican electric power is supplied at U.S.-standard 110 volts, 60 cycles. Plugs and sockets are generally two-pronged, nonpolar (like the pre-1970s U.S. ones). Bring adapters if you're going to use appliances with polar two-pronged or three-pronged plugs. A two-pronged polar plug has different-sized prongs, one of which is too large to plug into an old-fashioned nonpolar socket.

Pacific Mexico operates on central time except for the northwest states of Sinaloa and Nayarit, which operate on mountain time.

SPECIALTY TRAVEL

Bringing the Kids

Children are treasured like gifts from heaven in Mexico. Traveling with kids will ensure your welcome most everywhere. On the beach, take extra precautions to make sure they are protected from the sun.

A sick child is no fun for anyone. Fortunately, clinics and good doctors are available even in small towns. When in need, ask a storekeeper or a pharmacist, *"¿Dónde hay un doctor, por favor?"* ("¿DOHN-day eye oon doc-TOHR por fah-VOHR?"). In most cases, within five minutes you will be in the waiting room of the local physician or hospital.

Children who do not favor typical Mexican fare can easily be fed with always available eggs, cheese, *hamburguesas,* milk, oatmeal, corn flakes, bananas, cakes, and cookies.

Your children will generally have more fun if they have a little previous knowledge of Mexico and a stake in the trip. For example, help them select some library picture books and magazines so they'll know where they're going and what to expect, or give them responsibility for packing and carrying their own small travel bag.

Be sure to mention your children's ages when making air reservations; child discounts of 50 percent or more are often available. Also, if you can arrange to go on an uncrowded flight, you can stretch out and rest on the empty seats.

For more details on traveling with children, check out *Adventuring with Children* by Nan Jeffries. (See Suggested Reading.)

Travel for People with Disabilities

Mexican airlines and hotels are becoming increasingly aware of the needs of travelers with disabilities. Open, street-level lobbies and large, wheelchair-accessible elevators and rooms are available in most Pacific Mexico resort hotels.

The law of the United States forbids travel discrimination against otherwise qualified people with disabilities. As long as your disability is stable and not liable to deteriorate during passage, you can expect to be treated like any passenger with special needs.

Make reservations far ahead of departure and ask your agent to inform your airline of your needs, such as boarding a wheelchair or in-flight oxygen. Be early at the gate to take advantage of the preboarding call.

For many helpful details to smooth your trip, get a copy of *Traveling Like Everyone Else: A Practical Guide for Disabled Travelers* by Jacqueline Freeman and Susan Gerstein. Get it from the publisher, Lambda Publishing, 3709 13th Ave., Brooklyn, NY 11218, tel. 718/972-5449. Also useful is the book *The Wheelchair Traveler,* by Douglas R. Annand. Yet another helpful publication is *New Horizons,* available from the U.S. Department of Transportation or the Paralyzed Veterans of America, tel. 888/860-7244, www.pva.org.

Certain organizations both encourage and provide information about travel for those with disabilities. One with many Mexican connections is **Mobility International USA,** P.O. Box 10767, Eugene, OR 97440, tel. 541/343-1284 voice/TDD, fax 541/343-6812, www.miusa.org. A $35 membership gets you a semiannual newsletter and referrals for international exchanges and homestays.

Similarly, **Partners of the Americas,** 1424 K St. NW, Suite 700, Washington, D.C. 20005, tel. 202/628-3300, 800/322-7844, fax 202/628-3306, info@partners.net, with chapters in 45 U.S. states, works to improve understanding of disabilities and facilities in Mexico and Latin America. It maintains lists of local organizations and individuals whom travelers with disabilities may contact at their destinations. For more information see www.partners.net.

Travel for Senior Citizens

Age, according to Mark Twain, is a question of mind over matter: If you don't mind, it doesn't matter. Mexico is a country where entire extended families, from babies to great-grandparents, live together. Elderly travelers will benefit from the respect and understanding Mexicans accord to older people. Besides these encouragements, consider the number of retirees already in havens in Puerto Vallarta, Guadalajara, Lake Chapala, Acapulco, Oaxaca, and other Pacific Mexico centers.

Certain organizations support senior travel. Leading the field is **Elderhostel,** 11 Ave. de Lafayette, Boston, MA 02111-1746, tel. 877/426-8056. website www.elderhostel.org, which publishes extensive U.S. and international catalogs of special tours, study, homestays, and people-to-people travel programs.

A number of newsletters publicize Pacific Mexico vacation and retirement opportunities. Among the best is *Adventures in Mexico,* published six times yearly and filled with pithy hotel, restaurant, touring, and real estate information for independent travelers and retirees seeking the "real" Mexico. For information, write Adventures in Mexico, c/o Lloyd Guadalajara, P.O. Box 437090, San Ysidro, CA 92143-7090; or, in Mexico, P.O. Box 31-70, Guadalajara, Jalisco 45050. Back issues are $2; one-year subscription $16, Canadian $19.

Equally worthy is the *Mexico File* monthly newsletter that, besides featuring pithy stories by Mexico travelers and news updates, offers an opportunity-packed classified section of Mexico rentals, publications, services, and much more. Subscribe ($39/year) at Simmonds Publications, 5580 La Jolla Blvd. #306, La Jolla, CA 92037, tel./fax 858/456-4419 or 800/563-9345 (voice mail), mf@mexicofile.com, or www.mexicofile.com.

Seniors might also benefit from a subscription to *Mature Traveler,* a lively, professional-quality newsletter featuring money-saving tips, discounts, and tours for over-50 active senior and travelers with disabilities. Individual copies are $5, a one-year subscription $29.95. Editor Adele Mallot has compiled years of past newsletters and experience into the *Book of Deals,* a 150-page travel tip and opportunity book, which sells for $7.95, plus postage and handling. Order, with a credit card, by calling tel. 916/923-6346 or toll-free 800/460-6676 or writing John Stickler Publishing Group, P.O. Box 15791, Sacramento, CA 95852. You may also order through the website at www.thematuretraveler.com.

Houston-based Vacation Publications offers yet more possibilities. Check out the book *Special Report for Discount Travelers,* which lists a plethora of hotel, travel club, cruise, air, credit card, single, and off-season discounts. Also useful is the magazine *Where to Retire.* For information, a catalog, and to order, contact Vacation Publications, 1502 Augusta, Suite 415, Houston, TX 77057, tel. 713/974-6903, www.vacationsmagazine.com.

Health and Safety

STAYING HEALTHY

In Pacific Mexico, as everywhere, prevention is the best remedy for illness. For those visitors who confine their travel to the beaten path, a few basic common-sense precautions will ensure vacation enjoyment.

Resist the temptation to dive headlong into Mexico. It's no wonder that people get sick—broiling in the sun, gobbling peppery food, guzzling beer and margaritas, then discoing half the night—all in their first 24 hours. An alternative is to give your body time to adjust. Travelers often arrive tired and dehydrated from travel and heat. During the first few days, drink plenty of bottled water and juice, and take siestas.

Immunizations and Precautions

A good physician can recommend the proper preventatives for your Pacific Mexico trip. If you are going to stay pretty much in town, your doctor will probably suggest little more than updating your basic typhoid, diphtheria-tetanus, and polio shots.

For camping or trekking in remote tropical areas—below 4,000 feet or 1,200 meters—doctors often recommend a gamma-globulin shot against hepatitis A and a schedule of chloroquine pills against malaria. While in backcountry areas, always use other measures to discourage mosquitoes—and fleas, flies, ticks, no-see-ums, "kissing bugs" (see Chagas' Disease and Dengue Fever), and other tropical pesties—from biting you. Common precautions include sleeping under mosquito netting, burning *espirales mosquito* (mosquito coils), and rubbing on plenty of pure DEET (n,n dimethyl-meta-toluamide) "jungle juice," mixed in equal parts with rubbing (70 percent isopropyl) alcohol. Although super-effective, 100 percent DEET dries and irritates the skin.

Sunburn

For sunburn protection, use a good sunscreen with a sun protection factor (SPF) rated 15 or more, which will reduce burning rays to one-fifteenth or less of direct sunlight. Better still, take a shady siesta-break from the sun during the most hazardous midday hours. If you do get burned, applying your sunburn lotion (or one of the "caine" creams) after the fact usually decreases the pain and speeds healing.

Safe Water and Food

Although municipalities have made great strides in sanitation, food and water are still major potential sources of germs in Pacific Mexico. Do not drink local tap water. Drink bottled water only. Hotels, whose success depends vitally on their customers' health, generally provide *agua purificada* (purified bottled water). If, for any reason, the water quality is doubtful, add a water purifier, such as "Potable Aqua" brand (get it at a camping goods stores before departure) or a few drops per quart of water of *blanqueador* (household chlorine bleach) or *yodo* (tincture of iodine) from the pharmacy.

Pure bottled water, soft drinks, beer, and fresh fruit juices are so widely available it is easy to avoid tap water, especially in restaurants. Ice and *paletas* (iced juice-on-a-stick) may be risky, especially in small towns.

Washing hands before eating in a restaurant is a time-honored Mexican ritual that visitors should religiously follow. The humblest Mexican eatery will generally provide a basin to *lavar las manos* (wash the hands). If it doesn't, don't eat there.

Hot, cooked food is generally safe, as are peeled fruits and vegetables. Milk and cheese these days in Mexico are generally processed under sanitary conditions and sold pasteurized (ask, *"¿Pasteurizado?"*) and are typically safe. Mexican ice cream used to be both bad-tasting and of dubious safety, but national brands available in supermarkets are so much improved that it's no longer necessary to resist ice cream while in town.

In recent years, much cleaner public water and increased hygiene awareness has made salads—once shunned by Mexico travelers—generally safe to eat in tourist-frequented Pacific Mexico cafés and restaurants. Nevertheless, lettuce and cabbage, particularly in country villages, is more likely to be contaminated than tomatoes, carrots, cucumbers, onions, and green peppers. In any case, whenever in doubt, douse your salad in vinegar *(vinagre)* or plenty of sliced lime *(limón)* juice, the acidity of which kills bacteria.

First-Aid Kit
In the tropics, ordinary cuts and insect bites are more prone to infection and should receive immediate first aid. A first-aid kit with aspirin, rubbing alcohol, hydrogen peroxide, water-purifying tablets, household chlorine bleach or iodine for water purifying, swabs, bandages, gauze, adhesive tape, Ace bandage, chamomile *(manzanilla)* tea bags for upset stomachs, Pepto-Bismol, acidophilus tablets, antibiotic ointment, hydrocortisone cream, mosquito repellent, knife, and good tweezers is a good precaution for any traveler and mandatory for campers.

HEALTH PROBLEMS
Traveler's Diarrhea
Traveler's diarrhea (known in Southeast Asia as "Bali Belly" and in Mexico as turista or "Montezuma's Revenge") sometimes persists, even among prudent vacationers. You can suffer turista for a week after simply traveling from California to Philadelphia or New York. Doctors say the familiar symptoms of runny bowels, nausea, and sour stomach result from normal local bacterial strains to which newcomers' systems need time to adjust. Unfortunately, the dehydration and fatigue from heat and travel reduce your body's natural defenses and sometimes lead to a persistent cycle of sickness at a time when you least want it.

Time-tested protective measures can help your body either prevent or break this cycle. Many doctors and veteran travelers swear by Pepto-Bismol for soothing sore stomachs and stopping diarrhea. Acidophilus, the bacteria found in yogurt, is widely available in the United States in tablets and aids digestion. Warm *manzanilla* (chamomile) tea, used widely in Mexico (and by Peter Rabbit's mother), provides liquid and calms upset stomachs. Temporarily avoid coffee and alcohol, drink plenty of *manzanilla* tea, and eat bananas and rice for a few meals until your tummy can take regular food.

Although powerful antibiotics and antidiarrhea medications such as Lomotil and Imodium are readily available over *farmacia* counters, they may involve serious side effects and should not be

> *It's no wonder that people get sick—broiling in the sun, gobbling peppery food, guzzling margaritas, then discoing half the night—all in their first 24 hours. Give your body time to adjust. During the first few days, drink plenty of bottled water and juice, and take siestas.*

taken in the absence of medical advice. If in doubt, consult a doctor.

Chagas' Disease and Dengue Fever

Chagas' disease, spread by the "kissing" (or, more appropriately, "assassin") bug, is a potential hazard in the Mexican tropics. Known locally as a *vinchuca,* the triangular-headed, three-quarter-inch (two-centimeter) brown insect, identifiable by its yellow-striped abdomen, often drops upon its sleeping victims from the thatched ceiling of a rural house at night. Its bite is followed by swelling, fever, and weakness and can lead to heart failure if left untreated. Application of drugs at an early stage can, however, clear the patient of the trypanosome parasites that infect victims' bloodstreams and vital organs. See a doctor immediately if you believe you're infected.

Most of the precautions against malaria-bearing mosquitos also apply to dengue fever, which does occur (although uncommonly) in outlying tropical areas of Mexico. The culprit here is a virus carried by the mosquito species *Aedes aegypti.* Symptons are acute fever, with chills, sweating, and muscle aches. A red, diffuse rash frequently results, which may later peel. Sypmtoms abate after about five days, but fatigue may persist. A particularly serious but fortunately rare form, called dengue hemorrhagic fever, afflicts children and can be fatal. See a doctor immediately. Although no vaccines or preventatives, other than deterring mosquitos, exist, you should nevertheless see a doctor immediately.

For more good tropical preventative information, get a copy of the excellent pamphlet distributed by the International Association of Medical Advice to Travelers (IAMAT). (See Medical Care.)

Scorpions and Snakes

While camping or staying in a *palapa* or other rustic accommodation, watch for scorpions, especially in your shoes, which you should shake out every morning. Scorpion stings and snakebites are rarely fatal to an adult but are potentially very serious for a child. Get the victim to a doctor calmly but quickly. (For more snakebite details, see Reptiles and Amphibians under Flora and Fauna in the general Introduction.)

Sea Creatures

While snorkeling or surfing, you may suffer a coral scratch or jellyfish sting. Experts advise you to wash the afflicted area with ocean water and pour alcohol (rubbing alcohol or tequila) over the wound, then apply hydrocortisone cream available from the *farmacia.*

Injuries from sea urchin spines and stingray barbs are painful and can be serious. Physicians recommend similar first aid for both: remove the spines or barbs by hand or with tweezers, then soak the injury in as-hot-as-possible fresh water to weaken the toxins and provide relief. Another method is to rinse the area with an antibacterial solution—rubbing alcohol, vinegar, wine, or ammonia diluted with water. If none are available, the same effect may be achieved with urine, either your own or someone else's in your party. Get medical help immediately.

Tattoos

All health hazards don't come from the wild. A number of Mexico travelers have complained of complications from black henna tattoos. When enhanced by the chemical dye PPD, results can include an itchy rash that can lead to scarring. It's best to play it safe. If you must have a vacation tattoo, get it at an established, professional shop.

MEDICAL CARE

For medical advice and treatment, let your hotel (or if you're camping, the closest *farmacia*) refer you to a good doctor, clinic, or hospital. Mexican doctors, especially in medium-sized and small towns, practice like private doctors in the United States and Canada once did before health insurance, liability, and group practice. They will come to you if you request it; they often keep their doors open even after regular hours and charge reasonable fees.

You will receive generally good treatment at the many local hospitals in Pacific Mexico's tourist centers. (See individual destination chapters for details.) If you must have an English-speaking, American-trained doctor, the International Association for Medical Assistance to Travelers (IAMAT) publishes an updated booklet of qual-

MEDICAL TAGS AND AIR EVACUATION

Travelers with special medical problems might consider wearing a medical identification tag. For a reasonable fee, **Medic Alert,** P.O. Box 1009, Turlock, CA 95381, toll-free U.S. tel. 800/344-3226, www.medicalert.org, provides such tags, as well as an information hotline that will provide doctors with your vital medical background information.

For life-threatening emergencies, **Critical Air Medicine,** Montgomery Field, 4141 Kearny Villa Rd., San Diego, CA 92123, tel. 619/571-0482, toll-free U.S. tel. 800/247-8326 or (reachable from Mexico 24 hours) 800/010-0268, provides high-tech jet ambulance service from any Mexican locale to the United States. For a fee averaging about $15,000, it promises to fly you to the right U.S. hospital in a hurry.

Alternatively, for similar services, consider **Medjet Assistance,** toll-free U.S. tel. 800/963-3538. In emergencies worldwide, call U.S. tel. 205/595-6626 collect. For more information, visit the website www.medjetassistance.com.

CONDUCT AND CUSTOMS

Safe Conduct

Mexico is an old-fashioned country where people value traditional ideals of honesty, fidelity, and piety. Crime rates are low; visitors are often safer in Mexico than in their home cities.

Even though four generations have elapsed since Pancho Villa raided the U.S. border, the image of a Mexico bristling with *bandidos* persists. And similarly for Mexicans: despite the century and a half since the *yanquis* invaded Mexico City and took half their country, the communal Mexican psyche still views gringos (and, by association all white foreigners) with revulsion, jealousy, and wonder.

Fortunately, the Mexican love-hate affair with foreigners does not necessarily apply to individual visitors. Your friendly *"buenos dias"* or *"por favor,"* when appropriate, is always appreciated, whether in the market, the gas station, or the hotel. The shy smile you will most likely receive in return will be your small, but not insignificant, reward.

Women

Your own behavior, despite low crime statistics, largely determines your safety in Mexico. For women traveling solo, it is important to realize that the double standard is alive and well in Mexico. Dress and behave modestly and you will most likely avoid embarrassment. Whenever possible, stay in the company of friends or acquaintances; find companions for beach, sightseeing, and shopping excursions. Ignore strange men's solicitations and overtures. A Mexican man on the prowl will invent the sappiest romantic overtures to snare a gringa. He will often interpret anything but a firm "no" as a "maybe," and a "maybe" as a yes.

Men

For male visitors, alcohol often leads to trouble. Avoid bars and cantinas; and if, given Mexico's excellent beers, you can't abstain completely, at least maintain soft-spoken self-control in the face of challenges from macho drunks.

ified member physicians, several of whom practice in the Pacific Mexico centers of Mazatlán, Guadalajara, Puerto Vallarta, Ixtapa-Zihuatanejo, and Acapulco. IAMAT also distributes a very detailed *How to Protect Yourself Against Malaria* guide, together with worldwide malaria risk and communicable disease charts. Contact IAMAT, at 417 Center St., Lewiston, NY 14092, tel. 716/754-4883, or in Canada at 40 Regal Rd., Guelph, Ontario N1K 1B5, tel. 519/836-0102, or 1287 St. Clair Ave. W, Toronto, Ontario M6E 1B8, tel. 416/652-0137. You may also contact IAMAT at info@iamat.org or www.iamat.org.

For more useful information on health and safety in Mexico, consult Dr. William Forgey's *Traveler's Medical Alert Series: Mexico, A Guide to Health and Safety* (Merrillville, IN: ICS Books) or Dirk Schroeder's *Staying Healthy in Asia, Africa, and Latin America* (Emeryville, CA: Avalon Travel Publishing, 1999).

MACHISMO

I once met an Acapulco man who wore five gold wristwatches and became angry when I quietly refused his repeated invitations to get drunk with him. Another time, on the beach near San Blas, two drunk campesinos nearly attacked me because I was helping my girlfriend cook a picnic dinner. Outside Taxco I once spent an endless hour in the seat behind a bus driver who insisted on speeding down the middle of the two-lane highway, honking aside oncoming automobiles.

Despite their wide differences (the first was a rich criollo, the campesinos were *indígenas,* and the bus driver, mestizo), the common affliction shared by all four men was machismo, a disease that seems to possess many Mexican men. Machismo is a sometimes reckless obsession to prove one's masculinity, to show how macho you are. Men of many nationalities share the instinct to prove themselves. Japan's *bushido* samurai code is one example. Mexican men, however, often seem to try the hardest.

When confronted by a Mexican braggart, male visitors should remain careful and controlled. If your opponent is yelling, stay cool, speak softly, and withdraw as soon as possible. On the highway, be courteous and unprovocative; don't use your car to spar with a macho driver. Drinking often leads to problems. It's best to stay out of bars or cantinas unless you're prepared to deal with the macho consequences. Polite refusal of a drink may be taken as a challenge. If you visit a bar with Mexican friends or acquaintances, you may be heading for a no-win choice of a drunken all-night *borrachera* (binge) or an insult to the honor of your friends by refusing.

For women, machismo requires even more cautious behavior. In Mexico, women's liberation is long in coming. Although a handful of Mexican women have risen to positions of political or corporate power, they constitute a small minority.

Machismo requires that female visitors obey the rules or suffer the consequences. Keep a low profile; wear bathing suits and brief shorts only at the beach. Follow the example of your Mexican sisters: make a habit of going out, especially at night, in the company of friends or acquaintances. Mexican men believe an unaccompanied woman wants to be picked up. Ignore such offers; any response, even refusal, might be taken as a "maybe." If, on the other hand, there is a Mexican man whom you'd genuinely like to meet, the traditional way is an arranged introduction through family or friends.

Mexican families, as a source of protection and friendship, should not be overlooked—especially on the beach or in the park, where, among the gaggle of kids, grandparents, aunts, and cousins, there's room for one more.

The Law and Police

While Mexican authorities are tolerant of alcohol, they are decidedly intolerant of other substances such as marijuana, psychedelics, cocaine, and heroin. Getting caught with such drugs in Mexico usually leads to swift and severe results.

Equally swift is the punishment for nude sunbathing, which is both illegal in public and offensive to Mexicans. Confine your nudist colony to very private locations.

Although with decreasing frequency lately, traffic police in Pacific Mexico's resorts sometimes seem to watch foreign cars with eagle eyes. Officers seem to inhabit busy intersections and one-way streets, waiting for confused tourists to make a wrong move. If they whistle you over, stop immediately or you will really get into hot water. If guilty, say *"Lo siento"* ("I'm sorry") and be cooperative. Although he probably won't mention it, the officer is usually hoping that you'll cough up a $20 *mordida* (bribe) for the privilege of driving away.

Don't do it. Although he may hint at confiscating your car, calmly ask for an official *boleto* (written traffic ticket, if you're guilty) in exchange for your driver's license (have a copy), which the officer will probably keep if he writes a ticket. If after a few minutes no money appears, the officer will most likely give you back your driver's license rather than go to the trouble of writing the ticket. If not, the worst that will usually happen is you will have to go to the *presidencia municipal* (city hall) the next morning and pay the $20 to a clerk in exchange for your driver's license.

Pedestrian and Driving Hazards

Although Pacific Mexico's potholed pavements and "holey" sidewalks won't land you in jail, one of them might send you to the hospital if you don't watch your step, especially at night. "Pedestrian beware" is especially good advice on Mexican streets, where it is rumored that some drivers speed up rather than slow down when they spot a tourist stepping off the curb. Falling coconuts, especially frequent on windy days, constitute an additional hazard to unwary campers and beachgoers.

Driving Mexican country roads, where slow trucks and carts block lanes, campesinos stroll the shoulders, and horses, burros, and cattle wander at will, is hazardous—doubly so at night.

Socially Responsible Travel

Latter-day jet travel has brought droves of vacationing tourists to developing countries largely unprepared for the consequences. As the visitors' numbers swell, power grids black out, sewers overflow, and roads crack under the strain of accommodating more and larger hotels, restaurants, cars, buses, and airports.

Worse yet, armies of vacationers drive up local prices and begin to change native customs. While visions of tourists as sources of fast money replace traditions of hospitality, television wipes out folk entertainments, Coke and Pepsi substitute for fruit drinks, and prostitution and drugs flourish.

Some travelers have said enough is enough and are forming organizations to encourage visitors to travel with increased sensitivity to native people and customs. They have developed travelers' codes of ethics and guidelines that encourage visitors to stay at local-style accommodations, use local transportation, and seek alternative vacations and tours, such as language-study and cultural programs and people-to-people work projects.

What to Take

"Men wear pants, ladies be beautiful" was once the dress code of one of Pacific Mexico's region's classiest hotels. Men in casual Pacific Mexico can get by easily without a jacket, women with simple skirts and blouses.

Loose-fitting, hand-washable, easy-to-dry clothes make for trouble-free tropical vacationing. Synthetic or cotton-synthetic-blend shirts, blouses, pants, socks, and underwear will fit the bill everywhere in the coastal Pacific Mexico region. For breezy nights, bring a lightweight windbreaker. If you're going to the highlands (Guadalajara, Pátzcuaro, Taxco, Oaxaca), add a medium-weight jacket.

In all cases, leave showy, expensive clothes and jewelry at home. Stow items that you cannot lose in your hotel safe or carry them with you in a sturdy zipped purse or a waist pouch on your front side.

Packing

What you pack depends on how mobile you want to be. If you're staying the whole time at a self-contained resort, you can take the two suitcases and one carry-on allowed by airlines. If, on the other hand, you're going to be moving around a lot, you'd do better to condense everything to one easily carried bag with wheels that doubles as luggage and soft backpack. Experienced travelers accomplish this by packing prudently and tightly, choosing items that will do double or triple duty (such as a Swiss army knife with scissors).

Campers will have to be super-careful to accomplish one-bag packing. Fortunately, camping along the tropical coast requires no sleeping bag. Simply use a hammock (buy it in Mexico) or, if sleeping on the ground, a sleeping pad and a sheet for cover. In the winter, at most, you may have to buy a light blanket. A compact tent that you and your partner can share is a must against bugs, as is mosquito repellent. A first-aid kit is absolutely necessary (see Staying Healthy).

ON THE ROAD

PACKING CHECKLIST

Necessary Items
camera, film (expensive in Mexico)
clothes, hat
comb
guidebook, reading books
inexpensive watch, clock
keys, tickets
mosquito repellent
passport
prescription eyeglasses
prescription medicines and drugs
purse, waist-belt carrying pouch
sunglasses, sunscreen
swimsuit
toothbrush, toothpaste
tourist card, visa
traveler's checks, money
windbreaker

Useful Items
address book
birth control
checkbook, credit and ATM cards
contact lenses
dental floss
earplugs
first-aid kit
flashlight, batteries
immersion heater
lightweight binoculars
portable radio/cassette player
razor
travel booklight
vaccination certificate

Necessary Items for Campers
collapsible gallon plastic bottle
dish soap
first-aid kit
hammock (buy in Mexico)
insect repellent
lightweight hiking shoes
lightweight tent
matches in waterproof case
nylon cord
plastic bottle, quart
pot scrubber/sponge
sheet or light blanket
Sierra Club cup, fork, and spoon
single-burner stove with fuel
Swiss army knife
tarp
toilet paper
towel, soap
two nesting cooking pots
water-purifying tablets or iodine

Useful Items for Campers
compass
dishcloths
hot pad
instant coffee, tea, sugar, powdered milk
moleskin (Dr. Scholl's)
plastic plate
poncho
short candles
whistle

Mazatlán

Mazatlán (pop. 700,000) spreads for 15 sun-splashed miles along a thumb of land that extends southward into the Pacific just below the Tropic of Cancer. Mazatlán thus marks the beginning of the Mexican tropics: a palmy land of perpetual summer and a refuge from winter cold for growing numbers of international vacationers.

Mazatlán's beauty is renowned. Its coast sprinkled with beckoning islands and miles of golden beaches and blue lagoons, it aptly deserves its title as "Pearl of the Pacific."

Despite its popularity as a tourist destination, Mazatlán owes its existence to local industry. As well as being a leading manufacturing center in the state of Sinaloa, Mazatlán is home port for a huge commercial and sportfishing fleet, whose annual catch of shrimp, tuna, and swordfish amounts to thousands of tons.

Mazatlán, consequently, lives independently of tourism. The vacationers come and frolic on the beach beside their "Golden Zone" hotels, while in the old town at the tip of the peninsula, life goes on in the old-Mexico style: in the markets, the churches, and the shady plazas scattered throughout the traditional neighborhoods.

HISTORY
Before Columbus
For Mexico, Mazatlán is not an old city. Most of its public buildings have stood for less than 100 years. Evidence of local human settlement dates back before recorded history,

airy Playa Norte, a favorite Mazatlán strolling ground

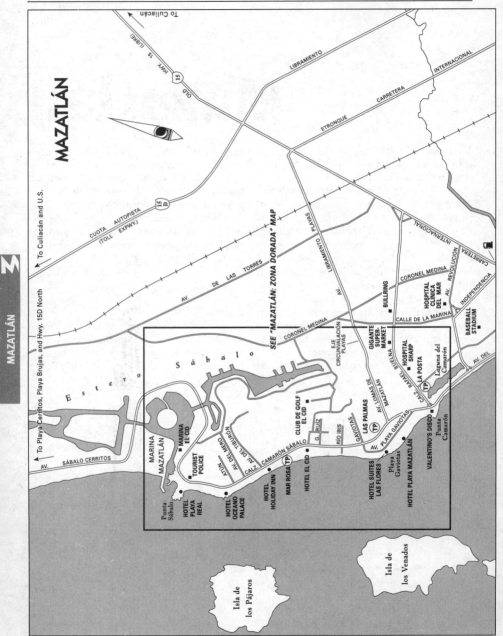

MAZATLÁN

MAZATLÁN

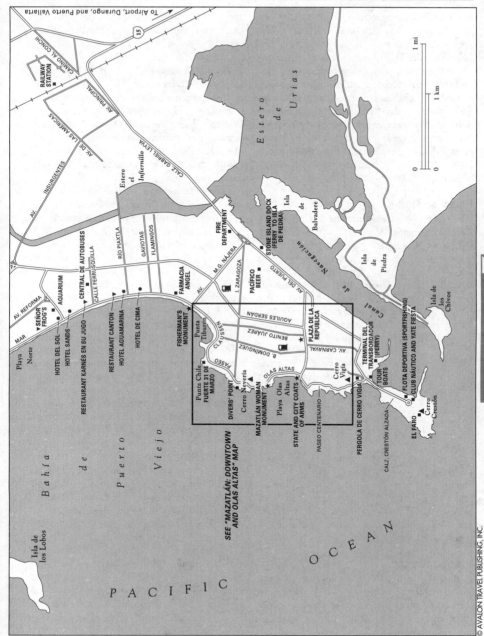

MAZATLÁN

© AVALON TRAVEL PUBLISHING, INC.

however. Scientists reckon petroglyphs found on offshore islands may be as much as 10,000 years old.

During the 1930s archaeologists began uncovering exquisite polychrome pottery, with elaborate black and red designs, indicative of a high culture. Unlike their renowned Tarascan, Aztec, and Toltec highland neighbors, those ancient potters, known as the Totorames, built no pyramids and left no inscriptions. They had been gone a dozen generations before conquistador Nuño de Guzmán burned his way through Sinaloa in 1531.

Colonial Times

The rapacious Guzmán may have been responsible for the name "Mazatlán," which, curiously, is a name of Náhuatl (Aztec language), rather than local origin. Since Aztecs rarely ventured anywhere near present-day Mazatlán, the name Mazatlán (Place of the Deer) presents an intriguing mystery. Historians speculate that a Náhuatl-speaking interpreter of Guzmán may have translated the name from the local language.

Mazatlán was first mentioned in 1602 as the name of a small village, San Juan Bautista de Mazatlán (now called Villa Union), 30 miles south of present-day Mazatlán, which was not yet colonized.

English and French pirates, however, soon discovered Mazatlán's benefits. They occasionally used its hill-screened harbor as a lair from which to pounce upon the rich galleons that plied the coast. The colonial government replied by establishing a small *presidio* on the harbor and watchtowers atop the *cerros*. Although the pirates were gone by 1800, legends persist of troves of stolen silver and gold buried in hidden caves and under windswept sands, ripe for chance discovery along the Mazatlán coast.

Independence

Lifting of foreign trade restrictions in 1820 and independence in 1821 seemed to bode well for the port of Mazatlán. However, cholera, yellow fever, and plague epidemics and repeated foreign occupations (the U.S. Navy in 1847, the French in 1864, and the British in 1871) slowed the growth of Mazatlán during the 19th century. It nevertheless served as the capital of Sinaloa from 1859 to 1873, with a population of several thousand.

The "Order and Progress" of dictator/president Porfirio Díaz (1876–1910) gave Mazatlán citizens a much-needed spell of prosperity. The railroad arrived, the port and lighthouse were modernized, and the cathedral was finished. Education, journalism, and the arts blossomed. The Teatro Rubio, completed in the early 1890s, was the grandest opera house between Baja California and Tepic.

The opera company of the renowned diva, Angela Peralta, the "Mexican Nightingale," arrived and gave a number of enthusiastically received recitals in Mazatlán in August 1883. Tragically, Peralta and most of her company fell victim to a disastrous yellow fever epidemic, which claimed more than 2,500 Mazatlán lives.

The revolution of 1910–1917 literally rained destruction on Mazatlán. In 1914, the city gained the dubious distinction of being the second city in the world to suffer aerial bombardment. (Tripoli, Libya, was the first.) General (later president) Venustiano Carranza, intent upon taking the city, ordered a biplane to bomb the ammunition magazine atop Nevería Hill, adjacent to downtown Mazatlán. But the pilot missed the target and dropped the crude leather-wrapped package of dynamite and nails onto the city streets instead. Two citizens were killed and several wounded.

Modern Mazatlán

After order was restored in the 1920s, Mazatlán soared to a decade of prosperity, followed by the deflation and depression of the 1930s. Recovery after World War II led to port improvements and new highways, setting the stage for the tourist "discovery" of Mazatlán during the 1960s and 1970s. The city limits expanded to include the strand of white sand (Playa Norte) north of the original old port town. High-rise hotels sprouted in a new "Golden Zone" tourist area, which, coupled with Mazatlán's traditional fishing industry, provided thousands of new jobs for an increasingly affluent population, which, by the 21st century, was approaching three-quarters of a million.

SIGHTS

Getting Oriented

Mazatlán owes its life to the sea. The city's main artery, which changes its name five times as it winds northward, never strays far from the shore. From beneath the rugged perch of El Faro (Lighthouse) at the tip of the Mazatlán peninsula, the *malecón* (seawall) boulevard curves northward past the venerable hotels and sidewalk cafés of the Olas Altas (High Waves) neighborhood. From there it snakes along a succession of rocky points and sandy beaches, continuing through the glitzy lineup of Zona Dorada (Golden Zone) beach hotels and restaurants. Next the boulevard loops inland for a spell, curving around a marina and back to the beach. The hotels thin out as it continues past condo complexes, venerable groves and finally, grassy dunes and a sheltered cove beneath Punta Cerritos hill, 15 miles from where it started.

Getting Around

A welter of little local buses run to and fro along identical main-artery routes. From the downtown central plaza they head along the *malecón,* continuing north through the Zona Dorada to various north-end destinations, which are marked on the windshields. Fares should run less than half a dollar.

Small, open-air taxis, called ***pulmonías,*** seating two or three passengers, provide quicker and more convenient service. The average *pulmonía* ("pneumonia," directly translated) ride should total no more than two or three dollars. Agree on the price before you get in, and if you think it's too high, hail another *pulmonía* and your driver will usually come to his senses. The same rules apply to taxi rides, which run about double the price of *pulmonías.*

You can also get around Mazatlán by joining a tour. Hotel travel desks or travel agencies

ANGELA PERALTA

Diva Angela Peralta (1845–1883) was thrilling audiences in Europe's great opera houses by the age of 16, when a Spanish journalist dubbed her the "Mexican Nightingale." On May 13, 1863, she brought down the house at La Scala in Milan with an angelic performance of *Lucia de Lammermoor.*

During Angela's second European tour she charmed maestro Guiseppi Verdi into bringing his entire company across the Atlantic so she could sing *Aida* in Mexico City. With Verdi conducting, Angela inaugurated the 1873 Mexico City season on a pinnacle of fame.

Legends abound of the fiercely nationalistic Peralta. She once got the last word in a tête-à-tête with Europe's most famous Italian soprano of the time. In an unforgettable joint recital, Angela courteously extended first bows to the haughty Italian diva, who remarked of her own performance, "That is the way we sing in Italy." Angela Peralta rejoined, "Mine was the way we sing in heaven."

Not content with mere performance, Angela Peralta went on to excel as a composer, librettist, and impresario, organizing her own opera companies. Her success and outspoken ways earned her enemies in high places, however. In 1873, Mexico City bluebloods were shocked to find out Angela was having an affair with her lawyer, Julian Montiel y Duarte. (It didn't seem to matter that Peralta was widowed and Montiel single at the time.) Much of Mexico City's high society boycotted her performances; when that didn't work, they sent hecklers to harass her. Liberals, however, defended her, and Peralta finally regained her audience in the early 1880s with a heartrending performance of *Linda de Chamounix.* She kept her vow, however, to never sing again in Mexico City.

Her star-crossed life came to an early end on August 30, 1883. Touring with her company in western Mexico, a Mazatlán yellow fever epidemic claimed her life and the lives of 76 of her 80-member company. On her deathbed, she married Montiel y Duarte, the only man she ever loved. Later, her remains were removed to Mexico City, where they now lie enshrined at the Rotunda de Hombres Ilustres (Rotunda of Illustrious Men).

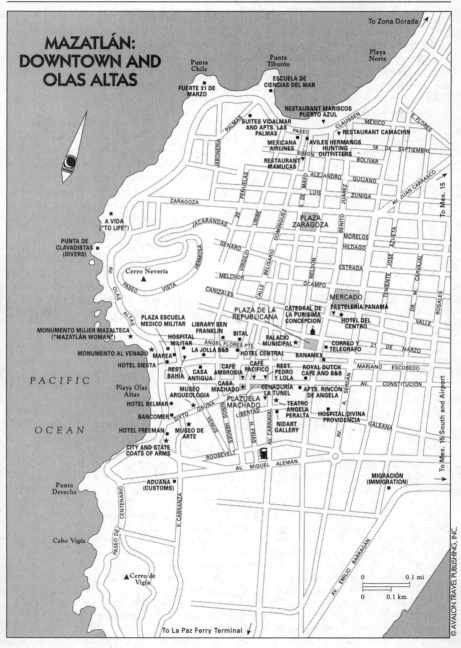

MAZATLÁN: DOWNTOWN AND OLAS ALTAS

To Zona Dorada

Punta Chile

Punta Tiburón

Playa Norte

ESCUELA DE CIENCIAS DEL MAR

FUERTE 31 DE MARZO

RESTAURANT MARISCOS PUERTO AZUL

SUITES VIDALMAR AND APTS. LAS PALMAS

PALMAS

JABONERIA

PASEO

CLAUSSEN

MEXICO

E. FLORES

RESTAURANT CAMACHIN

MEXICANA AIRLINES

AVILES HERMANOS HUNTING OUTFITTERS

SIMON

18 DE SEPTIEMBRE

BOLIVAR

RESTAURANT MAMUCAS

ALEJANDRO

QUIJANO

MORELOS

PENUELAS

5 DE MAYO

LUIS

JUAREZ

ZUNIGA

BENITO

AV. JUAN CARRASCO

To Mex. 15

ZARAGOZA

JACARANDAS

20

URIBE

BELISARIO

DOMINGUEZ

PLAZA ZARAGOZA

BENITO

MORELOS

HILDAGO

A VIDA ("TO LIFE")

PUNTA DE CLAVADISTAS (DIVERS)

GENARO

HERMOSA

VIRGILIO

ESTRADA

JOSE AZUETA

Cerro Nevería

AV. OLAS

PASEO

VISTA

MELCHOR

CALLE

OCAMPO

NELSON

MERCADO

PASTELERÍA PANAMA

DR. R. CARVAJAL

ROSALES

CANIZALES

PLAZA DE LA REPUBLICANA

CATEDRAL DE LA PURISIMA CONCEPCION

HOTEL DEL CENTRO

VALLE

TENIENTE

PLAZA ESCUELA MEDICO MILITAR

LIBRARY BEN FRANKLIN

BITAL

PALACIO MUNICIPAL

CORREO Y TELEGRAFO

21 DE MARZO

MONUMENTO MUJER MAZALTECA ("MAZATLÁN WOMAN")

HOSPITAL MILITAR

ANGEL FLORES PTE.

LA JOLLA B&B

HOTEL CENTRAL

BANAMEX

MONUMENTO AL VENADO

MAREA

REST. BAHIA

CASA ANTIGUA

CAFÉ AMBROSIA

CAFÉ PACIFICO

REST. PEDRO Y LOLA

ROYAL DUTCH CAFE AND B&B

MARIANO

ESCOBEDO

HOTEL SIESTA

CASA MACHADO

CENADURÍA LA TÚNEL

APTS. RINCÓN DE ANGELA

AV. CONSTITUCION

PACIFIC

Playa Olas Altas

MUSEO ARQUEOLOGIA

PLAZUELA MACHADO

TEATRO ANGELA PERALTA

HOSPITAL DIVINA PROVIDENCIA

AV. A. SERDAN

HOTEL BELMAR

SIXTO OSUNA

NINOS HEROES

VENUS

LIBERTAD

H. FRIAS

AV. CARNAVAL

NIDART GALLERY

GALEANA

OCEAN

BANCOMER

HOTEL FREEMAN

MUSEO DE ARTE

CITY AND STATE COATS OF ARMS

ROOSEVELT

AV. MIGUEL ALEMÁN

MIGRACIÓN (IMMIGRATION)

To Mex. 15/South and Airport

Punta Derecha

CENTENARIO

ADUANA (CUSTOMS)

V. CARRANZA

Cabo Vigía

PASEO DEL

Cerro de Vigía

AV. EMILIO BARRAGAN

0   0.1 mi

0   0.1 km

© AVALON TRAVEL PUBLISHING, INC.

To La Paz Ferry Terminal

MAZATLÁN

usually can set you up with one. Boat tours offer yet more options; for specifics, see below.

A Walk Around Downtown Mazatlán

Let the towering double spire of the **Catedral Basílica de la Purísima Concepción** guide you to the very center of old Mazatlán. Begun by the Bishop Pedro Loza y Pardave in 1856, the cathedral was built on the filled lagoon site of an original native temple. Mazatlán's turbulent history delayed its completion until 1899 and final elevation in 1937 to the status of a basilica.

Inside, the image of the city's patron saint, the Virgen de la Purísima Concepción (Virgin of the Immaculate Conception) stands over the gilded, baroque main altar, while overhead soar rounded Renaissance domes and pious, pointed gothic arches. On the left, as you exit, pause and notice the shrine to the popular Virgin of Guadalupe. The cathedral is open daily 6 A.M.–1 P.M. and 4–8 P.M.

In front of the cathedral, the verdant tropical foliage of the central **Plaza de la República** encloses the traditional wrought-iron Porfirian bandstand. To the right is the **Palacio Municipal** (City Hall), where on the eve before Independence Day, September 16, the *presidente municipal* (county mayor) shouts from the balcony the traditional Grito de Dolores above a patriotic and tipsy crowd.

After enjoying the sights and aromas of the colorful **Mercado Central** (Central Market) two blocks behind the cathedral, reverse your path and head down Juárez. Turn right at Constitución, one block to **Plazuela Machado,** Mazatlán's original central plaza. It was named in honor of Juan Nepomuceno Machado, a founding father of Filipino descent who donated the land. The venerable Porfirian buildings and monuments clustered along the surrounding streets include the **Teatro Angela Peralta,** completed around 1890 and recently restored and dedicated to diva Angela Peralta.

At the west end of the Plazuela, along Calle Heriberto Frías, walk beneath the **Portales de Cannobio,** the arcade of the 1846 estate house of apple grower Luis Cannobio, a 19th-century Italian-born resident. The Cannobio family occupied the upper floor while operating a pharmacy at street level beneath the portals.

In those days, Plazuela Machado was the hub of Mazatlán life. The activity that buzzed around a lineup of mining and assay offices on adjacent **Calle de Oro** (now Calle Sixto Osuna) bubbled over with merrymaking (and still does) during the yearly Carnaval Lenten celebration.

Present owners of the old Cannobio house, now renamed **Casa Machado,** have reopened it as a museum (open daily 10 A.M.–6 P.M., tel. 669/982-1440). They invite visitors to "find their way to the inner memories" of Mazatlán in the upper-floor rooms, decorated with antique reminders—polished provincial French furniture, bright Carnaval costumes, and lacey four-poster beds—of old Mazatlán.

For a shady break, take a seat at one of the small **sidewalk cafés** on the plaza's north side (or the refined **Café Memorial** across from the Teatro Angela Peralta); or go inside and sample the menu at restaurant **Lola and Pedro** at the plaza's northeast corner, Carnaval and Constitución.

Olas Altas

Continue west a few blocks toward the ocean from Plazuela Machado along Calle Sixto Osuna and step into the small **Museo Arqueología,** Sixto de Osuna 76, tel. 669/985-1455, and peruse its well-organized exhibits outlining Sinaloan prehistory and culture. The displays include case after case of petroglyphs, human and animal figurines, and the distinctive red- and black-glazed ancient polychrome pottery of Sinaloa. Open Tues.–Sun. 10 A.M.–1 P.M. and 4–7 P.M.

Half a block farther west and south around the corner of V. Carranza, take a look inside the **Museo de Arte,** which displays the works of noted local and nationally recognized painters, sculptors, and graphic artists. Open approx. Tues.–Sun. 10 A.M.–1 P.M. and 4–7 P.M.

Continue west one short block to the *malecón* (seawall) **Av. Olas Altas.** This airy, café-lined stretch of boulevard and adjacent beach was at one time *the* tourist zone of Mazatlán. It extends from the **Monumento al Venado** (Monument to the Deer) at its the north end, at Av. Ángel Flores, south a few blocks past the restored Hotel Freeman to the **Escudos de Sinaloa y Mazatlán** (State and City Coats of Arms of Sinaloa and Mazatlán). There, Av. Olas Altas changes names, in front of the distinguished 1889 school building at the foot of steep Cerro Vigía, where the boulevard, now **Paseo del Centenario,** climbs to it breezy south-end summit viewpoint.

Step inside the lobby of the restored 1940s-era **Hotel Freeman.** Perhaps more than any event, the Freeman's return to life in late 2002 signalled the resurgence of the vitality of old Mazatlán. The Freeman's shiny five-star reincarnation promises an impressive array of facilties, including an 11th-floor open-air swimming pool, a lavishly equipped gym, Internet access in each room, a business center, convention facilities, and much more. (For Hotel Freeman lodging details, see the Accommodations section.)

Outside, nearby, you might pause a while and soak up the flavor of old Mazatlán. Take a seat at one of the sidewalk cafés; later look around the lobby of the old Hotel Belmar. Notice the wall map a few steps inside the entrance door, dated 1948, when the entire state of Sinaloa had a population less than half of present-day Mazatlán, and the whole country had a population equal to Mexico City's today.

Cerro Vigía

Now, unless, you're in the mood for a steep hike, bargain for a *pulmonía* to take you up Paseo Centenario, the southern extension of Av. Olas Altas, to the **Pergola de Cerro Vigía** viewpoint at the top of the hill. There, next to the old cannon (stamped by its proud London maker, "Vavaseurno. 830, 1875"), you get the sweep of the whole city.

Cerro Vigía is the spot where, according to tradition, the colonial soldiers of the old Mazatlán presidio maintained their 200-year vigil, scanning the horizon for pirates. Step across the little hilltop plaza and down to the **Café El Mirador** and enjoy lunch, a drink, and the view; open daily noon–9 P.M.

Cerro Creston and El Faro

To the south rises Mazatlán's tallest hill, Cerro Creston, topped by the El Faro lighthouse, whose 515-foot (157-meter) elevation qualifies it as the world's highest natural lighthouse. Along the jetty/landfill that connects Cerro Creston to the mainland lie the docks and anchored boats of the several *flotas deportivas* (sport fleets). Every morning, in season, they take loads of anglers out in search of big fighting marlin and sailfish.

Boat Tours

Harbor tour boats also depart from the same docks. *Yate Fiesta* leaves regularly at 11 A.M. for a harbor and island cruise, passing the inner harbor shrimp fleet, circling past the lighthouse, sea lion island (winter only) and Mazatlán's offshore islands, Islas Chivos, Pájaros, and Venados. Tickets cost about $15 per person for the three-hour trip. For information and reservations, call tel. 669/981-7640, 669/913-0624, or 669/913-0625 (or go to the Zona Dorada office across from the Hotel Las Palmas on Camarón Sábalo).

Also, trimaran *Kolonahe* offers a pair of tours from the north-end Marina El Cid: A 9:30 A.M. island tour that includes part of the harbor tour as described above, as well as a landing at Isla Venados for swimming, hiking, lunch, and sunning on the beach, returning in early afternoon. Later in the afternoon, the *Kolonahe* heads seaward again for an open-bar sunset cruise (about $42). For more information and reservations, contact a travel agent or call the El Cid Marina, tel. 669/916-3468.

Across the south-side deep-water harbor entrance looms the bulk of **Isla de Piedra** (Stone Island), actually a peninsula. Its southern beach stretches to the horizon in a narrowing white thread, beneath the dark green plumes of Mexico's third-largest coconut grove. If you've a hankering to explore, ride the tour boat *Renegado,* which heads out mornings, first passing the world's biggest shrimp fleet, continuing through the harbor's far mangrove reaches to the Stone Island landing, where, after lunch at a *palapa* restaurant, you can explore the beach and coconut grove by foot, play in the waves, paddle a kayak, ride horses or a banana boat, or simply laze in the sun. Hotel pickup is included in the approximately $25 price. For information

© BRUCE WHIPPERMAN

The red bars add a bit of fiery realism to the Devil's Cave's decoration.

and reservations, call a travel agent or contact the *Renegado* directly at tel. 669/914-2477. (If the *Renegado* is full, you can alternatively go by the *Catamaran Sábalo,* tel. 669/982-8877, to Stone Island.)

(For more adventurous tours and activities, such as biking, snorkeling, scuba diving, hiking, and wildlife viewing, see Sports and Recreation.)

Cerro Nevería

The rounded profile of Cerro Nevería (Icehouse Hill) rises above the patchwork of city streets, south of the Olas Altas neighborhood. Its unique label originated during the mid-1800s, when the tunnels that pock the hill served for storage of ice imported from San Francisco, California. Now the hilltop holds a number of radio and microwave beacons. The northerly view from atop Cerro Nevería reveals a spectacular panorama of city, beach, and offshore islands. Get there via Calle Puebla, which climbs uphill, from the from the west end of downtown Calle Zaragoza. Keep going uphill at every fork. Before the summit, fol-

low the cobbled driveway to the summit, where you'll see the long, graceful sweep of wave-tossed Playa Norte, and the three offshore islands, basking in the blue Pacific.

Punta Camarón and Offshore Islands

The curving white ribbon of sand north of the downtown area traces the *malecón* northward to Punta Camarón and the Golden Zone, marked by the cluster of shoreline high-rise hotels. Offshore from Punta Camarón, Mazatlán's three islands—**Chivos** (Rams) and **Venados** (Deer), nearest, and **Pájaros** (Birds) on the horizon—seem to float offshore like a trio of sleeping whales.

Along Paseo Claussen

Return back downhill to Av. Olas Altas. Moving south from the Hotel Freeman, pass the Statue of the Deer in the middle of the intersection where the *malecón* becomes Paseo Claussen. Named for the rich German immigrant who financed the blasting of the scenic drive, Paseo Claussen continues around the wave-tossed foot of Cerro Nevería. First, you will pass a striking bronze sculpture, the ***Monumento Mujer Mazalteca,*** nearly erotic in its intensity. Nearby, a yawning cave (plugged by heavy bars), pierces the hill. Known by local people as the **Caverna del Diablo** (Devil's Cave), it served as an escape route for soldiers guarding the ammunition stored in caves farther up the hill.

Not far ahead, a four-story platform at the **Punta de Clavadistas** (Divers' Point) towers above the wave-swept tidepools. The divers—professionals who take their work very seriously, especially at low tide, when their dives must coincide with the arrival of a big swell—perform a number of times daily, more frequently on Sundays and holidays.

Moving north, you'll pass the new ***Continuity of Life*** sculpture, popular with crowds of local folks who arrive evenings to watch its colored fountains. Continue another block to the 1892 fort turned maritime office, **Fuerte 31 de Marzo,** named in honor of the heroic stand of the local garrison, which repelled a French invasion on March 31, 1864.

MAZATLÁN

BEACHES

Olas Altas to Punta Camarón

Exploration of Mazatlán's beaches can start at Av. Olas Altas, where narrow **Playa Olas Altas** offers some water sports opportunities. The strip is wide and clean enough for wading, sunning, bodysurfing, and boogie boarding. Swimmers take care: the waves often break suddenly and recede strongly. Locally popular intermediate surfing breaks angle shoreward along both north and south ends. Bring your own equipment, since there's rarely any for rent on this largely locals-only beach.

For fly and bait-casting—although the beach surf is too murky to catch much—casts from the rocks on either end may yield rewards worth the effort.

Continuing north around Paseo Claussen, past the fort, you'll come to a wave-tossed **Pinos** cove adjacent to the modern Ciencias del Mar (Marine Sciences) college. Although the narrow strand here is suitable for no more than wading, the rocks provide good casting spots, and the left-breaking swells challenge beginning and intermediate surfers.

Next comes the small boat cove where **Playa Norte** begins. Unfortunately, the first one-mile stretch is too polluted for much more than strolling (because of the waste from the fleet of fishing *lanchas*) along the beach.

A mile farther north beginning around the oafish **Monumento al Pescador** (Fisherman's Monument), where Paseo Claussen becomes Av. del Mar, a relatively wide, clean white strand extends for three miles. This stretch is popular with local families and is uncrowded except during holidays. On calm days the waves break gently and gradually; other times they can be rough. If so, stick by a lifeguard if you see one.

Beginning and intermediate surfers congregate at the north end of this beach, on both flanks of **Punta Camarón** (marked by the needle spires Valentino's disco), where the swells break gradually left. For fisherfolk, the rocks on the point provide good spots for casting.

Zona Dorada Beaches

At Punta Camarón (marked by the white spires of Valentino's disco) beachfront Av. del Mar becomes Calz. Camarón Sábalo, which winds northward through the clutter of Zona Dorada streetside eateries, crafts shops, travel agencies, and banks.

The way to enjoy and understand the Zona Dorada is not on the boulevard, but on the beach a few blocks away. The lineup of successful hotels immediately north of Punta Camarón testifies to the beauty of Playa Camarón and Playa Gaviotas. These shining strands—with oft-gentle rolling waves, crystal sand, and glowing, island-silhouetted sunsets—give meaning to the label "Golden Zone": golden memories for visitors and gold in the pockets of the Mazatlán folks lucky enough to own or work in the Zona Dorada. (Sometimes it seems as if half the town *is* trying to work there. During the low-season months of September and October, beachfront crafts and food vendors often outnumber the sunbathers.)

Although the **Playas Camarón** and **Gaviotas** are often lumped together, the beaches themselves contrast sharply. The more southerly Playa Camarón is oft-narrow and steep, with coarse, yellow sand. Its waves often break suddenly and recede strongly. At such times, bodysurfing on Playa Camarón is a thrilling but potentially hazardous pastime.

Despite the popularity of this strip, small shells, such as mother-of-pearl and lovely rust-brown-mottled little clams, are sometimes plentiful.

About 500 yards north of the point, near the Las Flores Hotel, Playa Camarón becomes Playa Gaviotas. There, the beach changes to Playa Gaviotas's silky smooth sand and lazy slope. Waves usually roll in gently and always for a long distance. They are not good for surfing, since they head straight into the beach and tend to break all at once along a long front, rather than angling left or right.

Another quarter mile north around Hotel El Cid, Playa Gaviotas becomes its identically lovely northward extension, **Playa Sábalo,** which stretches another mile to Punta Sábalo at the Hotel Playa Real (formerly Camino Real).

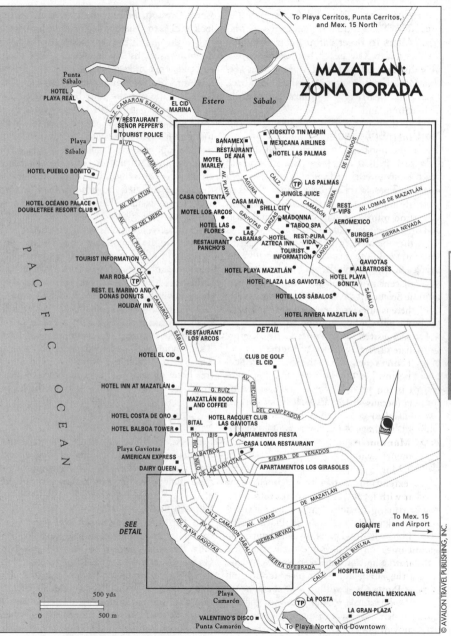

To Playa Cerritos, Punta Cerritos, and Mex. 15 North

MAZATLÁN: ZONA DORADA

Punta Sábalo

HOTEL PLAYA REAL

CALZ. CAMARÓN SÁBALO

EL CID MARINA

Estero   Sábalo

RESTAURANT SENOR PEPPER'S

TOURIST POLICE

AV. DE MARLIN

BLVD

Playa Sábalo

HOTEL PUEBLO BONITO

HOTEL OCÉANO PALACE
DOUBLETREE RESORT CLUB

AV. DEL ATÚN

AV. DEL MERO

AV. DEL PUERTO

P A C I F I C

TOURIST INFORMATION

MAR ROSA

CALZ. CAMARÓN

REST. EL MARINO AND
DONAS DONUTS

HOLIDAY INN

SÁBALO

RESTAURANT
LOS ARCOS

DETAIL

HOTEL EL CID

CLUB DE GOLF
EL CID

HOTEL INN AT MAZATLÁN

AV. G. RUIZ

AV. CIRCUITO

MAZATLÁN BOOK
AND COFFEE

DEL CAMPEADOR

HOTEL COSTA DE ORO

HOTEL RACQUET CLUB
LAS GAVIOTAS

HOTEL BALBOA TOWER

BITAL

RÍO IBIS

APARTAMENTOS FIESTA

RÍO

Playa Gaviotas
AMERICAN EXPRESS

CASA LOMA RESTAURANT

ALBATROS

RÍO NILO

DAIRY QUEEN

SIERRA DE VENADOS

AV. DE LAS GAVIOTAS

APARTAMENTOS LOS GIRASOLES

O C E A N

SEE DETAIL

CALZ. CAMARÓN SÁBALO

AV. LOMAS

DE MAZATLÁN

AV. R.T.

AV. PLAYA GAVIOTAS

SIERRA NEVADA

To Mex. 15
and Airport

GIGANTE

SIERRA QUEBRADA

CALZ. RAFAEL BUELNA

HOSPITAL SHARP

0   500 yds

0   500 m

Playa Camarón

LA POSTA

COMERCIAL MEXICANA

LA GRAN PLAZA

VALENTINO'S DISCO
Punta Camarón

To Playa Norte and Downtown

DETAIL

BANAMEX

KIOSKITO TIN MARIN

MEXICANA AIRLINES

RESTAURANT
DE ANA

HOTEL LAS PALMAS

MOTEL
MARLEY

AV. PLAYA

LAGUNA

CALZ.

DE VENADOS

TP   LAS PALMAS

JUNGLE JUICE

CASA CONTENTA

CASA MAYA

SHELL CITY

GAVIOTAS

GARZA

CAMARÓN

REST.
VIPS

AV. LOMAS DE MAZATLÁN

SIERRA

MOTEL LOS ARCOS

MADONNA

AEROMEXICO

SIERRA NEVADA

HOTEL LAS
FLORES

TABOO SPA

BURGER
KING

LAS
CABAÑAS

HOTEL
AZTECA INN

REST. PURA
VIDA

RESTAURANT
PANCHO'S

TOURIST
INFORMATION

GAVIOTAS

GAVIOTAS
ALBATROSES

HOTEL PLAYA MAZATLÁN

HOTEL PLAYA
BONITA

SÁBALO

HOTEL PLAZA LAS GAVIOTAS

HOTEL LOS SÁBALOS

HOTEL RIVIERA MAZATLÁN

MAZATLÁN

Past the rocks of Punta Sábalo, the waters of the **Estero Sábalo** tidal lagoon (now the Marina Mazatlán's outer harbor) ebb through a boat channel. The beach boulevard loops a mile inland, past the El Cid Marina, then Marina Mazatlán, curving north, then west, back to the beach, where it becomes Calz. Sábalo Cerritos.

Northern Beaches

The strand north of Punta Sábalo, called **Playa Cerritos,** in places begins to resemble a wild beach along undeveloped stretches of its northern reaches. Grass sways atop the dunes, flocks of sandpipers probe the wave-washed sand, pelicans and frigate birds glide overhead, and shells and driftwood accumulate.

At the northern end of Playa Cerritos, just south of the hill that marks Punta Cerritos, the beach becomes **Playa Brujas,** named for the *brujas,* female witch doctors, who used to perform their rituals there. If you're thirsty or hungry by that time, a seafood restaurant at the end of the beach will gladly accommodate you.

On the north side of Punta Cerritos, more seafood *palapa* restaurants perch at the very end of the beach boulevard. On the left, a rocky tidepool shelf juts out into the waves, forming a protected cove. This, some say, is the best fishing spot in Mazatlán. It appears so; half a dozen *lanchas* are usually pulled up on the rocky beach, while offshore, one or two divers hunt for oysters in the clear, calm waters.

Hikes

The best hike in Mazatlán leads right along the beach. Just walk any of your favorite stretches. You could do the whole thing (or just part of it) starting anywhere—Olas Altas, Playa Norte, Playa Gaviotas—and walking as far north (to avoid having the sun in your eyes) as you want. Other than a hat and sunscreen, you won't have to carry anything along; beach restaurants and stores along the way will provide the goodies. Neither will you have to walk back; just grab the bus or a *pulmonía* back to town whenever you decide you've walked enough.

Another good hike leads to the summit of **Cerro Creston** and provides a close, interesting look at **El Faro.** The trail begins at the foot of the hill, at the end of the pavement past the *flotas deportivas* (sportfishing fleet) docks. Wear a hat, and take some insect repellent, water, and maybe food for a breezy summit picnic.

Follow the initially wide track as it zigzags up the hill. Sometimes overhung by vines, leafy trees, and gnarled cacti, the trail narrows to a rocky path about halfway to the summit. Nearing the top, you wind your way beside rocky outcroppings until you come to the fence around the lighthouse. If your group is small, the keeper may let you in for a look around and to sign his book. He claims the lighthouse is 400 years old.

If you arrive around dusk (bring a flashlight), you will see the beacon in action. The dazzling 1.5-million-watt beacon rotates gradually, like the spokes of a heavenly chariot, with several brilliant, wheeling pencils of light focused by the great antique Fresnel lens atop the tower.

At least one local agency offers a city and **hiking tour** that includes a guided climb to the lighthouse summit. It customarily begins at 3 P.M., ending with a sunset view from the hilltop. The $19 tariff includes drinks on the bus and free hotel pickup. Call a travel agent or Vista Tours, tel. 669/986-8610, www.vistatours.com.

EXCURSIONS

Besides restful country ambience, the area around Mazatlán offers interesting history, attractive handicrafts, and rewarding wildlife viewing for the steady flow of visitors to its southern hinterland.

Copala and Concordia

The twin colonial towns of Copala and Concordia, in the lush Sierra Madre foothills, provide the focus for an unhurried day-trip. Concordia, about 12 miles inland along Highway 40 (27 miles, 44 km from Mazatlán), offers fine colonial-style furniture and an abundance of attractive pre-Columbian-motif pottery. A short side road leads to a mineral spring, where a number of women make a business of washing clothes. About a dozen miles farther up the road stands Copala (founded 1565), an antique mining town with hillside lanes winding to a petite plaza and old colonial church. Bring a picnic lunch or stop for refreshment beneath the shady veranda of one of the town's good restaurants.

Get there by tour, car, or bus (ride a Durango-bound first-class Transportes Chihuahenses or a second-class bus from the *central de autobuses*). For a tour (about $40, including lunch) contact an agency, such as Viajes Copala, tel. 669/986-2120, or Olé Tours, tel. 669/916-6287 or 669/916-6288, www.oletours.com.

Rosario and Teacapán

Rosario and Teacapán likewise provide an inviting, although contrasting day-trip option. Rosario (pop. about 10,000), on Highway 15, about 56 miles (90 km) south of Mazatlán, is famed for the towering, solid-gold baroque "Million Dollar Altar" in the town church. You also can visit the home of famous singer Lola Beltrán, on Lola Beltrán Street near the church. Beltrán's well-deserved fame flows from her dozens of songs and recordings of Mexican folk-style "Ranchera" music, which she popularized during many world tours.

> *You can nearly predict the room price of a hotel by its position on a Mazatlán map. The farther north, away from the old downtown, the newer and more expensive it's likely to be.*

Continue less than an hour (31 miles, 51 km) to Teacapán, where you can enjoy lunch, either at Wayne's Restaurant on the village bayfront, or at hacienda-style Rancho Los Angeles on the beach a few miles north of town. Top your day off by viewing the nesting swarm of pelicans, egrets, and cormorants at Bird Island, via hired launch on Agua Grande Lagoon. Get there by car, bus, or tour along Highway 15 south. The tour, sometimes called the "Bird Island" tour, costs about $50, including lunch. See a travel agent, or call Olé Tours, tel. 669/916-6287 or 669/916-6288, or Pronatours, tel. 669/916-7720 or 669/913-3333, ext. 3490.

(For more south of Mazatlán tour details, including lodgings, see the South to Puerto Vallarta and Inland to Guadalajara chapter.)

ACCOMMODATIONS

You can nearly predict the room price of a hotel by its position on a Mazatlán map. The farther north, away from the old downtown, the newer and more expensive it's likely to be.

Downtown Hotels and Bed-and-Breakfasts

At one time, all Mazatlán hotels were downtown. But, during the 1980s and 1990s the plush new hotels and condos on the Playa Norte-Zona Dorada luxury beach strip drew away most of the high-ticket vacationers, leaving the old Olas Altas tourist zone to the sprinkling of travelers who seek the charms of traditional Mexico and Mexican families on Sunday outings. The exception to this is the week after Christmas, the week before Easter, and, most of all, Carnaval (Mardi Gras, in late February or March), when Olas Altas is awash with merrymakers.

The new owners of the **Hotel Freeman** have taken a giant step toward the re-energizing old Mazatlán, with their two-year restoration of the original 1940s-era hostelry. Reopened in November 2002, the Hotel Freeman now gleams with a host of five-star amenities, including an 11-floor open air swimming pool, a lavishly equipped gym and spa, Internet access in each room, a business center and convention facilities. The approximately 100 rooms rent from about $110. Find it on Av. Olas Altas, corner of Sixto Osuna, Mazatlán, Sinaloa 82000. For information and reservations, email reservaciones@posadadelrio.com or ventas@posadadelrio.com or visit the website www.posadadelrio.com.

Two blocks south stands the venerable six-story oceanfront **Hotel Belmar,** Av. Olas Altas 166, Mazatlán, Sinaloa 82000, tel. 669/985-1112, fax 669/981-3428, faded but still welcoming the longtimers who remember when it was *the* hotel in Mazatlán. Belmar offers 200 rooms, with a/c, phones, and parking, from about $28 d, $33 with

MAZATLÁN ACCOMMODATIONS BY PRICE

Accommodations (area code 669, postal code 82000 unless otherwise noted) are listed in increasing order of approximate high-season, double-room rates.

Downtown

Hotel Belmar, Av. Olas Altas 166, tel. 985-1112, fax 981-3428, $20

Hotel del Centro, Canizales 18, tel. 981-2673, $25

Hotel Central, Belisario Domínguez 2 Sur, tel. 982-1888 or 982-1866, $25

Hotel Siesta, Av. Olas Altas 11, tel. 981-2640 or 981-2334, fax 982-2633, $40

Suites Vidalmar and Apts. Las Palmas, Calle Las Palmas 15, tel. 981-2190 or 981-2197, $50

Playa Norte

Hotel del Sol, Av. del Mar s/n, P.O. Box 400, tel./fax 985-1103, $32

Hotel Sands, Av. del Mar 1910, P.O. Box 309, tel. 982-0000, 982-0800, 982-0600, fax 982-1025, hotelsandsarenas@red2000.com.mx, $38

Hotel Aguamarina, Av. del Mar 110, P.O. Box 345, tel. 981-7080, fax 982-4624, info@aguamarina.com, $81

Zona Dorada and North

Fiesta Apartmentos, Ibis 502, postal code 82110, tel. 913-5355, 913-5313, or 913-1764, hudsontours@mazatlan.com.mx, $30

Racquet Club Las Gaviotas, Ibis at Bravo, P.O. Box 173, tel. 913-5939, $35

Bungalows Playa Escondida, Calz. Sábalo Cerritos 999, P.O. Boxes 682 and 202, postal code 82110, tel. 988-0077, $38

Los Girasoles, Av. Gaviotas 709 (postal code 82110), tel./fax 913-5288, $40

Hotel Plaza Las Gaviotas, Bugambilias 100, P.O. Box 970, postal code 82110, tel. 913-4496, fax 913-6685, $52

Hotel Azteca Inn, R. T. Loaiza 307, P.O. Box 841, tel. 913-4477, fax 913-4655, www.aztecainn.com.mx, $53

Hotel Las Flores, R.T. Loaiza 212, P.O. Box 583, postal code 82110, tel. 913-5011 or 913-5100, toll-free U.S. tel. 800/452-0627 or Can. tel. 877/529-7567, fax 914-3422, www.lasflores.com.mx, $65

Motel Los Arcos, R. T. Loaiza 214, P.O. Box 132, tel./fax 913-5066, $70

Motel Marley, R. T. Loaiza 226, P.O. Box 214, tel./fax 913-5533, $70

Casa Contenta, R. T. Loaiza 224, tel. 913-4976, fax 913-9986, $80

Hotel Tropicana, R. T. Loaiza 27, P.O. Box 501, postal code 82110, tel. 983-8000, fax 983-5361, tropican@prodigy.net.mx, $80

Hotel Riviera Mazatlán, Camarón Sábalo 51, P.O. Box 795, tel. 983-4722, fax 984-4532, $90

Hotel Playa Mazatlán, Av. R. T. Loaiza 202, P.O. Box 207, postal code 82110, tel. 989-0555, fax 914-0366, $110

Hotel Inn at Mazatlán, Camarón Sábalo 6291, P.O. Box 1292, postal code 82110, tel. 913-5500 or 913-5354, fax 913-4782, innatmazatlan@red2000.com.mx, $120

Hotel El Cid, Camarón Sábalo s/n, P.O. Box 335, postal code 82110, tel. 913-3333, fax 914-1311, $140

view; credit cards are accepted. Although now a bit tattered, its old amenities remain: pool, sidewalk restaurant, parking, and many ocean-view rooms, some carpeted and modern and some so old and makeshift they're quaint.

A block farther south, the popular **Hotel Siesta,** Av. Olas Altas 11, Mazatlán, Sinaloa 82000, tel. 669/981-2640 or 669/981-2334, fax 669/982-2633, provides a solid, moderately priced option for enjoying the flavor of the Olas Altas neighborhood. The 57 rooms have TV, a/c, and phones. (Some, however, are showing wear. Look at more than one before choosing.) For balcony views of Carnaval or lovely sunsets any time of the year, reserve one of the several ocean-front rooms. Another extra is the charming old inner patio, decorated by the colorful umbrellas of the El Shrimp Bucket restaurant and shaded by towering, leafy trees festooned with hanging air-roots. A combo plays traditional Latin melodies seasonally on the patio (weather permitting) most nights till around 10 P.M. From about $33 d ($38 with view) low season, $40 high ($46 with view); credit cards are accepted. For more information and reservations, email lasiesta@mazatlan.com.mx or visit the website www.lasiesta.com.mx.

About a half mile north, where Paseo Claussen bends around Cerro Nevería, a big sign on the hill above the Ciencias del Mar (Marine Sciences) college marks **Suites Vidalmar,** Calle Las Palmas 15, Mazatlán, Sinaloa 82000, tel. 669/981-2190 or 669/981-2197. Get information and reservations by email suitesvidalmar@yahoo.com. The modern stucco apartment complex clusters artfully above a blue designer swimming pool with a sweeping view of the nearby rocky bay and northward-curving shoreline. Ten immaculate one-bedroom suites—all spacious, tastefully furnished, with kitchenettes—can accommodate four in two double beds. One airy, two-story suite accommodates five. Amenities include a/c, phones, parking, pool, and kitchenette; rates run, low season, about $35 for two, $60 for four, and $80 for the big five-person suite, $50, $80 and $100 high season. This is a place for those who want a restful vacation while enjoying quiet pursuits: cooking, basking in the

sun, reading, and watching sunsets from the comfort of their own home in Mazatlán. For the high winter season, be sure to reserve early; credit cards are accepted.

The same management operates **Apartmentos las Palmas,** a stack of apartments and a penthouse, across the street. Although not nearly as luxurious as Suites Vidalmar, the kitchenette apartments are large, very clean, modern, and spartan but thoughtfully furnished and sleep up to four. Residents have access to the pool across the street. Same address and phone as Suites Vidalmar; the 11 one-bedroom apartments $30 d, low season, about $60 high; with a/c, and parking; credit cards are not accepted.

Budget travelers wanting to be near the center of colorful downtown bustle stay at the no-frills **Hotel del Centro,** Canizales 18, Mazatlán, Sinaloa 82000, tel. 669/981-2673, within sight of the cathedral, right around the corner from the market. (The hotel's streetfront, although busy, is too narrow for buses and is consequently not overly noisy.) The 24 rooms rent for about $22 d high season, $19 low, with a/c and TV. There's not much in the clean rooms but the basics. No matter; the attraction of this part of town is what's outside the door.

For a little more luxury in the downtown district, walk about four blocks to the opposite and quieter west side of the cathedral to the **Hotel Central,** Calle Belisario Domínguez 2 Sur at Calle Ángel Flores, Mazatlán, Sinaloa 82000, tel. 669/982-1888 or 669/982-1866. Past the upstairs lobby you'll find a small restaurant, a friendly place for meeting other travelers, and three floors of cool, clean, modern-style rooms. Rates for the 40 rooms, with a/c, TV, and phones, are from about $25 s, $28 d and $31 t year-round, except for Carnaval, Easter, and Christmas.

Old Mazatlán's revival has attracted a sprinkling of **bed-and-breakfast inns and apartments** in the city lanes just inland from Av. Olas Altas and around Plazuela Machado. Start half a block east of the Plazuela Machado, at **Royal Dutch Bed and Breakfast,** at Constitución 610, Mazatlán, Sinaloa 82000, tel. 669/981-4396. Here, the friendly hard-working Dutch expatriate owner (who's also owner of the next-door

Royal Dutch Cafeteria) offers three clean, comfortable homey rooms with bath for $60 d all year around, including breakfast, afternoon tea, fans, and cable TV. One day is free with a one-week rental; monthly discounts are negotiable. For more information and reservations, email reydutch@prodigy.net.mx or visit www.royal-dutch.cx.com.mx.

Walk across the street, to **Apartmentos Rincón de Angela,** adjacent and behind the Teatro Angela Peralta, at Constitución 610, Mazatlán, Sinaloa 82000, tel. 669/981-1551, cellular tel. 044-669/929-4833. Enterprising Mexican owners have created in inviting cluster of three attractively decorated rustic-chic kitchenette studio apartments around an quiet, inviting interior patio. All are fully furnished with a queen-sized beds, up-to-date appliances, cable TV and a/c. Rentals run about $400/week, $450 (about $35/day) for two weeks, and $650 ($23/day) per month. For more information and reservations, email angelaapartments@hotmail.com.

Walk west three blocks (toward the beach) and a block north, to **La Jolla Bed and Breakfast,** at Mariano Escobedo 219, Mazatlán, Sinaloa 82000, tel./fax 669/982-3301, 1.5 blocks from Av. Olas Altas. Here, North American owners offer three spacious rooms and a suite in their lovingly restored 19th-century family house. Amenities include queen-sized beds, all original tiles, private bathrooms, a lovely bougainvillea-decorated rear patio, a comfortable common living room with cable TV and Internet access, and a kitchen to share. The suite is especially large, with bedroom for parents (in queen-sized bed), a sleeping loft for kids, and an airy private balcony. The rooms rent for about $80 for two high season, the suite $140 for four. Half price low season (May 1 until mid-November). For more information and reservations, email harryeyer@hotmail.com or visit www.mazatlanlajolla.com.

Continue half a block west to Venus and north half a block to **Marea** silver workshop and gallery, at Venus 6, Mazatlán, Sinaloa 82000, tel. 669/982-0681, email siboli@prodigy.net.mx. Here, artists Siboli and Karen Valenzuela manage five clean, spacious upstairs one- and two-bedroom apartments for rental ranging from one day to long-term. The simply furnished but comfortable apartments rent from $25 daily low season, $30 high; $350 low and $400 high monthly.

Playa Norte Hotels

During the 1960s Mazatlán burst its old city limits at the end of Paseo Claussen and spilled northward along the long sand crescent called Playa Norte. Now, a three-mile string of 1960s-style hotels and motels lines the breezy beachfront of Av. del Mar, an extension of Paseo Claussen.

Moving north, first find the elegantly modern **Hotel Aguamarina,** Mazatlán at Av. del Mar 110, P.O. Box 345, Mazatlán, Sinaloa 82000, tel. 669/981-7080, fax 669/982-4624, info@aguamarina.com, www.aguamarina.com. With a low-rise stucco motel facade, built around a pool and patio, its rooms (either ocean- or garden-view) are large and gracefully decorated with native-style handmade wood furniture. The wall art hangs tastefully on colonial-style textured white interiors. The 101 rooms rent for about $90 d, with a/c, cable TV, phones, parking, an airy, high-ceilinged restaurant, and pool; credit cards are accepted. Reserve via toll-free Mex. tel. 800/716-9580.

A few blocks farther north, next to the popular Restaurant Señor Frog's, comes the **Hotel Sands,** Av. del Mar 1910, P.O. Box 309, Mazatlán, Sinaloa 82000, tel. 669/982-0000, 669/982-0800, or 669/982-0600, fax 669/982-1025, hotelsandsarenas@red2000.com.mx. It's clean, and if you don't mind a bit of traffic noise from the avenue, it has the ingredients for a pleasant beach vacation: sea-view rooms with balconies overlooking an inviting pool patio, a/c, phones, and TV. The 50 rooms usually rent for about $45 d, about $50 during holidays.

Farther north a few blocks (just past the Pizza Hut) appears the smallish facade of the motel-style, child-friendly **Hotel del Sol,** Av. del Mar s/n, P.O. Box 400, Mazatlán, Sinaloa 82000, tel./fax 669/985-1103. A few steps from the streetfront reception, you will find that the Motel del Sol is roomier than it looks. Its rooms cluster around an inviting pool and patio where, on one corner, a clownish plaster duck squirts water from his mouth. Inside, tasteful wood furniture, white walls, and spotless tile floors decorate the spacious rooms. Rooms run about $46 d with kitchenette, $30 without, $400/week (cash only), discount for monthly rentals, with a/c, phones, TV, and parking.

Zona Dorada Lodgings
$100 and Under

Along a six-mile strip of golden sand rise Mazatlán's newest, plushest hotels. But unlike some other world-class resorts, the Zona Dorada is not wall-to-wall high-rises. In the breezy, palm-fringed spaces between the big hotels, there are many excellent moderately priced hotels and apartment complexes.

For one of the most charming budget accommodations in Mazatlán, try **Fiesta Apartmentos,** three blocks directly inland from beachside landmark Balboa Tower, at Calle Ibis 502, Fracc. Gaviotas, Mazatlán, Sinaloa 82110, tel. 669/913-5355, 669/913-5313, 669/913-1764, or 669/913-5364, hudsontours@mazatlan.tm. This complex of studios and one- and two-bedroom apartments lies within a jungle-garden blooming with bushy guavas, hanging vines, squawking parrots, and slinking iguanas. Hardworking owner/manager Yolanda Olivera and her carpenter spouse built the place from the ground up while raising a family during the 1970s and 1980s. The units are each uniquely furnished with husband-made wooden chairs and tables, toilet, hot shower, and a double bed. Larger units have an additional bed, a sofa or two, and a kitchenette. While you may have to do some initial cleaning up, the price and ambience are certainly right: the 10 studios and one-bedroom apartments, all with kitchenettes, rent from about $25/day ($550/month); larger two-bedroom units go for about $62/day ($850/month). All apartments come with parking; reservations are necessary during the winter.

Right next door is the less personal but equally unique **Racquet Club Las Gaviotas,** on Calle Ibis at Bravo, P.O. Box 173, Mazatlán, Sinaloa 82000, tel. 669/913-5939, email gaviotas@mzt.megared.net.mx. Step inside the gate and find an inviting village of bungalow-type apartments and condominiums spread around a spacious palm-shaded swimming pool and garden. While a comfortable, moderately priced vacation lodging for anyone, this is a paradise for tennis buffs on a budget, with its row of seven well-maintained (three clay and four hard) courts. The bungalows themselves are spacious one- and two-bedroom units with a living room/dining room furnished in Spanish-style tile and wood and equipped with modern kitchenettes. The 20 units rent from about $650/month for a one-bedroom bungalow and $850/month for two bedrooms (with higher daily and weekly rates, fans and daily cleaning service included). Lower units are wheelchair-accessible. Reservations are mandatory year-round.

Even lovelier (but minus the tennis courts) is the nearby **Los Girasoles,** a stucco apartment complex built around an inviting pool patio and spacious garden at Av. Gaviotas 709, Mazatlán, Sinaloa 82110, tel./fax 669/913-5288, five blocks from the beach at the end of Gaviotas, next to Restaurant Casa Loma. When ripe, the fruit of the banana trees that fringe the garden becomes available to guests. Inside, the airy Mexican-style wood and tile kitchenette apartments are comfortably furnished and spotless. The 22 units (both one- and two-bedroom) rent from about $40/day or $600/month low season, $50 and $800 high season. Rental includes fans, parking, and daily cleaning service; credit cards are accepted.

On Mazatlán's loveliest beach stand a number of small, moderately priced lodgings along Av. Playa Gaviotas, which, about a block north of Valentino's, loops left, one way, away from noisy Calz. Camarón Sábalo. Among the best is **Casa Contenta,** a comfortable two-story complex that lives up to its name at Av. Playa Gaviotas 224, tel. 669/913-4976, fax 669/913-9986. Step past the off-street parking and you will find seven roomy, tastefully furnished kitchenette apartments tucked behind a luxurious family house, all within a manicured garden. Besides the creamy beach and small pool in the backyard, Casa Contenta residents can enjoy good restaurants and the entertainment of plush hotels within a few minutes' walk. Reserve early: about $90/day high season, $63 low, for an apartment, $210 high season, $152 low for the house. The apartments rent for about $1,700 monthly, about $3,000 for the house. All include daily cleaning service, a/c, cable TV, and parking. Credit cards are accepted, and lower-level units have limited wheelchair access. For information and reservations, email lacasacontenta224@hotmail.com or visit www.casacontenta.com.mx.

If Casa Contenta is full, you can try its plainer (but nevertheless comfortable and ideally situated) neighbors, Motel Marley and Motel Los Arcos. Guests at the two-story **Motel Marley,** Av. Playa Gaviotas 226, P.O. Box 214, Mazatlán, Sinaloa 82000, tel./fax 669/913-5533, can choose between upper-or ground-level one- or two-bedroom units, all with living rooms and fully furnished kitchenettes, with daily maid service and air-conditioned bedrooms. Extras include parking and attractive garden grounds that spread from an inviting pool patio. A few of the apartments are right on the beach. For the most privacy and best of views, reserve one of the beachfront upper units early. Rates run, yearround, about $70 d for one bedroom (with two double beds), $85 for two bedrooms (four double beds) for four people. One-month rentals receive an approximate 10 percent discount; add about $8 per additional person. Credit cards are accepted. For more information and reservations, email motmarley@mzt.megared.net.mx or visit www.travelbymexico.com/sina/marley.

Accommodations at **Motel Los Arcos,** a block south, next to Hotel Las Flores, at Playa Gaviotas 214, P.O. Box 132, tel./fax 669/913-5066, mlarcos@prodigy.net.mx, are similar to the Motel Marley. The lack of a pool doesn't seem to deter the many guests who return yearly to enjoy the sparkling sun, sea, and sand, right from their front doorsteps. The approximately 20 clean, brightly furnished kitchenette view apartments rent, year-round, for about $80 d for one bedroom, $95 d for two bedrooms for four people, $72 and $85 low season. Add about $10 per additional person; credit cards are accepted.

On the beachfront next door towers the **Hotel Las Flores,** Playa Gaviotas 212, P.O. Box 583, Mazatlán, Sinaloa 82110, tel. 669/913-5011, 669/913-5788, or 669/913-5100, fax 669/914-3422, h.flores@red2000.com.mx, www.lasflores.com.mx, very popular with North American

winter package vacationers. Most of the rooms and suites feature soothing blue and white decor. Many units have kitchenettes, while all enjoy expansive ocean views. Downstairs, the lobby spreads to an attractive restaurant, pool-bar, and tables beneath thatched-roof beachside *palapas.* During high season, the 119 accommodations rent for about $100 d standard ($140 w/kitchenette), $155 deluxe w/kitchenette; corresponding low-season asking rates are about $90, $125 and $140; bargain for a discount. Rentals include a/c, TV, phones, and parking; credit cards are accepted. For information and reservations, call toll-free U.S. tel. 800/452-0627 or Can. tel. 877/756-7529.

The owner of the Hotel Siesta downtown brings similar good management to the **Hotel Azteca Inn,** at Av. Playa Gaviotas 307, P.O. Box 841, Mazatlán, Sinaloa 82110, tel. 669/913-4477 or 669/913-4655, toll-free Mex. tel. 800/716-9770, fax 669/913-4655 or 669/913-7476, aztecainn@mazatlan.com.mx, www.aztecainn.com.mx, right in the middle of the Zona Dorada bustle, one short block from the beach. Here, guests enjoy about 40 comfortably furnished, immaculate semideluxe rooms, arranged motel-style, in two floors around an inviting inner pool patio. Rentals run about $60 s or d high season, $50 low, with a/c, TV, and parking; credit cards are accepted.

Half a block farther south, the low-rise **Hotel Plaza Las Gaviotas,** Bugambilias 100, P.O. Box 970, Mazatlán, Sinaloa 82110, tel. 669/913-4496, fax 669/913-6685, plazagaviotas@mzt.megared.net.mx, tucked just off Av. Playa Gaviotas, is easy to miss. The petite but attractive lobby leads to a leafy inner patio with a small pool. The surrounding rooms are clean, tiled and decorated in light pastels. (Maintenance, however, has not been a strong point in the past. Look at several rooms before choosing.) Prices run a reasonable about $36 d, low season, $68 d, high; bargain for an even better rate, especially weekdays or long-term. With cable TV, a/c, and lower-floor wheelchair access; credit cards are accepted.

The **Hotel Playa Bonita** (formerly Hotel Tropicana), Av. Playa Gaviotas 27, P.O. Box 501,

Mazatlán, Sinaloa 82110, tel. 669/983-8000, fax 669/983-5361, reservaciones@playabonita.com, www.playabonita.com, shares virtually everything—beach, shopping, restaurants, and nightlife—with Zona Dorada luxury hotels except prices. For many savvy vacationers, the hotel's other big pluses—spacious rooms, private ocean-view balconies, big marble baths—far outweigh the the half-block walk to the beach. To assure yourself of the best room (top floor, beachside) reserve early. Rooms go for about $70 s or d high season, $40 low. Amenities include a/c, phones, a small lobby-front pool, beach club, restaurant/bar, and full wheelchair access; credit cards are accepted.

The mostly young guests at the **Hotel Riviera Mazatlán,** Camarón Sábalo 51, P.O. Box 795, Mazatlán, Sinaloa 82000, tel. 669/983-4722, fax 669/984-4532, enjoy luxurious beach-front amenities at reasonable rates. The hotel's design makes the most of its already enviable location. The rooms, in a pair of sunny, breeze-swept tiers, enclose a spacious two-pool patio that looks out on a gorgeous beach, sea, and sunset vista. Upstairs, most guest rooms have private sea-view balconies and are tiled, clean, and simply but thoughtfully decorated in blues and whites. Rates run about $95 d high season, $50 low. Amenities include nightly pop music in the patio (be prepared with earplugs), TV, a/c, parking, and full wheelchair access; credit cards are accepted. For reservations and information, call toll-free Mex. tel. 800/716-9567 or U.S. tel. 800/762-5816, email riviera@mazatlan.com.mx, or visit www.riviera.com.mx.

Zona Dorada Luxury Hotels

A few blocks farther north along Av. Playa Gaviotas stands the landmark of the Zona Dorada—the first hotel built (despite many doubters) on what was once an isolated sand strip far from the city center. Even during the September and October low-occupancy months (when many Zona Dorada hotels and restaurants are virtually empty) everyone—Mexicans and foreigners alike—still flocks to the **Hotel Playa Mazatlán,** in the heart of the Zona Dorada at Av. Playa Gaviotas 202, P.O. Box 207, Mazatlán, Sinaloa, 82110, tel. 669/989-0555, fax 669/914-0366. The band

plays every night, the Fiesta Mexicana buffet show goes on every Saturday, and the fireworks boom and flash above the beach Sunday nights during high season. To enjoy the Playa Mazatlán, you don't have to stay there; just order something at the beachside *palapa* terrace restaurant and enjoy the music, the breeze, and the same ocean view shared by its luxurious rooms. The 408 rooms go for about $125 d for "standard" (but nevertheless deluxe) grade high season, $100 low; the larger one-bedroom junior suites go for about $250 high season, and $210 low, with a/c, cable TV, phones, pool, hot tub, parking, and full wheelchair access; credit cards are accepted. Low-season packages and promotional discounts are sometimes available.

For the classiest tropical retreat in town, step northward about a mile to the **Hotel Inn at Mazatlán,** right on silky Playa Camarón at Camarón Sábalo 6291, P.O. Box 1292, Mazatlán, Sinaloa 82110, tel. 669/913-5500 or 669/913-5354, fax 669/913-4782, innat-mazatlan@red2000.com.mx. Although mostly a time-share (buy a room for a specified week or two each year), it does rent out the vacant units hotel-style. All guests, whether owners or one-time renters, receive the same tender loving service. Every lovely feature of the Inn at Mazatlán shines with care and planning, from the excellent inside-outside beach-view restaurant and the artistically curved pool to the palms' sunset silhouettes and the spacious, luxuriously appointed sea-view rooms and suites. Asking rates for the 175 units begin at about $120 year-round, although you might be able to bargain for a low-season discount. For about $60 more, you can have a one-bedroom suite sleeping six, with kitchenette, extra person, about $25. All rentals enjoy a/c, phones, refrigerators, TV, tennis, and parking. Reservations are generally necessary; credit cards are accepted.

No discussion of Mazatlán hotels would be complete without mention of the **Hotel El Cid** megaresort, the hotel that tries to be everything, on Camarón Sábalo s/n, P.O. Box 335, Mazatlán, Sinaloa 82000, tel. 669/913-3333, fax 669/914-1311. The huge complex, which sprawls over the

MAZATLÁN

north end of Av. Camarón Sábalo, claims to be the biggest in Mexico—with 1,000 rooms in three separate hotels, 15 separate bars and restaurants, a health club, a giant glittering disco, a country club subdivision, a marina development, a world-class 18-hole golf course, and 17 tennis courts. Size, however, lends El Cid a definite institutional feeling—as if everyone, the 2,000 employees and 2,000 guests alike, were anonymous. The El Cid's saving grace (besides its lovely beachfront) may be its huge pool. It meanders among the three hotels, a palm-fringed blue lagoon complete with a fake (albeit very clever fake) rock water slide, waterfall, and diving platform straight from an old Tarzan movie. The poolside crowd of guests, from ages 4 to 90, enjoy watching each other slipping, sliding, and jumping into the cool water. Room rates start at about $150 d, year-round, with everything, including complete wheelchair access. El Cid often offers cheaper promotions, obtainable through travel agents or the reservations office. For more information and reservations, call toll-free U.S./Can. tel. 800/525-1925 or visit the website www.elcid.com.

Beyond the Zona Dorada

Vacationers who hanker for a more rustic downscale but kid-friendly beach atmosphere enjoy the **Bungalows Playa Escondida** on palmy Playa Cerritos, about five miles north of the Zona Dorada at Calz. Sábalo Cerritos 999, P.O. Boxes 682 and 202, Mazatlán, Sinaloa 82110, tel. 669/988-0077. Administered by the trailer park office across the boulevard, the 20 whitewashed bungalows laze beneath a swaying coconut palm grove. The clean, spartan, tile-kitchenette units, in parallel rows facing the ocean, sleep 2–8. The more heavily used beachfront row enjoys sweeping ocean views, while the others lie sheltered beneath the palms behind the dune. During the winter season you can enjoy plenty of friendly company at the trailer park pool across the street. Stores and restaurants are within a short drive. The bungalows rent from about $33 for the smaller units, sleeping four and $44 for the larger, sleeping 6–8, with a/c. One-month rentals customarily run about $900 and $1,100 per month, for the smaller and larger units, respectively.

Homestay Program

Besides offering Spanish classes, the privately owned **Centro de Idiomas** (Language Center) also runs a homestay program. Participants live with a Mexican family (about $180/week, including three meals). The center also offers person-to-person contacts, in which such visiting professionals as teachers, nurses, and doctors meet with and learn from their local counterparts. Contact the school downtown at Belisario Domínguez 1908, upstairs, tel. 669/985-5606, fax 669/982-2053, or via email info@spanishlink.org or thewebsite www.spanishlink.org.

Long-Term Rentals

One of the best sources of rentals is the classified (print or online) section of the *Pacific Pearl* tourist newspaper, tel./fax 669/913-0117 or 669/913-4411, www.pacificpearl.com.

Furthermore, a number of agents offer long-term apartment, condominium, or house rentals. For example, contact veteran English-speaking realtor **Lupita Bernal,** tel. 669/914-1753, fax 669/914-5082, bernal@red2000.com.mx, website www.pacificpearl.com/bernalre.

Alternatively, contact rental agent Carol Sinclair of Walfre Real Estate, tel./fax 669/983-0011 or 669/983-5077, walfre@red2000.com.mx, or website www.mazatlanrealty.com.

RV and Trailer Parks

Mazatlán's beachfront trailer space is an increasingly scarce commodity, victim to rising land values. If you're planning on a Christmas stay, phone or mail in your reservation and deposit by September or you may be out of luck, especially for the choice spaces.

One trailer park owner determined never to sell out is Gabriela C. Aguilar van Duyn, of **Mar Rosa Trailer Park,** just north of the Hotel Holiday Inn at Calz. Camarón Sábalo 702, P.O. Box 435, Mazatlán, Sinaloa 82000, tel./fax 669/913-6187. Besides being the on-the-spot manager, she's Mazatlán's informal one-woman welcoming committee and information source. "I will never sell. The people who come here are my friends—like my family." If you ask if she has a pool, she will probably point to the

© BRUCE WHIPPERMAN

Wilderness camping is allowed on offshore Isla Venados. Catch a ride to the island on the Hotel El Cid boat from the beach.

land from Valentino's Disco), the **Trailer Park La Posta,** P.O. Box 362, Mazatlán, Sinaloa 82000, tel. 669/983-5310, spreads beneath the shade of a banana, mango, and avocado grove (all-you-can-eat in season). Residents enjoy a plethora of facilities, including all hookups, showers and toilets, a big pool and sundeck, shaded picnic *palapas,* a small store, and the beach two blocks away. The 180 spaces rent for about $15–20/day or $350–420 per month. Early winter reservations are generally necessary.

In the quieter beach country a block from north-end Playa Cerritos, the **Playa Escondida Trailer Park,** Calz. Sábalo Cerritos 999, P.O. Box 682 or 202, Mazatlán, Sinaloa 82110, tel. 669/988-0077, spreads for acres beneath a lazy old coconut grove. Residents enjoy direct access to the long, uncrowded beach across the road and to nearby minimarkets and restaurants. They can also stay in the trailer park's Bungalows Playa Escondida across the street. The 200 spaces run $17/day or $350/month, with all hookups, a big saltwater pool, rec room, hot showers, and toilets; leashed dogs are okay.

Camping

Although there is no established public campground in Mazatlán, camping is allowed for a fee in all the trailer parks above except Mar Rosa.

If, however, you prefer solitary beach camping, there are empty grassy dunes on the northerly end of **Playa Cerritos** that appear ripe for tenting. If you are uncertain about the safety or propriety of a likely looking spot, inquire at a local business, such as the beachside Restaurant Playa Bruja.

Other, more isolated spots (be sure to bring water) lie along the long curve of sand on the south shore of **Stone Island;** catch a ride on the launch across from the Stone Island dock, at the foot of Av. Gutiérrez Najera on Playa Sur.

Camping is also permitted on **Isla Venados,** a mile off Playa Sábalo. Ride the boat from the El Cid beachfront. On Isla Venados, don't set up your tent on the narrow beach; it's under water at high tide. Carry out all of your trash.

beach a few feet away, and say, "one big pool." During high season, Gabriela offers about 55 spaces, some shaded, with all hookups, for $14–28/day, $13–21 low, depending on location. Discounts are negotiable for one-month or three-month rentals. With toilets, hot showers, a/c power, and cable TV; it's near markets and restaurants; leashed dogs are okay.

Another popular close-in (Zona Dorada, two blocks from the beach) trailer spot is the downscale **Trailer Park Las Palmas,** in a big, palm-shaded lot off busy Camarón Sábalo, about half a block south of the Dairy Queen at Calz. Camarón Sábalo 333, tel. 669/913-5311, manager Marina in charge. Spaces rent for about $15/day, $350/month, all hookups, toilets, showers, leashed dogs okay, and camping available, and it's near everything.

Nearby (on Calz. R. Buelna, two blocks in-

MAZATLÁN

FOOD

Mazatlán abounds in good food. The competition is so fierce that bad eateries don't survive. The best are easy to spot because they have customers even during the quiet Sept.–Nov. low season.

Snacks, Stalls, Bakeries, and Markets

With care, you can do quite well right on the street downtown. An afternoon cluster of folks around a streetside cart piled with oyster shells and shrimp is your clue that the fare is fresh, tasty, and reasonably priced. These carts usually occupy the same place every day and, for most of them, the quality of their food is a matter of honor. One of the best is **Santos El Burro Feliz,** which usually occupies a spot at 61 Calle Sixto Osuna, outside of the family house across from the Archaeological Museum. Try the dozen-oyster cocktail, enough for two, for $7.

If you're cooking your own meals, or simply hanker for some fresh fruit and vegetables, the best place to find the crispest of everything is the **Central Market,** corner of Calles Benito Juárez and Melchor Ocampo, two short blocks behind the cathedral. Open daily 6 A.M.–6 P.M.

After an hour of hard market bargaining, you may be in the mood for a cool, restful lunch. If so, step upstairs inside the market to the leafy balcony *fonda* over the corner of Juárez and Valle and enjoy the scene. Alternatively, walk one block down Juárez and enter the air-conditioned interior of **Pastelería Panamá,** Av. Juárez, corner of Canizales, tel. 669/985-1853, (or in the Golden Zone, on Camarón Sábalo, at Garzas, or its bakery branch near Plazuela Machado, corner of Sixto Osuna and B. Domínguez) and try one of the tasty lunch specials or treat yourself to the excellent *helado chocolate* (chocolate ice cream). Open daily 8 A.M.–10 P.M.

Afterward, just outside the door, you may see the *churro* cart that always seems to be parked at that corner. Try three of these uniquely Mexican, foot-long, thin sugar doughnuts for $1.

Downtown and Olas Altas Restaurants

The better downtown restaurants are concentrated around Plazuela Machado and the Olas Altas *malecón*. On Plazuela Machado, three stars for food and ambience go to **Restaurant Pedro and Lola,** named after the celebrated Mexican singers Pedro Infante and Lola Beltrán. Here, step into a cool, casual-chic bohemian atmosphere, take a table and choose from a menu long on salads and seafood and short on meat. Find it at the corner of Canalizo and Carnaval, tel. 669/982-2589, open 5 P.M.–midnight, with live jazz and nouveau classical music Friday, and Saturday. Moderate–expensive.

Nearby, one block east, **Royal Dutch Cafetería,** at 1307 Juárez, corner of Constitución, tel. 669/981-4596, specializes in breakfast. Besides the usual eggs, pancakes, and French toast, it offers baked-in-house pastries, including croissants, muffins, and brownies. The setting here is especially pleasant: tables around an art-decorated patio, blooming with leafy greenery and tropical birdcalls. Open Mon.–Sat. 8 A.M.–8 P.M. Moderate.

For a special local-style treat, you can return to the same neighborhood for supper and sample the homey fare of the **Cenaduría El Tunel.** Tucked just off the southeast corner of Plazuela Machado at Carnaval 1207 and open daily 6–10 P.M., El Tunel's entry leads you through to a narrow corridor where customers are enjoying the craft of a squad of grandmotherly chefs who carry out their mission at stoves in the interior dining room. Their delectable enchiladas, crunchy tacos, rich *pozole* (pork or chicken with hominy stew), and creamy refried beans are bound to please all devotees of true Mexican food. Budget–moderate.

Walk a block west of Plazuela Machado, to refined **Café Ambrosia,** at Sixto Osuna 26, corner of B. Domínguez, tel. 669/985-0333, for many healthy choices. Besides a fresh daily appetizer menu, Café Ambrosia offers a professionally prepared and served menu of wholesome salads (avocado and mixed vegetables), soups (tortilla), enchiladas, pastas, and veggie sandwiches. Open daily 8 A.M.–10 P.M. Moderate.

Continue west two blocks and north one block to **Restaurant Bahía,** at M. Escobedo 203, a block from Av. Olas Altas, behind the Hotel Siesta. What is arguably the best seafood cooking in town has earned the label "La Catedral de Ceviche" for the owner chef and her family who continue a tradition begun by her parents in 1950. Make up a party to share a maximum of their home-style regional specialties, such as *pescado zarondeado, pescado relleno de camarón,* and *filete de pescado al mojo.* Open Mon.–Sat. noon–8 P.M., tel. 669/981-2645, credit cards not accepted. Moderate–expensive.

If you're in a party mood, **El Shrimp Bucket,** Av. Olas Altas 11, bottom floor of Hotel La Siesta, tel. 669/981-6350, is open daily 6 A.M.–11 P.M.; credit cards are accepted. The restaurant, hung with a riot of taffeta flowers and balloons inside, with the marimba combo humming away by dinnertime in the tropical patio outside, is a *fiesta* waiting to happen. This is especially true when you call for the bounteous bucket of shrimp ($20, enough for two or three), which the kitchen will fix exactly as you wish—breaded, grilled, steamed, or barbecued. Breakfasts are also very popular here. Moderate–expensive.

Two more Mazatlán old-town eateries, very reliably recommended (but which I didn't have the time to visit) are **Bandidos y Gente Bien** regional cuisine restaurant-bar (at Heriberto Frias 1405, half a block north of the Plazuela Machado), and **La Puntilla** harbor view seafood *palapa* restaurant at the south-side Stone Island dock, tel. 669/982-8877, www.mariscoslapuntilla.com.

Playa Norte Restaurants

It's hard to imagine a restaurant closer to the source than the rough and ready family-style **Restaurant El Camachín,** 97 Paseo Claussen and 5 de Mayo, tel. 669/985-0197, located where the boats bring the fish in every morning. In true Mexican tradition, the restaurant augments many of its dishes with a number of flavorful sauces, which range from a mild salsa Oriental (onions, celery, and a bit of soy) to a peppery salsa ranchero. Pick your favorite and have it served with the recommended catch of the day. Open daily 10 A.M.–10 P.M. Moderate.

Another good seafood bet is **Mamucas,** Mazatlán's "King of Seafood" for more than a generation, at 404 Bolivar Poniente (west), two blocks from the Paseo Claussen *malecón,* tel. 669/981-3490. The specialties are *parillada de mariscos*—grilled seafood, you pick which—and *pescado zarandeado en brasero*—fish, toss-broiled in a wood-fired brazier. Open daily 10:30 A.M.–9:30 P.M. Moderate.

If you're in the mood for Chinese food, you'll find it at **Restaurant Canton,** a legacy of the significant local Chinese community, whose ancestors first migrated to these shores during the 19th century. The food here is pure 1940s-genre Cantonese: almond chicken, pork chow mein, broccoli beef, egg foo yung, and about 20 more very recognizable choices, all the way to the fortune cookies at meal's end. Restaurant Canton is a few blocks north of the Fisherman's Monument, just past Hotel Aguamarina, open noon–8 P.M., tel. 669/985-1247. Moderate.

A few blocks farther north along the *malecón,* a bright sign marks **Karnes en Su Jugo,** Av. del Mar 550, just south of the Hotel Sands, tel. 669/982-1322. If personable owner Jorge Pérez (who, with his red hair, looks more like a Swede than most Swedes do) is there, let him place your order: bounteous table, likely set with a plate of savory roast beef in juice, hot melted Chihuahua white cheese, refried beans, and enough salsa and hot corn tortillas for a dozen yummy tacos or tostadas. Open daily 1 P.M.–1 A.M.; credit cards not accepted. Moderate–expensive.

A stay in Mazatlán wouldn't be complete without a trip to **Señor Frog's,** Calz. Camarón Sábalo s/n, tel. 669/982-1925, the second (El Shrimp Bucket was the first), and perhaps the best, creation of late owner Carlos Anderson's worldwide chain. Many extreme adjectives—brash, bold, loud, risqué, funny, far-out—have been used to describe the waiters, patrons, and the music at Señor Frog's. Most everyone agrees the ribs are the best and the margaritas the most potent in town. Open daily noon–past midnight; credit cards are accepted. Expensive.

Zona Dorada Restaurants

Despite their Golden Zone locations, Zona Dorada restaurants aren't excessively expensive. When you're in a sweat from shopping, sunburn, and street vendors, and you're ready to escape from Mexico, try Mexico's first **Dairy Queen** instead, Camarón Sábalo 500, corner of Playa Gaviotas, tel. 669/916-1522. The regular hamburgers and soft ice cream goodies will taste better than at home. When you emerge, you'll feel like staying another couple of months. Open daily 10 A.M.–11 P.M. Budget.

For a pleasant surprise, especially for breakfast, walk two blocks south from the Dairy Queen corner to the Zona Dorada branch of the **Pastelería Panamá,** on Camarón Sábalo at Garzas, tel. 669/914-0612. Here, a legion of local middle- to upper-class folks flock for everything from ham and eggs and hamburgers to *enchiladas suizas* and chocolate malts. Open daily 7 A.M.–11 P.M. Moderate.

Much of the same is available at the refined coffee-shop–style **Restaurant VIPs,** a few blocks farther south on Camarón Sábalo, across from Cinemas Gaviotas y Albatroses, tel. 669/914-0754. Here, the Denny's-modeled food and cool a/c ambience beats Denny's by a mile, with crisp salads, hot entrées, and luscious desserts, appetizingly presented and professionally served. Moreover, the restaurant features a bookstore, where you can browse till midnight over Mazatlán's biggest assortment of English-language magazines. Open daily 7 A.M.–midnight. Moderate.

For good Mexican-style macrobiotic fare, step across to the beach side of Camarón Sábalo, to side street Gaviotas (across from Hotel Playa Mazatlán) and **Pura Vida** restaurant, tel. 669/916-5815. Here, in an airy air-conditioned space, a bustling cadre of waiters serves from a long list of fresh fruit drinks, veggie-light sandwiches, whole-wheat pizza, vegetable and fruit salads, yogurt, granola, omelettes, and much more. Open daily 8 A.M.–10 P.M. Moderate.

On the other hand, for those who frankly enjoy meat, the owner of Señor Pepper's (See Splurge Restaurants), has inaugurated stylishy decorated **Restaurant Green Chile,** at Av. Playa Gaviotas 63, right across the street from the Hotel Playa Mazatlán. In the cool dark *chile*-chic interior, light rock music bounces, silent TVs flash, while waiters scurry to display a menu tray of steak, chops, ribs, chicken and fish. Crisp house salad and veggies are included, however. Entrées range

from baby back ribs ($10) to one-pound New York steak, enough for two ($20). Expensive.

For a relaxed outdoor resort setting, go to the airy beach-view **Terraza Playa** restaurant at Hotel Playa Mazatlán, R.T Av. Playa Gaviotas 202, tel. 669/913-4455, so popular that tables are sometimes hard to get. This is frequently true some Sunday nights when families begin to arrive two hours early for the free 8 P.M. fireworks show. The Terraza Playa offers excellent entrées, such as *pescado Veracruzana* for $5–10. Open daily 7 A.M.–11 P.M.; credit cards are accepted. Moderate.

A spectacular beachfront view, cool breezes, snappy service, and fresh salads, sandwiches, and seafood at reasonable prices keep patrons coming to restaurant **Pancho's** year-round, at the beach end of the small complex across from Shell City, tel. 669/914-0911. During the winter season, when vacationers crowd in, come early. The dozen tables can fill by noon. Open daily 8 A.M.–11 P.M. Moderate.

Find one of the Zona Dorada's hidden culinary gems, **La Cocina de Ana,** at Laguna 49, near the Dairy Queen corner, behind Banamex, tel. 669/916-3119. Cooking is a labor of love of the friendly owner, and it shows, in her hearty, healthy daily buffet—chili, paella, Chinese, soup, fish—Mon.–Sat. noon–8 P.M. (Sept.–Oct. noon–4 P.M. only.)

For impeccable service and tranquil, palm-framed sunsets, try **Papagayo** restaurant at the Hotel Inn at Mazatlán, at Camarón Sábalo 6291, between Hotels El Cid and Costa de Oro, tel. 669/913-5500. The menu caters to the tastes of the mostly middle-aged North American clientele, with salad bar and reasonably priced complete dinner specials, notably a mouthwatering chicken-rib combo. Open daily 7 A.M.–10 P.M.; credit cards are accepted. Moderate.

North a few blocks, across from the Holiday Inn, the friendly family management of **Restaurant El Marino and Donas Donuts,** blends the best of both worlds, with dozens of comfortable American-style breakfasts and lunches (bacon and eggs, hamburgers, and malts), plus tamales, tacos, and enchiladas. Clean and bright; good for breakfast. Open daily 7 A.M.–10 P.M. Moderate.

Zona Dorada Splurge Restaurants

One of the most successfully exclusive restaurants in town is **Casa Loma,** Gaviotas 104, tel. 669/913-5398, which, besides tucking itself behind a wall on a quiet dead-end street, often manages to close July to October. (Call ahead to check.) The Casa Loma secret: a secluded location, subdued tropical atmosphere, excellent service, and a selection of tasty international specialties continue to attract a clubby list of affluent patrons. Open 1:30–10 P.M.; credit cards are accepted, and reservations recommended. Expensive.

The low-key facade of **Señor Pepper's,** Camarón Sábalo, north end, across from Hotel Playa Real, tel. 669/914-0101, gives little hint of what's inside: a flight of fancy away from Mexico to some Victorian polished brass, mirror, and wood-paneled miniplanet, more San Francisco than San Francisco ever was. When you sit down at a table and ask for a menu, the tuxedo-attired waiter will probably do a double take, scurry away, and return with a small tray of a few thick steaks, a pork chop huge enough for two, and a big lobster. You choose one of these as the basis for your dinner. The meal proceeds from there like a Mozart symphony, through each delectable course, until dessert, invariably served with a flourish. Señor Pepper's is open daily 6–11 P.M.; credit cards are accepted, and reservations recommended. Expensive.

ENTERTAINMENT AND EVENTS

Just Wandering Around

A good morning place to start is the little beach at the beginning of Playa Norte, at the north end of Av. 5 de Mayo, where the fishermen sell their daily catches. As the cluster of buyers busily bid for the choicest tuna, shrimp, *dorado* (mahimahi), and mackerel, pelicans and seagulls scurry after the leftovers.

Come back later, around supper time, to enjoy the end product: fresh-cooked seafood (try Restaurant Camachín), accompanied by the tunes of one of many strolling mariachi bands—perhaps even one of the famous Sinaloan-style brass bands. If someone else is paying, just sit back and enjoy, especially the tuba solo. If you are

paying, make sure that you agree upon the price, usually around $2 per selection, before the performance begins.

Around noon, the area around the central plaza downtown (Juárez and Ángel Flores) is equally entertaining. Take a seat beneath the shade of the big trees and have your shoes polished for about $1.

Shady Plazas

Downtown Mazatlán has a number of neighborhood squares within strolling distance of the central plaza. Five blocks north along Calle Guillermo Nelson lies **Plaza Zaragoza** and the colorful little flower market nearby.

West of the central plaza, two short blocks behind the Palacio Municipal, is the **Plazuela de Los Leones** (corner of Calles Ángel Flores and Niños Héroes), marked by a pair of brass lions guarding the city library. Upstairs, you can peruse the venerable collection of the all-English **Benjamin Franklin Library.**

In a southerly direction from the cathedral, stroll along Juárez three blocks; at Constitución turn right one block to **Plazuela Machado,** the gem of old Mazatlán. Depending upon the time, you may want to stop for a soda or juice at a sidewalk café or *refresquería* on the north side of plaza, or a drink and a round of billiards at the friendly, elegantly Victorian (or, in Mexico, Porfirian, after former President Porfirio Díaz) Café Pacífico at the adjacent corner. Across the square, in the midafternoons on school days, you can take a park bench seat and listen to the sounds of violin lessons that sometimes waft down from the upstairs chambers of the Academia Angela Peralta.

If you're in the mood for a little browsing late Saturday afternoon, take in the Plazuela Machado **Bazar del Sábado** (Saturday Bazaar). Beginning around 5 P.M., booths of local artists, artisans and entrepreneurs line the square, offering everything from fine handmade jewelry and art-to-wear, to antiques, books, and bric-a-brac.

Sidewalk Cafés

A few blocks west, on beachfront Av. Olas Altas, watch the passing parade from a table at one of the shady sidewalk cafés clustered around the old Hotel Belmar. If it's summer and you're lucky, you may get a chance to enjoy a Pacific Mexico rainstorm. It usually starts with a few warm drops on the sidewalk. Then the wind starts the palms swaying. Pretty soon the lightning is crackling and the rain is pouring as if from a million celestial faucets. But no matter; you're comfortably seated, and even if you happen to get a little wet it's so warm you'll dry off right away.

Late afternoons on Olas Altas yield a feast of quiet people-watching delights. Perch yourself on the old *malecón* and watch the sunset, the surfers tackling the high waves *(olas altas)* offshore, and the kids, old folks, and loving couples strolling along the sidewalk.

After dark, stroll a few blocks south along the oceanfront, past the divers' point and join the crowd at streetside enjoying the rainbow flutter and flash of the lights on the *Continuity of Life* fountain.

Later, if you're in the mood for livelier entertainment, return to the **Copa de Leche** sidewalk coffeehouse and restaurant where a live trio entertains patrons Thurs., Fri., and Sat. evenings (Av. Olas Altas, next to the Hotel Belmar.)

> *Mazatlán's century-old Carnaval is among Mexico's liveliest Mardi Gras celebrations. The merrymaking begins the week before Ash Wednesday and climaxes on Shrove Tuesday with a parade of floats and riotous revelers, which by this time includes everyone in town.*

Theater, Dance, and Concerts

Mazatlán's busy menu of permformances—drama, classical ballet, folkloric dance, symphony—centers around the **Teatro Angela Peralta** at the Plazuela Machado's southwest corner. (See Sights.) The schedule peridodically intensifies, notably around the Oct.–Nov. **Sinaloa Fiesta de los Artes.**

Fiestas

Mazatlán's century-old **Carnaval** is among Mexico's liveliest Mardi Gras celebrations. The merrymaking begins the week before Ash Wednesday (usually late February or early March, when the faithful ceremoniously receive ash marks on their foreheads), beginning the period of fasting called Lent. Mazatlán Carnaval anticipates all this with a vengeance in a weeklong series of folk dances, balls, ballets, literature readings, beauty contests, and "flower" games. The celebration climaxes on Shrove Tuesday (the day before the beginning of Lent) with a parade of floats and riotous revelers, which by this time includes everyone in town, culminating along Av. Olas Altas. If you'd like to join in, reserve your hotel room (streetfront rooms at the Hotels Freeman, Siesta and Belmar are best for Carnaval) at least six months in advance.

Fall visitors can enjoy events of the **Sinaloa Fiesta de los Artes,** which lately has begun around October 20 and continued through the first week in November. Find the list of programs, which include classical music and ballet and folkloric dance, in the tourist newspapers, *Pacific Pearl,* tel. 669/913-0117, or *Viejo Mazatlán,* tel./fax 669/985-3781.

Mazatlán heats up again for the December 8 patronal **Feast of the Immaculate Conception,** that kicks off two solid weeks of merrymaking, first, with the fiesta of the **Virgin of Guadalupe** on December 12 and later with traditional Christmas *posada* processions and midnight and early morning Masses *(mañanitas)* through December 25.

Bullfights, Rodeos, and Baseball

Every Sunday from mid-December through Easter, bullfights (not really "fights"), called *corridas de toros,* are held at the big bullring, Plaza Monumental (Av. R. Buelna at Av. de la Marina), about a mile from the beach. The ritual begins at 4 P.M. sharp. Get your tickets through a travel agency or at the bullring.

Once or twice a year the Mazatlán professional association of *charros* (gentleman cowboys) holds a rodeolike *charreada.* Some events (such as jumping from one racing, unbroken horse to another, or trying to flatten an angry

The white towers of Valentino's disco jut prominently atop Punta Camarón.

steer by twisting its tail!) make the garden-variety North American rodeo appear tame.

Los Venados (The Deer), Mazatlán's entry in the Mexican Pacific Coast Baseball (Béisbol) League (AAA), begins its schedule in early October and continues into the spring. Get your tickets at the stadium (Estadio Teodoro Mariscal), whose night lights are so bright that when the team is home you can't help but see a quarter mile inland from beachfront Av. del Mar. Baseball fever in Mazatlán heats up to epidemic proportions when Culiacán, Los Venados's arch-rival, is in town.

Tourist Shows

While a number of hotels present folkloric song and dance shows, the Hotel Playa Mazatlán's **Fiesta Mexicana** remains the hands-down favorite. The entire three-hour extravaganza, including a sumptuous buffet, begins at 7 P.M. sharp Tuesday and Saturday during high season (Sat. only during low). Call either the hotel (tel. 669/989-0555 or 669/913-5320) office (or a travel agent) for confirmation and tickets, which run about $30 per adult, kids half price. If you miss Fiesta Mexicana on Saturday, you might be able to get in on the gratis beach fireworks show Sunday (high season only) evening at 8 P.M. It's popu-

lar, so arrive an hour early to ensure a seat. Call the hotel to confirm.

Others are trying harder. Wednesday and Saturday nights at 7 P.M. Hotel El Cid succeeds in capturing the flavor of Mexico with a folkloric fiesta, including a bountiful buffet, followed by a succession of colorful extravaganzas, ranging from a choruses of whirling señoritas and their *charro* partners to rope-flinging *vaqueros*. Call the Hotel El Cid, tel. 669/913-3333, for information and reservations (about $30, half price for kids).

Movies

A number of Mazatlán cinemas screen first-run Hollywood movies. Try the six-screen **Cinemas Gaviotas,** Camarón Sábalo 218, a few blocks north of Valentino's disco; call tel. 669/983-7545 for programs.

Dancing and Discoing

Dance music is plentiful in Mazatlán. You can start out by enjoying drinks or dinner with the medium-volume bands that play from around 8 P.M. at the more popular Golden Zone hotels, especially the **Playa Mazatlán,** tel. 669/989-0555, and others, such as **El Cid,** tel. 669/913-3333, **Los Sábalos,** tel. 669/983-5409 or 669/983-8357, and on Áv. Olas Alas at **Hotel La Siesta.**

Then, after around 11 P.M., while the Mazatlán night is still young, go out and jump at one of several local discos. **Valentino's,** tel. 669/984-1666, with its jumble of white spires and turrets, perches on Punta Camarón, inspiring intense curiosity, if not wonder, among newcomers. Its three separate dance floors have the requisite flashing lights and speakers varying from loud and louder to loudest (with a booming bass audible for a couple of miles up and down the beach).

On the other hand, what **El Caracol,** at El Cid, tel. 669/913-3333, lacks on the outside, it makes up on the inside. Here, one huge dance floor is split beneath two upper levels, which patrons can navigate by exiting to the lower by sliding down a chute or slithering down a brass firehouse pole. Open seasonally Tues.–Sat.

The discos, which charge a cover of about $20 and expect you to dress casually but decently (slacks and shirts, dresses or skirts and blouses, and shoes), open around 10 P.M. and go on until 4 or 5 in the morning.

Bars and Hangouts

Mazatlán has a few romantic, softly lighted piano bars. Besides the suave **Mikonos** piano bar (right next to Valentino's at Camarón Sábalo and Rafael Buelna), you can sample the elegant sophistication of **Señor Pepper's,** tel. 669/914-1101, piano bar across from the Hotel Playa Real at the north end of Camarón Sábalo.

For high-volume 1970s rock and beer-and-popcorn camaraderie, **Jungle Juice** restaurant's upstairs bar on side street Garzas, off Av. Playa Mazatlán, one block inland from Hotel Playa Mazatlán, tel. 669/913-3315, is literally wall-to-wall customers during the high season. The same is true for disco-style **Pepe Toro** diagonally across the street and the open-air cantina **Gringo Lingo** around the corner (except, at Gringo Lingo, there's more air). If all these bore you, walk south three blocks and climax your evening rocking to the high-volume *salsa* offering at **Tony's,** at the corner of Av. Playa Gaviotas and Calz. Camarón Sábalo.

Child's Play

When your kids get tired of digging in the sand and splashing in the pool, take them to the **Aquarium,** Mexico's largest, with many big, well-maintained fish tanks—of flinty-eyed sharks, clownish wide-bodied box fish, and shoals of luminescent damselfish. It's on Av. de Los Deportes 111, just off Av. del Mar about a mile south of Valentino's (watch for the Acuario sign), tel. 669/981-7816 or 669/981-7817. Admission is about $5 adults, $2.50 kids; open daily 10 A.M.–6 P.M. Outside, don't miss the exotic tropical botanical garden, where you'll find a pair of monstrously large crocodiles. Time your arrival to take in one of the three daily sea lion shows around 1:30, 3:30, and 5:30 P.M.

For a different type of frolic, take the kids to **Mazagua** water park, Playa Cerritos s/n, tel./fax 669/988-0041, where they'll be able to slip down the 100-foot-long Kamikaze slide, swish along the toboggan, loll in the wave pool, or simply splash in the regular pool. Follow the right fork toward Highway 15 near the north end of Calz. Camarón Sábalo and you'll immediately see the water park on the left. Open daily 10 A.M.–6 P.M.; admission runs about $8 for everyone over three. The park has a restaurant and snack bar.

During the adult fun and games of Carnaval, there's no reason your kids have to feel left out if you take them to the **"Carnival"** (as known in North America). You'll find it by looking for the Ferris wheel (customarily near the bus terminal on Calle Tamazula and the Highway 15 downtown ingress boulevard) behind the Hotel Sands.

SPORTS AND RECREATION
Walking and Jogging

The Mazatlán heat keeps walkers and joggers near the shoreline. On the beaches themselves, the long, flat strands of Playa Norte (along Av. del Mar), Playa Gaviotas (north from about the Hotel Los Flores), and the adjoining Playa Sábalo (north from about El Cid) provide firm stretches for walking and jogging. If you prefer an even firmer surface, the best uncluttered stretch of the *malecón* seaside sidewalk is along Av. del Mar from Valentino's disco south about three miles to the Fisherman's Monument.

Swimming, Boarding, and Sailing

During days of calm water, you can safely swim beyond the gentle breakers, about 50 yards off **Playa Gaviotas** and **Playa Sábalo.** Heed the usual precautions. (See Water Sports in the On the Road chapter.)

On rough-water days you'll have to do your laps in a hotel pool, since there is no public pool in Mazatlán. If your hotel has no pool, some of the big hotels, such as El Cid, allow fee day-use by outside guests.

There are several challenging intermediate surfing spots along the Mazatlán shoreline, mostly adjacent to rocky points, such as **Pinos** (next to Ciencias del Mar off Paseo Claussen), **Punta Camarón** (at Valentino's disco), and **Punta Cerritos** at the far north end of the *malecón.*

Bodysurfing and boogie boarding are popular on calm days on Mazatlán's beaches. Boogie boards rent for about $3 an hour on the beachfronts of some Zona Dorada hotels, such as Los Sábalos, Playa Mazatlán, El Cid, and Hotel Playa Real.

© BRUCE WHIPPERMAN

Afternoon crowds often gather at Divers' Point.

Sailboarding is possible nearly anywhere along Mazatlán's beaches. An especially good, smooth spot is the protected inlet at the north end of Av. Sábalo Cerritos. Bring your own equipment, as there's little sailboarding rental gear available in Mazatlán.

Aqua Sports Center at El Cid, tel. 669/913-3333, and beach shops at other hotels rent Hobie Cats, small catamaran sailboats, for around $25 per hour (three-person limit) to sail from the beach.

Ecoadventuring

Mazatleco Sports Center guides a number of local nature adventure tours. Choose from kayaking offshore islands, birdwatching in mangrove wetlands, mountain biking through a thorn forest, snorkeling, scuba diving, sailing, and more. If you prefer, guide yourself via rental kayaks and sailboats. For more information, call tel./fax 669/916-5362 or 669/916-5933, or visit the website www.mazatleco.com.

Pronatur, affliated with the El Cid hotel, tel. 669/913-3333, ext. 3490 or 6581, also guides a number of ecoexcursions. These include a turtle hatchery, Bird Island in Teacapan, a Deer Island excursion, Stone Island, and more.

Snorkeling and Scuba Diving

The water near Mazatlán's beaches is generally too churned up for good visibility. Serious snorkelers and divers head offshore to the outer shoals of Isla Venados and Isla Chivos. A number of shops along the Zona Dorada beaches arrange such trips. The best equipped is **El Cid's Aqua Sports Center,** tel. 669/913-3333, ext. 341, marked by the clutter of equipment on the beach by Hotel El Cid. A three-hour scuba excursion, including equipment and instructor, runs $80 per person, while snorkelers can go along for about $20, including mask and fins.

Personal Watercraft Riding and Parasailing

The highly maneuverable snowmobile-like personal watercraft have completely replaced waterskiing at Mazatlán. Three or four of them can usually be seen tearing up the water, hotdogging over big waves, gyrating between the swells, and

M

MAZATLÁN

racing each other far offshore. For a not-so-cheap thrill, rent one of them at Aqua Sports Center at El Cid, tel. 669/913-3333, ext. 341, which has the best and most equipment, for about $40 per half hour for one, $50 for two people.

Parasailing chutes are continually ballooning high over Zona Dorada beaches. For about $25 for a 10-minute ride, you can fly like a bird; arrangements can be made at any of the following hotels: El Cid, Playa Mazatlán, or Playa Real.

Tennis and Golf

If you're planning on playing lots of tennis in Mazatlán, check into one of the several hotels, such as Playa Mazatlán, Inn at Mazatlán, or El Cid (which charges $13/hour even for guests), all of which have courts. If your lodging does not provide courts, you can rent one at **Racquet Club Las Gaviotas,** tel. 669/913-5939 (three clay, four hard courts, some lighted), for about $12/hour. They're popular and likely to be crowded during the winter season, however.

In-town Mazatlán golf is even more exclusive. The 18-hole course at **El Cid,** tel. 669/913-3333, is the only one within the city limits, and during the high winter-spring season it may allow only its guests (and those of a few other deluxe hotels) to play. On the other hand, during low season, outsiders may play for a $60 greens and a $15 caddy fee. Two-person carts rent for about $30.

Of Mazatlán's other golf courses, the closest is the nine-hole course at the **Club Campestre,** next to the Coca-Cola factory off the airport highway beyond the south edge of town. Fees run a total of about $20 for nine holes. Go by taxi. The other, the **Golf Club Estrella del Mar,** is accessible by taxi or car off the airport entrance road: About a quarter mile before the airport terminal, turn right at the signed side road; continue nine miles until the you get to the boat landing, where a launch will take you across to the golf course. Fees run about $80, cart included. The club runs a shuttle from its Zona Dorada office, next to Banamex, corner Gaviotas and Camarón Sábalo; call the golf course at tel. 669/982-3300 or its office, tel. 669/914-0362, for information and schedule.

Sportfishing

Competent captains and years of experience have placed Mazatlán among the world's leading billfish (marlin, swordfish, and sailfish) ports. The several licensed *flotas deportivas* (sports fleets) line up along the jetty road beneath the south-end El Faro point. They vary, mostly in size of fleet; some have two or three boats, others have a dozen. Boats generally return with about three big fish—one of them a whopping marlin or sailfish—per day.

The biggest is the **Bill Heimpel Star Fleet,** owned and operated by personable Bill Heimpel, a descendant of a German immigrant family. During the high season he organizes the groups so you can fish without having to rent a whole boat. One day's fishing runs about $80 (add $20 for a nonfishing guest) per person, complete. Entire boats for about eight passengers (five of whom can fish at a time) rent for around $320 per day, complete. During the May–Oct. low season, reservations only a few days in advance are all that is necessary; high-season reservations are mandatory. For more information, contact the fleet in Mazatlán, P.O. Box 129B, Camionera Central, Mazatlán, Sinaloa 82000, tel. 669/982-2665, fax 669/982-5155. Alternatively, email starfleet@mazatlan.com.mx, or visit the website www.starfleet.com.mx. From the United States, contact Star Fleet through the toll-free U.S. tel. 888/882-9614.

A bit farther down the scale, you can check out some of the local boats right at the dock, such as **Flota Neptuno,** owned and operated by captain Ricardo Salazar. He rents out a big 42-foot, six-person boat with skipper, bait, and poles for billfish for about $160 low season, $250 high. Ask him and he might also be able to furnish a group of four with a launch and skipper, fully equipped for half a day to catch smaller fry, such as 30-pound tuna, or *sierra,* for around $100.

On the other hand, if price is not a big factor, go to the **El Cid Marina,** at the north end of Calz. Camarón Sábalo, where the boulevard bends right around the lagoon, just after the Hotel El Camino. There, the **Aries Fleet,** which "proudly supports the Catch and Release program of the Billfish Foundation," offers either individual reservations in season at about $100 per person, or five elaborately equipped boats to rent. Complete charters run from about $375 (28 feet, five lines) to $450 (35 feet, six passengers, five lines). For information and reservations, call a travel agent or contact Aries Fleet directly, at tel. 669/916-3468, or write Naviera Aries, S.A. de C.V., Marina El Cid, Calz. Camarón Sábalo s/n, Fracc. El Cid C.P., Mazatlán, Sinaloa 82110.

If you're on a tight fishing budget, try negotiating with one of the fishermen on **Playa Norte** (at the foot of 5 de Mayo at Paseo Claussen) to take you and a few friends out in his *panga* for half a day. He can supply lines and bait enough to bring in several big mahimahi and red snapper for a total price of about $50, depending on the season.

Boat Launching

If you have your own boat, you can launch it at one of two official public ramps in Mazatlán. One ramp is at the **Ciencias del Mar** college (on the point just past the boat cove on Paseo Claussen). The school office (tel./fax 669/982-8656, ask for Gloria) inside sells tickets for about $20 to use the ramp for one day 7 A.M.–6 P.M. The tariff for a one-month permit is only about triple that. That would entitle you to anchor your boat, among a dozen neighbors, in the sheltered Playa Norte cove for a month. No facilities are available except the ramp, however.

The other boat ramp is at **Club Náutico,** Explanada del Faro s/n, Mazatlán, Sinaloa 82000, tel./fax 669/981-5195, at the far end of the line of sportfishing docks, below the lighthouse hill. A one-day launching permit runs about $20, plus $5 per day docking fee. The club has a first-class yacht harbor with hoists, a repair shop, and gasoline, but unfortunately little or no room for outsiders to store boats, either in or out of the water. You may, however, be able to get permission to park your boat and trailer on the road outside the gate.

Hunting Outfitters and Guides

The highest-profile outfitters in town are the **Aviles Hermanos** (Aviles Brothers) at 5 de Mayo 2605, at Paseo Claussen. Their business peaks during the winter duck season, when they drive or fly groups about 60 miles south to hunting grounds in the Marismas Nacionales near Esquinapa. Further options to other air-accessible sites may be possible. Contact their office, in old town, at the corner of 5 de Mayo and Paseo Claussen, P.O. Box 221, Mazatlán, Sinaloa 82000, tel. 669/981-3728 or 669/981-6060, fax 669/914-6598, across Paseo Claussen from the shorefront Marine Sciences College.

SHOPPING

Judging from the platoons of racks in the Zona Dorada and in the Mercado Central, T-shirts would seem to be the most popular sale item in Mazatlán. Behind the racks, however, Mazatlán's curio shops stock an amazing bounty of handicrafts from all over the country. The best route to quality purchases at reasonable prices is first to look downtown for the lowest prices, next search the Zona Dorada for the best quality, and then make your choice.

Central Market Shopping

The town *mercado* occupies one square block near the cathedral, between Calles Juárez, Ocampo, Serdan, and Valle. Here, bargaining is both expected and essential unless you don't mind paying $20 for a $5 item. (See Bargaining in the On the Road chapter.)

Although the colorful mélange of meat and vegetable stalls occupies most of the floor space, several small handicrafts shops are tucked inside on the Juárez and Valle sides (west and south) and along all four outside sidewalks. For example, nothing typifies Mexico more than huaraches. One of Mazatlán's best selections is the family-owned **Huarachería Internacional,** on the outside market sidewalk at Ocampo and Juárez. Its goods, much from the highlands of Michoacán, are all authentic and, with bargaining, very reasonably priced.

Old Town Shops and Saturday Bazaar

The restored Olas Altas (Old Town) district has attracted a number of worthy galleries, and silver, handicrafts, and antique shops. The original is

M

MAZATLÁN

Casa Antigua, two blocks from Olas Altas, at Mariano Escobedo 206 Poniente, tel. 669/982-5236, open Mon.–Sat. 10 A.M.–5 P.M. Peruse their eclectic all-Mexico assortment—shiny pâpier maché, glittering jewelry, Tlaquepaque stoneware, exquisite Talavera ware and much more.

Another worth visiting nearby is silver workshop and gallery **Marea** around the corner, at Venus no. 6 (behind Hotel La Siesta), tel. 669/982-0681, open Mon.–Sat. 10 A.M.–7 P.M. Husband-wife team of Siboli and Karen Valenzuela offer Siboli's gleaming one-of-a-kind silver jewelry selection (he'll execute your personal design), and more, including Huichol indigenous art—masks, dolls, yarn paintings—and handmade clothing.

Walk a few blocks east, near the Plazuela Machado and the Angela Peralta Theater and visit **Nidart** gallery and workshop, on Libertad, half a block south of the theater, at the corner of Carnaval. A labor of love of artist-founders Rak and Loa, Nidart showcases a museum of unique art-for-sale. Items ranges from whimsical ceramic figurines and silver kaleidoscopes to indigenous pottery curios and fanciful leather sculptures. An absolute must-see; it's very hard to visit without buying something.

Additional Old Town shops and galleries that might be worth a look include **Regalos Indio,** at Ángel Flores 206 Poniente, tel. 669/981-3753; **Elina Chauvet,** 21 de Marzo 416, corner Heriberto Frias, tel. 669/983-1498; **Viejo Mazatlán,** Sixto Osuna 309, tel. 669/982-2798; and **Casa del Rey** antiques, at Carnaval 1125, a block south of the Teatro Angela Peralta.

Community leaders have lately promoted the arts and crafts **Bazar del Sábado** (Saturday Bazaar), Saturday evenings, beginning around 5 P.M. Booths of local artists, artisans and entrepreneurs offer a wide range, from fine handmade jewelry and art-to-wear, to antiques and used books.

Zona Dorada Shopping

The Zona Dorada presents a bewildering variety of shops—in small shopping centers, hotel malls, and at streetside along Av. Camarón Sábalo. Nearly everything you're looking for, however, probably can be found in the concentration of many good and unusual shops along the side street Av. Playa Gaviotas, which forks left, one-way, off of Av. Camarón Sábalo a block north of Valentino's disco. The following are a few highlights, as you move north on Av. Playa Gaviotas.

One of your first stops should be at a trio of shops in the Hotel Playa Mazatlán shopping center on the beach side of Av. Playa Gaviotas. First, on the center's left corner, is **La Carreta,** open daily 9 A.M.–6 P.M., tel. 669/913-8320, an invitingly arranged museum of fine crafts, including bright Talavera pottery, gleaming handmade glassware, bright paper flowers, and hand-crocheted shawls *(rebozos),* napkins *(servilletas),* and tablecloths *(manteles).*

Next door, let the equally attractive selection of **Mexico, Mexico** lead you on, past its racks of colorful women's cotton resortwear, colorful Huichol *cuadras* (yarn paintings), eerie Guerrero masks, and shining Oaxaca tinware. Open Mon.–Sat. 9 A.M.–6 P.M., tel. 669/989-0555, ext. 1000.

Continue one door uphill to admire the glistening collection of the **Playa** silver store, tel. 669/989-0555, ext. 222. Virtually all Mexican silver jewelry (see Shopping in the On the Road chapter) is crafted far away in Taxco, Guerrero. Without bargaining, Mazatlán silver prices may be a bit steep. You can compare prices against other shops or ask them to weigh the piece. Many shops sell silver jewelry from one U.S. dollar per gram for simple pieces. If your choice costs significantly more than that, you'd better bargain.

Back on the street, head north half a block to the big **Señor Indio** all-Mexico crafts store next to the Azteca Inn, tel. 669/913-4923. Here, owners display an out-of-the ordinary selection, including bronze and ceramic sculpture and attractive classical fresco reproduction fragments. Open Mon.–Sat. 9 A.M.–7:30 P.M.

Continue half a block north to the corner of side-street Garzas (marked by Gringo Lingo Cantina). Head right a short block to **Madonna,** at the corner of Laguna, tel. 669/914-2839. Inside, enjoy the artfully selected all-Mexico jewelry and crafts assortment, including much reasonably priced (from $.80 per gram) silver from Taxco, a fetching collection of indigenous Huichol beaded artifacts, iridescent opals, and intriguing wood and stone masks.

Back on Av. Playa Mazatlán, a block north, step into **Shell City,** Av. Playa Gaviotas 407, tel. 669/913-1301, a de facto museum of shells (and perhaps the reason they've become so scarce on Mazatlán's beaches). Constellations of pearly curios—swirling conches, iridescent abalones, bushy corals, and in one single deviation, whimsical coconut faces—fill Shell City's seeming acres of displays. Open daily 9 A.M.–8 P.M.; credit cards are accepted.

After Shell City, move next door to **Centro Comercial Pancho's** and peruse the welter of goods—silver, *huipiles,* ceramics, onyx—for sale. Best here are probably **Rossana's Curios,** with its min-museum of huaraches and, across the aisle, **Huichol's,** with a treasury of Huichol art—bead masks, ceremonial cups, yarn paintings—and miniatures, wooden skeletons, and papier-mâché *alebrijes* (fanciful animals).

Cross the street, toward the beach, and continue your browsing in the intimate beachfront **Las Cabañas** mall. Some shops stand out: **Garcia's,** with a trove of pewter and fine ceramics; **Melissa and Mike,** with handsome Taxco silver; and farther back, where the ocean breeze blows through, **Yama María,** with a trove of hand-embroidered *traje* and *ropa típica huipiles* and dresses from Oaxaca. Beyond that, take a break at a breezy, sea-view table at **Restaurant Pancho's.**

Return across the street to **Casa Maya** fine leather store, tel. 669/916-7220, unmissable because of its replica Mayan pyramid looming above the Av. Playa Gaviotas. Casa Maya, which specializes in custom boot and leathercraft orders, also offers a fine ready-made selection of boots, coats, jackets, shoes, and purses so original that many are interesting as works of art. Lately, Casa Maya has widened its offerings to a fine all-Mexico assortment, including genuine Puebla Talavera ceramics, elaborate censers from Metepec, and Oaxaca *alebrijes* (fanciful wooden animals) and pearly black pottery. Casa Maya is open Mon.–Sat. 10 A.M.–8:30 P.M. and Sun. 10 A.M.–2 P.M.

Pardo Jewelry, a few doors north, at 411 Av. Playa Gaviotas, tel./fax 669/914-3354, specializes in fine gems and jewelry. The glittering silver- and gold-set diamonds, rubies, emeralds, lapis, opals, and amethysts are worth appreciating whether you're buying or not. Open Mon.–Sat. 9:30 A.M.–5:30 P.M.; credit cards are accepted.

Supermarkets

For a big, air-conditioned selection of everything, from hardware and cosmetics to film and groceries, local people and tourists flock to Mexico's Kmart look-alikes, **Gigante,** tel. 669/986-7298, on R. Buelna, about a mile inland from Valentino's disco, open daily 9 A.M.–9 P.M., and **Comercial Mexicana,** tel. 669/984-3090, at the Gran Plaza mall. Get there by following R. Buelna inland from Valentino's, turn right just past the La Posta trailer park, and continue for a quarter mile to Comercial Mexicana's big orange pelican emblem/sign.

Photography

Although many big hotel shops develop and sell film, their services are limited and expensive. Competition lowers the prices on "photo row," Calle Ángel Flores downtown, just west of the central plaza. For reasonable one-hour developing and jumbo printing, try **Photo Arauz,** Ángel Flores 607, tel. 669/982-2015, open Mon.–Sat. 8 A.M.–8 P.M., Sun. 8 A.M.–2 P.M. It does 35 mm rolls for about $12. Nearby **Photo de Llano,** Ángel Flores 820, tel. 669/981-6277, open Mon.–Sat. 9 A.M.–1:30 P.M. and 4–7 P.M., develops, prints, and enlarges in color on-site. It also stocks some professional sheet and 120 film, in addition to cameras, photo equipment, and supplies.

INFORMATION

Tourist Information Office

Mazatlán government tourism maintains two information centers. Most convenient is the booth on Playa Gaviotas, across from the Hotel Playa Mazatlán, by the U.S. consular office. If it's not open, go to the main office on Calz. Camarón Sábalo, corner of Tiburón, in the big Banrural building, 4th floor, tel. 669/916-5160 through 669/916-5165, fax 669/916-5166 or

669/916-5167, tursina@prodigy.net.mx. Office hours are Mon.–Fri. 9 A.M.–5 P.M.; Sat. (by telephone only) 9 A.M.–1 P.M.

Publications

Several stores in the Zona Dorado slake visitors' thirst for English-language books, newspapers, and magazines. Perhaps the most bountiful selection is at **Mazatlán Book and Coffee Company,** across from Hotel Costa de Oro, behind, Banco Santander Mexicano. Select from a small library of novels, magazines, maps, dictionaries (and a certified masseuse next door). Open 10 A.M.–3 P.M. low season, 10 A.M.–9 P.M. high, tel. 669/916-7899.

After hours, try the big book rack at **Restaurant VIPs,** tel. 669/914-0754 or 669/913-4016, open daily 7 A.M.–midnight, across Camarón Sábalo from the Cinemas Gaviotas. It stocks several dozen titles, mostly popular novels and many U.S. popular magazines.

During the November through Easter winter season, you will often find the *Los Angeles Times, USA Today,* and the daily English-language Mexico City *News* at **Kioskito Tin Marin,** open daily 9:30 A.M.–8 P.M., diagonally across Camarón Sábalo from the Dairy Queen.

Old Mazatlán's revival now includes an English-language rental **library,** at Sixto Osuna 115, open Mon.–Fri. 9 A.M.–noon high season, 9 A.M.–noon Tues., Wed., and Fri., low season.

The unique new-age **Evolución Bookstore** stocks many English-language occult/self-help/meditation/music/astrology titles, along with assorted used paperbacks, cards, crystals, incense, and oils. Evolución is open daily except Sunday about 10:30 A.M.–6:30 P.M. and is in the Coral shopping center, Playa Gaviotas 204, tel./fax 669/916-0839. Find it behind, right side, Señor Frog's store.

For announcements of local cultural events, tours, restaurants, and interesting "feature articles, pick up a copies of *Pacific Pearl* and *Viejo Mazatlán,* Mazatlán's visitors' monthlies, widely available at tourist shops, restaurants, and hotels. If you can't find copies, call or drop into their respective offices: *Pacific Pearl,* open

Mon.–Fri. 9 A.M.–5 P.M., Sat. 9 A.M.–2 P.M., in shopping Plaza San Jorge, just south of the Dairy Queen corner, tel./fax 669/913-0117, tel. 669/913-4411, webmaster@pacificpearl.com, www.pacificpearl.com (subscribe online for $13); *Viejo Mazatlán,* downtown, at Belasario Domínguez 1401A, tel. 669/985-3781, fax 669/982-2798, olincali@mzt.megared.net.mx.

Public Library

Mazatlán's respectable public library is downtown, at **Plazuela de Los Leones,** two short blocks behind the Palacio Municipal. Of special interest is the upper-floor **Benjamin Franklin Library:** row upon row of venerable volumes of classic American literature. Open Mon.–Fri. 8 A.M.–8 P.M., Sat. 9 A.M.–noon.

Ecology and Volunteer Work

Mazatlán has a small but growing ecological movement, which has coalesced under the acronym **CEMAZ** (Consejo Ecologico de Mazatlán). Its main focus has been on education by example—cleaning up and restoring Mazatlán's offshore islands and lagoons. It occasionally needs volunteers for projects. Look for announcements in the newspapers *Pacific Pearl* and *Viejo Mazatlán.*

The Mazatlán **Acuario** (Aquarium), Av. de Los Deportes, one block off Av. del Mar about a mile south of Valentino's disco (watch for the signs), tel. 669/981-7815, 669/981-7816, or 669/981-7818, is another center of ecological activity. Mainly through school educational programs, it is trying to save the marine turtles that come ashore to lay eggs along local beaches during the summer and early fall. It may be able to use volunteers to help with such efforts. Check with the Aquarium public-relations officer or contact the volunteer Friends of the Aquarium (Amigos del Acuario): call Kitty at tel. 669/983-9931 or Vicky at tel. 669/916-6210 for more details.

Another worthwhile effort is the **Amigos de los Animales,** the local volunteer humane society. For more information, call Judy at tel. 669/988-0911.

SERVICES

Money Exchange

All banks compensate for short hours by 24-hour ATMs, which have become the peso source of choice in Mazatlán. Otherwise, during bank hours, obtain the most pesos for cash and traveler's checks at **Banamex,** Camarón Sábalo 424, tel. 669/914-0000, 669/914-0001, or 669/914-0002, in the Zona Dorada across the corner, south, from Dairy Queen. Banamex has both an ATM and a special longer-hours cashier outside and to the right of the regular bank, which may be open Mon.–Fri. 8:30 A.M. to as late as 5 P.M. during the high winter season. The downtown main branch, also with ATM at the central plaza, corner of Juárez and Ángel Flores, tel. 669/982-7733, changes both Canadian and U.S. dollars and traveler's checks Mon.–Fri. 8:30 A.M.–4:30 P.M., closed weekends.

On the other hand, **Banco Internacional** (Bital) offers both ATM and much longer money-changing hours: Mon.–Fri. 8 A.M.–7 P.M., Sat. 8 A.M.–3 P.M. at two branches, on Camarón Sábalo, across from Balboa Tower, about three blocks north of Dairy Queen, tel. 669/916-3425, and downtown, corner of Belisario Domínguez and Ángel Flores, tel. 669/982-5579.

Furthermore, after a long absence, a bank, namely **Bancomer** is doing business on Av. Olas Altas (corner of Sixto Osuna), open Mon.–Fri. 8:30 A.M.–4 P.M., tel. 669/981-2090 or 669/985-0386.

After bank hours, change cash and traveler's checks at one of the many of *casas de cambio* by the banks along Calz. Camarón Sábalo (such as the counter at the north end of Playa Gaviotas, across from Dairy Queen, open daily 9 A.M.–7 P.M., Sun. 10 A.M.–4 P.M., tel. 669/913-9209).

American Express maintains a full-service Zona Dorada money counter and travel agency on Camarón Sábalo, half a block north of the Dairy Queen, open Mon.–Fri. 9 A.M.–6 P.M., Sat. 9 A.M.–1 P.M., tel. 669/913-0600, fax 669/916-5908. It gives bank rates for American Express U.S. dollar traveler's checks; no others are accepted, however.

Communications

For routine mailings, use one of the several post boxes *(buzones)* at the big hotels, such as Los Sábalos, Playa Mazatlán, El Cid, Playa Real, and others.

Otherwise, go to one of the branch **post offices.** The main branch *(correo)* is adjacent to the central plaza downtown, corner of Juárez and Ángel Flores, tel. 669/981-2121. Open Mon.–Fri. 9 A.M.–6 P.M., Sat. 8 A.M.–noon, philatelic services in the morning only. Alternatively, go to the bus station branch, open Mon.–Fri. 8 A.M.–6 P.M. (four blocks inland from Playa Norte, behind the Hotel Sands).

Telecomunicaciones (public telephone, fax, and money orders) has two Mazatlán branches, both open Mon.–Fri. 8 A.M.–7 P.M., Sat.–Sun. 8 A.M.–noon. Choose either the downtown branch, in the post office building, tel. 669/981-2220, or the central bus station branch, open Mon.–Fri. 8 A.M.–7:30 P.M., Sat. and Sun. 8 A.M.–noon, tel./fax 669/982-0354.

Post@Ship, on Calz. Camarón Sábalo, across from VIPs restaurant a few blocks south of Dairy Queen, provides many postal services and more, including stamps, mail box, Mexpost express mail, P.O. boxes (with a Laredo, Texas address), fax, Internet access, and word processing. Hours are Mon.–Fri. 9 A.M.–6 P.M., Sat. 9 A.M.–2 P.M., tel. 669/916-4010, fax 669/916-4011.

It's much cheaper and usually quicker to use Ladatel calling cards in **sidewalk public telephones.** The cards are widely available in denominations of about $3, $5, and $10 at streetfront liquor stores, pharmacies, and minimarkets. Street telephones charge Ladatel phone cards at the rate of about $1 per minute for a call to the United States or Canada (first dial 001 then the local area code and number).

Furthermore, operator-assisted long-distance telephone *(larga distancia)* service is generally available from sidewalk telephones in Mazatlán. For operator-assisted calls within Mexico, dial 020; for operator-assisted international calls, dial 090. For more options, see the easy to follow directions in the phone book (directorio telefónico).

Beware of the many prominently located but usually very expensive "Call U.S. with your Visa or MasterCard" or "Collect Calls to the U.S.A." telephones. Routinely, such telephones require a minimum three-minute call, which will typically cost you about $10 before even speaking a word. Ask the operator for the minimum three-minute toll; if it's too high, take your business elsewhere. It's best to buy an easy-to-use Ladatel phone card.

Hospitals and Pharmacies

If you get sick, it's probably best to let your hotel get you a physician. Otherwise, go to one of Mazatlán's several good hospitals: for example, its 24-hour on-duty staff of specialists earns the **Hospital Militar** high recommendations. Despite its exclusive-sounding title, anyone can receive for-fee treatment at the Hospital Militar, in the Olas Altas district at Malpica and Venus, tel. 669/981-2079, one block from the Hotel Siesta.

Another good place to be sick is the shiny, big **Hospital Sharp,** tel. 669/986-5676, at Rafael Buelna and Calz. Jesus Kumate (formerly Calz. Reforma), about a quarter mile along Buelna from Valentino's disco. One of Mexico's newest and best, Hospital Sharp has a cadre of highly trained specialists using its mountain of high-tech equipment to set new Mexican diagnostic and care standards. Prices, however, are generally much higher than other Mexican hospitals.

The **Cruz Roja** (private Red Cross), tel. 669/981-3690, operates ambulances and is usually called to auto accidents when the victims are incapacitated. The Cruz Roja hospital is not highly recommended, however. Tell the ambulance to take you to Hospital Militar or Sharp, if you can manage it.

If you prefer a bona fide American-trained doctor, try surgeon Dr. Gilberto Robles Guevara's **Clínica Mazatlán** (office tel. 669/981-2917, home tel. 669/985-1923) at Zaragoza 609, corner 5 de Mayo, on the downtown "doctors' row." Dr. Robles Guevara is the local affiliate of IAMAT, the International Association for Medical Assistance to Travelers.

Farmacias in Mexico are allowed wide latitude to diagnose illnesses and dispense medicines. For a physician and pharmacy all in one right on the *malecón*, try **Farmacia Ángel,** run by friendly

Dr. Ángel Avila Tirado, who examines, diagnoses, prescribes, and rings up the sale on the spot. Find him on Av. del Mar, one block from the Fisherman's Monument, tel. 669/982-4746 or 669/981-6831, open Mon.–Sat. 9 A.M.–1 P.M. and 4–9:30 P.M., Sun. 9 A.M.–1 P.M. and 4–7 P.M.

Another good pharmacy is **Farmacia Moderna,** with many Mazatlán branches: downtown, at the corner of 5 de Mayo and 21 Marzo, behind the Palacio Municipal, tel. 669/981-0202 or 669/981-6266; in the Zona Dorada, across from the Hotel Costa de Oro, tel. 669/914-0044, where a doctor is customarily available for advice Mon.–Fri. 6–9 P.M.; also next to Banamex, just south of Dairy Queen, tel. 669/913-4277 or 669/913-4333. After hours, call the 24-hour prescription number, tel. 669/916-5233 or 669/916-5867.

Police and Fire Emergencies

For police emergencies in the Zona Dorada, the special **Policía Turística,** which patrols the Zona Dorada exclusively, can respond quickly. Go to their substation, north end of the Golden Zone, across from the Hotel Playa (formerly Camino) Real. Alternatively, dial emergency number 080 or taxi to police headquarters in Colonia Benito Juárez.

For downtown police emergencies, contact the *preventiva* police, in the Palacio Municipal on the central plaza, tel. 669/983-4510.

In case of fire, call the *bomberos* (firefighters), tel. 669/981-2769. (If no one answers, dial the emergency number 080.)

Immigration and Customs

If you lose your tourist card, be prepared by having made a copy beforehand; next best is your airline ticket itinerary or receipt, indicating your arrival date in Mexico. Take one or both of these to **Migración** at the airport, tel. 669/981-6611, or at Aquiles Serdán and Playas Gemelas, on the south side of downtown, two blocks north of the ferry dock, tel. 669/981-3813. This is also the place to extend your visa (up to 180 days total). It is open Mon.–Fri. 8 A.M.–2 P.M., closed weekends.

For customs matters contact the **Aduana** (customs) at the airport, tel. 669/982-2461; or in the old historic building, at V. Carranza 107, corner of Cruz, in the Olas Altas district, tel. 669/981-6109 or 669/981-1570; open Mon.–Fri. 8 A.M.–3 P.M.

Consulates

The **United States Consular Agent** helps U.S. citizens with legal and other urgent matters, at the Golden Zone office, tel./fax 669/916-5889, mazagent@mzt.megared.net, open Mon.–Fri. 8 A.M.–4 P.M., on Av. Playa Gaviotas, directly across from the Hotel Playa Mazatlán. In emergencies, call the closest U.S. consulate, in Hermosillo, tel. 658/217-2375 or 658/217-2585, or in Mexico City, tel. 55/5080-2000.

The **Canadian Consular Office** on Av. Playa Gaviotas, just adjacent to the Hotel Playa Mazatlán, tel. 669/913-7320, fax 669/914-6655, is open Mon.–Fri. 9 A.M.–1 P.M. In an emergency, contact the consul through the Canadian Embassy, tel. 55/5724-7900, in Mexico City.

Belgium, Finland, Italy, Germany, and France customarily maintain Mazatlán consular officers. See the local telephone Yellow Pages, under *Embajadas, Legaciones, y Consulados,* for contact telephone numbers, or ask the U.S. or Canadian agents above.

Language Courses and Lessons

The downtown **Centro de Idiomas** (Language Center), owned and operated by very knowledgeable American resident Dixie Davis, offers good beginning and advanced Spanish courses. Registration and all materials run about $105; tuition is about $120/week for small, two-hour daily classes. The center also arranges homestay and person-to-person programs. For more information, contact the school downtown at Belisario Domínguez 1908, upstairs, tel. 669/985-5606, fax 669/982-2053, info@spanishlink.org, website www.spanishlink.org.

Alternatively, look into the highly recommended **Active English** Spanish instruction program, in the Golden Zone, at Calz. Camarón Sábalo 333D, a few doors north of the Pasteleria Panamá, open daily 8 A.M.–8 P.M. Drop by or call tel. 669/916-7223 or 669/913-0423, or email activeenglish@mzt.megared.net.mx.

Art, Music, and Dance Classes

The **Escuela Municipal de Arte** (Municipal School of the Arts) periodically offers ballet, instrumental and choral music, painting, and other instruction for adults and children. The sessions are conducted in the airy old-world buildings that cluster around the charming downtown Plazuela Machado. For more information, contact the director, Ricardo Urquijo, at Teatro Angela Peralta, tel. 669/982-4447, at the Plazuela Machado, or visit the website www.teatroangelaperalta.com, or see announcements in the *Pacific Pearl* and *Viejo Mazatlán* newspapers.

Massage

The **Centro de Massage of Mazatlán,** tel. 669/913-7666, open by appointment Mon.–Sat. 10 A.M.–7 P.M., provides massage therapy for around $25–40 per hour using a variety of techniques, such as shiatsu, neuromuscular, acupressure, Swedish, and cranial vascular, in a studio in the Paraíso Tres Islas shopping center, on Av. Playa Gaviotas, across from Shell City. It advertises itself as the "Land of the Deer Healing Center," quoting a Yaqui proverb: "In gentleness there is great strength." Local hotels refer many customers there.

Newcomer **Taboo Day Spa,** tel. 669/913-1110, offers massage plus other services, such as manicure, pedicure, facials, hairdressing, and more. Drop in to its Golden Zone center, on side street Laguna, behind the Azteca Inn; open approximately 9 A.M.–6 P.M.

GETTING THERE AND AWAY
By Air

A number of reliable U.S. and Mexican airlines connect Mazatlán with many destinations in Mexico and the United States.

Alaska Airlines flights connect daily with Los Angeles, San Francisco, Portland, and Seattle-Tacoma. The local flight information office is at the airport, tel. 669/985-2730. For reservations and tickets, call a travel agent, such as American Express, tel. 669/913-0600, fax 669/916-5908, or the central booking number, toll-free U.S. tel. 800/426-0333.

Mexicana Airlines flights connect daily with Los Angeles, Denver (via affliate Frontier Airlines), Tepic, Mexico City, and Los Cabos. The local reservations offices are in the Zona Dorada, tel. 669/913-0772. For flight information, call the airport at tel. 669/982-5666 or toll-free Mex. tel. 800/502-2000.

Aeroméxico and affiliated **Aerolitoral** flights connect daily with San Diego (high season only), Phoenix, Tijuana, Mexico City, Durango, Hermosillo, La Paz, Guadalajara, Torreón, and Monterrey. The local reservations/information offices are in the Zona Dorada, at Calz. Camarón Sábalo 310, tel. 669/914-1111 or 669/914-1609, and at the airport, tel. 669/982-3444, 669/982-4894, or 669/914-1621.

Aerocalifornia Airlines flights connect with Los Angeles, Tijuana, La Paz, Guadalajara, and Mexico City. For reservations, call a travel agent or the airline office at Hotel El Cid, tel. 669/913-2042. For flight information, call the airport office at tel. 669/985-2557.

America West Airlines flights connect with Phoenix. For reservations, call toll-free U.S. tel. 800/235-9292. For flight information, call tel. 669/981-1184.

Continental Airlines Express charter connects once a week with Houston. Call toll-free Mex. tel. 800/900-5000 for information and reservations.

CENCA International Airlines connects with Guadalajara and Ixtapa-Zihuatanejo. For reservations and flight information in Mazatlán, call tel. 669/981-4813.

Mazatlán Airport Arrival and Departure

For arrivees, the Mazatlán Airport (code-designated MZT, officially the General Rafael Buelna Airport) offers a modicum of services. Although, at this writing, a Banamex ATM was functioning, a money exchange office was operating seasonally 9 A.M.–5 P.M., and car rental agents meet flights, tourist information and hotel booking services were lacking. You should arrive with first-night hotel reservations and guidebook in hand. (Otherwise, you'll be at the mercy of the taxi driver, who will most likely collect a commission from the hotel where he deposits you.)

Local **car rental** agencies include: AGA, tel. 669/914-4405 or 669/981-3580, rentasaga @mzt.megared.net.mx; Budget, tel. 669/913-2000, fax 669/914-3611, budget_aeropuerto_mzt@hotmail.com; National, tel. 669/913-6000 or 669/986-4562, fax 669/913-9087, nationalmzt@grupoantyr.com.mx; Hertz, tel. 669/913-6060 or 669/913-4955, fax 669/914-2523; and Alamo, tel. 669/981-2266 or 669/913-1010, alamomzt@mzt.megared.net.mx.

Taxi and *colectivo* transportation for the 15-mile (25-km) ride into town is well organized. Booths (in the arrival hall, across from the car rentals) sell both kinds of tickets: *colectivo* about $6 per person, taxi about $25 per car. No public bus runs from town to the airport.

For departure, *colectivos* are harder to find around hotels than are departing tourists. Share a regular taxi and save on your return to the airport.

The **international airport departure tax** runs about $15. If your ticket price doesn't cover it, be prepared to pay up. If you've lost your tourist card and haven't had time to get a duplicate at immigration, you may be able to avoid the $20 departure fine by presenting a photocopy of your original tourist card.

By Car or RV

Three main highway routes reach Mazatlán: from the United States through Nogales and Culiacán; from the northeast, through Durango, and from the southeast, from Guadalajara or Puerto Vallarta through Tepic.

The quickest and safest way to drive to Mazatlán from the U.S. western border region is by Mexico National Highway 15, which connects with U.S. I-19 from Tucson, at Nogales, Mexico. A four-lane superhighway for nearly all the 743-mile (1,195-km) route, Highway 15 allows a safe, steady 55 mph (90 kph) pace. Although the tolls total about $60 for a car (more for trailers and big RVs) the safety and decreased wear and tear are well worth it. Take it easy and allow yourself at least two full days travel to or from Nogales.

Heading to Mazatlán from the northeast, the winding (but spectacular) two-lane National Highway 40 crosses the Sierra Madre Occidental from Durango. Steep grades over the 7,350-foot (2,235-meter) pass will stretch the trip into a better part of a day, even though it totals only 198 miles (318 km). During the winter, snow can (but rarely does) block the summit for a few hours.

From the southeast, heavy traffic slows progress along the mostly two-lane narrow northern section of National Highway 15, which connects with Tepic (182 miles, 293 km, four hours). At Tepic, toll (cuota) expressway Hwy 15 D smoothes the way to Guadalajara (141 miles, 227 km, 3 hours). Allow a full day for this trip.

About the same is required for the Mazatlán-Puerto Vallarta highway connection. Both legs, first two-lane National Highway 15 (182 miles, 293 km, four hours) connecting at Tepic with the second leg, two-lane Highway 200 (104 miles, 167 km, three hours) to Puerto Vallarta is subject to slowing by heavy traffic and requires a full day.

By Bus

Best hire a taxi to take you (and your luggage) to the *central de autobuses* (central bus terminal), at the corner of Highway 15 ingress boulevard and Calle Chachalulas, about two miles north of downtown and four blocks from Playa Norte beach, behind the Sands Hotel.

Although the terminal is divided into *primera-* (first) and *segunda-clase* (second-class), counters on both sides sell both tickets. First-class (with an a/c waiting room) is on the far right, around the inside terminal corridor corner. Facilities include a kept luggage section (*guarda de equipaje,* about $7/day), a post office, public phone and fax office, many public Ladatel card-operated long distance telephones (buy Ladatel cards in the Elite a/c first-class waiting room snack counter), and a few lunch stands and stores where travelers can buy food, pure water, and drinks. Stock up before you leave.

Several well-equipped bus lines provide frequent local departures. Go first- or luxury-class whenever possible. The service, speed, and reserved seats (*asientos reservados*) of first-class buses

far outweigh their small additional cost. Parent company **Estrella Blanca** (which includes Elite, Futura, Transportes Chihuahuenses, and luxury-class Turistar) provides the most departures and the widest range, connecting the entire Pacific corridor, all the way to Acapulco, with border points from California to the Gulf of Mexico. Independent line **Transportes del Pacífico** successfully competes in the northwest, offering both first- and luxury-class departures, connecting Puerto Vallarta with California and Arizona border crossings. All connections listed below are first class and depart locally (*salidas locales*) unless otherwise noted.

First-class **Elite** (EL) buses, tel. 669/981-3811 or 669/981-2335, connect with southeast destinations of Tepic, Guadalajara, Morelia, Aguascalientes, Queretaro, and Mexico City and intermediate points. At least one daily *salida de paso* (bus passing through) connects en route south with Tepic, Puerto Vallarta, Manzanillo, Zihuatanejo, and Acapulco; in the opposite direction many buses connect with northwest destinations of Culiacán, Los Mochis, Nogales, Mexicali, and Tijuana, including many intermediate points.

Transportes Chihuahuenses (TC) buses, tel. 669/981-2335, connect north via Durango, Chihuahua, Ciudad Juárez, and intermediate points.

Luxury-class **Futura** (FU) departures, tel. 669/981-2335, connect northeast with Monterrey, via Durango, Torreón, and Saltillo.

Transportes del Pacífico, tel. 669/982-0577, (TP) *salidas de paso* connect hourly en route northwest to Tijuana and southeast to Tepic, Guadalajara, Mexico City, and intermediate points. You can change buses at Tepic, however, and continue to Puerto Vallarta.

In the second-class section, to the left as you enter the terminal, many daily **Transportes Norte de Sonora** (TNS) buses, tel. 669/981-3811, connect with all points along the northwest Pacific route (including Culiacán, Agua Prieta, and Tijuana), southeast with Guadalajara, Queretaro, and Mexico City, and south with Tepic, San Blas, Puerto Vallarta, and intermediate points.

By Train

Privatization of the Pacific Railroad has put an

end to passenger service. Go by bus or airplane instead.

By Ferry

Mazatlán's passenger and automobile ferry service, which used to connect with La Paz, Baja California, has been cancelled until further notice. (At this writing, however, passenger and automobile ferry service was still connecting La Paz with mainland Pacific Mexico, via Topolobampo, near Los Mochis, a day's drive north of Mazatlán. (For details, see By Ferry in the Getting There section of the On the Road chapter.)

South to Puerto Vallarta and Inland to Guadalajara

Along the Road to San Blas

National Highway 15 winds southward from Mazatlán through a lush, palm-dotted patchwork of pasture, fields, and jungle-clad hills. To the east rise the sculpted domes of the Sierra Madre Occidental, while on the west, a grand, island-studded marshland stretches to a virtually unbroken barrier of ocean sand.

Although a few scattered fishing villages edge this 150-mile (250-km) coastline, it remains mostly wild, the domain of hosts of shorebirds and waterfowl, and, in the most remote mangrove reaches, jaguars and crocodiles. Its driftwood-strewn beaches invite adventurous trekkers, RV campers, and travelers who enjoy Pacific Mexico beaches at their untouristed best.

PLAYA CAIMANERO

A lineup of beachside *palapa* restaurants marks the southern end of Playa Caimanero, a 20-mile barrier dune that blocks **Laguna Caimanero** from the sea. (The salinity of Laguna Caimanero, however, is a mystery to local people, who speculate that the salt water migrates under the dune.)

Besides most of the low-key beach pastimes, both Playa Caimanero and its lagoon are a bird-watcher's heaven (bring your bird book, binoculars, and repellent). The broad, shallow Laguna Caimanero is less than a mile from the beach along any one of three dirt roads through the grove. Local people could probably point you to

the timeless classic façade of Guadalajara's Teatro Degollado

To Culiacán and U.S.A.

To Durango

Copala
DANIEL'S HOTEL

Mazatlán
Villa
Union
Concordia

MAZATLÁN TO SAN BLAS

Laguna
El Huizache
El Walamo
Teodoro Beltran
HOTEL YUACO
Rosario

Laguna
Caimanero
El Caimanero
Agua
Verde
Esquinapa
HOTEL IQ
L. Los Cerritos

L. Grande
Las Cabras

L. Agua
Grande

Río San Pedro

Río San Pedro

PACIFIC

HOTEL RANCHO LOS ANGELES
HOTEL VILLAS CORAL
Teacapan
HOTEL DENISSE

TP

15

Acaponeta

OCEAN

Isla del
Otro Lado
HOTEL PACÍFICO
Novillero

Tecuala

DETAIL

Union
San Andres
Mayorquin
Higuerita
EMBARCADERO TICHA
Los Patitos
San
Vicente
Colorabas
las Pesqueria
Mexcaltitán
Laguna
Grande
de
Mexcaltitán
El Mescal
EMBARCADERO
TECOCTA
EMBARCADERO
LA BATANGA
Tuxpán
Las
Cuatos
Las
Gallinas
Toluca
Las Tortugas
Campos de
los Limones
Sentispac

L. Agua
Brava
L. El Valle

15

Chilapa

L. Los
Pericos
Santa Cruz
Tuxpán

Mexcaltitán
La Punta

Santiago Ixcuintla

Villa Hidalgo

SEE DETAIL

Bocas de Camachin
Playa Cesteo
Playa Los Corchos
Toro Mocho
Villa
Juarez
Río Grande
de Santiago

74

0   20 mi
0   20 km

Barra Asadero
Laureles

San Blas
To Puerto Vallarta

To Tepic and Puerto Vallarta

© AVALON TRAVEL PUBLISHING, INC.

a boatman who could take you on a bird-watching excursion (especially at the south end, where the road edges the lagoon and an embarcadero.)

Besides birds, Playa Caimanero is a prime hatching ground for endangered species of sea turtles. They crawl ashore, especially during the later summer and fall, when volunteers patrol the sand, trying to protect the eggs from poachers and predators.

Beach Activities

Playa Caimanero offers possibilities, from a scenic, one-day excursion out of Mazatlán or a side loop from Highway 15, traveling either north or south, to a weeklong trekking-camping-fishing and wildlife-watching adventure. (Swimmers, however, must be careful of the rough waves and undertow.)

Although no beach facilities exist save the rustic seafood *palapas* at El Caimanero, small stores at two or three villages behind the dune carry basic food supplies. Furthermore, driftwood for the taking litters the beach, at least during the summer-fall rainy season. Water, however, is scarce along the beach; campers, bring your purification tablets or filter and some big plastic bottles to fill at the villages. If you get tired of walking, a truck bumps along the beach road every 5 or 10 minutes; stick out your thumb; and if one stops, offer to pay.

Getting There

At Villa Union, 15 miles (24 km) south of Mazatlán, stock up on gas and supplies. Then head west (or ride the local bus) along the street that passes the south side of the landmark town **20** church. Continue another 14 miles (23 km) along Sinaloa Highway D-6 through the dusty little town of El Walamo. At the west side of El Walamo, jog left one block and continue along the paved road to Teodoro Beltrán village. At Mile 17 (Km 27), turn right on to a bumpy gravel road and keep going two miles to the beach, at Mile 19 (Km 31). The graded gravel road continues atop the beach dune for about another 10 miles (16 km) to the seafood *palapas* at El Caimanero. The pavement resumes at the south end (where the road becomes

Sinaloa 5-19), heading along the southern edge of Caimanero lagoon to Agua Verde and rejoining Highway 15 at Rosario. The reverse, northbound trip could be done just as easily from Rosario. From the *cuota autopista* at Rosario, exit west, toward Agua Verde.

CONCORDIA, COPALA, AND ROSARIO

These easily accessible colonial-era towns offer charming off-the-beaten track glimpses of country Mexico. If driving, mark your odometer at the Highway 15-Highway 40 fork, where you head for Concordia and Copala, east along Highway 40, toward the mountains. After winding through lush, summer and fall wildflower–decorated foothills, you'll notice that roadside pottery factories begin appearing around Mile 10 (Km 16). Their offerings, all made in local family workshops, include many floral, animal, and human (some erotic) designs from local pre-Columbian tradition. Near the bridge at Mile 12 (Km 19), which marks the entrance to Concordia, shops make and sell a wealth of sturdy, chestnut-varnished, colonial-style furniture.

For an interesting side excursion, fork sharply right onto a dirt road at the west end of the bridge. After about 100 yards, turn left and continue another 200 yards, then bear left, off the road, to a tree-shaded hot spring (*manantial*—mah-NAHN-teeahl), where women wash clothes in big collecting basins. You can bathe, along with the local folks (with bathing suit, or your clothes on) in the last, coolest basin.

Continue through Concordia. Pass through a creek, inviting for picnicking and swimming, at Mile 20 (Km 32). Eight miles (13 km) farther, turn right at the signed Copala side road. Copala, an old gold-mining town, founded by conquistador Francisco Ibarra in 1565, continues in the present as a picture-perfect stop for the trickle of tourists who venture out from Mazatlán. However, when the last tour bus departs, at around 3 in the afternoon, you'll have the place nearly to yourself, save for a few local bench-warmers, a scattering of kids and dogs, and the obligatory chickens scratching around the plaza. The "new"

TO PV/GUADALAJARA

plaza-front church, built in 1624 and dedicated to San José, replaced the original. It presides over the few festivities (Easter, Virgin of Guadalupe on December 12, and Christmas), especially March 16, the day of San José, when Copala livens up.

For food, try the streetside *taquerías* or the pair of relaxing tourist spots, the **Copala Butter Company** or **Daniel's** restaurant and hotel, on the right, just as you enter town. Although Daniel, the friendly expatriate American owner, and his wife have leased the restaurant to other managers, they still offer lodging in comfortable hacienda-style rooms for about $22 d. Reserve, especially on weekends and holidays, by writing to Restaurant Daniel's, Copala, Concordia, Sinaloa 82650; or leave a message (in Spanish) with the Copala long-distance phone operator, tel. 669/985-4225.

Although Daniel's still probably has the best food, the Copala Butter Company (name taken from the ex-hacendado and mine owner Charles Butter) probably has the most personality. Friendly owner Jesús Morales and his wife have gathered a minimuseum of artifacts from the local mine diggings, which closed operations in 1980. Besides meals beneath their antique hacienda roof, they also offer five genuinely rustic rooms that open onto a long town- and valley-view porch. Step back 150 years and stay overnight for only about $20 d. Reserve at Plaza Juárez, Copala, Sinaloa 82650; by phone, leave a message (in Spanish) with the Copala long-distance phone operator, tel. 669/985-4225, or at Río Baluarte 412, Mazatlán, Sinaloa, tel. 669/981-3224.

Back on Highway 15, continue south to Rosario (pop. about 10,000), about 56 miles (90 km) south of Mazatlán. This dusty but historic town has two claims to fame: its colonial cathedral and its favorite daughter, singer Lola Beltrán. You pass the old church just after the town's entrance arch (off Highway 15, to the right). Inside rises the lofty, baroque gold altar, carved as a gilded foliage abode for a choir of angels and cherubs. After the church, stop at the house museum on Lola Beltrán street nearby, where world-renowned "Ranchera"-style singer Lola Beltrán lived. (Lola's sister, who runs the home as a museum, enjoys company.)

© BRUCE WHIPPERMAN

Copala's "new" church of San José was founded in 1624.

For a restful poolside *comida* and/or an overnight lodging in Rosario, try the **Hotel Yuaco,** (tel./fax 694/952-1222, about $30 d), on the highway, east side, a couple of blocks south of the entrance arch.

TEACAPÁN

The downscale little beach resorts of Teacapán and Novillero have not yet been "discovered." They remain quiet retreats for lovers of sun, sand, simple lodgings, and super-fresh seafood. Trucks travel from all over Sinaloa and Nayarit to buy their shrimp and fish.

Although Teacapán and Novillero are only a few miles apart, the Río San Pedro estuary that divides Sinaloa from Nayarit also divides Teacapán from Novillero. Novillero's south-side peninsula is identified by Teacapán residents as simply Isla del Otro Lado (Island on the Other Side).

The small town of Teacapán (pop. 3,000) lies along the sandy northeast edge of the estuary, which most residents know only as *la boca,* the river "mouth." Tambora, Teacapán's broad beach, borders a stately old palm grove on the open ocean a couple of miles north of the town.

Most restaurants, however, are on the estuary, a lazy place, where people walk very slowly. Here, a crumbling old dinghy returns to the sand; there, native-style *canoas* lie casually beneath the palms.

Accommodations and Food
Of the restaurants that line the estuary beach, most established is seafood **Restaurant Mr. Wayne** (from the name of an American friend of the enterprising Mexican owner). He employs his own fisherman to bring the best *pargo, robalo,* and *mero* to the barbecue every afternoon.

The most prominent of Teacapán's in-town hotel accommodations is **Hotel Denisse,** on the main plaza, diagonally adjacent to the church, and only three blocks from the beach. The owners revitalized a former private home, and now they offer six furnished rooms with bath spread around an inner patio. The rooms rent for about $22 d with a/c. Although reservations aren't usually necessary, it is best to write or fax the hotel in advance: Hotel Denisse, Calles R. Buelna y Morelos, Teacapán, Sinaloa 82560, tel./fax 695/452-66 or 695/954-5130.

A few miles back on the road to Teacapán, you may have noticed a sign in passing, advertising the **Hotel Rancho Los Angeles.** If you continue along the side road to the beach, you will find a restaurant (open until around 6 P.M.), bar, beautiful big pool, and an adjacent trailer park. Upstairs is a luxurious three-room suite that opens to a big deck overlooking a breezy, palm-fringed ocean vista. As the manager says, "The music we have here is the music of the waves." No TV, but plenty of sun, sand, and solitude; the upstairs rents for about $50/day. Other smaller but equally luxurious rooms downstairs rent for about $35 per day. A three-bedroom cottage beneath the palm grove a short walk away goes for about $100/day. The approximately 60 unshaded trailer spaces go for about $15 per day, $100 per week, $300 per month, including all hookups, toilets, showers,

and use of the pool. For reservations, contact the hotel directly in Teacapán, tel./fax 695/953-1344, email tvrivera@hotmail.com, or visit the website www.teacapan.com. (*Note:* During the high winter season, hotel residents enjoy lots of company in the restaurant, especially from the trailer park people. Summers, by contrast, are for those who prefer solitude.)

Rancho Los Angeles's personable owner, Ernesto River, M.D., and his son Jorge offer to guide small groups of guests to a unique nearby **archaeological site,** which they describe as a former pyramid, 100 feet high, made completely of sea shells. They say that an archaeologist, Dr. Stuart Scott of the University of Buffalo, New York, investigated the site, as yet undeveloped, in the 1970s. The trip, which they say takes a full day, leads through savannah and mangrove wetlands, habitat to a trove of wildlife, including crocodiles, dolphins, turtles, fish, and dozens of bird species. Bring your repellent, water, a hat, binoculars, and your bird identification book.

Development has arrived at Teacapán, in the form of **Hotel Villas Coral,** in the lovely green park beneath the estuary-front palm grove just before entering town. As an anchor to what appears to be a budding second-home development, owners have built and furnished four lovely rustic-chic tile and stucco minivillas around an inviting pool-patio. Rentals run about $65 for four, with a/c, kitchenettes, beach club restaurant, and tennis court. Tent camping is also allowed, beneath the palms by the estuary beach. Figure about $10 per tent or (self-contained only, no hookups) RV. For reservations (probably not necessary except for Christmas and Easter) call (in Spanish) tel. 695/954-5477.

RVers and trailer folks are welcome at the palm-shadowed 40-space beachfront **trailer park** (owned by Rancho Los Angeles, same prices and reservation numbers), adjacent to the north-end beach restaurant. Amenities include showers and hammocks for trailer park occupants, beneath a shady beachfront *palapa.* Get there along the signed road from the highway; turn right into the driveway just after the big white house on the right.

Camping is customary most anywhere, either on the sand or beneath the big palm grove that edges the shoreline, curving south back to the estuary. To the north, the beach stretches, wild and breeze-swept, for several miles.

Beach Activities

Despite depletion of the Teacapán lagoon, ocean fishing remains good off Tambora beach. Watch for the sign on the right about two miles before town. You can rent a *lancha* or shove off in your own boat right on the beach.

Tambora is a very broad silky sand beach where the waves normally roll in gently from about 100 yards out, breaking gradually both left and right for surfing. Sailboarding would also be good here, although the water is too sandy for snorkeling. Various clam, cowrie, and cockle shells turn up at seasonal times. Permanent beachside *palapa* restaurants serve fresh seafood and drinks. Other food and supplies are available in stores back in town.

Laguna Agua Grande

As it approaches the sea, the Río San Pedro, which forms the Sinaloa-Nayarit border, curves and broadens into a broad brackish lake, Laguna Agua Grande. Fisherfolk traditionally have made their living from the bounty of its waters, as have a host of waterbirds and myriad other creatures that inhabit its mangrove reaches. Overfishing has unfortunately forced the government to severely limit fish, shrimp, and shellfish catches. The government has had to enforce its rules with roadside inspections and military presence.

Consequently, an increasing number of boats have begun plying the waters, not hauling fish but ecotourists and bird-watchers. If you have your own boat, you can do the same, or hire a fisherman to take you. A convenient site for either boat launching or hiring is at the end of Av. Niños Héroes, just one block north of the Teacapán plaza. Follow the gravel road east

Little Novillero enjoys one of the longest (55 miles, 90 km), smoothest stretches of sand in Mexico. The waves roll in gently from 100 yards out and swish lazily along a velvety, nearly level beach.

for about 1.5 miles to the small fishing camp and improvised boat ramp.

Services

Along the main street back in Teacapán town, residents enjoy the services of a doctor, a pharmacy, a fairly well-stocked grocery, and a long-distance telephone office.

An estuary-front **boat ramp** is available for public use at the beachfront park back in town. Find it by turning right (heading south), at the official blue boat sign in the middle of town.

Getting There

Teacapán is accessible from Highway 15 by Sinaloa Highway 5-23 from Esquinapa. Ride either the local *urbano* or the red- and blue-striped Transportes Esquinapa buses from in front of the little park adjacent to the plaza cathedral or the bus station at the Teacapán turnoff at the north edge of town.

Southbound drivers, just before you enter downtown Esquinapa, a diversion funnels through traffic one-way to the right, then left within a block or two. Instead of following left, continue straight ahead for several blocks until you arrive at the asphalt westbound highway out of town, where you continue straight ahead for Teacapán. The all-paved 24 miles (38 km) passes quickly, through bushy thorn forest and past shallow lagoons dotted with waterbirds and rafts of wild lotus. Palm groves and broad fields of *chiles,* which make Sinaloa one of Mexico's top *chile*-producing states, line the roadside.

Esquinapa (pop. 40,000), a busy farm town, has a good overnight hotel, the **IQ de Esquinapa** (with restaurant), a block from the downtown plaza at Gabriel Leyva 7 Sur, tel./fax 695/953-0471, 695/953-0782, or 695/953-0396. The 30 semideluxe rooms around an enclosed courtyard rent for about $22 d, with TV, a/c, phones, and parking; credit cards are accepted.

M

TO PV/GUADALAJARA

NOVILLERO

Little Novillero (pop. about 1,000) enjoys one of the longest (55 miles, 90 km), smoothest stretches of sand in Mexico. The waves roll in gently from 100 yards out and swish lazily along a velvety, nearly level beach. Here, all of the ingredients for a perfect beach stay come together: *palapa* seafood restaurants, hotels, a big palm grove for RV or tent camping, ocean fishing, and a broad creamy strand for beachcombers and wilderness campers stretching from both ends of town.

Moreover, Novillero's mangrove hinterland, about a mile inland from the beach, is a yet-to-be-discovered wildlife-viewing wonderland. You might be able to enjoy such an opportunity by hiring a local boatman (expect to pay about $15 an hour after bargaining) to take your party on an excursion along the mangrove-laced jungle waterways. Ask at the hotel, around town, or in the fishing village beneath the estuary bridge (about two miles before town).

Accommodations and Food

Foremost among the three lodgings is the beachfront **Hotel Pacifico,** tel. 323/239-4648. Here, owners offer a score of beach-view rooms, with modern-standard baths and color-coordinated maroon bedspreads and curtains. The prices are certainly right, at $25 s or d, $45 t, with TV, a/c, big blue pool, parking, and restaurant.

In the unlikely eventuality that Hotel Pacifico is full, you can try downscale basic, family-run third-choice **Hotel Miramar** on the beach across the street, or **Hotel and Restaurant Puerto Azul,** back three blocks from the beach.

For food, Novillero offers a number of choices: a well-stocked country grocery (here called the "mini-super") and half a dozen *palapa* restaurants accustomed to serving a generation of vacationers. Try the big beachside **Hotel Miramar** *palapa,* or look into Lola's **La Gaera,** two blocks south, on the main (parallel to the beach) town street, where grandmotherly Lola has fashioned a vine-covered *palapa* with an assortment of chairs and oilcloth-covered tables. Her son sometimes arrives about 9 P.M. and belts out gratis serenades for customers on his guitar.

Getting There

Novillero is about halfway between Tepic and Mazatlán, a two-hour ride, either way, plus another half hour (22 miles, 35 km) by paved side road from Highway 15. Get there by bus via Transportes Victoria local bus from the highway to Tecuala, where you continue by minibus or *colectivo* van.

For drivers, Novillero is about halfway between Tepic and Mazatlán, a two-hour drive either way, plus a half hour (22 miles, 35 km) by paved side road from Highway 15. Turn west only a few hundred yards south of the Pemex station (and junction to Acaponeta), at the paved side road signed Tecuala. Continue about eight miles (13 km) and, as you're entering Tecuala, turn right just after the Pemex station. Continue another half mile and turn right at the paved highway, which continues west another 14 miles (22 km) west to Novillero.

MEXCALTITÁN

Mexcaltitán (pop. 2,000), the "House of the Mexicans," represents much more than just a scenic little island town. Archaeological evidence indicates Mexcaltitán may actually be the legendary Aztlán (Place of the Herons) where, in A.D. 1091, the Aztecs (who called themselves the Mexica—May-SHEE-kah) began their generations-long migration to the Valley of Mexico.

Each year on June 28 and 29, the feast days of St. Peter and St. Paul, residents of Mexcaltitán and surrounding villages dress up in feathered headdresses and jaguar robes and breathe life into their tradition. They celebrate the opening of the shrimp season by staging a grand regatta, driven by friendly competition between decorated boats carrying rival images of saints Peter and Paul.

Getting There

By car, the southbound Highway 15 turnoff for Mexcaltitán is 136 miles (219 km) miles south of Mazatlán, four miles (six km) after the village of Chilapa. The 25-mile (40-km) southbound side trip ends at La Ticha embarcadero. It passes its last half along a rough (but passable by ordinary automobile) gravel road-dike through the marsh,

Mexcaltitán, the "House of the Mexicans," is much more than a small island town.

edged by bushy mangroves and lotus ponds and inhabited by constellations of waterbirds and water lily–munching cattle.

By car, northbound from Highway 15, follow the signed Santiago Ixcuintla turnoff, 38 miles (60 km) north of Tepic; continue five miles past Santiago Ixcuintla (see below) to the signed and paved Mexcaltitán side road, which continues another 15 miles (25 miles total from Highway 15) to the La Batanga embarcadero (boat landing).

By bus, southbound, ask your bus driver to let you off at the Santiago Ixcuitla turnoff from Highway 15 where you can catch a local bus into town. If it's early, continue (about an hour) by local bus or *colectivo* to Mexcaltitán Embarcadero La Batanga.

Northbound, go from Tepic or San Blas bus stations by Transportes Noreste de Nayarit blue buses direct to Santiago Ixcuintla. Continue as described in previous paragraph.

Sights

From either of the Mexcaltitán road's-end embarcaderos, boatmen ferry you across (about $1 per person for *colectivo,* $5 for private boat, each way) to Mexcaltitán island-village, some of whose inhabitants have never crossed the channel to the mainland. The town itself is not unlike many Mexican small towns, except more tranquil, because of the absence of motor vehicles.

Mexcaltitán is prepared for visitors, however. Instituto Nacional de Arqueología y Historia (INAH) has put together an excellent **museum** with several rooms of artifacts, photos, paintings, and maps describing the cultural regions of pre-Columbian Mexico; open Tues.–Sun. 10 A.M.–2 P.M., 4–7 P.M. The displays climax at the museum's centerpiece exhibit, which tells the story of the Aztecs' epic migration to the Valley of Mexico from legendary Aztlán, now believed by experts to be present-day Mexcaltitán.

Outside, the proud village **church** (step inside and admire the heroic St. Peter above the altar) and city hall preside over the central plaza, from which the town streets radiate to the broad lagoon that surrounds the town.

At the watery lagoon-ends of the streets, village men set out in the late afternoon in canoes and boats for the open-ocean fishing grounds where, as night falls and kerosene lanterns are used, they attract shrimp into their nets. Occasionally during the rainy season, water floods

AZTLÁN

During their first meeting in imperial Tenochtitlán, the Aztec Emperor Moctezuma informed Hernán Cortés that "from the records which we have long possessed and which are handed down from our ancestors, it is known that no one, neither I nor the others who inhabit this land of Anahuac, are native to it. We are strangers and we came from far outer parts."

Although the Aztecs had forgotten exactly where it was, they agreed on the name and nature of the place from which they came: Aztlán, a magical island with seven allegorical caves, each representing an Aztec subtribe—of which the Mexica, last to complete the migration, had clawed its way to dominion. Aztlán, the Aztecs also knew, lay somewhere vaguely to the northwest, and their migration to Anahuac, the present-day Valley of Mexico, had taken many generations.

For centuries, historians puzzled and argued over the precise location of Aztlán, placing it as far away as Alaska and as near as Lake Chapala. This is curious, for there was an actual Aztlán, a chiefdom, well known at the time of the Spanish conquest. Renegade conquistador Nuño de Guzmán immediately determined its location, and three days before Christmas in 1529, he headed out with a small army of followers, driven by dreams of an Aztec empire in western Mexico. However, when Guzmán arrived at Aztlán—present-day San Felipe Aztatlán village, near Tuxpan in Nayarit—he found no golden city. Others who followed, such as Vásquez de Coronado and Francisco de Ibarra, vainly continued to scour northwestern Mexico, seeking the mythical "Seven Cities of Cíbola," which they confused with the legend of Aztlán's seven caves.

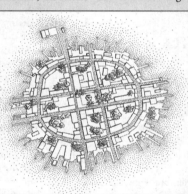

Guzmán probably came closest to the original site. Scarcely a dozen miles due west of his trail through San Felipe Aztatlán is the small island-town of Mexcaltitán, which a number of experts now believe to be the original Aztlán. Many circumstances compel their argument. The spelling common to Mexcaltitán and Mexica is no coincidence, they say. The name Aztlán, furthermore, is probably a contraction of Aztatlán, which translates as Place of the Herons—the birds flock in abundance around Mexcaltitán. Moreover, a 1579 map of New Spain by renowned cartographer Ortelius shows an "Aztlán" exactly where Mexcaltitán is today.

The argument goes on: the Codex Boturini, a 16th-century reconstruction of previous Aztec records, reveals a pictogram of Aztecs leaving Aztlán, punting a canoe with an oar. Both the peculiar shape of the canoe and the manner of punting are common to both old Tenochtitlán and present-day Mexcaltitán.

Most compelling, perhaps, is the layout of Mexcaltitán itself. As in a pocket-sized Tenochtitlán, north-south and east-west avenues radiate from a central plaza, dividing the island into four quadrant neighborhoods. A singular, circular plaza-centered street arcs through the avenues, joining the neighborhoods.

If you visit Mexcaltitán, you'll find it's easy to imagine Aztec life as it must have been in Tenochtitlán of old, where many people depended on fishing, rarely left their island, and, especially during the rainy season, navigated their city streets in canoes.

N
TO PV/GUADALAJARA

the entire town, so that folks must navigate the streets as Venice-style canals.

Accommodations and Food

At the view-edge of the lagoon behind the museum is Mexcaltitán's first official tourist lodging, the **Hotel Ruta Azteca.** More like a guesthouse than a hotel, it offers four clean, bare-bulb rooms with bath, renting from about $12. Except for the last week in June, reservations are not usually necessary. You may, however, be able to contact the hotel in advance by calling the town telephone operator (in Spanish), tel. 323/232-0426, and asking for the hotel extension 128.

On the town plaza opposite the church stands airy **El Camarón** seafood restaurant. (Better supplied, however, is the oft-raucous south-side embarcadero restaurant and bar.)

SANTIAGO IXCUINTLA

If you take the southern approach to Mexcaltitán, you get the added bonus of Santiago Ixcuintla (pop. 20,000—eeks-KOOEEN-tlah) on the north bank of the Río Grande de Santiago, Mexico's longest river. Get there via the signed turnoff from Highway 15, 38 miles (60 km) north of Tepic; continue five miles to the town.

Just past the solitary hill that marks the town, turn right at the first opportunity, on to the one-way main street 20 de Noviembre, which in a couple of blocks runs past the picturesque main plaza. Linger a bit to admire the voluptuous Porfirian nymphs who decorate the restored bandstand and the pretty colonial church. Stroll beneath the shaded porticos and visit the colorful market two blocks north of the plaza.

Although its scenic appeal is considerable, the Huichol people are the best reason to come to Santiago Ixcuintla. Hundreds of Huichol families migrate seasonally (late winter and early spring, especially) from their Sierra Madre high-country homeland to work for a few dollars a day in the local tobacco fields. For many Huichol, their migration in search of money includes a serious hidden cost. In the mountains, they have their homes, their friends and relatives around them, and the familiar rituals and ceremonies they have tenaciously preserved in their centuries-long struggle against Mexicanization. But when the Huichol come to lowland towns and cities, they often encounter the mocking laughter and hostile stares of townspeople, whose Spanish language they do not understand, and whose city ways seem alien. As strangers in a strange land, the pressure for the migrant Huichol to give up their old costumes, language, and ceremonies to become like everyone else is powerful indeed.

Centro Cultural Huichol

Be sure to reserve part of your time in Santiago Ixcuintla to stop by the Centro Cultural Huichol, 20 de Noviembre 452, Santiago Ixcuintla, Nayarit 63300, tel. 323/235-1171, fax 323/235-1006. The immediate mission of founders Mariano and Susana Valadez—he a Huichol artist and community leader, and she a U.S.-born anthropologist—is to ensure that the Huichol people endure, with their traditions intact and growing. Their instrument is the Centro Cultural Huichol—a clinic, dining hall, dormitory, library, craftsmaking shop, sale gallery, and interpretive center—which provides crucial focus and support for local migratory Huichol people.

Lately, Susana has opened another center high in the mountains in Huejuquilla, Jalisco, tel. 457/983-7000, while Mariano, with the help of their daughter Angélica, continues the original mission in Santiago Ixquintla. As well as filling vital human needs, the Huichol Cultural Center actively nurtures the vital elements of an endangered heritage. This heritage belongs not only to the Huichol, but to the lost generations of indigenous peoples—Aleut, Yahi, Lacandones, and myriad others—who succumbed to European diseases and were massacred in innumerable fields, from Wounded Knee and the Valley of Mexico all the way to Tierra del Fuego.

Although they concentrate on the immediate needs of people, Mariano, Susana, and Angélica and their volunteer staff also reach out to local, national, and international communities. Their center's entry corridor, for example, is decorated with illustrated Huichol legends in Spanish, especially for Mexican visitors. An adjacent gallery exhibits a treasury of Huichol art for sale—yarn paintings, masks, jewelry, gourds, God's eyes—adorned with the colorful deities and animated heavenly motifs of the Huichol pantheon.

The Centro Cultural Huichol invites volunteers, especially those with secretarial, computer, language, and other skills, to help with projects in the center. If you don't have the time, the center also solicits donations of money and equipment (such as a good computer or two).

Get to the Centro Cultural Huichol by heading away from the river, along 20 de Noviembre, the main street that borders the central plaza. Within a mile, you'll see the Centro Cultural Huichol, no. 452, on the right.

Accommodations

If you decide to stay overnight in Santiago Ixcuintla, consider the **Hotel Casino** near the plaza downtown, at Arteaga and Ocampo, Santiago Ixcuintla, Nayarit, tel./fax 323/235-0850, 323/235-0851, or 323/235-0852. It has a respectable downstairs restaurant/bar and about 35 basic rooms around an inner parking patio for $24 d, with a/c and parking.

Services

Santiago Ixcuintla is an important regional business center, with a number of services. Banks, all with 24-hour ATMs, include long-hours Bital (Banco Internacional), open Mon.–Sat. 8 A.M.–7 P.M., south side of the plaza, at Hidalgo and Zaragoza;

THE HUICHOL

Because the Huichol have retained more of their traditional religion than perhaps any other group of indigenous Mexicans, they offer a glimpse into the lives and beliefs of dozens of now-vanished Mesoamerican peoples.

The Huichol's natural wariness, plus their isolation in rugged mountain canyons and valleys, has saved them from the ravages of modern Mexico. Despite increased tourist, government, and mestizo contact, prosperity and better health swelled the Huichol population to around 20,000 by the late 1990s.

Although many have migrated to coastal farming towns and cities such as Tepic and Guadalajara, several thousand Huichol remain in their ancestral heartland—roughly 50 miles (80 km) northeast of Tepic as the crow flies. They cultivate corn and raise cattle on 400 *rancherías* in five municipalities not far from the winding Altengo River valley: Guadalupe Ocotán in Nayarit; and Tuxpan de Bolaños, San Sebastián Teponahuaxtlán, Santa Catarina, and San Andrés Cohamiata in Jalisco.

Although studied by a procession of researchers since Carl Lumholtz's seminal work in the 1890s, the remote Huichol and their religion remain enigmatic. As Lumholtz said, "Religion to them is a personal matter, not an institution and therefore their life is religion—from the cradle to the grave, wrapped up in symbolism."

Hints of what it means to be Huichol come from their art. Huichol art contains representations of the prototype deities—Grandfather Sun, Grandmother Earth, Brother Deer, Mother Maize—that once guided the destinies of many North American peoples. It blooms with tangible religious symbols, from green-faced Mother Earth (Tatei Urianaka) and the dripping Rain Goddess (Tatei Matiniera), to the ray-festooned Father Sun (Tayau) and the antlered folk hero Brother Kauyumari, forever battling the evil sorcerer Kieri.

The Huichol are famous for their use of the hallucinogen peyote, their bridge to the divine. The humble cactus—from which the peyote "buttons" are gathered and eaten—grows in the Huichol's Elysian land of Wirikuta, in the San Luis Potosí desert 300 miles east of their homeland, near the town of Real de Catorce.

To the Huichol, a journey to Wirikuta is a dangerous trip to heaven. Preparations go on for weeks and include innumerable prayers and ceremonies, as well as the crafting of feathered arrows, bowls, gourds, and paintings for the gods who live along the way. Only the chosen—village shamans, temple elders, those fulfilling vows or seeking visions—may make the journey. Each participant in effect becomes a god whose identity and very life are divined and protected by the shaman en route to Wirikuta.

TO PV/GUADALAJARA

Banamex at 20 de Noviembre and Hidalgo, tel. 323/235-0053, open Mon.–Fri. 9 A.M.–4 P.M.; and Bancomer, at 20 de Noviembre and Morelos, tel. 323/235-0535, open Mon.–Fri. 9 A.M.–4 P.M., Sat. 10 A.M.–2 P.M.

Find the *correo* (post office) at Allende 23, tel. 323/235-0214, east side of the plaza. *Telecomu-*nicaciones, including telegraph, long-distance phone, and public fax, is available at Zaragoza Ote. 200, tel. 323/235-0989.

Unleaded (Magna) gasoline is customarily available at the Pemex station on the east-side highway (toward Highway 15) as you head out of town.

San Blas and Vicinity

San Blas (pop. about 15,000) is a small town slumbering beneath a big coconut grove. Life goes on in the plaza as if San Blas has always been an ordinary Mexican village. But once San Blas was anything but ordinary. During its latter 18th-century glory days, San Blas was Mexico's burgeoning Pacific military headquarters and port, with a population of 30,000. Ships from Spain's Pacific Rim colonies crowded its harbor, silks and gold filled its counting houses, and noble Spanish officers and their mantilla-graced ladies strolled the plaza on Sunday afternoons.

Times change, however. Politics and San Blas's pesky *jejenes* (hey-HEY-nays, invisible "no-see-um" biting gnats) have always conspired to deflate any temporary fortunes of San Blas. The *jejenes'* breeding ground, a vast hinterland of mangrove marshes, may paradoxically give rise to a new, more prosperous San Blas. These thousands of acres of waterlogged mangrove jungle and savanna are a nursery-home for dozens of Mexico's endangered species. This rich trove is now protected by ecologically aware governments and admired (not unlike the game parks of Africa) by increasing numbers of ecotourists.

HISTORY
Conquest and Colonization
San Blas and the neighboring, southward-curving Bay of Matanchén were reconnoitered by gold-hungry conquistador Nuño de Guzmán in May 1530. His expedition noted the protected anchorages in the bay and the Estero el Pozo adjacent to the present town. Occasionally during the 16th and 17th centuries, Spanish explorers in their galleons and the pirates lying in wait for them would drop anchor in the *estero* or the adjacent Bay of Matanchén for rendezvous, resupply, or cargo-transfer.

By the latter third of the 18th century, New Spain, reacting to the Russian and English threats in the North Pacific, launched plans for the colonization of California through a new port called San Blas.

The town was officially founded atop the hill of San Basilio in 1768. Streets were surveyed; docks were built. Old documents record that more than 100 pioneer families received a plot of land and "a pick, an adze, an axe, a machete, a plow . . . a pair of oxen, a cow, a mule, four she-goats and a billy, four sheep, a sow, four hens and a rooster."

People and animals multiplied, and soon San Blas became the seat of Spain's eastern Pacific naval command. Meanwhile, simultaneously with the founding of the town, the celebrated Father Junípero Serra set out for California with 14 missionary-brothers on *La Concepción,* a sailing vessel built on Matanchén beach just south of San Blas.

Independence
New Spain's colonial grandeur, however, crumbled in the bloody 1810–1821 war for independence, taking San Blas with it. In December 1810, the *insurgente* commander captured the Spanish fort atop San Basilio hill and sent 43 of its cannons to fellow rebel-priest Miguel Hidalgo to use against the loyalists around Guadalajara.

After independence, fewer and fewer ships called at San Blas; the docks fell into disrepair, and the town slipped into somnolence, then complete slumber when President Lerdo de Tejada closed San Blas to foreign commerce in 1872.

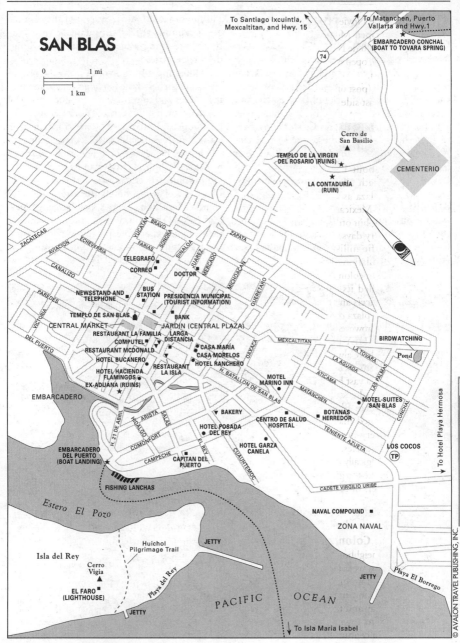

SAN BLAS

0   1 mi

0   1 km

To Santiago Ixcuintla,
Mexcaltitan, and Hwy. 15

To Matanchen, Puerto
Vallarta and Hwy.1

EMBARCADERO CONCHAL
(BOAT TO TOVARA SPRING)

74

Cerro de
San Basilio

TEMPLO DE LA VIRGEN
DEL ROSARIO (RUINS)

CEMENTERIO

LA CONTADURÍA
(RUIN)

ZACATECAS

AVIACIÓN

ECHEVERRIA

YUCATÁN

BRAVO

FARIAS

SONORA

SINALOA

JUAREZ

MERCADO

MICHOACAN

ZAPATA

CANALIZO

TELEGRAFO

CORREO

DOCTOR

QUERETARO

PAREDES

NEWSSTAND AND
TELEPHONE

BUS
STATION

PRESIDENCIA MUNICIPAL
(TOURIST INFORMATION)

VICTORIA

TEMPLO DE SAN BLAS

BANK

MEXCALTITAN

BIRDWATCHING

DEL PUERTO

CENTRAL MARKET

JARDIN (CENTRAL PLAZA)

RESTAURANT LA FAMILIA

COMPUTEL

LARGA
DISTANCIA

CASA MARÍA

LA TOVARA

Pond

RESTAURANT McDONALD

CASA MORELOS

LA AGUADA

HOTEL BUCANERO

HOTEL RANCHERO

RESTAURANT
LA ISLA

ATICAMA

LAS PALMAS

HOTEL HACIENDA
FLAMINGOS

H. BATALLON DE SAN BLAS

MOTEL
MARINO INN

EX-ADUANA (RUINS)

MATANCHEN

MOTEL-SUITES
SAN BLAS

EMBARCADERO

H. 21 DE ABRIL

HIDALGO

ARISTA

SALAS

CONCHAL

BAKERY

BOTANAS
HERREDOR

LOS COCOS

COMONFORT

CENTRO DE SALUD
HOSPITAL

TENIENTE AZUETA

TP

EMBARCADERO
DEL PUERTO
(BOAT LANDING)

HOTEL POSADA
DEL REY

CAMPECHE

CAPITAN DEL
PUERTO

EL REY

CUAUHTEMOC

HOTEL GARZA
CANELA

To Hotel Playa Hermosa

FISHING LANCHAS

CADETE VIRGILIO URIBE

Estero El Pozo

NAVAL COMPOUND

ZONA NAVAL

Isla del Rey

Huichol
Pilgrimage Trail

JETTY

Cerro
Vigia

Playa del Rey

JETTY

Playa El Borrego

EL FARO
(LIGHTHOUSE)

JETTY

PACIFIC   OCEAN

To Isla Maria Isabel

TO PV/GUADALAJARA

SIGHTS AND ACTIVITIES

Getting Oriented

The overlook atop the **Cerro de San Basilio** is the best spot to orient yourself to San Blas. From this breezy point, the palm-shaded grid of streets stretches to the sunset side of **El Pozo** estuary and the lighthouse-hill beyond it. Behind you, on the east, the mangrove-lined **San Cristóbal** river-estuary meanders south to the Bay of Matanchén. Along the south shore, the crystalline white line of San Blas's main beach, **Playa el Borrego** (Sheep Beach), stretches between the two estuary mouths.

Around Town

While you're atop the hill, take a look around the old *contaduria* counting house and fort (built in 1770), where riches were tallied and stored en route to Mexico City or to the Philippines and China. Several of the original great cannons still stand guard at the viewpoint like aging sentinels waiting for long-dead adversaries.

Behind and a bit downhill from the weathered stone arches of the *contaduria* stand the gaping portals and towering, moss-stained belfry of the old church of **Nuestra Señora del Rosario,** built in 1769. Undamaged by war, it remained an active church until at least 1872, around the time when poet Henry W. Longfellow was inspired by the silencing and removal of its aging bells.

Downhill, historic houses and ruins dot San Blas town. The old hotels **Bucanero** and **Hacienda Flamingos** on the main street, Juárez, leading past the central plaza, preserve some of their original charm. Just across the street from the Hacienda Flamingos, you can admire the crumbling yet monumental brick colonnade of

THE BELLS OF SAN BLAS

Renowned Romantic poet Henry Wadsworth Longfellow (1807–1882) most likely read about San Blas during the early 1870s, just after the town's door was closed to foreign trade. With the ships gone, and not even the trickle of tourists it now enjoys, the San Blas of Longfellow's time was perhaps even dustier and quieter than it is today.

San Blas must have meant quite a lot to him. Ten years later, ill and dying, Longfellow hastened to complete "The Bells of San Blas," his very last poem, finished nine days before he died on March 24, 1882. Longfellow wrote of the silent bells of the old Nuestro Señora del Rosario (Our Lady of the Rosary) church, which still stands atop the Cerro San Basilio, little changed to this day.

The Bells of San Blas

What say the Bells of San Blas
To the ships that southward pass
From the harbor of Mazatlán?
To them it is nothing more
Than the sound of surf on the shore,—
Nothing more to master or man.

But to me, a dreamer of dreams,
To whom what is and what seems
Are often one and the same,—
The Bells of San Blas to me
Have a strange, wild melody,
And are something more than a name.

For bells are the voice of the church;
They have tones that touch and search
The hearts of young and old;
One sound to all, yet each
Lends a meaning to their speech,
And the meaning is manifold.

They are a voice of the Past,
Of an age that is fading fast,
Of a power austere and grand;
When the flag of Spain unfurled
Its folds o'er this western world,
And the Priest was lord of the land.

the 19th-century former **Aduana,** now replaced by a nondescript new customshouse at the estuary-foot of Av. Juárez.

At that shoreline spot, gaze across El Pozo estuary. This was both the jumping-off point for colonization of the Californias and the anchorage of the silk- and porcelain-laden Manila *galeón* and the bullion ships from the northern mines.

El Faro (lighthouse) across the estuary marks the top of **Cerro Vigía,** the southern hill-tip of Isla del Rey (actually a peninsula). Here, the first beacon shone during the latter third of the 18th century.

Although only a few local folks ever bother to cross over to the island, it is nevertheless an important pilgrimage site for Huichol people from the remote Nayarit and Jalisco mountains. Huichol have been gathering on the Isla del Rey for centuries to make offerings to Aramara, their goddess of the sea. A not-so-coincidental shrine

to a Catholic virgin-saint stands on an offshore sea rock, visible from the beach-endpoint of the Huichol pilgrimage a few hundred yards beyond the lighthouse.

A large cave sacred to the Huichol at the foot of Cerro Vigía was sadly demolished by the government during the early 1970s for rock for a breakwater. Fortunately, President Salinas de Gortari (1988–1994) partly compensated for the insult by deeding the sacred site to the Huichols during the early 1990s.

Two weeks before Easter, Huichol people begin arriving by the dozens, the men decked out in flamboyant feathered hats. On the ocean beach, 10 minutes' walk straight across the island, anyone can respectfully watch them perform their rituals: elaborate marriages, feasts, and offerings of little boats laden with arrows and food, consecrated to the sea goddess to

The chapel that once looked down
On the little seaport town
Has crumbled into the dust
And on oaken beams below
The bells swing to and fro,
And are green with mould and rust.

"Is then, the old faith dead,"
They say, "and in its stead
Is some new faith proclaimed,
That we are forced to remain
Naked to sun and rain,
Unsheltered and ashamed?

"Once in our tower aloof
We rang over wall and roof
Our warnings and our complaints;
And round about us there
The white doves filled the air,
Like the white souls of the saints.

"The saints! Ah, have they grown
Forgetful of their own?
Are they asleep, or dead,
That open to the sky

Their ruined Missions lie,
No longer tenanted?

"Oh, bring us back once more
The vanished days of yore,
When the world with faith was filled;
Bring back the fervid zeal,
The hearts of fire and steel,
The hands that believe and build.

"Then from our tower again
We will send over land and main
Our voices of command,
Like exiled kings who return
To their thrones, and the people learn
That the Priest is lord of the land!"

O Bells of San Blas, in vain
Ye call back the Past again!
The Past is deaf to your prayer;
Out of the shadows of night
The world rolls into light;
It is daybreak everywhere.

—Henry Wadsworth Longfellow

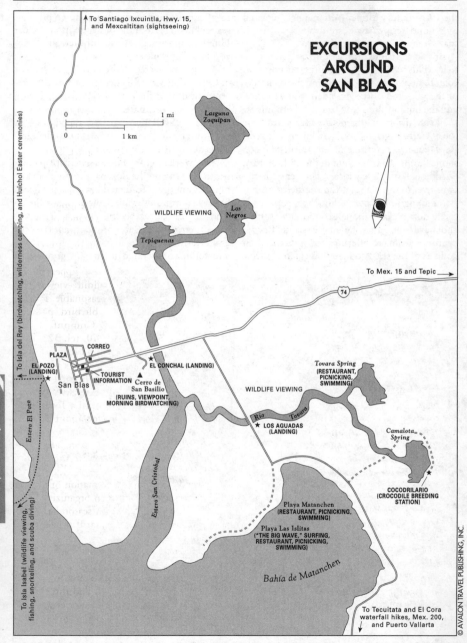

EXCURSIONS AROUND SAN BLAS

To Santiago Ixcuintla, Hwy. 15, and Mexcaltitan (sightseeing)

To Isla del Rey (birdwatching, wilderness camping, and Huichol Easter ceremonies)

Lasguna Zoquipan

Los Negros

WILDLIFE VIEWING

Tepiquenas

To Mex. 15 and Tepic

74

CORREO

PLAZA

EL POZO (LANDING)

TOURIST INFORMATION

San Blas

EL CONCHAL (LANDING)

Cerro de San Basilio (RUINS, VIEWPOINT, MORNING BIRDWATCHING)

Tovara Spring (RESTAURANT, PICNICKING, SWIMMING)

WILDLIFE VIEWING

Río Tovara

LOS AGUADAS (LANDING)

Camalota Spring

COCODRILARIO (CROCODILE BREEDING STATION)

Estero El Pozo

Estero San Cristobal

To Isla Isabel (wildlife viewing, fishing, snorkeling, and scuba diving)

Playa Matanchen (RESTAURANT, PICNICKING, SWIMMING)

Playa Las Islitas ("THE BIG WAVE," SURFING, RESTAURANT, PICNICKING, SWIMMING)

Bahía de Matanchen

To Tecuitata and El Cora waterfall hikes, Mex. 200, and Puerto Vallarta

0   1 mi
0   1 km

© AVALON TRAVEL PUBLISHING, INC.

TO PV/GUADALAJARA

ensure good hunting and crops and many healthy children.

Hotel Playa Hermosa

For a glimpse of a relic from San Blas's recent past, head across town to the crumbling Hotel Playa Hermosa. Here, one evening in 1951, President Miguel Alemán came to dedicate San Blas's first luxury hotel. As the story goes, the *jejenes* descended and bit the president so fiercely the entire entourage cleared out before he even finished his speech. Rumors have circulated around town for years that someone's going to reopen the Playa Hermosa, but—judging from the vines creeping up the walls and the orchids blossoming on the balconies—they'd better hurry or the jungle is going to get the old place first. To get there follow H. Batallón toward the beach, turn left just after the Los Cocos Trailer Park, and continue along the jungle road for about half a mile.

La Tovara Jungle River Trip

On the downstream side of the bridge over Estero San Cristóbal, launches-for-hire will take you up the Río Tovara, a side channel that winds about a mile downstream into the jungle.

The channel quickly narrows into a dark tree-tunnel, edged by great curtainlike swaths of mangrove roots. Big snowy *garza* (egrets) peer out from leafy branches; startled turtles slip off their soggy perches into the river, while big submerged roots, like gigantic pythons, bulge out of the inky water. Riots of luxuriant plants—white lilies, green ferns, red *romelia* orchids—hang from the trees and line the banks.

Finally you reach Tovara Springs, which well from the base of a verdant cliffside. On one side, a bamboo-sheltered *palapa* restaurant serves refreshments, while on the other families picnic in a hillside pavilion. In the middle, everyone jumps in and paddles in the clear, cool water.

You can enjoy this trip either of two ways: the longer, three-hour excursion as described ($40 per boatload of six to eight) from El Conchal landing on the estuary, or the shorter version (two hours, $30 per boatload) beginning upriver at road-accessible Las Aguadas near

Matanchén village. Take the hourly Matanchén bus from the San Blas central plaza. *Note:* Sometimes a tourist crowd draws all of the boats away from La Conchal to Las Aguadas (to go there instead, see map "Excursions Around San Blas").

The more leisurely three-hour trip allows more chances (especially in the early morning) to spot a jaguar or crocodile, or a giant boa constrictor hanging from a limb (no kidding). Many of the boatmen are very professional; if you want to view wildlife, tell them, and they'll go more slowly and keep a sharp lookout.

Some boatmen offer more extensive trips to less-disturbed sites deeper in the jungle. These include the Camalota spring, a branch of the Río Tovara (where a local *ejido* maintains a crocodile breeding station) and the even more remote and pristine Tepiqueñas, Los Negros, and Zoquipan lagoons in the San Cristóbal Estero's upper reaches.

In light of the possible wildlife-viewing rewards, trip prices are very reasonable. For example, the very knowledgeable bird specialist Oscar Partida Hernández, Comonfort 134 Pte., San Blas, Nayarit 63740, tel. 323/285-0324, will guide a four-person boatload to La Tovara for about $60. If Oscar is busy, call "Chencho," tel. 323/285-0716, for a comparably excellent trip. More extensive options include a combined Camalota-La Tovara trip (allow four to five hours) for about $90, or Tepiqueñas and Los Negros (six hours) for about $100. For each extra person, add about $8, $12, and $16, respectively, to the price of each of these options.

The San Blas tourist information office (see under Information) has been organizing daily money-saving, collective high-season La Tovara boat tours for visitors. The tariff usually runs about $6 per person.

Isla Isabel

Isla Isabel is a two-mile-square offshore wildlife study area 40 miles (65 km) and three hours north by boat. The cone of an extinct volcano, Isla Isabel is now home to a small government station of ecoscientists and a host of nesting boobies, frigate birds, and white-tailed tropic

Birds are sometimes so thick in San Blas's mangrove wetland that they appear as snow on trees.

birds. Fish and sea mammals, especially dolphins, and sometimes whales, abound in the surrounding clear waters. Although it's not a recreational area, local authorities allow serious visitors, accompanied by authorized guides, for a few days of camping, snorkeling, scuba diving, and wildlife-viewing. A primitive dormitory can accommodate several people. Bring everything, including food and bedding. Contact English-speaking Tony Aguayo or Armando Navarrete for arrangements and prices, which typically run $200 per day for parties of up to four people. Two- and three-day extensions run about $250 and $300, respectively. Stormy summer and fall weather limits most Isla Isabel trips to the sunnier, calmer winter-spring season. Tony and Armando's "office" is the little *palapa* to the left of the small floating boat dock at the El Pozo estuary end of Juárez. Tony can also be reached by tel. 323/285-0364 or cellular tel. 01-311/102-3107; Armando at home, at Sonora 179, in San Blas. Also recommended for the Isla Isabel trip is Antonio Palma, whom you can contact by asking Josefina Vasquéz at the Hotel Garza Canela front desk.

Bird-Watching

Although San Blas's extensive mangrove and mountain jungle hinterlands are renowned for their birds and wildlife, rewarding bird-watching can start in the early morning right at the edge of town. Follow Calle Conchal right (southeast) one block from Suites San Blas, then left (northeast) to a small pond. With binoculars, you might get some good views of local species of cormorants, flycatchers, grebes, herons, jacanas, and motmots. A copy of Chalif and Petersen's *Field Guide to Mexican Birds* or Steve Howell's *Bird-Finding Guide to Mexico* (see Suggested Reading) will assist in further identification.

Rewarding bird-watching is also possible on **Isla del Rey.** Bargain for a launch (from the foot of Juárez, about $2 round-trip) across to the opposite shore. Watch for wood, clapper, and Virginia rails, and boat-billed herons near the estuary shore. Then follow the track across the island (looking for warblers and a number of species of sparrows) to the beach where you might enjoy good views of plovers, terns, Heerman's gulls, and rafts of pelicans.

Alternatively, look around the hillside cemetery and the ruins atop **Cerro de San Basilio** for good early morning views of hummingbirds, falcons, owls, and American redstarts.

You can include serious bird-watching with your boat trip through the mangrove channels branching from the **Estero San Cristóbal** and the **Río Tovara.** This is especially true if you obtain the services of a wildlife-sensitive guide, such as Oscar Partida, tel. 323/285-0324, "Chencho," tel. 323/285-0716, or Juan "Bananas" Garcia, tel. 323/285-0462.

For more details on bird-watching and hiking around San Blas, get a copy of the booklet *Where to Find Birds in San Blas, Nayarit* by Rosalind Novick and Lan Sing Wu, at the shop at Garza Canela Hotel ($4). Or order from them directly at 178 Myrtle Court, Arcata, CA 95521. The American Birding Association Bookstore, P.O. Box 6599, Colorado Springs, CO 80934, and the Los Angeles and Tucson Audubon Society bookstores also may stock it.

Waterfall Hikes

A number of waterfalls decorate the lush jungle foothills above the Bay of Matanchén. Two of these, near Tecuitata and El Cora villages, respectively, are accessible from Highway 74 about 10 miles (16 km) south of San Blas. The local white bus *(autobús blanco)* will take you most of the way. It runs south to Santa Cruz every two hours 8:30 A.M.–4:30 P.M. from the downtown corner of Juárez and Paredes. (See the access details under Waterfall Hikes in Around the Bay of Matanchén.)

While rugged adventurers may guide themselves to the waterfalls, others rely upon guides Armando Navarrette (Sonora 179, San Blas), and local ecoleader Juan "Bananas" Garcia, who works out of his café-shop, at H. Batallón 219 (tel. 323/285-0462), four blocks south of the plaza, or Lucio Rodríguez (inquire at Tourist Information, on Mercado, one block south, half a block east of the plaza, or with Josefina Vasquéz at the Hotel Garza Canela).

Besides the above, Armando Navarette offers bird-watching hikes, especially around Singayta in the foothills, where birders routinely identify 30–40 species in a two-hour adventure. Such an excursion might also include a coffee plantation visit, hiking along the old royal road to Tepic, and plenty of tropical fauna and flora, including butterflies, wildflowers, and giant vines and trees, such as *ceiba, arbolde,* and the peeling, red *papillo* tree. Armando's fee for such a trip, lasting around five hours, runs about $12 per person, plus your own or rented transportation.

Beach Activities

San Blas's most convenient beach is **Playa el Borrego,** at the south end of Calle Cuauhtémoc about a mile south of town. With a lineup of *palapas* for food and drinks, the mile-long, broad, fine-sand beach is ripe for all beach activities except snorkeling (because of the murky water). The gradually breaking waves provide boogie boarding and intermediate surfing challenges. Bring your own equipment, as no one rents on the beach; although Juan "Bananas" Garcia rents snorkels, surfboards, and boogie boards at his café-shop, at H. Battallón 219, four blocks south of the town plaza.

Shoals of shells—clams, cockles, mother-of-pearl—wash up on Borrego Beach during storms. Fishing is often good, especially when casting from the jetty and rocks at the north and south ends.

ACCOMMODATIONS

Hotels

San Blas has several hotels, none of them huge, but all with personality. They are not likely to be full even during the high winter season (unless the surf off Mantanchén Beach runs high for an unusually long spell).

At the low end, the family-run *casa de huéspedes* (guesthouse) **Casa María,** tel. 323/285-0820, makes a reality of the old Spanish saying, *"Mi casa es tu casa."* It is at the corner of Canalizo and Michoacán, three blocks from the plaza. There are about eight rooms around a homey, cluttered patio, and María offers to do everything for the guests except give them baths (which she would probably do if someone got sick). Not too clean, but very friendly and with kitchen privileges. Rooms rent for about $20 s or d, with fans, hot water showers, kitchen and washing machine included.

SAN BLAS ACCOMMODATIONS BY PRICE

Accommodations (area code 323, postal code 63740) are listed in increasing order of approximate high-season, double-room rates.

Casa Morelos, H. Batallón 108, tel. 285-0820, $15

Hotel Ranchero, Esquina Batallón y Michoacán, tel. 285-0820, $15

Casa María, Esquina Canalizo y Michoacán, tel. 285-0820, $20

Hotel Bucanero, Juárez 75, tel. 285-0101, $25

Motel-Suites San Blas, Aticama and Las Palmas, tel. 285-0505, $27

Hotel Posada del Rey, Campeche 10, tel. 285-0123, $32

Motel Marino Inn, H. Batallón s/n, tel. 285-0303, $35

Hotel Hacienda Flamingos, Juárez 105, tel. 285-0485, technica@red2000.com.mx, $72

Hotel Garza Canela, Paredes 106 Sur, tel. 285-0112 or 285-0480, fax 285-0308, hotel@garzacanela.com, $115

Alternatively, you can try María's original guesthouse, **Casa Morelos** at 108 Heróico Batallón, operated by her daughter, Magdalena, who accepts no reservations, or **Hotel Ranchero,** operated by her ex-husband Alfredo, right across the street. They each offer about five rooms around homey plant-filled patios for similar rates (about $15 s or d). María, Magdalena, and Alfredo all cooperate for the benefit of guests; if one is full, they'll probably be able to find a room next door for you.

Back in the middle of town, newly renovated **Hotel Hacienda Flamingos** lives on as a splendid reminder of old San Blas. It's at Juárez 105, San Blas, Nayarit 63740, three blocks down Juárez from the plaza, tel. 323/285-0485, technica@red2000.com.mx. Owners have spared little in restoring this 1863 German consulate to its original graceful condition. Now, the fountain flows once more in the tranquil, tropical inner patio, furnished with period chairs and tables

and a gallery of old San Blas photos on the walls. A side door leads outside to a luxuriously spacious adjoining garden, sprinkled with recliners, a grass badminton court, and a croquet set ready for service. Inside, the rooms are no less than you'd expect: luxuriously airy and high-ceilinged, with elegantly simple decor, replete with Porfirian-era touches and wall art; with baths, gleaming with polished traditional-style fixtures. Year-round rates for the 10 rooms run about $72 d ($92 weekends).

Half a block along Juárez, the **Hotel Bucanero** appears to be living up to its name at Calle Juárez 75, San Blas, Nayarit 63740, a block from the plaza, tel. 323/285-0101. A stanza from the *Song of the Pirate* emblazons one wall, a big stuffed crocodile bares its teeth beside the other, and a crusty sunken anchor and cannons decorate the shady patio. Despite peeling paint the rooms retain a bit of spacious, old-world charm, with high-beamed ceilings under the ruddy roof tile. (High, circular vent windows in some rooms cannot be closed, however. Use repellent or your mosquito net.) Outside, the big pool and leafy old patio/courtyard provide plenty of nooks for daytime snoozing and socializing. A noisy nighttime (winter-spring seasonal) bar, however, keeps most guests without earplugs jumping till about midnight. The 32 rooms run, low season, about $15 s, $20 d; with ceiling fans and hot water.

San Blas's modern-era hotels are nearer the water. Foremost is the excellent, resort-style **Hotel Garza Canela,** Paredes 106 Sur C.P., San Blas, Nayarit 63740, tucked away at the south end of town, two blocks off H. Batallón, tel. 323/285-0112, 323/285-0307, or 323/285-0480, fax 323/285-0308, hotel@garzacanela.com, www.garzacanela.com. The careful management of its Vásquez family owners (Señorita Josefina Vasquez in charge) shows everywhere: manicured palm-shaded gardens, crystal-blue pool, immaculate sundeck, and centerpiece restaurant. The 60 cool, air-conditioned rooms are tiled, tastefully furnished, and squeaky clean. Rates run about $92 s, $115 d high season, $65 and $96 low, with a hearty breakfast included and credit cards accepted. The family also runs a travel agency and an outstanding crafts and gift shop on the premises.

The lively family-operated **Hotel Posada del Rey,** Calle Campeche 10, San Blas, Nayarit 63740, tel. 323/285-0123, seems to be trying hardest. It encloses a small but inviting pool and patio beneath a top-floor viewpoint bar (and high-season-only restaurant) that bubbles with continuous soft rock and salsa tunes. Year-round asking rates for the 13 rooms are about $32 s or d, with a/c; credit cards are not accepted. Bargain for a low-season discount.

In the palm-shadowed, country fringe of town not far from Playa Borrego is the **Motel-Suites San Blas.** at Calles Aticama and Las Palmas, San Blas, Nayarit 63740, tel. 323/285-0505, left off H. Batallón a few blocks after the Motel Marino. Its pool, patio, playground, game room, and spacious but somewhat worn suites with kitchenettes (dishes and utensils *not* included) are nicely suited for active families. The 23 fan-only suites include 16 one-bedrooms for two adults and kids renting for about $27, and seven two-bedrooms accommodating four adults with kids for about $60; credit cards are accepted.

Although the facilities of the four-star **Motel Marino Inn** look fine on paper, the place is bare of most usual hotel amenities. Rooms, however, although plain and mostly bare-bulb, are comfortable enough for a few nights. You'll find it at Av. H. Batallón s/n, San Blas, Nayarit 63740, tel. 323/285-0303. The 60 rooms go for about $35 s or d except holidays, with a/c and a pool (when it's working) and private balconies. Credit cards are accepted.

Trailer Park

San Blas's only trailer park, the **Los Cocos,** at H. Batallón s/n, San Blas, Nayarit 63740, tel. 323/285-0055, is a two-minute walk from the wide, yellow sands of Playa el Borrego. Friendly management, spacious, palm-shaded grassy grounds, pull-throughs, unusually clean showers and toilet facilities, a laundry next door, fishing, and a good, air-conditioned bar with satellite TV all make this place a magnet for RVers and tenters from Mazatlán to Puerto Vallarta. The biting *jejenes* require the use of strong repellent for residents to enjoy the balmy evenings. The 100 spaces rent for about $13/day for two people,

$2 for each additional person, with all hookups, one day free per week for longer-term stays.

Camping

The *jejenes* and occasional local toughs and Peeping Toms make camping on close-in Borrego Beach only a marginal possibility. However, **Isla del Rey** (across Estero El Pozo, accessible by *lancha* from the foot of Calle Juárez) presents possibilities for prepared trekker-tenters. The same is true for ecosanctuary **Isla Isabel,** three hours by hired boat from San Blas. For those less equipped, the palm-lined strands of **Playa las Islitas, Playa Matanchén,** and **Playa Cocos** on the Bay of Matanchén appear ripe for camping.

FOOD

Snacks, Stalls, and Market

During the mornings and early afternoons try the fruit stands, groceries, *fondas,* and *jugerías* in and around the **Central Market** (behind the plaza church). Late afternoons and evenings, many semipermanent streetside stands around the plaza, such as the **Taquería Las Cuatas** on the corner of Canalizo and Juárez, offer tasty *antojitos* and drinks.

For sit-down snacks every day till midnight, drop in to the **Lonchería Ledmar** (also at the Canalizo-Juárez corner) for a hot *torta,* hamburger, quesadilla, tostada, or fresh-squeezed *jugo* (juice). For a change of venue, you can enjoy about the same at the **Terraza** café on the opposite side of the plaza.

For basic **groceries** and deli items nearby, try the plaza-front **Centro San Blas** store, corner of Juárez and H. Batallón San Blas.

Get your fresh cupcakes, cookies, and crispy *bolillos* at the **bakery** *(panadería)* at Comonfort and Cuauhtémoc, around the uptown corner from Hotel Posada del Rey, closed Sunday. You can get similar (but not quite so fresh) goodies at the small bakery outlet across from the plaza, corner of Juárez and Canalizo.

Restaurants

Family-managed **Restaurant McDonald,** 36 Juárez, half a block from the plaza, is one of the

TO PV/GUADALAJARA

gathering places of San Blas. Its bit-of-everything menu features soups, meat, and seafood in the $5–7 range, besides a hamburger that beats no-relation U.S. McDonald's by a mile. Open daily 7 A.M.–10 P.M.

As an option, step across the street to the TV-free **Wala Wala,** restaurant, tel. 323/285-0863, for breakfast, lunch, or dinner daily 8 A.M.–10 P.M. except Sunday. Its long menu of offerings—tasty salads, pastas, seafood, and fish fillets—crisply prepared and served in a simple but clean and inviting setting, will never go out of style. Everything is good; simply pick out your favorite.

Another alternative is to step into the airy plaza-front (southeast plaza corner) **Restaurant Cocodrilo.** Here you can choose from a sandwich, or full dinner, such as a professionally prepared and served fresh fish fillet or spaghetti *a la Bolognese.* Open daily 8 A.M.–10 P.M. Moderate.

For TV with dinner, the **Restaurant La Familia** is just the place at H. Batallón between Juárez and Mercado. American movies, serape-draped walls, and colorful Mexican tile supply the ambience, while a reasonably priced seafood and meat menu furnishes the food. For dessert, step into its luminescent-decor bar next door for giant-screen American baseball or football. Open for lunch and dinner daily except Sunday. Moderate.

For a refined marine atmosphere and good fish and shrimp, both local folks and visitors choose **Restaurant La Isla,** at Mercado and Paredes, tel. 323/285-0407. As ceiling fans whir overhead and a guitarist strums softly in the background, the net-draped walls display a museum-load of nautical curiosities, from antique Japanese floats and Tahitian shells to New England ship models. Open Tues.–Sun. 2–10 P.M. Moderate.

San Blas's class-act restaurant is the **El Delfín** at the Hotel Garza Canela, Cuauhtémoc 106, tel. 323/285-0112. Potted tropical plants and leafy planter-dividers enhance the genteel atmosphere of this air-conditioned dining room-in-the-round. Meticulous preparation and service, bountiful breakfasts, savory dinner soups, and fresh salad, seafood, and meat entrées keep customers returning year after year. Open daily 8–10 A.M. and 1–9 P.M.; credit cards accepted. Moderate–expensive.

ENTERTAINMENT

Sleepy San Blas's entertainment is of the local, informal variety. Visitors content themselves with strolling the beach or riding the waves by day, and reading, watching TV, listening to mariachis, or dancing at a handful of clubs by night.

Nightlife

Owner/manager Mike McDonald works hard to keep **Mike's Place,** Juárez 36, on the second floor of his family's restaurant, the classiest club in town. He keeps the lights flashing and the small dance floor thumping with blues, Latin, and '60s rock tunes from his own guitar, accompanied by his equally excellent drum and electronic-piano partners. Listen to live music Friday, Saturday, and Sunday nights and holidays 9 P.M.–midnight. There's usually a small cover; drinks are reasonably priced.

A few other places require nothing more than your ears to find. During high season music booms out of low-life **Botanas Herredor** (down H. Batallón, a block past the Marino Inn). The same is true seasonally at the bar at the **Hotel Bucanero,** Calle Juárez 75, tel. 323/285-0101.

SPORTS AND RECREATION
Walking and Jogging

The cooling sea breeze and the soft but firm sand of **Playa Borrego** at the south end of H. Batallón make it the best place around town for a walk or jog. Arm yourself against *jejenes* with repellent and long pants, especially around sunset.

Water Sports

Although some intermediate- and beginner-level surf rolls in at Borrego Beach, nearly all of San Blas's action goes on at world-class surfing mecca Matanchén Beach. (See Around the Bay of Matanchén.)

The mild offshore currents and gentle, undertow-free slope of Borrego Beach are nearly always safe for good swimming, bodysurfing, and boogie boarding. Conditions are often right for good sailboarding. Bring your own equipment, as no rentals are available.

Sediment-fogged water limits snorkeling and scuba diving possibilities around San Blas to the offshore ecopreserve Isla Isabel. (See under Sights and Activities for details.)

Sportfishing

Tony Aguayo and Abraham "Pipila" Murillo are highly recommended to lead big-game deep-sea fishing excursions. Tony's "office" is the *palapa* shelter to the left of the little dock at the foot of Calle Juárez. You can reach Abraham—distinguished winner of six international tournament grand prizes—at his home, Comonfort 248, tel. 323/285-0719. Both Tony and Abraham regularly captain big-boat excursions for tough-fighting marlin, *dorado,* and sailfish. Their fee will run about $250 for a five-hour expedition for up to three people, including boat, tackle, and bait.

On the other hand, a number of other good-eating fish are not so difficult to catch. Check with other captains, such as Antonio Palmas at the Hotel Garza Canela or one of the owners of the many craft docked by the estuary shoreline at the foot of Juárez. For perhaps $100, they'll take three or four of you for a *lancha* outing, which most likely will result in four or five hefty 10-pound snapper, mackerel, tuna, or yellowtail; afterward you can ask your favorite restaurant to cook them for a feast.

During the last few days in May, San Blas hosts its long-running (30-plus years) **International Fishing Tournament.** The entrance fee runs around $350; prizes vary from automobiles to Mercury outboards and Penn International fishing rods. For more information, contact Tony Aguayo or Pipila Murillo, tel. 323/285-0719, or the local tourist information office, downtown, at the Presidencia Municipal. (See Information.)

SHOPPING

San Blas visitors ordinarily spend little of their time shopping. For basics, the stalls at the **Central Market** offer good tropical fruits, meats, and staples. Hours are daily 6 A.M. until around 2 P.M.

For used clothes and a little bit of everything else, a **flea market** (known in Mexico as a *tianguis*) operates on Calle Canalizo a block past the bus station (away from the *jardín*) Saturday morning and early afternoon.

The plaza-corner store, **Comercial de San Blas,** corner of Juárez and H. Batallón, open daily 9 A.M.–2 P.M. and 5–9 P.M. except Sunday, offers a unique mix of everything from film developing and Hohner harmonicas to fishing poles. Hooks, sinkers, and lines are available.

Handicrafts

Although San Blas has relatively few handicrafts sources, the shop at the **Hotel Garza Canela** has one of the finest for-sale handicrafts collections in Nayarit state. Lovingly selected pieces from the famous Pacific coast crafts centers—Guadalajara, Tlaquepaque, Tonalá, Pátzcuaro, Olinalá, Taxco, Oaxaca, and elsewhere—decorate the shop's cabinets, counters, and shelves.

You'll find many common but nevertheless attractive handicrafts assortments in the **crafts stalls** that daily occupy the San Blas main plaza.

INFORMATION

Tourist Information Office

The local tourist office is at the Presidencia Municipal, inside, at the interior patio's southeast corner. Although the officer in charge is sometimes out on business, volunteers sometimes staff the office during the official hours, Mon.–Fri. 9 A.M.–2 P.M. and 4–7 P.M., Sat. 10 A.M.–2 P.M.

For tickets, tours, and information, see **Josefina Vasquez,** both the desk manager and travel agent, at the Hotel Garza Canela (see Accommodations).

Alternatively, contact downtown travel agent **Tacua,** at Sinaloa 20, tel. 323/285-0487 or 323/285-0720, behind and north of the *presidencia municipal,* open Mon.–Sat. 9 A.M.–2 P.M. and 4–7 P.M.

Publications

English-language reading material in San Blas is as scarce as tortillas in Tokyo. The newsstand, on the north side of the plaza, a block past the bus station, may carry some publications, such as *Newsweek, Time, Life,* and *Cosmopolitan.*

As for English-language books, the **tourist**

TO PV/GUADALAJARA

information office, in the *presidencia municipal,* east side of the plaza, has a shelf of used English and American paperbacks for sale.

SERVICES
Bank
Banamex, with a 24-hour ATM, one block east of the plaza at Juárez 36 Ote., tel. 323/285-0031, exchanges U.S. traveler's checks and cash weekdays 9 A.M.–4 P.M.

Communications
The *correo* and *telégrafo* stand side by side at Sonora and Echeverría (one block behind, one block east of the plaza church). The *correo,* tel. 323/285-0295, is open Mon.–Fri. 8 A.M.–3 P.M.; the *telégrafo,* tel. 323/285-0115, is open Mon.–Fri. 8 A.M.–2 P.M.

In addition to the new long-distance public phone stands that sprinkle the town, there are a number of old-fashioned *larga distancia* stores. Most prominent is the **Computel** on Juárez, just west of the plaza, across from Restaurant Mc-Donald, open daily 8 A.M.–9 P.M.

Internet access has arrived in San Blas at **Café Net San Blas,** the hole-in-the wall store near the plaza's southwest corner, on H. Batallón.

Health and Police
One of San Blas's most highly recommended **physicians** is Dr. Alejandro Davalos, available at his office on Juárez, corner of Farias, three blocks east of the plaza.

If you prefer a female physician, consult with general practitioner Doctora Dulce María Jácome Camarillo, at her office in the small off-street complex on Sinaloa, a block east of the new plaza-front church.

Alternatively, you can go to San Blas's respectable local hospital, the government **Centro de Salud,** at Yucatán and H. Batallón (across the street from the Motel Marino Inn), tel. 323/285-0232.

For over-the-counter remedies, go to one of San Blas's many pharmacies, such as **Farmacia Economica,** tel. 323/285-0111, a block south of the plaza southwest corner, at H. Batallón and

Mercado. Open daily 8:30 A.M.–2 P.M. and 4:30–9:30 P.M. For **police** emergencies, contact the headquarters on the left side behind the Presidencia Municipal (City Hall), on Canalizo, east side of the central plaza, tel. 323/285-0221.

Immigration and Customs
San Blas no longer has either Migración (Immigration) or Aduana (Customs) offices. If you lose your tourist card, you'll have to go to the Secretaria de Gobernación, at Oaxaca no. 220 Sur, in Tepic, or, better, to Migración at the airport in Puerto Vallarta a day before you're scheduled to fly home. For customs matters, such as having to leave Mexico temporarily without your car, go to the Aduana in Puerto Vallarta for the necessary paperwork (see Services in the Puerto Vallarta: Town, Bay, and Mountains chapter).

GETTING THERE AND AWAY
By Car or RV
To and from Mazatlán and Tepic, National Highway 74 (formerly National Highway 11) connects San Blas to main-route National Highway 15. Highway 74 winds 19 miles (31 km) downhill from its Highway 15 junction 161 miles (260 km) south of Mazatlán and 22 miles (35 km) north of Tepic. From the turnoff (marked by a Pemex gas station), the road winds through a forest of vine-draped trees and tall palms. Go slowly; the road lacks a shoulder, and cattle or people may appear unexpectedly around any blind, grass-shrouded bend.

To and from Puerto Vallarta, the new Highway 161 cutoff at Las Varas bypasses the slow climb to Tepic, shortening the San Blas-Puerto Vallarta connection to about 94 miles (151 km), or about 2.5 hours.

From Tepic, Highway 76 leaves Highway 15 at its signed "Miramar" turnoff at the northern edge of town. The road winds downhill about 3,000 feet (1,000 meters) through a jungly mountain forest to Santa Cruz and Miramar villages. It continues along the Bahía de Matanchén shoreline to San Blas, a total of 43 miles (70 km) from Tepic. Although this route generally has more shoulder than Highway 74, frequent pedestrians and occasional unexpected cattle necessitate caution.

By Bus

The **San Blas bus terminal** stands adjacent to the new plaza church, corner of Calles Sinaloa and Canalizo. First-class **Transportes Norte de Sonora (TNS),** tel. 323/285-0043, buses connect more than a dozen times a day with Tepic, one continuing to Guadalajara. Additionally, a few departures connect north with Mazatlán and south with Puerto Vallarta. Two afternoon Mazatlán departures continue all the way to Tijuana, at the U.S. border.

Two daily morning second-class navy blue and white **Transportes Noroeste de Nayarit** departures (about 8 and 10 A.M.), connect south with Las Varas, via Bay of Matanchén points of Matanchén, Los Cocos, and Santa Cruz de Miramar. Other departures connect east with Tepic, north with Santiago Ixcuintla, via intermediate points of Guadalupe Victoria and Villa Hidalgo.

A local white *(autobús blanco)* bus connects San Blas with the Bay of Matanchén points of Las Aguadas, Matanchén, Aticama, Los Cocos, Miramar, and Santa Cruz. It departs from the downtown corner of Paredes and Sinaloa (a block west of the church) four times daily, approximately every two hours between 8:30 A.M. and 4:30 P.M.

From Puerto Vallarta, bus travelers have three ways to get to San Blas. Quickest is via one of the four **Transportes Norte de Sonora** (TNS) departures that connect daily with San Blas. They depart from the new Puerto Vallarta bus station, north of the airport; get your ticket at the Elite-Estrella Blanca desk, tel. 322/221-0848.

On the other hand, many more second-class **Transportes Pacífico** buses connect Puerto Vallarta with Las Varas, on Highway 200, where you can transfer to one of the two daily second-class **Transportes Noroeste de Nayarit** (morning and early afternoon) navy blue and white and white buses that connect with San Blas (see the big sign) at the Highway 161 junction.

If you're too late for that connection, continue to the Tepic bus station, where you might be early enough to catch the last of the several

Transportes Norte de Sonora and Transportes Noroeste de Nayarit that connect daily with San Blas.

AROUND THE BAY OF MATANCHÉN

The shoreline of the Bahía de Matanchén sweeps southward from San Blas, lined with an easily accessible, pearly crescent of sand, ripe for beachcombers and tent campers. In the luxuriant foothill forest above the bay, trails lead to bubbling waterfalls and idyllic jungle pools, fine for picnicking or wilderness camping. The villages of Matanchén, Aticama, Los Cocos, and Santa Cruz del Miramar dot this strand with *palapa* restaurants and stores offering food and basic supplies. A pair of trailer parks and two good small hotels provide accommodations.

Beaches and Activities

The beaches of **Matanchén** and **Las Islitas** make an inseparable pair. Las Islitas (if heading south, turn right at the Matanchén village junction) is dotted by little outcroppings topped by miniature jungles of swaying palms and spreading trees. One of these is home for a colony of surfers waiting for the Big Wave, the Holy Grail of surfing. The Big Wave is one of the occasional gigantic 20-foot breakers that rise off Playa Las Islitas and carry surfers as much as a mile and a quarter—an official Guinness world record—to the soft sand of Playa Matanchén.

About three miles (five km) south of Matanchén village, a sign marks a side road to a *cocodrilario* (crocodile farm). At the end of the two-mile track (truck okay, car-negotiable with caution when dry), you'll arrive at El Tanque, a spring-fed pond, home of the **Ejido de la Palma crocodile farm.** About 50 toothy crocs, large and small, snooze in the sun within several enclosures. Half the fun is the adjacent spring-fed freshwater lagoon, so crystal clear you can see half a dozen big fish wriggling beneath the surface. Nearby, ancient trees swathed in vines and orchids tower overhead, butterflies flutter past, and turtles sun themselves on mossy logs. Bring a picnic lunch, your binoculars, bird book, insect repellent, and bathing suit.

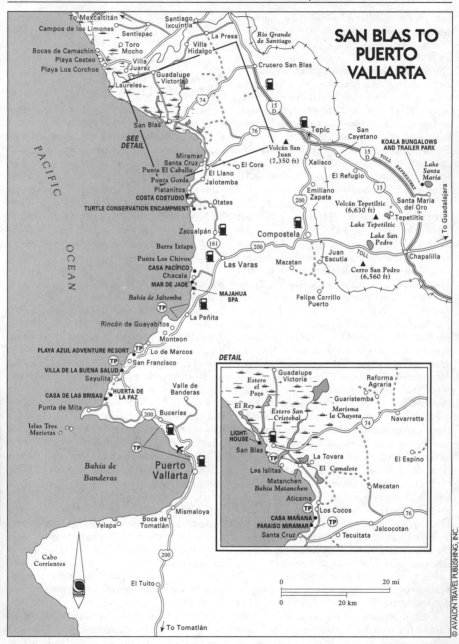

SAN BLAS TO PUERTO VALLARTA

To Mexcaltitán
Campos de los Limones
Santiago Ixcuintla
Sentispac
La Presa
Río Grande de Santiago
Toro Mocho
Villa Hidalgo
Bocas de Camachin
Playa Cesteo
Playa Los Corchos
Villa Juárez
Crucero San Blas
Guadalupe Victoria
Laureles
74
San Blas
SEE DETAIL
76
15 D
Tepic
San Cayetano
KOALA BUNGALOWS AND TRAILER PARK
Volcán San Juan (7,350 ft)
Miramar
Santa Cruz
Punta El Caballo
El Cora
Xalisco
15 D
Lake Santa Maria
El Llano
El Refugio
15
Jalotemba
Punta Gorda
Platanitos
COSTA COSTUDIO
Emiliano Zapata
200
Santa Maria del Oro
To Guadalajara
TURTLE CONSERVATION ENCAMPMENT
Otates
Volcán Tepetiltic (6,630 ft)
Tepetiltic
Zacualpán
Lake Tepetiltic
Compostela
Lake San Pedro
161
200
Barra Ixtapa
Juan Escutia
Chapalilla
Punta Los Chivos
Mazatan
CASA PACÍFICO
Cerro San Pedro (6,560 ft)
Chacala
Las Varas
MAR DE JADE
Bahía de Jaltemba
MAJAHUA SPA
Felipe Carrillo Puerto
TP
Rincón de Guayabitos
La Peñita
Monteon
PLAYA AZUL ADVENTURE RESORT
Lo de Marcos
TP
VILLA DE LA BUENA SALUD
San Francisco
Sayulita
Valle de Banderas
CASA DE LAS BRISAS
HUERTA DE LA PAZ
Punta de Mita
200
Bucerias
Islas Tres Marietas
TP
Bahía de Banderas
Puerto Vallarta
Mismaloya
Cabo Corrientes
Yelapa
Boca de Tomatlán
200
El Tuito
To Tomatlán

PACIFIC OCEAN

DETAIL

Estero el Pozo
Guadalupe Victoria
Reforma Agraria
El Rey
Guaristemba
Estero San Cristobal
Marisma la Chayota
Navarrette
74
LIGHTHOUSE
San Blas
La Tovara
El Espino
TP
Las Islitas
El Camalote
Matanchen
Bahía Matanchen
Mecatan
Aticama
TP
Los Cocos
76
CASA MAÑANA
PARAISO MIRAMAR
TP
Jalcocotan
Santa Cruz
Tecuitata

0   20 mi
0   20 km

MOON

Accommodations and Food

For camping, the intimate, protected curves of sand around Playa Islitas are ideal. Although few facilities exist (save for a few winter-season food *palapas*), the beachcombing, swimming, fishing from the rocks, shell-collecting, and surfing are usually good even without the Big Wave. The water, however, isn't clear enough for good snorkeling. Campers, be prepared with plenty of good insect repellent.

In surfing season (Aug.–Feb.), the Team Banana and other *palapa*-shops open up at Matanchén and Las Islitas to rent surfboards and sell what each of them claims to be the "world's original banana bread."

Getting Around the Bay of Matanchén

Drive, taxi, or ride the local *autobús blanco* Santa Cruz del Miramar–bound bus, which departs several times a day from the corner of Paredes and Sinaloa, a block west of the San Blas church. Also, you can ride the second-class navy blue and white Noroeste de Nayarit bus, which leaves from the San Blas bus station twice in the morning and goes around the bay, past Santa Cruz, all the way to Highway 200 at Las Varas.

South from Matanchén

Bending south from Playa Islitas past a lineup of beachfront *palapa* restaurants, the super-wide and shallow (like a giant kiddie-pool) Playa Matanchén stretches to a palm-fringed ribbon of sand, washed by gentle rollers and frequented only by occasional fisherfolk and a few Sunday visitors.

Continuing down the road a mile farther, past the crocodile farm and a marine sciences school, the beach sand gives way to rocky shoals beneath a jungle headland. The road curves and climbs to shoreline **Aticama** village (small stores and restaurants) and continues along a beachside coconut grove, name-source of the bordering Playa Los Cocos. Unfortunately, the ocean is eroding the beach, leaving a crumbling, 10-foot embankment along a mostly rocky shore.

The place is, nevertheless, balmy and beautiful enough to attract a winter RV colony to **Trailer Park Playa Amor,** overlooking the waves, right in the middle of Playa Los Cocos. Besides excellent fishing, boating, boogie boarding, swimming, and sailboarding, the park offers about 30 grassy spaces for very reasonable prices. Rentals run $9, $10, and $11 for small, medium, and large RVs, respectively, with all hookups, showers, and toilets; pets are okay. Write Trailer Park Playa Amor, c/o gerente Javier López, Playa Los Cocos, San Blas, Nayarit 63740. Although you can expect plenty of friendly company during the winter months, reservations are not usually necessary.

Casa Mañana

About 2.5 miles farther south (or eight miles, 13 km, south of San Blas), the diminutive shoreline retreat Casa Mañana perches at the south end of breezy Los Cocos beach. Owned and managed by an Austrian man, Reinhardt, and his Mexican wife, Lourdes, Casa Mañana's two double-storied tiers of rooms rise over a homey, spic-and-span, beach-view restaurant and pool deck and garden. Very popular with Europeans and North Americans seeking South Seas tranquility on a budget, Casa Mañana offers fishing, beachcombing, hiking, and swimming right from its palm-adorned front yard. The 26 rooms rent for about $49 d high season, $38 low, with a/c and ocean view, $35 d, with a/c but no view, with one day free per week stay. Longer-stay discounts are negotiable, and winter reservations are strongly recommended. For reservations, write P.O. Box 49, San Blas, Nayarit 63740, call tel./fax 323/254-9080, 323/254-9090, or toll-free Mex. tel. 800/202-2079, email reinhard@prodigy.net.mx, or visit www.casa-manana.com.

Paraíso Miramar

Continue south another 2.5 miles and you will pass through rustic Manzanilla village, where a right-side sign marks the driveway to Paraíso Miramar. The spacious green bay-view park is bedecked by palms and sheltered by what appears to be the grandmother of all banyan trees. Beneath the great tree on a cliff-bottom beach the surf rolls in gently, while the blue bay, crowned by jungle-covered ridges, curves gracefully northward toward San Blas.

TO PV/GUADALAJARA

Paraíso Miramar's owner/family, most of whom live in Tepic, and their personable, hardworking staff offer a little bit for everyone: six simple but clean and comfortable rooms with bath facing the bay; behind that, 12 grassy RV spaces with concrete pads and all hookups, and three kitchenette bungalows sleeping up to six. A small view restaurant and blue pools—swimming, kiddie, and hot tub—complete the lovely picture.

Rooms rent from about $35 d, low season, $45 high; bungalows, about $45 low, and $85 high, with hot-water showers and a/c. RV spaces go for about $14/day. For a week's stay, you customarily get one day free. If, on the other hand, you'd like to set up a tent, the shady hillside palm grove on the property's south side appears just right. Make reservations by writing Paraíso Miramar directly at Km 1.2 Carretera a San Blas, Playa La Manzanilla, Santa Cruz de Miramar, Nayarit, or by calling the family at home in Tepic (in Spanish), tel./fax 323/254-9030 or 323/254-9031.

Waterfall Hikes

A number of pristine creeks tumble down boulder-strewn beds and foam over cliffs as waterfalls *(cataratas)* in the jungle above the Bay of Matanchén. Some of these are easily accessible and perfect for a day of hiking, picnicking, and swimming. Don't hesitate to ask for directions: *"¿Dónde está el camino a la catarata, por favor?"* ("Where is the path to the waterfall, please?") If you would like a guide, ask, *"¿Hay guía, por favor?"* One (or all) of the local crowd of kids may immediately volunteer.

You can get to within walking distance of the waterfall near **Tecuitata** village either by car, taxi, or the Tepic-bound bus; it is only a few miles out of Santa Cruz along Nayarit Highway 76. A half-mile uphill past the village, a sign reading Balneario Nuevo Chapultepec marks a dirt road heading downhill a half-mile to a creek and a bridge. Cross over to the other side ($3 entrance fee), where you'll find a *palapa* restaurant, a hillside water slide, and a small swimming pool.

Continue upstream along the right-hand bank of the creek for a much rarer treat. Half the fun are the sylvan jungle delights—flashing butterflies, pendulous leafy vines, gurgling little cascades—along the meandering path. The other half is at the end, where the creek spurts through a verdure-framed fissure and splashes into a cool, broad pool festooned with green, giant-leafed *chalata* (taro in Hawaii, tapioca in Africa). Both the pool area and the trail have several possible campsites. Bring everything, especially your water-purification kit and insect repellent. Known locally as Arroyo Campiste, it is popular with kids and women who bring their washing.

Another waterfall, the highest in the area, near the village of **El Cora,** is harder to get to but the reward is even more spectacular. Again, on the west-east Santa Cruz-Tepic Highway 76, a negotiable dirt road to El Cora branches south just before Tecuitata. At road's end, after about eight km, you can park by a banana-loading platform. From here, the walk (less than an hour) climaxes with a steep, rugged descent to the rippling, crystal pool at the bottom of the waterfall.

While rugged adventurers may find their own way to the waterfalls, others rely upon guides Armando S. Navarrete and Juan "Bananas" Garcia, founder of Grupo Ecologio in San Blas, tel. 323/285-0462, or at his café, "La Tumba de Yaco" at H. Battllón 173. Contact Armando at home at Sonora 179 in San Blas, Nayarit 63740.

Shortcut South to Puerto Vallarta

All-paved Nayarit Highway 161 allows Puerto Vallarta–bound drivers to bypass the old route—the slow, roundabout climb and descent—via Tepic. Instead, Highway 161 forks right, south, from Tepic-bound Highway 76 (about 11 miles, 18 km, south of San Blas), a mile past Santa Cruz village. It continues through lush foothill farms and tropical forest, joining Highway 200 at Las Varas, about 53 miles (85 km) north of Puerto Vallarta.

Travelers who wish to explore Tepic, Nayarit's colonial state capital, and its lush, volcano-rimmed valley, should continue uphill along Highway 76.

Tepic

Tepic (elev. 3,001 feet, 915 meters) basks in a lush highland valley beneath a trio of giant, slumbering volcanoes: 7,600-foot Sanganguey and 6,630-foot Tepeltiltic in the east and south, and the brooding Volcán San Juan (7,350 feet, 2,240 meters) in the west. The waters that trickle from their cool green slopes have nurtured verdant valley fields and gardens for millennia. The city's name reflects its fertile surroundings; it's from the Náhuatl *tepictli,* meaning "land of corn."

Resembling a prosperous U.S. county seat, Tepic (pop. 200,000) is the Nayarit state capital and the service, manufacturing, and governmental center for the entire state. Local people flock to deposit in its banks, shop in its stores, and visit its diminutive main-street state legislature.

The Huichol people are among the many who come to trade in Tepic. The Huichol fly in from their remote mountain villages, loaded with crafts—yarn paintings, beaded masks, ceremonial gourds, God's eyes—which they sell at local handicrafts stores. Tepic has thus accumulated troves of their intriguing ceremonial art, whose animal and human forms symbolize the

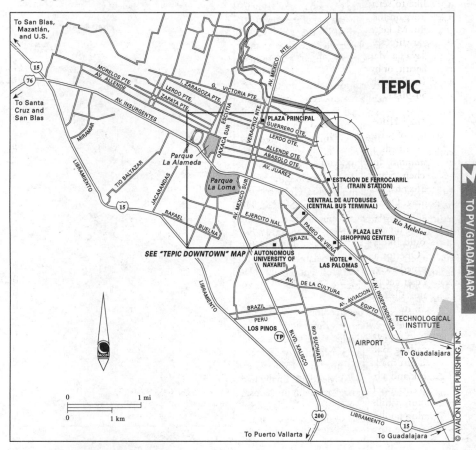

Huichol's animistic world view. (See the special topic "The Huichol.")

Beyond the city limits, the Tepic valley offers an unusual bonus for lovers of the outdoors. About 45 minutes from town by car, sylvan mountain-rimmed lake Santa María de Oros offers comfortable bungalow lodgings and a modest RV park and campground, fine for a relaxing day or week of camping, hiking, swimming, kayaking, rowboating, and wildlife viewing.

HISTORY

Scholars believe that, around A.D. 1160, the valley of Tepic may have been a stopping place for a generation of the Mexica (Aztecs) on their way to the Valley of Mexico. By the eve of the conquest, however, Tepic was ruled by the kingdom of Xalisco (whose capital occupied the same ground as the present-day city of Jalisco, a few miles south of Tepic).

In 1524, the expedition headed by the great conquistador's nephew, Francisco Cortés de San Buenaventura, explored the valley in peaceful contrast to those who followed. The renegade conquistador Nuño de Guzmán, bent on accumulating gold and *indígena* slaves, arrived in May 1530 and seized the valley in the name of King Charles V. After building a lodging house for hoped-for future immigrants, Guzmán hurried north, burning a pathway to Sinaloa. He returned a year later and founded a settlement near Tepic, which he named, pretentiously, Espíritu Santo de la Mayor España. In 1532 the king ordered his settlement's name changed to Santiago de Compostela. Today it remains Nayarit's oldest municipality, 23 miles (37 km) south of present-day Tepic.

Immigrants soon began colonizing the countryside of the sprawling new dominion of Nueva Galicia, which today includes the modern states of Jalisco, Nayarit, and Sinaloa. Guzmán managed to remain as governor until 1536, when the new viceroy, Antonio Mendoza, finally had him arrested and sent back to Spain in chains.

With Guzmán gone, Nueva Galicia began to thrive. The colonists settled down to raising

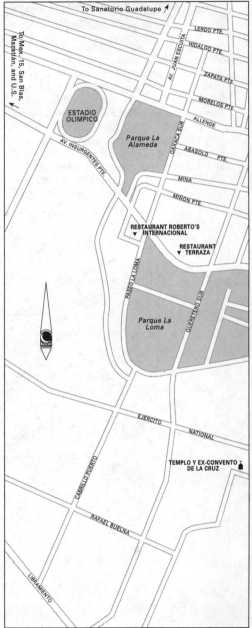

TO PV/GUADALAJARA

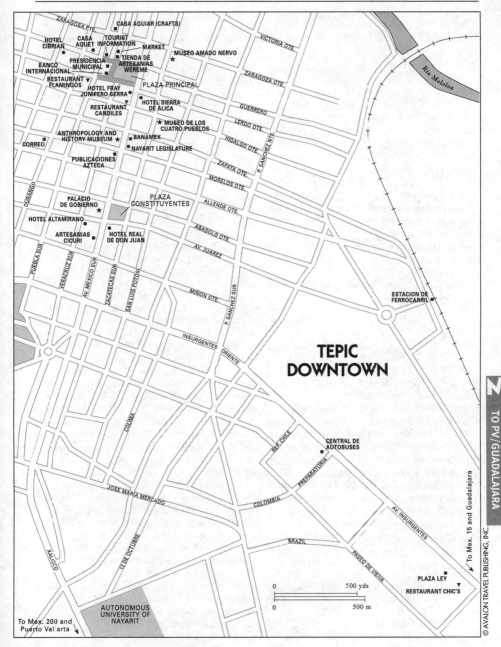

TEPIC
DOWNTOWN

Río Mololoa

TO PV/GUADALAJARA

To Mex. 15 and Guadalajara

ZARAGOSA PTE.

CASA AGUIAR (CRAFTS)

HOTEL CIBRIAN

CASA AGUET

TOURIST INFORMATION

MARKET

MUSEO AMADO NERVO

VICTORIA OTE.

BANCO INTERNACIONAL

PRESIDENCIA MUNICIPAL

TIENDA DE ARTESANIAS WEREME

ZARAGOZA OTE.

RESTAURANT FLAMINGOS

HOTEL FRAY JUNIPERO SERRA

PLAZA PRINCIPAL

RESTAURANT CANDILES

HOTEL SIERRA DE ALICA

GUERRERO

MUSEO DE LOS CUATRO PUEBLOS

LERDO OTE.

ANTHROPOLOGY AND HISTORY MUSEUM

BANAMEX

HIDALGO OTE.

CORREO

NAYARIT LEGISLATURE

P. SANCHEZ NTE.

PUBLICACIONES AZTECA

ZAPATA OTE.

DURANGO

MORELOS OTE.

PALACIO DE GOBIERNO

PLAZA CONSTITUYENTES

ALLENDE OTE.

HOTEL ALTAMIRANO

ARTESANIAS CICURI

HOTEL REAL DE DON JUAN

ABASOLO OTE.

AV. JUAREZ

PUEBLA SUR

VERACRUZ SUR

AV. MEXICO SUR

ZACATECAS SUR

SAN LUIS POTOSI

MINON OTE.

P. SANCHEZ SUR

ESTACION DE FERROCARRIL

INSURGENTES ORIENTE

COLIMA

REP. CHILE

CENTRAL DE AUTOBUSES

PREPARATORIA

JOSE MARIA MERCADO

COLOMBIA

AV. INSURGENTES

BRAZIL

XALISCO

12 DE OCTUBRE

PASEO DE VIEJA

PLAZA LEY

RESTAURANT CHIC'S

0   500 yds

0   500 m

AUTONOMOUS UNIVERSITY OF NAYARIT

To Mex. 200 and Puerto Vallarta

JUNÍPERO SERRA: APOSTLE OF CALIFORNIA

His untiring, single-minded drive to found a string of missions and save the souls of native Californians has lifted Junípero Serra to prominence and proposed sainthood. Not long after he was born—on November 24, 1713, to illiterate parents on the Spanish island of Mallorca—he showed a fascination for books and learning. After taking his vows at the Convent of St. Francis in Palma on September 15, 1731, he changed his name to Junípero, after the beloved friend and "merry jester of God" of St. Francis Assisi.

Ordained in 1738 into the Franciscan order, Junípero soon was appointed professor of theology at the age of 30. He made up for his slight five foot, two inch height with a penetrating intelligence, engaging wit, and cheery disposition. Serra was popular with students, and, in 1748, when he received the missionary call, two of them—Francisco Palóu and Juan Bautista Crespi—accompanied Serra to Mexico, beginning their lifelong sojourn with him.

Serra inspired his followers by example, sometimes to the extreme. On arrival at Veracruz in December 1749, he insisted on walking the rough road all the way to Mexico City. The injuries he suffered led to a serious infection that plagued him the rest of his life. During his association with the Mexico City College of San Fernando (1750–1767), which included an extensive mission among the Pames Indians around Jalpan, in Querétaro state, he practiced self-flagellation and wore an undercoat woven with sharp bits of wire. Often he would inspire his indigenous flock during Holy Week, as he played the role of Jesus, lugging a ponderous wooden cross through the stations. Afterward, he would humbly wash his converts' feet.

Serra's later mission to the Californias was triggered by the June 24, 1767, royal decree of King Carlos III, which expelled the Jesuit missionaries from the New World. The king's inspector general of the Indies, José de Galvez, prevailed upon Serra, at age 55, to fulfill a double agenda: organize a Franciscan mission to staff the former Jesuits' several Baja California missions, then push north and found several more in Alta California.

From the summer of 1767 to the spring of 1768, Serra paused in Guadalajara, Tepic, and San Blas with his fellow missionaries en route to the Californias. They sailed north from San Blas on March 12, 1768.

They found the Baja California missions in disarray. The soldiers, left in custody of the missions, were running amok—raping native women, murdering their husbands, and squandering supplies. With the cooperation of military commander and governor Gaspar de Portolá, Serra managed to set things straight within a year and continue northward. On March 25, 1769, Serra, weak with fever, had two men lift him onto his mule, beginning the 1,000-mile desert trek from Loreto to San Diego. On May 17 Serra's leg became so infected that Portolá insisted he return to Loreto. Serra refused. "I shall not turn back. . . . I would gladly be left among the pagans if such be the will of God."

Serra, however, was always practical. He asked the mule driver's advice. "Imagine I am one of your mules with a sore on his leg. Give me the same treatment." The mule driver applied the ordinary remedy, a soothing ointment of herbs mixed with lard. Serra resumed the trip and reached San Diego, where, on July 16, 1769, he founded San Diego Mission.

The following years would see Serra laboring on, trekking by muleback up and down California, founding eight more missions, encouraging the padres whom he assigned, and teaching and caring for the welfare of the Native Americans in his charge. Given the few padres (only two per mission) and the few stores brought by the occasional supply ship from San Blas, it was a monumental, back-breaking task.

In the end, Serra's sacrifices probably shortened his life. On August 18, 1784, at his beloved headquarters mission in Carmel, Serra spent his last days with Palóu, his companion of 40 years. Palóu gave the last sacrament, and two days afterward, Serra, in pain, retraced the stations of the cross with his congregation for the last time. He died peacefully in his cell eight days later.

Whatever one believes about Spain's colonial role, the fate of the indigenous inhabitants, and sainthood, it is hard not to be awed by this compassionate, gritty little man who would not turn back.

cattle, wheat, and fruit; the padres founded churches, schools, and hospitals. Explorers set out for new lands: Coronado to New Mexico in 1539, Legazpi and Urdaneta across the Pacific in 1563, Vizcaíno to California and Oregon in 1602, and Father Kino to Arizona in 1687. Father Junípero Serra stayed in Tepic for several months en route to the Californias in 1767. Excitement rose in Tepic when a column of 200 Spanish dragoons came through on their way to establishing the port of San Blas in 1768.

San Blas's glory days were numbered, as were Spain's. Insurgents captured its fort cannons and sent them to defend Guadalajara in 1810, and finally President Lerdo de Tejada closed the port to foreign commerce in 1872.

Now, however, trains, jet airplanes, and a seemingly interminable flow of giant diesel trucks carry mountains of produce and manufactures through Tepic to the Mexican Pacific and the United States. Commerce hums in suburban factories and in banks, stores, and shops around the plaza, where the aging colonial cathedral rises, a brooding reminder of the old days that few have time to remember.

SIGHTS
Getting Oriented
Tepic has two main plazas and two main highways. Approaching along Highway 15 at the north edge of town, you'll arrive at an overpass that diverts traffic either west (right) to Miramar-Santa Cruz and San Blas via Nayarit Highway 76, or southeast, toward downtown Tepic along Av. Insurgentes. If you're only passing through, keep going straight ahead south, on the *libramiento* Highway 15 throughway, which efficiently conducts traffic around the city-center congestion. Still on the *libramiento* about six miles (nine km) farther south, a second interchange at the south edge of town distributes traffic southeast (continuing along *libramiento* Highway 15 toward Guadalajara), or south toward Puerto Vallarta, or northeast, toward downtown along Blvd. Xalisco.

Av. México, Tepic's main north-south downtown street, angles from Blvd. Xalisco just south of big **Parque La Loma.** A few blocks farther north, it crosses Av. Insurgentes and continues downtown past the two main plazas: first Plaza Constituyentes, and then Plaza Principal, about a half mile farther north.

A Walk Around Downtown
The **cathedral,** adjacent to Av. México, at the east side of the Plaza Principal, marks the center of town. Dating from 1750, the cathedral was dedicated to the Purísima Concepción (Immaculate Conception). Its twin neogothic bell towers rise somberly over everything else in town, while inside, cheerier white walls and neoclassic gilded arches lead toward the main altar. There, the pious, all-forgiving Virgin de la Asunción appears to soar to heaven, borne by a choir of adoring cherubs.

The workaday **Presidencia Municipal** (City-County Hall) stands on the plaza opposite the cathedral, while the **municipal tourist information office,** with many good brochures, is just north of it, at the corner of Puebla and Amado Nervo. Back across the plaza, behind the cathedral and a half block to the north at 284 Zacatecas Nte., the **Museo Amado Nervo,** tel. 311/212-2916, occupies the house where the renowned poet was born on August 27, 1870. The four-room permanent exhibition displays photos, original works, a bust of Nervo, and paintings donated by artists J. L. Soto, Sofía Bassi, and Erlinda T. Fuentes. The museum is open Mon.–Fri. 9 A.M.–2 P.M. and 4–7 P.M., Sat. 9 A.M.–2 P.M.

Return to the plaza and join the shoppers beneath the arches in front of the Hotel Fray Junípero Serra on the plaza's south side, where a platoon of shoe shiners ply their trade.

Head around the corner, south, along Av. México. After about two blocks you will reach the venerable 18th-century former mansion that houses the **Regional Anthropology and History Museum,** Av. México 91 Nte., tel. 311/212-1900, open Mon.–Fri. 9 A.M.–7 P.M., Sat. and Sun. 9 A.M.–3 P.M. The palatial residence was built in 1762 with profits from sugarcane, cattle, and wheat. Since then, the mansion's spacious, high-ceilinged chambers have echoed with the voices of generations of

TO PV/GUADALAJARA

occupants, including the German consul, Max-imiliano Delius, during the 1880s. Now, its downstairs rooms house a changing exhibition of charming, earthy, pre-Columbian pottery arti-facts from the museum's collection. These have included dancing dogs, a man scaling a fish, a boy riding a turtle, a dog with a corncob in its mouth, and a very unusual explicitly amorous couple. In an upstairs room, displays illustrate the Huichol symbolism hidden in the *cicuri* (eye of God) yarn sculptures, yarn paintings, cere-monial arrows, hats, musical instruments, and other pieces. Also upstairs, don't miss the mon-strous, 15-foot stuffed crocodile, captured near San Blas and donated by ex-president Carlos Salinas de Gortari in 1989.

If you have time, cross Av. México and con-tinue one block along Hidalgo to take a peek in-side a pair of other historic homes, now serving as museums. Within the restored colonial-era house at the southwest corner of Hidalgo and Zacatecas is the **Museo de los Cuatro Pueblos** (Museum of the Four Peoples), tel. 311/212-1705, which exhibits traditional costumes and crafts of Nayarit's four indigenous peoples—Huichol, Cora, Tepehuan, and Mexica. The museum is open Mon.–Fri. 9 A.M.–2 P.M. and 4:30–7 P.M., Sat. 10 A.M.–2 P.M. Afterward, walk three doors farther on Hidalgo and cross the street, to the **Casa de Juan Escuita,** a colonial house furnished in original style. It's named after a Tepic-born boy who was one of Mex-ico's beloved six "Niños Héroes"—cadets who fell in the futile defense of Chapultepec Castle (the "Halls of Montezuma") against U.S. Marines in 1846.

Continue south along Av. México; pass the state legislature across the street on the left and, two blocks farther, on your right, along the west side of the plaza, spreads the Spanish classical facade of the State of Nayarit **Palacio de Gob-ierno.** Inside, in the center, rises a cupola deco-rated with a 1975 collection of fiery murals by artist José Luis Soto. In a second, rear building, a long, unabashedly biased mural by the same artist portrays the historic struggles of the Mex-ican people against despotism, corruption, and foreign domination.

Continuing about a mile south of Plaza Con-stituyentes past Insurgentes, where Av. Méx-ico crosses Ejército Nacional, you will find the **Templo y Ex-Convento de la Cruz de Za-cate** (Church and Ex-Convent of the Cross of Grass). This venerable but lately restored mon-ument has two claims to fame: the rooms where Father Junípero Serra stayed for several months in 1767 en route to California, and the mirac-ulous cross that you can see in the open-air en-closure adjacent to the sanctuary. According to chroniclers, the cross-shaped patch of grass has grown for centuries (from either 1540 or 1619, depending upon the account), needing neither water nor cultivation. While you're there, pick up some of the excellent brochures at the **Nayarit State Tourism** desk at the build-ing's front entrance.

Crater Lake Santa María

Easily accessible by car and about 45 minutes south of town, by either old Highway 15 or the new toll *autopista,* Laguna Santa María, tucked into an ancient volcanic caldera, offers near-per-fect opportunities for outdoor relaxation. The lake itself, reachable via a good paved road, is big, blue, and rimmed by forested, wildlife-rich hills. You can hike trails through shady woods to ridgetop panoramic viewpoints. Afterward, cool off with a swim in the lake. On another day, row a rental boat across the lake and explore hidden, tree-shaded inlets and sunny, secluded beaches. Afterward, sit in a palm-fringed grassy park and enjoy the lake view and the orange blossom–scented evening air.

The driving force behind this seemingly too-good-to-be-true scene is Chris French, the per-sonable owner/operator of lakeshore Koala Bungalows and Trailer Park. He's dedicated to preserving the beauty of the lake and its sur-roundings. It seems a miracle that, lacking any visible government protection, the lake and its forest hinterland remain lovely and pristine. The answer may lie partly in its isolation, the rela-tively sparse local population, and the enlightened conservation efforts of Chris and his neighbors. (For accommodations and access details, see Trailer Park, Bungalows, and Camping.)

ACCOMMODATIONS

Downtown Hotels

Tepic has a pair of good deluxe and several acceptable moderate downtown hotels. Starting in the north, near the Plaza Principal, the **Hotel Cibrián** is on Amado Nervo, 1.5 blocks behind the Presidencia Municipal, Amado Nervo 163 Pte., Tepic, Nayarit 63000, tel. 311/212-8698, fax 311/221-6146 or 311/221-1461. It offers clean, no-frills rooms with bath, ceiling fans, telephones, parking, and a pretty fair local restaurant. The Cibrián's small drawback is the noise that might filter into your room through louvered windows facing the tile (and therefore sound-reflective) hallways. Nevertheless, for the price, it's a Tepic best buy. The 46 rooms go for about $16 s, $19 d, $22 t; credit cards are not accepted.

Right on the Plaza Principal stands the five-story tower of Tepic's **Hotel Fray Junípero Serra,** Lerdo 23 Pte., Tepic, Nayarit 63000, tel. 311/212-2525, fax 311/212-2051. The hotel offers spacious, tastefully furnished view rooms with deluxe amenities, efficient service, convenient parking, and a cool plaza-front restaurant. The 90 rooms run a reasonable $50 s and $53 d and have satellite TV, a/c, and phones; no pool or parking, limited wheelchair access; credit cards are accepted. For more information, visit the website www.frayjunipero.com.mx.; reserve by telephone or email frayjunipero@tepic.megared.net.mx.

On Av. México, half a block to the right (south) of the cathedral, the **Hotel Sierra de Alica** (AH-lee-kah), Av. México 180 Nte., Tepic, Nayarit 63000, tel. 311/212-0325, fax 311/212-1309, remains a longtime favorite of Tepic business travelers. Polished wood paneling downstairs and plain but comfortable rooms upstairs reflect the Sierra de Alica's solid unpretentiousness. The 60 rooms rent for $26 s, $38 d all with a/c, satellite TV, phones, and parking; credit cards are accepted.

The **Hotel Real de Don Juan,** Av. México 105 Sur, Tepic, Nayarit 63000, tel./fax 311/216-1880 or 311/216-1828, on Plaza Constituyentes appears to be succeeding in its efforts to become Tepic's class-act hotel. A plush, tranquil lobby and adjoining restaurant/bar matches the luxury of the king-sized beds, thick carpets, marble baths, and soft pastels of the rooms. Rates for the 48 rooms are $58 s or d, with a/c, TV, parking, and limited wheelchair access; credit cards are accepted.

Nearby on Mina, half a block from the Av. México plaza corner, the **Hotel Altamirano,** Mina 19 Pte., Tepic, Nayarit 63000, tel. 311/212-7131 or 311/218-0225, offers basic bare-bulb rooms with bath at budget rates. The hotel, although clean, is drab. The 31 rooms with fans rent for $15 s, 25 d; parking available.

Suburban Motels

If you prefer to stay out of the busy downtown, you have at least two good options. On the north end, three miles from the city center, try the graceful, 50-room **Hotel Bugam Villas,** Insurgentes and Libramiento Pte., Tepic, Nayarit 63000, tel./fax 311/218-0225, 311/218-0226, or 311/218-0227. From the lobby, the grounds extend past lovely, spreading *higuera* (native wild fig) trees to the two-story stucco and red-tile-roofed units. Inside, the rooms are clean with high ceilings, huge beds, marble shower baths, TV, a/c, and phone. The restaurant, elegant, cool, and serene within, leads outside to an airy dining veranda that overlooks a manicured shady garden. The food is appealing, professionally presented (but slowly served), and moderately priced. The only blot on this near-perfect picture is the noise—which choice of room can moderate considerably—from the trucks on the expressway nearby. Rates run $50 s or d, with parking; credit cards are accepted.

On the opposite side of town, another good choice is the motel-style **Hotel Las Palomas,** Av. Insurgentes 2100 Ote., Tepic, Nayarit 63000, tel. 311/214-0239 or 311/214-0948, fax 311/214-0953, about two miles southeast of the city center. The two stories of double rooms and suites surround a colonial-chic pool and parking patio. The reception opens into an airy solarium restaurant, especially inviting for breakfast. The 67 clean and comfortable Spanish-style, tile-floored rooms rent for $58 s or d, with a/c, satellite TV, and phones; credit cards are accepted. For more information visit the website www.laspalomashotel.com.mx, reserve by telephone or email hpalomas@prodigy.net.mx.

Trailer Park, Bungalows, and Camping

The demise of the former Trailer Park Los Pinos has left Tepic city with no trailer park. Nevertheless, RV and tent camping and comfortable rooms are available at the **Koala Bungalows and Trailer Park** at the gorgeously rural, semitropical mountain lake Santa María (see Sights), about 45 minutes via Highway 15 southeast of Tepic. Owner Chris French maintains a tranquil, palm-studded lakeside park, with bungalow-style rooms, houses, RV and tent sites, a snack bar, kiddie pool, small swimming pool, and rowboat rentals. For reservations, call tel. 311/212-3772, or write P.O. Box 493, Tepic, Nayarit 63000. The four spartan but clean and comfortable garden kitchenette apartments, for up to four people, with bath, rent for about $39 daily, $250 weekly, and $800 monthly. A small house and a larger two-bedroom house are also available for $64 and $80 per day, respectively. About 20 well-maintained shady RV sites rent for $15 daily, $100 weekly, and $300 monthly, with all hookups, toilets, and showers. Add $2 per day for a/c power. Campsites go for about $4 per adult, $3 per child, per night. Weekends at Koala Bungalows tend to bustle with local families; weekdays, when the few guests are middle-class European, North American, and Mexican couples, are more tranquil.

Those who yearn for even more serenity and privacy opt for one of the fully furnished semi-luxurious **view apartments,** built by Chris's daughter Hayley and her husband on the opposite side of the lake. The apartments' overall plan, on four separate levels, stair-stepping up the hillside among ancient, spreading trees, blends thoughtfully into the pristine lakeside setting. Here, all the ingredients—individual lake-vista *terrazas,* kitchenettes (bring your food), king-sized beds, swimming pool—seem to come together for a perfectly tranquil weekend, week, or month of Sundays. Apartments rent for about $60/day; reserve through the same numbers and address as Koala Bungalows.

Get there by bus or by driving, either along Highway 15 *libre* (nontoll) or the new toll road *(cuota autopista)* to Guadalajara, which begins at the far southeast suburb. From *libre* Highway 15, about 16 miles (26 km) east of Tepic, between roadside kilometer markers 194 and 195, follow the signed turnoff left (north) toward Santa María del Oro town. Keep on five more miles (eight km) to the town (pop. 3,000). Continue another five miles (eight km), winding downhill to the lake. For a breathtaking lake view, stop at the roadside viewpoint about a mile past the town. At the lakeshore, head left a few hundred yards to Koala Bungalows and Trailer Park. From the *autopista* follow the signed "Santa María del Oro" exit. Proceed to the town and continue, winding downhill to the lake, as described above.

Laguna Santa María is directly accessible by bus from the second-class bus terminal in downtown Tepic (from the Cathedral, walk four blocks north along Av. Mexico; at Victoria, turn east a few steps to #9, at the station driveway). The relevant ticket office (*taquiila* of Transportes Noroeste de Nayarit, tel. 311/212-2325) is inside at the back. Buses leave for Laguna Santa María three times daily, around 6 A.M., 7 A.M., and 1 P.M. On return, they depart from the lake around 9 A.M., 10 A.M., and 3 P.M.

You can also ride a long-distance second-class Guadalajara-bound bus from the Central Camionera (Central Bus Station, on Insurgentes, southeast of the Tepic town center; see Getting There and Away) to Santa María del Oro town, where you can catch a taxi, local bus, or collective van the remaining five miles downhill to the lake.

FOOD

Traffic noise and exhaust smoke sometimes sully the atmosphere in downtown restaurants. The **Hotel Fray Junípero Serra** restaurant does not suffer such a drawback, however, in air-conditioned serenity behind its plate glass, plaza-front windows at Lerdo 23 Pte., tel. 311/212-2525. Open daily 7 A.M.–10 P.M.; credit cards are accepted. Moderate–expensive.

A much humbler but colorful and relatively quiet lunch or supper spot is the downtown favorite **Lonchería Flamingos,** tel. 311/212-1560, on Puebla Nte., half a block north behind the Presidencia Municipal, where a cadre of spirited female chefs puts out a continuous supply of steaming *tortas,* tostadas, tacos, *hamburguesas,* and *chocomiles.* The *tortas,* although tasty, are small. Best try the tostada, which is served on a huge, yummy, crunchy corn tortilla. Open daily except Wed., 10 A.M.–10:30 P.M. Budget.

For authentic Mexican cooking, go to Tepic's clean, well-lighted place for tacos, **Tacos Mismaloya,** southwest plaza corner, across from the Banco Internacional. Pick from a long list of tacos in eight styles, as well as *pozole,* enchiladas, tamales, quesadillas, and much more. Open daily 8 A.M.–10 P.M., tel. 311/216-9024.

Another popular downtown restaurant choice is the **Restaurant Altamirano,** at Av. México 109 Sur, in the big Hotel Real de Don Juan at the southeast corner of Plaza Constituyentes. Here, in a clean rustic-chic atmosphere, businesspeople lunch in the daytime, and middle- and upper-class Tepic families stop for snacks after the movies. The appetizing menu includes a host of Mexican entrées plus a number of international favorites, including spaghetti, hamburgers, omelettes, and pancakes; open Mon.–Sat. 8 A.M.–8 P.M., Sun. 8 A.M.–4 P.M. Moderate.

About a mile south of downtown, across Insurgentes from Parque La Loma, a loyal cadre of middle- and upper-class patrons keep the coffee shop–style **Restaurant Terraza,** tel. 311/213-2180, bustling morning till night. A major attraction, besides the food, is the racks of books and magazines that patrons enjoy reading, along with the good omelettes, spaghetti, and sandwiches. Open daily 7 A.M.–11 P.M. Moderate.

Tepic people enjoy a number of good suburban restaurants. On the north side of town, one of the best is the **Restaurant Higuera** at the Hotel Bugam Villas (see Suburban Motels). In the southeast suburb, **Chic's,** a Mexican version of Denny's, on Av. Insurgentes, by the big Plaza Ley shopping center, about 1.5 miles from downtown, tel. 311/214-2810, offers a bit of everything for the travel-weary: tasty American-style specialties, air-conditioned ambience, and a mini-playground for kids around back; open daily 7 A.M.–10:30 P.M. Moderate.

If Chic's is not to your liking, go into Plaza Ley nearby for about half a dozen more alternative pizzerias, *jugerías, taquerías,* and *loncherías.*

For a deluxe treat, go to **Restaurant Roberto's Internacional,** at Paseo de La Loma 472, at the corner of Av. Insurgentes, west side of La Loma park, tel. 311/213-2085. Here, attentive waiters, subdued 1960s-style decor, crisp service, and good international specialties set a luxurious but relaxing tone. Open daily except Sun. 1–11 P.M. Expensive.

SHOPPING

Its for-sale collections of Huichol art provide an excellent reason for stopping in Tepic. At least four downtown shops specialize in Huichol goods, acting as agents for more than just the commissions they receive. They have been involved with the Huichol for years, helping them preserve their religion and traditional skills in the face of expanding tourism and development. (See the special topic "The Huichol.")

Starting near the Plaza Principal, the **Casa Aguet,** on Amado Nervo, a block behind the Presidencia Municipal (look for the second-story black and white "Artesanías Huichol" sign) has an upstairs attic-museum of Huichol art. It's at 132 Amado Nervo, tel. 311/212-4130; open Mon.–Sat. 9 A.M.–2 P.M. and 4–8 P.M., Sun. 9 A.M.–2 P.M. The founder's son, personable Miguel Aguet, knows the Huichol well. Moreover, he guarantees the "lowest prices in town." His copy of *Art of the Huichol Indians* furnishes authoritative explanations of the intriguing animal and human painting motifs. He sells wholesale to dealers.

The small government handicrafts store, **Tienda de Artesanías Wereme,** corner of Amado Nervo and Mérida, next to the Presidencia Municipal, open Mon.–Fri. 9 A.M.–2 P.M. and 4–7 P.M., Sat. 9 A.M.–2 P.M., stocks some Huichol and other handicrafts. The staff, however, does not appear as knowledgeable as the private merchants.

TO PV/GUADALAJARA

© BRUCE WHIPPERMAN

Huichol people sell their handicrafts beneath the city hall portal by Tepic's Plaza Principal.

TO PV/GUADALAJARA

If you can manage only one stop in Tepic, make it one block north of the plaza at **Casa Aguiar,** Zaragoza 100 Pte., corner of Mérida, tel. 311/220-6694, where elderly Alicia and Carmela Aguiar carry on their family tradition of Huichol crafts. There, in the parlor of their graceful old ancestral home, they offer a colorful galaxy of artifacts, both antique and new. Eerie beaded masks, venerable ceremonial hats, votive arrows, God's eyes, and huge yarn *cuadras,* blooming like Buddhist *tankas,* fill the cabinets and line the walls. Open Mon.–Sat. 10 A.M.–2 P.M. and 4–7:30 P.M.

Several blocks south on Av. México, at no. 122 Sur, just past Plaza Constituyentes and across from the Hotel Real de Don Juan, **Artesanías Cicuri,** tel. 311/212-3714, 311/212-1466, or 311/216-7416, names itself after the renowned *cicuri,* the "eye of God" of the Hui-

chol. Its collection is both extensive and particularly fine, especially the beaded masks; open Mon.–Sat. 9 A.M.–2 P.M. and 4–8 P.M.

INFORMATION

Tepic's **municipal tourist information office,** tel. 311/212-8036, is at the Plaza Principal's northwest corner, just north of the Presidencia Municipal (city hall), at the corner of Amado Nervo and Puebla. It dispenses information and a tableful of excellent brochures, many in English. Hours are daily 9 A.M.–8 P.M.

Nayarit State Tourism offices, tel. 311/214-1017, is in the Convento de la Cruz at Av. Mexico and Calzado Ejercito, about a mile south of the cathedral. Stop by its information booth, open Mon.–Fri. 9 A.M.–2 P.M. and 6–8 P.M., Sat. 9 A.M.–2 P.M., which stocks excellent brochures. Altenatively, visit the website www.visitnayarit.gob.mx.

English-language books and magazines are scarce in Tepic. **Newsstands** beneath the plaza portals just west of the Hotel Fray Junípero Serra and the bookstore **Publicaciones Azteca** on Av. México, corner Morelos (open daily 7 A.M.–11 P.M.), tel. 311/216-0811, usually have the *News* from Mexico City in the afternoon. Also, the Restaurant Terraza, tel. 311/213-2180, open daily 7 A.M.–11 P.M., on Insurgentes, across from Parque La Loma, between Querétaro and Oaxaca, also generally has the *News* and a couple of dozen popular American magazines, such as *Time, Newsweek,* and *National Geographic.*

SERVICES

For best money exchange rates, go to a bank (all with ATMs), such as the main **Banamex** branch on Av. México at Zapata. It's open Mon.–Fri. 9 A.M.–4 P.M. If the lines at Banamex are too long, go to **Bancomer,** tel. 311/212-0260, open Mon.–Fri. 9 A.M.–4 P.M., Sat. 10 A.M.–2 P.M. across the street, or long-hours **Banco Internacional,** tel. 311/212-4238 or 311/212-4338, on the main square next to the Presidencia Municipal (Mérida 184 Nte., open for U.S. dollar money exchange Mon.–Sat. 8:30 A.M.–7 P.M.).

After hours, use a bank ATM, or try one of the many *casas de cambio* (money exchange counters) on Av. Mexico, such as the **Lidor,** just north of the Palacio de Gobierno, tel. 311/212-3384; or **Mololoa,** at 49 Mexico Nte., tel. 311/216-7416, near the corner of Morelos, open Mon.–Fri. 8:30 A.M.–2 P.M. and 4:30–6:30 P.M., Sat. 9 A.M.–2 P.M.

Tepic's **post office** is downtown at Durango Nte. 27, tel. 311/212-0130, corner of Morelos Pte., open Mon.–Fri. 8 A.M.–5 P.M., Sat. 8 A.M.–11:30 P.M., about two blocks west and three blocks south of the Plaza Principal.

Telecomunicaciones, which provides telegraph, telephone, and public fax, likewise has both a downtown branch on Av. México, corner of Morelos, tel./fax 311/212-9655, open Mon.–Fri. 8 A.M.–7 P.M., Sat. 8 A.M.–4 P.M., and a Central de Autobuses branch, tel./fax 311/213-2327, open Mon.–Fri. 8 A.M.–2 P.M., Sat. 8 A.M.–noon.

If you need a doctor, contact the **Sanatorio Guadalupe,** Juan Escuita 68 Nte., tel. 311/212-9401 or 311/212-2713, seven blocks west of the Plaza Principal. It has a 24-hour emergency room and a group of specialists on call. A fire-department paramedic squad is also available by calling tel. 311/213-1809.

For **police** call the emergency number tel. 066; for **fire** emergencies, call the *bomberos* (firefighters), tel. 311/213-1607.

GETTING THERE AND AWAY

By Car or RV

Main highways connect Tepic with Puerto Vallarta in the south, San Blas in the west, Guadalajara in the east, and Mazatlán in the north.

Two-lane Highway 200 from Puerto Vallarta is in good condition for its 104-mile (167-km) length. Curves, traffic, and the 3,000-foot Tepic grade, however, usually slow the northbound trip to about three hours, a bit less southbound.

A pair of routes (both about 43 miles, 70 km) connect Tepic with San Blas. The more scenic of the two takes about 1.5 hours, heading south from San Blas along the Bay of Matanchén to Santa Cruz, then climbing 3,000 feet west to Tepic via

Nayarit Highway 74. The quicker route leads west from San Blas along National Highway 11, climbing through the tropical forest to Highway 15, where four lanes guide traffic rapidly to Tepic.

To and from Mazatlán, traffic, towns, and rough spots slow progress along the 182-mile (293-km), two-lane stretch of National Highway 15. Expect four or five hours of driving time under good conditions.

The same is true of the winding, 141-mile (227-km) continuation of Highway 15 eastward over the Sierra Madre Occidental to Guadalajara. Fortunately, a *cuota autopista* (toll superhighway 15D), which begins at Tepic's southeastern edge, eliminates two hours of driving time. Allow about three hours by *autopista* and at least five hours without.

By Bus

The shiny, modern **Central Camionera** on Insurgentes Sur about a mile southeast of downtown has many services, including a **tourist information office,** left-luggage lockers, a cafeteria, a post office, long-distance telephone, and public fax. Booths *(taquillas)* offering higher-class bus service are generally on the station's left (east) side; the lower class is on the right (west) side as you enter.

Transportes Pacífico (TP), tel. 311/213-2320 or 311/213-2313, has many first- and second-class local departures, connecting south with Puerto Vallarta, east with Guadalajara and Mexico City, and north with Mazatlán, and the U.S. border at Tijuana and Nogales.

Estrella Blanca (EB), tel. 311/213-2315, operating through its subsidiaries, provides many second-class, first-class, and super-first-class direct connections north, east, and south. First-class Elite (EL) departures connect north with the U.S. border (Nogales and Tijuana) via Mazatlán, and south with Acapulco via Puerto Vallarta, Barra de Navidad, Manzanillo (with connections through Colima east to Michoacán and Mexico City), and Zihuatanejo. First-class Transportes Norte (TN) departures connect, through Guadalajara, north with Saltillo and Monterrey. Super-first-class Futura (FU) connects, through Guadalajara, with Mexico City.

First-class Transportes Chihuahuenses (TC) connects north with the U.S. border (Ciudad Juárez) via Aguascalientes, Zacatecas, and Torreón. Second-class Transportes Norte de Sonora (TNS) departures connect north, through Mazatlán and Nogales, Mexicali, and Tijuana, at the U.S. border.

Transportes Norte de Sonora, tel. 311/213-2315, sells tickets for hourly daytime second-class connections with San Blas and with Santiago Ixcuintla, where you can continue by local bus to the Mexcaltitán embarcadero.

Besides providing many first-class connections with Guadalajara, independent **Omnibus de Mexico (OM),** tel. 311/213-1323, provides a few departures that connect, via Guadalajara, north with Fresnillo, Torreón, and the U.S. border at Ciudad Juárez, and northeast with Aguascalientes, Zacatecas, Saltillo, Monterrey, and the U.S. border, at Matamoros.

By Train

The recently privatized Mexican Pacific Railway no longer offers passenger service. Until further notice, trains, which clickety-clacked along the rails for generations, connecting Guadalajara, Tepic, and the U.S. border at Nogales and Mexicali, are mere fading memories.

Guadalajara

Pacific Mexico residents often go to Guadalajara (pop. three million, elev. 5,214 feet, 1,589 meters), the capital of Jalisco, for the same reason Californians frequently go to Los Angeles: to shop and choose from big selections at correspondingly small prices.

But that's only part of the fascination. Although Guadalajarans like to think of themselves as different (calling themselves, uniquely, "Tapatíos"), their city is renowned as the "most Mexican" of cities. Crowds flock to Guadalajara to bask in its mild, springlike sunshine, savor its music, and admire its grand monuments.

HISTORY

Before Columbus

The broad Atemajac Valley, where the Guadalajara metropolis now spreads, has nurtured humans for hundreds of generations. Discovered remains date back at least 10,000 years. The Río Lerma-Santiago—Mexico's longest river, which meanders across six states—has nourished Atemajac Valley cornfields for at least three millennia.

Although they built no pyramids, high cultures were occupying western Mexico by A.D. 300. They left sophisticated animal- and human-motif pottery in myriad bottle-shaped underground tombs of a style found in Jalisco, Nayarit,

and Colima. Intriguingly, similar tombs are also found in Colombia and Ecuador.

During the next 1,000 years, waves of migrants swept across the Valley of Atemajac: Toltecs from the northeast; the Aztecs much later from the west. As Toltec power declined during the 13th century, the Tarascan civilization took root in Michoacán to the south and filled the power vacuum left by the Toltecs. On the eve of the Spanish conquest, semiautonomous local chiefdoms, tributaries of the Tarascan Emperor, shared the Atemajac valley.

Conquest and Colonization

The fall of the Aztecs in 1521 and the Tarascans a few years later made the Valley of Atemajac a plum ripe for the picking. In the late 1520s, while Cortés was absent in Spain, the opportunistic Nuño de Guzmán vaulted himself to power in Mexico City on the backs of the native peoples and at the expense of Cortés's friends and relatives. Suspecting correctly that his glory days in Mexico City were numbered, Guzmán cleared out three days before Christmas 1529, at the head of a small army of adventurers seeking new conquests in western Mexico. They raped, ravaged, and burned for half a dozen years, inciting dozens of previously pacified tribes to rebellion.

Hostile Mexican attacks repeatedly foiled Guzmán's attempts to establish his western Mexico capital, which he wanted to name after his Spanish hometown, Guadalajara (from the Arabic *wad al hadjarah,* or river of stones). Ironically, it wasn't until the year of Guzmán's death in Spain, in 1542, six years after his arrest by royal authorities, that the present Guadalajara was founded. At the downtown Plaza de Los Fundadores, a panoramic bronze frieze shows cofounders Doña Beátriz de Hernández and governor Cristóbal de Oñate christening the soon-to-become-capital of the "Kingdom of Nueva Galicia."

The city grew; its now-venerable public buildings rose at the edges of sweeping plazas, from which expeditions set out to explore other lands. In 1563, Legazpi and Urdaneta sailed west to conquer the Philippines; the year 1602 saw Vizcaíno sail for the Californias and the Pacific Northwest. In 1687 Father Kino left for 27 years of mission-building in Sonora and what would be Arizona and New Mexico; finally, during the 1760s, Father Junípero Serra and Captain Gaspar de Portola began their arduous trek to discover San Francisco Bay and found a string of California missions.

During Spain's Mexican twilight, Guadalajara was a virtual imperial city, ruling all of northwest Mexico, plus what would become California, Nevada, Arizona, and Utah—an empire twice the size of Britain's 13 colonies.

Independence

The cry, "Death to the *gachupines,* Viva México" by insurgent priest Miguel Hidalgo ignited rebellion on September 16, 1810. Buoyed by a series of quick victories, Hidalgo advanced on Mexico City in command of a huge ragtag army. But, facing the punishing fusillades of a small but disciplined Spanish force, Hidalgo lost his nerve and decided to occupy Guadalajara instead. Loyalist General Felix Calleja pursued and routed Hidalgo's forces on the bank of the Lerma-Santiago, not far east of Guadalajara. Although Hidalgo and Allende escaped, they were captured in the north a few months later. It wasn't for another dozen bloody years that others—Iturbide, Guerrero, Morelos—from other parts of Mexico realized Hidalgo's dream of independence.

Guadalajara, its domain reduced by the republican government to the new state of Jalisco, settled down to the production of corn, cattle, and tequila. The railroad came, branched north to the United States and south to the Pacific, and by 1900, Guadalajara's place as a commercial hub and Mexico's second city was secure.

Modern Guadalajara

After the bloodbath of the 1910–1917 revolution, Guadalajara's growth far outpaced the country's in general. From a population of around 100,000, Guadalajara ballooned to more than three million by 2000. People were drawn from the countryside by jobs in 1,000 new factories, making everything from textiles and shoes to chemicals and soda pop.

Handicraft manufacture, always important in Guadalajara, zoomed during the 1960s, when waves of jet-riding tourists came, saw, and bought mountains of blown glass, leather, pottery, and metal finery.

During the 1980s, Guadalajara put on a new face while at the same time preserving the best part of its old downtown. An urban-renewal plan of visionary proportions created Plaza Tapatía—acres of shops, stores, and offices beside fountain-studded malls—incorporating Guadalajara's venerable theaters, churches, museums, and government buildings into a single grand open space.

During the 1990s the digital revolution in the United States spilled over into Guadalajara. Dozens of giant new plants—Hewlett-Packard, Sony, Intel, Motorola—added substance to the claim that, by 2000, Guadalajara had become the Silicon Valley of Mexico.

SIGHTS

Getting Oriented

Although Guadalajara sprawls over a 100 square miles, the treasured mile-square heart of the city is easily explorable on foot. The cathedral corner of north-south Av. 16 de Septiembre and Av. Morelos marks the center of town. A few blocks south, another important artery, east-west Av. Juárez, runs above the new metro subway line through the main business district, while a few

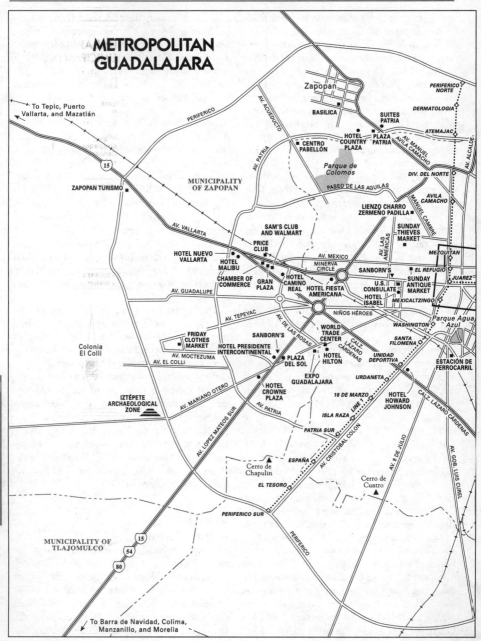

METROPOLITAN GUADALAJARA

Zapopan

PERIFERICO NORTE

DERMATOLOGIA

BASILICA

SUITES PATRIA

ATEMAJAC

To Tepic, Puerto Vallarta, and Mazatlán

PERIFERICO

AV. ACUEDUCTO

HOTEL COUNTRY PLAZA

PLAZA PATRIA

AV. MANUEL AVILA CAMACHO

AV. ALCALDE

CENTRO PABELLON

15

AV. PATRIA

Parque de Colomos

DIV. DEL NORTE

ZAPOPAN TURISMO

MUNICIPALITY OF ZAPOPAN

PASEO DE LAS AGUILAS

AVILA CAMACHO

LIENZO CHARRO ZERMEÑO PADILLA

MANUEL CAMBRE

AV. VALLARTA

SAM'S CLUB AND WALMART

PRICE CLUB

SUNDAY THIEVES MARKET

AV. LAS AMERICAS

MEZQUITAN

HOTEL NUEVO VALLARTA

HOTEL MALIBU

AV. MEXICO

MINERVA CIRCLE

SANBORN'S

EL REFUGIO

JUAREZ

CHAMBER OF COMMERCE

GRAN PLAZA

HOTEL CAMINO REAL

SUNDAY ANTIQUE MARKET

AV. GUADALUPE

HOTEL FIESTA AMERICANA

U.S. CONSULATE

HOTEL ISABEL

MEXICALTZINGO

NIÑOS HÉROES

Parque Agua Azul

AV. TEPEYAC

AV. DE LAS ROSAS

WORLD TRADE CENTER

WASHINGTON

Colonia El Colli

FRIDAY CLOTHES MARKET

SANBORN'S

CALZ. LAZARO CARDENAS

SANTA FILOMENA

HOTEL PRESIDENTE INTERCONTINENTAL

HOTEL HILTON

UNIDAD DEPORTIVA

ESTACIÓN DE FERROCARRIL

AV. MOCTEZUMA

PLAZA DEL SOL

AV. EL COLLI

EXPO GUADALAJARA

URDANETA

CALZ. LAZARO CARDENAS

IZTÉPETE ARCHAEOLOGICAL ZONE

HOTEL CROWNE PLAZA

18 DE MARZO

HOTEL HOWARD JOHNSON

AV. MARIANO OTERO

AV. PATRIA

ISLA RAZA

LINE 1

AV. LOPEZ MATEOS SUR

PATRIA SUR

AV. CRISTOBAL COLON

AV. 8 DE JULIO

AV. GOB. LUIS CUREL

Cerro de Chapulin

ESPAÑA

Cerro de Cuatro

EL TESORO

MUNICIPALITY OF TLAJOMULCO

15

54

80

PERIFERICO SUR

PERIFERICO

To Barra de Navidad, Colima, Manzanillo, and Morelia

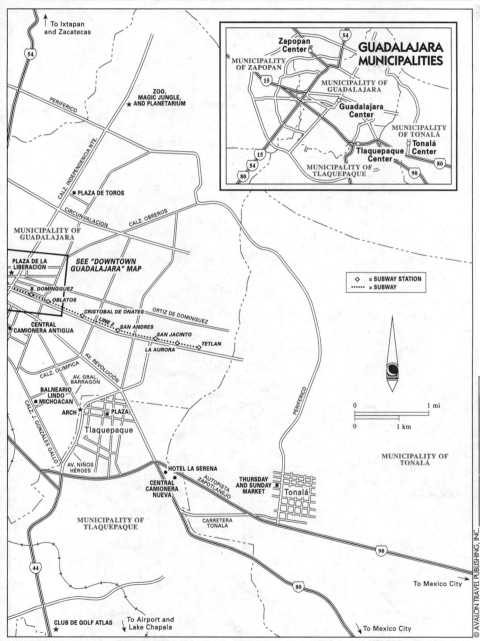

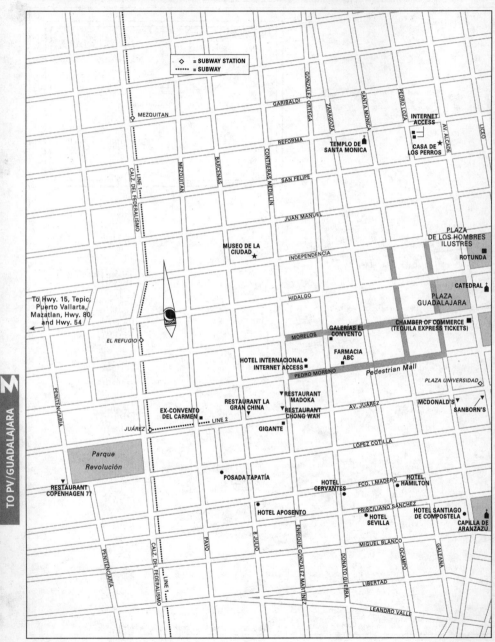

◇ = SUBWAY STATION
••••• = SUBWAY

MEZQUITAN

GONZALEZ ORTEGA
GARIBALDI
ZARAGOZA
SANTA MONICA
PEDRO LOZA

INTERNET ACCESS
AV. ALCADE
LICEO

REFORMA

TEMPLO DE SANTA MONICA
CASA DE LOS PERROS

MEZQUITAN
BARCENAS
CONTRERAS MEDELLIN
SAN FELIPE

JUAN MANUEL

MUSEO DE LA CIUDAD ★
INDEPENDENCIA

PLAZA DE LOS HOMBRES ILUSTRES
ROTUNDA

CALZ. DEL FEDERALISMO
LINE 1

To Hwy. 15, Tepic,
Puerto Vallarta,
Mazatlan, Hwy. 80,
and Hwy. 54

HIDALGO

CATEDRAL

PLAZA GUADALAJARA

EL REFUGIO ◇

MORELOS

GALERÍAS EL CONVENTO

CHAMBER OF COMMERCE (TEQUILA EXPRESS TICKETS)

HOTEL INTERNACIONAL ●
INTERNET ACCESS ■

FARMACIA ABC

PEDRO MORENO

Pedestrian Mall

PLAZA UNIVERSIDAD ◇

PENITENCIARIA

EX-CONVENTO DEL CARMEN ■
LINE 2

▼ RESTAURANT MADOKA
▼ RESTAURANT LA GRAN CHINA
▼ RESTAURANT CHONG WAH

AV. JUAREZ

MCDONALD'S ▼
SANBORN'S ▼

JUAREZ ◇

GIGANTE

LÓPEZ COTILLA

Parque Revolución

POSADA TAPATÍA ●

RESTAURANT COPENHAGEN 77 ●

HOTEL CERVANTES ●
FCO. I. MADERO
HOTEL HAMILTON ●

PENITENCIARIA

CALZ. DEL FEDERALISMO
LINE 1

8 JULIO

PAVO

ENRIQUE GONZALEZ MARTINEZ

HOTEL APOSENTO ●

PRISCILIANO SANCHEZ
HOTEL SEVILLA ●

HOTEL SANTIAGO DE COMPOSTELA ●
CAPILLA DE ARANZAZÚ

DONATO GUERRA

MIGUEL BLANCO

OCAMPO

GALEANA

LIBERTAD

LEANDRO VALLE

MOON

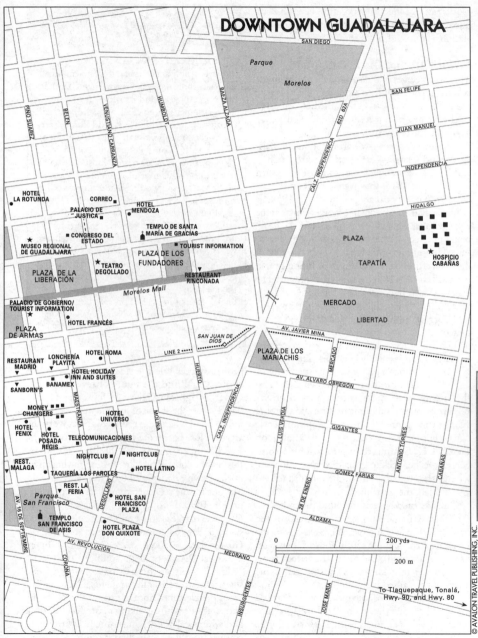

DOWNTOWN GUADALAJARA

SAN DIEGO

Parque
Morelos

SAN FELIPE

JUAN MANUEL

INDEPENDENCIA

HIDALGO

HOTEL
LA ROTUNDA

CORREO

HOTEL
MENDOZA

PALACIO DE
JUSTICA

CONGRESO DEL
ESTADO

TEMPLO DE SANTA
MARÍA DE GRACIAS

MUSEO REGIONAL
DE GUADALAJARA

TOURIST INFORMATION

PLAZA DE LOS
FUNDADORES

PLAZA
TAPATÍA

HOSPICIO
CABAÑAS

TEATRO
DEGOLLADO

PLAZA DE LA
LIBERACIÓN

RESTAURANT
RINCONADA

Morelos Mall

MERCADO

LIBERTAD

PALACIO DE GOBIERNO/
TOURIST INFORMATION

HOTEL FRANCÉS

PLAZA
DE ARMAS

AV. JAVIER MINA

SAN JUAN DE
DIOS

LINE 2

PLAZA DE LOS
MARIACHIS

RESTAURANT
MADRID

LONCHERÍA
PLAYITA

HOTEL ROMA

AV. ALVARO OBREGÓN

HOTEL HOLIDAY
INN AND SUITES

BANAMEX

SANBORN'S

MONEY
CHANGERS

HOTEL
UNIVERSO

GIGANTES

HOTEL
FENIX

HOTEL
POSADA
REGIS

TELECOMUNICACIONES

NIGHTCLUB

NIGHTCLUB

REST.
MALAGA

TAQUERÍA LOS FAROLES

HOTEL LATINO

GÓMEZ FARÍAS

REST. LA
FERIA

Parque
San Francisco

HOTEL SAN
FRANCISCO
PLAZA

ALDAMA

TEMPLO
SAN FRANCISCO
DE ASIS

HOTEL PLAZA
DON QUIXOTE

AV. REVOLUCIÓN

0   200 yds

0   200 m

MEDRANO

To Tlaquepaque, Tonalá,
Hwy. 90, and Hwy. 80

TO PV/GUADALAJARA

© AVALON TRAVEL PUBLISHING, INC.

182 South to Puerto Vallarta and Inland to Guadalajara

blocks east, Av. Independencia runs beneath Plaza Tapatía and past the main market to the railway station a couple of miles south.

A Walk Around Old Guadalajara

The twin steeples of the **cathedral** serve as an excellent starting point to explore the city-center plazas and monuments. The cathedral, dedicated to the Virgin of the Assumption when it was begun in 1561, was finished about 30 years later. A potpourri of styles—Moorish, Gothic, Renaissance, and Classic—make up its spires, arches, and facades. Although an earthquake demolished its steeples in 1818, they were rebuilt and resurfaced with cheery canary yellow tiles in 1854.

Inside, side altars and white facades climax at the principal altar, built over a tomb containing the remains of several former clergy, including the mummified heart of renowned Bishop Cabañas. One of the main attractions is the **Virgin of Innocence,** in the small chapel just to the left of the entrance. The glass-enclosed figure contains the bones of a 12-year-old girl who was martyred in the 3rd century, forgotten, then rediscovered in the Vatican catacombs in 1786 and shipped to Guadalajara in 1788. The legend claims she died protecting her virginity; it is equally likely that she was martyred for refusing to recant her Christian faith.

Somewhere near the main altar you'll find either a copy of or the authentic **Virgin of Zapopan.** Between sometime in June and October 12, the tiny, adored figure will be the authentic "La Generala," as she's affectionately known; on October 12, a tumultuous crowd of worshippers escorts her back to the cathedral in Zapopan, where she remains until brought back to Guadalajara the next June.

Outside, broad plazas surround the cathedral: the **Plaza Guadalajara,** in front (west) of the cathedral, then as you move counterclockwise, the **Plaza de Armas** to the south, **Plaza Liberación** to the east (behind), and the **Plaza de los Hombres Ilustres** (also known as La Rotonda) to the north of the cathedral.

Across Av. Morelos, the block-square Plaza de los Hombres Ilustres is bordered by 15 sculptures of Jalisco's eminent sons. Their remains lie beneath the stone rotunda in the center; their

SUBWAY, GUADALAJARA STYLE

Since the early 1990s, Guadalajarans have enjoyed a new underground train system, which they call simply the **Tren Ligero** (Light Train). It's nothing fancy, a kind of Motel 6 of subway lines—inexpensive, efficient, and reliable. A pair of intersecting lines, Línea 1 and Línea 2, carry passengers in approximately north-south and east-west directions, along a total of 15 miles (25 km) of track. The station most visitors see first is the Plaza Universidad (on line 2), accessible by staircases that descend near the city-center corner of Juárez and Colón. Look for the Denny's restaurant nearby.

Downstairs, if you want to take a ride, deposit the specified number of pesos in machines, which will give you in exchange a brass *ficha* token, good for one ride and one transfer. If you opt to transfer, you have to do it at Juárez station, the next stop west of Plaza Universidad, where lines 1 and 2 intersect. (Hint: It's best to begin your Guadalajara subway adventure before 9 P.M.; the Tren Ligero goes to sleep by about 11 P.M.)

bronze statues line the sidewalk. Right at the corner you'll find the figure of revered Jalisco Governor Ignacio Vallarta; a few steps farther north stands the statue of José Clemente Orozco, legally blind when he executed his great works of art. (See Jose Clemente Orozco Art Museum.)

Adjacent to and east of the Plaza Hombres Ilustres, the colonial building behind the lineup of horse-drawn *calandrias* housed the Seminario de San José for the six generations after its construction in 1696. During the 1800s it served variously as a barracks and a public lecture hall, and, since 1918, it has housed the **Museo Regional de Guadalajara,** 60 Liceo, tel. 33/3614-6521, open Tues.–Sat. 9 A.M.–6:30 P.M., Sun. 9 A.M.–5 P.M.

Inside, tiers of rooms surrounding a tree-shaded interior patio illustrate local history. Exhibits depict scenes from as early as the Big Bang and continue with a hulking mastodon skeleton and whimsical animal and human figurines recovered from the bottle-shaped tombs of Jalisco,

Nayarit, and Colima. Upstairs rooms contain life-sized displays of contemporary but traditional fishing methods at nearby Lake Chapala and costumes and culture of regional Cora, Huichol, Tepehuan, and Mexica peoples.

Back outside, head east two blocks down Av. Hidalgo, paralleling the expansive Plaza Liberación behind the cathedral. On your left you will pass the baroque facades of the *congreso del estado* (state legislature) and the *palacio de justicia* (state supreme court) buildings. Ahead at the east end of the plaza rises the timeless silhouette of the **Teatro Degollado.**

The theater's classic, columned facade climaxes in an epic marble frieze, depicting the allegory of Apollo and the nine muses. Inside, the Degollado's resplendent grand salon is said to rival the gilded refinement of Milan's renowned La Scala. Overhead, its ceiling glows with Gerardo Suárez's panorama of canto IV of Dante's *Divine Comedy,* complete with its immortal cast—Julius Caesar, Homer, Virgil, Saladin—and the robed and wreathed author himself in the middle. Named for the millionaire Governor Degollado who financed its construction, the theater opened with appropriate fanfare on September 13, 1866, with a production of *Lucia de Lammermoor,* starring Angela Peralta, the renowned "Mexican Nightingale." An ever-changing menu of artists still graces the Degollado's stage. These include an excellent local folkloric ballet troupe every Sunday morning (see Entertainment and Events).

Walk behind the Degollado, where a modern bronze frieze, the *Frisa de Los Fundadores,* decorates its back side. Appropriately, a mere two blocks from the spot where the city was founded, the 68-foot sculpture shows Guadalajara's co-founders facing each other on opposite sides of a big tree. Governor Cristóbal de Oñate strikes the tree with his sword, while Doña Beátriz de Hernández holds a fighting cock, symbolizing her gritty determination (and that of dozens of fellow settlers) that Guadalajara's location should remain put.

Plaza Tapatía

Turn around and face east. The 17 acres of the Plaza Tapatía complex extend ahead for several blocks across subplazas, fountains, and malls. Initially wide in the foreground of Plaza de Los Fundadores, the Tapatía narrows between a double row of shiny shops and offices, then widens into a broad esplanade and continues beside a long pool/fountain that leads to the monumental, domed Hospicio Cabañas a third of a mile away. Along the Tapatía's lateral flanks, a pair of long malls—continuations of Avs. Hidalgo and Morelos—parallel the central Paseo Degollado mall for two blocks.

The eastern end of the Morelos mall climaxes with the striking bronze *escudo* (coat of arms) of Guadalajara. Embodying the essence of the original 16th-century coat of arms authorized by Emperor Charles V, the *escudo* shows a pair of lions protecting a pine tree (with leaves, rather than needles). The lions represent the warrior's determination and discipline, and the solitary pine symbolizes noble ideals.

Continue east, to where the Plaza Tapatía widens, giving berth for the sculpture-fountain **Imolación de Quetzalcoatl,** designed and executed by Víctor Manuel Contreras in 1982. Four bronze serpent-birds, representing knowledge and the spirit of humankind, stretch toward heaven at the ends of a giant cross. In the center, a towering bronze spiral represents the unquenchable flame of Quetzalcoatl, transforming all that it touches. Locals call the sculpture the "big corkscrew," however.

At this point, Av. Independencia runs directly beneath Plaza Tapatía, past the adjacent sprawling **Mercado Libertad,** built in 1958 on the site of the traditional Guadalajara *tianguis* (open-air market), known since pre-Columbian times. Follow the elevated pedestrian walkway to explore the Libertad's produce, meat, fish, herbs, food, and handicrafts stalls. (For more Mercado Libertad details, see the shopping section.)

On Independencia, just beyond the market, musicians at the **Plaza de los Mariachis** continue the second century of a tradition born when mariachi (cowboy troubadour) groups first appeared during the 1860s in Guadalajara. The musical hubbub climaxes Saturday nights and Sunday afternoons, as musicians gather, singing while they wait to be hired for serenades and parties.

Behind the long pool/fountain at the east end of Plaza Tapatía stands the domed neoclassic **Hospicio Cabañas,** the largest and one of the most remarkable colonial buildings in the Americas, designed and financed by Bishop Juan Ruiz de Cabañas; construction was complete in 1810. The purpose of the "Guadalajara House of Charity and Mercy," as the good bishop originally named it, a home for the sick, helpless, and homeless, was fulfilled for 170 years. Although still successfully serving as an orphanage during the 1970s, time had taken its toll on the Hospicio Cabañas. The city and state governments built a new orphanage in the suburbs, restored the old building, and changed its purpose. It now houses the **Instituto Cultural Cabañas,** a center for the arts at Cabañas 8, tel. 33/3617-4440. Open Tues.–Sat. 9 A.M.–8 P.M., Sun. 10 A.M.–3 P.M. Public programs include classes and films, and instrumental, chorale, and dance concerts. For more information, call 33/3617-4440 (in Spanish).

Inside, seemingly endless ranks of corridors pass a host of sculpture-decorated patios. Practice rooms resound with the clatter of dancing feet and the halting strains of apprentice violins, horns, and pianos. Exhibition halls and studios of the **José Clemente Orozco Art Museum** occupy a large fraction of the rooms, while the great muralist's brooding work spreads over a corresponding fraction of the walls. Words such as dark, fiery, nihilistic, even apocalyptic, would not be too strong to describe the panoramas that Orozco executed (1938–1939) in the soaring chapel beneath the central dome. On one wall, an Aztec goddess wears a necklace of human hearts; on another, armored, automaton-soldiers menace Indian captives; while in the cupola overhead, Orozco's *Man of Fire,* wreathed in flame, appears to soar into a hellishly red-hot sky.

Out-of-Downtown Sights

The former villages of Zapopan, Tlaquepaque, and Tonalá, now parts of metropolitan Guadalajara, make interesting day-trip destinations from the city center. Although local buses or your own wheels can get you there, crowds of bus commuters and congested city streets increase the desirability of the local tour option. Contact your hotel travel desk, a travel agent, or a well-equipped agency such as Panoramex, at Federalismo Sur 944, tel. 33/3810-5057 or 33/3810-5005, which conducts reasonably priced bilingual tours daily from the city center. (For more suggestions, see Guides in the Information and Services section.)

Zapopan, about six miles northwest of downtown, is famous for its soaring baroque (1730) basilica, home of the renowned Virgin of Za-

THE THREE SISTERS OF MEXICO

In all of Mexico, only the Virgin of Guadalupe exceeds in adoration the all-Jalisco trio—the "Three Sister" Virgins of Talpa, Zapopan, and San Juan de los Lagos. Yearly they draw millions of humble Mexican pilgrims who bus, walk, hitchhike, or in some cases crawl, to festivals honoring the virgins. Each virgin's popularity springs from some persistent, endearing legend. The Virgin of Talpa defied a haughty bishop's efforts to cage her; the Virgin of Zapopan rescued Guadalajara from war and disaster; the Virgin of San Juan de los Lagos restored a dead child to life.

Talpa, Zapopan, and San Juan de los Lagos townsfolk have built towering basilicas to shelter and honor each virgin. Each small and fragile figurine is draped in fine silk and jewels and worshipped by a continuous stream of penitents. During a virgin festival the image is lifted aloft by a platoon of richly costumed bearers and paraded to the clamor, tumult, and cheers of a million or more of the faithful.

Even if you choose to avoid the crowds and visit Talpa, Zapopan, or San Juan de los Lagos on a nonfestival day, you'll soon see the hubbub continues. Pilgrims come and go, bands and mariachis play, and curio stands stuffed with gilded devotional goods crowd the basilica square.

popan. The legendary image, one of the beloved "three sisters" virgins of Mexico, has enjoyed generations of popularity so enormous that it must be seen to be believed. Local folks, whenever they happen by, often stop to say a prayer (or at least make the sign of the cross as they pass) in front of the cathedral gate. Inside, the faithful crawl the length of the sanctuary to pay their respects to the diminutive blue and white figure. The adoration climaxes on October 12, when a rollicking crowd of hundreds of thousands accompanies the Virgin of Zapopan from the downtown Guadalajara cathedral home to Zapopan, where she stays from October 13 until June.

Afterward, look over the displays of Huichol indigenous handicrafts in the adjacent museum-shop **Artesanías Huichola Wirrarica,** tel. 33/3636-4430, on your left as you exit the basilica; open Mon.–Sat. 9:30 A.M.–1:30 P.M., Sun. 9:30 A.M.–2 P.M. Sale items include eerie beaded masks, intriguing yarn paintings, and *ojos de dios* (God's eyes) yarn sculptures. Later, browse for bargains among the handicrafts stalls in front of the basilica and in the municipal market in the adjacent plaza on the corner of Av. Hidalgo and Calle Eva Briseño.

Getting There: From downtown Guadalajara, local Zapopan-marked (275 diagonal or air-conditioned Tur) buses depart from the southside Camionera Antigua (Old Bus Station) on Av. Estadio, just north of Parque Agua Azul, and continue through the downtown, stopping at the corner of López Cotilla and 16 de Septiembre. By car, follow Av. Manuel Avila Camacho, which diagonals northwest for about four miles from the city center to Zapopan, marked by the old baroque arch on the left. After one block, turn left onto Av. Hidalgo, the double main street of Zapopan. Within four blocks you'll see the plaza and the basilica on the left.

Zapopan town is the *cabecera* (headquarters) of the sprawling *municipio* of Zapopan, farm and mountain hinterland, famous for **La Barranca,** the 2,000-foot-deep canyon of the Río Grande de Santiago. At the viewpoint past San Isidro, around Km 15, Saltillo Highway 54 north of Guadalajara, motorists stop at the viewpoint, **Mirador Dr. Atl,** to admire the canyon vista

and the waterfall **Cola del Caballo** (Horse's Tail) as it plummets hundreds of feet to the river below.

Past that, a small paradise of springs decorates the lush canyonland. First, at Km 17, comes **Los Camachos,** a forest and mountain-framed *balneario* (bathing park) with pools and restaurants; a few miles farther along is the hot spring bathing complex, **Balneario Nuevo Paraíso,** at Km 24. A kilometer farther (follow the left side road from the highway about a half kilometer) you can visit colonial-era **Ixcatán** village. Don't miss the precious old village church, and the stones bearing maplike inscriptions in the church-front park. Historians speculate that these served as directions to safe havens during the Mixtón war that blazed around Ixcatán in 1541–1542. Get there by car via Highway 54, the Saltillo-Zacatecas highway, which heads northward along Av. Alcalde from the city-center cathedral. Bus riders can board the "Los Camachos" bus, which leaves the Glorieta Normal (on Av. Alcalde about a mile north of the downtown cathedral) about every hour from 5 A.M. until the early afternoon.

For more information about Zapopan sights, drop by the Zapopan tourist information office at Plaza Centro, just inside the west-side *periférico* (peripheral boulevard), open Mon.–Sat. 9 A.M.–7:30 P.M., at Av. Vallarta 6503. Call before you come, tel. 33/3100-0755, ext. 113, or 33/3110-0754, ext. 59. Ask to speak with the friendly English-speaking director, Gabriel Delgado. Alternatively, contact him by fax 33/3110-0383, or email jdelgado@zapopan.gob.mx. For more information, visit the Zapopan tourism website, www.zapopan.gob.mx.

Tlaquepaque and **Tonalá,** in the southeast suburbs, are among Mexico's renowned handicrafts villages. Tlaquepaque (tlah-kay-PAH-kay) (now touristy, but still interesting), about five miles from the city center, is famous for fine stoneware and blown glass; Tonalá, another five miles farther, retains plenty of sleepy, colorful country ambience. Shops abound in celebrated ceramic, brass, and papier-mâché animal figurines. The most exciting, but crowded, time to visit is during the Thursday and Sunday open-air markets. (For more Tlaquepaque and Tonalá details, see Shopping.)

ACCOMMODATIONS

Downtown Hotels

Several good hotels, from budget to plush, dot the center of Guadalajara, mostly in the Av. Juárez business district, a few blocks from the cathedral and plazas. Many have parking garages; a desirable downtown option for auto travelers. Hotels farthest from the cathedral plazas are generally the most economical.

The **Posada San Rafael,** López Cotilla 619, Guadalajara, Jalisco 44100, tel. 33/3614-9146, sanrafael@avantel.net, one block off Juárez, near the corner of Calle 8 Julio, is about 10 blocks from the cathedral. Its simple but gaily decorated rooms with bath are spread around a light, colorfully restored central patio. Tightly managed by the friendly on-site owner, the Tapatía's prices are certainly right. Try for a room in the back, away from the noisy street. The 12 rooms rent for $19 s, $22 d, with fans.

Three blocks closer in, at the northeast corner of Prisciliano Sánchez and Donato Guerra, step up from the sidewalk and enter the cool, contemporary-classic interior of the **Hotel Cervantes** at 442 Prisciliano Sánchez, tel./fax 33/3613-6686 or 33/3613-6846. Here, everything, from the marble-and-brass lobby, the modern-chic restaurant and bar, pool, and exercise room downstairs to the big beds, plush carpets, and shiny marble baths of the rooms upstairs, seems perfect for the enjoyment of its predominately business clientele. For such refinement, rates, at about $54 s, $59 d, are surprisingly moderate; with TV, phones, parking, and a/c; credit cards are accepted.

Across the street, on Prisciliano Sánchez between Ocampo and Donato Guerra, the old standby **Hotel Sevilla,** Prisciliano Sánchez 413, Guadalajara, Jalisco 44100, tel./fax 33/3614-9354 or 33/3614-9037, fax 33/3614-9172, offers basic accommodations at budget prices. Its 80 rooms, furnished in dark brown wood and rugs to match, are plain but comfortable. For more light and quiet, get an upper-story room away from the street. Amenities include a lobby with TV, parking, a hotel safe for storing valuables, and a restaurant open daily except Sunday.

Rates run $18 s, $20 d, $33 t; fans and telephones included.

One block away, on Madero, the even plainer **Hotel Hamilton,** Madero 381, Guadalajara, Jalisco 44100, tel. 33/3614-6726, offers a rock-bottom alternative. The 32 bare-bulb, not-so-clean rooms border on dingy; their steel doors seem to enhance the drabness more than increasing security. Store your valuables in the hotel safe. For less noise and more light, get a room in back, away from the street. Rooms rent for $9 s or d, $15 t, with fans but no parking.

Cheerier and closer in, where the pedestrian strolling mall begins on Moreno, stands the big, 110-room **Hotel Internacional,** Pedro Moreno 570, Guadalajara, Jalisco 44100, tel. 33/3613-0330, fax 33/3613-2866. Downstairs, a small lobby with comfortable chairs adjoins the reception area. In the tower upstairs, the 1960s-style rooms, most with city views, are clean and comfortable, but varied. Look at more than one before moving in. Try for a discount below the asking prices of $56 s or d, which are high compared to the competition. (The hotel does, however, offer a 15 percent discount for a one-week rental). Amenities include fans, some a/c, phones, TV, a café, and parking; credit cards are accepted.

Equally well-situated but shinier, **Hotel Fénix,** Corona 160, Guadalajara, Jalisco 44100, tel. 33/3614-5714, fax 33/3613-4005, ventas@fenixgdl.com.mx, lies on Corona, smack in the downtown business center, a short walk from everything. The owners have managed to upgrade this rather basic small-lobby hotel into something more elaborate. The somewhat cramped result, while not unattractive, is often very busy. During the day, tour groups traipse in and out past the reception desk, while at night guests crowd the adjacent lobby bar for drinks and live combo music. Upstairs the 200 air-conditioned rooms are spacious and comfortably furnished with American-standard motel amenities. Walk-in rates, which run about $80 s or d, are high for a hotel with neither pool nor parking. You might try for a better deal in advance by book-

GUADALAJARA ACCOMMODATIONS BY PRICE

Accommodations (telephone area code 33, postal code 44100 unless otherwise noted) are listed in increasing order of approximate high-season, double-room rates. Unless specified otherwise, 800 numbers are for toll-free reservations from the United States and Canada.

Downtown Hotels

Hotel Hamilton, F. Madero 381, tel. 3614-6726, $9

Hotel Sevilla, P. Sánchez 413, tel./fax 3614-9037, 3614-9354, fax 3614-9172, $20

Hotel Latino, P. Sánchez 74, tel. 3614-4484 or 3614-6214, $21

Posada San Rafael, L. Cotilla 3619, tel. 3614-9146, sanrafael@avantel.net, $22

Hotel Posada Regis, R. Corona 171, tel. 3614-8633, tel./fax 3613-3026, $30

Hotel Universo, L. Cotilla 1361, tel. 3613-2815, fax 3613-4734, $42

Hotel San Francisco Plaza, Degollado 267, tel. 3613-8954, fax 3613-3257, $46

Hotel Frances, Maestranza 35, tel. 3613-1190 or 3613-0936, fax 3658-2831, hfrances@hotel-frances.com, $53

Hotel Internacional, P. Moreno 570, tel. 3613-0330, fax 3613-2866, $56

Hotel Cervantes, 442 P. Sánchez, tel./fax 3613-6686, 3613-6846, or 3613-6816, $59

Hotel Roma, Juárez 170, tel. 3614-8650, fax 3613-2629, $70

Hotel Fénix, R. Corona 160, tel. 3614-5714, fax 3613-4005, ventas@fenixgdl.com.mx, $80

Hotel de Mendoza, V. Carranza 16, tel. 3613-4646 or 3614-6752, fax 3613-7310, hotel@demendoza.com.mx, $90

Holiday Inn Hotel and Suites, Juárez 211, tel. 3613-1763, 800/465-4329, fax 3614-9766, holidaycentro@prodigy.net.mx, $120

Suburban Hotels

Hotel La Serena, Carretera Zapotlanejo 1500, tel. 3600-0910, fax 3600-1974, $30

Hotel Isabel, J. Guadalupe Montenegro 1572, tel./fax 3826-2630, hotelisa@telmex.net.mx, $53

Hotel Sun, Aeropuerto Internacional, postal code 45640, tel./fax 3678-9099 or 3678-9000, reservas@hotmail.udg.mx, $130

Hotel Camino Real, Av. Vallarta 5005, postal code 45040, tel. 3134-2424 or 800/903-2100 (within Mexico), 800/7CAMINO (800/722-6466), fax 3134-2404, gdl@caminoreal.com, $160

Hotel Fiesta Americana, Aurelio Aceves 225, tel. 3825-3434, 800/FIESTA1 (800/343-7821), fax 3630-3725, $180

Hotel Crowne Plaza, L. Mateos Sur 2500, postal code 45050, tel. 3634-1034, 800/272-9273, fax 3631-9393, crownegd@crownegdl.com.mx, $200

ing a package through a travel agent. Frequently, for a three-night stay, it offers a fourth night free. For more information, visit the website www.fenixgdl.com.mx.

With the same prime location right across the street, the second-floor **Hotel Posada Regis** offers both economy and a bit of old-world charm, at Corona 171, Guadalajara, Jalisco 44100, tel. 33/3614-8633 or tel./fax 33/3613-3026. Its clean and comfortable high-ceilinged rooms enclose a gracious Porfirian-era indoor lobby/atrium. Evening videos, friendly atmosphere, and a good breakfast/lunch café provide

opportunities for relaxed exchanges with other travelers. The 19 rooms cost $25 s and $30 d, with phones, fans, and optional TV, but no parking; credit cards are accepted.

Central location, comfortable though a bit worn rooms, and moderate prices explain the popularity of the nearby **Hotel Universo,** López Cotilla 161, Guadalajara, Jalisco 44100, tel. 33/3613-2815, fax 33/3613-4734, corner of Cotilla and Degollado, just three blocks from the Teatro Degollado. Guests enjoy renovated, carpeted, and draped air-conditioned rooms with wood furniture and ceiling-to-floor tiled bathrooms. The 137 rooms and suites rent for $39 s, $42 d, suites from about $45, with TV, phones, and parking; credit cards are accepted.

The Universo's competent owner/managers also run a pair of good-value hotels nearby. Their graceful, authentically colonial **Hotel San Francisco Plaza,** Degollado 267, Guadalajara, Jalisco 44100, tel. 33/3613-8954, fax 33/3613-3257, is replete with traditional charm. The reception area opens to an airy and tranquil inner patio, where big soft chairs invite you to relax amid a leafy garden of potted plants. In the evenings, the venerable arched stone corridors gleam with antique, cut-crystal lanterns. Upstairs, the rooms are no less than you would expect: most are high-ceilinged, with plenty of polished wood, hand-made furniture, rustic brass lamps by the bed, and sentimental old-Mexico paintings on the walls. Each room has a phone, TV, fan, and a large, modern-standard bathroom with marble sink. You'll find an elegant restaurant with high ceilings and chandeliers downstairs in front and plenty of parking. All this for $43 s, $46 d; credit cards are accepted.

The same owners run the **Hotel Latino,** one of Guadalajara's better cheap hotels, just around the corner at Prisciliano Sánchez 74, Guadalajara, Jalisco 44100, tel. 33/3614-4484 or 33/3614-6214. Although it's a plain hotel with a small lobby, the Latino's guests nevertheless enjoy a modicum of amenities. The 57 rooms in four stories (no elevator) are clean, carpeted, and thoughtfully furnished, albeit a bit worn around the edges. Baths are modern-standard, with shiny-tile showers and marble sinks. Rates are certainly right, at about $18 s, $21 d, including a/c, TV, parking, and phones.

Guests at the nearby **Hotel Roma,** Av. Juárez 170, Guadalajara, Jalisco 44100, tel. 33/3614-8650, fax 33/3614-2629, enjoy luxurious amenities—plush lobby, shiny restaurant/bar, rooftop rose garden, and pool—usually available only at pricier hostelries. Owners, however, have upped the tariffs; whether they can make them stick is another question. Try bargaining for discounts below the $70 s or d asking rates; with TV, phones, a/c, parking, and limited wheelchair access; credit cards are accepted. Some rooms, although clean and comfortable, are small. Look before moving in.

Across the street, the **Holiday Inn Hotel and Suites** offers a host of luxuries, at Juárez 211, tel./fax 33/3613-1763, holidaycentro@prodigy.net.mx. Upstairs, rooms are luxuriously appointed in soothing pastels, marble baths, plush carpets, and large beds. For all this and more, you'll pay from about $120 d, with cable TV, phones, a/c, parking, classy restaurant, gym, but no pool; credit cards are accepted.

The three-story, authentically baroque **Hotel Frances,** Maestranza 35, Guadalajara, Jalisco 44100, tel. 33/3613-1190 or 33/3613-0936, fax 33/3658-2831, hfrances@hotelfrances.com, rises among its fellow monuments on a quiet side street within sight of the Teatro Degollado. The Frances, Guadalajara's first hotel, built in 1610, has been restored to its original splendor. The 40-odd rooms, all with bath, glow with polished wood, bright tile, and fancy frosted cut-glass windows. Downstairs, an elegant chandelier illuminates the dignified, plant-decorated interior patio and adjacent restaurant. However, to increase business, owners have installed nightly live music downstairs (Mon.–Sat. until 10 P.M., Fri., mariachis until 11:30 P.M.), which for some may not fit with the hotel's otherwise old-world ambience. Rates, however, run a very reasonable $53 s or d; credit cards are accepted, fans only, and parking is included.

The big colonial-facade **Hotel de Mendoza,** V. Carranza 16, Guadalajara, Jalisco 44100, tel. 33/3613-4646, fax 33/3613-7310, hotel@demendoza.com.mx, www.demendoza.com.mx, only a couple of blocks north of the Teatro Degollado, is a longtime favorite of Guadalajara repeat visitors. Refined traditional embellishments—neo-Renaissance murals and wall portraits, rich dark paneling, glittering candelabras—grace the lobby, while upstairs, carpeted halls lead to spacious, comfortable rooms furnished with tasteful dark decor, including large baths, thick towels, and many other extras. The 100 rooms and suites rent from $80 s, $90 d, with American cable

TV, phones, a/c, a small pool, refined restaurant, parking, and limited wheelchair access; third night (by reservation only) often free, credit cards are accepted.

Although not in the immediate downtown area, the **Hotel Isabel,** J. Guadalupe Montenegro 1572, Guadalajara, Jalisco 44100, tel./fax 33/3826-2630, hotelisa@telmex.net.mx, in the west-side embassy neighborhood, offers a flowery garden setting at reasonable prices. The Isabel's 1960s-era amenities—comfortably furnished semideluxe rooms with phones, small blue pool, popular restaurant, and parking—have long attracted a loyal following of Guadalajara return visitors and local businesspeople. Buses (10 minutes to the city center) run nearby. Its 50 rooms rent for $48 s, $53 d, with ceiling fans and limited wheelchair access.

West-Side Luxury Hotels
During the 1980s the Plaza del Sol, a large American-style hotel, shopping, and entertainment complex, mushroomed on west-side Av. Adolfo López Mateos. The Holiday Inn and its plush neighboring hostelries that anchor the development have drawn many of the high-ticket visitors away from the old city center to the Plaza del Sol's shiny shops, restaurants, and clubs.

The **Hotel Crowne Plaza,** at Av. López Mateos Sur 2500, Guadalajara, Jalisco 45050, tel. 33/3634-1034, fax 33/3631-9393, a quarter-mile south on López Mateos (past the traffic circle), offers a relaxed resort setting. The rooms, most with private view balconies, rise in a 10-story tower above the pool and garden. Their luxurious furnishings, in soothing earth tones, include spacious, marble-accented baths. The 285 rooms start at about $200 s or d, with everything: spa, sauna, gym, children's area, miniature golf, tennis courts, and wheelchair access. Besides the local numbers above, you can reserve at toll-free U.S./Can. tel. 800/272-9273 or by email at crownegd@crownegd.com.mx. For more information, visit the website www.crownegd.com.mx.

About a mile north of Plaza del Sol, the **Hotel Fiesta Americana,** Aurelio Aceves 225, Guadalajara, Jalisco 44100, tel. 33/3825-3434, fax 33/3630-3725, towering above Av. Vallarta, the

Highway 15 Blvd. Ingreso, offers another luxury hotel option. From the reception area, a serene, carpeted lobby spreads beneath a lofty, light atrium. The 396 plush view rooms are furnished in pastel tones with soft couches, huge beds, and a host of luxury amenities. Rooms rent from about $180 d, with tennis courts, spa, restaurants, pool, and sundeck. For more information and reservations, dial toll-free U.S./Can. tel. 800/FIESTA1 (800/343-7821) or visit Fiesta Americana's website www.fiestaamericana.com.mx.

Along the same boulevard, about a mile farther west, is the **Hotel Camino Real,** Av. Vallarta 5005, Guadalajara, Jalisco 45040, the graceful queen of Guadalajara luxury hotels. In contrast to its high-rise local competitors, the Camino Real spreads through a luxurious park of lawns, pools, and shady tropical verdure. Guests enjoy tastefully appointed bungalow-style units opening onto semiprivate pools and patios. Rates start at $160 s or d and include cable TV, phone, four pools, tennis courts, and a nearby golf course. Reserve through its local number, tel. 33/3134-2424, or toll-free at Mex tel. 800/903-2100 or U.S./Can. tel. 800/7-CAMINO (800/722-6466), fax 33/3134-2404, gdl@caminoreal.com. For more information, visit the website www.caminoreal.com.

Bus-Station and Airport Hotels
Two hotels on the edge of town offer interesting bus- and air travel–related options, respectively. For bus travelers, the big long-distance Central Camionera bus station is at Guadalajara's far southeast edge, at least 20 minutes by taxi (figure $8) from the center. Bus travelers might find it convenient to stay at the sprawling, two-pool, moderately priced modern **Hotel La Serena**, Carretera Zapotlanejo 1500, Guadalajara, Jalisco 45625, tel. 33/3600-0910, fax 33/3600-1974. It's adjacent to the big bus terminal and has a restaurant. Bus and truck noise, however, may be a problem. Ask for a quiet *(tranquilo)* room. The 600 tidy and comfortable rooms, all with bath, rent for about $30 s or d. Rooms vary; look at more than one before moving in.

For air travelers, the luxuriously spacious and

airy **Hotel Sun** (formerly Hotel Casa Grande), outside the airport terminal exit door, at Calle Interior, Aeropuerto Internacional Miguel Hidalgo s/n, Guadalajara, Jalisco 45640, tel./fax 33/3678-9000 or 33/3678-9099, toll-free Mex. tel. 800/366-4200, reservashc@hotmail.com. Rates run about $130 (ask for a discount) for a comfortable double room with TV, phone, big bed, a/c, and a pool, restaurant, and bar downstairs.

Trailer Park

Guadalajara's last surviving in-town trailer park, the west-side Hacienda Trailer Park, has been sold and replaced by new apartments and condominiums.

One good out-of-town alternative exists, however. Check out the southwest-side **San José del Tajo** Trailer Park, tel. 33/3686-1738, about a mile north of the Santa Anita Country Club and Golf Course. Its very adequate facilities include many shady spaces with all hookups, toilets, showers, pool, clubroom, and tennis court. RV spaces run about $18/day, $125/week, $360/month or $11/day (for a three-month stay). Find it on the southern extension of Av. López Mateos Sur (Highways 15, 54, and 80) about three miles (five km) south of the *periférico*. Northbound, it's about half a mile (one km) north of the Santa Anita village exit.

FOOD
Breakfast and Snacks

Local folks flock to the acres of *fondas* (permanent foodstalls) on the second floor of the **Mercado Libertad** at the east end of Plaza Tapatía; open daily about 7 A.M.–6 P.M. Hearty home-style fare, including Guadalajara's specialty, *birria*—pork, goat, or lamb in savory, spiced tomato-chicken broth—is at its safest and best here. It's hard to go wrong if you make sure your choices are hot and steaming. Market stalls, furthermore, depend on repeat customers and are generally very careful that their offerings are wholesome. Be sure to douse fresh vegetables with plenty of lime *(lima)* juice, however.

Downtown Guadalajara is not overloaded with

restaurants, and many of them close early. For long-hours breakfast or supper, however, you can always rely on **Sanborn's,** which retains the 1950s' ambience and menu of its former Denny's owners. Find it right in the middle of town, at the corner of Juárez and 16 de Septiembre, open daily 7:30–1 A.M., open 24 hours Fri. and Sat., tel. 33/3613-6283.

For a local variation, head directly upstairs to **Restaurant Esquina** on the same corner, open 7 A.M.–10:30 P.M., or to the other **Sanborn's** across the street, open daily 7:30 A.M.–11 P.M., tel. 33/3613-6264. Besides a tranquil, refined North American–style coffee shop, it has a big gift shop upstairs and a bookstore, offering English-language paperbacks and magazines, downstairs.

For a light breakfast or a break during a hard afternoon of sightseeing, stop in at **Croissants Alfredo** bakery, north side of Plaza Liberación (in front and east of the Teatro Degollado). Here, a trove of luscious goodies—flaky croissants, crisp cookies, tasty tarts, and good coffee—can keep you going for hours. Open daily 8 A.M.–9:30 P.M.

If, on the other hand, you need a little break from Mexico, go to **McDonald's** for breakfast (at Juárez and Colón, one short block west of Denny's). There you can get an Egg McMuffin with ham, coffee, and hash browns for about $4 until noon daily.

For melt-in-your-mouth doughnuts and good coffee, try **Dunkin' Donuts,** open daily 8 A.M.–9 P.M., across Corona from the Hotel Fénix.

Downtown Restaurants

As you move west across downtown from the Plaza Tapatía, first comes the airy, restored Porfirian **Restaurant Rinconada,** 86 Morelos, across the plaza behind the Teatro Degollado, tel. 33/3613-9914. The mostly tourist and upper-class local customers enjoy Rinconada for its good meat, fish, and fowl entrées plus the mariachis who wander in from the Plaza Mariachi nearby. By 4 P.M. many afternoons, two or three groups are filling the place with their melodies. Open Mon.–Sat. 8 A.M.–8 P.M., Sun. 10–6 P.M. Moderate–expensive.

Nearby, a pair of clean places for good local food stand out. Try **La Chata,** open daily

8 A.M.–11 P.M., on Corona, between Cotilla and Juárez, next to Bancomer, tel. 33/361-0588. Although plenty good for breakfast, *cena* (supper) is when the cadre of female cooks come into their own. Here you can have it all: tacos, *chiles rellenos,* tostadas, enchiladas, *pozole, moles,* and a dozen other delights you've probably never heard of, all cooked the way *mamacita* used to. Recent renovations have attracted a gentrified clientele and have consequently led to higher prices. Moderate–expensive.

If La Chata's jump upscale has put it beyond your budget, go instead to **La Playita,** open daily 8 A.M.–11 P.M. half a block north, on Juárez, near Corona. Budget–moderate.

Two blocks south and one block west is the no-nonsense but worthy **Restaurant Málaga,** 16 de Septiembre 210, whose hard-working owner really does come from Málaga, Spain. The food shows it: an eclectic list of hearty breakfasts, which include hand-squeezed orange juice and good coffee. Additionally, it offers many salads, sandwiches, and desserts, and savory espresso coffee. Besides the food, customers enjoy live semiclassical piano solos, daily afternoons 2–4:30 P.M. or evenings 7–9 P.M. Open daily 7 A.M.–10:30 P.M. Credit cards accepted. Moderate–expensive.

(The Restaurant Málaga's prices seem to have risen lately. You can get similar fare and good service at the **Restaurant Madrid,** a few blocks north, on Juárez, between Corona and 16 de Septiembre, open daily 7:30 A.M.–10:30 P.M., tel. 33/3614-9504. Moderate.)

A few blocks farther south, at Corona 291, across from Parque San Francisco, you'll find **La Feria** (The Fair), tel. 33/3613-7150 or 33/3613-1812, which, true to its name, is a party ready to happen: ceilings hung with a rainbow of piñatas and tassels flowing in the breeze of overhead fans, and tables piled high with goodies. Here, vegetarian pretensions must be suspended temporarily, if only for time to sample the enough-in-themselves barbecued appetizers—spicy chorizo sausage, tacos, *ahogado* (hot dipped sandwich), ribs, and much more. Actually, vegetarians needn't go hungry—

try the mixed salads, guacamole, or soups, for example. Go for it all and share a big *parrillada* specialty of the house appetizer plate with some friends. By the time the food has gone down, the next course—a mariachi concert, complete with rope tricks, singers, with maybe a juggler or magic act thrown in for good measure, will keep you entertained for hours. Open daily 1:30 P.M.–midnight. The complete show starts around 9 P.M. Expensive.

Return a few blocks west, by the cathedral, to **Sandy's,** at mezzanine level, above the plaza, northeast corner of Colón and P. Moreno, tel. 33/3614-5871. Here, snappy management, service with a flourish, and weekend evening live music make the typical, but tasty, coffee shop menu of soups, salads, meat, pasta, Mexican plates, sandwiches, and desserts seem like an occasion. Open daily 8 A.M.–10:30 P.M. Moderate.

If you're in the mood for a restful lunch or dinner, head west a few blocks to the airy interior patio of **Restaurant San Miguel,** at the northwest corner of Morelos and Donato Guerra, open Tues.–Sat. 8:30 A.M.–11 P.M., Sun.–Mon. 8:30 A.M.–6 P.M.; tel. 33/3613-0809. Here, you can enjoy salad, soup (if too salty, send it back), or a full meal and take in the tranquil, traditional ambience. Around you rise the walls of Guadalajara's oldest convent for women, founded by the sisters of Santa Teresa de Jesús, in 1694. Moderate–expensive.

Continue a few blocks west along Juárez to **Restaurant La Gran China,** Juárez 590, between Martinez and 8 Julio, tel. 33/3613-1447, where the Cantonese owner/chef puts out an authentic and tasty array of dishes. Despite the reality of La Gran China's crisp bok choy, succulent spareribs, and smooth savory noodles, they nevertheless seem a small miracle here, half a world away from Hong Kong. Open daily noon–9 P.M. Budget–moderate.

For a variation, try Gran China's plainer but equally authentic neighboring **Restaurant Chong Wah,** Juárez 558, half a block east, at the corner of E. G. Martinez, tel. 33/3613-9950; open noon–8 P.M. Budget–moderate.

TO PV/GUADALAJARA

ENTERTAINMENT AND EVENTS

Just Wandering Around

Afternoons any day, and Sunday in particular, are good for people-watching around Guadalajara's many downtown plazas. Favorite strolling grounds are the broad Plaza Tapatía west of the cathedral and, especially in the evening, the pedestrian mall-streets, such as Colón, Galeana, Morelos, and Moreno, which meander south and west from cathedral-front Plaza Guadalajara.

In your wanderings, don't forget to stop by the **Plaza de Los Mariachis,** just east of the Plaza Tapatía, adjacent to the Mercado Libertad and the big boulevard, Insurgentes, which runs beneath the Plaza Tapatía. Take a sidewalk table, have a drink or snack and enjoy the mariachis' sometimes soulful, sometimes bright, but always enjoyable, offerings.

If you time it right you can enjoy the concert, which the **Jalisco State Band** has provided since 1898, in the Plaza de Armas adjacent to the cathedral (Thursday and Sunday at 6:30 P.M.), or take in an art film at the Hospicio Cabañas (Mon.–Sat. 4, 6, and 8 P.M.). If you miss these, climb into a *calandria* (horse-drawn carriage) for a ride around town; carriages are available on Liceo between the rotunda and the history museum, just north of the cathedral, for about $15/hour.

Parque Agua Azul

Some sunny afternoon, hire a taxi (about $2 from the city center) and find out why Guadalajara families love Parque Agua Azul. The entrance is on Independencia, about a mile south of Plaza Tapatía. It's a green, shaded place where you can walk, roll, sleep, or lie on the grass. When weary of that, head for the bird park, admire the banana-beaked toucans and squawking macaws, and continue into the aviary where free-flying birds flutter overhead. Nearby, duck into the *mariposario* (butterfly farm) and enjoy the flickering rainbow hues of a host of *mariposas*. Continue to the orchids in a towering hot-house, festooned with growing blossoms and misted continuously by a rainbow of spray from the center. Before other temptations draw you away, stop for a while at the open-air band or

symphony concert in the amphitheater. The park is open Tues.–Sun. 10 A.M.–6 P.M.

Music and Dance Performances

The **Teatro Degollado** is host to world-class opera, symphony, and ballet events. While you're in the Plaza Liberación, drop by the theater box office and ask for a *lista de eventos.* You can also call (or ask your hotel desk clerk to call) the theater box office at tel. 33/3614-4773 or 33/3616-4991, for reservations and information. Pick up tickets 4–7 P.M. on the day of the performance. For a very typical Mexican treat, attend one of the regular 10 A.M. Sunday University of Guadalajara folkloric ballet performances. They're immensely popular; get tickets in advance.

You can also sample the offerings of the **Instituto Cultural Cabañas,** Sun.–Mon. 8:30 A.M.–6 P.M.; tel. 33/3617-4440. It sponsors many events, both experimental and traditional. For more information, ask at the Hospicio Cabañas admission desk. Open Tues.–Sun. 10 A.M.–5 P.M., tel. 33/3615-2177.

Right in the center of town, the **Hotel Fénix** restaurant offers live music after about 7 P.M. nightly. Call tel. 33/3614-5714 to confirm.

Restaurant/club **Peña Cuicalli** (House of Song) offers a varied menu of rock, Latin, blues, jazz, reggae Tues.–Sunday. It's at west-side Av. Niños Héroes 1988, tel. 33/3825-3272, near the Niños Héroes monument.

For some very typically Mexican fun, plan a night out for the dinner and mariachi show at **La Feria** restaurant, at Corona 291, across from Parque San Francisco.

Fiestas

Although Guadalajarans always seem to be celebrating, the town really heats up during its three major annual festivals. Starting the second week in June, the southeast neighborhood, formerly the separate village of Tlaquepaque, is host to the **National Ceramics Fair.** Besides its celebrated stoneware, Tlaquepaque shops and stalls are stuffed with a riot of ceramics and folk crafts from all over Mexico, while cockfights, regional food, folk dances, fireworks, and mariachis fill its streets.

MARIACHIS

Mariachis, those thoroughly Mexican troubador bands, have spread from their birthplace in Jalisco throughout Mexico and into much of the United States. The name itself reveals their origin. "Mariachi" originated with the French *mariage,* or marriage. When French influence peaked during the 1864–1867 reign of Maximilian, Jaliscans transposed *mariage* to "mariachi," a label they began to identify with the five-piece folk bands that played for weddings.

The original ensembles, consisting of a pair of violins, *vihuela* (large eight-stringed guitar), *jarana* (small guitar), and harp, played exclusively traditional melodies. Song titles such as "Las Moscas" (The Flies), "El Venado" (The Stag), and "La Papaya," thinly disguised their universal themes, mostly concerning love.

Although such all-string folk bands still play in Jalisco, notably in Tecalitlán and other rural areas, they've largely been replaced by droves of trumpet-driven commercial mariachis. The man who sparked the shift was probably Emilio Azcárraga Vi-daurreta, the director of radio station XEW, which began broadcasting in Mexico City in 1930. In those low-fidelity days, the subdued sound of the harp didn't broadcast well, so Azcárraga suggested the trumpet as a replacement. It was so successful the trumpet has become the signature sound of present-day mariachis.

Still, mariachis mostly do what they've always done—serenade sweethearts, play for weddings and parties, even accompany church Masses. They seem to be forever strolling around town plazas on Saturday nights and Sunday afternoons, looking for jobs. Their fees, which should be agreed upon before they start, often depend on union scale per song, per serenade, or per hour.

Sometimes mariachis serve as a kind of live jukebox which, for a coin, will play your old favorite. And even if it's a slightly tired but sentimental "Mañanitas" or "Cielito Lindo," you can't help but be moved by the singing violins, bright trumpets, and soothing guitars.

A few months later, the entire city, Mexican states, and foreign countries get into the **Festival of October.** For a month, everyone contributes something, from ballet performances, plays, and soccer games to selling papier-mâché parrots and sweet corn in the plazas. Concurrently, Guadalajarans celebrate the traditional **Festival of the Virgin of Zapopan.** Church plazas are awash with merrymakers enjoying food, mariachis, dances (don't miss the Dance of the Conquest), and fireworks. The merrymaking peaks on October 12, when a huge crowd conducts the Virgin from the downtown cathedral to Zapopan. The merrymakers' numbers often swell to a million faithful who escort the Virgin, accompanied by ranks of costumed saints, devils, Spanish conquistadores, and Aztec chiefs.

Bullfights and Rodeos

Winter is the main season for *corridas de toros,* or bullfights. The bulls charge and the crowds roar *"Olé"* (oh-LAY) Sunday afternoons at the Guadalajara Plaza de Toros (bullring), on Calz. Independencia about two miles north of the Mercado Libertad.

Local associations of *charros* (gentleman cowboys) stage rodeolike Sunday *charreadas* at Guadalajara *lienzos charro* (rodeo rings). Oft-used Guadalajara rodeo rings include Lienzo Charro de Jalisco, 477 Calz. Las Palmas, tel. 33/3619-3232, just beyond the southeast side of Parque Agua Azul. Watch for posters, or ask at your hotel desk or the tourist information office, tel. 33/3688-1600, for *corrida de toros* and *charreada* details and dates.

The Tequila Express

Ride the tourist train to the town of Amatitán, an hour west of Guadalajara, for a tour of the tequila liquor factory in the historic ex-Hacienda San José. Included are viewing of the blue *agave* harvesting process, a Mexican buffet, and a folkloric show, including dances, mariachis, a roping exhibition, and handicrafts.

Tequila Express tickets cost $55 per adult, kids $35. Get them at the Chamber of Commerce

TO PV/GUADALAJARA

CHARREADAS

The many Jalisco lovers of *charrera*, the sport of horsemanship, enjoy a long-venerated tradition. Boys and girls, coached by their parents, practice riding skills from the time they learn to mount a horse. Privileged young people become noble *charros* or *charras* or *"coronelas"*—gentleman cowboys and cowgirls—whose equestrian habits follow old aristocratic Spanish fashion, complete with broad sombrero, brocaded suit or dress, and silver spurs.

The years of long preparation culminate in the *charreada*, which entire communities anticipate with relish. Although superficially similar to an Arizona rodeo, a Jalisco *charreada* differs substantially. The festivities take place in a *lienzo charro*, lit-

erally, the passageway through which the bulls, horses, and other animals run from the corral to the ring. First comes the *cala de caballo*, a test of the horse and rider. The *charros* or *charras* must gallop full speed across the ring and make the horse stop on a dime. Next is the *piales de lienzo*, a roping exhibition during which an untamed horse must be halted and held by having its feet roped. Other bold performances include *jineteo de toro* (bull riding and throwing) and the super-hazardous *paso de la muerte*, in which a rider tries to jump upon an untamed bronco from his or her own galloping mount. *Charreadas* often end in a flourish with the *escaramuza charra*, a spectacular show of riding skill by *charras* in full, colorful dress.

downtown branch, at Morelos 395, corner of 16 de Septiembre, tel. 33/3614-3145, open Mon.–Fri. 9 A.M.–2 P.M., 4–6 p.m. Ticketmaster also sells Tequila Express tickets for a commission, by credit card. Call tel. 33/3818-3800. For more information, visit the website www.tequilaexpress.com.mx.

Entertainment and Events Listings
For more entertainment ideas, pick up the events schedule at the Hospicio Cabañas, behind the long pool/fountain at the east end of Plaza Tapatía, or the tourist information office, in the Plaza Tapatía, on Paseo Morelos, the mall-extension of Av. Morelos, behind the Teatro Degollado at Morelos 102. Another good source of entertaining events is the weekly English-language Guadalajara *Reporter*. If you can't find a newsstand copy, call the office, at Duque de Rivas 254, Guadalajara, tel. 33/3615-2177.

SPORTS AND RECREATION
Walking and Jogging
Walkers and joggers enjoy several spots around Guadalajara. Close in, the **Plaza Liberación** behind the cathedral provides a traffic-free (although concrete) jogging and walking space. Avoid the crowds with morning workouts. If you prefer

grass underfoot, try **Parque Agua Azul** (entrance $3) on Calz. Independencia about a mile south of the Libertad Market. An even better jogging-walking space is the **Parque de los Colomos**—hundreds of acres of greenery, laced by special jogging trails—four miles northwest from the center, before Zapopan; take a taxi or bus 51C, which begins at the old bus terminal, near Parque Agua Azul, and continues along Av. 16 de Septiembre, through downtown Guadalajara.

Tennis, Golf, and Swimming
Although Guadalajara has few, if any, public tennis courts, the west-side **Hotel Camino Real,** Av. Vallarta 5005, tel. 33/3134-2424, rents its tennis courts to the public, by appointment, for about $10 per hour. Also, the Hotels Fiesta Americana, Aurelio Aceves 225, Glorieta Minerva, tel. 33/3825-3434, and the Hotel Crowne Plaza, Av. López Mateos Sur 2500, tel. 33/3634-1034, have courts for guests.

The 18-hole **Atlas Country Club Golf Course** welcomes nonmembers from dawn to dusk Tues.–Sunday, tel. 33/3689-2620. Greens fee runs $80 Tues.–Fri. and $100 Sat. and Sunday. Clubs and carts rent for about $14 and $23; a caddy will cost about $12. Get there via Chapala Highway 44, the south-of-town extension of Calz. J. Gonzales Gallo. The golf course is 1.1

miles (1.8 km) south of the *periférico* on the east
side of the expressway.

Nearly all the luxury hotels have swimming
pools. Two of the prettiest (but unheated) pools
perch atop moderately priced hotels downtown:
the **Roma,** tel. 33/3614-4484, in the heart of
downtown (corner Juárez and Degollado), and
the **Cervantes,** at 442 Prisciliano Sáchez, tel.
33/3613-6686, a few blocks west of the cathedral.
(See Accommodations.)

If your hotel doesn't have a pool, go to the very
popular public pool and picnic ground at Balneario
Lindo Michoacán, Rio Barco 1614, corner Calz. J.
Gonzalez Gallo, tel. 33/3635-9399. Find it about
two miles along Gallo southeast of Parque Agua
Azul. Open daily 8 A.M.–6 P.M.; entrance about
$4 adults, $2 kids.

Farther out but even prettier are the canyon-
country *balnearios* **Los Camachos** and **Nuevo
Paraíso** on Highway 54 north toward Saltillo.
(For more details, see Out-of-Downtown Sights.)

SHOPPING
Downtown

The sprawling **Mercado Libertad,** at the east
end of Plaza Tapatía, has several specialty areas
distributed through two main sections. Most
of the handicrafts are on the bottom, downstairs floor, north side. While selection varies,
from guitars, jewelry, and trinkets, to piñatas,
sweets, baskets, and sombreros, leather pre-
dominates—in jackets, belts, saddles, and the
most huaraches you'll ever see under one roof.
Here, bargaining *es la costumbre.* Competition,
furthermore, gives buyers the advantage. If the
seller refuses your reasonable offer, simply turning in the direction of another stall will often
bring him to his senses.

On the adjacent south side, peruse the produce, meat, and the especially intriguing herb
stalls, stuffed with mounds of forest-gathered
wild dried natural barks, flowers, leaves, mushrooms, and much more.

When you get hungry, mount the stairway
(photographers, note the photogenic view of the
produce floor below) to the upstairs acre of food
stalls *(fondas)* and enjoy a snack or a wholesome

© BRUCE WHIPPERMAN

**Besides having colorful fruits and vegetables,
Mercado Libertad stalls stock a trove of
leather, silver, and woven handicrafts.**

(for sure, if it's steaming) meal of tacos, enchiladas, *guisado* (stew), or *chiles rellenos.*

Finally, be sure to step out the rear, east, door
to the courtyard, where a lineup of bird-sellers,
with their caged charges, wait for customers.

Of the few downtown handicrafts shops, a
few stand out. Right near the city center, try the
Galerías El Convento complex, in a big restored
mansion, on Donato Guerra, corner of Morelos, four blocks west of the cathedral front, between Morelos and Pedro Moreno. Inside, a
sprinkling of shops offer fine arts and handicrafts, from leather furniture and Tlaquepaque
glass to baroque religious antiques and fine silver.
Stop for a restful drink or meal at the Restaurant San Miguel (See Downtown Restaurants).

You might also find what you're looking for
at the government **Casa de Artesanías Agua
Azul,** by Parque Agua Azul, tel./fax 33/3619-
4664 or 33/3619-5179. Here, you can choose
from virtually everything—brilliant stoneware,

TO PV/GUADALAJARA

handsome gold and silver jewelry, and endearing ceramic, brass, and papier-mâché animals—short of actually going to Tonalá, Tlaquepaque, or Taxco. Find it at Calz. Gonzales Gallo 20, next to Parque Agua Azul (off of Independencia); hours are Mon.–Fri. 10 A.M.–6 P.M., Sat. 10 A.M.–5 P.M., Sun. 10 A.M.–2 P.M.

Two other promising, but less extensive, downtown handicrafts sources in the Plaza Tapatía vicinity are at the **tourist information office** at Morelos 102, and the native, mostly Huichol, vendors in the adjacent alley, called Rincón del Diablo.

Tlaquepaque

Tlaquepaque was once a sleepy village of potters miles from Guadalajara. Attracted by the quiet of the country, rich families built palatial homes during the 19th century. Now, entrepreneurs have moved in and converted them into upscale restaurants, art galleries, and showrooms, stuffed with quality Tonalá and Tlaquepaque ceramics, glass, metalwork, and papier-mâché.

In spite of having been swallowed by the city, Tlaquepaque still has the feel and look of a small colonial town, with its cathedral and central square leading westward onto the mansion-decorated main street, now mall, Av. Independencia.

> *To the visitor, everyone in Tonalá seems to be making something. Tonalá family patios are piled with their specialties, whether they be pottery, stoneware, brass, or papier-mâché.*

Although generally pricier than Tonalá, Tlaquepaque still has bargains. Proceed by finding the base prices at the more ordinary crafts stores in the side streets that branch off the main mall-street Independencia. Then, price out the showier, upscale merchandise in the galleries along Independencia itself. For super-fine examples of traditional Tlaquepaque and Tonalá crafts, be sure to stop by the **Museo Regional de Cerámica y Arte Popular,** 237 Independencia, open Tues.–Sat. 10 A.M.–6 P.M., Sun. 10 A.M.–3 P.M., tel. 33/3635-5404.

From the *museo,* cross the street to the **Sergio Bustamante** store, tel. 33/3639-5519, upscale outlet for the famous sculptor's arresting, whimsical studies in juxtaposition. Bustamante supervises an entire Guadalajara studio-factory of artists who put out hundreds of one-of-a-kind variations on a few human, animal, and vegetable themes. Prices seem to depend mainly on size; rings and bracelets may go for as little as $200, while a two-foot humanoid chicken may run $2,000. Don't miss the restroom. Open Mon.–Sat. 10 A.M.–7 P.M., Sun. noon–4 P.M.

Half a block west, at the intersection of Independencia and Alfarareros (Potters), a pair of regally restored former mansions, now galleries, enjoy a dignified retirement facing each other on opposite sides of the street. **La Casa Canela,** Independencia 258, tel. 33/3657-1343, takes pride in its museum-quality religious art, furniture, paper flowers, pottery, blown glass, and classic, blue-on-white Tlaquepaque stoneware. Open Mon.–Fri. 10 A.M.–2 P.M. and 3–7 P.M., Sat. 10 A.M.–6 P.M., Sun. 11 A.M.–3 P.M.

Across the street, **Antigua de Mexico,** Independencia 255, tel. 33/3635-3402, specializes in baroque gilt wood antiques and reproductions, being one of the few studios in Mexico to manufacture fine 17th century–style furniture. Open Mon.–Fri. 10 A.M.–2 P.M. and 3–7 P.M., Sat. 10 A.M.–6 P.M. For more information, visit antiguadademexico@infosel.net.mx.

Getting to Tlaquepaque: Most conveniently, hire a taxi (about $12 round-trip and well worth it) or ride the usually crowded city bus 275 (look for "Tlaquepaque" scrawled on the front window) from stops (such as at Madero) or the air-conditioned "Turquesa" bus along downtown Av. 16 de Septiembre. By car, from the center of town, drive Av. Revolución southeast about four miles to the Niños Héroes traffic circle. From Av. Niños Héroes, the first right off the traffic circle, continue about a mile to the west end of Av. Independencia, on the left.

Tonalá

About five miles past Tlaquepaque, Tonalá perches at Guadalajara's country edge. When the Spanish arrived in the 1520s, Tonalá was dominant among the small kingdoms of the Atemajac Valley. Tonalá's widow-queen and her royal court were adorned by the glittering handiwork of an honored class of silver and gold crafters. Although the Spaniards carted off the valuables, the tradition of Tonalá craftsmanship remains today. To the visitor, everyone in Tonalá seems to be making something. Tonalá family patios are piled with their specialties, whether they be pottery, stoneware, brass, or papier-mâché.

Right at the source, bargains couldn't be better. Dozens of shops dot the few blocks around Tonalá's central plaza corner at Av. Hidalgo (north of the plaza; called Av. Madero south of it) and Av. Juárez (east-west). For super-bargaining opportunities and *mucho* holiday excitement and color, visit the Thursday and Sunday *tianguis* (markets), which spreads along the tree-lined *periférico* highway about four blocks west of the Tonalá plaza.

Tonalá Shopping Tour

Start at the north end, north end, past the plaza on Hidalgo, where several shops stand out. Among the most outstanding is factory shop **Galería Bernabe,** at Hidalgo 83, open Mon.–Fri. 10 A.M.–6 P.M., Sat.–Sun. 10 A.M.–3 P.M., tel./fax 33/3683-0877 or 33/3683-0040. Celebrated founders of the 200-year *petalillo* (little petal) double-fired technique, Bernabe specializes in intricate, fetching animal and plant designs in black, green, and white. Some of the best pieces are reminiscent of fine ancient Chinese ceramics. Offerings vary, from glistening vases, pitchers, and bowls, to gorgeous table settings for a dozen or more. If you can't find exactly what you want, Bernabe will execute your own design to order.

Half a block farther south, don't miss **El Bazar de Sermel,** at Hidalgo 67, tel. 33/3683-0010. Here, master craftspeople have stretched the Tonalá papier-mâché tradition to the ultimate. Stop in and pick out the life-sized flamingo, pony, giraffe, or zebra you've always wanted for your living room. Open Mon.–Fri. 9 A.M.–6:30 P.M., Sat. 9 A.M.–2 P.M., Sun. 10 A.M.–3 P.M.

Walk back to the Pplaza corner, to **La Mexicanía,** at 13 Hidalgo, tel. 33/3683-0152, north corner of Juárez. In the 10 years that I've been coming to Tonalá, La Mexicanía has prospered

and expanded, by virtue of its diverse, all-Mexico collection. This is heaven for Mexico handicrafts lovers. If you've wanted a particular item—a weaving or a *huipil* from Oaxaca, a jaguar mask from Guerrero, a guitar from Michoacán, an ironwood sailfish from Sonora, a Huichol indigenous yarn painting, or a Guanajuato papier-mâché clown, it's here. Open Mon.–Sat. 10 A.M.–7 P.M., Sun. 10 A.M.–3 P.M.

Back outside, continuing south, turn west at the corner of Juárez and walk a few steps to **La Flor de Yahuac** paper flower store, at Juárez 80, open Mon.–Sat. 10 A.M.–7 P.M., Sun. 10 A.M.–5 P.M., tel. 33/3683-0017. Inside, select your heart's content from the festoons of realistically lovely lilies, sunflowers, roses, and more.

Cross the street to **Artesanías Nuño,** Juárez 59, tel. 33/3683-0011. Here, pick from a fetching menagerie, including parrots, monkeys, flamingos, and toucans, in papier-mâché, brass, and ceramics. Open Mon.–Sat. 10 A.M.–7 P.M., Sun. 10 A.M.–5 P.M.; bargain for very reasonable buys.

Many interesting shops dot Av. Madero, south of the plaza. Be sure to stop in at **Antiguas Santiago,** at Madero 42, for a museum of designer glass—lamps, vases, bowls—in a myriad of fantastic colors, shapes and sizes, too lovely to resist. Open Mon.–Sat. 9 A.M.–6:30 P.M., Sun. 10 A.M.–3 P.M., tel. 33/3683-0641.

More pleasant surprises are in store a few steps farther south, at **Vidrios Soplado** (Blown Glass), at Madero 57. Here, admire all the lovely *esferas* (colored glass balls), vases, tumblers, and goblets that you'll ever need. Open Mon.–Sat. 10 A.M.–6 P.M., Sun. 10 A.M.–4 P.M., tel. 33/3683-0641.

Half a block farther south, step into **Artesanías Alba,** at Madero 85B, for a trove of fetching high-fired Guanajuato-made Talavera look-alike high-fired pottery (but with prices much more reasonable than the genuine Puebla Talavera ware.) Choose among a large selection of lovely urns, vases, bowls, and bathroom sinks. Find it open Mon.–Sat. 10 A.M.–7 P.M., Sun. 10 A.M.–5 P.M., tel. 33/3683-1414.

Finally, a few doors farther, don't miss **Carousel,** at Madero 88, open Mon.–Sat. 9 A.M.–6 P.M.,

Sun. 9 A.M.–3 P.M., on the west side of the street. Here, owners specialize in the rustic but decorative, such as merry-go-round horses, quixotic Don Quijotes, and bright chandeliers.

Getting to Tonalá: From downtown Guadalajara, by far the best option is to go by taxi (about $20 round-trip). Alternatively, ride the oft-crowded city bus 275 (look for "Tonalá" scrawled on the windshield or the more expensive but much more comfortable air-conditioned bus) from the stops, such as the corner of Madero, on downtown Av. 16 de Septiembre. By car, drive Av. Revolución about six miles southeast of the city center to the big Plaza Camachines (New Bus Station—Camionera Central Nueva). Follow the Highway 90 Carretera Zapotlanejo expressway (Mexico City direction, east). After about two miles, exit right at the signed Tonalá off ramp (then turn left and cross over the expressway), then right at the first street; three blocks farther turn left and within a few blocks you'll be at the Tonalá central plaza.

Guadalajara Photo, Grocery, and Department Stores

The several branches of the **Laboratorios Julio** chain offer quick photofinishing and a big stock of photo supplies and film, including professional 120 transparency and negative rolls. Its big downtown branch is at Colón 125 between Juárez and Cotilla, tel. 33/3614-2850; open Mon.–Sat. 10 A.M.–8 P.M., Sun. 10 A.M.–6 P.M. Its west-side store, at Av. Americas 50, corner of Manuel Acuña, tel. 33/3344-5470, is open daily 9 A.M.–2:30 P.M., 4–7:30 P.M. Find dozens more branches in the Guadalajara Yellow Pages, under "Fotografía."

For convenient, all-in-one shopping, including groceries, try **Gigante,** downtown on Juárez, corner of Martínez, tel. 33/3344-5470. Open daily 8 A.M.–11 P.M. For even more under one air-conditioned roof, try the big **Comercial Mexicana** at Plaza del Sol, Av. López Mateos Sur 2077. Open daily 9 A.M.–9 P.M.

A pair of good department stores, **Suburbia** and **Fábricas de Francia,** anchor the town-center corner of Juárez and 16 de Septiembre.

INFORMATION AND SERVICES

Tourist Information Office

The main Guadalajara tourist information office is in the Plaza Tapatía, on Paseo Morelos, the mall-extension of Av. Morelos, behind the Teatro Degollado, at Morelos 105, tel. 33/3668-1600 or 33/3668-1601, fax 33/3668-1686; open Mon.–Fri. 9 A.M.–8 P.M. and Sat.–Sun. 9 A.M.–1 P.M. For lots of online information, visit the website www.visitajaliscotour.gob.mx.

Guadalajara Municipal Tourism maintains an information booth in the Palacio de Gobierno, just adjacent, east, of the Plaza de Armas (marked by the bandstand.) Hours are Mon.–Fri. 9 A.M.–2:30 P.M. and 5–7 P.M. and Sat.–Sun. 10 A.M.–12:30 P.M. For more information, visit the website www.jaliscotour.com.

Publications

Among the best Guadalajara sources of English-language magazines is **Sanborn's,** a North American–style gift, book, and coffee shop chain. It's downtown, corner Juárez and 16 de Septiembre, open 7:30 A.M.–11 P.M.; at Plaza Vallarta, Av. Vallarta 1600, open 7–1 A.M.; and Plaza del Sol, 2718 López Mateos Sur, open 7–1 A.M.

You can usually get the excellent *News* from Mexico City at one of the newsstands edging the Plaza Guadalajara, across from the cathedral.

While you're downtown, if you see a copy of the informative local weekly, the ***Colony Reporter,*** buy it. Its pages will be stuffed with valuable items for visitors, including local events calendars, restaurant and performance reviews, meaty feature articles on local customs and excursions, and entertainment, restaurant, hotel, and rental listings. (If you can't find one, call the *Reporter,* tel. 33/3615-2177, to find out where you can get a copy.)

Additionally, suburban southwest-side **Librería Sandi,** at Tepeyac 718, Colonia Chapalita, Guadalajara, tel. 33/3121-4210, fax 33/3647-4600, open Mon.–Fri. 9:30 A.M.–7 P.M. and Sat. 9:30 A.M.–2 P.M., has one of the best selections of English-language books and magazines in the Guadalajara area.

TO PV/GUADALAJARA

Language and Cultural Courses

The University of Guadalajara's **Centro de Estudios Para Extranjeros** (Study Center for Foreigners) conducts an ongoing program of cultural studies for visitors. Besides formal language, history, and art instruction, students may also opt for live-in arrangements with local families. Write the center at Tomás S. V. Gómez 125, P.O. Box 1-2130, Guadalajara, Jalisco 44100, or call tel. 33/3616-4399 or 33/3616-4382, fax 33/3616-4013, or email cepe@corp.udg.mx.

Money Exchange

Change more types of money (U.S., Canadian, German, Japanese, French, Italian, and Swiss) for the best rates at the downtown streetfront **Banamex** office and ATM (Juárez, corner of Corona, open Mon.–Fri. 9 A.M.–4 P.M.). Alternatively, go to **Bancomer,** on Corona, with ATM, one block south of Banamex, open Mon.–Fri. 8:30 A.M.–4 P.M., Sat. 10 A.M.–2 P.M. After hours, go to one of the dozens of *casas de cambio* (money changers) nearby, a block east of Banamex, on Cotilla between Maestranza and Corona.

The Guadalajara **American Express** branch is on the west side, at Plaza Los Arcos, Av. Vallarta 2440, about three miles west of the city center, tel. 33/3818-2323, fax 33/3616-7665. It provides both travel-agency and member financial services, including personal-check and traveler's-check cashing, Mon.–Fri. 9 A.M.–6 P.M., Sat. 9 A.M.–1

Guides

A good guide can provide a hassle-free route to seeing Guadalajara. Very accessible right downtown is friendly American expatriate **Lynn Mendez,** who staffs the tourist information booth mornings in the Palacio de Gobierno (on Corona), adjacent to the bandstand. Afternoons, Lynn leads walking tours of the city center, beginning at 2:30 P.M. Tues.–Friday. Her fee is $15 per person for two, $10 per person, for three to six. If you can't contact her, Lynn recommends some local guides: Roberto Arellano, of the Sindicato de Guias de Guadalajara, tel. 33/3657-8376, and Octavio Estrada, tel. 33/3632-7306.

Consulates

The **U.S. Consulate** is at Progreso 175 (between Cotillo and Libertad) about a mile west of the town center; open Mon.–Fri. 8 A.M.–4:30 P.M., tel. 33/3825-2020 or 33/3825-2250. The **Canadian Consulate** is in the Hotel Fiesta Americana at Aurelio Aceves 225, local 31, near the intersection of Av. López Mateos and Av. Vallarta, tel. 33/3615-6215; open Mon.–Fri. 8:30 A.M.–2 P.M. and 3–5 P.M.

Consular agents from many other countries maintain Guadalajara offices. Consult the local Yellow Pages, under *"Embajadas, Legaciones y Consulados."*

Health, Police, and Emergencies

If you need a doctor, follow your hotel recommendation; otherwise, contact the **Hospital Mexico Americano,** Colomos 2110, tel. 33/3641-3141, ambulance emergency 33/3642-7152, with many specialists on call.

If you must have an English-speaking doctor, IAMAT (International Association for Medical Assistance to Travelers) has two American-trained Guadalajara affiliates. Contact either J. Jaime Ramírez Parra, M.D., at Tarascos 3514, suite 14, tel. 33/3813-0440, 33/3813-0700, or 33/3813-1025; or pediatrician Roberto A. Dumois, M.D., at Francisco Zarco 2345, Colonia Ladrón de Guevara, tel. 33/3616-9616, fax 33/3615-9542, email rdumois@infosel.net.mx.

For ordinary remedies and medications, one of the best sources is the Guadalajara chain **Farmacia ABC,** with many branches. For example, downtown, at 518 P. Moreno between M. Ocampo and D. Guerra, tel. 33/3614-2950, open daily 8 A.M.–10 P.M. See the Guadalajara Yellow Pages, under "Farmacias," for more branches, including 24-hour home delivery numbers.

For **police** emergencies, call the radio patrol (dial 080) or the police headquarters at tel. 33/3617-6060. In case of **fire,** call the *servicio bomberos* fire station at tel. 33/3619-5155 or 33/3619-0794.

Communications

The downtown Guadalajara post office is two blocks west of the Teatro Degollado, just past

TO PV/GUADALAJARA

the Hotel Mendoza, at Independencia and V. Carranza. **Telecomunicaciones** offers public telephone and fax in the city center, at Degollado and Madero, below the city *juzgado* (jail), Mon.–Fri. 8 A.M.–6 P.M., Sat. 9 A.M.–2 P.M.

Guadalajara has many downtown Internet stores. For example, at the travel agency Ramos Ramírez (at the street entrance of Hotel Internacional), at Pedro Moreno 570, five blocks west of the cathedral; call ahead, at tel. 33/3613-7318. Open Mon.–Sat. 9 A.M.–9 P.M., Sun. 9 A.M.–3 P.M.

GETTING THERE AND AWAY
By Air

Several air carriers connect the **Guadalajara Airport** (officially, the Miguel Hidalgo International Airport, code-designated GDL) with many U.S. and Mexican destinations.

Mexicana Airlines flights, reservations tel. 33/3837-7070, arrivals and departures tel. 33/3688-5775, connect with U.S. destinations of Los Angeles, San Francisco, San Jose, Oakland, Sacramento, Las Vegas, and Chicago, and Mexican destinations of Los Cabos, Puerto Vallarta, Tijuana, Mexicali, and Mexico City.

Aeroméxico and partner line **Aerolitoral** flights (reservations, arrivals and departures toll-free Mex. tel. 800/621-4000), connect with U.S. destinations of Los Angeles, Ontario, Las Vegas, Phoenix, and New York, and Mexican destinations of Juárez, Hermosillo, Chihuahua, Veracruz, Torreón, Puerto Vallarta, Acapulco, Culiacán, Monterrey, Tijuana, and Mexico City.

Aerocalifornia, reservations tel. 33/3616-2525, flight information tel. 33/3688-5514, connects with U.S. destinations of Los Angeles and Tucson, and Mexican destinations of Tijuana, Mazatlán, La Paz, Los Cabos, Culiacán, Los Mochis, Durango, Monterrey, Puebla, and Mexico City.

Aviacsa Airlines, reservations toll-free Mex. tel. 800/006-2200, flight information 33/3123-1751 or 33/3123-1752, connects with the U.S. destination of Los Angeles and Mexican destinations of Monterrey and Mexico City.

Azteca Airlines, reservations toll-free Mex. tel. 01-800/229-8322, flight information tel.

33/3630-4616, connects with Mexican destinations of Tijuana, Mexico City, and Cancún.

Other carriers include: **American Airlines,** reservations toll-free Mex. tel. 800/904-6000, which connects daily with Los Angeles and Dallas; **Delta Air Lines,** reservations tel. 33/3630-3530 or toll-free Mex. tel. 800/123-4710, which connects daily with Los Angeles; **Continental Airlines,** reservations toll-free Mex. tel. 800/900-5000, which connects twice daily with Houston; and **America West Airlines,** toll-free U.S. tel. 800/235-9292 (reachable also from Mexico), which connects seasonally with Phoenix. For information and reservations for all of the above, you may also contact a travel agent, such as American Express, tel. 33/3818-2323 or 33/3818-2325.

Airport arrival is simplified by money exchange counters and a Bital (Banco Internacional) bank with 24-hour ATM just outside the terminal door (open Mon.–Sat. 8 A.M.–7 P.M.).

Many **car rental agencies** maintain arrival hall booths: Avis, tel. 33/3688-5656 or 33/3688-5874; Alamo, tel. 33/3613-5551 or 33/3613-5560, alamogdl@ibm.net; Aries, tel. 33/3688-5400 or 33/3688-5272, fax 33/3345-8050; Arrasa, tel. 33/3615-0522; Budget, tel. 33/3613-0027 or 33/3613-0286, fax 33/3688-5216 or 33/3688-5531; Dollar, tel. 33/3688-5956 or 33/3688-5958, dollar@megared.net.mx; Hertz, tel. 33/3688-5633 or 33/3688-6080, fax 33/3688-6070; National, tel. 33/3614-7175 or 33/3614-7994, fax 33/3688-6070, natrent@prodigy.net.mx; Optima, tel. 33/3688-5532 or 33/3812-0437; Ohama, tel./fax 33/3614-6902; and Thrifty, 33/3825-5080, ext. 121.

Ground transportation is likewise well organized for shuttling arrivees the 12 miles (19 km) along Chapala Highway 44 into town. Private taxis have preempted ground transportation into both Guadalajara downtown and Lake Chapala shore destinations. Tickets for *taxis especiales* (individual taxis, $15 for one to four people) are sold at a booth just outside the terminal door.

However, a red and white Autotransportes Guadalajara-Chapala bus (designed for local people, but usable by everyone) stops in front of the terminal (on the right side, in front of Hotel

Sun) and continues to Zapote village, where, on the highway, you can wave down another similar bus, bound for either Guadalajara or Chapala.

Many simple and economical card-operated public telephones are also available; buy telephone cards at the snack bar by the far right-hand terminal exit. Also you'll find a newsstand (lobby floor), bookstore (upstairs), and many crafts and gift shops convenient for last-minute business and purchases.

Airport departure is equally simple, as long as you save enough for your international departure tax of $19 ($12 federal tax, $7 local), unless it's already included in your ticket. A post office, a (secure mail) Mexpost office, and *telecomunicaciones* office (telegraph, fax, long-distance phone) are inside the terminal, right of the entrance as you enter. A public telephone and fax office operates midterminal, by the car rental counters.

Don't lose your tourist card. If you do, be prepared with a copy or some evidence (such as a ticket stub to verify your Mexico arrival date) to airport Migración, tel. 33/3688-8664, to avoid a fine and red tape.

By Car or RV

Four major routes connect Guadalajara to the rest of Pacific Mexico. From Tepic in the west, federal Highway 15 winds about 141 miles (227 km) over the Sierra Madre Occidental crest. The new *cuota* (toll) expressway, although expensive ($30 for a car, RVs more), greatly increases safety, decreases wear and tear, and cuts the Guadalajara-Tepic driving time to three hours. The *libre* (free) route, by contrast, has two oft-congested lanes that twist steeply up and down the high pass and bump through towns. For safety, allow around five hours to and from Tepic.

To and from Puerto Vallarta, bypass Tepic via the toll *corta* (cutoff) that connects Highway 15 (at Chapalilla) with Highway 200 (at Compostela). Figure on four hours total if you use the entire toll expressway (about $20), six hours if you don't.

From Barra de Navidad in the southwest, traffic curves and climbs smoothly along two-lane Highway 80 for the 190 miles (306 km) to Guadalajara. Allow around five hours.

An easier road connection with Barra de Navidad runs through Manzanillo along *autopistas* (superhighways) 200, 110, and 54 D. Easy grades allow a leisurely 55 mph (90 km/hour) most of the way for this 192-mile (311-km) trip. Allow about four hours from Manzanillo; add another hour for the additional smooth (follow the Manzanillo town toll bypass) 38 miles (61 km) of Highway 200 to or from Barra de Navidad.

By Bus

The long-distance Guadalajara *camionera central* (central bus terminal) is at least 20 minutes by taxi (about $8) from the city center. The huge modern complex sprawls past the southeast-sector intersection of the old Tonalá Highway (Carretera Antigua Tonalá) and the Zaplotanejo Autopista (Freeway) Highway 90. The *camionera central* is sandwiched between the two highways. Tell your taxi driver which bus line you want or where you want to go, and he'll drop you at one of the terminal's seven *modulos* (buildings). For arrival and departure convenience, you might consider staying at the adjacent, moderately priced Hotel La Serena.

Each of the seven *modulos* is self-contained, with restrooms, cafeteria or snack bar, stores offering snack foods (but few fruits or veggies), bottled drinks, common medicines and drugs, and handicrafts. Additionally, *modulos* 1, 3, and 7 have public long-distance telephone and fax service. *Modulos* 2 and 3 have kept luggage service, and *modulo* 3 has hotel ($70 and up, Guadalajara, Mazatlán, Acapulco, Puerto Vallarta, and Mexico City) reservations agent Sendetur.

Dozens of competing bus lines offer departures. The current king of the heap is **Estrella Blanca,** a holding company that operates a host of subsidiaries, notably Elite, Turistar, Futura, Transportes del Norte, Transportes Norte de Sonora, and Transportes Chihuahenses. Second-largest and trying harder is **Flecha Amarilla,** which offers "Servicios Coordinados" through several subsidiaries. Trying even harder are the biggest independents: **Omnibus de Mexico, Enlaces Terrestres Nacionales** (National Ground Network), **Transportes Pacífico,** and **Autobuses del Occidente,** all of whom would very much like to be your bus company.

To northwest Pacific Coast destinations, go

TO PV/GUADALAJARA

to *modulo* 4. Take first-class Elite, tel. 33/3679-0485, via Tepic and Mazatlán, to the U.S. border at Nogales, Mexicali, and Tijuana. Alternatively, ride first-class Transportes Pacífico, tel. 33/3600-0211, for the same northwest Pacific destinations as Elite.

For southwest Pacific Coast destinations, go by Transportes Pacífico, tel. 33/3600-0211, 33/3600-0854, or 33/3600-0194, ext. 230 or 234, in *modulo* 3 or *modulo* 4, for the small southwest Nayarit coastal towns and villages, such as Las Varas, La Peñita, and Rincón de Guayabitos, en route to Puerto Vallarta. Moreover, you can ride second-class Transportes Norte de Sonora west and northwest, tel. 33/3679-0463, *modulo* 4, to smaller northern Nayarit and Sinaloa towns, such as Tepic, San Blas, Santiago Ixcuintla-Mexcaltitán, Acaponeta-Novillero, and Escuinapa-Teacapan.

Additionally, in *modulo* 3, second-class Autotransportes Guadalajara-Talpa-Mascota, tel. 33/3600-0098, offers connections to the non-touristed western Jalisco mountain towns of Talpa and Mascota, where you can connect to Puerto Vallarta by the rugged super-scenic back-country route via the antique mining village of San Sebastián.

For far southern Pacific destinations of Zihuatanejo, Acapulco, and the Oaxaca coast you can go one of two ways: direct to Acapulco by Futura (*modulo* 3) east to Toluca, then south, all in one day, bypassing Mexico City (one or two buses per day). Alternatively, go less directly via Elite (*modulo* 3) west to Tepic or Puerto Vallarta (or by a Flecha Amarilla affiliate, tel. 33/3600-0770, *modulo* 1, south to Tecomán), where you must transfer to a Zihuatanejo-Acapulco southbound Elite bus. This may necessitate an overnight in either Tepic, Puerto Vallarta, or Tecomán and at least two days traveling (along the scenic, un-touristed Pacific route, however), depending upon connections. Finally, in Acapulco, connections will be available southeast to the Oaxaca coast.

If you're bound southeast directly to the city of Oaxaca, go conveniently by Futura (*modulo* 3) to Mexico City Norte (North) station, where you transfer, via ADO (Autobuses del Oriente), southeast direct to Oaxaca city.

Also at *modulo* 4 allied lines Autocamiones del Pacífico and Transportes Cihuatlán, tel. 33/3600-0076 (second-class), tel. 33/3600-0598 (first class), together offer service south along scenic mountain Highway 80 to the Pacific via Autlán to Melaque, Barra de Navidad, and Manzanillo.

For eastern to southern destinations in Jalisco, Guanajuato, Aguascalietes, Michoacán, and Colima, go to either *modulos* 1 or 2. In *modulo* 2, ride first-class ETN, tel. 33/3600-0501, east to Celaya, León, and Aguascalientes, or west and southwest to Uruapan, Morelia, Colima, Manzanillo, and Puerto Vallarta. Also in *modulo* 1, Flecha Amarilla subsidiary lines, tel. 33/3600-0398, offer service to a swarm of northeast destinations, including León, Guanajuato, and San Miguel de la Allende, and southeast and south to Uruapan, Morelia, Puerto Vallarta, Manzanillo, Barra de Navidad, and untouristed villages—El Super, Tomatlán, and El Tuito—on the Jalisco coast. Also, from *modulo* 2, La Linea and La Linea Plus (formerly Autobuses del Occidente), tel. 33/3600-0055, offers departures southeast to Michoacán destinations of Zamora, Zitácuaro, Quiroga, Pátzcuaro, Uruapan, and Morelia. Additionally, in *modulo* 2, Autotransportes Sur de Jalisco second-class buses offer southern departures, via old Highway 54 or *autopista* 54 D, via Sayula, Ciudad Guzman, Colima, to Tecomán, thence southeast via the Michoacán coast to Lazaro Cardenas, or northwest via the via Cuyutlán, to Manzanillo.

In *modulo* 5, a number of lines offer connections with north and northeast destinations. Rojo de los Altos, tel. 33/3679-0404, second-class departures connect northeast with Tepatitlán, San Juan de Los Lagos, and Lagos de Moreno. Others connect north with Nochixtlán, Zacatecas, and Fresnillo. Additionally in *modulo* 5, small independent Linea Azul tel. 33/3679-0453, offers departures northeast, via San Juan de Los Lagos and San Luis Potosí, to Tampico and the U.S. border, at Matamoros and Reynosa.

Omnibus de Mexico, tel. 33/3600-0184 or 33/3600-0469, dominates *modulo* 6, offering broad service in mostly north and northeast directions: to the U.S. border at Juárez via Zacatecas, Saltillo, Durango, Torreón, Fresnillo, and

Chihuahua; and Monterrey via Saltillo; and northeast, via Tampico, to the U.S. border at Reynosa and Matamoros.

Additionally, Omnibus de Mexico offers first class connections south, with Ciudad Guzmán, Colima, and Manzanillo, and north with regional destinations of Nochistlán and Colotlán.

The Estrella Blanca subsidiary lines operating out of *modulo* 7 also mostly offer connections north. Ride first-class Transportes Chihuahuenses, tel. 33/3679-0404, via San Juan de los Lagos, Zacatecas, Durango, Torreon, Chihuahua, and Juárez; luxury-class Turistar, tel.

33/3679-0404, along the same routes as Transportes Chihuahuenses; or first-class Transportes del Norte, tel. 33/3679-0404, via San Juan de los Lagos, Zacatecas, Saltillo, Monterrey, and Matamoros, at the U.S. border.

By Train
Passenger rail service to and from Guadalajara has been stopped by the privatization of the Mexican Railways' Pacific route. Unless future government subsidies offset private losses, Pacific passenger trains will have gone the way of buggy whips and Stanley Steamers.

Along the Road to Puerto Vallarta

The lush, 100-mile stretch between Tepic and Puerto Vallarta is a Pacific Eden of flowery tropical forest and pearly palm-shaded beaches, largely unknown to the outside world. The gateway Mexican National Highway 200 is still relatively new; development has just barely begun. Only a few towns and a scattering of villages, with their pastures, tobacco fields, and tropical fruit orchards, encroach upon the vine-strewn jungle.

PLAYA CHACALA
Side roads off Highway 200 provide exotic, close-up glimpses of Nayarit's tangled, tropical woodland, but rarely will they lead to such a delightful surprise as the green-tufted golden crescent of Playa Chacala and its diminutive neighbor, Playa Chacalilla.

Just a mile or two south of Las Varas (43 miles, 69 km, south of Tepic; 61 miles, 97 km, north of Puerto Vallarta) follow the six-mile, newly paved road to the great old palm grove at Chacala. Beyond the line of rustic *palapa* seafood restaurants lies a heavenly curve of sand, enfolded on both sides by palm-tipped headlands.

A mile farther north, past Chacala village on the headland, the road ends at Playa Chacalilla, Playa Chacala's miniature twin. (The status of public access to Playa Chacalilla is lately in doubt, however, because of hotel construction on the site.)

Beach Activities and Food
Playa Chacala's gentle surf is good for close-in bodysurfing, boogie boarding, swimming, and beginning-to-intermediate surfing. Furthermore, the water is generally clear enough for snorkeling off the rocks on either side of the beach. If you bring your equipment, kayaking, sailboarding, and sailing are possible. Moreover, the sheltered north end cove is nearly always tranquil and safe, even for tiny tots. Fishing is so good local people make their living at it. Chacala Bay is so rich and clean that tourists eat oysters right off the rocks.

Supplied by the beachside restaurants (especially recommended: Restaurant Las Brisas, for good breaded shrimp, and Restaurant El Amigo, for special *El Tlaxtihuille* shrimp broth soup) and the stores in the village, Playa Chacala is ideal for tent or small RV camping. Now that the road is paved, motorhomes and trailers should be able to get there routinely. Chacalilla would be similarly good for camping, except new development now limits access.

Boatmen on the beach offer **excursions** (figure about $20 per hour) to nearby secluded beaches, such as **Playa la Caleta** for surfing; and Playa Las Cuevas (the Caves), for picnicking, swimming, and snorkeling. Be prepared with your own drinks, food and equipment, however.

Horseback rides along local jungle trails are also available from providers at the beach.

TO PV/GUADALAJARA

Few beaches in Pacific Mexico can match the beauty of Playa Chacala's gentle half-moon curve.

Mar de Jade

The Mar de Jade, a holistic-style living center at the south end of Playa Chacala, offers unique alternatives. Laura del Valle, Mar de Jade's personable and dynamic physician/founder, has worked hard since the early 1980s building living facilities and a learning center while simultaneously establishing a local health clinic. Now, Mar de Jade offers Spanish-language and work-study programs for people who enjoy the tropics but want to do more than laze in the sun. The main thrust is interaction with local people. Spanish, for example, is the preferred language at the dinner table.

Its thatched, cool, and clean adobe and brick cabins, adjacent two-story lodging complex (with concrete floors, showers, restrooms, and good water) nestle among a flowery, palm-shaded garden of fruit trees. Stone pathways lead to the beach-side main center, which consists of a dining room, kitchen, offices, library, and classroom overlooking the sea.

While Mar de Jade's purpose is serious, it has nothing against visitors who *do* want to laze in the sun, beachcomb, and soak in their beachfront pool and whirlpool tub. Mar de Jade invites travelers to make reservations (or simply drop in) and stay as long as they like, for adults from about $120 d year-round, including breakfast. Discounts are available for children.

The core educational program is a three-week Spanish course (fee about $300 for three weeks), although it does offer one- and two-week options for those who can't stay the full three weeks. Work-study programs, such as gardening, kitchen assistance, carpentry, and maintenance can possibly be arranged. Sometimes participants join staff in local work, such as at the medical clinic or on construction projects.

For more information about the course schedule and fees, contact Mar de Jade directly in Puerto Vallarta, at tel./fax 322/222-1171 or tel. 322/222-3524, info@mardejade.com, www.mardejade.com.

Majahua Spa

Laura del Valle's brother, civil engineer and builder José Enrique del Valle, who owns the jungle forest parcel above Mar de Jade, has worked hard to put his land to good use. His dream-made-true, Majahua Spa, is now receiving guests. José and his wife, Carmen Ramírez, chef of their in-house restaurant, offer a small cluster of luxuriously rustic and private accommodations, deluxe camping, and full spa services. The three lodgings, which blend artfully into the verdant tropical forest hillside, are all lovingly designed and hand-built of stucco and tile, with both king-sized and kid-sized beds, modern-standard baths, and luxurious *palapa* roofs.

Accommodations vary, from the La Puerta honeymoon suite just above the restaurant, to the "Penthouse," big enough for six at the top of a winding hillside path. In the middle, a spa section offers all services, including massage, facials, and aromatherapy. High-season (Dec. 15–April 30) rates begin at about $105 for two, and run upward to about $260 for the "penthouse" suite. Super-luxurious tents for camping are also available in an upper garden, for about $40. All lodging prices include breakfast. For more information, visit www.majahua.com; reserve by telephoning Nayarit Adventures in Tepic at tel. 311/212-4011 or by email reservations@majahua.com.

For his more active guests, José offers to lead (or get a guide to lead) all-day wildlife viewing and hiking excursions, including a nearby extinct volcano (elev. 750 feet) crater lake.

Techos de Mexico

Jorge shares his sister Laura's vision of community building through teaching, help, and leadership. He, Laura, and Susana Escobido (see Casa Pacifica) have led Chacala's transition from drowsy subsistence fishing village to growing tourism destination through the past few years. Now, under the government- and business-sponsored **Techos de Mexico** (Roofs of Mexico) program, local people have built modern-standard tourist accommodations into their homes. They invite travelers to come and stay at very reasonable rates, ranging $20–40 for two, usually including breakfast.

Nearly all of the Techos de Mexico lodgings can be reserved through Susan Escobido's email, sescobido@aol.com. The growing list at present includes seven accommodations. All are within three blocks of the beach and fresh seafood *palapa* restaurants. For more information, visit the Techos de Mexico website www.playachacala.com/techos.htm.

Casa Pacifica

Sparkplug Susan Escobido collaborates with both Laura and José in leading the Chacala community transition. Moreover, Susan offers her own lodging, the lovely sea-view Casa Pacifica and airy Mauna Kea Restaurant, on a breezy sunset-view hillside above petite Chacalilla Bay. Choose from three invitingly comfortable modern-standard rooms, for about $45 d, with fan, hot-water shower bath, and breakfast. For more information, visit her website, www.playachacala.com; for reservations, email sescobido@aol.com.

Rincón de Guayabitos and La Peñita

Rincón de Guayabitos (pop. about 3,000 permanent, maybe 8,000 in winter) is a relaxed beachside resort town. It lies about an hour and a half's drive south of Tepic, and about the same north of Puerta Vallarta, at the tiny south-end *rincón* (wrinkle) of the broad, mountain-rimmed Bay of Jaltemba. The full name of Rincón de Guayabitos's sister town, La Peñita (Little Rock) de Jaltemba, comes from its perch on the sandy edge of the bay.

Once upon a time, Rincón de Guayabitos (or simply Guayabitos, meaning Little Guavas) lived up to its diminutive name. During the 1970s, however, the government decided Rincón de Guayabitos would become both a resort and one of three places in the Puerto Vallarta region where foreigners could own property. Today Rincón de Guayabitos is a summer, Christmas, and Easter haven for Mexicans, and a winter retreat for Canadians and Americans weary of glitzy, pricey resorts.

SIGHTS

Getting Oriented

Guayabitos and La Peñita (pop. around 10,000) represent practically a single town. Guayabitos has the hotels and the scenic beach village ambience, while two miles north La Peñita's main street, Emiliano Zapata, bustles with stores, restaurants, a bank, and a bus station.

Guayabitos's main street, **Av. del Sol Nuevo,** curves lazily for about a mile parallel to the beach. From the Av., several short streets and *andandos* (walkways) lead to a line of *retornos* (cul-de-sacs). The choicest of Guayabitos's community of small hotels, bungalow complexes, and trailer parks lie here within a block of the beach.

Isla Islote

Only a few miles offshore, the rock-studded humpback of Isla Islote may be seen from every spot along the bay. A flotilla of wooden glass-bottomed launches plies the Guayabitos shoreline, ready to whisk visitors across to the island.

For about $20 per hour, parties of up to six or eight can view fish through the boat bottom and see the colonies of nesting terns, frigate birds, and boobies on Islote's guano-plastered far side. You might see dolphins playing in your boat's wake, or perhaps a pod of whales spouting and diving nearby.

BEACHES AND ACTIVITIES

The main beach, **Playa Guayabitos-La Peñita,** curves two miles north from the rocky Guayabitos point, growing wider and steeper at La Peñita. The shallow Guayabitos cove, lined by *palapa* restaurants and dotted with boats, is a favorite of Mexican families on Sunday and holidays. They play in the one-foot surf, ride the boats, and eat barbecued fish. During busy times, the place can get polluted from the people, boats, and fishing.

Farther along toward La Peñita, the beach broadens and becomes much cleaner, with surf good for swimming, bodysurfing, and boogie boarding. Afternoon winds are often brisk enough for sailing and sailboarding, though you must bring your own equipment. Scuba and snorkeling are good near offshore Isla Islote, accessible via rental boat from Guayabitos. Local stores sell inexpensive but serviceable masks, snorkels, and fins.

A mile north of La Peñita, just past the palm-dotted headland, another long, inviting beach begins, offering good chances for beginning and intermediate surfing.

Cerro de la Santa Cruz

Some afternoon, you might enjoy following the (May 3 and Easter) 225-step pilgrimage path to the summit of Cerro de la Santa Cruz (Hill of the Holy Cross). From the top of La Cruz, as it's locally known, appreciate the ocean, beach, and cloud-tipped mountain panorama of the Bay of Jaltemba. Find the trail at the south end of Guayabitos's main steet, Av. del Sol Nuevo. Turn left at the crossroad, and look for the path heading uphill.

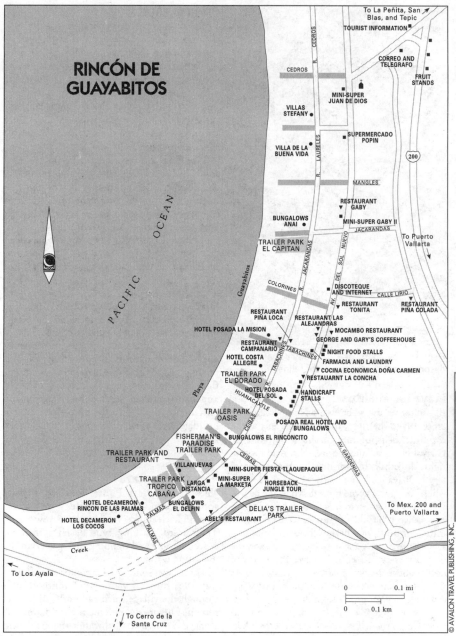

RINCÓN DE GUAYABITOS

To La Peñita, San Blas, and Tepic
TOURIST INFORMATION

R. CEDROS

CEDROS

CORREO AND TELEGRAFO

FRUIT STANDS

MINI-SUPER JUAN DE DIOS

VILLAS STEFANY

R. LAURELES

SUPERMERCADO POPIN

200

VILLA DE LA BUENA VIDA

MANGLES

OCEAN

RESTAURANT GABY

BUNGALOWS ANAI

MINI-SUPER GABY II

JACARANDAS

To Puerto Vallarta

TRAILER PARK EL CAPITAN

Guayabitos

R. JACARANDAS

AV. DEL SOL NUEVO

CALLE LIRIO

PACIFIC

COLORINES

R. COLORINES

DISCOTEQUE AND INTERNET

RESTAURANT TONITA

RESTAURANT PIÑA COLADA

RESTAURANT PIÑA LOCA

RESTAURANT LAS ALEJANDRAS

HOTEL POSADA LA MISION

MOCAMBO RESTAURANT

GEORGE AND GARY'S COFFEEHOUSE

RESTAURANT CAMPANARIO

R. TABACHINES

NIGHT FOOD STALLS

FARMACIA AND LAUNDRY

HOTEL COSTA ALLEGRE

COCINA ECONOMICA DOÑA CARMEN

Playa

TRAILER PARK EL DORADO

RESTAUARNT LA CONCHA

HOTEL POSADA DEL SOL

HANDICRAFT STALLS

R. HUANACAXTLE

TRAILER PARK OASIS

POSADA REAL HOTEL AND BUNGALOWS

R. CEIBAS

FISHERMAN'S PARADISE TRAILER PARK

BUNGALOWS EL RINCONCITO

TRAILER PARK AND RESTAURANT

R. CEIBAS

AV. GARDENIAS

VILLANUEVAS

MINI-SUPER FIESTA TLAQUEPAQUE

TRAILER PARK TROPICO CABAÑA

LARGA DISTANCIA

MINI-SUPER LA MARKETA

HORSEBACK JUNGLE TOUR

HOTEL DECAMERON RINCON DE LAS PALMAS

BUNGALOWS EL DELFIN

R. PALMAS

To Mex. 200 and Puerto Vallarta

HOTEL DECAMERON LOS COCOS

DELIA'S TRAILER PARK

ABEL'S RESTAURANT

R. PALMAS

Creek

To Los Ayala

To Cerro de la Santa Cruz

0   0.1 mi
0   0.1 km

TO PV/GUADALAJARA

© AVALON TRAVEL PUBLISHING, INC.

© BRUCE WHIPPERMAN

Fishing nets, boats, and a drowsy palm decorate La Peñita's sandy shoreline.

TO PV/GUADALAJARA

Playa los Muertos

Also at the south end of Av. Sol Nuevo, follow the crossroad to the right, to Los Ayala. Just as the road reaches its summit, curving left around the Guayabitos headland, notice a dirt road forking right, downhill. It continues through a cemetery to Playa los Muertos (Beach of the Dead), where the graves come right down to the beach.

Ghosts notwithstanding, this is a scenic little sandy cove. On fair days get your fill of safe swimming, sunning on the beach, or tidepooling among the clustered oysters and mussels and the skittering crabs. (Recently, however, the owners of houses above the beach have placed a gate across the private entrance road to discourage cars. They cannot legally bar people from the beach, so, even if you have to hire a launch to drop you off and pick you up there, Playa los Muertos is worth it. Please be sure to carry away all your trash.)

Playa los Ayala

Continue along the road about another mile to the once sleepy but now up-and-coming settlement and one-mile yellow strand of Playa los Ayala. Although local-style beachside *palapa* restaurants and bungalow accommodations are blossoming, the long, lovely, Los Ayala beach retains its Sunday popularity among local families. All of the beach sports possible at Guayabitos are possible here, with the added advantage of a much cleaner beach.

Like Guayabitos, Los Ayala has its secluded south-end cove. Follow the path up the beach-end headland. Ten minutes' walk along a tropical forest trail leads you to the romantic little jungle-enfolded sand crescent called **Playa del Beso** (Beach of the Kiss). Except during holidays, for hours on end few if any people come here.

Among the best of Los Ayala's new accommodations is **Bungalows Quinta Mina,** Los Ayala, Nayarit 63727, tel./fax 327/274-1141. This three-story stack of modern-standard kitchenette apartments enfolds an inviting beachfront pool and patio. Here, adults lounge around the small pool, while their kids frolic in a beachside kiddie pool. Upstairs, the dozen or so one-bedroom units, sleeping four, are simply but attractively furnished, with large rustic floor tiles, soft couches, white stucco walls, and shiny shower bathrooms. Low-season rentals run about $50 for up to four, except holidays and *puentes* (long weekends.) Add about 20 percent during the winter-spring high season.

Playa Punta Raza

The road to Playa Punta Raza, while only about three miles long, requires a maneuverable high-clearance vehicle and dry weather. The reward is a long, wild beach perfect for beachcombing and camping. Bring everything, including water.

Three miles south of Guayabitos along Highway 200, turn off west at El Monteón; pass through the village, turn right at Calle Punta Raza just before the pavement ends. Continue along the rough road through the creek and over the ridge north of town. At the summit, stop and feast your eyes on the valley view below, then continue down through the near-virgin jungle, barely scratched by a few poor cornfields. About a mile downhill from the summit, stop to see if the seasonal hillside Hotel and Restaurant Rincón del Cielo on the right is open. This site has recently been used as head-quarters for "Campo de Tortugas de Playa Punta Raza," a group of plucky volunteers who camp out on the beach trying to save endangered turtle eggs from poachers.

At the bottom of the steep grade, the track parallels the beach beneath big trees; sandy trails run through the brush to the beach—four-wheel drive and experienced sand drivers only—it's very easy to get stuck. You have two straight miles of pristine, jungle-backed sand virtually to yourself.

The beach itself slopes steeply, with the resulting close-in crashing waves and undertow. The water would be fine for splashing, but swimmers be careful. Because of the jungle hinterland, birds and other wildlife are plentiful here. Bring your insect repellent, binoculars, and identification books.

Turtles arrive seasonally, mostly in late summer and fall, to lay eggs here. Look for their obvious tracks in the sand. The turtles attract predators—cats, iguanas, birds, and human poachers. If you find an egg nest, either report it to the volunteers or keep watch over it; your reward may be to witness the birth and return to the ocean of dozens of baby turtles.

If the **Hotel and Restaurant Rincón del Cielo** is open, it affords the opportunity of enjoying an overnight at Playa Punta Raza without the effort of camping. Pioneering owners María Zavala and Juan Bernal offer four immaculate, simply but lovingly decorated rooms at the jungle's edge and two others perched right above the surf. Without electricity, Maria and Juan and their nighttime guests manage well by gas for light and refrigeration in their (seafoods, salads and pasta) restaurant and candlelight in the rooms. Room rentals run $40 d. Make reservations (not usually necessary) by leaving a message with the telephone operator in Monteón, tel. 327/274-7070.

ACCOMMODATIONS

Guayabitos Hotels

Rincón de Guayabitos has more far more hotels than any other town in Nayarit, including the capital, Tepic. Competition keeps standards high and prices low. During the low season (Sept.–Dec. 15), most places are less than half full and ready to bargain. During the winter season, the livelier part of town is at the south end, where most of the foreigners, mostly Canadian and American RV folks, congregate.

Guayabitos has many lodgings that call themselves "bungalows." This generally implies a motel-type suite with kitchenette with less service, but more spacious and more suited to families than a hotel room. For long stays or if you want to save money by cooking your own meals, bungalows can provide a good option.

Perhaps the cheapest good lodging in town is the homey 32-room **Posada Real Hotel and Bungalows,** Retorno Ceibas and Andando Huanacaxtle, Rincón de Guayabitos, Nayarit 63727, tel./fax 327/274-0177, built around a cobbled parking courtyard jungle of squawking parrots and shady palms, mangoes, and bamboo. The bungalow units are on the ground floor in the courtyard; the hotel rooms are stacked in three plant-decorated tiers above the lobby in front. The 26 four-person bungalows with kitchenette rent for about $37; the 20 two-person hotel rooms rent for about $33/day year-round, with discounts possible for longer-term stays. Amenities include ceiling fans, a small pool and a kiddie pool, water slide, racquetball, and parking; credit cards are accepted.

Immediately north, across Andando Huanacaxtle, best-buy **Hotel Posada del Sol,** tel. 327/274-0043, fax 327/273-1319, offers 18 tastefully furnished bungalows around a palmy garden patio, for about $30/day, $600/month. This charming place, as you would expect, is very popular and full in winter. Get your reservations in early.

One of the most appealing off-beach Guayabitos lodgings is **Bungalows El Delfín,** managed by friendly owners Francisco and Delia Orozco at Retorno Ceibas and Andando

TO PV/GUADALAJARA

RINCÓN DE GUAYABITOS
ACCOMMODATIONS BY PRICE

Accommodations (area code 327, postal code 63727) are listed in increasing order of approximate high-season, double-room rates.

Motel Russell (in La Peñita), Ruben C. Jaramillo 24, tel. 274-0959, $25.
Posada Real Hotel and Bungalows, Retorno Ceibas s/n, tel./fax 274-0177, $33
Hotel Posada del Sol, Retorno Tabachines s/n, tel./fax 274-0043, $35
Bungalows El Delfín, Retorno Ceibas s/n, P.O. Box 12, tel. 274-0385, www.bungalowsdelfin.com.mx, $37
Hotel Posada La Misión, Retorno Tabachines 6, tel./fax 274-0357, $38
Bungalows El Rinconcito, Retorno Ceibas s/n, P.O. Box 19, tel. 274-0229, $46
Hotel Costa Alegre, Retorno Tabachines s/n, tel./fax 274-0241, 274-1141, 274-0242, or 274-0243, $47
Bungalows Quinta Mina (in Playa Los Ayala), postal code 63727, tel./fax 274-1141, $60
Bungalows Anai, Retorno Jacarandas, P.O. Box 44, tel./fax 274-0245, anaisuites@prodigy.net.mx, $70
Villas Steffany, Retorno Laureles 12 Poniente, tel. 274-0536 or 274-0537, fax 274-0963, sales@steffanyvillas.com.mx, $75
Villas Buena Vida, Retorno Laureles 2, P.O. Box 62, tel. 274-0231, fax 274-0756, www.villasbuenavida.com, $90

Cocoteros, Rincón de Guayabitos, P.O. Box 12, Nayarit 63727, tel./fax 327/274-0385. Amenities include an intimate banana- and palm-fringed pool and patio, including recliners and umbrellas for resting and reading. Chairs on the shaded porch/walkways in front of the three room-tiers invite quiet relaxation and conversation with neighbors. The spacious four-person suites are large and plainly furnished, with basic stove, refrigerator, and utensils, rear laundry porches, and big, tiled toilet-showers. The 23 bungalows with kitchenette sleep four and rent for about $37 year-round, except for holidays, with ceiling fans, pool, and parking; pets are allowed. For more details, visit the website www.bungalows-delfin.com.mx.

Right-on-the-beach **Bungalows El Rinconcito,** Retorno Ceibas s/n and Calle Ceibas, P.O. Box 19, Rincón de Guayabitos, Nayarit 63727, tel./fax 327/274-0229, remains one of the best buys in Guayabitos. The smallish white-washed complex set back from the street offers large, tastefully furnished units with yellow and blue tile kitchens and solid, Spanish-style dark-

wood chairs and beds. Its ocean-side patio opens to a grassy garden overlooking the surf. Three two-bedroom bungalows rent for about $55 year-round, and seven one-bedroom bungalows for about $46 year-round, with fans and parking. Discounts are generally negotiable for longer-term stays.

One of the fancier Guayabitos lodgings is the colonial-style **Hotel Posada La Misión,** Retorno Tabachines 6, Rincón de Guayabitos, Nayarit 63727, tel./fax 327/274-0357, whose centerpiece is a beachside restaurant/bar/patio nestled beneath a spreading, big-leafed *hule* (rubber) tree. Extras include a luxurious shady garden veranda and an inviting azure pool and patio, thoughtfully screened off from the parking. Its rooms are high-ceilinged and comfortable except for the unimaginative bare-bulb lighting; bring your favorite bulb-clip lampshades. Rentals go for about $38 d, $65 for four, and $65 for suites sleeping six. Two kitchenette bungalows go for $47. Amenities include a pool, good restaurant in front, ocean-view bar, ceiling fans, and parking; credit cards are accepted.

Another good alternative is the family-oriented **Hotel Costa Alegre,** Retorno Tabachines s/n at Calle Tabachines, Rincón de Guayabitos, Nayarit 63727, tel./fax 327/274-0241, 327/274-0242, or 327/274-0243, where the Guayabitos beach broadens. Its pluses include a big, blue pool and patio on the street side and a broad, grassy, ocean-view garden on the beach side. Although the rooms are adequate, the kitchenette bungalows are set away from the beach with no view but the back of neighboring rooms. The best choices are the several upper-tier oceanfront rooms, all with sliding glass doors leading to private sea-view balconies. Some rooms are in better repair than others; look at more than one before paying. The 30 view rooms run about $47 d, the 43 kitchenette bungalows $66. Amenities include a/c, pool, parking, and restaurant/bar; credit cards are accepted. Reserve by email at costaalegre@guayabitos.com.

Most of Guayabitos' upscale lodgings are at the north end. For peace and quiet in a luxurious tropical setting, the **Bungalows Anai,** at Calle Jacarandas and Retorno Jacarandas, P.O. Box 44, Rincón de Guayabitos, Nayarit 63727, tel./fax 327/274-0245, is just about the best on the beach. The approximately 15 apartments, in two-story tiers, each with private ocean-view balcony, stand graciously to one side. They overlook a spacious, plant-bedecked garden, shaded by a magnificent grove of drowsy coconut palms. The garden leads to an ocean-view patio where a few guests read, socialize, and take in the beachside scene below. Inside, the two-bedroom suites are simply but thoughtfully furnished in natural wood, bamboo, and tile and come with bath, three double beds, furnished kitchen, fans, a/c, and TV. Rentals run about $70 for up to four people, one-week minimum stay. Discounts (approximately 33 percent for one week, 50 percent for one month) are available for long-term stays. For more information, visit the website www.anaisuites.com; reserve by telephone or email anaisuites@prodigy.net.mx.

About a block farther north, at Retorno Laureles 2, the new, deluxe **Villas Buena Vida** ranks among Guayabitos's most luxurious lodgings. About 40 tastefully appointed, ocean-view suites rise in three stories above a palm-shaded pool and patio right on the beach. For Guayabitos, the high-season asking rates are correspondingly luxurious: two-bed "villa" apartments run about $90 d high season, junior suites $110, master suites $146. Discounts are customarily available for long-term stays. Reserve at P.O. Box 62, Rincón de Guayabitos, Nayarit 63727, tel. 327/274-0231, toll-free Mex. tel. 800/640-3388, fax 327/274-0756, www.villasbuenavida.com.

A few doors north, **Villas Steffany,** Retorno Laureles 12 Poniente, Rincón de Guayabitos, Nayarit 63727, tel. 327/274-0536 or 327/274-0537, fax 327/274-0963, sales@steffanyvillas.com.mx, www.steffanyvillas.com.mx, offers another attractive deluxe alternative. Guests in the 34 suites enjoy private balconies overlooking a lush pool, patio, and garden and ocean vista. The apartments, simply but comfortably furnished in pastels, wood, and tile, have a living room with furnished kitchenette and one bedroom with two double beds and a bath; other extras include cable TV, telephone, and a/c. Rentals run about $75 d year-round. Discounts are negotiable for stays of two weeks or more. There are a restaurant, pool, and lobby bar, with street parking only, and credit cards are accepted.

Guayabitos Trailer Parks

All Guayabitos trailer parks are customarily wall-to-wall RVs most of the winter. Some old-timers have painted and marked out their spaces for years of future occupancy. The best spaces of the bunch are all booked by mid-October. And although the longtime residents are polite enough, some of them are clannish and don't go out of their way to welcome new kids on the block.

This is fortunately not true at **Delia's,** Guayabitos's homiest trailer park, Retorno Ceibas 4, Rincón de Guayabitos, Nayarit 63727, tel. 327/274-0398. Friendly owner Delia Bond Valdez and her daughter Rosa Delia have 12 spaces, some often unfilled even during the high season. Their place, alas, is not right on the beach, nor is it as tidy as some folks would like. On the other hand, Delia offers a little store and a long-distance phone service right next to the premises. She also rents three bungalows for about $450 a month. Spaces run about $11/night, $300/month all year, with all hookups, room for big rigs (but insufficient power for a/c), showers, and toilets; pets are okay, extra person $2.50. Camper vans cost $230 with all hookups, tent spaces go for $7/day, $180/month.

The rest of Guayabitos's trailer parks line up right along the beachfront. As you move from the south end, first comes **Trailer Park Trópico Cabaña,** built with boats and anglers in mind. One woman, the manager says, has been coming for more than 20 years running. It must be for the avocados—bulging, delicious three-pounders—which hang from a big shady tree. Other extras are a boat launch and storage right on the beach, with an adjacent fish-cleaning sink and table. This is a prime, very popular spot; get your reservation in early to Retorno Las Palmas, P.O. Box 3, Rincón de Guayabitos, Nayarit 63727. The 28 cramped spaces, six 38-footers and 22 33-footers, rent for about $19/day with all hookups, discounts possible for longer stays, with showers, toilets, and barbecue; pets are okay. Reserve at tel. 327/274-0662.

A block to the north comes **Fisherman's Paradise Trailer Park,** which is also popular as a mango-lover's paradise, Retorno Ceibas s/n, Rincón de Guayabitos, Nayarit 63727, tel. 327/274-0014, fax 327/274-0525. Several spreading mango trees shade the park's 33 concrete pads, and during the late spring and summer when the mangoes ripen, you'll probably be able to park under your own tree. Winter-season spaces rent for about $15/day for two people, minimum 15-day rental (or $14 for a three-month rental), with all hookups, showers, toilets, and lovely pool and patio; pets are okay, and add $3.50 per extra person.

Neighboring **Trailer Park Oasis** is among Guayabitos's most deluxe and spacious trailer parks, Retorno Ceibas s/n, Apdo. 52, Rincón de Guayabitos, Nayarit 63727, tel. 327/274-0361. Its 19 all-concrete, partly palm-shaded spaces are wide and long enough for 40-foot rigs. Pluses include green grassy grounds, beautiful blue pool, a designer restaurant, and a luxury ocean-view *palapa* above the beach. Spaces rent for about $18/day, with all hookups, showers, toilets, fish-cleaning facility, beautiful beachfront pool, and boat ramp; pets okay.

If you can't (or don't want to) get into any of the above, try nearby **Trailer Park Villanuevas,** at Retorno Ceibas s/n, P.O. Box 25, Rincón de Guayabitos, Nayarit 63727, tel. 327/274-0391 or 327/274-0606, or **Trailer Park El Capitán,** Retorno Jacarandas at Andando Jacarandas, Rincón de Guayabitos, Nayarit 63727, tel./fax 327/274-0304, www.elcapitanbungalows.com, sfcapitan@yahoo.com.

La Peñita Motel and Trailer Park

It will be good news to many longtime Mexico vacationers that **Motel Russell** remains open and ready for guests. The scene is vintage tropical Mexico—peeling paint, snoozing cats, lazy palms, and a beautiful beach with boats casually pulled onto the sand a few steps from your door—all for rock-bottom prices. Come and populate the place while octogenarian owner Mary Cárdenas Nichols is still around to tell stories about "the way things used to be." Reserve at Calle Ruben C. Jaramillo no. 24, La Peñita de Jaltemba, Nayarit, tel. 327/274-0959. There are about 15 spartan, one-bedroom apartments (most in need of repair) with fans for $25 d, $30 (two bedrooms $50), 30 percent discount for one month rental, with fans, kitchenette, and refrigerator. Great fishing from the front yard, and it's two blocks from practically everything else in La Peñita. For a fee, you may also be able to set up a tent or park your RV on one of the old beachfront trailer spaces. Get there by driving to the beach end of La Peñita's main street, Emiliano Zapata. Turn right and parallel the beach for about two blocks.

The big **Trailer Park Hotelera La Peñita,** P.O. Box 22, La Peñita, Nayarit 63727, tel. 327/274-0996, enjoys a breezy ocean-view location one mile north of La Peñita; watch for the big highway sign. Its 128 grassy spaces cover a tree-dotted, breezy hillside park overlooking a golden beach and bay. Rates run $15/day, $400/month, with all hookups; closed May through October. The many amenities include a pool, hilltop terrace club, Internet connection, restaurant, laundry, showers, and toilets; fine for tenting ($10 per tent for two), surfing, and fishing. Get your winter reservations by telephone, or email cthacker@oberon.ark.com. For more information, visit the website www.geocities.com/lapenitarvpark.

FOOD
Fruit Stands and Supermarkets
The farm country along Highway 200 north of Puerto Vallarta offers a feast of tropical fruits. Roadside stands at Guayabitos, La Peñita, and especially at Las Varas, half an hour north, offer mounds of papayas, mangoes, melons, and pineapples in season. Watch out also for more exotic species, such as the *guanabana,* which looks like a spiny mango, but whose pulpy interior looks and smells much like its Asian cousin, the jackfruit.

A number of Guayabitos minisupermarkets supply a little bit of everything. Try **Mini-Super La Marketa,** Retorno Ceibas across from Trailer Park Villanueva, on the south end, for vegetables, a small deli, and general groceries. Open daily 7 A.M.–2:30 P.M. and 4–7:30 P.M. Competing next door is **Mini-Super Tlaquapaque Fiesta,** open daily 8 A.M.–8 P.M. On the north end of Av. del Sol Nuevo, second branches of each of these, opposite the church and Hotel Peñamar, respectively, stock more, including fresh baked goods. Both are open daily, 8 A.M.–9 P.M.

For larger, fresher selections of everything, go to one of the big main-street *fruterías* or supermarkets in La Peñita, such as **Supermercado Lorena,** tel. 327/274-0255, across from Bancomer, open daily 8 A.M.–10 P.M.

For a good breakfast or sandwich, don't miss **George and Gary's Coffee House,** run by friendly, knowledgeable former professor of veterinary medicine and civic leader Jorge Castuera. Find his place on Av. del Sol Nuevo, beach side, near the corner of Tabachines. If there's something you want to know about Guayabitos, Jorge is the person to ask.

Restaurants
Several Guayabitos restaurants offer good food and service during the busy winter, spring, and August seasons. Hours and menus are often restricted during the midsummer and Sept.–Nov. low seasons.

By location, moving from the Guayabitos south end, first comes tidy, budget **Abel's Restaurant** *palapa,* at the south end of Av. del Sol Nuevo, behind Bungalows Delfín. Start off your day right, with a home-cooked North American–style breakfast, such as French toast, pancakes, or eggs any style, or finish it in style, with one of Abel's hearty soups, followed by a tasty meat, fish, and or chicken plates. Open daily 7 A.M.–9 P.M. in season.

For supper, you can't enjoy a homier option than the family-run **Cocina Económica Doña Carmen,** smack in the middle of Av. Sol Nuevo, east side, corner of Tabachines. Here, dedicated cooks put out hearty tacos, enchiladas, spicy *pozole* (shredded pork roast and hominy vegetable stew), and the catch of the day at budget prices. Open every day from early morning till about 10 p.m. year-round.

Across the street, the clean, local-style **Restaurant Las Alejandras,** tel. 327/274-0488, offers good breakfasts and a general Mexican-style menu; on Av. del Sol Nuevo, just north of the pharmacy, open daily in season 8 A.M.–9 P.M.

Similar good home-style food and service is available at **Restaurant Tonita,** half a block north, near the corner of Andando Colorines. Open Mon.–Fri. 7:30 A.M.–9:30 P.M. in season.

One of Guayabitos's best, the moderately priced restaurant **Campanario** in front of the Hotel Posada la Misión, Retorno Tabachines 6 at Calle Tabachines, tel. 327/274-0357, is a longtime favorite of the North American trailer colony. The menu features bountiful fresh seafood, meat, and Mexican plates at reasonable prices, open 8 A.M.–9 P.M. high season, 2–9 P.M. low; credit cards are accepted. For a variation on a similar comfort food theme, try equally popular **Restaurant La Piña Loca** across the street.

Also highly recommended (although I didn't have time to eat there) is **Restaurant Pina Colada** of friendly local guide Estaban Valdivia. Find it, on the Highway 200 lateral road, end of Calle Lirio, east of Av. Sol Nuevo, tel. 327/274-1211 or 327/274-1172.

SPORTS AND ENTERTAINMENT

Sports

Aquatic sports concentrate around the south end of Guayabitos beach, where launches ply the waters, offering banana (towed-tube) rides and **snorkeling** at offshore Isla Islote. Rent a **sportfishing** launch (*panga*, say PAHN-gah) along the beach. If you want to launch your own boat, ask one of the trailer parks if you can use its ramp for a fee. (For more beach sports details, see Beaches and Activities under Sights.)

Nightlife

Although Guayabitos is a resort for those who mostly love peace and quiet, a few nightspots, findable by the noise they emanate, operate along Av. del Sol Nuevo. One of the liveliest and longest-lasting is Charley's live music cabaret, at the corner of Tabachines.

INFORMATION AND SERVICES

Nayarit State Tourism maintains an **information office,** tel. 327/274-0693, open Mon.–Fri. 9 A.M.–2 P.M. and 4–7 P.M., Sat. and Sun. 9 A.M.–5 P.M. at the north end of Av. del Sol Nuevo, by the highway. If it's closed, an excellent alternative source is **Jorge Castuera,** the well-informed, personable, English-speaking former professor of veterinary medicine and owner of George and Gary's Coffee House, on Av. del Sol Nuevo, corner of Tabachines.

Another possible information source is the **Christoper Travel Agency,** tel. 327/274-0447, fax 327/274-0475.

Communications

The *correo* (post office), tel. 327/274-0717, open Mon.–Fri. 9 A.M.–1 P.M., and the *telecom* (public fax and money orders), open Mon.–Fri. 8 A.M.–2 P.M., stand side by side in the park, just north of the town church.

Long-distance telephoning is most conveniently and economically done on public street telephones, with Ladatel phone cards, widely available in stores along Av. del Sol Nuevo. A $5 Ladatel card will get you about 10 minutes of time to the United States or Canada (dial 001, then the area code and local number) on a street telephone.

Money Exchange

Although Guayabitos has no money-exchange agency as such, some of the minisupermarkets may exchange U.S. or Canadian dollars or traveler's checks. More pesos for your cash or traveler's checks are available at the **Bancomer** branch (with ATM) in La Peñita, E. Zapata 22, tel. 327/274-0237; it's open for U.S. and Canadian money exchange, Mon.–Fri. 9 A.M.–4 P.M.

Hospitals, Doctors, and Pharmacy

Although Guayabitos has no hospital, La Peñita at least has a small clinic. For medical consultations, go to the highly recommended, small, private 24-hour **Clínica Rentería,** on Calle Valle de Acapulco in La Peñita, tel. 327/274-0140, with a surgeon, gynecologist, and a general practitioner (Raul Rentería, M.D.) on call.

Alternatively, you can drive or taxi 14 miles (22 km) south to the small general hospital, tel. 311/258-4077, in San Francisco (known locally as "San Pancho"). It offers X-ray, laboratory, gynecological, pediatric, and internal medicine consultations and services both during regular office hours, weekdays 10:30 A.M.–noon and 4–6 P.M., and on 24-hour emergency call.

For medical consultations in Guayabitos, see Dr. Alfredo Rentería, M.D., at his pharmacy, at Av. del Sol Nuevo at Tabachines, tel. 327/274-0400.

Tours and Guides

A few local guides lead tours into the lush, wildlife-rich Guayabitos hinterland. Most accessible is **Indalesio Muñoz,** who leads horseback nature trail rides directly from his corral on the south end of Av. del Sol Nuevo, across from the Hotel Bugambilias. Tariff is $18 per person for a two-hour ride.

Highly recommended English-speaking guide **Estaban Valdivia** offers more extensive tours to unusual, untouristed local sites. His itinerary can include such intriguing destinations as hidden Las Miñitas bay and beach near Lo de Marco, Jamurca hot mineral pools near Las Varas, the jungle river boat tour to La Tovara spring in San Blas and the sylvan volcanic Crater Lake Laguna Santa María, in the Sierra southeast of Tepic. Contact him at home, tel. 327/274-1172, or at his Restaurant Pina Colada, tel. 327/274-1211 (on the Highway 200 lateral road, go east from Av. del Sol Nuevo along Calle Lirio).

GETTING THERE AND AWAY

Puerto Vallarta– and Tepic-bound Transportes Pacífico (TP) first- and second-class buses routinely stop (about once every daylight hour, each direction) on the main highway entrance to Guayabitos's Av. del Sol Nuevo. Additionally, several daily first-class buses pick up Puerto Vallarta– and Tepic-bound passengers at the Transportes Pacífico station, tel. 327/274-0001, at the main street highway corner in La Peñita.

Transportes Norte de Sonora (TNS) and Elite (EL) buses routinely stop at the small La Peñita station, one block south of the main street highway corner, inland side. Northern destinations include Tepic, San Blas, Mazatlán, and the U.S. border; southern, Puerto Vallarta, Manzanillo, Zihuatanejo, and Acapulco. **Primera Plus** luxury buses en route between Puerto Vallarta and Guadalajara stop at a small station on the same side, a few doors north of the TNS and Elite station.

The Guayabitos coast is easily accessible by bus or taxi from the **Puerto Vallarta International Airport,** the busy terminal for flight connections with U.S. and Mexican destinations. Buses and taxis cover the 39-mile (62-km) distance to Guayabitos in less than an hour. (For more details, see Getting There and Away in the Puerto Vallarta: Town, Bay, and Mountains chapter.)

South of Guayabitos

PLAYA LO DE MARCO

Follow the signed Lo de Marco (That of Marco), turnoff, eight miles (13 km) south of Rincón de Guayabitos (or 31 miles, 49 km, north of the Puerto Vallarta airport). Continue about a mile through the town to the long, sandy beach, dotted with a dozen seafood *palapa* restaurants. Playa Lo de Marco is popular with Mexican families; on Sunday and holidays they dig into the fine golden sand and frolic in the gentle, rolling waves. The surf of the nearly level, very wide Playa Lo de Marco is good for all aquatic sports except surfing. The south end has a rocky tidepool shelf, fine for bait-casting. Equipped scuba divers can rent boats to go to offshore Isla Islote, where water during the dry winter season, is passably clear.

Accommodations

The constant flow of vacationing Mexican families supports a pair of moderately priced hotels on the main street, on the right, about a quarter-mile from the highway. Best by far is **Hotel Bungalows Las Tortugas,** at Luis Echevarría 28, Lo de Marco, Nayarit, tel./fax 327/275-0092. The major

attraction is the layout of about 18 kitchenette apartments in two stories around a broad, invitingly tropical, designer pool and patio, with kiddie pool and hot tub. Inside, the units, all with kitchenettes, are bare-bulb (bring your own lampshade), sparely but comfortably furnished, spacious, and clean. The upper apartments, with king-sized beds, are more inviting than some others. Look at more than one before deciding. Asking rates run a high $36, with TV, dishes and utensils, and fans. Except during holidays and some weekends, discounts may be negotiable. Be sure to ask for a *descuento* (days-koo-AYN-toh).

Alternatively, take a look at the Bungalows Padre Nuestro (Our Father), tel. 327/275-0025, fax 327/275-0055, a few doors back toward the highway, with pool and a big family-friendly grassy picnic *palapa* and patio in back. Although the approximately 20 kitchenette apartments are plain, they're clean and the prices are right, at about $25 except for holidays, when rentals go for about $50.

For something fancier, consider the big **Villas and Bungalows Tlaquepaque,** Pie de Av. Luís Echeverría, Lo de Marco, Nayarit, tel./fax

TO PV/GUADALAJARA

327/275-0080, email villastlaquepaque_02@hot-mail.com. Past the imposing neocolonial front gate and reception spreads a manicured, grassy park, with luxurious blue-pool patio, basketball court, soccer field, kiddie playground, inter-spersed among handsome accommdations tiers. Lodgings vary from one-bedroom studios to big three-bedroom, three-bath extended family suites. Rooms are deluxe and comfortable; prices are right, beginning at about $40 d for the smaller and ranging up to $120 for two-bed-room family suites.

Beachfront Trailer Parks, Bungalows, and Camping

Lo de Marco has a number of beachfront trailer parks, popular during the winter with a regi-ment of American and Canadian RV retirees. Best of the bunch is the superb trailer park/bun-galow complex **El Caracol**, owned and operated by German expatriate Gunter Maasan and his Mexican wife and daughter. The nine luxuri-ously large "little bit of Europe in the tropics" motel-style bungalows sleep four to six people with all the comforts of Hamburg. Rents begin at about $45 d low season, $55 high, with fans or a/c, and complete kitchenettes. Add about $10 per extra person, $10 for a/c.

The trailer park is correspondingly luxurious, with concrete-pad spaces in a palm- and banana-shaded grassy park right on the beach. With small beachfront pool-patio, all hookups, and immac-ulate hot-shower and toilet facilities, the 15 spaces rent for about $15 per day, $13 per day monthly. Add $5 per extra person. Dogs are not generally welcome. It's popular, so make winter reservations by September. Write P.O. Box 89, La Peñita de Jal-temba, Nayarit 63726, or call tel./fax 327/275-0050, or in Guadalajara tel. 33/3686-0481.

Tent, RV camping, and lodging are also avail-able at the trailer park **Pequeña Paraíso** (Little Paradise) beside the jungle headland at the south end of the beach. Here, the friendly family man-ager welcomes visitors to the spacious, palm-shaded beachside grove. Basic but clean apartments rent for about $27 d ($38 d with kitchenette), with hot-water showers and fans. RV spaces, with all hookups, rent for about $15/day,

$90/wk, $330/month, with showers and toilets. Dozens of grass-carpeted, palm-shaded tent spaces rent for about $4 per person per day. Stores in town nearby can furnish basic supplies. Re-serve, especially during the winter, at tel. 327/275-0089, or in writing to Parque de Trailer Pequeío Paraíso, Carretera Las Miñitas no.1938, Lo de Marco, Nayarit.

Alternatively, a few other nearby trailer parks are recommendable. Check out **Pretty Sunset** trailer park, tel. 327/275-0024 or 327/275-0055, or **Trailer Park and Bungalows Huerta de Igua-nas,** tel. 327/275-0089, or last choice huge over-flow-style **Trailer Park and Campground El Refugio,** operated by the big Hotel Villas and Bungalows Tlaquepaque. (See contact informa-tion under Accommodations.)

Get to the trailer parks by turning left just before the beach, at the foot of the town main street (which leads straight from the highway). Continue about another mile to El Caracol, on the right, and El Pequeño Paraíso, a hundred yards farther.

Continuing south along the Lo de Marco beach road past the trailer parks, you will soon come to two neighboring pearly sand paradises, **Playa Las Miñitas** and **Playa El Venado.** Bring your swimsuit, picnic lunch, and, if you crave isolation, camping gear.

PLAYA SAN FRANCISCO

The idyllic beach and drowsy country ambience of the little mango-processing town of San Fran-cisco (San Pancho, locals call it) offers yet an-other bundle of pleasant surprises. Exit Highway 200 at the road sign six miles (nine km) south of Guayabitos (25 miles, 40 km, north of the Puerto Vallarta airport) and continue straight through the town to the beach.

The broad, golden-white sand, enclosed by palm-tipped green headlands, extends for a half-mile on both sides of the town. Big, open ocean waves (take care—there's an undertow) pound the beach for nearly its entire length. Offshore, flocks of pelicans dive for fish while frigate birds sail overhead. At night during the rainy months, sea turtles come ashore to lay their egg clutches,

© BRUCE WHIPPERMAN

The shoreline trail north of San Francisco leads to a wild, hidden beach, ripe for trekkers.

which a determined group of volunteers tries to protect from poachers. Beach *palapa* restaurants provide food and drinks. If all this entices you to stay, several comfortable lodgings offer accommodations.

Accommodations

A sign on the right a couple of blocks before the beach marks the bumpy road to the **Costa Azul Adventure Resort.** In-hotel activity centers around the beach and palm-shaded pool/bar/restaurant/patio. Farther afield, hotel guides take guests on kayaking, biking, surfing, and snorkeling trips and naturalist-guided horseback rides along nearby coves, beaches, and jungle trails.

The hotel itself, at the foot of a hillside of magnificent Colima palms, offers 20 large, comfortable suites and eight villas (six one-bedroom and a pair of two-bedroom)—all with both fans and a/c—respectively, for about $90 d, $136 d, and $200 for up to six, high season. Corre-

sponding low-season rates run about $75, $95, and $160. Up to two children 12 and under stay free. Make reservations through the U.S. booking agent at 224 Av. del Mar, Suite D, San Clemente, CA 92672, tel. 949/498-3223 or toll-free U.S./Can. tel. 800/365-7613, fax 949/498-6300, getaway@costaazul.com, www.costaazul.com. Reservations are strongly recommended, especially in the winter.

Continue north past the Costa Azul Adventure Resort a mile and a fraction (about two km) along the gravel coastal road to a signed driveway leading through the shady, vine-hung tropical forest. At road's end, find **Bungalows Lydia,** mini-Eden and life dream-made-true of spritely and welcoming Lydia (whose surname I forgot to ask). Her offering consists of four spic-and-span kitchenette studios set in a charming oceanfront garden on a spectacularly rocky point buffeted by wild, foaming surf.

The accommodations themselves, while not fancy, are sturdily built, clean and simply but thoughtfully decorated in whites and pastels. Situated overlooking the surf, the place is kept nearly bug-free by the ocean breeze. Lydia asks $55 for two ($80 for a larger two-bedroom for up to six), discounts negotiable for longer-term rentals, with small kitchenettes and hot water shower baths. No phones, no TV, but plenty of fresh air, sunsets, and peace and quiet. Reserve by mail, at Bungalows Lydia, San Francisco, Km 111, Carreterra Puerto Vallarta-Tepic, Nayarit 63732, by telephone to Lydia's family agent in Guadalajara, tel. 33/3811-6979, or email bungalowslydia@hotmail.com.

Back in town, American owners have rebuilt a side-street house, thus creating the **Hotel Los Amigos** bed-and-breakfast, seemingly perfect for those who appreciate quiet relaxation. Find it on Calle Asia 6, San Francisco, Nayarit 63732, tel./fax 311/258-4155. A tiled entrance walkway guides visitors indoors, through an artfully decorated small lobby to a flowery breakfast garden patio, partially sheltered by a gracefully traditional (but water-tight) *palapa* roof. A hot tub for guests' enjoyment is tucked on one side.

Stairs lead upward to two luxuriously airy upper room stories, of six luxurious, crafts-decorated

TO PV/GUADALAJARA

double rooms and two studio suites. The rooms (with either queen-sized beds, or two twins) rent from about $75 d, high season, $60 low; the larger studio suites (with one queen, one twin each), go for about $95 high season, $80 low; all with ceiling fans and continental breakfast included. For more information visit the website www.losamigoshotel.com.

Also lovely, at the edge of a shady palm grove, only half a block from the beach, are **Palapas Las Iguanas**, on main street Calle Tercer Mundo, San Francisco, Nayarit 63732, tel. 311/258-4015. Owners Dar Peters and Angela López Garcia, who also operate the excellent Los Arcos Restaurant next door, offer eight accommodations, divided between a luxurious, thatched open- air (but mosquito-netted) *palapa* complex and a more conventional, but nevertheless attractive, enclosed bungalow apartment section. Units vary, from a spacious two-bedroom, two-bath apartment with full kitchen, all the way down to a petite, one-bedroom studio with small kitchenette. Rentals begin at about $40 d for the smallest studio, running up to about $100 for the largest two-bedroom. Reserve by telephone or email peters@pvnet-com.mx; for more information, visit the website www.sanpanch.net.mx.

For other San Francisco **rentals,** consult friendly real estate agent Gino Lamphier, at San Pancho Real Estate, on the main street, at 23 Av. Tercer Mundo, tel. 311/258-4250, or email ginolamphier@hotmail.com.

Food

The growing local community of middle-class Americans, Canadians,and Mexicans and burgeoning numbers of Puerto Vallarta day-trippers support a number of recommendable in-town eateries. Among the best is **Restaurant Los Arcos,** whose sparkplug owner-chef Angela López Garcia serves a delicious menu of hearty country Mexican cuisine, with plenty of fresh seafood, salads, and fine wines to boot. Find it at the beach end of the main town thoroughfare, Av. Tercer Mundo. Open daily 8:30–11 A.M. and 4–10:30 P.M., tel. 311/258-4015. Moderate–expensive.

Also on the same main street, in the middle of

town, **La Ola Rica Restaurant and Bar** offers fresh seafood and Mexican supper specialties daily, 8:30–11 A.M. and 6–10 P.M. Oct.–May, shorter hours June–Sept., tel. 311/255-4123. Moderate–expensive.

For Italian specialties, go to *palapa* **Restaurant Pizzeria Galloly,** on the south side of the main street, about four blocks from the beach, tel. 311/258-4135. Moderate.

Alternatively, for breakfast, lunch or dinner, you can retreat a mile north, to the palm-shaded beachside ambience of **Wahoo Bar and Grill** at the Costa Azul Adventure Resort. Open daily 8 A.M.–9 P.M. Moderate–expensive.

Shopping

A few arts and crafts gallery-shops now sprinkle main street Av. Tercer Mundo. In the middle of town, the **Oasis** gift shop sells crafts and T-shirts, profits from which go to the local turtle protection project. Also **Galería del Tercer Mundo,** a block from the beach, features Huichol indigenous art and ceremonial handicrafts; open Mon.–Sat. 9 A.M.–5 P.M.

Hospital

San Francisco residents enjoy a modest local general hospital, tel. 311/258-4077, with ambulance, emergency room, and doctors on call 24 hours. Find it off the main street, to the right (north), about a quarter-mile from the highway.

SAYULITA

Little Sayulita (pop. 3,000), nine miles (14 km) south of Guayabitos (22 miles, or 35 km, north of the Puerto Vallarta airport), was once the kind of spot that romantics hankered for: a drowsy village on a palmy arc of sand, a hidden retreat for those who enjoy the quiet pleasures and local color of Mexico. And while Sayulita during low season still resembles that former description, it's become much busier during the fall surfing and winter vacation seasons.

Once only a destination for a handful of Puerto Vallarta day-trippers, Sayulita is being discovered by a growing host of sun-seeking retirees and youthful Americans, Canadians, Europeans, and

Japanese who have made it their fall-winter destination of choice.

Nevertheless, Sayulita's amenities remain: clean waters, fine for swimming, surfing, bodysurfing, and fishing, relaxed country ambience, and plenty of warm sun during the day and cooling offshore breezes at night. What's changed is the high-season bustle of the newcomers lining the beach and the crop of real estate agents, stores, crafts shops, restaurants, bungalows, bed-and-breakfasts, and hotels that have turned up to serve them.

Accommodations

Adrienne Adams, owner/manager of the bed-and-breakfast **Villa de la Buena Salud,** rents six comfortable upstairs rooms with bath from about $50 d, including breakfast for two, minimum three days. Her airy, art-draped, three-story house is a few steps from the Sayulita beach. Although her six upper rooms are for adults only, families with children are welcome in a downstairs apartment sleeping five, with kitchen, VCR, and TV, for about $85 per night. Get your winter reservations in early. Adrienne's daughter Lynn, at 1495 San Elijo, Cardiff CA 92007, tel. 760/942-9640, handles reservations year-round. Adrienne also takes reservations July–Oct. in California, at tel. 760/632-7716 or toll-free tel. 888/221-9247, fax 760/632-8585, tia@tiaadrianas.com, or by mail, at 1495 B San Elijo, Cardiff, CA 92007. She returns to Sayulita in November. You can contact her in Sayulita until June, by writing her at P.O. Box 5, La Peñita de Jaltemba, Nayarit 63727, phoning her directly in Sayulita at tel. 329/291-3029, or by email. Also, you might take a look at Tía Adriana's website www.tiaadrianas.com. She also rents a cluster of deluxe hillside suites. For details, visit Tía Adriana's website www.tiaadrianas.com.

Nearby, the newish, *palapa*-chic **Bungalows Aurinko** (Sun in the Finnish language), Calle Marlin, Sayulita, Nayarit 63727, tel. 329/291-3150, info@sayulita-vacations.com, www.sayulita-vacations.com, offers an excellent alternative. Labor of love of its friendly owner-builder Nazario Carranza, Aurinko glows with his handiwork: hand-crafted natural wood bedstands and dressers, rustically luxurious whitewashed walls, adorned with native arts and crafts, all beneath a handsome, towering *palapa* roof, only half a block from the beach. The five one-bedroom units rent from about $68 d, high season, $60 low. A pair of two-bedroom units go for about $106 each high, $85 low, all with modern-standard bathrooms, airy patio kitchens, and ceiling fans.

At the end of the south-side beach road, the designer cabanas of newcomer hotel **Villa Amor** grace the leafy headland. Villa Amor offers about 30 (soon to be about 50) owner-designed architecture-as-art rustic *palapa*-chic view dwellings. Accommodations, many open air (thus sometimes winter-night-cool, and summer damp) range from two-bedroom, 2.5-bath house-sized full kitchen suites, down to modest but still deluxe refrigerator-and-sink studios, all enjoying panoramic vistas of Sayulita's petite bay. Most beds are king- or queen-sized, colors range from soft pastels to white. Rental tariffs run from about $60, up to $300, high season, $55 to $250 low. Credit cards are not accepted. Fans only, no phones, no TV. Reserve by tel. 329/291-3010, fax 329/291-2018, or email info@villaamor.com. For more information, visit the website www.villaamor.com.

More modest, but still comfortably appointed, beachfront bungalows are also available at the **Sayulita Trailer Park**, on the opposite, north side of town. A cadre of long-time returnees enjoy about 10 clean, two-bedroom bungalows with kitchen, four of them smack on the beach. Rates begin at about $60/day, $400/week, $1,400/month for two; add about $8 per extra person per day. During the two weeks before Easter and December 15–31, rates run about 20 percent higher and reservations must include a minimum seven-day stay and a 50 percent deposit. For reservations—in winter, get them in six months early—contact the owners, Thies and Cristina Rohlfs, at Sayulita directly, at P.O. Box 11, La Peñita de Jaltemba, Nayarit 63727, tel./fax 329/291-3126.

Also on the north side of town, find luxuriously lovely **Villas Sayulita,** on a quiet side street about two long blocks uphill from the beach. Guadalajara owner-architect Oscar Limón offers about a dozen spacious kitchenette suites. They occupy lower and upper floors, adjacent to an invitingly intimate tropical pool patio, with picnic *palapa*. The suites themselves are lovingly designed and immaculately maintained, with attractive rustic tile floors, deluxe, modern-standard baths, and soaring arched ceilings. Some beds are king-sized, with pullout for kids, others with two double beds. Rentals are a very reasonable $55 d high season, $45 low, with TV and a/c. Reserve directly by tel./fax 329/291-3064, 329/291-3065, or 329/291-3067, oscarlimon4@yahoo.com.mx.

Back near the center of town, and much farther down the economic ladder, is 1940s auto court–style (occasional auto noise and exhaust, but a block from the beach) **Bungalows Las Gaviotas,** at Calle Gaviotas 12, Sayulita, Nayarit 63727. Here, you have a choice of three fan-only rooms sleeping two, and five bungalows, with two beds and kitchenette, sleeping at least four. All units are clean, with a reading lamp, and bright blue and white tile floors. The rooms go for about $25, the kitchenette bungalows, about $50. Reservations, usually not necessary except for holidays, might be possible by writing the hotel long ahead of time, or by calling the owner (in Spanish) in Guadalajara, at 33/3616-3402.

Last choice in Sayulita goes to the scruffy, oft-empty **Hotel Sayulita** right on the beach. Although the owner, at the hardware store next door, asks about $17 d, $22 t, for 33 very basic rooms that surround a cavernous interior courtyard, you might be able to bargain for a better price.

Trailer Park and Campground

RV folks love the north-side **Sayulita Trailer Park,** in a big shady sandy lot, with about 36 hookups (some for rigs up to 40 feet) right on the beach. Guests enjoy just about everything—good clean showers and toilets, electricity, water, a bookshelf, concrete pads, dump station, pets okay—for about $15/day for two pe people, one day free per week, discounts available for extended stays. Add about $3 per extra person. Reserve through owners Thies and Cristina Rohlfs, P.O. Box 11, La Peñita de Jaltemba, Nayarit 63727, tel./fax 329/291-3126.

Trying harder is Sayulita's new campground, gated and enclosed **Palmar del Camarón,** in a big former palm grove, on the north-side beachfront. The owner, known locally as "Camarón," offers lots of grassy spots for tents and smaller self-contained RVs needing no hookups. Spaces, first-come, first-served, cost $3.50 per person, including showers, toilets, and individual *palapas* for shelter against sun and rain. Camarón also rents rustic *palapa* cabanas, with mosquito nets and private toilet and shower, for $30 d. Find it as you enter town, by turning right at the lane that borders the baseball field. After a block and a half, turn right in to the campground gate.

Rental Agent

Drawn by the quiet pleasures of country Mexico, a number of American, Canadian, and Mexican middle-class folks have built comfortable vacation homes in and around Sayulita and are renting them out. **Propiedades Sayulita** (Sayulita Properties), at Calle Delfin 9, Sayulita, Nayarit 63732, tel./fax 329/291-3076, sayulitaproperties@yahoo .com or sayulitapropiedades@pvnet.com.mx, www.sayulita.com, lists such properties for rental or sale.

Food

Vegetables, groceries, and baked goods are available at a pair of stores by the town plaza, or at Abarrotes Doria, just south of the bridge, on Revolución, the main ingress street from the highway. Local cuisine is supplied by a lineup of plaza taco stand at night, a pair of beachfront *palapa* restaurants, and breakfast, lunch, and dinner at **Restaurant Las Blancas,** beach side of the plaza.

Higher up the economic scale, a few recommendable restaurants dot Sayulita's streets and beachfront. Best established is **Pedro's** once humble, but now elegant, fresh seafood *palapa,* on the south end beachfront. Here, the main events are the freshest catches of the day, such as *dorado* (mahimahi), oysters, octupus, shrimp, all professionally prepared and presented. Expensive.

In town, on the main street Revolución, family-owned **La Fiesta** restaurant is a party ready to happen nearly every night. The whole family, including the waiters, and the audience sometime get into the act. Moreover, their Mexican food, with bottomless hot, handmade tortillas, is just about the best on the Nayarit coast. Moderate–expensive.

Return another evening, across Revolución, to restaurant-pizzeria **"Si Hay Olitas"** ("Yes, there are some little waves"), for your choice of of ribs, hamburgers, chicken, or good in-house pizza in a dozen varieties. Moderate.

Sports Rentals and Tours
Mario "Papa" Rubio, co-owner of **Propiedades Sayulita** also operates "Papa's *Palapa*" hotel on the beach (and Bungalows Duendes Vista on the hillside three blocks above the beach). Right in front of his beach hotel, Mario rents beach chairs, umbrellas, boogie boards, snorkel gear, surfboards, kayaks, offers surfing lessons, and more. He also arranges jungle tours, horseback rides, or guided foot hikes, and hotel-surfing packages. Contact him through Propiedades Sayulita (see Rental Agent).

TO PV/GUADALAJARA

Puerto Vallarta: Town, Bay, and Mountains

Puerto Vallarta

The town of Puerto Vallarta (pop. 350,000) perches at the most tranquil recess of one of the Pacific Ocean's largest, deepest bays, the Bay of Banderas. The bay's many blessings—golden beaches, sparkling sunshine, blue waters, and the seafood that they nurture—are magnets for a million seasonal visitors.

Visitors find that Puerto Vallarta is really two cities in one—a new town strung along the hotel strip on its northern beaches, and an old town nestled beneath jungly hills on both sides of a small river, the Río Cuale. Travelers arriving from the north, whether by plane, bus, or car, see the modern Puerto Vallarta first—a parade of luxury hotels, condominiums, apartments,

and shopping centers. Visitors can stay for a month in a slick new Vallarta hotel, sun on the beach every day, disco every night, and return home, never having experienced the old Puerto Vallarta.

HISTORY
Before Columbus
For centuries before the arrival of the Spanish, the coastal region that includes present-day Puerto Vallarta was subject to the indigenous kingdom of Xalisco, centered near the modern Nayarit city of Xalisco. Founded around A.D. 600, the Xalisco civilization was ruled by chiefs who worshipped a trinity of gods: foremost, Naye, a legendary former chief elevated to a fierce god of war, followed by the more benign Teopiltzin, god of rain and fertility, and finally by wise Heri, the god of knowledge.

south end of Playa Los Muertos

© BRUCE WHIPPERMAN

Recent archaeological evidence indicates another influence: the Aztecs, who probably left Náhuatl-speaking colonies along the southern Nayarit coastal valleys during their centuries-long migration to the Valley of Mexico.

Conquest and Colonization

Some of those villages still remained when the Spanish conquistador Francisco Cortés de Buenaventura, nephew of Hernán Cortés, arrived on the Jalisco-Nayarit coast in 1524.

In a broad mountain-rimmed green valley, an army of 20,000 warriors, their bows decorated by myriad colored cotton banners, temporarily blocked the conquistador's path. So impressive was the assemblage that Cortés called the fertile vale of the Ameca River north of present Puerto Vallarta the Valle de las Banderas (Valley of the Banners), and thus the great bay later became known as the Bahía de Banderas.

The first certain record of the Bay of Banderas itself came from the log of conquistador Don Pedro de Alvarado, who sailed into the bay in 1541 and disembarked (probably at Mismaloya) near some massive sea rocks. He named these Las Peñas, undoubtedly the same as the present "Los Arcos" rocks that draw daily boatloads of snorkelers and divers.

For 300 years the Bay of Banderas slept under the sun. Galleons occasionally watered there; a few pirates hid in wait for them in its jungle-fringed coves.

Independence

The rebellion of 1810–1821 freed Mexico, and finally, a generation later, the lure of gold and silver led, as with many of Mexico's cities, to the settlement of Puerto Vallarta. Enterprising merchant Don Guadalupe Sanchez made a fortune (ironically, not from gold, but from salt, for ore processing), which he hauled from the beach to the mines above the headwaters of the Río Cuale. In 1851 Don Guadalupe built a hut and brought his wife and children. Their tiny trading station grew into a little town, Puerto de Las Peñas, at the mouth of the river.

Later, the local government founded the present municipality, which, on May 31, 1918, of-

The Las Peñas sea rocks were first recorded in the 1541 log of explorer Pedro de Alvarado.

ficially became Puerto Vallarta, in honor of the celebrated jurist and former governor of Jalisco, Ignacio L. Vallarta.

However, the Cuale mines eventually petered out, and Puerto Vallarta, isolated, with no road to the outside world, slumbered again.

Modern Puerto Vallarta

But not for long. Passenger planes began arriving sporadically from Tepic and Guadalajara in the 1950s; a gravel road was pushed through from Tepic in the 1960s. The international airport was built, the highway was paved, and tourist hotels sprouted on the beaches. Meanwhile, in 1963, director John Huston, at the peak of his creative genius, arrived with Richard Burton, Elizabeth Taylor, Ava Gardner, and Deborah Kerr to film *Night of the Iguana*. Huston, Burton, and Taylor stayed on for years, waking Puerto Vallarta from its long slumber. It hasn't slept since.

PUERTO VALLARTA

SIGHTS

Getting Oriented

Puerto Vallarta is a long beach town, stretching about five miles from the Riviera-like Conchas Chinas condo headland at the south end. Next, as you head north, comes the popular Playa Los Muertos beach and the intimate old Río Cuale neighborhood, which join, across the river, the busy central *malecón* (seawall) shopping and restaurant (but beachless) bayfront. North of there, the beaches resume again at Playa Camarones and continue past the Zona Hotelera string of big resorts to the Marina complex, where tour boats and cruise liners depart from the Terminal Maritima dock. In the Marina's northern basin lie the Peines (pay-EE-nays) sportfishing and Club de Yates docks. A mile farther north, the city ends at the bustling International Airport.

One basic thoroughfare serves the entire beachfront. Officially Búlevar Francisco Medina Ascencio, but commonly called the **Carretera Aeropuerto** (Airport Highway) as it conducts express traffic south past the Zona Hotelera, it changes names three times. Narrowing, it becomes the cobbled Av. México, then Paseo Díaz Ordaz along the seafront *malecón* with tourist restaurants, clubs, and shops, changing finally to Av. Morelos before it passes the Presidencia Municipal (city hall) and central plaza.

When southbound traffic reaches Isla Río Cuale, the tree-shaded, midstream island where the city's pioneers built their huts, traffic slows to a crawl and finally dissipates in the colorful old neighborhood on the south side of the river.

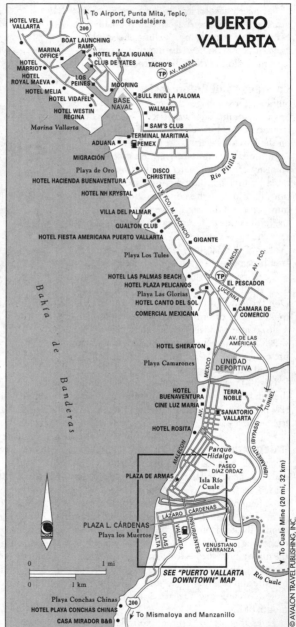

There being little traffic south of the Cuale, people walk everywhere, and slowly, because of the heat. Every morning men in sombreros lead burros down to the mouth of the river to gather sand. Little *papelerías, miscelaneas,* and streetside *taquerías* serve the local folks while small restaurants, hotels, and clubs serve the visitors.

Getting Around

Since nearly all through traffic flows along one thoroughfare, Puerto Vallarta transportation is a snap. Simply hop on one of the frequent (but usually crowded) city buses (fare about $.40), virtually all of which end up at Plaza Lázaro Cárdenas on Av. Olas Altas a few blocks south of the river. Northbound, the same buses retrace the route through the Zona Hotelera to one of several destinations scrawled across their windows. Taxis, while much more convenient, are all individual and rather expensive (about $2–6 per trip within the city limits; don't get in until the price is settled).

Drivers who want to quickly travel between the north and the south ends of town often take

NIGHT OF THE IGUANA: THE MAKING OF PUERTO VALLARTA

The idea to film Tennessee Williams's play *Night of the Iguana* in Puerto Vallarta was born in the bar of the Beverly Hills Hotel. In mid-1963, director John Huston, whose movies had earned a raft of Academy Awards, met with Guillermo Wulff, a Mexican architect and engineer. For the film's location Wulff proposed Mismaloya, an isolated cove south of Puerto Vallarta. On leased land, Wulff would build the movie set and cottages for staff housing, which he, Huston, and producer Ray Stark would later sell for a profit as tourist accommodations.

Most directors would have been scared away by the Mismaloya jungle, where they would find no roads, phones, or electricity. But, according to Alex Masden, one of Huston's biographers, Huston loved Mismaloya: "To me, *Night of the Iguana* was a picnic, a gathering of friends, a real vacation."

A "gathering of friends," indeed. The script required most of the cast to be dissolute, mentally ill, or both: a blonde nymphet tries to seduce an alcoholic defrocked minister while his dead friend's love-starved, hard-drinking widow keeps a clutch of vulturous biddies from destroying his last bit of self-respect—all while an iguana roped to a post passively awaits its slaughter.

Huston's casting was perfect. The actors simply played themselves. Richard Burton (the minister) came supplied with plenty of booze. Burton's lover, Elizabeth Taylor, who was not part of the cast and still married to singer Eddie Fisher, accompanied him. Sue Lyon (the nymphet) came with her lovesick boyfriend, whose wife was rooming with Sue's mother; Ava Gardner (the widow) became the toast of Puerto Vallarta while romping with her local beach paramour; Tennessee Williams, who was advising the director, came with his lover Freddy; while Deborah Kerr, who acted the only prim lead role, jokingly complained that she was the only one not having an affair.

With so many mercurial personalities isolated together in Mismaloya, the international press flew to Puerto Vallarta in droves to record the expected fireworks. Huston gave each of the six stars, as well as Elizabeth Taylor, a velvet-lined case containing a gold derringer with five bullets, each engraved with the names of the others. Unexpectedly, and partly because of Huston's considerable charm, none of the bullets was used. Bored by the lack of major explosions, the press corps discovered Puerto Vallarta instead.

As Huston explained later to writer Lawrence Grobel: "That was the beginning of its popularity, which was a mixed blessing." Huston nevertheless returned to the area and built a home on the Bay of Banderas, where he lived the last 11 years of his life. Burton and Taylor bought Puerto Vallarta houses, got married, and also stayed for years. Although his Mismaloya tourist accommodations scheme never panned out, Guillermo Wulff became wealthy building for the rich and famous many of the houses and condominiums that now dot Puerto Vallarta's jungly hillsides and golden beaches.

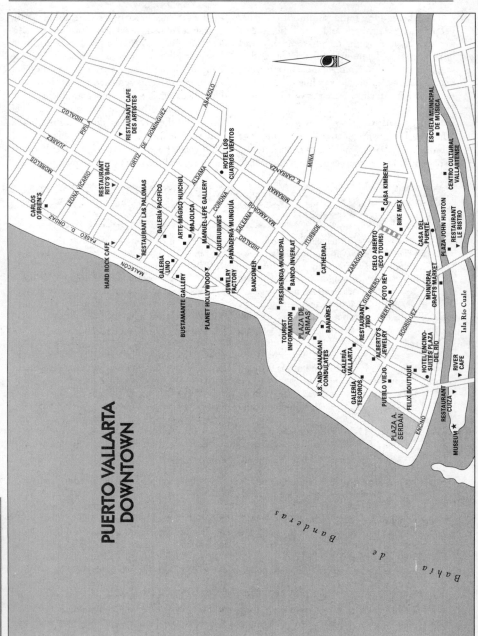

PUERTO VALLARTA
DOWNTOWN

Bahía de Banderas

PUERTO VALLARTA

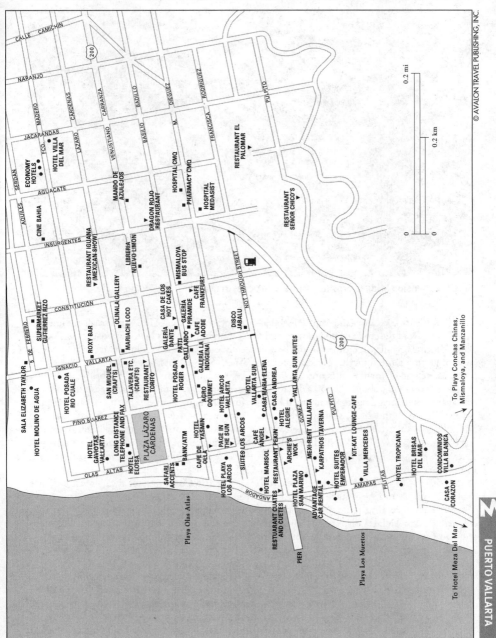

© AVALON TRAVEL PUBLISHING, INC.

0.2 mi

0.2 km

CALLE CAMICHIN

NARANJO

200

JACARANDAS

SERDAN

ECONOMY HOTELS

HOTEL VILLA DEL MAR

AGUACATE

AQUILES

CINE BAHIA

MADERO

CARDENAS

CARRANZA

BADILLO

DIEGUEZ

RODRIGUEZ

PULPITO

FCO.

LAZARO

VENUSTIANO

BASILIO

M.

FRANCISCA

RESTAURANT EL PALOMAR

MANDO DE AZULEJOS

HOSPITAL CMQ

PHARMACY CMQ

HOSPITAL MEDASIST

RESTAURANT SEÑOR CHICO'S

INSURGENTES

RESTAURANT IGUANA (MEXICAN SHOW)

LIBRERIA NUEVO-LIMON

DRAGON ROJO RESTAURANT

MISMALOYA BUS STOP

SALA ELIZABETH TAYLOR

SUPERMARKET GUTIERREZ RIZO

CONSTITUCIÓN

OLINALA GALLERY

CASA DE LOS HOT CAKES

CAFE FRANKFURT

5 DE FEBRERO

ROXY BAR

MARIACHI LOCO

GALERÍA DANTE

GALERÍA PIRAMIDE

PATTI GALLARDO

CAFE ADOBE

DISCO JABALU

NOT THROUGH STREET

HOTEL MOLINO DE AGUA

IGNACIO

VALLARTA

HOTEL POSADA RIO CUALE

SAN MIGUEL (CRAFTS)

TALAVERA ETC. (CRAFTS)

RESTAURANT TORITO

HOTEL POSADA ROGER

GALERÍA LA INDIGENA

AGRO GOURMET

HOTEL ARCOS VALLARTA

HOTEL VALLARTA SUN

CASA MARIA ELENA

CASA ANDREA

HOTEL ALEGRE

VALLARTA SUN SUITES

PINO SUÁREZ

HOTEL GAVIOTAS VALLARTA

LONG DISTANCE TELEPHONE AND FAX

PLAZA LÁZARO CÁRDENAS

HOTEL YASMIN

BANK/ATM

PAGE IN THE SUN

SUITES LOS ARCOS

CAFE ANGEL

GOMEZ

HOTEL MARISOL

RESTAURANT PEKIN

MEXI-RENT VALLARTA

KARPATHOS TAVERNA

PULPITO

KIT-KAT LOUNGE-CAFE

HOTEL ELOISA

OLAS ALTAS

SAFARI ACCENTS

HOTEL PLAYA LOS ARCOS

CAFE DE OLLA

ARCHIE'S WOK

HOTEL PLAZA SAN MARINO

ADVANTAGE CAR RENTAL

HOTEL SUITES EMPERADOR

AMAPAS

VILLA MERCEDES

HOTEL TROPICANA

HOTEL BRISAS DEL MAR

CONDOMINIOS VILLA BLANCA

ANDADOR

RESTAURANT CUATES AND CUETES

PILITAS

CASA CORAZON

PIER

Playa Olas Atlas

Playa Los Muertos

To Hotel Meza Del Mar

To Playa Conchas Chinas, Mismaloya, and Manzanillo

200

PUERTO VALLARTA

Small suspension bridges provide picturesque pedestrian paths over the Río Cuale.

the *libramiento* bypass (see the map "Puerto Vallarta") and avoid the crowded downtown traffic.

Car rentals, while expensive, are an efficient way of getting around locally, especially for independent out-of-town excursions north and south. Expect to pay about $40–50 a day for the cheapest rental, including legally required liability insurance. Cut the cost by sharing with others.

In Puerto Vallarta, the gang's all there: contact Avis, tel. 322/221-1112; Budget, toll-free Mex. tel. 800/700-1700; Dollar, tel. 322/223-1354; Hertz, tel. 322/221-1413; National, tel. 322/209-0356; Thrifty, toll-free Mex. tel. 800/021-2277; and Advantage, tel. 322/221-1499. (For more auto rental contact details, see the Puerto Vallarta airport car rental section in Getting There and Away.) You might also save money with an air-car package or by reserving a discount (ask for AARP, AAA, senior, airline, credit card, or other) rental car before you leave for Mexico.

A Walk Along Isla Cuale

Start at the **Museo Río Cuale,** a joint government-volunteer effort near the very downstream tip of Isla Río Cuale. Inside is a small but fine collection of paintings by local artists as well as locally excavated pre-Columbian artifacts (open Tues.–Sun. 10 A.M.–2 P.M. and 4–7 P.M.).

Head upstream beneath the bridge and enjoy the shady *paseo* of shops and restaurants. For fun, stroll out on one of the two quaint suspension bridges over the river. Evenings, these are the coolest spots in Puerto Vallarta. A river of cool night air often funnels down the Cuale valley, creating a refreshing breeze along the length of the clear, tree-draped stream.

The **Río Cuale** was not always so clean. Once upon a time, a few dozen foreign residents, tired of looking down upon the littered riverbank, came out one Sunday and began hauling trash from the riverbed. Embarrassed by the example, a neighborhood crowd pitched in. The river has been much cleaner ever since.

Farther upstream, on the adjacent riverbank, stands the **Mercado Municipal Río Cuale,** a honeycomb of stalls stuffed with crafts from all over Mexico. Continue past the upriver (Av. Insurgentes) bridge to **Plaza John Huston,** marked by a pensive bronze likeness of the renowned

Hollywood director who helped put Puerto Vallarta on the map with his filming of Tennessee Williams's *Night of the Iguana* in 1963.

About 50 yards farther on, stop in at the small gallery of the **Centro Cultural Vallartense,** a volunteer organization that conducts art classes, sponsors shows of promising artists, and sometimes invites local artists to meet the public and interested amateurs for informal instruction and idea exchange. Ask the volunteer on duty for more information or see the community events listings in *Vallarta Today* or the *Vallarta Tribune,* the local English-language newspapers.

A few more steps upstream, at a small plaza, stands the round stucco headquarters and practice room of the **Escuela Municipal de Música.** On the left side are the classrooms of the **Instituto de Allende.** They, along with the Centro Cultural Vallartense, offer courses to the general public. (See Arts and Music Courses.)

Walk a few steps farther to the boulder-strewn far upstream point of the island, where you can enjoy the airy river panorama: clear (in dry season) rushing water, framed by great riverbank trees, verdant canyon ramparts, and distant, cloud-capped mountains.

Gringo Gulch

The steep, villa-dotted hillside above the island's upper end is called Gringo Gulch for the colony of rich *norteamericanos* who own big homes there. It's an interesting place for a stroll.

Get there by heading downstream, back over the Insurgentes bridge. Turn north, toward the center of town. After the bridge, bear right to the end of one-block Calle Emilio Carranza and continue up a steep, bougainvillea-festooned staircase to Calle Zaragoza one block above.

At the corner of Zaragoza and the upper level of Emilio Carranza, you are at the gateway to Gringo Gulch. Wander through the winding, hillside lanes and enjoy the picturesque scenes that seem to appear around each rickety-chic corner. For example, note the luxurious *palapas* perched atop the tall villa on Carranza, half a block above Zaragoza.

During your meanderings, don't miss the Gringo Gulch centerpiece mansion at Zaragoza

446, once owned by Elizabeth Taylor. (You'll scarcely be able to miss it, for it has a pink passageway arching over the street.) The house was a gift to Taylor from Richard Burton. After they were married, they also bought the house on the other side of Zaragoza, renovated it, and built a pool; thus the passageway became necessary. The house across the street, no. 446, is now the **Casa Kimberly,** a private Elizabeth Taylor-Richard Burton museum, which offers public tours for about $8 per person. Call tel. 322/222-1336 for details.

The **Club Internacional de la Amistad** (International Friendship Club) conducts very popular weekly seasonal tours of some of Puerto Vallarta's showplace homes. Conducted between Thanksgiving and Easter, tours customarily begin at the Hotel Molino de Agua, tel. 322/222-1907, mornings around 10:30 A.M. The club asks $25 per person as a contribution for its charitable activities. For confirmation and details, call the hotel, or the club, at tel. 322/222-5466. (See Volunteer Work under Information.)

Another worthwhile Puerto Vallarta guided stroll is the regular "Art Walk" tour of noted local galleries. For more information, contact Barbara Peters, personable owner of Galería Vallarta, tel. 322/222-0290 (see Shopping).

On the Malecón

Head back down Zaragoza, and let the church belfry be your guide. Named **La Parroquia de Nuestra Señora de Guadalupe,** for the city's patron saint, the church is relatively new (1951) and undistinguished except for the very unusual huge crown atop the tower. Curiously, it was modeled after the crown of the tragic 19th-century Empress Carlota, who went insane after her husband was executed. On the church steps, a native woman sometimes sells textiles, which she weaves on the spot with a traditional backstrap loom (in Mexican Spanish, *tela de otate,* loom of bamboo, from the Náhuatl *otlatl,* bamboo).

Continue down Zaragoza past the Presidencia Municipal at one side of the central Plaza de Armas, straight toward Los Arcos (The Arches) right at the water's edge. They have formed a backdrop for frequent free weekend evening music and dance performances. From there, the *malecón* seawall-walkway stretches north toward the Zona Hotelera hotels, which you can see along the curving northern beachfront.

The *malecón* marks the bay's innermost point. From there the shoreline stretches and curves westerly many miles on both sides, adorned by dozens of sandy beaches until it reaches its wave-washed extremities at Punta Mita (on the distant horizon, at the bay's northwest extremity) and Punta La Iglesia to the far southwest.

Terra Noble

The dreamchild of owner-artist Jorge Rubio, Terra Noble, on a vista hilltop above the middle of town, is at least unique and at best exhilarating. It's a New Age–style retreat, spreading downhill over a breathtakingly scenic tropical deciduous forested hillside at the western edge of the big Agua Azul Nature Reserve hinterland. The headquarters building is a latter-day interpretation of a traditional Mexican stick-and-mud wattle house. The inside view, of curving ceilings and passageways dotted with round window-holes, leaves the impression of the interior of a huge hunk of Swiss cheese. For more architectural details, see the Terra Noble feature story in *Architectural Digest,* July 1996.

Besides its singular building and parklike grounds, Terra Noble is a serious healing center, featuring massage ($50 per hour) or an all-day treatment ($150), including massage, a saunalike *temascal* sweat bath and shamanistic ceremony, tarot reading, and more. It also offers day sculpture and painting workshops.

Regardless of whether you get the full treatment or not, Terra Noble would be worth a visit, if for nothing more than a look around and a picnic. (Bring your own food.) It's generally open daily 9 A.M.–4 P.M.; admission is about $5. Contact Terra Noble ahead of time, tel. 322/223-3530 or 322/222-4058, fax 322/222-5400, shantihc@prodigy.com.mx, to verify hours. Get there by car, taxi, or any local bus that follows the bypass *(libramiento)* through the hills east of town. Follow the side road, signed "Par Vial Zona Centro," about 100 yards south of the summit tunnel (not the short tunnel at the south

end), on the west (ocean) side of the *libramiento.* After about a half mile, curving uphill, you'll see the Terra Noble entrance sign on the view side of the road.

BEACHES
Playa Los Muertos

Generations ago, when Puerto Vallarta was a small, isolated town, there was only one beach, Playa Los Muertos, the strand of yellow sand that stretches for a mile south of the Cuale River. Old-timers still remember the Sundays and holidays when it seemed as if half the families in Puerto Vallarta had come south of the Río Cuale, to Los Muertos Beach especially, to play in the surf and sand.

This is still largely true, although now droves of winter-season North American vacationers and residents have joined them. Fortunately, Playa Los Muertos is much cleaner than during the polluted 1980s. The fish are coming back, as evidenced by the flocks of diving pelicans and the crowd of folks who drop lines every day from the **New Pier** (foot of Francisca Rodriguez).

Fishing is even better off the rocks on the south end of the beach. *Lisa* (mullet), *sierra* (mackerel), *pargo* (snapper), and *torito* are commonly caught anywhere along close-in beaches. On certain unpredictable occasions, fish (and one memorable time even giant 30-pound squids) swarm offshore in such abundance that anyone can pick them out of the water barehanded.

Gentle waves and lack of undertow make Playa Los Muertos generally safe for wading and good for swimming beyond the close-in breakers. The same breakers, however, eliminate Los Muertos for bodysurfing, boogie boarding, or surfing (except occasionally at the far south end).

Playa Conchas Chinas

Playa Conchas Chinas (Chinese, or "Curly," Shells Beach) is not one beach but a series of small sandy coves dotted by rocky outcroppings beneath the condo-clogged hillside that extends for about a mile south of Playa Los Muertos. A number of streets and driveways lead to the beach from the Manzanillo Highway 200 (the extension of Insurgentes) south of town. Drive, taxi, or ride one of the many the minibuses marked "Mismaloya" or "Boca" that leave from Calle Basilio Badillo, just below Insurgentes, or hike along the tidepools from Los Muertos Beach.

Fishing off the rocks is good here; the water is even clear enough for some snorkeling. Bring your gear, however, as there's none for rent. The usually gentle waves, however, make any kind of surfing very doubtful.

Beaches Just South of Town

Beach lovers can spend a month of Sundays poking around the many little beaches south of town. Drive, taxi, or take a Mismaloya- or Boca-marked minibus from the corner of Badillo and Constitución.

Just watch out the window, and when you see a likely spot, ask the driver to stop. Say *"Pare* (PAH-ray) *por favor."* The location will most likely be one of several lovely *playas:* **El Gato** (Cat), **Los Venados** (Deer), **Los Carrizos** (Reeds), **Punta Negra** (Black Point), **Garza Blanca** (White Heron), or **Gemelas** (Twins).

Although many of these little sand crescents have big hotels and condos, it doesn't matter because beaches are public in Mexico up to the high-tide line. There is always some path to the beach used by local folks. Just ask *"¿Dónde está el camino* (road, path) *a la playa?"* and someone will probably point the way.

Mismaloya and Los Arcos

If you ride all the way to Playa Mismaloya, you will not be disappointed, despite the oversized Hotel Mismaloya crowding the beach. Follow the dirt road just past the hotel to the intimate little curve of sand and lagoon where the cool, clear Mismaloya stream meets the sea. A rainbow array of fishing *lanchas* lie beached around the lagoon's edges, in front of a line of beachside *palapa* restaurants.

Continue a few hundred yards past the *pala-*

Snorkeling near the wave-washed Los Arcos is a Puerto Vallarta "must do." Swirling bunches of green algae and branching ruddy corals attract schools of grazing parrot, angel, butterfly, and goat fish. Curious pencil-thin cornet fish may sniff you out as they pass.

pas to the ruins of the movie set of the *Night of the Iguana.* Besides being built for the actual filming, the rooms behind those now-crumbling stucco walls served as lodging, dining, and working quarters for the dozens of crew members who camped here for those eight busy months in 1963.

North, offshore beyond the Mismaloya cove, rise the green-brushed Los Arcos sea rocks, a federal underwater park and ecopreserve. The name comes from the arching grottoes that channel completely through the bases of some of the rocks. Los Arcos is one of the best snorkeling grounds around Puerto Vallarta. Get there by hiring a glass-bottomed boat in the lagoon.

Snorkeling near the wave-washed Los Arcos is a Puerto Vallarta "must do." Swirling bunches of green algae and branching ruddy corals attract schools of grazing parrot, angel, butterfly, and goat fish. Curious pencil-thin cornet fish may sniff you out as they pass, while big croakers and sturgeon will slowly drift, scavenging along the coral-littered depths.

Fishing, especially casting from the rocks beneath the movie set, and every other kind of beach activity are good at Mismaloya, except surfing and boogie boarding, for which the waves are generally too gentle. Stop for food (big fish fillet plate, any style, with all the trimmings, $8, or breakfast eggs from the restaurant's own hens) or a drink at the **Restaurant Las Gaviotas** *palapas* across the river.

Alternatively, for food and nostalgia, go to the viewpoint **John Huston Café** or the neighboring showplace **Night of the Iguana Restaurant,** off the highway, ocean side, on Mismaloya Bay's south headland. Both are open daily—the restaurant for breakfast, lunch, and dinner, the café for lunch and dinner. Both are designed around the Night of the Iguana legend, replete with old Hollywood photos and mementos and a daily video screening of the original *Night of the Iguana* film at the restaurant.

For still another treat, visit nearby **Chino's Paradise.** Follow the riverside lower road that forks upstream at the north end of the bridge across the road from the hotel. Arrive in the late morning (around 11) or late afternoon (around 3) to avoid the tour-bus rush. Chino's stream-side *palapas* nestle like big mushrooms on a jungle hillside above a cool, cascading creek. Adventurous guests enjoy sliding down the cascades (be careful—some have injured themselves seriously), while others content themselves with lying in the sun or lolling in sandy-bottomed, clear pools. Beneath the *palapas,* Chino's serves respectable but uninspired seafood and steak plates and Mexican *antojitos.* Open daily 11 A.M.–5 P.M.

For a more rustic alternative, follow the road another mile uphill to **El Eden,** a jungle swimming hole, complete with food *palapas,* a natural pool, and Tarzan-style rope swing; open daily until about 5 P.M.

Beaches Farther South

Three miles south of Mismaloya is **Boca de Tomatlán,** a tranquil country village overlooking a broad strip of yellow sand bordering a petite, blue bay. *Palapa* restaurants supply enough food and shade for days of easy relaxation.

If you decide to linger, contact **Agustín Bas,** a personable, English-speaking Argentinian expatriate who provides lodging in his gorgeous two-bedroom, two-bath jungle hillside **Casa Tango.** Tariffs run about $80 per day, $550 weekly for four, including airport pickup. Contact him at home, tel. 322/228-0057, or at his Puerto Vallarta office, tel. 322/222-7454, vallarta@casa-tango.com. (Agustín also offers personalized guided tours, specializing in the verdant Bay of Banderas southern shoreline. Visit his website, www.casatango.com, or stop by his conveniently located office, at 367 Olas Altas, upstairs.)

You can continue by *colectivo* water taxi (about $3 per person) to the pristine paradises of Las Animas, Quimixto, and Yelapa farther south. **Las Animas** has seafood *palapas,* an idyllic beach, and snorkeling; the same is true for **Quimixto,** which also has a waterfall nearby for splashing.

Yelapa, a settlement nestled beneath verdant, palm-crowned hills beside an aquamarine cove, is home for perhaps a hundred local families and a small colony of foreign expatriates. For visitors, it offers a glimpse of South Seas life as it was before the automobile. Accessible only by sea, Yelapa's residents get around on foot or horseback. A waterfall cascades through the tropical forest above the village, and a string of *palapa* restaurants lines the beach. Lodging is available in the *palapa-*roofed cabanas of the rustic **Hotel Lagunita.** Rooms run about $35 d low season, $65 high, and, although generally not necessary, you can reserve by calling its agent at tel. 329/298-0554, hotellagunita@prodigy.com.mx, www.hotella-gunita.com.mx.

North-End (Zona Hotelera) Beaches

These are Puerto Vallarta's cleanest, least-crowded in-town beaches, despite the many hotels that line them. Beginning at the Hotel Rosita at the north end of the *malecón,* **Playas Camarones, Las Glorias, Los Tules,** and **de Oro** form a continuous three-mile strand to the Marina. Stubby rock jetties about every quarter-mile have succeeded in retaining a 50-yard-wide strip of golden-cream sand most of the way.

The sand is midway between coarse and fine; the waves are gentle, breaking right at the water's edge; and the ocean past the breakers is relatively clear (10- or 20-feet visibility) and blue. Stormy weather occasionally dredges up clam, cockle, limpet, oyster, and other shells from the offshore depths.

Fishing by pole, net, or simply line is common along here. Surfing, bodysurfing, and boogie boarding, however, are not. All other beach sports, especially the high-powered variety, are available at nearly every hotel along the strand (see Sports and Recreation).

Farther north, along the shore past the Maritime Terminal-Marina Harbor entrance, the beach narrows to a seasonally rocky strip at the oceanfronts of a row of big resort hotels.

Beach Hikes

A pair of good close-in hikes are possible. For either of them, don't forget a sun hat, sunscreen, bug repellent, a shirt, and some light shoes. On the south side, walk from Playa Los Muertos about 1.5 miles along the little beaches and tide-pools to Playa Conchas Chinas. Start at either end and take half a day swimming, snorkeling, sunning, and poking among the rocks.

More ambitiously, you can hike the entire three-mile beach strip from the northern end of the *malecón* to the Marina. If you start by 9 A.M. you'll enjoy the cool of the morning with the sun at your back. Stop along the way at the showplace pools and beach restaurants of hotels such as the Sheraton, the Plaza Las Glorias, the Fiesta Americana Vallarta, and Krystal. Walk back, or opt for a return by taxi or city bus.

WATER TAXIS AND DAY CRUISES

Puerto Vallarta visitors can also reach the little southern beaches of Quimixto, Las Animas, and Yelapa from Puerto Vallarta itself. You have two options: fast water taxis or one of several all-day tourist cruises. The water taxis, which allow you more time at your destination, customarily leave the Playa Los Muertos New Pier twice in the morning, usually at about 9:45 and 11 A.M. (returning at 4 P.M.), and once in the afternoon, at about 4 P.M., for those staying overnight. The morning departures allow about three hours for lunch and swimming at either the Quimixto or Yelapa waterfalls. The round-trip tariff runs about $20.

The more leisurely tourist cruises leave around 9 A.M. (return by 4 P.M.) from the dock at the Puerto Vallarta Maritime Terminal. They also customarily pick up additional passengers at the New Pier on Playa Los Muertos downtown.

One of the most popular of these excursions is aboard the big *Princess Yelapa,* a tripled-decked steel tub with room for a hundred. The route follows the coastline, stopping at Los Arcos for snorkeling, and continues for Las Animas and Quimixto. At Quimixto, passengers disembark for a few hours, just long enough for the short waterfall hike (or by horseback, if desired) and lunch at a beach *palapa.* The package includes light breakfast, lunch, and no-host bar for about $40 per person.

Princess Cruises also runs the *Sarape,* a sail-boat accommodating around 30, for snorkeling at Los Arcos, continuing to Yelapa for a hike (or horseback ride) and swimming at the waterfall. Open bar, live music, and lunch are included, for about $40 per person.

For romantics, the *Princess Vallarta,* a scaled-down version of the *Princess Yelapa,* offers a 6:30–9 P.M. sunset cruise, with snacks, open bar, and live music for dancing, for about $35 per person.

For information and reservations for all of the above cruises and more, contact a travel agent, your hotel tour desk, or Princess Cruises directly at tel. 322/224-4777 or crucerosprincesa@pvnet.com.mx.

If you tend toward seasickness, fortify yourself with Dramamine before these cruises. Destination disembarkation at Las Animas, Quimixto, and Yelapa is by motor launch and can be difficult for the physically disabled.

ACCOMMODATIONS

In Puerto Vallarta you can get any type of lodging you want at nearly any price. The location sets the tone, however. The relaxed, relatively tranquil but interesting neighborhood south of the Río Cuale (especially around Av. Olas Altas) has many budget and moderately priced hotels, apartments, and condos within easy walking distance of restaurants, shopping, and services. Many of them are very close, if not right on, lively Playa Los Muertos. While no strict dividing line separates the types of available lodgings, hotels (listed first, below) generally offer rooms with maximum service (desk, daily cleaning, restaurant, pool) without kitchens for shorter-term guests, while apartments and condos virtually always offer multiple-room furnished kitchen units for greatly reduced per diem rates for longer-term rentals. If you're staying more than two weeks, you'll save money and also enjoy more of the comforts of home in a good apartment or condo rental.

Hotels—Río Cuale and South

Although landmark **Hotel Molino de Agua** (Water Mill), at the corner of Ignacio Vallarta and Aquiles Serdán, Puerto Vallarta 48380,

PUERTO VALLARTA ACCOMMODATIONS BY PRICE

Accommodations (telephone area code 322; postal code 48300 unless otherwise noted) are listed in increasing order of approximate high-season, double-room rates. Toll-free numbers are for reservations from the United States and Canada; "all-inclusive" means all in-house food, drinks, and entertainment are included in the lodging price, quoted for two, double-occupancy.

Hotels—Río Cuale and South

Hotel Bernal, Madero 427, 222-3605, $18

Hotel Analiz, Madero 429, 222-1757, $20

Hotel Villa del Mar, Fco. I. Madero 440, postal code 48380, tel. 222-0785, hvilladelmar@hotmail.com, $24

Hotel Yasmin, Basilio Badillo 168, postal code 48380, tel. 222-0087, $32

Casa Corazón, Amapas 326, P.O. Box 66, tel./fax 222-6364, 222-2738, or U.S. tel./fax 505/523-4666, corazon@zianet.com, $50

Hotel Suites Emperador, Amapas 114, postal code 48380, tel. 222-5243, fax 222-3329, info@hotelemperadorpv.com, $50

Hotel Alegre, F. Rodríguez 168, postal code 48380, tel./fax 222-4793, wl@alegre-pv.com, $55

Hotel Posada Río Cuale, A. Serdán 242, P.O. Box 146, tel./fax 222-0450, riocuale@pvnet.com.mx, $55

Hotel Vallarta Sun, Francisca Rodríguez 169, tel./fax 223-1523, $55

Hotel Eloisa, Lázaro Cárdenas 170, tel./fax 222-6465 or 222-0286, info@hoteleloisa.com, $60

Hotel Arcos Vallarta, M. Diéguez 171, postal code 48380, same contact numbers as Hotel Playa Los Arcos, $60

Casa del Puente, sobre Puente Av. Insurgentes, postal code 48380, tel. 222-0749 or U.S. tel. 415/648-7245, casadelpuente@yahoo.com, $60

Hotel Posada Roger, Basilio Badillo 237, postal code 48380, tel. 222-0836, fax 223-0482, pvroger@pvnet.com.mx, $60

Hotel Gaviotas Vallarta, Fco. I. Madero 176, P.O. Box 497, tel. 222-1500 or 222-5518, fax 222-5516, $68

Hotel Brisas del Mar, Privada Abedul 10, tel. 222-1821, fax 222-1800, $75

Hotel Playa Conchas Chinas, P.O. Box 346, postal code 48390, tel./fax 221-5770 or 221-5733, hconchaschinas@pvnet.com.mx, $85

Hotel Playa Los Arcos, Olas Altas 380, postal code 48380, tel. 222-0583, 800/648-2403, 888/729-9590, fax 222-7104, reservaciones@playalosarcos.com, $88

Hotel Encino-Suites Plaza del Río, Juárez 122, tel. 222-0051 or 222-0280, fax 222-2573, encino@prodigy.net.mx, $90

Hotel San Marino Plaza, Rudolfo Gómez 111, postal code 48380, tel. 222-1555 or 222-3050, fax 222-2431, $90

Suites Los Arcos, M. Diéguez s/n, postal code 48380, tel. 222-0717, 800/648-2403, fax 222-2418; same contact numbers as Hotel Playa Los Arcos, $90

Hotel Tropicana, Amapas 214, postal code 48380, tel. 222-0912, fax 222-6737, $92

Hotel Meza del Mar, Amapas 380, tel. 222-4888, U.S. tel. 303/321-7779, 888/694-0010, fax 222-2308, $95 all-inclusive

Hotel Molino de Agua, I. Vallarta at A. Serdán, postal code 48380, tel. 222-1907, fax 222-6056, hotelmolino@prodigy.net.mx, $100

Casa Mirador, Km 2, Carretera Puerto Vallarta-Manzanillo, tel./fax 222-5597, U.S. tel. 616/349-5933, 800/910-2272, $150

Hotel Sun Resort Puerto Vallarta, Km 4, Carretera a Barra de Navidad, tel. 221-5500, 800/713-3020, fax 221-5105, $190 all-inclusive

Hotel Camino Real, P.O. Box 95, Playa de las Estacas, Puerto Vallarta, tel./fax 221-6000, 800/7CAMINO (800/722-6466), pvr@caminoreal.com, $240

Hotels—North of Río Cuale

Hotel Rosita, Díaz Ordaz 901, P.O. Box 32, tel./fax 223-2000, tel. 223-2177, 223-2151, or 223-2185, $45

Hotel Los Cuatros Vientos, Matamoros 520, P.O. Box 83, tel./fax 222-0161 or 222-2831, fourwinds@pvnet.com.mx, $65

Hotel Hacienda Buenaventura, Paseo de la Marina, P.O. Box 95B, postal code 48310, tel. 224-6667, fax 224-6242, ventas@haciendaonline.com.mx, $105

Hotel Plaza Pelícanos, Km 2.5, Plaza Las Glorias, tel. 224-1010, fax 224-3618, reservapelicanos@hotelesgdlplaza.com.mx, $120 per person all-inclusive

Hotel Buenaventura, México 1301, P.O. Box 8B, postal code 48350, tel. 226-7000, fax 222-3546, ventas@buenaventuraonline.com, $120

Las Palmas Resort, Blv. Fco. Ascencio, Km 2.5, tel. 224-0650, fax 226-1268, laspalmasresort@pvnet.com, $125 all-inclusive

Hotel Fiesta Americana Puerto Vallarta, P.O. Box 270, tel. 224-2100, 800/FIESTA1 (800/343-7821), fax 224-2108, favsale@pvnet.com.mx, $170

Hotel NH Krystal, Av. de las Garzas s/n, tel. 224-0202, 800/231-9860, fax 224-0111, www.nh-hoteles.com, $190

Hotel Canto del Sol Plaza Vallarta, Blv. Fco. Ascencio, Km 2.5 Plaza Las Glorias, tel. 226-0123 (reservations ext. 4143, 4144, 4145), fax 224-4437, reservaciones@cantodelsol.com, $200 all-inclusive

Hotel Qualton Club and Spa, Blv. Fco. Ascencio, Km 2.5, tel. 224-4446, 800/327-1847, fax 224-4447, qualton@pvnet.com.mx, $250 all-inclusive

Apartments and Condominiums

Prices listed are the approximate high-season monthly rental rates for a studio or one-bedroom unit.

Hotel Villa del Mar, Fco. I. Madero 440, postal code 48380, tel. 222-0785, hvilladelmar@hotmail.com, $500

Vallarta Sun Suites, R. Gómez 169, tel. 222-6200, fax 222-1626, vallartasun@usa.net, $1,100

Casa María Elena, F. Rodríguez 163, tel. 222-0113, fax 223-1380, mariazs@prodigy.net.mx, $1,200

Hotel Suites Emperador, Amapas 114, postal code 48380, tel. 222-5243, fax 222-3329, info@hotelemperadorpv.com, $1,200

Hotel Encino-Suites Plaza del Río, Juárez 122, tel. 222-0051 or 222-0820, fax 222-2573, encino@prodigy.net.mx, $1,220

Villa Mercedes, Amapas 175, tel. 222/2148 or 223-4543, villamercedes@yahoo.com, $1,500

Hotel Brisas del Mar, Privada Abedul 10, tel. 222-1821, fax 222-1800, $1,500

Condominios Villa Blanca, Amapas 349, tel./fax 222-6190, $1,500

Casa Andrea, F. Rodríguez 174, tel./fax 222-1213, casaandrea@aol.com, $1,800

tel. 322/222-1907, fax 322/222-6056, hotel-molino@prodigy.net.mx, www.molinodeagua.com, occupies two riverfront blocks right on the beach, many visitors miss it completely. Its very tranquil colony of rustic-chic cabanas hides in a jungle-garden of cackling parrots, giant-leafed vines, and gigantic, spreading *hule* (rubber) trees. Most of the cabanas are at ground level and unfortunately don't feel very private inside unless you close the shutters—which seems a shame in a tropical garden. The very popular beachside upstairs units remedy this problem. The hotel's 40 garden rooms rent for about $75 d low season, $100 high, while the upstairs beachside rooms go for about $115 d low season, $160 high season; amenities include two pools, restaurant, a/c, credit cards accepted.

Adjacent to the Hotel Molino de Agua, as you head south, away from the river, at the corner of I. Vallarta and A. Serdán, the diminutive **Hotel Posada Río Cuale** packs a lot of hotel into a small space. Find it at Av. Aquiles Serdán 242, P.O. Box 146, Puerto Vallarta 48300, tel./fax 322/222-0450 or 322/222-0914, riocuale@pvnet.com.mx. Good management is the key to this picturesque warren of rooms that clusters beside its good restaurant/bar and a small but pleasant pool and patio. Tasteful brown and brick decor makes the rooms somewhat dark, especially on the ground floor. Artful lighting, however, improves this. Unless you like diesel-bus noise, try to avoid getting a room on the busy Av. Vallarta side of the hotel. The 41 a/c rooms rent for about $45 d low season, about $55 high season; credit cards are accepted.

Nearby, the high-rise but moderately priced **Hotel Gaviotas Vallarta** is curiously hidden, though nearly right on the beach at Fco. I. Madero 176, P.O. Box 497, Puerto Vallarta, Jalisco 48300, tel. 322/222-1500 or 322/222-5518, fax 322/222-5516. Clean, well managed, and newly decorated, the hotel rises in eight tile-and-brick tiers around an inviting, plant-decorated interior pool/patio. A small restaurant and Internet snack bar serves guests downstairs, while, upstairs, guests enjoy ocean vistas directly from their room windows or from arch-framed breezeways just outside their doorways. The 84 semi-

deluxe, clean and comfortable rooms rent for about $45 s, $50 d low season, $60 and $68 high; add about $7 for TV, $10 for a/c.

Recent renovations have boosted the nearby venerable **Hotel Eloisa** from ho-hum to invitingly attractive. Find it, on the quiet, bus-free north (cul-de-sac) side of Plaza Lázaro Cárdenas, at Calle Lázaro Cárdenas 170, Puerto Vallarta, Jalisco 48300, tel./fax 322/222-6465, 322/222-0286, or 322/223-3650, info@hoteleloisa.com, www.hoteleloisa.com. The hotel's five floors of approximately 75 rooms and kitchenette studios and suites enclose an appealingly light and airy inner atrium. Downstairs, past the small lobby, guests enjoy a modest restaurant-bar and a small but inviting pool patio. Upstairs, standard-grade rooms are decorated with white tile floors, bright pastel bedspreads, king-sized (or a pair of double) beds, shiny, modern-standard shower baths, and pleasingly traditional wood furniture and doors. Many rooms open to sunny, plaza-view balconies. Studios and suites are similarly decorated but larger, with kitchenettes, one or two bedrooms and a living room-dining room. A breezy, view rooftop sundeck completes the attractive picture. Rentals for rooms start at about $50 low season, $60 high, with satellite TV, a/c or fans (or both), and only a block from the beach. Discounts for long-term rentals are negotiable.

Head directly upstream, to the upper (Av. Insurgentes) river bridge, and you'll find **Casa del Puente** tucked uphill behind the sidewalk café by the bridge. The elegant villa-home of Molly Stokes, grandniece of celebrated naturalist John Muir, Casa del Puente is a lovely home-away-from-home. Antiques and art adorn the spacious, high-beamed-ceiling rooms, while outside its windows and around the decks great trees spread, tropical birds flit and chatter, jungle hills rise, and the river gurgles, hidden from the city hubbub nearby. Molly offers three lodging options: an upstairs river-view room with big bath and double bed for around $40 low season, $60 high, and a pair of spacious apartments (a one-bedroom/one-bath and a two-bedroom/two-bath) for around $50 low season, $90 high, for two people, and about $60 low, $110 high, for four in the two-bedroom. Discounts may be negotiated, depending upon season and length of stay. Reserve early for the winter season. For more information contact Molly Stokes, Casa del Puente, Av. Insurgentes, Puerto Vallarta, Jalisco 48380, tel. 322/222-0749, www.casadelpuente.com. In the United States or Canada, reserve through Molly's daughter, María, tel. 415/648-7245, casadel puente@yahoo.com.

Nearby, across the river and two more blocks upstream, along Av.s Aquiles Serdán and Fco. I. Madero, stand a few economy hotels. These bare-bulb, but respectable and clean, one-star hostelries have tiers of interior rooms with few amenities other than four walls, a shower bath (check for hot water), and a double bed. The prices, however, at about $16 s, $20 d, are certainly right. The best of the bunch are probably Hotel Analiz, at Madero 429, Puerto Vallarta, Jalisco 48300, tel. 322/222-1757, or Hotel Bernal, tel. 322/222-3605, next door. Although I didn't check it out, the Hotel Cartagena (New Carthage), at Madero 426 across the street, might be considering.

Especially worthy is Hotel Villa del Mar, whose longtime loyal patrons swear by it as the one remnant of Puerto Vallarta "like it used to be," at Fco. I. Madero 440, corner of Jacarandas, Puerto Vallarta, Jalisco 48300, tel. 322/222-0785, hvilladelmar@hotmail.com. The austere dark-wood, street-corner lobby leads to a double warren of clean upstairs rooms, arranged in a pair of separate "A" and "B" wings. (Above that is a top-floor cluster of attractive studio kitchenette apartments; for details, see Apartments and Condominiums.) The "A" wing rooms are generally the best, with nondeluxe but comfortable amenities, including queen-sized beds, traditional-style dark wood decor, ceiling fans, and, in some cases even private street-view balconies. Section "A," with exterior-facing windows, has the triple advantage of more privacy, light, and quiet. "B" rooms, by contrast, have windows that line walkways around a sound-reflective, and therefore oft-noisy, interior tiled atrium, where guests must draw curtains for quiet and privacy. Year-round rates for the approximately 30 "A" rooms run about $20 s, $24 d, $28 t. "B" rooms rent, year-round, for about $15 s, $19 d, $23 t. Rooms vary, so inspect a few before you decide. No TV,

phones, or pool are available, and credit cards are not accepted.

The Hotel Yasmin, downhill a block from the beach, at Basilio Badillo 168, at Pino Suárez, Puerto Vallarta, Jalisco 48380, tel. 322/222-0087, offers another budget alternative. The Yasmin's positives are its verdant, plant-festooned inner patio and outstanding Mexican food at Café de Olla next door. Although the three tiers of fan-only rooms are clean, many are small. Inspect before you pay. You can compensate by renting one of the lighter, more secluded sunny-side upper rooms. Rates for all 30 rooms run about $32 d year-round.

Head downhill toward the beach and left around the Av. Olas Altas corner and you are in the popular Olas Altas neighborhood. At the hub of activity is the Hotel Playa Los Arcos (middle of the block between Calles Basilio Badillo and M. Dieguez), a favorite of a generation of savvy American and Canadian winter vacationers. The Playa Los Arcos is the flagship of a triad that includes the nearby Hotel Arcos Vallarta and the apartments Suites Los Arcos, both of whose guests are welcome to enjoy all of the Playa Los Arcos's leisurely beachfront facilities.

All three of these lodgings have swimming pools and many comfortable, tastefully decorated, air-conditioned rooms with TV, phones, and small refrigerators in many rooms. The mecca, however, is the bustling Playa Los Arcos, with its (small) but palm- and vine-decorated inner pool/patio sundeck, restaurant with salad bar, live music every night, and beach chairs in the sand beneath shady palms or golden sun. The Hotel Playa Los Arcos is at Olas Altas 380, Puerto Vallarta, Jalisco 48380, reservations tel. 322/222-0583 or 322/222-7100, toll-free U.S. tel. 800/648-2403 or Can. tel. 888/729-9590, fax 322/222-7104, hoteles@playalosarcos.com, website www.playalosarcos.com. The 175 rooms rent from about $70 d low season, approximately $88 high season, for standard-grade rooms. More spacious, some with ocean views, superior-grade rooms run about $90 d low season, $112 high season, with credit cards accepted.

The Hotel Arcos Vallarta (formerly Hotel Fontana) is half a block away, around the corner, on a quiet cul-de-sac, at M. Dieguez 171, Puerto Vallarta, Jalisco 48380, tel. 322/222-0712, same reservations numbers and email as Playa Los Arcos. Its amenities include a rooftop pool/patio with a city and hill view. The Arcos Vallarta's 42 thoughtfully furnished pastel rooms, built around a soaring interior atrium, rent from about $50 d low season, $60 d high season; credit cards are accepted.

Right across the street, on M. Dieguez (contact information is the same as the Hotel Arcos Vallarta), are the apartment-style **Suites Los Arcos,** with a long blue pool/patio and an airy sitting area to one side of the lobby. Upstairs are 15 studio apartments, simply but attractively furnished in tile, wood furniture, and pastel-blue sofas and bedspreads. All have baths (some with tub-shower), king-sized beds, furnished kitchenette, a/c, TV, and private balcony. The apartments rent (daily rate only) for about $70 d low season, and $90 high.

The Hotels Playa Los Arcos, Arcos Vallarta, and Suites Los Arcos all accept bookings through travel agents. (In fact, many guests pay much less than the above rates, *because* they prebook bargain air-hotel packages, typically $500/week per person, high season, $300 low, through travel agents or the Internet.) Moreover, during low season (May, June, July, September, October, November, and sometimes even January), all three hotels often offer special promotions, such as 20 percent senior discount, two kids under 12 free when sharing a room with parents, long-term discounts, or fourth night free. See the website for further information.

A block farther up Olas Altas, on a quiet uphill side street, at Francisca Rodríguez 168, Puerto Vallarta, Jalisco 48380, tel./fax 322/222-4793, wl@alegre-pv.com, www.alegre-pv.com, stands the modest but well-managed **Hotel Alegre.** The small lobby leads to an intimate, leafy pool/patio, enclosed by three tiers of rooms simply decorated in rustic wood, tile, and stucco, with TV, a/c, and shower bath. Rates are about $35 s, $40 d, $50 t (with two beds) low season, $50, $55, and $65 high, add $6 for kitchenette; credit cards are accepted. During times of low occupancy, the Alegre sometimes offers promotions, such

as kids free with parents or fourth day free. Ask before you reserve. (*Note:* The new owner has plans to renovate the Hotel Alegre; prices may have risen by the time you read this.) For more information and reservations, see the website.

Another good choice, three doors uphill and across the street from the Alegre, is the **Hotel Vallarta Sun,** at Francisca Rodríguez 169, tel./fax 322/223-1523. Here, about 20 spacious rooms with balconies overlook a sunny pool patio. Inside, rooms are clean, attractive, and comfortable, with modern-standard bathrooms and queen-sized beds. Rentals run about $45 d, $850/month low season, $55 and $1,000 high.

Farther south on Playa Los Muertos, **Hotel-Suites Emperador** offers ocean-view lodgings at moderate prices. Although the seven-story beachfront section of the apartment-style Hotel-Suites Emperador, at Amapas 114, Puerto Vallarta, Jalisco 48380, tel. 322/222-5143, fax 322/222-4689, has no beach facilities, it has an inviting small pool and patio for guests half a block away. The hotel (formerly Hotel Las Glorias and Suites Emperador, respectively), on opposite sides of Amapas, offers either ocean or hill views. For the cheaper hill-view suites, expect to pay $40 d low season, $50 high; for ocean view, $56 and $70, with a/c, phones, TV, and credit cards accepted. If you want cheaper long-term rates, they're negotiable. For more information, call the additional numbers tel./fax 322/222-3329, 322/222-5143, or 322/222-1767, email info@hotelemperadorpv.com, or visit the website www.hotelemperadorpv.com.

The **Hotel Tropicana,** Amapas 214, Puerto Vallarta, Jalisco 48380, tel. 322/222-0912, fax 322/222-6737, once the plushest hotel on Playa Los Muertos, is trying hard to regain that status through extensive and savvy renovations. It will probably succeed, since the hotel's airy pool patio and spacious beachfront amenities—sundeck, restaurant, volleyball court, and shady *palapas*—spread all the way to the surf. Upstairs, virtually all of the comfortable, older semideluxe and newer deluxe rooms enjoy private balconies and ocean vistas. Asking prices for the 160 rooms run about $70 d low-season, $92 high, with a/c, and credit cards are accepted. Try to reserve in the deluxe new section ("sección nueva"). Moreover, it won't hurt to ask for a discount, especially weekdays and low season.

About a block south along Amapas, the breezy, plant-decorated room tiers of **Casa Corazón** spread artfully down its beachfront hillside at Amapas 326, P.O. Box 66, Puerto Vallarta, Jalisco 48300, tel./fax 322/222-6364 or 322/222-2738. Tucked on one of the middle levels, a homey open-air restaurant and adjacent soft-couch lobby with a shelf of used paperbacks invite relaxing, reading, and socializing with fellow guests. No TVs, ringing phones, or buzzing air-conditioners disturb the tranquility; the people and the natural setting—the adjacent lush garden and the boom and swish of the beach waves—set the tone. The 14 rooms, while not deluxe, are varied and comfortably decorated with tile, brick, and colorful native arts and crafts. Guests in some of the most popular rooms enjoy spacious, sunny beach-view patios. Tariffs for smaller rooms run about $25 s, $35 d low season, $60 s or d high; larger run $35 and $40 low season, $70 high. You may book directly by contacting either the hotel above or owner George Tune, P.O. Box 937, Las Cruces, NM 88004, tel./fax 505/523-4666 or 505/523-7694. For more information, email corazon@zianet.com or herlinda@prodigy.net.mx or visit the website www.zianet.com/corazon.

The all-inclusive **Hotel Meza del Mar,** Amapas 380, Puerto Vallarta 48300, tel. 322/222-4888, fax 322/222-2308, on the beachview hillside, two blocks farther south, offers a contrasting alternative. A host of longtime returnees swear by the hotel's food, service, and friendly company of fellow guests, who, during the winter, seem to be divided equally between Americans and English- and French-speaking Canadians. The Meza del Mar's 127 rooms and suites are distributed among two adjacent buildings: the Main Tower, a view high-rise overlooking the pool deck, and the Ocean Building, a three-story tier with views right over the beach. Guests in the preferred rooms, most of which are in the Ocean Building, enjoy private balconies and the sound of the waves outside their window. Other guests are quite happy with the expansive ocean view from the top floors of the Main Tower.

The rooms themselves, while not super-deluxe, are comfortably furnished, many in the Mexican *equipal* style of handcrafted leather furniture. Although all rooms are clean and semideluxe, they vary. Ask to see others if your assignment isn't satisfactory.

Rates vary sharply according to season and grade of room and include all food (not gourmet, but wholesome), drinks, and entertainment in the hotel's restaurants, bars, pools, and beachfront club. Rates, quoted per person double occupancy, for a minimum three-night stay, run from about $36 low season, $41 high, for a smallish but comfortable room (some with views), to $72 low season, $85 high for a choice view suite. All rooms have a/c, but no TV nor phones, and only limited wheelchair access. Add $7 per person in lieu of tipping. Although the hotel does accept walk-in guests, individual reservations outside of Mexico must be through its Denver-based reservations office, tel. 303/321-7779, 888/694-0010, fax 303/322-1939, www.club-meza.com.

Other South-of-Cuale Hotels: A number of other recommendable hotels sprinkle the south-end downtown. All have pools, a/c, cable TV, restaurants, and accept credit cards. Starting at the River Cuale north bank and moving south, begin at the renovated **Hotel Encino-Suites Plaza del Río** at Av. Juárez 122, Puerto Vallarta, Jalisco 48300, tel. 322/222-0051 or 322/222-0280, fax 322/222-2573, encino@prodigy.net.mx. The 75 tastefully decorated rooms and suites rent from about $35 s, $50 d low season, $45 and $60 high. One- and two-bedroom kitchenette suites begin at about $60 low season, $90 high; discounts for long-term rentals are customary.

Continue south six blocks to tourist mecca **Hotel Posada Roger,** Basilio Badillo 237, Puerto Vallarta, Jalisco 48380, tel. 322/222-0836, fax 322/223-0482, pvroger@pvnet.com.mx, with three stories of about 50 smallish rooms at $27 s, $30 d low season, $50 s, $60 d high, with a/c, and pool. Stow all valuables in the house safe.

Three blocks farther south and on the beachfront, find **Hotel San Marino Plaza,** at Rudolfo Gómez 111, Puerto Vallarta, Jalisco 48380, tel.

322/222-1555 or 322/222-3050, fax 322/222-2431; 160 rooms and suites, from about $70 d low season, about $90 high, with a/c, TV, and phones.

Hotels South of Town

Bus or drive the Manzanillo Highway 200 (the southward extension of Insurgentes) about a mile south of town and your reward will be the **Hotel Playa Conchas Chinas,** which offers a bit of charm at moderate rates, P.O. Box 346, Puerto Vallarta, Jalisco 48390, tel./fax 322/221-5770 or 322/221-5733. The stucco and brick complex rambles down a palm-shaded hillside (with dozens of stairs to climb) several levels to an intimate cove on Conchas Chinas beach. Here, sandy crescents nestle between tidepool-dotted sandstone outcroppings.

The 39 lodgings themselves come in two grades. "Studio superior" rooms are spacious, decorated in Mexican traditional tile-brick and furnished in brown wood with kitchenette and tub bath; most have an ocean view. "Studio deluxe" grade adds a bedroom, ocean-view patio/balcony and a whirlpool tub. The studio superior rooms begin at about $74 d low season, $105 high; studio deluxe, $90 low, $112 high. Amenities include a/c, phones, with restaurant and café, credit cards accepted, but no pool. Low-season discounts may be available. For more information, email hconchaschinas@pvnet.com.mx or visit the website www.conchaschinas.com.

Two doors south (adjacent to the big Lindo Mar condo), the **Casa Mirador** bed and breakfast decorates the ocean cliffside, at Km 2, Carretera Puerto Vallarta-Manzanillo, Puerto Vallarta, Jalisco 48300, tel./fax 322/221-5597. The four luxuriously private view studio apartments are elegantly furnished with blond *primavera* native wood doors and paneling, big beds, modern-standard baths, and up-to-date kitchenettes. Rentals for studios run $105 low season, $150 high; and $150 and $225 for a fan-only suite sleeping four, with airy pool-patio, common living-dining room, library and Internet access. For more information and reservations, call tel. 616/349-5933 or toll-free U.S./Can. tel. 800/910-CASA (800/910-2272) 8 A.M.–8 P.M. Central time only.

© BRUCE WHIPPERMAN

A number of lodgings overlook Playa Conchas Chinas's intimate rocky coves.

Another mile south, you can enjoy the extravagant isolation of the **Hotel Camino Real**, at correspondingly extravagant prices. Reserve at P.O. Box 95, Playa de las Estacas, Puerto Vallarta, Jalisco 48300, tel. 322/221-5000, toll-free U.S./Can. tel. 800/7-CAMINO (800/722-6466), fax 322/221-6000, pvr@caminoreal.com, www.caminoreal.com.

Puerto Vallarta's first world-class hotel, the Camino Real has aged gracefully. It is luxuriously set in a lush tropical valley, with polished wooden walkways that wind along a beachside garden intermingled with blue swimming pools. A totally self-contained resort on a secluded, sometimes seasonally narrow, strip of golden-white sand, the twin-towered Camino Real offers every delight: luxury view rooms, all water sports, restaurants, bars, and live music every night. The 250 rooms of the main tower begin at about $180 d low season, $240 high, while the 150 hot tub–equipped rooms of the Royal Beach Club tower go for about $240 d low season, $360 high, with everything, including wheelchair access.

For folks who prefer activity over serenity, the all-inclusive **Hotel Sun Resort Puerto Vallarta** (formerly Blue Bay) about 2.5 miles south of town, may be the right choice for a hassle-free tropical vacation. Find it at Km 4, Carretera a Barra de Navidad, P.O. Box 385, Puerto Vallarta, Jalisco 48300, tel. 322/221-5500, U.S./Can. toll-free tel. 800/713-3020, fax 322/221-5105. The deluxe rooms, all with private view balcony, run about $90 s, $150 d low season, $110 s, $190 d high, including all in-house food, drinks, sports, games, and entertainments. Kids under five free; kids 6–12, $30 low season, $45 high.

Hotels North of Río Cuale

Hotels generally get more luxurious and expensive the farther north of the Río Cuale you look. The far northern section, on the Marina's ocean side, the site of several huge international chain hotels, is both isolated several miles from downtown (and Mexico) and has only a small, rocky beach, usually with little, if any, sand. Most of the central part of town, which stretches for a mile along the *malecón*, has no good beach either and is too noisy and congested for comfortable lodgings.

A notable exception, however, is the **Hotel Los Cuatros Vientos,** Matamoros 520, P.O. Box 83, Puerto Vallarta, Jalisco 48300, tel./fax 322/222-0161 or 322/222-2831, fourwinds@pvnet.com .mx, perched in the quiet, picturesque hillside neighborhood above and behind the main town church. The 16 rooms and suites are tucked in tiers above a flowery patio and restaurant Chez Elena. The fan-only units are simply but attractively decorated in colonial style, with tile, brick, and traditional furniture and crafts. Rates (excluding Dec. 15–Jan. 5) run about $65 s or d Oct. 15–June 15, $35 other times, with continental breakfast and a small pool; credit cards are accepted. (Rooms vary, however; check more than one before paying your money.)

Near the north end of the downtown *malecón*, where the good beach resumes at Playa Ca-

marones, so do the hotels. They continue, dotting the tranquil, golden strands of Playa las Glorias, Playa los Tules, and Playa de Oro. On these beaches are the plush hotels (actually, self-contained resorts) from which you must have wheels to escape to the shopping, restaurants, and the piquant sights and sounds of old Puerto Vallarta.

At the north end of the *malecón* (at 31 de Octubre) stands one of Puerto Vallarta's popular old mainstays, the homey beachfront **Hotel Rosita,** Díaz Ordaz 901, P.O. Box 32, Puerto Vallarta, Jalisco 48300, tel./fax 322/223-2185, 322/223-2000, 322/223-2151, or 322/223-2177. The Rosita centers on a grassy, palm-shadowed oceanview pool, patio, and restaurant, with plenty of space for relaxing and socializing. About half of the spacious rooms, of *típica* Mexican tile, white stucco, and wood, look down upon the tranquil patio scene, while others, to be avoided if possible, border the noisy, smoggy main street. An unfortunate wire security fence mars the ocean view from the patio. Egress to the beach, Playa Camarón, is through a side door. The Rosita's 90 rooms range, depending on location, $33–80 d low season, $45–100 high, including fans or a/c, security boxes, and a bar; credit cards are accepted.

The **Hotel Buenaventura,** Av. México 1301, P.O. Box 8B, Puerto Vallarta, Jalisco 48350, tel. 322/226-7000, fax 322/222-3546, ventas@buenaventuraonline.com, on the beach several blocks farther north, where the airport boulevard narrows as it enters old town, is one of Puerto Vallarta's few north-side close-in deluxe hotels. The lobby rises to an airy wood-beamed atrium and then opens toward the beach through a jungle walkway festooned with giant hanging leafy philodendrons and exotic palms. At the beachfront Los Tucanes Beach Club, a wide, palm-silhouetted pool/patio borders a line of shade *palapas* along the creamy-yellow sand beach. Most of the smallish rooms, decorated in wood, tile, and earth-tone drapes and bedspreads, open to petite, private, ocean-facing balconies. The 206 rooms go for about $95 d low season, $120 high, including a/c, phones, buffet breakfast, restaurant, bar, and live music nightly in season; credit cards accepted. For reservations call toll-free Mex. tel. 800/713-2888 or U.S. tel. 888/859-9439.

PUERTO VALLARTA

Zona Hotelera Luxury Hotels

Puerto Vallarta's plush hostelries vary widely, and higher tariffs do not guarantee quality. Nevertheless, some of Pacific Mexico's best-buy luxury gems glitter among the 20-odd hotels lining Puerto Vallarta's north-end Zona Hotelera beaches. The prices listed are "rack rates"—the highest prices paid by walk-in customers. Much cheaper—as much as a 50 percent discount—airfare/lodging packages are often available, especially during low seasons, which are January, May–July, and Sept.–November. Get yourself a good buy by shopping around among hotels and travel agents several weeks before departure.

Heading north, about two miles from downtown, you'll find the **Hotel Canto del Sol Plaza Vallarta** (formerly Hotel Continental Plaza) at Km 2.5 Blv. Fco. Ascencio, Plaza Las Glorias, Puerto Vallarta, Jalisco 48300, tel. 322/226-0123 (reservations ext. 4143, 4144, 4145), fax 322/224-4437, reservaciones@cantodelsol.com, www.cantodelsol.com. During the high winter season, Hotel Canto del Sol bustles all day with tennis in the adjacent eight-court John Newcombe Tennis Club next door, aerobics, water polo, and volleyball in the big pool, and parasailing, jetboating, and sailboarding from the golden Playa las Glorias beach. The luxurious but not large rooms, decorated in soothing pastels, open to balconies overlooking the broad, palmy patio. The hotel's 434 room tariffs run about $100 s or d low season, $130 high, or $140 for two, low season, $200 high, all-inclusive (all in-house food, drinks, and entertainment included) with a/c, some sports, restaurants, bars, sauna, hot tub, exercise room, wheelchair access, and parking.

SPLENDID ISOLATION

A sprinkling of luxuriously secluded upscale miniresorts, perfect for a few days of quiet tropical relaxation, have opened in some remote corners corners of the Puerto Vallarta region. Being hideaways, they are not easily accessible. But for those willing to make an extra effort, the rewards are rustically luxurious accommodations in lovely natural settings.

In order of accessibility, first comes the minihaven **Majahuitas Resort,** tucked into a diminutive palm-shaded golden strand on the bay between Quimixto and Yelapa. Here, guests have their choice of seven uniquely decorated cabanas, including a honeymoon suite. Solar panels supply electricity, and a luxuriously appointed central house serves as dining room and common area. A spring-fed pool, sunning, snorkeling, and horseback and hiking excursions into the surrounding tropical forest provide diversions for guests. Rates run about $200 for two, including all meals. For reservations and information, call tel. 322/221-5808 or U.S. tel. 831/336-5036 or visit www.mexicoboutiquehotels.com or call toll-free U.S. tel. 877/278-8018 or Can. tel. 866/818-8342. Get there by water taxi, from the beach at Boca de Tomatlán, accessible by car or the Boca-marked buses, from the south-of-Cuale corner of Basilio Badillo, one block downhill from Insurgentes.

Farther afield but nevertheless car-accessible, **Hotelito Desconocido** (Undiscovered Little Hotel) basks in luxurious isolation on a pristine lagoon and beach two hours south of Puerto Vallarta. Here, builders have created a colony of thatched designer houses on stilts. From a distance, it looks like a native fishing village. However, inside the houses (called *palafitos* by their Italian creator), elegantly simple furnishings—antiques, plush bath towels, and artfully draped mosquito nets—set the tone. Lighting is by candle and oil lantern only. Roof solar panels power ceiling fans and warm showers. Outside, nature blooms, from squadrons of pelicans wheeling above the waves by day to a brilliant overhead carpet of southern stars by night. In the morning, roll over in bed and pull a rope that raises a flag, and your morning coffee soon arrives. For the active, a full menu, including volleyball, billiards, bird-watching, kayaking, and mountain biking, can fill the day. Rates, which include all food and activities, begin at about $200 per person during the April 15–Dec. 20 low season, and rise to about $300 during the winter-spring high season. Reservations are strongly recommended. For reservations,

Next door, the **Hotel Plaza Pelícanos** (formerly Hotel Plaza Las Glorias), Km 2.5, Blv. Fco. Medina Ascencio, Puerto Vallarta, Jalisco 48300, tel. 322/224-1010, fax 322/224-3618, once a Mexican-oriented hotel, now caters to a majority of North American clientele, except during Mexican national holidays, pre-Easter week, and August. At the Hotel Plaza Pelícanos, a blue swimming pool meanders beneath a manicured patio/grove of rustling palms. The rooms, behind the Spanish-style stucco, brick, and tile facade, overlook the patio and ocean from small view balconies. The South-Seas ambience ends, however, in an adjacent jogging track. Inside, the luxurious rooms are tile-floored, in dark wood, white stucco, and blue and pastels. The 237 rooms rent low season for about $100 per person, double occupancy, all-inclusive, or about

$115 s or d, for room only, with a/c, cable TV, two pools, bars, restaurants, and parking. Add about 20% during high winter season and holidays. For reservations call toll-free Mex. tel. 800/509-0588 or U.S. tel. 866/837-7557. For more information on reservations, email reservapelicanos@hotelesgdlplaza.com.mx or visit www.hotelesgdlplaza.com.mx.

At the north side of the Hotel Plaza Pelícanos, the **Las Palmas Resort**, Km 2.5, Blv. Fco. Medina Ascencio, Puerto Vallarta, Jalisco 48300, tel. 322/224-0650, fax 322/226-1268, offers an attractive beachfront option. An airy, renovated *palapa* shelters the lobby, which continues to a palm-adorned beachside pool/patio. Here, on the wide, sparkling Playa las Glorias, opportunities for aquatic sports are at their best, with the hotel's sport shop (snorkeling, fishing, Hobie

call toll-free Mex. tel. 800/013-1313 or U.S./Can. tel. 800/851-1143, email hotelito@pvnet.com.mx, or visit the website www.hotelito.com.

Get there, at the side road, to El Gargantino and Cruz de Loreto, at Km 131, via Hwy 200 south of Puerto Vallarta. Continue west several miles via good gravel road to Cruz de Loreto village. Follow the signs to Hotel Desconocido from there.

About 30 miles farther south, the small sign at Km 83 gives no hint of the pleasant surprises that **Las Alamandas** conceals behind its guarded gate. Solitude and elegant simplicity seem to have been the driving concepts in the mind of Isabel Goldsmith, daughter of the late British tycoon Sir James Goldsmith, when she acquired control of the property in the latter 1980s. Although born into wealth, Isabel has not been idle. She converted her dream of paradise—a small, luxuriously isolated resort on an idyllic beach in Puerto Vallarta's sylvan coastal hinterland—into reality. Now, her guests (22 maximum) enjoy accommodations that vary from luxuriously simple studios to entire villas that sleep six. Activities include a health club, tennis, horseback riding, bicycling, fishing, and lagoon and river excursions. Daily rates begin at about $350 low season, $450 high for garden-view studios, to beachfront villas for about $900 low, $1,400 high;

all with full breakfast. Three meals, prepared to your order, cost about $200 additional per day per person. For more information and reservations, contact Las Alamandas in Mexico directly, at Quémaro, Km. 83 Carretera Puerto Vallarta-Barra de Navidad, Jalisco 48854, tel. 322/285-5500, or call the hotel's agents at toll-free U.S./Can. tel. 888/882-9616, fax 322/285-5027, email info@las-alamandas.com, www.las-alamandas.com. Don't arrive unannounced; the guard will not let you through the gate unless you have reservation in hand or have made an appointment.

Alternatively, about three hours south of Puerto Vallarta, you can choose the holistic retreat **Punta Serena,** perching on a hill overlooking the blue Bay of Tenacatita. Here, guests soak it all in—enjoying meditation, massage, hot tub, traditional *temascal* hot room, and healthy food. Expect to pay about $115 low season, $155 high, per person per day, all included. For more information, call tel. 315/351-5020 or toll-free U.S. and Can. tel. 866/807-5205 or visit www.puntaserena.com. Get there via the side road signed Sun Resort, at Km 20 (120 miles south of Puerto Vallarta, 15 miles north of Barra de Navidad). Be sure to call ahead for a reservation or an appointment; otherwise the guard at the gate will, most likely, not let you pass.

Cat sailboats, parasailing) right on the beach-front. The 240 rooms, most with private ocean-view balconies, are comfortable but not luxurious. Rates run about $100 per person low season, $125 per person high, all-inclusive, or $95 s or d low, $130 high, for room only, with a/c, phones, TV, restaurant, snack bar, bars, pool, and parking; credit cards are accepted. For information and reservations, email laspalmasresort@pvnet.com or visit www.laspalmasresort.com.

Another quarter-mile north, the **Hotel Fiesta Americana Puerto Vallarta,** P.O. Box 270, Puerto Vallarto, Jalisco 48300, tel. 322/226-2100, toll-free U.S./Can. tel. 800/FIESTA-1 (800/343-7821), fax 322/224-2108, favsale@pvnet.com.mx, www.fiestaamericana.com.mx, is, for many, the best hotel in town. The lobby-*palapa,* the world's largest, is an attraction unto itself. Its 10-story palm-thatch chimney draws air upward, creating a continuously cool breeze through the open-air reception. Outside, the high-rise rampart of ocean-view rooms overlooks a pool and garden of earthly delights, complete with a gushing pool fountain, water volleyball, swim-up bar, and in-pool recliners. Beyond spreads a 150-foot-wide strip of wave-washed yellow sand. The 291 super-deluxe view rooms run about $140 d low season, rising to $250 high, with a/c, TV, phones, all sports, three restaurants, huge pool, three bars, wheelchair access, and parking.

Next door, the all-inclusive **Hotel Qualton Club and Spa,** Km 2.5, Av. de las Palmas s/n, Puerto Vallarta, Jalisco 48300, tel. 322/224-4446, toll-free U.S./Can. tel. 800/327-1847, fax 322/224-4447, qualton@pvnet.com.mx, offers an attractive all-inclusive option for vacationers who enjoy lots of food, fun, and company. On a typical winter-season day, hundreds of fellow sun-bathing guests line the rather cramped poolside, while, a few steps away, dozens more relax beneath shady beachfront *palapas.* Nights glow with beach buffet theme dinners—Italian, Mexican, Chinese, and more—for hundreds, followed by shows where guests often become part of the entertainment. The list goes on—constant food, open bars, complete gym and spa, tennis by night or day, scuba lessons, volleyball, water sports, free discos, golf privileges, stress therapy, yoga, aerobics

galore—all included at no extra charge. If you want relief from the hubbub, you can always escape to the greener, more spacious Fiesta Americana poolside next door. The Qualton Club's 320 rooms, all with private view balconies, are luxuriously decorated in pastels and include a/c, cable TV, and phone. All-inclusive low-season rates run around $90 per person, double occupancy, about $125 high season, with wheelchair access; credit cards are accepted.

Another half-mile north, the **Hotel NH Krystal,** Av. de las Garzas s/n, Puerto Vallarta, Jalisco 48300, tel. 322/224-0202, fax 322/224-0111, is more than a hotel, it's a palmy, manicured resort-village, exactly what a Mexican Walt Disney would have built. The Krystal is one of the few Puerto Vallarta ultraluxury resorts designed by and for Mexicans.

Instead of being put off by the rather gloomy lobby (the new owners are trying to save electricity) feast your eyes on the amenities spread over its 34 beachside acres: a flock of deluxe garden bungalows that open onto private pool/patios, a Porfirian bandstand that stands proudly at the center, while nearby a colonial-style aqueduct gushes water into a pool at the edge of a serene spacious palm-shaded park. Guests who prefer a more lively environment can have it. Dancing often goes on in the lobby or beside the huge, meandering beachside pool, where the music is anything but serene. The NH Krystal's 460 rooms and suites rent from about $170 d low season, $190 high (with low-season promotions as low as $100 d); with a/c, phones, TV, 44 pools—no joke—multiple restaurants, and all sports. For information and reservations, call toll-free Mex. tel. 800/903-3300 or U.S./Can. tel. 800/231-9860, or visit the website www.nh-hoteles.com.

Next door to the north, the neocolonial **Hotel Hacienda Buenaventura,** Paseo de la Marina, P.O. Box 95B, Puerto Vallarta, Jalisco 48310, tel. 322/226-6667, fax 322/226-6242, ventas@haciendaonline.com.mx, offers a load of luxurious amenities at moderate rates. Its 150 rooms, arranged in low-rise tiers, enfold a leafy-green patio/garden, graced by a blue free-form pool and a slender, rustic *palapa.* On one side, water spills from a neo-antique aqueduct, while guests linger at the adjacent airy restaurant. The rooms are spacious, with high, hand-hewn-beam ceilings, marble floors, and rustic-chic tile and brick baths. The only drawback to all this is guests must walk a couple of short blocks to the beach. Rates run around $90 d low season, $105 d high (all-inclusive option, about $75 per person), with a/c, phones, cable TV, some wheelchair access, and credit cards accepted. Be sure to ask for a discount.

Apartments and Condominiums

Puerto Vallarta abounds with apartments and condominiums, mostly available for rentals of two weeks or more. A number of U.S.-based agencies specialize in the more luxurious rentals scattered all over the city. See Apartments, Bunglalows, Condominiums and Villas, in the On the Road Chapter.

The best-buy Puerto Vallarta apartments and condos are concentrated in the colorful Olas Altas-Conchas Chinas south-side district and are generally available only through local owners, managers, or rental agents. Among the most helpful of local rental agencies is **Mexi-Rent Vallarta,** the brainchild of friendly Dutch expatriate John Dommanschet, who works from his little Olas Altas neighborhood office at R. Gómez 130, across from the Hotel San Marino Plaza, tel./fax 322/222-1655 or tel. 322/225-1462, toll-free U.S./Can. tel. 800/656-5555, john@mexirent.com, www.mexirent.com. His rentals, largely confined to the Olas Altas neighborhood, include apartments, condos, and houses rentable by day, week, or month. High-season rates run from about $600/month for modest studios to $1,200 and more for three-bedroom houses.

Other well-established south-of-Cuale rental agencies you may want to contact are **Tropicasa Realty,** at Pulpito 45A, corner of Olas Altas, tel. 322/222-6505, fax 322/222-2555, rentals@tropicasa.com, www.tropicasa.com; and **Bayside Properties,** at F. Rodríguez 160, a few doors uphill from Av. Olas Altas. Call tel. 322/223-4424 or 322/223-4418, www.baysidepropertiespv.com.

Many apartments are rentable only through local owners or managers. The following short list, by location, moving south from the Río Cuale, includes some of the best-buy Olas Altas apartments and condominiums.

Among the most economical are the top-floor studio apartments at the **Hotel Villa del Mar,** at Fco. I. Madero 440, Puerto Vallarta, Jalisco 48300, tel. 322/222-0785, a block south of the Río Cuale and four blocks uphill from Av. Insurgentes. The several apartments, which cluster around a sunny top-floor patio, are clean and thoughtfully furnished in attractive rustic brick, dark wood, and tile. A living area, with furnished kitchenette in one corner, leads to an airy, city- and hill-view private balcony. A comfortable double bed occupies an adjacent alcove. Four stories (no elevator) above an already quiet street, guests are likely to enjoy peace and tranquility here. Rents run about $40/day, $500/month high season, $34 and $450 low. Get your winter reservations in early.

Downhill and south, on Av. Olas Altas, from the Hotel Playa Los Arcos, walk south two short blocks to Francisca Rodríguez, then left a few steps uphill to the **Casa María Elena,** owned and operated by articulate, English-speaking María Elena Zermeño Santana. Her address is Francisca Rodríguez 163, Puerto Vallarta, Jalisco 48380, tel. 322/222-0113, fax 322/223-1380, mariazs@prodigy.net.mx. The eight attractive fan-only brick-and-tile units stand in a four-story stack on a quiet, cobbled side street just 1.5 blocks from the beach. The immaculate, light, and spacious units have living room with TV, bedroom, and modern kitchenettes (toaster oven and coffeemaker) and are all comfortably decorated with folk art chosen by María Elena herself. Although the units have neither swimming pool nor phones, daily maid service and breakfast are included. She offers studio or one-bedroom apartments. The studios rent for about $50/day high season, $35 low; the one-bedrooms, $70 and $50 low. A one-week rental gets a 10 percent discount; longer-term discounts are negotiable. Guests also enjoy the option of three weekly hours of free Spanish lessons taught by María Elena.

One door uphill and across the street from María Elena, other attractive options are available at **Casa Andrea,** at Francisca Rodríguez 174,

Puerto Vallarta, Jalisco 48380, tel./fax 322/222-1213, casaandrea@aol.com, www.casaandrea.com. Here, friendly and helpful, on-site owner Andrea offers 10 gorgeous one- and two-bedroom balcony apartments and a view penthouse, overlooking an invitingly tropical pool patio. The apartments themselves are immaculate, airy, and artfully decorated in whites and pastels and Andrea's tasteful selection of native crafts and paintings. Rooms include king- or queen-sized beds and fully equipped, modern-standard kitchens, with use of a library, small exercise room with treadmill and weights, and a community TV down by the pool. The eight one-bedroom units rent for about $300/week low season, $450 high; the two two-bedroom/two-bath units, about $600 and $800, more for the penthouse, if available; with fans, and maid service. Children under five aren't allowed. For the winter, get reservations in by June.

Six blocks farther south, the path to the 59-unit condo-style **Hotel Brisas del Mar** winds uphill through its view restaurant, across its expansive pool/deck to the big white main building perched a short block below the highway. If this place weren't such a climb, the builders would have sold all the units long ago. Now, however, it's owned and operated by the downhill Hotel Tropicana, whose attractive beachside facilities Brisas del Mar guests are invited to enjoy. At the Brisas del Mar, Privada Abedul 10, Puerto Vallarta, Jalisco 48300, tel. 322/222-1821, fax 322/222-1800, comfortable kitchenette suites with view rent from about $65/night or $700/month low season to $75 and $1,500 high season, with a/c, restaurant, and credit cards accepted. Get there either by car or taxi from the highway, or by climbing the stairs from Amapas through the doorway at no. 307, labeled "Casa del Tigre."

Downriver several blocks, at the north foot of the Av. I. Vallarta bridge, stands the renovated **Hotel Encino-Suites Plaza del Río,** at Av. Juárez 122, Puerto Vallarta, Jalisco 48300, tel. 322/222-0051 or 322/222-0280, fax 322/222-2573, encino@prodigy.net.mx. The hotel lobby opens into a pleasant, tropical fountain-patio, enfolded by tiers of rooms. The suites are in the adjacent Suites Plaza del Río. Here you'll find three stories

of spacious, comfortable kitchenette units. An additional bonus is the Hotel Encino's rooftop pool and sundeck, where both hotel and suite guests enjoy a panoramic view of the surrounding green jungly hills above the white-stucco-and-tile old town, spreading to the blue, mountain-rimmed bay. The approximately 25 suites rent for $67/day ($1,050/month) low season, $90/day ($1,220/month) high; with a/c, phones, security boxes, and restaurant/bar.

If you can't get into Casa Andrea, try **Vallarta Sun Suites,** behind Casa Andrea, on the next street south, at Gómez 169, Puerto Vallarta, Jalisco 48380, tel. 322/222-6200, fax 322/222-1626, vallartasun@usa.net. Perched on a quiet side street, four stories of comfortably furnished new one-bedroom kitchenette apartments overlook a sunny pool patio just two blocks from the beach. Rentals run about $80/day, $1,200/month high season, $60 and $1,000, low season.

Two blocks toward the beach, on Amapas, between Gomez and Pulpito, **Hotel Suites Emperador,** tel. 322/222-5243, fax 322/222-3329, offers simply furnished but clean and comfortable kitchenette studio or one-bedroom apartments from about $1,000 per month low season, $1,200 high; with phones and a/c, and a pool-patio for guest use half a block away; credit cards accepted. For more information, email info@hotelemperadorpv.com or visit the website www.hotelemperadorpv.com.

Half a block farther south on Amapas, find restored **Villa Mercedes,** at Amapas 175, Puerto Vallarta, Jalisco, 48350, tel. 322/222-2148 or 322/223-4543, villamercedes@yahoo.com. Past the small hotel-style front desk, guests enjoy an inviting inner patio garden. Upstairs, the 16 kitchenette apartments are divided about equally between studios and junior suites, all renovated to deluxe modern standards throughout. High-season rentals run about $70 for studios, $92 for junior suites, with a/c, fans, cable TV, and a 25 percent discount for a one-month rental. Ask for a low-season discount.

A block farther south, the 10 white designer units of the **Condominios Villa Blanca,** Amapas 349, Puerto Vallarta, Jalisco 48300, tel./fax 322/222-6190, stair-step artfully above the street.

These light, attractive, air-conditioned luxury apartments vary from studios to two-bedroom units, all with ocean views, modern kitchenettes, and rustic decorator vine-entwined palm trunks adorning the doors and walls. Daily-rate rentals, for studios run about $50 low season, $60 high; for a one-bedroom, $50 low, $70 high, two-bedroom, $70 and $110. Long-term discounts are customary.

Trailer Parks and Camping

Puerto Vallarta visitors enjoy two good trailer parks. The smallish, palm-shaded **Trailer Park El Pescador,** Francia 143, P.O. Box 141, Puerto Vallarta, Jalisco 48300, tel. 322/224-2828, is two blocks off the highway on Francia, corner of Lucerna, a few blocks north of the *libramiento* downtown bypass fork. The 65 spaces (four blocks from the Playa Las Glorias) rent for about $16 per day, with one free day per week, one free week per month; with all hookups, including showers, toilets, long-distance phone access, and launderette. Pets are okay. Luxury hotel pools and good restaurants are nearby.

Farther out, but much more spacious, is **Tacho's Trailer Park,** half a mile from Highway 200 on Av. Aramara, the road that branches inland across the airport highway from the cruise ship dock. Tacho's, P.O. Box 315, Puerto Vallarta, Jalisco 48300, tel. 322/224-2163, offers a large grassy yard with some palms, bananas, and other trees for shade. The 100 spaces run $16/day (one free week on a monthly rental), including all hookups and use of showers, toilets, laundry room, pool and *palapa,* and shuffleboard courts. Pads are paved, and pets are okay.

Other than the trailer parks, Puerto Vallarta has precious few campsites within the city limits. Plenty of camping possibilities exist outside the city, however. Especially inviting are the pearly little beaches, such as Las Animas, Quimixto, Caballo, and others that dot the verdant, wild coastline between Boca de Tomatlán and Yelapa. *Colectivo* water taxis regularly head for these beaches for about $5 per person from Boca de Tomatlán (see Beaches). Local stores at Quimixto, Las Animas, and Boca de Tomatlán can provide water (bring water purification tablets or filter)

and basic supplies. (For more camping possibilities, see Around the Bay of Banderas.)

FOOD

Puerto Vallarta is brimming with good food. Dieters beware: light or nouvelle cuisine, tasty vegetables, and bountiful salads are the exception, as in all Mexico. In the winter, when the sun-hungry vacationers crowd in, a table at even an average restaurant may require a reservation. During the low season, however, Puerto Vallarta's best eateries are easy to spot. They are the ones with the customers. (*Note:* If you're coming to Puerto Vallarta mainly for its gourmet offerings, avoid September and October, when a number of the best restaurants are closed.)

Stalls, Snacks, and Breakfast

Good Puerto Vallarta eating is not limited to sit-down restaurants. Many foodstalls offer wholesome, inexpensive meals and snacks to hosts of loyal repeat customers. It's hard to go wrong with hot, prepared-on-the-spot food. Each stand specializes in one type of fare—seafood, *tortas,* tacos, hot dogs—and occupies the same location daily, beginning around 6 P.M. For example, a number of them concentrate along Av.s Consitución and Pino Suárez just south of the Río Cuale; several others cluster on the side-street corners of Av. Olas Altas a few blocks away.

Other tasty late-night options are available at many of the eateries along main street Av. Insurgentes, just south of the upstream Río Cuale bridge. For example, drop into the no-name *jugería* a few doors north from the Cine Bahía. Try one of the luscious *tortas de pierna,* roast leg of pork smothered in avocado on a bun, $1.75. Top it off with a banana *licuado,* with a touch of *(un poquito de)* chocolate. It's at Insurgentes 153 and open daily 7 A.M.–midnight.

Similar is **Tuti Fruti,** a good spot for a refreshing snack, especially while sightseeing or shopping around the *malecón.* Find it at the corner of Morelos and Corona, one block from the *malecón;* open Mon.–Sat. 8 A.M.–11 P.M. You could even eat breakfast, lunch, and dinner there, starting with juice and granola or eggs in the morning, a *torta* and a *licuado* during the afternoon, and an *hamburguesa* for an evening snack.

Some of the most colorful, untouristed places to eat in town are, paradoxically, at the tourist-mecca **Mercado Municipal** on the Río Cuale, at the Av. Insurgentes (upstream) bridge. The *fondas* tucked on the upstairs floor (climb the streetside staircase) specialize in steaming, home-style soups, fish, meat, tacos, *moles,* and *chiles rellenos.* Point out your order to the cook and take a seat at the cool, river-view seating area. Open daily 7 A.M.–6 P.M.

For breakfast, **La Casa de Los Hot Cakes,** skillfully orchestrated by personable travel writer-turned-restaurateur Memo Barroso, has become a Puerto Vallarta institution, at Basilio Badillo 289, between I. Vallarta and Constitución, tel. 322/222-6272. Breakfast served Tues.–Sun. 8 A.M.–2 P.M. Besides bountiful Mexican and North American breakfasts—orange juice or fruit, eggs, toast, and hash browns for about $4—Memo offers an indulgent list of pancakes. Try his nut-topped, peanut butter–filled "O. Henry" chocolate pancakes, for example. Add his bottomless cup of coffee and you'll be buzzing all day. For lighter eaters, vegetarian and less indulgent options are available.

Memo's latest love is **coffee.** If you're lucky enough to be near Casa de Los Hot Cakes at the right time, simply follow your nose to the source of the heavenly aroma of his roasting beans—premium estate-grown only, from Oaxaca, Chiapas, and Veracruz.

If Casa de Los Hot Cakes is too crowded, you can get a reasonable facsimile at Freddy's **Tucán** restaurant half a block downhill (which Memo inaugurated in the 1980s) at Hotel Posada Roger, corner B. Badillo and I. Vallarta, tel. 322/222-0836. Open daily 8 A.M.–2 P.M.

Another good spot for breakfast served 7–11:30 A.M. is the airy beachfront terrace of the **Hotel Playa Los Arcos** restaurant at 380 Olas Altas. Here the ambience—tour boats arriving and leaving, the passing sidewalk scene, the swishing waves, the swaying palms—is half the fun. The other half is the food, either a hearty $7 buffet, or a briskly served à la carte choice of your heart's desire, from fruit and oatmeal to eggs, bacon, and hash browns.

Shorter on scenery but longer on food and service is **Café Tizoc,** on Olas Altas, between Rodríguez and Gómez, tel. 322/223-2554. Here the main event is great hashbrowns and "slam" breakfasts, introduced by the friendly, semiretired headwaiter, who worked for a dozen years at Denny's in Las Vegas, Nevada. Food and service are so good that you'll most likely return to try lunch and supper. Open daily 8 A.M.–11 P.M.

Coffeehouses

Good coffee has arrived at Puerto Vallarta, where some cafés now roast from their own private sources of beans. Just a block from Los Muertos Beach, coffee and book lovers get the best of both worlds at **Page in the Sun,** corner Olas Altas and M. Dieguez, diagonally across from Hotel Playa Olas Altas. There, longtimers sip coffee and play chess while others enjoy their pick of lattes, cappuccinos, ice cream, muffins, and walls of used paperbacks and magazines. Open daily 8 A.M.–9 P.M.

Exactly one block farther up Olas Altas, at the corner of Rodríguez, take a table at the **Café San Ángel** and soak up the sidewalk scene. Here, you can enjoy breakfast or a sandwich or dessert and good coffee in a dozen varieties, 8 A.M.–10 P.M.

For fancier offerings and upscale ambience, go to the **Café Maximilian** on the sidewalk-front of Hotel Playa Los Arcos, at 380 Olas Altas, open daily (except Sunday in low season).

Restaurants—Río Cuale and South

Archie's Wok, Francisca Rodríguez 130, between Av. Olas Altas and the beach, tel. 322/222-0411, is the founding member of a miniature "gourmet ghetto" that is flourishing in the Olas Altas neighborhood. The founder, now deceased, was John Huston's longtime friend and personal chef. However, Archie's wife, Cindy Alpenia, carries on the culinary mission. A large local following swears by her menu of vegetables, fish, meat, and noodles. Favorites include Thai coconut fish, barbecued ribs Hoi Sin, and spicy fried Thai noodles. Make up a party of three or four, and each order a favorite. Arrive early; there's usually a line by 7:30 P.M. for dinner. Open

Mon.–Sat. 2–11 P.M.; Visa accepted. Moderate–expensive.

Next door to Archie's Wok, **Restaurant Pekin,** at F. Rodríguez 136, adds a new, refined version of Chinese cooking to Puerto Vallarta's already rich gastronomic treasury. Perhaps the promise of "the only Chinese-born chef in Puerto Vallarta" is its secret to success, but whatever, the food, whether a light lunch of spring rolls and wonton soup, or a dinner of stir-fried scallops, kung pao chicken, and a whole fish, is bound to please. Open daily, noon until around 10 P.M. Moderate–expensive.

One block due north, across from the Hotel Plaza San Marino, **Karpathos Taverna,** R. Gomez 110, tel. 322/223-1562, has acquired a considerable local following by creating a little corner of Greece here in Puerto Vallarta. Although the ambience comes, in part, from very correct service and the Greek folk melodies emanating from the sound system, the food—genuine Greek olives, feta cheese, rolled grape leaves, savory moussaka (layered eggplant), piquant roast lamb, garlic-rubbed fish with olive oil—seems a small miracle here, half a world from the source. Open Mon.–Sat. 4–11 P.M. Moderate–expensive.

Head back down Olas Altas to **Restaurant Kaiser Maximilian,** a prominent member of the growing roll of Olas Altos gourmet gems. Here, the Austrian expatriate owner skillfully orchestrates a cadre of chefs and waiters to produce a little bit of Vienna with a hint of California cuisine. From his long list of appetizers, consider starting off with prune-stuffed mountain quail in nine-spice sauce with polenta, continue with organic salad greens in vinaigrette, and finish with scalloped *rahmschnitzel* with noodles in a cream mushroom sauce, accompanied with a Monte Xanic Baja California chenin blanc. If you have room, top everything off with Viennese apple strudel. Alas, the only thing missing at Café Maximilian is zither music playing softly in the background. At the Hotel Playa Los Arcos, Olas Altas 380B, tel. 322/222-5058; open daily 4–11 P.M. Reservations, tel. 322/223-0760, strongly recommended. Expensive.

Mexican food is well represented south of Cuale by a trio of good restaurants (Tres Huastecas,

Café de Olla, and Los Arbolitos, below, near the end of the restaurant section). Restaurant **Tres Huastecas**'s charming, pure-blooded Huastec owner calls himself "El Querreque," -while others call him the "Troubador of Puerto Vallarta." His poetry, together with sentimental Mexican country scenes, covers the walls, while everything from soft-boiled eggs and toast to frog legs and enchiladas Huastecas fills the tables. Find it at Olas Altas, corner of F. Rodríguez, tel. 322/222-4525; open daily 8 A.M.–8 P.M. Moderate.

Nearby, the **Café de Olla,** B. Badillo 168, tel. 322/223-1626, a few doors uphill from the Olas Altas corner, draws flocks of evening customers with its bountiful plates of scrumptious local delicacies. It serves Mexican food the way it's supposed to be, starting with enough salsa and *totopes* (chips) to make appetizers irrelevant. Your choice comes next—either chicken, ribs, and steaks from the streetfront grill—or the savory *antojitos* platters piled with tacos, tostadas, *chiles rellenos,* or enchiladas by themselves, or all together in its unbeatable *plato Mexicano.* Prepare by skipping lunch and arriving for an early dinner to give your tummy time to digest it all before bed. Open daily 8 A.M.–11 P.M. Budget–moderate.

As Archie's Wok did in the Olas Altas neighborhood years ago, Memo Barroso's Casa de Los Hot Cakes has sparked a small restaurant and café renaissance on Basilio Badillo, now so popular it's becoming known as the "Calle de Cafes."

One of the Badillo originals still going strong is **Café Adobe,** at the corner of Basilio Badillo and I. Vallarta, tel. 322/222-6720. Here, diners escape from the colorful but insistent Puerto Vallarta street-bustle into the Adobe's cool, refined American Southwest ambience. You'll enjoy soft music, flowers, and white table linens while you make your choice from a short but tasty menu of soups, fettuccine, poultry, seafood, and meats. Open daily except Tuesday 6–11 P.M., closed June, July, and August; reservations recommended. Expensive.

Noisy, smoky bus traffic mars daytime dining at Av. Basilio Badillo sidewalk cafés. Fortunately, this is not true in the evening or any time at both Café Adobe and Casa de Los Hot Cakes as both have inside seating. Another such tranquil refuge, just one block east, uphill, of Café Adobe, is **Café Frankfurt,** the closest thing to a German *biergarten* south of New Braunfels, Texas. Brainchild of master chef Michael Pohl, who started out with a budget hotel in 1995 (which still operates) and expanded to a garden restaurant a few years later, works his miracle with aplomb. Besides all of the German favorites (smoked pork chops with sauerkraut, Wiener schnitzel, *bratwurst,* and melt-in-your-mouth *apfel strudel,* Michael also offers popular French, Italian, and vegetarian specialties. If you can manage it, best of all is Michael's all-out effort, a geniune Bavarian buffet (Nov.–April, Mon., Wed., and Sat., 6–10 P.M.) Find him open daily 11 A.M.–10 P.M., at Basilio Badillo 300, corner of Constitución, tel. 322/222-3403.

For atmosphere, the showplace **Le Bistro** is tops, at Isla Río Cuale 16A, tel. 322/222-0283, just upstream from the Av. Insurgentes bridge. Renovations with lots of marble and tile have replaced some of the old bohemian-chic atmosphere with European-elegant. Nevertheless the relaxed, exotic ambience still remains: the river gurgles past outdoor tables, and giant-leafed plants festoon a glass ceiling, while jazz CDs play so realistically that you look in vain for the combo. Its hours are Mon.–Sat. 9 A.M.-11:30 P.M., first come, first served—reservations not accepted. Expensive.

If, on the other hand, you're hungry for Chinese food, go to **Dragon Rojo,** at Insurgentes 323, uphill side, between V. Carranza and B. Badillo, tel. 322/222-0175. Here, competent chefs put out a respectable line of the usual San Francisco–style Cantonese specialties. Open daily 1–11 P.M. Moderate.

Los Arbolitos, Camino Rivera 184, tel. 322/223-1050 (bear right at the upper end of Av. Lázaro Cárdenas, way upstream along the Río Cuale), remains very popular, despite its untouristed location. Here, home-style Mexican specialties reign supreme. The house pride and joy is the Mexican plate, although it serves dozens of other Mexican and international favorites. Colorful decor, second-floor river-view location, and attentive service spell plenty of satisfied customers. Open daily 8 A.M.–11 P.M. Moderate.

Your stay in Puerto Vallarta would not be complete without sunset cocktails and dinner beneath the stars at one of Puerto Vallarta's south-of-Cuale hillside view restaurants. Of these, **Señor Chico's,** Púlpito 377, tel. 322/222-3535, remains a longtime favorite, despite its average (but professionally presented) food. The atmosphere—soft guitar solos, flickering candlelight, pastel-pink tablecloths, balmy night air, and the twinkling lights of the city below—is memorable. Open daily 5–11 P.M.; reservations recommended. Expensive. (Best get there by taxi. If not, turn left at Púlpito, the first left turn possible uphill past the gasoline station as you head south on Highway 200 out of town. After about two winding blocks, you'll see Sr. Chico's on the left as the street climaxes atop a rise.)

Restaurants North of Río Cuale

The success of up-and-coming **Restaurant Trio** at 264 Guerrero (between Hidalgo and Matamoros), two short blocks north of the Río Cuale, flows from an innovative Mediterranean menu and its cool, elegant candlelit atmosphere. Imaginative combinations of traditional ingredients, attentive service, and satisfying desserts topped off with savory espresso will keep customers coming back for years. Open noon–3:30 P.M. and 6 P.M.–midnight; reservations recommended, tel. 322/222-2196. Moderate–expensive.

Within the bustle of the *malecón* restaurant row stands the longtime favorite **Las Palomas,** *malecón* at Aldama, tel. 322/222-3675. Soothing suppertime live marimba music and graceful colonial decor, all beneath a towering big-beamed ceiling, afford a restful contrast from the sidewalk hubbub just outside the door. Both the breakfasts and the lunch and dinner entrées (nearly all Mexican style) are tasty and bountiful. Open Mon.–Sat. 8 A.M.–10 P.M., Sun. 9 A.M.–5 P.M. Moderate.

If, however, you hanker for home-cooked Italian food, stop by **Rito's Baci,** tel. 322/222-6448, the labor of love of the sometimes taciturn but warmhearted owner-chef, who stays open seven days a week because his "customers would be disappointed if I closed." His establishment, as plain as Kansas in July, requires no atmosphere other than Rito himself, a member of the Mexican football league hall of fame. All of his hearty specialties, from the pestos through the pastas and the eggplant Parmesan, are handmade from traditional family recipes. Rito's Baci is on the corner of Juárez and Ortíz de Dominguez. Open daily 1–11 P.M. Moderate.

A choice pair of romantic hillside restaurants concludes the list of north-of-Cuale dining options. Highest on the hill is the longtime favorite **Restaurant Chez Elena,** Matamoros 520, tel. 322/222-0161, on a quiet side street a few blocks above and north of the downtown church. Soft live guitar music and flickering candlelight in a colonial garden terrace set the tone, while a brief but solid Mexican-international menu, augmented by an innovative list of daily specialties, provides the food. On a typical evening, you might be able to choose between entrées such as *cochinita pibil* (Yucatecan-style shredded pork in sauce), banana leaf–wrapped Oaxacan tamales, or *dorado* fillet with cilantro in white sauce. Chez Elena guests often arrive early for sunset cocktails at the rooftop panoramic view bar and then continue with dinner downstairs. Open nightly 6–10 P.M.; reservations are recommended. Moderate–expensive.

A few blocks downhill and north, the striking castle-tower of **Restaurant Café des Artistes** rises above the surrounding neighborhood at 740 Guadalupe Sanchez at Leona Vicario, tel. 322/222-3228 or 322/222-3229. Romantics only need apply. Candlelit tables, tuxedoed servers, gently whirring ceiling fans, soothing live neoclassical melodies, and gourmet international cuisine all set a luxurious tone. You might start with your pick of soups, such as chilled cream of watercress or cream of prawn and pumpkin, continue with a salad, perhaps the smoked salmon in puff pastry with avocado pine nut dressing. For a finale, choose honey- and soy-glazed roast duck or shrimp sautéed with cheese tortellini and served with a carrot custard and a spinach-basil puree. Open daily 6–11:30 P.M.; reservations recommended. Expensive.

Vegetarian Restaurants

Good macrobiotic and vegan cuisine is getting a foothold in Puerto Vallarta in at least three locations. Downtown, off the malecón, you'll find **Papaya 3,** at Abasolo 169, tel. 322/222-0303, uphill 1.5 blocks from the Hard Rock Cafe. Here, owners have succeeded with a dazzlingly varied repertoire for Puerto Vallarta's growing cadre of health-conscious visitors and locals. The list begins with dozens of creamy tropical fruit *licuados,* which they call "shakes," but which contain no ice cream, and continues through a host of salads, pastas, omelettes, sandwiches, Mexican specialties, and chicken and fish plates. The atmosphere, augmented with plants and soft music, is refined but relaxed. Moderate. (You can also enjoy the same at its second location, on upper Olas Altas, at no. 485, near the corner of Gómez, open Mon.–Sat. 8 A.M.–10:30 P.M., tel. 322/223-1692.)

For a very worthy alternative, go to up-and-coming **Planeta Vegetariana** downtown, near the south side of the church, at 270 Iturbide, by the corner of Hidalgo, tel. 322/222-3073, open 8 A.M.–10 P.M.

ENTERTAINMENT AND EVENTS
Wandering Around

The *malecón,* where the sunsets seem the most beautiful in town, is a perfect place to begin the evening. Make sure you eventually make your way to the downtown central plaza by the Presidencia Municipal (City Hall). On both weekday and weekend nights, the city often sponsors free music and dance concerts beginning around 8 P.M. at the bayside **Los Arcos** amphitheater. (For current listings, see the events calendar pages of tourist newspapers *Vallarta Today* or *Vallarta Tribune.*)

After the concert, join the crowds watching the impromptu antics of the *mimos*(mimes) on the amphitheater stage and the nearby street artists painting plates, watercolor country scenes, and fanciful, outer-galaxy spray-can spacescapes.

If you miss the Los Arcos concert, you can usually console yourself with a balloon, *palomitas* (popcorn), and sometimes a band concert in the plaza. If you're inconsolable, buy some peanuts, a roasted ear of sweet corn *(elote),* or a hot dog from a vendor. After that, cool down with an *agua* or *jugo* fruit juice from the *juguería* across the bayside plaza corner, or a cone of ice cream from Baskin-Robbins just north of the city hall.

A tranquil south-of-Cuale spot to cool off evenings is the **Muelle Nuevo** (New Pier) at the foot of Francisca Rodríguez (beach side of Hotel Playa Los Arcos). On a typical evening you'll find a couple of dozen folks—men, women, and kids—enjoying the breeze, the swish of the surf, and, with nets or lines, trying to catch a few fish for sale or dinner.

Special Cultural Events

Puerto Vallarta residents enjoy their share of local fiestas. Preparations for **Semana Santa** (Easter week) begin in February, often with a **Carnaval** parade and dancing on Shrove Tuesday, and continue for the seven weeks before Easter. Each Friday until Easter, you might see processions of people bearing crosses filing through the downtown for special Masses at neighborhood churches. This all culminates during Easter week, when Puerto Vallarta is awash with visitors, crowding the hotels, camping on the beaches, and filing in somber processions, which finally brighten to fireworks, dancing, and food on Domingo Gloria (Easter Sunday).

The town quiets down briefly until the May **Fiesta de Mayo,** a countrywide celebration of sports contests, music and dance performances, art shows, parades, and beauty pageants.

On the evening of September 15, the Plaza de Armas (City Hall plaza) fills with tipsy merrymakers, who gather to hear the mayor reaffirm Mexican independence by shouting the Grito de Dolores—"Long Live Mexico! Death to the Gachupines!"—under booming, brilliant cascades of fireworks.

Celebration again breaks out seriously during the first 12 days of December, when city groups—businesses, families, neighborhoods—try to outdo each other with music, floats, costumes, and offerings all in honor of Mexico's patron, the Virgin of Guadalupe. The revelry climaxes on December 12, when people, many in native garb to celebrate their indigenous origins, converge on the downtown church to receive the Virgin's blessing. If you miss the main December Virgin of Guadalupe fiesta, you can still enjoy a similar, but smaller-scale celebration in El Tuito (see Cabo Corrientes Country in the Coast of Jalisco chapter), a month later, on January 12.

Visitors who miss such real-life fiestas can still enjoy one of several local **Fiesta Mexicana** tourist shows, which are as popular with Mexican tourists as foreigners. The evening typically begins with a sumptuous buffet of salads, tacos, enchiladas, seafood, barbecued meats, and flan and pastries for dessert. Then begins a nonstop program of music and dance from all parts of Mexico: a chorus of revolutionary *soldaderas* and their Zapatista male compatriots; raven-haired señoritas in flowing, flowered Tehuantepec silk dresses; rows of dashing Guadalajaran *charros* twirling

© BRUCE WHIPPERMAN

The Fiesta Mexicana show at the Hotel Playa Los Arcos nearly always includes a skilled *vaquero.*

their fast-stepping *chinas poblanas* sweethearts, climaxing with enough fireworks to swab the sky red, white, and green.

The south-of-Cuale **Restaurant Iguana,** Calle Lázaro Cárdenas 311, between Insurgentes and Constitución, tel. 322/222-0105, stages a very popular and *auténtico* such show Thursday and Sunday around 7 P.M. (Sunday only in the low season, call ahead to confirm). Another safe bet is the **Hotel NH Krystal** show, tel. 322/224-0202, Tuesday and Saturday (Saturday only during the low season) at 7 P.M.

Other such shows are held seasonally at the **Sheraton** on Thursday, tel. 322/226-0404; the **Qualton Club** on Wednesday, tel. 322/224-4446; and the **Playa Los Arcos** on Saturday, tel. 322/222-0583.

The tariff for these shows typically runs $40 per person with open bar—except for the more modest Playa Los Arcos show, which runs about $20, drinks extra. During holidays and the high winter season reservations are generally necessary; best to book through a travel or tour desk agent.

Movies

Puerto Vallarta's "art" movie house is **L'Opera.** at Encino 287, 2nd floor, in the central downtown district. Screenings, which include titles such as *The Unbearable Lightness of Being, Sabina* and the *Caveman,* with English subtitles, when necessary, customarily begin around 6 P.M.For programs, call tel. 322/222-7378.

In a more popular vein, the south-of-Cuale **Cine Bahía,** at Insurgentes 189, between Madero and Serdán, tel. 322/222-1717, remains a typical '50s-style small-town movie house. Managers run a mixture of Mexican and American pop horror, comedy, and action, such as *The Lord of the Rings* and *Men in Black II.* Another similar neighborhood movie house on the north side of town is the **Cine Luz María,** at Av. México 227, across the street from the Pemex *gasolinera,* tel. 322/222-0705.

Live Music

Cover charges are not generally required at the hotel bars, many of which offer nightly live music and dancing. For example, the band at **Hotel NH Krystal,** tel. 322/224-0202, plays Mexican-romantic-pop in season, 8 P.M.–midnight, directly adjacent to the hotel reception desk. (For up-to-date listings, see the nightlife and events pages in *Puerto Vallarta Today* and the *Vallarta Tribune.*

The **Hotel Westin Regina,** tel. 322/221-1100, has seasonal live guitar music nightly, 7–8 P.M., while the **Hotel Fiesta Americana,** tel. 322/224-2010, has Mexican trio and tropical music groups (nightly 7 P.M.–1 A.M.) guaranteed to brighten the spirits of any vacationer after a hard day on the beach.

The **Hotel Playa Los Arcos,** tel. 322/222-0583, offers a combo in the *palapa* restaurant bar with a little bit of everything nightly from oldies-but-goodies to including the patrons in the act, nightly 8–10 P.M.

Other hotels with similar music offerings are the Sheraton, tel. 322/223-0404; the Westin Regina, tel. 322/221-1100; and the Canto del Sol (formerly Continental Plaza), tel. 322/226-0123.

Discos

Discos open quietly around 10 P.M., begin revving up around midnight, and usually pound on till about 5 in the morning. They have dress codes requiring shoes, shirts, and long pants for men, and dresses or blouses and skirts or pants, or modest shorts, for women. Often they serve only (expensive) soft drinks. Discos that cater to tourists (all of the following) generally monitor their front doors very carefully; consequently they are pleasant and, with ordinary precautions, secure places to have a good time. If you use earplugs, even the high-decibel joints needn't keep you from enjoying yourself. Listings below are grouped by Zona Hotelera (north side), *malecón,* and south-of-Cuale locations, in approximate order of increasing volume.

Zona Hotelera: In front of Hotel NH Krystal stands **Christine,** the showplace of Puerto Vallarta discos, tel. 322/224-0202. This disco entices customers to come and pay the $15 cover charge early (11 P.M.) to see its display of special fogs, spacy gyrating colored lights, and sophisticated woofers and tweeters, which, even when loud as usual, are supposed to leave you with minimum hearing impairment.

Malecón: Many popular *malecón* spots regularly pound out a continuous no-cover repertoire of recorded rap and rock. One of the longtime standouts, popular with all generations, is **Carlos O'Brian's,** *malecón* at Pípila, tel. 322/222-1444. High-volume recorded rock, revolutionary wall-photos, zany mobiles, zingy margaritas, and "loco" waiters often lead patrons to dance on the tables by midnight. Folks who generally shy away from loud music can still have fun at Carlos O'Brian's, since the place is big and the high-volume speakers are confined to one area.

Since most *malecón* discos are trying to imitate the **Hard Rock Cafe,** you might as well go right to the source at *malecón* at Abasolo, tel. 322/222-5532.

The **Zoo,** however, across Abasolo from the Hard Rock Cafe, tel. 322/222-4945, appears not to be imitating anyone. While animals—hippos, swooping birds, zebras, even a circulating gorilla—entertain the customers, reggae, rap, and rock thunder from overhead speakers.

South of Cuale: Longtime favorite disco Cactus's new reincarnation is salsa disco club **Jabalu,** at the south end of I. Vallarta, tel. 322/222-0391. Here, Friday and Saturday evenings (cover $10) a youngish crowd gyrates to live Latin rock until around three in the morning.

Newcomer **Paco Paco,** one block north at I. Vallarta, between Badillo and Carranza, is trying harder to do the same thing by charging no cover.

Club **Santa Barbara,** on Olas Altas, across the street from Hotel Playa Los Arcos, gives the older generation a chance for fun, with nightly programs, varying from games shows and bingo to karaoke and dinner theater cabaret. Drop in (at Olas Altas 351, tel. 322/223-2048) and see how the club accomplishes it.

Malecón Cafés, Bars, and Hangouts

One of the simplest Puerto Vallarta entertainment formulas is to walk along the *malecón* until you hear the kind of music at the volume you like.

Young film buffs like the glitz and neon of **Planet Hollywood,** at the spot of former Restaurant Brazz, near the *malecón's* south end, at Morelos 518, at Galeana.

On the other hand, traditionalists enjoy

Restaurant Las Palomas, which features seasonal live marimba music, 7–9 P.M., at the corner of Aldama, tel. 322/222-3675.

Another block north, the African safari–decorated **Mogambo,** between Ortíz and Abasolo, offers seasonal low-volume live music, often piano or jazz, nightly during high season, tel. 322/222-3476.

A few blocks farther north, corner of Allende, **La Dolce Vita** entertains dinner customers with live programs such as reggae, flamenco, jazz, or folk, 9 P.M.–midnight in season, tel. 322/222-3852.

Those who desire a refined, romantic ambience go to **Restaurant Café des Artistes,** tel. 322/222-3228, and take a table for dinner or a seat at the bar, where they enjoy soothing neoclassical flute–accompanied melodies nightly during high season, Friday and Saturday during low season. Find it by walking three blocks along Leona Vicario inland from the *malecón.*

South-of-Cuale Cafés, Bars, and Hangouts

The increasingly popular small entertainment district, spread along I. Vallarta, near the corner of L. Cárdenas, has acquired a number of lively spots, among them the **Mariachis Locos** bar/restaurant. Inside, a mostly local clientele enjoys a lively nonstop mariachi show nightly from about 8 P.M. to the wee hours.

On the same side of Vallarta, half a block north, folks crowd in nightly 9 P.M.–1 A.M. at **Roxy** "Rhythm and Blues Bar" for its unique brand of live, loud, and jazzy rock and roll.

Across the street, 1.5 blocks north, corner of Vallarta and Carranza, the longtime favorite, friendly **Restaurant El Torito,** tel. 322/222-3784, has good ribs, reasonable prices, and seasonal live music from around 10 P.M., bar open till around 5 A.M.

Many folks' nights wouldn't be complete without stopping in at the **Andale** Mexican pub, Olas Altas 425, tel. 322/222-1054, whose atmosphere is so amicable and lively that few even bother to watch the nonstop TV. Restaurant upstairs; open till around 2 A.M.

If the night is still young, continue downhill one block to the foot of Francisca Rodríguez, to beachfront restaurant **Cuates and Cuetes,** for innovative live "tropical" Latin music, beginning around 7:30 nightly.

SPORTS AND RECREATION
Jogging and Walking
Puerto Vallarta's cobbled streets, high curbs (towering sometimes to six feet!), and "holey" sidewalks make for tricky walking around town. The exception is the *malecón,* which can provide a good two-mile round-trip jog when it is not crowded. Otherwise, try the beaches or the big public sports field, Unidad Deportiva, on the airport boulevard across from the Sheraton.

Swimming, Surfing, and Boogie Boarding
While Puerto Vallarta's calm waters are generally safe for swimming, they are often too tranquil for surfing, bodysurfing, and boogie boarding. Sometimes, strong, surfable waves rise along the southern half of **Playa Los Muertos.** Another notable possibility is at the mouth of the Ameca River (north of the airport) where, during the rainy summer season, the large river flow helps create bigger than normal waves. Surfing is also common at **Bucerías** and **Punta Mita.** (For details, see under Around the Bay of Banderas.)

Sailboarding and Sailboating
A small but growing nucleus of local sailboarding enthusiasts practice the sport from Puerto Vallarta's beaches. They sometimes hold a **sailboarding tournament** during the citywide Fiesta de Mayo in the first week in May.

Sail **Vallarta,** which operates from Marina Vallarta, takes parties out on sailing excursions. For more information, call tel. 322/221-0096. **Vallarta Adventures,** tel. 322/221-0657, does the same for $150 for two. Bargain for a discount.

Snorkeling and Scuba Diving
The biggest scuba instructor-outfitter in town is **Chico's Dive Shop,** on the *malecón* at Díaz Ordaz 770, between Pípila and Vicario, tel. 322/222-1895, fax 322/222-2010; open daily 9 A.M.–10 P.M. Chico's offers complete lessons, arranges and leads dive trips, and rents scuba equipment to qualified divers (bring your certificate). A beginning scuba lesson in the pool runs about $20, after which you'll be qualified to dive at Los Arcos. A day boat trip, including one 40-minute dive, costs $65 per person (two tanks, $80), gear included. Snorkelers on the same trip pay about $30. Chico's takes certified divers only to the **Marietas Islands,** the best site in the bay, for $100, including gear and two dives, and sandwiches and sodas for lunch.

Alternatively, try **Vallarta Adventures** at tel. 322/221-0657, another well-established outfit that offers scuba diving services (and much more).

Personal Watercraft Riding, Water-Skiing, and Parasailing
These are available right on the beach at a number of the northside resort-hotels, such as the Sheraton, Las Palmas Resort, Fiesta Americana Puerto Vallarta, and NH Krystal.

The same sports are also seasonally available south of Cuale on Playa Los Muertos, in front of the Hotels Playa Los Arcos and Tropicana.

Expect to pay about $50 per half hour for a Jet Ski personal watercraft, $75/hour for water-skiing, and $25 for a 10-minute parasailing ride.

Tennis and Golf
The eight—four outdoor clay, four indoor—courts at the friendly **John Newcombe Tennis Club,** Hotel Canto del Sol, tel. 322/226-0123, rent all day for about $20/hour. A sign-up board is available for players seeking partners. It also offers massage, steam baths, equipment sales and rentals, and professional lessons ($38/hour).

The several night-lit courts at the **Hotel NH Krystal,** tel. 322/224-0202 or 322/224-2030, rent for about $15/hour. The Krystal club also offers equipment sales, rentals, and professional lessons. Other clubs, such as at the **Sheraton,** tel. 322/223-0404, also rent their courts to the public.

The 18-hole, par-71 **Marina Vallarta Golf Course,** tel. 322/221-0545, designed by architect Joe Finger, is one of Mexico's best. It is open to the public for $100, which includes greens fee, caddy, and cart. It's open daily 7:30 A.M. to dusk.

The green, palm-shaded 18-hole **Los Flamingos Golf Course,** at Km 145, Highway 200, eight miles (13 km) north of the airport, tel. 329/296-5006, offers an alternative. Open to the public daily 7 A.M.–5 P.M., the Los Flamingos services include carts ($28), caddies ($10), club rentals ($20), a pro shop, restaurant, and locker rooms. The greens fee runs about $50. Its white shuttle bus leaves daily during the high season from the Zona Hotelera (in front of the Sheraton) at 7, 8, and 9 A.M. daily except Sunday, picking up passengers (keep your eyes peeled) everywhere northbound along the boulevard, and returning in the afternoon, by 5 P.M. Telephone to confirm.

Bicycling

Bike Mex offers mountain bike adventures in surrounding scenic country locations. It tailors trips from beginning to advanced levels according to individual ability and interests. More advanced trips include outback spots Yelapa and Sayulita and mountain destinations, such as San Sebastián, Mascota, and Talpa. Participants enjoy GT Full Suspension or Kona mountain bikes (27-gear), helmets, gloves, purified water, and bilingual guides. Drop by or call the downtown office at 361 Guerrero, tel. 322/223-1680 or visit www.bikemex.com.

Alternatively, contact **Ecoride,** at 382 Miramar, tel. 322/222-7912, which offers approximately the same services.

Horseback Riding

A pair of nearby ranches give visitors the opportunity to explore scenic tropical forest, river, and mountainside country. Options include English or Western saddles, and rides ranging from two hours to a whole day. Contact either **Rancho Ojo de Agua,** tel. 322/224-0607 or 322/224-8240 or **Rancho El Charro,** tel. 322/224-0114, aguirre@pvnet.com.mx, www.ranchoelcharro.com.

Adventure Tours

A number of nature-oriented tour agencies lead off-the-beaten-track Puerto Vallarta–area excursions. **Vallarta Adventures** offers boat tours to the Islas Marietas wildlife sanctuary (sea turtles, manta rays, dolphins, whales, seabirds) and air-

plane excursions and a rugged all-day Mercedes-Benz truck ride (canyons, mountains, crystal streams, rustic villages) into the heart of Puerto Vallarta's backyard mountains. Contact a travel agent or tel. 322/221-0657 or 322/221-0658, fax 322/221-2845, info@vallarta-adventures.com, or www.vallarta-adventures.com for information and reservations.

The offerings of unusually ecologically aware **Expediciones Cielo Abierto** (Open Sky Expeditions), downtown at 339 Guerrero, two blocks north of the riverside Municipal Crafts Market, tel. 322/222-3310, fax 322/223-2407, openair@vivamexico.com, include snorkeling around Punta Mita, hiking in the Sierra Cuale foothill jungle, bird-watching, cultural tours, dolphin encounters, and whale-watching.

Viva Tours, tel. 322/224-0410 or 322/224-8026, fax 322/224-0182, viva2000@prodigy.net.mx, organizes a number of relaxing adventures, including an excursion to a hot spring on the idyllic Mascota River, just half an hour from downtown Puerto Vallarta. Options include a hike or horseback ride and an overnight at a cozy, rustic Rancho Canastilla at the hot spring.

Puerto Vallarta's only **jungle canopy adventure** (for the fearless and fit only: ride at treetop heights like a bird through the tropical forest) is up and operating. The inventor is ecologically aware Jeff Coates (Gringo Bob as he's known to local folks), who's set to receive adventurers at his jungle preserve near Boca de Tomatlán. For information, call tel. 322/224-0719 or 322/223-6060.

Gyms

Puerto Vallarta has a number of good exercise gyms. One of the best is the women only **Total Fitness Gym** (ays-PAH) at the Marina, Tennis Club Puesta del Sol, tel. 322/221-0770, offering 40 machines, complete weight sets, professional advice, and aerobics workouts.

Similar facilities and services are available for both sexes at the **Hotel Qualton Club and Spa,** tel. 322/224-4446, for about $10 day use fee.

Sportfishing

You can hire a *panga* (outboard launch) with skipper on the beach in front of several hotels, such as Los Arcos on Playa Los Muertos; the Buenaventura and Sheraton on Playa los Camarones; the Plaza Pelícanos, Las Palmas Resort, and Fiesta Americana Puerto Vallarta on Playa las Glorias; and NH Krystal on Playa de Oro. Expect to pay about $25/hour for a two- or three-hour trip that might net you and a few friends some jack, bonito, *toro,* or *dorado* for dinner. Ask your favorite local-style restaurant to fix you a fish banquet with your catch.

Another good spot for *panga* rentals is near the **Peines** (pay-EE-nays) docks, where the fishermen keep their boats. You may be able to negotiate a good price, especially if you or a friend speaks Spanish. Access to the Peines is along the dirt road to the left of the Isla Iguana entrance (just adjacent, south, at the fake roadside lighthouse a mile north of the Marina cruise ship terminal). The fishermen, a score or so members of the Cooperativa de Deportes Aquaticos Bahía de Banderas, have their boats lined up along the roadside channel to the left, a few hundred yards from the highway.

At the end-of-road dock complex (the actual Peines), behind the entrance gate lie the big-game sportfishing boats that you can reserve only through agents back in town or at the hotels. Agents, such as American Express, tel. 322/223-2910, 322/223-2927, or 322/223-2955, fax 322/223-2926, customarily book reservations during high season on the big 40-foot boats. They go out mornings at 7:30 and return about seven hours later with an average of one big fish per boat. The tariff runs around $100 per person; food and drinks are available but cost extra. Big boats generally have space for 10 passengers, about half of whom can fish at any one time. Most everyone usually gets something, if not a big sailfish or marlin.

Another agency that rents sportfishing boats is the **Sociedad Cooperativa Progreso Turístico,** which has 10 boats, ranging 32–40 feet. Rentals run $250–350 per day for a completely outfitted boat. For more information, drop by or call the office on the north end of the *malecón* at 31 de Octubre, across the street from the Hotel Rosita, tel. 322/222-1202. It's best to talk to the man-

ager, Apolinar Arce Palomeres, who is usually there Mon.–Sat. 8 A.M.–noon and 4–8 P.M.

A number of local English-speaking captains regularly take parties out on their well-equipped sportfishing boats. Alex Gómez, known as **Mr. Marlin,** record-holder of the biggest marlin catch in Puerto Vallarta, acts as agent for more than 40 experienced captains. Prices begin at about $480 per boat for a full day, including bait, ice, and fishing tackle. Call tel. 322/221-0809 at the Tennis Club Puesta del Sol (at the deli), local 16.

Alternatively, go **Fishing with Carolina** and Captain Juan, who offer sportfishing, whale-watching, and snorkeling expeditions on their fully equipped twin-engine diesel boat. For information and reservations, call Candace Caroline Shaw at tel. 322/224-7250, cellular tel. 01-044-322/292-2953, or email caroline@hotmail.com.

If you'd like to enter the Puerto Vallarta **Sailfish Tournament,** held annually in November (2005 marks the 50th), call Mr. Marlin (see above), tel. 322/221-0809, email inscription@pvfishtournament.com, or visit the website www.pvfishtournament.com. The registration fee runs about $600 per participant, which includes the welcome dinner and the closing awards dinner. The five grand prizes usually include automobiles. The biggest sailfish caught was a 168-pounder in 1957.

At their present rate of attrition, sailfish and marlin will someday certainly disappear from Puerto Vallarta waters. Some captains and participants have fortunately seen the light and are releasing the fish after they're hooked in accordance with IFGA (International Fish and Game Association) guidelines.

Freshwater bass fishing is also an option, at lovely foothill Cajón de Peñas Reservoir (see the Coast of Jalisco chapter), on your own or by **Viva Tours,** at tel. 322/224-0410 or 322/224-0826, fax 322/224-0182. For about $100 per person, you get all transportation, breakfast and lunch, fishing license, guide, and gear. The lake record is 13 pounds.

Boating

The superb 350-berth **Marina Vallarta** has all possible hookups, including certified potable water, metered 110–220-volt electricity, phone, fax, showers, toilets, laundry, dock lockers, trash collection, pump-out. Other amenities include 24-hour security, a yacht club, and complete repair yard. It is surrounded by luxurious condominiums, tennis courts, a golf course, and dozens of shops and offices. Slip rates run around $.75 per foot per day for 1–6 days, $.60 for 7–29 days, and $.50 for 30 or more days. For information, write the Marina at P.O. Box 350-B, Puerto Vallarta, Jalisco 48300, tel. 322/221-0275, fax 322/221-0722.

The Marina also has a **public boat-launching ramp** where you can float your craft into the Marina's sheltered waters for about $5. If the guard isn't available to open the gate, call the marina office, tel. 322/221-0275, for entry permission. To get to the launch ramp, follow the street marked "Proa," next to the big pink and white disco, one block south of the main Marina Vallarta entrance (below the monumental Neptune statue on the corner building).

Sporting Goods Stores

Given the sparse and pricey local sporting goods selection, serious sports enthusiasts should pack their own equipment to Puerto Vallarta. A few stores carry some items. Among the most reliable is **Deportes Gutiérrez Rizo,** corner of south-of-Cuale Av.s Insurgentes and A. Serdán, tel. 322/222-2595. Although fishing gear—rods, reels, line, sinkers—is its strong suit, it also stocks a general selection including sleeping bags, inflatable boats, tarps, pack frames, wet suits, scuba tanks, and water skis. Open Mon.–Sat. 9 A.M.–2 P.M. and 4–8 P.M.

SHOPPING

Although Puerto Vallarta residents make few folk crafts themselves, they import tons of good—and some very fine—pieces from the places where they *are* made. Furthermore, Puerto Vallarta's scenic beauty has become an inspiration for a growing community of artists and discerning collectors who have opened shops filled with locally crafted sculpture, painting, and museum-grade handicrafts gathered from all over Mexico.

Furthermore, resortwear needn't cost a bundle in Puerto Vallarta, where a number of small boutiques offer racks of stylish, comfortable Mexican-made items for a fraction of stateside prices.

South-of-Cuale Shopping

The couple of blocks of Av. Olas Altas and side streets around the Hotel Playa Los Arcos are alive with a welter of T-shirt and *artesanías* (crafts) stores loaded with the more common items—silver, onyx, papier-mâché, pottery—gathered from all over Mexico.

A few shops stand out, however. On Av. Olas Altas, a block north of Hotel Playa Los Arcos, find **Safari Accents,** at Olas Altas 224, tel. 322/223-2660. Inside, peruse a delightful trove of the baroque, including brilliant designer candles, angelic icons, bright metal-framed mirrors, a rainbow of glass lampshades, and gleaming candelabras.

For a different kind of excellence, head uphill along Badillo. After a block and a half, on the south side of the street, step into **Galería La Indígena,** tel./fax 322/222-3007, for a brilliant display of fine native ceremonial crafts. Here, you can appreciate bright Huichol yarn paintings and masks; Tarascan art from Ocumichu, Michoacán; Nahua painted coconut faces from Guerrero; a host of masks, both antique originals and new reproductions; pre-Columbian replicas; and Oaxaca fanciful wooden *alebrijes* animal figures. Open Mon.–Sat. 10 A.M.–3 P.M. and 7–9 P.M.; in winter, Mon.–Sat. 10 A.M.–9 P.M.

Continue uphill half a block to the corner of I. Vallarta to admire the eclectic collection of designer **Patti Gallardo,** 250 B. Badillo, tel./fax 322/222-5712 or 322/224-9658. Although Patti's creations extend from fine art and jewelry to clothing and metal sculptures, she's especially proud of her collection of colorfully designed, handmade carpets. Find her open Mon.–Sat. 10 A.M.–2 P.M. low season, and Mon.–Sat. 10 A.M.–6 P.M. high season.

Walk a few doors uphill and across the street to view the eclectic sculpture collection at Galería Dante, at 269 B. Badillo, tel. 322/222-2477, fax 322/222-6284, www.galleriadante.com. Exquisite wouldn't be too strong a description of the many museum-quality pieces, from neoclassic to abstract modern. Open Mon.–Sat. 10 A.M.–5 P.M.

Across the street, step into **Pirámide,** which specializes in fine Huichol pre-Columbian reproductions, open Mon.–Sat. 10 A.M.–2 P.M. and 6–9 P.M.

Next to Pirámide, look into **Viva,** the life project of designer Mary Sue Morris, at 274 B. Badillo, tel. 322/222-4078, open Mon.–Sat. 10 A.M.–10 P.M. Take your pick from dozens of distiguished designs, based on famous originals of such luminary Taxco silver-crafting families as Aguilar, Castillos, and Piñedas. For more examples, visit the website www.vivacollection.com.

Head north on Vallarta two blocks and take a look inside a pair of shops, **Talavera, Etc.,** and **San Miguel,** near the corner of Lázaro Cárdenas. As its name suggests, Talavera, Etc., displays a selection of Talavera-style pottery. The label comes from the town in Spain from which the potters, who eventually settled in Puebla, Mexico, emigrated. The style, a blend of Moorish, Chinese, and Mediterranean traditions, is sometimes called Majolica, from the island city of Majorca, an early center, where the tradition emerged and spread through the Mediterranean during the Middle Ages. San Miguel, on the other hand, specializes in fine glass as art—elegant vases, colorful lampshades, mirrors, and much more. Both stores are open Mon.–Sat. approximately 10 A.M.–2 P.M. and 4–7 P.M.

Continue north to **Santa María,** at I. Vallarta 226, for a display of shiny Taxco silver jewelry, and next door, to **Serendipity,** for a carefully selected all-Mexico handicrafts collection.

Walk half a block east (uphill) along Lázaro Cárdenas to **Olinalá Gallery,** 274 Lázaro Cárdenas, tel. 322/222-4995, originally created by Mexico lovers and collectors Nancy and John Erickson. Here, you can peruse the Ericksons' minimuseum of intriguing masks and fine lacquerware. Although their "Olinalá" name originated from the famed Mexican lacquerware village where they got most of their pieces, ceremonial and festival masks—devils, mermaids, goddesses, skulls, crocodiles, horses, and dozens more—now dominate their fascinating selection. (Now, although the Ericksons have retired,

personable new owners Brewster and Carmen Brockman continue the Ericksons' woodcrafts tradition in addition to exhibiting the work of noted local artists upstairs.) All offerings, moreover, are priced to sell; open Mon.–Sat. 10 A.M.–2 P.M. and 5–9 P.M.

Tucked away on a quiet residential street is **Mando de Azulelos,** at Carranza 374, a block uphill from Insurgentes, tel. 322/222-2675, fax 322/222-3292. It offers a treasury of made-on-site tile and Talavera-style pottery at reasonable prices. Unique, however, are the custom-made tiles—round, square, oval—inscribed and fired as you choose, with which you can adorn your home entryway or facade. Open Mon.–Fri. 9 A.M.–7 P.M., Sat. 9 A.M.–2 P.M. For more information, email info@talavera-tile.com or visit www.talvera-tile.com.

Shopping Along the River: Mercado Municipal and Pueblo Viejo

For more ordinary, yet attractive, Mexican handicrafts, head any day except Sunday (when most shops are closed) to the Mercado Municipal at the north end of the Av. Insurgentes bridge. Here, most shops begin with prices two to three times higher than the going rate. You should counter with a correspondingly low offer. If you don't get the price you want, always be prepared to find another seller. If your offer is fair, the shopkeeper will often give in as you begin to walk away. Theatrics, incidentally, are less than useful in bargaining, which should merely be a straightforward discussion of the merits, demerits, and price of the article in question.

The Mercado Municipal is a two-story warren of dozens upon dozens of shops filled with jewelry, leather, papier-mâché, T-shirts, and everything in between. The congestion can make the place hot; after a while, take a break at a cool river-view seat at one of the *fondas*—permanent food stalls on the second floor.

One of the most unusual Mercado Municipal stalls is **Cabaña del Tío Tom** (Uncle Tom's Cabin), whose menagerie of colorful papier-mâché parrots are priced a peg or two cheaper than at the tonier downtown stores.

It's time to leave when you're too tired to distinguish silver from tin and Tonalá from Tlaquepaque. Head downstream to the Pueblo Viejo complex on Calle Augustín Rodríguez between Juárez and Morelos, near the Av. I. Vallarta lower bridge. This mall, with individual stores rather than stalls, is less crowded but generally pricier than the Mercado Municipal. Some shopkeepers will turn their noses up if you try to bargain. If they persist, take your business elsewhere.

Downtown Shopping: Along Juárez and Morelos

A sizable fraction of Puerto Vallarta's best boutiques and arts and crafts stores lie along the six downtown blocks of Av. Juárez, beginning at the Río Cuale. The **Felix Boutique** heads the parade at Juárez 132, half a block north of the river. The friendly, outgoing owner offers reasonably priced women's resortwear of her own design. (Also find much of the same next door at María Bonita, Juárez 136.) Both open approximately Mon.–Sat. 11 A.M.–2 P.M. and 4–7:30 P.M.

Another block north, cross the west side of the street to **Galería Vallarta,** at Juárez 263, tel./fax 322/222-0290. Through the years, arts and crafts lovers Barbara Peters and her late husband, Jean, collected so many Mexican handicrafts that they had to find a place to store their finds. Galería Vallarta, a small museum of singular paintings, ceremonial masks, lampshades, art-to-wear, and more, is the result. Open Mon.–Sat. 10 A.M.–8 P.M., Sun. 10 A.M.–2 P.M.

A few doors farther up the street, the store of renowned **Sergio Bustamante** (who lives in Guadalajara), Juárez 275, tel. 322/222-1129, contains so many unique sculptures it's hard to understand how a single artist could be so prolific. (The answer: he has a factory-shop full of workers who execute his fanciful, sometimes unnerving, studies in juxtaposition.) Bustamante's more modest faces on eggs, anthropoid cats, and double-nosed clowns go for as little as $200; the largest, most flamboyant works sell for $10,000 or more. Open Mon.–Sat. 10 A.M.–9 P.M.

Back across the street, the government **Instituto de Arte Jaliscense** store, Juárez 284, tel. 322/222-1301, displays examples of nearly every

Jalisco folk craft, plus popular items from other parts, such as Oaxaca *alebrijes* (ahl-BREE-hays), fanciful wooden animals. Open daily, except Sun., 9 A.M.–9 P.M. Since it has a little bit of everything at relatively reasonable prices, this is a good spot for comparison shopping.

A few blocks farther on, at the corner of Galeana, an adjacent pair of stores, the **Querubines** (Cherubs) and **La Reja** (Grillwork), display their excellent traditional merchandise—riots of papier-mâché fruit, exquisite blue pottery vases, gleaming pewter, clay trees of life, rich Oaxaca and Chiapas textiles, shiny Tlaquepaque hand-painted pottery—so artfully they are simply fun to walk through. The stores are at Juárez 501A and 501B. Queribines, tel. 322/222-2988, is open Mon.–Sat. 9 A.M.–9 P.M.; La Reja, tel. 322/222-2272, is open Mon.–Sat. 10 A.M.–2 P.M. and 4–8 P.M., winter season 10 A.M.–6 P.M.

Half a block farther north, at 533 Juárez, you'll find the **Manuel Lepe** shop, tel. 322/222-0515, fax 322/222-5515, run by the family of the man who put Puerto Vallarta art on the map. His paintings and prints reflect his vision that "Puerto Vallarta is a Paradise," a sentiment to which Manuel Lepe's choirs of angels and little children still testify. Manuel Lepe was proclaimed "National Painter of Mexico" by President Echevarría not long before he died prematurely in 1982 at the age of 46. Find the shop open Mon.–Sat. 10 A.M.–3 P.M., 5–9 P.M., Sat. 10 A.M.–6 P.M. For more information, visit the website www.manuellepe.com.

Another half-block north, on the short block of Corona (downhill between Juárez and Morelos), are a number of interesting fine crafts stores. First is the ceramics gallery **Majolica,** 183 Corona, tel. 322/222-5118, which uses the older name from the Mediterranean island of Majorca, where the Talavera pottery style originated before migrating to Spain and Mexico. The personable owner/manager hand-selects the pieces, all of which come from the Puebla family workshops that carry on the Talavera tradition. Her prices reflect the high demand that the Talavera style of colorful classic elegance has commanded for generations. Open Mon.–Sat. 10 A.M.–2 P.M. and 4–9 P.M.

Downhill a few doors, **Arte Mágico Huichol**

displays an unusually fine collection of Huichol yarn paintings by renowned artists such as Mariano Valadéz, Hector Ortíz, and María Elena Acosta, at Corona 179, tel. 322/222-3077. Open Mon.–Sat. 10 A.M.–2 P.M. and 4–8 P.M.; winter season also open Sun. 10 A.M.–2 P.M.

Downhill, one door before the corner of Morelos, you'll find the unusual collection of **Casa de Fung Shui,** which specializes in the mysteriously quirky but glittering collectibles—onyx pyramids, geodes, blown glass spheres, glass crystals—of the trendy Chinese *feng shui* (fuhng shooway) vogue.

Step west, across Morelos, to **Galería Uno,** one of Puerto Vallarta's longest-established fine art galleries, at Morelos 561, tel. 322/222-0908, galeriauno@pvnet.com.mx. The collection—featuring internationally recognized artists with whom the gallery often schedules exhibition openings for the public—tends toward the large, the abstract, and the primitive. Open Mon.–Fri. 10 A.M.–8 P.M. and Sat. 10 A.M.–2 P.M.

For a similarly excellent collection, step one block north and around the uphill corner of Aldama, to **Galería Pacifico,** at Aldama 174 upstairs, tel./fax 322/222-1982 or 322/222-5502, gary@artmexico.com, www.artmexico.com. Here, in an airy upstairs showroom, personable owner Gary Thompson offers a fine collection of paintings, prints, and sculptures of Mexican artists, both renowned and up-and-coming. The mostly realistic works cover a gamut of styles and feelings, from colorful and sentimental to stark and satirical. Gary often hosts Friday meet-the-artist openings, where visitors are invited to socialize with the local artistic community. Open Mon.–Sat. 10 A.M.–2 P.M. and 5–9 P.M. Low-season hours may be shorter.

Finally, head a few blocks back south along Morelos to the **Regina Jewelry Factory** (Fábrica de Joyería Regina), at Morelos 434, on the *malecón,* tel. 322/222-2487, for just about the broadest selection and best prices in town. Charges for the seeming acres of gold, silver, and jeweled chains, bracelets, pendants, necklaces, and earrings are usually determined simply by weight; from a dollar per gram for silver. Open daily 10 A.M.–10 P.M.

One more unique store, outside the downtown area, is **Ric** jewelry, which displays the gleaming one-of-a-kind master works of silver artist Erika Hult de Corral. Find it in the Villas Vallarta Shopping Center, Km 2.5, Highway 200, local C-8, tel. 322/224-4598, directly across the interior street from the Hotel Canto del Sol.

Department and Warehouse Stores

Puerto Vallarta's best department stores are **Comercial Mexicana** and locally owned **Supermarket Gutiérrez Rizo.** Comercial Mexicana's Puerto Vallarta branch is at **Plaza Marina,** Km 6.5, Highway 200, just before the airport, beneath the McDonald's sign, tel. 322/221-0053 or 322/221-0490, open daily 7 A.M.–11 P.M. Gutiérrez Rizo is downtown, at Constitución and Vallarta, just south of the Río Cuale, tel. 322/222-0222. Open 365 days a year, 6:30 A.M.–10 P.M.

Warehouse stores **Wal-Mart** and **Sam's Club** have arrived in Puerto Vallarta. Find them on the inland side of the north-side cruise ship basin-dock, Terminal Maritima.

Supermarkets, Bakeries, Organic Groceries, and Produce

The king of national supermarket chains is **Comercial Mexicana,** Mexico's Kmart with groceries. The quality is generally good to excellent, and the prices match those in the United States and Canada. Comercial Mexicana's Puerto Vallarta branch is at **Plaza Marina,** Km 6.5, Hwy. 200, just before the airport, beneath the McDonald's sign, tel. 322/221-0053 or 322/221-0490, open daily 7 A.M.–11 P.M.

Both **Wal-Mart** and **Sam's Club** have arrived in Puerto Vallarta. Find them on the inland side of the cruise ship dock, Terminal Maritima.

Much closer to downtown is the big, locally owned **Supermarket Gutiérrez Rizo,** a remarkably well-organized dynamo of a general store at Constitución and Vallarta, just south of the Río Cuale, tel. 322/222-0222. Besides vegetables, groceries, film, socks, spermicide, and sofas, it stocks one of the largest racks of English-language magazines (some you'd be hard-pressed to find back home) outside of Mexico City. Open 365 days a year 6:30 A.M.–10 P.M.

Panadería Mungía is nearly worth the trip to Puerto Vallarta all by itself. The three branches are: downtown at Juárez and Mina; south-of-Cuale, corner Insurgentes and A. Serdán; and Francisca Rodríguez, uphill from Olas Altas, next to Hotel Alegre. Big, crisp cookies, flaky fruit tarts, hot fresh rolls, and cool cream cakes tempt the palates of visitors, locals, and resident foreigners alike. Open Mon.–Sat. 7 A.M.–9 P.M.

Rival **Panadería Los Chatos** offers an equally fine selection, also at two locations: downtown, at north-end Plaza Hidaldgo, Av. México 995; and in the Hotel Zone, across from the Hotel Sheraton, Fco. Villa 359, tel. 322/223-0485. Both are open Mon.–Sat. 7 A.M.–9 P.M.

South of Cuale, don't miss stopping by the charming neighborhood bakery, **Pays de Catalina** (Catalina's Pies), at 317 Basilio Badillo, north side, a few doors up the street from Casa de Los Hot Cakes. Here, the longtime owner-baker continues to put out a scrumptious menu of goods, from big, crunchy cookies and cinnamon rolls, to get-'em-while-they're-there croissants and crisp apple tarts. Find her open daily, 8 A.M.–10 P.M., tel. 322/223-2682.

South of Cuale, health food devotees have at least two choices: **La Panza Es Primero,** at Constitución 204, tel. 322/223-0090, open Mon.–Sat. 9 A.M.–9 P.M., and a competing store nearby, on Insurgentes, east side, near the corner of Badillo.

For organic produce go nearby to **Agro Gourmet,** at the south-of-Cuale corner of Basilio Badillo and Pino Suárez. Besides home-grown lettuces and other vegetables and herbs, it also offers a trove of hard-to-get cheeses, breads, ravioli, pesto, tahini, hummus, and much more.

Photofinishing, Cameras, and Film

Although a number of downtown stores do one-hour developing and printing at U.S. prices, **Foto Rey,** Libertad 330, tel. 322/222-0937 (and a second branch a few blocks away, at Morelos 490), is one of the few in town that develops and prints black and whites. Open Mon.–Sat. 9 A.M.–10 P.M., Sun. 9 A.M.–3 P.M.

Right across the street, **Laboratorios Vallarta,** Libertad 335, tel. 322/222-5070, stocks the most cameras, accessories, and film of any Vallarta store: lots of Fuji and Kodak color negative (print) film in many speeds and sizes plus transparency, professional 120 rolls, and black and white. Open Mon.–Sat. 9 A.M.–8 P.M. If this store doesn't have what you need, perhaps you'll find it at its second branch, around the corner at Morelos 101.

Cameras are an import item in Mexico and consequently very expensive. Even the simplest point-and-shoot cameras cost twice as much as in the United States or Canada. You're better to bring your own.

INFORMATION

Tourist Information Offices

Two tourist information offices serve Puerto Vallarta visitors. The downtown branch is on the central plaza, northeast corner (at Juárez) on the central plaza, customarily open Mon.–Fri. 8 A.M.–4 P.M., tel. 322/223-2500, ext. 230 or 232, fax ext. 233. The other tourist information office, tel. 322/221-2676, fax 322/221-2678, is in the Marina shopping plaza (marked by the big McDonald's sign), with about the same hours as the plaza branch. Both offices provide assistance, information, and dispense whatever maps, pamphlets, and copies of *Vallarta Today* and *Puerto Vallarta Lifestyles* they happen to have.

Another source of local information (in Spanish) is the Puerto Vallarta branch of the **Cámara Nacional de Comercio** (chamber of commerce), which publishes an excellent *Directorio Comercial Turístico,* a directory to everything you are likely to need in Puerto Vallarta. Find the chamber at Morelia 138, 2nd floor, tel. 322/224-2708, one block off the *libramiento* downtown bypass boulevard, four blocks from the airport highway, open Mon.–Fri. 9 A.M.–5 P.M.

Publications

New books in English are not particularly common in Puerto Vallarta. However, a number of small stores and stalls, such as the no-name **newsstand** at 420 Olas Altas, regularly sells newspapers, including Mexico City *News* and sometimes *USA Today* and the *Los Angeles Times.* Both are open daily until 9 or 10 P.M.

Supermercado Gutiérrez Rizo, just south of

the Río Cuale, corner Constitución and F. Madero, offers an excellent American magazine selection and some new paperback novels; open daily 6:30 A.M.–10 P.M. **Señor Book,** on upper Olas Altas, at Gómez, has perhaps the best English-language for-sale book collection in Puerto Vallarta.

Vallarta Today and *Vallarta Tribune,* an unusually informative tourist daily, are handed out free at the airport and travel agencies, restaurants, and hotels all over town. Besides detailed information on hotels, restaurants, and sports, both include a local events and meetings calendar and interesting historical, cultural, and personality feature articles. Call them if you can't find a copy: *Vallarta Today,* at tel. 322/225-3323, fax 322/224-1186, vallartatoday@yahoo.com; and *Vallarta Tribune,* at tel. 322/223-0585 or tel. 322/223-1302, pvtribune@hotmail.com.

Equally excellent is *Puerto Vallarta Lifestyles,* the quarterly English-language magazine, which also features unusually detailed and accurate town maps. Equally useful is its briefer sister publication *Vallarta Now.* If you cannot find a copy of either at the airport or your hotel, contact *Lifestyles* at tel. 322/221-0106, Mon.–Fri. 9 A.M.–7 P.M., or at Calle Timon #1, in the Marina.

The local **public library** (actually the "DIF" federally supported library) has a small general collection, including Spanish-language reference books and a dozen shelves of English-language paperbacks, at Parque Hidalgo, one block north of the end of the *malecón,* in front of the church. Open Mon.–Fri. 8 A.M.–8 P.M., Sat. 9 A.M.–5 P.M.

A second public library, established and operated by a volunteer committee, has accumulated a sizable English and Spanish book collection, at Francisco Villa 1001, in Colonia Los Mangos. Get there by taxi or car, several blocks along Villa, which diagonals northerly and inland past the sports field across the airport boulevard from the Hotel Sheraton. By bus, take the "Pitillal" and "biblioteca"-marked bus.

Spanish Instruction

The **University of Guadalajara Study Center for Foreigners** offers one-, two-, and four-week total immersion Spanish language instruction, including homestays with local families. For more information, visit the office, at Libertad 105 downtown or call tel. 322/223-2082, fax 322/223-2982, email cepv@prodigy.net.mx, or see the website www.cepe.udg.mx.

Volunteer Work

A number of local volunteer clubs and groups invite visitors to their meetings and activities. Check with the tourist information office or see the events calendar pages in *Vallarta Today* or *Vallarta Tribune.*

The **Club Internacional de la Amistad** (International Friendship Club), an all-volunteer service club, sponsors a number of health, educational, and cultural projects. It welcomes visitors to the (usually second Monday) monthly general membership meeting. For more information, see the events calendar section of *Vallarta Today,* or *Vallarta Tribune,* call tel. 322/222-5466, email ifcpv@prodigy.net.mx, or drop by the office, at Parian del Puente office complex, local 13, (above Banco Internacional, just north of the Río Cuale Av. Insurgentes (upper) bridge, open Mon.–Fri. 9:30 A.M.–1:30 P.M. Alternatively, you can write P.O. Box 604, Puerto Vallarta, Jalisco 48350.

The **Ecology Group of Vallarta,** a group of local citizens willing to work for a cleaner Puerto Vallarta, welcomes visitors to its activities and regular meetings. Call Ron Walker, tel. 322/222-0897, or email rc_walkermx@yahoo.com.mx, for more information.

The **Animal Protection Association** is working to humanely reduce the number of stray and abandoned animals on Puerto Vallarta streets. For more information, see the events calendar sections of the *Vallarta Today* and *Vallarta Tribune* newspapers.

SERVICES

Money Exchange

Banking has come to the Olas Altas district, with the branch of **Banorte,** on Av. Olas Altas, beach side, between B. Badillo and Carranza. Hours are Mon.–Fri. 9 A.M.–4 P.M. and Sat. 10 A.M.–2 P.M. After hours, use its ATM.

Additionally, you can use the Banco Internacional (Bital) ATM on upper Olas Altas, corner of Rodríguez, two blocks south of Hotel Playa Los Arcos.

Most **downtown banks** cluster along Juárez, near the plaza. Avoid long lines by using your card in their 24-hour ATMs for cash. One exception is **Banco International**, just north of the Insurgentes bridge, and open the longest hours of all, Mon.–Sat. 8 A.M.–7 P.M.

The **National Bank of Mexico** (Banamex), at the southeast corner of the town plaza, tel. 322/222-5377 or 322/222-1998, changes U.S. and Canadian cash and traveler's checks at the best rates in town. Money exchange hours (go to the special booth at 176 Zaragoza, left of the bank main entrance) are approximately Mon.–Fri. 9 A.M.–4 P.M., Sat. 10 A.M.–2 P.M.

If the lines at Banamex are too long, try **Banco Inverlat,** on Juárez, half a block north, tel. 322/223-1224, money exchange hours approximately Mon.–Fri. 9 A.M.–5 P.M., Sat. 9 A.M.–1 P.M., or **Bancomer,** half a block farther north, approximately the same hours.

Additionally, scores of little *casas de cambio* (exchange booths) dot the cobbled old town streets, especially along the *malecón* downtown, and along Av. Olas Altas and Insurgentes south of the Río Cuale. Although they generally offer about $2 per $100 less than the banks, they compensate with long hours, often daily 9 A.M.–9 P.M. In the big hotels, cashiers will generally exchange your money at rates comparable to the downtown exchange booths.

The local **American Express** agency cashes American Express traveler's checks and offers full member travel services, such as personal-check cashing (up to $1,000, every 21 days; bring your checkbook, your ID or passport, and your American Express card). The office is downtown, at Morelos 160, corner of Abasolo, tel./fax 322/223-2927, 322/223-2955, 322/223-29101, or 322/223-2926, one block inland from the Hard Rock Cafe. Business hours are Mon.–Fri. 9 A.M.–6 P.M., Sat. 9 A.M.–1 P.M.

Communications

Puerto Vallarta has a number of branch post of-fices. The main *correo* is downtown, two blocks north of the central plaza, just off Juárez, at Mina 188, tel. 322/222-1888, open Mon.–Fri. 8 A.M.–3 P.M., Sat. 9 A.M.–1 P.M. The branch at the Edificio Maritima (Maritime Building), near the cruise liner dock, is open Mon.–Fri. 8 A.M.–3 P.M., Sat. 9 A.M.–1 P.M., tel. 322/224-7219. The airport has lost its post office branch; deposit postcards and letters in the airport mailbox *(buzón.)*

Secure express mail, telegraph, fax, telex, and money orders *(giros)* are available at the **Mexpost** office, 584 Juárez, four blocks north of the central plaza, tel. 322/223-1360; open Mon.–Fri. 9 A.M.–6 P.M., Sat. 9 A.M.–1 P.M.

The cheapest and often most convenient telephone option is to buy a public phone card (*tarjeta de teléfono*: say tar-HAY-tah day tay-LAY-foh-noh) and use it at street telephones. They're widely available at stores, in denominations of 30, 50, and 100 pesos. Telephone card calling rates to the United States and Canada are much cheaper than AT&T and Sprint. Lacking a telephone card, call from your hotel. Lacking a hotel (or if you don't like its extra charges), go to one of the many *casetas de larga distancia,* long-distance telephone offices, sprinkled all over town.

Puerto Vallarta has a flock of public **Internet** stores. However, they change as often as the Puerto Vallarta breeze. At this writing, I saw many, mostly concentrated downtown: several south of the Río Cuale, along Av. Olas Altas and several more, north of the Río Cuale along Juárez. Ask your hotel desk clerk for the closest.

Health, Police, and Emergencies

If you need medical advice, ask your hotel desk for assistance, or go to one of Puerto Vallarta's several good small hospital-clinics. One of the most respected is the **CMQ** (Centro Médico Quirúrgico) south of the Río Cuale at 366 Basilio Badillo, between Insurgentes and Aguacate, tel. 322/223-1919 (ground floor) or 322/223-0011 (second floor).

Right around the corner on Insurgentes, across from the gas station, is the bilingual-staffed **Hospital Medasist,** at M. M. Dieguez 358, tel./fax 322/223-0444. The hospital (which has advertised that it accepts major medical insurance), with emergency room, lab, diagnostic equipment, and a staff of specialists, appears to be another good place to go when you're sick.

If you must have an English-speaking doctor, **IAMAT** (International Association for Medical Assistance to Travelers) has U.S.-trained Alfonso Rodríguez L., M.D., at north downtown Lucerna 148, Colonia Versalles, tel. 322/293-1919, Mon.–Fri. 10 A.M.–2 P.M. and 5–8 P.M.

The hottest new high-tech hospital in the whole state of Jalisco is **Ameri+Med Hospital,** in the Marina, Plaza Neptuno, tel. 322/221-0023 or 322/221-0024. I have heard no testimonials, good nor bad, about its services. It advertises that all U.S. medical insurance is accepted. For details, check it out on website www.amerimed.com.mx.

For round-the-clock prescription service, call one of the five branches of **Farmacia CMQ;** for example, south of Cuale, at B. Badillo 367, tel. 322/222-1330 or 322/222-2941, or on the north side, at Peru 1146, tel. 322/222-1110.

A legion of loyal customers swears by the diagnostic competence of Federico López Casco, of **Farmacia Olas Altas,** Av. Olas Altas 365, two blocks south of Hotel Playa Los Arcos, tel. 322/222-2374, whom they simply know as "Freddy." Although a pharmacist and not a physician, his fans say he is a wizard at recommending remedies for their aches and pains.

For **police** emergencies, call the emergency number, 06. In case of **fire**, call the *bomberos* (fire department), at tel. 322/222-2551.

Immigration, Customs, and Consulates

If you need an extension to your tourist card, you can get a total of 180 days at the local branch of **Instituto Nacional de Migración.** Present your existing tourist card at the office, on the maritime terminal entrance road (cruise ship dock), next to the Pemex gas station, at street number 2755 (upstairs), tel. 322/224-7719, 322/224-7653, or 322/224-7970, open Mon.–Fri. 9 A.M.–4 P.M. (or longer hours, at the airport.)

If you lose your tourist card, go to Migración with your passport or identification, and some

proof of the day you arrived in Mexico, such as a copy of the original permit or your airplane ticket.

The small local **United States Consular Office** issues passports and does other essential legal work for U.S. citizens at Zaragoza 160, room 18, 1st floor, adjacent to the town plaza, south side, open Mon.–Fri. 10 A.M.–2 P.M. (except closed every third Wednesday). Write P.O. Box 395, Puerto Vallarta, Jalisco 48300, or call tel./fax 322/222-0069 or 322/223-0074. In an emergency after hours, call the U.S. Consul General in Guadalajara, tel. 33/3826-5553.

The **Canadian honorary consul,** tel. 322/222-5398 or 322/223-0858, fax 322/222-3517, provides similar services for Canadian citizens Mon.–Fri. 9 A.M.–4 P.M., at the same plaza-front address, room 10, 1st floor. In an emergency, after hours call the Canadian Embassy in Mexico City at toll-free Mex. tel. 800/706-2900.

Arts and Music Courses

The private, volunteer **Centro Cultural Vallartense** periodically sponsors theater, modern dance, painting, sculpture, aerobics, martial arts, and other courses for adults and children. From time to time it stages exhibition openings for local artists, whose works it regularly exhibits at the gallery/information center at Plaza del Arte on Isla Río Cuale. For more information, look for announcements in the events pages of *Vallarta Today* or the *Vallarta Tribune,* or drop by and talk to the volunteer in charge at the Plaza del Arte gallery and information center, at the upstream end of Isla Río Cuale (see Sights).

Sharing the Plaza de Arte is the round **Escuela Municipal de Música** building, where, late weekday afternoons, you may hear the strains of students practicing the violin, guitar, piano, flute, and pre-Columbian instruments. Such lessons are open to the general public; apply in person during the late afternoon or early evening.

Trying harder is the private **Instituto de Arte,** which offers classes in painting (watercolor, oil, acrylic) and printmaking. For more information, contact Cherie at tel. 322/222-1866, or cellular tel. 01-044-322/294-5915, stop by south-of-Cuale

Aquiles Serdán 369, or visit the website www.artin-stitutevallarta.com.

GETTING THERE AND AWAY

By Air

Several major carriers connect Puerto Vallarta by direct flights with United States and Mexican destinations.

Mexicana Airlines flights connect daily with Chicago, Mexico City, and Guadalajara. In Puerto Vallarta, call for reservations, tel. 322/221-1266 or toll-free Mex. tel. 800/366-5400, for airport flight information, tel. 322/221-1138.

Aeroméxico flights connect daily with Los Angeles, Tijuana, Guadalajara, Acapulco, León, Monterrey, and Mexico City; for reservations and flight information, call tel. 322/224-2777.

Alaska Airlines flights connect with Los Angeles, San Francisco, San Jose, Portland, Seattle, and Anchorage; for reservations, call a local travel agent or, from Puerto Vallarta, call toll-free U.S. tel. 800/426-0333; for arrival and departure information, call the airport, tel. 322/221-2610.

American Airlines flights connect with Dallas-Ft. Worth and Chicago; call tel. 322/221-1799 or 322/221-1927, toll-free Mex. tel. 800/362-7000 for reservations and information.

Continental Airlines flights connect daily with Houston; call tel. 322/221-1025, toll-free Mex. tel. 800/900-5000 for reservations.

America West Airlines flights connect with Phoenix; for reservations and information, call a travel agent, such as American Express, tel. 322/223-2910, or America West at toll-free U.S. tel. 800/235-9292 (reachable also from Mexico).

Aerocalifornia Airlines connects with Los Angeles and Mexico City. For reservations, call a travel agent, such as American Express, tel. 322/223-2910 or 322/223-2955.

Canada 3000 charter flights connect with Toronto, Winnipeg, Saskatoon, Regina, Calgary-Edmonton, and Vancouver (mostly during the winter); for information, call a travel agent, such as American Express, tel. 322/223-2910 or 322/223-2955.

Puerto Vallarta Airport Arrival and Departure

Air arrival at Puerto Vallarta (code-designated PVR, officially the Gustavo Díaz Ordaz International) Airport is generally smooth and simple. After the cursory (if any) customs check, arrivees can avail themselves of a long-hours **24-hour ATM** and a Banco Internacional (Bital) **money-exchange counter,** open Mon.–Fri. 8 A.M.–8 P.M., Sat. 8 A.M.–3 P.M.

A lineup of **car rental booths** includes Advantage, tel. 322/221-1499, advantagepvr@prodigy .net.mx; Alamo, tel. 322/221-3030; Avis, 322/221-1112 or 322/221-3150; Budget, toll-free Mex. tel. 800/700-1700, reservaciones@bud-get.com.mx; Dollar, tel. 322/223-1354, dollarpvr@prodigy.net.mx; Hertz, tel. 322/221-1413; National, tel. 322/221-1226 or 322/209-0352, natpvr@pvnet.com.mx; and Thrifty, toll-free Mex. tel. 800/021-2277.

Transportation to town is easiest by *colectivo* (collective taxi-vans) or *taxi especial* (individual taxi). Booths sell tickets at curbside. The *colectivo* fare runs about $4 per person to the northern hotel zone, $5 to the center of town, and $7 or more to hotels and hamlets south of town. Individual taxis (for up to four passengers) run about $20, $26, and $30 for the same rides.

Taxis to more distant northern destinations, such as Rincón de Guayabitos (39 miles, 62 km) and San Blas or Tepic (100 miles, 160 km), run about $80 and $120, respectively. A much cheaper alternative is to hire a taxi (no more than $3) from the airport to the new bus terminal a mile north of the airport, where you can continue by very frequent **Transportes Pacifico** northbound second-class bus. The Bucerías bus fare should run less than $2, Sayulita $4, Guayabitos about $5, and Tepic or San Blas $7 (for San Blas, go by Transportes Norte de Sonora direct or Transportes del Pacifico second-class and transfer at Las Varas). The buses are usually crowded; don't tempt people with a dangling open purse or a bulging wallet in your pocket.

Airport departure is as simple as arrival. Save by sharing a taxi with departing fellow hotel guests. Agree on the fare with the driver before you get in. If the driver seems too greedy (see airport arrival fares above), hail another taxi. Once at the airport, you can do last-minute shopping at a number of airport shops, or mail a letter at the airport *buzón* (mailbox).

If you've lost your tourist card, arrive early and be prepared with a copy or you may have to pay a fine unless you've gotten a duplicate through Immigration (Migración; see Immigration, Customs, and Consulates). In any case, be sure to save enough pesos or dollars to pay your **$12 departure tax** (unless your ticket already includes it).

By Car or RV

Three road routes connect Puerto Vallarta north with Tepic and San Blas, east with Guadalajara, and south via Melaque-Barra de Navidad with Manzanillo.

To Tepic, **Mexican National Highway 200** is all asphalt and in good condition most of its 104 miles (167 km) from Puerto Vallarta. Traffic is ordinarily light to moderate, except for some slow going around Tepic, and over a few low passes about 20 miles north of Puerto Vallarta. Allow three hours for the southbound trip and half an hour longer in the reverse direction for the winding 3,000-foot climb to Tepic.

A shortcut connects San Blas directly with Puerto Vallarta, avoiding the oft-congested uphill route through Tepic. Heading north on Highway 200, at Las Varas turn off west on to Nayarit Highway 161 to Zacualpan and Platanitos, where the road continues through the coastal tropical forest to Santa Cruz village on the Bay of Matanchén. From there you can continue along the shoreline to San Blas. In the opposite direction, heading south from San Blas, follow the signed "Puerto Vallarta" turnoff to the right (south) a few hundred yards after the Santa Cruz de Miramar junction. Allow about three hours, either direction, for the entire San Blas-Puerto Vallarta trip.

The story is similar for Mexican National Highway 200 along the 172 miles (276 km) to Manzanillo via Barra de Navidad (134 miles, 214 km). Trucks and a few potholes may cause slow going while climbing the 2,400-foot Sierra Cuale summit south of Puerto Vallarta, but light traffic should prevail along the other stretches. Allow about four hours to Manzanillo, three from Barra de Navidad, and the same in the opposite direction.

The Guadalajara route is a bit more complicated. From Puerto Vallarta, follow Highway 200 as if to Tepic, but, just before Compostela (80 miles, 129 km from Puerto Vallarta) follow the 22-mile (36-km) Guadalajara-bound toll *(cuota)* shortcut east, via Chapalilla. From Chapalilla, continue east via **Mexican National Highway 15 D** toll *(cuota)* expressway *autopista*. Although expensive (about $20 per car, much more for motor homes) the expressway is a breeze, compared to the old, narrow, and congested *libre* Highway 15. Allow around five hours at the wheel for the entire 214-mile (344-km) Guadalajara-Puerto Vallarta trip, either way. (Seven hours by the old *libre route*.)

By Bus

Many bus lines run through Puerto Vallarta. The major long-distance bus action is at the new **Camionera Central** (Central Bus Station) a few miles north of the airport. Reservations and ticketing are efficiently computerized, and the major lines accept credit cards.

The shiny, air-conditioned complex resembles an airline terminal, with a cafeteria, juice bars, a travel agency, a long-distance telephone and fax service, luggage storage lockers, a gift shop, and a hotel reservation booth.

Mostly first- and luxury-class departure ticket counters line one long wall. First-class **Elite** (EL) line and its parent **Estrella Blanca** (EB), with its affiliated lines Turistar (TUR), Futura (FU), Transportes Norte de Sonora (TNS) and Transportes Chihuahenses (TC), tel. 322/221-0848 or 322/290-1001, connect the entire northwest-southeast Pacific Coast corridor. Northwesterly destinations include La Peñita (Rincón de Guayabitos), Tepic, San Blas, Mazatlán, all the way to Nogales or Mexicali and Tijuana on the U.S. border. Other departures head north, via Tepic, Torreón, and Chihuahua to Ciudad Juárez, at the U.S. border. Still others connect northeast, via Guadalajara, Aguascalientes, Zacatecas, and Saltillo, with Monterrey, where quick connections are available with east Texas border points of Nuevo Laredo and Matamoros. In the opposite direction, departures connect with the entire southeast Pacific Coast, including Melaque-Barra de Navidad, Manzanillo, Playa Azul, Lázaro Cárdenas, Ixtapa-Zihuatanejo, and Acapulco (where you can transfer to Oaxaca-bound departures.) Additionally **Transportes Norte de Sonora** (TNS) departures connect north with San Blas via the coastal (Tepic bypass) shortcut.

Transportes Pacífico, tel. 322/290-1008, offers first-class departures that also travel the northwest Pacific route, via Tepic and Mazatlán to Nogales, Mexicali, and Tijuana. Transportes Pacifico provides additional first-class connections, east with Guadalajara and Mexico City direct, and others to Guadalajara by expressway shorcut *(corta)*.

Transportes Pacifico also provides very frequent second-class daytime connections, north with Tepic, stopping everywhere, notably, Bucerías, Sayulita, Guayabitos, La Peñita, Las Varas, and Compostela en route.

Affiliated lines **Autocamiones del Pacífico** and **Transportes Cihuatlán,** tel. 322/221-0994, provide many second-class and some first-class departures along the Jalisco coast. Frequent second-class connections stop at El Tuito,

Tomatlán, El Super, Careyes, Melaque, Barra de Navidad, and everywhere in between. They also connect with Guadalajara by the long southern route, via Melaque, Autlán, and San Clemente (a jumping-off point for interesting mountain hamlets of Talpa, Mascota, and San Sebastián). Primera Plus, its luxury-class line, provides a few daily express connections southeast with Manzanillo, with stops at Melaque and Barra de Navidad.

A separate luxury-class service, a subsidiary of Flecha Amarilla, also called **Primera Plus,** tel. 322/290-0716, also provides express connections, southeast, with Melaque, Barra de Navidad, Manzanillo, and Colima. Other such Primera Plus departures connect east with Guadalajara, continuing to Aguascalientes, Irapuato, Celaya, Querétaro, and León. Affiliated line **Autobuses Costa Alegre** provides frequent second-class connections southeast along the Jalisco coast, via El Tuito, El Super, Careyes, Melaque, Barra de Navidad, and all points in between.

Additionally, **ETN (Enlaces Transportes Nacional),** tel. 322/290-0996 or 322/290-0997, provides first-class departures connecting east with Guadalajara and Mexico City, offering continuing connections in Guadalajara with several Michoacán destinations.

Around the Bay of Banderas

As a destination city, Puerto Vallarta is packed with all the services, food, and accommodations a quality resort can supply. What Puerto Vallarta often cannot offer, however, is peace and quiet.

But an out exists. The diadem of rustic retreats—fishing villages, palm-shadowed sandy beaches, diminutive resorts—that ring the Bay of Banderas can provide a day-, week-, or month-long respite from the citified tourist rush.

The Southern Arc — Mismaloya

The southern-arc beach gems of Mismaloya, Boca de Tomatlán, Las Animas, Quimixto, and Yelapa are described in the Puerto Vallarta section under Beaches.

The Northern Arc — Nuevo Vallarta, Bucerías, and Punta Mita

The northern curve of the Bay of Banderas begins as Highway 200 crosses the Ameca River and enters the state of Nayarit. Here clocks shift from central to mountain time; heading north, set your watch back one hour. Just after you cross over the bridge, you might want to stop at the **Nayarit tourist information office,** tel./fax 329/297-0018, which (if it's open) supplies several excellent brochures of Nayarit's interesting but mostly untouristed destinations.

NUEVO VALLARTA

The Nuevo Vallarta development, just north of the river, is Nayarit's design for a grand resort, comparable to the Zona Hotelera 10 miles south. For years, however, miles of boulevard parkways dotted with streetlights and empty cul-de-sacs remained deserted, waiting for homes, condos, and hotels that were never built. The spurt of activity that began in the early mid-1990s has continued until Nuevo Vallarta now has a green golf course, a marina, a flock of luxurious new homes, and a dozen-odd beachfront resort hotels. Much remains undeveloped at this writing, however. At some spots, construction continues, with the associated noise and dust competing with the swish of the waves on Nuevo Vallarta's creamy beachfront.

Nevertheless, the **Club de Playa Nuevo Vallarta,** the core of the original development, finished for years, is indeed a pretty place—perfect for a relaxing beach afternoon. Get there by turning left at Av. Nuevo Vallarta about five miles (eight km) north of the airport at the Nuevo Vallarta signed monument (beach side of highway), one mile past the north end of the Ameca bridge. At the end of the 1.4-mile driveway entrance you will come to the Club de Playa, with a parking lot, small regional art and artifacts museum, pool, snack bar, and seemingly endless beach.

The miles-long beach is the main attraction. The nearly level golden white sand is perfect for beachcombing, and the water is excellent for surf fishing, swimming, bodysurfing, and boogie boarding. Beginning or intermediate surfing might be possible for those who bring their own boards. You may still be able to enjoy isolated beach camping during the temperate winter on the seemingly endless dune past the north end beach boulevard of Paseo Cocoteros. Bring everything, including water and a tarp for shade.

Accommodations

Adjacent to the Club de Playa is the palmy, Mediterranean-style, French-Canadian–owned twin development, with its older section (formerly the Club Oasis Marival, now the **Suites Marival** beside the new, shinier **Grand Marival,** which sometimes invites the public to drop in on its continuous party, which includes sports, crafts, games, and food and drink for about $50 per person, per day. If you take a room in the Grand Marival, the all-inclusive food, lodging, and activities run about $140 per day for two in low season, $260 high. The Club section, being a half a block from the beach, is cheaper by about $20 per person. Make reservations (ask for a discount) through an agent or at the hotel, Blvd. Nuevo Vallarta, esq. Paseo Cocoteros, Nuevo Vallarta, Nayarit 63573, or through its

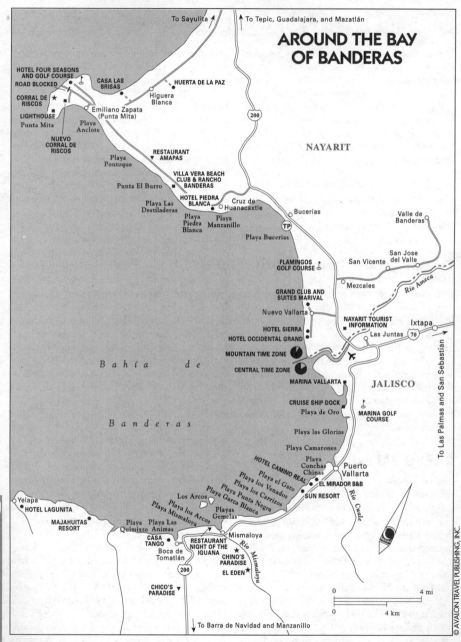

AROUND THE BAY OF BANDERAS

To Sayulita

To Tepic, Guadalajara, and Mazatlán

HOTEL FOUR SEASONS AND GOLF COURSE
ROAD BLOCKED
CASA LAS BRISAS
HUERTA DE LA PAZ
Higuera Blanca
CORRAL DE RISCOS ★
LIGHTHOUSE
Punta Mita
Emiliano Zapata (Punta Mita)
Playa Anclote
NUEVO CORRAL DE RISCOS

NAYARIT

200

Playa Pontoque
RESTAURANT AMAPAS
VILLA VERA BEACH CLUB & RANCHO BANDERAS
Punta El Burro
HOTEL PIEDRA BLANCA
Cruz de Huanacaxtle
Playa Las Destiladeras
Playa Piedra Blanca
Playa Manzanillo
Bucerias
Valle de Banderas
Playa Bucerias
TP

FLAMINGOS GOLF COURSE
San Vicente
San Jose del Valle
Mezcales
Río Ameca

GRAND CLUB AND SUITES MARIVAL
Nuevo Vallarta
NAYARIT TOURIST INFORMATION
Ixtapa
HOTEL SIERRA
Las Juntas
70
HOTEL OCCIDENTAL GRAND
MOUNTAIN TIME ZONE
CENTRAL TIME ZONE
MARINA VALLARTA
JALISCO

Bahía de

Banderas

CRUISE SHIP DOCK
Playa de Oro
MARINA GOLF COURSE
Playa las Glorias
Playa Camarones
Playa Conchas Chinas
HOTEL CAMINO REAL
Playa el Gato
Playa los Venados
Playa los Carrizos
EL MIRADOR B&B
Puerto Vallarta
SUN RESORT
Playa Punta Negra
Playa Garza Blanca
Los Arcos
Playa los Arcos
Playas Gemelas
Río Cuale

Yelapa
HOTEL LAGUNITA
MAJAHUITAS RESORT
Playa Quimixto
Playa Las Animas
Playa Mismaloya
CASA TANGO
Boca de Tomatlán
RESTAURANT NIGHT OF THE IGUANA
Mismaloya
Río Mismaloya
CHINO'S PARADISE
EL EDEN ★
200
CHICO'S PARADISE ▼

To Las Palmas and San Sebastian

To Barra de Navidad and Manzanillo

0   4 mi
0   4 km

© AVALON TRAVEL PUBLISHING, INC.

local booking number, tel. 322/297-0100, or toll-free Mex. tel. 800/326-6600, fax 322/297-0160, email ventas@clubmarival.com, or the website www.cameleonmarival.com.

Along the beach boulevard, about two miles south of the original development, a line of big new hotels woo vacationers with a plethora of facilities and long, velvety beaches. The 344-room **Hotel Sierra Nuevo Vallarta** seems to be one of the most successful, Paseo de Cocoteros 19, Nuevo Vallarta, Nayarit 63732, tel. 322/297-1300, fax 322/297-0266. Arriving at the Sierra feels like approaching a small, Elysian planet. You drive for miles, finally pulling up to a huge, apparently deserted structure, where, inside, to your surprise, droves of relaxed, well-fed tourists are socializing in half a dozen languages. Above the reception area rises a towering, angular atrium. Nearby, a garden of lovely ceramic fruits decorates whitewashed stairs leading down to a buffet loaded with salads, fruit, poultry, fish, meats, and desserts spread on one side of an airy, guest-filled dining area. Outside are pools beneath palm trees along the beach, where crowds enjoy nightly dancing and shows. By day, guests lounge, swim, and frolic amid a varied menu of activities, from water aerobics and yoga to beach volleyball, bicycling, and kayaking.

Rates include all food, drinks, activities, and a deluxe ocean-view room with everything. For walk-in guests, prices begin at about $200 s, $250 d low season, about $240 and $300 high. Children under seven stay free; add $34 tariff for kids 7–12, and those over 12 are considered adults. If the season is right, a travel agent may be able to secure a reduced-rate package. For information and reservations, call toll-free U.S./Can. tel. 800/515-4321 or 800/544-4686, email info@mtmcorp.com, or see the website www.hsnvr1@sidek.com.

Next door the **Occidental Grand Nuevo Vallarta** (formerly the Allegro Resort), Paseo de los Cocoteros 18, Nuevo Vallarta, Nayarit 63732, tel. 322/297-0400, fax 322/297-0626, offers a similar all-inclusive vacation package for about $170 s, $226 d low season, $230 and $275 high. Children under seven free, 7–12, $53 low, $70 high. Day passes, including all in-house, food, drinks, sports and entertainment, run about $35 per adult; night about $40. Bargain packages are usually available by reservation or through agents during nonpeak seasons.

BUCERÍAS

The scruffy roadside clutter of Bucerías (Place of the Divers) is deceiving. Situated 12 miles (19 km) north of the Puerto Vallarta airport, Bucerías (pop. 5,000) has the longest, creamiest beach on the Bay of Banderas. Local people flock there on Sunday for beach play, as well as for fresh seafood from one of several beachfront *palapa* restaurants (which, however, may be mostly closed weekdays).

For arrivees seeking at least a quiet week in the sun or at most, a relaxing retirement, Bucerías offers a number of excellent options. It has developed continuously from a country town of four long streets running for three miles parallel to the beach. The town features small businesses and grocery stores and a sprinkling of local-style restaurants. Bucerías furthermore has lots of old-fashioned local color, especially in the evenings around the lively market at the south end of the business district.

Now, however, the wealth brought in by the growing resident expatriate colony supports several excellent restaurants and many good lodgings, from moderate hotel rooms to luxurious beachfront villas.

The beach—seemingly endless and nearly flat, with slowly breaking waves and soft, golden-white sand—offers swimming, bodysurfing, boogie boarding, beginning and intermediate surfing, and surf fishing. Tent camping is customary beyond the edges of town, especially during the Christmas and Easter holidays.

Accommodations

At the town's serene north end is the Playas de Huanacaxtle subdivision, with big flower-decorated homes owned by rich Mexicans and North Americans. Sprinkled among the intimate, palm-shaded *retornos* (cul-de-sacs) are a number of good bungalow-style beachside lodgings. As you move southward from the north edge of town, the top accommodations begin with the **Condo-Hotel Vista Vallarta,** at Av. de los Picos s/n,

Playas de Huanacaxtle, Bucerías, Nayarit 63732, tel. 329/298-0361 or 329/298-0360. Here, three stories of stucco and tile apartments cluster intimately around a palm-tufted beachside pool and patio. A loyal cadre of longtime guests—mostly U.S. and Canadian retiree-couples—return year after year to enjoy the big blue pool, the *palapa* restaurant, walks along the beach, and the company of fellow vacationers. All enjoy fully furnished two-bedroom suites with dining room, kitchenette, living room, cable TV, and private ocean-view balconies. Maids clean rooms daily, while downstairs, friendly, English-speaking clerks manage the desk and rent cars, boogie boards, and surfboards. High-season rates, for up to six people per suite, run $98/nightly, $75/night monthly; bargain for a big discount (to as little as $50 per night) during the summer-fall low season, when the place is nearly empty. For more information, email vistavallarta@prodigy.net.mx or visit the website www.vistavallarta.com.

A block south, the family-style **Bungalows Princess** looks out on the blue Bay of Banderas beneath the rustling fronds of lazy coco palms. The two-story, detached beachfront bungalows provide all the ingredients for a restful vacation for a family or group of friends. Behind the bungalows, past the swimming pools a stone's throw from the beach, a motel-style lineup of suites fills the economy needs of couples and small families. Reserve in writing or by phone at Retorno Destiladeras, Playas Huanacaxtle, Bucerías, Nayarit 63732, tel. 329/298-0100 or 329/298-0110, fax 329/298-0068. It has a total of 36 bungalows and suites. The big semideluxe bungalows (ask for a beachfront unit) rent, high season, for about $150 d; off-beach suites, about $95 d. Bargain for discounts and long-term rates, especially during low Jan.–Feb., May–June, and Sept.–Nov. months. All rooms feature TV with HBO, phone, and a/c; hotel amenities include desk service, a minimarket and two pools, and credit cards are accepted. For more information, email bungalowsprincess@prodigy.net.mx or visit the website www.bungalowsprincess.com.

Continuing south, nearby **Bungalows Pico,** Av. Los Pico and Retorno Pontoque, Playas Huanacaxtle, Bucerías, Nayarit 63732, tel. 329/298-0470, fax 329/298-0131, shares the same palm-shadowed Bucerías beachfront. A rambling, Mexican family-style complex, Bungalows Pico clusters around a big inner pool/patio, spreading to a second motel-style bungalow tier beside a breezy beachside pool area. These units, which enjoy ocean views, are the most popular. During low season, the management offers such promotions as three nights for the price of two; discounts for long-term rentals are usually available. Bargain under all conditions. The beachfront, three-bedroom kitchenette bungalows for up to eight rent from about $115; two-bedroom poolside kitchenette apartments for six cost $85. Adjacent smaller, four-person kitchenette suites run $70. Smaller nonkitchenette studios go for about $40. Corresponding low-season rates run about $80, $70, $60, and $25, with TV, a/c, snack restaurant, and two pools; credit cards are accepted. For more information and reservations, email lospicos@lospicos.com.mx or visit the website www.lospicos.com.mx.

About a mile away, on the opposite, or south, side of town, right across the street from the Bucerías trailer park, stands popular **Bungalows Arroyo,** at 500 Lázaro Cárdenas, Bucerías, Nayarit 63732, tel. 329/298-0288, fax 329/298-0076. The dozen-odd roomy, two-bedroom apartments are clustered beside a verdant, palmy pool and garden half a block from the beach. The units are comfortably furnished, each with king-sized beds, private balcony, kitchen, and living and dining room. Units rent for about $85 a day low season, $100 high, with discounts available for monthly rentals. They're popular; get your winter reservations in months early.

Nearby, consider the inviting, moderately priced **Hotel Villa Serena,** sharing the same quiet, plumy beach neighborhood, at 35 Lázaro Cárdenas, Bucerías, Nayarit 63732, tel. 329/298-1288. Here you have all the basics for a cozy tropical beach vacation: about a dozen comfortable (if some slightly dark) rooms, some with with king-sized beds, built around a tranquil, tropical pool-patio, just a block from the beach, with several excellent nearby restaurants. Ask for an upstairs room for more light and privacy. Prices, moreover, are right, beginning at about $45 d low season, with a/c. Book through the toll-free U.S./Can. tel. 888/349-3566 or email wwserena@prodigy.net.mx.

Trailer Park

Across the street from Bungalows Arroyo in a flowery, palm-shaded beachside garden is **Bucerías Trailer Park,** P.O. Box 148, Bucerías, Nayarit 63732, tel. 329/298-0265, fax 329/298-0300. The property was once owned by Elizabeth Taylor. At last writing, the 48 spaces rented for about $18/day or $400/month; add $1 a day for a/c power. (This time the owner refused to tell me the new prices because I arrived at 8 P.M.) With all hookups, showers, toilets, new blue pool, nearby boat ramp, and good drinkable well water. Get your winter reservations in early.

Even if only passing through Bucerías, don't miss Pie in the Sky; its chocolate-nut cookies have to be tasted to be believed.

Rental Agents

If you can't find your ideal Bucerías vacation retreat by yourself, try savvy and personable Bucerías resident Victoria Pratt, at Retorno Flamingos 20, on the north side of town, a block north of the big Decameron resort complex. She manages rentals for a number of choice Bucerías villas, houses, and apartments. Contact her at tel. 329/298-1644, fax 329/298-0932, or by email vlpratt@pvnet.com.mx.

Other competent local real estate agencies are easy to contact through the Internet. For more information, visit the websites www.las_palmas_travel.com, www.move2mexico.com, and www.casasbucerias.com.

Alternatively, look up the English-speaking real estate team of Carlos and Mina González, who also rent a number of deluxe Bucerías beachfront homes and vacation apartments. Drop by their office on the highway, beach side, a few blocks south of town, or call tel. 329/298-0265, fax 329/298-0300, or write them at González Real Estate, Héroes de Nacozari 128, Bucerías, Nayarit 63732.

Food

A number of good restaurants serve Bucerías's cadre of discriminating diners. Most of the restaurants lie along Calle Lázaro Cárdenas, just south of the center of town, between the cross streets of Galeana and Morelos. As you move from south to north, the two best and most popular are probably **Sandrina's** and ocean view **Claudio's.** Find Sandrina's just south of Hotel Villa Serena, between Galeana and Morelos, tel. 329/298-0273. The labor of love of Victoria, B.C., expatriates Andrew and Sandra Neumann, Sandrina's serves a varied breakfast, lunch, and dinner menu in an inviting inside-outside garden setting. Offerings vary from hearty North American egg and hash brown late breakfasts to exquisite catch of the day *dorado* (mahimahi) fillet dinners. Find them open during the high winter season daily except Tuesday, 10 A.M.–10 P.M.; they're closed May–September. Moderate–expensive.

Especially popular and enjoyable for lunch or dinner, Claudio's is a block farther north on the beach side. Here the welcoming owner has everything in place: a large airy beachfront *palapa,* perfect for evening happy hour sunsets. Here, you can test: super-fresh catch of the day fish, lobster, prawns, clams and oysters, plus a bountiful meat barbecue, plus generous salad bar. This all climaxes every Wednesday night with an overflowing all-you-can-eat barbecue. Open daily 2–10 P.M., tel. 329/298-1634. Moderate–expensive.

After trying the above, you might also check out a number of other reliably recommended restaurants in the same neighborhood. Moving south to north, first comes **Karen's Place** (late breakfast, lunch, early dinner, Sunday champagne brunch, in the big Costa Dorada condo complex), corner of Lázaro Cárdenas and Juárez. Continue north a block to gourmet **Expressions,** (across Lázaro Cárdenas from Hotel Villa Serena); next door comes the **Red Apple,** corner of Morelos; then **Café Magna** (ribs, fish and chips sports bar) just north of Morelos. Moreover, for popcorn and beer camaraderie, try the **Gecko Pub,** half a block east on Morelos.

Even if only passing through Bucerías, don't miss **Pie in the Sky,** the little bakery of entrepreneurs Don and Teri Murray, who've developed a thriving business soothing the collective sweet tooth of Puerto Vallarta's expatriate and retiree colony. Their chocolate-nut cookies have to be tasted to be believed. Watch for the sign on the inland side of the highway just south of town; open Mon.–Fri. 9 A.M.–5 P.M.

PUNTA MITA COUNTRY

A day trip on the road to Punta Mita takes you past white-sand beaches, fishing villages, and waterfront *palapa* restaurants. A few miles north of Bucerías the Punta Mita highway splits left, west, and passes over Highway 200. Drivers, mark your mileage (or reset your odometer). Within a mile (two km), look downhill on the left and you'll see the formerly drowsy, now developing, little town of **Cruz de Huanacaxtle** above a small fishing harbor. Although the town has stores, a good café, a few lodgings, and a protected boat and yacht anchorage, it lacks a decent beach.

Playa Manzanilla and Hotel Piedra Blanca

Half a mile (at around Mile 2, Km 3) farther on, a rough side road to the left leads to beautiful Playa Manzanilla and the Hotel Piedra Blanca. The beach itself, a carpet of fine, golden-white coral sand, stretches along a little cove sheltered by a limestone headland—thus Piedra Blanca (White Stone). This place was made for peaceful vacationing: snorkeling at nearby **Playa Piedra Blanca** on the opposite side of the headland; fishing from the beach, rocks, or by boat launched on the beach or hired in the Cruz de Huanacaxtle harbor.

The hotel is a small, unpretentious, family-managed resort. The best of the big comfortable suites offer upstairs ocean views. All the ingredients—a good tennis court, a shelf of used novels, and a rustic *palapa* restaurant beside an inviting beach-view pool and patio—perfect for tranquil relaxation. The 41 suites with kitchenettes, a/c, and TV rent from $40 d in the low season, $50 high; credit cards are not accepted. Reserve by writing directly to the hotel, at Alcatraz 36, Cruz de Huanacaxtle, Nayarit 63732, or by calling tel. 329/295-5489 or 329/295-5493. (*Note:* The trailer park that the hotel once managed is now closed.)

Past Piedra Blanca, the highway winds for 12 miles (19 km) to Punta Mita through the bushy green jungle country at the foot of the Sierra Vallejo. Although once wild, this stretch is now pocked with condo and villa developments that unfortunately restrict access to the emerald-forested and coral-studded shoreline. Let's hope aroused local citizens will coax authorities to allow public access.

Rock coral, the limestone skeleton of living coral, becomes gradually more common as you move west along the Punta Mita coast, thus tinting the water aqua and the sand white. As the highway approaches Punta Mita, the living reef offshore becomes intact and continuous.

Playa Destiladeras

A pair of rustic ocean-side *palapa* restaurants (at Mile 5, Km 8) mark Playa Destiladeras, a beach-lover's heavenly mile of white sand. Two- to five-foot waves roll in gently, providing good conditions for bodysurfing and boogie boarding. Surfing gets better the closer you get to the end of the headland at **Punta el Burro** (known also as Punta Veneros), where good left-breaking waves make it popular with local surfers.

The intriguing label *destiladeras* originates with the fresh water dripping from the cliffs past Punta el Burro, collecting in freshwater pools right beside the ocean. Campers who happen upon one of these pools may find their water problems solved.

Villa Vera Beach Club and Rancho Banderas

About a mile past Playa Destiladeras, you'll see the Villa Vera (formerly Los Veneros) Beach Club entrance. A fee of $12 per person gets you a beach towel and entitles you to enjoy the attractive facilities, which include pools, a beach-view snack bar, and changing rooms. The half-mile-long white coral sand beach, although with waves often too tranquil for surfing, will most likely be fine for wading, swimming, and boogie boarding. In addition, the resort rents horses and mountain bikes and furnishes guides for beach excursions or along its "archaeological" trail through the nearby tropical deciduous forest.

If you decide to stay overnight, the neighboring timeshare Rancho Banderas might be able to put you up in a deluxe suite for perhaps $100 overnight, with bargaining. For more information and reservations, call the Villa Vera Puerto Vallarta office, tel. 322/227-2782.

Restaurant Amapas

For a treat, stop in at the friendly, family-run Restaurant Amapas (Mile 8, Km 13). Homesteaded when the Punta Mita road was a mere path through the jungle, Restaurant Amapas still retains a country flavor. Ducks waddle around the yard, javelina (wild pigs) snort in their pen, while sometimes in the evening twilight when the work is all done, the elderly owner recalls her now-deceased husband hunting food for the table: "We ate deer, javelina, ducks, coatimundi, rattlesnake, iguana . . . whatever we could catch." Although local hunters now provide most of the food, she and her daughter-in-law do all the cooking, and their many loyal customers still enjoy the same wild fare. The restaurant is open every day 9 A.M. to sunset.

Punta Mita

In the early 1990s, the Mexican government concluded a deal with private interests to build the Four Seasons resort development at Corral de Riscos, at the end of the Punta Mita highway. The idyllic Corral de Riscos inlet, however, was *ejido* (communally owned) land and base of operations for the local fishing and boating cooperative, Cooperativa Corral de Riscos. In 1995 the government moved the people, under vigorous protest, into modern housing beside a new anchorage at nearby Playa Anclote. Now the *ejido* people seem to have grudgingly accepted their new housing and harbor (which they've even named "Nuevo Corral de Riscos"). At approximately Mile 12,

a private gate on the right leads to the super-exclusive 18-hole golf course and 100-room Four Seasons Hotel.

The Hotel Four Seasons was only the first step in government plans for Punta Mita development. Real estate offices show (with pride) a map of about five projected large hotels and several condominium complexes (some already built, others under construction.) Although all of this ferment bodes well for employment prospects of local people, the question of whether it will transform Punta Mita for the better of the worse will become more apparent after the dust of construction settles.

The name Punta Mita (actually Punta de Mita) encompasses the entire northwestern headland of the Bay of Banderas. Important sections include the Emiliano Zapata village (pop. about 1,000) on the bluff above the beach; Nuevo Corral de Riscos (pop. about 500), the new town that the government built for the displaced *ejido* people, adjacent, west of Emiliano Zapata; and the boat harbor and beachfront *palapa* restaurant strip, called Playa Anclote, or simply "Anclote," by local folks.

The hotel people are trying to erase Corral de Riscos, the lovely west-side fishing inlet and location of the original *ejido* village, from memory. "Corral de Riscos doesn't exist," they claim.

Corral de Riscos

I'm hopeful that someday, public access will be restored to the lovely sand crescent that borders the petite, gorgeous Corral de Riscos inlet, former anchorage of the Corral de Riscos fishing cooperative.

When that happens, families will again be able to swim and picnic on the golden sand, in view of the two small bare-rock islands, **Isla del Mono** on the left, and **Isla de las Abandonadas** on the right, that shelter the scenic lagoon. The name of the former comes from a *mono* (monkey) face people see in one of the outcroppings; the latter label springs from the legend of the fishermen who went out to sea and never returned. Las Abandonadas were their wives, who waited on the islet for years, vainly searching the horizon for their lost husbands.

Playa Anclote

Head left, downhill, at the highway's end (Mile 13, Km 21) toward Playa Anclote (Anchor Beach), which gets its name from the galleon anchor displayed at one of the beachside *palapa* restaurants. The beach itself is a broad, half-mile-long curving strand of soft, very fine, coral sand. The water is shallow for a long distance out, and the waves are gentle and long-breaking, good for beginning surfing, boogie boarding, and bodysurfing.

A few hundred yards downhill from the highway, a block left of the road "T" at the bottom, stands the **Caseta Cooperativa Corral de Riscos Servicios Turísticos,** at Av. Anclote 17, tel./fax 329/291-6298. This former fishing cooperative, now tourism provider, offers a number of services, such as sightseeing and snorkel tours at the Marietas Island, an hour offshore, fishing for $40 per hour, whale-watching Dec.–March, and surf instruction.

Alternatively, look up the original veteran surf instructor Jesús "Chuy" Casilla, who welcomes visitors daily next door, on the beach, west of the *cooperativa* office. Chuy rents boogie boards, snorkel gear, and surfboards for about $6 per day. He also arranges sportfishing launches (three-hour trip, about $100 complete) and snorkeling, wildlife-viewing, and photography boat tours to the pristine offshore wildlife sanctuaries of Islas Las Marietas. During a typical half-day trip, visitors may glimpse dolphins, sea turtles, and sometimes whales, as well as visit breeding grounds for brown and blue-footed boobies, Heerman's gulls, and other birds.

When he's not working, Chuy follows his love of surfing, which he also loves to teach. He claims the best surfing in the Bay of Banderas is on the left breaks off Isla del Mono, off the lighthouse point about a half mile to the west.

Yet another surf lessons option is **Tranquilo Surf Adventures** of veteran surfers Josea Villagas and Kemi Vernon. Find them at Calle Pez Vela 130, in Emiliano Zapata, Nayarit 63734, tel. 329/291-6475, surf-adventures@yahoo.com.

An especially knowledgable local lover of Punta Mita is personable California expatriate resident Susan Ingle, who offers **guide and orientation service** for visitors interested in a close look around at Punta de Mita and environs. She also offers bed and breakfast in her comfortable house. (For Susan's contact information, see Accommodations.)

Punta Mita Accommodations

If you decide to stay, Punta Mita offers a number of comfortable accommodations. In the town of Emiliano Zapata, on the bluff above Playa Anclote, you have your choice of two apartment complexes, a small bed-and-breakfast, and a modest hotel. Most comfortable is **Casa Las Palmas,** tucked on a quiet side street, at Calle Francisco Madero, Emiliano Zapata (Punta de Mita), Nayarit 63734, tel. 329/291-6340. Owner-builders David and Irene Forbes offer five spacious apartments, built around an inviting inner garden. Inside, the immaculate, commodious one- and two-bedroom apartments are finished in pleasingly rustic brick and stucco, with soft chairs, gleaming bathrooms, and comfortable beds. Rates begin at $50 d low season, $60 high, with discounts available for long-term rentals. Reserve most conveniently by email: elas_palmas72@hotmail.com.

Equally welcoming is local American resident Susan Ingle, who offers a comfortable room with breakfast, in her art-decorated house, on quiet Calle Otelia Montaña, Emiliano Zapata (Punta de Mita), Nayarit 63734. She asks $35 for two, including breakfast, during the winter-spring-fall. She's customarily closed June through September. Reserve through telephone, tel. 329/291-6414, or email single@pvnet.com.mx.

Another option are the apartments **Quinta del Sol** of resident expatriate Anna Seals, formerly of Muncie, Indiana. She offers eight studios, with bed-sitting rooms, furnished kitchens, and wide verandas overlooking the bay, in Emiliano Zapata. (Although I didn't get a chance to look at these, they were highly recommended to me by Susan Ingle.) Rates will run about $40/day or $200/week. For more information, contact Anna Seals, tel. 329/291-6299, annaseals@pvnet.com.mx. During the low summer-fall season, Ulrika Kuhnert (see Food) manages Anna's apartments.

Finally, consider the modest **Hotel Punta de Mita,** also overlooking the bay, in Emiliano Zapata, at Hidalgo 5, Fracc. E. Zapata, Punta de Mita, Nayarit 63734, tel. 329/291-6269. Here, what you see is what you get: about 15 small, motel-style rooms around an inviting, kid-friendly grassy pool-patio. Rates run about $40 per room, with a/c, with bunk bed for children, and small kitchenette. (On the other hand, by the time you read this, the Hotel Punta de Mita may have been destroyed by the condominium fever that seems to have gripped Punta Mita lately.)

Tent camping is possible when not prohibited by the government because of local construction; ask at the restaurants if it's okay to camp under big trees at either end of the beach. Stores nearby and on the highway in Emiliano Zapata (commonly known as Punta Mita) back on the highway a quarter-mile east can furnish the necessities, including drinking water.

Punta Mita Deluxe Accommodations

Increased visitor arrivals now support a sprinkling of mid- to high-end accommodations. Among the most successful is **Casa Las Brisas** of friendly owner-manager-builder Mark Lindskog. Mark personally makes sure that his guests enjoy the best of all possible worlds: a breezy creamy-sand beach, gourmet cuisine, fine wines, spacious art- and antique-decorated rooms, and plenty of peace and quiet, around an azure pool-patio. For the active, Mark provides a universal gym station, and optional fishing, horseback riding, surfing, golf, and more. All this for about $340 for two, all lodging, food, and drinks included. Reserve at Casa Las Brisas, Playa Cayero, Punta de Mita, Nayarit 63734, tel. 322/225-4364, casalasbrisas@mexicoboutiquehotels.com. Or, reserve through Boutique Hotels of Mexico toll-free at U.S. tel. 877/278-8018 or Can. tel. 866/818-8342. For more information, visit the Boutique Hotels of Mexico website at www.mexicoboutiquehotels.com. (See access directions after Huerta de la Paz.)

For an equally unusual, but completely different, lodging experience, look into the **Huerta de la Paz** ecoretreat and life project of artist-pioneer Sandra Richards, formerly of San Francisco, California. In 10 years of solid work, Sandra has carved her version of paradise out of the Punta

Casa Las Brisas guests enjoy a superbly serene beachfront location.

Mita foothill tropical forest. Now, her bucolic acreage encompasses minigroves of mandarin orange and mango trees, and an all-organic vegetable garden. Besides her horticultural work, Sandra enjoys both cooking and company, so she has added four comfortable guest cabanas to her paradise. Two of the cabanas she describes as "rustic-elegant." Indeed; they are spacious, art- and antique-decorated and enjoy luxurious panoramic forest and ocean views. The other two cabanas are also comfortable, with panoramic views, but are not so large or elegantly appointed. Sandra asks $125 with breakfast (fruit, baked bread, scones, coffee, tea, juice) for two for the larger cabanas, $55 and $85, with breakfast, for the smaller. She closes down during the buggier, rainy season, July 1–Oct. 15. Reserve by mail, at Km 4, Carretera Higuera Blanca, Punta de Mita, Nayarit 63764, or by email at rnchpaz@hotmail.com; for more information, visit www.huertalapaz.com.

Access directions for both Casa Las Brisas and Huerta de la Paz are similar. For both, from

PUERTO VALLARTA

the Punta Mita Highway at Mile 11 (Km 18) follow the Higuera Blanca road fork north. (If you reach the Four Seasons Hotel gate, turn around; you've gone too far.) Heading north, within a mile, cross two bridges. For Casa Las Brisas, turn left after the second bridge. Continue about half a mile to the beach, where you bear left at the fork. Continue another approximately quarter mile to Casa Las Brisas, marked by only a tile plaque, on the right.

For Huerta de la Paz, continue straight ahead after the second bridge. Pass Ejido Higuera Blanca village on the left and continue ahead a total of about 2.5 miles (4 km) from the Punta Mita Highway, where a sign directs you right, up the Higuera de la Paz entrance driveway.

Rental Agent

A number of real estate agents handle house, condo, and apartment rentals in Punta Mita. Among the best established is **Punta Mita Realty,** tel. 329/291-6420, fax 329/291-6421, on beachfront Av. Anclote, by the restaurant El Dorado. For more information, visit website www.puntarealty.com.

Food

Right in the middle of Playa Anclote is one of Playa Anclote's best seafood restaurants, **El Dorado,** tel. 329/291-6296 or 329/291-6297, open daily 11 A.M. to sunset. The menu is based on meat, poultry, and the bounty of super-fresh snapper, scallops, oysters, and lobsters that local fisherfolk bring onto the beach. If El Dorado is too full, you have your choice of a number of other beachfront *palapas* that share the same coral-studded strand.

For good comfort food, try **Galería and Internet Café Paquima,** competently managed by friendly German expatriate Ulrika Kuhnert, at Av. Las Pangas 2, tel. 329/291-6292. Ulrika's specializes in hearty breakfasts, with home-fried potatoes, bacon, and scrambled eggs. For lunch, try her bountiful sandwiches, cappuccino, or banana milkshakes, in half a dozen flavors. Find her open daily (high season) from about 8 A.M. until 5 P.M.

GETTING TO NUEVO VALLARTA, BUCERÍAS, AND PUNTA MITA

Autotransportes Medina buses complete a flood of daily round-trips between Playa Anclote (Restaurant El Dorado terminal) and its Puerto Vallarta station, north of the *malecón,* at 1410 Brasil, tel. 322/222-4732. In Puerto Vallarta, walk or hire a taxi to the terminal, or catch the bus as it heads north along the airport boulevard through the Zona Hotelera. Stops en route include Bucerías, Cruz de Huancaxtle, Piedra Blanca, and Destiladeras. The last bus returns to Puerto Vallarta at about 9 P.M.

The Jalisco Coast

The Road to Barra de Navidad

The country between Puerto Vallarta and Barra de Navidad is a landscape ripe for travelers who enjoy getting away from the tourist track. Development has barely begun to penetrate its vast tracts of mountainous jungle, tangled thorny scrub, and pine-clad summit forests. Footprints rarely mark miles of its curving, golden beaches.

Fortunately, everyone who travels south of Puerto Vallarta doesn't have to be a Daniel Boone. The coastal strip within a few miles of the highway has acquired some comforts—stores, trailer parks, campgrounds, hotels, and a scattering of small resorts—enough to become well known to Guadalajara people as the Costa Alegre (Happy Coast).

This modicum of amenities makes it easy for all visitors to enjoy what local people have for years: plenty of sun, fresh seafood, clear blue water, and sandy beaches, some of which stretch for miles, while others are tucked away in little rocky coves like pearls in an oyster.

Heading Out

If you're driving, note your odometer mileage (or reset it to zero) as you pass the Pemex gas

the Barra de Navidad lagoon landing

© BRUCE WHIPPERMAN

station at Km 214 on Highway 200 at the south edge of Puerto Vallarta. In the open southern country, mileage and roadside kilometer markers are a useful way to remember where your little paradise is hidden.

If you're not driving, simply hop on to one of the many southbound Autocamiones del Pacífico or Transportes Cihuatlán second-class buses just before they pass at the south-end gas station. Let the driver know a few minutes beforehand where along the road you want to get off.

CHICO'S PARADISE

The last outpost on the Puerto Vallarta tour-bus circuit is Chico's Paradise, 13 miles (22 km, at Km 192) from the south edge of Puerto Vallarta in the lush jungle country. Here, the clear, cool Río Tuito cascades over a collection of smooth, friendly granite boulders. Chico's restaurant is a

big multilevel *palapa* that overlooks the entire beautiful scene—deep green pools for swimming, flat warm rocks for sunning, and gurgling gentle waterfalls for splashing. Although a few homesteads dot the streamside nearby, the original Chico's still dominates, although its reputation rests mainly on the beauty of the setting rather than the quality of its pricey menu.

The forest-perfumed breezes, the gurgling, crystal stream, and the friendly, relaxed ambience are perfect for shedding the cares of the world. Although as yet there are no formal lodgings, a number of potential camping spots border the river, both up- and downstream. Stores at either the nearby upstream village or Boca de Tomatlán, three miles downhill, can provide supplies.

Adventurers can hire local guides (ask at Chico's restaurant) for horseback rides along the river and overnight treks into the green, jungly **Sierra Lagunillas** that rises on both

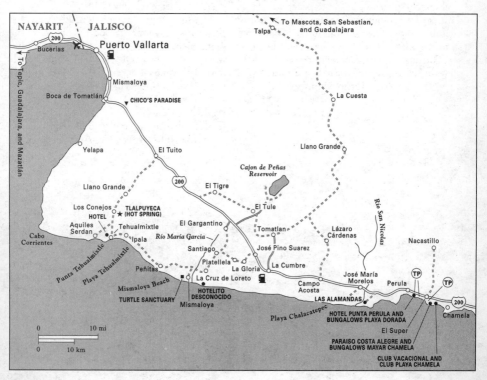

sides of the river. If you're quiet and aware, you may be rewarded with views of chattering parrots, dozing iguanas, feisty javelinas (wild pigs), clownish *tejones* (coatimundis), and wary *gatos de montaña* (wildcats). If you're especially lucky, you might even get a glimpse of the fabled *tigre* (jaguar).

CABO CORRIENTES COUNTRY
El Tuito

The town of El Tuito, at Km 170 (27 miles, 44 km, from Puerto Vallarta), appears from the highway as nothing more than a bus stop. It doesn't even have a gas station. Most visitors pass by without even giving a second glance. This is a pity, because El Tuito (pop. 3,000) is a friendly little colonial-era town that spreads along a long main street to a pretty square about a mile from the highway.

El Tuito enjoys at least two claims to fame: besides being the *mescal* liquor capital of western Jalisco, it's the jumping-off spot for the seldom-visited coastal hinterland of Cabo Corrientes, the southernmost lip of the Bay of Banderas. This is pioneer country, a land of wild beaches and sylvan forests, unpenetrated by electricity, phone, and paved roads. Wild creatures still abound: Turtles come ashore to lay their eggs, hawks soar, parrots swarm, and the faraway scream of the jaguar can yet be heard in the night.

The rush for the ***raicilla,*** as local connoisseurs call El Tuito *mescal,* begins on Saturday when men crowd into town and begin upending bottles around noon, without even bothering to sit down. For a given individual, this cannot last too long, so the fallen are continually replaced by fresh arrivals all weekend.

Although El Tuito is famous for the *raicilla,* it is not the source. *Raicilla* comes from the sweet

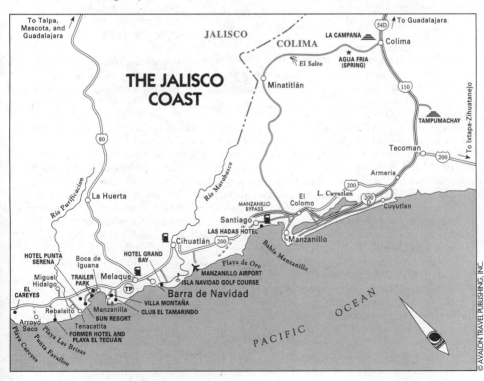

sap of the maguey plants, a close relative of the cactuslike century plant, which blooms once and then dies. The *ejido* (cooperative farm) of Cicatan (see-kah-TAHN), six miles out along the dirt road as you head to the coast west of town, cultivates the maguey.

Along the Road to Aquiles Serdán

You can get to the coast with or without your own wheels. If you're driving, it should be a strong, high-clearance vehicle (pickup, jeep, very maneuverable RV, or VW van) filled with gas; if you're not driving, trucks and VW taxi-vans (*combis* or *colectivos*) make daily trips. Their destinations include the coastal hamlet of Aquiles Serdán, the storied fishing cove of Tehualmixtle, and the farming village of Ipala beside the wide Bahía de Tehualmixtle. Fare runs a few dollars per person; inquire at the Highway 200 crossing or the west end of the El Tuito central plaza.

Getting there along the bumpy, rutted, sometimes steep 23-mile (37-km) dirt track is half the fun of Aquiles Serdán (pop. 200). About six miles (10 km) from Highway 200, you'll pass through the lands of the *mescal* cooperative, Cicatan, marked only by a crumbling whitewash-and-thatch house in front of a tiny school on the right. On the left, you'll soon glimpse a field of maguey in the distance. A few dozen families (who live in the hills past the far side of the field) quietly go about their business of tending their maguey plants and extracting, fermenting, and distilling the precious sap into their renowned *raicilla*.

The road dips up and down the rest of the way, over sylvan hillsides dotted with oak *(robles)*, through intimate stream valleys perfect for parking an RV or setting up a tent, and past the hardscrabble rancho-hamlets of Llano Grande (Broad Plain, 14 miles, 22 km), with stores, *comedores* (places to eat), and a *Centro de Salud* (health center), and Los Conejos (The Rabbits, 19 miles, 30 km).

> *This is pioneer country, unpenetrated by electricity, phone, and paved roads. Wild creatures still abound: Turtles come ashore to lay their eggs, hawks soar, parrots swarm, and the faraway scream of the jaguar can yet be heard in the night.*

You can't get lost, because there's only one route until a few miles past Los Conejos, where a fork (23 miles, 37 km) marks your approach to Aquiles Serdán. The left branch continues south to Maito and Tehualmixtle. A mile and a half to the north along the right branch you will arrive at the Río Tecolotlán. Aquiles Serdán stands on the far bank, across 100 yards of watery sand. Fortunately the riverbed road is concrete-bottomed, and (if it's in good repair, which it wasn't at this writing) you can drive right across the streambed any time other than after a storm. If you can't drive across, roll up your pant legs and walk across, like most of the local folks do.

Aquiles Serdán

The Aquiles Serdán villagers see so few outsiders that you will become their attraction of the week. Wave and say *hola,* buy a *refresco,* stroll around town, and, after a while, the kids will stop crowding around and the adults will stop staring when they've found out you, too, are human. By that time, someone may even have invited you into his or her tree branch–walled, clean dirt–floored house for some hot fish-fillet tacos, fresh tomatoes, and beans. Accept, of course.

Aquiles Serdán basks above the lily-edged river lagoon, which during the June–Oct. rainy season usually breaks through the beach-sandbar and drains directly into the surf half a mile below the town. During the dry season, the lagoon wanders lazily up the coast for a few miles. In any case, the white-sand beach is accessible only by boat, which you can borrow or hire at the village.

If you do, you'll have miles of untouched white sand and surf all to yourself for days of camping, beachcombing, shell collecting, surf fishing, wildlife-viewing, and, if the waves permit, swimming, surfing, boogie boarding, and snorkeling. The town's two stores can provide your necessities.

Back at the fork (23 miles, 37 km from the highway) continue along the left branch about two miles through Maito (pop. 100), which has two stores. A right fork just after Maito leads half a mile to **Playa Maito,** a surf fishing and beachcombers' rustic paradise, where you can either park your RV or tent on the beach or stay at a rough small beachfront hotel with "water and a washing machine" (bring all your food) for about $15 per night.

Tehualmixtle

Back on the main road, you arrive at another fork (at 26 miles, 42 km). The right branch goes steeply up and then down a rough track to the right, which soon levels out on the cliff above the idyllic fishing cove of Tehualmixtle. Here, a headland shelters a blue nook, where a few launches float, tethered and protected from the open sea. To one side, swells wash over a submerged wreck, while an ancient, moss-stained warehouse crumbles above a rocky little beach. At the end of the road downhill, a pair of beachside *palapas* invite visitors with drinks and fresh-out-of-the-water oysters, lobster, *dorado,* and red snapper.

Candelario, owner/operator of the right-side *palapa,* is the moving force behind this pocket-sized paradise. After your repast, and a couple of bottles more beer for good measure, he might tell you his version of the history of this coast—of legends of sunken galleons, or of the days when the old warehouse stored cocaine for legal shipment to the United States, when Coca-Cola got its name from the cocaine, which, generations ago, was added to produce "the pause that refreshes."

Nowadays, however, Tehualmixtle serves as a resting point for occasional sailboaters, travelers, fisherfolk, and those who enjoy the rewards of clear-water snorkeling and scuba diving around the sunken shrimp trawler and the rocky shoreline nearby. Several level spots beside the cove invite camping or RV parking. Candelario will gladly supply you with your stomach's delight of choice seafood and drinks.

Furthermore, Candelario and his family, led by his friendly, outgoing English-speaking daughter Gaby, have built a small **hotel.** They offer four clean, simply furnished rooms with shiny white bathrooms, view windows, and ceiling fans. Asking rates are about $25 s, $30 d, $36 t. Additionally, they rent out a comfortable view

bungalow sleeping five, fine for groups, with a kitchenette, good bathroom, and ceiling fans for $45 nightly, discount for one-week stay.

For those who stay a few days, Candelario offers his services as a **guide** for equipped snorkelers and scuba divers to investigate nearby sites, especially the submerged wreck right offshore. Farther afield, he also can lead parties inland a few miles, by foot or horseback, to hot spring **Tla-puyeca,** where, years ago, a French company operated a logging concession.

Southeast of Tehualmixtle

Returning back up the road above the cove, glimpse southward toward the azure Bay of Tehualmixtle washing the white-sand ribbon of the Playa de Tehualmixtle. The village of **Ipala,** three miles down the road, is supply headquarters (unleaded gasoline available) for the occasional visitors drawn by the good fishing, surfing, beachcombing, and camping prospects of the Playa de Tehualmixtle. Being on the open ocean, its waves are usually rough, especially in the afternoon. Only experienced swimmers who can judge undertow and surf should think of swimming here.

From Ipala (29 miles, 47 km), you can either retrace your path back to the highway at El Tuito, or continue down the coast (where the road gets rougher before it gets better) through the hamlet and beach of **Peñitas** (36 miles, 58 km; a few stores, restaurants), past **Mismaloya** (46 miles, 74 km), site of a University of Guadalajara turtle-hatching station. To get there, turn right onto the rough dirt road just before the concrete bridge over the broad Río María Garcia.

From Mismaloya, return to the bridge, continue over the river three miles farther, and you will soon be back to the 21st century at **Cruz de Loreto** (49 miles, 79 km; many stores, sidewalks, electric lights, and phones).

After all the backcountry hard traveling, treat yourself to a few nights at luxury ecoresort **Hotelito Desconocido** (inquire locally for directions, or follow the signs west to the hotel, at the lagoon and beach nearby); reservations are strongly recommended. For reservations, call toll-free U.S./Can. tel. 800/851-1143 or Mex. tel. 800/013-1313, email hotelito@pvnet.com.mx, or visit the website www.hotelito.com. (For more Hotelito details, see the special topic "Splendid Isolation" in the Puerto Vallarta: Town, Bay, and Mountain chapter.)

If you decide not to stay at Hotelito Desconocido, return to Highway 200 directly from Cruz de Loreto, by heading east 10 miles (via Santiago and El Gargantino) to the highway at the Km 133 marker, just 23 miles (37 km) south of where you started at El Tuito.

CAJÓN DE LAS PEÑAS RESERVOIR

The lush farms of the Cabo Corrientes region owe much of their success to the Cajón de Peñas dam, whose waters enable farmers to profit from a year-round growing season. An added bonus is the recreation—boating, fishing, swimming, camping, and hiking—the big blue lake behind the dam makes possible.

With a car, the reservoir is easy to reach. Trucks and cars are frequent, so hikers can easily thumb rides. At Highway 200 Km 131, about a mile

south of the Cruz de Loreto turnoff, head left (east) at a signed, paved road. After about five miles the road turns to gravel. Continue another four miles to a road fork atop a complex of three rock-fill dams, separated by a hill. The left road continues over the smaller two dams to a dead end. The right fork leads to a sign reading Puerto Vallarta Bass Club and a left fork just before the largest dam. Turn left and continue downhill to **La Lobina,** a humble family-run restaurant *palapa* and boat landing. The friendly husband-wife team maintains the little outpost in hopes of serving the trickle of mostly holiday and weekend visitors. Besides their children, who help with chores, their little settlement consists of two parrots, a brood of turkeys, and a flock of chickens that flies into the nearby forest to roost at night. Their cooking, based mostly upon freshly caught *lobina* (large-mouth bass) is basic but wholesome. Their parking lot above the lake has room for a number of self-contained RVs, while the forested knoll nearby might serve for tent camping. They offer their boat for lake sightseeing and fishing excursions for about $15 an hour.

Bass fishing is a main attraction of Cajón de las Peñas Reservoir.

© BRUCE WHIPPERMAN

Otherwise, you could swim, kayak, or launch your own motorboat right from the lakeshore below the restaurant.

Head back, turn left at the uphill fork and continue over the larger dam, counterclockwise around the forested, sloping lakeshore. Within about two miles (three km) you'll arrive at the boat-cooperative village, where several down-scale *palapa* restaurants and boat landings provide food and recreational services for visitors. For a fee—ask at one of the restaurants, *"¿Hay una tarifa para campar?"* ("Is there a fee to camp?")—you can usually set up a tent or park your RV under a nearby lakeside tree.

PLAYA CHALACATEPEC

Playa Chalacatepec (chah-lah-kah-tay-PEK) lazes in the tropical sun just six miles from the highway at Km 88. Remarkably few people know of its charms except a handful of local youths, a few fishermen, and occasional families who come on Sunday outings, and the resident volunteers of the beachfront Tortuguera Verde Valle (Green Valley Turtle Encampment).

Playa Chalacatepec, with three distinct parts, has something for everyone: on the south side, a wild, arrow-straight, miles-long strand with crashing open-ocean breakers; in the middle, a low, wave-tossed, rocky point; and on the north, a long, tranquil, curving fine-sand beach.

The north beach, shielded by the point, has gently rolling breakers good for surfing, body-surfing, and safe swimming. Shells seasonally carpet its gradual white slope, and visitors have even left a pair of *palapa* shelters. These seem ready-made for camping by night and barbecuing fish by day with all of the driftwood lying around for the taking.

The point, Punta Chalacatepec, which separates the two beaches, is good for pole fishing on its surf-washed flanks and tidepooling in its rocky crevices.

Folks with RVs can pull off and park either along the approach road just above the beach or along tracks (beware of soft spots) downhill in the tall acacia scrub that borders the sand.

One of the few natural amenities that Playa Chalacatepec lacks is drinking water, however. Bring your own from the town back on the highway.

Getting There

Just as you're entering little José María Morelos (pop. 2,000), 100 feet past the Km 88 marker, turn right toward the beach at the corner. (Note the telephone booth.) If you're planning to camp, stock up with water and groceries at the stores in the town down the road, south.

The road, although steep in spots, is negotiable by passenger cars in good condition and small-to-medium RVs. Owners of big rigs should do a test run. On foot, the road is an easy two-hour hike—much of which probably won't be necessary because of the many passing farm pickups.

Mark your odometer at the highway. Continue over brushy hills and past fields and pastures, until Mile 5.2 (Km 8.4), where the main road veers right. Instead, continue straight ahead, over the dune, to the beach, at mile 5.4 (Km 8.7), where the road turns left (south) and parallels the beach. Pass turtle encampment Tortuguera Verde Valle, at mile 5.9 (Km 9.5). Steer right downhill to Playa Chalactepec at mile 6 (Km 9.7). The present bad news is that a squad of poor fisherman have junked up the beach; the good news is twofold: that several choice parking sites are available in the high brush bordering the beach (be careful of soft sand) and you'll have the good company of the turtle-saving volunteers, who would probably appreciate any help you can give them.

LAS ALAMANDAS

After roughing it at Playa Chalacatepec, you can be pampered in the luxurious isolation of Las Alamandas, a deluxe 1,500-acre retreat a few miles down the road.

The small Quémaro village sign at Km 83 gives no hint of the pleasant surprises that Las Alamandas conceals behind its guarded gate. Solitude and elegant simplicity seem to have been the driving concepts in the mind of Isabel Goldsmith when she acquired control of the property in the late 1980s. Although born into wealth (her grandfather was the late tin tycoon Antenor Patiño, who developed Manzanillo's renowned Las Hadas; her father, the late multimillionaire Sir James Goldsmith, who bought the small kingdom her family now owns at Cuitzmala, 25 miles south), she was not idle. Isabel converted her dream of paradise—a small, luxuriously isolated resort on an idyllic beach in Puerto Vallarta's sylvan coastal hinterland—into reality. Now, her guests (28 maximum) enjoy accommodations that vary from luxuriously simple studios to a villa sleeping six. Activities include a gym, tennis, horseback riding, bicycling, fishing, kayaking, snorkeling, and lagoon and river excursions.

The hotel's luxurious facilities—dining restaurant and veranda, bars, book and video library, sitting and reading areas, pool-patio, gym, pavilions, and much more—are gracefully sprinkled throughout a plumy, grass-carpeted, beachfront palm grove. Powerful waves, good for intermediate and advanced surfing, on the south and north shoals, rise about 100 yards out and break rather quickly at the creamy, yellow-sand beach. With about twice as many employees as guests, hotel service is personal. Staff are attentive and focused on the goal of complete guest relaxation.

Daily rates range from about $400 low season ($500 high), for garden-view studios, up to about $1,100, low season ($1,800 high), for a three unit beach-front villa for six; all with full breakfast. Three meals, prepared to your order, cost about $200 additional per day per person.

For more information and reservations, contact Las Alamandas directly at Mex. tel. 315/285-5500 or U.S./Can. tel. 888/882-9616, fax 315/285-5027; by email at info.alamandas.com; or by mail, at Quémaro, Km. 83 Carretera Puerto Vallarta-Barra de Navidad, Jalisco 48854. For additional information, visit the website www.alamandas.com.

Alternatively, reserve through Las Alamandas's agent, Mexico Boutique Hotels, toll-free U.S. tel. 877/278-8018 or Can. tel. 866/818-8342, email info@mexicoboutiquehotels.com, or visit the website www.mexicoboutiquehotels.com.

Get there by car, taxi (about $100), or rental car from the Puerto Vallarta airport via Highway 200. At the Km 83 highway marker, 81 miles (130 km) south of Puerto Vallarta, turn right at the signed Quémaro village side road. Continue about three miles west, passing through Quémaro village, to the Alamandas gate. Don't arrive unannounced; unless you are a recognizable celebrity, the guard will not let you through the gate without a reservation in hand or unless you have made an appointment. (Alternatively, you can arrive by charter airplane, using the Las Alamandas's private airstrip. Contact a travel agent, such as American Express, in Puerto Vallarta, tel. 322/223-2910, 322/223-2927, or 322/223-2955, fax 322/223-2926.)

CHAMELA BAY

Most longtime visitors know Jalisco's Costa Alegre through Barra de Navidad and two big, beautiful, beach-lined bays: Tenacatita and Chamela. Tranquil Bahía de Chamela, the most northerly of the two, is broad, blue, dotted with islands, and lined by a strip of fine, honey-yellow sand.

Stretching five miles south from the sheltering Punta Rivas headland near Perula village, Chamela Bay is open but calm. A chain of intriguingly labeled rocky *islitas,* such as Cocinas (Kitchens), Negrita (Little Black One), and Pajarera (Place of Birds), scatter the strong Pacific swells into gentle billows by the time they roll onto the beaches.

Besides its natural amenities, Chamela Bay has three bungalow-complexes, one mentionable motel, two trailer parks, and an unusual "camping club." The focal point of this low-key resort area is the Km 72 highway corner (88 miles, 142 km, from Puerto Vallarta; 46 miles, 74 km, to Barra de Navidad). This spot, which on many maps is incorrectly marked "Chamela" (actually the village at Km 63), is known simply as "El Super" by local people. Though the supermarket and neighboring bank have closed and are filled with the owner's dusty antique car collection, El Super, nevertheless, lives on in the minds of the local folks.

Beaches and Activities

Chamela Bay's beaches are variations on one continuous strip of sand, from Playa Rosadas in the south through Playa Chamela in the middle to Playas Fortuna and Perula at the north end.

Curving behind the sheltering headland, **Playa Perula** is the broadest and most tranquil beach of Chamela Bay. It is best for children and a snap for boat launching, swimming, and fishing from the rocks nearby. A dozen *pangas* usually line the water's edge, ready to take visitors on fishing excursions (figure $15 per hour, after bargaining) and snorkeling around the offshore islets. A line of seafood *palapas* provides the food and drinks for the fisherfolk and mostly Mexican families who know and enjoy this scenic little village/cove.

Playas Fortuna, Chamela, and Rosada: As you head south, the beach gradually changes character. The surf roughens, the slope steepens, and the sand narrows from around 200 feet at Perula to perhaps 100 feet at the south end of the bay. Civilization also thins out. The dusty village of stores, small eateries, vacation homes, and beachfront *palapa* restaurants that line Playa Fortuna give way to farmland and scattered houses at Playa Chamela. Two miles farther on, grassy dunes above trackless sand line Playa Rosada.

The gradually varying vigor of the waves and the isolation of the beach determine the place where you can indulge your own favorite pastimes. For bodysurfing and boogie boarding, Rosada and Chamela are best; and while sailboarding is usually possible anywhere on Chamela Bay, it will be best beyond the tranquil waves at La Fortuna. For surf fishing, try casting beyond the vigorous, breaking billows of Rosada. And Rosada, being the most isolated, will be the place where you'll most likely find that shell-collection treasure you've been wishing for.

The five-mile curving strand of Chamela Bay is perfect for a morning hike from Rosada Beach. To get there, ride a Transportes Cihuatlán second-class bus to around the Km 65 marker, where a dirt road heads a half-mile to the beach. With the sun comfortably at your back, you can walk all the way to Perula if you want, stopping for refreshments at any one of several *palapas* along the way.

The firm sand of Chamela Bay beaches is likewise good for jogging, even for bicycling, provided you don't mind cleaning the sand out of the gears afterwards.

El Super Accommodations

Three accommodations serve travelers near the El Super corner: an emergency-only motel on the highway, bungalows, and a "camping club." The owners of the "camping club," **Paraíso Costa Alegre,** who live in Guadalajara, don't call it a campground because, curiously, in the past their policy has been, instead of allowing campers to use their own tents, to rent out one of their stuffy, concrete, tent-shaped constructions. Unfortunately these have fallen out of repair and are unusable. Nevertheless, it's worth asking about it, for Paraíso Costa Alegre would be a beautiful tent camping spot, where the beach and bay set the mood: soft, golden sand, island-silhouetted sunsets, tranquil surf, abundant birds and fish, sometimes whales and dolphins, and occasionally great manta rays leaping from the water offshore.

Even without your own tent you can still enjoy staying in the outdoors by renting one of Paraíso Costa Alegre's several recently renovated open-air oceanfront Swiss Family Robinson–style cabanas, each with a cooking and eating area and toilet and shower downstairs, and a pair of thatch-roofed bedrooms with soft floor-sleeping pads upstairs.

In addition, you could rent one of the 15 shady spaces in its trailer park with all hookups, right next to the communal showers and toilet. Moreover, the lovely, palm-shadowed complex has two tall, elaborate *palapa* restaurant/bars, a minimarket, drinkable water, hot water, communal showers, toilets, and a laundry.

A minor drawback to all this, besides there being no pool, are the somewhat steep rates: the open-air cabanas go for the same price as a moderate hotel room: about $32 for one or two, $49 for four; the trailer spaces go for about $15 per day or $400 per month. These prices, however, are subject to bargaining and discounts any time other than peak holidays. For reservations and more information contact Paraíso Costa Alegre at tel. 315/333-9778, fax 315/333-9777, email (visit the website www.paraisocostalegre.com.mx), or by mail, at Km 72, Carretera 200, Barra de Navidad a Puerto Vallarta, El Super, Jalisco 48854.

Right across the lane from Paraíso Costa Alegre stands the **Bungalows Mayar Chamela,** Km 72, Carretera Puerto Vallarta, El Super, Jalisco

48854, tel. 315/333-9711. The 18 spacious kitchenette-bungalows with fans (no a/c) surround an attractive inner garden and a palmy, banana-fringed pool and patio. Although the blue meandering pool and palmy grounds are very inviting, the bungalows themselves have suffered from past neglect. Look inside three or four and make sure that everything is in working order before moving in. If so, the bungalows' pool and garden setting and the long, lovely Chamela beach just a block away might be perfect for a week or month of tranquil relaxation. If you're passing through, it might be worthwhile to take a look. Rentals run about $30 d, $60 for four; monthly discounts are available. For reservations, write or fax the owner, Gabriel Yañez G., at Obregón 1425 S.L., Guadalajara, Jalisco, tel. 33/3644-0044, fax 33/3643-9318. (*Note:* The summer-fall season is pretty empty on the Chamela Bay beaches. Consequently, food is scarce around Paraíso Costa Alegre and Bungalows Mayar Chamela. Meals, however, are available at the restaurant at the El Super corner, and a few groceries at small stores along the highway nearby, or in San Mateo village a mile south.)

Perula Hotels and Trailer Parks

At Km 74, a sign marks a paved road to Playas Fortuna and Perula. About two miles downhill, right on the beach, you can't miss the bright yellow stucco **Hotel, Bungalows, and Trailer Park Playa Dorada,** Perula, Km 76, Carretera 200 Melaque-Puerto Vallarta, Jalisco 48854, tel. 315/333-9710. More a motel than bungalows, its three tiers of very plain rooms and suites with kitchenettes are nearly empty except on weekends and Mexican holidays.

Playa Dorada's two saving graces, however, are the beach, which curves gracefully to the scenic little fishing nook of Perula, and its inviting palm-shaded pool and patio. The best-situated rooms are on the top floor, overlooking the ocean. The 46 plain rooms sleeping two or three rent for about $35; 15 kitchenette units sleeping four go for about $60, all with parking. Although a 20 percent discount for weekly rentals is routinely available, you might be able to bargain for an even better deal any time other than peak holidays.

Folks who take one of the dozen trailer spaces in the bare lot across the street are welcome to lounge all day beneath the palms of the pool and patio. Spaces rent for about $10, with all hookups, and brand-new showers and toilets. For reservations, call or email pdorada@cyber-cable.net.mx; for more information, visit the website www.geocities.com/pdorada.

It's easy to miss the low-profile **Hotel Punta Perula,** just one block inland from the Bungalows Playa Dorada, at Perula, Km 76, Carretera 200, Melaque-Puerto Vallarta, Jalisco 48854, tel. 315/333-9782. This homey place seems like a scene from Old Mexico, with a rustic white stucco tier of rooms enclosing a spacious green garden and venerable tufted grove. Its 14 clean, gracefully decorated, colonial-style, fan-equipped rooms go for about $25 d, $30 t, except for Christmas and Easter holidays. Bargain for lower, long-term rates. (Being out of Old Mexico, it has no pool, of course.)

Also occupying the same luscious beachfront is **Red Snapper RV Park and Restaurant,** life project of friendly North American owners Harry, Carmen, and Bonnie Adams. Here, what you see is what you get: about 10 shadeless, fenced-in spaces with all hookups, showers, toilets, washing machine, beachfront restaurant *palapa* on gorgeous Chamela Bay, ripe for surf or boat fishing (launch right from the beach), surfing, and sailboarding. Spaces rent for $10 per day, $65/week, $250/month. Electricity (30-amp receptacle) runs $.16 per kilowatt-hour (about $2–3/day) extra. A 15-foot, 25 horsepower Zodiac is available for fishing. Reserve by mail, with Harry Adams, P.O. Box 42, Melaque, Jalisco 48980, or by phone, tel. 315/333-9784.

Centro Vacacional Chamela Sección 47 and Club Playa Chamela

Four miles south of El Super, at Rosada Beach, sharing the same luscious Chamela Bay strand, is the **Centro Vacacional Chamela Sección 47,** a teachers' vacation retreat that rents its unoccupied units to the general public. The two modern, apartment-style tiers enfold an inviting, grassy pool-patio and park. An outdoor *palapa* stands by the pool and another airy open room

© BRUCE WHIPPERMAN

A blue oceanview pool at Centro Vacacional Chamela invites relaxation.

invites cards and conversation. The units themselves are large, bright one-bedrooms, sleeping four, with sea views and kitchens. They rent for about $60, drop-in only. Call tel. 315/333-9878 or arrive before about 4 P.M., when the manager is usually around to check things before going home for the night. On nonholiday weekdays the place is often nearly empty. Have a look by following the upper of two side roads at the big "47" sign near the Km 66 marker. Within a few hundred yards you'll be there. Ask one of the teachers to explain the significance of "47."

If the teachers' retreat is full, try next door at the **Club Playa Chamela,** perhaps the most downscale timeshare in Mexico, if not the world. The manager said that, for a one-time fee of about $1,200, you can get one idyllic week for each of 20 years there. In the meantime, while the units are being sold, the owner is renting them out. All 12 of the pink and blue, bare-bulb cottages have two bedrooms, a kitchenette, and small living room. Although plainly furnished, they're reasonably clean and have ceiling fans and hot water. Outside, beyond a shady palm

grove, is a blue pool, a *palapa* sometimes-restaurant, and a long, pristine, sunset-view beach. The asking rate is about $32/day, $300/week, or $700/month. Try bargaining for a better price anytime other than the popular Christmas, Easter, and August seasons. Contact the manager, Martin Palafox, directly on-site, or owner Jose A. Santana Soto in Guadalajara, at tel. 33/3343-4061, for information and reservations.

Camping

For RVs, the best spots are the trailer parks at **Paraíso Costa Alegre,** the **Hotel, Bungalows, and Trailer Park Playa Dorada,** and **Red Snapper RV Park and Restaurant** (see above).

If you can walk in, you can probably set up a tent anywhere along the bay you like. One of the best places would be the grassy dune along pristine Playa Rosada a few hundred yards north of the Centro Vacacional Chamela Sección 47 (Km 66; see above). Water is available from the manager (offer to pay) at the Centro Vacacional.

Playa Negrita, the pristine little sand crescent that marks the southern end of Chamela

Bay, offers still another picnic or camping possibility. Get there by following the dirt road angling downhill from the highway at the south end of the bridge between Km 63 and Km 64. Turn left at the Chamela village stores beneath the bridge, continue about two miles, bearing left to the end of the road, where the *palapa* of an old restaurant stands at beachside. This is the southernmost of two islet-protected coves flanking the low Punta Negro headland. With clear, tranquil waters and golden-sand beaches, both coves are great for fishing from the rocks, snorkeling, sailboarding, and swimming. The gorgeous south-end beach, Playa Negrita, is offered as a campground, with plenty of room for tenting and RV parking; a friendly caretaker collects about $2.50 per day per car. A *palapa* restaurant provides drinks and seafood lunches and dinners.

Food

Groceries are available at stores near the **El Super** corner (Km 72) or in the villages of **Perula** (on the beach, turn off at Km 74), **San Mateo** (Km 70), and **Chamela** (walk north along the beach, or follow the side road, downhill, at the south end of the bridge between Km 64 and 63).

Hearty country Mexican food, hospitality, and snack groceries are available at the **Tejeban** truck stop/restaurant at the El Super corner; open daily from breakfast time until 10–11 P.M. Two popular local roadside seafood spots are the **La Viuda** (The Widow, Km 64) and **Don Lupe Mariscos** (Km 63), on opposite ends of the Río Chamela bridge. They both have their own divers who go out daily for fresh fish ($5), octopus *(pulpo)* ($7), conch, clams, oysters, and lobster ($10). Open daily 8 A.M. until around 9 P.M.

Information and Services

The closest **bank** is 34 miles north at Tomatlán (turnoff at La Cumbre, at Km 116). *Casetas de larga distancia* operate at the Tejeban restaurant at El Super corner, daily 8 A.M.–9 P.M., and at Pueblo Careyes, the village behind the soccer field at Km 52.

Until someone resurrects the **Pemex** *gasolinera* at El Super, the closest unleaded Magna Sin gas is

SAVING TURTLES

Sea turtles were once common on Pacific Mexico beaches. Times have changed, however. Now a determined corps of volunteers literally camps out on isolated beaches, trying to save the turtles from extinction. This is a tricky business, because their poacher opponents are invariably poor, determined, and often armed. Since turtle tracks lead right to the eggs, the trick is to get there before the poachers. The turtle-savers dig up the eggs and hatch them themselves, or bury them in secret locations where they hope the eggs will hatch unmolested. The reward—the sight of hundreds of new hatchlings returning to the sea—is worth the pain for this new generation of Mexican ecoactivists.

Once featured on a thousand restaurant menus

green turtle

BOB RACE

from Puerto Angel to Mazatlán, turtle meat, soup, and eggs are now illegal commodities. Though not extinct, Pacific Mexico's three main sea turtle species—green, hawksbill, and leatherback—have dwindled to a tiny fraction of their previous numbers.

The **green turtle** *(Chelonia mydas),* known locally as *tortuga verde* or *caguama,* is named for the color of its fat. Although officially threatened, the prolific green turtle remains relatively numerous. Females can return to shore up to eight times during the year, depositing 500 eggs in a single season. When not mating or migrating, the vegetarian greens can be spotted most often in lagoons and bays, especially the Bay of Banderas, nipping at seaweed with their beaks. Adults,

27 miles north at La Cumbre (Km 116) or 50 miles (80 km) south at Melaque (Km 0).

If you get sick, the closest health clinic is in Perula (Km 74, one block north of the town plaza, no phone, but a pharmacy) or at Pueblo Careyes at Km 52 (medical consultations daily 8 A.M.–2 P.M.; doctor on call around the clock in emergencies).

Local special **police,** known as the Policia Auxiliar del Estado, are stationed in a pink roadside house at Km 46, and also in the house above the road at Km 43. The local *preventiva* (municipal police) are at the El Super corner.

EL CAREYES BEACH RESORT

El Careyes Beach Resort, one of the little-known gems of the Pacific Coast of Mexico, is really two hotels in one. After Christmas and before Easter it brims with well-to-do Mexican families letting their hair down. The rest of the year the hotel is a tranquil, tropical retreat basking at the edge of a pristine, craggy cove.

The natural scene sets the tone: a majestic palm grove opens onto a petite sandy beach set between rocky cliffs. Offshore, the water, deep and crystal clear, is home for dozens of kinds of fish. Overhead, hawks and frigate birds soar, pelicans dive, and boobies and terns skim the waves. Seasonally, at night nearby, sea turtles carry out their ancient ritual by silently depositing their precious eggs on nearby beaches where they were born.

As if not to be outdone by nature, the hotel itself is an elegant, tropical retreat. A platoon of gardeners manicure lush spreading grounds that lead to gate and reception area. Past the desk, tiers of ochre-hued Mediterranean-chic lodgings enclose an elegant inner courtyard where a blue pool meanders beneath majestic, rustling palms. At night, the grounds glimmer softly with lamps. They illuminate the tufted grove, light the path to a secluded beach, and lead the way up through the cactus-sprinkled hillside thorn forest to a romantic restaurant high above the bay.

Hotel Activities

Hotel guests enjoy a plethora of sports facilities, including tennis courts, riding stables, and a polo field. Aquatic activities include snorkeling, scuba

usually three or four feet long and weighing 100–200 pounds, are easily identified out of water by the four big plates on either side of their shells. Green turtle meat was once prized as the main ingredient of turtle soup.

The endangered **hawksbill** (*Eretmochelys imbricata*) has vanished from many Pacific Mexico beaches. Known locally as the *tortuga carey*, it was the source of both meat and the lovely translucent tortoiseshell that has been supplanted largely by plastic. Adult *careys*, among the smaller of sea turtles, run two to three feet in length and weigh 30–100 pounds. Their usually brown shells are readily identified by shingle-like overlapping scales. During late summer and fall, females come ashore to lay clutches of eggs (around 100) in the sand. *Careys*, although preferring fish, mollusks, and shellfish, will eat most anything, including seaweed. When attacked, *careys* can be plucky fighters, inflicting bites with their eagle-sharp hawksbills.

You'll be fortunate indeed if you glimpse the rare **leatherback** (*Dermochelys coriacea*), the world's largest turtle. "Experts" know so little about the leatherback, or *tortuga de cuero*, it's impossible to determine just how endangered it is. Tales are told of fisherfolk netting seven- or eight-foot leatherbacks weighing nearly a ton apiece. If you see even a small one you'll recognize it immediately by its back of smooth, tough skin, creased with several lengthwise ridges.

BOB RACE

hawksbill turtle

diving, kayaking, sailing, and deep-sea fishing. Boats are additionally available for picnic-excursions to nearby hidden beaches, wildlife-viewing, and observing turtle nesting in season. A luxury spa with view pampers guests with massage, facials, sauna, whirlpool tub, and exercise machines. Evenings, in season, live music brightens the cocktail and dinner hours at the elegant beach-view restaurant/bar.

The hotel was named for *carey* (kah-RAY), the native word for an endangered species of sea turtle (the hawksbill) that used to lay eggs on the little beach of Careyitos that fronts the hotel. Saving the turtles at nearby Playa Teopa, accessible only through hotel property, has now become a major hotel mission. Guards do, however, allow access to serious outside visitors during hatching times; follow the dirt road between Km 49 and 50 to gate and beach; no camping, please. Check with the hotel desk for information and permission.

Hotel Information

The luxurious rooms and suites, depending on location and size, run between approximately $335 d and $510 d, low season; $365–621 d high. All accommodations have a/c, TV, and direct-dial phones. Additional hotel facilities and services include fiber-optic telecommunications, a 100-person meeting room, several shops and boutiques, library, small theater, babysitters, heliport, private landing strip, and a number of business services.

For reservations and information, contact the hotel directly at tel. 315/351-0000, toll-free Mex. tel. 800/909-4800, fax 315/351-0100, email careyes@careyeshotel.com.

You may also contact the El Careyes through its agent, the Mexico Boutique Hotels, toll-free U.S. tel. 877/278-8018 or Can. tel. 866/818-8342, email info@mexicoboutiquehotels.com, or visit the website www.mexicoboutiquehotels. Otherwise, contact the hotel's other agent, the Luxury Collection, at toll-free U.S./Can. tel. 800/325-3589 or website www.luxurycollection.com.

Getting There

The El Careyes is a few minutes' drive down a cobbled entrance road (bear left all the way) at Km 53.5 (100 miles, 161 km, from Puerto Val-

larta; 34 miles, 55 km, from Barra de Navidad; and 52 miles, 84 km, from the Manzanillo International Airport).

PLAYA CAREYES AND CUITZMALA

At Km 52, just south of a small bridge and a bus stop, a dirt road leads to the lovely honey-tinted crescent of Playa Careyes. Here, a car-accessible track (be careful for soft spots) continues along the dune, where you could enjoy a day or week of beach camping. Beyond the often powerful waves (swim with caution), the intimate, headland-framed bay brims with outdoor possibilities. Bird-watching and wildlife-viewing can be quite rewarding; notice the herons, egrets, and cormorants in the lagoon just south of the dune. Fishing is good either from the beach, by boat (launch from the sheltered north end), or the rocks on either side. Water is generally clear for snorkeling and, beyond the waves, good for either kayaking or sailboarding. If you have no boat, no problem, for the local fishing cooperative (boats beached by the food *palapa* at north end) would be happy to take you on a fishing trip. Figure about $20 per hour, with bargaining. Afterward, they might even cook up the catch for a big afternoon dinner at their tree-shaded *palapa*. Nearby Pueblo Careyes (behind the soccer field at Km 52) has a store, a **Centro de Salud** (Health Center), and *larga distancia*.

Access to the neighboring **Playa Teopa** is, by contrast, carefully guarded. The worthy reason is to save the hatchlings of the remaining *carey* turtles (see the special topic "Saving Turtles") who still come ashore during the late summer and fall to lay eggs. For a closer look at Playa Teopa, you could walk south along the dune-top track, although guards might eventually stop you. They will let you through (entry gate on dirt road between Km 49 and 50) if you get official permission at the desk of the El Careyes Beach Resort.

The pristine tropical deciduous woodlands that stretch for miles around Km 45 are no accident. They are preserved as part of the **Fideicomiso Cuitzmala** (Cuitzmala Trust), the local kingdom of beach, headland, and forest held by the family of late multimillionaire Sir James Gold-smith. Local officials, many of who were not privy to Sir James's grand design (which includes a sprawling sea-view mansion complex), say that a team of biologists are conducting research on the property. A ranch complex, accessible through a gate at Km 45, is Fideicomiso Cuitzmala's most obvious highway-visible landmark.

PLAYA LAS BRISAS

For a tranquil day, overnight, or weeklong beach camping adventure consider Playa Las Brisas, a few miles by the dirt road (turnoff sign near Km 36) through the village of Arroyo Seco.

About two miles long, Playa Las Brisas has two distinct sections: first comes a very broad, white sandy strand decorated by pink-blossomed verbena and pounded by wild, open-ocean waves. For shady tent camping or RV parking, a regal co-conut grove lines the beach. Before you set up, however, you should offer a little rent to the owner/caretaker, who may soon show up on a horse. Don't be alarmed by his machete; it's for husking and cutting fallen coconuts.

To see the other half of Playa Las Brisas, con-tinue along the road past the little beachside va-cation home subdivision (with a seasonal store and snack bar). You will soon reach an open-ocean beach and headland, backed by a big, level, grassy dune, perfect for tent or RV camping. Take care not to get stuck in soft spots, however.

The headland borders the El Tecuán lagoon, part of the Rancho El Tecuán, whose hilltop hotel you can see on the far side of the lagoon. The la-goon is an unusually rich fish and wildlife habitat (see Former Hotel and Playa El Tecuán for details).

Getting There

You reach the village of Arroyo Seco, where stores can furnish supplies, 2.3 miles (3.7 km) from the highway at Km 36. At the central plaza, turn left, then immediately right at the Conasupo rural store, then left again, heading up the steep dirt road. In the valley on the other side, bear right at the fork at the mango grove, and within another mile you will be in the majestic beach-bordering palm grove.

FORMER HOTEL AND PLAYA EL TECUÁN

Little was spared in perching the Hotel El Tecuán above its small kingdom of beach, lagoon, and palm-brushed rangeland. It was to be the cen-terpiece of a sprawling vacationland, with marina, golf course, and hundreds of houses and con-dos. Although those plans have yet to materialize, the hotel, unoccupied and for sale, still stands proudly, with an ambience more like an African safari lodge than a Mexican beach resort.

Masculinity bulges out of its architecture. Its corridors are lined with massive, polished tree trunks, fixed by brawny master joints to thick, hand-hewn mahogany beams. The view restau-rant was patterned after the midships of a Manila galleon, complete with a pair of varnished tree-trunk masts reaching into the inky darkness of the night sky above. If the restaurant could only sway, the illusion would have been complete.

Wildlife-Viewing, Hiking, and Jogging

It is perhaps fortunate that the former hotel and its surroundings, part of the big **Rancho Tecuán,** may never be developed into a residential com-munity. Being private, public access has always been limited, so the Rancho has become a de facto habitat-refuge for the rapidly diminishing local animal population. Wildcats, ocelots, small crocodiles, snakes, and turtles hunt in the man-groves edging the lagoon and the tangled forest that climbs the surrounding hills. The lagoon itself nurtures hosts of waterbirds and shoals of *robalo* (snook) and *pargo* (snapper).

At this writing, visitors were still being al-lowed to pass along the entrance road and enjoy wildlife-viewing opportunities. If such visitors tread softly, clean up after themselves, start no fires, and refrain from fishing or hunting, the present owners may continue to allow access. This would be ideal, because wildlife-viewing opportunities are superb. First, simply walk along the lagoon-front below the hotel hilltop, where big white herons and egrets perch and preen in the mangroves. Don't forget your binoculars, sun hat, mosquito repellent, telephoto camera, and identification book. Try launching your own rowboat, canoe, or inflatable raft for an even more rewarding outing.

The environs offer plenty of jogging and walking opportunities. For starters, stroll along the lagoonside entrance road and back (three miles, 4.8 km) or south along the beach to the Río Purificación and back (four miles, 6.4 km). Take water, mosquito repellent, sunscreen, a hat, and something to carry your beachcombing treasures in.

Tecuán Beach

The focal point of the long, wild, white-sand Playa Tecuán is at the north end, where, at low tide, the lagoon's waters stream into the sea. Platoons of waterbirds—giant brown herons, snowy egrets, and squads of pelicans, ibises, and grebes—stalk and dive for fish trapped in the shallow, rushing current.

On the beach nearby, the sand curves southward beneath a rocky point, where the waves strew rainbow carpets of limpet, clam, and snail shells. There the billows rise sharply, angling shoreward, often with good intermediate and advanced surfing breaks. Casual swimmers beware; the surf is much too powerful for safety.

Getting There

The former Hotel El Tecuán is six miles (10 km) along a paved entrance road marked by a white lighthouse at Km 33 (112 miles, 181 km, from Puerto Vallarta; 22 miles, 35 km, from Barra de Navidad).

PLAYA TENACATITA

Imagine an ideal tropical paradise: free camping on a long curve of clean white sand, right next to a lovely little coral-bottomed cove, with all the beer you can drink and all the fresh seafood you can eat. That describes Tenacatita, a place that old Mexican Pacific hands refer to with a sigh: Tenacatitaaaahhh . . .

Folks usually begin to arrive sometime in November; by Christmas, some years, there's room only for walk-ins. Which anyone who can walk can do: carry in your tent and set it up in one of the many RV-inaccessible spots.

Tenacatita visitors enjoy three distinct beaches:

the main one, Playa Tenacatita; the little one, Playa Mora; and Playa la Boca, a breezy, palm-bordered sand ribbon stretching just over three km north to the *boca* (mouth) of the Río Purificación.

Playa Tenacatita's strand of fine white sand curves from the north end of Punta Tenacatita along a long, tall packed dune to **Punta Hermanos,** a total of about two miles. The dune is where most visitors—nearly all Americans and Canadians—park their RVs. The water is clear with gentle waves, fine for swimming and sailboarding. Being so calm, it's easy to launch a boat for fishing—common catches are *huachinango* (red snapper) and *cabrilla* (sea bass)—especially at the very calm north end.

The sheltered north cove is where a village of *palapas* has grown to service the winter camping population. One of the veteran establishments is **El Puercillo,** run by longtimer José Bautista. He and several other neighbors take groups out in his launches ($80 total per half-day, bring your own beer) for offshore fishing trips and excursions.

Trouble at Tenacatita

Tenacatita is headed for changes, however. In the early 1990s, the federal government made a deal with private interests to develop a hotel at Tenacatita. The trouble began when the 50-odd squatter-operators of the Tenacatita *palapas* refused to leave. One night in November 1991, after giving the squatters plenty of warning, federal soldiers and police burned and smashed the *palapas*. Nevertheless, the squatters, backed by the Rebalsito *ejido,* the traditional owner of Tenacatita, have vowed to have their day in court. Despite further destruction by an earthquake and 10-foot tidal wave in October 1995, the squatters have tenaciously rebuilt their *palapas*.

Lately, government authorities have adopted a friendlier attitude toward the beach community. The hotel plans, so far not realized, have been scaled back to a low-profile, ecofriendly development, something like Hotelito Desconocido, north at Cruz de Loreto. (See the special topic "Splendid Isolation" in the Puerto Vallarta: Town, Bay, and Mountains chapter.)

Playas Mora and La Boca

Jewel of jewels Playa Mora is accessible by a steep, but short, uphill dirt road running north from Playa Tenacatita, past the *palapas*. Playa Mora itself is salt-and-pepper, black sand dotted with white coral, washed by water sometimes as smooth as glass. Just 50 feet from the beach the reef begins. Corals, like heads of cauliflower, some brown, some green, and some dead white, swarm with fish: iridescent blue, yellow-striped, yellow-tailed, some silvery, and others brown as rocks. (Be careful. Moray eels like to hide in rock crannies, and they bite. Don't stick your hand anywhere you can't see.)

If you get to Playa Mora by December you may be early enough to snag one of the roughly dozen car-accessible camping spots. If not, plenty of tent camping spaces accessible on foot exist; also, a few abandoned *palapa* thatched huts are usually waiting to be resurrected.

North-side Playa la Boca (fronting the palm grove by the ingress road) is the overflow campground for Tenacatita. It's not as popular because of its rough surf and steep beach. Its isolation and vigorous surf, however, make Playa la Boca the best for driftwood, beachcombing, shells, and surf fishing.

Wildlife-Viewing

Tenacatita's hinterland is a spreading, wildlife-rich mangrove marsh. From a landing behind the Tenacatita dune, you can float a boat, rubber raft, or canoe for a wildlife-viewing excursion. Local guides also furnish boats and lead trips from the same spot. Take your hat, binoculars, camera, telephoto lens, and plenty of repellent.

Tenacatita Bugs

That same marshland is the source for swarms of mosquitoes and *jejenes*, "no-see-um" biting gnats, especially around sunset. At that time no sane person at Tenacatita should be outdoors without having slathered on some good repellent.

Food and Services

The village of **El Rebalsito,** on the Highway 200-Tenacatita road, 1.5 miles back from the beach, is Tenacatita's supply and service center. It has two or three fair *abarroterías* (groceries) that carry meat and vegetables. Best of all these is friendly **Minisuper "La Morenita,"** on the highway, with a little bit of everything and a long-distance tel./fax 315/351-5224.

Additional services include a *gasolinera* that dispenses gasoline from drums, a water *purificadora* that sells drinking water retail, and even a bus stop. A single Transportes Cihuatlán bus makes one run a day between El Rebalsito and Manzanillo, leaving El Rebalsito at the crack of dawn (inquire locally) and returning from the Manzanillo central bus station around 3 P.M., arriving at El Rebasito around 6 P.M.

If you want a diversion from the fare of Tenacatita's seafood *palapas* and El Rebalsito's single restaurant, you can drive or thumb a ride seven miles (11 km) to **Restaurant Yoly** at roadside Miguel Hidalgo village (Km 30 on Highway 200) for some country-style enchiladas, tacos, *chiles rellenos*, tostadas, and beans. Open daily 7 A.M.–8 P.M.

Getting There

Leave Highway 200 at the big Tenacatita sign and interchange (at Km 27) half a mile south of the big Río Purificación bridge. El Rebalsito is 3.7 miles (six km), Tenacatita 5.4 miles (8.7 km), by a good paved road.

SUN RESORT

Despite new owners, who have changed its name to Sun Resort, the former Hotel Los Angeles Locos (which had nothing to do with crazy people from Los Angeles) lives on in minds of local people. Once upon a time, a rich family built an airstrip and a mansion by a lovely little beach on pristine Tenacatita Bay and began coming for vacations by private plane. The local people, who couldn't fathom why their rich neighbors would go to so much trouble and expense to come to such an out-of-the-way place, dubbed them *los angeles locos* (the crazy angels), because they always seemed to be flying.

The beach is still lovely and Tenacatita Bay, curving around Punta Hermanos south from Tenacatita Beach, is still pristine. Now the Sun

Resort makes it possible for droves of sun-seeking vacationers to enjoy it en masse.

Continuous music, open bar, plentiful buffets, and endless activities set the tone at Sun Resort—the kind of place for folks who want a hassle-free week of fun in the sun. The guests are typically working-age couples and singles, mostly Mexicans during the summer, Canadians and some Americans during the winter. Very few children seem to be among the guests, although they are welcome.

Hotel Activities

Although all sports and lessons—including tennis, snorkeling, sailing, sailboarding, horseback riding, volleyball, aerobics, exercises, water-skiing—plus dancing, disco, and games cost nothing extra, guests can, if they want, do nothing but soak up the sun. Sun Resort simply provides the options.

A relaxed attitude will probably allow you to enjoy yourself the most. Don't try to eat, drink, and do too much to make sure you get your money's worth. If you do, you're liable to arrive back home in need of a vacation.

Although people don't come to the tropics to stay inside, Sun Resort's rooms are quite comfortable—completely private, in pastels and white, air-conditioned, each with cable TV, phone, and private balcony overlooking either the ocean or palmy pool and patio.

Hotel Information

For information and reservations, contact a travel agent or the hotel at Km 20, Carretera Federal 200, Melaque, Jalisco, tel./fax 315/351-5020, toll-free Mex. tel. 800/713-3020 or U.S./Can. tel. 800/713-3020, website www.sun-resorts.com. Low-season rates for the 201 rooms and suites run about $155 per person per day, double occupancy, $200 high season. Children under seven with parents go free; kids 7–12, $30. For a bigger, better junior suite, add about $30 per room; prices include everything except transportation.

Getting There

The Sun Resort is about four miles (six km) off Highway 200 along a signed cobbled entrance road near the Km 20 marker (120 miles, 194 km, from Puerto Vallarta; 14 miles, 23 km, from Barra de Navidad; and 32 miles, 51 km, from the Manzanillo International Airport).

If you want to simply look around the resort, don't drive up to the gate unannounced. The guard won't let you through. Instead, call ahead and make an appointment for a "tour." After your guided look-see, you have to either sign up or mosey along. The hotel doesn't accept day guests.

Hotel Punta Serena

Part of the original development, but separate in concept and location, is Punta Serena, reachable through Sun Resort tel. 315/351-5020 (dial 0 for operator), www.puntaserena.com, perched on a breezy hilltop overlooking the entire broad sweep of Tenacatita Bay. Here, the idea is a holistic summit meditation retreat, for lovers of contemplation and tranquility. Activities—sauna, ocean-view hot tub, native Mexican *temazcal*, yoga, drumming, martial arts, gym, and more—centers on the main hilltop reception-restaurant-pool-patio building.

Paths radiate to the tile-roofed lodging units, spread over the palmy summit-park like a garden of giant mushrooms. The units themselves are designer spartan, in white and blue, with modern baths, luxuriously high ceilings, and broad ocean vistas from view balconies.

The 70 rooms, all with a/c, rent for the same as Sun Resort, about $115 per person low season, $155 high, with all in-house food and activities included.

Directions and address are identical to Sun Resort above. Turn right at the signed Punta Serena entrance driveway before heading downhill to Sun Resort.

PLAYA BOCA DE IGUANAS

Plumy Playa Boca de Iguanas curves for six miles along the tranquil inner recess of the Bay of Tenacatita. The cavernous former beachfront Hotel Bahía Tenacatita, which slumbered for years beneath the grove, is being reclaimed by the jungle and the animals that live in the nearby mangrove marsh.

The beach, however, is as enjoyable as ever: wide, level, with firm white sand, good for hiking, jogging, and beachcombing. Offshore, the gently rolling waves are equally fine for bodysurfing and boogie boarding. Beds of oysters, free for those who dive for them, lie a few hundred feet offshore. A rocky outcropping at the north end invites fishing and snorkeling while the calm water beyond the breakers invites sailboarding. Bring your own equipment.

Accommodations

First choice goes to **Camping Trailer Park Boca Beach,** with about 50 camping and RV spaces shaded beneath a majestic, rustling grove at Km 16.5 Carretera Melaque-Puerto Vallarta, P.O. Box 18, Melaque, Jalisco 48987, tel. 317/381-0393, fax 317/381-0342, bocabeach@hotmail.com. In 10 years, friendly owners Michel and Bertha Billot (he's French, she's Mexican) have built up their little paradise, surviving hurricanes and a 1995 tidal wave by trying harder. Their essentials are in place: electricity, water, showers, toilets, and about 40 spaces with sewer hookups. Much of their five acres is undeveloped and would be fine for tent campers who prefer privacy with the convenience of fresh water, a small store, and congenial company at tables beneath a rustic *palapa*. Rates run about $15/day ($13 with no hookups) $300 per month, for motor home, trailer, van, plus $.20 per kilowatt-hour for electricity. Camping runs about $6.50 per day per group; add $3 for two kids.

The original local pocket paradise, **Camping and Trailer Park Boca de Iguanas,** Km 16.5, Carretera Melaque-Puerto Vallarta, P.O. Box 93, Melaque, Jalisco 48987, seems to be succeeding where the old hotel down the beach failed. Instead of fighting the jungle, the manager is trying to coexist with it. A big crocodile lives in the mangrove-lined lotus marsh at the edge of the trailer park.

"When the crocodile gets too close to my ducks," the manager says, "I drive him back into the mangrove where he belongs. This end of the mangrove is ours, the other side is his."

The trailer park offers 40 sandy, shaded (but smallish) spaces for tents and RVs, including electricity, well water for showering, flushing, and laundry, bottled water for drinking, and a dump station. The manager runs a minimarket that supplies the necessities for a relaxed week or month on the beach. A loyal cadre of American and Canadian regulars stay here all winter. The trailer park includes a genuinely rustic kitchenette bungalow that sleeps four for $28/day. Reserve by mail, generally necessary only during Christmas or Easter week. Rates run about $14 per RV for two persons. Add $5 per additional person. Tent camping runs $5 per person.

A third-choice lodging, the nearby **Hotel and Campamento Entre Palmeras,** offers six plain rooms with fans for one to four people for about $25. The grounds feature much tent or RV camping space, electricity, showers, toilets, a simple restaurant, and a big, funky swimming pool. Its location, closer to the mangrove marsh and farther from the beach, is buggier, however.

Get to Playa Boca de Iguanas by following the signed paved road at Km 17 for 1.5 miles, 2.4 km.

PLAYA LA MANZANILLA

The little fishing town of La Manzanilla (pop. 2,000) drowses at the opposite end of the same long, curving strip of sand that begins at the Boca de Iguanas trailer parks. Here the beach, Playa La Manzanilla, is as broad and flat and the waves are as gentle, but the sand is several shades darker. Probably no better fishing exists on the entire Costa Alegre than at La Manzanilla. A dozen seafood *palapas* on the beach manage to stay open by virtue of a trickle of foreign visitors and local weekend and holiday patronage.

A very notable addition to La Manzanilla accommodations is the beautiful **Posada Tonalá,** life project of kindly owner-builder Alfonso Torres López. You must, at least, come and look at his handiwork: the graceful teak (*granadillo*) stairway, the vines cascading on one side of the airy lobby, all topped by a uniquely lovely overhead *palapa* roof.

Señor López retired from his auto parts business in Guadalajara and returned to realize his lifelong dream, to contribute to his hometown. His rooms are immaculate and spacious, with modern shower baths and plenty of attractive tile, as well as handsome, dark, hand-carved furniture and colorful, handmade bedspreads. All this for only $45 s or d, $53 t, with fans. Add about $10 during Christmas and Easter holidays. Reserve at Posada Tonalá, María Asunción 75, La Manzanilla, Jalisco, tel. 315/351-5474, fax 315/351-5318, posada-tonala@hotmail.com, website www.posada-tonala.com. Find it on the town's main street, about three blocks past the edge of town.

For an equally pleasurable but completely different experience, stay at private, secluded, sea-view **Villa Montaña,** on the hillside above and behind the town, at 46 Calle Los Angeles Locos, La Manzanilla, Jalisco 48988. Accommodations start at $89 d. For more information and reservations, contact Dan Clarke, owner-operator of Outland Adventures, P.O. Box 16343, Seattle, WA 98116, tel./fax 206/932-7012, www.choice1.com/villamontana.htm, outlandadventures@foxinternet.net. (Look for Outland Adventures under Special Tours and Study Options in the On the Road chapter.)

A handful of more basic hotels also accommodate guests. At **Hotel Posada del Cazador** (The Hunter), visitors enjoy friendly husband-wife management, a lobby for sitting and socializing, a shelf of used paperback novels, and a long-distance telephone. Find it on the main street on the left, as you enter town, at María Asunción 183, La Manzanilla, Jalisco 48988, tel. 315/351-5000, fax 630/982-8130. It has seven plain but clean rooms for $15 s or d, low season; $15 s, $22 d high. Kitchenette suites sleeping four rent for $35 low, $42 high; a larger suite, sleeping eight, $50 low, $62 high, all with fans and hot-water showers.

On the opposite, even sleepier country edge of town, the **Hotel Puesta de Sol** (Sunset), Calle Playa Blanca 94, La Manzanilla, Jalisco, tel./fax 315/351-5033, offers 17 basic rooms around a cool, leafy central patio. Rates run about $15 s, $15 d, $25 t low season; $20 s or d, $40 t high, with discounts for longer-term rentals.

Get to La Manzanilla by following the signed paved road at Km 13 for one mile. The Hotel Cazador is on the left, one block after you turn left onto the main beachfront street. The Hotel Puesta de Sol is a quarter-mile farther along; bear right past the town plaza for a few blocks along the beachfront street, Calle Playa Blanca.

EL TAMARINDO

The Costa Alegre's newest big development, El Tamarindo, occupies the lush, green peninsula that forms the southernmost point of Tenacatita Bay. Plans project a giant jungle country club, based on sales of about 100 parcels averaging 20 acres apiece. Owners will have access to extensive resort facilities, including golf course, tennis courts, hotel, restaurants, heliport, skeet range, equestrian paths, beach club, and small marina. Plans apparently include owner commitment to leaving a sizable fraction of the present forest in its original, pristine state.

The plan seem to be on track. The Tamarindo hinterland remains home to hundreds of wild creatures, from possumlike armadillos and snorting *javelines* (wild pigs) to feisty raccoons and warm and fuzzy but wily *coatimundis.*

Virtually all of the resort facilities have been installed. The golf course is a wonder all in itself, designed by renowned Robert Trent Jones and David Fleming. It meanders for thousands of yards, traversing lush lawns, tricky sand traps, serene ponds, and verdant, vine-hung thickets. Greens fee runs $150 for in-house guests, $205 for outside guests, of such plush hotels as Grand Bay, Cabo Blanco, Sun Resort, Las Alamandas, El Careyes, and Las Hadas.

Accommodations, at El Tamarindo, tel. 315/351-5032 or 315/351-5052, toll-free Mex. tel. 800/021-7526, fax 315/351-5070, tamarindo@grupoplan.com, www.grupoplan.com, are in airy, pastel stucco and tile, super-deluxe jungle-edge housekeeping villas. Rates for the several secluded lodgings run between about $500 and $800 d per day. For reservations, call Starwood Resorts, toll-free U.S./Can. tel. 800/909-4800, or Mexico Boutique Hotels, toll-free U.S. tel. 877/278-8018 or Can. tel. 866/818-8342, or email info@mexicoboutiquehotels.com, or visit the website www.mexicoboutiquehotels.

Get there via the signed side road at Km 8, five miles north of Melaque. After about two miles of winding through the sylvan tropical forest, you arrive at the gate, where you must have either a reservation in hand or an appointment before the guard will let you through.

Barra de Navidad, Melaque, and Vicinity

The little country beach town of Barra de Navidad, Jalisco (pop. 5,000), whose name literally means "Bar of Christmas," has unexpectedly few saloons. In this case, "Bar" has nothing to do with alcohol; it refers to the sandbar upon which the town is built. That lowly spit of sand forms the southern perimeter of the blue Bay of Navidad, which arcs to Barra de Navidad's twin town of San Patricio Melaque (pop. 10,000), a few miles to the west.

Barra and San Patricio Melaque, locally known as "Melaque" (may-LAH-kay), are twin, but distinct, towns. Barra has the cobbled, shady lanes and friendly country ambience; Melaque is the metropolis of the two, with most of the stores and services.

HISTORY

The sandbar is called "Navidad" because the Viceroy Antonio de Mendoza, the first and arguably the best viceroy Mexico ever had, disembarked there on December 25, 1540. The occasion was auspicious for two reasons. Besides being Christmas Day, Don Antonio had arrived to personally put down a bloody rebellion raging through western Mexico that threatened to burn New Spain off the map. Unfortunately for the thousands of native people who were torched, hung, or beheaded during the brutal campaign, Don Antonio's prayers on that day were soon answered. The rebellion was smothered, and the lowly sandbar was remembered as Barra de Navidad from that time forward.

A generation later, Barra de Navidad became the springboard for King Philip's efforts to make the Pacific a Spanish lake. Shipyards built on the bar launched the vessels that carried the expedition of conquistador Miguel López de Legazpi and Father André de Urdaneta in search of God and gold in the Philippines. Urdaneta came back a hero one year later, in 1565, having discovered the northern circle route, whose favorable easterly winds propelled a dozen subsequent generations of the fabled treasure-laden Manila galleon home to Mexico.

By 1600, however, the Manila galleon was landing in Acapulco, with its much quicker land access to the capital to transport their priceless Asian cargoes. Barra de Navidad went to sleep and didn't wake up for more than three centuries.

Now Barra de Navidad only slumbers occasionally. The townsfolk welcome crowds of beachgoing Mexican families during national holidays, and a steady procession of North American and European budget vacationers during the winter.

SIGHTS

Exploring Barra and Melaque

Most Barra hotels and restaurants lie on one oceanfront street named, uncommonly, after a conquistador, Miguel López de Legazpi. Barra's other main street, Veracruz, one short block inland, has most of the businesses, groceries, and small, family-run eateries.

Head south along Legazpi toward the steep Cerro San Francisco in the distance and you will soon be on the palm-lined walkway that runs atop the famous sandbar of Barra. On the right, ocean side, the Playa Barra de Navidad arcs northwest to the hotels of Melaque, which spread like white pebbles along the far end of the strand. The great blue water expanse beyond the beach, framed at both ends by jagged, rocky sea stacks, is the **Bahía de Navidad.**

Opposite the ocean, on the other side of the bar, spreads the tranquil, mangrove-bordered expanse of the **Laguna de Navidad,** which forms the border with the state of Colima, whose

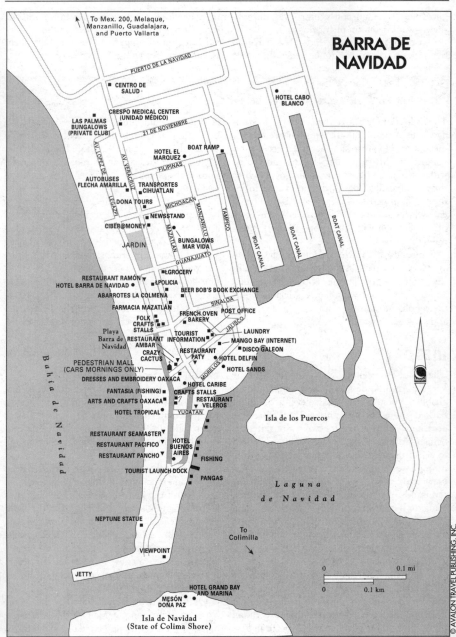

To Mex. 200, Melaque, Manzanillo, Guadalajara, and Puerto Vallarta

BARRA DE NAVIDAD

PUERTO DE LA NAVIDAD

CENTRO DE SALUD

HOTEL CABO BLANCO

CRESPO MEDICAL CENTER (UNIDAD MÉDICO)

LAS PALMAS BUNGALOWS (PRIVATE CLUB)

21 DE NOVIEMBRE

AV. LÓPEZ DE LEGAZPI

AV. VERACRUZ

HOTEL EL MARQUEZ

BOAT RAMP

FILIPINAS

AUTOBUSES FLECHA AMARILLA

TRANSPORTES CIHUATLAN

MICHOACAN

MANZANILLO

TAMPICO

DONA TOURS

NEWSSTAND

CIBER@MONEY

MAZATLAN

BOAT CANAL

BOAT CANAL

BOAT CANAL

BOAT CANAL

JARDIN

BUNGALOWS MAR VIDA

GUANAJUATO

LGROCERY

RESTAURANT RAMÓN

HOTEL BARRA DE NAVIDAD

LPOLICIA

ABARROTES LA COLMENA

BEER BOB'S BOOK EXCHANGE

FARMACIA MAZATLAN

SINALOA

FOLK CRAFTS STALLS

FRENCH OVEN BAKERY

POST OFFICE

Playa Barra de Navidad

RESTAURANT AMBAR

TOURIST INFORMATION

JALISCO

LAUNDRY

MANGO BAY (INTERNET)

CRAZY CACTUS

RESTAURANT PATY

DISCO GALEON

HOTEL DELFIN

Bahía de Navidad

PEDESTRIAN MALL (CARS MORNINGS ONLY)

MORELOS

HOTEL SANDS

DRESSES AND EMBROIDERY OAXACA

HOTEL CARIBE

FANTASIA (FISHING)

CRAFTS STALLS

ARTS AND CRAFTS OAXACA

RESTAURANT VELEROS

HOTEL TROPICAL

YUCATAN

Isla de los Puercos

RESTAURANT SEAMASTER

RESTAURANT PACIFICO

HOTEL BUENOS AIRES

RESTAURANT PANCHO

FISHING

TOURIST LAUNCH DOCK

PANGAS

Laguna de Navidad

NEPTUNE STATUE

To Colimilla

VIEWPOINT

JETTY

HOTEL GRAND BAY AND MARINA

MESÓN DOÑA PAZ

Isla de Navidad (State of Colima Shore)

0   0.1 mi

0   0.1 km

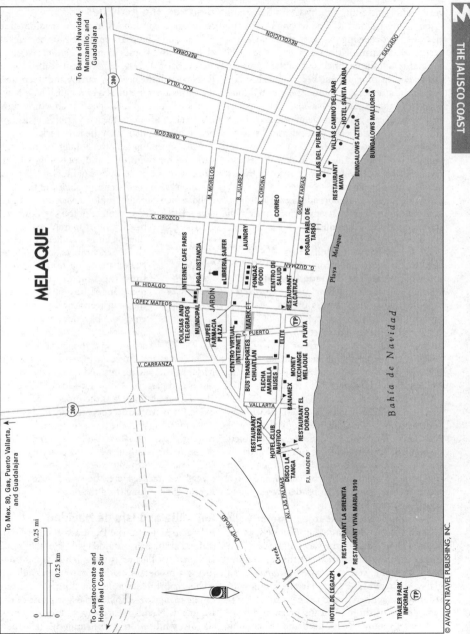

MELAQUE

To Barra de Navidad, Manzanillo, and Guadalajara →

To Mex. 80, Gas, Puerto Vallarta, and Guadalajara →

0   0.25 mi

0   0.25 km

To Cuastecomate and Hotel Real Costa Sur

200

200

REVOLUCION

A. SALGADO

REFORMA

FCO. VILLA

VILLAS CAMINO DEL MAR

HOTEL SANTA MARIA

BUNGALOWS MALLORCA

A. OBREGON

M. MORELOS

B. JUAREZ

R. CORONA

GOMEZ FARIAS

VILLAS DEL PUEBLO

BUNGALOWS AZTECA

RESTAURANT MAYA

C. OROZCO

CORREO

POSADA PABLO DE TARSO

INTERNET CAFE PARIS

LARGA DISTANCIA

LIBRERIA SAIFER

LAUNDRY

G. GUZMAN

M. HIDALGO

LOPEZ MATEOS

MUNICIPAL

JARDIN

FONDAS (FOOD)

CENTRO DE SALUD

RESTAURANT ALCATRAZ

Playa Melaque

POLICIAS AND TELEGRAFOS

SUPER FARMACIA PLAZA

MARKET

P. PUERTO

TP

V. CARRANZA

CENTRO VIRTUAL (INTERNET)

ELITE

LA PLAYA

BUS TRANSPORTES CHUATLAN

FLECHA AMARILLA BUSES

BANAMEX

MONEY EXCHANGE MELAQUE

Bahía de Navidad

VALLARTA

RESTAURANT LA TERRAZA

HOTEL CLUB NAUTICO

RESTAURANT EL DORADO

DISCO LA TANGA

F.I. MADERO

AV. LAS PALMAS

DEL FARO

RESTAURANT LA SIRENITA

RESTAURANT VIVA MARIA 1910

Creek

HOTEL DE LEGAZPI

TRAILER PARK INFORMAL

TP

© AVALON TRAVEL PUBLISHING, INC.

mountains (including nearby Cerro San Francisco) loom beyond it. The lagoon's calm appearance is deceiving, for it is really an *estero* (estuary), an arm of the sea, which ebbs and flows through the channel beyond the rock jetty at the end of the sandbar. Because of this natural flushing action, local folks still dump fishing waste into the Laguna de Navidad. Fortunately, new sewage plants route human waste away from the lagoon, so with care, you can usually swim safely in its inviting waters. Do not, however, venture too close to the lagoon-mouth beyond the jetty or you may get swept out to sea by the strong outgoing current.

On the sandbar's lagoon side, a *panga* (fishing launch) mooring and passenger dock hum with daytime activity. From the dock, launches ferry loads of passengers for less than half a dollar to the Colima shore, which is known as **Isla de Navidad,** where the marina and hotel development has risen across the lagoon. Back in the center of town, **minibuses** enter town along Veracruz, turn left at Sinaloa, by the crafts market, and head in the opposite direction, out of town, along Mazatlán, Veracruz, and Highway 200, three miles (4.8 km) to Melaque.

The once-distinct villages of San Patricio and Melaque now spread as one along the Bay of Navidad's sandy northwest shore. The business district, still known locally as San Patricio (from the highway, follow a small "San Patricio" sign two blocks toward the beach), centers around a plaza, market, and church bordering the main shopping street López Mateos.

Continue two blocks to beachfront Calle Gómez Farías, where a lineup of hotels, eateries, and shops cater to the vacation trade. From there, the curving strand extends toward the quiet Melaque west end, where *palapas* line a glassy, sheltered blue cove. Here, a rainbow of colored *pangas* perch upon the sand, sailboats rock gently offshore, pelicans preen and dive, and people enjoy snacks, beer, and the cooling breeze in the deep shade beneath the *palapas.*

A boat trip across the lagoon for super-fresh seafood at the palm-studded village of Colimilla is a primary Barra pastime.

Beaches and Activities

Although a continuous strand of medium-fine golden sand joins Barra with Melaque, it changes character and names along its gentle, five-mile arc. At Barra de Navidad, where it's called **Playa de Navidad,** the beach is narrow and steep, and the waves are sometimes very rough. Those powerful swells often provide good intermediate surfing breaks adjacent to the jetty. Fishing by line or pole is also popular from the jetty rocks.

Most mornings are calm enough to make the surf safe for swimming and splashing, which, along with the fresh seafood of beachside *palapa* restaurants, make Barra a popular Sunday and holiday picnic-ground for local Mexican families. The relatively large number of folks walking the beach unfortunately makes for slim pickings for shell collectors and beachcombers.

For a cooling midday break from the sun, drop in to the restaurant of the Hotel Tropical at the south end of Legazpi and enjoy the bay view, the swish of the waves, and the fresh breeze streaming through the lobby.

As the beach curves northwesterly toward Melaque, the restaurants and hotels give way to dunes and pasture. At the outskirts of Melaque, civilization resumes, and the broad beach, now called **Playa Melaque,** curves gently to the west.

Continuing past the town center, a lineup of rustic *palapas* and *pangas* pulled up on the sand decorate the tranquil west-end cove, which is sheltered from the open sea behind a tier of craggy sea stacks. Here, the water clears, making for good fishing from the rocks.

Colimilla and Isla de Navidad

A boat trip across the lagoon for super-fresh seafood at the palm-studded village of Colimilla is a primary Barra pastime. While you sit enjoying a moderately priced oyster cocktail, ceviche, or broiled whole-fish dinner, gaze out on the mangrove-enfolded glassy expanse of the Laguna de Navidad. Far away, a canoe may drift silently, while white herons quietly stalk their prey. Now and then a launch will glide in and deposit its load of visitors, or a fisherman will head out to sea.

One of the most pleasant Colimilla vantage spots is the **Restaurant Susana,** whose broad *palapa* extends into the lagoon; open daily 8 A.M.–8 P.M. Take mosquito repellent, especially if you're staying for dinner. Launches routinely ferry as many as six passengers to Colimilla from the Barra lagoonside docks for about $5 round-trip. Tell them when you want to return, and they'll pick you up.

From the same Barra lagoonside dock, launches also shuttle passengers for $1.50 round-trip across the lagoon to Isla de Navidad and its new Hotel Grand Bay marina, vacation home development, and golf course.

Playa de Cocos

A trip to wild, breezy Playa de Cocos, hidden just behind the Cerro San Francisco headland south of Barra, makes an interesting afternoon outing, especially when combined with the trip to Colimilla. A wide, golden sand beach curves miles southward, starting beneath a cactus-dotted jungly headland. The beach, although broad, is steep, with strong shorebreakers. Although swimming is hazardous, fishing off the rocks and beachcombing are the delights here. A feast of driftwood and multicolored shells—olives, small conches, purple-striated clams—litters the sand, especially on an intimate, spectacular hidden cove, reachable by scampering past the waves at low tide.

There are two ways to get to Playa de Cocos. Through Colimilla, walk uphill to the road above the La Colimilla restaurants. Head left (east) for about a quarter-mile. Turn right at the palm-lined boulevard and continue along the golf course about a mile and a quarter to the beach beneath the tip of the Cerro San Francisco headland.

You can also taxi or drive there by turning off Highway 200 at the Ejido La Culebra (or Isla Navidad) sign as the highway cuts through the hills at Km 51 a few miles south of Barra. Mark your odometer at the turnoff. Follow the road about three miles (4.8 km) to a bridge, where you enter the state of Colima. From there the road curves right, paralleling the beach. After about two more miles (3.2 km), you pass through

the golf course gate. After winding through the golf course another mile, fork left at the intersecting boulevard and traffic circle at the north edge of the golf course. Continue another mile to the end of the road and beach.

Playa Coastecomate

Playa de Cocos has its exact opposite in Playa Coastecomate (kooah-stay-koh-MAH-tay), tucked behind the ridge rising beyond the northwest edge of Melaque. The dark, fine-sand beach arcs along a cove on the rampart-rimmed big blue **Bahía de Coastecomate.** Its very gentle waves and clear waters make for excellent swimming, sailboarding, snorkeling, and fishing from the beach itself or the rocks beneath the adjacent cliffs. A number of *palapa* restaurants along the beach serve seafood and drinks.

The Coastecomate beachside village itself, home for a number of local fisherfolk and a few North Americans in permanently parked RVs, has a collection of oft-empty bungalows on the hillside, a small store, and about three times as many chickens as people.

To get there, drive, taxi, or bus via the local minibus or Transportes Cihuatlán to the signed Melaque turnoff from Highway 200. There, a paved side road marked Hotel Real Costa Sur heads northwest into the hills, winding for two miles (3.2 km) over the ridge through pasture and jungle woodland to the village. If you're walking, allow an hour and take your sun hat, insect repellent, and water.

Barra-Melaque Hike

You can do this four-mile stroll either way, but starting from Barra in the morning, with the sun behind you, the sky and the ocean will be at their bluest and best. Take insect repellent, sunscreen, and a hat. At either end, enjoy lunch at one of the seaside restaurants. At the Melaque end you can continue walking north to the cove on the far side of town. The trail beneath the cliff leads to spectacular wave-tossed tidepools and rugged sea rocks at the tip of the bay. At the Barra end, you can hire a launch to Colimilla. End your day leisurely by taxiing or busing back from the bus station at either end.

Bird-Watching and Wildlife-Viewing

The wildlife-rich upper reaches of the Laguna de Navidad stretch for miles and are only a boat ride away. Besides the ordinary varieties of egrets, terns, herons, pelicans, frigate birds, boobies, ducks, and geese, patient bird-watchers can sometimes snare rainbow flash-views of exotic parrots and bright tanagers and orioles.

As for other creatures, quiet, persistent observers are sometimes rewarded with mangrove-edge views of turtles, constrictors, crocodiles, coatimundis, raccoons, skunks, deer, wild pigs, ocelots, wildcats, and, very rarely, a jaguar. The sensitivity and experience of your boatman/guide is, of course, crucial to the success of any nature outing. Ask at the dock-office of the **Sociedad Cooperativa de Servicios Turísticos**, 40 Av. Veracruz on the lagoon front. You might also ask Tracy Ross at Crazy Cactus (on Jalisco, next door to the church, near the corner of Veracruz) to recommend a good guide, or even a complete wildlife-viewing excursion.

ACCOMMODATIONS

Barra Hotels

Whether on the beach or not, all Barra hotels (except the world-class Hotel Grand Bay) fall in the budget or moderate categories. One of the best, the family-run **Hotel Sands,** offers a bit of class at moderate rates at Morelos 24, Barra de Navidad, Jalisco 48987, tel./fax 315/355-5018. Two tiers of rooms enclose an inner courtyard lined with comfortable sitting areas opening into a lush green garden of leafy vines and graceful coconut palms. A side-corridor leads past a small zoo of spider monkeys, raccoons, and squawking macaws to a view of Barra's colorful lineup of fishing launches. On the other side, past the swim-up bar, a big curving pool and outer patio spreads to the placid edge of the mangrove-bordered Laguna de Navidad. The pool-bar (happy hour daily 4–6 P.M., winter season) and the sitting areas afford inviting places to meet other travelers. The rooms, all with fans (but with sporadic hot water in some rooms—check before moving in) are clean and furnished with dark varnished wood and tile. Light sleepers should wear earplugs or book a room in the wing farthest from the disco down the street, whose music thumps away until around 2 A.M. most nights during the high season. Its 43 rooms and bungalows rent from $28 s, $36 d low season, $42 s, $57 d high (bargain for a better rate); bungalows sleeping four with kitchenette run $100 low season, $150 high. Credit cards (with a 6 percent surcharge) are accepted, and parking is available.

Across the street, its loyal international clientele swears by the family-operated **Hotel Delfín,** Morelos 23, Barra de Navidad, Jalisco 48987, tel. 315/355-5068, fax 315/355-6020, mmadrigal@nautilus.melaque.udg.mx. Its four stories of tile-floored, balcony-corridor rooms (where curtains, unfortunately, must be drawn for privacy) are the cleanest and coziest of Barra's moderate hotels. The Delfín's tour de force, however, is the cheery patio buffet where guests linger over the breakfast offered every morning ($3–5, open daily 8:30–10:30 A.M.) to all comers. Overnight guests, like those of the Sands, must put up with the moderate nighttime noise of the disco half a block away. For maximum sun and privacy take one of the top-floor rooms, many of which enjoy lagoon views. The Delfín's 30 rooms rent for $29 s, $35 d, $45 t low season, $50 s or d, $60 t high; with fans, small pool, and parking; credit cards are accepted.

One block south and a notch down the economic scale is **Casa de Huéspedes Caribe,** Sonora 15, Barra de Navidad, Jalisco 48987, tel. 315/355-5952, tucked along a side street. The family owners offers 11 clean, plain rooms, all with bath and hot water, to a devoted following of long-term customers. Amenities include a homey downstairs garden sitting area, and more chairs and a hammock for snoozing on an upstairs porch. Rates run $14 s, $22 d, and $25 t in rooms with twin, double, or both types of beds.

Continue south two blocks along Morelos (and jog half a block uphill, west, to Veracruz), to new, white-stuccoed **Hotel Buenos Aires,** at Veracruz 209, Barra de Navidad, Jalisco 48987, tel./fax 315/355-6967, hotelbuenos airesmx@yahoo.com.mx. The savvy but friendly Argentine expatriate on-site owner offers eight simply but comfortably furnished modern ac-

BARRA AND MELAQUE ACCOMMODATIONS BY PRICE

Accommodations (area code 315) are listed in increasing order of approximate high-season, double-room rates.

Barra (postal code 48987)

Casa de Huéspedes Caribe, Sonora 15, tel. 355-5952, $22

Hotel Delfín, Morelos 23, tel. 355-5068, fax 355-6020, $33

Hotel Buenos Aires, Veracruz 209, tel./fax 355-6967, hotelbuenosaires@yahoo.com.mx, $55

Hotel Sands, Morelos 24, tel./fax 355-5018, $57

Bungalows Mar Vida, Mazatlán 168, tel. 355-5911, fax 355-5349, marsha@marshaewing.com, $60

Hotel Tropical, Legazpi 96, tel. 355-5020, fax 355-5149, $60

Hotel El Márquez, Filipina and Manzanillo, tel/fax 355-5304, www.geocities.com/barradenavidad-hotelmar.html, $70

Hotel Cabo Blanco, P.O. Box 31, tel. 355-5103 or 355-5136, fax 355-6494, $70

Hotel Barra de Navidad, Legazpi 250, tel. 355-5122, fax 355-5303, hotel_barradenavidad@yahoo.com, $72

Mesón Doña Paz P.O. Box 20, tel. 355-6441, toll-free U.S. tel. 877/278-8018 or Can. tel. 866/818-8342, reservaciones@mesondonapaz.com, $330

Hotel Grand Bay, P.O. Box 20, tel. 355-5050, fax 355-6070, reservaciones@islaresort.com.mx, $450

Melaque (postal code 48980)

Hotel Santa María, Abel Salgado 85, P.O. Box 188, tel. 355-5677, fax 355-5553, $23

Hotel de Legazpi, Av. de las Palmas s/n, P.O. Box 88, tel./fax 355-5397, hlegazpi@prodigy.net.mx, $35

Posada Pablo de Tarso, Gómez Farías 408, tel. 355-5117, fax 355-5268, $42

Villas Camino del Mar, P.O. Box 6, tel. 355-5207, fax 355-5498, thevillas@prodigy.net.mx, $46–105

Bungalows Azteca, P.O. Box 57, tel./fax 355-5150, $50

Bungalows Mayorca, Abel Salgado 133, P.O. Box 157, tel. 355-5219, bungalowsmayorca@prodigy.net.mx, $60

Hotel Club Náutico, Gómez Farías 1A, tel. 355-5770 or 355-5766, fax 355-5239, club_nauticomx@yahoo.com, $60

Hotel Real Costa Sur, P.O. Box 12, tel./fax 355-5085, $70

Villas del Pueblos, P.O. Box 6, tel. 355-5207, fax 355-5498, thevillas@prodigy.net.mx, $85–120

---

commodations in three floors, topped by a view penthouse. The building's height affords upper-floor accommodations the benefit of either lagoon or ocean sunset views and cooling afternoon westerly breezes. Rooms rent from $30 s, $35 d low season for the bottom floor, $40 and $45 for the second floor. The third-floor penthouse goes for $60. Add about $10 for high season. With fans, a/c; credit cards accepted. Make your winter season reservations early. For more information, visit the website www.go.to/barradenavidad.com.

(*Note:* The longtime **Hotel Tropical,** near the south, "bar" end of Legazpi, at Av. L. de Legazpi 96, Barra de Navidad, Jalisco 48987, sustained serious damage in the October 9,

1995, earthquake. Alas, at this writing, it is not yet open, but repairs appear largely completed. It seems that, by the time you read this, the Tropical will be an improved version of the old hotel. In previous editions, I wrote: "guests in many of its renovated oceanfront tiers of comfortable, high-ceilinged rooms enjoy luxuriously private ocean-view balconies. Downstairs, the natural air-conditioning of an ocean breeze often floods the sea-view lobby-restaurant." The 57 rooms will probably rent for about $40 s, $60 d, with fans and a tiny pool; credit cards are accepted. For reservations, write, or, if the phone numbers remain the same, call tel. 315/355-5020, fax 315/355-5149.)

Sharing the same beachfront by the town plaza a few blocks away is the white stucco three-story **Hotel Barra de Navidad** at Av. L. de Legazpi 250, Barra de Navidad, Jalisco 48987, tel. 315/355-5122, fax 315/355-5303, hotel_barradenavidad@yahoo.com. Guests in the seaside upper two floors of comfortable (but not deluxe) rooms enjoy palm-fringed ocean vistas from private balconies. An inviting pool and patio on one side and good Bananas Restaurant upstairs complete the attractive picture. Rates for the 57 rooms run a pricey $62 s, $72 d, $78 t high season, $56, $65, $70 low, all with a/c. Ask for one of the sunnier, quieter, ocean-view rooms, with a/c. Credit cards are accepted. (The Barra de Navidad waves during fall storm season sometimes hit the sand with a boom. If you're a light sleeper, best come prepared with earplugs.)

The heavy surf of hurricane Kenna, in October 2002, unfortunately destroyed Barra oceanfront favorite twin lodgings **Hotel Bogavante** and **Bungalows Karelia.** At this writing, a stark sandy lot is all that remains. I hope the owners will some day restore them to the attractive conditions that I described in previous editions.

Given the consequent scarcity of Barra de Navidad beachfront lodgings, you might consider switching to increasingly popular Melaque, where the waves are more tranquil (see Melaque Hotels), or staying in one of several good Barra off-beach lodgings.

For example, consider three-star **Hotel El Márquez,** at Calles Filipinas and Manzanillo, Barra de Navidad, Jalisco 48987, tel./fax 315/355-5304, on the north end, four short blocks from the beach. Inside the gate, guests enjoy about 20 comfortable, semideluxe rooms, around an invitingly intimate inner pool patio. Rates begin at about $50 low season, $70 high. Reserve either by telephone or emailing elmarquez@esmas.com. For more information, visit the website www.geocities.com/barrdenavidad-hotelmar.html.

If the Márquez is full, try nearby similar three-star neighbor **Bungalows Mar Vida,** one block west and one block south, at Mazatlán 168, Barra de Navidad, Jalisco 48987. Reserve by tel. 315/355-5911, fax 315/355-5349, or email marsha@marshaewing.com. For more information, visit website www.tomzap.com/marvida.html.

Barra's original deluxe lodging is the peach-hued, stucco-and-tile, four-star **Hotel Cabo Blanco,** P.O. Box 31, Barra de Navidad, Jalisco 48987, tel. 315/355-5103 or 315/355-5136, fax 315/355-6494. The 125-room low-rise complex (named after the 1970s Barra de Navidad–filmed Hollywood thriller *Cabo Blanco,* starring Charles Bronson) anchors the vacation home development along the three marina-canals that extend about five blocks north from the Barra lagoon. Within its manicured garden-grounds, Hotel Cabo Blanco offers night-lit tennis courts, restaurants, bars, two pools, kiddie pools, and deluxe sportfishing yachts-for-hire. The deluxe, pastel-decorated rooms run about $70 d high season, $50 d low, all with a/c, cable TV, and phones; with a folkloric dance show, many water sports, and credit cards accepted. Bring your repellent; during late afternoon and evening mosquitoes and gnats from the nearby mangroves seem to especially enjoy the Cabo Blanco's posh ambience. For more information, visit the website www.hotelcaboblanco.com.

Barra's plushest hotel by far is the class-act **Hotel Grand Bay,** P.O. Box 20, Barra de Navidad, Jalisco 48987, tel. 315/355-5050, fax 315/355-6070, reservaciones@islaresort.com.mx, a short boat ride across the lagoon. Builders spared little expense to create the appearance of a *gran epoch* resort. The 198 rooms are elaborately furnished in marble floors, French provincial furniture, and jade-hued Italian marble bathroom sinks. Accommodations run from spacious "superior" rooms for $450 d high season, $380 low, and master suites ($800 high, $700 low) through grand four-room executive suites that include their own steam rooms, from $2,300. With all conveniences, including three pools, three elegant restaurants, tennis, volleyball, children's club, marina, and a wonderfully breezy oceanfront golf course. (Don't be put off by the high quoted rates. The hotel customarily offers deep discounts and packages and promotions by reservation, either directly or through travel agents. For more information, visit the website www.islanavidad.com.)

© BRUCE WHIPPERMAN

Villas Camino del Mar is one of the most relaxing of Melaque's many beachfront hotels.

The owners of the Hotel Grand Bay also offer a more private, personal option, the **Mesón Doña Paz.** Originally built as the owners' private manor house (which they now use only at Christmas), the Mesón Doña Paz is a maharaja's mansion of spacious super-luxurious suites, elegantly decorated in the marble-French Provincial mode of the neighboring Hotel Grand Bay. The load of amenities include elaborate telephone-equipped bathrooms (with separate rooms for tubs and showers), airy, private, view patios, an exclusive restaurant, dining veranda, and bar, and a private boat landing. Upstairs, a regal penthouse view salon, perfect for executive meetings (up to about 50 people) adds an interesting business-friendly option. Offering rates, beginning at $235 d low season, $330 high ($350 and $470 for junior suites; $470 and $600 for master suite), considering the luxury facilities, are very reasonable.

Reserve for Mesón Doña Paz either directly, tel./fax 315/355-6441; toll-free Mex. tel. 800/012-9887; by email at reservaciones@meson-donapaz.com; or through its agent, Mexico Boutique Hotels, toll-free U.S. tel. 877/278-8018 or Can. tel. 866/818-8342, or email info@mex-icoboutiquehotels.com. For more information, visit the website www.mexicoboutiquehotels. (If all these fail, use the Hotel Grand Bay contact numbers, above.)

Note: Security is tight at Hotel Grand Bay. Guards at the hotel lagoon-side boat dock (and the separate Mesón Doña Paz dock) only allow entrance to guests and prospective guests. If you want to look around, you have to be accompanied by an in-house guide. Call the desk beforehand for an appointment.

Melaque Hotels

In contrast to Barra de Navidad, San Patricio-Melaque has many beachfront hotels. Although some, especially in the old San Patricio town center, are mediocre at best, visitors enjoy a number of well-managed, comfortable, even luxurious exceptions, especially in the quiet south-side neighborhood.

Hotels South of Town: Classy in its unique way is the **Villas Camino del Mar**, whose owner doesn't believe in much advertising. A few signs in the humble beach neighborhood about a quarter-mile on the Barra side of the Melaque town center furnish the only clue that this gem of a lodging hides among the Melaque dross at Calle Francisco Villa, corner Abel Salgado, P.O. Box 6, San Patricio-Melaque, Jalisco 48980, tel. 315/355-5207, fax 315/355-5498, thevillas@prodigy.net.mx. (Note: Recently, owners have added an annex across the street, which, although inviting, crams in more accommodations in a smaller space than the original building. Specifically ask for a room in the original building in your written or faxed reservation request.) A five-story white stucco monument draped with fluted, neoclassic columns and hanging pedestals, the original Villas Camino del Mar hotel offers a lodging assortment from simple double rooms through deluxe suites with kitchenettes to a rambling penthouse. The upper three levels have sweeping ocean views, while the lower two overlook an elegant blue pool and patio bar and shady beachside palm grove. The clientele is split between Mexican middle-class families who come for weekends all year around, and quiet Canadian and American couples who come to soak up the winter sun for weeks and months on end. Reserve early, especially for the winter. Year-round rates for the 37 rooms and suites (all with kitchenettes) run as little as $46 ($42 per day weekly, $32 monthly) for small but comfortable ocean-view doubles; $75 ($65 weekly, $47 monthly) for one-bedroom kitchenette studios, and $105 ($95 weekly, $70 monthly) for deluxe two-bedroom, two-bath suites with kitchen; all with fans only.

Camino del Mar's nearby new, upscale **Villas del Pueblo**, set in a spacious, grassy beachfront compound, with its own pool, offers much more luxury and space. The nine one- and two- bedroom kitchenette apartments go for $85–125; a one-week rental gets an 8 percent discount; one month 25 percent. Reserve early, through the Villas Camino del Mar contact numbers, above.

If the Camino del Mar is full or not to your liking, you can choose from a trio of acceptable lodgings around the corner that share the same golden sunset-view strand. The plainer but priced-right **Hotel Santa María** offers 46 rooms and kitchenette apartments with bath, close enough to the water for the waves to lull guests to sleep at Abel Salgado 85, P.O. Box 188, San Patricio-Melaque, Jalisco 48980, tel. 315/355-5677, fax 315/355-5553. Rooms, popular with budget-conscious Canadians and Americans in winter, are arranged in a pair of motel-style stucco tiers around an invitingly green inner patio. Units vary; upper rooms are brighter, so look at a few before you move in. All-season prices for the spartan but generally tidy rooms begin at about $23 d per day, $130/week, $350/month, with fans, and sunny beach-front pool. Credit cards not accepted.

Right next door, the sky-blue and white **Bungalows Azteca** auto court–style cottages line both sides of a cobbled driveway courtyard garden that spreads to a lazy beachfront patio. The 14 spacious kitchenette cottages, in small (one-bedroom) or large (three-bedroom) versions, are plainly furnished but clean. The nine one-bedroom units rent, low season, for about $50/day, $200/week, $500/month (high season, $60, $300, $600). The two three-bedrooms rent for about $130/day, $500/week, $1,500/month. Send your reservation request to P.O. Box 57, San Patricio-Melaque, Jalisco 48980, or tel./fax 315/355-5150. Get your reservation in early, especially for the winter.

Less than a block away, the open, parklike grounds, spacious blue pool, and beachside palm garden of the **Bungalows Mayorca** invite unhurried outdoor relaxation. Its stacked, Motel 6–style layout, now draped with tropical greenery, has aged gracefully. Here, groups and families used to providing their own atmosphere find the kitchens and spacious (but dark) rooms of the Bungalows Mayorca appealing. The 24 two-bedroom bungalows with a/c and TV rent for about $57 d, $200/week, $700/month low season ($60, $280, and $920 high). Ask for one of the beachfront units, with view balconies. Reserve directly, at Abel Salgado 133, Colonia Villa Obregón, P.O. Box 157, San Patricio-Melaque, Jalisco 48980, tel. 315/355-5219, or by email bungalowsmayorca@prodigy.net.mx.

Closer toward town is the well-kept, colonial-chic **Posada Pablo de Tarso,** Av. Gómez Farías 408, San Patricio-Melaque, Jalisco 48980, tel. 315/355-5117, fax 315/355-5268, named after the apostle Paul of Tarsus. This unique label, along with the many classy details, including art-decorated walls, hand-carved bedsteads and doors, and a flowery beachside pool and patio, reflect an unusual degree of care and devotion. The only drawback lies in the motel-style corridor layout, which requires guests to pull the dark drapes for privacy. Year-round rates for the 27 rooms and bungalows begin at about $42 d; a kitchen raises the tariff to about $55 d, with fans only, TV, and phones. You can also reserve through the owner in Guadalajara, at tel. 33/3616-4850 or tel./fax 33/3616-6688.

Hotels North of Town: If you prefer hotel high-rise ambience with privacy, a sea-view balcony, and a disco next door, you can have it right on the beach at the in-town **Hotel Club Náutico,** Av. Gómez Farías 1A, San Patricio-Melaque, Jalisco 48980, tel. 315/355-5770 or 315/355-5766, fax 315/355-5239, club_nauticomx@yahoo.com. The 40 deluxe rooms, in blue, pastels, and white, angle toward the ocean in sunset-view tiers above a smallish pool and patio. The upper-floor rooms nearest the beach are likely to be quieter with the best views. The hotel also has a good beachside restaurant whose huge *palapa* both captures the cool afternoon sea breeze and frames the blue waters of the Bay of Navidad. The hotel's main drawback is lack of space, being sandwiched into a long, narrow beachfront lot. Rentals run about $40 s, $60 d high season. Ask for a discount during times of low occupancy. With a/c, TV, phones, and restaurant/bar; credit cards are accepted.

In contrast, the friendly, downscale-modern, white stucco **Hotel de Legazpi** in the drowsy beach-end neighborhood nearby offers a more personal and tranquil ambience, at P.O. Box 88, San Patricio-Melaque, Jalisco 48980, tel./fax 315/355-5397, hlegazpi@prodigy.net.mx. A number of the hotel's spacious, clean, and comfortable front-side rooms have balconies with palmy ocean and sunset views. Downstairs, guests enjoy use of a homey restaurant and a rear-court pool and patio. The hotel's beachside entrance leads through a jungly front garden straight to the idyllic Melaque west-end sand crescent. Here, good times bloom among an informal club of longtime winter returnees beneath the *palapas*

of the popular La Sirenita and Viva María restaurants. The hotel's 16 fan-only rooms (two with kitchenette) rent for $28 s, $32 d, $35 t low season, $33, $35 $39 high.

The five-star **Hotel Real (Royal) Costa Sur** on Playa Coastecomate a few miles north offers a local resort alternative at P.O. Box 12, San Patricio-Melaque, Jalisco 48980, tel./fax 315/355-5085. The hotel's low-rise view guest cabanas spread like a giant mushroom garden in the jungly palm-forest hillside above the beach. Patrons—mostly Canadians and Americans in winter, Mexicans in summer and holidays—enjoy deluxe air-conditioned view rooms with cable TV, tennis courts, sailing, sailboarding, pedalboats, snorkeling, volleyball, and a broad pool and sundeck right on the beach. All-inclusive rates, including all food, beverages, and in-house entertainment, run about $50 per person, double occupancy; for room only, about $70 d high season, $55 d low). During times of low occupancy the hotel may accept day guests for a set fee. (*Note:* A reader complained that she got sick from musty mildew in her room here. Although new management seems competent and seems to have corrected such problems, be sure to choose a clean, satisfactorily ventilated room before moving in.)

Apartments, Houses, and Long-Term Rentals

If you're planning on a stay longer than a few weeks, you'll get more for your money if you can find a long-term house or apartment rental. Peggy and Tracye Ross, at Crazy Cactus store in Barra (on Jalisco, corner of Veracruz, next to Restaurant Ambar) specialize in finding local rentals for visitors. Call tel./fax 315/355-6099, or drop by, or write them several weeks in advance, at Tienda Crazy Cactus, Calle Jalisco 8, esquina Veracruz, Barra de Navidad, Jalisco 48987.

(Alternatively, see the websites in Internet Resources at the end of this book. Notable for vacation rentals is **www.choice1.com** with information and reservations links to individual owners.)

Trailer Parks and Camping

Barra-Melaque's best trailer park is **La Playa,**

right on the beach in downtown Melaque at P.O. Box 59, Av. Gómez Farías 250, San Patricio-Melaque, Jalisco 48980, tel. 315/355-5065. Although the park is a bit cramped and mostly shadeless, longtimers nevertheless get their winter reservations in early for the choice beach spaces. The better-than-average facilities include a small store, fish-cleaning sinks, showers, toilets, and all hookups. The water is brackish—drink bottled. Boat launching is usually easy on the sheltered beach nearby. The Trailer Park La Playa's 45 spaces rent for about $19/day, $120/week, $400/month.

Scores of winter returnees enjoy Melaque's **informal RV-trailer park/campground** with room for about 50 rigs and tents. The cliff-bottom lot spreads above a calm rocky cove, ripe for swimming, snorkeling, and sailboarding. Other extras include super fishing and a sweeping view of the entire Bay of Navidad. All spaces are usually filled by Christmas and remain that way until March. The people are friendly, the price is certainly right, and the beer and water trucks arrive regularly throughout the winter season. Please dump your waste in sanitary facilities while staying here; continued pollution of the cove by irresponsible occupants has led to complaints, which may force local authorities to close the campground. Get there by the dirt road that splits left, toward the bay, about two blocks west (toward Coastecomate), from the Highway 200 intersection at Melaque's northwest edge.

Wilderness campers will enjoy **Playa de Cocos,** a miles-long golden sand beach, accessible by launch from Barra via Colimilla, or directly from the open ocean, or by road the long way around. Playa de Cocos has an intimate hidden south-end sandy cove, perfect for an overnight or a few barefoot days of bird-watching, shell collecting, beachcombing, and dreaming around your driftwood campfire. The restaurants at the village of Colimilla or the stores (by launch across the lagoon) in Barra are available for food and water. Mosquitoes come out around sunset. Bring plenty of good repellent and a mosquito-proof tent.

FOOD
Breakfast, Snacks, and Stalls
An excellent way to start your Barra day is at the intimate *palapa*-shaded patio of the **Hotel Delfín,** Av. Morelos 23, tel. 315/357-0068. While you dish yourself fruit and pour your coffee from its little countertop buffet, the cook fixes your choice of breakfast options, from savory eggs and omelettes to French toast and luscious, tender banana pancakes; a complete breakfast costs $4–6, daily 8:30–10:30 A.M.

In Melaque, the restaurant at Club Náutico and *palapa* Restaurant Pelícanos are also good places to start your day.

Also, plenty of good daytime eating in Melaque goes on at the lineup of small, permanent *fondas* (foodstalls) in the alley that runs south from Av. Hidalgo, half a block toward the beach from the southwest plaza corner. You can't go wrong with *fonda* food, as long as it's made right in front of you and served piping hot.

For evening light meals and snacks, Barra has plenty of options. Here, families seem to fall into two categories: those who sell food to sidewalk passersby, and those who enjoy their offerings. The three blocks of Av. Veracruz from Morelos to the city *jardín* (park) are dotted with tables that residents nightly load with hearty, economical food offerings, from tacos *de lengua* (tongue) and pork tamales to *pozole Guadalajara* and *chiles rellenos*. The wholesomeness of their menus is evidenced by their devoted followings of longtime neighbor and tourist customers.

On the other hand, you can enjoy the strictly North American fare—hamburgers, salads, sandwiches, malts—of Tessa's Malt Shop, between the Barra church and Café Ambar.

Restaurants
One local family has built its sidewalk culinary skills into a thriving Barra storefront business, the **Restaurant Paty,** at the corner of Veracruz and Jalisco, tel. 315/357-0743. It offers the traditional menu of Mexican *antojitos*—tacos, quesadillas, tostadas—plus roast beef, chicken, and very tasty *pozole* soup. Open daily 8 A.M.–11 P.M.

© BRUCE WHIPPERMAN

A sprinkling of good restaurants perch on Barra's picturesque lagoon edge.

Budget. For a variation on the same theme, try **Restaurant Chela,** across the street, on the corner.

Restaurant Ambar, Veracruz 101A, corner Jalisco, one of Barra's most refined eateries, stands beneath a luxuriously airy upstairs *palapa* diagonally across from the Paty. The unusual menu features lighter fare—eggs, fish, whole-wheat *(harina integral)* tortillas, and bread. Besides a large selection of sweet and savory crepes, it also serves a number of seafood and vegetable salads and Mexican plates, including scrumptious *chiles rellenos.* The wine list, which features the good Baja California Cetto label, is the best in town. Open daily, in season, 8 A.M.–noon for breakfast, 5–10 P.M. for dinner; American Express accepted. Moderate.

Among Barra's best eateries is the **Restaurant Ramon,** tel. 315/355-6485, tucked beneath its tall *palapa* at 260 Legazpi, across the street from the Hotel Barra de Navidad. Completely unpretentious and making the most of the usual list of international and Mexican specialties, friendly owner/chef Ramon and his hardworking staff continue to build their already sizable following. Choose whatever you like—chicken, fish,

chiles rellenos, guacamole, spaghetti—and you'll most likely be pleased. Meals include gratis salsa and chips to start, hearty portions, and often a healthy side of cooked veggies on your plate. Open daily 7 A.M.–11 P.M. Moderate.

One of Barra's most entertainingly scenic restaurants is **Veleros,** right on the lagoon at Veracruz 64, tel. 315/355-5838. If you happen to visit Barra during the full moon, don't miss watching its shimmering reflection from the restaurant *palapa* as it rises over the mangrove-bordered expanse. An additional Veleros bonus is the fascinating darting, swirling school of fish attracted by the spotlight shining on the water. Finally comes the food, which you can select from a menu of carefully prepared and served shrimp, lobster, octopus, chicken, and steak entrées. The brochettes are especially popular. Open daily noon–10 P.M.; credit cards are accepted. Moderate.

For change of scene, try **Restaurant Sea-master,** one block away, on the beach side of the sandbar, where guests enjoy a refreshing sea breeze every afternoon and a happy-hour sunset every evening at López de Legazpi 140. Besides super-fresh seafood selections, it features savory barbecued chicken and rib plates. Open daily 8 A.M.–11 P.M. Moderate.

Restaurant Pancho, three doors away at Legazpi 53, is one of Barra's original *palapas,* which old-timers can remember from the days when *all* Barra restaurants were *palapas.* The original Pancho, who has seen lots of changes in the old sandbar in his 80-odd years, still oversees the operation daily 8 A.M.–8 P.M. Moderate.

In **Melaque,** jazz and nouvelle cuisine have arrived, at hot new **Restaurant Maya,** favorite of a loyal cadre of American and Canadian vacationers and expatriates. Its private, sheltered beachfront (foot of south-side Calle Obregon) garden and the murmur of the Melaque surf set the stage, while the music and the food provide the shadow and act. For example, start out with a Maya Martini, continue with curried fish cakes, follow up with linguine with pesto, cream, and prawns, and finish off with the chef's dessert creation of the day. Expensive. Winter high season reservations highly recommended. Find it open Tues.–Sat. 6 P.M.–11 P.M.; Sun. brunch 10:30 A.M.–11 2 P.M. Expensive.

In the middle of Melaque town, corner of López Mateos and Gomez Farías, across from the trailer park, **Restaurant Alcatraz** keeps the customers coming with an airy upstairs *palapa* setting and good, professionally prepared and served food. Choose from a broad, very recognizable menu of soups, creams, salads, hamburgers, fish, steaks, and chicken. Although North American selections occupy most of the menu, Mexican country cooking is the house specialty. (*Note:* The name "Alcatraz" refers to the flower of the lily family for which the infamous California island prison was named.)

Restaurant El Dorado, under the big beachside *palapa* in front of the Hotel Club Náutico, provides a cool breezy place to enjoy the beach scene during breakfast or lunch at Calle Gómez Farías 1A, tel. 315/355-5770. Service is crisp and the specialties are carefully prepared. Open daily 8 A.M.–11 P.M.; credit cards are accepted. Moderate–expensive.

ENTERTAINMENT AND EVENTS

Most entertainments in Barra and Melaque are informal and local. ***Corridas de toros*** (bullfights) are occasionally held during the winter-spring season at the bullring on Highway 200 across from the Barra turnoff. Local *vaqueros* (cowboys) sometimes display their pluck in spirited ***charreadas*** (Mexican-style rodeos) in neighboring country villages. Check with your hotel desk or the Barra tourist information office, near the east end of Jalisco, at no. 67, across the street from the Terraza upstairs bar, tel./fax 315/355-5100, for details.

The big local festival occurs in Melaque during the St. Patrick's Day week of March 10–17. Events include blessing of the local fishing fleet, folk dancing, cake eating, and boxing matches.

Nightlife

Folks enjoy the Bahía de Navidad sunset colors evenings during the happy hours at Restaurant Seamaster, Hotel Tropical (if it's open), or Sunset Restaurant-bar (across Legazpi from the church).

The same is true at the beachside Restaurant Maya (see Restaurants) and Restaurant Dorado at Hotel Club Náutico in Melaque, north end of main street Gómez Farías. You can prepare for this during the afternoons (December, January, and February mostly) at the very congenial 4–6 P.M. happy hour around the swim-up bar at Barra's Hotel Sands.

Lovers of pure tranquility, on the other hand, enjoy the breeze and sunset view from the end of Barra's rock jetty.

After dinner, in season, huge speakers begin thumping away, lights flash, and the fogs ooze from the ceilings around 10 P.M. at disco **El Galeón** of the Hotel Sands, tel. 315/355-5148 (young local crowd), and **La Tanga,** tel. 315/355-5472, across the street from Hotel Club Náutico, north end of beachfront street Gómez Farías (entrance $7, mixed young and older, local and tourist crowd). Hours vary seasonally; call for details.

SPORTS AND RECREATION

Swimming, Surfing, and Boogie Boarding

The roughest surf on the Bahía de Navidad shoreline is closer to Barra, the most tranquil closest to Melaque. Swimming is consequently best and safest toward the Melaque end, while, in contrast, the only good surfing spot is where the waves rise and roll in beside the Barra jetty. Bodysurfing and boogie boarding are best somewhere in between. At least one shop in Barra—Crazy Cactus on Jalisco, corner of Veracruz, next to (and below) upstairs Restaurant Ambar—rents surfboards and boogie boards.

Sailing and Sailboarding

Sailing and sailboarding are best near the Melaque end of the Bay of Navidad and in the Bay of Coastecomate nearby. Bring your own equipment, however; none is available locally.

Snorkeling and Scuba Diving

Local snorkeling is often good, especially at Playa Tenacatita several miles north. The Crazy Cactus beach shop, near the corner of Jalisco and Veracruz, next to Restaurant Ambar, organizes snorkeling excursions.

Although no commercial dive shops operate out of Barra or Melaque, Susan Dearing, the very professional Manzanillo-based instructor, outfits and leads dives in the Barra-Melaque area. Susan, a veteran certified YMCA-method instructor with a record of many hundreds of accident-free guided dives, and her partner, NAUI-certified instructor Carlos Cuellar, can be contacted by mail, at P.O. Box 295, Santiago, Colima 28860, or at their office by tel./fax 314/333-0642, Carlos's cellular tel. 044-314/358-0327, or Susan's cellular tel. 044-314/358-5042. For more information, visit the websites www.divemanzanillo.com or www.gomanzanillo.com/scubamex/index.htm.

Tennis and Golf

The Hotel Cabo Blanco tennis courts, tel. 315/355-5182 or 315/355-5103, fax 315/355-64-94, are customarily open for public rental for about $5 per hour. Call ahead to check. Lessons

may also be available. The Hotel Costa Sur, tel. 315/355-5085, has tennis courts for guests and day members.

The plumy, breezy 18-hole **Isla de Navidad Golf Course** is available to the public for a fee of around $100 per person. Call the Hotel Grand Bay (see Accommodations) for information. Get there by regular launch from the Barra launch dock on the lagoon (to the Casa Club landing, about $5 round-trip). By car, turn right from Highway 200 at the Ejido La Culebra (or Isla de Navidad) sign as the highway cuts through the hills at Km 51 a few miles south of Barra. Follow the road about three miles (4.8 km) to a bridge, where the road curves right, paralleling the beach. After about two more miles (3.2 km), you pass through the golf course gate. After winding through the golf course another mile (1.6 km), turn right at the traffic circle at the north edge of the golf course. Continue another mile (1.6 km), between the golf course and the adjacent hillside, to the big golf clubhouse on the right.

Sportfishing

Big-game fishing boat rentals are available from friendly Captain Eduardo Castellos, at his shop, **Fantasia,** on Legazpi, corner of Jalisco, diagonally across from the church, at López de Legazpi 213, Barra de Navidad, Jalisco 48987, tel./fax 315/355-6824, pati21@prodigy.net.mx. Eduardo has three boats: a launch and two medium-sized craft, one with cabin and toilet. His all-day fee runs about $180 (six hours, three people fishing) for the *lancha* and $360 for the biggest boat (six hours, four people fishing) complete with bait, tackle, and soft drinks.

The captains of the Barra Boat Cooperative **Sociedad Cooperativa de Servicios Turístico** routinely take parties on successful marlin and swordfish hunts for about $22 per hour, including bait and tackle. Their lagoonside office-dock is at Av. Veracruz 40.

There are many other fish in the sea besides deep-sea marlin and swordfish, both of which often make tough eating. Half-day trips arranged through Fantasia, the Sociedad Cooperativa de Servicios Turístico, or others will typically net a number of large *dorado,* albacore, snapper, or other delicious eating fish. Local restaurants will generally cook a banquet for you and your friends if you give them the extra fish caught during such an outing.

If you'd like to enter one of a pair of annual Barra de Navidad **International Fishing Tournaments** (billfish, tuna, and *dorado* in January and May) and father and son/daughter tournament in August, contact Eduardo Castellos or the tourist information office for information.

Boat Launching

If you plan on mounting your own fishing expedition, you can do it from the Barra boat-launching ramp at the end of Av. Filipinas near the Hotel Cabo Blanco. The fee, about $10 per day, covers parking your boat in the canal and is payable to boatkeeper, whose headquarters is inside the boatyard adjacent to the ramp, Mon.–Fri. 8 A.M.–4 P.M.

Sports Equipment Sales and Rentals

Barra's sport shop, **Crazy Cactus,** tel. 315/355-6099, run by friendly, English-speaking mother-daughter team of Peggy and Tracye Ross, offers rental surfboards, boogie boards, bicycles, and snorkels, masks, and fins. It's on Jalisco, corner of Veracruz, next to (and below) upstairs Restaurant Ambar.

SHOPPING
Handicrafts

While Melaque has many stores crammed with humdrum commercial tourist curios, Barra has a few interestingly authentic sources. For example, a number of Nahua-speaking families from Guerrero operate small individual shops on Legazpi. Some of the shops, near the corner of Sinaloa and Legazpi, behind the church, are minimuseums of delightful folk crafts, made mostly by *indígena* country craftspeople. Pick what you like from among hundreds—lustrous lacquerware trays from Olinalá, winsome painted pottery cats, rabbits, and fish, a battalion of wooden miniarmadillos, and glossy dark-wood swordfish from Sonora.

You can pick from an equally attractive selection south two blocks, at **Arts and Crafts of**

Oaxaca, across Legazpi diagonally southwest from the church. Besides a fetching collection of priced-to-sell Oaxacan *alebrijes* (crazy wooden animals), *tapetes* (wool rugs), and masks, you'll also find a host of papier-mâché and pottery from Tlaquepaque and Tonalá, *sombreros* from Zitácuaro in Michoacán, and much more.

Across the street, many more shops have similarly attractive offerings, on the south end of Veracruz, around the corner of Morelos. Although bargaining is customary, don't bargain too hard. Many of these folks, far from their country villages, are strangers in a strange land. Their sometimes-meager earnings often support entire extended families back home.

Fruit, Vegetable, and Grocery Stores

There are no large markets, traditional or modern, in Barra or Melaque. However, a number of good minisupers and *fruterías* stock basic supplies. In Barra, your best bet for groceries is **Abarrotes La Colmena,** east side of Veracruz, three doors south of the plaza, open daily until around 8 P.M.

Half a block north, northeast corner of Veracruz and Michoacán, **Frutería Ixtapa,** tel. 315/355-6443, stocks piles of good fruits and veggies. Find out the day of arrival, so you can get them when they're fresh; open Mon.–Sat. 8 A.M.–10 P.M.

In Melaque, nearly all grocery and fruit shopping takes place at the central market or at several good stores on main street López Mateos, which runs away from the beach past the west side of the central plaza.

INFORMATION
Tourist Information Office

The small Barra-Melaque regional office of the Jalisco Department of Tourism is tucked in a little office near the east end of Jalisco, at no. 67, across the street from the Terraza upstairs bar, which is on the east end of the south end of Veracruz. Staff distributes maps and literature and answers questions during office hours (Mon.–Fri. 9 A.M.–5 P.M., Sat. 9 A.M.–2 P.M., tel./fax 315/355-5100, email www.costalege.com. The office is a good source of information about local civic and ecological issues and organizations.

Publications

The Barra **newsstand,** open daily 7 A.M.–10 P.M., at the corner of Veracruz and Michoacán, customarily stocks the Mexico City *News,* which usually arrives by 4 P.M.

Perhaps the best English-language lending library in all of the Mexican Pacific is **Beer Bob's Book Exchange** on a Barra back street, 61 Mazatlán, near Sinaloa. Thousands of vintage paperbacks, free for borrowing or exchange, fill the shelves. Chief librarian and Scrabble devotee Bob (actually Robert Baham, retired counselor for the California Youth Authority) manages his little gem of an establishment just for the fun of it. "It's not a store," he says. Just drop your old titles in the box and take away the equivalent from his well-organized collection. If you have nothing to exchange, simply return whatever you borrow before you leave town.

In Melaque, the **Librería Saifer,** open Mon.–Sat. 2–11 P.M. and Sun. 6–11 P.M., on the central plaza, southwest corner, by the church, also stocks the *News.*

Ecology Groups

The informal community **Grupo Ecobana** accomplishes ecological improvement through practical examples, which include beach-cleaning sessions with schoolchildren and camping out at secluded local beaches in order to discourage turtle egg poachers. For more information, contact the Tourist Information Office, in Barra, at Jalisco 67, open Mon.–Fri. 9 A.M.–5 P.M.

The University of Guadalajara also runs the local **Centro Estudios Ecológicos de la Costa,** which, through research, education, and direct action, is trying to preserve local animal and plant species and habitats. Now and then you may spot one of its white vans on the highway or around town. At the wheel might be the director, Enrique Godinez Domínguez, one of whose better-known efforts is the turtle-hatching station at Mismaloya, about 72 miles (115 km) north of Barra, near Cruz de Loreto. The local headquarters is in Melaque at V. Gómez Farías 82, tel.

315/355-6330, fax 315/355-6331, across from the Hotel Pablo de Tarso in Melaque.

SERVICES

Money Exchange

Although Barra has no bank, it does have a Banamex **ATM,** at the Barra plaza, southeast corner. Melaque does have a bank, **Banamex,** with ATM, across the street and half a block north of the main bus station. It's open Mon.–Fri. 9 A.M.–3 P.M. Barra's friendliest *casa de cambio* is **Ciber@Money,** (see Communications.) With even longer hours, the **Vinos y Licores Barra de Navidad,** on Legazpi, across from the Hotel Barra de Navidad, exchanges both Canadian and American traveler's checks and cash; open daily 8:30 A.M.–11 P.M.

After bank hours in Melaque, use the Banamex ATM, or go to **Money Exchange Melaque,** Gómez Farías 27A, across from the bus terminal, tel. 315/355-5343. It exchanges both American and Canadian traveler's checks and cash Mon.–Sat. 9 A.M.–2 P.M. and 4–7 P.M., Sun. 9 A.M.–2 P.M. The tariff, however, often amounts to a steep $3 per $100 above bank rate.

Communications

Barra and Melaque each have a small **post office** *(correo).* Barra has a *telégrafo.* The Barra post office is at the southside corner of Sinaloa and Jalisco, a block east of the church, open Mon.–Fri. 8 A.M.–3 P.M., Sat. 9 A.M.–1 P.M.

The Melaque post office is three blocks south of the plaza, at 13 Clemente Orozco, between G. Farías and Corona, 1.5 blocks from the beach, tel. 315/355-5230. Open Mon.–Fri. 8 A.M.–3 P.M., Sat. 9 A.M.–1 P.M.

The Barra *telégrafo,* which handles money orders, is on Veracruz, half a block north of the Barra plaza, open Mon.–Fri. 9 A.M.–3 P.M.

In Barra, go to friendly, **Ciber@Money** for public telephone, Internet access, and money exchange. Find it at 212 Veracruz, east side, open Mon.–Sat. 8 A.M.–2 P.M., 4–8 P.M., closed Sun., tel. 315/355-6177. In Melaque, go to the **long-distance telephone office** on the *jardín* northeast corner, at the intersection of Morelos and Hidalgo, tel. 315/355-6250, open daily 9 A.M.–2 P.M., 4–10 P.M.

Connect with the Internet connection in Barra at **Mango Bay** café, at 70 Jalisco, across the street from *turismo,* or **Ciber@Money.**

In Melaque, you have a pair of Internet choices: **Ciber@Net** across from the bus terminal on Gómez Farías, interior hall, next to the money exchange, open Mon.–Sat. 9 A.M.–2:30 P.M. and 4–8 P.M., or **Centro Virtual** in the Melaque market, opposite the food stalls, half a block toward the beach from the plaza, cellular tel. 315/355-5044; open Mon.–Sat. 9 A.M.–2 P.M. and 4–10 P.M.

Health

In Barra, the government **Centro de Salud** (health clinic), corner Veracruz and Puerto de La Navidad, four blocks north of the town plaza, tel. 315/355-6220, has a doctor 24 hours a day. The **Melaque Centro de Salud,** Calle Gordiano Guzman 10, tel. 315/355-5080, off main beachside street Gómez Farías two blocks from the trailer park, also offers access to a doctor 24 hours a day.

In a medical emergency, dial local number tel. 315/355-2300 for a Red Cross (Cruz Roja) **ambulance** to whisk you to the well-equipped hospitals in Manzanillo.

For routine medical consultations, follow your hotel's recommendation. Otherwise, in Barra, contact **Dr. Pedro Crespo, M.D.,** family medicine, at Unidad Médica Crespo, at Veracruz 45, tel. 315/355-8082, or at home, at tel. 315/355-6869.

For ordinary medicines and remedies, in Barra, try **Farmacia Crespo,** at Veracruz 45, tel. 315/355-8082. In Melaque, go to **Super Farmacia Plaza,** on López Mateos, northwest corner of the town plaza, tel. 315/355-5167.

Police

The Barra police, tel. 315/355-5399, are on 24-hour duty at the city office at 179 Veracruz, adjacent to the *jardín.*

For the Melaque police, either call tel. 315/355-5080 or go to the headquarters behind the plaza-front *delegación municipal* (municipal agency) at the plaza corner of L. Mateos and Morelos.

Travel Agent

For airplane tickets, fishing trips, tours, and other vacation arrangements in Barra, contact **Viajes Dona Tours,** at Veracruz 220, corner of Michoacán, open Mon.–Fri. 11 A.M.–8 P.M., Sat. 11 A.M.–4 P.M., tel. 315/355-5667, fax 315/355-5666. In Melaque, go to its second branch office, at Gómez Farías 27A, tel. 315/355-5615.

Laundries

Barra and Melaque visitors enjoy the services of a number of *lavanderias.* In Barra, try **Lavandería Jardín,** at Jalisco 69, next to *turismo,* open Mon.–Fri. 9 A.M.–2 P.M. and 4–7 P.M., Sat. 9 A.M.–noon. In Melaque, step one block east (parallel to beach) along Juárez from the plaza, to **Lavandería Francis.**

GETTING THERE AND AWAY
By Air

Barra de Navidad is air-accessible either through **Puerto Vallarta Airport** (see Getting There and Away in the Puerto Vallarta: Town, Bay, and Mountains chapter) or the **Manzanillo Airport,** only 19 miles (30 km) south of Barra-Melaque. While the Puerto Vallarta connection has the advantage of many more flights, transfers to south coast are time-consuming. If you can afford it, the quickest option from Puerto Vallarta is to rent a car. Alternatively, ride a local bus or hire a taxi from the airport to the new central bus station, north of the airport. There, catch a bus, preferably **Autocamiones del Pacífico,** tel. 322/290-0716, or Flecha Amarilla's luxury service **Primera Plus,** tel. 322/221-0994, to Barra or Melaque (three hours).

On the other hand, arrival via the Manzanillo airport, half an hour from Barra-Melaque, is much more direct, provided that good connections are obtainable through the relatively few carriers that serve the airport.

Manzanillo Airport Flights

Aerocalifornia Airlines flights connect with Los Angeles and Mexico City. For local reservations and flight information, call tel. 314/334-1414.

America West Airlines flights connect with

Phoenix during the winter-spring season. For local reservations and flight information, call tel. 314/334-1140.

Aeroméxico Airlines' subsidiary carrier **Aerolitoral** flights connect Manzanillo airport with Zihuatanejo and Guadalajara (where many U.S. connections are available). For reservations, contact a travel agent, such as Viajes Dona Tours, in Barra de Navidad, tel. 315/355-5667, fax 315/355-5666; or Aeroméxico's reservation number, toll-free Mex. tel. 800/621-4000. For flight information, contact Aeroméxico's Manzanillo office, tel. 314/334-1226.

Mexicana Airlines flights connect daily with Mexico City, where many U.S. connections are available. For reservations and flight information, contact its airport office, tel. 314/333-2323, the Manzanillo reservations numbers, tel. 314/334-0800 or 314/355-8159, or toll-free Mex. tel. 800/502-2000 or 800/501-9900.

Canada 3000 charter flights connect with Toronto, Calgary-Edmonton, and Vancouver during the winter-spring season. Contact a travel agent for information and reservations.

Airport Arrival and Departure

The terminal, although small for an international destination, does have an ATM for cash, a few gift shops for last-minute purchases, snack stands, an upstairs restaurant, some car rentals, and a *buzón* (mailbox) just outside the front entrance. However, it has no hotel booking service, so you should arrive with a hotel reservation or you'll be at the mercy of taxi drivers who love to collect fat commissions on your first-night hotel tariff. Upon departure, be sure to save enough cash to pay the approximate $12 **departure tax,** (if your ticket doesn't already include it.)

After the usually rapid immigration and customs checks, independent arrivees have their choice of a car rental or taxi tickets from a booth just outside the arrival gate. *Colectivos* head for Barra de Navidad and other northern points seasonally only. Taxis, however, will take three passengers to Barra, Melaque, or Hotel Real Coastecomate for about $30 total; to El Tamarindo, $35; Hotel Sun, $48; El Careyes, $67; Chamela-El Super, $67; or Las

Alamandas, $105. *Colectivo* tickets run about $7–9 per person to any Manzanillo hotel, while a *taxi especial* runs about $22–29, depending on destination.

No public buses service the Manzanillo airport. Strong, mobile travelers on tight budgets could save pesos by hitching or hiking the three miles to Highway 200 and flagging down one of the frequent north or southbound second-class buses (fare about $2 to Barra or Manzanillo). Don't try it at night, however.

As for airport **car rentals,** you have a choice of National, tel. 314/333-0611, fax 314/333-1140, interent@bay.net; Hertz tel. 314/333-3191, 314/333-3141, or 314/333-3142; and Budget, tel./fax 314/333-1445. Unless you don't mind paying upward of $50 per day, shop around for your car rental by calling the car rentals' U.S. and Canada toll-free numbers at home *before* you leave (see the chart "Car Rental Agencies" in the On The Road chapter).

By Car or RV

Three highway routes access Barra de Navidad: from the north via Puerto Vallarta, from the south via Manzanillo, and from the northeast via Guadalajara.

From Puerto Vallarta, Mexican National Highway 200 is all asphalt and in good condition (except for some potholes), along its 134-mile (216-km) stretch to Barra de Navidad. Traffic is generally light, but it may slow a bit as the highway climbs the 2,400-foot Sierra Cuale summit near El Tuito south of Puerto Vallarta, but the light traffic and good road make passing safely possible. Allow about three hours for this very scenic trip.

From Manzanillo, the 38-mile (61-km) stretch of Highway 200 is nearly all countryside and all level. It's a snap in under an hour.

The longer but quicker and easier Barra de Navidad-Guadalajara road connection runs through Manzanillo along *autopistas* (superhighways) 54D, 110, and 200 D. Start out at the Minerva Circle (at the intersection of Av. López Mateos and Guadalajara west-side Av. Vallarta). Mark your odometer and follow Av. López Mateos south. After about 10 miles (32 km), at Guadalajara's country edge, continue, following the signs for

Colima that direct you along the four-lane combined Mexican National Highways 15, 54, and 80 heading southwest. Nineteen miles (30 km) from the Minerva Circle, as Highway 15 splits right for Morelia and Mexico City, continue straight ahead, following the signs for Colima and Barra de Navidad. Very soon, follow the Highway 80-Highway 54 D right fork for Barra de Navidad-Colima. Two miles farther, follow the Highway 54 D branch left toward Colima. Continue on Highway 54 D straight ahead for about two hours, bypassing Colima. About 10 miles south of Colima Highway 54 D changes, continuing as Highway 110 expressway. At Tecoman, Highway 110 becomes Highway 200 D expressway, which you follow another hour, bypassing Manzanillo (via the Manzanillo Highway 200 *cuota* toll bypass) all the way to Barra de Navidad. Easy grades allow a leisurely 55 mph (90 km/hour) most of the way for this 192-mile (311-km) trip. Allow about 4.5 hours, either direction.

The same is not true of the winding, two lane, 181-mile (291-km) Highway 80 route between Barra de Navidad and Guadalajara. Start out from the Minerva Circle, as described above, but south of the city, instead of forking left on Highway 54 D to Colima, continue straight ahead on Highway 80 toward Barra de Navidad. The narrow, two-lane road continues through a dozen little towns, over three mountain ranges, and around curves for another 160 miles (258 km) to Melaque and Barra de Navidad. To be safe, allow about six hours' driving time uphill to Guadalajara, five hours in the opposite direction.

By Bus

Various regional bus lines cooperate in connecting Barra and Melaque north with Puerto Vallarta; south with Cihuatlán, Manzanillo, Colima, Playa Azul, Zihuatanejo, and Acapulco; and northeast with Guadalajara, via Highway 80. They arrive and leave so often (about every half-hour during the day) from the little Barra de Navidad station, on Av. Veracruz 1.5 blocks north past the central plaza, tel. 315/355-5265, that they're practically indistinguishable.

Of the various companies, affiliated lines **Transportes Cihuatlán** and **Autocamiones del Pacífico** provide the most options: super-first-class "Primera Plus" buses connect (several per day) with Guadalajara, Manzanillo, and Puerto Vallarta. In addition to this, they offer at least a dozen second-class buses per day in all three directions. These often stop anywhere along the road if passengers wave them down.

Other lines, affiliated with bus giant Flecha Amarilla, provide similar services, including a different "Primera Plus" luxury-class service to Manzanillo, Puerto Vallarta, Guadalajara, and León, out of its separate little station at Veracruz 269, across and half a block up the street, tel. 315/355-6111.

The buses that stop in Barra also stop in Melaque; all Autocamiones del Pacífico and Transportes Cihuatlán buses stop at the Melaque main terminal, **Central de Autobúses** on Gómez Farías at V. Carranza, tel. 315/355-5003; open 24 hours daily.

Flecha Amarilla maintains its own fancy new a/c station in Melaque across the street, tel. 315/355-6110, where you can ride its luxury-class "Primera Plus" buses, in addition to regular second-class Autobuses Costas Alegre, north to Puerto Vallarta, south to Manzanillo, and with expanded service, to Guadalajara, León, and Mexico City.

However, one line, **Elite (EL),** does not stop in Barra. It maintains its own little Melaque station a block south of the main station, across from the Melaque Trailer Park, at Gómez Farias 257, tel. 315/355-5177. From there, Elite connects by first-class express north (two daily departures) all the way to Puerto Vallarta, Mazatlán, and Tijuana, and south (two daily departures) to Manzanillo, Zihuatanejo, and Acapulco.

Note: All Barra de Navidad and Melaque bus departures are *salidas de paso,* meaning they originate somewhere else. Although seating cannot be ascertained until the bus arrives, seats are generally available, except during super-crowded Christmas and Easter holidays.

Manzanillo and Inland to Colima

Manzanillo

Manzanillo (pop. 100,000) is a small city tucked at the southern corner of a large bay, so broad that it has room for a pair of five-mile-wide junior bays. From the north spreads the **Bahía de Santiago,** separated by the jutting Peninsula de Santiago from its twin **Bahía de Manzanillo** on the south.

Manzanillo's importance as a port has continued since the conquest. Even its name comes from its fortunate harborfront location, where

manzanillos—trees whose inedible yellowish-red fruit resembles a small apple, or *manzanillo*—flourished beside the original wharves.

Splendid local fishing led to an unexpected bonus: flocks of visitors, drawn by Manzanillo's annual International Sailfish Tournament. During three days in 1957, for example, tournament participants brought in 336 sailfish. The word soon got around. The balmy winters and the golden sand beaches drew even more visitors. By the 1980s, a string of small hotels, condos, and resorts lined Manzanillo's long, soft strands,

© BRUCE WHIPPERMAN

continuously erupting 13,000-foot Volcán de Fuego

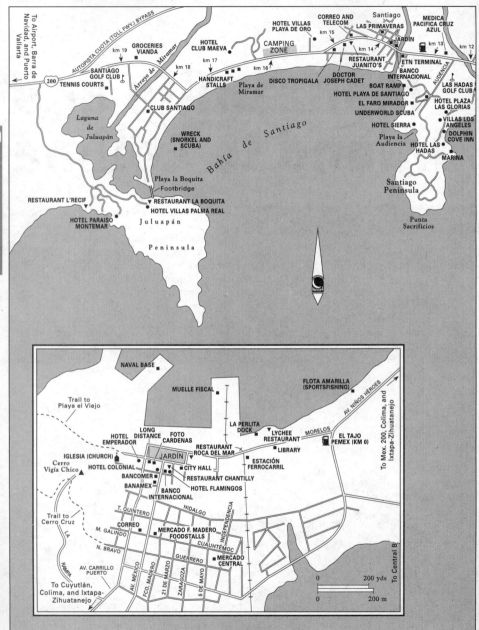

To Airport, Barra de Navidad, and Puerto Vallarta

AUTOPISTA CUOTA (TOLL FWY.) BYPASS

200

km 19

GROCERIES VIANDA

SANTIAGO GOLF CLUB
TENNIS COURTS

Arroyo de Miramar

km 18

HOTEL CLUB MAEVA

km 17

HANDICRAFT STALLS

Playa de Miramar

CLUB SANTIAGO

Laguna de Juluapán

WRECK (SNORKEL AND SCUBA)

km 16

HOTEL VILLAS PLAYA DE ORO

CAMPING ZONE

DISCO TROPIGALA

km 15

CORREO AND TELECOM

Santiago

LAS PRIMAVERAS

km 14

JARDÍN

RESTAURANT JUANITO'S

DOCTOR JOSEPH CADET

MEDICA PACIFICA CRUZ AZUL

km 13

km 12

ETN TERMINAL

BANCO INTERNACIONAL

BOAT RAMP
HOTEL PLAYA DE SANTIAGO
EL FARO MIRADOR
UNDERWORLD SCUBA

AUDIENCIA

LAS HADAS GOLF CLUB

HOTEL PLAZA LAS GLORIAS

HOTEL SIERRA

Playa la Audiencia

HOTEL LAS HADAS

VILLAS LOS ANGELES

DOLPHIN COVE INN

MARINA

Bahía de Santiago

Playa la Boquita
Footbridge

RESTAURANT L'RECIF

RESTAURANT LA BOQUITA
HOTEL VILLAS PALMA REAL

HOTEL PARAISO MONTEMAR

Juluapán

Peninsula

Santiago Peninsula

Punta Sacrificios

MOON

NAVAL BASE

Trail to Playa el Viejo

MUELLE FISCAL

FLOTA AMARILLA (SPORTSFISHING)

AV. NIÑOS HÉROES

To Mex. 200, Colima, and Ixtapa-Zihuatanejo

LA PERLITA DOCK

LYCHEE RESTAURANT

MORELOS

EL TAJO PEMEX (KM 0)

HOTEL EMPERADOR

LONG DISTANCE

FOTO CARDENAS

RESTAURANT ROCA DEL MAR

LIBRARY

IGLESIA (CHURCH)

JARDÍN

Cerro Vigía Chico

HOTEL COLONIAL

BANCOMER

BANAMEX

CITY HALL

RESTAURANT CHANTILLY

HOTEL FLAMINGOS

ESTACIÓN FERROCARRIL

BANCO INTERNACIONAL

To Central B

Trail to Cerro Cruz

LA RAMPA

T. QUINTERO

CORREO

M. GALINDO

N. BRAVO

AV. CARRILLO PUERTO

To Cuyutlán, Colima, and Ixtapa-Zihuatanejo

HIDALGO

INDEPENDENCIA

MERCADO F. MADERO FOODSTALLS

CUAUHTÉMOC

GUERRERO

MERCADO CENTRAL

AV. MÉXICO

FCO. MADERO

21 DE MARZO

ZARAGOZA

5 DE MAYO

0   200 yds

0   200 m

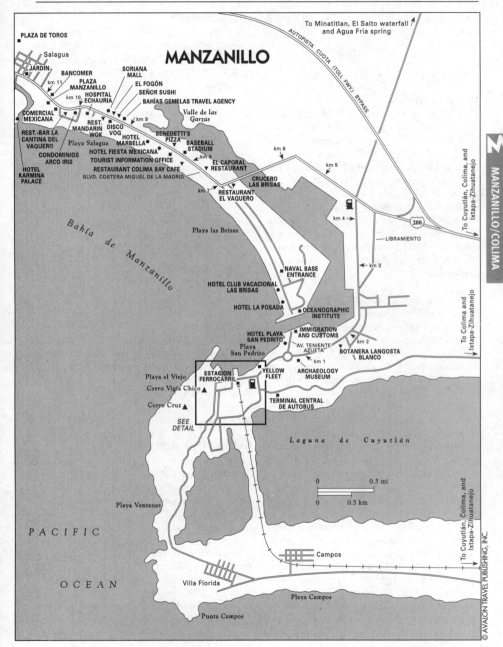

MANZANILLO

To Minatitlan, El Salto waterfall and Agua Fria spring

AUTOPISTA CUOTA (TOLL FWY.) BYPASS

PLAZA DE TOROS

Salagua

JARDIN

BANCOMER

km 11

PLAZA MANZANILLO

HOSPITAL ECHAURIA

km 10

SORIANA MALL

EL FOGÓN

SEÑOR SUSHI

BAHÍAS GEMELAS TRAVEL AGENCY

COMERCIAL MEXICANA

REST.-BAR LA CANTINA DEL VAQUERO

REST. MANDARIN WOK

DISCO VOG

HOTEL MARBELLA

km 9

BENEDETTI'S PIZZA

Valle de las Garzas

CONDOMINIOS ARCO IRIS

HOTEL KARMINA PALACE

Playa Salagua

HOTEL FIESTA MEXICANA

TOURIST INFORMATION OFFICE

RESTAURANT COLIMA BAY CAFE

BLVD. COSTERA MIGUEL DE LA MADRID

BASEBALL STADIUM

km 8

EL CAPORAL RESTAURANT

km 7

RESTAURANT EL VAQUERO

CRUCERO LAS BRISAS

km 6

km 5

km 4

200

Bahía de Manzanillo

Playa las Brisas

LIBRAMIENTO

km 3

NAVAL BASE ENTRANCE

HOTEL CLUB VACACIONAL LAS BRISAS

HOTEL LA POSADA

OCEANOGRAPHIC INSTITUTE

IMMIGRATION AND CUSTOMS

HOTEL PLAYA SAN PEDRITO

Playa San Pedrito

AV. TENIENTE AZUETA

km 2

BOTANERA LANGOSTA BLANCO

km 1

Playa el Viejo

Cerro Vigía Chico

Cerro Cruz

ESTACIÓN FERROCARRIL

YELLOW FLEET

ARCHAEOLOGY MUSEUM

TERMINAL CENTRAL DE AUTOBUS

SEE DETAIL

Laguna de Cuyutlán

0   0.5 mi

0   0.5 km

PACIFIC

Playa Ventanas

OCEAN

Villa Florida

Campos

Playa Campos

Punta Campos

To Cuyutlán, Colima, and Ixtapa-Zihuatanejo

To Colima and Ixtapa-Zihuatanejo

To Cuyutlán, Colima, and Ixtapa-Zihuatanejo

MANZANILLO/COLIMA

© AVALON TRAVEL PUBLISHING, INC.

providing jobs and opportunities in the previously sleepy bayside communities of Santiago and Salagua.

HISTORY
Before Columbus
One of the earliest records of Manzanillo comes from a story of Ix, king of ancient Coliman, now the state of Colima. The legend states that Ix received visits from Chinese trader-emissaries at a shore village, which became the present town of Salagua, on Tzalahua Bay (now the Bay of Manzanillo). It's not surprising the dream of riches gained by trade propelled the Chinese across the Pacific hundreds of years before the Spanish conquest. The same goal drew Columbus across the Atlantic and pushed Hernán Cortés to this gateway to Asia a generation later.

Conquest and Colonial Times
Cortés heard of the legend of the Chinese at Manzanillo Bay from the emperor of the Tarascan kingdom in Michoacán. With the riches of China tantalizingly within his grasp, Cortés sent his lieutenants to conquer Pacific Mexico, on whose sheltered beaches they would build ships to realize Columbus's elusive quest.

In 1522, Gonzalo de Sandoval, under orders from Cortés, reconnoitered Manzanillo Bay, looking for safe anchorages and good shipbuilding sites. Before he left a year later, Sandoval granted an audience to local chieftains at the tip of the Santiago Peninsula, which to this day retains the name Playa Audiencia.

Cortés himself visited Manzanillo Bay twice, in pursuit of a Portuguese fleet rumored to be somewhere off the coast. Cortés massed his forces at the northern bay of Manzanillo, which he christened Bahía de Santiago on July 24, 1535. Although Cortés's enemy failed to appear, the foreign threat remained. Portuguese, English, Dutch, and French corsairs menaced Spain's galleons as they repaired, watered, and unloaded their rich cargoes for 10 generations in Manzanillo and other sheltered Pacific harbors.

Independence
The hope generated by independence in 1821 soon dissipated in the turbulent civil conflicts of the next half century. Manzanillo languished until President Porfirio Díaz's orderly but heavy-handed rule (1876–1910) finally brought peace. The railroad arrived in 1889; telephone, electricity, drainage, and potable water soon followed. During the 1950s and '60s the harbor was modernized and deepened, attracting ships from all over the Pacific and capital for new industries. Anticipating the demand, the government built a huge, oil-fueled (but unfortunately smelly and smoky) generating plant, which powered a fresh wave of factories. By the 1970s, Manzanillo had become a major Pacific manufacturing center and port, providing thousands of local jobs in dozens of mining, agricultural, and fishing enterprises.

Recent Times
Although Mexican tourists had been coming to Manzanillo for years, international arrivals grew rapidly after the opening of the big Club Maeva and Las Hadas resorts in the 1970s. The new jetport north of town increased the steady flow to a flood; then came the 1980s, with Bo Derek starring in her fabulously successful movie *10,* which rocketed Las Hadas and Manzanillo to the stars as an international vacation destination.

SIGHTS
Getting Oriented
Longtimers know two Manzanillos: the old downtown, clustered around the south-end harborfront *jardín* and the rest—greater Manzanillo—spread northerly along the sandy shores of Manzanillo and Santiago Bays. The downtown has the banks, the government services, and the busy market district, while most of the hotels, restaurants, and tourist businesses dot the northern beachfronts.

Everything north of downtown is measured from the **El Tajo** junction (Km 0), marked by the downtown Pemex station. Here, along bayfront **Av. Niños Héroes,** the Barra de Navidad-Puerto Vallarta highway starts north just a few blocks from the *jardín.*

The shoreline highway curves past foothills and marshland, crossing the mirror-smooth waters of the **Valle de Las Garzas** (Valley of the Herons) between Km 5 and Km 7. The soaring white concrete sailboat sculpture at the traffic circle (Km 7) marks the *crucero* Las Brisas, known locally as the "suicide crossing." Here, the **Las Brisas Highway** forks left, curving southward, through a quiet neighborhood of condos, homes, and small hotels fronting Playa las Brisas.

Back on the main highway, now the **Boulevard Costera Miguel de la Madrid,** continue north past the hotels and restaurants that dot the long Playa Azul beachfront. Just after the dusty little town *jardín* of **Salagua** around Km 11, a golf course and big white gate mark the Las Hadas *crucero* (crossing) at Km 12. There, **Av. Audiencia** leads uphill along the plush, condo-dotted **Santiago Peninsula,** flanked by the Las Hadas resort on its south side and Hotel Sierra Manzanillo on Playa Audiencia on the north.

Back on the main road, continuing north, you pass the **Pemex** gas station at Km 13. Soon comes the Río Colorado creek bridge, then the **Santiago** town *jardín,* on the right, across from the restaurants, banks, and stores of Plaza Santiago shopping center (Km 13.5) on the left.

From there, traffic thins out, as you pass scattered beachfront condos along Playa Olas Altas (Km 15–16). Soon the **Club Maeva** spreads, like a colony of giant blue and white mushrooms, along the hill above Playa de Miramar at Km 17. Finally, another golf course and entrance gate at Km 19 mark the vacation-home community of **Playa Santiago.**

Getting Around

Visitors can easily drive, taxi (share to make it affordable), or bus to their favorite stops along Manzanillo's long shoreline. Dozens of **local buses** run along the highway through Las Brisas, Salagua, and Santiago (destinations marked on the windshields), all eventually returning to the downtown *jardín.* Fares (in pesos) run less than half a dollar. Hop on with a supply of small change and you're in business.

A Walk Around Downtown

A pair of busy north-south streets—Av. México and Av. Carrillo Puerto—dominate the downtown. Avenida Carrillo Puerto traffic runs one-way from the *jardín,* while Av. México traffic does the reverse. The corner of Av. México and Av. Juárez, adjacent to the *jardín,* is a colorful slice of old Mexico, crowded with cafés, storefronts, and street vendors. A dignified Porfirian kiosk presides nearby at the center of the *jardín,* while, on the far side, boats queue obediently at dockside Av. Morelos. In the distance, drab gray cutters and destroyer escorts line the **Base Naval** (BAH-say nah-VAHL) wharfs.

Walk a pair of blocks along Av. Juárez (which becomes B. Dávalos) past Av. México to the cathedral, officially the **Parroquia Nuestra Señora de Guadalupe,** after Manzanillo's patron saint. Inside, four shining stained-glass panels flanking the main altar tell the story of Juan Diego and the miracle of the Virgin of Guadalupe.

During the first 12 days of December, a colorful clutter of stalls lines the streetfront, where families bring their children, girls in embroidered *huipiles* and *chinas poblanas,* and boys in sombreros and serapes. After paying their respects to the Virgin, they indulge in their favorite holiday foods and get themselves photographed in front of a portrait of the Virgin. (See Fiesta de Guadalupe for more details.)

Town Hills and Market

Steep knolls punctuate Manzanillo's downtown. Residents climb precipitous cobbled alleyways, too narrow for cars, to their humble (yet luxuriously perched) homes overlooking the city. For an interesting little detour, climb one of the staircase lanes that angle uphill off Av. Juárez, around the city hall.

An even steeper hill rises behind the cathedral—the brushy slope of **Cerro Vigía Chico**— where colonial soldiers kept a lookout for pirates. Above and beyond that towers the cross-decorated summit of **Cerro Cruz,** the highest point (about 1,000 feet) above the Bay of Manzanillo. Every May 3, the **Día de la Santa Cruz,** pilgrims climb to its summit.

A Manzanillo downtown walk wouldn't be

complete without including a stroll down Av. México, past a dozen old-fashioned little shops—*papelerías, farmacias, dulcerías, panaderías*—to the **Mercado** (turn left at Cuauhtémoc) at Calle 5 de Mayo. Here you can wander among the mounds of bright produce, admire the festoons of piñatas, say a good word to the shrimp-sellers, and stop to listen to the harangue of a sidewalk politician or evangelist.

Archaeology Museum

Manzanillo's new museum, the Museo Universitario de Arqueología, on the waterfront boulevard about a mile, Puerto Vallarta direction, from downtown, displays a wealth of finds from recent investigations, especially around Salagua. Displays include painted ceramic bowls, jars, and a load of decorative shellwork, especially bracelets, earrings, and necklaces, some dating as far back as 2,000 years.

They also display some of the remains recently discovered at Los Ortices, south of present-day Colima (see Southern Excursion in the Colima and Vicinity section), including charming human and animal figurines—a man with a headache, flutes, dogs, whistles—some masterfully crafted to an alabaster-like stoneware finish.

The museum, tel. 314/332-2256, is on Av. Niños Héroes, near the San Pedrito traffic circle, and is open Tues.–Sat. 10 A.M.–2 P.M. and 5–8 P.M.

BEACHES AND HIKES
Playa San Pedrito

Manzanillo's closest-to-downtown beach, Playa San Pedrito, although now a bit polluted, remains a tranquil little strip of sand right on the harbor along Av. Teniente Azueta (which angles off Niños Héroes half a mile from the El Tajo junction Pemex station). The perfect Mexican Sunday beach, San Pedrito has lots of

OWNING PARADISE

Droves of repeat visitors have fled their northern winters and bought or permanently rented a part of their favorite Pacific Mexico paradise. They happily live all or part of the year in beachside developments that have mushroomed, especially in Mazatlán, Puerto Vallarta, Manzanillo, Ixtapa-Zihuatanejo, and Acapulco. Deluxe vacation homes, which foreigners can own through special trusts, run upward from $100,000; condos begin at about half that. Time shares, a type of rental, start at about $5,000.

Trusts
In the past, Mexicans have feared, with some justification, that foreigners were out to buy their country. As a consequence, present laws prohibit foreigners from holding direct title to property within 30 miles (50 km) of a beachfront or within 60 miles (100 km) of a national border.

However, Mexican law does permit *fideicomisos* (trusts), which substitute for outright foreign ownership. Trusts allow you, as the beneficiary, all the usual rights to the property, such as use, sale, improvement, and transfer, in exchange for paying

an annual fee to a Mexican bank, the trustee, which holds nominal title to the property. Trust ownership has been compared to owning all the shares of a corporation, which in turn owns a factory. While not owning the factory in name, you have legal control over it.

Although some folks have been bilked into buying south-of-the-border equivalents of the Brooklyn Bridge, Mexican trust ownership is a happy reality for growing numbers of American, Canadian, and European beneficiaries who simply love Mexico.

Bienes raíces (real estate) in Mexico works a lot like in the United States and Canada. Agents handle multiple listings, show properties, assist negotiations, track paperwork, and earn commissions for sales completed. If you're interested in buying a Mexican property, work with one of the many honest and hardworking agents in Mexico, preferably recommended through a reliable firm back home or trustworthy, property-savvy friends in Mexico.

Once you find a good property and have a written sales agreement in hand, your agent should recommend a *notaria pública* (notary) who, unlike a U.S. notary public, is an attorney skilled and

golden sand, seafood *palapas,* and a few big trees for shade. Although its very gentle waves are fine for swimming and sailboarding (with your own equipment), Playa San Pedrito is too close to the harbor for much good fishing or snorkeling.

Manzanillo Bay Beaches

From either the *jardín* or the Las Brisas *crucero,* ride a Las Brisas-marked bus to end-of-the-line Hotel La Posada at the southern end of **Playa Las Brisas.** From the jetty, which marks the entrance to the Puerto Interior (Inner Harbor), a 100-foot-wide sand ribbon seems to curve north without end. It changes its name to **Playa Azul,** then **Playa Salagua** along its five-mile length, ending finally at Las Hadas at the base of the Santiago Peninsula. The beach, while wide, is also steep. The usually gentle waves break suddenly at the sand, allowing little chance for surfing, bodysurfing, or boogie boarding. Sailboarding

(bring your own equipment) and surf fishing, however, are popular, as are snorkeling and scuba diving among the fish that swarm around the corals and rocks of the south-end jetty.

A number of restaurants along the beaches provide refreshments. They include the Hotel La Posada, Carlos'n Charlie's, the big adobe-colored Fiesta Mexicana on Playa Azul, and Hotel Marabella on Playa Salagua.

The Santiago Peninsula and Playa Audiencia

One of Manzanillo's loveliest views is from the hillside, topped by **El Faro,** the white tower at the summit of the Santiago Peninsula. At the Highway 200 Las Hadas *crucero* (Km 12) turn onto the cobbled Av. Audiencia. Continue past the golf course to the top of the rise, turn right at Calle La Reyna, and keep winding upward as far as possible.

Unfortunately, the condo community has

---

licensed in property transactions. A Mexican notary, functioning much as a title company does in the United States, is the most important person in completing your transaction. The notary traces the title, ensuring that your bank-trustee legally receives it, and making sure the agreed-upon amounts of money get transferred between you, seller, bank, agent, and notary.

You and your agent should meet jointly with the notary early on to discuss the deal and get the notary's computation of the closing costs. For a typical trust-sale, closing costs (covering permit, filing, bank, notary, and registry fees) are considerable, typically 8–10 percent of the sale amount. After that, you will continue to owe property taxes and an approximately 1 percent annual fee to your bank-trustee.

Time-Sharing

Started in Europe, time-sharing has spread all over the globe. A time-share is a prepaid rental of a condo for a specified time period per year. Agreements usually allow you to temporarily exchange your time-share rental for similar lodg-

ings throughout the world.

Your first contact with time-sharing will often be someone on a resort street corner who offers you a half-price tour for "an hour of your time." Soon you'll be attending a hard-sell session offering you tempting inducements in exchange for a check written on the spot. The basic appeal is your investment—say $10,000 cash for a two-week annual stay in a deluxe beach condo—will earn you a handsome profit if you decide to sell your rights sometime in the future. What they don't mention is that, in recent years, time shares have become increasingly difficult to sell and the interest you could get for your $10,000 cash would go far toward renting an equally luxurious vacation condo every year without entailing as much risk.

And risk there is, because you would be handing over your cash for a promise only. Read the fine print. Shop around, and don't give away anything until you inspect the condo you would be getting and talk to others who have invested in the same time-share. It may be a good deal, but don't let them rush you into paradise.

MANZANILLO/COLIMA

© BRUCE WHIPPERMAN

The mansion-decorated Santiago Peninsula (background) adorns the bay view from Playa Olas Altas.

fenced off the El Faro tower, but the views, especially from the topmost accessible lane beneath the summit's north side, are nevertheless memorable. From the emerald ridge of the **Juluapan Peninsula** and the 4,000-foot (1,300-meter) Cerro Toro bull's hump on the north, the panorama sweeps past green sierra and the blue bays to the white downtown spread beneath the pyramid-peak of Cerro Cruz on the southern horizon. On the ocean side, due west, the Hotel Sierra Manzanillo rises above the diminutive sand ribbon of Playa Audiencia.

Once an idyllic downscale cove, Playa Audiencia is now dominated by the ultramodern gleaming white tower of the Hotel Sierra Manzanillo. Families still come on Sunday to play in the fine golden-black sand, drink coconut milk, eat tacos, and leave everything on the beach. The beach concessionaire, **Deportes Aquáticos del Pacífico y Recreaciones del Pacífico,** tel. 314/331-0101, ext. 3804, rents kayaks, sailboarding boards, water skis, personal watercraft, banana boats, and boogie boards right on the beach; open daily 9 A.M.–6 P.M. Instructors from the hotel often guide snorkeling

and scuba diving parties from the beach to the shoals on either side.

Santiago Bay Beaches

The beaches of Santiago Bay stretch for five golden miles north of the Santiago Peninsula to Playa la Boquita, the lagoon-mouth beneath the Juluapan Peninsula's headland. The beaches are all continuous variations of the same wide carpet of yellow, semicoarse sand.

First, at around Km 14, **Playa Santiago** reaches the Río Colorado creek, where it becomes **Playa Olas Altas.** Here, although the sand drops steeply into the surf, it levels out offshore, so the waves roll in gradually, providing excellent surfing, bodysurfing, and boogie boarding breaks.

Playa Miramar continues past Club Maeva, marked by the highway pedestrian overpass. The beach itself is popular and cluttered with umbrellas, horses for rent, and vendors. The usually gentle surf is good for bodysurfing and boogie boarding. Concessionaires rent boogie boards for about $3 an hour.

Finally, at Club Santiago, the beach curves

past a village of seafood *palapas* and fishing boats called **La Boquita** (The Little Mouth). The sand is wide and firm, and the surf is as tranquil as a huge kiddie pool. Offshore, a 200-foot wreck swarms with fish a few feet beneath the surface, excellent for snorkeling and scuba diving. On the other side of the beach, the **Laguna de Juluapan,** a wildlife-rich tidal wetland, winds along miles of forest-edged shallows and grassy marshes.

Hikes

The adventurous can seek out Manzanillo's many hidden corners, beginning right downtown. **Playa Viejo** is often missed, tucked in a little cove over the hill and accessible by path only. Wear walking shoes and a hat, and take your bathing suit, water, and a picnic lunch. Follow Calle Balbino Dávalos past the cathedral. Bear left up the narrow street and climb the steep concrete staircase (on the left) to the hilltop schoolyard. Continue down the other side along a wooded arroyo trail to the beach. The dark sand beach is strewn with shells and surf-rounded rocks. If you're fortunate, you may find a dry, grassy perch, good for camping above the surf.

Also beginning from downtown, the steep trail to Cerro Vigía Chico and Cerro Cruz will challenge fit hikers. It leads to the top of the highest point in Manzanillo for a breezy panoramic view of the city, bay, and ocean below. Allow about 1.5 hours round-trip for Cerro Vigía Chico, about twice that for the steep continuation to Cerro Cruz. Take plenty of water, and avoid midday heat by going early in the morning or late afternoon.

Cerro Vigía Chico: Head south along Av. Carrillo Puerto from the *jardín.* Notice the *sastrería* (tailor shop) Aguayo at no. 223 on the left-hand side, where the master tailor sews suits by hand. Turn the corner at the *tortillería* at Nícolas Bravo and head along the upward lane, past little hillside-perched houses. Ask the local people if you get lost. Say *"¿A Cerro Vigía, por favor?"* They'll help keep you on the right track.

You'll know you've arrived when you see the white FM radio transmitter station atop the hill.

Cerro Cruz: Unfortunately the direct old route has been blocked by a fence. An easier route is accessible by proceeding downhill along the stone and concrete automobile access road. After about 100 yards, you'll see a trail angling right from the road. Go about 4 P.M. to both avoid the midday heat and enjoy the sunset. From the summit, a majestic panorama spreads below: from the Gibraltar-like headland of Juluapan in the north, past golden beaches, over the villa-studded Santiago Peninsula, past the white city to the huge expanse of the Laguna de Cuyutlán, where power stanchions leapfrog across the lagoon from the gargantuan, smoke-spewing seaside power plant.

EXCURSIONS

Manzanillo provides a convenient base for some rewarding excursions. Although sharing a rental car is the easiest way to go, you can also get most anywhere quickly via early-morning buses from the Central de Autobuses. (Ride a taxi, or a bus labeled Central de Autobus or Caminonera Central, or walk, from the El Tajo junction downtown, follow the rail tracks south about three blocks, bear left at the busy Calle Hidalgo traffic fork and continue another six or eight blocks to the bus station on the right.) Some of the most enjoyable excursions lead to Cuyutlán and El Paraíso southeast beaches and El Salto waterfall, Minatitlán, and Agua Fria spring in the northeast foothills.

Cuyutlán and El Paraíso

Cuyutlán is a small, antique resort, unique in Pacific Mexico. It began as a beach haven for upper and middle-class Guadalajarans when Porfirio Díaz's government pushed the rail route through around 1900. Some of the old Porfirian-era hotels remain, as do the quaint wooden walkways to the umbrella-festooned beach. The town has a number of claims to fame, notably a mysterious giant "Green Wave," a Salt Museum that keeps Cuyutlán's ancient salt-harvesting tradition alive, and a latter-day turtle sanctuary and eco-education center. El Paraíso, a more typical, but nevertheless relaxingly lovely minihaven for lovers of sun, surf, sand, and seafood, is a few miles southwest, along Cuyutlán's long, dark-sand strand. (For lots more specifics, see the Cuyutlán and El Paraíso sections in the South to Ixtapa-Zihuatanejo and Inland to Pátzcuaro chapter.)

Excursion to El Salto, Minatitlán, and Agua Fria

Start out early by rental car or by Minatitlán-bound bus from the Manzanillo Central de Autobus. Drivers, set your odometer to zero at the northbound all-paved Minatitlán highway, across the big traffic circle near the Km 4 Pemex gas station.

The road quickly rises, winding past ranches and farms that soon give way to lush, summer-green tropical deciduous forest. Along the way, you pass a **double spring** that cascades by the road on the right (at Mile 26, Km 42). At the same spot, on the left, you can view the scar of the **Peña Colorada** (Red Rock) iron strip mine on a mountain-top to the north. An entire mountain

El Salto Waterfall provides a relaxing excursion from Manzanillo or Colima.

© BRUCE WHIPPERMAN

MANZANILLO/COLIMA

of iron ore is currently being extracted and sent via a 17-mile (27-km) conveyor belt to the processing mill on Manzanillo's north side. There, the ore is pelletized and sent by ship to the giant Las Truchas mill in Lázaro Cárdenas, Michoacán, and other Pacific Rim locations to be made into steel.

Continue another three miles (five km) to the prim company town, Peña Colorada, with all up-to-date facilities—bank, hospital, schools, houses—for the miners' families, built by the Japanese-Mexican consortium that developed the mine.

In another mile (at Mile 30, Km 48) you come to **El Salto Park** and new picnic ground to the right, below the highway. Bear left after you enter, another 100 yards, to the more intimate old park just overlooking the waterfall. Here, butterflies flutter and orchids grow among great mossy rock outcroppings. A rustic swimming pool and kiddie pool delight picnicking families.

Follow the steps down to the base of the El Salto (the Jump) fall, that cascades in a pair of 30-foot leaps to a turbulent pool below. The best time to arrive is during the dry late autumn, winter, and spring. During the rainy summer and early autumn El Salto may be a muddy brown. From the base of the falls, adventurers can float down the deep, slow creek, 100 yards to a beach downstream. Bring a picnic, or maybe even a tent or your RV for an overnight. Weekdays the park isn't usually crowded. Sundays and holidays, however, are for those who like company. Then, the place will likely be crowded with frolicking families, mariachis and taco vendors.

From El Salto, continue to **Minatitlán,** half a mile off the highway intersection at Mile 32 (Km 53). It's a typically pleasant Mexican mountain *municipio,* with a modicum of stores and services. Stop for a break or lunch at the very clean **Cocina Herradura** (in midtown, beneath the Coca-Cola sign on the right).

Continue ahead downhill toward Agua Fria spring. Another eight miles (13 km) along, at Mile 40 (Km 64), a sign marks a gateway to the **Manantlán Biosphere,** a unique ice-age remnant cloud forest habitat. A rough, jeep-negotiable road leads uphill, through **El Sauz Rancho** a total of at least 20 miles (32 km) to **Terrero** hamlet in the cloud forest around the 7,000-foot summit. Under the best dry conditions allow at least five hours at the wheel for the round-trip. Be prepared to camp overnight in the rain. (Don't try driving all the way unless you're back-road experienced, emergency-equipped, and stocked with food, gas, and water. Backpackers should be similarly prepared.)

Continue ahead another 13 miles (21 km) downhill, where a sign (at Mile 53, 85 km from Manzanillo) marks Agua Dulce. (Here, an old timer told me that *Agua Dulce*—Sweet Water—got its name from the single potable natural spring—among the many foul ones—discovered here.)

Finally, another mile later, you reach **Agua Fría** on the right, an idyllic cluster of cool, clear ponds that meander among rustic picnic *palapas*. Here, you can have it all: food and drinks from restaurants, plenty of relaxing shade, space for camping, and when so much pleasure gets boring, you can slip, for a cooling break, into a crystal spring-fed pool.

ACCOMMODATIONS
Downtown Hotels
Near cafés, shopping, and transportation, Manzanillo's downtown is colorful and lively, but often noisy.

The **Hotel Colonial,** Bocanegra 28, at Av. México, Manzanillo, Colima 28200, tel./fax 314/332-0668, 314/332-1134, or 314/332-1230, Manzanillo's best downtown hotel, is built around dignified interior courtyard Restaurant Candiles. Dating from the 1940s, the Colonial, one block from the *jardín,* is replete with old-fashioned touches—bright-hued tile staircases,

MANZANILLO ACCOMMODATIONS BY PRICE

Accommodations (area code is 314, postal code is 28200) are listed in increasing order of approximate high-season, double-room rates. The toll-free 800, 877, and 866 numbers are dialable only from either the United States and Canada or both.

Hotel Flamingos, Madero 72, tel. 332-1037, $14

Hotel Emperador, B. Dávalos 69, tel. 332-2374, $14

Hotel Playa San Pedrito, Teniente Azueta 3, tel. 332-0535, $30

Hotel Colonial, Bocanegra 28, tel./fax 332-0668, 332-1134, or 332-1230, $30

Club Vacacional Las Brisas, L. Cárdenas 207, tel. 333-1747, fax 334-0086, $43

Condominios Arco Iris, P.O. Box 359, tel./fax 333-0168, irisarc@col1.telmex.net.mx, $47

Hotel Marbella, Km 8.5, Playa Azul, P.O. Box 554, tel. 333-1103 or 333-1105, fax 333-1222, $47

Hotel Fiesta Mexicana, Km 8.5, Blvd. Miguel de la Madrid, P.O. Box 808, tel./fax 333-2180, tel. 333-1100, fiestmz@prodigy.net.mx, $50

Hotel Playa de Santiago, P.O. Box 147, Santiago, Colima 28860, tel./fax 333-0055 or 333-0344, hoplsan@prodigy.net.mx, $59

Hotel La Posada, L. Cárdenas 135, tel. 333-1899, posada@bay.net.mx, $70

Villas Los Angeles, Av. de Cima, Peninsula de Santiago, tel. 333-1702 or 333-1703, fax 334-0283, $80

Dolphin Cove Inn, tel. 334-1692, fax 334-1689, dolphin_cove_inn@hotmail.com, $100

Hotel Villas Palma Real, La Boquita, tel. 33/3880-0700, $170

Hotel Sierra Manzanillo, Av. La Audiencia 1, tel. 333-2000, 800/515-4321, or 800/544-4686, fax 333-2272, hszlo@sidek.com.mx, $260 (two adults, all-inclusive)

Club Maeva, P.O. Box 440, tel./fax 331-0800, 331-0891, or 866/275-8392, $320 (two adults, all-inclusive)

Hotel Las Hadas, P.O. Box 158, tel. 334-0000, 331-0101, 800/226-3161, fax 331-0121, reserv.hada@brisas.com.mx, $200

Karmina Palace, Av. Vista Hermosa 13, Peninsula de Santiago, tel. 334-1313, 877/KARMINA (877/527-6462), fax 334-1108, reservations@karminapalace.com, $420 (two adults, all-inclusive, two children free)

stained-glass windows, and sentimental tile wall scenes. The rooms, although worn, have traditional high ceilings, hand-hewn leather chairs, and wrought-iron lamp fixtures. They open to shady, street-view corridors, lined with chairs for sitting. Try for a room on the relatively quiet Bocanegra Street side of the hotel. The 38 rooms rent for about $24 s, $30 d, with baths and a/c. Credit cards accepted.

A prime budget stop is the **Hotel Emperador,** at B. Dávalos 69, Manzanillo, Colima 28200, tel. 314/332-2374, a stack of 28 rooms around a dim interior patio, which, at first glance, appears uninviting. Inside, however, the grandmotherly owner, María Trinidad Bautista, her son and their staff keep the corridors and stairways shining. The rooms too, although very plain, are very clean. Furthermore, the price is certainly right: rates run about $12 s, $14 d, $21 t, with baths, ceiling fans, and a good restaurant downstairs. Half a block from the *jardín,* on the quiet westward extension of B. Dávalos, just before the church.

If Hotel Emperador is full try the good budget alternative, **Hotel Flamingos,** at Madero 72, Manzanillo, Colima 28200, tel. 314/332-1037. Find it on the dead-end street, Madero, that leads inland uphill from the *jardín.* Its quiet side-street location makes the Hotel Flamingos very worthy of consideration. Upstairs, past the small front desk, the approximately 30 rooms in four floors are clean, mostly spacious, and simply but thoughtfully decorated with maroon Asian-motif bedspreads to match the ruddy tile floors and handsome rustic wood furniture and doors. Rates are a bargain at the ordinary (nonfestival) rates of about $11 s, $14 d. The only drawback here is lack of privacy and ventilation of the hotel's inside rooms, whose only windows face the hallways. Ask for an outside room for more air, quiet, and privacy.

If, on the other hand, you prefer a beach location, walk or taxi a mile east of downtown along the waterfront about .6 mile (one km) to the **Hotel Playa San Pedrito.** The hotel offers a homey close-in alternative, right on locally popular (but somewhat polluted) Playa San Pedrito, at Av. Teniente Azueta 3, Manzanillo, Colima 28200, tel. 314/332-0535. This unpretentious

Mexican family hotel rambles amid a flowery garden, edged with colorful tropical plants and centering on a free-form blue swimming pool. A tennis court stands at one side, and beyond that, waves lap the sandy beach. With all those outdoor attractions, the plainness of the rooms and the dust in their corners matter little. Request one of the *piso arriba* (upper-floor) rooms for privacy and sea views from a front balcony-corridor. The 33 fan-only rooms go for about $20 s or d, $30 t low season, $30 s, d, or t high, with parking. Credit cards not accepted.

Las Brisas–Playa Azul Hotels

The swish of the waves on the sand, long walks at dusk, and good restaurants nearby summarize the attractions of the "passionate pink" **Hotel La Posada,** a durable jewel among Manzanillo's small hotels, Av. Lázaro Cárdenas 135, P.O. Box 201, Manzanillo, Colima 28210, tel. 314/333-1899, posada@bay.net.mx. Every detail—leafy potted plants, rustling palms, brick arches, airy beach-view *sala,* resplendent bay-view sunsets— adds to La Posada's romantic (although now somewhat faded) ambience. La Posada's clientele, mostly middle-aged North American winter vacationers, tend to prefer the upstairs rooms, some of which have private balconies and bay views. Get your winter reservations in early. Rates for the 24 comfortable semideluxe rooms run year-round, about $46 s, $70 d, some with a/c, including a good breakfast. Ask for a discount or special price during the low summer-fall season. The hotel has a bar-cart, snack restaurant, comfortable sitting area, good pool, and street parking, and accepts credit cards.

A few doors north along the beach, the family-friendly **Club Vacacional Las Brisas** likewise enjoys platoons of repeat customers, at Av. L. Cárdenas 207, Fracc. Las Brisas, Manzanillo, Colima 28200, tel. 314/333-1747, fax 314/334-0086. Attentive on-site management keeps the garden manicured, the pool inviting, and the beach beyond the gate clean and golden. The best rooms, white-walled and comfortable but not deluxe, are on the ocean-view upper floors. The 35 rooms and suites, all with kitchenettes, rent for about $37 s, $43 d, except for Christmas and Easter holidays, when prices rise to about $50s, $60 d. With both fan and a/c, parking, and credit cards accepted.

The **Hotel Fiesta Mexicana,** Km 8.5, Carretera Manzanillo-Santiago, Blvd. Miguel de la Madrid, P.O. Box 808, Manzanillo, Colima 28200, tel./fax 314/333-2180 or 314/333-1100, fiestmz@prodigy.net.mx. From the outside, the hotel, right on Playa Azul, appears as a big white box perched on the beach. Inside, however, the rooms rise in graceful tiers, which enclose a lovely patio with a meandering blue pool. On one side is a big restaurant with an ocean-vista veranda. The 190 smallish but comfortable rooms look out on sea views on the ocean side. They rent for about $50 d normally, about $100 during holidays; all with TV, phones, and a/c. Alternatively, all-inclusive lodging (meals and in-house sports and entertainment included) runs about $100 for two low season, $200 high; promotions are sometimes available. With street parking and pool; credit cards are accepted.

Less than a quarter mile farther west, the neighboring **Hotel Marbella,** Km 8.5, Playa Azul, P.O. Box 554, Manzanillo, Colima 28200, tel. 314/333-1103 or 314/333-1105, fax 314/333-1222, offers a breezy beachfront location at moderate prices. All the ingredients seem to be in place—a beachfront pool, rustling palms, a good breakfast restaurant, sand and surf—for a tranquil Manzanillo week in the sun. Of the approximately 150 rooms, the best are the oceanview balcony rooms on the upper floor of the original two-story low-rise beachfront wing. A pair of new wings added many more deluxe rooms, but most without ocean views. All rooms (most in the new wings) run about $40 s, $47 d year-round except holidays (when rates begin at around $60). If an airy ocean view balcony is what you want, specify reservations in the old wing with an ocean view *(sección vieja con vista del mar)*. Parking is available, and credit cards are accepted.

The **Condominios Arco Iris,** Km 9.5, P.O. Box 359, Manzanillo, Colima 28200, tel./fax 314/333-0168, irisarc@col1.telmex.net.mx, half a mile north, is more like a garden apartment complex than condominiums. The setting, a spacious, leafy manicured tropical park, with inviting blue pool-patio and *palapa,* nicely complements the apartments themselves. The units, most at ground level, with kitchenettes and either one or two bedrooms, are immaculate and attractively furnished in 1970s-modern style. The two-bedroom, two-bath units, which sleep four, rent for about $105. The one-bedrooms go for about $47. Discounts are generally available for monthly (or perhaps even weekly) rentals. A block from the beach and a favorite of many Manzanillo longtimers. Get your winter reservation in early.

Santiago Peninsula Hotels

The Santiago Peninsula's sea-view villas, condo developments, and resorts for the rich and famous are luxuriously isolated, generally requiring a car or taxi to get anywhere.

Hotel Las Hadas Golf Resort and Marina, P.O. Box 158, Manzanillo, Colima 28200, tel. 314/334-0000 or 314/331-0101, fax 314/331-0121, reserv.hada@brisas.com.mx, is a self-contained city with a host of pleasurable amenities. Las Hadas, now operated by the big Mexican Las Brisas hotel chain, spreads over so much ground that only a fraction of its rooms are near the water, and most are a small hike to the beach. Furthermore, when guests finally get there, they find no waves on the sheltered Las Hadas cove, and their views are cluttered by the white Arabian-style tents of a regiment of fellow vacationers. Las Hadas nevertheless offers plenty of interest, at extra charge: three restaurants, a sport-fishing marina, a sunset cruise, horseback riding, a golf course, a squadron of tennis courts, and a dozen aquatic sports. The approximately 300 luxurious white-and-blue motif suites, villas, and standard rooms rent from about $200 d; larger "Camino Suites" run from about $250 d. All amenities included, including complete wheelchair access. For reservations dial toll-free Mex. tel. 800/227-4727 or U.S./Can. tel. 866/226-3161. For more information, visit the website www.brisas.com.mx.

On the other, west, side of the peninsula, the shining white **Hotel Sierra Manzanillo,** Av. La Audiencia 1, Peninsula Santiago, Manzanillo, Colima 28200, tel. 314/333-2000, fax

314/333-2272, hszlo@sidek.com.mx, towers futuristically above the gemlike Playa Audiencia. The hotel's large size, however, doesn't seem to bother the guests, whose activities focus upon the spreading ocean-view pool and patio. There, around the swim-up bar, drinks flow, music bounces, and water volleyball and polo fill the sunny days. No matter if guests tire of pool frolicking; every hotel corner, from the indulgent pastel-appointed rooms (each with sea-view balcony) to **Hidra,** the airy, rustic-chic restaurant-in-the-round, abounds with style. Bars offer nightly live music; fine crafts and designer clothes fill the boutiques, while dozens of books and the latest U.S. magazines line the shop shelves. The all-inclusive rates, which include all in-house lodging, food, and entertainment, for the 350 rooms run about $180 for two, low season, about $260 high. Children under six free, 6–12, about $40 per day. All rooms have a/c, cable TV, phones, and mini-bars; all water sports, tennis, golf, and wheelchair access included; credit cards are accepted. For reservations, dial toll-free U.S./Can. tel. 800/515-4321 or 800/544-4686. For more information, visit the website www.mexicoissoeasy.com.

A relatively recent, worthy addition to the Santiago Peninsula's list of luxury hotels is the **Karmina Palace,** on the beachfront, just south of Las Hadas, at Av. Vista Hermosa 13, Peninsula de Santiago, Manzanillo, Colima 28200, tel. 314/334-1313, fax 314/334-1108, reservations@karminapalace.com. Here, the owner (a prominent U.S. hotelier) built a palace in honor of his wife, Karmina. And so it is, a neo-Mayan super-mansion, like the kings of old Uxmal never even dreamed of. Little was spared in creating this ultraresort; from an artificial ocean minibay and kiddie lagoon and luxuriously isolated bay-point restaurant to 10 lighted tennis courts and eight swimming pools, all set within spreading, grassy, palm-tufted grounds. Add a kids' club, spa, gym, three restaurants, five bars, and a complete theater with shows, and you have the equivalent of a very spacious luxury liner on land. The super-deluxe rooms, equipped with all the newest amenities and tastefully dec-

orated in creamy pastels, are no less than you would expect. Everything, including all food and drinks and in-house facilities, costs about $100 for one, $160 for two, low season; $210 and $420 high. One child up to 12 per adult goes free, 12–16, half price. For reservations, dial toll-free U.S./Can. tel. 877/KARMINA (877/527-6462). For more information, visit the website www.interclubresorts.com.

Manzanillo visitors weary of luxury hotel rates but who still crave a luxurious location can choose the hilltop **Villas Los Angeles,** on Av. de Cima, Peninsula de Santiago, Colima 28200, tel. 314/333-1702 or 314/333-1703, fax 314/334-0283. Here, owners Patricia and Michael La Pointe have built a hilltop cluster of deluxe rooms and suites perched artfully above an airy panoramic view pool and patio. Inside, rooms are immaculate, luxuriously light and private, comfortably furnished, and decorated with handicrafts and original wall art. Guests in most rooms enjoy sweeping bay or mountain vistas. Daily rates run about $80 d for studios; $120 gets you a larger one-bedroom apartment with kitchenette. Stays of more than a week receive a 10 percent discount; all with a/c, TV, and parking. Reserve early, especially during the winter. For more information, visit the website www.villaslosangeles.com.

Nearby, moderately priced **Dolphin Cove Inn,** tel. 314/334-1692, fax 314/334-1689, dolphin_cove_inn@hotmail.com, offers super-deluxe view lodgings, spread artfully above a rocky but spectacularly scenic shorefront, right next to Las Hadas. Inside, guests in the approximately 30 low-rise studios and suites enjoy attractive designer white and blue decor, with luxuriously marbled baths and floors, 1990s-standard kitchenettes and baths and panoramic bay views. Moreover, a short walking path leads to Las Hadas Resort shops, restaurants, and beach sports. (To get through the Las Hadas Resort gate from Dolphin Cove Inn, however, guests must buy a $25 day pass per adult, kids under 12 free, $10 usable toward food and beverages.) Dolphin Cove Inn room rates cost a very reasonable $82 d low season, $100 high; seniors over 60 customarily get a 20 percent

MANZANILLO/COLIMA

The view from the Dolphin Cove Inn encompasses the broad, blue sweep of Manzanillo Bay.

low-season discount. Amenities include a/c, cable TV, lovely ocean-front pool-patio, restaurant, and kiddie pool. Credit cards are accepted. For more information, visit the website www.dolphincoveinn.com.

Santiago Bay Hotels

The once-grand but now relatively humble 1950s-genre **Hotel Playa de Santiago,** Balneario de Santiago s/n, Bahía de Santiago, P.O. Box 147, Santiago, Colima 28860, tel./fax 314/333-0055 or 314/333-0344, hoplsan@prodigy.net.mx, on the south side of Santiago Bay nevertheless offers much for budget-conscious travelers. Besides spacious, private balcony sea-view rooms overlooking the hotel's placid cove and beach, guests enjoy a palmy, seaside pool and sundeck, sunset views, a tennis court, a boat ramp, and friendly management. High-season prices for the 105 rooms and suites begin at about $59 d; two-bedroom suites go for about twice these rates; all with phones and fans only; credit cards are accepted. For more information, visit the website www.playadesantiago.com.

The **Club Maeva,** P.O. Box 440, Manzanillo,

Colima 28200, tel./fax 314/331-0800, 314/331-0875, or 314/331-0891, Manzanillo's all-inclusive fun-in-the-sun colony, spreads for a whitewashed quarter mile on the hillside above Santiago Bay. Club Maeva, whose clientele is mostly Mexican in the summer, Canadian and American during the winter, demonstrates the power of numbers. Its staff of 700 services upward of 1,000 guests who enjoy a plethora of aquatic, field, court, and gym activities at no extra cost. Months would be needed to take full advantage of the endless sports menu, which includes pool, scuba, snorkeling, tennis, horseback riding, volleyball, softball, aerobics, and basketball. Besides sports, Club Maeva guests enjoy continuous open bar and restaurant service, nightly theme shows, a disco, a miles-long beach, sunning beside Latin America's largest pool, and a complete water-slide park. Inclusive rather than exclusive, Club Maeva resembles a huge comfortable summer camp. Children are more than welcome, with a special miniclub for ages 4–12. Club Maeva seems to offer options for everyone, such as table games—cards, backgammon, checkers, and chess—Spanish lessons, and a tranquil adults-only solarium and pool-bar. The rooms, actually clusters of small villas, are an unusual luxurious-spartan combination, snow white and royal blue with private view balconies and marble floors, but with no movable furniture. With the exception of stoves and refrigerators in some units, all shelves, cabinets, bed platforms, and seats are attractive but indestructible white concrete built-ins. The 550 rooms and suites rent for the all-inclusive rate of about $110 per person, low season double occupancy, about $160 high. Children under seven free, 7–12 pay $50, over 12 pay adult rates; all rooms with a/c, but no phones or TV; credit cards accepted. For reservations and information, dial toll-free Mex. tel. 800/523-8450 or U.S./Can. tel. 866/275-8392. For more information, visit the website www.maevaresort.com.

At the sylvan northernmost corner of Santiago Bay, guests at **Hotel Villas Palma Real** enjoy Santiago Bay's entire beach, ocean, and mountain panorama from the comfort of their private, shaded balconies. A 100-unit hybrid condo, time-share, and hotel tucked at the foot of a jungly mountain ridge, Villas Palma Real offers luxurious tropical living at relatively modest rates. Apartments range from spacious one-bedroom junior suites without kitchens to huge three-bedroom, three-bath apartments sleeping eight. All suites and apartments are simply but elegantly appointed, with creamy tile floors, decorator pastel sofas and bedspreads, designer lamps, king-size beds, and modern tiled baths. All but the junior suites have full kitchenettes. Here, you can have Las Hadas luxury for half the price. Rates for the one-bedroom junior suites run about $130 low season, $170 high, one-bedroom suites with kitchenette, about $150 low season, $195 high. Two-bedroom apartments run about $250 low season, $290 high. The hotel is adjacent to scenic La Boquita beach and wildlife-rich Laguna de Juluapan; bring your binoculars and bird book. No public transportation is available from the hotel; if you don't have your own wheels, moderately priced taxis are available. Amenities include cable TV, phones, a/c, fans, view balconies, pool, good open-air *palapa*

restaurant, minimarket, and laundry. Reserve through the hotel's reservation office, tel./fax 333/880-0700.

Rental Agent

If you're interested in the comfort of a longer-term stay, contact Real Tur Real Estate, tel. 314/334-1600 or 314/333-2288, fax 314/333-0623, or email realtur@bay.net.mx.

Trailer Park and Camping

At this writing, the manager of the downscale **Trailer Park La Marmota** (a block from Highway 200, along the Minatitlán highway that heads north from near the Pemex station at approximately Km 4.4.) says that the owner has closed it. (You might write Marmota Trailer Park, Km 0.1, Carretera Manzanillo-Minatitlán, Manzanillo, Colima 28200, or drop by or call tel. 314/336-6248 to see if he changed his mind.)

Condos, hotels, and restaurants have crowded out virtually all camping prospects along Manzanillo beaches. However, authorities allow tent camping and overnight RV parking in the quarter-mile-long open space on the inland side of the highway (watch for the dirt road angling from the highway), just north of Hotel Villas Playa de Oro between Km 15 and Km 15.5.

The closest good country campsites are about a dozen miles north, three miles off Highway 200, at **Playa de Oro,** from the signed cobbled (but rough in parts) side road near Km 31, five miles north of El Naranjo. Pablo, the friendly caretaker, at the entrance portal, told me that the owners welcome campers. He pointed out some good camping and parking spaces and a shady ramada, by the south-side headland.

A land development turned sour, Playa de Oro has returned to the wild: an endless sandy beach with many drive-in sites, good for RVs and tents. The surf, while often not too rough, has some undertow—don't swim alone. Boogie boarding and surfing are possible for cautious beginners and intermediates. Surf fishing is excellent, and the waves deposit carpets of shells and miles of driftwood, perfect for a week of beachcombing. You'll share the beach with a colony of sand crabs, which, like a legion of arthropodic prairie dogs, jealously guard their individual sand holes. Bring everything; the closest stores are in El Naranjo.

Although the Mexican name Playa de Oro (Beach of Gold) is as common as tacos in Taxco, this particular Playa de Oro is not just another developer's label. The story goes back to 1862, when the paddle-wheeled steamship *Golden Gate*, loaded with 337 passengers and more than a million dollars in California gold, caught fire and, sank not far off the beach. Only 80 people were saved and none of the gold. Although a salvage operation two years later netted some of the treasure, most remained until an enterprising American, a now-retired former hotel owner, arrived on the scene during the 1950s. He promoted a powerful suction dredge, brought from the United States, which harvested the lost treasure. Despite the giant underwater vacuum cleaner's efficiency, local folks tell stories of occasional shiny coins still washing up on the "Beach of Gold."

Note: The cobbled access road, excellent when new years ago, appears unmaintained and consequently has developed a number of rough spots, especially on steep sections. These make the road marginally usable by bulky RVs and passenger cars. It's best to be prepared to drive in with a maneuverable, high-clearance, preferably four-wheel-drive truck or SUV.

FOOD

Downtown Snacks and Stalls

The cluster of *fondas* (permanent foodstalls) at the **Mercado Francisco Madero** is the downtown mecca for wholesome homestyle cookery. Each *fonda* specializes in a few favorite dishes, which vary from rich *pozole* and savory stewed pork, beef, or chicken, to ham and eggs and whole grilled fish.

One of the favorites, the **Menudería Paulita,** open daily 5 A.M.–10 P.M., is tended by a jolly squad of women off Av. México, at the F. Madero and Cuauhtémoc corner, five short blocks from the *jardín.* One of them enjoys the singular job of crafting and baking unending stacks of hot tortillas, which their mostly workingmen customers use to scoop up the last delectable morsels.

Besides sit-down meals, the same downtown neighborhood is a source of on-street desserts. These include *churros* (long doughnuts) and pastries, sold from carts late afternoons along Av. México about four blocks from the *jardín,* and velvety ice cream from the **Bing** ice cream chain's downtown branch on the east end of the *jardín.*

North-End Breakfast and Snacks

No local vacation would be complete without breakfast or lunch at **Juanito's,** Manzanillo's friendly refuge from high prices, in Santiago, Km 13.5, a few blocks north of Santiago Plaza, tel. 314/333-1388. The longtime American expatriate owner and his family feature tasty, modestly priced hometown fare, such as ham and eggs any style, hotcakes, hamburgers, milk shakes, and apple pie. For a generation of repeat customers, Juanito's is home away from home, with satellite TV, a shelf of used paperbacks, a long-distance telephone, and bottomless cups of coffee. Open daily 8 A.M.–10 P.M.

Another excellent spot to start the day is the restaurant at the **Hotel Marbella,** at around Km 8.5 on Playa Azul, tel. 314/333-1103. Here, bright sun streams into the ocean-view bay windows while waitresses bring hearty breakfasts of eggs with potatoes, pancakes with maple syrup, and bottomless cups of coffee.

On the other hand, regulars flock nightly to tiny **Pepe's,** also around Km 8.5, on the beach side, which specializes in mouthwatering barbecued beef, roast chicken, and pork loin tacos; open daily 7 P.M.–1 A.M.

Equally popular is **Julio's** Mexican food in Santiago (which a number of folks recommended but I haven't yet checked out personally).

Downtown Restaurants

One of Manzanillo's prime people-watching cafés is the **Restaurant Chantilly** on the *jardín* corner adjacent to city hall, tel. 314/332-0194. The completely unpretentious Chantilly offers its mostly local clientele prompt service, an extensive economical menu, and long moments lingering over several varieties of café espresso. The *comida corrida* (five-course set lunch, $4.50) highlights many patrons' downtown day. Open daily except Saturday 7 A.M.-10:30 P.M. Budget—moderate.

The dignified, airy ambience of the **Los Candiles** restaurant of the Hotel Colonial on Av. México, just south of the *jardín*, offers another attractive option. Besides its high-beamed ceiling, softly whirring ceiling fans, and a tranquil adjoining open-air patio, the lunch and dinner menu offers an unusually long selection of seafood, from broiled marlin and tuna to jumbo butterflied shrimp and pan-fried squid. A live duo sometimes adds to the enjoyment with soft guitar music afternoons and evenings. Open daily 7 A.M. to 10 P.M. Moderate.

The crowd of midafternoon customers alerts budget-minded diners to the value and quality of the restaurant at the **Hotel Emperador,** at B. Dávalos 69, half a block west of the *jardín*, tel. 314/332-2374. Although *desayuno, comida,* and *cena* are all good at the Emperador, the favorite is the $3 *comida corrida* set lunch, beginning around 1 P.M. Budget.

A different cadre of loyal customers enjoys the **Café Roca del Mar,** tel. 314/332-0302, at the east end of the *jardín*. With approximately the same menu and prices as the Chantilly, the Roca del Mar, whose tables spread to the shady sidewalk, is a bit more refined and relaxed. Open daily 7 A.M.–11 P.M. Moderate.

Around the corner, **Restaurant Lychee,** on the dock-front, two blocks east, at Niños Héroes 397, tel. 314/332-1103, serves bountiful plates of tasty Chinese-style specialties. Although the meat and fish dishes are tasty enough, it's the mounds of stir-fried broccoli, bean sprouts, snow peas, and bok choy that spell welcome relief for vegetable-hungry palates. Unfortunately, present government plans include demolishing the Lychee and much else along the waterfront to make way for a new Puerto-Vallarta–style *malecón* walkway. Open Tues.–Sun. 2–10 P.M. Moderate.

Crucero Las Brisas–Playa Azul Restaurants

Right at the Crucero Las Brisas, a few doors east of the intersection, south side of the street, stands **El Vaquero,** Manzanillo's enduring cowboy B-movie set. An apparently exact replica of a 1900 Arizona (or maybe Sonora?) mining town saloon, all that El Vaquero seems to have missing is the tinkling of an old upright piano. Leave all dietary pretensions aside and enjoy the hearty chuck-wagon cuisine: grill-roasted onions, real-thing chili and beans (*frijoles charros*), and a load of meat, from mere hamburgers and *arrachera* (ordinary sirloin steak), to choice two-pound fillets mignon and porterhouse steaks, all grilled to order in the outside patio. Open daily, from about noon until midnight, tel. 314/333-1654. Moderate–expensive.

Among the most modest of the Las Brisas-Playa Azul good restaurants is the Las Brisas branch of the Mexican **Benedetti's Pizza** chain, on the inland side of the highway, just west of the baseball stadium, tel. 314/333-1592. The hard-working, friendly staff offers respectable Italian fare, good service, a friendly family atmosphere, and reasonable prices. The cool salad bar plate—carrots, tomato, beets, mushrooms, lettuce, and fresh bread, $3—seems like heaven on a warm afternoon. Open daily 10 A.M.–10 P.M. Budget–moderate. Visit or order pizza from other Benedetti's branches on the *jardín*, downtown, and by Comercial Mexicana in Salagua.

Across the street, and with much more personality, is Carlos'n Charlie's **Colima Bay Café,** the Manzanillo branch of late owner Carlos Anderson's goofy worldwide chain at Highway 200, Km 8. Although open Mon.–Sat. 1:30 P.M.–1 A.M. during high season, low-season hours may be shorter; call tel. 314/333-1150 or 314/333-1890. The fun begins at the entrance where a sign announces: "Colima Bay Café, since 1800." Inside, the outrageous decorates the ceilings while a riot of photos—romantic, poignant, sentimental, and brutal—covers the walls. Meanwhile, the waiters (who, despite their antics, are gentle sorts) entertain the customers. The menu, with items such as "Moo," "Peep," and "Pemex," cannot be all nonsense, since many of them, such as Oysters 444, TBC Salad, and the tangy barbecued ribs, are delicious. Moderate–expensive.

Many new restaurants have arisen to replace the several that couldn't afford to stay open during the post-September 11, 2001, tourism lull. Past the Colima Bay Café, continuing west, find **Señor Sushi**, on the inland side of Highway 200, at Km 9.5, just half a block past the Chrysler dealer. Although it specializes in about 30 kinds of sushi, it also offers a full Japanese food menu. Enter the open-air *palapa*-roofed enclosure, and soon the colorul, flutterering banners, the waiters, garbed as if out of old Osaka, and apertif cups of warm *o-sake* begin to create an illusion of Japan. The impression becomes more vivid, with the arrival of the food: *gyoza* (pot stickers), yakitori (chicken kebabs), tempura (breaded, french-fried vegetables), and *teppanyaki*, (diced-in-front-of-you grilled meat and vegetables), all of which seems a minor miracle half a world away from the source. Appearances, however, are only the beginning. The miracle becomes complete as you taste the sticky rice, with its grains individual yet just exactly sticky enough, and very correctly served with a dab of pungent green *wasabi* (horseradish sauce).

Across the street, west, at **El Fogón**, another, but completely different illusion awaits. It's best to go at night, when the very artful, subdued lighting enhances the effect: of an old-time Rancho Grande somewhere up north, where meat was (and is) both the staple and king. Appetizers (chorizo, or spicy sausage), fondue, quesadillas, salads (shrimp, mixed), and soups *(Azteca)*, quickly lead to meats, from tongue *(lengua,)* and pork loin *(lomo)*, to main events, such as *arrachera* (steak, often tough), several styles of *molcajetes* (steaming meat and vegetables), and T-bone steaks. Open daily noon–11 P.M., tel. 314/333-1654. Moderate–expensive.

Cross the street to **Mandarin Wok,** with pretty fair Chinese cuisine—good hot and sour soup, sweet and sour pork, and spring rolls, and nothing bad—when a friend and I ate there. Mandarin Wok's customers enjoy the added plus of handsome decorations and a refined, but festive atmosphere and attentive, very professional service. Open daily approximately noon–midnight, tel. 314/334-0590. Expensive.

Newest on the list of Manzanillo newcomer restaurants is **Manos Morenos** (Brown Hands), whose owner's mission is to demonstrate the best of Mexican culture—arts and crafts, music, and cuisine. She's certainly proved herself by her cuisine, which is gourmet Mexican at its best. Such as *chiles,* stuffed with cheese and potato, fish fillet with mango sauce, and *arrachera* in mushroom sauce. But never mind, close your eyes and put your forefinger to the menu and whatever you touch will be bound to please. Make up a party of four to share and sample as much as possible. Good for breakfast, too. Open daily 8 A.M. to 10 P.M.

For romantics, a Manzanillo trip wouldn't be complete without a visit to the showplace **Restaurant L'Recife**, end of Av. Cerro de Cenicero, at the breezy tip of north-end Peninsula Juluapan. Although its dazzling clifftop location is at least half the attraction, the tasty food—salads, seafood, and steaks—would alone make the trip worthwhile. Taxi or drive northwest along the beach boulevard. Pass the Club Santiago; within a mile, turn left at the La Boquita road. After about two miles winding along the lagoon, follow the signed L'Recife road fork uphill right. Continue another quarter mile to road's end. Be sure to arrive before 5:30 P.M., in time to enjoy the sunset. Reservations, tel. 314/335-0900, are mandatory; open daily 5–11 P.M. Expensive.

ENTERTAINMENT AND EVENTS
Botaneras
A number of *botaneras,* beer and entertainment halls, have big local followings. One of the best is **Langosto Blanco** (White Lobster) that provides a class-act dancing, singing, and comedy show for patrons nightly. As soon as you order a drink, the *botanas*—small plates of ceviche, beans, pickled vegetables, and guacamole—begin to flow. Although the clientele is mostly male, a sprinkling of accompanied wives, girlfriends, sisters, and cousins make the atmosphere comfortable for women also. Find Langosto Blanco on bayfront Blv. Niños Héroes, not far from the Archaeological Museum, about a mile and a half from downtown, at about Km 1.5; open nightly until around midnight.

Farther northwest, near the Crucero Las Brisas, afternoon *botanero* **El Caporal** opens quietly at around 1 P.M. By 3 P.M., mariachis begin strumming away, more bottles pop open, and more *botanas* arrive. By 4 P.M., the place is often packed; if you stay till 6 P.M. you'll probably need someone to stuff you into a taxi home. El Caporal is behind the Superior beer distributor at Km 8, across the highway from the beach; open daily noon–7 P.M.

Sunsets, Strolling, and Sidewalk Cafés

Playa Las Brisas and Playa Azul provide the best vantage for viewing Manzanillo's often spectacular sunsets. For liquid refreshment and atmosphere to augment the natural light show, try one of the romantic beachside spots, such as Hotel La Posada, Carlos'n Charlie's Colima Bay Café, Hotel Sierra, Hotel Playa Santiago, and especially L'Recife restaurant. Sunset views from the plush terraces at Hotels Las Hadas and Karmina Palace are unfortunately obstructed by intervening headlands.

> *Playa Las Brisas and Playa Azul provide the best vantage for viewing Manzanillo's often spectacular sunsets.*

Las Hadas provides an out, however. Its motorboat catamaran *Explorer* departs daily high season (Mon., Thurs., Sat. low), from the hotel marina (at around 4:30 P.M.) for a *crucero de atardecer* (sunset cruise). The $36 per-person tariff includes drinks. For tickets, contact the hotel, tel. 314/334-0000, or a travel agent, such as Agencia Bahías Gemelas, tel. 314/333-1000.

Early evenings are great for enjoying the passing parade around the downtown *jardín*. Relax over dessert and coffee at bordering sidewalk cafés, such as **Chantilly,** corner Av. México, closed Saturday, or **Roca del Mar,** east side of the *jardín*, next to Bing ice cream.

A major unmissable downtown entertainment is the swarms of swallows (*golondrinas*) who fly in around sunset and crowd upon the overhead telephone and power lines around the *jardín*. They first scream and squack as they squabble for the choice perches. Later, after much cackling and preening, they settle down for the night.

North of downtown, the **Salagua** (Km 11.5) and **Santiago** (Km 14) village plazas offer similar, even more *típica*, sidewalk diversions.

Movies

Television, recession, and the October 1995 earthquake have demolished all but one of Manzanillo's movie houses. Remaining is the **Cine Club Fiesta,** Km 9.5, across from Vog disco, which screens first-run Mexican and U.S. films beginning around 4 P.M. Admission is $3.

Fiestas

Manzanillo's longest yearly party is the **Fiesta de Mayo,** celebrated for two weeks, beginning late April and ending around May 10. A continuous schedule of events, including sports tournaments, art exhibitions, parades, concerts, folkloric dancing in the *jardín,* and a carnival by the downtown market, brightens Manzanillo days and nights.

The **Fiesta de Guadalupe** honors Manzanillo's—and all Mexico's—patron saint, the Virgin of Guadalupe. Shrines to the Virgin, with flower and food offerings beneath her traditional portrait, begin appearing everywhere, especially downtown, by the end of November. For 12 evenings beginning December 1, floats parade and native-costumed dancers twirl around the *jardín*. Afternoons, people (women and girls, especially) proudly display their ancestry by dressing up in Indian *huipiles, enredos,* and *fajas* and heading to the cathedral. Nearing their destination, they pass through lanes crowded with stalls offering Indian food, curios, toys, souvenirs of the Virgin, and snapshots of people beside the Virgin's portrait.

Sporting Events

Manzanillo hosts an occasional winter-season *corrida de toros* (bullfight) at either the Salagua or the El Coloma bullring (on Highway 200, four miles south of town). Watch for posters. For dates, call a travel agent, such as Bahias Gemeleas, tel. 314/333-1000, or Manzanillo city tourism, at the booth in front of the city hall on the *jardín,* open daily 9 A.M.–7 P.M.

The renowned Manzanillo **International Sailfish Tournament** kicks off annually during the last half of November (see under Sportfishing).

Tourist Shows

The **Club Maeva** seasonally hosts a lively Saturday **Mexican Fiesta,** including swirling dancers, mariachis, rope dance, and rooster fights. Other nights, it stages theme parties where guests become part of the entertainment, such as International Gala Night, a journey to the world's great cities; or Brazilian Night, a glittering Río de Janeiro Carnaval; or amateur Night of the Stars, your chance to shine on the stage. Club Maeva parties, customarily open to the public, begin with a big buffet at 8 P.M. and cost about $35 per person, half price for kids under 12. For reservations, phone the hotel at tel. 314/331-0800, or a travel agency, such as Agencia Bahías Gemelas, tel. 314/333-1000.

Dancing and Live Music

The big hotels, such as Las Hadas, tel. 314/334-0000, and Hotel Sierra, tel. 314/333-2000, offer seasonal no-cover live dance music in their lobby bars and restaurants. Call for times and programs.

Mexican rancho atmosphere at its welcoming best fills low-key *botanas* restaurant-bar **Cantina del Vaquero,** at beach Highway 200 Km 10, a block east of Comercial Mexicana in Salagua. Relax with friends over drinks and/or ranch-style supper plates to the soothing live melodies of strolling guitarists. Open daily 2–11 P.M.

Discos

Discomania reigns regularly at a number of clubs along beach boulevard Highway 200. Call to verify hours, which vary with season. Bring earplugs, just in case. Some of the longer-lasting spots, from south to north:

The very popular **Bar Felix,** Km 9 on Playa Azul, tel. 314/333-1875 or 314/334-1444, has relatively low-volume recorded music, soft couches, and no cover, with a two-drink minimum at $3 apiece. Music is much less subdued, however, at its companion club, **Disco Vog,** next door, tel. 314/334-1660, 314/334-1875, or 314/334-1444. There, lights begin gyrating and the woofers begin thumping around 10:30 P.M.; cover is $10.

Kitzias Disco, beach side, Km 10.5, tel. 314/333-1414, customarily offers recorded music, often alternating between louder tropical rock and softer Latin-romantic. Call to confirm schedule.

At disco **Tropigala** ("fun guaranteed") in Santiago, Km 15, patrons gather in its soaring black-walled interior to sway to live salsa "tropical" rock; call tel. 314/333-2474 or 314/333-2475 to confirm hours. Cover is about $5. While the night is still young, continue to bar-discoteque **Enjoy** next door.

The round, spacey interior of **Disco Solaris,** at Km 15.5, Hotel Villas Playa de Oro, tel. 314/333-2540, feels like a trip in a big flying saucer. Lights begin flashing, colored fogs descend, and music begins booming around 11 P.M.; there's about a $6 cover charge.

SPORTS AND RECREATION

Walking and Jogging

All of the beaches of Manzanillo and Santiago bays are fine for walking. The sand, however, is generally too soft for jogging, except along the wide, firm, north-end Playa de Miramar. On the south side, the last mile of the no-outlet Las Brisas Highway Asphalt serves as a relatively tranquil and popular jogging course.

Swimming, Surfing, and Bodysurfing

With the usual **safety** precautions, Manzanillo's beaches are generally safe for swimming, except on occasional days of high waves, when all but the most foolhardy avoid the surf. The safest swimming beaches are Playa San Pedrito and Playa de Miramar at the protected south and north ends, respectively.

The best surfing breaks occur along Playa Olas Altas (High Waves Beach), where, most any day, a sprinkling of surfers ride the swells 100 yards offshore.

Bodysurfing and boogie boarding are much more common, especially on Playas Audiencia, Olas Altas, and Miramar, where concessionaires often rent boogie boards.

Sailing, Sailboarding, and Kayaking

Manzanillo's waters are generally tranquil enough for kayaking, but also windy enough for good sailing and sailboarding. A few concessionaires rent equipment at fairly hefty prices. At **Playa Audiencia,** the beach concessionaire, Deportes Aquáticos del Pacífico, tel. 314/331-0101 (Las Hadas Resort number), ext. 3804, rents kayaks ($16/hour) to any able body. The same concessionaire, at **Las Hadas Resort** beachside, rents sailboard outfits and kayaks to Las Hadas guests and those of other hotels who buy a Las Hadas beach day pass ($25).

Snorkeling and Scuba Diving

Manzanillo waters are generally clear. Visibility runs from about 30 feet onshore to 60–80 feet farther out. Manzanillo has three standout shore-accessible spots: the jetty rocks (depth 5–25 feet) at the south end of Playa las Brisas; rocks in mid-bay and shoals on both sides of Playa Audiencia; and the wrecked (1959 hurricane) frigate 200 yards off north-end Playa la Boquita. All of these swarm with schools of sponge- and coral-grazing fish.

The veteran YMCA-method certified dive director Susan Dearing and her NAUI-certified partner, Carlos Cuellar, operate **Underworld Scuba** from their shop on Av. Audiencia (Hotel Sierra Manzanillo-Las Hadas entrance road) two blocks from the Las Hadas crossing. With thousands of accident-free dives between them, Susan and Carlos rank among Pacific Mexico's best-qualified scuba instructors. They offer all levels and types of certification, including PADI, YMCA, CMAS, NAUI, and SSI.

Susan and Carlos start you out with a free qualifying lesson at the pool. After enough free practice, they'll guide you in onshore dives (for about $60 for a two-hour outing, including one half-hour fully equipped dive). They guide experienced divers (bring your certificate) much farther afield, including super sites such as Roca Elefante at the Juluapan Peninsula's foamy tip.

Contact them at their office on Av. Audiencia (the street that heads west from *crucero* Las Hadas, in Salagua at Km 12.5) on the right, two blocks from the *crucero,* tel./fax 314/333-0642. Additionally, you can reach them by Carlos's cellular tel. 314/358-0327, or Susan's, cellular tel.

314/358-5042 (if cell phones don't respond, dial 044, or 01-044, then the number). For their current email address, visit their website www.dive manzanillo.com, or alternate website www.go manzanillo.com/scubamex/index.htm; or if all else fails, write P.O. Box 295, Santiago, Colima 28860.

Power Sports

At Playa Audiencia, *motos* (small motorboats) and water-ski towing are available at about $40 per half hour from the beach concessionaire, **Deportes Aquaticos del Pacífico,** tel. 314/331-0101, ext. 3804. Wave-runners are available at $45 per half hour.

The same concessionaire, at Las Hadas beach, offers similar equipment and services to guests of Hotels Las Hadas, Club Maeva, Sierra Manzanillo, Villa del Palmar, Dolphin Cove Inn, and others.

Tennis and Golf

Manzanillo has no free public tennis courts. **Hotel Sierra Manzanillo,** tel. 314/333-2000, rents its six superb courts to nonguests for $8 hourly during the day and $10 at night. The hotel's teaching pro offers lessons for about $25 per hour. Most other large hotels, notably Club Maeva and Las Hadas, have many courts but do not rent them to the public.

You might also be able to take advantage of the three excellent tennis courts of the **Club Santiago,** tel. 314/335-0370, open about 7 A.M.–6 P.M., about $6/hour. Get there by turning off Highway 200 at the side road, signed Canchas de Tenis, just north of the golf course. The Club Santiago nine-hole golf course (office just inside the Club Santiago gate at Highway 200, Km 19) is available for public use daily 8 A.M.–5 P.M. The 18-hole greens fee runs about $45 ($38 for nine holes), clubs rent for about $22 a set, and a golf cart is about $24 ($20 for nine holes). Caddies work 18 holes for about $10 ($7 for nine holes).

The renowned 18-hole **Las Hadas** course, off Av. Audiencia, at the Km 12.5, Highway 200, *crucero Las Hadas* is open to the public. The greens fee runs about $100 for 18 holes and about $60 for nine holes. Carts cost about $50, clubs $25, and a caddy about $15. Call Las

Hadas, tel. 314/331-0101, for details and reservations.

Ecoadventuring

A number of providers guide groups on outdoor explorations of Manzanillo's wildlife-rich mountain, tropical forest, and coastal hinterlands.

Check with guides **Fernando Hernández** (tel. 314/333-2067) and **Walter Oldenburg** (tel. 314/313-0834), for wildlife-sensitive open ocean and mangrove lagoon kayaking trips.

Robert Sandoval, cellular tel. 044-314/358-3431, of the Guides Association of Manzanillo,tel. 314/332-1185, leads discovery trips into the La Floreña stalagmite and stalactite-rich cave and the neighboring pristine tropical forest.

Horseback adventures are the specialty of **Eugenio Caligari,** tel. 314/334-2744, cellular tel. 044-314/357-1801, who leads groups for wildlife-viewing along tropical forest trails out from nearby Rancho de Don Tomás.

The Association of Guides of Manzanillo, tel. 314/332-1185, collectively specializes in a Mountain Tour Adventure, leading hikers through mountain tropical forest where they visit a coffee plantation, catch their own fresh-water prawns and shrimps, and swim in a waterfall-fed natural pool.

Sportfishing

Manzanillo's biggest sportfishing operation is the **Flota Amarilla** (Yellow Fleet), whose many captains operate cooperatively through their association, Sociedad Cooperativa de Prestación de Servicios Turísticos Manzanillo. You can see their bright yellow craft anchored off their dockside office on Av. Niños Héroes, a long block east (away from downtown) of the El Tajo Pemex gas station. Their five-person boats run about $300 for a day's billfish (marlin, sailfish) hunting, completely equipped with three fishing lines. Larger, plusher 12-person, six-line boats go for about $400, complete with ice and no-host bar. All of their boats are insured and equipped with CB radios and toilets. For information and reservations, call tel. 314/332-1031, or write Flota Amarilla-Soc. Coop. de P. de Servicios Turísticos Manzanillo, Niños Héroes frente al 638,

Manzanillo, Colima 28200, or drop into the dockside office.

A local Texas-bred couple, Sam and Marilyn Short, offer a duo of highly recommended sportfishing boats. The smaller is the 28-foot **Rosa Elena;** the larger is the 38-foot **S.F. Marlin.** The captains, Hector and Hugo, veteran trophy winners in past fishing tournaments, try hard to get their clients big catches. The *Rosa Elena,* which can handle up to five passengers and three lines, runs about $220 per day, complete. The *S.F. Marlin* can handle 10 passengers, six lines, and costs about $275. For reservations, call Sam and Marilyn at tel. 314/334-0784 or 314/335-0605, or email them at fish@bay.net.mx. For more information, see their websites www.mexonline.com/opafish.htm or www.gomanzanillo.com/fish/index/fishing.htm.

Other alternatives are available through travel agents, such as the Agencia Bahías Gemelas, tel. 314/333-1000.

Manzanillo hosts two annual **billfish tournaments** in early February and late November. Competing for automobiles as top prizes, hundreds of contestants ordinarily bring in around 300 big fish in three days. The complete entry fee runs several hundred dollars, which includes the farewell awards dinner. For more information, contact Guillermo Gómez, prominent Club de Yates (Yacht Club) officer, at the Nissan dealership, tel. 314/336-5252, or visit the tournament website, www.pescamanzanillo.com.mx, or write the sponsors, the Deportivo de Pesca Manzanillo, P.O. Box 89, Manzanillo, Colima 28200.

It's to be hoped that sponsors of such tournaments will soon be able to devise competitions that will preserve, rather than wipe out, the species upon which their sport depends. Some progressive captains have seen the light and encourage their clients to release the caught fish.

Yacht Berthing and Boat Launching

Las Hadas Hotel's excellent marina has about 100 berths (up to 80 feet) rentable for about $.65 per foot per day, including potable water and 110/220-volt electrical hookup. Reservations recommended, especially during the winter; write Manager, Las Hadas Marina, P.O. Box 158,

Manzanillo, Colima 28200, or call tel, 314/331-0101 (ask for the marina, ext. 3706), send your reservation request via fax 314/331-0129, or email eduardo.llamas@brisas.com.mx.

Las Hadas marina also has a boat ramp, available for a fee. Make arrangements with the marina before you arrive, however, or you might have to do some fast talking to get past the guard at the gate. At Highway 200, Km 12, follow Av. Audiencia past the hilltop, turn left at the Las Hadas sign. At the gate, the guard will direct you.

On north-side Santiago Bay, you can also use the steep ramp (smaller boats only) at the **Hotel de Playa Santiago,** tel./fax 314/333-0055 or 314/333-0344, hoplsan@prodigy.net.mx, for a $4 fee. Get there from Highway 200, Km 13.5, just south of the Los Colorados creek bridge, just north of the gas station, follow the side road running next to the ETN bus terminal, along the peninsula's north shore to the hotel at road's end.

SHOPPING
Markets and Downtown
Manzanillo's colorful, untouristed **Mercado Municipal** district clusters around the main market at Cuauhtémoc and Independencia (five short blocks along Av. México from the *jardín,* turn left and go four blocks). Southbound Mercado-marked buses will take you right there.

Wander through the hubbub of fish stalls, piled with dozens of varieties, such as big, fresh-caught *sierra* (mackerel) or slippery *pulpo* (octopus). Among the mounds of ruby tomatoes, green melons, and golden papayas, watch for the exotic, such as nopales (cactus leaves) or spiny green *guanábanas,* the mango-shaped relative of the Asian jackfruit. On your way out, don't miss the spice stalls, with their bundles of freshly gathered aromatic cinnamon bark and mounds of fragrant dried *jamaica* flower petals (for flavoring *aguas* drinks). Be sure to arrive a few hours before 3 P.M., when the inside section shuts down.

Salagua and Santiago Shopping
Salagua has a pair of worthwhile handicrafts stores, diagonally west, across the Highway 200

beach boulevard, from shopping Plaza Manzanillo (and Comercial Mexicana.) First, take a look inside **Arte de Mi Gente,** a little corner of Tonalá in Manzanillo. Enjoy perusing the attractive selection, including rustic furniture, in leather *equipal* or handcrafted wood styles, and a small village of charming *nacimientos* Christmas Nativity figurines.

Continue next door to **Tienda de Artesanías Tepeyac,** for beach clothes, a collection of handsome ironwood sculptures from the Sonoran desert, a load of painted pottery, and plenty of sombreros. Both stores are open daily, approximately 10 A.M.–8 P.M.

Saturday morning, join the folks who gather for the **Santiago Market,** beneath *tianguis* (awnings) that spread along Av. V. Carranza, two blocks north of the town plaza. Although merchandise tends toward dime-store-grade clothes and hardware, it's worth a stroll if only for the color and the occasional exotica (wild herbs and fruits, antiques, bright parrots) that may turn up.

For a host of genuine folkcrafts, head to nearby **Centro Artesanal Las Primaveras,** at Juárez 40, tel. 314/333-1699, two blocks from the highway, a couple of blocks north of the Santiago town *jardín.* There, scattered amid a rambling dusty clutter, a warehouse of many attractive handicrafts—blown glass, crepe flowers, pre-Columbian-motif pottery, leatherwork, papier-mâché clowns and parrots—languish, waiting for someone to rescue them. Open Mon.–Sat. 8 A.M.–8 P.M., Sun. 8 A.M.–2 P.M.

Back on the highway, just a few doors north of the Santiago *jardín,* take a look inside **El Palacio de Las Conchas y Caracoles** shell emporium, tel. 314/333-0260. Bring your shell book. Hosts of glistening, museum-quality specimens—iridescent silver nautiluses, luscious rose conches, red and purple corals—line a multitude of shelves. Buy them (from $1,000 on down) singly or choose from an array of jewelry—necklaces, earrings, brooches, and rings. Open Mon.–Sat. 9 A.M.–2 P.M. and 4–9 P.M., Sun. 9 A.M.–2 P.M.

As you near Club Maeva on the highway, stop about 100 yards south of the Club Maeva pedestrian overpass and look over the offerings of the **Mercado de Artesanías** (Flea Market) on the beach side of the highway. Here, a dozen families sell crafts, many made by family and friends in their native villages in the mountains of Guerrero, Michoacán, Oaxaca, and Chiapas. They're poor but proud people. You should bargain, but gently.

Supermarket, Photo, and Health-Food Stores

The big **Soriana** Kmart look-alike department store is Manzanillo's latest big shopping venue, unmissable, in Salagua, Km 9.5, inland side of Highway 200. Everything, from motor scooters and computers to screwdrivers, socks, and groceries seems to be on sale. Also in the same complex are banks (Banamex, BaNorte, and Bital) all with ATMs, and fast food lunch spots serving tacos, cookies, ice cream and much more.

At the Soriana complex's northwest corner, a **handicrafts** store sells much, from Tlaquepaque, Tonalá (stoneware, papier mâché, and brass), and Colima, including a fetching assortment of Colima's lovable ceramic dogs.

Also in Salagua, the Manzanillo branch of the big **Comercial Mexicana,** tel. 314/333-0005, marked by the orange pelican sign, anchors the American-style Plaza Manzanillo shopping center at Km 10.5. It offers everything—from appliances and cosmetics to produce, groceries, and a bakery—spread along shiny, efficient aisles. Open daily 9 A.M.–9 P.M.

At the entrance to the same Plaza Manzanillo complex, drop off your film for quick finishing at up-to-date **Foto Sol,** tel. 314/333-1860. Foto Sol also sells popular films and stocks some camera accessories. Open Mon.–Sat. 9 A.M.–9 P.M., Sun. 9 A.M.–8 P.M.

Downtown, **Photo Studio Cárdenas** offers film, and some cameras and accessories on the jardín, at Balvino Dávalo 52, tel. 314/332-1160; open daily 9:30 A.M.–2 P.M. and 4:30–9 P.M. Alternatively, go to the downtown branch of **Foto Sol,** two blocks south (away from the harbor) from the jardín, tel. 314/332-3395, open Mon.–Sat. 8 A.M.–8 P.M.

Manzanillo's health-food store, **Yacatecuhtli,**

downtown at Av. México 249, urges customers to "watch your health" with yogurt, granola, natural vitamins, ginseng, alfalfa tablets, soy burgers, and cheese. Open Mon.–Sat. 8 A.M.–11 P.M., Sun. 8 A.M.–3 P.M. and 5–10 P.M. Its small branch, tel. 314/333-5670, in Santiago, on the highway, about a block west of the Santiago town jardín, is open Mon.–Sat. 8 A.M.–2 P.M. and 5–8 P.M. and stocks a modest supply of health foods and products.

INFORMATION
Tourist Information Office

The city of Manzanillo maintains a tourist information modulo (booth) in front of the the city hall, on the south side of the jardín, open daily 9 A.M.–7 P.M.

Publications

Downtown, **Revistas Saifer,** Av. México 117, tel. 314/332-5435, across from the Hotel Colonial, and Av. México 207, open daily one block down the street from the jardín, sometimes stocks the Mexico City News and many American magazines, such as Time, Life, Newsweek, Computer, National Geographic, Popular Science and Bride; open daily 9 A.M.–10 P.M. The same is approximately true for its Plaza Manzanillo shopping center branch in Salagua, Km 11, open daily 8 A.M.–10 P.M.

The tabaquería shop at **Hotel Sierra,** tel. 314/333-2000, has the most extensive stock of U.S. newspapers, magazines, and English-language paperbacks in Manzanillo.

The Manzanillo **Biblioteca Municipal** (historical archive section) is open Tues.–Sun. 9 A.M.–3 P.M. on the third floor of the Presidencia Municipal on the jardín downtown. The regular city biblioteca (library) is also downtown, on waterfront street Morelos, two blocks north of the jardín, approximately across from pierfront Restaurant Lychee.

Additionally, the **Supermarket Vianda,** open Mon.–Sat. 8 A.M.–9 P.M., Sun. 8 A.M.–6 P.M., across Highway 200 from Club Santiago (at the northwest end of town), stocks some many American magazines and the News from Mexico City.

SERVICES

Money Exchange

Several banks, all with ATMs, serve downtown customers. **Banamex** (Banco Nacional de Mexico) exchanges both U.S. and Canadian traveler's checks and cash, Av. México 136, three blocks from the *jardín,* tel. 314/332-0115; open Mon.–Fri. 9 A.M.–4 P.M., Sat. 10–2 P.M. The **Bancomer** next door, Av. México 122, does the same; open Mon.–Fri. 9 A.M.–4 P.M. Sat. 10–2 P.M. If both are closed or too crowded, the **Banco Internacional,** tel. 314/332-0809, across the street a block toward the *jardín,* changes U.S. traveler's checks and cash and has even longer hours, Mon.–Sat. 8 A.M.–7 P.M.After hours and on Sunday, use the banks' ATMs or go to **Casa de Cambio El Puerto,** at Av. Mexico 118, across from Bancomer, tel. 314/332-4759, open Mon.–Sat. 9 A.M.–7 P.M., Sun. 9 A.M.–1 P.M.

Banks, all with ATMs, along the Highway 200 suburbs also change money. In Salagua, try the **Banco Serfin,** or **Banamex**, both in the Manzanillo Plaza shopping center west of Comercial Mexicana. Alternatively, go across the highway and a block west to **Bancomer,** tel. 314/334-0102. In Santiago, you can choose from **Banco Internacional,** tel. 314/333-0813 (open Mon.–Fri. 8 A.M.–7 P.M., Sat. 8 A.M.–3 P.M.), on the highway, or **Banco Santander Mexicano,** tel. 314/333-0738 (open Mon.–Fri. 9 A.M.–4 P.M.), on Juárez, two blocks inland from the highway. Both banks have ATMs.

Travel Agencies

The former Manzanillo American Express agency **Agencia de Viajes Bahías Gemelas,** Highway 200 Km 9, next to Chrysler Motor, tel. 314/333-1000, fax 314/333-0649, bahias@prodigy.net.mx., no longer offers any American Express financial services. However, it remains a full-service travel agency, booking air tickets, local tours, hotel reservations, and more. Open Mon.–Fri. 9 A.M.–2 P.M. and 4–6 P.M., Sat. 9 A.M.–2 P.M.

Alternative travel agency options are **Acuario,** at Av. Mexico 207, downtown, tel. 314/332-

4577, acuario@wspanmex.com.mx; or **Expo-Manzanillo** in Santiago, at Km 14.5, tel. 314/334-0788, expozlo@prodigy.net.mx.

Communications

The downtown combined *correo* and express mail **Mexpost** is on Calle Galindo, between Av.s Mexico and Carrillo, about four blocks inland from the jardín. The *correo,* tel. 314/332-0022, is open Mon.–Fri. 9 A.M.–5 P.M. and Sat. 9 A.M.–1 P.M.; Mexpost is open Mon.–Fri. 9 A.M.–3 P.M.

Telecomunicaciones, the high-tech telegraph office in the Presidencia Municipal on the *jardín,* bottom floor, sends telegrams, telexes, fax messages, and money orders. Open Mon.–Fri. 8 A.M.–6 P.M., Sat.–Sun. 9 A.M.-12:30 P.M. *Giros* (money order) hours are shorter: Mon.–Fri. 9 A.M.–1 P.M. and 3–5 P.M. only.

In Santiago, the post office, tel. 314/334-1130, and *telecomunicaciones* offices stand side by side on Venustiano Carranza nos. 2 and 4, across Highway 200 from Juanito's restaurant. Post office hours are Mon.–Fri. 9 A.M.–3 P.M., while *telecomunicaciones* hours are Mon.–Fri. 9 A.M.–3 P.M., Sat. 9 A.M.–1 P.M.

Manzanillo's *larga distancia* telephone offices are conveniently spread from the downtown north along Highway 200. Everyone's favorite downtown is homey **Restaurant del Río,** 330 Av. Mexico, tel. 314/337-2525 or 314/332-2515, about three blocks inland from the *jardín,* where you can enjoy a country-style enchilada, *torta,* or *hamburguesa* while you await your call. Open daily 8 A.M.–9 P.M.

However, if you're in the mood for efficiency, go to computer-assisted **Computel,** with a number of convenient locations: downtown, at Av. México 302, tel. 314/332-3926; on the *malecón* at Morelos 196, one block east of the *jardín,* tel. 314/332-0205, open daily 8 A.M.–9 P.M.; at *crucero* Las Brisas, tel. 314/334-0680, open daily 8 A.M.–9:30 P.M. In Santiago, make your long-distance call or fax at **Juanito's Restaurant,** tel. 314/333-1388, tel./fax 314/333-2010, open daily 7 A.M.–10 P.M.

Internet access stores are popping up all over town. For example, at **Juanito's** restaurant, at Km 15 in Santiago, tel. 314/333-1388, $4 per hour; and **Cyber Café Enredos,** in the Manzanillo Plaza Shopping Center (marked by the big Comercial Mexicana sign), in Salagua, open daily 11 A.M.–10 P.M., about $3.50 per hour.

Hospital, Police, and Emergencies

In a medical emergency, call a taxi to take you to either **Centro Médico Quirúrgico Echauri** at Km 9.7, Blvd. Miguel de la Madrid, tel. 314/334-0001, or **Médica Pacífico Cruz Azul** (and Super-Farmacia, tel. 314/333-3047), at Av. Palma Real 10, Km 13, a block just south of the gas station, tel. 314/334-0385. Manzanillo's newest and best-equipped private hospitals, they each have round-the-clock service, including a laboratory and several specialists on call you can also visit for routine consultations.

For both medical consultations and a good pharmacy in Santiago, contact French- and English-speaking **Dr. Joseph Cadet Jr.** at his office next to Juanito's at Highway 200, Km 14.5, open Mon.–Sat. 11 A.M.–2 P.M. and 5–9 P.M., or his adjacent **Farmacia Continental,** tel. 314/333-0286, open Mon.–Sat. 9 A.M.–2 P.M. and 4–9 P.M. Call the pharmacy number if you wish to see the doctor.

For police emergencies, call the **Policía Municipal,** tel. 314/332-1004, in the city hall on the *jardín.*

Although Manzanillo no longer has any foreign consulates, it does have **HELP!,** of the Manzanillo Foreign Community Association, run by friendly director Bonnie Sumlin, who gives advice and assistance to travelers. Contact her at P.O. Box 65, Santiago, Colima 28860, tel./fax 314/334-0977, help!@bay.net.mx.

Immigration and Customs

Both Migración and the Aduana occupy the upper floors of the **Edificio Federal Portuario** (Federal Port Building) on San Pedrito Beach, at the foot of Av. Teniente Azueta.

The cooperative, efficient **Migración** staff, third floor, tel. 314/332-1730, fax 314/332-0030, can replace a lost tourist card. (Make a copy of it beforehand, just in case. Lacking this, go to them with your passport and some proof, such as an airline ticket, of your arrival date in Mexico.) Open Mon.–Fri. 9 A.M.–2 P.M. for business and around the clock for questions.

Contact the **Aduana,** 2nd floor, tel. 314/332-0087 or 314/332-1182, for import-export rules. If your Spanish is rusty, ask your hotel desk clerk or the tourist information office to call for you. Open Mon.–Fri. 8 A.M.–3 P.M.

Both the Aduana and Migración also have offices at the Manzanillo airport, open daily 8 A.M.–8 P.M.

GETTING THERE AND AWAY
By Air

The **Manzanillo airport,** officially the Playa de Oro International Airport (code ZLO), is 28 easy highway miles (44 km) from downtown Manzanillo, and only about 22 miles (35 km) from most Manzanillo beachside hotels. From the other direction, the airport is 19 miles (30 km) south of Barra de Navidad.

Aerocalifornia Airlines flights connect with Los Angeles and Mexico City. For local reservations and flight information, call tel. 314/334-1414.

America West Airlines flights connect with Phoenix during the winter-spring season. For local reservations and flight information, call tel. 314/334-1140, or toll-free U.S. tel. 800/235-9292 (reachable also from Mexico).

Aeroméxico Airlines' subsidiary carrier **Aerolitoral** flights connect Manzanillo airport with Zihuatanejo and Guadalajara (where many U.S. connections are available). For reservations, call Aeroméxico's national reservation number, toll-free Mex. tel. 800/621-4000. For flight information, contact Aeroméxico's Manzanillo office, tel. 314/334-1226.

Mexicana Airlines flights connect daily with Mexico City, where many U.S. connections are available. For reservations and flight information, contact its airport office, tel. 314/333-2323, the Manzanillo reservations numbers, tel. 314/334-0800 or 314/355-8159, or the national numbers, toll-free Mex. tel. 800/502-2000 or 800/501-9900.

Canada 3000 charter flights connect with Toronto, Calgary-Edmonton, and Vancouver during the winter-spring season. Contact a travel agent for information and reservations.

Manzanillo Airport Arrival and Departure

The terminal, although small for an international destination, does have an ATM for cash, a few gift shops for last-minute purchases, snack stands, an upstairs restaurant, some car rentals, and a *buzón* (mailbox) just outside the front entrance. However, it has no hotel booking service, so you should arrive with a hotel reservation or you'll be at the mercy of taxi drivers who would love to collect a fat commission on your first-night hotel tariff. Upon departure, be sure to save enough cash to pay the approximate $12 **departure tax** (if your ticket doesn't already include it.)

After the usually rapid immigration and customs checks, independent arrivees have their choice of a car rental (see below), or *colectivo,* and taxi tickets from a booth just outside the arrival gate.

Colectivo tickets run about $7–9 per person to any Manzanillo hotel, while a *taxi especial* runs about $22–29, depending on destination.

Colectivos take passengers to Barra de Navidad and other northern points seasonally only. Taxis, however, will take three passengers to Barra, Melaque, or Hotel Real Coastecomate for about $30 total; to El Tamarindo, $35; Hotel Sun, $48; El Careyes, $67; Chamela-El Super, $67; or Las Alamandas, $105.

No public buses service the Manzanillo airport. Strong, mobile travelers on tight budgets could save pesos by hitching or hiking the three miles to Highway 200 and flagging down one of the frequent north or southbound second-class buses (fare about $2 to Barra or Manzanillo). Don't try it at night, however.

As for airport **car rentals,** you have a choice of National, tel. 314/333-0611, fax 314/333-1140, interent@bay.net; Hertz, tel. 314/333-3191, 314/333-3141, or 314/333-3142; and Budget, tel./fax 314/333-1445. Unless you don't mind paying upward of $50 per day, shop around for your car rental by calling the car rentals' U.S. and Canada toll-free numbers at home *before*

you leave (see the chart "Car Rental Agencies" in the On The Road chapter).

By Car or RV

Three main highway routes connect Manzanillo with the outside world: from the north via Puerto Vallarta and Barra de Navidad; from the northeast via Guadalajara and Colima; and from the southeast via Ixtapa-Zihuatanejo and Playa Azul (Lázaro Cárdenas).

From the north, Mexico National Highway 200 glides 172 smooth asphalt miles (276 km) from Puerto Vallarta via Barra de Navidad. Neither steep grades nor crowds of traffic slow progress along this foothill-, forest-, and beach-studded route. Allow about four hours to or from Puerto Vallarta, about one hour to or from Barra.

The safety and ease of the Guadalajara-Colima *autopista* (combined National Highways 54 D, 110, and 200) more than compensates for the (approximately $20 per car) tolls. Head southwest from the Glorieta Minerva circle in Guadalajara along Av. López Mateos south (Highway 15, 54, and 80) for around 27 miles (45 km) until Acatlán de Juárez, and follow the *cuota* toll) Highway 54 D freeway south for Colima. Two or three highway hours later, after bypassing, Colima, the expressway 54 D continues as expressway Highway 110, continuing south to just before Tecomán, where Highway 110 becomes Highway 200 as it splits off right, northwest, to Manzanillo. Figure about 4.5 driving hours for this easy, 190-mile (311-km) trip, either way.

The same cannot be said for the winding 238 miles (390 km) of coastline Highway 200 between Zihuatanejo and Manzanillo. Keep your gas tank filled; the spectacularly scenic but sparsely populated 100-mile stretch from the Colima border to Caleta de Campos has no gas stations. Allow a full eight-hour day, in broad daylight, either way. Don't try it at night.

Drivers just passing through who want to avoid the long, sometimes congested Manzanillo Bay beachfront strip should follow the *cuota* (toll) bypass. Watch for signs around Km 20, at the village of Naranjo. Follow the Cihuatlán sign after you cross the Laguna Cuyutlán bridge on the Highway 200 *cuota* freeway.

By Bus

Several bus lines serve Manzanillo from the *Central de Autobús* (central bus station) at Hidalgo and Aldama (taxi or walk south from the El Tajo Pemex gas station corner, following the rail tracks three blocks; bear left and continue about a quarter mile to the station on the right). Unfortunately, the October 1995 earthquake destroyed the terminal building. The bus lines are operating out of makeshift ticket booths where the old terminal once stood. There is talk of a new terminal, but no one knows when it will be finished. As of this writing the agents and drivers are making do as best they can.

All departures listed below are local *(salidas locales)* unless noted as *salidas de paso*. Choose first class whenever you can; its service, speed, and *asientos reservados* (reserved seats) far outweigh the small additional ticket cost. The bus lines divide roughly into northwest-southeast (coastal) and northeast (Mexico City-Michoacán) categories.

Northwest-Southeast Bus Lines: Elite (EL), tel. 314/332-4243, provides first-class *salidas de paso* service north with Puerto Vallarta, Mazatlán, and Tijuana, and south with Playa Azul junction, Lázaro Cárdenas, Zihuatanejo, and Acapulco. Other first-class Futura departures also connect northeast with Colima and Mexico City.

Autocamiones del Pacífico (AP), tel. 314/332-0515, and associated line Transportes Cihuatlán provide Manzanillo's most frequent service northwest and north. A few first-class departures connect along the coast, with Puerto Vallarta; several first-class departures connect with Guadalajara via Highway 80 (through Melaque and Autlán) daily. Many other second-class buses follow the same routes, stopping everywhere.

Autotransportes Sur de Jalisco second-class buses, tel. 314/332-1003, connect round the clock with Guadalajara via Colima. A few buses per day also connect south with the Playa Azul junction and Lázaro Cárdenas.

The interurban second-class **Sociedad Cooperativo de Autotransportes** buses connect half-hourly with south Colima destinations of Armería, Cuyutlán, Tecomán, and Colima.

Northeast Buses: More than a dozen **Autovías del Occidente** (AO) second-class buses, tel. 314/332-0123, connect round the clock with Mexico City through Michoacán via Morelia. At Morelia, you can continue to Pátzcuaro. Many second-class buses connect daily with subsidiary Michoacán destinations of Apatzingan, Zamora, and Uruapan.

Also in the same booth as AO, **Autobúses de Jalisco** connect with Colima, Guadalajara, and Mexico City and Michoacán destinations of Morelia, Uruapan, Nueva Italia, and Apatzingan.

Flecha Amarilla, tel. 314/332-0210, and its subsidiary lines combine under the "Servicios Coordinados" blanket to offer a host of departures. Many luxury-class "Primera-plus" buses connect direct with Guadalajara and Mexico City. Other "Primera-plus" connections continue past Guadalajara as far as Aguascalientes and Querétaro. A few departures connect with Mexico City (Norte) through Colima and Morelia. Several second-class departures connect north with Minatitlán, Colima, Zamora, Salamanca, Irapuato, and Morelia. Other departures connect northwest with Barra de Navidad-Melaque and Puerto Vallarta and all intermediate Highway 200 points.

Independent, airline-style luxury **Enlaces Transportes Nacionales** (ETN), tel. 314/334-1060, operates out of its terminal in Santiago, across from the Pemex station. ETN provides frequent connections northwest with Puerto Vallarta, and east through Colima, Michoacán, all the way to Mexico City.

By Train

President Porfirio Díaz's once-plush 19th-century passenger service that carried Guadalajara's elite to frolic on Manzanillo's beaches withered over the years and was finally discontinued in 1998.

Colima and Vicinity

From atop their thrones of fire and ice high above the Valley of Colima, legends say that the gods look down upon their ancient domain. The name "Colima" itself echoes the tradition: from the Náhuatl "Colliman" (*colli:* ancestors or gods, and *maitl:* domain of).

Approaching from Manzanillo, visitors seldom forget their first view of the sacred mountains of Colima: the dignified, snowcapped 14,220-foot (4,334-meter) Nevado de Colima, above his fiery, tempestuous younger brother, the 13,087-foot (3,989-meter) Volcán de Fuego (Volcano of Fire). The heat from that heavenly furnace rarely reaches down the green slopes to the spring-fed valley, where the colonial city invites coastal visitors to its more temperate (1,600-foot) heights for a refreshing change of pace.

HISTORY

Before Columbus

Although Colima (pop. 180,000) is the smallish capital of a diminutive agricultural state, it is much more than a farm town. Visitors can enjoy the residents' obvious appreciation of their arts and their history—twin traditions whose roots may extend as far south as Ecuador and Peru and as far west as the Gulf coast's mystery-shrouded monument builders, the Olmecs.

Colima's museums display a feast of ceramic treasures left behind by the many peoples—Nahua, Tarascan, Chichimec, Otomi—who have successively occupied the valley of Colima for upwards of 3,000 years. Much more than mere utilitarian objects, the Colima pottery bursts with whimsy and genius. Acrobats, musicians, and dancers frolic, old folks embrace, mothers nurse, and most of all, Colima's famous dogs scratch, roll, snooze, and play in timeless canine style, as if they could come alive at any moment.

Conquest and Colonization

By 1500, the ruler of Colima, in order to deter his aggressive Tarascan neighbors to the north, had united his diminutive kingdom with three neighboring coastal provinces. This union, now known as the Chimalhuacan Confederation, did not prevail against Spanish horses and steel,

© BRUCE WHIPPERMAN

The ruins at La Campana, dating from around A.D. 800, show strong Teotihuacán influence.

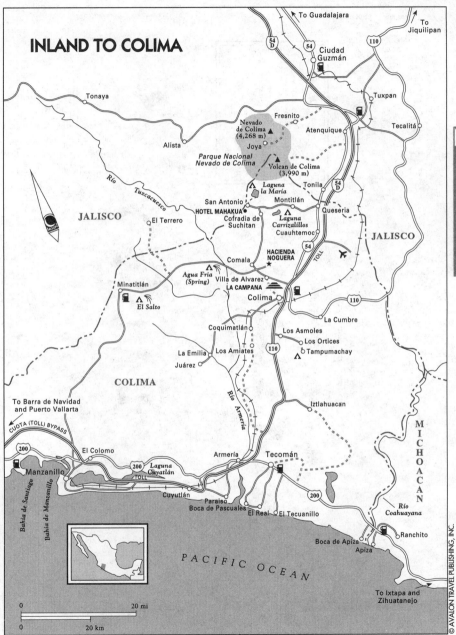

INLAND TO COLIMA

To Guadalajara

To Jiquilipan

Ciudad Guzmán

Tuxpan

Tecalitá

Tonaya

Nevado de Colima (4,268 m)

Fresnito

Atenquique

Alista

Joya

Parque Nacional Nevado de Colima

Volcan de Colima (3,990 m)

Tonila

Laguna la María

Montitlán

Queseria

San Antonio

HOTEL MAHAKUA

JALISCO

El Terrero

Cofradia de Suchitan

Laguna Carrizalillos

Cuauhtemoc

JALISCO

Comala

HACIENDA NOGUERA

Agua Fría (Spring)

Villa de Alvarez

LA CAMPANA

Minatitlán

Colima

La Cumbre

El Salto

Coquimatlán

Los Asmoles

Los Ortices

Tampumachay

La Emilia

Los Amiates

Juárez

COLIMA

Río Tuxcacuesco

Río Armería

Iztlahuacan

To Barra de Navidad and Puerto Vallarta

CUOTA (TOLL) BYPASS

MICHOACAN

El Colomo

Manzanillo

Laguna Cuyutlán

TOLL

Armería

Tecomán

Bahía de Santiago

Bahía de Manzanillo

Cuyutlán

Paraiso

Boca de Pascuales

El Real

El Tecuanillo

Río Coahuayana

Boca de Apiza

Apiza

Ranchito

PACIFIC OCEAN

To Ixtapa and Zihuatanejo

0   20 mi

0   20 km

MANZANILLO/COLIMA

© AVALON TRAVEL PUBLISHING, INC.

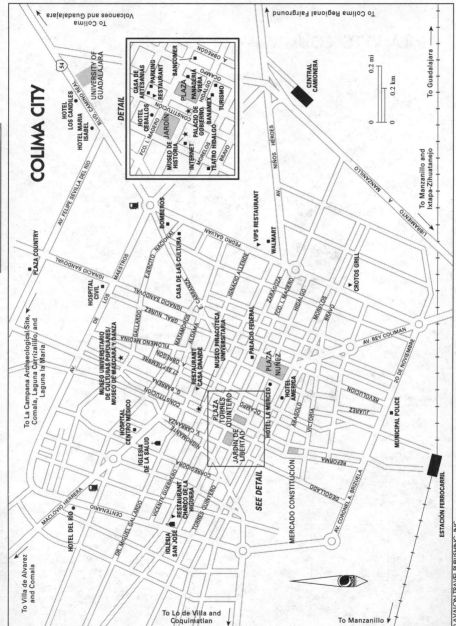

COLIMA CITY

To Colima Volcanoes and Guadalajara

To Colima Regional Fairground

To Guadalajara

To Manzanillo and Ixtapa-Zihuatanejo

CENTRAL CAMIONERA

0.2 mi
0.2 km

UNIVERSITY OF GUADALAJARA

HOTEL LOS CANDILES

HOTEL MARIA ISABEL

BLVD. CAMINO REAL

DETAIL

CASA DE ARTESANÍAS
PARKING
RESTAURANT
BANCOMER
PLAZA
PANADERÍA VERA
HIDALGO
OBREGÓN
OCAMPO

HOTEL CEBALLOS
MORELOS
CONSTITUCIÓN
BANAMEX
TURISMO

FCO. I. MADERO
PALACIO DE GOBIERNO

MUSEO DE HISTORIA
INTERNET
TEATRO HIDALGO
BRAVO

AV. FELIPE SEVILLA DEL RÍO

BOMBEROS

PLAZA COUNTRY

IGNACIO SANDOVAL

HOSPITAL CIVIL

LOS MAESTROS

EJERCITO NACIONAL

CASA DE LA CULTURA

E. CARRANZA

VIPS RESTAURANT
WALMART
PEDRO GALVAN

IGNACIO ALLENDE

ZARAGOZA

CROTOS GRILL

AV. NIÑOS HÉROES

To La Campana Archaeological Site, Comala, Laguna Carrizalillo, and Laguna la María

AV. DE

MUSEO UNIVERSITARIO DE CULTURAS POPULARES/ MUSEO DE MASCARA Y DANZA

FILOMENO MEDINA

GALLARDO

GRAL. NUÑEZ

MATAMOROS

ALDAMA

G. BARRERA

OBREGÓN

27 DE SEPTIEMBRE

RESTAURANT CASA GRANDE

MUSEO PINACOTECA UNIVERSITARIA

PALACIO FEDERAL

FCO. I. MADERO

HIDALGO

MORELOS

BRAVO

AV. REY COLIMAN

HOSPITAL CENTRO MÉDICO

CONSTITUCIÓN

V. CARRANZA

RESTAURANT

IGLESIA DE LA SALUD

NIGROMANTE

PLAZA NUÑEZ

HOTEL AMERICA

20 DE NOVIEMBRE

REVOLUCIÓN

JUAREZ

PLAZA TORRES QUINTERO

OCAMPO

HOTEL LA MERCED

ABASOLO

VICTORIA

MACLOVIO HERRERA

CORREGIDORA

JARDÍN DE LIBERTAD

SEE DETAIL

REFORMA

HOTEL DEL RÍO

CENTENARIO

VICENTE GUERRERO

TORRES QUINTERO

RESTAURANT CHARCO DE LA HIGUERA

MERCADO CONSTITUCIÓN

DR. MIGUEL GALLARDO

IGLESIA SAN JOSÉ

DEGOLLADO

AV. CORONELA A. BRIZUELA

MUNICIPAL POLICE

ESTACIÓN FERROCARRIL

To Villa de Alvarez and Comala

To Lo de Villa and Coquimatlan

To Manzanillo

© AVALON TRAVEL PUBLISHING, INC.

MANZANILLO/COLIMA

however. Many local folks take ironic pride that Colima is one of Mexico's earliest provinces. Their ancestors fell to the swords of conquistador Gonzalo de Sandoval and his 145 soldiers, who, in an anticlimax to their bloody campaign, founded the city on July 25, 1523.

Two years later, Cortés appointed his nephew, Francisco Cortés de Buenaventura, mayor and head of a settlement of about 100 Spanish colonists and 6,000 native tributaries.

Cortés himself, in search of Chinese treasure in the Pacific, repeatedly visited Colima on his way to and from the Pacific coast during the 1530s, most notably during January 1535, en route to his exploration of Baja California.

Scarcely a generation after the Great Circle route to the Orient was finally discovered in the 1560s, the Spanish king bypassed Colima by designating Acapulco as the prime Pacific port. This, along with a series of disasters—earthquakes, volcanic eruptions, hurricanes, and pirates—kept Colima in slumber until President Porfirio Díaz began building the railroad to the beaches and from the port of Manzanillo during the 1890s.

Modern Times

The destructive 1910–1917 Revolution and the hard economic times of the 1930s kept Colima quiet until the 1950s, when burgeoning mining and Pacific Rim shipping, fishing, and tourism brought thousands of new jobs. Manzanillo became a major port and manufacturing center, boosting Colima to a government and university headquarters and trading hub for the bounty (meat, hides, milk, fruit, vegetables, copra, sugar) of rich valley and coastal plantations, farms, and ranches.

SIGHTS

Getting Oriented

Colima's central district is a simple, one-mile square. The street grid runs north-south (north, toward the volcanoes; south, toward the coast) and east-west. Nearly all sights and services are reachable by a few minutes' walk or short taxi ride from the central plaza, the **Jardín de Libertad.**

A Walk Around Downtown

An ambience of refined prosperity—fashionable storefronts, shady portals, and lush, manicured greenery—blooms in the blocks that spread from Jardín de Libertad. The landmark **Catedral de San Felipe de Jesús** and **Palacio de Gobierno** statehouse stand side by side on Av. Constitución, bordering the *jardín.* For a colonial town, the buildings are not old, having replaced the original earthquake-weakened colonial-era structures generations ago. Most prominent is the cathedral, the latest (1894) incarnation of a succession of churches built on the same spot since 1527.

A number of local celebrations begin from the *jardín,* the hub of commercial and community activities. The mayor shouts the **Grito de Dolores** (independence cry, evening of September 15), and crowds celebrate the **Fiesta Charrotaurina** (February 7–23—see below).

Other landmarks dot the portals around the square. As you move counterclockwise from the cathedral, next comes the renovated **Hotel Ceballos,** corner of Constitución and Av. Francisco I. Madero. At the succeeding corner (Madero and north-south Av. V. Carranza) rises the **Presidencia Municipal.** And finally, on the south side, stands the state and city **Museo de Historia** on Av. 16 de Septiembre, corner of Constitución. Step into the museum, tel. 312/312-9228, for excellent examples of Colima's famous pre-Columbian pottery and go next door to a good bookstore offering a number of excellent local art, history, and picture guidebooks. Open Tues.–Sat. 9 A.M.–6 P.M.

Next stroll across the *jardín* corner to the **Palacio de Gobierno** and head through its big, open front door and enjoy the calm, classic elegance of the inner patio. Take a minute or two to admire the stairwell mural, completed in 1953, by muralist Jorge Chaves Carrillo, to commemorate the 200th anniversary of *insurgente* Miguel Hidalgo's birth. Continue out the other side and into Colima's second square, named after Torres Quintero (1866–1934), a beloved Colima teacher whose statue decorates the tree-shaded park.

Back on the Jardín de Libertad, at the cathedral-front, head north across Madero and explore the little blocklong **Andando Constitución** pedestrian mall, one of Colima's charming little corners. Here you will find several interesting shops, a restaurant, and, at the far end, a little doughnut and coffee shop and a good crafts store with a bountiful selection of reasonably priced folk crafts. These include fine ceramic reproductions of Colima's dogs.

Continue one block farther on Constitución to the corner of Guerrero and the University of Colima's **Pinocoteca Universitaria** art museum, tel. 312/312-2228. Besides a permanent collection of historical works by local and nationally noted artists, including Sofía Bassi, José Clemente Orozco, and Dr. Atl, the museum schedules showings of contemporary paintings and photography; open Tues.–Sat. 10 A.M.–2 P.M. and 5–8 P.M., Sun. 10 A.M.–1 P.M.

Two Good Museums

For a look at more excellent regional crafts, continue along Constitución three more blocks north to Gallardo then east a block to G. Barrera to the **Museo de Culturas Populares,** tel. 312/312-6869. Besides a folk-art sales shop (pottery, gourds, baskets, a loom, glassware) and several intriguing displays of masks (don't miss the scary horned crocodile-man) and ceremonial costumes, you can often watch potters and other artisans at work in the little house to the right of the museum entrance on Gallardo. The museum, the full name of which is Museo Universitario de Culturas Populares María Teresa Pomar, is at Av.s Aldama and 27 de Septiembre; open Tues.–Sat. 10 A.M.–2 P.M. and 5–8 P.M.

The prime repository of Colima's archaeological treasures is the landmark **Museo de Culturas del Occidente** (Museum of Cultures of the West), tel. 312/312-8431 or 312/312-3155. Walk or taxi along the diagonal street E. Carranza to side street Ejercito Nacional, about a mile from the town center. Inside the modern building, a spiral walkway leads you past artifact-illustrated displays of the history of Colima and surrounding regions. The exposition climaxes on the top floor with choirs of delightful classical Colima figurines: musicians tapping drums and fingering flutes, dancers circling, wrestlers grappling, and hosts of animals, in-

cluding the all-time favorites, Colima dogs. Open Tues.–Sat. 9 A.M.–6:30 P.M.

EXCURSIONS

The valley and mountainsides surrounding the city offer a variety of scenic diversions, from relaxing in colonial villages and camping on sylvan mountainsides to exploring tombs, examining petroglyphs, and descending into limestone caverns.

La Campana Archaeological Zone

If you're not driving, walk or take a taxi a couple of miles northwest of the city center to the recently restored La Campana (The Lookout) Archaeological Zone. Head north about a mile from the city center; at main street Av. Tecnología, turn left and continue about another mile, past the technological institute, to the archaeological zone on the right (north) side of the boulevard.

Although untold generations of local people, especially those of Villa Alvarez, have known that La Campana was a special place, serious studies of the site didn't get under way until about 1920. Engineer José María Gutiérrez first mapped the site in 1917, clearing the way for archaeologist Miguel Galindo, who led the first systematic excavation in 1922. Now, with the perspective of half a century of digging, investigators believe that La Campana reached its heyday around A.D. 800, when it was a complete town with ceremonial platforms, markets, a commercial area, schools, priests' and nobles' quarters, and residential zones for several thousand commoners. From physical remains—mainly pottery shards, implements, and small stone sculptures—experts furthermore conclude that the predominant culture of Campana's former inhabitants was Nahua (Aztec-speaking), although signs of other cultures are present.

The entire archaeological zone, open daily except Mon., 9 A.M.–5 P.M., extends over an approximately square area of more than 120 acres, although the restored structures cover only about one-tenth of that. The main monument, the Adoritorio Central, is a 15-foot-high (five-meter),

50-foot (15-meter) square-based stone platform. Here, archaeologists uncovered a ritually interred skeleton, apparently a human sacrifice. A pair of secondary (lower, but larger in area) rectangular platform-complexes flank the Adoritorio. Experts believe that all of these platforms supported shrines dedicated to yet unknown gods or goddesses. Earthquakes, most investigators believe, led to the abandonment of La Campana by the time of the conquest.

Plenty is yet to be uncovered here, however. From atop the Adoritorio, between 100 and 300 yards toward the northeast, you might be able to make out the approximately eight additional unexcavated mounds scattered over the archaeological zone.

Northside Foothill Country Tour

By car, head out the Comala road toward the foothills northwest of the city, where your first reward will be ever-closer views of the volcanoes. **Comala** town, nestling above a lush stream valley about six miles from Colima, has always been a local Sunday favorite.

Just before town, be sure to stop at the roadside stalls of the local woodworkers' cooperative **Cooperativa Artesanal Pueblo.** Their specialty is furniture, adorned with the flower-, bird-, and children-motif decorations of painter Alejandro Rangel Hidalgo.

Continue uphill to the town center, where cares seem to float away in the orange blossom–scented air around the picture-perfect old plaza. Mariachis stroll every afternoon and restaurants (try Los Portales right on the plaza) serve *botanas* free with drinks, which should include at least one obligatory glass of local *ponche* fruit wine.

If you have an extra hour, reverse your path downhill and turn left at the **Hacienda Noguera** signed road that heads left (east) just downhill from town. In a few miles, you'll come to the venerable 18th-century Hacienda Noguera, where the University of Colima is setting up a new campus, centering on historical, archaeological, and anthropological studies. An especially exquisite small museum, open Tues.–Fri. 10 A.M.–2 P.M., 4:30–7 P.M., Sat. and Sun. 10 A.M.–6 P.M., features artifacts and art from the collection of Comala collector/artist Alejandro Rangel Hidalgo. The exhibitions climax in a collection of Colima ceramic dogs finer than you'll see most anywhere.

Perhaps after a refreshment at the museum's inviting outdoor café, be sure to visit the adjacent handicrafts store, **La Iguana Encantada** tel. 312/314-8484. Enjoy perusing the excellent selection of huipiles, embroidered purses, dolls, framed Rangel prints, and more. Open Tues.–Fri. 10 A.M.–2 P.M., 4:30–7 P.M., Sat. 10 A.M.–6 P.M., Sun. 10 A.M.–2 P.M.

Continuing uphill from Comala, the road leads past green pastures and groves, through the village of Cofradia de Suchitlán. Soon the road divides. Take the left fork and continue down a jungly, lava-cliffed canyon to **Ex-hacienda San Antonio**, about 20 miles (32 km) from Colima. (Unfortunately, the recently restored hacienda is marked only by a guarded gate. A roadside earth levee hides a trove of charming old-Mexico scenes inside: water gurgles from the ancient aqueduct, a stone chapel dedicated to San Antonio, stands intact, and a massive gate and wall, like a medieval keep, still protect the inhabitants from long-forgotten marauders.)

The latecomer owners, family of the late British multimillionaire Sir James Goldsmith, have recently renovated the hacienda into a superexclusive hotel which they have named **Mahakua**, replete with restored old-world details. Paying guests, of course, may enjoy all of the hidden treasures. Low-season rates (Feb. 1–Sept. 30) run about $1,100 d (about $1,400 d other times), including all meals, beverages, and in-house activities. Reserve directly at the hotel at tel. 312/313-4411, or toll-free at Mex. tel. 800/624-2582, U.S. tel. 888/809-9127, or Can. tel. 877/631-6286, fax 312/314-3727, or email hacienda@mahakua.com.mx, or reserve@mahakua.com.mx. For more information, visit the website www.mahakua.com.

A gravel road continues uphill from San Antonio a few miles farther to the mountainside Shangri-La **Ejido la María**. Past a gate (where you pay a small admission to park), a walking trail downhill leads past tidy vegetable fields to the idyllic shoreline of natural Laguna la María. Here, weekend and holiday visitors enjoy creekside picnicking and camping beneath the spreading boughs of a venerable lakeside grove. At other times, walk-in campers often enjoy nearly complete solitude. Bring everything, including water-purifying tablets, insect repellent, and tents for possible rain, especially during the summer. The 4,000-foot (1,200-meter) elevation produces usually balmy days and mild nights.

For noncampers, the ejido (communal farm) offers five clean, rustic bungalows on the hillside above the lake, with complete kitchens (bring your food), flush toilets, and hot water for a pricey $50–60 per night. Reserve (ask for a discount), at tel. 312/320-8891. Additionally, self-contained RVs may park hereabouts for a fee. Given the general friendliness of the local ejido folks, visitors who enjoy the sunny outdoors by day and mountain stillness by night could spend a few very enjoyable days at Laguna la María.

Centro Turístico Carrizalillos (Little Reeds Tourist Center) offers yet another outdoor possibility. Back at the fork, two miles uphill past Cofradia de Suchitlán, head right. After about two more miles, follow the signed driveway off to the right. The Carrizalillos campsites spread for about a mile around the circumference of an oak-studded ridge that encloses a small natural lake. The few dozen developed campsites (picnic tables, water, pit toilets), some suitable for small-to-medium RVs, rent for about $5 a day. A rustic view Restaurant Portales del Volcán occupies a lakeside hilltop, and a dozen unkempt housekeeping cabins overlook the lake. (The cabins may be in usable shape; the tariff used to be about $20 for two, but take a look before paying.) In season—Easter and Christmas weeks, and August—horses ($10/hour) and boats ($4/hour) are available. Given the magnificent mountain and valley views, the volcano's reflections in the azure lake (if the water level is up), and the fresh air, Carrizalillos might be just right for a cool, restful change of pace.

> *The Volcán de Fuego, one of the world's most active volcanoes, has erupted more than a dozen times since the conquest, continuously belching a stream of smoke and ash and frequently burping up red-hot boulders.*

The Volcanoes

Although taller by about 1,100 feet, Nevado (Snowy One) de Colima is far quieter than his younger brother, Volcán de Fuego, one of the world's most active volcanoes. The **Volcán de Fuego** has erupted more than a dozen times since the conquest, continuously belching a stream of smoke and ash and frequently burping up red-hot boulders. The government seals the access road when a serious eruption is imminent.

If you want a close-up look at Volcán de Fuego, check with the state tourism office, at Hidalgo 96, downtown Colima, tel./fax 312/312-4360, for advice, pack everything you're going to need, and head out along Highway 54 *libre* (old nontoll route) northeast of Colima. Drive a high-clearance truck or van or ride a second-class bus from the Colima bus station. Pass Tonila (19 miles, 30 km from Colima) to a dirt turnoff road 35 miles (near the Km 56 marker) from Colima. There, at a Telmex (Teléfonos de Mexico) *microndas* (microwave relay station) sign, take a sharp left toward the mountain. The Volcanic National Park boundary is a bumpy 17 miles (27 km) farther. How far you can go after that depends upon the authorities.

The approach to the much quieter **Nevado de Colima** is considerably more certain. The clear, dry winter months, when the views and the weather are the best, are Colima climbers' season of choice. This is wilderness mountain country, so you'll need to pack everything—winter sleeping bags, tents, alpine equipment, water, and food—that you'll require.

The ascent, which begins at La Joya hut at around the 11,000-foot level, is not particularly difficult for experienced, fit hikers. The trail starts out leading for an easy hour to the microwave station at the tree line. Then it continues for a few hours of steep walking, except for a bit of scrambling at the end. Ice is a possibility all year-round, however, so carry crampons and ice axes and be prepared to use them. Climbers often tent overnight at La Joya, get an early morning start, and arrive at the summit before noon.

To get to Nevado de Colima, go by bus or drive a jeep, pickup, or rugged, high-clearance van. Head out northeast along Highway 54 *libre,* past Tonila. Continue 39 miles (63 km) from Colima (a couple of miles past the Atequique mining village), where Highway 54 *libre* interchanges with the Colima-Guadalajara *cuota* (toll) freeway 54 D. Fork left on Highway 54 *libre* toward Ciudad Guzmán (rather than straight ahead, toward Jiquilipan). After paralleling the freeway for about two miles, a small sign reading Fresnito at Km 66 marks a good gravel uphill road (about eight miles) to Fresnito. At Fresnito, head left another 17 very rough miles (27 km) farther to La Joya.

Alternatively, on Highway 54, you can continue past the Fresnito sign several miles. Pass over the freeway 54 D. After a few more miles, turn left at the El Grullo sign. Pass under the freeway 54 D and continue until you see a Parque Nacional Nevado de Colima sign, where you turn left and continue 17 rough miles to La Joya.

By bus, from the Colima bus station, ride an early Autotransportes Sur de Jalisco or other bus to Ciudad Guzmán; transfer to a local bus to Fresnito, where you can thumb your way by truck uphill to La Joya.

Southern Excursion

The valley of Colima has a number of important archaeological sites. One of the most accessible and scenic is at Tampumachay, near the village of **Los Ortices,** eight miles south of Colima city.

The **Centro Turístico Tampumachay,** a shady green miniresort, accommodates visitors with a modest five-room hotel, two swimming pools, a rope bridge, a restaurant, and a camping area. It was developed originally by archaeologist Fidencio Perbez of Colima, and the present owners continue his policy of careful custodianship of the nearby ruins.

The archaeological zone surrounds the hotel, whose grounds perch at the edge of a spectacularly deep, rock-studded gorge. The staff members lead visitors on tours of the scenic, cactus-dotted cliffside plateau. Paths wind past intriguing ani-

mal- and human-motif petroglyph-sculptures and descend into tombs littered with grave pottery and human bones. Guides point out the remains of an unexcavated ceremonial platform on the opposite side of the canyon. The tombs and petroglyphs are well preserved, since local people, fearing dire ghostly consequences, generally leave the site alone.

Other local excursions include exploration of a limestone cave a couple of miles past the archaeological zone and wildlife-viewing hikes down into the gorge by a trail near the hotel. The Tampumachay resort itself is a lovely, tree-shaded garden, with artifact-dotted paths, a rope bridge, view gazebos, and pool-decks perfect for snoozing.

The five thoughtfully decorated, rustic beamed-ceilinged rooms rent for about $25 d (in one double bed), $45 (two double beds for up to four people), with shower and fan. A four-room cabin with communal kitchen and campsites for tents and (self-contained) RVs are also available. Reservations are usually not necessary except during holidays; write Centro Turístico Tampumachay, P.O. Box 149, Colima, Colima 28000. You can also contact the center through the Los Ortices local operator, tel. 312/314-7225 (in Spanish), who will forward your message to Tampumachay.

Getting There: Eight miles (13 km), at the Km 12 marker, along the Highway 110 expressway south of Colima city, just past the gasoline station, turn left, east, at the big Los Asmoles sign. Head uphill toward Los Ortices for 2.5 miles (four km), then turn right at a dirt road just before Los Ortices village. After about 200 yards, a sign directs you left to Tampumachay.

Northbound, toward Colima, take the right turnoff near Km 14, signed Los Asmoles. Continue about one mile (1.5 km), past the signed Rancho; turn right at the next paved side road.

ACCOMMODATIONS

Untouristed Colima has a sprinkling of good hotels. Some are city-style, downtown near the central plaza, and others are motel-style, in the suburbs. The prices quoted may be subject to discounts, which, under any conditions, you should always ask for: Say *"¿Hay descuento?"*

Downtown Hotels

Many business travelers stay at **Hotel América,** Morelos 162, Colima, Colima 28000, tel. 312/312-9596, fax 312/314-4425, hamerica@prodigy.net.mx, three blocks from the city center. Outside, the facade is colonial; inside a two-story warren of rooms hides among a maze of glass-and-steel tropical terrariums. The rooms are spacious, carpeted, and comfortable. Lack of a pool is partially compensated for by a sauna (use of which is limited to mornings, however). One of Hotel América's pluses is its good restaurant, where patrons enjoy snappy service and tasty food at reasonable prices. The 70 rooms rent for about $65 s or d with king-sized or two beds, cable TV, a/c, phones, and parking; credit cards are accepted, and there is limited lower-level wheelchair access. For more information, visit the website www.hotelamerica.com.mx.

Hotel Ceballos, Portal Medillin 12, Colima, Colima 28000, tel. 312/312-4444, fax 312/312-0645, principal@hotelceballos.com, right on the central plaza, offers a best-buy alternative. Although recently renovated, the hotel retains its high ceilings and graceful colonial ambience. Ceballos offers tastefully decorated, clean, and comfortable air-conditioned rooms with TV. Rates for the 63 rooms run about $33. Rooms vary in size and ventilation; ask to see more than one before choosing. The owners have recently upgraded the hotel amenities considerably, adding a lovely top-floor sundeck, petite pool, airy sitting room and small kiddie playground. Parking is included and credit cards are accepted. For more information, visit the website www.hotelceballos.com.

Travelers looking for old-Mexico ambience on a budget might enjoy staying at *posada*-style **Hotel La Merced,** at 188 Hidalgo, tel. 312/312-6969 or 312/312-1421, email divisioncuartos@hotelmariaisable.com.mx, just off shady Plaza Nuñes, five blocks west of the city center. Here, travelers have a choice of two connected sections: at Hidalgo 188, a dozen plainly furnished high-ceilinged rooms with baths around a homey, traditional inner patio, and at Juárez 82, a more conventional, modest, but still clean hotel with reception desk. Look at rooms in both sections. Rates run about $17 s or $19 d.

If the Merced is full, for another budget choice, go about four blocks north (to Aldama), about eight blocks diagonally northwest (along Maclovio Herrera) to Centenario and the motel-style ("Don't look for stars") basic but clean **Hotel Río,** at Centenario 289, tel./fax 312/312-9607. Rooms, built around an inner garden patio, run a very reasonable $22 s or d, $25 t, with a/c ($13 s, $20 with fans only) with hot water and parking.

Suburban Hotels

Motel-style **Hotel María Isabel,** Blvd. Camino Real at Av. Felipe Sevilla del Río, Colima, Colima 28010, tel./fax 312/312-6464 or 312/312-6262, divisioncuartos@hotelmariaisable.com.mx, about two miles northeast of the city-center, appeals to families and RV and car travelers. Moreover, desk management, general hotel cleanliness and accommodation quality have greatly improved in recent years.

The double-story room tiers line a long parking lot edged on one side by a lawn and tropical foliage. A large pool and airy restaurant occupy one side near the entrance. The rooms come in standard and luxury versions. The standard rooms, although smaller, are nevertheless clean and deluxe. The luxury rooms are larger, with tonier decor. The 90 rooms go for about $70 standard s or d, $90 luxury (ask for a discount) with credit cards accepted and parking. For more information, visit the website www.hotelmariaisabel.com.mx.

Neighboring **Hotel Los Candiles,** Blvd. Camino Real 399, Colima, Colima 28010, tel. 312/312-3212, fax 312/313-1707, avoids the usual cluttered motel parking lot atmosphere by putting the swimming pool and patio at the center and the cars off to the side. An attractive tropical garden-style hotel is the result. Recently increased prices have led to greatly improved room quality, especially in the lower-priced standard-grade economy rooms. You more or less get what you pay for: standard rooms, while clean and comfortable, are about Motel 6 size and decor. The deluxe grade are larger and more plush. The 60 rooms rent for about $53 economy s or d, $80 deluxe, suite $90 (ask for a discount), with TV, phones, restaurant, and restaurant breakfast included; credit cards are accepted.

FOOD

Breakfast, Snacks, and Bakery

A good place to start out the day is the restaurant at the **Hotel América,** Morelos 162, tel. 312/312-9596, open daily at 7 A.M. for breakfast, dinner served till 10 P.M., where the servers greet you with hot coffee and a cheery *"Buenos días."* The menu affords plenty of familiar fare, from fresh eggs any style to pancakes and fruit, at reasonable prices.

After a few hours among the downtown sights, take a break at one of the sidewalk cafés bordering the Jardín de Libertad. First choice goes to the airy **Café de la Plaza,** open daily 7 A.M.–10 P.M., at the Hotel Ceballos on the Jardín de Libertad. Here, high ceilings, graceful arches, and, if you choose, sidewalk tables, add a touch of leisurely refinement to your breakfast or midday lunch break. The relatively short menu—of breakfasts, sandwiches, tacos, *tortas,* juices, desserts, and coffees—is crisply served and reasonably priced.

Alternatively, you can sample the possibilities on the opposite, or south, side of the *jardín,* such as **Restaurant Portales,** where patrons enjoy either shady sidewalk tables or an upstairs balcony perch from which to take in the passing scene.

If you're in the mood for dessert, head east two blocks to the east side of Plaza Torres Quintero and sample the luscious baked offerings of **Panadería Viera,** tel. 312/313-0017, open Mon.–Sat. 9 A.M.–9 P.M.

Restaurants

Starting downtown, at the southwest *jardín* corner (of Degollado and Torres Quintero), the strictly local **Restaurant El Trébol** offers hearty breakfasts, lunches, and dinners daily 8 A.M.–8 P.M. Especially popular with the downtown shopping and business crowd is the *comida corrida* (traditional multiple-course set lunch, about $2), served daily from around noon–3 P.M. Budget.

Equally good for breakfast, lunch, or dinner is the mid- to upper-class **Los Naranjos** (The Orange Trees), 2.5 blocks away at 34 Gabino Barreda, between Madero and Zaragoza, tel. 312/312-7316. Los Naranjos's relaxed, refined ambience—

try the airy back patio—and eclectic menu (salads, sandwiches, tacos, enchiladas, meats, and poultry), professionally prepared and presented, have ensured a legion of loyal customers since 1956. Open daily 8 A.M.-11:30 P.M. Moderate.

Nearby, the popularity of **Restaurant Colima 88** (formerly Casa Grande), 129 Av. 27 de Septiembre, near the corner of Allende, tel. 312/311-2786, is due to its tasty regional specialties, refined ambience, and very correct service. Patrons enjoy shady seating beneath a hacienda roof beside a sun-splashed patio with a fountain. The house specialties are Colima regional lunch and supper dishes, such as Pepena roast beef in sauce and Tatemado roast pork. Vegetable lovers, on the other hand, order the excellent tomato, onion, and avocado salad. Open daily 4-11 P.M., two blocks east and three blocks north of the *jardín.* Moderate.

Unpretentiously lovely restaurant **El Charco de la Higuera,** tel. 312/313-0192, is a perfect spot for soaking up the charm of traditional Mexico. Its graceful amenities—at the leafy edge of an old church plaza, a bubbling fountain, a shady veranda—and its long list of *típico* Mexican specialties provide all the ingredients for a leisurely breakfast, lunch, or dinner. At old San José church, six blocks from the *jardín,* along the westward extension of Madero. Open daily 8 A.M.–midnight. Moderate.

If, however, you hanker for familiar food in polished, air-conditioned surroundings, head for the local branch of **VIPs,** tel. 312/313-2238, the Mexican (although classier) version of Denny's. Also on east-side Calz. Galvan, just a block downhill from Allende, in front of the big, shiny Auerrera department store. Open Sun.–Thurs. 7 A.M.–11 P.M., Fri.–Sat. 7–2 A.M. Moderate.

ENTERTAINMENT AND EVENTS

Local folks compensate for the lack of nightlife by whooping it up during Colima's major local festivals. Don't miss them if you happen to be in town.

For nine days beginning January 23, people celebrate the **Fiesta de La Virgen de La**

Salud, which climaxes on February 2. The church (Iglesia de La Salud) neighborhood near Av.s Gallardo and Corregidora blooms with colorful processions, bands, food, and crafts stalls, and the church plaza resounds with music, folk dancing, and fireworks.

Ever since 1820 the Villa de Alvarez (a suburb a few miles northwest of the city center) has staged **Fiesta Charrotaurina,** a 10-day combination rodeo/bullfight/carnival. The celebration wouldn't be as much fun if the Villa de Alvarez people stayed to themselves. Every day, however, February 7–23 around noon, a troupe of Villa de Alvarez musicians, cowboys, cowgirls, papier-mâché bulls, and a pair of *mojigangos* (giant effigies of the Colima governor and spouse) assemble on Colima's downtown Jardín de Libertad. The music begins, the *mojigangos* start whirling, and a big crowd of bystanders follows them back to Villa de Alvarez.

Visitors who miss the Virgen de La Salud in January can get in on the similar **Fiesta de San José,** which culminates on March 19 in the westside neighborhood of the Iglesia de San José (corner Quintero and Suárez) with a host of traditional foodstalls, regional folk dancing, and religious processions.

During the fall, Colima heats up again for the **Todos Santos/Día de los Muertos** (All Saints/Day of the Dead) fair about Oct. 20–Nov. 10. Most events and merrymaking take place at the La Estancia Fairground, about two miles (three km) east of town along the extension of Av. Niños Héroes.

Music and Dance

Right downtown, a few cafés and restaurants offer live music around the plaza. Try the Café La Plaza, tel. 312/312-4444, at the Hotel Ceballos, weekend evenings, and Colima 88 Restaurant, 129 Av. 27 de Septiembre, near corner of Allende, tel. 312/311-2786, which has a similar offering. Call to verify programs.

The University of Colima has an active folkloric ballet group that performs seasonally. Check with the tourist information office (see succeeding) or call the director, at tel. 312/312-5140, for information.

SHOPPING

Reliable downtown shops sell reproductions of Colima's charming pre-Columbian animal and human figurines.

Handicrafts

The state-operated **Casa de Las Artesanías,** Av. Zaragoza and Andando Constitución, tel. 312/314-4790, near the Jardín de Libertad, stocks a number of locally made figurines, plus shelves of handicrafts gathered from all over Mexico, such as sombreros, *huipiles,* serapes, toys, and Christmas decorations. Other local items include Colima coffee beans, regional cuisine cookbooks, and coconut candy. Open Mon.–Fri. 10 A.M.–2 P.M. and 5–8 P.M., Sat. 10 A.M.–2 P.M.

A few doors down the Andador Constitución, a pair of privately owned shops, **Mexicanía,** tel. 312/312-8350, and **Casa México** also offer attractive handicrafts selections. Both are customarily open approximately Mon.–Sat. 10 A.M.–2 P.M. and 5–8:30 P.M., Sun. 10 A.M.–2 P.M.

Also, across the *andador,* take a look inside **Artesanías Ceballos,** for a selection of many unusual local handicrafts. For example, eerie masks from Suchitlán, small framed prints, rustic woodcrafts, ingenious purses made of coconuts, and whimsical coconut carvings. Open daily 11 A.M.–9 P.M., tel. 312/314-044.

If you prefer to buy your ceramics directly from the artisan, go to the **Museo de Culturas Populares,** Avs. Gallardo and Barreda, tel. 312/312-6869, open four blocks north of the *jardín.* Here, you can see potters reproducing Colima's captivating animal and human figurines. If no artisans are available, the museum shop inside sells their work, plus many other folk crafts, both local and national. Open Tues.–Sat. 10 A.M.–2 P.M. and 5–8 P.M., Sun. 10 A.M.–1 P.M.

Photography

Get your film developed in an hour and buy film and basic camera supplies at **Foto Carmen,** on the *jardín,* northwest corner of Degollado and Madero, tel. 312/314-0066. Open Mon.–Sat. 9 A.M.–2 P.M. and 4:30–8 P.M.

© BRUCE WHIPPERMAN

Restaurants, hotels, shops, and skateboarding draw both young and old to the Colima central *jardín*.

INFORMATION AND SERVICES

Tourist Information Office

The efficient and helpful staff of the *oficina de turismo,* southwest corner of Hidalgo and Ocampo, adjacent to Banamex, a block east of the Jardín de Libertad, tel. 312/312-4360, fax 312/312-8360, turiscol@correo.col.gob.mx, answers questions and offers a Colima map and excellent color brochures. Open Mon.–Fri. 9 A.M.–8:30 P.M., Sat. 10 A.M.–2 P.M. For more information, visit the website www.visitacolima.com.mx.

Publications

English newspapers and magazines are rare in Colima. The newsstand next to the Hotel Ceballos stocks the English-language Mexico City *News*; it's open daily 8 A.M.–9 P.M.

Money Exchange

Several banks, all with ATMs, serve downtown customers. The **Banamex** downtown branch, at Hidalgo 90, just two blocks east of the *jardín,* tel. 312/312-9820, exchanges U.S.

and Canadian currency and traveler's checks Mon.–Fri. 9 A.M.–4 P.M. If Banamex lines are too long, walk a block north to **Bancomer,** at Madero 106, corner of Obregón, tel. 312/314-6843, open Mon.–Fri. 9 A.M.–4 P.M., Sat. 10 A.M.–2 P.M.; or another block east to **Banco Internacional,** at Madero 183, tel. 312/312-3623 or 312/312-3624, open Mon.–Sat. 8 A.M.–7 P.M.

After bank hours, try one of the nearby *casas de cambio,* on Madero, such as **Casa de Cambio USA-Mex.,** tel. 312/312-9230, at the corner of 27 de Septiembre and Madero, open Mon.–Sat. 9 A.M.–8 P.M. and Sun. 9 A.M.–2 P.M.

Communications

The main *correo* (post office) is open Mon.–Fri. 8 A.M.–6 P.M., Sat. 8 A.M.–noon, on Madero at Plaza Nuñez, four blocks east of the *jardín,* by the Palacio Federal, tel. 312/312-0033. For simple letter mailing, use the *buzón* (mailbox) on the Andador Constitución.

For **telephone,** local or long-distance, buy a Ladatel card (look for the small blue and yellow signs) on the plaza and use it in the public street telephone. (For long-distance in Mexico, first dial 01, then the area code and local number. For Canada and the United States, first dial "001," then the number.)

Alternately, you can use the *larga distancia* and fax in the little office (open daily 7 A.M.–10 P.M.) beneath the portal on the south side of the *jardín;* or the Caseta Colima in the Andador Constitución, tel. 312/314-1664, open Mon.–Sat. 8:30 A.M.–8:30 P.M.

Connect to the Internet at **CIA Internet,** Reforma 63 upstairs, just downhill from the southwest plaza corner, tel. 312/330-1547, open daily 8 A.M.–9 P.M.

Hospital, Police, and Emergencies

The respected private hospital, **Centro Médico,** at Maclovio Herrera 140, a quarter mile north of Jardín de Libertad, tel. 312/312-4044, 312/312-4045, or 312/312-4046, has emergency service and many specialists on 24-hour call.

The **Super Farmacia,** tel. 312/312-0031 or 312/312-5537, on the *jardín,* offers a large stock of medicines and drugs. Open Mon.–Sat. 9 A.M.–11 P.M., Sun. 9 A.M.–10 P.M.

The **Cabercera Policia** (police headquarters), tel. 312/313-1434, is on the north side of town, at (take a taxi) Roberto Esperón 1152, in Colonia Trabajadores.

For **fire** emergencies, call the *bomberos* (firefighters), tel. 312/312-5858, off Ejercito Nacional, a block north of the Museum of the Cultures of the West.

Travel Agency

For tickets, tours, and car rentals, go to the excellent **Vamos A** (We're Going) travel agency, tel. 312/314-9600 or 312/314-9700, open Mon.–Fri. 9 A.M.–2 P.M. and 4–7:30 P.M., Sat. 9 A.M.–2 P.M., at Independencia 51, two blocks south of the *jardín.* Alternatively, try **Turisste Colima** on the Andador Constitución, northeast corner of the *jardín,* tel. 312/314-3592 or 312/314-3593; open Mon.–Fri. 9 A.M.–7 P.M.

GETTING THERE AND AWAY

By Car or RV

The Manzanillo-Colima combined Highways 200 and 110 *autopista* makes Colima safely accessible from Manzanillo in about 1.5 hours. From Manzanillo, follow the *cuota* (toll) Highway 200 (34 miles, 54 km) southeast to the Highway 110 junction near Tecomán. Branch north, continuing on Highway 110 for another 25 miles (40 km) to Colima.

To Guadalajara from Colima, drive to the east side of town, where entrance ramps lead you on to the combined Highway 110-54D *autopista* freeway for an easy drive three hours north to Guadalajara.

For southeast coastal destinations, such as Playa Azul and Zihuatanejo, follow Highway 110 south, then fork southeast to Highway 200 at Tecomán and continue along the coast about six hours to Playa Azul (eight to Zihuatanejo). (For more driving details, see the Manzanillo section.)

By Bus

The airy, airport-style *central camionera* (central bus station), on the Highway 110 *libramiento* (bypass) east of town, is the Colima point of departure for several good first- and luxury-class bus lines. The terminal has a number of services, including a tourist information booth, hotel reservations, trinket shops, travel agent, and luggage storage. The ticketing is efficiently computerized and major lines accept credit cards. A continuous procession of **local** and **semilocal buses,** destinations marked on their windshields, stop out in front.

Estrella Blanca and it associated lines, **Elite,** and **Futura** tel. 312/312-8499, provide connections northwest, with Mexicali and Tijuana at the U.S. border via Ciudad Guzman, Tepic, and Mazatlán, and northeast with Mexico City direct.

First-class **Omnibus de Mexico** buses, tel. 312/314-7190 or 312/312-1630, connect north with Guadalajara. From there they continue north via Durango to the U.S. border at Ciudad Juárez, or northeast via Aguascalientes, Monterrey, and Matamoros and Nuevo Laredo at the U.S. border.

Autovías del Occidente, tel. 312/314-8179, provides frequent first-class connections with Manzanillo in the southwest, Guadalajara in the north and Mexico City, via Michoacán destinations of Uruapan and Morelia. It also provides first-class connections, via Tecomán, southeast, with La Mira (Playa Azul) and Lázaro Cárdenas. Autovias del Occidente, furthermore, provides connections northeast, through northern Michoacán, via Mazamitla, Jiquilipan, Zamora, Quiroga, and Morelia.

Flecha Amarilla, tel. 312/314-8067, and its subsidiary *servicios coordinados* lines provide "Primera-plus" luxury-class and first-class direct connections north with Guadalajara, Aguascalientes, and León, northeast with Mexico City, and southwest with Manzanillo, continuing, via Barra de Navidad-Melaque, to Puerto Vallarta. Second-class departures also connect frequently northwest with Jalisco and Michoacán destinations of Tamazula, Mazamitla, Jiquilipan, Zamora, Irapuato, continuing via Queretero, to Mexico City. Other second-class departures connect southwest via Tecomán, with Manzanillo, and southeast, with San Juan de Alima.

The airline-style, luxury-class buses of **Enlaces Transportes Nacionales** (ETN), tel. 312/312-5899 or 312/314-1060, connect directly north with Guadalajara, southwest with Manzanillo and Puerto Vallarta, and east with Michoacán destinations of Uruapan and Morelia, continuing to Mexico City.

Autotransportes Sur de Jalisco, tel. 312/312-0316, provides regional second-class connections northeast with Guadalajara via Ciudad Guzman, southwest with Manzanillo, and southeast with La Mira (Playa Azul) and Lázaro Cárdenas, where you can continue to Zihuatanejo and Acapulco.

Galeana, tel. 312/313-4785, provides "Ruta Paraíso" second-class connections with Michoacán destinations of Uruapan and Morelia and the southeast coast with Tecomán and San Juan de Lima.

By Train
Privatization has ended Colima passenger train service. Until further notice, drive, fly, or ride the bus.

South to Ixtapa-Zihuatanejo and Inland to Pátzcuaro

Along the Road to Playa Azul

Heading southeast out of Manzanillo, the Mexican Pacific coast highway winds for 200 miles, hugging the shorelines of two states. First, it follows the southern Colima coast, well known for its beaches, surf, and abundant fresh seafood. After that the road pierces the little-traveled wild coast of Michoacán.

That last lonely Michoacán coastal link was completed in 1984. Local people still remember when, if they wanted to travel to Manzanillo, they had to walk half the way. What they saw along the path is still there: moun-

tainsides of great vine-draped trees and seemingly endless pearly, driftwood-strewn beaches, fringed by verdant palm groves and enfolded by golden sandstone cliffs. From ramparts high above the foaming surf, gigantic headlands seem to file in procession along the shore and fade into the sea-mist a thousand miles away. Along the highway, coatimundis peer from beneath bushes, iguanas scurry along the shoulder, and, in the spring, a rainbow of blossoms—yellow, red, pink, and violet—blooms beside the roadside.

© BRUCE WHIPPERMAN

view from Isla Janitzio

HISTORY

Before Columbus

The great Río Balsas, whose watershed includes Michoacán and five other Mexican states, has repeatedly attracted outsiders. Some of the first settlers to the Río Balsas basin came thousands of years ago, from perhaps as far away as Peru. They left remains—pottery, of unmistakable Andean influence—and their language, roots of which remain in the native dialects of highland Michoacán.

The major inheritors of this ancient Andean heritage became known as the Tarascans. They founded a powerful Michoacán empire, centered at highland Lake Pátzcuaro, which rivaled the Aztec empire at the time of the conquest.

Conquest and Colonial Era

Although the Tarascans were never subdued by the Aztecs, they quickly fell prey to the Spanish conquistadores, who were also drawn to the River Balsas. In search of the riches of the Southern Sea (as the Pacific was known to him), Hernán Cortés sent his captains Juan Rodríguez and Ximón de Cuenca to the mouth of the Río Balsas, where they founded the Villa de La Concepción de Zacatula in 1523. But, like all the early Pacific ports, Zacatula was abandoned in favor of Acapulco by 1600.

Recent Times

The Michoacán-Colima coast slumbered until the 1880s, when railroad building began at the reawakened port of Manzanillo. By 1887 trains from Manzanillo were stopping at Cuyutlán, a village of salt harvesters, who soon became prosperous by lodging and feeding droves of rich seashore vacationers from Guadalajara.

Neighboring coastal Michoacán had to wait for the dust of the 1910–1917 Revolution to settle before getting its own development project. Again the Río Balsas drew outsiders. Dam builders came to harness the river's hydropower to make steel out of a mountain of Michoacán iron ore. In succession came the new port, Lázaro Cárdenas, the railroad, the dam, then finally the huge Las Trucas steel mill. Concur-

rently, Playa Azul, Michoacán's planned beach resort on the Pacific, was developed nearby.

The new facilities, however, never quite lived up to expectations. Although a few ships and trains still arrive, and some tourists come weekends and holidays, Lázaro Cárdenas and Playa Azul drowse fitfully, dreaming of their long-expected awakening.

CUYUTLÁN

Little Cuyutlán (pop. 2,000) is heaven for lovers of nostalgia and tranquility. No raucous hangouts clutter its lanes; no rock, techno, or rap bounces from its few cafés. Sun, sand, and gentle surf are its prime amenities. Rickety wooden walkways lead across its hot dark sands to a line of beachfront umbrellas, where you can rent a chair for the day, enjoy the breeze, and feast on the seafood offerings of seaside kitchens.

Most of Cuyutlán's hotels, restaurants, and services lie along a single street: Hidalgo, which runs from the *jardín* (on the Manzanillo-Armería road) a few blocks, crossing Av. Veracruz and ending at the beachfront *malecón*.

The shady, cobbled side streets of Cuyutlán invite impromptu exploring. Near the beach, lanes lead past weathered wooden houses and *palapas* (some for rent). On the inland side of the *jardín* near the rail station, kerosene lamps flicker at night through the wood-stick walls of village houses. The station itself is an antique out of the Porfirian age, with the original iron columns still supporting its moss-streaked, gabled platform roof. Nearby, hulking wooden (exotically unusual in Mexico) salt warehouses line an earthen street. Those ancient repositories are reminders of the old tradition of salt harvesting at the edges of nearby Cuyutlán lagoon. Peek through the cracks in the rickety warehouse walls and you'll see the salt—huge white piles, looking exactly like *nieve* (snow) from the heights of the Nevado de Colima.

The Salt Museum

Local authorities have, very appropriately, turned one of those old warehouses into a museum, the **Museo de Sal,** a block north of the *jardín*.

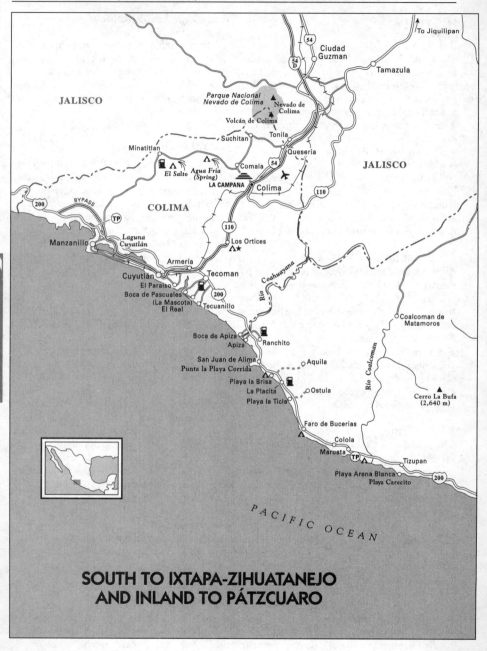

TO IXTAPA/PÁTZCUARO

SOUTH TO IXTAPA-ZIHUATANEJO
AND INLAND TO PÁTZCUARO

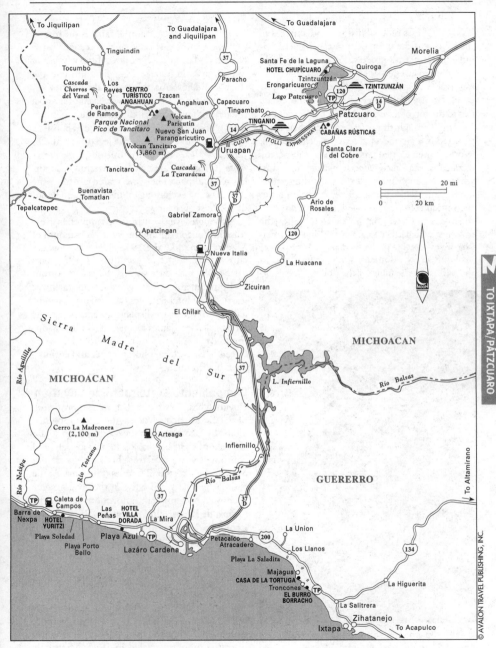

Around the walls inside, displays describe the last 1,000 years of local history, and a model in the middle of the room demonstrates the laborious salt-extraction process. First, workers filled pottery jars with salt-laden brine from *tajos* (shallow wells) near the naturally salty Laguna de Cuyutlán. By hand, they lifted the brine several feet to the top of a *cujete* (leaching bed). After percolating through the *cujete,* the enriched brine gathered in a ground-level *toza* (collection basin). Workers then carried jars full of brine to nearby rectangular salt-diked *planes* (concentration pans) where the sun evaporated the remaining water, leaving pure white sea salt. They sell bags of it in the museum for less than a dollar. A kindly octogenarian salt worker who watches after the museum will gladly explain everything (in Spanish), if you ask. He probably makes a large part of his living off the donations that people leave in the basket on the table by the door.

© BRUCE WHIPPERMAN

Weathered wooden salt warehouses decorate Cuyutlán's quiet back streets.

The Green Wave

Cuyutlán's latter-day claim to fame is the mysterious Green Wave, which is said to occasionally rise offshore and come crashing down from a height of 20, 30, or even 50 feet. (The later at night the story is told, it seems, the greater the height.)

The source of the Green Wave's color is also a mystery, although some local aficionados speculate that an offshore algae bloom might be responsible.

The probable source of the legend is real. On June 22, 1932, a gigantic 60-foot high *maremoto* (tsunami) came close to washing Cuyutlán off the map. The wave reared up from the sea, smashing everything on the beach and flooding the rest of the town.

Although several faithful still apprehensively scan the horizon during the most likely month of May, nothing like the 1932 tidal wave has occurred since. Some suggest that the 1978 local earthquake may have shifted the ocean bottom and quieted the Green Wave (temporarily, at least). The Hotel Morelos, at the corner of Hidalgo and Veracruz, displays, in addition to its lobby gallery of James Dean and Marilyn Monroe photos, a snapshot of an alleged 20-foot Green Wave by local photographer and enthusiast Eduardo Lolo.

Campamento Tortuguero de Cuyutlán

Cuyutlán has its own member of the growing roll of Pacific Mexico turtle-saving encampments. Find it by following main street Av. Veracruz south; after about eight blocks, jog right, then left, and continue (where the street becomes Av. López Mateos) for a total of 2.5 miles (four km). At the end of the road you'll arrive at the government-sponsored encampment, known officially as the **Centro de Desarrollo Productivo, Recreativo, y Ecológico de Cuyutlán** (Cuyutlán Center for Productive, Recreative, and Ecological Development). It's open Tues.–Sat. 8:30 A.M.–5:30 P.M., admission about $2 per person.

Inside the gate, the center staff gladly explain their manifold educational, scientific, economic, and ecological mission. They have made an excellent start. They have been returning more than 50,000 hatchling turtles to the sea annually since the program started in 1995. The turtle

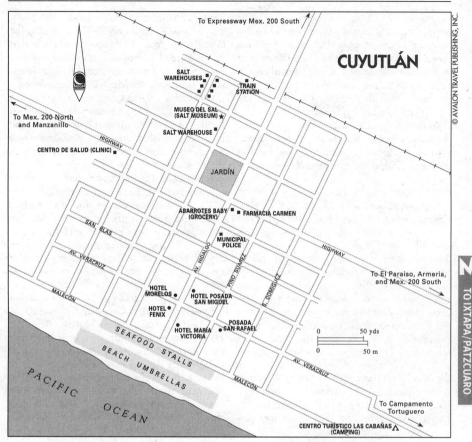

hatchery, where they incubate the eggs that they rescue from poachers, is beneath the big tent on the beach.

Three turtle species arrive during the July–Nov. hatching season: the **olive ridley** *(golfina), Lepidochelys olivacea)*; the **Pacific green** *(tortuga negra*—black turtle, as it's known in Mexico), *Chelonia agassizi*; and, most notably, the **leatherback** *(tortuga de cuero), Dermochelys coriacea.* (See the special topic "Saving Turtles" in the Road to Barra de Navidad section.)

Project staff also try to educate everyone—most important, a steady flow of local schoolchildren and teachers—both about saving turtles specifically

and threatened plants and wildlife in general. Animal enclosures and tanks of a (thankfully) few fish, turtles, crocodiles, iguanas, and more serve as examples. Their effort also extends to guiding visitors on wildlife-viewing boat tours in the adjacent lagoon ($5 per person—watch for the 10-foot crocodiles!) during the Dec.–May waterfowl season. Moreover, visitors are invited to take a dip in the blue swimming pools, have a *refresco*, and enjoy a picnic lunch beneath the *palapa*.

Beach Activities

Cuyutlán's wide and seemingly endless beach invites a number of activities and sports. The nearly level offshore slope produces little undertow, so wading and swimming conditions are ideal. The waves, which roll in gradually, are fine for boogie boarding, bodysurfing, and all levels of surfing, depending on the size of the swells. Bring your own surfboard, although boogie board rentals are available on the beach. Shells become more common the farther you stroll away from the few picked-over blocks of beach.

As for fishing, the shallow slope decreases the chances for successful surf-casts. Hire or launch your boat (easy in calm weather) and head to the happy fishing grounds beyond the waves.

Accommodations

The **Hotel Morelos,** Hidalgo 185, Cuyutlán, Colima 28350, tel./fax 313/326-4013, founded in the 1890s, continues Cuyutlán's turn-of-the-20th-century tradition with a long (quaintly downhill-sloping) lobby, decorated with plastic flowers and white Grecian columns. The hotel has added an inviting new patio, built around a designer blue pool. Rooms, moreover, have been redecorated with elegant, hand-carved wooden beds and doors. Most rooms, however, are dark; look at more than one before moving in. The family owners top all this off with hearty local-style food, which they serve in the hotel restaurant. The Morelos's 40 rooms rent for about $12 s, $24 d with hot water and fans. During the super-high Christmas and Easter weeks, rates run $30 per day per person, including three meals.

Across the street toward the beach stands the equally venerable **Hotel Fénix,** Hidalgo 201, Cuyutlán, Colima 28350, tel./fax 313/326-4082, whose patrons likewise enjoy a good open-air, street-level restaurant. Olivia and Jeffry, husband-wife owners (she's Mexican, he's American) have completely redecorated the 25-odd rooms, scattered along upstairs corridors, in attractive natural wood with billowing white cotton curtains. The result is pleasingly light, airy, and traditional. Rates run about $20 s or d for the more deluxe upstairs rooms, and $7 s, $14 d for the downstairs rooms.

New owners have likewise rejuvenated Cuyutlán's newest hostelry (formerly the Hotel Ceballos), now the **Hotel María Victoria,** at Veracruz 10, Cuyutlán, Colima 28350, tel. 313/326-4004, fax 313/326-4023, fronting the beach at the foot of Hidalgo. Inside, the airy, cream-tinted lobby towers to a fluted concrete roof-shell like a giant spaceship hangar. It encloses a curious cylindrical central tier of rooms that resemble a flying saucer waiting to whisk a few chosen guests to an Encounter of the Third Kind. But never mind; simply rent one of the many comfortable, attractive pink-and-white pastel rooms that surround the entire lobby in three tiers. Ask for a room on the oceanfront (*frente el mar*) side, and enjoy your own breezy sea-view balcony. The 80 rooms rent for about $21 s, $42 d all year, except around Christmas and Easter, when tariffs rise to about $80 per room for up to four people, with hot water, fans, beachview restaurant, and a small pool. Try bargaining for a discount during times of low occupancy, such as weekdays, Jan., and Sept.–November.

Back uphill, bargain-rate **Hotel Posada San Miguel,** Av. Hidalgo, Cuyutlán, Colima 28350, tel. 313/326-4062, across Hidalgo from the Hotel Morelos, has bright, comfortable upstairs rooms that open onto a shady sitting porch overlooking the street. The eight rooms run about $10 per person low season, $13 high ($20 during the Christmas and Easter holidays), with hot water and fans. (The owner says that customers who arrive with the *Moon Handbooks Pacific Mexico* get a 10 percent discount.)

Down the beach, a block south of the Hotel María Victoria, stands the luxuriously situated beachfront **Hotel San Rafael,** Av. Veracruz y Piño Suárez, Cuyutlán, Colima 28350, tel. 313/326-4015, fax 312/312-0319. Besides its inviting big blue swimming pool, the hotel offers 30 simply furnished rooms (a few with hand-carved wood and reading lamps), six of which have spacious, breezy, semiprivate second- and third-floor ocean-view porches. Downstairs, a shady open-air restaurant overlooks the beach and waves beyond. Rooms rent for about $20 s, $30 d all year around—bargain for a lower long-term rate—with fans and hot water. Reserve your room *arriba con vista del mar* (upstairs with ocean view).

Long-Term Apartment and House Rentals

If you'd like to linger in Cuyutlán a few weeks or more, contact Olivia Ramírez, co-owner of the Hotel Fenix, tel./fax 313/326-4082, who manages a number of beachfront rental properties.

Camping and RV Parking

Tent campers who desire company stay at the beachfront **Centro Turístico Las Cabañas,** about six blocks southeast of the town center, on the way to the Campamento Tortuguero (see above). Tariffs run about $10 per group, with showers, toilets, shady picnic *palapas*, a kiddie pool, and a store.

On the other hand, campers who hanker for privacy can follow dirt roads that lead to miles of open beach, good for camping or parking, on both sides of town. (Be careful of soft sand, however.) Cuyutlán, being a generally friendly, upright country place, will ordinarily present no security problem. If in doubt, however, don't hesitate to ask local shopkeepers. Say, *"¿Está bueno acampar acá?"* (ehs-TAH boo-EY-noh ah-kam-PAHR ah-KAH?).

Food

Besides the good restaurants at the Hotels Morelos, Fénix, and María Victoria, the main Cuyutlán eateries are the many seafood vendors, whose semipermanent umbrella-covered establishments do big busines on holidays and weekends. Quality of the fare—oyster cocktails, grilled or boiled shrimp and lobster, and fried fish—is generally excellent, since many of them depend on loyal repeat customers.

For groceries, try **Abarrotes Baby,** at the *jardín*, corner Hidalgo.

Information and Services

Most of Cuyutlán's businesses are spread along Hidalgo between the beach and the *jardín*. At the *jardín,* corner Hidalgo, is the **Farmacia Carmen,** open daily 9 A.M.–2 P.M. and 4–9 P.M. Up the street, at 144 Hidalgo, the municipal *policía* (police), tel. 313/326-4114, are on duty round the clock. Downhill, a block from the *jardín,* Manzanillo direction, is the **Centro de Salud** (Health Center), open routinely until 5 P.M., but only in emergencies after that.

Getting There and Away

By car or RV from Manzanillo, follow the Highway 200 *cuota* (toll) branch superhighway 17 miles (28 km) to Cuyutlán. Or, for a more scenic alternative, from Manzanillo, follow main street Av. Carrillo Puerto south from the *jardín* through downtown Manzanillo and continue along the west end of placid Laguna Cuyutlán. This route curves southeasterly, past the giant smoking power plant chimneys, through miles of *ciruela* orchards, then along a breezy barrier dune and wild beach, eventually joining the toll highway about 10 miles before Cuyutlán. For the same scenic route, in the reverse direction, follow Av. Hidalgo east, past the Cuyutlán *jardín* to the Highway 200 expressway entrance, Manzanillo direction. Continue about 10 miles to the first exit, and proceed west.

Southeasterly-bound drivers not in a hurry simply head in the opposite direction, along the old highway, that passes the Cuyutlan jardín. After a few miles, past lush pastures and palm groves, turn right at the fork for El Paraíso beach (see below), or continue ahead, eventually joining Highway 200 at Armería. Alternatively, if you want to get away in a hurry, get on the Highway 200 *cuota* (toll) expressway southbound by following the extension of Av. Hidalgo, north, past the *jardín* and over the railroad tracks a few hundred yards to the expressway entrance on the right.

Manzanillo taxis take three or four passengers to and from Cuyutlán for about $30 one way. If this is too expensive, local **buses** make the Manzanillo-Cuyutlán connection approximately every hour until around 8 P.M. via Armería (transfer point on Highway 200), half an hour by bus from Manzanillo's **Central de Autobús** bus station.

Although freight trains still run between Cuyutlán and both Manzanillo and Colima, passenger service has been discontinued until further notice.

TO IXTAPA/PÁTZCUARO

SOUTH COLIMA BEACHES

El Paraíso

El Paraíso (pop. 1,000) is just seven miles southeast from Cuyutlán, via the local highway; turn at the right fork, four miles from the Cuyutlán *jardín*. Its beach is especially popular on Sunday and holidays with families, who eat their fill at the dozen shorefront seafood *palapas* lining the bumpy main street. El Paraíso's long strand, which extends for miles on both sides, is similar to Cuyutlán's: warm (sometimes hot), dark sand and generally gentle, rolling surf, with little or no undertow, excellent for safe wading, swimming, bodysurfing, boogie boarding, and surfing.

The good beach and seafood account for the success of the **Hotel Paraíso** and restaurant, Playa Paraíso, Armería, Colima 28300, which perches above the surf at the south end (left as you arrive) of the beachfront street. Many of the hotel's plain but clean rooms enjoy the same airy oceanfront vista as the popular restaurant. The adjacent pool and sundeck is yet another reason for spending a day or two there. The 54 rooms in the older section by the ocean rent from about $25 d (room-temperature water only). The 26 rooms in the new section across the street rent for about $29 d, with hot water and fans. Credit cards are accepted. Reserve, especially during holidays and weekends, by writing or calling the hotel, or contacting its agent in Colima, tel./fax 312/312-1032 or 312/312-4787; or directly at the hotel, tel. 313/322-4305.

Guided **mangrove jungle boat trips** take off from the dock (on the right, just before entering town) daily at about 9 A.M., 11 A.M., 1 P.M., and 3 P.M. For about $5 per person, kids half price, you're likely to see crocodiles and turtles, and (during the high winter bird season) swarms of ducks, geese, egrets, herons, cormorants, anhingas, ibis, lily walkers, parrots, and more. How much you see depends upon the sensitivity of the boatman. If he insists on plowing ahead, scattering droves of animals and birds, take control and tell him to slow down. Bring your repellent, a hat, binoculars, and your copy of Steve Howell's *Bird-Finding Guide to Mexico*. (See Suggested Reading.)

Boca de Pascuales, El Real, Tecuanillo, and Boca de Apiza

Local folks know this quartet of downscale beachside *palapa* heavens well for their gentle surf, abundant seafood, and wide-open spaces for tent and RV camping. Drivers can get to them along good paved roads from Highway 200. For bus travelers, Tecomán's town market, adjacent to the *camionera central* central bus station is the point of departure for local buses, which run frequently until around 6 P.M. After that, you might have to take a taxi.

Boca de Pascuales, eight paved miles (13 km) from Highway 200, is literally the *boca* (mouth) of the Armería River, whose waters, which begin on the snowy slope of Nevado de Colima, widen to a broad estuary. Here, they nourish schools of fish and flocks of seabirds—pelicans, cormorants, herons—which dive, swoop, and stalk for fry in the rivermouth lagoon. Fishermen wade in and catch the very same prey with throw-nets.

The beach itself is broad, with semicoarse gray sand. The waves roll gradually shoreward over a near-level, sandy shelf, and recede with little or no undertow. Consequently, swimming, boogie boarding, and bodysurfing are relatively safe, and surfing is not uncommon during the fall hurricane season. A lot of driftwood litters the sandbar, and several rentable fishing *lanchas* lay pulled up along the beach. A quarter-mile lineup of seafood *ramadas* provide shade and food for the local families who crowd in on Sundays and holidays. Find Boca de Pascuales by heading south on Highway 200 to just before Tecomán. Follow the signed turnoff road, right, southbound, about seven miles to the beach, turn right, and continue a quarter mile past the *ramadas* to the lagoon and sandbar. If you decide to stay overnight, the downscale beachfront **Hotel Perla del Real** will probably have plenty of room to accommodate you.

For more lovely beach and surf, head from Boca de Pascuales along the two miles of beachfront road to El Real (marked La Mascota on some maps). The paved road passes a file of hurricane-battered shoreline homes, separated by open spaces, good for camping or RV parking (if you don't mind occasional company). Ask if it's okay before setting up camp. Bring all of your supplies, including water; the few stores along this stretch are meagerly stocked.

Several restaurants (notably, the popular **En Ramada Boca de Río**), many of which have added pools and water slides, dot the two miles to El Real. There, a few more seafood *ramadas* crowd the corner where the road heads back about seven miles (11 km) to Highway 200 at Tecomán.

For **Tecuanillo,** head seaward at the paved Highway 200 turnoff road about a mile south of the Tecomán (south end) Pemex station. Continue about five miles to the roadside ponds of the **La Granja** restaurant, open Tues.–Sun. noon–6 P.M., just before the beach. About six acres of ponds supply loads of *langostinas* (prawns or crayfish) and *pargo* (sea bass) for on-the-spot consumption—broiled, boiled, *ranchera,* garlic, *diabla,* ceviche—any way you prefer, $6–10.

Besides its long, wide beach and good surf fishing, visitors to the hamlet of Tecuanillo enjoy the fresh offerings of a long lineup of seafood *ramadas.* Stores can supply food and drinks for picnickers, tenters, and RVers, and a hotel, the modern local-style beachfront **Hotel Las Palmas,** tel. 313/329-9222 or 313/328-8089, will most likely be able to put you up for the night.

Boca de Apiza, at the mouth of the Río Coahuayana (which forms the Colima-Michoacán border), has surfing potential, driftwood, and possible tenting spots next to a wild, mangrove jungle-lined beach. Get there by following Colima Highway 185, the signed, paved turnoff road about 21 miles (34 km) south of Tecomán. About three miles from the highway, past a mangrove channel bridge, the road splits. Ahead is a beach with some informal camping spots. Follow the left fork through a mangrove jungle (bring insect repellent) for about a mile to a second beach, where powerful surfing waves rise sharply and break both left and right. In the rainy summer and early fall, river outflow unfortunately stains the water an uninviting brown, but during the rest of the year, parking, tenting, fishing, beachcombing, and surfing might be fine here, providing it's safe. If in doubt, check with storekeepers back on the highway.

Although the fishing hamlet of **Apiza** is in Mi-

choacán, it's barely so, being just south of the Río Coahuayana. It's reachable by the paved side road about a mile south of the river bridge. A dozen seafood *ramadas,* complete with tables and hammocks, spread along the road's end 2.5 miles from the highway. The long, dark-sand beach spreads seemingly without limit on the south side, while on the other, a bamboo-hut village spreads quaintly along the boat-lined estuary bank. With a store for supplies, tenters and self-contained RV campers could fish, beachcomb, and bodysurf here for a month of Sundays.

If you'd prefer a hotel stay, try the **Hotel Sarahi,** on the road as you enter town. Owners offer clean but plain rooms with toilet and shower, for about $20 d, with fans.

TECOMÁN

Tecomán (pop. 80,000), on Highway 200, 37 miles (59 km) southeast of Manzanillo, three miles south of the Colima (Highway 110) junction, is south Colima's service center. All services are not far from Av. Insurgentes, the Highway 200 through-town main boulevard, which splits, diverting city-center traffic into a pair of one-way northbound (Manzanillo-Colima) and southbound (Michoacán) streams.

Accommodations

If you're planning to stay overnight, Tecomán offers a pair of good hotels. First choice goes to the refined and comfortable four-star **Real Motel,** on Av. Insurgentes, corner of Lic. M. Gudiño, Tecomán, Colima 28110, tel. 313/324-0100, about eight blocks north of the city center. Rates for the 80 rooms run about $46 s, $56 d, with a/c, phones, satellite TV, pool, and parking.

Alternatively, you'll find approximately the same semideluxe amenities at the **Hotel Plaza,** at Insurgentes 502, tel. 313/324-3574 or 313/324-2648, fax 313/324-2675, two blocks closer to town. Here, doubles run about $28, with a/c, TV, parking, restaurant, and phone.

Information and Services

A number of banks, all with ATMs, dot the downtown plaza-front streets. **Bital** (Banco

Internacional), tel. 313/324-6364 or 313/324-6641, with the longest hours (Mon.–Fri. 8 A.M.–6 P.M. and Sat. 8 A.M.–3 P.M.), changes money on the north side of the main plaza. Alternately, try **Banamex,** one block west of the plaza's north side, tel. 313/324-1413; or **Bancomer,** on Av. Insurgentes, tel. 313/324-0568 or 313/324-0026, about three blocks northwest of the main plaza.

For a doctor, go to 24-hour diagnostic **Clínica Centro Médico,** at 592 E. Zapata, a block off Insurgentes, about six blocks north of the main plaza, tel. 313/324-3560. Alternatively, try the **Clínica de Especialidades,** tel. 313/324-0533, with many specialists on call.

Otherwise, for simple remedies and medicines, go to one of the plaza-front *farmacias,* such as **Farmacia America,** southeast side, next to the church, tel. 313/324-0071, or **Farmacia Moderna,** on the opposite, northeast, side, tel. 313/324-1094.

The *correo,* tel. 313/324-1939, is at B. Dávalos 35, two blocks north of the main plaza. Long-distance telephone service is available from many Ladatel card–operated telephones around the central plaza. Buy a card ($3, $5, or $10) from one of many local minimarkets or drugstores. Otherwise, **Computel** long-distance telephone and public fax, tel. 313/324-3899 or 313/324-5130, open 7 A.M.–10 P.M., is at the main bus terminal.

Bus Service

A trio of cooperating bus networks operates out of the long-distance *camionera central* (central bus terminal), at the Plaza Progreso shopping mall, about four blocks west and two blocks north of the main plaza. (Local buses, which connect to nearby communities, such as Armería, Cuyutlán, El Paraíso, Tecuanillo, and Boca de Pasquales, line up on the curb in front of the town market, adjacent to the central bus terminal.

Autotransportes Sur de Jalisco (ASJ), tel. 313/324-0795, offers many daily first- and second-class departures, connecting north with Colima, Ciudad Guzmán, and Guadalajara. Northwest-southeast departures connect with with Manzanillo in the northeast end and Lázaro

Cárdenas in the southeast. Companion line **Autovias del Occidente** (AO), same phone number, offers first-class connections northeast with Michoacán, via Jiquilpan, Paracho, Uruapan, and Morelia. Cooperating line **La Linea** offers luxury-class connections with Guadalajara, and with Michoacán destinations of Nueva Italia, Uruapan, Morelia, continuing all the way to Mexico City.

In an adjacent booth, agents, tel. 313/324-6166, sell tickets for first-class Flecha Amarilla (FA) and "Primera-plus" luxury-class departures, which connect, along both northerly routes, with Colima, Manzanillo, Guadalajara, Celaya, and Querétaro and northeasterly routes, with Michoacán destinations, of Jiquilpan and Zacapu, continuing to Mexico City.

Next door, first-class **Elite** (EL), tel. 313/324-6027, coordinates its services with its Estrella Blanca companion lines. It offers several *salidas de paso* that connect daily along the Highway 200 corridor, southeast with Acapulco (via Playa Azul and Zihuatanejo) and northwest, with the U.S. border (via Manzanillo, Melaque, Puerto Vallarta, and Mazatlán).

Operating from a supplementary booth (at this writing, just outside of the main ticketing hall), first-class **Ruta Paraiso** and second-class **Galeana** buses offer connections northwest, with Manzanillo, and southeast along the Michaoacán coast via Caleta de Campos, Playa Azul-La Mira, and Lázaro Cárdenas (thence inland, north with, Nueva Italia, Uruapan, Pátzcuaro, and Morelia).

NORTHERN MICHOACÁN BEACHES

Adventure often draws travelers along the thinly populated, pristine northwestern Michoacán coast. Mostly lacking telephones and electricity, people live by natural rhythms. They rise with the sun, tend their livestock, coconuts, and papayas, take shady siestas during the heat of the day, and watch the ocean for what the tides may bring.

Outsiders often begin to enjoy the slow pace. They stop at little beaches, sit down for a soda beneath a *ramada,* ask about the fishing and the waves, and stroll along the beach. They wander, picking up shells and driftwood and saying hello to the kids and fisherfolk along the way. Charmed and fully relaxed, they sometimes linger for months.

Heading Out

If driving, fill up with unleaded gas at the Tecomán south side Pemex or the La Mira Pemex on Highway 200 a few miles south of Playa Azul (if traveling in the opposite direction). The road's empty middle section stretches 93 miles (149 km) between La Placita and Caleta de Campos with no gas station except only a few village stores selling unleaded Magna from drums. If you're driving south, note your odometer mileage at the Río Coahuayana bridge (Highway 200, Km 231) at the Colima-Michoacán border. (The northbound kilometer markers, incidentally, begin with zero at the junction with Highway 37 near Playa Azul, thus giving the distance directly from that point.) In such undeveloped, untouristed country, road mileage will help you find and remember your own favorites among Michoacán's dozens of lovely beach gems.

Bus travelers enjoy the best connections at Manzanillo *camionera central,* or Tecomán in the northwest, or Lázaro Cárdenas or La Mira (near Playa Azul) in the southeast. Bus lines, such as Autotransportes Sur de Jalisco, Ruta Paraíso, Flecha Amarilla, and Elite, run a few daily first-class local departures from both Manzanillo and Lázaro Cárdenas. Second-class Autotransportes Galeana buses run from the same terminals approximately hourly during the day, stopping everywhere and giving adventurers the option of getting off wherever they spot the palmy little heaven they've been looking for.

San Juan de Alima

Once-sleepy San Juan de Alima has now been discovered and is developing. Paralleling the highway, city fathers have built an entire wide new concrete main street where none ever was. Energized by growing numbers of visitors, especially fall-season surfers, enterprising residents have built new stores, added tiers of shiny new rooms to old hotels and opened brand new hotels on the beachfront.

San Juan de Alima's popularity comes from its long, creamy sand beach, framed between a pair of rocky headlands. Very surfable breakers roll in from about 50 yards out and recede with little undertow. All beach sports are relatively safe, except during the fall hurricane season, when the waves are 10 or 15 feet tall and surfers are as common as coconuts.

Fishing is probably best off the rocks at the sheltered north-end beach, **Playa la Punta Corrida** (see Getting There), where the very gentle waves allow easy boat launching. (Be on your guard for soft sand.) The same spot appears ripe for RV or tent camping.

Accommodations and Food: The side-by-side south-end hotels Parador and Miramar, each with about 25 rooms and its own sea-view *palapa* restaurant, are open all year. Mutual rivalry keeps their standards and prices on an approximate par. At the hotel **Miramar** (on the left as you face the beach), tel. 312/302-1355 or 313/328-8077, about $15 in either hotel gets you a spartan but clean bare-bulb room for two with toilet and shower. More deluxe rooms, with a/c, go for about $25 d. The **Hotel Parador,**, tel. 313/328-8712, besides its rooms, has the most popular restaurant in town. The family members who run it take special pride in the cooking, which invariably includes the fresh catch of the day. They're friendly, and the view from their shady tables is blue and breezy.

In third place is the rival motel-style **Hotel San Juan** and beach *palapa* restaurant, which has gained a niche on the north side of town. The 20 simply furnished but clean rooms with showers rent for about $22 d, with fan only, $35 d for a/c.

Trying harder to become San Juan de Alima's upscale destination of choice is the new **Hotel Puerta del Mar** at the far north edge of town. Watch for the hotel sign and dirt road turnoff on the highway, right side, as you're heading south. Guests in all of the simply furnished but comfortable rooms enjoy panoramic ocean views from private balconies. (However, bring your own clippable lamp shade, book light, or reading lamp—bare bulbs predominate here.) Downstairs, past the reception is a patio (with a pool maybe to be built) that leads past a small restaurant overlooking the beach and waves beyond.

TO IXTAPA/PÁTZCUARO

For reservations (not generally necessary), contact the owner in Ranchito, tel. 313/327-0564. Expect to pay about $17 d, with fans and hot water, $30 with a/c.

Getting There: San Juan de Alima is at Km 211, 12 miles (19 km) southeast of the Colima border. Get to the north-end beach, Playa la Punta Corrida, by turning off onto the dirt road at Km 212.5 north of town. After a third of a mile (.5 km), follow the left fork. Continue past the oceanography station at Mile 1.6 (Km 2.6) to the beach a half mile farther.

Playa La Brisa

At Km 207, 16 miles (26 km) south of the Colima-Michoacán line, Highway 200 reaches a breezy vista summit, where a roadside *mirador* (viewpoint) affords a look southeast. Far below, a foam-bordered white strand curves from a little palm grove, past a lagoon to a distant misty headland. This white strand is Playa La Brisa, where, beneath the little grove, the Rentería-Álvarez family members manage their miniature utopia.

Their shady grove is made for tent or self-contained RV camping. People often ask them how much they charge. "Nothing," they say. "As long as you have a little lunch or dinner in our *palapa* here, stay as long as you like."

On the very broad beach beyond the grove, the waves roll in, breaking gradually both right and left. With little or no undertow, the surf is good for swimming, boogie boarding, and bodysurfing. Furthermore, taking your clue from the name "La Brisa," you know that sailboarding is frequently good here, too.

Additionally, the lagoon a mile down the beach affords opportunities for wildlife viewing, aided by your own kayak or portable rubber boat. Fishing is also often rewarding either from the rocks beneath the headland, or by boat (your own or local *panga*) launched from the beach.

The large **Hotel El Paraíso Las Brisas** crowds the beach, 100 paces north of the Rentería-Álvarez grove. From the outside, it's a big, white stucco motel of about 30 rooms (uppers have sea-view balconies) around an inner parking patio with a kiddie pool. Inside, the rooms are thoughtfully decorated in 1990s-mode pastels and shiny,

modern-standard bathrooms with shower. However, they are smallish and lack light and natural ventilation. Consequently, some rooms are usually musty and in need of airing out. Look until you find one that satisfies you. Rentals run about $45 d, $60 t high season, with good cable TV, hot water, and restaurant; credit cards are accepted. Reserve by calling the hotel directly by cellular tel. 01-313/328-8036, or the owner's agency, tel. 313/327-4033 or 313/324-4034, in Ranchito. If you need air-conditioning, a soft bed, and a hot-water bathroom at a reasonable price on a gorgeous, secluded beach, this may be the place for you.

Getting There: Follow the dirt road at Km 205 at the base of the hill one mile to the beachfront palm grove at Playa la Brisa.

La Placita

The dusty town of La Placita (pop. 3,000) sits at Km 199 four miles south of Playa la Brisa. If it's past your bedtime, bare-bones rooms are available in the **Reyna,** a small hotel next to the north-end bridge. A restaurant, the **Zuñiga,** and pharmacies are on the highway at the central plaza; a government **Centro de Salud** (health center) is on the street that borders the south edge of the plaza; a *larga distancia* phone is on the plaza; and a new *gasolinera,* at the south end of town, if it's successful, will have unleaded gasoline.

Playa La Ticla

The broad, gray-white sands of La Ticla attract visitors—mostly surfers—for one good reason: its big, right-breaking rollers. Besides the surfing waves, a clear, sandy-banked river, fine for freshwater swimming, divides the beach in two. The town has stores and a health center. The beach has plenty of room for RV parking and tents and appears fine for camping. Unfortunately, drugs have led to problems in the past, but lately the situation appears to have improved. Check with a local storekeeper to see if this is still true.

Getting There: Turn off at the signed (notice the big La Ticla government billboard) dirt side road at Km 183, 31 miles from the Colima border. At mile 1.7 (Km 2.7), just past the big warehouse, fork left downhill to the village square.

Jog right, then left, around the square, and continue downhill, passing the red Playa sign at the next corner. Continue to the beach at Mile 2.2 (Km 3.5).

Faro de Bucerías

Idyllic perfectly describes Faro de Bucerías: a crystalline yellow-sand crescent and clear blue waters sheltered by offshore islets. The name Bucerías (Divers) suggests what local people already know: Faro de Bucerías is a top snorkeling location. Favorable conditions, such as minimal local stream runoff and a nearly pure silica-sandstone shoreline, combine to produce unusually clear water. Chance intervened to make it even better, in the form of a wreck beside the offshore Morro Elefante (Elephant Isle), where multicolored fish swarm among the corals.

Several petite sandstone bays and beaches dot the coast around the main beach, Playa de Faro de Bucerías, which has all the ingredients for a relaxing stay. The beach itself is a lovely half-mile arc, where the waves rise and crash immediately at the water's edge and recede with strong undertow. Wading is nevertheless generally safe and swimming ideal in a calm south-end nook, protected by a rocky, tidepool-laced outcropping.

For food and accommodations, beachside *palapas* serve seafood during holidays, while the well-organized **Kalaki Alt Tlayekantik** restaurant/campground at the middle of the beach serves visitors on a daily basis. You set up your tent or park your self-contained RV beneath its beachfront camping *ramada* for about $3 per person per night, toilets, freshwater showers, and drinking water.

Alternatively, try the nearby government-sponsored **Parador Turístico,** with a beach restaurant and cabanas at Playa Manzanillo, a quarter mile north.

Faro de Bucerías is heaven for fresh seafood lovers. Local divers (their spots marked by their floating offshore inner tubes) bring up daily troves of octopus, conches, clams, oysters, and lobsters, which you can buy on the spot and have cooked in the restaurant. If you prefer, catch your own from the rocks or hire a local fisherman to take you out for half a day.

For more local diversions, you can poke around in tidepools or climb to the white lighthouse *(faro)* perched atop the southeast rocky point. Another day you can walk in the opposite direction and explore little Playa Manzanilla and other hidden coves beyond the stony northeast headland.

Getting There: A big El Faro sign over the highway at Km 173 marks the Faro de Bucerías turnoff, 37 miles (60 km) from the Colima border. Just before the village store, Abarrotes Mauricia, on the right, .9 mile (1.4 km) from the highway, turn right. Pass the school on the left and continue about 300 yards to a T intersection. Turn left and continue another 200 yards to the Kalaki Alt Tlayekantik campground, at the end of the track.

Playa Maruata

This unique seaside refuge has formed where a mountain river tries to empty into the sea but is partially blocked by a pair of big rocks. Sand has collected, so the rocks appear as islands in sand rather than water. The ocean has worn away sea tunnels, which surging waves penetrate, pushing air and water, gushing and spouting onto the shore. At times, a dry sand beach builds up next to the rocks, where campers can build an evening fire and be soothed to sleep by the gurgling, booming, and whistling lullaby of Maruata.

Maruata visitors enjoy three distinctly different beaches. On the northwest, right-side, thunderous, open-ocean breakers (advanced surfing) pound a long, steep beach. A small middle beach, protected between the rocks, has oft-swimmable (with caution) water. The southeast, left-side beach is long and sheltered by the sea rocks, enclosing a shallow rivermouth lagoon. Its usually gentle waves are generally safe for wading, swimming, and boat launching. In addition, snorkeling off the rocks is often very good during the winter-spring dry season.

What's even better, the Náhuatl-speaking *ejido* owners of Playa Maruata, who once fished for turtles for living, have joined the green revolution and now maintain a turtle sanctuary, protecting the turtle from poachers. The local community has organized, under the banner of **Maruata 2000,** with the goal of preserving and protecting local wildlife and habitat in the 21st century and beyond. They back up their ideals with deeds by not allowing personal watercraft and other power sports, which, they write, "could alter the view and freedom for swimmers and scuba divers."

As part of their plan, they encourage visitors to stay in their improved facilities. They run a number of permanent *palapa* restaurants beneath the sleepy beachfront grove and rent rustic tourist *palapas* ($4 per person). They've developed a campground, where tenters can set up for about $3 per person per night and motorized folks can set up their self-contained RV for about the same.

Moreover, community members are ready with horse rentals ($10 per person), motor *lanchas* for fishing or snorkeling ($50 per trip), and boat tours ($5 per person).

Getting There: Playa Maruata is 50 miles (80 km) southeast of the Colima line at Km 150. Just south of a big bridge, a dirt turnoff road descends from the southbound lane. Continue straight across the airstrip to a gravel road, heading into the village. Turn right (north) at the village square, go about 100 yards, then left at the road that borders the village square's north side. Continue through a stream to the palm grove and *palapa* restaurant-campgrounds by the beach.

Playas Arena Blanca, Carecitos, and Pichilinguillo

Near Km 93, the rugged coastal mountains open to a stream valley, where (by a small roadside store) a narrow dirt lane winds down from the highway through a small village to Playa Arena Blanca. Here a creamy strand faces a broad blue bay, which arcs gracefully for a mile to a wave-splashed south-end headland. Prospects appear excellent for swimming, beachcombing, and surf- and rock-casting. During calm mornings boat-launching wouldn't be difficult, as evidenced by the *pangas* pulled up on the beach. Seafood lovers are in heaven here, with the fish, octopuses, and oysters that local fisherfolk and divers bring in and sell right on the beach. For water and limited additional supplies, little stores and restaurants in the village and on the highway (a half mile north at the truck stop) are available.

Even prettier and more intimate is neighboring Playa Carecitos, a crescent of yellow sand enfolded by sandstone cliffs, accessible from Playa Arena Blanca by ducking around the north-end cliff corner. Big rolling surfable breakers rise in the middle of a petite bay, while tranquil billows lap the sand on the sheltered northwest end. The sand curves a few hundred yards past scattered shoreline rocks, where snorkeling and fishing (by either surf- or rock-casting) appear promising, while shells, driftwood, and even a semipermanent sand volleyball court enrich the beach possibilities. On one side, a food *palapa* appears ready to be renovated to serve holiday visitors.

Playa Carecitos might be good for at least a pleasant afternoon, perhaps more. Temporary palm-thatch *ramadas,* apparently ready for new camper-occupants, usually stand on the beach.

If you get to Carecitos, check out petite **Pichilinguillo** bay and beach just half a mile north. Enterprising owner-builder Lazio has built a restaurant and four view cabanas, ready for visitors, on the slope above the beach.

Barra de Nexpa

While well known as one of Pacific Mexico's best surfing beaches, Barra de Nexpa's appeal is not limited to surfers. Don Gilberto, the grandfatherly founder of this pocket paradise, will gladly tell you all about it (in Spanish, of course). As more people arrived, facilities were added. First, Don Gilberto built *palapas*, a well, and showers. Then he built a restaurant, which his son now runs. Next door, another family, the Mendozas, built a laid-back RV and tenting park along the palmy shoreline of the adjacent freshwater lagoon. Gradually they put together a line of Robinson Crusoe–like rustic driftwood beach houses along the sandbar.

Although Don Gilberto's and the Mendozas' enterprises grew, the natural setting remained unchanged. The breakers (10-footers are common) still roll in, often curling into tubes, to the delight of both surfers and surf-watchers. Nexpa's big waves, however, need not discourage waders and swimmers, who splash and paddle in the freshwater lagoon instead. Beachcombers savor many hours picking through driftwood and shells, while birdwatchers enjoy watching dozens of species preen, paddle, stalk, and flap in the lagoon. And finally, when tired of all of these, everyone enjoys the hammocks, which seem to hang from every available Nexpa post and palm.

At the height of the fall-winter season, when lots of surfers and campers crowd in, the atmosphere is generally communal and friendly. At the *palapa* restaurant, on the beach, or in the shade beneath the palms and the *ramadas,* you won't lack company. (*Note:* Palmy surfing havens such as Barra de Nexpa are sometimes marred by one or two light-fingered individuals. Don't forget to safely stow your valuables.)

Although Don Gilberto and his son are still renting only rustic *palapas* for about $7 per person, with shared toilet and showers, Jorge Mendoza and his American wife, Helen, next door (left as you enter) offer more. Besides their driftwood beach *palapas,* they've built comfortable, modern-standard hotel rooms, each with room-temperature shower baths, all beside a green, grassy beachfront garden, a kiddie playground, and *palapa* restaurant. Rentals for the beachfront *palapas* are about $8 d, the hotel rooms, with two beds about $20. The adjacent RV-camping park, managed by Jorge's brother Chicho, charges about $2 per person per night. Additionally, Jorge and Chicho rent surfboards, kayaks, boogie boards, and arrange fishing excursions by *lancha,* from the beach. For reservations and more information, email helennex@hotmail.com, or visit the website www.surf-mexico-rio-nexpa.com.

Getting There: At Km 56, 109 miles (175 km) southeast of the Colima border, follow the unmarked dirt road, which curves sharply from the highway, following an uphill slope. It continues, bumping and winding downhill about half a mile to the beach. The road appears negotiable when dry by ordinary cars and RVs, even perhaps big motor homes. If in doubt, do a preliminary run.

Caleta de Campos

Caleta de Campos (pop. 3,000) is at the signed turnoff of Km 50, 112 miles (181 km) southeast of the Colima border. Sometimes called Bahía de Bufadero (Blowhole Bay), Caleta de Campos

is the metropolis and service center for this corner of Michoacán. With a long, golden-sand beach beside a blue bay, the beach is a haven for both touring visitors and commercial fishing launches. Snorkeling and pole casting prospects appear excellent, off the rocky shelf and breakwater jetty beneath the north-side headland. Likewise, tenting, RV parking, beachcombing, surfing, and surf-fishing prospects appear equally fine, on the beach's palm-shaded far south end.

A lineup of seafood *palapas* in the middle of the beach supply fresh seafood meals for visitors. Fishing *pangas* may be hired on the beach. A half-day excursion (about $50) typically returns with 50 pounds of *huachinango* (snapper), *cabrilla* (sea bass), *sierra* (mackerel), *robalo* (snook), and *atún* (tuna). Anyone can launch a boat on the beach's protected northwest end. Get to the beach, via the access road, right, southbound, about a quarter mile south of the main signed town entrance.

Accommodations: Caleta's most visible hotel, the **Hotel Yuritzi,** perches on the hill above the beach. The family owners have remodeled and rebuilt their originally plain establishment into something more upscale and comfortable, adding about 10 modern-standard rooms and an inviting view pool-patio and a restaurant. A big yard within the fenced hotel compound can also accommodate large RVs (no hookups, however). The 26 rooms, all with hot-water shower baths, rent for about $20 s, $25 d, with fan, $33 s, $40 d, with a/c. Reservations are generally necessary only during Christmas and Easter holidays; contact the hotel at tel. 753/531-5010, fax 753/531-5020, or write the hotel a few weeks in advance, address simply Caleta de Campos, Michoacán.

The friendly family owners of Hotel Yuritzi take special pride in their don't-miss-it **homemade ice cream,** which they make in luscious chocolate, vanilla, coconut, and strawberry flavors. If you do nothing else, be sure to stop by for a sample.

Lower profile **Hotel Los Arcos** stands on the hillside downhill, one block west, of the Hotel Yuritzi, at Heróica Escuela Naval 5, Caleta de Campos, Michoacán, tel. 753/531-5038. The on-site husband-wife owners offer three breezy floors of 32 clean but simply furnished bare-bulb rooms, many with panoramic ocean views, some even with a view of the famous spouting *bufadora* (blowhole). Rooms, all with hot water showers, rent for about $20 d low season, $25 d high, with fan; $40 d with a/c.

Across the street from Hotel Yuritzi, American expatriate-surfer "Gringo John" and his Mexican wife, Alfa, operate **Surf y Espuma** (Surf and Foam) laundry and surfing shop. Besides surfboard ($8) and boogie board ($6) rentals and sales, beach clothes, hats, and friendly information, they offer accommodations—four comfortable rooms and a one-bedroom kitchenette apartment—in a house with pool, luxuriously perched on an ocean-vista slope nearby. Rooms rentals begin at $35 for two in double bed, ($45 d for king-sized bed), with fans and kitchen privileges; and about $60 d for the apartment. For more information and reservations, dial tel./fax 753/531-5255. (Get to Hotels Yuritzi and Los Arcos via the main town entrance street. Turn left after two blocks, then after a block, turn right at the Los Arcos sign, continue straight ahead another block to Hotel Yuritzi.)

Another local American expatriate property owner, Eric Kaufman, told me that he offers his nearby three-bedroom, three-bath deluxe house, **Casa de Caleta** for rent for $400 per night. For reservations and more information, call tel. 753/539-1715, email ekaufman007@yahoo.com, or visit his website www.casadecaleta.com,

Food and Services: Most of Caleta's stores and institutions are scattered along its single main street, which leads directly from the signed highway entrance. A new pavement, which replaced the former bumpy, dusty surface, is a source of so much community pride that shopkeepers sweep the storefront concrete clean both morning and night. There you'll find a *larga distancia* telephone office, tel./fax 753/531-5004 through 753/531-5006, a *farmacia*, a grocery, a dentist, doctors, and a Centro de Salud (health center) on a side street nearby. Of the several streetfront eateries, Alfa, knowledgeable co-owner of the Surf and Espuma shop, recommends **Restaurant Las Adelitas.**

Buses stop frequently at either the Highway 200 crossing or the small station on the dirt main street a block uphill. They include Ruta Paraíso first-class, Galeana second-class, and Sur de Jalisco second-class, all running between Manzanillo and Lázaro Cárdenas, and first-class Elite, running the nearly the entire Pacific coast route, U.S. border to Acapulco. Executive-class "Plus" buses run between Lázaro Cárdenas and Guadalajara; and local minibuses run to and from Lázaro Cárdenas, via La Mira and the Playa Azul junction. Drivers of mini- and second-class buses will generally let you off anywhere along the highway you request.

Around Caleta de Campos: A number of plumy havens north and south of Caleta are lately offering more reasons to stop, take a look, and perhaps linger. Worth investigating is **Playa Las Cabañas,** at Km 52, beneath a long, gorgeous beach and grove. At this writing there were several thatched *palapas* (with permanent concrete hotel rooms under construction) around an invitingly blue pool-patio. A restaurant now and and maybe a store in the near future will supply picnickers, tenters, and RVers who decide to set up beneath the beachfront palms.

Also consider **Playa Soledad,** at Km 36, about nine miles (14 km) south of Caleta. Visible a few hundred yards below the highway, a creamy, rock-enfolded beach decorates the shoreline. Several permanent *palapa* restaurants laze in the shade beneath the palms. Rustic cabanas or hotel rooms will probably soon join them.

Three miles (four km) farther south, at Km 32, at Chuquiapan (choo-kee-AH-pan), a beach road leads a quarter mile to **Playa Porto Bello,** a beach village of several permanent *palapa* seafood restaurants beneath a shorefront palm grove. Rollers from 100 yards out break gradually on a soft grey-sand beach. No hotel had yet been built at this writing, but one fenced-in *ramada* and plenty of open space was available for tenting and RV parking.

Hotel Villa Dorada

Developers, working to establish a luxury beach vacation-home community, have built Hotel Villa Dorada as the anchor of a big planned shoreline subdivision, a few miles north of Playa

Azul. The hotel, envisioned as a beach club for a regiment of well-heeled retirees and vacationers, offers 21 palm-shaded modern kitchenette bungalows, built around a gorgeously spacious beachfront pool-patio. The attractive deluxe units are decorated with white stucco walls, colorful Mexican tile, and furnished with handsome hand-hewn wood furniture and up-to-date appliances. Guests in beachfront units enjoy ocean views.

The lavish facilities include tennis and basketball courts, a soccer field, table games, a kiddie pool and playground, and a restaurant. This is a great spot for families with kids, who stay free with parents, for about $100 per night (ask for a discount, especially May–June, and Sept.–Dec. 15). The main drawback to Hotel Villa Dorada

appears to be isolation; weekdays, the place is often nearly empty. However, you can easily drive or taxi into Playa Azul for the excitement and color of real Mexico, then retire to the peace and quiet of your Hotel Villa Dorada refuge.

Reserve by contacting the hotel directly, at tel. 753/535-1084, toll-free Mex. tel. 800/719-8587, or at its Morelia office, tel. 443/314-8102, fax 443/314-8309.

Get to Hotel Villa Dorada by car or local bus, at the signed side road at Km 7.5, about 25 miles (42 km) south of Caleta de Campos, about five miles (7.5 km) north of Playa Azul. Continue 1.4 miles (2.5 km), to a village; jog left, then right, toward the beach. Continue another mile south along the beach to the hotel.

Playa Azul

It's easy to see how Playa Azul (Blue Beach) got on the map of Pacific Mexico. The beach is long and level, the sand is yellow and silky. The waves roll in slowly, swish gently, and stop, leaving wet, lazy arcs upon the sand. At sunset, these glow like medallions of liquid gold.

Around Town

Playa Azul (pop. 5,000) is a small town on a big beach with a mile of *palapa* seafood restaurants. Four bumpy streets, Carranza, Madero, Independencia, and Justo Sierra, parallel the beach-front *malecón* walkway. Much of the activity clusters on or near a fifth street (actually a dirt lane), Aquiles Serdán, which bisects the other four and ends at the *malecón*. Here the atmosphere—piquant aromas of steaming *pozole* and hot tacos, the colorful mounds of papayas and tomatoes, the language and laughter of the people—is uniquely and delightfully Mexican.

Note: Playa Azul is so far south and east in Pacific Mexico, that the Pacific Ocean lies to the south. The reason is that on the map of western Mexico, the Pacific coastline bends easterly the farther south it runs, until in Acapulco and Oaxaca, the coastline runs nearly due east-west. You can best observe this in Playa Azul at sunset, when you will see the sun in a direction roughly

parallel to the shoreline. Since the sun, world-wide, virtually always sets in a westerly direction, you notice that the direction south, 90 degrees counterclockwise from west, is where you see the Pacific Ocean.

Beach Activities

Geography nothwithstanding, the Playa Azul beach is good for just about everything. The waves, big enough for surfing as they break far offshore, roll shoreward, picking up boogie boarders and bodysurfers along the way, finally rippling around the ankles of waders and splashers at the sand's edge. Concessionaires rent chairs, umbrellas, and boogie boards, but few, if any, surfboards. The weekend crowds keep the beach relatively free of shells and drift-wood, although pickings will be better farther out along the beach (which stretches many miles in either direction).

Eating is another major Playa Azul beach occupation. Fruit vendors stroll the sand, offering luscious cut pineapple, watermelon, and man-goes-on-a-stick, while semipermanent beach stands and dozens of *malecón* restaurants offer fresh *cócktel de ostión* (oyster cocktail, $6), *langostina al gusto* (prawns any style, $9), and *langosta al vapor* (steamed lobster, $12).

Laguna Pichi

Playa Azul's long, creamy beach is interrupted only during the summer rainy season, when the Laguna Pichi (follow main street Independencia about a mile east of town) overflows and spills into the ocean. Most of the time, however, it's a big blue freshwater lake, bordered by palms and *palapa* restaurants. The lagoon provides visitors with a variety of diversions, such as super-fresh seafood, wading and swimming, fishing, and viewing the battalion of waterbirds that cackle, paddle, and preen in the clear lagoon. The prepared can set up tents for camping along the sandy shore (bring repellent) and venture out in their kayaks and rubber boats (or lacking those, hire a boat) for bird-watching and wildlife-viewing in the lagoon's mangrove wilderness reaches.

ACCOMMODATIONS

Playa Azul has about half a dozen hotels, one with a trailer park. Four of them stand out.

One block from the beach, the triple-tiered main building of the **Hotel Playa Azul and Trailer Park,** Av. V. Carranza s/n, Playa Azul, Michoacán 60982, tel./fax 753/536-0024 or 753/536-0091, fax 753/536-0090, surrounds a lovely patio with tall palms, rubber trees, and giant-leafed vines. A spacious blue swimming pool curves artfully in the middle, while the bar and restaurant are tucked beneath a soaring beamed *palapa* on one side. The shady patio invites quiet relaxation; other rooms offer TV and Ping-Pong. Families especially enjoy the hotel's water-slide minipark (beachside, behind the main building past the trailer park). The 70 rooms, spacious and comfortable but a bit worn, come in economy and standard versions. Economy rooms (with fan only, on the ground floor by the parking lot) rent for about $30 s or d; standard rooms go for about $36 s or d, with fan only, about $54 with a/c, add $5 per extra person. Ask for a low-season discount. Parking is available, credit cards are ac-

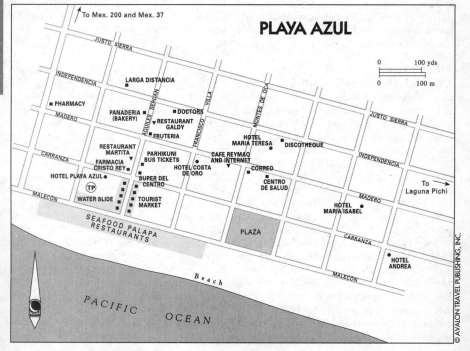

PLAYA AZUL

THE MAR DEL SUR

It's surprising to many travelers that Pacific Mexico runs farther east than it does south. From the Michoacán coast southward (or more accurately, eastward) the Pacific Mexico coastline, instead of running mostly north-south as in Mazatlán and Puerto Vallarta, runs essentially east-west. Here, the Pacific Ocean becomes truly the Mar del Sur (Ocean of the South) that the early Spanish explorers named it. Consequently, in Playa Azul, Zihuatanejo, Acapulco, and on the entire Oaxaca coast, streets that run parallel to the shore run east-west, and those perpendicular to the shore run north-south.

You can convince yourself of this by simply observing sunrise or sunset on the beach. For example, in Playa Azul and points south, notice that the sun rises and sets in direction roughly parallel to the shoreline. Since it's true that the sun rises generally in the east and sets in the west, worldwide, it follows that the southerly compass direction, 90 degrees counterclockwise from west, must coincide with the direction of the Pacific Ocean.

cepted, and some ground-level rooms are wheelchair-accessible.

The trailer park, with about a dozen spaces crowded behind the hotel, is nevertheless popular, since guests have access to the hotel pools and restaurant. Cramped spaces (up to about 30 feet) rent for about $18 per day with all hookups, including power for air-conditioning, toilets, and hot showers. Discounts for lower power and weekly and monthly stays are available. Contact the hotel for reservations, which are mandatory for the trailer park during the winter.

The **Hotel María Teresa,** Av. Independencia 626, Playa Azul, Michoacán 60982, tel. 753/536-0005 or 753/536-0150, fax 753/536-0055, three blocks east of Aquiles Serdán and three short blocks from the beach, stands within an airy garden compound, with parking on one side and an attractive *palapa* restaurant and sunny pool and patio tucked on the other. Its discotheque, Playa Azul's only one, is nearly always quiet, but may occasionally heat up on the hol-

idays. If this is the case, request a room on the relatively *tranquilo* wing farthest from the disco. The 42 comfortable, near-deluxe rooms, all with TV, phones, and a/c, rent for about $39 s, $45 d, and $54 t; credit cards are accepted, and there's limited wheelchair access.

Most of Playa Azul's cheaper accommodations lack hot water, a serious drawback for many winter vacationers. One exception is the **Hotel María Isabel,** four blocks east of the center of town, at Av. F. Madero s/n, Playa Azul 60982, Michoacán, tel. 753/536-0016, fax 753/532-0369. Its two stories of approximately 20 simply but comfortably furnished motel-modern rooms cluster around an interior pool and patio one block from the beach. Rooms rent for about $15 s, $25 d, with fans (and $35 and $45 with a/c), and hot water.

If the María Isabel is full, fourth choice goes to the closer-in **Hotel Costa de Oro,** a block east of A. Serdán, at Av. F. Madero s/n, Playa Azul, Michoacán 60982, no phone, two blocks from the beach. The 14 spartan rooms rent from about $10 s or d, $15 t, with fans and hot water.

The new **Hotel Andrea,** at the corner of Librado Rivera and E. Zapata, closer to the beach, will probably be open by the time you read this. Priced right, at $10 s, $15 d, with hot water, it might be worth checking out. For reservations and information, call the owners Benigno Villa Rios and María Guadalupe Sánchez Lucatero, at tel. 753/536-0251.

FOOD

Avenida Aquiles Serdán (at the Hotel Playa Azul corner) offers several possibilities. Evenings, a squad of taco stalls open. Their steaming tacos—of *res* (roast beef), chorizo (spicy sausage), and *lengua* (tongue)—wrapped in hot tortillas and spiced with piquant salsas make perfect appetizers.

For an equally tasty second course, walk down Serdán past the corner of Madero and take a streetside table at **Restaurant Galdy,** begun in 1968. Now retired, the original Galdy rests while her daughter Alexandra continues Galdy's tradition. Alejandra recommends that her customers order the house specialty, *frijoles*

TO IXTAPA/PÁTZCUARO

charros, a rich meat, vegetable, *chile,* and bean stew, simmered to perfection. Served Friday, Saturday, and Sunday only. For a final course any day, pick one of the hearty country specialties for which Galdy's hard-working all-women cadre of cooks and waitresses is well-known: such as its hearty *pozole* (soup), *pierna* (roast pork), and *platos Mexicanos* (combination plates). Open daily 7 A.M.–11 P.M.

For dessert, step back to the Madero corner to **Frutería Berenice** for a succulent selection of fruit. Local mangoes (spring, summer), pineapple, and *platanos* (bananas) will be familiar, but *guanabanas* (green and scaly, like an artichoke) and *ciruelas* (yellow and round, like a plum) probably will not. Open daily 6:30 A.M.–9 P.M.

To top everything off, cross Serdán to the *panadería* and pick up some cake, cookies, or *donas;* open Mon.–Sat. 7 A.M.–10 P.M.

For a change of scene, go to the fanciest restaurant in town, beneath the big inner-patio *palapa* of the **Hotel Playa Azul.** Your reward will be tasty appetizers, salads, pizza, pasta, meat, seafood, and chicken entrées, professionally prepared and served. Open daily 7:30 A.M.–10 P.M.

ENTERTAINMENT AND SHOPPING

Playa Azul's evening entertainment begins with the sunset, views of which are unobstructed year-round. The effect is doubly beautiful, for the sky's golden glow is reflected from both the ocean and Playa Azul's shoreline swaths of flat wet sand. Sunset is also an excellent time for joggers and walkers to take advantage of the cool sea breeze and Playa Azul's level, firm sand.

The **tourist market,** beneath the awnings stretched over Aquiles Serdán next to the Hotel Playa Azul, has several stands that offer beach balls, T-shirts, and bathing suits. Some of the more common crafts, such as painted ceramic animals and papier-mâché, may be available also.

The friendly **Super del Centro** grocery, Av. Aquiles Serdán (at the Hotel Playa Azul corner), has a little bit of everything, from cheese and milk to mops and *espirales mosquitos* (mosquito coils). Open daily 7:30 A.M.–9 P.M.

INFORMATION AND SERVICES

Playa Azul has only a few services. Go to Lázaro Cárdenas, 14 miles (22 km) east along Highway 200, for what Playa Azul lacks.

If you get sick, consult one of the town **doctors,** either Dr. Mayolo Martínez Razo or gyecologist Dr. Mauro Irra Hernany, who maintain offices on Independencia, a few doors east of the Aquiles Serdán corner, or go to the very modest Centro de Salud on the town plaza. Alternatively, hire a taxi to take you to either the **Centro de Salud,** tel. 753/535-0004, in La Mira (five miles, at the Highway 200 and Highway 37 intersection), or the big **Seguro Social General Hospital,** tel. 753/532-0900, 753/532-0901, or 753/532-0902, in Lázaro Cárdenas.

For routine drugs and medications, go to the **Farmacia Cristo Rey,** corner of Carranza and Aquiles Serdán, across the street from the Hotel Playa Azul, open Mon.–Sat. 9 A.M.–9 P.M.

The Playa Azul *correo* (post office) is open Mon.–Fri. 8 A.M.–3 P.M., next to the Centro de Salud, two blocks from the beach and two blocks from Aquiles Serdán. For telephone, go to the private *larga distancia* on Independencia, one block west of the Aquiles Serdán corner.

Connect to the **Internet,** at Café Rey Maq, tel. 753/536-0209, at the corner of Madero and Montes de Aca, two blocks east of Aquiles Serdán, before the post office; open daily 9 A.M.–10 P.M.

GETTING THERE AND AWAY

By Bus: Just before bus arrival at Playa Azul, ask your driver to drop you at the Highway 200-Highway 37 Playa Azul junction (three miles from Playa Azul, two miles from La Mira), where a taxi or local minibus can take you the rest of the way.

Long-distance bus departure has been greatly simplified by **Parhikuni** buses that leave twice daily for Morelia, via Uruapan and Pátzcuaro (at 7 A.M. and 10:30 P.M. respectively), from the corner of Aquiles Serdán and Carranza. Get reserved tickets at Cynthia Restaurant, tel. 753/536-0111, a few doors north of the same corner.

For other departures, go to La Mira (five miles by local minibus or taxi) and wait at the intersection of Highways 200 and 37. Although most Manzanillo-, Pátzcuaro-, and Zihuatanejo-bound buses stop and pick up passengers frequently at La Mira during daylight hours, reserved seats are available only from the Lázaro Cárdenas stations.

By Car or RV: Paved Highway 200 connects Playa Azul with Manzanillo in the northwest (195 miles, 314 km). Although the route is in good condition and lightly traveled most of the way, its twists and turns through rugged oceanside canyons and along spectacular shoreline ridges make it considerably slow going. Allow at least six hours for safety. If the Playa Azul Pemex is open, fill up with gasoline as you start out (otherwise gas up at La Mira or maybe Caleta), since the first reliably available Magna (unleaded) heading northeast is in Tecomán, about 167 miles (240 km) from Playa Azul (or if you're lucky, in La Placita, 125 miles or 199 km from Playa Azul).

Between Playa Azul and Ixtapa-Zihuatanejo in the southeast, the route is relatively short and straight, although trucks sometimes slow progress. Allow 2.5 hours for the 76-mile (122-km) trip.

For Pátzcuaro and central Michoacán in the north, you have a pair of options: either the new toll *autopista* 37 D, about 3.5 hours (157 miles, 253 km) to Uruapan, four hours (196 miles, 317 km) to Pátzcuaro, and five hours (239 miles, 384 km) to Morelia. Connect with the *autopista* in the northern outskirts of Lázaro Cárdenas. Drive east from Playa Azul along Highway 200 about 12 miles (19 km); fork right on to the signed Lázaro Cárdenas entrance boulevard. Continue approximately one mile to the first signalled intersection. Turn left, and after another mile you arrive at the expressway entrance toll gate, at the first Río Balsas bridge.

Alternatively, old Highways 37 and 14 connect Pátzcuaro and Central Michoacán in the north, with Playa Azul, over 191 miles (307 km) of winding mountain highway. Although paved all the way, this route—through fertile valleys and over pine-shadowed crests—is potholed in places and occasionally congested. Allow at least seven hours for safety. Magna unleaded gasoline is available only at Arteaga, Nueva Italia, and Uruapan, so keep filled. As for *bandidos,* stick to the main highway for security. Many mountain folks cultivate marijuana and opium. They're understandably suspicious of wandering strangers.

Pátzcuaro

The high road from Playa Azul leads inland to Pátzcuaro (pop. 70,000), a city brimming with inspirations. Pine- and cedar-brushed mountains ring it, an islet-studded lake borders it. Its air is fresh and clean and the sky always seems blue. Visitors come from all over the world to wander through narrow colonial lanes, buy fine copper and lacquerware, and gaze at grand, mystery-shrouded monuments of long-forgotten emperors.

HISTORY

Before the Conquest

The valley and lake of Pátzcuaro, elev. 7,500 feet (2,280 meters), have nurtured civilizations for millennia. The Tarascans, whose king, Tariácuri, rebuilt the city during the 1370s, were the last and the greatest dynasty. To them the lake and surrounding grounds were sacred: the door to the land of their ancestors. They chose the venerated foundation stones of already-ancient temples as the new city's cornerstones, marking the symbolic door to the land of the dead: *tzacapuamúcutin-pátzcuaro* (stone door where all changes to blackness). The last part of that original name remains in use today.

The founders of Pátzcuaro did not call themselves Tarascans. This was from the Spanish word, meaning "son-in-law." Before the conquest, Pátzcuaro people called (and still call) themselves the Purépecha (poo-REH-peh-chah). After they arrived in 1521, the Spanish increasingly applied their own label as they intermarried with the Pátzcuaro people.

Before the conquest, the Valley of Pátzcuaro was the center of a grand Purépecha empire, which extended beyond the present-day borders

To Lago Pátzcuaro, Boat Dock,
Isla Janitzio, Jaracuaro,
Erongaricuaro, and
West Lakeshore

To Hotel San Carlos

14

120

To Uruapan and Playa Azul

To El Pozo Trailer Park, Ihuatzio, Tzintzuntzán,
Morelia, Guadalajara, and Mexico City

AV. LÁZARO CÁRDENAS

MOTEL DEL LAGO

HOTEL VILLA
PÁTZCUARO

HOTEL DON VASCO

PÁTZCUARO

CALZ. DE LAS AMÉRICAS

HOSTERÍA
SAN FELIPE

RESTAURANT
LA COCINA DE
LOS ANGELES

AHUMADA

EFREN   URICHO

CRUZ   VERDE

DEL PANTEON

SAN JOSE

ÁLVARO

OBREGON

INDUSTRIAS

CORREO
TELEGRAFO

TITERE

CALLE

LARGA
DISTANCIA

CINE
EMPERADOR

HOTEL FIESTA PLAZA

EX-TEMPLO SAN AGUSTIN

HOSTAL DEL
VALLE

LIBERTAD

CALLE PADRE   LLOREDA

DEGOLLADO

MERCADO

CALLE VOLADOR

HOTEL CONCORDIA

BANAMEX

PLAZA
GERTRUDIS
BOCANEGRA

HOTEL
VALMEN

TURISMO
(INFORMATION)

HOTEL POSADA DE
LA BASÍLICA

AHUMADA

ARCIGA

BASÍLICA

RAMOS REGULES

EL SANTUARIO

BENITO   JUAREZ

GRAN
HOTEL

RESTAURANT
DON RAFA

JANITZIO TOURS

INTERNET

LA PAZ

TURBE

PUNTOCOM (INTERNET)

BANCO INTERNACIONAL

BANCOMER

HOTEL RINCÓNDE JOSEFA

BENIGNO   SERRATO

HOTEL
POSADA DE
LA SALUD

INTERNET

RAM TOURS

RESTAURANT
LA CASONA

BANCO
SERFIN

EX-COLEGIO SAN
NICOLAS

ENSEÑANZA

POLICE STATION

IBARRA

ABARROTES
LA SURTIDORA

HOTEL MANSIÓN
ITURBE

QUIROGA

ALCANTARILLAS

RESTAURANT
LA COMPANIA

EX-COLEGIO
JESUITO

To Hospital

HOTEL LOS
ESCUDOS

PLAZA DON
VASCO

CALLE PORTUGAL

LA COMPAÑIA DE
JESUS CHURCH

EMILIO

PLAZA
REVOLUCION

ABARROTES ROSY

HOTEL MISIÓN
SAN MANUEL

REST. LA
ESCALERA

LERIN

POSADA MANDALA

LAUNDRY

TERAN

PONCE   DE   LEON

FEDERICO TENO

CAFE BOTE FUMEIRA

HOTEL POSADA SAN RAFAEL

CRAFTS
STORES

JOSE M. COS

CARRANZA

RESTAURANT
EL PATIO

RESTAURANT MISTONGO

CASA BRUNSON B&B

To Central Camionera,
Santa Clara del Cobre,
Lake Zirahuen, and
Playa Azul

CONSULTORIO
DEL CENTRO

HOTEL MESON
DEL GALLO

CASA DE ONCE
PATIOS

NAVARRETE

DR. NAVARRETE

0   200 yds

0   200 m

© AVALON TRAVEL PUBLISHING, INC.

of the state of Michoacán. Local folk are still proud that their ancestors were never subjects of the Aztecs, whose armies they defeated and slaughtered by the tens of thousands on the eve of the conquest.

Conquest and Colonization

As Hernán Cortés approached the Valley of Mexico, the jittery Aztec emperor Moctezuma sent ambassadors to Tzintzuntzán (seen-soon-SAHN), the Purépecha capital on the shore of the lake a dozen miles northwest of Pátzcuaro. The ambassadors implored King Zuangua, known by his imperial title *caltzonzin*, to send an army to help repel Cortés. The *caltzonzin* refused, hastening Moctezuma's downfall and perhaps his own.

The first Spaniards, a few seemingly harmless travelers, wandered into the Valley of Pátzcuaro in 1521. The smallpox they unwittingly brought, however, was far from harmless. Zuangua soon succumbed to the ugly disease, along with tens of thousands of his subjects.

The Spanish military threat, in the person of conquistador Cristóbal de Olid and 70 mounted cavalry, 200 foot soldiers, and thousands of native allies, arrived at Tzintzuntzán in 1522. As the new *caltzonzin*, Tangaxoan II, fled to Uruapan, Olid quickly appropriated the imperial treasure and the gold and jewels from the temples. After a short resistance, Tangaxoan II pledged his homage to Cortés and was soon baptized, accepting the Christian name of Pedro. By 1526, most of his subjects had followed suit.

Peace reigned, but not for long. Cortés was called back to Spain, and the gold-hungry opportunist Nuño de Guzmán took temporary control in Mexico City. In late 1528, Guzmán had the *caltzonzin* tortured and killed. The Spanish royal government, alarmed by Guzmán's excesses, sent an official panel, called the Second Audiencia, to replace him. Guzmán, one jump ahead of them, cleared out in command of a battalion of like-minded adventurers, hell-bent to find another Tenochtitlán in western Mexico. They pounced upon the Purépecha, burning, raping, and pillaging the Valley of Pátzcuaro.

Vasco de Quiroga

The Purépecha fortunes began to improve when Father Vasco de Quiroga, a member of the Second Audiencia, arrived in 1533. At the age of 63 he began his life's work on the shore of Lake Pátzcuaro. Through his kindness, compassion, and tireless energy, Don Vasco gained the confidence of the Purépecha. He immediately established a hospital for the care of the poor. Named Santa Fe de la Laguna, it still stands by the lakeshore.

Appointed bishop in 1538, Don Vasco moved the episcopal seat from Tzintzuntzán to Pátzcuaro, which had already become the provincial government headquarters. Pressing ahead, he immediately began the Colegio San Nicolas. Its features became the model for many more: a hospital for the care of the poor, a school to educate young Tarascans, and a seminary for training bilingual Tarascan priests.

Pátzcuaro's rich handicrafts heritage is partly due to Don Vasco. He moderated the Tarascans' *encomienda* obligations so that they had time to become self-sustaining on their communal and individual plots. Entire villages became centers of specific skills and trades. Such traditions remain: Santa Clara turns out fine copperware; Tzintzuntzán, furniture. Other valley communities produce elaborate baskets, delicate lacquerware, and handsome saddles.

Don Vasco toiled until his death in 1565 at the age of 95. Pátzcuaro people still adore him. Children often leave flowers at the foot of his statue in the plaza at the very heart of the city.

IN-TOWN SIGHTS
Getting Oriented

From the good bishop's tree-shaded bronze image in the main **Plaza Don Vasco de Quiroga,** the city spreads out along half a dozen north-south and east-west main streets. **Av. Mendoza** runs from the northwest plaza corner one long block north to the city's second square, **Plaza Gertrudis Bocanegra,** named for the city's renowned independence heroine. The **market** spreads from the northwest side of Plaza Bocanegra, while past the south end, Av. La Paz runs uphill (east) two blocks to the **basilica.**

Back at the main plaza's northeast corner, a second main thoroughfare, **Av. Amuhada,** runs north, becoming Av. Lázaro Cárdenas, the main highway-access route. It continues about two miles to the east-west Uruapan-Morelia highway and the railroad station. Crossing the railroad tracks at the station, a branch road leads about a mile north to the **Lake Pátzcuaro** embarcadero, where boats depart for Janitzio and other islands.

Getting Around

Virtually everything downtown is within a few blocks of the Plaza Don Vasco de Quiroga. For trips out of the city, hail a taxi or ride a white *colectivo* van of your choice, for about $.30 (read the destinations on the windows), from in front of the Hotel Los Escudos at the Plaza Don Vasco de Quiroga corner of Ibarra and Mendoza or on the Plaza Bocanegra in front of the market.

A Walk Around Old Pátzcuaro

The natural place to start is at the center of the

GERTRUDIS BOCANEGRA, HEROINE OF PÁTZCUARO

Independence heroine Gertrudis Bocanegra de Lazo de la Vega was born into a well-to-do Pátzcuaro family on April 11, 1765. Her outspoken nature emerged at an early age. Once, as a young child, on her family balcony overlooking Pátzcuaro's main plaza, she was horrified at the sight of an unruly mob beating a helpless beggar with sticks. She cried out from the top of her lungs, but the crowd took little notice. She retreated inside, sobbing, to her mother's arms. The incident indelibly marked her; from then on, the oppressed had a ready defender in Gertrudis Bocanegra.

As she was growing up, young Gertrudis, like many of her Mexican criollo generation, was inspired by the European liberal ideas of liberty and justice and the daring deeds that led to the American Revolution.

When she arrived at marriageable age, more than just a few young suitors competed for her affections. Pedro Lazo de la Vega, a young criollo second lieutenant of the local army garrison, won Gertrudis's heart with a secret note, declaring his fervent admiration. Soon he proposed marriage, but she imposed one severe condition: she would not marry someone in the service of Mexico's colonial oppressors; in exchange for her consent, her fiancée would have to resign his military commission.

For young Pedro, this was no small matter. Criollos (Mexican-born of pure Spanish descent) such as he had few good professional career options; the most prestigious positions were traditionally reserved for *peninsulares,* Spanish-born colonists, derisively known as *gachupines.* Even after Pedro promised to quit the army, Gertrudis's father refused to give the couple his blessing, citing no better reason than the fact that Pedro had black hair and a swarthy complexion. Finally, however, the father was unable resist his daughter's pleadings and Pedro's obvious love for her.

Seven children resulted from their union, four sons and three daughters. For 20 years, the young family enjoyed the modicum of success accorded Mexican criollos under the rule of the Spanish-born colonials.

But they chafed under the *peninsular* yoke. On September 15, 1810, when Father Miguel Hidalgo cried "Viva Mexico! Death to the *gachupines!*" he had immediate allies in hundreds of thousands of criollos, including Pedro and Gertrudis. Pedro and their teenage son Manuel quickly joined the insurgent army, which suffered disastrous defeat on January 17, 1811, at the Puente de Calderón, east of Guadalajara. They returned and joined the guerrilla campaign being waged against the Spanish forces in Michoacán.

Meanwhile, Gertrudis never wavered in her support for them and the *insurgente* cause. She made their Pátzcuaro house a secret rebel intelligence, finance, and supply headquarters. She promoted contributions of money and a small mountain of food and ammunition for the *insurgente* fighters. Although authorities suspected her activities, she avoided arrest for years as the increasingly bitter war ground on. Rebel guerrillas attacked, killed, and tortured Spanish soldiers and their sympathizers; the royalists responded with equal ferocity. Eventually both Pedro and Manuel died of battle wounds.

main plaza, beneath the statue of the revered Don Vasco de Quiroga (1470–1565). As first bishop of Pátzcuaro he reversed the despair and destruction wrought by the conquistadores.

Colonial buildings, some dating to the 17th century, rise behind the portals that spread around the square. The portals are themselves named and localize individual addresses (such as the Hotel Los Escudos, Portal Hidalgo 73).

Walk east, uphill, one block to Pátzcuaro's oldest colonial building, the former **Colegio San Nicolás,** begun by Don Vasco in 1540. Pass in-

side beneath its quaint three-bell Spanish classic facade to the venerable inner garden. Now called the Museo de Arte Popular, tel. 434/342-1029, its corridors lead past rooms filled with fine regional crafts. In a rear courtyard, be sure to see the stair-step foundations of the original Tarascan temple, exposed on the hillside. Turn around and inspect a wall inscribed with the marks of prisoners counting the days. Open Tues.–Sat. 9 A.M.–7 P.M., Sun. 9 A.M.–2:30 P.M.

As you exit the museum, glance left at the curious little doorway emerging from the outside

TO IXTAPA/PÁTZCUARO

Gertrudis nevertheless redoubled her efforts. She traveled tirelessly, gathering support for her compatriots. On one such trip, she left a family friend, a retired sergeant whom she had once saved from the gallows, to watch her house. When she returned, Gertrudis found some valuables missing. She questioned him, and, in retaliation, he denounced her to the authorities.

The local military commander quickly arrived at her house. During a chess party, before her compatriot-guests, he took Bocanegra into custody, placing her under arrest in the house at 14 Calle Ibarra, just around the corner from her childhood home. Her execution was summarily ordered; on October 10, 1817, a military guard escorted her, blindfolded, to the corner square (now Plaza Revolución) in front of San Francisco church. The priest accompanying her asked that she be allowed to stop and pray for a few moments. His request was granted, but she was not allowed to go inside the church to her family altar, for it traditionally had been a place where the persecuted had found refuge from civil authorities.

The guards conducted her to gallows that had been set up in the adjacent small plaza. The streets were empty of passersby; neighbors shut their windows, refusing to witness the execution. Bells rang out in protest from every church tower. At the last moment, the official in charge received an order to take Gertrudis to the main town plaza and execute her by firing squad. There, in front of the jail, she was to become an example for many of her comrades who were being held inside.

First the soldiers tried to rope her to a tree, but she protested such a humiliation. Left standing free, she removed her shawl, then a fine comb from her hair. This, along with a gold watch, Bocanegra handed over to her executioner, requesting that they be given to her three daughters so that they would remember her and not be shamed by their mother, who had been executed for defending the cause of liberty. Then Bocanegra produced a gold peso, saying, "Here's all I have left," as she threw it to the soldiers of her execution squad. She pulled off her blindfold and began addressing the small crowd of friends and compatriots. Her fervent message so stirred the onlookers that the official in charge was forced to disperse the gathering.

A single fusillade ended her life. Her body fell and lay for hours, until her blood caked and crusted in the sun and a swarm of flies gathered on the corpse. Guards finally had to douse it with a bucket of water and cover it with her shawl. The next day, her family was allowed to take her body home for vigil, then burial at the nearby church of the Compañía de Jesús.

The people of Pátzcuaro have never forgotten Bocanegra's sacrifice. During his 1934–1940 presidency, Lázaro Cárdenas ordered that a statue of the defiant Gertrudis at her moment of execution be erected in Plaza San Agustín (now Plaza Bocanegra) in Pátzcuaro. Every year, on the October 10 anniversary of her death, the people of Pátzcuaro gather beside her statue and honor Gertrudis Bocanegra's memory with overflowing bouquets of flowers.

uphill lane. Behind that door, Pátzcuaro people say, is an aqueduct that Don Vasco built to supply the poor with water during times of drought.

Walk ahead past the big courtyard and church on the left, a former Jesuit College, now restored as a community cultural center. It maintains an art museum upstairs and offers classes in theater, painting, drawing, and music, both instrumental and choral. Watch for posters announcing events. The old church at the far end of the bare courtyard, **La Parroquia de la Compañía de Jesús,** is the final resting place of renowned Pátzcuaro independence heroine Gertrudis Bocanegra, who was executed on October 10, 1817, for her staunch defense of the *insurgente* cause.

Continue along Calle Enseñanza. After two blocks, turn right, downhill, to the former Dominican Convent of Santa Catarina de Sena, commonly known as the **Casa de Once Patios** (House of 11 Patios) on the left. Most of its inner labyrinth of gardens, corridors, and rooms are restored and open to the public. Dozens of artisans have set up display workshops where they paint, weave, polish, and carve handicrafts for sale. (For more details, see the Shopping section.) Open daily 9 A.M.–2 P.M. and 4–7 P.M.

Return past the former Colegio San Nicolas and continue two blocks along Calle Arciga to the big **Basílica María Inmaculada de la Salud,** begun by Don Vasco during the mid-16th century. In addition to Don Vasco's tomb, the basilica is noted for its four-century-old main altar image of the Virgin, made according to a pre-Columbian recipe of cornstalk paste and orchid glue.

Follow diagonal Av. Buenavista downhill and continue a block along Lloreda to the former monastery, **Ex-Templo San Agustín,** now housing the public library, **Biblioteca Gertrudis Bocanegra,** at the northeast corner of Plaza Bocanegra; open Mon.–Fri. 9 A.M.–7 P.M., Sat. 9 A.M.–1 P.M. The library's main attraction is its huge mural, the first by Juan O'Gorman, completed in 1942. In this panorama of the history of the Valley of Pátzcuaro, O'Gorman is nearly as critical of the Tarascans' slaughter of 30,000 Aztec pris-

© BRUCE WHIPPERMAN

The antique belfry dates from the 1540 founding of the Colegio San Nicolás by Don Vasco de Quiroga.

oners as of Nuño de Guzmán (scowling like a demon in armor) as he tortures the last *caltzonzin* (emperor). All is not lost as O'Gorman shows the murdered emperor's niece, Erendira, riding out (and becoming the first Native American to ride a horse) to warn the people. Don Vasco, the savior, appears at the bottom, assuring a happy ending as he brings utopia to Pátzcuaro.

The librarian has a Spanish copy of the mural guide, signed by O'Gorman, who appears with his wife at the mural's left side. Additionally, the librarian will duplicate a copy of a brief but informative Spanish biography of independence heroine Gertrudis Bocanegra, whose statue stands in the adjoining plaza. The library's respectable book collection includes many Spanish-language reference works and several shelves of English-language fiction and nonfiction.

JANITZIO AND YUÑUEN ISLANDS

An excursion to the island of Janitzio (hah-NEET-seeoh) is de rigueur for first-time Pátzcuaro visitors. The breezy launch trip takes about half an hour. Waves splash, spray, and rock the bow; gulls wheel above the stern as the pyramidal volcanic island-village of Janitzio grows upon the horizon. The Janitzio villagers believe themselves to be the purest of the Purépecha. Only the young speak Spanish; the old—some of whom have never visited the mainland—hold fast to their language and traditional ways.

Fishing for the tasty Pátzcuaro *pescado blanco* (whitefish) used to be the major Janitzio occupation. Overfishing has unfortunately reduced the famous *mariposas* (butterfly nets), which Don Vasco introduced long ago, to mere ceremonial objects. Long, cumbersome nets are now needed for the increasingly meager catches. The price (about $10) of a succulent whitefish platter—the specialty of the dozen-odd embarcadero restaurants—has inflated beyond the reach of most Pátzcuaro families.

Fortunately, government and local cooperative conservation measures show promise of eventually replenishing the whitefish population. Progressive rules limit the commercial fishing season to the months of January through April, during which only fish larger than nine inches (23 centimeters) are allowed to be taken. Meanwhile, the *mariposas* still come out for display only during tourist-show regattas on weekends and holidays.

A steady procession of handicrafts shops lines the steep lane that winds to the island's summit. Although many items are common, some unusual finds in baskets, masks, papier-mâché, lacquerware, cottons, and woolens await those willing to look and bargain.

From the hillcrest, you can see the still more isolated islets of Tecuen, Yuñuen, and La Pacanda dotting the lake's northern reaches, while in the opposite direction, the city of Pátzcuaro basks at the foot of a distant pine-tufted green sierra. If you have the energy, climb to the tip-top of the colossal José María Morelos statue, lined inside with a continuous mural of scenes from the fiery independence hero's life.

Lake Pátzcuaro's other islands, notably Yuñuen, also welcome visitors. The community maintains an cluster of rustic *troje* native-style wooden kitchenette guest cabins in an airy hilltop poinsettia-adorned garden. Inside, the cabins are immaculate, cozy, and comfortable. Rates run about $35 d, with a number of amenities, including a good pool table in a handsome game room, and a small store, but no cars, no noise except the crowing of roosters and sunrise and sunset for entertainment. Active visitors can stroll around the island, go fishing (in season) or kayaking, and learn the Purépecha language. For reservations and more information, contact Alfredo Menocal or Laura Acuña, tel. 434/342-4473, fax 434/342-3969. Alternatively, you may make reservations at the Yuñuen booth at the the main dock *(muelle general),* daily approximately 9 A.M.–5 P.M.

Getting There: If you're driving, head downhill (north) a couple of miles along Av. Lázaro Cárdenas and turn left at the Uruapan-Morelia highway. Within a few hundred yards, turn right at the road crossing the rail tracks at the rail station. After about half a mile, bear right at a fork, and soon you'll see the parking lot (about $1). If you're not driving, take a taxi or ride the white *colectivo* VW van (about $.40, from the corner by the Hotel Los Escudos on Plaza Don Vasco de Quiroga, or the Mercado corner, Plaza Bocanegra) to the embarcadero. Round-trip boat tickets, available from a dock-front booth, cost about $2 for Janitzio, $5 or more for Yuñuen, Pacanda, and Tecuen, in advance of departure. The last boat returns from the islands around 5 P.M.

IHUATZIO

Pre-Columbian ruins dot the Pátzcuaro Valley. Most remain unexcavated grassy mounds except the most famous: Ihuatzio (ee-WAHT-seeoh) and Tzintzuntzán, both near the lakeshore northeast of the city.

Pátzcuaro dominated the valley during the latter-1300s golden-era reign of King Tariácuri. When he died the valley was divided between his younger son and his nephews, Hiripan and Tangaxoan (ancestor of Tangaxoan II, the last Tarascan emperor). According to Vasco de

TO IXTAPA/PÁTZCUARO

Quiroga's 16th-century narrative, *Relación de Michoacán,* squabbling broke out among the heirs. Hiripan won out, and, by A.D. 1400, had concentrated power at Ihuatzio.

Exploring Ihuatzio

The remains of Ihuatzio (literally, Place of the Coyotes) spread over a rectangular area about half a mile long by a quarter mile wide. Nearly all ruins are mound-dotted unexplored fields, closed to the public. The open part, the so-called **Parade Ground,** is about the size of four football fields and enclosed by a pair of ceremonial stepped-wall raised causeways. These lead toward a pair of hulking truncated pyramids that tower above the Parade Ground's west end. These, Ihuatzio's most prominent structures, lost nearly all of their original stone sheathing to colonial construction projects, although a remnant appears on the right pyramid's face as you approach from the Parade Ground.

Climb carefully (the steps are steep) to the top for a view of the surrounding unexcavated ruins. Along the Parade Ground's north and south sides, notice the **King's Causeways,** a pair

of long stepped mounds, presumably used as the *caltzonzin's* ceremonial approach road.

About a quarter mile due south rises another mound, which marks the **Observatory,** a mysterious 100-foot-wide cylindrical structure whose name merely represents an educated guess about its possible function. In nearly the same direction as the Observatory, but much closer, stands the rubbly mound of the *yácatas,* three half-cylindrical truncated pyramids, whose original forms are unrecognizable because of repeated ransackings. Their shapes, however, are certain, because of a number of other excavated local examples, most notably Tzintzuntzán, five miles to the north. The Ihuatzio site is open daily around 10 A.M.–5 P.M.; entry fee about $2, no facilities except a lavatory. Bring your hat and drinking water.

Getting There: By car or taxi, take Highway 120 from Pátzcuaro northeast (Morelia direction) about five miles (eight km) to the signed Ihuatzio turnoff. Turn left and continue 3.1 miles (five km) to a small plaza on the left. Turn right on to the rough dirt entrance road and continue another .7 mile (one km) to the site parking lot.

IHUATZIO ARCHAEOLOGICAL ZONE

WALL-CAUSEWAY

WALL-CAUSEWAY

WALL-CAUSEWAY

OBSERVATORY

YÁCATAS

RECONSTRUCTED PYRAMIDS

KING'S CAUSEWAYS

PARADE GROUND

PARKING

0   150 yds
0   150 m

To Pátzcuaro

By bus, ride one of the blue and white *urbano* buses, which all pass the central bus station front entrance on the south edge of town and continue to the north edge of town to Highway 120 at the foot of Av. Lázaro Cárdenas. Hop on the bus marked Ihuatzio on the windshield. About 20 minutes later, when the bus turns from the highway on to the Ihuatzio side road, tell the driver *"ruinas, por favor"* and you'll soon get dropped off at the small plaza on the left near town. Follow the dirt entrance road across from the plaza, about a kilometer to the site.

TZINTZUNTZÁN

Ihuatzio's power waned during the 1400s, gradually giving way to nearby Tzintzuntzán (Place of the Hummingbirds). Within a generation, Tzintzuntzán (seen-soon-SAHN) became the hub of an expanded Tarascan empire, which included nearly all of present Michoacán and half of Jalisco and Guanajuato. When the Spanish arrived in 1521, authority was concentrated entirely in Tzintzuntzán, an imperial city whose population had swelled to perhaps as much as 100,000.

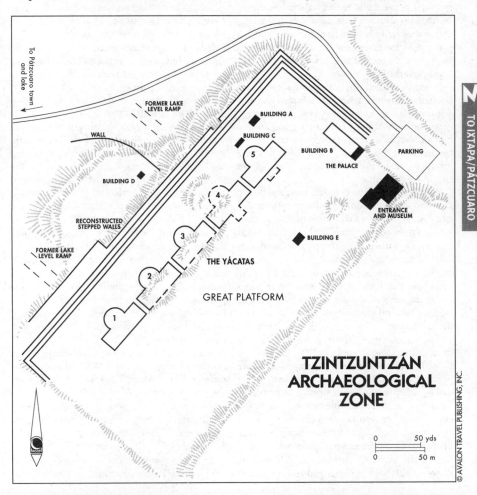

TZINTZUNTZÁN ARCHAEOLOGICAL ZONE

To IXTAPA/PÁTZCUARO

© AVALON TRAVEL PUBLISHING, INC.

The present town (pop. 5,000), a dozen miles northeast of Pátzcuaro, is a mere shadow of its former glory. The Great Platform, although long abandoned, still towers in proud relief on the hill above the dusty modern town.

Exploring the Archaeological Site

The entire archaeological zone—of which the **Great Platform** occupies a significant but very small area—spreads over nearly three square miles. The excavated part, open to the public, represents only a 50th of the total, being confined within a rectangle perhaps 500 yards long and half that in width. The visitor's entrance leads you toward the rear of the Great Platform from the east through a grassy park. You first see the Great Platform spreading from right (north) to left, with the town and lake below the far front side.

The Great Platform is singularly intriguing because of its five side-by-side *yácatas:* massive, semicylindrical ceremonial platforms. The *yácatas* are built of huge cut basalt (lava) stones, like a giant child's neat stacks of black building blocks. When the Spanish arrived, a temple to the legendary god-king Curicaueri perched upon the *yácata* summit.

Although the Great Platform itself was purely ceremonial in function, excavations in outer sections of the zone reveal that imperial Tzintzuntzán was an entire city, housing all classes from kings to slaves. Within the city, people lived and worked according to specialized occupations— farmers, artisans, priests, and warriors. Most experts agree that such urban organization required a high degree of sophistication, including excess wealth, laws and efficient government, and a reliable calendar.

Tzintzuntzán grew through a number of stages from its founding around A.D. 900. Excavations beneath the Great Platform masonry reveal earlier *yácatas* overlaid, like layers of an onion, above earlier constructions with similar, but smaller, features. (Look, for example, at the archaeological test hole between *yácatas* 4 and 5.)

Other intriguing structures dot the Great Platform. **Entrance ramps,** apparently built as boat-traffic terminals, appear beneath the Great Platform's 20-foot-high stepped retaining wall.

Records reveal that, at the time of the conquest, lake waters lapped beaches at the foot of these ramps.

The Palace, a group of rooms surrounding an inner patio, stands about 100 yards northeast of the first *yácata.* Because thousands of human bones and an altar were found here, some archaeologists speculated that it may have been a ceremonial depository for the remains of vanquished enemies.

About 75 yards in front of *yácatas* 4 and 5 is Building E, a puzzling L-shaped group of rooms. Although archaeologists speculate that they may have been storerooms or granaries, excavations, curiously, revealed no entrances.

The site is open daily about 10 A.M.–5 P.M.; facilities include a small museum, lavatories, and a picnic park. Entry fee is about $3; bring your hat and drinking water.

Modern Tzintzuntzán

The buildings the Spanish colonials erected still stand at the far (west) end of the town park, which spreads from the crafts stalls bordering the Highway 120 main street. Clustered at the park's far end you will find the **Franciscan monastery and church.** Inside the church are several paintings and murals dedicated to the Señor de Rescate, whose festival the townspeople celebrate with Purépecha music and regional dances. The adjacent monastery, dedicated to Santa Ana, is known for its plateresque facade (richly ornamented baroque style taken from the elaborate designs silversmiths used to craft fine plates, candlesticks, and utensils) and courtyard, containing some of the world's oldest olive trees, which somehow survived the royal ban on olive trees in Mexico.

Back on the main street, handicrafts stores and shops offer some unusual woodwork. Especially noteworthy are the **Artesanías Colibrí** and the warren of shops behind it. Wander among the riots of wooden crafts—giant masks, baskets, headboards, cabinets—where you can select from a potpourri of pre-Columbian, gothic, baroque, and neoclassic motifs.

Even more woodcrafts are available on the road back to Pátzcuaro, a mile or two from Tzintzuntzán, where a village of woodcarvers' shops has sprouted on both sides of the road.

Getting There: By car head northeast along Highway 120, Morelia direction, continuing past the Ihuatzio turnoff about five miles (eight km) to the signed Tzintzuntzán right fork, which leads to the ruins on the hill above the highway. By bus, from the Pátzcuaro *camionera central* (south side of town), ride one of the several Ruta Paraíso (tel. 434/342-0808) second-class bus departures to Tzintzuntzán. A few minutes after the Ihuatzio turnoff (note the road sign), tell the driver *"ruinas, por favor"* and you'll probably get dropped off at the highway fork to the ruins (or, if you're lucky, at the ruins parking lot a quarter mile farther on).

EXCURSIONS SOUTH AND WEST OF PÁTZCUARO

An auto excursion to the copper-crafting town of Santa Clara de Cobre can be conveniently extended into a half-day loop that includes the tranquil, storied mountain lake Zirahuén and the mysterious pre-Tarascan ruins at the Tinganio archaeological site.

Santa Clara de Cobre

Santa Clara de Cobre (pop. 5,000) is tucked on a gently sloping mountainside about half an hour (13 miles, 21 km by Highway 120) south of Pátzcuaro. The present town, completely devoted to the manufacture, display, and sale of copperware, gives no hint of the historical implications of the Santa Clara metalworking craft, product of an ancient pre-Columbian tradition. The Purépecha are proud of their historic independence from the the Aztec domination that befell nearly all Mexican peoples by A.D. 1500. But how did the Purépecha prevail against the Aztec legions that vanquished nearly everyone else? The answer may be in the very handicraft technology that produced the gleaming copperwares displayed around the Santa Clara plaza. That technology, of extraction, alloying, and forging metals was the closely guarded secret of the Purépecha. It probably resulted in superior metal weapons, not unlike those of bronze age

Europeans, which enabled Purépechan warriors to defeat and slaughter numerically superior (but technically inferior) Aztec armies time and again up to the eve of the conquest.

The town itself clusters around an intimate plaza, where most everything you see—the benches, the bandstand, and the lampposts—seems to be made of copper. A look at the shiny contents of the plaza shops—galaxies of gleaming utensils, curios, and art objects—confirms the impression. Although the old mines are all played out, the livelihoods of many Santa Clara families are still based on the fine copperware (now made from copper from other parts of Mexico), which they turn out in their workshop-homes.

If you decide to linger, acceptable colonial-style restaurants and hotels on the plaza can provide food and lodging. For example, try the **Hotel Real de Cobre** at the plaza's west side, Portal Hidalgo 19, Santa Clara de Cobre, Michoacán 61800, tel. 434/343-0205. It offers tidy but mostly dark bare-bulb rooms, good for an overnight, for about $20 d, with hot water, parking, and a restaurant. For more light, ask for room 18, 19, or 20.

A copper museum, the **Museo del Cobre** and a number of uniquely interesting factory stores dot the main street, Morelos, east (Pátzcuaro direction) from the town plaza. Stop by the museum first, at the first corner (uphill side) one block east of the plaza. Inside, admire the superfine copper-as-art: a trove of prizewinning vases, plates, pitchers and more, in a dozen masterful variations. Finally, continue to the back courtyard and watch the artisans at work, hewing and hammering their marvels in copper. Find the museum, tel. 434/343-0254, open Mon.–Fri. 9 A.M.–3 P.M. and 5–7 P.M., Sat. 10 A.M.–3 P.M. and 5–7 P.M., and Sun. 10 A.M.–4 P.M.

Of the private factories, at least two stand out. Across and farther down the street, find **Galería de Arte y Diseña,** at Morelos Ote. 363, tel. 434/343-0189. Enter and meet friendly, prizewinning designer-artisan Ignacio Punzo, who's happy to demonstrate and discuss (in Spanish) his masterworks on display. For much more, continue across the street, to **El Arte del Cobre,** at Morelos Ote. 449, tel. 434/343-0124 or 434/343-0225.

TO IXTAPA/PÁTZCUARO

Step inside and admire the wealth of prizewinning art-in-metal of master Abdón Punzo and Brothers that fills their museum-store. Later, continue to the big workshop-factory in the rear and be awed by the skill of Abdón and his workers as they mold, anneal, hammer, and polish their pieces into gleaming works of art.

Lake Zirahuén

From Highway 120, just past the southwestern fringe of Santa Clara, a cobbled road forks right about seven miles (12 km) to reed-lined Lake Zirahuén. According to Purépecha legend, the lake resulted from the river of tears that Princess Zirahuén wept after losing her true love. Although Zirahuén died of sorrow, her spirit still lives in the lake. Men who set out upon the water in their canoes must beware, for the spirit appears as a lovely, beckoning young maiden. And alas for the one who cannot resist, for the spirit will take him, never to be seen again.

Ghosts notwithstanding, Lake Zirahuén is a jewel set among emerald, pine-clad summits and lush communal fields ripe for relaxed exploring, or maybe even renting a local house and soaking in backcountry Michoacán for a week or month. Fisherfolk paddle dugout canoes across Zirahuén's mirror surface; local-style wooden houses known as *trojes* cluster near the lakeshore. Village kids play in the street; old men sit and talk about the "way things used to be." A rough but passable road circles the lake, and excursion boats take parties out from a pair of embarcaderos at sleepy, colonial Zirahuén town (pop. 1,000). Restaurants at both embarcaderos offer whitefish dinners for reasonable prices.

Accommodations and Food: The more upscale of the embarcaderos, the first you pass (on the left, en route from Santa Clara), has attractive lakeside **Restaurant "Zirah-Bar,"** and four clean housekeeping cabins with fireplace, sleeping 2–6. Weekday rates are about $40 for two, $72 for four. Weekends and holiday rates run upward from about $85 d.

The Zirah-Bar concessionaire also manages two other deluxe rustic lodging sites on the forested lakeshore, accessible by road or boat a few miles from the Zirahuén embarcaderos: **Agua Verde,** with six two-bedroom "Alpine" cabins (from about $50 d, weekdays low season Jan. 4–June and Sept. 1–Dec. 15), and four three-bedroom "Residential" cabins (from about $72 d, weekdays) all with kitchens, fireplaces, and some king-sized beds; and **Arcoiris** (Rainbow), with four one-bedroom (two with kitchens), two-story cabins with fireplaces and some king-sized beds (from about $50 d). Weekend and holiday rates are higher, beginning at about $100 d for both the Alpine and Arcoiris lodgings.

If you do get to the Arcoiris lodge (from Zirahuén town, drive or walk a few miles clockwise, about a quarter of the way around the lakeshore, to the adjacent side, be sure not to miss seeing the **Casa Grande** antique late-colonial (1817) wooden mansion, now repository of a museum of fine copper and lacquerware. For information and reservations, contact Impulsora de Zirahuén at its office in Morelia, Michoacán, tel. 443/326-3301 or 443/327-3624, fax 443/327-3998, izirahuen@infosel.net.mx, www.zirahuen.com.

Folks who enjoy Zirahuén's idyllic lakeside ambience and are willing to forgo some luxury for more modest prices in a quiet, forested lakeside setting should check out *troje*-style **Cabañas Rústicas de Zirahuén.** Find it in its own pine-shaded park, about half a mile (along the Santa Clara road) from embarcadero Zirah-Bar. Here, owners have creatively built about six rustic, petite log-house chalets, complete with a sprinkling of 20th-century comforts—carpet, hot-water baths, inside toilets, and plenty of extras, such as big lake-view windows, airy porches, barbecue decks, and cozy sleeping lofts. Rentals begin at about $30 d, add $5 per extra person. Some of the chalets have modestly equipped kitchenettes. These might be perfect for a couple, either solo or with kids, or a group of three or four. Drop in or reserve at Obregon 19, Pátzcuaro, Michoacan 61600, tel. 434/342-0280, fax 434/342-0758.

The other route to Lake Zirahuén is via the well-signed turnoff road at Km 17 (10 miles west of Pátzcuaro) on Highway 14 to Uruapan. If you go that way, you'll pass the Hotel Zirahuén on the left just as you enter Zirahuén town. For embarcadero and Restaurant "Zirah-Bar," continue ahead for about 50 yards, then bear left on the cobbled lakeshore road.

Alternatively, you might consider the **Hotel Zirahuén,** Av. Vicente Guerrero s/n, Zirahuén, Michoacán 61810, tel. 434/353-4131, fax 434/353-4132, an unusual family project a couple minutes' walk from the lakeshore. It features 12 deluxe rooms, including a super-deluxe, two-bedroom (king-sized) "presidential suite," with a sauna and a grand indoor spa that would accommodate about eight. All this for about $140 for two, three, or four. Smaller but nevertheless luxurious options, all with spa, include a "master" suite, minus the sauna, $100 for up to four; a one-bedroom "junior" suite, about $54 d, and a "super" room, about $40 d. Regular rooms, still deluxe but without spa, run about $30 d. (Hotel Zirahuén's major drawback is its ugly parking lot, with an old, hulking unfinished concrete structure that will be completed who knows when.)

Getting There: Travel to Zirahuén either by car, taxi, or second-class Autovias del Occidente (AO) bus, tel. 434/342-1243, which provides several daily Zirahuén departures from the Pátzcuaro south-side central bus station.

Tinganio Archaeological Zone

If instead of turning toward Zirahuén you stay on Highway 14, you'll arrive at **Tingambato,** at Km 37 (23 miles, 37 km from Pátzcuaro; 16 miles, 26 km from Uruapan). Turn at the small roadside archaeological sign and continue through the town about a mile to the Tinganio archaeological site parking lot.

The excavated section, uncovered during the late 1970s, constitutes a small, albeit very important part of the entire archaeological zone. Modern dating methods show construction occurred in two phases, the first beginning around A.D. 450 and the second continuing between A.D. 600 and A.D. 900. The second stage culminated in the visible reconstructions, which surround a central sunken plaza: on the east side, a 25-foot, six-step pyramid; a tomb complex on the north; and a sunken ball court on the west. The pyramid, reached by a ritual stairway, is reminiscent of classic Teotihuacán style. Opposite is

the ceremonial ball court (see the special topic "*Tlatchtli:* The Ball Game" in the Acapulco and Inland to Taxco chapter) in which players tried to bat a solid, natural rubber ball past their opponents with their torsos, shoulders, and heads. Stakes for ritually important contests sometimes ran as high as the lives of the participants.

Although much of the site had been looted before the arrival of the Spanish, excavators discovered an unopened tomb (note the descending staircase) on the north side. Finds included a host of skulls and skeletons—although only one complete, seated at the entrance—and a trove of artifacts, enough for a generation of archaeologists to sort out.

LAKE PÁTZCUARO WEST SHORELINE

The smooth 30-mile (50-km) road that follows Lake Pátzcuaro's rural west shoreline provides a path for a leisurely half-day exploration by car or taxi (or by bus—allow a full day).

Although the folks along this route are accustomed to seeing foreign visitors when they go into the city, the same foreign visitors seldom come to where they live. People are going to wonder why you came. A wave of the hand, a smile, and a simple *"Hola," "Buenos días,"* or *"Buenas tardes"* on your part will go a long way toward breaking the ice.

Some of the villages en route are known for certain handicrafts. Few, if any, families have formal shops to sell their goods, but people will tell (or lead you) where to find them if you ask.

Getting There: By car, the route begins as if you're going to the Janitzio excursion boat dock (see above), except at the fork past the rail station, instead of heading right to the boat dock, you head left. By bus, from the *camionera central,* south side of town, take one of the early, very frequent Autobuses del Occidente (ADO) second-class buses headed for Jarácuaro and/or Erongarícuaro, the biggest towns on the west shore. Hop off at the first likely spot along the way, and continue with a succeeding bus. At Erongarícuaro, if it isn't too late, you can continue by different, but connecting buses, to Quiroga, at the lake's north end, where you can connect with a Ruta Paraíso bus back to Pátzcuaro, via Tzintzuntzán.

Tócuaro and Jarácuaro

After about five miles (eight km) along the lakeshore from Pátzcuaro, you pass scruffy Tócuaro village on the left, known for its good papier-mâché and masks (*máscaras;* MAHS-cah-rahs). About two miles farther you'll see Jarácuaro town, on the offshore island. Head right at the paved fork to the causeway and bridge. Here, you can first visit the rustically serene old Señor San Pedro de Jarácuaro church and garden in the middle of town. Then head around to the back side of town, behind the church, where,

instead of the lake, you see a 500-yard-wide grassy "beach" being grazed by a herd of apparently very contented cows. By this time you probably will have noticed what seems to be the townfolks' main occupation: weaving reeds for *petates* (all-purpose straw mats) in their spare time. The whole town—tots, men, women, old folks—do it nimbly, automatically, and often collectively, passing the time of day together.

Erongarícuaro, Opongio, and Chupícuaro

About three miles farther, you'll arrive at the biggest west-shore town, Erongarícuaro (pop. about 3,000), known for its *bordado* (hand em-

AROUND LAKE PÁTZCUARO

broidery). About two miles (three km) before the town, you might stop for refreshment at the German-owned and operated **Restaurant Campestre Alemán** and try the specialty, trout, German-style. Continue to the town, whose inviting green plaza, grocery stores, and restaurant (one block north, past the plaza) at the roadside rate at least a stop and a stroll around.

The road winds another five or six miles (8–10 km) past cornfields and pastures to a crest and broad vista point, just before Opongio village. Pause and view the giant arms of the lake spread south and north, separated by a looming, pine-tufted 10,000-foot extinct volcanic peak. On the right, the islands of Pacanda, Yuñuen, Tecuen, and Janitzio appear as a procession of turtles, paddling toward the lake's shallow southern shore. On the left, Pátzcuaro's deeper northern arm extends to a misty-blue, mountain-rimmed shoreline.

If you want to see the lake close up, you can easily do so at Chupícuaro, several miles farther along. Just before joining the main Zacapu-Quiroga highway, turn right at a paved fork, which leads downhill to a cedar-shaded grassy park right at the lakeshore. A restaurant sells drinks and snacks, and the lake provides plenty of cool water for wading.

Hotel Chupícuaro

On a lakeview knoll above the park stands the Hotel Chupícuaro, just right for a for a day or week of quiet relaxation. The longtime hotel is a family project of three Jalisco brothers and their mother, Dulce María Orozco, whose pride and joy is a beautiful new separate building. The recent addition is a delightfully rustic collection of about six rooms and suites, with shiny hand-carved furniture, polished hardwood floors, beamed ceilings, and a host of other charming architectural details. The building's larger units, sleeping up to six, rent for about $125; smaller (nos. 27 and 28), with airy lake views, go for $30 s, $46 d, all with private hot water baths. A separate cluster of plainer and older but clean and spacious cabins, with toilets and hot water showers, run $16 s, $25 d. **Camping** spaces, with your own tent or self-contained RV, cost $4 per adult. Except for weekends and holidays, reservations (tel. 455/354-

0400 or 455/354-0707, claudio@mail.com.mx) are not generally necessary.

Santa Fe de La Laguna

Finally, be sure to leave enough time to stop at Santa Fe de La Laguna, marked by the roadside pottery shops, two miles farther east (toward Quiroga), on the left. Follow the street dividing the shops to the picturesquely restored town plaza, two blocks from the highway. Past the door on the plaza's far side stands the venerable **Iglesia Santa Fe de La Laguna** church and former hospital, behind the church. Built by the singular energy of Bishop Vasco de Quiroga more than four centuries ago, both church and hospital live on in his spirit, even though the hospital has become a museum and library.

Inside, a librarian shepherds flocks of eager young scholars, while next door in the museum, Don Vasco looks down from his portrait. The good bishop's chair stands sedately on one side, and next to the entrance is the remarkable first page of Don Vasco's rules for the hospital. Loosely translated, the document declares that Hospital Santa Fe de La Laguna is not only for visiting priests, pilgrims, and dignitaries, but for *all* the people. Judging from the devotion that Pátzcuaro people still show for him, Bishop Vasco de Quiroga must have been a man of his word.

PÁTZCUARO ACCOMMODATIONS

Downtown Hotels

Although prices have risen sharply at most Pátzcuaro hotels, visitors can still enjoy comfortable, reasonably priced colonial-decor hotels clustered near the plazas. By all means ask for a discount, especially nonholidays and weekdays, when most hotels are minimally occupied. Because of the mild, dry climate, rooms generally have neither air-conditioning nor central heating. Fans and *chimeneas* (fireplaces, a cozy winter plus), noted below, are sometimes available.

Hotels Around the Plaza Don Vasco: The family-owned and managed **Hotel Los Escudos,** Portal Hidalgo 73, Pátzcuaro, Michoacán 61600, tel. 434/342-0138 or 434/342-1290, fax 434/342-0649, west side of the Plaza Don Vasco de Quiroga, is a longtime Pátzcuaro favorite. Its rooms rise in three tiers around a cool, serene inner patio, wrapped in wrought iron, tile, and bright greenery. The homey, dark-paneled rooms come with lacy curtains, wood floors, and fireplaces (wood included). The wood-paneled café downstairs, one of Pátzcuaro's favorite meeting places, is a good spot for lingering over dessert with friends or with a good book after a hard day on the lake. The hotel's 30 rooms rent for about $35 s and $45 d, with TV and parking; credit cards are accepted. Rooms in the next-door annex are a bit cheaper, about $30 s, $40 d. Reservations, recommended any time, are mandatory weekends and holidays. The annex *(nueva sección)*, although authentically colonial and inviting, lacks the charming and light inner courtyard of the old hotel. If you can afford the higher tariff, specify the "old section," *(sección viejo)* when reserving.

Moving counterclockwise around the plaza, at the next corner, enter the lobby of the **Hotel Misión San Manuel,** Portal Aldama 12,

Pátzcuaro, Michoacán 61600, tel. 434/342-1050, fax 434/342-1313, which appears as if you've returned to colonial times. Owner-manager Clementina Tovar lovingly maintains her authentic mansion of about 30 rooms in two stories that rise above the polished, wood-paneled lobby and enfold an adjacent grand but dark hall. Fortunately, lovers of light can choose a room off the intimate and sunny rear patio. Inside, rooms are immaculate and regally spacious, with towering beamed ceilings, shiny flowered tile bathrooms, and (nearly all) with fireplaces, wood included. Turn off the room lamps, light candles, and let their warm glow and the long shadows transport you back to the 18th century. Asking rates are high, however, at about $60 s or d, $83 t; ask for a discount. Credit cards are not accepted.

Hotel Posada San Rafael, Portal Aldama 15, Plaza Don Vasco de Quiroga, Pátzcuaro, Michoacán 61600, tel./fax 434/342-0770, on the adjacent plaza-front block, offers an alternative. Greatly expanded during the 1980s from an original colonial mansion core, its 104 rooms spread along three stories of corridors facing a narrow

---

PÁTZCUARO ACCOMMODATIONS BY PRICE

Downtown

Hotel Valmen, Lloreda 34, tel. 434/342-1161, $16

Hotel Concordia, Portal Juárez 31, Plaza Bocanegra, tel. 434/342-0003, $16

Hotel Posada de la Salud, Av. Serrato 9, tel./fax 434/342-0058, $22

Gran Hotel, Portal Regules 6, Plaza Bocanegra, tel. 434/342-0443, fax 434/342-3090, granhotel@yahoo.com, $24

Hotel Posada San Rafael, Portal Aldama 15, tel. 434/342-0770, $25

Posada Mandala, Lerin 14, tel. 434/342-4176, matiasag@hotmail.com, $28

Hotel Misión San Manuel, Portal Aldama 12, tel./fax 434/342-1313, tel. 434/342-1050, $37

Hotel Los Escudos, Portal Hidalgo 73, tel. 434/342-0138 or 434/342-1290, fax 434/342-0649, $45

Posada de la Basílica, Arciga 6, tel. 434/342-1108, fax 434/342-0659, $47

Hotel Mesón del Gallo, Dr. Coss 20, tel. 434/342-1474, fax 434/342-1511, $48

Hotel Fiesta Plaza, Plaza Bocanegra 24, tel./fax 434/342-2515 or 434/342-2516, $54

Av. Lázaro Cárdenas

Motel del Lago, L. Cárdenas 509, tel./fax 434/342-1471, $20

Hotel San Carlos, Calle Caltzonzín s/n, Colonia Morelos, tel. 434/342-1359, $30

Hotel Villa Pátzcuaro, L. Cárdenas 506, tel. 434/342-0767, fax 434/342-2984, vpatzcuara@yahoo.com, $35

Hostería San Felipe, L. Cárdenas 321, tel./fax 434/342-1298, $60

Hotel Posada de Don Vasco, L. Cárdenas 450, tel. 434/342-0227 or 434/342-2704, U.S./Can. tel. 800/528-1234, fax 434/342-0262, posva@yrevi.crefal.edu.mx, $85

Many Pátzcuaro hotels, such as the Hotel Los Escudos (shown), are authentically colonial.

inner parking courtyard. While the parked cars detract, the neocolonial decor—traditional tile, big-beamed ceilings, and hand-carved oak doors—lend a touch of charm. The paneled rooms, with throw rugs, wood floors, and fluffy curtains, if not deluxe, are at least clean and comfortable. Hot-water hours are limited to 7–11 A.M. and 6:30–11 P.M. Rates run about $36 s, 40$ d for all rooms; but with no fireplaces, and no credit cards accepted.

Much more personal and lovely is **Casa Brunson,** life dream of Phyllis and John Skaglund, tucked around the plaza Don Vasco's southeast corner, at Dr. Coss 13, Pátzcuaro, Michoacán 61600, tel. 434/342-3903, phyllis@mail.ml.com.mx. They offer a trio of (all nonsmoking) accommodations, immaculate and elegantly decorated with John's polished handmade furniture. Amenities include a graceful and comfortable common living room, with fireplace, books and magazines, and an invit-

ingly tranquil inner patio-garden. Room prices (two-night minimum, reservations required) are $100 d for two of the rooms (called Verde and Azul), and $130 for a larger super comfortable, large one-bedroom suite, with its own private garden. All rentals include full made-to-order breakfast, parking available but extra, and no TV, no children, no phones, and no credit cards.

Across the street, find **Hotel Mesón del Gallo,** at Dr. Coss 20, Pátzcuaro, Michoacán 61600, tel. 434/342-1474, fax 434/342-1511. Once one of Pátzcuaro's most comfortable and popular lodgings, some of its formerly attractive amenities have been allowed to deteriorate. Moreover, the entire place could use a thorough top-to-bottom dusting and scrubbing.

Nevertheless, the hotel offers many tastefully appointed colonial-decor rooms with bath (but with dim, drab lighting), and manicured green gardens on both sides of the building. Rooms, which have the definite minus of neither heat nor fireplaces, do vary, so look before you pay. Other amenities include a (dark) dining room and a sitting room right out of *Don Quixote* with a big fireplace (where, however, I've never seen a fire in a dozen years) that would feel mighty cozy on a cool Pátzcuaro winter night. The once blue and beautiful pool has been out of operation for a long time. It might be worth checking to see if it's going again. Asking prices for the 25 rooms and suites are modest, at about $25 s, $41 d, with breakfast, and parking and limited wheelchair access, but no TV; credit cards are accepted.

Back on the Plaza Don Vasco, the **Hotel Mansión Iturbe,** at Portal Morelos 59, Pátzcuaro, Michoacán 61600, tel. fax 434/342-5502, mansioniturbe@yahoo.com, offers a deluxe, ideally situated option, at the middle of the plaza's north side. Owner Margarita Arreaga, descendant of the original Iturbe family, has fashioned the venerable colonial-era family mansion into an attractive 14-room bed and breakfast. In doing so, she has conserved and refurbished the attractive old-world high-beamed ceilings, massive planked floors, authentically antique, hand-hewn dressers, commodes, and writing desks. Thoughtful lighting, designer reading lamps, gleaming modern-standard shower baths, king-sized beds (in five of the rooms) and a luxuriously tranquil top-floor patio and adjacent solarium, with books, magazines, and soft chairs for sitting, all complete the attractive picture. Prices, moreover, are very reasonable, at $46 s or d, $65 triple (higher holidays, especially Nov. 1–2, Day of the Dead), with parking and full a la carte breakfast included, but no credit cards accepted. For more information, visit the website www.mexonline.com/iturbe.htm.

Moving north on Calle Iturbe, away from the plaza half a block, find large but attractive Hotel Rincón de Josefa, at Calle Iturbe 29, Pátzcuaro, Michoacán 61600, tel. 434/342-5502, fax 434/342-1143. Nicely situated on a quiet side street, midway between Pátzcuaro's two plazas, Rincón de Josefa's approximately 60 rooms rise in three floors, around a long, leafy, and light interior patio. Rooms are immaculate, comfortable, and thoughtfully decorated with colorful Mexican tile, hand-woven bedspreads, attractively rustic wooden furniture, and shiny, modern-standard bathrooms. Rooms rent for about $46 s or d, $65 t, with parking, but credit cards not accepted. For more information, visit the website www.rincondejosefa.com.

Hotels Around the Plaza Gertrudis Bocanegra: The plainer but competently managed, modern-style **Gran Hotel** on Plaza Bocanegra, at Portal Regules 6, Plaza Bocanegra, Pátzcuaro, Michoacán 61600, tel. 434/342-0443, fax 434/342-3090, granhotel@yahoo.com, offers a moderately priced alternative. Its 20 rooms, stacked in two stories, are clean, comfortable, and thoughtfully decorated in 1960s-motel style. For minimum noise, get a room away from the busy street. Rates run about $35 s or d, and $55 t, with restaurant, phones, parking, TV, and credit cards are accepted. For more information, visit the website www.galeon.com/granhotel.

Moving counterclockwise around Plaza Bocanegra, find the **Hotel Fiesta Plaza,** Plaza Bocanegra 24, Pátzcuaro, Michoacán 61600, tel./fax 434/342-2515 or 434/342-2516, on the opposite, north side of Plaza Bocanegra. A 1990 renovation of a colonial house, Fiesta Plaza's

three stories of comfortable rooms surround a fountain-decorated inner patio. The restaurant, convenient for breakfast, spreads into the patio, while just outside the door the colorful Plaza Bocanegra hubbub—the market, the movie theater, a dozen taco stands, bus and minivan traffic—buzzes from morning to midnight. Guests who require relief should pick an upper-tier room away from the street. The sharply increased asking rates run about $63 s or d, $72 t (ask for a discount), with TV, phones, and parking; credit cards are accepted.

Continue past the market to budget travelers' haven **Hotel Concordia,** Portal Juárez 31, Plaza Bocanegra, Pátzcuaro, Michoacán, 61600, tel. 434/342-0003, on the plaza's west side. Here, 33 clean, comfortable rooms in two stories surround the parking-patio of a colonial-era family house. Noise, however, may sometimes be a problem; get an upstairs room away from the street and/or wear earplugs. Prices, however, are reasonable: $22 s and $36 d with private bath, $11 s, $22 d without; with restaurant, 24-hour hot water, and parking. Credit cards not accepted.

The **Hotel Valmen,** Lloreda 34, Pátzcuaro, Michoacán 61600, tel. 434/342-1161, on the corner of Lloreda and Ahumada two blocks uphill from the north side of Plaza Bocanegra, offers another budget alternative. Plants, light, and attractive tile soften the Valmen's otherwise spartan ambience. Two upper tiers of plain but tidy rooms with hot showers spread around the interior patio. Avoid the street noise by choosing an interior room. Rates run a very reasonable $10 s, $20 d, $30 t; credit cards are not accepted.

Hotels Around the Basilica: Continue uphill, east, a block up Lloreda, to Hostal del Valle, at Lloreda 27, Pátzcuaro, Michoacán 61600, tel/fax 434/342-0512, reservaciones@hostaldelvalle.com. Friendly welcoming husband-wife owner-managers have modernized their old family house into a simple but inviting inn, with about eight comfortable, clean art-decorated, modern-standard rooms, clustered around a soaring covered, but light, inner patio. Five of the rooms are accessible by a quaint spiral staircase; the others by conventional stairs. Rentals run $35 s, $45 d, $60 t, except for Easter, Christmas, and especially Day of the

Dead holidays. For more information, visit the website www.hostaldelvalle.com.

Guests at the very popular **Posada de la Basílica,** Arciga 6, Pátzcuaro, Michoacán 61600, tel. 434/342-1108, fax 434/342-0659, one block farther uphill, across Arciga from the basilica, enjoy a very attractive view restaurant. The panorama (also visible from the hotel's adjoining patio) of colonial city, lake, and mountains adds a bit of luxury to the hotel's authentically colonial atmosphere. The rooms, furnished in hand-carved, hand-woven, and hand-wrought 17th-century chic, add even more. Prices unfortunately have steeply increased during the past few years. (When I told the desk clerk that that my readers might take their business elsewhere rather than pay the higher rates, he explained rather smugly that the hotel is now a member of the upscale "Tesoros de Michaocán"—Treasures of Michoacán—marketing group.) The 12 rooms (seven with fireplaces), all with hot water, run about $52 s, $62 d or t, with parking; credit cards are accepted. Reservations are generally necessary.

The **Hotel Posada de la Salud,** Av. Serrato 9, Pátzcuaro, Michoacán 61600, tel./fax 434/342-0058, on the basilica's south side, is especially popular with female basilica visitors. The 15 plain but very clean rooms spread around a sunny, conventlike courtyard. The typical guest, while not saintly, is at least probably in bed reading by 9 P.M. at the latest. Rooms rent for about $19 s, $25 d, $30 t; reservations are recommended, especially during religious holidays, such as the Fiesta de la Virgen de La Salud (Dec. 1–Dec. 8) and Semana Santa (week preceding Easter Sunday). Hot-water hours are limited to 6:30–11 A.M. and 5–10 P.M.

Continue west along Arciga, past the museum and the church on the left, three blocks to **Posada Mandala,** at 14 Lerin, Pátzcuaro, Michaoacán 61600, tel. 434/342-4176, email matiasag@hotmail.com. Here, artist owners have transformed a former family house into a rustic, art-decorated guesthouse. Bathrooms are artfully tile-adorned and a quaint wrought-iron spiral staircase rises from an inviting interior patio to a trio of upstairs rooms. The total of five rooms rent for $20 s, $35 d with private bath, $28 d with shared bath.

Avenida Lázaro Cárdenas Hotels

A number of comfortable motel-style accommodations cluster along Av. Lázaro Cárdenas, about a mile from downtown and half a mile uphill from the Uruapan-Morelia Highway. As you head downhill from town, first comes the **Hostería San Felipe,** on the left, at Av. L. Cárdenas 321, Pátzcuaro, Michoacán 61600, tel. 434/342-1298, fax 434/342-1955. Behind the roadside restaurant, 11 motel-style cottages surround a patio parking lot. Clean, comfortable, and carpeted, the units have colonial-style wrought-iron fixtures and brick fireplaces. Rooms rent for about $60 s or d, $70 t ($100 s or d, Christmas, Easter, and Day of the Dead holidays); credit cards are accepted. Some rooms are wheelchair-accessible. For reservations, dial toll-free Mex. tel. 800/714-1522.

A few blocks farther along spreads the 130-room resort-style Best Western **Hotel Posada de Don Vasco,** Av. Lázaro Cárdenas 450, Pátzcuaro, Michoacán 61600, tel. 434/342-0227 or 434/342-2704, fax 434/342-0262, bwposada@prodigy.net.mx. Here, guests enjoy old-world decor, comfortable, high-beamed room ceilings, spreading lawns, quiet patio nooks, a chapel, a big pool, tennis, billiards, bowling, a bar, and a good restaurant with breakfast buffet and folkloric dance shows. Lodgings come in three grades. The colonial-style, high-ceilinged rooms in the older, original building go for about $100 s or d. Large and luxurious modern-decor garden-view balcony rooms in a resort-style wing run about $120 s or d. Bargain third choice goes to rooms renting for about $85 s or d, in an attractive new colonial-style annex across the boulevard. All lodgings come with TV, phones, heat, seasonal discotheque, parking, and limited wheelchair access to lower floors; credit cards are accepted. Reserve at Best Western toll-free U.S./Can. tel. 800/528-1234. For more information, visit the website www.bestwestern.com.

Head a few blocks farther downhill to the **Motel del Lago,** at Av. L. Cárdenas 509, Pátzcuaro, Michoacán 61600, tel./fax 434/342-4992. The choice of families with wheels, the del Lago's 12 brick units surround a central parking area garden, bordered by leafy avocado, rubber, and peach trees. The somewhat worn but reasonably clean, rustic wood-and-tile cottages have fireplaces, wood $2 extra, and hot water. There's limited wheelchair access. Rooms run a bargain-basement $12 s, $20 d, $24 t; credit cards are not accepted. (*Note:* A new friendly, hard-working owner plans to add a restaurant and renovate Motel del Lago—the evening I arrived she was sewing new drapes. Prices will probably rise to about $20 s, $35 d, $45 t.)

Cross Av. Lázaro Cárdenas to **Hotel Villa Pátzcuaro,** Av. L. Cárdenas 506, Pátzcuaro, Michoacán 61600, tel. 434/342-0767, fax 434/342-2984, info@villapatzcuaro.com, a homey cluster of a dozen cottages set half a block back from the road. It was built a generation ago by longtime lovers of Pátzcuaro, Obdulia and the late Arturo Pimentel Ramos; Obdulia and her family now manage the complex of cottages, attractively furnished in rustic browns, knotty-pine paneling, and brick fireplaces. The grassy grounds spread past a blue swimming pool (not maintained in winter) and a tennis court to an acre of tent and RV (self-contained only) sites on the adjacent gentle hillside. A kitchen is available for guests' use. The cottages rent for a refreshingly moderate $30 s, $35 d, $50 t. Guests with a big RV pay about $6 per person per night. Tent campers and small RV guests pay about $5 per person per night. The cottages are often filled— make reservations. Limited wheelchair access. For more information, visit the website www.villapatzcuaro.com.

Finally, follow Av. Lázaro Cárdenas across the Morelia-Uruapan highway downhill, bear left after the railroad tracks, and continue to road's-end **Hotel San Carlos,** Colonia Morelos, Calle Caltzonzín s/n, Pátzcuaro, Michoacán 61600, tel./fax 434/342-1359. The 10 rooms are tucked along a long covered veranda adjoining an elegantly tranquil orchard/garden planted with avocado, peach, pear, and fragrant orange and lemon trees. Paths among the trees lead past a graceful, colonial-style restaurant and a big blue, beautiful (but unheated) pool and kiddie pool, finally heading, via country lanes, a few blocks to the Janitzio boat dock and the reed-lined lakeshore. Back at the hotel, the simply but thoughtfully furnished beam-ceiling rooms rent, nonholiday weekdays, for about $25 s, $30 d, $40 t; $30, $40 and $50 weekends and Christmas, Easter, and Day of the Dead (Nov. 1–2) holidays.

Trailer Park and Camping

Visitors who enjoy RV and tent camping near the lakeside opt for **Trailer Park El Pozo** (The Well). Watch for the sign on the highway about a mile in the Morelia direction past the Av. Lázaro Cárdenas intersection. The 20 RV spaces spread downhill in a grassy park about a quarter mile from the reed-lined lakeshore. The friendly, family-run park provides all hookups, a picnic table with each space, some shade, toilets, and hot showers for about $12 per day for two, $14 for three, $16 for four, with one day free per week for weekly and monthly stays. Tenters are also welcome, at about $4 per person. While reservations are generally not necessary, it's best to call or write ahead of time for weekends and holidays: Trailer Park El Pozo, P.O. Box 142, Pátzcuaro, Michoacán 61600, tel. 434/342-0937, elpozorv@yahoo.com.mx.

FOOD
Breakfast and Snacks

A pair of good spots to start out your day with coffee or tea and breakfast are either of the locally popular **Cafetería Los Escudos** and the **Restaurant La Casona.** They're both open from 8 A.M., on the west and north sides, respectively, of the Plaza Don Vasco de Quiroga.

For quick cooling energy during the heat of the day, try the *neverías* (ice-cream stands) in front of the Hotel Los Escudos on Plaza Don Vasco de Quiroga. The fruit ices are so popular you may have to wedge your way in. Just point to what you want. Eat without worry—its offerings are pure; the stand depends on repeat customers. Open daily 9 A.M.–6 P.M.

For a hot pick-me-up, go for a cup of freshly ground Michoacán mountain-grown coffee at **Café Bote Fumeiro** (Café Smoking Censer) beneath Portal Aldama at the adjacent corner of the plaza. It also sells pastries, cookies, and fresh-roasted beans for around $5 per pound ($11 per kilo). Open daily 8 A.M.–10 P.M., if business warrants.

At night at the market corner of Plaza Bocanegra, a very professional lineup of taco stands steams with hearty offerings. Among the best is **Tacos Rápido,** run by Jorge, whose fingers fly as if they could wrap 1,000 chorizo (spiced sausage), *res* (roast beef), *pastor* (roast lamb, pork or beef), and *lengua* (tongue) tacos a night.

For tasty late-night international-style fare, try the popular **Viejo Gaucho** club and restaurant, behind the Hotel Mansion Iturbe, two doors north of the Plaza Don Vasco. Their long menu includes favorites, such as onion rings, Caesar salad, spaghetti Bolognese, pizza, hamburgers, and baked potato. Open daily except Sun. and Mon., 6 P.M. until about midnight, at Iturbe 10, tel. 434/342-0368.

Restaurants

Pátzcuaro has a sprinkling of good restaurants, many on or near the Plaza Don Vasco de Quiroga.

At the **Cafetería Los Escudos** in the Hotel Los Escudos, northwest plaza corner of Mendoza and Ibarra, tel. 434/342-0138, conversation and café espresso sometimes seem as important as the menu. A broad list of regional and international favorites (try the taco soup) keeps customers satisfied. Open daily 8 A.M.–9:30 P.M.; credit cards are accepted. Moderate.

As you continue counterclockwise around the plaza, next comes the **Restaurant El Patio,** at 19 Plaza Don Vasco de Quiroga, near the Hotel Posada San Rafael, tel. 434/342-0484, where soft music, muted lighting, and tasteful handicrafts decor set the tone. Despite the mostly tourist clientele, many are longtime repeat customers (who know to start out with the excellent Tarascan soup). Open daily 8 A.M.–9:30 P.M.; credit cards are accepted. Moderate–expensive.

Head south around the southeast plaza corner, half a block on Dr. Coss, to **Restaurant Mistongo** with an Argentinian flair, tel. 434/342-6332, open daily except Mon., 8:30 A.M.–10 P.M. Specialties of friendly owner-chef Suzie Santiago include made-in-house pastas, Argentine-style *ensalada criolla,* and ostrich fillet, cooked with wine.

Added pluses are the frequent evenings of live music and dance; call for progams. Moderate–expensive.

Perhaps the best restaurant on the Plaza Bocanegra is at the **Hotel Fiesta Plaza.** Hearty breakfasts and strong, fragrant espresso head an interestingly varied menu of appetizers, salads, and a number of house specialties such as Tarascan soup, *crema conde,* trout with white wine, and lake whitefish *al gusto.* Open daily 8 A.M.–10 P.M.; credit cards are accepted. Moderate–expensive.

Uphill from the Plaza Bocanega, romantics congregate at the restaurant of the **Hotel Posada de la Basílica** on Arciga, opposite the basilica, tel. 434/342-1108. Diners enjoy Pátzcuaro's famous whitefish and wine (ask for Cetto label sauvignon blanc) while feasting on the gleaming view of the old city, the lake, and the mountains beyond. Open daily for breakfast and lunch only, 8 A.M.–5 P.M.; credit cards are not accepted. Moderate–expensive.

Far downhill, at Av. Las Americas 158, on the left side as you go downhill, three cheers for **La Cocina de los Angeles,** probably Pátzcuaro's best restaurant. (I hope it will still be open when you read this. The out-of-downtown location is difficult.)

Regardless, the cooking of chef David Jourde, of Carcassone, the renowned French castle town, is splendid. When I was there I enjoyed a simple but delicious lunch of vegetable potage, *cassoulet* (country bean and ham stew), custard and coffee for dessert. My wife had a delicious salmon fillet on a bed of vegetables and rice. Our selections were so delicious we had to return the next day. Find it open daily except Sat., 2–8 P.M.

Nothing to rave about, but good enough to recommend, is the restaurant of the **Hotel Posada de Don Vasco,** a quarter mile farther downhill, on the left, at Av. Lázaro Cárdenas 450, tel. 434/342-0227 or 434/342-2704, open daily 7 A.M.–5 P.M. The breakfast buffet is probably the best bet here, although the lunch-dinner menu is very recognizable, tasty, and professionally presented and served. (The same cannot be said, however, for the folkloric dance-and-mariachis entertainment buffet, which seemed a

TO IXTAPA/PÁTZCUARO

bland prelude to the Los Viejos dancers, who were excellent.)

ENTERTAINMENT AND EVENTS

Pátzcuaro's one must-see entertainment is the famous **Viejecitos** (Little Old Men) dance. Said to have been invented during the early colonial period to mock the Spanish colonists, a troupe of dancers put on wrinkle-faced pink masks and campesino-style dress and dance as if every stumbling step were about to send them to the hospital. Perhaps the most reliable of the local Los Viejos performances is in the Casa de Once Patios (see In-Town Sights) Sat. and Sun. at noon. Hotels and restaurants also stage the Los Viejos periodically. Check with the Hotel Posada de Don Vasco, tel. 434/342-0227 or 434/342-2704, the Hotel Los Escudos, tel. 434/342-0138 or 434/342-1290, and Restaurant El Patio, tel. 434/342-0484.

Local people celebrate a number of fiestas and holidays. During the first two weeks in December, dance, music, processions, fireworks, and foodstalls fill Pátzcuaro streets and plazas in celebration of the **Fiesta de La Virgen de La Salud,** the city's patron saint.

Later, Semana Santa festivities climax on **Viernes Santa** (Good Friday), when townsfolk carry big Christ-figures through the packed downtown streets.

Finally, on Nov. 1 and 2, Pátzcuaro (and many neighboring towns) stage Mexico's most spectacular **Día de los Muertos** (Day of the Dead) festivals. Crowds converge on the *panteón* (cemetery) on the old Morelia road with loads of food offerings and decorations for the graves of their beloved deceased. They keep candles burning next to the tombstones all night, illuminating their ancestors' return path to feast with the family once again. To get there, walk or ride a taxi a half mile northeast of the basilica.

The big movie house and theater **Cine Emperador** screens Mexican and American movies Sunday and stages occasional concerts and cultural events. Drop by (north end of Plaza Bocanegra, next to the Hotel Fiesta Plaza) and check the schedule.

For after-hours nightlife a couple of café-bars, such as the **El Viejo Gaucho Restaurant,** at Iturbe 10, tel. 434/342-0368, **Restaurant La Compañía,** on the Plaza Don Vasco de Quiroga, east side, and **Restaurant Mistongo,** on Dr. Coss, half a block south of the Plaza Don Vasco's southeast corner, tel. 434/342-6332, offer live music often until around 11 P.M.

SHOPPING

The Valley of Pátzcuaro is rich in handicrafts. Visitors need only travel to the *mercado* (which extends a long block, beginning at the Plaza Bocanegra) to find good examples. Copperware from the village of Santa Clara de Cobre and locally crafted woolens are among the most plentiful and bargainable items.

In the fish stalls, in season, Jan.–April, you'll see mounds of Pátzcuaro whitefish (at about $5 a pound!) and, farther on, among the piles of produce, unusual fruits from around Uruapan (such as the brown, puckery *mamey* and the greenish-pink *anona,* which is creamy like a Southeast Asian custard apple).

For a uniquely rich selection of fine handicrafts, don't miss the former convent, **Casa de Once Patios,** one block east and one block south of the Plaza Don Vasco de Quiroga. In a dozen separate shops, artisans paint, carve, weave, and polish excellent work for sale. In the *local de paja* (straw shop), for example, workers fashion Christmas decorations—candy canes, trees, wreaths, bells—entirely of strands of colored straw. Nearby, the *local de cobre* (copper shop) displays shelves and cases of brilliant copper and silver plates, vases, cups, and jewelry.

Although other *locales* craft and display fine furniture, textiles, papier-mâché, and masks, the climax comes in the *local de laca,* with lacquerware so fine it resembles the rich cloisonnés of Europe and Asia. In the especially excellent shop of the brothers Alozo Meza, artisans finish wares in a myriad of animal, human, and floral motifs in sizes and complexities to fit every pocketbook. Open daily 9 A.M.–2 P.M. and 4–7 P.M.

On your way to or from the Casa de Once Patios, be sure to browse some of the dozen-odd

© BRUCE WHIPPERMAN

A number of stalls at the Pátzcuaro market offer attractive baskets.

streetfront private **handicrafts shops** that have sprouted like mushrooms around the southeast corner of the Plaza Don Vasco de Quiroga.

On Friday, the small plaza, **Jardín Revolución,** blooms with ceramics from all over Michoacán (corner Ponce de Leon and Tena, one block west of the Plaza Don Vasco de Quiroga).

Grocery and Photo Stores

Two old-fashioned grocery stores, **Abarrotes Rosy** and **La Surtidora,** offer very basic grocery items, including cheese, milk, and deli meats, on opposite ends of Portal Hidalgo, west side of Plaza Don Vasco de Quiroga. You'll find them open Mon.–Sat., about 9 A.M.–2 P.M. and 4–8 P.M. When you enter La Surtidora (near the Hotel Los Escudos), which advertises "since 1916" in its sign, you'll probably agree that it's scarcely changed since then.

The local Kodak dealer, **Foto 30,** has two stores on Plaza Bocanegra, one on the southwest plaza corner, at Mendoza, tel. 434/342-1925, and the

other, larger, branch at the adjacent southeast plaza corner, of Iturbe. Besides a fair stock of film (including 120 black-and-white and color negative) and photo equipment, they offer 30-minute color developing and printing, three-day transparency, and five-day black-and-white photofinishing services. Open Mon.–Sat. 9:30 A.M.–2 P.M. and 4–8 P.M., Sun. 9:30 A.M.–2 P.M.

INFORMATION AND SERVICES

The helpful **Michoacán Tourism Office** is at 7 Calle Buena Vista, the short street that diagonals northwest downhill, from the basilica park, northwest side. The friendly tourism staff, tel. 434/342-4765, fax 434/342-4771, turismopatzcuaro@hotmail.com, answers questions and offers a number of excellent brochure-guides, some in English, of out-of-the-way Michoacán towns, scenic points of interest, and ecoadventure touring. Office hours are Mon.–Sat. 9 A.M.–3 P.M. and 4–7 P.M., Sun. 9 A.M.–2 P.M.

The Pátzcuaro municipality also has a tourist information office, open Mon.–Fri. 9 A.M.–3 P.M. and 4–7 P.M., Sat. 9 A.M.–2 P.M. and 4–7 P.M., Sun. 9 A.M.–2 P.M., at the Presidencia Municipal (City Hall), west side of the Plaza Don Vasco, tel. 434/342-0215.

Several banks, all with ATMs, serve downtown Pátzcuaro. **Banco Internacional** (Bital) is trying hardest, with the longest hours of all, on Iturbe, midway between Plaza Bocanegra and Plaza Don Vasco, open Mon.–Fri. 8 A.M.–7 P.M., Sat. 9 A.M.–2:30P.M., tel. 434/342-3456. **Banamex,** on Plaza Bocanegra (Portal Juárez, west side), tel. 434/342-1550 or 434/342-1031, is open Mon.–Fri. 9 A.M.–4 P.M., Sat. 10 A.M.–4 P.M., for changing U.S., Canadian, French, German, Spanish, and Japanese currency and traveler's checks. Alternatively, go to **Bancomer,** open Mon.–Fri. 8:30 A.M.–4 P.M., Sat. 10 A.M.–2 P.M., half a block south, at 23 Mendoza; or **Banco Serfin,** around the corner, beneath the north portal on Plaza Don Vasco de Quiroga. A number of small Plaza Bocanegra *casas de cambio* change money after bank hours and Saturday and Sunday.

Health and Emergencies

For medical advice, go to the very professional **Consultorio Médicos del Centro,** at Navarrete 44-A, corner of Nicolas Romero, two blocks south of the southwest corner of Plaza Don Vasco de Quiroga, tel. 434/342-4533. You'll have the choice of at least three physicians: Dr. Marlon La Cayo, orthopedist; Dr. Fidel Orozco, pediatrician; and Dr. Jorge Alberto Ochoa, internal medicine.

Alternatively, go to **Hospital Guadalupana,** at Ibarra 36, three blocks west of Plaza Don Vasco de Quiroga, tel. 434/342-2194, with internist, surgeon, gynecologist, pediatrician, neurologist, and pharmacy, and 24-hour emergency service.

Pátzcuaro has many pharmacies; one of the most convenient and best stocked is the **Farmacia Moderna,** which, wryly, has an ancient snake-oil preventative advertisement on the wall outside and shelves filled with old-fashioned apothecary bottles inside. On the Iturbe lane-corner, middle of the north side of Plaza Don Vasco de Quiroga, open daily 9 A.M.–3 P.M. and 4–9 P.M., tel. 434/342-1731.

For police emergencies, contact the ***preventiva,*** on Ibarra, 2.5 blocks west of Plaza Don Vasco de Quiroga, tel. 434/342-0004.

Communications

The *correo* (post office), tel. 434/342-0128, is open Mon.–Fri. 8 A.M.–4 P.M., Sat. 9 A.M.–1 P.M., at Obregón 13, one block north of the Plaza Bocanegra.

For computer-assisted *larga distancia* and public fax, go to **Computel,** fax 434/342-2756, open daily 6 A.M.–midnight, on the Plaza Bocanegra next to the Cine Emperador movie house. Alternatively, go to the government ***telecomunicaciones,*** fax 434/342-0010, open Mon.–Fri. 8 A.M.–7 P.M. and Sat.–Sun. 9 A.M.–noon, next to the post office, at Obregon 13.

Among the very few sources of English-language news is the **newsstand** on the Plaza Bocanegra, at Portal Juárez 30, a few doors north of Banamex, which, around midday, gets the *News* from Mexico City and sometimes stocks *Time* magazine.

Internet connection is available at the **Meganet Café,** at Mendoza 5, half a block north of the northwest corner of Plaza Don Vasco. Find it open daily, 9 A.M.–9 P.M. Alternatively, go to **Puntocom,** tel. 434/342-3596, puntocom_soporte@hotmail.com, open Mon.–Sat. 10 A.M.–8 P.M.

GETTING THERE AND AWAY
By Air

Although the **Morelia International Airport,** code MLM, is a long 1.5-hour car or taxi ride east from Pátzcuaro, a number of its flights conveniently connect directly with several key U.S. and Mexico gateway destinations.

Mexicana Airlines flights connect with Mexico City and U.S. destinations of Los Angeles, San Francisco, San Jose, and Chicago. For reservations, call Mexicana's toll-free Mex. tel. 800/710-5089; for flight information, call the airport, at tel. 443/312-4725.

Aeromexico Airlines flights connect with Tijuana. For reservations, call Aeromexico's toll-free Mex. tel. 800/621-4000; for flight information, call the airport, at tel. 443/324-2424.

Mexicana affiliate **Aeromar Airlines** flights connect with Mexico City. For reservations, call tel. 443/324-6777 or Mexicana's toll-free Mex. tel. 800/710-5089; for flight information, call the airport, at tel. 443/313-6886.

Azteca Airlines flights connect with Tijuana. For reservations, call a travel agent, such as Ram Tours in Pátzcuaro, at Ibarra 1, tel. 434/342-4765, or email ramtours@hotmail.com.

Airport arrival and departure is straightforward. Although the Morelia terminal is small for an international destination, it does have an ATM for cash, a small gift shop, and some snack bars serving tacos, *tortas,* hot dogs, and drinks. Taxis and *colectivos* connect ($50 for four or $17 per person, respectively) to Pátzcuaro. Buy tickets at the booth next to the arrival exit gate. Plenty of public Ladatel card-operated telephones (buy cards at the gift shop) are available. The airport, however, has no hotel booking service, so arrive with a hotel reservation or you may be at the mercy of an unscrupulous taxi driver who would like to collect a commission from the hotel where he deposits you. I didn't see any **auto rental** booths, but auto rentals agents customarily meet arriving air passengers who have car rental reservations.

As for departure, don't lose your tourist card. If you do, arrive early and be prepared with a copy to avoid immigration red tape delay and perhaps a fine.

Travelers without wheels can get to the Morelia airport by either taxi (about $50 for three or four), or by **Herradura de Plata bus,** tel. 434/342-1045, from the Pátzcuaro *camionera central* (central bus terminal; see By Bus).

Get to the Morelia airport, from Pátzcuaro, via four-lane Highway 120 east, about 36 miles (58 km) to the (very ill-marked at this writing) interchange before downtown Morelia. Here, you avoid downtown by following the Highway 120, northern (Salamanca-Mexico City direction) town bypass, called *periférico* Independencia. This switches to *perférico* Republica as it passes the big Av. Francisco Madero intersection, where it begins its circuit around the north side of town for about six miles (10 km). Continue following the Highway 120-Salamanca-Mexico City signs

as you pass the big signalled Av. del Pedregal, Av. Cerro Quincero, and Av. Prospero Cristobal Vega intersections in succession. Finally, turn left at the big signalled Highway 43 intersection, also signed Av. Technologia. Now heading north, continue, still following the Mexico City and Salamanca signs, but also following the airport (aeropuerto), airplane logo, Highway 120, and Zinapecuaro signs. After another six miles (10 km) turn right at the signed Zinapecuaro-Highway 120-airport exit. After another 10 miles (15 km), or a total of about 58 miles (93 km) and 1.5 hours, from Pátzcuaro, you'll be at the airport. Whew.

By Car or RV

The quickest auto connection between Pátzcuaro to the Pacific Coast is via the new *cuota* (toll) *autopista* 37 D, that enables drivers to safely travel the 166 miles to Highway 200 in about 3.5 hours, thence another (47 miles, 76 km) southeast to Zihuatanejo, or another 45 minutes (30 miles, 47 km) northwest to Playa Azul. (Find the Highway 37 D Pátzcuaro entrance, by following the the road to Santa Clara del Cobre, about two miles east of town.)

Although I don't recommend it you can alternatively follow the old north-south National Highways 14 and 37 that connect Pátzcuaro with the Pacific coast Highway 200 at Playa Azul. The 192-mile (307-km) scenic but winding and sometimes potholed route requires around seven hours of careful driving. Fill with gasoline wherever you can. Magna unleaded is routinely available only at Uruapan, Nueva Italia, and Arteaga en route.

In the opposite direction, four-lane National Highway 120 will connect you with the state capital, Morelia, in about an hour. To continue east, follow the southern bypass around town and continue on the winding but very scenic two-lane Highway 15, which will eventually lead you to Mexico City in about eight hours.

A much easier eastbound alternative is the toll expressway 90 D *(autopista cuota)* with which you can connect half an hour north of Morelia. Follow the airport access directions above but instead continue straight ahead on Highway 43 instead of exiting right on Highway 120 toward the airport and Zinapecuaro. In 15 minutes you'll be at the 90 D expressway entrance and five hours later you can be in Mexico City. Make sure to arrive on a day permitted by your license plate number. (See the special topic "Mexico City Driving Restrictions" in the Acapulco chapter.)

To and from Lake Chapala and Guadalajara, the scenic route is the relatively level, aging Highway 15 Lake Chapala south-shore route. Head north 17 miles (27 km) to the Highway 15 junction at Quiroga. Turn left (west) onto Highway 15, continuing through Zacapu, Sahuayo, the Chapala shore, and Acatlán, to Guadalajara, a total of 210 miles (338 km). Congestion around the several towns en route slows progress. Allow about six hours' driving time, either direction. You can cut the Pátzcuaro-Guadalajara driving time to about four hours by picking up the *cuota* (toll) *autopista* 90 D near Villa Jiménez, about 10 miles north of Highway 15 from Zacapu.

By Bus

The spacious, modern long-distance *camionera central,* on the *libramiento* (peripheral boulevard) south of town offers a number of services, including a snack bar, luggage lockers (open daily 7 A.M.–9 P.M.) and Computel public long-distance telephone and fax (open daily 7 A.M.–10 P.M.).

From an ajacent terminal, many local **urbano** buses depart to dozens of local and regional towns and villages, such as Santa Clara del Cobre, Ihuatzio, Tzintzunzán, and Zirahuen.

From the long-distance terminal, several first- and second-class bus lines connect frequently with a host of regional and national destinations. Longest-distance daily service is provided by **Estrella Blanca** subsidiaries Elite (EL) and Turistar (TUR), tel. 434/342-1460, (departing from Morelia, however; reservations only in Pátzcuaro) northwest, via Guadalajara, continuing north either by the Pacific route to the U.S. border at Tijuana, or by the central route to Monterrey and the U.S. border at Nuevo Laredo, Matamoros, and Reynosa.

Several **Autovías del Occidente** (AO) buses, tel. 434/342-1243, with first- and second-class departures, connect west with Guadalajara, east with Morelia and Mexico City, and locally west with Lake Zirahuén, and north, with Lake Pátzcuaro west-shore towns of Jarácuaro and Erongarícuaro.

Frequent **Galeana** and **Ruta Paraíso** first- and second-class departures, tel. 434/342-0808, connect with regional destinations: north with Tzintzuntzán, east with Morelia; south with Uruapan, Apatzingan, Nueva Italia, Playa Azul (La Mira), and Lázaro Cárdenas on the Pacific coast.

Parhikuni first-class and luxury-class departures, tel. 434/342-1060, also connect east, with Morelia, and west, with Uruapan.

Flecha Amarilla (FA) second-class and first-class "Primera-plus" departures, tel. 434/342-0960, offer broad service east via Morelia to Mexico City; north with Irapuato, León, Querétaro, and San Luis Potosí; west, via the *autopista,* with Guadalajara; and south with Lake Zirahuen and Uruapan.

Herradura de Plata buses, tel. 434/342-1045, offer first- and luxury-class connections along Highway 120, with the Morelia airport, and Zinapecuaro, and Mexico City.

By Train

Although Pátzcuaro lies on the rail line connecting Lázaro Cárdenas on the Pacific coast to Morelia, privatization has erased train passenger service from the Pátzcuaro travel menu.

Uruapan

En route to or from Lake Pátzcuaro, Uruapan (pop. 200,000), Michoacán's second city, is well worth a day or two, if only to bask for a while in its springlike weather and enjoy a stroll through its luxuriantly lovely spring-fed river park.

Uruapan's mile-high (1,610-meter) elevation places it squarely on the delightfully balmy border between the warm tropics and the cool highlands, where a bounty of fruit—citrus, *mamey, chirimoya,* and a million acres of avocados—have earned Uruapan the semiofficial title of "avocado capital of the world."

HISTORY

Some of the most important clues to Uruapan's pre-Columbian past have been unearthed beneath the pyramids and platforms in the **Tinganio archaeological zone,** at Tingambato, about 16 miles (26 km) from Uruapan. Here, between A.D. 450 and 950, a highly cultured people built a ceremonial center, with plazas, a ball court, and tombs reminiscent of classic Teotihuacán style. Where those builders originated and why they abandoned their city remains a mystery. Their pyramids were rubble by the time the Tarascans arrived, around A.D. 1200.

The great Tarascan kings Tariácuri, Hiripan, and Tangaxoan, who ruled from the shore of Lake Pátzcuaro, controlled a vast western empire, which included Uruapan (oo-roo-AH-pahn). The name itself comes from the Tarascan (more correctly, Purépecha) language, translating as "Place of Fruit and Flowers."

Although the Purépecha emperors ruled, collecting tribute from the Uruapan tribes, only a small minority of Purépecha-speaking people actually lived in Uruapan; most inhabitants belonged to other indigenous groups—Otomi, Nahua, Chontal, Chichimec, and more—scattered through the mountains and valleys of the Uruapan basin.

In 1522, when conquistador Cristóbal de Olid and his battalion arrived at Lake Pátzcuaro, the last Purépecha emperor, Tangaxoan II, fled to Uruapan. There, after a short resistance, Tangaxoan II was captured and taken to Mexico City, where he pledged fealty to Hernán Cortés. Unfortunately, Cortés had to return to Spain; while he was gone, renegade conquistador Nuño de Guzmán's gold-crazed outlaw army rampaged over all Michoacán—killing, raping, burning, and sending the villagers fleeing into the mountains.

Ruin and desolation confronted Franciscan Father Juan de San Miguel when he arrived in Uruapan in early 1532. His first task was to coax those remaining of the original inhabitants to rebuild their homes and return to their fields. Proceeding with care and compassion, much as Father Vasco de Quiroga did in Pátzcuaro, Father Juan gained the confidence of the Uruapan people. He founded the town in December 1533, organizing it in eight *barrios,* each with its patron saint, church, school, and cemetery. In the center of town, Father Juan laid out the present town plaza, where, in 1533, he began building the Church of San Francisco, the Chapel of the Holy Sepulchre, and the "Huatapera" community hospital, all of which still stand on the plaza.

During succeeding generations, events of historical note occasionally occurred in sleepy Uruapan. During the mid-18th century, local citizens rebelled, refusing to billet Spanish troops without compensation. In retaliation, the Spanish flogged an indigenous chief, igniting a revolt. The local people overran the garrison and were about to massacre the soldiers when a priest interceded; the locals won the day, however, by throwing the soldiers into the river.

During the 1810–1821 War of Independence, Uruapan was the seat of the Congress of Anahuac, the insurgent shadow government led by José María Morelos, the father of Mexican independence.

Uruapan briefly served as the Michoacán state capital three times: during the Mexican-American war in 1847, the War of the Reform in 1859, and the French imperialist War of the Intervention in 1863. During the last, the French army surprised and defeated Mexican troops in a battle

TO IXTAPA/PÁTZCUARO

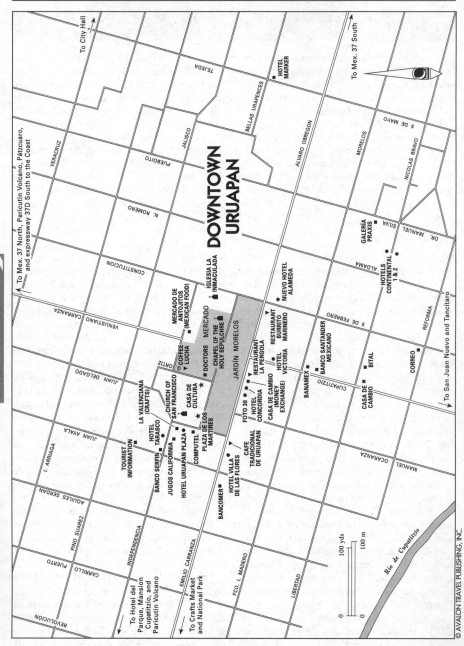

DOWNTOWN URUAPAN

TO IXTAPA/PÁTZCUARO

To City Hall

To Mex. 37 North, Paricutin Volcano, Pátzcuaro, and expressway 37D South to the Coast

To Mex. 37 South

HOTEL MARKER

TEJEDA

BELLAS URAPENCES

ALVARO OBREGON

MORELOS

5 DE MAYO

NICOLAS BRAVO

JALISCO

PUEBOITO

VERACRUZ

N. ROMERO

CONSTITUCION

VENUSTIANO CARRANZA

DR. MANUEL SILVA

GALERÍA PRAXIS

ALDAMA

HOTELS CONTINENTAL 1 & 2

REFORMA

5 DE FEBRERO

NUEVO HOTEL ALAMEDA

IGLESIA LA INMACULADA

MERCADO DE ANTOJITOS (MEXICAN FOOD)

MERCADO

COFFEE LUCHA

DOCTORS

CHAPEL OF THE HOLY SEPULCHRE

JARDÍN MORELOS

RESTAURANT BURRITO MARINERO

BANCO SANTANDER MEXICANO

BITAL

CORREO

CUPATITZIO

To San Juan Nuevo and Tancitaro

JUAN DELGADO

ORTIZ

LA VALENCIANA (CRAFTS)

CHURCH OF SAN FRANCISCO

CASA DE CULTURA

RESTAURANT LA PERGOLA

HOTEL VICTORIA

CASA DE CAMBIO (MONEY EXCHANGE)

BANAMEX

CASA DE CAMBIO

JUAN AYALA

HOTEL TARASCO

PLAZA DE LOS MARTIRES

FOTO 30

HOTEL CONCORDIA

I. ARRIAGA

TOURIST INFORMATION

BANCO SERFIN

JUGOS CALIFORNIA

HOTEL URUAPAN PLAZA

COMPUTEL

CAFE TRADICIONAL DE URUAPAN

OCARANZA

MANUEL

AQUILES SERDAN

BANCOMER

HOTEL VILLA DE LAS FLORES

PINO SUAREZ

INDEPENDENCIA

EMILIO CARRANZA

FCO. I. MADERO

LIBERTAD

Rio de Cupatitzio

CARRILLO PUERTO

REVOLUCION

To Hotel del Parque, Mansion Cupatitzio, and Paricutin Volcano

To Crafts Market and National Park

100 yds

100 m

0

0

© AVALON TRAVEL PUBLISHING, INC.

at nearby Santa Ana Amatlán. The leading five Mexican officers, including General José Arteaga, were brought to Uruapan and executed on October 21, 1865. They became known as the "Martyrs of Uruapan." A small square and monument in their honor stands in front of the Church of San Francisco on the town plaza.

On February 20, 1943, Mother Nature put Uruapan permanently on the world map by pushing a volcano up through a cornfield near Angahuan town, about 20 miles northwest of Uruapan. The volcano, which the local Purépecha folks call "Parhikútini" (Paricutín in Spanish), sent villagers fleeing in fear, buried their church with lava, and blanketed their fields with ash. The fiery mountain roared, smoked, and hissed for years, building up a 1,350-foot (410-meter) cone before going dormant in 1952. Since then, the government has established a national park, which draws thousands of yearly visitors, who hike the cinder-strewn fields, peer inside the lava-choked church, and climb to the top of the Paricutín's gray cone of ash.

SIGHTS

Getting Oriented

Uruapan, walled by mountains on its north and west sides, spreads southeast, down the valley of the **Río Cupatitzio** (koo-pah-TEET-zeeoh). Traveling to or from Pátzcuaro on Highway 37, you can easily miss Uruapan completely by continuing north or south along the highway's main truck route, which skirts Uruapan's eastern suburb. That would be a pity, for a stroll around the shady downtown plaza can provide relaxed glimpses of the charms of old Mexico. The very center of town is at the "T," where north-south Av. Cupatitzio ends at the town plaza, officially **Jardín Morelos.** At the corner of Av. Cupatitzio, face north, toward the *jardín.* The main east-west boulevard, which changes names at Av. Cupatitzio, is called Av. Emilio Carranza on your left and Av. Alvaro Obregón on your right. If you follow Av. Obregón, you'll be heading east, where after about half a mile, you'll reach a traffic circle and the railroad tracks and antique rail station, a block to the south. On the other hand, if you

walk west along Carranza in the opposite direction, after about seven blocks you'll arrive at the luxuriantly leafy gorge of the Río Cupatitzio, preserved for public enjoyment as Uruapan's renowned national park.

A Walk Around the Plaza

Back at the center of town, at the Av. Cupatitzio corner, look north, directly across the *jardín,* and you'll see a pair of big, old Renaissance-style churches on the *jardín's* far side. The right-hand one is the 18th-century **Iglesia La Inmaculada** (Church of the Immaculate Conception); on the left stands the **Parroquia de San Francisco** (Parish Church of San Francisco), founded by Father Juan de San Miguel in 1533. Step across to the north side of the *jardín,* where, in front of the San Francisco church, a gothic arch leads to a small square, the **Plaza de los Mártires de Uruapan.** Inside the church, in the *sacristía,* you can view a renaissance painting of founder Father Juan de San Miguel.

Next, head east toward La Inmaculada church, along the lane that borders the *jardín's* north side. Before the first corner, on your left, you pass the **Casa de Cultura,** a modest government-supported museum and performing arts center, open Mon.–Fri. 10 A.M.–2 P.M. and 5–8 P.M. Three exhibit halls display artifacts including an 1899 gold and silver bell, paintings of President Benito Juárez and Father Miguel Hidalgo, pre-Columbian pottery, sculptures, jewelry, stone hatchets, and jade masks, and 1910-era revolutionary memorabilia. One of the rooms houses a minimuseum of one of Michoacán's favorite sons, historian Eduardo Ruiz, with photos, personal effects, autographed books, and military mementos. The Casa de Cultura, moreover, sponsors occasional films, lectures, art exhibits, and performances; look for posters announcing programs, or stop at the desk for information before you leave.

Outside, continue east across the adjacent lane another 50 yards, where, on the left, a walkway, the Paseo Vasco de Quiroga, leads into an arcade. Along the walkway dozens of stalls offer a multitude of handicrafts—lacquerware, guitars, woolens, sombreros, serapes, copperware, and chocolate stirrers *(molinillos).* Deeper inside, lanes diverge into the main **town market,** a block-square warren of shops displaying a galaxy of everyday items.

Back outside, continue east to the courtyard, just before La Inmaculada church. Here a venerable chapel, La Capilla del Santo Sepulcro (Chapel of the Holy Sepulchre), adjoins the picturesque Huatápera, the former community hospital, founded by Father Juan de San Miguel in 1533. Inside (open Tues.–Sun. 9:30 A.M.–1:30 P.M. and 3:30–6 P.M.), three spacious rooms gleam with museum-quality Michoacán ceramics, lacquerware, copperware, masks, and textiles.

National Park

For a memorable finale, stroll through Uruapan's lovely **Parque Nacional Lic. Eduardo Ruiz.** Head west to the end of E. Carranza, about seven blocks from the *jardín,* to Av. Fray Juan de San Miguel. At the corner, walk right, uphill, another two blocks to the big curbside crafts market. Across the street, behind the fence, is the leafy ravine of the Río Cupatitzio, a botanist's paradise of bright flowers, twisting vines, and grand spreading trees. Lush trails lead you across bridges and past waterfalls, picnic grounds, and small restaurants nestled beneath the leafy canopy. Along the way, be sure not to miss the **Rodilla del Diablo** (Devil's Knee) spring, at the top end near the Hotel Mansión Cupatitzio; the **Cascada de Golgota** waterfall, 100 yards farther downstream; and the **Fuente de Janintzizic** fountain, on the left bank, about a quarter mile farther downstream. Stop by the adjacent riverside **Granja Truticola,** trout farm, where you can rent a fishing rod. If you catch a fish, you get to keep it for $5. (*Note:* After heavy upstream rains the Río Cupatitzio often becomes a muddy brown.)

The park has two entrances: the main lower entrance, across Av. Fray Juan de San Miguel from the crafts market; and the upper entrance, at the far end of the parking lot by the Hotel Mansión Cupatitzio, about five blocks farther up Av. Fray Juan de San Miguel. Either entrance has its advantages. From the crafts market entrance, you walk gradually uphill, ending at the river's crystal-blue source, the Rodilla del Dia-

blo spring. From there you could continue to the adjacent graceful Hotel Mansion Cupatitzio patio restaurant for a relaxing drink or lunch. From the upper entrance, you could start with lunch at the Hotel de Cupatitzio and begin your downhill stroll at the Rodilla del Diablo spring. In either case, bring along your bathing suit for a swim in the hotel's big blue pool.

Waterfall La Tzararacua

Visitors hankering for a small out-of-town adventure will probably enjoy La Tzararacua (Tsar-rah-RAH-kooa), the renowned falls of the Río Cupatitzio, about five miles south of town. Part of the fun is getting down to the falls. The 1.5-mile foot trail leads downhill through wildlife-rich highland tropical forest. If it's too hot to walk, concessionaires rent horses. Stands also provide food and drinks. Bring walking shoes and a hat. Get there by second-class buses running along Highway 37 west of downtown, by taxi, or by car. After about five miles (eight km) from the edge of town, watch for a signed turnoff on the right.

ACCOMMODATIONS

Uruapan visitors have their choice of several good budget-moderate hotels, mostly around the central *jardín.* The major exception, in the west suburb, about half a mile from the *jardín,* stands the queen of Uruapan lodgings, the **Hotel Mansión Cupatitzio,** adjacent to the lush canyon of the gushing Río Cupatitzio. The hotel's hacienda-style wings enfold a tranquil, flowery pool patio. Tucked on one side, the shady poolside tables of the excellent restaurant lead to an elegant inside dining room. In the hotel, guests enjoy light, spacious rooms, many with patio views, equipped with modern-standard tub baths and furnished with original wall art, hand-painted furniture, fresh flowers, and mints on the pillows. All this for about $80 s, $100 d, with a/c, cable TV, and telephones. Stay if you can possibly manage it. Be sure to reserve at P.O. Box 63, Uruapan, Michoacán 60000, tel. 452/523-2100, fax 452/524-6772, or email reservaciones@mansioncupatitzio.com. For more information, visit website www.mansioncu-patitzio.com.

Visitors who prefer the livelier downtown atmosphere have many good choices. By location, moving from the northwest to the southeast, first comes the homey, *posada*-like **Hotel del Parque** at 124 Independencia, Uruapan, Michoacán 60000, tel. 452/524-3845, six blocks west of the *jardín*, one block east of the national park. Here, past the lobby, furnished with soft couches for reading and conversation, tile stairs rise to three stories of 14 clean, comfortable rooms with baths and hot water. The top floor opens to a light, view patio porch for relaxing. Rates, moreover, are right, at $13 s, $16 d, $19 t, with parking; credit cards are not accepted.

Five blocks farther east, **Villa de las Flores,** a block from the *jardín,* at E. Carranza 15, Uruapan, Michoacán, tel. 452/524-2800, offers old-world atmosphere with an unpretentious touch of class. Most rooms surround a spacious, azalea-decorated, portal-shaded front patio. Continuing inside, you pass the restaurant (closed at this writing), tucked to one side. Beyond that is an intimate, bougainvillea-adorned rear patio, enfolded by several rooms in two stories. If you're going to stay, reserve one of these (upstairs, numbers 23–29). Inside, they're clean and thoughtfully furnished in natural wood and tile. Rates run about $29 s, $38 d, $41 t, with bath, phones, and TV. Privateparking is available nearby for about $3 per day. Credit cards are accepted.

A block farther, on the west side of the *jardín,* rises multistory **Hotel Plaza Uruapan,** at M. Ocampo 64, Uruapan, Michoacán, 60000, tel. 452/523-3599 or 452/523-3700, fax 452/523-3980, reservaciones@hotelplazauruapan.com.mx. The downstairs reception adjoins an atrium, opening to an oft-busy double level shopping mall that includes a travel agent at lobby level and a coffee shop and restaurant at the lower level. Upstairs, the 103 rooms are modern, clean, and tastefully decorated with beige carpets, drapes, and bedspreads. Rentals run $64 s, $77 d, $92 t, with a/c, TV, phones, bar, disco, live music, parking, and gym, but no pool. Credit cards are accepted. Reserve via toll-free Mex. tel. 800/420-0200.

Half a block farther north, at the *jardín's*

northwest corner, stands the 1960s-modern **Hotel Tarasco,** best-buy deluxe lodging of local business travelers, at Independencia 2, Uruapan, Michoacán 60000, tel./fax 452/524-1500. Downstairs, guests enjoy an airy lobby, good restaurant, and inviting outside pool and patio. Elevators lead upstairs to six stories of clean, modern-standard rooms, comfortably furnished with dark red carpets and bedspreads. Rooms rent for about $49 s, $59 d, with cable TV, a/c, parking, and phones.

For more choices, head south to Carranza, on the *jardín's* southwest side, to reliable standby **Hotel Concordia,** at Portal Concordia 8, Uruapan, Michoacán 60000, tel./fax 452/523-0400, toll-free Mex. tel. 800/420-0400. Right in the middle of *jardín* action but with the inviting lobby cleverly elevated from street noise, the hotel offers about 100 clean, tastefully decorated deluxe rooms for a sharply increased $38 s, $52 d, $59 t, (but Mon., Tues., Wed. 15 percent discount) including resrtaurant, parking, and TV; credit cards are accepted.

Continue west along Carranza, turn right at Cupatitzio. At midblock on the left rises the modern **Hotel Victoria,** at Cupatitzio 11, Uruapan, Michoacán 60000, tel. 452/523-6611 or 452/523-6700, fax 452/523-9662. Downstairs, guests have a convenient restaurant and upstairs, very clean modern rooms with bath, tastefully decorated in blues and grays. Rates run a high $49 s, $57 d, $64 t (if you can't get a discount, go to the Hotel Tarasco); with TV, phones, fans, a/c, and parking.

Around the block, economy business-class high-rise **Nuevo Hotel Alameda,** at 11 Cinco de Febrero, Uruapan, Michoacán 60000, tel. 452/523-4100, fax 452/523-3645, offers 50 rooms at modest rates. Here, what you see is what you get: a clean, smallish, modern, beige-carpeted and -draped room, a good value for about $28 s, $36 d, $44 t, with a/c, heat, TV, telephone, and parking, but no restaurant.

Two blocks south, and two blocks east of the southeast *jardín* corner, **Hotels Continental I and II,** at N. Bravo 33 and 34, Uruapan, Michoacán, 60000, tel./fax 452/523-5028 or 452/523-9793, offer still more options. Plainest is Hotel II, where creative management has upgraded a very lackluster layout into something with a bit of charm. Rooms with baths, in a pair of parallel, interior, motel-style two-story tiers, are clean and simply but thoughtfully decorated. Rates run a high $35 s, $40 d, $47 t, with fans, parking, and a restaurant in Hotel Continental I, across the street. Credit cards are accepted.

Across the street, brother Hotel Continental I offers about the same, except that it's larger, fancier, and the rooms are quite attractively furnished. Rooms in Hotel Continental I, with fans, private baths, parking, and restaurant in the lobby, run $40s, $46 d, and $53 t. Reserve both hotels by phone or email at hotelesucasa@yahoo.com.mx. For more information, visit the website www.sucasahoteles.com.mx.

Much more economical but still inviting is **Hotel Monarca,** a few blocks east of the *jardín,* at 18 Tejada, Uruapan, Michocán 60000, tel. 452/528-6959. Here, guests enjoy three stories of modern-standard deluxe rooms in color-coordinated brown and yellow decor and attractively tiled hot-water bathrooms. A bargain at about $15 s or d, $25 t, with fans, but street parking only. Get there by walking four blocks east of the *jardín* along Obregón to Tejada; turn left a block to the hotel at the corner of Bellas Uruapan and Tejada.

> *Uruapan's mile-high (1,610-meter) elevation places it on the border between the warm tropics and the cool highlands, where a bounty of fruit—citrus,* mamey, *chirimoya,* and a million acres of avocados—*have earned Uruapan the semiofficial title of "avocado capital of the world."*

FOOD

Plenty of tasty snacks are available around the *jardín.* The aroma of roasted coffee beans will probably draw you to the coffeehouse **Lucha,** at Garcia Ortíz 20, on the north side of the *jardín,* tel. 452/524-0375, sandwiched between the market and Parroquia de San Francisco. Here, refined atmosphere, quiet conversation, excellent coffee, and good pastries draw customers daily, 9 A.M.–9 P.M.

Nearby, wholesome homestyle food is the main event at the big **Mercado de Antojitos,** at the interior end of handicrafts lane Paseo de Vasco de Quiroga, in the market, north side of *jardín.*

Late at night, you can usually get a hot dog, hamburger, French fries, or tacos at stalls and carts around the *jardín,* especially on the south side, corner of Cupatitzio.

One of the most successful downtown restaurants is **Restaurant La Pérgola,** south side of the *jardín,* west of Cupatitzio, next to Hotel Concordia, tel. 452/523-5087. Polished dark wood furniture, colorfully executed wall murals, genteel ambience (ask the staff to turn down the TV), and a good, professionally served menu draw a steady stream of business and professional-class customers. Open daily 8 A.M.–11:30 P.M.

For similar good food and welcoming atmosphere but in a more spacious, more relaxed setting, join the host of middle- and upper-class clients at the coffeehouse restaurant **Café Tradicional de Uruapan,** at Emilio Carranza 5B, just west of the *jardín*'s southwest corner. Open daily 8 A.M.-10:30 P.M. Good for breakfast. Moderate.

A contrasting but also worthy spot for good eating is **Restaurant Burrito,** upstairs, overlooking the *jardín,* a block east of Cupatitzio, tel. 452/527-2395. Here, cooks put out a mixed menu of Mexican and American breakfasts and a little bit of everything else, including seafood, hamburgers, milk shakes, juices, and a host of tacos, burritos, *flautas,* enchiladas, and *chiles rellenos.* Open for breakfast and lunch daily 8 A.M.–5 P.M.

About the same juice, breakfast, sandwich, and Mexican snack menu is served in the clean *lonchería* atmosphere of **Jugos California,** across the street from Hotel Tarasco, northwest corner of the *jardín,* open daily 7 A.M.–10 P.M.

For a treat, go to one of Uruapan's finest, the **Hotel Mansión Cupatitzio** restaurant, on Av. Fray Juan de San Miguel, seven blocks west and five blocks north of the *jardín,* tel. 452/523-2100. Breakfast outside in the shady patio by the pool, and dinner inside, in the elegant, dignified dining room, are equally excellent. Arrive early enough to enjoy the live grand piano melodies in the dining room, Sat. and Sun. 9–11 A.M. and 8–10 P.M. Open daily 8 A.M.–10 P.M.

ENTERTAINMENT, EVENTS, AND SHOPPING

In addition to national (especially the Sept. 15 and 16 Independence and the Dec. 12 Virgin of Guadalupe) fiestas, Uruapan folks celebrate with an abundance of local festivals. Before Easter, around the Domingo de Ramos (Palm Sunday) usually in late March, campesinos flood into town in their traditional dress. Originally celebrated by artisans of palm-leaf handicrafts, the festival now attracts hundreds of vendors whose stalls mushroom around the *jardín,* filled with an all-Michoacán galaxy of pottery, musical instruments, woolens, baskets, and copperware.

Later, the **Fiesta de Santa María Magdalena** kicks off on July 22, continuing for eight days of colorful processions of decorated, yoked mules and oxen and climaxing in favorite dances, including Los Viejitos, Cristianos y Moros, and Los Negros. The fiesta centers around the Magdalena church, at the corner of Acapulco and González Ortega, about a mile southeast of the *jardín.*

Other locally important festivals include the July 25 **Día de Santiago Apostól** (Day of St. James the Apostle), with fireworks, carnival, and dances, at Capilla (Chapel) Santiago (end of E. Carranza, about seven blocks west of the *jardín*).

On Oct. 4, all the townsfolk celebrate the day of **San Francisco,** Uruapan's patron saint, with handicrafts, regional food, and favorite dances, around the Parroquia de San Francisco, on the *jardín.* For three days, Oct. 24–26, a swarm of local people enjoy the **Fiesta de Coros y Danzas** (Chorus and Dance). Performances, limited to folks of native Purépecha blood only, are highlighted by the all-female Danza de las Canacuas.

In addition to Uruapan's yearly fiestas, the government-funded **Casa de Cultura** sponsors cultural events and performances. Stop by Mon.–Fri. 10 A.M.–2 P.M. and 5–8 P.M. (north side of *jardín,* next to Parroquia de San Francisco) for information.

Handicrafts

Uruapan draws craftspeople from all over Michoacán. Goods made from wood—lacquerware, masks, guitars and other musical instruments, and furniture—are among the most widely available. Also, in addition to lots of wool jackets and sweaters, you'll find woven goods—hats, baskets, mats, and raffia decorations and utensils—and much shiny copperware.

The best places to start shopping are Uruapan's two main **crafts markets,** one on the Paseo Vasco de Quiroga, in the arcade, north side of the *jardín,* and the other, seven blocks west, on Av. Fray Juan de San Miguel, adjacent to the Río Cupatitzio National Park.

If you can't find everything you want in the markets, continue downhill, toward *jardín* along Independencia a block downhill past the Hotel del Parque one block to **Artesanías Lupita,** open Mon.–Sat. 10 A.M.–7 P.M. and Sun. 10 A.M.–2 P.M., at Indepencia 112. The specialty is woodcrafts, made to please—baskets, toys, small desks and tables, knickknack shelves, spice and CD racks—and much more festoon every corner of the store.

Continue downhill to the *jardín,* and **Artesanías La Valenciana,** which offers plenty of Paracho-made guitars, embroidery, baskets, and lacquerware. Find it on the west side of the *jardín,* a few doors south of the Hotel Plaza Uruapan, open Mon.–Sat. 10 A.M.–2 P.M. and 4–9 P.M., Sun. 10 A.M.–2 P.M., tel. 452/523-1762.

For an especially fine all-Mexico crafts collection, be sure to visit the shop at the **Hotel Mansión Cupatitzio** (open daily except Tues. 10 A.M.–6 P.M.), before or after you stroll the Río Cupatitzio park.

Photography

At least one store sells photo supplies and equipment and develops film on the south side of the *jardín.* Try **Photo 30,** tel. 452/523-6322, open Mon.–Sat. 9 A.M.–2 P.M. and 4–8:30 P.M., Sun. 9 A.M.–2 P.M., on Carranza, a few doors west of the Restaurant Pergola.

TOIXTAPA/PÁTZCUARO

INFORMATION AND SERVICES

Information and Guides

The competent local state of Michoacán **tourist information office** hands out maps and brochures and answers questions at its downtown office, on Juan Ayala, behind the Hotel Tarasco, adjacent to the hotel parking lot. Hours are Mon.–Sat. 9 A.M.–2 P.M. and 4–7 P.M., Sun. 9 A.M.–2 P.M., tel./fax 452/524-7199 or 452/524-7850, delregdetururuapan@prodigy.net.mx.

The tourism information office staff recommends a number of certified local guides. Choose from Edgar Avarez Herrera, at the Hotel Palacio, tel. 452/524-3192, Marta Elvia Bejar Maldonado (who works in the tourist information office, cellular (long distance from Uruapan) tel. 01-452/567-4938 or cellular (local in Uruapan) tel. 044-452/525-6749, or Guadalupe Avila, tel. 452/524-4517.

English-language reading matter is not easy to find in Uruapan. Nevertheless, the hotel shop at Hotel Plaza Uruapan customarily stocks a few popular American magazines, paperback novels, and a newspaper or two. The newsstand, on the adjacent northwest *jardín* corner, beneath Portal Aldama, across from the Hotel Tarasco, may have the daily English-language *News* from Mexico City, after it arrives around 2 P.M.

Money Exchange

You can change money at a number of banks, all with ATMs, near the *jardín*. These include **Banamex,** tel. 452/523-4966, 452/523-9290, or 452/524-1023, open Mon.–Fri. 9 A.M.–4 P.M. and Sat. 10 A.M.–2 P.M., at the corner of Cupatitzio, one block south of the *jardín;* or the **Banco Santander Mexicano,** a few steps downhill from Banamex, open Mon.–Fri. 9 A.M.–4 P.M., and **Banco International** (which has very long Mon.–Sat. 8 A.M.–7 P.M. hours), downhill and around the corner east, on Bravo. Additionally, you can go to **Bancomer,** near the southwest *jardín* corner, open Mon.–Fri. 8:30 A.M.–4 P.M. and Sat. 10 A.M.–3 P.M., at 7 E. Carranza, corner 20 de Noviembre, tel. 452/523-6522 or 452/524-1460. On Sunday, try one of the small *casas de cambio* (money-changers) scattered around the *jardín.*

Travel Agents

For tickets, tours, and information, go to one of the travel agents near the *jardín,* such as **Viajes Tzitzi,** in the Hotel Plaza Uruapan, tel. 452/523-3419 or 452/523-3452, fax 452/523-1578, tzitzi@prodigy.net.mx; or **Viajes Cupatitzio,** tel. 452/524-1185 or 452/523-5633, fax 452/524-1636, cupatitzio-i@wspanmex.com.mx, open Mon.–Fri. 9 A.M.–2 P.M., 4–7:30 P.M., Sat. 10 A.M.–2 P.M., in the Hotel Tarasco; both hotels are on the west side of the *jardín.*

Communications and Emergencies

Find the local *correo* (post office) three blocks south of the *jardín,* on Reforma, at the corner of 5 de Febrero. Efficient long-distance telephone and fax is available at the **Computel** office, open daily 6 A.M.–10 P.M., tel. 452/524-5482, at the west side of the *jardín* in front of Hotel Plaza Uruapan.

Read your email at **Internet Café Azul,** at Portal Santos Degollado 15, on the *jardín,* tel. 452/524-7917, open Mon.–Fri. 9 A.M.–9 P.M., Sat. 10 A.M.–7 P.M., Sun. 10 A.M.–3 P.M.

For **police** emergencies, call the municipal *preventiva,* tel. 452/524-0620 or 452/523-2733; for the **firefighters** *(bomberos),* call tel. 452/524-0616.

Doctors, Pharmacies, and Hospitals

If you get sick, ask your hotel desk to call a physician. Otherwise, a trio of good doctors, internist Dr. G. Fernando Hernández Zarco, pediatrician Dr. Julio Torres Farías, and surgeon Efren Castro Carrillo, maintain offices, tel. 452/523-0800, at 10 Garcia Ortiz, on the lane just north of the *jardín,* across Ortiz from the Casa de Cultura, offer routine advice and medicines daily 8 A.M.–9:30 P.M.

If you need hospitalization and/or expert diagnostic services, go to 24-hour emergency **Hospital El Ángel,** tel. 452/524-8030, at the corner of Juan N. López and Hilanderos, about seven blocks east, eight blocks south of the *jardín.* Alternatively, go to the government **Centro de Salud,** at 3 M.P. Coronado, in the same southeast

"IMPORTANTE"

- Este recibo es el comprobante de su transacción, consérvelo para verificar su operación en su estado de cuenta.
- En caso de aclaración, deberá presentar el recibo que corresponda.
- Las operaciones efectuadas durante días no laborables, ó después de las 22:00 hrs. serán consideradas o realizadas en el siguiente día hábil bancario.

"IMPORTANTE"

- Este recibo es el comprobante de su transacción, consérvelo para verificar su operación en su estado de cuenta.
- En caso de aclaración, deberá presentar el recibo que corresponda.
- Las operaciones efectuadas durante días no laborables, ó después de las 22:00 hrs. serán consideradas o realizadas en el siguiente día hábil bancario.

"IMPORTANTE"

- Este recibo es el comprobante de su transacción, consérvelo para verificar su operación en su estado de cuenta.
- En caso de aclaración, deberá presentar el recibo que corresponda.
- Las operaciones efectuadas durante días no laborables, ó después de las 22:00 hrs. serán consideradas o realizadas en el siguiente día hábil bancario.

"IMPORTANTE"

- Este recibo es el comprobante de su transacción, consérvelo para verificar su operación en su estado de cuenta.
- En caso de aclaración, deberá presentar el recibo que corresponda.
- Las operaciones efectuadas durante días no laborables,

neighborhood; or, in an emergency, the excellent local **Hospital Fray Juan de San Miguel,** at Mazatlán 75, tel. 452/524-4447, with 24-hour emergency service.

GETTING THERE AND AWAY
By Car or RV
North-south National Highway 37 connects Uruapan with the Pacific coast Highway 200 at La Mira (near Playa Azul). The 157-mile (253-km) scenic but winding and sometimes potholed route requires at least five hours of alert driving. Fill your car with gasoline; Magna unleaded be available only at Nueva Italia and Arteaga en route.

In the opposite direction, the spectacular but curving and sometimes steep 39-mile (62-km) Highway 14 will lead you to Pátzcuaro uphill in about 1.5 hours; allow one hour in the opposite direction, downhill. Alternatively, you can cut your Pátzcuaro driving time to 45 minutes and your driving time to the Pacific coast to about 3.5 hours by going via the Highway 37 D *cuota* toll expressway that takes off from the northeast edge of town.

Get to the Highway 37 D expressway entrance via the Uruapan north-side *libramiento* (downtown bypass). From downtown, follow one-way thoroughfare Venustiano Carranza (behind the plaza churches) about half a mile north to the *libramiento* traffic signal. Turn right and continue about two miles to old Highway 14 four-lane divided boulevard. Turn right, south and continue about a mile to the overpass where you pass under the overpass and immediately turn left. Continue approximately another mile to the 37 D toll expressway entrance. Follow the signs (to Highway 200, 128 miles, 206 km; Zihuatanejo, 174 miles, 280 km; Lázaro Cárdenas 147 miles, 237 km; and Playa Azul, 158 miles, 254 km).

The scenic route west to Lake Chapala and Guadalajara is the old two-lane, winding but relatively level Lake Chapala south-shore Highway 15. Head north, 48 miles (77 km), via Paracho, to the Highway 15 junction at Carapan. Turn left (west) onto Highway 15, continuing past Zamora, Sahuayo, along the Chapala shore to Acatlán, then Guadalajara, a total of 232 miles (373 km).

Congestion around the towns en route slows progress. Allow about six hours driving time, either direction. You can cut the Uruapan-Guadalajara driving time to about four hours by following Highway 37 north, past its Highway 15 junction about 20 miles (32 km) to the Churintzio entrance to the toll *autopista* to Guadalajara.

A paved, fairly rapid, and very scenic mountain highway route connects Uruapan southwest with Colima and Manzanillo on the Pacific coast. Head north along Highway 37, 48 miles (77 km) to the Highway 15 junction. Turn left (west), continuing on Highway 15, 22 miles (36 km) to Zamora, then another 38 miles (61 km) to the Highway 110 junction at Jiquilipan. Follow Highway 110, via Mazamitla, another 116 miles (187 km) to Colima. Allow about seven hours for the entire 224-mile (361-km) Uruapan-Colima trip, either way. Add another hour for the extra 54 miles (88 km) via the Highway 54-Highway 110-Highway 200 toll expressway to or from Manzanillo.

By Bus
A host of well-equipped long-distance buses connect directly with many western Mexico destinations from the big, modern *camionera central,* on the northeast side Highway 37 ingress boulevard. Besides the buses, the station has Computel long-distance telephone service, tel. 452/524-9694, government Telecom public fax and telephone, left luggage lockers, a pharmacy, bakery, a snack bar and minisuper for drinks, and canned and packaged foods.

First-class **Elite,** tel. 452/523-4450 or 452/523-4467, provides service north, either by the Pacific route via Mazatlán to the U.S. border at Mexicali and Tijuana, the northern route to Ciudad Juárez, or the northeast route to Monterrey and the U.S. border at Matamoros. Elite also offers connections south, with Lázaro Cárdenas and Ixtapa-Zihuatanejo.

Frequent **Galeana** and **Ruta Paraíso** first- and second-class departures, tel. 452/523-0300 or 452/524-4154, connect with many local and regional destinations: northeast, with Pátzcuaro and Morelia; north with Angahuan and Tancítaro, south with Apatzingan, Nueva Italia, La

Mira (Playa Azul), and Lázaro Cárdenas; and southwest with Colima and Manzanillo.

Parhikuni first-class and luxury-class departures, tel. 452/523-8754, also connect north with Morelia and south with Nueva Italia, Playa Azul (La Mira), and Lázaro Cárdenas on the Pacific coast.

Flecha Amarilla second-class, first-class and "Primera-plus" luxury-class departures, tel. 452/524-3982, offer broad service east via Morelia to Mexico City; north with Irapuato, León, and San Luis Potosí; and northwest with Guadalajara, and southwest, with Colima and Manzanillo.

Many **Autovías del Occidente** (AO) first- and second-class departures, tel. 452/523-1871, connect east with Mexico City via Morelia; south with La Mira (Playa Azul) and Lázaro Cárde-

nas; southwest with Colima and Manzanillo; west with Guadalajara via Jiquilipan along the slow but scenic Highway 15 route; and east, via Morelia and Toluca, with Mexico City.

Second-class **Auto Transportes Tancítaro** offers regional connections west, via San Juan Nuevo, with Tancítaro.

By Train

As with other Mexican railways, privatization has eliminated all passenger service on the rail line connecting Lázaro Cárdenas on the Pacific coast with Uruapan, Pátzcuaro, Morelia, and Mexico City. As in the United States and Canada many years ago, improved highways, cars, airlines, and fast, economical bus service are converting passenger train service all over Mexico to a vanishing memory.

West of Uruapan

Paricutín volcano's spectacular 1943 birth, the world's first volcanic eruption known to be witnessed at its very origin, added to the attraction of its dormant big brother Tancítaro (elev. 12,670 feet, 3,860 meters). The government established a National Park (Parque Nacional Pico Tancítaro); a private volcano visitor center, with cabins, campsites, and a restaurant followed. Now, new paved roads further encourage the adventurous to explore the pine-tufted backcountry of this sylvan, Purépecha native heartland, less than an hour's drive northwest of Uruapan.

ANGAHUAN VILLAGE, VOLCÁN PARICUTÍN, AND VICINITY

Before Paricutín there was Angahuan village, about 24 miles (38 km) by road northwest of Uruapan. The name, locals say, was originally "Andanhuan," which means "The Place That the People Reached," or perhaps, simply, "Resting Place." It's also said that the Spanish couldn't pronounce the original name, so it got changed to the present Angahuan (ahn-GAH-wahn).

Although now the gateway to Paricutín, An-

gahuan (pop. about 3,000) is interesting in its own right. When you arrive, men will probably crowd around, offering to be your guide. Whether you accept their services or not, your first stop should be the main square, by the old plaza church, on the left, at the town center.

Even though the Spanish arrived in 1527, in the person of the rapacious renegade conquistador Nuño de Guzmán, the church, dedicated to Santiago (St. James), wasn't begun until the Franciscan missionaries could gain the confidence of the local folks, who had been victims of Guzmán's reign of terror. By 1577, the church finally was finished, under the guidance of Father Jacobo Daciano. He commissioned a Spanish-Moorish stonemason to supervise the work. The flowery patterns, similar to those on the famous Talavera ceramics, that the stonemason executed resulted in the unmistakable Moorish style that blooms, like an ornate Persian carpet, both on the arched front facade and on the nave ceiling inside.

A Stroll Around Angahuan

Much of the fun of Angahuan is the old-Mexico scenes—a backyard lumber mill, bright *huipiles*

© BRUCE WHIPPERMAN

The 1577 Angahuan village church is decorated with an unmistakably Moorish-motif facade.

hanging out to dry on a clothesline, kids playing kickball—you might glimpse while strolling its back lanes. Among the most picturesque of Angahuan sights are the log houses, called *trojes* in the Purépecha tongue. Their steep shake roofs come in two forms: with two slopes, called "two waters," or with four slopes, "four waters."

As you stroll out from the church be sure to look for a house, about 100 yards on and a door or two to the right of the grocery store, across the other side of the plaza from the church front. Eight prize-winning carved panels tell the story of **Volcán Paricutín,** from the moment, one afternoon in 1943, when farmer Dionisio Pulido became the first person in the world to witness a volcano's birth. (Owners have moved the panels inside. Maybe if you ask, they will let you see them.)

If you want to see Paricutín's smoky eruption as it appeared at the time, try to get a video or catch a cable-TV presentation of the epic movie *Captain from Castile* (1947), starring Tyrone Power, Susan Peters, Lee J. Cobb, and César Romero. It was filmed on location, near Angahuan, with scenes of

the erupting Paricutín in the background. The volcano appears during the last 10 minutes of the movie. You might want to record the volcano scenes with a VCR so you can replay them.

By car, get to Angahuan by heading from Uruapan north along Highway 37. After about 19 miles (31 km) turn left at the westbound paved road and continue another 14 miles (23 km) to the Angahuan side road on the left. By bus, go early in the morning by second-class regional Galeana or Ruta Paraíso bus from the *camionera central,* on the Highway 37 ingress boulevard, about a mile northeast of the *jardín.* Alternatively, catch a local bus at the highway stop where Highway 37 heads north of town, uphill from the Hotel Mansion Cupatitzio.

You can also go by **local tour;** contact Viajes Cupatitzio, tel. 452/523-5633 or 452/524-1185, fax 452/524-1636, cupatitzio-i@wspanmex.com.mx at the Hotel Tarasco, at 2 Independencia, on the *jardín,* northwest corner.

Centro Turístico Angahuan

Continue from the Angahuan plaza along the extension of the main ingress street. After about three blocks, follow the sign left about another mile, up a low hill, to the private Centro Turístico Angahuan tourist center. An attendant collects a nominal entrance fee at the gate. The office is on the right; after that comes the interpretive center and museum, then the cabins, restaurant, and camping area. Behind the restaurant is the *mirador* (viewpoint), where, above the southern horizon, beyond the lava-choked villages and fields, you can see Paricutín's hulking, truncated cone. On a clear day, more likely during the Dec.–May dry season, you might see the gargantuan, cedar-crested bulk of Tancítaro mountain rising high above the horizon slightly to the right (west) of Paricutín.

Exploring the Paricutín Volcanic Zone

An overnight stay, followed by an early morning start, is the best strategy for exploring Paricutín's ash-strewn wasteland. Along the way you'll pass lava-covered fields, buried village houses and a church, a burned forest, active steam vents, and, finally, dark, forbidding Paricutín and Sapichi, the parasite vent that belched forth the

DIONISIO PULIDO AND VOLCÁN PARICUTÍN

On the afternoon of March 4, 1943, campesino Dionisio Pulido was the first person to witness the birth of a live volcano and live to tell the tale. He said that, around 3 in the afternoon, he was plowing his field with his yoke of bullocks, when the earth beneath his feet began to shift, shudder, and roar. Soon steam began rising from the animals' hoofprints. When Dionisio grabbed his hoe and desperately tried to fill the steamy holes, more holes appeared. His wife arrived with a dozen villagers, who worked like demons with sticks, hoes, shovels, and picks, struggling to fill the ever-widening hot fissures. But it was no use; a terrifying fiery explosion blew huge rocks into the air, and most people simply knelt down in the field, weeping and praying.

BOB RACE

Over the next few weeks, the smoke and explosions gradually became more violent. People ran for their lives as choking ash blanketed their fields and red-hot boulders rained down for half a mile around. Within six months, lava began oozing from the crater and formed huge flows 10 feet deep that burned the forest and buried the villages of Paricutín and San Juan Parangaricutiro, including their church.

When Volcán Paricutín's fires finally sputtered out on March 4, 1952, a grand 10,000-acre moonscape of burnt embers and hardened lava lay at the foot of a dark cinder mountain nearly a third of a mile in height. The entire displaced population of both villages resettled in a new town, San Juan Nuevo Parangaricutiro, where the people rebuilt their church, six miles west of Uruapan.

Local resident Simón Lázaro Jiménez heard Dionisio tell his story scarcely two days after the volcano had burst from the ground beneath his feet. Lázaro Jiménez later related the story in his 1993 book, *Paricutín a Cincuenta Años de su Nacimiento* (Paricutín, Fifty Years After Its Birth). Guadalajara, Jalisco: Editorial Agata, 1993.

lava that drowned San Juan Parangaricutiro. The 12-mile round-trip to the top of the volcano requires an entire day. Bring plenty of water, sturdy walking shoes, a hat, and food. The trail is at times vague, and the lava is sharp and pocked with holes. For safety, hire a guide in Angahuan or at the Centro Turístico. Rental horses are also available to ease your adventure.

Accommodations

Although most of the time the place is only lightly occupied, during the high July–Aug. season and weekends and holidays reservations are generally needed to spend a night in one of the center's dozen rustic family-style cabins or in the men's or women's dormitory. Cabins, which sleep six, have fireplaces, wood included, with bunk beds, attractive locally woven blankets, tile floors and bath with hot shower. They cost about $35 for up to three people, $60 for six. Although not immacu-

late, the cabins are clean enough for a night or two. Dormitory guests pay $11 tariff per person.

Also consider the center's two native-style *troje*, log cabins: **Trojecito,** with bed and electric light and outside toilet and hot water shower, for $17 d, and **Troje Grande,** sleeping up to four, with kitchenette and inside toilet and hot-water shower, for $43.

Camping in your own tent costs about $3 per person per night. Roofed fixed shelters for camping cost the same. RVers may also park their (self-contained) rigs for the same prices.

As for reservations, contact agent Jesús Angeles, tel. 452/523-3934, in Uruapan. If that fails, try getting a reservation message to the cellular number, tel. 044-452/529-0971 in Angahuan, or the on-site cellular long distance tel. 01-333/203-8527, in Centro Turistico Angahuan. The surest but slowest method is to write for a reservation, at least a month in advance, to J. Guadalupe Amado Bravo, Gerente, Centro Turístico Angahuan, Camino al Volcán Paricutín, Angahuan, Michoacán.

PARQUE NACIONAL PICO DE TANCÍTARO

The Parque Nacional Pico de Tancítaro encompasses the small kingdom of de facto high-country wilderness that climaxes at **Tancítaro Peak,** which rises to its 12,670-foot (3,860-meter) peak just 17 miles (28 km), as the crow flies, due west of downtown Uruapan. Like many Mexican national parks, the 90-square-mile (60,000-acre) Tancítaro has little government presence—no public campgrounds, no maintained trails, few if any rangers, and no visitors' center.

Adventurous travelers nevertheless can safely explore the park and climb the peak, accompanied by a guide. The best—actually the only—

time to go is during the clear Dec.–May dry season. Two major routes are customary for Tancítaro climbers, one on the south side, the other on the north. The north-side approach is shortest and easiest, requiring only a rugged high-clearance vehicle, such as a pickup truck, jeep, or other strong sport utility vehicle. Begin at the rugged dirt road that takes off from the south side of the highway, a bit more than a mile (two km) east of Angahuan. Continue about another 1.5 miles (two km), passing Rancho Choritiro. Another 11 miles (18 km) brings you to Rancho la Escondida (Hidden Ranch). Continue three miles (five km) to San Salvador mountain hamlet, where the jeep road ends. The peak is another three hours of rugged walking after that. Light snow (that often melts quickly) is possible during the winter. Be prepared with adequate food, water, water purification tablets, insect repellent, good boots, layers against the cold, a hat, emergency shelter, and sleeping

AROUND PARQUE NACIONAL PICO DE TANCÍTARO

© AVALON TRAVEL PUBLISHING, INC.

bags. For a guide, either inquire among the volunteer guides in Angahuan, ask at San Salvador, or (in Spanish) consult the Centro Turístico Angahuan manager, Prodigio Bravo Bravo.

The other route to Tancítaro peak begins on the mountain's south slope, at Tancítaro town (pop. 4,000), about 32 miles (51 km), 1.5 hours by paved road west of Uruapan. (For details, see Tancítaro Town.)

Around-the-Mountain Excursion

Tancítaro town (pop. 4,000) is a good halfway stopping point on a scenic excursion through the lush foothills around Tancítaro mountain. Starting early from Uruapan, drivers could do the all-paved route in one leisurely day. By bus, if you start early enough, you could do it in a long day. The clockwise route begins by following Av. Cupatitzio west from the Uruapan *jardín*. Fill up with gas and set your odometer at the Pemex *gasolinera* at the west edge of town. Bus riders, walk along Cupatitzio and hop on the first Nuevo San Juan- or Tancítaro-signed bus that comes along.

At Mile 5 (Km 8) comes bustling **Nuevo San Juan Parangaricutiro** (pop. about 10,000). The town was built, beginning in 1946, by the villagers displaced by Paricutín. Their pride is the big Templo del Señor de los Milagros, which contains the original patronal image of Jesus, saved from the eruption. Their eight-day patronal fiesta begins on Sept. 13; they also celebrate the fiesta of the Tres Reyes Magos (Three Magi Kings) on Jan. 7, 8, and 9.

After several up-and-down miles through luxuriant foothill avocado groves, you pass Parícuari village (a few stores and a local-style restaurant) at Mile 23.5 (Km 38) and larger Condembaro at Mile 27 (Km 43). You might stop for refreshment and a good word with friendly Dr. Rosendo Zamora Tamaya, who runs his practice out of his pharmacy (turn left on to the main side street; his pharmacy is immediately on the right). Continue as the road bends right (northwest), toward Tancítaro, at Mile 32 (Km 52). Alternatively, visit the pharmacy of Doctora Maribel Carrillo, M.D., on the right, right on the highway.

Tancítaro Town

This is an old colonial-era settlement, the present-day "Authentic Avocado Capital of the World," with venerable church, town plaza, post and telecommunications offices, and a few restaurants. The town's ordinarily sleepy ambience is interrupted by Sunday's big *tianguis* native market.

The **Hotel Saint Louis** (*not* San Luis), at 35 Morelos, offers accommodation on the main plaza-front thoroughfare, a block uphill from the plaza. At the hotel, you should introduce yourself to the friendly owner, Dr. Carlos Navarro, who can put you in contact with a reliable mountain trekking guide. His modest hotel offers eight clean rooms with hot-water showers, television, and phones, for about $5 s, $10 d. Although usually not necessary, you can reserve a room by writing or better, calling, the hotel (in Spanish) at tel. 425/591-5054, fax 425/591-5049. If it's full, other alternatives are **Hotel Villa Tancítaro,** on the opposite, southeast side of town, and **Hotel GH,** uphill three blocks from the Hotel Saint Louis.

The customary climbing route to Tancítaro peak takes off from Zirimóndiro village, several miles uphill from Tancítaro town. The entire trek requires about 15 hours of hiking and two nights, three days, round-trip. Net elevation gain is about 6,000 feet (from about 6,500 feet at Zirimóndiro, to the 12,670-foot summit). Although horses are available, most guides do not recommend using them, because of the difficulty of the route. This trek is only for fit, prepared, and experienced hikers. Be equipped with everything—water, purifying tablets or iodine, food, clothing layers against the cold, cooking utensils, small stove with fuel, matches, insect repellent, sleeping bag and pad, a hat, socks, and sturdy, broken-in hiking boots.

Doctor Navarro recommends experienced local mountain man Francisco Mendoza to lead your trek. (If he is unavailable, Mendoza recommends two more: Francisco Monte Longo and Benjamin Mesa.) Mendoza will lead a trek to the top, minimum three days, for a fee of about $15 or $20 per day. Although he doesn't expect it, as a courtesy you should carry enough food for him, too. He's a kindly, modest, slender but wiry man, sixtyish, with a twinkle in his eye. He's probably been to the top more than a dozen times in a generation of living on the Tancítaro mountainside.

You can usually find Mendoza at his rancho, about two miles uphill, on the road to Zirimóndiro, from town. From Hotel Saint Louis, go two blocks uphill, turn right at Domínguez, go four blocks, turn left at the end of the street, Taria, continue one long block to Rayón, and turn right. Continue 1.2 miles (1.9 km) to Mendoza's rancho, where the road bends left.

Back in town, continuing on your round-the-mountain excursion, go uphill from Hotel Saint Louis on Morelos several blocks and turn left on to the highway, at Bravo. From there, you'll pass a number of colonial-era towns and villages: Apo del Rosario, with stores and *troje* log houses at Mile 41 (Km 66), and a junction (bear right) at Mile 53 (Km 85) at the farming town Peribán de Ramos, (pop. 5,000), with a gas station, restaurants, a bank with ATM, doctors, and pharmacies.

Continue through Tzacan village, containing many *troje* log houses, at Mile 65 (Km 105) and Angahuan at Mile 70 (Km 105) and back to Uruapan and Hotel Mansion Cupatitzio at Mile 103 (Km 166).

Lázaro Cárdenas

The new industrial port city of Lázaro Cárdenas, named for the Michoacán-born president famous for expropriating American oil companies, is Michoacán's Pacific transportation and service hub. Most of its services, including banks, bus stations, post office, hospitals, hotels, and restaurants, are clustered along north-south Av. Lázaro Cárdenas, the main ingress boulevard, about three miles from its Highway 200 intersection.

ACCOMMODATIONS AND FOOD

Take a break from the sun beneath the shady streetfront awning of the **Restaurant Las Sombrillas,** open daily 8 A.M.–8 P.M., across from Banamex. (Don't be afraid to ask the staff to turn the TV off or at least lower the volume.)

For cheaper but wholesome country cooking, check out the *fondas* (foodstalls) on the side street, Constitución de 1814, adjacent to the Galeana station bus lot, and on side street Corregidora, the next block, north.

If you must stay overnight, a number of nearby hotels offer reasonably priced lodging. The most convenient is the **Hotel Delfín,** 1633 L. Cárdenas, Lázaro Cárdenas, Michoacán 60950, tel. 753/532-1418, fax 753/532-1419, across the street from the Galeana bus station. The approximately 20 rooms with baths, in three stories, cluster around an inner pool and patio. Rates run about $20 d, fan only, $30 with a/c, with hot water, TV, and telephone.

For more class, go to the high-rise **Hotel Casablanca** (on Bravo, a block east from Lázaro Cárdenas, visible behind Bancomer.) It offers about six stories of light and comfortable modern-standard deluxe rooms with panoramic, private balcony views. Downstairs, past the lobby, a restaurant overlooks an inviting rear pool and patio. Rooms cost $36 s, $52 d, with a/c, TV, and parking. For reservations, call tel. 753/537-3480 through 753/537-3484, fax 753/532-4036.

An even fancier hotel option is the **NH Krystal Express,** on the ingress boulevard, Av. Lázaro Cárdenas, west side, about a quarter mile from the town center. It offers 120 deluxe rooms, for about $80 d, with continental breakfast, restaurant, exercise gym, and whirlpool tub. Reserve at the hotel directly, at tel. 753/533-2900 or 753/533-2941, toll-free at U.S. tel. 800/231-9860, or email nhlazaro@nh-hoteles.com.mx. For more information, visit the website www.nh-hoteles.com.

INFORMATION AND SERVICES

Tourist Information Office

For information and a selection of excellent maps and brochures, stop by the local branch of Michoacán state tourism, at N. Bravo 475, front of the Casablanca Hotel, open Mon.–Fri. 9 A.M.–6 P.M., Sat.–Sun. 10 A.M.–2 P.M.

TO IXTAPA/PÁTZCUARO

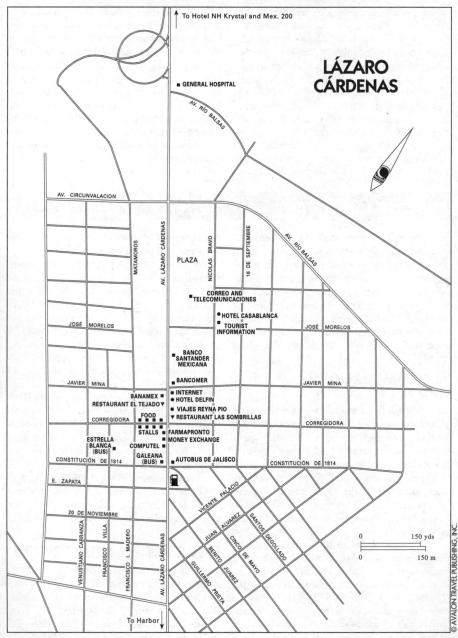

Travel Agents

A competent and conveniently situated travel agency (and possible information source) is **Viajes Reyna Pio,** on L. Cárdenas, right across from the Galeana bus station and Banamex, tel. 753/532-3868 or 753/532-3935, fax 753/532-0723. Alternatively, try **Chinameca Viajes,** on N. Bravo, one block east from L. Cárdenas and two blocks north of the Casablanca Hotel, tel. 753/537-0253.

Money Exchange

Three banks, all with ATMs, are available nearby. **Banamex,** at Av. L. Cárdenas 1646, tel. 753/532-2020, is open for money exchange Mon.–Fri. 9 A.M.–4 P.M., Sat. 10 A.M.–2 P.M. If it's too crowded, try **Bancomer,** open Mon.–Fri. 9 A.M.–4 P.M., Sat. 10 A.M.–2 P.M., a block north and across the street, at 1555 L. Cárdenas, tel. 753/532-3888; or **Banco Santander Mexicano,** tel. 753/532-0032, at no. 1681, on the same side, half a block farther north.

Communications

The *correo* (post office), tel. 753/537-2387, is in the middle of the big grassy town plaza; look for it on the left as you arrive at the town center, two long blocks after the big traffic circle.

Telecomunicaciones, with telegraph, money orders, telephone, and public fax 753/532-0273, is next door to the post office. For telephone, plenty of public street phones accept widely available Ladatel telephone cards. More expensive, but with long hours, **Computel,** the computer-assisted long-distance telephone and fax agency, operates daily 7:30 A.M.–10 P.M., tel./fax 753/532-4806, fax 753/532-4807, next to the Galeana bus terminal, at 1810 L. Cárdenas, corner of Constitución de 1814.

Connect to the **Internet** at the small store, tel. 753/532-1480, corner of Javier Mina, across the street, south of Bancomer; open Mon.–Sat. 9 A.M.–9 P.M., Sun. 10 A.M.–2 P.M.

Hospital, Doctor, and Pharmacies

The **General Hospital,** known locally as "Seguro Social," tel. 753/532-0900 through 753/532-0904, is on the boulevard into town, left side,

corner of H. Escuela Naval, a block before the big right-side traffic circle. Alternatively, visit highly recommended Doctor Gustavo Cejos Pérez, at Melchor Ocampo 475, tel. 753/532-3902. For routine medicines and drugs, go to conveniently situated **Farmacia Pronto,** tel. 753/537-5002, open daily 8 A.M.–10 P.M., a few doors north of the Galeana bus station; or **Droguería Moderna,** tel. 753/532-0246, on the main street, across from the Galeana bus station, open daily 7:30 A.M.–9 P.M.

GETTING THERE AND AWAY

By Car or RV

The driving options to and from Lázaro Cárdenas are virtually the same as those for Playa Azul.

By Bus

A trio of long-distance bus terminals serves Lázaro Cárdenas. From the Galeana (officially, Lineas Unidas del Sur) terminal at 1810 Av. L. Cárdenas, tel. 753/532-0262 or 753/537-3868, **Ruta Paraíso** first- and second-class local-departure buses connect daily north with Apatzingán, Uruapan, Pátzcuaro, and Morelia. Very frequent local departures connect northeast along the coast with La Mira, Playa Azul, and Caleta de Campos. Additionally, several more first- and second-class departures connect northwest with Manzanillo and intermediate points. In an adjacent booth, tel. 753/532-3006, agents sell tickets for **Parhikuni** luxury-class buses (with a/c waiting lounge), connecting north with Michoacán destinations of Nueva Italia, Uruapan, Pátzcuaro, and Morelia.

Directly across the street, **Autobúses de Jalisco** and associated lines, tel. 753/537-1850, maintains a small streetfront station. It offers four types of departures: executive class "Plus," connecting northeast with Guadalajara via Tecomán and Colima; first-class Autobuses de Jalisco, connecting north, then west, with Uruapan, Zamora, and Guadalajara; first-class Via 2000 buses, connecting north, then east, via Uruapan, Morelia, and Toluca, with Mexico City; and second-class Autobuses Sur de Jalisco, connecting northwest with Manzanillo and also with Guadalajara, via Colima and Ciudad Guzmán.

TO IXTAPA/PÁTZCUARO

The big **Estrella Blanca** terminal, tel. 753/532-1171, is two short blocks away, directly behind the Galeana terminal, on Fco. Villa, between Constitución de 1814 and Corregidora. From there, one or two daily first-class buses local departures connect north with Michoacán destinations of Uruapan, Pátzcuaro, and Morelia. Three first-class buses stop, en route southeast to Zihuatanejo, Acapulco, and the Oaxaca coast, and northwest to Manzanillo, Puerto Vallarta, Mazatlán, and the U.S. border. In the opposite direction southeast, many first and second-class local departures connect with Zihuatanejo, Acapulco, and intermediate points, in addition to three Futura first-class departures that connect daily with Mexico City.

By Train

Privatization has erased passenger service on the Lázaro Cárdenas-Uruapan-Pátzcuaro-Morelia rail line. Ride the bus instead.

Along the Road to Ixtapa-Zihuatanejo

It's hard to remain unimpressed as you cross over the **Río Balsas Dam** for the first time. The dam, which marks the Michoacán-Guerrero state boundary, is huge and hulking. Behind it a grand lake mirrors the Sierra Madre mountains, while on the opposite side, Mexico's greatest river spurts from the turbine exit gates hundreds of feet below. The river's power, converted into enough electric energy for a million Mexican families, courses up great looping transmission wires, while the spent river meanders toward the sea.

Heading Out

The middle of the dam (Highway 200, Km 103 north of Zihuatanejo) is a good point at which to reset your odometer. Your odometer reading and the roadside kilometer markers may be your best way to find the several little hideaways between the Río Balsas and Zihuatanejo.

As for bus travelers, having gotten aboard at La Mira or Lázaro Cárdenas (or Zihuatanejo, if traveling northwest), ask the driver to let you off at your destination.

Playas Atracadero and La Saladita

Both of these little havens are especially for shellfish lovers who yearn for their fill of uncrowded swimming, surfing, splashing, fishing, and beachcombing. Atracadero is the less frequented of the two. Except for the fishing family's house down the beach, you probably would have the entire place to yourself most of the time. The beach *palapa* restaurant appears to operate only seasonally. Crowds must gather sometimes, however: the main *palapa* has, over time, accumulated a five-foot pile of oyster shells!

The beach sand itself is soft and gray. The waves, with good surfing breaks, roll in from far out, arriving gently on the sand. Boat launching would be easy during calm weather. Little undertow menaces casual swimmers, bodysurfers, or boogie boarders. Lots of driftwood and shells—clams, limpets, snails—cover the sand. The beach extends for at least three miles past palm groves on the northwest. A fenced grove and house occupies the southeast. A grassy lot on the northwest side could accommodate some tents and RVs. Bring your own food and water.

To get to Playa Atracadero, turn off at the hamlet of Joluta, at Km 64, 24 miles (39 km) from the Río Balsas and 40 miles from Zihuatanejo. Bear left all the way, 2.1 miles (3.3 km) to the beach.

At La Saladita (The Little Salty One), the day used to climax when the oyster divers would bring in their afternoon catches. Now, the oysters are all fished out. While the oysters recover, divers now go for octupus and lobster which, broiled and served with fixings, sell for about $10 for a one-pounder. You can also do your own fishing via rentable (offer $15/hour) beach *pangas,* which go out daily and routinely return with three or four 20-pound fish.

The beach itself is level far out, with rolling waves fine for surfing, swimming, boogie boarding, and bodysurfing. There's enough driftwood and shells for a season of beachcombing. The

THE ECUADOR CONNECTION

During recent years some historians and archaeologists have been wondering why preconquest Michoacán people (who still call themselves the Purépecha) wore clothes very different than those common to other Mexican people, possessed unique metal technology, and kept dogs identically as hairless as those kept by people on the Pacific coast of Ecuador.

One key to this mystery may be a letter written to Spanish King Carlos V by his accountant in December 1525. The letter related that, in the recent past, alien traders had been arriving, from time to time, by sea, at the mouth of the Río Balsas. They customarily stayed for several months, while trading their exotic goods, until weather and ocean conditions permitted them to return to their home country somewhere on the far shore of the southern sea.

The mystery goes deeper. Archaeologists have discovered other evidence in Western Mexico that points to the Ecuadoran Pacific province of Manabi, more than 2,000 miles southeast of Michocán, as the mysterious traders' homeland. Thousand-year-old bottle-shaped tombs, found in Mesoamerica only in Jalisco, Nayarit, and Colima, are very similar to shaft tombs commonly used by Andean peoples from Peru to Panama. Moreover, figurines found in such tombs in both Nayarit and Manabi province demonstrate remarkably similar clothing, notably, of the checkered weave and short breeches worn both in Manabi province and (uniquely in Mexico) in preconquest Michoacán.

The Purépecha's singularly superior knowledge of metallurgy helps clinch the case for a Michoacán-Ecuador connection. During the 1990s historians were documenting that the superior mining and metal technology skills—ore recognition, smelting, and alloying techniques—that produced brasslike and bronzelike alloys unique to Michoacán, were so similar to Andean techniques that someone from South America must have been there to teach the Purepécha metalsmiths. (That the presumed teacher imparted knowledge and not the ores or alloys is certain, since the chemical signatures of the Michoacán and Ecuadorian alloys differ markedly.)

Lastly, since all detectives must seek a motive, archaeologists have speculated about the Manabi traders' motivation for sailing so far north to trade. Historian Patricia Rieff Anawalt, in her article "Traders of the Ecuadorian Littoral" (*Archaeology*, Nov.–Dec. 1997), writes that "the traders may have needed to augment their most lucrative stock, spondylyus *[Spondylus princeps oyster]* shell." She goes on to note that the spondylus was "a profoundly sacred and necessary religious commodity" for the high Andean cultures, such as the Inca. Since the needed oysters did not grow in the cold Ecuadorian waters, Rieff Anawalt speculates that the traders had to sail far afield, to the warmer waters of western Mexico, for a solid source of supply.

TO IXTAPA/PÁTZCUARO

beach spreads for hundreds of yards on both sides of the road's end. Permanent *palapa* restaurants supply shade, drinks, and seafood.

Beach camping is common and popular, especially during the Christmas and Easter holidays. Other times, you may have the whole place to yourself. Bring your own food and water; the small stores at the highway village may help add to your supplies.

Although it's popular, camping is no longer necessary at La Saladita. **Indio's Bar and Grill** offers a two-story beachfront bungalow rental, past the gate at the beach.

To get to La Saladita, at Km 40, 39 miles (63 km) southeast of the Río Balsas and 25 miles (40 km) northwest of Zihuatanejo, turn off at the village of Los Llanos. At .2 mile, turn right, at the church, and continue another 3.1 miles (5.1 km) to the beach, where a left fork leads you to Indio's, and a right leads you to the so-called Embarcadero sector of the beach and Paco's and Ibañez *palapa* restaurants.

Playas Majagua and Troncones

This pair of palmy nooks basks on a pristine coastal stretch, backed by a jungly, wildlife-rich hinterland. While Playa Troncones has acquired a trailer park, a number of restful inns, and some

© BRUCE WHIPPERMAN

Jagged limestone outcroppings decorate the beach at Troncones.

good beachside restaurants, Playa Majagua remains very rustic.

Playa Majagua, at Km 33 north of Zihuatanejo, is a fishing hamlet with palmy shade, stick-and-wattle houses, and about half a dozen hammock-equipped *ramadas* scattered along the beach. One of the *ramadas* is competently run by a friendly family who calls it Restaurant Los Angeles. Next door, *palapa* Restaurant Las Brisas is also locally recommended. Camping is safe and welcomed by local folks (although space, especially for RVs, is limited). Water is available, but campers should bring purifying tablets and food.

The beach curves from a rocky southeast-end point, past the lagoon of Río Lagunillas, and stretches miles northwest past shoreline palm and acacia forest. The sand is soft and dark yellow, with mounds of driftwood but few shells. Waves break far out and roll in gradually, with little undertow. Fine left-breaking surf rises off the southern point. Boats are easily launchable (several *pangas* lie along the beach) during normal good weather.

To get to Playa Majagua, turn off at the sign just south of the Río Lagunillas bridge, at Km 33, 44 miles (70 km) southeast of Río Balsas, 20 miles northwest of Zihuatanejo. Continue 2.9 miles (4.7 km) to the beach.

Nearby Playa Troncones has a little bit of everything: shady seafood ramadas, cozy seaside inns, restaurants, a small trailer park, and room to park your RV or set up a tent. Most folks arriving get there from Ixtapa-Zihuatanejo via the side road at km 30. (See Getting There). For camping spots, turn left, south (left) at the beach and follow the road half a mile past several likely spots to pull off and camp. At the far southern end, a lagoon spreads beside a pristine coral-sand beach, which curls around a low hill toward a picture-perfect little bay. Stores can supplement your food and water supplies.

But that's just the beginning. Troncones has acquired a growing colony of North Americans, some of whom operate small beachside accommodations for lovers of peace, quiet, and the outdoors. Besides lazing in hammocks and sunning on the sand, guests at all Troncones lodgings share the same luscious shoreline. You can swim, surf, bodysurf, and boogie board the waves, jog along the sand, and explore a limestone cave in the adjacent jungle hinterland. Back by the shore, you can beachcomb to your heart's content while enjoying views of the wildlife trove—fish, whales (Dec.–March), dolphins, turtles (Nov.–Jan.), swarms of herons, boobies, egrets, and cormorants—that abounds in the ocean and in nearby lagoons.

Accommodations and Food: As you move northwest (from the entrance road, turn right at the beach) after the bridge, first comes **Casa Ki,** the life project of Ed and Ellen Weston, P.O. Box 405, Zihuatanejo, Guerrero 40880, tel. 755/553-2815, casaki@yahoo.com. Casa Ki (named after the Japanese word for energy and wholeness), offers three immaculate, charmingly rustic cottages, tucked in the Westons' lovingly tended seaside garden compound. Each cottage sleeps approximately two adults and two children and comes with shower, toilet, fans, and a refrigerator. Guests share a shady outside cooking and dining *palapa*. High-season (Nov. 15–April 30) rentals run $75 s, $85 d ($65, $60 low) for the three cottages, including full breakfast. Ed and Ellen also rent a lovely two-bedroom, two-bath house that sleeps four, with full kitchen and daily maid service, for about $165 high, $140 low. Get your winter reservations in early.

After another quarter mile comes **Casa de la Tortuga,** the original Troncones lodging, built by friendly pioneer Dewey McMillin during the late 1980s. Now, his guests enjoy a clean room (some with shared bath) and breakfast in their modern beach house, a restful patio with plenty of shade, quiet, and opportunities for delighting in the outdoors. During the Nov. 1–April 30 high season, room rentals run $50 s or d, with shared bath; $75 s or d, private bath, all with breakfast. A kitchen is available for guest use. No children under 12, unless you rent the whole place. The entire layout (sleeping a dozen or more) rents for $350/day, $2,100/week, $8,000/month; guests supply their own food. Rates during the low May through October season are half the above. Write, fax, or email early for reservations (mandatory during the winter) at P.O. Box 37, Zihuatanejo, Guerrero 40880, tel./fax 755/553-2812, casadelatortuga@yahoo.com. If business is too slow, Casa de la Tortuga closes June, July, and August. For more information, visit website www.casadelatortuga.com.

Continuing another half mile, you'll find one of the newer additions to Troncones, the **Inn at Manzanillo Bay,** owner-chef Michael Bensal's pocket paradise of eight rustic-style *palapa*-roofed cabanas, comfortably furnished with deluxe amenities, set around a luscious blue swimming pool and leafy patio. Here you can have it all: a gently curving, wave-washed shoreline, with the murmur of the billows at night and plenty of hammock time by day. There's a good restaurant and even TV if you want it. All this from about $88 d high season, $68 low. Reserve by tel./fax 755/553-2883, or email manzanillobay@aol.com. For more information, visit the website www.manzanillobay.com.

Finally, 100 yards farther northwest, you arrive at the six-room **Eden Beach Hacienda and Caña del Sol Restaurant,** which shares the same luscious tropical forest oceanfront as all the other lodgings. The amenities include 10 immaculate rooms, six in the main house and four open to the air in the beachfront house, decorated in stucco and Talavera tile, with king-sized beds and private hot-water bathrooms. High-season rates run about $65 s, $75 d, $50 low, including breakfast. Star of the Eden show is chef Christian Shirmer, American graduate of the Baltimore culinary academy, whose menus feature traditional Mexican cuisine with a nouveau flair, focusing on fresh ingredients and seasonal foods. At least, stop in for lunch or dinner and meet Christian and Eva Robbins and Jim Garrity, the builder-owners. Make reservations directly at tel. 755/556-5879, or cellular tel. 755/556-5879, or in the United States by mail at 41 Riverview Dr., Oak Ridge, TN 37830, fax 801/340-9883, evaandjim@aol.com, www.edenmex.com.

At the opposite, southeast end of the Troncones beach, **El Burro Borracho** (The Drunken Burro) beachfront *palapa* restaurant and inn has become a favorite stopping place for the growing cadre of daytime visitors who are venturing out from Ixtapa and Zihuatanejo. Here, owner Dewey McMillin continues the standard set by former owner/chef Michael Bensal, with spicy shrimp tacos, rum-glazed ribs, jumbo shrimp grilled with coconut-curry sauce, and broiled pork chops with mashed potatoes. Besides the

TO IXTAPA/PÁTZCUARO

shady ocean-view *palapa* restaurant, Burro Borracho offers six "simply elegant" airy rooms, each with bath, in three stone duplex beachfront cottages. Extras include king-sized bed, rustic-chic decor, hot water, and fans. Shared cooking facilities are also available. Sports and activities include swimming, surfing, and boogie boarding, plus kayaks for use of guests. Room rentals run about $60 d high season, $35 low, with continental breakfast. Facilities also include five (shadeless) **RV spaces,** with all hookups, adjacent to the cottages for about $15 per night. Discounts are negotiable for long-term rentals. Write, telephone, or fax for reservations (mandatory in winter) at P.O. Box 37, Zihuatanejo, Guerrero 40880, tel./fax 755/553-2834, cellular tel. 755/553-0732.

For more information for all Troncones lodgings, restaurants, and more, see the Troncones website www.troncones.com.mx. Also check the excellent **www.zihuatanejo.net** website for additional information and updates on lodgings listed here.

Sports, Recreation and Shopping: Dewey McMillin and partners Bill and Kat Moore have established **Jaguar Tours,** across the road from Casa de Tortuga. Beside surf and boogie board and bicycle rentals they offer a number of ecoadventure tours. These include bird-watching and wildlife-viewing walks, a jungle canopy tour along a cable hitched to the treetops, a trip into nearby Majagua limestone cave, replete with rocky gardens of stalagmites and stalactites, in a towering floodlighted chamber. For more information, call tel. 755/553-2862 or cellular tel. 044-755/7189, email jaguartours@hotmail.com, or visit the website www.jaguartours.net.

Michael Bensal at the Inn at Manzanillo Bay also arranges sealife-viewing tours and fully equipped launches for four hours of fishing for 2–4 people for about $135.

Michael also runs a shop at his inn, selling fine wines, Taxco silver, and Cuban cigars. Eva Robbins, at Eden Beach Hacienda, also has a shop with an eclectic collection of mostly Guerrero country crafts: baskets, toys, silver jewelry, silk scarves, and much more.

Getting There: Follow the (signed southbound) paved turnoff, to Playa Troncones from Highway 200, around Km 30, about 42 miles (73 km) south of the Río Balsas (about 18 miles north of Zihuatanejo). Continue 2.2 miles to the Playa Troncones beachfront *ramadas.* Turn left for the camping spots, the main part of the beach and El Burro Borracho; turn right for the other listed lodgings, beginning with Casa Ki, about a mile farther along the beachfront forest road. From there, the car-negotiable dry-weather track continues about 1.5 miles along the beach to Playa Majagua.

Ixtapa-Zihuatanejo and South to Acapulco

Ixtapa-Zihuatanejo

The Costa Grande, the "Big Coast," of the state of Guerrero angles 200 miles southeast from the Río Balsas to Acapulco. Before the highway came in the 1960s, this was a land of corn, coconuts, fish, and fruit. Although it's still that, the road added a new ingredient: a trickle of visitors seeking paradise in Zihuatanejo, a sleepy fishing village on a beautiful bay.

During the 1970s, planners decided to create the best of all possible worlds by building Ixtapa, a luxurious resort on a pearly beach five miles away. Now, Ixtapa-Zihuatanejo's clear, rich waters, forested ecosanctuaries, pearly little beaches, pristine offshore islets, good food, comfortable hotels, and friendly local folks offer visitors the ingredients for memorable stays any time of the year.

HISTORY

Zihuatanejo's azure waters attracted attention long before Columbus. Local legend says the Tarascans (whose emperor ruled from now-Michoacán and who was never subject to the Aztecs) built a royal bathing resort on Las Gatas Beach in Zihuatanejo Bay.

© BRUCE WHIPPERMAN

Zihuatanejo's Playa La Ropa

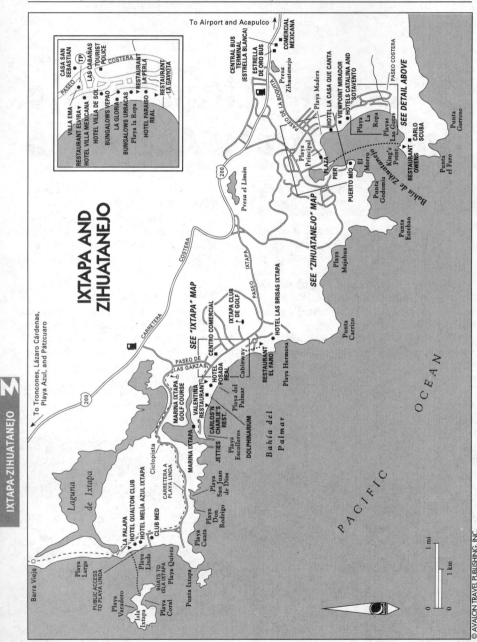

To Airport and Acapulco

CASA SAN SEBASTIAN
VILLA EMA
RESTAURANT ELVIRA
HOTEL VILLA MEXICANA
HOTEL VILLA DE SOL
BUNGALOWS VEPAO
LA GLORIA
BUNGALOWS URRACAS
Playa la Ropa
HOTEL PARAISO REAL
LAS CABAÑAS
TOURIST POLICE
RESTAURANT LA PERLA
RESTAURANT LA GAVIOTA
COSTERA
PASEO

CENTRAL BUS TERMINAL (ESTRELLA BLANCA)
ESTRELLA DE ORO BUS
COMERCIAL MEXICANA

Presa Zihuatanejo
Playa Madera
HOTEL LA CASA QUE CANTA
VIEWPOINT MIRADOR
HOTELS CATALINA AND SOTAVENTO
PASEO COSTERA
SEE DETAIL ABOVE

Playa Principal
PLAZA
PIER
PUERTO MIO
El Morro
Punta Godomia
King's Point
Playa La Ropa
Playas Las Gatas
RESTAURANT OWENS
CARLO SCUBA
Punta Garroso
Punta el Faro

Punta Esteban

IXTAPA AND ZIHUATANEJO

Presa el Limón

SEE "ZIHUATANEJO" MAP

Bahía de Zihuatanejo

Playa Majahua

To Troncones, Lázaro Cárdenas, Playa Azul, and Pátzcuaro

CARRETERA

COSTERA

SEE "IXTAPA" MAP

CENTRO COMERCIAL
IXTAPA CLUB DE GOLF
HOTEL LAS BRISAS IXTAPA

IXTAPA

PASEO

Punta Carrizo

PASEO DE LAS GARZAS

MARINA IXTAPA GOLF COURSE
VALENTINA RESTAURANT
HOTEL POSADA REAL
Playa del Palmar
RESTAURANT EL FARO
Playa Hermosa

CARLOS'N CHARLIE'S REST.
MARINA IXTAPA
JETTIES
Playa Escolleros
DOLPHINARIUM
Cableway

Bahía del Palmar

Laguna de Ixtapa

Ciclopista

LA PALAPA
HOTEL QUALTON CLUB
HOTEL MELIA AZUL IXTAPA
CLUB MED
CARRETERA A PLAYA LINDA

Playa San Juan de Dios
Playa Don Rodrigo
Playa Cuata

PACIFIC OCEAN

Barra Vieja

Playa Larga

Playa Linda
Playa Quieta

PUBLIC ACCESS TO PLAYA LINDA

BOATS TO ISLA IXTAPA

Playa Varadero
Isla Ixtapa
Playa Coral
Playa Ixtapa
Punta Ixtapa

1 mi
1 km
0

© AVALON TRAVEL PUBLISHING, INC.

IXTAPA-ZIHUATANEJO

That was sometime around A.D. 1400. People had been attracted to the Costa Grande much earlier than that: archaic pottery has been un-covered at a number of sites, left by artists who lived and died as long as 5,000 years ago. Later, around 1000 B.C., the Olmecs (famous for their monumental Gulf coast sculptures) left their un-mistakable stamp on local ceramics. After them came waves of settlers, including the barbaric Chichimecs (Drinkers of Blood), the agricul-tural Cuitlatecs, and an early invasion of Aztecs, perhaps wandering in search of their eventual homeland in the Valley of Mexico.

None of those peoples were a match for the armies of Tarascan emperor Hiripan, who during the late A.D. 1300s invaded the Costa Grande and established a coastal province, headquar-tered at Coyuca, between Zihuatanejo and pre-sent-day Acapulco.

Three generations later the star of the Aztec emperor Tízoc was rising over Mexico. His armies invaded the Costa Grande and pushed out the Tarascans. By A.D. 1500 the Aztecs ruled the coast from their provincial town capital at Zi-huatlán (Place of Women; so named because the local society was matriarchal), not far from pre-sent-day Zihuatanejo.

Conquest and Colonization

Scarcely months after Hernán Cortés conquered the Aztecs, he sent an expedition to explore the "Southern Sea" and find a route to China. In November 1522 Captain Juan Álvarez Chico set sail with boats built on the Isthmus of Tehuan-tepec and reconnoitered the coast to the Río Bal-sas, planting crosses on beaches, claiming the land for Spain.

An oft-told Costa Grande story says, when Chico was exploring at Zihuatanejo, he looked down on the round tranquil little bay, lined with flocks of seabirds and women washing clothes in a freshwater spring. His Aztec guide told him that this place was called Zihuatlán (Place of Women). When Chico described the little bay, Cortés tacked *nejo* (little) on to the name, giv-ing birth to "Zihuatlanejo," which later got short-ened to the present Zihuatanejo.

Cortés, encouraged by the samples of pearls and gold that Chico brought back, sent out other expeditions. A shipyard and town were estab-lished at Zacatula, at the mouth of the Río Balsas in 1523; then, in 1527, Captain Alvaro Saavedra Cerón set sail for China from Zihuatanejo Bay. Not knowing any details of the Pacific Ocean and its winds and currents, it is not surprising that (although he did arrive in the Philippines) Saavedra Cerón failed to return to Mexico. A number of additional attempts would be neces-sary until finally, in 1565, Father André de Ur-daneta coaxed Pacific winds to give up their secret and returned, in triumph, from Asia.

By royal decree, Acapulco became Spain's sole port of entry on the Pacific in 1561. Except for an occasional galleon (or pirate caravel) stopping for repairs or supplies, all other Pacific ports, includ-ing Zihuatanejo, slumbered for hundreds of years.

Zihuatanejo was one of the last to wake up. The occasion was the arrival of the highway from Acapulco during the 1960s. No longer isolated, Zihuatanejo's headland-rimmed aqua bay at-tracted a small colony of paradise-seekers.

Zihuatanejo had grown to perhaps 5,000 souls by the late 1970s when Fonatur, the gov-ernment tourism-development agency, decided Ixtapa (which means "White Place," for its bril-liant sand beach five miles north of Zihuatanejo) was a perfect site for a world-class resort. In-vestors agreed, and the infrastructure—drainage, roads, and utilities—was installed. The jetport was built, hotels rose, and by the 1990s the dis-tinct but inseparable twin resorts of Ixtapa and Zihuatanejo (combined pop. 70,000) were at-tracting a steady stream of Mexican and foreign vacationers.

SIGHTS
Getting Oriented

Both Ixtapa and Zihuatanejo are small and easy to know. Zihuatanejo's little Plaza de Armas town square overlooks the main beach, Playa Munici-pal, just beyond the palm-lined pedestrian walk-way, Paseo del Pescador. From the plaza looking out toward the bay, you are facing south. On

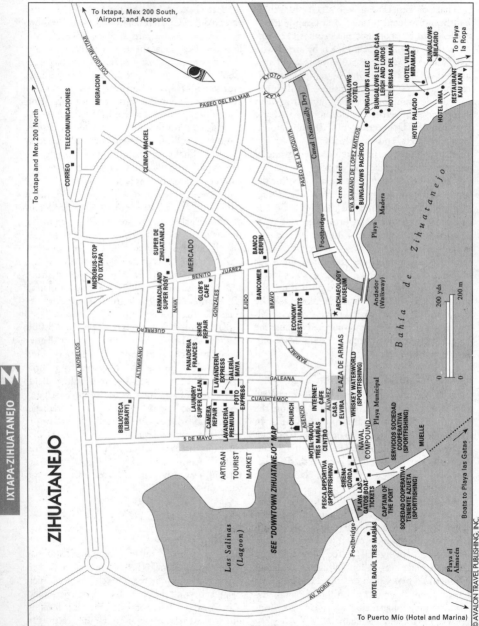

ZIHUATANEJO

To Ixtapa, Mex 200 South,
Airport, and Acapulco

To Ixtapa and Mex 200 North

COLEGIO MILITAR

MIGRACION

TELECOMUNICACIONES

CORREO

CLINICA MACIEL

PASEO DEL PALMAR

KYOTO
PLAZA

PASEO DE LA BOQUITA

Canal (Seasonally Dry)

Cerro Madera

EVA SAMANO DE LÓPEZ MATEOS

BUNGALOWS SOTELO

BUNGALOWS PACÍFICO

BUNGALOWS ALLEC

BUNGALOWS LEY AND CASA
LEIGH AND LOROS

HOTEL BRISAS DEL MAR

HOTEL VILLAS
MIRAMAR

BUNGALOWS
MILAGRO

To Playa
la Ropa

HOTEL PALACIO

HOTEL IRMA

RESTAURANT
KAU KAN

Playa
Madera

Footbridge

Playa
Madera

Bahía de Zihuatanejo

ARCHAEOLOGY
MUSEUM

Andador
(Walkway)

200 yds

200 m

0

0

AV. MORELOS

MICROBUS-STOP
TO IXTAPA

SUPER DE
ZIHUATANEJO

MERCADO

FARMACIA AND
SUPER ROSY

BENITO   JUAREZ

GLOB'S
CAFE

NAVA

GONZALES

GUERRERO

ALTIMIRANO

BIBLIOTECA
(LIBRARY)

PANADERIA
FRANCES

SHOE
REPAIR

LAVANDERIA
EXPRESS

GALERIA
MAYA

FOTO
EXPRESS

LAUNDRY
SUPER CLEAN

CAMERA
REPAIR

LAVANDERIA
PREMIUM

5 DE MAYO

BANCO
SERFIN

BANCOMER

BRAVO

EJIDO

RAMIREZ

GALEANA

CUAUHTÉMOC

ALVAREZ

ASENCIO

ECONOMY
RESTAURANTS

PLAZA DE ARMAS

INTERNET
CAFE

CHURCH

CASA
ELVIRA

WHISKEY WATERWORLD
(SPORTFISHING)

Playa Municipal

SERVICIOS SOCIEDAD
COOPERATIVA
(SPORTFISHING)

MUELLE

SEE "DOWNTOWN ZIHUATANEJO" MAP

ARTISAN
TOURIST
MARKET

Las Salinas
(Lagoon)

Footbridge

HOTEL RAOUL TRES MARÍAS

HOTEL RAOUL
TRES MARÍAS
CENTRO

SIRENA
GORDA

PLAYA LAS
GATOS BOAT
TICKETS

PESCA DEPORTIVA
(SPORTFISHING)

CAPTAIN OF
THE PORT

SOCIEDAD COOPERATIVA
TENIENTE AZUETA
(SPORTFISHING)

NAVAL
COMPOUND

Boats to Playa las Gatas

AV. NORIA

Playa el
Almacén

To Puerto Mío (Hotel and Marina)

© AVALON TRAVEL PUBLISHING, INC.

IXTAPA-ZIHUATANEJO

your right is the *muelle* (moo-AY-yay), and on the left, the bay curves along the outer beaches Playas La Ropa, Madera, and finally Las Gatas beneath the far Punta El Faro (Lighthouse Point).

Turning around and facing inland (north), you see a narrow waterfront street, Juan Álvarez, running parallel to the beach past the plaza, crossing the main business streets (actually tranquil shady lanes) Cuauhtémoc and Guerrero. A third street, busy Benito Juárez, one block to the right of Guerrero, conducts traffic several blocks to

and from the shore, passing the market and intersecting a second main street, Av. Morelos. There, a right turn will soon bring you to Highway 200 and, within five miles, Ixtapa.

Nearly everything in Ixtapa lies along one three-mile-long boulevard, Paseo Ixtapa, which parallels the main beach, hotel-lined Playa del Palmar. Heading westerly from Zihuatanejo, you first pass the Club de Golf Ixtapa, then the big Barceló on the left, followed by a succession of other high-rise hotels. Soon come

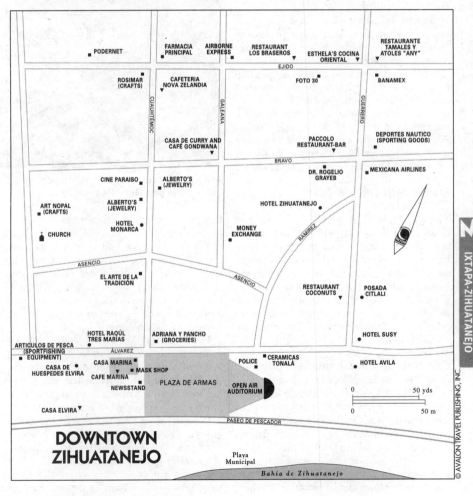

the Zona Comercial shopping malls and the Paseo de las Garzas corner on the right. Turn right for either Highway 200 or the outer beaches, Playas Cuata, Quieta, Linda, and Larga. At Playa Linda, boats continue to heavenly Isla Ixtapa.

If, instead, you continued straight ahead back at the Paseo de las Garzas corner, you would soon reach the Marina Ixtapa condo development and yacht harbor.

Getting Around

In downtown Zihuatanejo, shops and restaurants are within a few blocks' walking distance of the plaza. For the beaches, walk along the beachfront *andador* (walkway) to Madera, take a taxi ($3) to La Ropa, and a launch from the pier ($4) to Las Gatas. For Ixtapa or the outer beaches, take a taxi (about $5) or ride one of the very frequent minibuses, labeled by destination, which leave from the east corner of Juárez and Morelos. A taxi ride between central Ixtapa and Zihuatanejo runs about $4. In Ixtapa itself, walk or ride the minibuses that run along Paseo Ixtapa.

Museo Arqueología de la Costa Grande

The small Museo Arqueología de la Costa Grande on the beachfront side of Álvarez, near the Guerrero corner, details the archaeological history of the Costa Grande. Maps, drawings, small dioramas, and artifacts—many donated by local resident and innkeeper Anita Rellstab—illustrate the development of local cultures, from early hunting and gathering to agriculture and, finally, urbanization by the time of the conquest. Open Tues.–Sun. 9 A.M.–8 P.M.

Beaches around Zihuatanejo Bay

Ringed by forested hills, edged by steep cliffs, and laced by rocky shoals, Zihuatanejo Bay would be beautiful even without its beaches. Five of them line the bay. On the west side is narrow, tranquil **Playa el Almacén** (Warehouse Beach), mostly good for fishing from its nearby rocks. Moving past the pier toward town comes the colorful, bustling **Playa Municipal.** Its sheltered waters are fine for wading, swimming, and boat

Playa Madera stretches for a mile along Zihuatanejo Bay's innermost sandy edge.

launching (which fishermen, their motors buzzing, regularly do) near the pier end.

For maximum sun and serenity, walk away from the pier along Playa Municipal past the usually dry creek outlet where a concrete *andador* winds about 200 yards along the beachfront rocks that mark the beginning of Playa Madera. If you prefer, you can also hire a taxi to take you to Playa Madera, about $1.

Playa Madera (Wood Beach), once a loading point for lumber, stretches about 300 yards, decorated with rocky nooks and outcroppings, and backed by the lush hotel-dotted hill, **Cerro Madera.** The beach sand is fine and gray-white. Swells enter the facing bay entrance, breaking suddenly in two- or three-foot waves, which roll in gently and recede with little undertow. Madera's usually calm billows are good for child's play and easy swimming. Bring your mask and snorkel for glimpses of fish in the clear waters. Beachside restaurant/bars Kau Kan, La Bocana, and the

Hotel Irma, above the far east end, serve drinks and snacks. (Lately some pollution overflow has fouled Playa Madera; authorities, however, are at work enlarging waste-treatment facilities.)

Zihuatanejo Bay's favorite resort beach is **Playa La Ropa** (Clothes Beach), a mile-long crescent of yellow-white sand washed by oft-gentle surf. The beach got its name centuries ago from the apparel that once floated in from a galleon wrecked offshore. From the bay's best *mirador* (viewpoint) at the summit of **Paseo Costera,** the La Ropa approach road, the beach sand, relentlessly scooped and redeposited by the waves, appears as an endless line of half-moons.

On the 100-foot-wide beach, vacationers bask in the sun, personal watercraft buzz beyond the breakers, rental sailboats ply the waves, and sailboard outfits recline on the sand. The waves, generally too gentle and quick-breaking for surf sports, break close-in and recede with little undertow. Joggers come out mornings and evenings. Restaurants at the several beachfront hotels provide food and drinks.

Secluded **Playa Las Gatas** (Cat Beach), reachable by very rough shoreline rock-hopping or easily by launch from the town pier, lies sheltered beneath the south-end Punta El Faro headland. Once a walled-in royal Tarascan bathing pool, the beach got its name from a species of locally common, small, whiskered nurse sharks. Generally calm and quiet, often with super-clear offshore waters, Playa Las Gatas is both a snorkeling haven and a jumping-off spot for dive trips headed for prime scuba sites. Beach booths rent gear for beach snorkelers, and a professional dive shop, **Carlos Scuba** right on the beach, instructs and guides both beginner and experienced scuba divers. (For more diving details, see Sports and Recreation.)

For a treat, pass the beach restaurant lineup and continue to **Owen's** *palapa* restaurant, visible on **King's Point,** the palm-shaded outcropping past the far curve of the beach. There, enjoy some refreshment, watch the surfers glide around the point, and feast on the luscious beach, bay, and hill view.

Ixtapa Beaches

Ixtapa's 10 distinct beaches lie scattered like pearls along a dozen miles of creamy, azure coastline. Moving from the Zihuatanejo direction, **Playa Hermosa** comes first. The elevators of the super-luxurious clifftop Hotel Brisas Ixtapa make access to the beach very convenient. At the bottom you'll find a few hundred yards of seasonally broad white sand, with open-ocean (but often gentle) waves usually good for most water sports except surfing. Good beach-accessible snorkeling is possible off the shoals at either end of the beach. Extensive rentals are available at the beachfront aquatics shop. A poolside restaurant serves food and drinks. Hotel access is only by car or taxi.

For a sweeping vista of Ixtapa's beaches, bay, and blue waters, ride the *teleférico* (cable tramway, open daily 7 A.M.–7 P.M.) to El Faro restaurant, at the south end of Ixtapa's main beach, Playa del Palmar, tel. 755/553-1027. Open daily 8 A.M.–10 P.M. (hours may be seasonally shortened).

Long, broad, and yellow-white, **Playa del Palmar** could be called the "Billion-Dollar Beach" for the investment money it attracted to Ixtapa. The confidence seems justified. The broad strand stretches for three gently curving miles. Even though it fronts the open ocean, protective offshore rocks, islands, and shoals keep the surf gentle most of the time. Here, most sports are of the high-powered variety—parasailing ($15), personal watercraft riding and water-skiing ($40), banana-boating ($10)—although boogie boards are rentable for $5 an hour on the beach.

Challenging surfing breaks roll in consistently off the jetty at **Playa Escolleros,** at Playa del Palmar's far west end. Bring your own board.

Ixtapa Outer Beaches

Ixtapa's outer beaches spread among the coves and inlets a few miles northwest of the Hotel Zone. Drive, bicycle (rentals by bank Bital, in front of the Hotel Riviera), taxi, take a "Playa Linda" minibus along the Paseo de las Garzas (drivers, turn right just past the shopping mall), then fork left again after less than a mile. After the Marina Golf Course (watch out for crocodiles crossing the road, no joke), the road turns toward the shoreline, winding past a trio of development-blocked beach gems,

IXTAPA-ZIHUATANEJO

Playa San Juan de Dios, Playa Don Rodrigo, and **Playa Cuata.**

Although Mexican law theoretically allows free public oceanfront access, guards might try to shoo you away from Playa Cuata, on the open-ocean side, even if you arrive by boat. If somehow you manage to get there, you will discover a cream-yellow strip of sand, nestled between rocky outcroppings, with oft-gentle waves with correspondingly moderate undertow for good swimming, bodysurfing, and boogie boarding. Snorkeling and fishing are equally good around nearby rocks and shoals.

On the peninsula's sheltered northern flank, **Playa Quieta** (Quiet Beach) is a place that lives up to its name. A ribbon of fine yellow sand arcs around a smooth inlet dotted by a regatta of Club Med kayaks and sailboats plying the water. Get there via the north-end access stairway from the parking lot, signed Playa Quieta Acceso Público. Stop by the beachfront restaurant for refreshment or fresh seafood lunch.

Playa Linda

Playa Linda, an open-ocean yellow-sand beach, extends for miles beyond the road's end. Flocks of sandpipers and plovers skitter at the surf's edge; pelicans and cormorants dive offshore, while gulls, terns, and boobies skim the wavetops. Driftwood and shells decorate the sand beside a green-tufted palm grove that seems to stretch endlessly to the north.

In addition to the beach, mangrove-fringed **Laguna de Ixtapa** an arm of which extends to the bridge before the Playa Linda parking lot, is becoming attraction. The lagoon's star actors are **crocodiles** who often sun and doze in the water and along the bank beneath the bridge.

Officially, the bicycle path ends at the bridge, but you can continue on foot or by bicycle about 1.5 miles to Barra Vieja village. Take a hat, water, insect repellent, your binoculars, and your bird-identification book. (For more bicycling information, see the Sports and Recreation section.)

The friendly downscale **La Palapa** beach restaurant, at pavement's end, offers beer, sodas, and seafood, plus showers, toilets, and free parking. Neighboring stable **Rancho Playa Linda,** managed by friendly "Spiderman" Margarito, provides horseback rides at about $15 per hour.

The flat, wide Playa Linda has powerful rollers often good for surfing. Boogie boarding and bodysurfing—with caution, don't try it alone—are also possible. Surf fishing yields catches, especially of *lisa* (mullet), which locals have much more success netting than hooking.

Isla Ixtapa

Every few minutes a boat heads from the Playa Linda embarcadero to mile-long Ixtapa Island daily 9 A.M.–5 P.M.; $3 round-trip. Upon arrival, you soon discover the secret to the preservation of the island's pristine beaches, forests, and natural underwater gardens. "No trash here," the *palapa* proprietors say. "We bag it up and send it back to the mainland."

It shows. Great fleshy green orchids and bromeliads hang from forest branches, multicolored fish dart among offshore rocks, shady native acacias hang lazily over the shell-decorated sands of the island's little beaches. Boats from Playa Linda arrive at **Playa Cuachalatate** (koo-ah-chah-lah-TAH-tay), the island's most popular beach, named for a local tree whose bark is said to relieve liver ailments. Many visitors stay all day, splashing, swimming, and eating fresh fish, shrimp, and clams cooked at any one of a dozen *palapas*. Visitors also enjoy the many sports rentals: water skis, banana boat rides, boats for fishing, aquatic bicycles ($6/hour), snorkel gear ($3/hour), and kayaks ($5/hour).

For a change of scene, follow the short concrete walkway over the west-side (right as you arrive) forested knoll to **Playas Varadero and Coral** on opposite flanks of an intimate little isthmus. Varadero's yellow-white sand is narrow and tree-shaded, its waters are calm and clear. Behind it lies Playa Coral, a steep coral-sand beach fronting a rocky blue bay. Playa Coral is a magnet for beach lovers, snorkelers, and the scuba divers who often arrive by boat to explore the waters around the offshore coral reef.

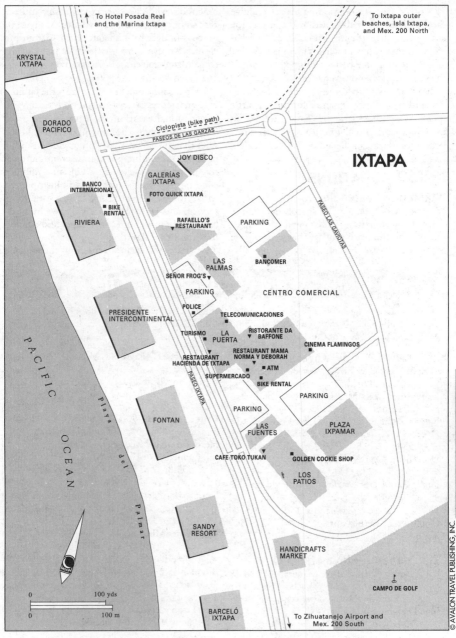

To Hotel Posada Real
and the Marina Ixtapa

To Ixtapa outer
beaches, Isla Ixtapa,
and Mex. 200 North

KRYSTAL
IXTAPA

DORADO
PACIFICO

Ciclopista (bike path)
PASEOS DE LAS GARZAS

IXTAPA

JOY DISCO

GALERÍAS
IXTAPA

BANCO
INTERNACIONAL

FOTO QUICK IXTAPA

BIKE
RENTAL

RIVIERA

RAFAELLO'S
RESTAURANT

PARKING

PASEO LAS GAVIOTAS

LAS
PALMAS

BANCOMER

SEÑOR FROG'S

PARKING

CENTRO COMERCIAL

POLICE

PRESIDENTE
INTERCONTINENTAL

TELECOMUNICACIONES

TURISMO

LA
PUERTA

RISTORANTE DA
BAFFONE

CINEMA FLAMINGOS

RESTAURANT
HACIENDA DE IXTAPA

RESTAURANT MAMA
NORMA Y DEBORAH

ATM

SUPERMERCADO

BIKE RENTAL

PACIFIC

PARKING

Playa

FONTAN

PARKING

del

PLAZA
IXPAMAR

OCEAN

LAS
FUENTES

Palmar

CAFE TOKO TUKAN

GOLDEN COOKIE SHOP

LOS
PATIOS

SANDY
RESORT

HANDICRAFTS
MARKET

0   100 yds

0   100 m

CAMPO DE GOLF

BARCELÓ
IXTAPA

To Zihuatanejo Airport and
Mex. 200 South

PASEO IXTAPA

MOON

IXTAPA-ZIHUATANEJO

© AVALON TRAVEL PUBLISHING, INC.

Scuba diving is so rewarding here that a dive shop, **Oliverio,** is maintained by the sons of the late founder, near the west end of Playa Cuachalatate. Other shops in Zihuatanejo (see Sports and Recreation) are better equipped to provide the same services, however.

Isla Ixtapa's fourth and smallest beach, secluded **Playa Carey,** is named for the sea-turtle species (see the special topic "Saving Turtles" in the Coast of Jalisco chapter). For access, hire a boat from Playa Cuachalatate.

ACCOMMODATIONS

Ixtapa or Zihuatanejo?

Your choice of local lodging sharply determines the tone of your stay. Zihuatanejo still resembles the colorful seaside village that visitors have enjoyed for years. Fishing *pangas* decorate its

beachside, while *panaderías, taquerías,* and *papelerías* line its narrow shady lanes. Many of its hotels—budget to moderate, with spartan but clean fan-only rooms—reflect the tastes of the bargain-conscious travelers who "discovered" Zihuatanejo during the 1960s.

Ixtapa, on the other hand, mirrors the fashionwise preferences of new-generation Mexican and international vacationers. A broad boulevard fronts your Ixtapa hotel, while on the beach side, thatch-shaded chairs on a wide strand, a palmy garden, blue pool, and serene outdoor restaurant are yours to enjoy. Upstairs, your air-conditioned room—typically in plush pastels, with private sea-view balcony, marble bath, room service, and your favorite TV shows by satellite—brings maximum convenience and comfort to a lush tropical setting.

Actually, you needn't be forced to choose. Split

IXTAPA-ZIHUATANEJO ACCOMMODATIONS BY PRICE

Accommodations (area code 755, postal code 40880) are listed in increasing order of approximate high-season, double-room rates. Toll-free 800, 888, 866, and 877 telephone numbers are dialable only from the United States or Canada or both.

Zihuatanejo—Downtown
Casa de Huéspedes Elvira, Paseo de la Pescador 9, tel. 554-2061, $15
Hotel Raoul Tres Marías, Noria 4, Col. Lázaro Cárdenas, tel. 554-2591, $35
Posada Citlali, Guerrero 3, tel./fax 554-2043, $35
Hotel Zihuatanejo, Ramírez 2, tel. 554-2669, fax 554-6987, zihuacenter@prodigy.net.mx, $40
Hotel Susy, Guerrero and Alvarez, tel. 554-2339, fax 554-4739, $40
Hotel Raoul Tres Marías Centro, Alvarez and Cinco de Mayo, tel./fax 554-6706, garroboscrew@prodigy.net.mx, $50
Hotel Ávila, Alvarez 8, tel. 554-2010, fax 554-8592, $50

Zihuatanejo—Playa Madera
Bungalows Allec, Cerro Madera, Calle Eva Samano de López Mateos, tel./fax 554-2002, josesanro@yahoo.com.mx, $40
Hotel Palacio, Av. Adelita (P.O. Box 57), tel./fax 554-2055, $46

Bungalows El Milagro, Av. Marina Nacional s/n, tel./fax 554-3045, $50
Bungalows Sotelo, Cerro Madera, Calle Eva Samano de López Mateos 13, tel./fax 554-6307, $60
Hotel Irma, Av. Adelita, tel./fax 554-3738, 800/262-4500, info@mcrx.com, $70
Hotel Brisas del Mar, Cerro Madera, Calle Eva Samano de López Mateos s/n, tel./fax 554-8332 or 554-2142, brisamar@prodigy.net.mx, $70
Bungalows Pacífico, Cerro Madera P.O. Box 12, tel. 554-2112, bungalowspacifico@yahoo.com, $82
Hotel Villas Miramar, Av. Adelita (P.O. Box 211), tel. 554-2106, fax 554-2149, villasm@prodigy.net.mx, $85
Bungalows Ley, Cerro Madera, tel. 554-4087, fax 554-4563, bungalowsley@prodigy.net.mx, $92
Casa Leigh y Loros, Cerro Madera, tel. 554-3755, zihua01@earthlink.net, $250

your hotel time between Ixtapa and Zihuatanejo and enjoy both worlds.

Zihuatanejo Downtown Hotels

Zihuatanejo's hotels divide themselves by location (and largely by price) between the budget–moderate downtown and moderate–expensive Playas Madera-La Ropa. For more information and updates on many of the following lodgings, in Ixtapa, Zihuatanejo, Troncones, and Barra de Potosí, visit the excellent website www.zihuatanejo.net.

Starting on the west side near the beach, begin at the **Hotel Raoul Tres Marias,** across the lagoon-mouth by footbridge from the end of Paseo del Pescador, at Noria 4, Colonia Lázaro Cárdenas, Zihuatanejo, Guerrero 40880, tel. 755/554-2191, fax 755/554-2591. Its longtime popularity derives from its low prices and the colorful la-

goonfront boat scene, visible from porches outside some of its 25 rooms. Otherwise, facilities are strictly bare-bones, without even hot water. Rooms rent for the same modest prices, however: $15 s, $20 d, $25 t, low season, and $25, $35, $40, high season, with fans.

Guests at the hotel's more upscale brother branch, **Hotel Raoul Tres Marias Centro,** Juan Álvarez and Cinco de Mayo, Zihuatanejo, Guerrero 40880, tel./fax 755/554-6706, garrobos crew@prodigy.net.mx (owned by brother Raoul, near the end of Álvarez), enjoy a few more amenities and the long-popular Restaurant Garrobos downstairs. Some of the 18 rooms have private balconies looking out on the usually quiet street below. Being close to the pier, the new branch is popular with fishing parties. Newcomers might pick up some local fishing pointers around the tables after dinner. Rooms go for

---

La Casa Que Canta, Carretera Escénica a Playa La Ropa, tel. 555-7030, 888/523-5050, fax 554-7040, casaquecanta@prodigy.net.mx, $450

Zihuatanejo—Playas La Ropa and Las Gatas

Hotel Sotavento, P.O. Box 2, tel. 554-2032 or 554-2024, 888/523-5050, fax 554-2975, info@hotelsotavento.com.mx, $58

Catalina Beach Resort, Playa La Ropa, tel. 554-2137 or 554-9321 through 554-9325, 877/387-2411, fax 554-9327, info@catalinabeachresort.com, $60–140

Bungalows Vepao, Playa La Ropa, tel. 554-3619 or 554-2631, www.ixtapa-zihuatanejo.com, $65

Bungalows Urracas, Playa La Ropa, tel. 555-2053, fax 554-2049, www.ixtapa-zihuatanejo.com, $70

Villas Ema, Playa La Ropa, c/o Posada Citlali, Guerrero 3, tel. 554-2043, $90

Hotel Villa Mexicana, tel./fax 554-3776 or 554-3636, 800/262-4500, info@mcrx.com, $100

Hotel Paraíso Real, Playa La Ropa, tel./fax 554-3873, 554-8156, or 554-2147, divemexico@email.com, $90

Casa La Gloria, Playa La Ropa, tel. 554-3619 or 554-2631, $105
Casa San Sebastián, tel./fax 554-3755, $175
Hotel Villa del Sol, Playa La Ropa, P.O. Box 84, tel. 554-5500 or 554-3239, 888/389-2645, 877/278-8018, 866/818-8342, fax 554-2758 or 554-4066, info@hotelvilladelsol.com, $450

Ixtapa

Hotel Posada Real, Paseo Ixtapa s/n, tel. 553-1625, 553-1745, 800/528-1234, fax 553-1805, $140

Hotel Barceló Ixtapa, Paseo Ixtapa s/n, tel. 555-0000, 866/485-4312, fax 553-2438, reservas@barceloixtapa.com.mx, $180

Hotel NH Krystal Ixtapa, Paseo Ixtapa s/n, tel. 553-0333, 800/231-9860, fax 553-0216, nhkrystalixtapa@nh-hoteles.com.mx, $320

Hotel Las Brisas Ixtapa, Paseo de la Roca, P.O. Box 97, tel. 553-2121, 866/226-3161, fax 553-0751, $340

Hotel Dorado Pacífico, Paseo Ixtapa s/n, P.O. Box 15, tel. 553-2025, fax 553-0126, reserv@doradopacifico.com.mx, $180

about $40 s or d, $47 t low season, $50 and $57 high, with hot water and a/c.

Right across the street is **Casa de Huéspedes Elvira,** Paseo del Pescador 9, Zihuatanejo, Guerrero 40880, tel. 755/554-2061, operated since 1956 by its founder, Elvira R. Campos. Every day, Elvira looks after her little garden of flowering plants, feeds rice to her birds—both wild and caged—and passes the time of day with friends and guests. She tells of the "way it used to be" when all passengers and supplies arrived from Acapulco by boat, local *almejas* (clams) were as big as cabbages, and you could pluck fish right out of the bay with your hands. Her petite eight-room lodging divides into an upper section, with more light and privacy, and a lower, with private baths. The leafy, intimate lower patio leads upward, via a pair of quaint, plant-decorated spiral staircases to the airy upper level. The 22 rooms themselves are small, authentically rustic, and clean. The four upper rooms share a bathroom and toilet. Rates run about $10 s or d, $20 t low season, $11 $15, $22 high. If nighttime noise bothers you, bring earplugs; TV and music from Elvira's adjoining restaurant continues until about 11 P.M. most evenings during the winter season.

A few blocks east, along the beach on Álvarez is the **Hotel Ávila,** Juan Álvarez 8, Zihuatanejo, Guerrero 40880, tel. 755/554-2010, fax 755/554-8592, downtown Zihuatanejo's only beachfront hostelry, mostly popular for its location rather than its management. Rooms, although simply decorated are comfortable, recently cleaned up and repainted. Of its 27 rooms, the several beachfront rooms, with luxurious private-patio bay and beach views, are the best. If possible avoid taking a room on the noisy streetfront side. Rooms rent, low season, for about $65 s or d with view and $40 without. Corresponding high-season rates are about $70 with view, $50 without. All rooms have fans, TV, a/c, phones, and hot water. Credit cards are accepted.

Hotel Susy, Guerrero and Álvarez, Zihuatanejo, Guerrero 40880, tel. 755/554-2339, fax 755/554-4739, viajesbravo@yahoo.com, across the street, has three tiers of rooms surrounding a shady inner patio. The seven upper-floor bayside rooms have private view balconies. Inside corridors unfortunately run past room windows, necessitating closing curtains for privacy, a drawback in these fan-only rooms. Avoid traffic noise by requesting an upper-floor room away from the street. The 20 clean but plain rooms go for $25 s, $30 d, $40 t low season, and $30, $40, $50 high, including fans and hot water.

A better choice, if you don't mind a bit of morning noise from the adjacent school, is the popular **Posada Citlali** (Star in Náhuatl), at Guerrero 3, tel./fax 755/554-2043. The hotel rises in a pair of three-story tiers, around a shady, plant-decorated inner courtyard. The 20 plain, rather small but clean rooms are all thankfully removed from direct street traffic hubbub. Guests on the upper floors have less corridor traffic and consequently enjoy more privacy. Reservations are mandatory during the high winter season and strongly recommended at other times. Rates run about $25 s, $30 d, $35 t low season, $30 s, $35 d, $40 t high, with hot water and fans.

Right in the middle of everything is **Hotel Zihuatanejo,** favorite of Mexican families, at Ramírez 2, Zihuatanejo, Guerrero 40880, tel. 755/554-2669, fax 755/554-6897, zihuacenter@prodigy.net.mx. Although right smack downtown, guests are nevertheless sheltered from the hubbub by rooms that face inward, on to an inviting inner pool-courtyard. The 79 rooms rising in four stories are clean and simply but comfortably furnished in pastels and vinyl floor tile. Some rooms have two double beds, others have one king- or queen-sized bed. For more air and light, ask for a room with a balcony. Rates run about $40 d year-round, with a/c, fans, TV, hot water showers, parking, and restaurant; credit cards are accepted. For more information, visit the website www.ixtapa-zihuatanejo.com/zihuacenter.

Zihuatanejo Playa Madera Hotels

Another sizable fraction of Zihuatanejo's lodgings spreads along Playa Madera on the east side of the bay, easily reachable during the dry season, by foot from the town plaza, via the scenic beachfront *andador* (walkway). Several hotels cluster on Cerro Madera, the bayside hill just east of town. Due to Zihuatanejo's one-way streets (which fortunately direct most noisy traffic away from downtown), getting to Cerro Madera is a bit tricky. The key is **Plaza Kyoto,** the traffic circle-intersection of Paseo de la Boquita and Paseo del Palmar a quarter mile east of downtown. If you're driving, keep a sharp eye out and follow the small Zona Hotelera signs. At Plaza Kyoto, marked by a big Japanese *torii* gate, bear right across the canal bridge and turn right at the first street. Continue straight ahead for another block to Av. Adelita, the address of several Playa Madera hotels, which runs along the base of Cerro Madera. At Adelita, jog right, then left at the first street, which will lead you uphill to the lane, Calle Eva Samano de López Mateos, that runs atop Cerro Madera.

By location, moving from west to east, start at **Bungalows Pacífico,** the labor of love of long-time local resident Anita Rellstab Hahner, at Cerro Madera, P.O. Box 12, tel./fax 755/554-2112, bungalowspacifico@yahoo.com. Her guests enjoy six spartan but spacious hillside apartments with broad bay-view patios and complete furnishings, including kitchenettes and daily maid service. Anita, herself an amateur archaeologist, ecologist, bird-watcher, and community leader, is a friendly, forthright, and knowledgeable hostess. She's more than happy to inform other bird- and animal-watching enthusiasts of good local viewing spots. Flower-bedecked and hammock-draped, Anita's retreat is ideal for those seeking quiet relaxation. No matter for lack of a pool; lovely Playa Madera is a short walk down the leafy front slope. Get your reservations in early, especially for winter. The apartments rent for about $58 d low season, $82 high, with hot water, fans only, and street parking; monthly discount possible during the May 1–Dec. 15 low season; get there via the short street uphill from Av. Adelita.

(If Bungalows Pacífico is full, you have a pair of similarly attractive lodging options on the same lane nearby: **Casa Lagartijas,** tel. 755/554-9391, larbym41@bigplanet.com; and **Casa Azul,** tel. 755/554-3534, U.S. tel. 303/458-8630, marsha_gould@msn.com, website www.mexonline.com/sucasita.htm)

Several more bungalow complexes cluster a block farther south, along the same rustic-scenic hilltop street. Although their details differ, their basic layouts—which stair-step artfully downhill to private beachfront gardens—are similar. First comes **Bungalows Sotelo,** at Calle Eva Samano de López Mateos 13, Zihuatanejo, Guerrero 40880, tel./fax 755/554-6307. Guests in a number of the clean stucco-and-tile apartments enjoy spacious private or semiprivate terraces with deck lounges and bay views. Rents for the smaller units without kitchenette run about $40 d low season, $60 high; larger one- and two-bedroom kitchenette suites rent for about $60 d low season, $80 high (for one bedroom) and $100 low season, $140 high (for two bedrooms). However, the management at times leaves something to be desired and rentals vary. Look at more than one before moving in. No pool, street parking only, but with a/c; get your winter reservations in early.

Next door but a notch down the economic scale is the aging circa-1960s **Bungalows Allec,** at Cerro Madera, Calle Eva Samano de López Mateos, Zihuatanejo, Guerrero 40880, tel./fax 755/554-2002. Comfortable, light, and spacious, although worn, the 12 clean fan-only apartments have and breezy bay views from private balconies. Six of the units are very large, sleeping up to six, with kitchenettes. The others are smaller doubles without kitchenette. No pool, but Playa Madera is a few steps downhill. The kitchenette apartments go for about $50 low season, $150 high; the smaller doubles are about $25 low, $40 high. Long-term discounts may be available. For more information, visit the website www.ixtapa-zihuatanejo.com/bun_allec.

Smaller but more attractive next door is **Bungalows Ley,** Calle Eva Samano de López Mateos s/n, Playa Madera, P.O. Box 466, Zihuatanejo, Guerrero 40880, tel. 755/554-4087, fax 755/554-4563, bungalowsley@prodigy.net.mx. Here, several white stucco studio apartments stair-step directly downhill to heavenly Playa Madera. Their recent decorations show nicely. Bathrooms shine with flowery Mexican tile, hammocks hang in spacious, rustic-chic, *palapa*-roofed view patios, and bedrooms glow with wall art, native wood details, and soothing pastel bedspreads. Except for a two-bedroom kitchenette unit at the top,

IXTAPA-ZIHUATANEJO

all are kitchenette studios. No pool, but the beach is straight down the steps from your door. The fan-only studios run for a steeply increased $75 d low season, $92 high. The beautiful two-bedroom unit with a/c runs $150 low season, $170 high. Long-term low-season discounts (of 15–30 percent for 6–21 night stays) are available.

Perched atop Bungalows Ley, with the same address, but completely separate, is upscale **Casa Leigh y Loros,** the lovely life project of friendly California resident Leigh Roth and her pet parrot, Loros. Casa Leigh y Loros, which Leigh rents when she's away, is a multilevel, art-decorated, white-stucco-and-tile, two-bedroom, two-bath villa with roof garden, airy bay-view balconies, and up-to-date kitchen appliances. High winter season (except Christmas) rent runs about $250/day, $1,500/week; during low season, Leigh charges $175/day, $1,150/week. With a/c, fans, TV, and daily maid service; cooking is available at extra charge.

Leigh also rents five smaller but similarly luxurious apartments from about $95/day, $570/week low season ($175/day, $1,000/week high) in villa **Casa San Sebastián** on the hillside, a mile away, above Playa La Ropa. For a more economical option, ask Leigh (or Lila, as she's known locally) about **Casa de Bambu,** which she also rents, across the street from Casa Leigh y Loros. Contact her or her agents at tel. 755/554-3755, email zihua01@earthlink.net. For more information, visit her website www.zihuatanejo-rentals.com.

Two doors away is yet another Cerro Madera option, **Hotel Brisas del Mar,** at Calle Eva Samano de López Mateos s/n, Cerro Madera, Zihuatanejo, Guerrero 40880, tel./fax 755/554-8332 or 755/554-2142, brisamar@prodigy.net.mx. New owners have completely renovated the original hotel and have added a big new wing of a dozen spacious, rustic-chic, native Mexico decor, view suites to the original 20 apartments. The bright spot of this entire complex is that about eight of the original apartments and all 12 of the new suites have sweeping bay views overlooking the hotel's lovely beach club, with its shady *palapas,* lounge chairs, and big blue pool. Brisas del Mar rents its original (but upgraded) apartments for about the same rates as its neighbors: about $60 d

low season, $70 high, with hot water and fans. For the spacious new-wing junior suites, expect to pay about $86 low season, $98 high, all with a/c and cable TV. For more information, visit the website www.brisasdelmar.net.

Downhill on Av. Adelita, right above the beach, is the longtime Mexican family–run **Hotel Palacio,** Av. Adelita, Playa Madera, P.O. Box 57, Zihuatanejo, Guerrero 40880, tel./fax 755/554-2055, a beachfront maze of rooms connected by meandering, multilevel walkways. Room windows along the two main tiers face corridor walkways, where curtains must be drawn for privacy. Upper units fronting the quiet street avoid this drawback. The rooms themselves are clean, renovated, brightly decorated and comfortable, with fans or a/c and hot water. Guests enjoy a small but very pleasant bay-view pool, kiddie pool, and sundeck, which perches above the waves at the hotel beachfront. Low season rentals run about $36 s, $46 d with fan, $42 and $52 with a/c but street parking only. High season, add about 20 percent.

Next door, the **Hotel Villas Miramar,** Playa Madera, Av. Adelita, P.O. Box 211, Zihuatanejo, Guerrero 40880, tel. 755/554-2106, fax 755/554-2149, villasm@prodigy.net.mx, clusters artfully around gardens of pools, palms, and leafy potted plants. The gorgeous, manicured layout makes maximum use of space, creating both privacy and intimacy in a small setting. The designer rooms have high ceilings, split levels, built-in sofas, and large, comfortable beds. The street divides the hotel into two different but equally lovely sections, each with its own pool. The restaurant, especially convenient for breakfast, is in the shoreside section but still serves guests who sun and snooze around the luxurious, beach-view pool patio on the other side of the street. The garden rooms rent for about $60 d low season, $85 high; the ocean-view apartments, about $75 low, $95 high; all have phones and a/c, and credit cards are accepted. Additional discounts may be available during May–Dec. 15 low seasons. Reservations strongly recommended during the winter season.

The **Hotel Irma,** Av. Adelita, Playa Madera, Zihuatanejo, Guerrero 40880, tel./fax 755/554-3738, half a block farther uphill, is a favorite for

© BRUCE WHIPPERMAN

Hotel Irma's prime location affords panoramic sunrise-to-sunset Zihuatanejo Bay views.

longtime lovers of Zihuatanejo, if for no reason other than its location. The good news is that fresh, revitalized management has renovated the hotel throughout. Now, guests enjoy very comfortable upgraded deluxe rooms, a passably pleasant sunset-view terrace restaurant and bar, and a pair of blue pools perched above the bay. A short walk downhill and you're at creamy Madera beach. Best of all, many of the front-tier rooms have private balconies with just about the loveliest view on Playa Madera. The 70 rooms rent for about $60 s or d low season, $80 high, with view ($45 and $60 without view), all with a/c, TV, and hot water. Low-season packages and discounts may be available May–June and Sept.–November.

Nearby, a couple of blocks off the beach, is the downscale but homey **Bungalows El Milagro,** Av. Marina Nacional s/n, P.O. Box 71, Playa Madera, Zihuatanejo, Guerrero 40880, tel. 755/554-3045, the project of late Dr. Niklaus Bührer and his wife, Lucina Gomes. A hacienda-like walled compound of cottages and apartments clustering around a shady pool, the

Bungalows El Milagro is winter headquarters for a cordial group of German longtime returnees. The friendly atmosphere and the inviting pool and garden account for the El Milagro's success, rather than the plain but clean kitchenette lodgings, which vary in style from rustic to 1940s motel. Look at several before you choose. The 17 units rent, high season, between about $50/day ($500/month) for two for the smaller rooms to about $90/day ($1,100/month) for the larger, six-person suites. All have kitchenettes, hot water, fans, pool, and parking.

A few hundred yards farther south along the Paseo Costera is **La Casa Que Canta,** Camino Escénico a Playa La Ropa, Zihuatanejo, Guerrero 40880, tel. 755/555-7030, fax 755/554-7040, casaquecanta@prodigy.net.mx, which is as much a work of art as a hotel. The pageant begins at the lobby, a luxurious soaring *palapa* that angles gracefully down the cliffside to an intimate open air view dining-room. Suite-clusters of natural adobe sheltered by thick *palapa* roofs cling artfully to the craggy precipice decorated with riots of bougainvillea and gardens of cactus. From petite pool terraces perched above foamy shoals, guests enjoy a radiant aqua bay panorama in the morning and brilliant ridge-silhouetted sunsets in the evening. The 18 art-bedecked, rustic-chic suites, all with private view balconies, come in three grades: super deluxe "terrace" rooms, and more spacious "grand suite," and even more spacious and luxurious "master suites" the latter two options with their own small pools. Rentals run about $450, $580, and $800; low-season discounts may be available, all with a/c, fans, phone, no TV, and no kids under 16 allowed. (*Note:* Casa Que Canta now offers the best of all possible upscale worlds within its present grounds: El Murmullo super-private 10,000-square-foot four-villa inner sanctum compound, built for a maharaja, with complete all-exclusive staff, from gardener, chambermaids, and butler, to waiters, kitchen staff, and gourmet chefs, all for only $4,000 daily.)

Make winter reservations very early toll-free at Mex. tel. 800/710-9345 or U.S. tel. 888/523-5050. For more information, visit the website www.lacasaquecanta.com.

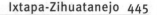

IXTAPA-ZIHUATANEJO

Zihuatanejo Playa La Ropa and Playa Las Gatas Hotels

Luscious Playa La Ropa begins at **Hotel Sotavento,** P.O. Box 2, Zihuatanejo, Guerrero 40880, tel. 755/554-2032 or 755/554-2024, fax 755/554-2975, email info@hotelsotavento.com.mx. Good hands-on owner management keeps the rambling complex, which perches on a leafy bayview hillside, healthy. The Sotavento is a 70-room mod-style warren that stair-steps five stories down the slope. Each floor of rooms opens to a broad, hammock-hung communal terrace overlooking the beach and bay. Inside, the Sotavento's rooms are spartan 1960s-style, clean and comfortable, most opening onto the view terrace, with king- or queen-sized beds and ceiling fans. High season rates begin at about $52 d, for a nonview, $58 d for view, to the largest deluxe family-sized bungalows, for about $100. Subtract about 20 percent during the low post-Easter–Dec. 15 low season. (*Note:* Views, light, and shade depend on your room's vertical position in the layout. Guests in upper rooms enjoy expansive bay and sunset vistas, while guests in less pricey lower-level rooms nevertheless enjoy intimate tropical verdure-framed sunset vistas of the bay beyond. Look at both kinds of rooms before choosing.)

The Hotel Sotavento's amenities include two beachside pools, room fans, and parking, restaurants, and a beach aquatics shop (see Catalina Beach Resort) but no elevator or wheelchair access; credit cards are accepted. For reservations, call toll-free U.S./Can. tel. 888-523/5050. For more information, visit the website www.hotelsotovento.com.mx.

By contrast, the 30 cabanas of the neighboring **Catalina Beach Resort** next door are scattered picturesquely beneath shady hillside trees all the way down to the beach. The Catalina's comfortably appointed tropical-rustic cabanas maximize privacy, being mostly separate units with individual view terraces and hammocks. Cabana lodgings vary, from huge to simply large; look until you find the one that most suits you. At the bottom of the hill, a beach aquatics shop offers sailing, sailboarding, snorkeling, and other rentals; those who want to simply rest enjoy chairs beneath the shady boughs of a beachside grove. A trio of restaurants, accessible by clients of both the Sotavento and Catalina, include an ordinary breakfast-lunch cafeteria at the beach level, a fancier dinner restaurant upstairs, and an airy upper-level terrace restaurant-bar.

The Catalina's high-season double-occupancy rents for two range as follows: economy room $60, standard room $80, casita $120, deluxe housekeeping bungalow $140 (low season, $55, $65, $77, and $90, respectively.) Reserve directly, at tel. 755/554-2137 or 755/554-9321 through 755/554-9325, or toll-free at U.S. tel. 877/387-2411, Can. tel. 866/485-4312, Germany tel. 0800/181-5405, fax 755/554-9327, or email info@catalinabeachresort.com. For more information, visit the website www.catalinabeachresort.com.

A dozen-odd hotels, bungalow complexes, and restaurants spread a mile farther along La Ropa Beach. The **Hotel Villa Mexicana,** Playa La Ropa, Zihuatanejo, Guerrero 40880, tel./fax 755/554-3776 or 755/554-3636, seems to be popular for nothing more than its stunning location right in the middle of the sunny beach hubbub. Its 75 rooms, comfortable and air-conditioned are packed in low-rise stucco clusters, around an inviting beachfront pool-patio-restaurant. This seems just perfect for the mostly North American winter package-vacation clientele, who ride personal watercraft, parasail, and boogie board from the beach, snooze around the pool, and socialize beneath the *palapa* of the beachside restaurant. Asking high-season rates begin at about $100 d ($145 d for a room with private view balcony). Low-season package three-night rates run about $200 d. Parking is available; credit cards are accepted. Reserve through toll-free tel. 800/262-4500 or email info@mcrx.com.

Up the street a few steps, a stone's throw from the beach, **Villas Ema** perches at the top of a flowery hillside garden. Here, the enterprising husband-wife owners of downtown Posada Citlali have built kitchenette apartments, beautifully furnished with white tile floors, matching floral drapes and bedspreads, modern-standard shower baths, plenty of windows for light, and sliding doors leading to private view porches for reading and relaxing. Amenities include a/c or fans, hot water, a beautiful blue pool, and the murmur of the waves on Playa La Ropa a block away. Rates for the nine smaller units, with kitchen in common, run about $60 d low season, $90 high. The three top-level units, although sunnier and consequently warmer, have the best views and most privacy. A pair of larger "villitas," each with its own kitchen and patio, sleeping four, rent for about $100 low season, $120 high. For reservations, highly recommended in winter, contact the owners through Posada Citlali, Av. Guerrero 3, Zihuatanejo, Guerrero 40880, tel./fax 755/554-2043, or at home (in Spanish) tel. 755/554-4880. To avoid confusion, be sure to specify your reservation is for Villas Ema.

German expatriate Helmut Leins sold out in Munich and came to create paradise on Playa La Ropa in 1978. The result is Playa La Ropa's luxury **Hotel Villa del Sol,** Playa La Ropa, P.O. Box 84, Zihuatanejo, Guerrero 40880, tel. 755/554-5500 or 755/554-3239, fax 755/554-2758 or 755/554-4066, info@hotelvilladel-sol.com. Here, in Helmut's exquisite beachside mini-Eden, a corps of well-to-do North American, European, and Mexican clients return yearly to enjoy tranquility and the elegance of the Villa del Sol's crystal-blue pools, palm-draped patios, and classic *palapas.* The lodgings themselves are spacious, with shining floor tile, handcrafted wall art, tropical-canopy beds, and private patios with hammocks. The plethora of extras includes restaurants, bars, pools, night tennis courts, a newsstand, art gallery boutique, beauty salon, and meeting room for about 30 people. The least expensive of the approximately 90 accommodations begin at $300 s or d, low season, $450 high. Super-plush options include more bedrooms and baths, ocean views, and small private pool for around $600 and up; with a/c and parking. Credit cards are accepted, but children only in two-bedroom suites. For reservations, call toll-free U.S./Can. tel. 888/389-2645, or contact the agent, Mexico Boutique Hotels, toll-free at U.S. tel. 877/278-8018 or Can. tel. 866/818-8342, email villa delsol@mexicoboutiquehotels.com. For more

information, visit the websites www.villasol.com or www.mexicoboutiquehotels.com/villadelsol.

A pair of good housekeeping bungalow-type complexes share the same luxuriously lovely beachfront as the Hotel Villas del Sol, but at greatly reduced prices. First comes **Bungalows Vepao,** address simply Playa La Ropa, Zihuatanejo, Guerrero 40880; reserve by calling either owner Gonzalo Ramírez, tel. 755/554-3619, or manager Margarita Castro, tel. 755/554-2631. Here they have created your basic clean and pleasant beach lodging, simply but architecturally designed, with floor-to-ceiling drapes, modern-standard kitchenettes, tiled floors, shower baths, white stucco walls, and pastel bedspreads and shaded lamps. Guests in each apartment enjoy front patios (upper ones have some bay view) that lead right to the hotel's private beachfront row of *palapas* a few steps away. Rates run about $50 d low season, $65 high, with parking, fans, and long-term discounts possible. For more information, visit www.ixtapa-zihuatanejo.com.

The same owner also rents four apartments in **Casa La Gloria,** a designer white stucco beachfront house, on the same property. Each of the deluxe units (two upstairs and two down) is attractively decorated with native rustic tile floors, bright floral tile baths, and whimsical hand-painted wall designs at the head of the two queen-sized beds. Each unit has its own kitchenette on an outdoor beachview patio. For more breeze and privacy, ask for one of the top-floor units. Rentals run about $85 low season, $105 high, with parking and fans. For reservations, see the Bungalows Vepao contacts.

Nearby, but as distinct as day from night, is **Bungalows Urracas,** about 15 petite brick cottages, like proper rubber planter's bungalows out of Somerset Maugham's *Malaysian Stories,* nestling in a shady jungle of leafy plants, trees, and vines. Inside, the illusion continues: dark, masculine wood furniture, spacious bedrooms, shiny tiled kitchenettes and baths, and overhead, rustic beamed ceilings. From the bungalows, short "jungle" paths lead to the brilliant La Ropa beachfront. About eight additional bungalows occupy beachfront view locations in front. Amenities include private, shady front porches (use insect repellent in the evenings), hot water, and fans. Rentals run a bargain $60 d low season, $70 high. Ask for a long-term discount. Get your winter reservations in early. Write Bungalows Urracas, Playa La Ropa, Zihuatanejo, Guerrero 40880, or call tel. 755/555-2053, fax 755/554-2049. For more information, visit www.ixtapa-zihuatanejo.com.

Go to the end of the road at Playa La Ropa and you'll find the **Hotel Paraíso Real,** the personal project of the friendly husband-wife team of scuba master Juan Barnard Avila and his wife, Margo. Their example reveals their strong commitment to sustainable ecotourism. In the mid-1990s, Juan and Margo renovated an old hotel, cleaned up the adjacent mangrove lagoon, and nurtured its wildlife (dozens of bird species and a number of crocodiles) back to health. They added 14 units, around a rear jungle-garden and golf putting green. Now, they run a combined hotel, restaurant, and scuba center, where guests may stay and relax for a week or a season, enjoy wholesome food and friendly people, perhaps get a massage, putt a little golf, and sample the good snorkeling, scuba diving, kayaking, turtle-hatching, and fishing available right from the beach.

Choose your room from one of two sections: beachview in front, or garden view in back. All rooms are immaculate and simply but comfortably furnished with handsomely handcrafted wooden beds, lamps, and cabinets. Rentals cost about $90 d year-round, with hot water, parking, and fans. For reservations (mandatory in winter) contact Hotel Paraíso Real, Playa La Ropa, Zihuatanejo, Guerrero, 40880, tel./fax 755/554-3873, 755/554-8156, or 755/554-2147, divemexico@email.com, www.divemexico.com.

Ixtapa Hotels

Ixtapa's dozen-odd hotels line up in a luxurious strip between the beach and boulevard Paseo Ixtapa. Best buy among them is the Best Western **Hotel Posada Real,** Paseo Ixtapa s/n, Ixtapa, Guerrero 40880, tel. 755/553-1625 or 755/553-1745, fax 755/553-1805, pr1ixt@prodigy.net.mx, at Paseo Ixtapa's far west end. Get there via the street, beach side, just past Valentine Restaurant. With a large grassy football field instead of tennis courts, the hotel attracts a seasonal following of soccer enthusiasts. Other amenities include a large airy beachfront restaurant and two luscious pools. Although the 110 (rather small) rooms are clean and comfortable, many lack ocean views. Rooms rent for about $117 d low season, $140 high, often with extended-stay or low-season discounts, such as third night free. Kids under 12 with parents are free; with a/c, satellite TV, phones, wheelchair access, and parking; credit cards are accepted. Reserve at Best Western toll-free U.S./Can. tel. 800/528-1234.

Nearer the middle of the hotel zone, the Spanish-owned **Hotel NH Krystal Ixtapa,** Paseo Ixtapa s/n, Ixtapa, Guerrero 40880, tel. 755/553-0333, fax 755/553-0216, nhkrystalixtapa@nh-hoteles.com.mx, towers over its spacious garden compound. Its innovative wedge design ensures an ocean view from each room. A continuous round of activities—a Ping-Pong tournament, handicrafts and cooking classes, and aerobics and scuba lessons—fills the days, while buffets, theme parties, and dancing fill the nights. Unscheduled relaxation centers on the blue pool, where guests enjoy watching each other slip from the water slide and duck beneath the waterfall all day. The 260 tastefully appointed deluxe rooms and suites have private view balconies, satellite TV, a/c, and phones. Rooms rent from a low of about $92 d low season, about $320 high. Check for additional discounts through extended-stay or other packages. Extras include tennis courts, racquetball, an exercise gym, parking, and wheelchair access; credit cards are accepted. For reservations, dial toll-free U.S./Can. tel. 800/231-9860. For more information, visit the website www.nh-hoteles.com.

If the NH Krystal is full, try the nearly-as-good **Hotel Dorado Pacífico,** Paseo Ixtapa s/n, P.O. Box 15, Ixtapa, Guerrero 40880, tel. 755/553-2025, fax 755/553-0126, reserv@doradopacifico.com.mx, next door. Although fewer organized activities fill the day, three palm-shaded blue pools, water slides, a swim-up bar, and three restaurant/bars seem to keep guests happy. Upstairs, the rooms, all with sea-view balconies, are pleasingly decorated with sky-blue carpets and earth-tone designer bedspreads. The 285 rooms rent from $145 d low season, $180 high, with a/c, phones, and TV. Low-season and extended stay discounts may be available. Other extras include tennis courts, parking, and wheelchair access; credit cards are accepted. For more information, visit the website www.doradopacifico.com.mx.

The **Hotel Barceló Ixtapa,** Paseo Ixtapa s/n, Ixtapa, Guerrero 40880, tel. 755/555-0000, fax 755/553-2438, reservas@barceloixtapa.com.mx; across from the golf course at the east end of the beach, rises around a soaring lobby/atrium. The Barceló, formerly the Sheraton, offers a long list of resort facilities, including pools, all sports, an exercise gym, several restaurants and bars, cooking and arts lessons, nightly dancing, and a Fiesta Mexicana. The 332 rooms in standard (which include mountain-view balconies only), ocean view, and junior suite grades, are spacious and tastefully furnished in designer pastels and include a/c, phones, and satellite TV. The Barceló operates both on a room only or all-inclusive basis. Room-only tariffs run about $162 d low season, $180 high, including breakfast, kids under 12 free; all-inclusive (all drinks, food, and entertainment) $220 d low, $250 d high, kids 6–12 $33. For more information, visit the website www.barcelo.com.

From the adjacent jungly hilltop, the **Hotel Las Brisas Ixtapa,** Paseo de la Roca, P.O. Box 97, Ixtapa, Guerrero 40880, tel. 755/553-2121, fax 755/553-0751, slopes downhill to the shore like a latter-day Aztec pyramid. The monumentally stark hilltop lobby, open and unadorned except for a clutch of huge stone balls, contrasts sharply with its surroundings. The hotel's severe lines immediately shift the focus to the adjacent jungle. The fecund forest aroma wafts into the lobby and the terrace restaurant, where, at breakfast, during the winter and early spring, guests sit watching iguanas munch hibiscus blossoms in the nearby treetops. The hotel entertains guests with a wealth of luxurious resort facilities, including pools, four tennis courts, a gym, aerobics, an intimate shoal-enfolded beach, restaurants, bars, and nightly piano bar music. The standard rooms, each with its own spacious view patio, are luxuriously spartan, floored with big designer tiles, furnished in earth tones, and equipped with big TVs, small refrigerators, phones, and a/c. More luxurious options include suites with individual pools and hot tubs. The 427 rooms begin at about $210 for a standard low-season double, $340 high, and run about twice that for super-luxury suites. June–Oct., bargain packages can run as low as $160 d per night. For reservations, dial toll-free Mex. tel. 800/227-4727 or U.S./Can. tel. 866/226-3161. For more information, visit the website www.brisas.com.mx.

Trailer Parks and Camping

Ixtapa-Zihuatanejo has one small, very basic trailer park. At south-end **Trailer Park Las Cabañas,** a block from La Ropa Beach, P.O. Box 197, Zihuatanejo, Guerrero 40880, tel. 755/554-4718, you can find out what it's like to park or camp in someone's shady backyard. Friendly, retired owner-managers María Elena and Hernán Cabañas, in order to make ends meet, decided to rent out their front and back yards. The result is enough space for a dozen tents or four medium-sized RVs in back, and one in front, with electricity, water, showers, and toilets. The price is certainly right—about $4 per person for tents, RVs $12—and it's only a block from one of the loveliest resort beaches in Pacific Mexico.

If Trailer Park Las Cabañas is too small for you, go to El Burro Borracho at Playa Troncones. (See Playa Majagua and Playa Troncones, at the end of the South to Ixtapa-Zihuatanejo and Inland to Pátzcuaro chapter.)

House, Apartment, and Condo Rentals

Zihuatanejo residents sometimes offer their condos and homes for temporary lease through agents. Among the better known is **Elizabeth Williams,** a longtime local realtor. Contact her at P.O. Box 169, Zihuatanejo, Guerrero 40880, tel. 755/554-2606, fax 755/554-4762, for a list of possible rentals.

Alternatively, try highly recommended realtor **Judith Whitehead** at tel. 755/554-6226, cellular tel. 044-755/557-0078, fax 755/5531212, or email jude@prodigy.net.mx. For more information, visit her website www.paradiseproperties.com.mx.

IXTAPA-ZIHUATANEJO

FOOD

Snacks, Bakeries, and Breakfast

For something cool in Zihuatanejo, stop by the **Paletería y Nevería Michoacana** ice shop across from the plaza. Besides ice cream, popcorn, and safe *nieves* (ices), it offers delicious *aguas* (fruit-flavored drinks, $.50), which make nourishing, refreshing non-Pepsi alternatives.

Downtown Zihuatanejo has at least two good bakeries. The long-time standby is **Panadería Francesa,** tel. 755/554-2742, tucked away on Galeana, the lane paralleling Cuahtémoc, a few doors north (uphill) from Gonzales, which turns out a daily acre of fresh goodies, from *pan integral* (whole-wheat) and black bread loaves to doughnuts and rafts of Mexican-style cakes, cookies, and tarts. It's open Mon.–Sat. 7 A.M.–9 P.M., Sun. 7 A.M.–2 P.M. Alternatively, sample the baked offerings of bakery **Buen Gusto,** at Guerrero 11, on the east side of the street, a few doors up the street from Coconuts Restaurant. Choose from a simply delicious assortment of fruit and nut tarts and cakes: pineapple, coconut, peach, strawberry, pecan, with coffee to go with them all. Open daily 8 A.M.–10 P.M.

Tasty, promptly served breakfasts are the specialty of the downtown **Cafetería Nova Zelandia** on Cuauhtémoc, corner of Ejido. Favorites include hotcakes, eggs any style, fruit, juices, and espresso coffee. Nova Zelandia serves lunch and supper also. Open daily 8 A.M.–10 P.M. Moderate.

For hot sandwiches and good pizza on the downtown beach, try the **Café Marina** on Paseo del Pescador, just west of the plaza. The friendly, hardworking owner features a spaghetti party—either bolognesa, pesto, or primavera—Wednesday night and chili on Friday. The shelves of books for lending or exchange are nearly as popular as the food. Open Mon.–Sat. noon–10 P.M., closed approximately June to mid-September. Moderate.

A local vacation wouldn't be complete without dropping in to the **Sirena Gorda** (Fat Mermaid), daily except Wed., 9 A.M.–11 P.M., near the end of Paseo del Pescador across from the naval compound, tel. 755/554-2687. Here the fishing crowd relaxes, trading stories after a tough day hauling in the lines. The other unique attractions, besides the well-endowed sea nymphs who decorate the walls, are tempting shrimp-bacon and fish tacos, juicy hamburgers, fish *mole,* and conch and nopal (cactus leaves, minus the spines) plates.

In Ixtapa, the **Café Toko Tucán,** tel. 755/553-0717, offers a refreshing alternative to hotel breakfasts. White cockatoos and bright toucans in a leafy patio add an exotic touch as you enjoy the fare, which, besides the usual juices, eggs, hotcakes, and French toast, includes lots of salads, veggie burgers, and sandwiches. Open daily 9 A.M.–10 P.M., on the west front corner of the Los Patios shopping complex, across the boulevard from Hotel Sandy Resort.

The perfume wafting from freshly baked European-style yummies draws dozens of the faithful to the nearby **Golden Cookie Shop,** brainchild of local longtimers Helmut and Esther Walter. He, a German, and she, an East Indian from Singapore, satisfy homesick palates with a continuous supply of scrumptious cinnamon rolls, pies, and hot buns, and hearty American-style breakfasts daily. In recent years, Helmut and Esther have served an authentic German buffet every Friday; call tel. 755/553-0310 to confirm. Open Mon.–Fri. 8 A.M.–3 P.M., Sat. 8 A.M.–1 P.M., on the inner patio, upper floor of the Los Patios shopping complex.

Zihuatanejo Restaurants

Local chefs and restaurateurs, long accustomed to foreign tastes, operate a number of good local restaurants, mostly in Zihuatanejo (where, in contrast to Ixtapa, most of the serious eating occurs *outside* of hotel dining rooms). Note, however, that a number of the best restaurants are closed during low season months of September and October.

All trails seem to lead to **Glob's Restaurant,** corner of west-side Juárez and Ejido, three blocks from the beach. Here the cool, coffee-shop atmosphere is refined but friendly, and the food is strictly for comfort—good American breakfasts, hamburgers, spaghetti, and salads. Open daily 8 A.M.–9 P.M. year-round. Moderate.

Zihuatanejo has a pair of good, genuinely local-style restaurants in the downtown area. **Tamales y Atoles "Any,"** tel. 755/554-7303, Zihuatanejo's clean, well-lighted place for Mexican food, is the spot to find out if your favorite Mexican restaurant back home is serving the real thing. Tacos, tamales, quesadillas, enchiladas, *chiles rellenos,* and such goodies are called *antojitos* in Mexico. At Tamales y Atoles "Any," they're savory enough to please even demanding Mexican palates. Open daily 9 A.M.–11 P.M., corner Guerrero and Ejido. Budget–Moderate. Incidentally, "Any" (AH-nee) is the co-owner, whose perch is behind the cash register, while her friendly husband cooks and tends the tables.

Restaurant Los Braseros, half a block along Ejido, at Ejido 21, between Cuauhtémoc and Guerrero, tel. 755/554-4858, is similarly authentic and popular. Waiters are often busy after midnight even during low season serving seven kinds of tacos and specialties such as Gringa, Porky, and Azteca from a menu it would take three months of dinners (followed by a six-month diet) to fully investigate. Open daily 4 P.M.–1 A.M. Moderate.

In the preface to their menu, the English owners of **Casa de Curry and Café Gondwana,** write that "in ancient times the European and Asian continents were part of one larger continent called Gondwana. And we are re-uniting the continents together again through our cooking." And they're making a good show of it. Indian food lovers will easily recognize and enjoy the result, which seems a major achievement here in Zihuatanejo so far from Madras and Mumbai. They also provide some familiar international specialties for those who do not indulge. Find them at the corner of Bravo and Galeana, two blocks from the beach; open daily 4 P.M.–midnight, tel. 755/554-6016. Moderate–expensive.

Longtime **Casa Elvira,** on waterfront Paseo del Pescador, by the naval compound, tel. 755/554-2061, founded long ago by now-octogenarian Elvira Campos, is as popular as ever, still satisfying the palates of a battalion of loyal Zihuatanejo longtimers. Elvira's continuing popularity is easy to explain: a palm-studded beachfront, strumming guitars, whirling ceiling fans, and a list of super-fresh salads, soups, fish, meat, and Mexican specialties, expertly prepared

and professionally served. Open daily 1–10 P.M.; reservations recommended during the high season. Moderate–xpensive.

If Elvira's is full, an excellent alternative would be **Porto de Mare,** the labor of love of its Italian architect owner, who designed and crafted its elegant open-air interior himself. As would be expected, his specialties are Italian-style pastas blended with the superbly fresh local seafood. Open daily noon–11 P.M. Expensive.

No guide to Zihuatanejo restaurants would be complete without mention of **Coconuts** restaurant, on Guerrero, a block from the beach, across from Posada Citlali, tel. 755/554-2518. Here, the food, although good, appears to be of lesser importance than its airy garden setting and good cheer generated among the droves of Zihuatanejo longtimers who return year after year. Open daily in season noon to midnight; closed approximately July–October. Expensive.

Walk to Juárez, two blocks east, to **Paul's** airy *palapa,* tel. 755/554-6528, where Swiss Chef Paul Karrer has attracted a following with gourmet specialties such as fettuccine with shrimp and mussels, pork chops with new potatoes, artichokes, and quail grilled with wine and herb sauce. Open Mon.–Sat. 2 P.M.–midnight. Expensive.

Restaurant Kau Kan, on the road above Playa Madera, half a block uphill from Hotel Irma, tel. 755/554-8446, continues to be popular for both its romantic view location and its excellent food and service. While music plays softly and bay breezes gently blow, waiters scurry, bringing savory appetizers, romaine Caesar salad, and cooked-to-perfection *dorado,* lobster, steak, and shrimp. Open daily noon–6 P.M. and 7 P.M.–midnight; high-season reservations mandatory, closed Sept.–October. Expensive.

Ixtapa Restaurants
Restaurants in Ixtapa have to be exceptional to compete with the hotels. One such, the **Bella Vista,** tel. 755/553-2121, *is* in a hotel, being the Las Brisas Ixtapa's view-terrace café. Breakfast is the favorite time to watch the antics of the iguanas in the adjacent jungle treetops. These black, green, and white miniature dinosaurs crawl up and down the trunks, munch flowers, and sunbathe on the

branches. The food and service, incidentally, are quite good. Open daily 7 A.M.–11 P.M. Call ahead to reserve a terrace-edge table; credit cards are accepted. Moderate–expensive.

An Ixtapa restaurant that has customers when most others don't is **Restaurant Mama Norma and Deborah,** in La Puerta shopping center, in the rear, by Da Baffone Italian restaurant, tel. 755/553-0274. Canadian expatriate proprietor Deborah Thompson manages with aplomb, working from a menu of delicious specialties familiar to North American and European palates. Whatever your choice, be it Greek salad, lobster, steak or fettuccine Alfredo, Deborah makes sure it pleases. For more information, visit the website www.restaurantmamanorma.com; open Mon.–Sat. 11 A.M.–11 P.M., Sun. 3–11 P.M. Moderate–expensive.

Those hankering for Italian-style pastas and seafood walk next door to **Ristorante Da Baffone,** tel. 755/553-1122. The friendly owner, a native of the Italian isle of Sardinia, claims his restaurant is the oldest establishment in Ixtapa. He's probably right: he served his first meal here in 1978, simultaneous with the opening of Ixtapa's first hotel, right across the boulevard. While Mediterranean-Mex decor covers the walls, marinara-style shrimp and clams with linguini, calamari, ricotta- and spinach-stuffed cannelloni, and glasses of Chianti and chardonnay load the tables. Open daily about noon–midnight during high season; call for reservations. Moderate–expensive.

If Da Baffone is full or closed, try the highly recommended gourmet Italian restaurant **Becco Fino** in the Marina Ixtapa. Reservations, tel. 755/553-1770, are usually necessary. Expensive.

(Other Ixtapa restaurants, popular for their party atmosphere, are described under Entertainment and Events).

ENTERTAINMENT AND EVENTS

In Zihuatanejo, visitors and residents content themselves mostly with quiet pleasures. Afternoons, they stroll the beachfront or the downtown shady lanes and enjoy coffee or drinks with friends at small cafés and bars. As the sun goes down, however, folks head to Ixtapa for its sunset vistas, happy hours, shows, clubs, and dancing.

Sunsets

Sunsets are tranquil and often magnificent from the **Restaurant/Bar El Faro,** tel. 755/553-1027, which even has a cableway, south end of the Ixtapa beach, open 7 A.M.–7 P.M., leading to it. Many visitors stay to enjoy dinner and the relaxing piano bar. The restaurant is open daily around 5:30–10 P.M.; reservations are recommended winter and weekends. Drive or taxi via the uphill road toward the Hotel Las Brisas Ixtapa, east of the golf course; at the first fork, head right for El Faro.

For equally brilliant sunsets in a lively setting, try either the lobby bar or Bella Vista terrace restaurant of the **Las Brisas Ixtapa.** Lobby bar happy hour runs 6–7 P.M.; live music begins around 7:30 P.M. Drive or taxi, following the signs, along the uphill road at the golf course, following the signs to the crest of the hill just south of the Ixtapa beach.

The west-side headland blocks most Zihuatanejo sunset views, except for spots at the far end of Playa La Ropa. Here, guests at the longtime favorite **Restaurant La Perla,** open 4–10 P.M., tel. 755/554-8700, and especially **Restaurant Elvira,** tel. 755/554-2588, at the opposite, inner, end of the beach, delight in Zihuatanejo's most panoramic sunset vistas.

Sunset and Sunshine Cruises

Those who want to experience a sunset party while at sea ride the trimaran *Tri Star,* which leaves from the Zihuatanejo pier around 5 P.M. daily, returning around 7:30 P.M. The tariff runs about $40 per person, including open bar.

The *Tri Star* also heads out daily on a Sunshine Cruise around 10 A.M., returning around 2:30 P.M. Included are open bar, lunch, and snorkeling, for about $50 per person. Book tickets for both of these cruises, which customarily include transportation to and from your hotel, through a hotel travel agent, such as American Express, tel. 755/553-0853, at Hotel NH Krystal in Ixtapa. Tickets are also available at the *Tri Star* office, tel. 755/554-2694, ydelsol@prodigy.net.mx, at

Puerto Mío, the small marina about half a mile across the bay from town. Get there via the road that curves around the western, right-hand shore of Zihuatanejo Bay.

Movies

Head over to the petite **Cine Paraíso,** on Cuauhtémoc, three blocks from the beach in downtown Zihuatanejo, to escape into American pop, romantic comedy, and adventure. About the same is available daily from 4:30 P.M. at **Cine Flamingos,** tel. 755/553-2490 in the shopping plaza, behind Señor Frog's, across the boulevard from the Hotel Presidente Intercontinental.

Tourist Shows

Ixtapa hotels regularly stage **Fiesta Mexicana** extravaganzas, which begin with a sumptuous buffet and go on to a whirling skirt-and-sombrero folkloric ballet. After that, the audience becomes part of the act, with piñatas, games, cockfights, dancing, while enjoying drinks from an open bar. In the finale, fireworks often boom over the beach, painting the night sky in festoons of reds, blues, and greens.

Entrance runs about $30–40 per person, with kids under 12 usually half price. Shows (often seasonally only) at the **Presidente Intercontinental,** tel. 755/553-0018; Tues. at the **Dorado Pacífico,** tel. 755/553-2025; and Wed. at the **Barceló,** tel. 755/555-0000, are the most reliable and popular. Usually open to the public; call ahead for confirmation and reservations.

Clubs and Hangouts

Part restaurant and part wacky seasonal nightspot, **Carlos'n Charlie's,** tel. 755/553-0085, is as wild and as much fun as all of the other Carlos Anderson restaurants from Puerto Vallarta to Paris. Here in Ixtapa you can have your picture taken on a surfboard in front of a big wave for $3, or have a fireman spray out the flames from the chili sauce on your plate. You can also enjoy the food, which, if not fancy, is innovative and tasty. Loud rock music ($10 minimum) goes on 10 P.M.–4 A.M. during the winter season. The restaurant serves daily noon–midnight. On the beachfront about half

a block on the driveway road west past the Hotel Posada Real.

For more of the same, but even more loud and outrageous, go to **Señor Frog's** in the shopping plaza, across from the Hotel Presidente Intercontinental.

In Zihuatanejo, at **Paccolo** bar, Bravo 38, just west of the corner of Guerrero, tel. 755/554-9116, a guitarist plays jazz melodies, from about 7 P.M. Thurs., Fri., and Sat. in season.

Dancing and Discoing

Many Ixtapa hotel lobbies blossom with dance music from around 7 P.M. during the high winter season. Year-round, however, good medium-volume groups usually play for dancing nightly from about 7 P.M. at the **Dorado Pacífico,** tel. 755/553-2025, the **Presidente Intercontinental,** tel. 755/553-0018; the **Barceló,** tel. 755/555-0000, and the **Las Brisas,** tel. 755/553-2121. Programs change, so call ahead to confirm.

Christine, Ixtapa's big-league discotheque in the Hotel NH Krystal, offers fantasy for a mere $10 cover charge. From 10 P.M., the patrons warm up by listening to relatively low-volume rock, watch videos, and talk while they can still hear each other. That stops around 11:30 P.M., when the fogs descend, the lights begin flashing, and the speakers boom forth their 200-decibel equivalent of a fast freight train roaring at trackside. Call to verify times, tel. 755/553-0333.

SPORTS AND RECREATION
Walking and Jogging

Zihuatanejo Bay is strollable from the Playa Madera all the way west to Puerto Mío. A relaxing half-day adventure could begin by taxiing to the Hotel Irma, Av. Adelita, on Playa Madera, for breakfast. Don your hats and follow the stairs down to Playa Madera and walk west toward town. At the end of the Playa Madera sand, head left along the *andador* (walkway) that twists along the rocks, around the bend toward town. Continue along the beachfront Paseo del Pescador; at the west end, cross the lagoon bridge, head left along the bayside road to **Puerto Mío** for a drink at the hotel café and perhaps a dip in the pool.

Allow three hours, including breakfast, for this two-mile walk; do the reverse trip during late afternoon for sunset drinks or dinner at the Irma.

Playa del Palmar, Ixtapa's main beach, is good for similar strolls. Start in the morning with breakfast at the Restaurant/Bar El Faro, atop the hill at the south end of the beach; open daily, mornings 6–11 A.M. (low season, 8:30–11 A.M.), evenings 6–10 P.M. Ride the cableway or walk downhill. With the sun at your back stroll the beach, stopping for refreshments at the hotel pool patios en route. The entire beach stretches about three miles to the marina jetty, where you can often watch surfers challenging the waves and where taxis and buses return along Paseo Ixtapa. Allow about four hours, including breakfast. The reverse walk would be equally enjoyable during the afternoon. Time yourself to arrive at the El Faro cableway (call ahead, tel. 755/553-1027, to make sure the cableway is running) about half an hour before sundown to enjoy the sunset over drinks or dinner. Get to El Faro by driving or taxiing via Paseo de la Roca, which heads uphill off the Zihuatanejo road at the golf course. Follow the first right fork to El Faro.

Adventurers who enjoy ducking through underbrush and scrambling over rocks might enjoy exploring the acacia forest and pristine beaches of the uninhabited west side of **Isla Ixtapa.** Take water, lunch, and a good pair of walking shoes.

Joggers often practice their art either on the smooth, firm sands of Ixtapa's main beachfront or on Paseo Ixtapa's sidewalks. Avoid crowds and midday heat by jogging early mornings or late afternoons. For even better beach jogging, try the flat, firm sands of uncrowded Playa Quieta about three miles by car or taxi northwest of Ixtapa. Additionally, mile-long Playa La Ropa can be enjoyed by early morning and late-afternoon joggers.

Golf and Tennis

Ixtapa's 18-hole, professionally designed **Campo de Golf** is open to the public. In addition to its manicured, 6,898-yard course, patrons enjoy full facilities, including pool, restaurant, pro shop, lockers, and tennis courts. Greens fee runs $50, cart $30, club rental $22, 18 holes with caddy $16, and golf lessons $25 an hour. Play goes on

daily 7 A.M.–3 P.M. The clubhouse, tel. 755/553-1062, is off Paseo Ixtapa, across from the Barceló. No reservations are accepted; morning golfers, get in line early during the high winter season.

The **Marina Golf Course,** tel. 755/553-1410 or 755/553-1424, offers similar services (greens fee $73, cart $68 for two, club rental $25, caddy $20) for higher prices.

Ixtapa has nearly all of the local **tennis** courts, all of them private. The Campo de Golf has some of the best. Rentals run about $5/hour days, $9 nights. Reservations, tel. 755/553-1062, may be seasonally necessary. A pro shop rents and sells equipment. A teaching professional offers lessons for about $25 per hour.

Several hotels also have tennis courts, equipment, and lessons. Call the **Barceló,** tel. 755/555-0000; **Dorado Pacífico,** tel. 755/553-2025; **NH Krystal,** tel. 755/553-0333; and the **Las Brisas,** tel. 755/553-2121, for information.

Horseback Riding

Rancho Playa Linda on Playa Linda rents horses daily for beach riding for about $15 per hour. Travel agencies and hotels offer the same, though for higher prices.

Bicycling

Ixtapa's hot new activity is bicycling along the new 10-mile round-trip *ciclopista* bike path to Playa Linda. Rental stations are along Paseo Ixtapa: in front of the Hotel Riviera by Banco Internacional, and east a couple of blocks, at the Las Fuentes shopping center parking lot, across from Hotel Fontana. Bargain for a discount from the steep $10/hour asking rate.

The *ciclopista* takes off north, across the street from the Banco Internacional rental station, at the Paseo Las Garzas intersection. Officially the *ciclopista* ends five miles west, at the wooden bridge and crocodile-viewing point at the Playa Linda parking lot, but you can go another 1.5 miles farther to Barra Vieja village at the lagoon's edge. Be sure to take a hat, water, and insect repellent.

Swimming and Surfing

Calm Zihuatanejo Bay is fine for swimming and sometimes good for boogie boarding and bodysurfing at Playa Madera. On Playa La Ropa, however, waves generally break too near shore for either bodysurfing or boogie boarding. Surfing is generally good at Playa Las Gatas, where swells sweeping around the south-end point give good, rolling left-handed breaks.

Heading northwest to more open coast, waves improve for bodysurfing and boogie boarding along Ixtapa's main beach Playa del Palmar, while usually remaining calm and undertow-free enough for swimming beyond the breakers. As for surfing, good breaks sometimes rise off the Playa Escolleros jetty at the west end of Playa del Palmar.

Along Ixtapa's outer beaches, swimming is great along very calm Playa Quieta; surfing, bodysurfing, and boogie boarding are correspondingly good but hazardous in the sometimes mountainous open-ocean surf of Playa Larga farther north.

Snorkeling and Scuba Diving

Clear offshore waters (sometimes up to 100-foot visibility during the dry winter-spring season) have drawn a steady flow of divers and nurtured professionally staffed and equipped dive shops. Just offshore, good snorkeling and scuba spots, where swarms of multicolored fish graze and glide among rocks and corals, are accessible from **Playa Las Gatas, Playa Hermosa,** and **Playa Carey** (on Isla Ixtapa).

Many boat operators take parties for offshore snorkeling excursions. On Playa La Ropa, contact the aquatics shop at the foot of the hill beneath Hotel Sotavento. Playa Las Gatas, easily accessible by boat for $4 from the Zihuatanejo pier, also has snorkel and excursion boat rentals. In Ixtapa, similar services are available at beachside shops at the Hotels Las Brisas, Barceló, NH Krystal, and seasonally at other hotels.

Other even more spectacular offshore sites, such as Morros de Potosí, El Yunque, Bajo de Chato, Bajo de Torresillas, Piedra Soletaria, and Sacramento, are accessible with the help of professional guides and instructors.

A pair of local scuba dive shops stand out. In Zihuatanejo, marine biologist-instructor Juan M. Barnard Avila coordinates **Zihuatanejo Scuba**

Center, at his Hotel Paraíso Real, on Playa La Ropa, tel./fax 755/554-3873, 755/554-8156, or 755/554-2147, divemexico@email.com, www.divemexico.com. Licensed for instruction through NAUI (National Association of Underwater Instructors), Avila is among Pacific Mexico's best-qualified professional instructors. Aided by loads of state-of-the-art equipment and several experienced licensed assistants, his shop has accumulated a long list of repeat customers. Avila's standard resort dive package, including a morning pool instruction session and an afternoon offshore half-hour dive, runs about $70 per person ($60 with your own gear) complete. Other services for beginners include open-water certification (one week of instruction, $450) and advanced NAUI certification up to assistant instructor. For certified divers (bring your certificate), Avila offers night, shipwreck, deep-water, and marine-biology dives at more than three dozen coastal sites. He's open Mon.–Sat. about noon–8 P.M.

Carlo Scuba, at Playa Las Gatas, also offers professional scuba services. The PADI-trained instructors offer a resort course, including one beach dive, for $60; a five-day open-water certification course, $450; and a two-tank dive trip for certified participants, $70, one-tank $55. It also conducts student referral courses and night dives. Contact the manager-owner, friendly Jean-Claude Duran (known locally as Jack Cousteau), on Las Gatas beach, tel. 755/554-3570, fax 755/554-2811, carloscuba@yahoo.com.

Sailing, Sailboarding, and Kayaking

The tranquil waters of Zihuatanejo Bay, Ixtapa's Playa del Palmar, and the quiet strait off Playa Quieta are good for these low-power aquatic sports. Shops on Playa La Ropa (at Hotel Sotavento and Catalina) in Zihuatanejo Bay and in front of Ixtapa hotels, such as the Las Brisas Ixtapa, the Barceló, and the NH Krystal, rent small sailboats, sailboards, and kayaks hourly.

Fishing

Surf or rock casting with bait or lures, depending on conditions, is generally successful in local waters. Have enough line to allow casting beyond the waves (about 50 feet out on Playa La Ropa, 100 feet on Playa del Palmar and Playa Linda).

The rocky ends of Playas La Ropa, La Madera, del Palmar, and Las Gatas on the mainland, and Playa Carey on Isla Ixtapa are also good for casting.

For deep-sea fishing, you can launch your own boat or rent one. *Pangas* are available for rent from individual fishermen on the beach, the boat cooperative (see below) at Zihuatanejo pier, or aquatics shops of the Hotel Sotavento on Playa La Ropa or the Hotels Las Brisas Ixtapa, Barceló, NH Krystal, and others on the beach in Ixtapa. Rental for a seaworthy *panga,* including tackle and bait, should run about $20 per hour, depending upon the season and your bargaining skill. An experienced boatman can help you and your friends hook, typically, six or eight big fish in about four hours, which local restaurants are often willing to serve as a small banquet for you in return for your extra fish.

Big-Game Sportfishing

Zihuatanejo has long been a center for billfish (marlin, swordfish, and sailfish) hunting. Most local captains have organized themselves into cooperatives, which visitors can contact either directly or through town or hotel travel agents. Trips begin around 7 A.M. and return 2–3 P.M. Fishing success depends on seasonal conditions. If you're not sure of your prospects, go down to the Zihuatanejo pier around 2:30 P.M. and see what the boats are bringing in. During good times they often return with one or more big marlin or swordfish per boat (although captains are increasingly asking that billfish be set free after the battle has been won). Fierce fighters, the sinewy billfish do not make the best eating and are often discarded after the pictures are taken. On average, boats bring in two or three other large fish, such as *dorado* (dolphinfish or mahimahi), yellowfin tuna, and roosterfish, all more highly prized for the dinner table.

The biggest local sportfishing outfitter is the blue and white fleet of the **Sociedad Cooperativa Teniente Azueta,** tel./fax 755/554-2056, named after the naval hero Lieutenant José Azueta. You can see adjacent to the Zihuatanejo pier many of its several dozen boats bobbing at anchor. Arrangements for fishing parties can be made through hotel travel desks or at its office, open daily 6 A.M.–6 P.M., at the foot of the pier. The largest 36-foot boats, with four or five lines, go out for a day's fishing for about $250 low season, $500 high. Twenty-five-foot boats with three lines run about $120 per day low season, $250 high. Smaller *pangas* go out for about $100 low season, $150 high.

The smaller (18-boat) **Servicios Sociedad Cooperativa Benito Juárez,** tel./fax 755/554-3758, tries harder by offering similar boats for lower prices. Its 36-foot boats for six start around $300; a 25-foot for four, about $150. Contact the office across from the naval compound near the end of Paseo del Pescador, open daily 9 A.M.–7 P.M.

On the adjacent corner, next door, at Paseo El Pescador 20, newest and trying even harder, is **Whiskey Water World,** Paseo del Pescador 20, tel./fax 755/554-0147, fax 755/554-0146, whiskey@prodigy.net.mx, www.zihuatanejosportfishing.com and www.ixtapasportfishing.com, which claims to employ only sober captains. Its top-of-the-line-only boats run from 30 feet and $250, including license, bait, and drinks. Jack Daniels is extra. Captains will take two people fishing, from 7 A.M. to 2 P.M., for $40 apiece (six-person minimum). Proud members of the IGFA (International Game Fishing Association), captains follow sailfish, tuna, and *dorado* catch-and-release policy.

Prices quoted by providers often (but not necessarily) include fishing licenses, bait, tackle, and amenities such as beer, sodas, ice, and on-board toilets. Such details should be pinned down (ideally by inspecting the boat) before putting your money down.

Sportfishing Tournament

Twice a year, usually in May and January, Zihuatanejo fisherfolk sponsor the **Torneo de Pez Vela,** with prizes for the biggest catches of sailfish, swordfish, marlin, and other varieties. Entrance fee runs around $800, and the prizes usually include a new Dodge pickup, cars, and other goodies. For information, contact the local sportfishing cooperative, Sociedad Cooperativa Teniente José Azueta, Muelle Municipal, Zihuatanejo, Guerrero 40880, tel. 755/554-2056, or the fishing tournament coordinator, Crecencio Cortés, tel. 755/554-8423.

Marinas and Boat Launching

Marina Ixtapa, at the north end of Paseo Ixtapa, offers excellent boat facilities. The slip charge runs about $.75 per foot per day, for 1–6 days ($.55 for 7–29 days), subject to a minimum charge per diem. This includes use of the boat ramp, showers, pump-out, electricity, trash collection, mailbox, phone, fax, and satellite TV. For reservations and information, contact the marina daily 9 A.M.–2 P.M. and 4–7 P.M., at the harbormaster's office in the marina-front white building on the right a block before the big white lighthouse, tel./fax 755/553-2180, marina0@prodigy.net.mx, or write Harbormaster, Marina Ixtapa, Ixtapa, Guerrero 40880.

The smooth, gradual Marina Ixtapa **boat ramp,** open to the public for an approximately $10 fee, is on the right-hand side street leading to the water, just past the big white lighthouse. Get your ticket beforehand from the harbormaster.

Sports Equipment Shops

Deportes Náuticos, corner of N. Bravo and Guerrero in downtown Zihuatanejo, tel. 755/554-4411, sells snorkel equipment, boogie boards, tennis racquets, balls, and a load of other general sporting goods. Open Mon.–Sat. 10 A.M.–2 P.M. and 4–9 P.M.

Pesca Deportiva (Sportfishing), on the other hand, specializes in fishing rods, reels, lines, weights, and lures. Open Mon.–Sat. 9 A.M.–2 P.M. and 4–7 P.M., at the far west end of Álvarez, corner of Armada de Mexico.

SHOPPING
Zihuatanejo

Every day is market day at the Zihuatanejo **Mercado** on Av. Benito Juárez, four blocks from the beach. Behind the piles of leafy greens, round yellow papayas, and huge gaping sea bass, don't miss the sugar and spice stalls. There you will find big cones of raw *panela* (brown sugar), thick, home-

Guerrero-made pottery animals make good gifts to take home.

made golden honey, mounds of fragrant *jamaica* petals, crimson dried *chiles,* and forest-gathered roots, barks, and grasses sold in the same pungent natural forms as they have been for centuries.

For more up-to-date merchandise, go to the nearby **Super de Zihuatanejo,** tel. 755/554-3634, on the side street bordering the market's north side. It's a typical sleepy Mexican country grocery, with shelves of canned vegetables, lots of good in-season fruit, and dusty back aisles piled with bags of sugar, beans, and salt; open Mon.–Sat. 7 A.M.–8 P.M. Next door, you can get about the same thing plus medications, at the **Super y Farmacia Rosy,** tel. 755/554-8617.

For convenience shopping, the grocery **Adriana y Pancho** at the plaza-front corner of Juan Álvarez and Cuauhtémoc, is one of the only stores in downtown Zihuatanejo with any food. Open Mon.–Sat. 9 A.M.–9 P.M.

Zihuatanejo's first supermarket-department

store is the big **Comercial Mexicana** behind the Central Bus Station, on Highway 200, about a mile east of downtown, open daily 9 A.M.–9 P.M.

Ixtapa

Ixtapa's **Centro Comercial** complex stretches along the midsection of Paseo Ixtapa across from the hotels. It has four viable (of about 10 planned but still not functioning) and attractive subcomplexes, all fronting the boulevard. Moving east to west, first come the Los Patios and Fuentes subcomplexes, where minimarts, T-shirt and trinket shops, and super-expensive designer stores, such as Bill Blass, Ralph Lauren, and Gucci, occupy the choice boulevard frontages. Behind them, dozens of mostly small and ordinary crafts and jewelry shops languish along back lanes and inside patios. More of the same occupies the La Puerta subcomplex 100 yards farther on. Next comes the police station, and, after that, the Galerías Ixtapa subcomplex at the corner of Paseo de las Garzas.

> *Don't miss the sugar and spice stalls at the Zihuatanejo Mercado. There you will find big cones of raw panela (brown sugar), thick, homemade golden honey, mounds of fragrant jamaica petals, crimson dried chiles, and forest-gathered roots, barks, and grasses.*

Handicrafts

Although some stores in the Ixtapa Centro Comercial shopping center and the adjacent tourist market (across from the Hotel Barceló) offer handicrafts, Zihuatanejo offers the best selection and prices.

The Zihuatanejo **tourist market** stalls display a flood of crafts brought by families who come from all parts of Pacific Mexico. Their goods—delicate Michoacán lacquerware, bright Tonalá birds, gleaming Taxco silver, whimsical Guerrero masks, rich Guadalajara leather—spread for blocks along Av. Cinco de Mayo on the downtown west side. Compare prices; although bargaining here is customary, the glut of merchandise makes it a one-sided buyer's market, with many sellers barely managing to scrape by. If you err in your bargaining, kindly do it on the generous side.

Prominent among downtown shops nearby is

the **Casa Marina** shopping center, tel. 755/554-2373, a family project of late community leader Helen Krebs Posse. Her adult children and spouses own and manage stores in the two-story complex, just west of the beachfront town plaza.

Their original store, **Embarcadero,** on the lower floor, streetside, has an unusually choice collection of woven and embroidered finery, mostly from Oaxaca. In addition to walls and racks of colorful, museum-quality traditional blankets, flower-embroidered dresses, and elaborate crocheted *huipiles,* she also offers wooden folk-figurines and a collection of intriguing masks.

Other stores in the Casa Marina include **La Zapoteca** on the bottom floor, specializing in weavings from Teotitlán del Valle in Oaxaca. Others include **Metzli,** with all-Mexico resort wear, **Arte de la Tradición,** with a trove of lovely Talavera pottery, tel. 755/554-4625. Upstairs are upstairs are **El Jumil** (silver and masks), **Latzotil** (Mayan art), **El Calibria** (leather), and, on the ground floor, facing the beach, the Café La Marina (pizza and used paperbacks). Local weavers demonstrate in the Embarcadero and La Zapoteca stores mornings and afternoons. The entire complex is open Mon.–Sat. approximately 10 A.M.–2 P.M. and 5–9 P.M.; credit cards are generally accepted.

A block toward the pier, **La Tienda de Ropa Típica,** on Paseo del Pescador, across from the naval compound, would be easy to pass because of its mounds of ho-hum T-shirts. But if you look inside, you'll find racks of many fetching hand-crocheted *huipiles* and blouses from back-country Guerrero and Oaxaca. Open daily 8 A.M.–10 P.M.

Walk away from the beach, along Cinco de Mayo, past the church, to **Nopal** handicrafts, the labor of love of the owner, who likes things from Oaxaca, especially baskets. He fills his shop with an organized clutter, including unique woven goods and ceramics. Open Mon.–Sat. 9 A.M.–3 P.M. and

4:30–9 P.M. low season, Mon.–Sat. 9 A.M.–9 P.M. high season, tel./fax 755/554-7530.

Head back along Álvarez two blocks, past the plaza, to **Cerámicas Tonalá**, 12B Álvarez, beach side, to view one of the finest Tonalá pottery collections outside of the renowned source itself. Here, friendly owner Eduardo López's graceful glazed vases and plates, decorated in traditional plant and animal designs, fill the cabinets, while a menagerie of lovable owls, ducks, fish, armadillos, and frogs, all seemingly poised to spring to life, crowd the shelves. Open Mon.–Sat. 9 A.M.–2 P.M. and 4–8 P.M., tel. 755/554-2161; credit cards are accepted.

A few steps up Cuauhtémoc, **Alberto's** pair of shops, on opposite sides of the street, tel. 755/554-2161, offer an extensive silver jewelry collection. As with gold and precious stones, silver prices can be reckoned approximately by weighing, at between $1 and $1.25 per gram. The cases and cabinets of shiny earrings, chains, bracelets, rings, and much more, are products of a family of artists, taught by a master craftsman, now semiretired, in Puerto Vallarta. Many of the designs are original, and, with bargaining, reasonably priced. Open Mon.–Sat. 9 A.M.–8 P.M.; credit cards are accepted.

A block farther, at the corner of Ejido, step into **Rosimar,** the creation of Josefina and Manuel Martínez. Manuel's intriguing outside murals lead you inside to their eclectic, priced-to-sell collection of Tonalá and Tlaquepaque pottery, papier-mâché, and glassware.

At **Galería Maya,** on Cuauhtémoc, farther from the beach, past Ejido, on the right, tel. 755/554-4606, owner Tania Scales has accumulated a multitude of one-of-a-kind folk curios from many parts of Mexico. Her wide-ranging, carefully selected collection includes masks, necklaces, sculptures, purses, blouses, *huipiles,* ritual objects, and much more. Open Mon.–Sat. 10 A.M.–2 P.M. and 5–9 P.M. Furthermore, be sure not to miss Tania's labor of love, several regal sculptures that represent a number of indigenous female deities: Ixta Bay, Mayan jungle goddess; Coyolxauhqui, Aztec moon goddess; and Cihuateteo, representing all the women of Zihuatanejo.

Photography

In Zihuatanejo, **Foto 30** on Ejido, between Galeana and Guerrero, two blocks from the plaza, tel. 755/554-7610, offers 30-minute develop-and-print service and stocks lots of film and accessories. These include a host of cameras, including SLRs, and film, including 120 print, 35mm slide, and sheet film, plus filters, tripods, and flashes. Open Mon.–Sat. 9 A.M.–8 P.M., Sun. 10 A.M.–2 P.M.

In Ixtapa, **Foto Quick,** in shopping center Galerías Ixtapa, across the boulevard from Hotel Riviera, offers approximately the same products and services.

INFORMATION
Tourist Information Office

The Ixtapa state-federal office of **Turismo,** tel. 755/553-1967 or 755/553-1968, also answers questions and dispenses literature and maps Mon.–Fri. 8 A.M.–8 P.M., Sat. 8 A.M.–2 P.M. Find it in the Ixtapa La Puerta shopping complex, across the boulevard from the Hotel Presidente Intercontinental.

Publications

The best local English-language book and magazine selection fills the many shelves of the **Hotel Las Brisas** shop. Besides dozens of new paperback novels and scores of popular U.S. magazines, it stocks *USA Today* and the *News* of Mexico City and a small selection of Mexico coffee table books of cultural and historical interest. Open daily 9 A.M.–9 P.M.

The **newsstand,** west side of the Zihuatanejo plaza, is a customary source of popular U.S. magazines, such as *Vogue, Time,* and *Sports Illustrated,* plus the newspapers *News* of Mexico (around 1 P.M.) and *USA Today.* Open daily 8 A.M.–8 P.M.

The friendly, small Zihuatanejo bookstore **Librería Byblos,** on Galeana, between Ejido and Bravo, tel. 755/554-2281, despite its mainly Spanish inventory, does have some used English-language paperbacks. It also stocks English-Spanish dictionaries and a number of good maps of Mexico. Open Mon.–Sat. 9 A.M.–9 P.M.

Many used paperbacks fill the bookshelf at

friendly **Café Marina** adjacent to the beach just west of the plaza; open Mon.–Sat. till 10 P.M., closed June to mid-September.

The small Zihuatanejo **Biblioteca** (public library) also has some shelves of English-language paperbacks. Open Mon.–Fri. 9 A.M.–8 P.M., Sat. 9 A.M.–5 P.M.; on Cuauhtémoc, five blocks from the beach.

Ecological Association and Humane Society

The grassroots **Asociación de Ecologistas** sponsors local cleanup, tree-planting, save-the-turtles, and other projects. For information, contact the society's president, architect Edgar Morales, tel. 755/553-1858, or Anita Rellstab Hahner, owner of Bungalows Pacífico, tel. 755/554-2112.

In Ixtapa, volunteers of **Eco-Ixtapa** concentrate their efforts on a community recycling project. For information, contact leader Carmen Huras, tel. 755/553-1758.

The family of the late Helen Krebs Posse are the guiding lights of the **Sociedad Protectora de Animales,** tel. 755/555-7227 or 755/555-6191, fax 755/555-3533, www.zihuatanejo.net/spaz, which is working hard to educate people about animal issues. Contact one of the family members, at the family's shop complex, Casa Marina, just west of the Zihuatanejo plaza, tel. 755/554-2373.

SERVICES

Money Exchange

Several banks, all with ATMs, clustered east of downtown of Juárez, serve customers. Go to **Banamex,** tel. 755/554-7293 or 755/554-7294, at the corner of Guerrero and Ejido, two blocks from the beach, open for money exchange Mon.–Fri. 9 A.M.–5 P.M., Sat. 9 A.M.–2 P.M. If the Banamex lines are too long, use the ATM or walk three blocks east, to **Bancomer,** tel. 755/554-7492 or 755/554-7493, open Mon.–Fri. 9 A.M.–5 P.M., Sat. 10 A.M.–2 P.M., or **Banco Serfin,** tel. 755/554-3941, open Mon.–Fri. 9 A.M.–4 P.M., both near the corner of Bravo and Juárez.

After hours, go around the corner to the **Casa de Cambio Guibal,** tel. 755/554-3522, fax 755/554-2800 (with long-distance telephone and fax), at Galeana and Ascencio, two blocks from the beach, to change U.S., Canadian, French, German, Swiss, and other currencies and traveler's checks. For the convenience, it offers you a few percent less for your money than the banks. Open daily 8 A.M.–9 P.M.

In Ixtapa, for long money-changing hours, go to **Banco Internacional,** in front of the Hotel Riviera right on Paseo Ixtapa, tel. 755/553-0641, 755/553-0642, or 755/553-0646. Open Mon.–Fri. 8 A.M.–7 P.M., Sat. 8 A.M.–3 P.M. Alternatively, go to **Bancomer** in the Los Portales complex behind the shops across the boulevard from the Hotel Presidente Intercontinental, tel. 755/553-2112, 755/553-0535, or 755/553-0525, open Mon.–Fri. 8:30 A.M.–4 P.M.

The local **American Express** branch in the Hotel NH Krystal sells and and cashes American Express traveler's checks and provides travel agency services to the public. For card-carrying members, it provides full money services, such as check-cashing. Hours are Mon.–Sat. 9 A.M.–6 P.M., Sat. 9 A.M.–1 P.M. Money services hours may be shorter. Call for confirmation, tel. 755/553-0853, fax 755/553-1206.

Communications

The only *correo* (post office), tel. 755/554-2192, serving both Zihuatanejo and Ixtapa is in Zihuatanejo at the Centro Federal, in the northeast corner of downtown, five blocks from the beach about three blocks east of the Ixtapa minibus stop at Juárez and Morelos. Open Mon.–Fri. 8 A.M.–3 P.M., Sat. 9 A.M.–1 P.M. Also in the post office is a sub-office of the very reliable government **Mexpost** (like U.S. Express Mail) upgraded, secure mail service.

Next door is **Telecomunicaciones,** which offers long-distance telephone, public fax 755/554-2163, telegrams, and money orders Mon.–Fri. 8 A.M.–7 P.M. Another similar telecommunications office serves Ixtapa, in the La Puerta shopping center (rear side), across Paseo Ixtapa from the Hotel Presidente Intercontinental.

Money changer Casa de Cambio Guibal is also downtown Zihuatanejo's private *larga distancia* telephone and fax office, on Galeana, the lane parallel to Cuauhtémoc, corner of Bravo, tel./fax 755/554-3522. Open daily 8 A.M.–9 P.M.

In both Ixtapa and Zihuatanejo, many streetside public phone booths provide economical national and international (call the United States for about $1 per three minutes) long-distance service, using a Ladatel telephone card. Cards are readily available in grocery, drug, and liquor stores everywhere. First dial 001 for calls to the United States and Canada, and 01 for Mexico long-distance. Lacking a Ladatel card, use your personal telephone credit card. Dial tel. 001-800/462-4240 for the English-speaking AT&T international operator, tel. 001-800/674-6000 for MCI.

Beware of certain private "To Call Long Distance to the U.S.A. Collect and Credit Card" telephones installed prominently in airports, tourist hotels, and shops. Tariffs on these phones can run as high as $30 for three minutes. Always ask the operator for the rate, and if it's too high, take your business elsewhere.

Health, Police, and Emergencies

For medical consultations in English, contact U.S.-trained **IAMAT associate** Dr. Rogelio Grayeb, in Zihuatanejo, at Bravo 71A, beach side, between Guerrero and Galeana, tel. 755/554-3334, 755/553-1711, or 755/554-2040, cellular tel. 044-755/551-3335, fax 755/554-5041.

Another Zihuatanejo medical option is the very professional **Clínica Maciel,** which has a dentist, pediatrician, gynecologist, surgeon, and general practitioner on 24-hour call, at 12 Palmas, two blocks east, one block north of the market, tel. 755/554-2380 or 755/554-0517.

Neither Ixtapa nor Zihuatanejo has any state-of-the art private hospitals. However, many local people recommend the state of Guerrero *hospital general,* on Av. Morelos, corner of Mar Egeo, just off from Highway 200, tel. 755/554-3965, 755/554-3650, or 755/554-3436, for its generally competent, dedicated, and professional staff.

For medicines and drugs in Ixtapa, ask your hotel desk to put you in contact with a pharmacy. Alternatively, call one of the many pharmacies in downtown Zihuatanejo, such as the **Farmacia La Principal,** corner of Cuauhtémoc

and Ejido, two blocks from the beachfront plaza, tel. 755/554-4217; open Mon.–Sat. 9 A.M.–9 P.M.

For police emergencies in Ixtapa and Zihuatanejo, contact the *cabercera de policía* headquarters in Zihuatanejo, on Calle Limón, near Highway 200, tel. 755/554-2040. Usually more accessible are the police officers at the *caseta de policía* 24-hour police booth at the Zihuatanejo plaza-front, and in Ixtapa on Paseo Ixtapa, across from the Hotel Presidente Intercontinental. On Playa La Ropa, go to the small police station on the Paseo Costera, at the north-end intersection by the Hotel Villa del Sol.

Immigration and Customs

If you lose your tourist permit, go to **Migración,** on Colegio Militar, about five blocks northeast of Plaza Kyoto, on the northeast edge of downtown, tel. 755/554-2795; open Mon.–Fri. 9 A.M.–3 P.M. Bring your passport and some proof of the date you arrived in Mexico, such as your airline ticket, stamped passport, or a copy of your lost tourist permit. Although it's not wise to let such a matter go until the last day, you may be able to accomplish the needed paperwork at the airport Migración office (open daily 8 A.M.–6 P.M.). Call first, however, tel. 755/554-8480.

The **Aduana** (Customs) office, tel. 755/554-3262, is at the airport, off Highway 200 about seven miles south of Zihuatanejo, open daily 9 A.M.–7 P.M. If you have to temporarily leave the country without your car, have someone fluent in Spanish call about the required paperwork, if any.

Laundry and Dry Cleaning

In Zihuatanejo, take your laundry to the **Laundry Super-Clean** at Gonzáles and Galeana, just off Cuauhtémoc, four blocks from the plaza, tel. 755/554-2347; open Mon.–Sat. 8 A.M.–8 P.M. Alternatively, go to **Lavandería Express,** on Cuauhtémoc, around the corner, a few doors toward the beach, open daily 8 A.M.–8 P.M.

If you also need something dry-cleaned, take both it and your laundry items to **Lavandería Premium,** on Cuauhtémoc, across the street from Super Clean, open daily 8:30 A.M.–8 P.M.

GETTING THERE AND AWAY

By Air

Four major carriers connect Ixtapa-Zihuatanejo directly with U.S. and Mexican destinations year-round; two more operate during the fall-winter season.

Many **Aeroméxico** flights connect daily with Mexico City, and one with Guadalajara, where connections with U.S. destinations may be made. For reservations, call tel. 755/554-2018 or 755/554-2019; for flight information, call tel. 755/554-2237 or 755/554-2634.

Mexicana Airlines flights connect directly with Mexico City. For reservations, call tel. 755/554-2208 or 755/554-2209; for flight information, call tel. 755/554-2227.

Alaska Airlines connects with Los Angeles, San Francisco, and Seattle. Call a travel agent or toll-free U.S. tel. 800/426-0333 (reachable also from Mexico) for flight information and reservations.

America West Airlines connects with Phoenix. Call a travel agent or toll-free U.S. tel. 800/235-9292 (reachable also from Mexico) for flight information and reservations.

Continental Airlines connects with Houston seasonally during the late fall, winter, and spring. Call a travel agent or toll-free Mex. tel. 800/900-5000 for flight information and reservations.

Canadian World of Vacations charter flights connect with Toronto and perhaps other Canadian gateways during the fall, winter, and spring. Call a travel agent, such as American Express, tel. 755/553-0853, for reservations.

Air Arrival and Departure

Ixtapa-Zihuatanejo is quickly accessible, only seven miles (11 km) north of the airport via Highway 200. Arrival is generally simple—if you come with a day's worth of pesos and hotel reservations. Although terminal does have an ATM (by the exit door near the car rentals), it has neither tourist information booth, nor hotel-reservation service. Best arrive with a hotel reservation, and not leave the choice up to your taxi driver who will probably deposit you

at the hotel that pays him a commission on your first night's lodging.

Transportation to town is usually by *taxi especial* (private taxi) or *colectivo* van. Tickets are available at booths near the terminal exit. Tariff for a *colectivo* is $6–9 per person (depending on destination); for a taxi, $19–26 for three or four people. Taxis to Troncones run about $48. Mobile budget travelers can walk the few hundred yards to the highway and flag down one of the frequent daytime Zihuatanejo-bound buses (very few, if any, continue to Ixtapa, however). At night, spend the money on *colectivo* or taxi.

Several major **car rental** companies staff airport arrival booths. Avoid problems and save money by negotiating your car rental through the agencies' toll-free numbers (see the chart "Car Rental Agencies" in the On the Road chapter) before departure. Agents include Hertz, tel. 755/554-3050 or 755/554-2590; Budget, tel. 755/554-4837 or 755/553-0397; and Alamo, tel. 755/553-0206.

Departure is quick and easy if you have your passport, tourist permit (which was stamped on arrival), and $19 cash (or the equivalent in pesos) international departure tax if your air ticket doesn't already cover it. Departees who've lost their tourist permits can avoid trouble and a fine by either getting a duplicate at Zihuatanejo Immigration or (perhaps) by having a passport, a copy of the lost permit, or at least some proof of their date of arrival, such as an airline ticket.

For last-minute postcards and shopping, the airport has a mailbox and a several gift shops and a pretty fair magazine stand.

By Car or RV

Three routes, two easy and one unsafe and not recommended, connect Ixtapa-Zihuatanejo with Playa Azul and Michoacán to the northwest, Acapulco to the southeast, and Ciudad Altamirano and central Guerrero to the northeast.

Traffic sails smoothly along the 76 miles (122 km) of Highway 200, either way, between Zihuatanejo and Lázaro Cárdenas/Playa Azul. Allow about two hours. Several miles before Lázaro Cárdenas the new Highway 37 D *cuota* toll expressway allows easy access to highland central

Michoacán (190 miles, 312 km, 4.5 hours to Uruapan, add another hour to Pátzcuaro) from Zihuatanejo. The same is true of the 150-mile (242-km, allow four hours) Highway 200 southern extension to Acapulco.

The story is much different, however, for the winding, sparsely populated, cross-Sierra Highway 134 (intersecting with Highway 200 nine miles north) from Zihuatanejo to Ciudad Altamirano. Rising along spectacular, jungle-clad ridges, the paved but sometimes potholed road leads over cool, pine-clad heights and descends to the Altamirano high, dry valley after about 100 miles (160 km). The continuing leg to Iguala on the Acapulco-Mexico City highway is longer, about 112 miles (161 km), equally winding, and often busy. Allow about eight hours westbound and nine hours eastbound for the entire trip. Keep filled with gasoline, and be prepared for emergencies, especially along the Altamirano-Zihuatanejo leg, where no hotels and few services exist. *Warning:* This route, unfortunately, has been plagued by robberies and nasty drug-related incidents. Inquire locally—your hotel, the tourist information office, the bus station—to see if authorities have secured the road before attempting this trip.

By Bus

Zihuatanejo's big, shiny long-distance Estrella Blanca *Central de Autobús* bus station is on Highway 200, Acapulco-bound side, about a mile southeast of downtown Zihuatanejo. Travelers have the use of a Sendatel public long-distance phone/fax and hotel reservations agency (for certain hotels only), a left-luggage service, and a small snack bar. You should prepare by stocking up with water and goodies before you depart.

Estrella Blanca (EB), tel. 755/554-3477, the major carrier, computer-coordinates the service of its subsidiaries Flecha Roja (FR), Elite (EL), Futura (FU), and Autotransportes Cuauhtémoc. Tickets are available with cash or credit cards for all departures from computer-assisted agents. In total, they offer luxury class (infrequent, super-first-class, reserved), first class (frequent, reserved), and second class (very frequent, unreserved) service.

Most buses run along the Highway 200 corridor, connecting with Lázaro Cárdenas/Playa Azul and northwestern points, and with Acapulco and points south and east.

Several luxury- and first-class buses and many (every half hour) second-class buses connect daily with Acapulco. Several of them continue to Mexico City, and at least one other continues east along the Oaxaca coast, all the way to Salina Cruz. In the opposite direction, many luxury-, first-, and second-class buses (at least one an hour) connect daily with Lázaro Cárdenas, Playa Azul, and northwest points.

A number of departures also connect, along the Pacific coast Highway 200 corridor, southeast with Acapulco and the Oaxaca coast, and northwest via Manzanillo, Puerto Vallarta, and Mazatlán, to the U.S. border at Mexicali and Tijuana. At least one daily departure connects north with Michoacán points of Uruapan and Morelia, via the new expressway.

Another major bus carrier, **Estrella de Oro**, tel. 755/554-2175, offers a few competing long-distance first-class departures from its station on the highway, just west of the Estrella Blanca Central de Autobus.

Along the Road to Acapulco

Although the 150-mile (242-km) Zihuatanejo-Acapulco stretch of Highway 200 is smooth and easy, resist the temptation to hurry through. Your reward will be a bright string of little pearls— idyllic South Seas villages, miles of strollable and fishable beaches, wildlife-rich *esteros,* lovely small hotels, and a tranquil little beach resort on the hidden edge of Acapulco.

Heading Out

If you're driving, mark your odometer at the Zihuatanejo southside Pemex, near Km 240 on Highway 200. Or, if driving north, do the same at the Acapulco *zócalo* (old town square) Km 0, and head out on the northbound coast road past Pie de la Cuesta. Road mileages and kilometer markers are helpful in finding the paths to hidden little beaches.

Bus travelers, take a second-class bus from the Zihuatanejo or the Acapulco Estrella Blanca *central de autobús.* Ask the driver to drop you at your chosen haven.

PLAYA LAS POZAS AND PLAYA BLANCA

These pocket paradises have arrived on the map of Guerrero. Las Pozas, a surf-fishing paradise, is reachable via the Zihuatanejo airport road. The reward is a lagoon full of bait fish, space for RV or tent camping (be careful of soft sand), a wide beach, and friendly beachside *palapa* restaurants. Farther east, the beach changes to Playa Blanca, where a delightfully luxurious new hotel welcomes travelers willing to stray a few miles off the beaten track.

But first, back at Playa Las Pozas, the beach itself is 100 yards wide, of yellow-white sand, and extends for miles in both directions. It has driftwood but not many shells. Fish thrive in its thunderous, open-ocean waves. Consequently, casts from the beach can yield five-pound catches by either bait or lures. Local folks catch fish mostly by net, both in the surf and the nearby lagoon. During the June–Sept. rainy season, the lagoon

breaks through the bar. Big fish, gobbling prey at the outlet, can be netted or hooked at the same spot themselves.

Camping is popular here on weekends and holidays. Other times you may have the place to yourself. As a courtesy, ask the friendly Neto family restaurant (on the west end, by the lagoon), the best of the *palapa* restaurants, if it's okay to camp nearby.

Rustic accommodations have arrived at Las Pozas, through the ingenuity of builder Jeffry Meyers, who has erected a few tropical "Treetops" cabanas beside a beachside swimming pool. For food, he offers either meals or use of a communal kitchen. Figure about $30–40 per night double. Contact him at tel. 755/554-8278 or email beach@hotmail.com for reservations. For more information, visit the website www.zihuatanejo.net/treetops. In the past he's been closed part of the summer and fall.

Get to Playa Las Pozas by following the well-marked airport turnoff road at Km 230. After one mile, turn right at the cyclone fence just before the terminal and follow the bumpy but easily passable straight level road 1.1 miles (1.8 km) to the beach. Continue one mile (1.6 km) two miles along the beach road to Playa Blanca and Hotel Las Palmas.

In 2001, friendly but savvy and hard-working owner-builders from Phoenix, Arizona, decided to create heaven on lazy, lovely Playa Blanca. The result, only a year later, was **Hotel Las Palmas,** replete with precious architecture-as-art, such as polished natural tree trunk beamed ceilings, elegant Mexican hardwood shutters, and massive overhanging thatched *palapa* roofs. A recipe for Paradise? Yes, but even more: a big blue pool, good restaurant and bar, all set in cool green grassy grounds overlooking a long, creamy, yellow-white strand.

Their six super-comfortable, hand-crafted rooms, four with a/c, two with ceiling fans, rent for $175 d high season, $125 low (June–Oct.), with breakfast, but without TV, phones, credit cards, or kids under 18. Reserve directly at the

Barra de Potosí boatmen offer wildlife-viewing lagoon tours and ocean fishing excursions.

hotel, tel. 755/557-0634, or email hotellaspal-mas@hotmail.com. Reservations are also possible through the owners' Arizona agent, Gold Coast Travel, at fax 602/253-3487 or email goldcoast-travel@hotmail.com. For more information, visit the website www.zihuatanejo.net.

BARRA DE POTOSÍ

At Achotes, on Highway 200, nine miles (15 km) south of Zihuatanejo, a Laguna de Potosí sign points right to Barra de Potosí, a picture-perfect fishing hamlet at the sheltered south end of the Bahía de Potosí. After a few miles through green, tufted groves, the road parallels the bayside beach, a crescent of fine white sand, with a scattering of houses and one small beachfront hotel.

The **Hotel Resort Barra de Potosí,** tel. 755/554-8290, cellular tel. 044-755/557-7259, fax 755/554-3445, perches right on the beach. The surf is generally tranquil and safe for swimming near the hotel, although the waves, which do not roll but break rather quickly along long fronts, do not appear good for surfing. The hotel is, happily, in the process of being restored. Most

rooms have been renovated and the pool has been returned to a brilliant blue. The owner says that the restaurant will be open during the high winter season, but will close during the low summer and fall. The beach, nevertheless, will remain inviting year-round. Kitchenette apartments rent for about $50, studios $40, but with only tepid room-temperature (not hot, not cold) water. All lamps are bare-bulb; bring your own lamp-shade or booklight.

The waves become even more tranquil at the beach's southeast end, where a sheltering headland rises beyond the village and the adjacent lagoon. Beneath its swaying palm grove, the hamlet of Barra de Potosí (pop. 1,000) has the ingredients for weeks of tranquil living. Several broad, hammock-hung *palapa* restaurants (here called *en-ramadas*) front the bountiful lagoon.

Home for flocks of birds and waterfowl and shoals of fish, the **Laguna de Potosí** stretches for miles to its far mangrove reaches. Adventure out with your own boat or kayak, or go with Orlando, who regularly takes parties out for fishing or wildlife-viewing tours.

Bait fish, caught locally with nets, abound in the

lagoon. Fishing is fine for bigger catches (jack, snapper, mullet) by boat or casts beyond the waves. Launch your boat easily in the lagoon, then head, like the local fishermen, past the open sandbar.

Rooms and breakfast are available in the charming flower-bedecked **Casa del Encanto** (House of Enchantment) on a village side street; ask for owner Doña Laura Nolo, tel. 755/556-8199, lauragecko2@hotmail.com. (Also in the village, try **Casa Frida,** tel. 755/556-3944, casa -frida@zihuatanejo.net.)

Camping is common by RV or tent along the uncrowded edge of the lagoon. Village stores can provide basic supplies. For more information about Barra de Potosí, visit its website www.cdnet.com.mx/zihua/barra.

Prepared food is available at about a dozen lagoon-side *palapa* restaurants. **Restaurant Teresita** is especially recommended

Get there by following the signed turnoff road at Km 225, nine miles (14 km) south of Zihuatanejo, just south of the Los Achotes River bridge. Continue along the good (trailer-accessible) dirt road for 5.5 miles (8.9 km) to the hotel and the village half a mile farther south.

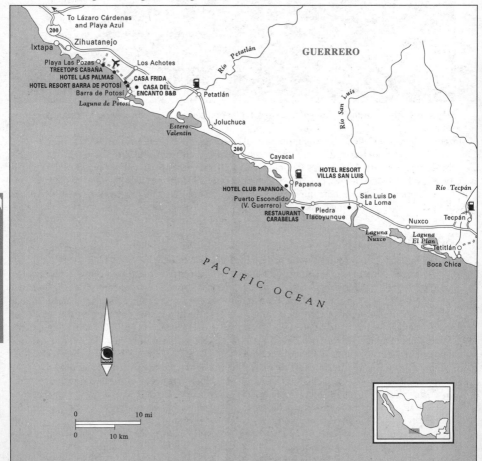

(Alternatively, get to Barra de Potosí by continuing east about three miles along the beach road, from Hotel Las Palmas—see the Playa Las Pozas and Playa Blanca section.)

PAPANOA

The small town of Papanoa (pop. 3,000) straddles the highway 47 miles (75 km) south of Zihuatanejo and 103 miles (165 km) north of Acapulco. Local folks tell the tongue-in-cheek story of its Hawaiian-sounding name. It seems that there was a flood, and the son of the local

headman had to talk fast to save his life by escaping in a *canoa*. Instead of saying "Papa . . . canoa," the swift-talking boy shortened his plea to "Papa . . . noa."

The town itself has a few snack restaurants, a pharmacy, a doctor, groceries, a *gasolinera* that stocks unleaded gas, first-class bus stops, a long-distance telephone, and one resort-style lodging, the **Hotel Club Papanoa,** Papanoa, Guerrero 40907, tel. 742/422-0150.

Near the beach about a mile south of town, the hotel has about 30 large rooms, a restaurant, and a big pool set in spacious ocean-view garden

SOUTH TO ACAPULCO

to Taxco and Mexico City

Corral de Bravo

Chilpancingo

95

SIERRA MADRE DEL SUR

Puerto del Gallo

Cerro Tlacotepec (2,700 m)

Río Atoyac

Río Atoyac

Tierra Colorada

Atoyac de Alvarez

200

San Jerónimo

Cacalutla

Laguna Mitla

El Payapo

200

Coyuca

ACAPULCO BYPASS

Bajos de Ejido

95

Laguna Coyuca

Barra de Coyuca

HOTEL CLUB PUESTA DEL SOL

Pie de la Cuesta

Acapulco

Puerto Marqués

Laguna Tres Palos

200

Barra Vieja

IXTAPA-ZIHUATANEJO

© AVALON TRAVEL PUBLISHING, INC.

grounds. Intended to be luxurious but now a bit worn around the edges, the hotel is nearly empty most nonholiday times. Rooms rent for about $40 s or d low season, $50 high. All with a/c. Ask for a discount.

The hotel grounds adjoin the beach, **Playa Cayaquitos.** The wide, breezy, yellow-gray strand stretches for two miles, washed by powerful open-ocean rollers with good left and right surfing breaks. Additional attractions include surf fishing beyond the breakers and driftwood along the sand. Beach access is via the off-highway driveway just north of the hotel. At the beach, a parking lot borders a seafood restaurant. Farther on, the road narrows (but is still motor-home accessible) through a defunct beachside home development, past several brush-bordered informal RV parking or tent camping spots.

PIEDRA TLACOYUNQUE

At Km 150 (56 miles, 90 km from Zihuatanejo or 94 miles, 151 km from Acapulco) a signed Restaurant Las Carabelas side road heads seaward to Piedra Tlacoyunque and the **Carabelas Restaurant.** About a mile down the paved road, the restaurant appears, perching on a bluff overlooking a monumental sandstone rock, Piedra Tlacoyunque. Below, a wave-tossed strand, ripe for beachcombing and surf fishing, stretches for miles. Powerful breakers with fine right-hand surfing angles roll in and swish up the steep beach. For fishing, buy some bait from the net fishermen on the beach and try some casts beyond the billows crashing into the south side of the Piedra. Later, stroll through the garden of eroded rock sea stacks on the north side. There you can poke among the snails and seaweeds in a big sheltered tidepool, under the watchful guard of the squads of pelicans roosting on the surrounding pinnacles.

The *palapa*-house (in need of repair) on the beach is the seasonal headquarters of the government-funded **Campamento Playa Piedra de Tlacoyunque,** whose mission is to rescue, incubate, and hatch as many turtle eggs as possible. Several staff members patrol the beach during the summer-fall hatching (and egg-poaching) season. Although they are dedicated to their task,

their vigil is a lonely one, and they generally welcome visitors and contributions of drinks and food.

At the Carabelas Restaurant on the bluff above, you can take in the whole breezy scene while enjoying the recommended catch of the day. The name Carabelas (Caravels) comes from the owner's admiration of Christopher Columbus. He christened his restaurant's three petite ocean-view gazebos after Columbus's three famous caravels: the *Niña*, the *Pinta*, and the *Santa María*.

For an overnight or a short stay, ask the restaurant owners if it's okay to set up your tent or park your (self-contained) RV in the restaurant lot or by the beach below the restaurant. For shower and dishwashing water, drop your bucket down into their well, at the bottom of the rise, before the restaurant.

HOTEL RESORT VILLAS SAN LUIS

Little was spared to embellish this pretty hacienda-like corner of a big mango, papaya, and coconut grove. It appears as if the owner, tiring of all work and no play, built a park to entertain his friends. Now, his project blooms with lovely swimming and kiddie pools, a big *palapa* restaurant, a smooth *palapa*-covered dance floor, a small zoo, basketball and volleyball courts, and an immaculate hotel.

Ideal for a lunch/swim break or an overnight or a respite from hard Mexico traveling, the 40 immaculate and attractively furnished hotel rooms rent for about $50 s or d, with a/c and hot water included; credit cards are not accepted. Add about 10 percent during holidays. If you'll be arriving on a weekend or holiday, write, phone, or fax for a reservation: Hotel Resort Villas San Luis, Carretera Zihuatanejo-Acapulco, Km 143, Buenavista de Juárez, Guerrero 40906, tel. 742/427-0228, fax 742/427-0235.

It's on the southbound side of the road near Km 142, 61 miles (98 km) southeast of Zihuatanejo, 89 miles (143 km) northwest of Acapulco.

San Luis de la Loma

The pleasant little market town of San Luis de la Loma (pop. 5,000) runs along a hilltop main street that angles off Highway 200 near Km 140. Besides a number of groceries, fruit stalls, and pharmacies, San Luis has a guesthouse—**Hotel Hermanos Ruiz**—a post office, a health center, a *larga distancia,* a dentist, and a doctor, gynecologist José Luis Barrera Garcia, tel. 742/427-0193 or 742/427-0025, on the plaza, three blocks from the highway. First-class buses also stop and pick up passengers at the main street-highway intersection.

BOCA CHICA

For the fun and adventure of it, visit Boca Chica, a beach village accessible by boat only. Here, camping is de rigueur, since even permanent residents are doing it. It makes no sense to pour concrete on a sandbar where palm fronds are free and the next wave may wash everything away anyway.

The jumping-off spot is near Km 98 (88 miles, 142 km south of Zihuatanejo and 61 miles, 98 km north of Acapulco), where a sign marks the dirt road to **Tetitlán** (pop. 2,000). In about three miles, turn left at the T intersection at the town plaza (with long-distance phone, pharmacy, groceries) and continue a couple of miles along a rough—but negotiable when dry—road to the Laguna Tecpán, which, during the dry season, may have narrowed to a river or dried completely. Here, launches will ferry you (or you can walk) the mile across to the village on the sandbar. Bargain the *viaje redondo* (return-trip) price with your boatman before you depart, unless of course you have your own kayak or boat.

On the other side, the waves thunder upon the beach and sand crabs guard their holes, while the village's four separate societies—people, dogs, pigs, and chickens—each go about their distinct business. Shells and driftwood decorate the sand, and surf fishing with bait from the lagoon couldn't be better.

Most visitors come for the eating only: super-fresh seafood charcoal-broiled in one of the dozen *palapas* along the beach. If, however, you plan to camp overnight, bring drinking water, a highly prized Boca Chica commodity.

During the summer rainy season, the Tecpán River, which feeds the lagoon, breaks through the bar. Ocean fish enter the lagoon, and the river current sometimes washes Boca Chica, *palapas* and all, out to sea.

PIE DE LA CUESTA

The translation of the name Pie (pee-YAY) de la Cuesta (Foot of the Hill), aptly describes this downscale resort village. Tucked around the bend from Acapulco, between a wide, open-ocean beach and placid Laguna Coyuca, Pie de la Cuesta appeals to those who want the excitement the big town offers and the tranquility it doesn't.

Laguna Coyuca, kept full by the sweet waters of the Río Coyuca, has long been known for its fish, birdlife, and tranquil, palm-lined shores. During the early 1400s, the Purépecha kings (who ruled from the Michoacán highlands) established a provincial capital near the town of Coyuca. After the Aztecs drove out the Purépecha a century later (and the Aztecs in turn were defeated by the Spanish), Pie de la Cuesta and its beautiful Laguna Coyuca slumbered in the shadow of Acapulco.

Sights

Laguna de Coyuca is a large sandy-bottomed lake, lined by palms and laced by mangrove channels. It stretches 10 miles along the shoreline, west from Pie de la Cuesta, which occupies the southeast (Acapulco) side. The barrier sandbar, wide Playa Pie de la Cuesta, separates the lagoon from the ocean. It extends a dozen miles west to the river outlet, which is open to the sea only during the rainy season. A road runs along the beach west the length of Laguna Coyuca to the tourist hamlet of Barra de Coyuca. There, *palapas* line the beach and serve seafood to busloads of Sunday visitors.

Playa Pie de la Cuesta, a seemingly endless, 100-yard-wide stretch of yellow sand, is fine for surf fishing, beachcombing, jogging, and long sunset walks. However, its powerful open-ocean waves are unsuited for surfing and frequently hazardous for swimming. They often break thunderously near the sand and recede with strong, turbulent undertow.

On the other side of the bar, the tranquil Acapulco (east) end of Laguna Coyuca is an embarkation point for lagoon tours and the center for water-skiing and personal watercraft riding. Among the best equipped of the shoreline clubs that offer powerboat services is the **Restaurant and Club de Skis Tres Marías.** Besides a pleasant lake-view shoreline *palapa* restaurant, it offers water-skiing at about $43/hour and personal watercraft for about $75/hour.

If you want to launch your own boat, you can do so easily at Club Tres Marias and others for about $15. The boat traffic, which confines itself mostly to midlagoon, does not deter swimming in the lagoon's clear waters. Slip on your bathing suit and jump in anywhere along the sandy shoreline.

Lagoon tours begin from several landings dotting the Pie de la Cuesta end of the lagoon. Half-day regular excursions (maximum 10 people, about $10 per person) push off daily around 11 A.M., noon, and 1:30 P.M. Along the way, they pass islands with trees loaded with nesting cormorants, herons, and pelicans. In midlake, gulls dip and sway in the breeze behind your boat while a host of storks, ducks, avocets, and a dozen other varieties paddle, preen, and forage in the water nearby. Other times, your boat passes through winding channels hung with vines and lined with curtains of great mangrove roots. At midpoint, tours usually stop for a bite to eat at Isla Montosa. (Ask ahead of time, because you shouldn't miss it.) Here, roosters crow, pigs root, bougainvillea blooms, and a colony of fishing families live, unencumbered by 20th-century conveniences, beneath their majestic shoreline palm grove.

On another day, drive your car or ride one of the frequent buses that head from Pie de la Cuesta to **Barra de Coyuca** village at the west end of the lagoon. Along the way, you will pass several scruffy hamlets and a parade of fenced lots, some still open meadows where horses graze while others are filled with trees and big houses. Lack of potable water, local residents complain, is a continuing problem on this dry sandbar.

At road's end, 10 miles from Pie de la Cuesta, a few tourist stores, a platoon of T-shirt vendors, and hammock-equipped beach *palapa* restaurants serve holiday crowds. Boats head for tours from lagoonside, where patrons at the **Restaurant Dos Vistas** enjoy a double view of both beach and lagoon.

Hotels and Guesthouses

Approximately 20 basic bungalows, *casas de huéspedes* (guesthouses), and hotels line the Pie de la

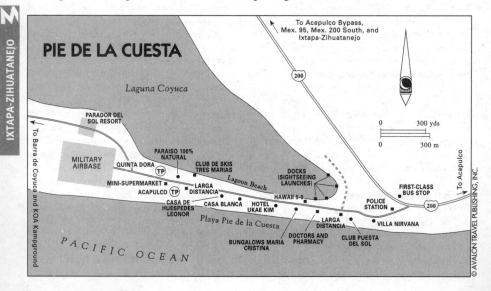

Cuesta's single beachside road. Competition keeps cleanliness high, management sharp, and prices low. They all cluster along a one-mile roadfront, enjoying highly visible locations right on the beach. Telephone, fax, or email for reservations, especially for the winter season and holidays. Many, but not all of them, have tepid, room-temperature bath water only and do not accept credit cards; exceptions are noted below.

Note: Some unscrupulous Acapulco taxi drivers are trying to squeeze commissions from Pie de la Cuesta lodgings in return for bringing customers to their doorsteps. Typical tactics include outright refusing to take customers to places that don't pay commissions, or telling customers that the hotel they request *"no sirve"* ("is not running"). You can combat this on the spot by making sure, before you get into the taxi, that the driver agrees to take you to the hotel of your choice, and, once in Pie de la Cuesta, making sure that he follows through or don't pay. Daytime taxi fares from Acapulco shouldn't run more than about $5 from old town, $7 from the Costera; nighttime tariffs should be no more than double those amounts. Plenty of daytime buses run there for less than half a dollar. All lodgings recommended below are marked on the Pie de la Cuesta map.

In approximate order of increasing price, first comes **Casa de Huéspedes Playa Leonor,** which is very popular with a loyal cadre of Canadian winter returnees, 63 Carretera Pie de la Cuesta, Guerrero 39900, tel. 744/460-0348. They enjoy camaraderie around the tables of the *palapa* restaurant that occupies the beachside end of a large parking-lot garden. The several breezy, more private, upper-floor, plain but clean units are most popular. All 10 rooms have two beds, showers, and fans, and rent for about $25 d low season, $32 high, with approximately 20 percent discount for monthly rentals.

More picturesque are the **Bungalows María Cristina,** P.O. Box 607, Acapulco, Guerrero 39300, tel. 744/460-0262, with eight units (four rooms, four kitchen-equipped bungalows) set between a streetside parking lot and a palmy beachside restaurant/garden. The clean, fixed-up and painted rooms with toilets and hot-water showers

rent for about $30 d low season, $35 high. The kitchenettes, most of which face the ocean, run about $60 low season, $70 high, for up to four people. Negotiate for long-term discounts.

Guests at the nearby **Hotel and Restaurant Casa Blanca,** Av. Fuerza Aerea 370, Pie de la Cuesta, Guerrero 39900, tel. 744/460-0324 or 744/460-4028, casablanca@prodigy.net.mx, enjoy a tranquil, car-free tropical garden, small blue beachfront pool and restaurant and new French management. Rents for approximately 15 very clean and comfortable rooms, all with toilets and hot-water showers and a/c run around $30 for one to four people, all year round. Discounts may be available for monthly or low season (May–Oct.) rentals. Credit cards are accepted.

Cooperating on-site owner-managers account for the relaxed atmosphere of the combined yet distinct **Villa Nirvana** and **Villa Roxana,** at 302 Playa Pie de la Cuesta, P.O. Box 950, Acapulco, Guerrero 39300. Additional pluses include two pools, respectively, at the inner and beach ends of lovely high-fenced garden and *palapa* restaurant compound. Cars park in an adjacent lot. Rooms in both complexes occupy two-story tiers bordering the garden, upper floors being more private. The Villa Nirvana, tel. 744/460-1631, nirvana@acabtu.com, is operated by Daniel Reams and Pamela Fox, with help from the former owner's son Tomás. It occupies the beachfront half of the property. Their 14 clean, comfortable rooms rent from about $20 s or d low season, $35 high. Discounts for monthly rentals run about 15 percent. The original owner, Roxana, with her daughter Alexis, manage the Villa Roxana, tel. 744/460-3252. Their 14 similarly clean and comfortable rooms rent for about $20 d, low season, $25 high, except for four rooms with kitchenettes, which go for about $25 d low, $35 high. Guests get to choose which they prefer between the two equally attractive options. Facilities of both hotels are shared by all guests.

The most spacious and among the prettiest of Pie de la Cuesta beach accommodations is the **Hotel Club Puesta del Sol,** Manzana 57, Pie de La Cuesta, Guerrero 39900, tel. 744/460-0412, where guests enjoy an airy beach dining area, a gorgeous blue pool, and a rough (but playable)

Guests at the Pie de la Cuesta KOA RV park and campground enjoy lavish beachfront facilities, including an attractive palmy pool area.

tennis court within roomy, sculpture-decorated garden grounds. Tasty food from the kitchen of the amiable comanagers Alba Garcia and Nestor Cisneros and hours spent socializing, relaxing, and reading around the restaurant tables account for the hotel's loyal North American, European, and Mexican clientele. The 24 spartan but clean rooms are spread among two double-story buildings, one at beachfront. Doubles by the beach go for about $25 low season and $30 high; away from the beach, the same run $20 and $25. Kitchen-equipped beachside apartments for six rent for about $40 low season, $60 high. All accommodations come with fans and include parking.

Trying hard to be luxurious is the **Hotel Ukae Kim,** Av. de Fuerza Aerea 356, Pie de la Cuesta 39900, tel./fax 744/460-2187. Unfortunately, the builder crammed the 21 rooms into a small, albeit palmy space, rendering them private but generally dark. Amenities include a small, inviting pool and patio and *palapa* restaurant at the hotel's beachfront end. The clean, tastefully decorated rooms with hot water and a/c go, low sea-

son, for about $40 s or d, $60 for ocean view, $100 with ocean view and hot tub. Corresponding high season rates are about $60, $80 and $120. Credit cards are accepted.

Finally, you might consider **Paraíso 100% Natural,** a project of the Acapulco family that runs several "100% Natural" restaurants. It offers eight clean, comfortable rooms with bath, on the luscious lagoon-front, across the road from the Acapulco Trailer Park. Rates run about $40 d, with fans, good restaurant, and an inviting lake-view pool and patio. Reserve at Pie de la Cuesta 410, Guerrero, tel. 744/460-2577.

Trailer Parks and Camping

RV-equipped Pie de la Cuesta vacationers have three recommendable trailer park choices. First to consider is the homey and popular **Acapulco Trailer Park,** with about 60 palm-shaded beachfront and choice lagoonside spaces, with all hookups, P.O. Box 1, Acapulco, Guerrero 39300, tel. 744/460-0010, fax 744/460-2457, acatrailerpark@hotmail.com. A congenial atmosphere, good management, and many extras, including a secure fence and gate, keep the place full most of the winter. Facilities include a boat ramp, blue pool, a store, a security guard, and clean restrooms and showers. The spaces rent for about $15 or $300 per month; tent spaces, $10. Get your winter reservation in early.

The security guard at the Acapulco Trailer Park is a reminder of former times, when muggings and theft were occurring with some frequency on Playa Pie de la Cuesta. Although bright new night lights on the beach (which marines patrol while local police patrol the streets) have greatly reduced the problem, some (but not all) local folks still warn against camping or walking on the beach at night.

Next in line is homey **Quinta Dora Trailer Park,** tel. 744/460-1138 or 744/460-0600, across the road from the Acapulco Trailer Park. Its pluses are an azure, palm-shaded lagoonfront location and boat ramp. Spaces rent for about $9 with electricity and water only, no sewer connection.

KOA Kampgrounds has come to Pie de la Questa, in the form of a large park, about a mile out of the Pie de la Cuesta village, along the west-bound Barra de Coyuca road. Undoubtedly the best-equipped on the beach, the KOA Kampground, tel./fax 744/444-4062, tel. 744/483-7830, 744/483-2281, or 744/444-4277, koaaca@acabtu.com.mx, offers some shade in a big lot, with most spaces not right on the beach. Nevertheless, everyone is a stone's throw from the long, silky Pie de la Cuesta beach, fine for shells, beachcombing, and surf fishing. Facilities include a snack restaurant, ministore, security fence, laundry, playground, pool, and kiddie pool. Big motor home spaces with all hookups run $30 by the beach, $22 in the shade away from beach, tent spaces go for $16; all get a 20 percent discount for monthly rentals. Tents rent for $15. For more information, visit the website www.koa.com.

Food

A number of restaurants have appeared in Pie de la Cuesta during recent years. Nearly all, however, are nondescript beachfront *palapas*. Of the few restaurants along the Pie de la Cuesta road,

the class-act is the lakeview *palapa* of the **Restaurant and Club de Skis Tres Marías.** Also, try the open-air dining room of the **Hotel Casablanca,** the beachfront *palapa* of the **Villa Nirvana,** and the poolside beachfront **Hotel Ukae Kim** for good prospects for a relaxing light meal.

Entertainment and Events

Pie de la Cuesta's big fiesta honors the local patron, the **Virgin of Guadalupe,** with Masses, processions, fireworks, and dances on Dec. 10, 11, and 12. The fiesta's climax, de rigueur for visitors, is the mass pilgrimage around the lake by boat.

At least one local discotheque, **Hawaii 5-O,** fires up seasonally and occasionally on weekends. Brightly painted signs on the roadside at midvillage make it impossible to miss.

The deluxe **Parador del Sol** all-inclusive resort (about a mile west of Pie de la Cuesta village—turn right at the Barra de Coyuca fork) invites visitors to buy day and/or evening guest memberships for about $35 per adult (children ages 4–11, half price) per eight-hour day session (10 A.M.–6 P.M.) and evening session (7 P.M.–2 A.M.). Day guests enjoy breakfast (10–11 A.M.), lunch (1–2 P.M.), open bar, and free use of the pools, beach club, kiddie playground, exercise gym, and basketball, volleyball, minigolf course, and tennis courts. The evening program kicks off at 7, with sports (including night-lit tennis) and swimming, continuing with supper (8:30–9:30 P.M.), open bar, and dancing at the discotheque until after midnight. If after a day you haven't had your fill, you might want to accept the invitation to stay overnight for about $80 per person, double occupancy, low season, $100 high. For details, inquire at the front desk, or at tel./fax 744/444-4050 or 744/444-4125, or check the website www.acabtu.com.mx/parador.

Services

Although most services are concentrated half an hour away in Acapulco, Pie de la Cuesta nevertheless provides a few essentials. For **medical consultations,** see either Doctora Patricia Villalobos or her husband, Doctor Luis Amados Rios, tel. 744/460-0923, at their pharmacy where the lagoon begins, right in the middle of the village.

Between them, they understand both English and French.

A scattering of minimarkets supply food. Two public **long-distance phones** are available, one in front of the Acapulco Trailer Park and the other on the highway by the doctors' pharmacy. In emergencies, go to the *policía,* at the small station near the intersection of the Pie de la Cuesta road and the highway to Acapulco.

Getting There and Away

Pie de la Cuesta is accessible via the fork from Highway 200 near Km 10, 144 miles (232 km) southwest of Zihuatanejo. First-class buses drop passengers at the roadside, where they can either walk, taxi, or ride one of the very frequent Acapulco microbuses half a mile to the hotels.

From the same intersection, the Acapulco old town plaza is six miles (10 km) by car, taxi ($5), or local bus.

Acapulco and Inland to Taxco

Acapulco

All over Mexico and half the world, Acapulco (pop. 1.5 million) means merrymaking, good food, and palm-shaded beaches. Despite half a century of continuous development, its reputation is as deserved as ever. The many Acapulcos—the turquoise bay edged by golden sands and emerald hills, the host of hotels, humble and grand, the spontaneous entertainments, the colorful market, the shady old town square—continue to draw millions of yearly visitors from all over the world.

HISTORY

Before Columbus

Despite its modern facade, Acapulco has been well known as a traveler's crossroads for at least a millennium. Its name comes from the Náhuatl (Aztec) words that mean "Place of Dense Reeds."

The earliest discovered local remains, stone metates and pottery utensils, were left behind by seaside residents around 2500 B.C. Much later, sophisticated artisans fashioned curvaceous female figurines, which archaeologists unearthed at Las Sabanas near Acapulco during the mid-20th century. Those unique finds added fuel to speculation

Rocky outcroppings add interest to Acapulco's already lovely beaches.

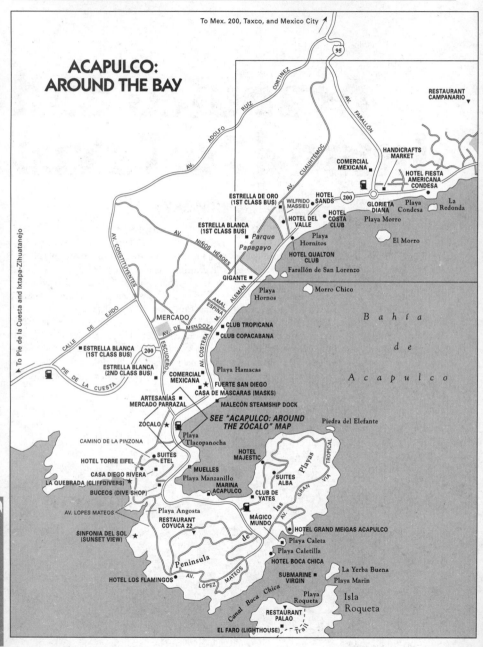

ACAPULCO: AROUND THE BAY

To Mex. 200, Taxco, and Mexico City

95

AV. CORTINEZ
AV. RUIZ
AV. ADOLFO
AV. CUAUHTEMOC
AV. FARALLÓN

RESTAURANT CAMPANARIO

HANDICRAFTS MARKET

COMERCIAL MEXICANA

HOTEL FIESTA AMERICANA CONDESA

ESTRELLA DE ORO (1ST CLASS BUS)
WILFRIDO MASSIEU
HOTEL SANDS
200
GLORIETA DIANA
Playa Condesa
La Redonda

HOTEL DEL VALLE
HOTEL COSTA CLUB
Playa Morro

ESTRELLA BLANCA (1ST CLASS BUS)
Parque Papagayo
AV. NIÑOS HEROES

Playa Hornitos

El Morro

HOTEL QUALTON CLUB
Farallón de San Lorenzo

GIGANTE

AV. ESPINA
M. ALEMÁN
AMAL

Playa Hornos

Morro Chico

AV. CONSTITUYENTES
CALLE DE EJIDO
MERCADO
AV. DE MENDOZA
AV. ESCUDERO
AV. COSTERA M. ALEMÁN

To Pie de la Cuesta and Ixtapa-Zihuatanejo

ESTRELLA BLANCA (1ST CLASS BUS)
200
ESTRELLA BLANCA (2ND CLASS BUS)
PIE DE LA CUESTA

CLUB TROPICANA
CLUB COPACABANA

Playa Hamacas

Bahía
de
Acapulco

COMERCIAL MEXICANA
FUERTE SAN DIEGO
CASA DE MASCARAS (MASKS)

ARTESANÍAS MERCADO PARRAZAL

MALECÓN STEAMSHIP DOCK

ZÓCALO ★

SEE "ACAPULCO: AROUND THE ZÓCALO" MAP

Piedra del Elefante

CAMINO DE LA PINZONA
Playa Tlacopanocha

HOTEL MAJESTIC

HOTEL TORRE EIFEL
SUITES ETEL

CASA DIEGO RIVERA
MUELLES
Playa Manzanillo
SUITES ALBA

LA QUEBRADA (CLIFFDIVERS) ★
MARINA ACAPULCO
BUCEOS (DIVE SHOP)
CLUB DE YATES

Playas
de las
GRAN VIA TROPICAL

AV. LOPES MATEOS
Playa Angosta
RESTAURANT COYUCA 22
MÁGICO MUNDO

SINFONIA DEL SOL (SUNSET VIEW) ★
HOTEL GRAND MEIGAS ACAPULCO

Playa Caleta
Playa Caletilla

Peninsula
HOTEL BOCA CHICA

HOTEL LOS FLAMINGOS
AV. LÓPEZ MATEOS
SUBMARINE VIRGIN
La Yerba Buena
Playa Marin

Canal Boca Chica
Playa Roqueta
Isla Roqueta

RESTAURANT PALAO
EL FARO (LIGHTHOUSE)
Trail

ACAPULCO/TAXCO

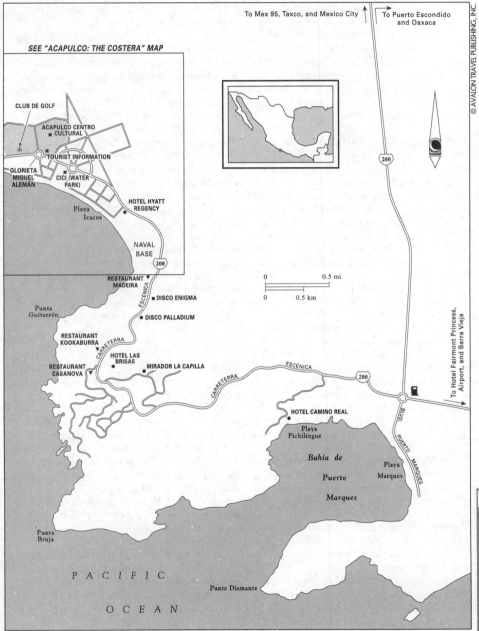

SEE "ACAPULCO: THE COSTERA" MAP

To Mex 95, Taxco, and Mexico City

To Puerto Escondido and Oaxaca

© AVALON TRAVEL PUBLISHING, INC.

CLUB DE GOLF

ACAPULCO CENTRO CULTURAL

TOURIST INFORMATION

GLORIETA MIGUEL ALEMÁN

CICI (WATER PARK)

Playa Icacos

HOTEL HYATT REGENCY

NAVAL BASE

200

RESTAURANT MADEIRA

ESCÉNICA

DISCO ENIGMA

DISCO PALLADIUM

Punta Guitarrón

RESTAURANT KOOKABURRA

CARRETERRA

RESTAURANT CASANOVA

HOTEL LAS BRISAS

MIRADOR LA CAPILLA

CARRETERRA

ESCÉNICA

200

To Hotel Fairmont Princess, Airport, and Barra Vieja

0   0.5 mi

0   0.5 km

HOTEL CAMINO REAL

Playa Pichilingue

Bahía de

Puerto

Marques

Playa Marques

BLVD. PUERTO MARQUES

Punta Bruja

PACIFIC

OCEAN

Punta Diamante

of early Polynesian or Asian influences in Pacific Mexico as early as 1,500 years before Columbus.

Other discoveries, however, resemble artifacts found in highland Mexico. Although undoubtedly influenced by Tarascan, Mixtec, Zapotec, and Aztec civilizations and frequented by their traders, Acapulco never came under their direct control but instead remained subject to local chieftains until the conquest.

Conquest and Colonization

The Aztecs had scarcely surrendered when Cortés sent expeditions south to build ships and find a route to China. The first such explorers sailed out from Zacatula, near present-day Lázaro Cárdenas on the coast 250 miles northwest of Acapulco. They returned, telling Cortés of Acapulco Bay. By a royal decree dated April 25, 1528, "Acapulco and her land . . . where the ships of the south will be built . . ." passed directly into the hands of the Spanish Crown.

Voyages of discovery set sail from Acapulco for Peru, the Gulf of California, and to Asia. None returned from the across the Pacific, however, until Father Andrés de Urdaneta discovered the northern Pacific tradewinds, which propelled him and his ship, loaded with Chinese treasure, to Acapulco in 1565.

From then on, for more than 200 years, a special yearly trading ship, renowned as the Nao de China and in England as the Manila galleon, set sail from Acapulco for the Orient. Its return sparked an annual merchant fair, swelling Acapulco's population with traders jostling to bargain for the Manila galleon's shiny trove of silks, porcelain, ivory, and lacquerware.

Acapulco's yearly treasure soon attracted marauders, too. In 1579, Francis Drake threatened, and in 1587, off Cabo San Lucas, Thomas Cavendish was the first to capture the Manila galleon, the *Santa Ana.* The cash booty alone, 1.2 million gold pesos, severely depressed the London gold market.

After a Dutch fleet invaded Acapulco in 1615, the Spanish rebuilt their fort, which they christened Fort San Diego in 1617. Destroyed by an earthquake in 1776, the fort was rebuilt by 1783. But Mexico's War of Independence (1810-21)

stopped the Manila galleon forever, sending Acapulco into a century-long slumber.

Modern Acapulco

In 1927, the government paved the Mexico City-Acapulco road; the first cars arrived on November 11. The first luxury hotel, the Mirador, at La Quebrada, went up in 1933; soon airplanes began arriving. During the 1940s President Miguel Alemán (1946–1952) fell in love with Acapulco and thought everyone else should have the same opportunity. He built new boulevards, power plants, and a superhighway. Investors responded with a lineup of high-rise hostelries. Finally, in 1959, Presidents Dwight Eisenhower and Adolfo López Mateos convened their summit conference in a grand Acapulco hotel.

Thousands of Mexicans flocked to fill jobs in the shiny hotels and restaurants. They built shantytowns, which climbed the hills and spilled over into previously sleepy communities nearby. The government responded with streets, drainage, power, housing, and schools. By 2000, more than 1.5 million people were calling Acapulco home.

SIGHTS
Getting Oriented

In one tremendous sweep, Acapulco curves around its dazzling half-moon bay. Face the open ocean and you are looking due south. West will be on your right hand, east on your left. One continuous beachfront boulevard, appropriately named the **Costera Miguel Alemán** (the "Costera," for short), unites old Acapulco, west of the Parque Papagayo amusement zone, with new Acapulco, the lineup of big beach hotels that stretches around the bay to the Las Brisas condo headland. There, during the night, a big cross glows and marks the hilltop lookout, Mirador La Capilla, above the bay's east end.

On the opposite, old-town side of Parque Papagayo, the Costera curves along the palmy, uncluttered *playas* Hornos and Hamacas to the steamship dock. Here the Costera, called the *malecón* as it passes the *zócalo* (town plaza), continues to the mansion-dotted hilly jumble of Peninsula de las Playas.

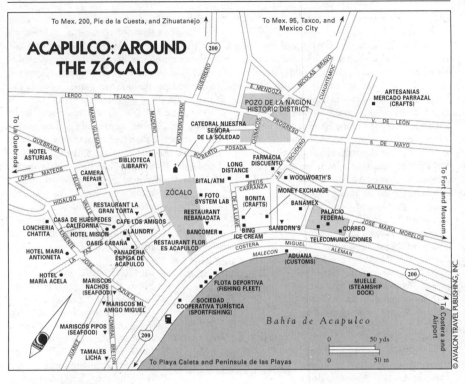

ACAPULCO: AROUND THE ZÓCALO

To Mex. 200, Pie de la Cuesta, and Zihuatanejo

To Mex. 95, Taxco, and Mexico City

To La Quebrada

To Fort and Museum

To Costera and Airport

© AVALON TRAVEL PUBLISHING, INC.

GUERRERO

LERDO DE TEJADA

MARIA IGLESIAS

MADERO

INDEPENDENCIA

E. MENDOZA

NICOLAS BRAVO

CUAUHTEMOC

ARTESANIAS MERCADO PARRAZAL (CRAFTS)

POZO DE LA NACIÓN HISTORIC DISTRICT

CATEDRAL NUESTRA SEÑORA DE LA SOLEDAD

CHINACOS

PROGRESO

V. DE LEÓN

QUEBRADA

HOTEL ASTURIAS

FELIPE VALLE

CAMERA REPAIR

BIBLIOTECA (LIBRARY)

ROBERTO POSADA

ESCUDERO

J.R.

S DE MAYO

FARMACIA DISCUENTO

LONG DISTANCE

BITAL/ATM

WOOLWORTH'S

MONEY EXCHANGE

GALEANA

HIDALGO

ZÓCALO

FOTO SYSTEM LAB

JESÚS CARRANZA

BONITA (CRAFTS)

BANAMEX

PALACIO FEDERAL

RESTAURANT LA GRAN TORTA

CASA DE HUÉSPEDES CALIFORNIA

CAFE LOS AMIGOS

RESTAURANT REBANADATA

DE LA LLAVE

JOSE MARIA MORELOS

LONCHERIA CHATITA

HOTEL MISIÓN

LAUNDRY

BANCOMER

SANBORN'S

CORREO

TELECOMUNICACIONES

OASIS CABAÑA

RESTAURANT FLOR ES ACAPULCO

BING ICE CREAM

MIGUEL

ALEMAN

HOTEL MARIA ANTIONETA

PANADERIA ESPIGA DE ACAPULCO

LA PAZ

JOSE AZUETA

COSTERA

MALECON

ADUANA (CUSTOMS)

HOTEL MARÍA ACELA

MARISCOS NACHOS (SEAFOOD)

FLOTA DEPORTIVA (FISHING FLEET)

MUELLE (STEAMSHIP DOCK)

MARISCOS MI AMIGO MIGUEL

SOCIEDAD COOPERATIVA TURÍSTICA (SPORTFISHING)

Bahía de Acapulco

MARISCOS PIPOS (SEAFOOD)

JUAREZ

ADMIRAL BRETON

TAMALES LICHA

To Playa Caleta and Peninsula de las Playas

LOPEZ MATEOS

TENIENTE

0   50 yds
0   50 m

Getting Around

Buses run nearly continuously along the Costera. Fare averages the equivalent of about $.30. Bus routes—indicated by such labels as Base (BAH-say, the naval base on the east end), Centro (*zócalo*), Caleta (the beach, at the far west end), Cine (movie theater near the beach before the *zócalo*), and Hornos (the beach near Parque Papagayo)—run along the Costera.

Taxis, on the other hand, cost between $1.50 and $5 for any in-town destination. They are not metered, so agree upon the price *before* you get in. If the driver demands too much, hailing another taxi often solves the problem.

A Walk Around Old Acapulco

In old Acapulco, traffic slows and people return to traditional ways. Couples promenade along the *malecón* dockfront, fishing boats leave and return, while in the adjacent *zócalo*, families stroll

past the church, musicians play, and tourists and businessmen sip coffee in the shade of huge banyan trees.

Start your walk beneath those *zócalo* trees. Under their pendulous air roots, browse the bookstalls, relax in one of the cafés; at night, watch the clowns perform, listen to a band concert, or join in a pitch-penny game. Take a look inside the mod-style **cathedral** dedicated to Our Lady of Solitude. Admire its angel-filled sky-blue ceiling and visit the Virgin to the right of the altar.

Outside, cross the boulevard to the *malecón* dockside; in midafternoon, you may see huge marlin and swordfish being hauled up from the boats.

Head out of the *zócalo* and left along the Costera past the steamship dock a few blocks to the 18th-century fort, **Fuerte San Diego,** atop its bayside hill; open Tues.–Sun. 10:30 A.M.–4:30 P.M. Engineer Miguel Costansó completed the massive, five-pointed maze of moats, walls, and battlements in 1783.

Inside, galleries within the original fort storerooms, barracks, chapel, and kitchen illustrate local pre-Columbian, conquest, and colonial history. The excellent, unusually graphic displays include much about pirates (such as Francis Drake and John Hawkins, known as "admirals" to the English-speaking world); Spanish galleons, their history and construction; and famous visitors, notably Japanese Captain Hasekura, who in 1613 built a ship and sailed from Sendai, Japan, to Acapulco; thence he continued overland to Mexico City, by sea to Spain, to the Pope in Rome, and back again through Acapulco to Japan.

Fuerte San Diego puts on a regular sound and light show that dramatizes Acapulco's history. Showtimes are at 8 P.M. Sat. low season, Thurs.–Sat. high. Confirm at the museum, tel. 744/482-3828, or at the tourist information office, tel. 744/484-4416 or 744/484-4583.

Just outside the old fort's exit, on the opposite side of the street, Calle José María Morelos, don't miss visiting the **Casa de Máscaras** (House of Masks). Inside the door, enjoy a fascinating museum of indigenous masks, from squinting pink El Viejitos and grinning red devils, to scary crocodiles and angelic cherubs, all hand-crafted for the myriad age-old traditional *fiestas* celebrated in towns and villages all over Mexico.

If you'd like to learn still more of Acapulco history, visit the **Naval Historical Museum of Acapulco,** in the Plaza Bahía shopping center, local 33, on the Costera in front of, west of the towering Hotel Costa Club. Exhibits detail famous voyages, display historic nautical maps and charts, ship models, and memorabilia of the Manila galleons. For more information, call tel. 744/463-2984.

Palma Sola Archaeological Site
On a high hillside, above Acapulco's west-side neighborhood, a trove of recently excavated pet-

roglyphs have been excavated for public viewing. The site, at an elevation of about 1,200 feet, adjacent to ridgetop El Veladero ecological park, displays a number of big (3–20 feet) geometric-, animal- and human-form petroglyphs. Created by an ancient people, known generically as "Los Yopes," the stone carvings date from between 200 B.C. and A.D. 600. Get there most easily by taxi, up Av. Palma Sola to road's end before the hilltop, where a path leads you the last few hundred yards. Take a hat, water, and walking shoes. Local guides will, most likely be available on-site. You may also want to arrange a tour through a travel agent, such as American Express, tel. 744/469-1121 through 744/469-1124. For more information, contact the tourist information office, tel. 744/484-4416.

La Quebrada
From the Fuerte San Diego, head back to the *zócalo* and continue past the cathedral. After three short blocks to Av. López Mateos, continue uphill to the La Quebrada diver's point, marked by the big parking lot at the hillcrest. There, Acapulco's energy focuses five times a day (at 1 P.M. and evenings hourly 7:30–10:30 P.M.) as tense crowds watch the divers plummet more than 100 feet to the waves below. Admission is about $2, collected by the divers' cooperative. Performers average less than $100 per dive from the proceeds. The adjacent Hotel Plaza Las Glorias (the former Hotel Mirador) charges about $5 cover to view the dives from its terrace.

Old Town Beaches
These start not far from the *zócalo*. At the foot of the Fuerte San Diego, the sand of **Playa Hamacas** begins, changing to **Playa Hornos** (Ovens) and curving northeast a mile to a rocky shoal-line called Farallón de San Lorenzo. Hornos is the Sunday favorite of Mexican families, where boats buzz beyond the very tranquil waves and retirees stroll the wide, yellow sand while vendors work the sunbathing crowd.

> *At La Quebrada, Acapulco's energy focuses five times a day (at 1 P.M. and evenings hourly 7:30–10:30 P.M.) as tense crowds watch the divers plummet more than 100 feet to the waves below.*

Moving south past the *zócalo* and the fishing boats, you'll find **Playa Tlacopanocha,** a petite strip of sand beneath some spreading trees. Here, bay-tour launches wait for passengers, and kids play in the glassy water, which would be great for swimming if it weren't for the refuse from nearby fishing boats.

From there, cross the Costera and hop on a bus marked Caleta to gemlike **Playa Caleta** and its twin **Playa Caletilla** on the far side of the hilly peninsula (named, appropriately, Peninsula de las Playas). With medium-coarse yellow sand and blue ripples for waves, Caleta and Caletilla are for people who want company. They are often crowded, sometimes nearly solid on Sundays. Boats offer banana-tube rides, and snorkel gear is rentable from beach concessionaires. Dozens of stalls and restaurants serve food and refreshments. Prominent among them is the stall of Arturo "Chocolate" Castro and his oyster divers, who serve their own catch-of-the-day mussels, oysters, and octopus right on the west end of the beach.

Mágico Mundo water park, tel. 744/483-1215—with an aquarium, museum, restaurant, water slides, cascades, and more—perches on the little peninsula between the beaches. Open daily 9 A.M.–5 P.M.; admission $3 adult, $2 child.

Isla Roqueta

A Roqueta Island ticket tout will often try to snare you as you get off the Caleta bus. The round-trip, which runs around $3, is usually in a boat with a glass bottom, through which you can peer at the fish as they peer back from their aqua underwater world. On the other side, you can relax on sunny little Playa Roqueta, have lunch at one of several beachside *palapas,* and swim, snorkel, and sun on some of the island's intimate beaches or take a hike through the shady mixed acacia-deciduous hillside forest above Playa Roqueta. Past the hillcrest, on the island's east side, a trail leads steeply downhill to tiny, secluded **Playa Marin,** where you can loll to your heart's content in the waves that funnel into the narrow channel. (Be prepared to avoid sunburn, however.)

A **boat tour** from Playa Tlacopanocha is an-

other way to get to Isla Roqueta. The glass-bottomed boats *Maryvioli, Santa María,* and *Tequila* leave several times daily for 90-minute tours (about $5 per person). Trips include viewing underwater life, shoreline vistas, the *Virgen Submarina* (a statue submerged in the Isla Roqueta channel), a stop on the island, and snorkeling. Beer and soft drinks are sold onboard.

Playa Angosta

Back on the mainland, you can visit another hidden beach nearby, Playa Angosta (Narrow Beach), the only Acapulco strand with an unobstructed sunset horizon. A breezy dab of a beach, sandwiched between a pair of sandstone cliffs, Angosta's ocean waves roll in, swishing upon the sand. A food *palapa* occupies one side of the beach and a few fishing launches and nets are on the other. With caution, swimming, bodysurfing, and boogie boarding are sometimes possible here; otherwise, Angosta is best for scenery and picnics.

Just uphill, a few hundred yards along the southbound cliffside boulevard, is **Sinfonía del Sol** sunset amphitheater. Here, local folks begin gathering around 5 P.M. daily during the winter (6:30 P.M. in the summer) to watch the sun go down.

Costera Beaches

These are the hotel-lined golden shores where affluent Mexicans and foreign visitors stay and play in the sun. They are variations on one continuous curve of sand. Beginning at the west end with **Playa Hornitos** (also known as Playa Papagayo), they continue, changing names from **Playa Morro** to **Playa Condesa** and finally, **Playa Icacos,** which curves and stretches to its sheltered east end past the naval base. All of the same semicoarse golden silica sand, the beaches begin with fairly broad 200-foot-wide Playas Papagayo and Morro. They narrow sharply to under 100 feet at Playa Condesa, then broaden again to more than 200 feet along Playa Icacos.

Their surf is mostly gentle, breaking in one- or two-foot waves and receding with little undertow. This makes for safe swimming within float-enclosed beachside areas, but it's too tranquil for bodysurfing, boogie boarding, or surfing. Beyond the swimming floats, motorboats hurry along, pulling parasailers and banana-tube riders, while personal watercraft cavort and careen over the swells.

Such motorized hubbub lessens the safety and enjoyment of quieter sports off most new town beaches. Sailboaters and sailboarders with their own equipment might try the remote, more tranquil east end of Playa Icacos, however.

Water-skiing, officially restricted to certain parts of Acapulco Bay, has largely moved to Coyuca Lagoon northwest of the city. Coyuca Lagoon also has enough space for many good motorboat-free spots for sailboaters and sailboarders (see Pie de la Cuesta in the Ixtapa-Zihuatanejo and South to Acapulco chapter).

Rocky outcroppings along Playas Papagayo, Morro, and Condesa add interest and intimacy to an already beautiful shoreline. The rocks are good for tidepooling and fishing by pole-casting (or by net, as locals do) above the waves.

Beaches Southeast of Town

Ride a Puerto Marquez- or Lomas-marked bus or drive along the Costera eastward. Past the naval base entrance on the right, the road climbs the hill, passing a number of panoramic bay viewpoints. After the Las Brisas condo-hotel complex, the road curves around the hill shoulder and heads downward past picture-perfect vistas of **Bahía de Puerto Marquez.** At the bottom-of-the-hill intersection and overpass, a road branches right to Puerto Marquez.

The little bayside town is mainly a Sunday seafood and picnicking retreat for Acapulco families. Dozens of *palapa* restaurants line its motorboat-dotted sandy beach. One ramshackle hotel, at the far south end of the single main beachfront street, offers lodgings.

If you're driving, mark your odometer at the hill-bottom intersection and head east toward the airport. If traveling by bus, continue via one of the Lomas buses, which continue east from Acapulco about once an hour. About a mile farther, a turn-off road goes right to the Fairmont Acapulco Princess and the Pierre Marquez hotels and golf course on Playa Revolcadero.

Beach access is by side roads or by walking directly through the hotel lobbies. If you come by bus, hail a taxi from the highway to the Hotel Princess door for the sake of a good entrance.

Playa Revolcadero, a broad, miles-long, yellow-white strand, has the rolling open-ocean billows that Acapulco Bay doesn't. The sometimes-rough waves are generally good for boogie boarding, bodysurfing, and even surfing near the rocks on the northwest end. Because of the waves and sometimes hazardous currents, the hotel provides lifeguards for safety. The Playa Revolcadero breeze is also brisk enough for sailing and sailboarding with your own boat or board. Some rentals may be available from the hotel beach concession.

Playa Larga and Barra Vieja

About seven miles (11 km) from the Puerto Marquez traffic intersection, the Barra Vieja road forks

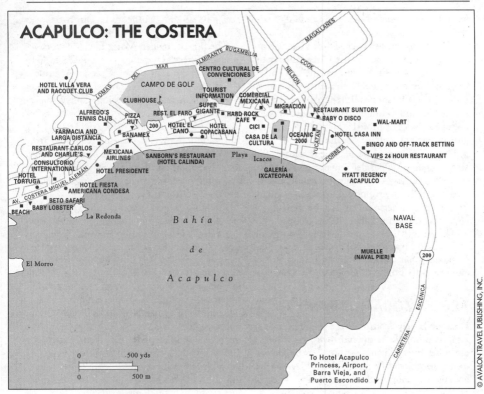

ACAPULCO: THE COSTERA

© AVALON TRAVEL PUBLISHING, INC.

right and heads along breezy, wild Playa Larga. About two miles from the fork, you will pass the lovely retreat Villas San Vicente, a collection of five small villas and two studio cottages, all nestled in their own palmy, private beachside park. (For details and rental information, see Out of Town Hotels in the Accommodations section.)

For the past several years a hardy group of ecovolunteers has patrolled Playa Larga (Long Beach), Playa Revolcadero's dozen-mile-long eastern extension to Barra Vieja. At this writing, they were camped out at around 10 miles (16 km) from the fork for the summer-fall turtle season at "Campamento Tortuguero Playa Larga." If you see them, stop and say a word of encouragement and perhaps donate some food or money to help them sustain their lonely vigil. Even better, set up your own tent nearby and volunteer your help recovering,

incubating, and finally releasing the turtle hatchlings.

If you do camp, you'll be able to share in enjoying the wide, breezy strand, whose rolling waves, with ordinary precautions, appear to be good for boogie boarding, bodysurfing, and possibly surfing. The sun sets on an unobstructed horizon, and the crab-rich beach is good for surf fishing (or by boat if you launch during morning calm). Additionally, the firm, level sand is excellent for jogging, walking, and beachcombing.

About 18 miles (32 km) from the traffic intersection (11 miles from the fork) a sign marks the former Playa Encantada resort and restaurant, which unfortunately is returning to ruin.

About a mile farther on, the stores (groceries and long-distance phone) and modest houses of fishing village Barra Vieja dot the roadside. Many seafood *palapas* line the beachside. The better

ACAPULCO/TAXCO

among them include Don Beto's and Gloria del Mar, both with pools.

In addition to the beach, Barra Vieja visitors enjoy access to the vast **Laguna Tres Palos** mangrove wetland from the *estero* at the east end of town before the bridge. From there, boatmen (ask for José Organes or Felipe Sala) take parties on fishing and wildlife-viewing excursions for about $25 per hour for six. Horseback rides are also available, for about $17/hour.

Despite its steady flow of Sunday tourists, this sleepy lagoonside hamlet remains an Acapulco few people know—like a faraway South Seas village—with drowsy palms, rolling waves, pleasant breezes, and fisherfolk who live by the ancient rhythms of sun and tide.

The road (which maps routinely show going through to Highway 200) crosses a rickety lagoon bridge and ends about two miles farther east at scruffy Lomas de Chapultepec village.

ACCOMMODATIONS

Location largely determines the price and style of Acapulco hotels. In the old town, most hotels are either clustered around the *zócalo* or perched on the hillsides of Peninsula de las Playas. They are generally not on the beach and are cheaper and less luxurious. Most new town hotels, by contrast, lie mostly along the Costera Miguel Alemán right on the beach. Guests often enjoy a wealth of resort amenities and luxury view rooms at correspondingly luxurious prices.

Many lodgings, however, defy categorization. Acapulco offers numerous choices to suit individual tastes and pocketbooks. In all cases, and especially in the luxury hotels, you can often save money by requesting low-season, package, and weekly or monthly discounts. For winter high-season lodgings, call or write for early reservations.

Hotels near the Zócalo

A number of clean, moderately priced hotels cluster in the colorful working-class neighborhood between La Quebrada and the *zócalo*. The most charming is the authentically colonial-era **Hotel Misión,** Felipe Valle 12, Acapulco, Guerrero 39300, tel. 744/482-3643,

fax 744/482-2076, corner of La Paz, two blocks from the *zócalo*.

The present owner, María Elena Sayago, relates the history of her hotel-home. From 1930 to 1966, it was a school, the Colegio Acapulco. When she began repairs several years ago, her workers uncovered broken antique Chinese porcelain, most likely brought from Asia by the colonial-era Manila galleons. Before the 1910–1917 Revolution, she says that the place housed army offices, and before that, it was a banklike *estango* (depository) for valuables. The front-section walls and rooms were preserved in the original adobe, and the columns in the original stone.

Most of the guest rooms, however, she had rebuilt, of concrete, in two stories around a plant-decorated patio, shaded by a spreading mango tree. When the mangos ripen in April guests get their fill of the fragrant fruit. Her 24 attractively decorated rooms rent for about $20 s, $40 d, low season, $25 and $50 high. With fans, hot water, and parking, in an adjacent lot.

Around the corner, behind the Hotel Misión, on quiet side-street La Paz stands good budget buy **Casa de Huéspedes California,** at La Paz 12, Acapulco, Guerrero 39300, tel. 744/482-2893. Guest enjoy about 20 plainly decorated, but clean rooms, in two stories, around a quiet inner tropical patio. Rentals run about $9 s, $18 d low season, $10 and $20 high.

One block farther away, along La Paz, from the *zócalo*, the 1960s-modern **Hotel María Antioneta** fronts the busy shop- and restaurant-lined Av. Azueta, at Teniente Azueta 17, Acapulco, Guerrero 39300, tel. 744/482-5024. The 34 plainly furnished, somewhat worn rooms are nevertheless light, especially on the upper floor. Bathrooms, especially, could use a good scrubbing, however. Most rooms are fortunately recessed along the leafy inner courtyard, away from street noise. Guests have the use of a handy communal kitchen and an unfurnished, but potentially attractive upstairs terrace (that I suggested to the manager would be greatly improved with some tables and chairs). Rates run about $17 d low season, $22 high, with hot water and fans. Credit cards are not accepted.

A block away, on the quiet cul-de-sac end of

ACAPULCO ACCOMMODATIONS BY PRICE

Accommodations (telephone area code 744, postal code 39300 unless otherwise noted) are listed in increasing order of approximate high-season, double-room rates. Toll-free 800, 866, and 877 telephone numbers listed here are dialable only from either the United States, Canada, or both.

Zócalo and Peninsula de las Playas Hotels

Hotel María Acela, La Paz 19, tel. 482-0661, fax 484-3121, enava99@prodigy.net.mx, $12

Casa de Huéspedes California, La Paz 12, tel. 482-2893, $20

Hotel María Antioneta, Teniente Azueta 17, tel. 482-5024, $22

Hotel Asturias, Quebrada 45, tel./fax 483-6548, ceradoancera@aol.com, $26

Hotel Torre Eifel, Inalambrica 110, tel. 482-1683, $30

Hotel Misión, Felipe Valle 12, tel. 482-3643, fax 482-2076, $50

Hotel Etel Suites, Pinzona 92, tel. 482-2240 or 482-2241, etelsuites@terra.com.mx, $50

Hotel Boca Chica, Playa Caletilla s/n, tel./fax 483-6601 or 483-6741, bocach@acabtu.com.mx, $70

Hotel Los Flamingos, P.O. Box 70, tel. 482-0690, 482-0691, or 482-0692, fax 483-9806, flamingo@acabtu.com.mx, $82

Hotel Grand Meigas Acapulco, Cerro San Martin 325, tel. 483-9334, 483-9234, or 483-9140, fax 483-9125, meigaca@prodigy.net.mx, $85

Suites Alba, Gran Via Tropical 35, postal code 39390, tel. 483-0073, fax 483-8378, alba@suitesalba.com.mx, $140

Costera Hotels

Hotel del Valle, G. Gomez Espinosa 8, postal code 39670, tel. 485-8336 or 485-8388, $55

Hotel Sands, Calle Juan de la Cosa 178, P.O. Box 256, postal code 39670, tel. 484-2261, 484-2262, 484-2263, or 484-2264, fax 484-1053, sands@sands.com.mx, $55

Hotel Monaco, Costera Miguel Alemán 186, postal code 39670, tel./fax 485-6467, tel. 485-6415, $59

Auto-Hotel Ritz, Costera M. Alemán and Wifrido Massieu, postal code 39670, tel. 486-2081, tel./fax 484-0984, panoramil@aca-novenet.com.mx, $90

Hotel Maris, Costera M. Alemán 59, postal code 39670, tel./fax 485-8440 or 485-8492, $110

Casa Inn, Costera M. Alemán 130, postal code 39860, tel./fax 435-2000 or 435-2037, reserva@acabtu.com.mx, $150

Hotel Maralisa, Alemania s/n, postal code 39670, tel. 485-6677, fax 485-9228, maralisa@aca-novenet.com.mx, $153

Hotel Elcano, Costera M. Alemán 75, postal code 39690, tel./fax 435-1500, elcano@hotel-elcano.com.mx, $200

Hotel Villa Vera and Racquet Club, Lomas del Mar 35, P.O. Box 3964, postal code 39690, tel. 484-0333, 484-0334, 484-0335, 877/278-8018, or 866/818-8342, fax 484-7479, $220

Hotel Fiesta Americana Condesa, Costera M. Alemán 1220, tel. 484-2828, 484-2355, or 800/ FIESTA-1 (800/343-7821), fax 484-1828, reslfaca@posadas.com, $250

Hyatt Regency Acapulco, Costera M. Alemán 1, postal code 39860, tel. 469-1234 or 800/233-1234, fax 484-3087, $360

Out-of-Town Hotels

Villas San Vicente, c/o Casa y Villas Real Estate, 180 Costera Miguel Alemán, Acapulco, Guerrero 39300, tel. 484-7600 or 484-2500, fax 484-8500, casas@casasyvillas.com.mx, $120–300

Vidafel Mayan Palace, Av. Costera de las Palmas, Fracc. Playa Diamante, tel./fax 469-0201, 800/VIDAFEL (800/843-2335), or 800/996-2926, $350

Hotel Fairmont Acapulco Princess, Playa Revolcadero, tel. 469-1000 or 800/866-5577, fax 469-1016, $400

Av. La Paz, stands the spartan three-story **Hotel María Acela,** Av. La Paz 19, Acapulco, Guerrero 39300, tel. 744/482-0661, fax 744/484-3121, anava99@prodigy.net.mx. Its family management lends a homey atmosphere more like a guesthouse than a hotel. The austerely furnished rooms, although clean enough (but not immaculate), lack hot water. Guests enjoy a small lobby library of paperback books. The 21 rooms rent for a bargain $8 s, $12 d, with fan.

The **Hotel Asturias,** Quebrada 45, Acapulco, Guerrero 39300, tel./fax 744/483-6548, cerardoancera@aol.com, on Av. Quebrada a few blocks uphill from the *zócalo,* offers a relaxing atmosphere at budget rates. Its two stories of plain but tidy rooms surround a plant-decorated pool and patio with chairs for sunning. Get an upper room for more light and privacy. Rates for the 15 rooms are about $9 s, $18 d, $26 t low season, $13, $26, and $34 high, with fans; four short blocks from the cathedral, between Ramirez and Ortiz.

A few blocks farther uphill, **Hotel Torre Eifel,** Inalambrica 110, Acapulco, Guerrero 39300, tel. 744/482-1683, rises above its hillside garden overlooking the La Quebrada diver's point tourist mecca. The 25 simply but comfortably furnished rooms rise in four motel-modern tiers above an inviting pool and patio. Guests in the uppermost rooms enjoy breezy sea views and a sunset horizon. Rooms rent for a bargain-basement $10 s, $15 d, $20 t low season, and $15, $30, $45 high, with fans, hot water, and parking; at the corner of Av. Pinzona, one block uphill from the La Quebrada parking lot.

Two more blocks up winding Av. Pinzona, the **Hotel Etel Suites** stands on the hillside above old Acapulco, Av. Pinzona 92, Acapulco, Guerrero 39390, tel. 744/482-2240 or 744/482-2241, etelsuites@terra.com.mex. Well managed by friendly owner Etel Sutter Álvarez (great-granddaughter of renowned California pioneer John A. Sutter) and her daughter, the three-building complex stair-steps downhill to a luxurious view garden and pool. Its airy hillside perch lends the Etel Suites a tranquil, luxurious ambience unusual in such an economical lodging. Chairs and sofas in a small street-level lobby invite relaxed conversation with fellow guests. The primly but thoughtfully furnished and well-maintained rooms range from singles to multibedroom view apartments. The dozens of rooms and suites rent from about $30 s or d low season, $50 high, with fans, a/c, and hot water. Completely furnished view apartments with kitchens go for about $50 low season, $70 high, with discounts negotiable for monthly rentals. Some parking, and credit cards are accepted.

Peninsula de las Playas Hotels

Many of these lodgings are spread along one continuous boulevard that winds through this plush hillside neighborhood. The boulevard starts as the Costera Miguel Alemán as it heads past the *zócalo* toward the peninsula. There it veers left as the Gran Via Tropical, rounding the peninsula clockwise. Passing Caleta and Caletilla beaches, the boulevard changes to Av. López Mateos and continues along the peninsula's sunset (southwest) side past Playa Angosta and La Quebrada diver's point before ending back in the *zócalo* neighborhood.

(*Note:* The once-grand hillside **Hotel Majestic,** Av. Pozo del Rey 73, Acapulco, Guerrero 39390, is in such a state of disrepair that I can't continue to recommend it. Present owners promise, however, that they will soon completely restore the hotel to its formerly attractive condition.)

A couple of blocks farther along Gran Via Tropical, the multistory **Suites Alba,** Gran Via Tropical 35, Acapulco, Guerrero 39390, tel. 744/483-0073, fax 744/483-8378, alba@suites alba.com.mx, apartment-style complex rambles through its well-kept hilltop garden of palms and pools. The mostly Canadian and American middle-class guests enjoy many facilities, including a pair of pools, a hot tub, a restaurant, a minimart, and a downhill bayside beach club with its own salt-water pool. The 292 comfortably furnished apartments have kitchenettes, a/c, and private garden-view balconies. Rentals begin at about $85 d low season, $140 high, with discounts available for monthly rentals; credit cards are accepted, and parking is available. For more information, visit the website www.suitesalba.com.mx.

Around on the opposite side of the peninsula, guests at the **Hotel Boca Chica,** Playa Caletilla s/n, Acapulco, Guerrero 39300, tel./fax 744/483-6601 or 744/483-6741, bocach@acabtu.com.mx, enjoy views of Playa Caletilla on one hand and the green Isla Roqueta beyond an azure channel on the other. The hotel perches on a rocky point, invitingly close to the clear aqua water from the pool deck and surrounding garden paths. The light, comfortably furnished rooms vary; if you have the option, look at two or three before you choose. Early reservations year-round are strongly recommended. Rates for the 45 rooms with phones and a/c run about $64 d low season, $70 high, with breakfast; credit cards are accepted, and parking is available.

If you like the gorgeous location but can't get into the Hotel Boca Chica immediately, try the best-buy **Hotel Grand Meigas Acapulco,** Cerro San Martin 225, Playa Caleta, Acapulco, Guerrero 39300, tel. 744/483-9334, 744/483-9234, or 744/483-9140, toll-free Mex. tel. 800/716-2159, fax 744/483-9125, meigaca@prodigy.net.mx, on the opposite side of nearby Playa Caleta. Hotel guests enjoy a big blue pool and view sundeck, an intimately private rock-enfolded open-ocean beach, lush green garden, and deluxe comfortable rooms, with private panoramic view balcony. Although renovated in the mid-1990s, the hotel is now showing a bit of wear around the edges. Nevertheless, rates for the 260 rooms, however, are very reasonable, at about $60 per person low-season double occupancy, $85 high, including all meals, drinks, and in-house sports and entertainment. Room-only rental runs about $60 d low season, $85 high; with a/c, phones, cable TV, and parking; credit cards are accepted. For more information, visit the website www.meigashoteles.com.

Hotel Los Flamingos, P.O. Box 70, Acapulco, Guerrero 39300, tel. 744/482-0690, 744/482-0691, or 744/482-0692, fax 744/483-9806, flamingo@acabtu.com.mx. The Los Flamingos, uphill about a mile west from Playa Caleta, along Av. López Mateos, is where oldsters reminisce and youngsters find out who John Wayne, Johnny Weissmuller, and Rory Calhoun were. Personable owner-manager and musician Adolfo Santiago González enjoys occasionally playing his guitar and relating his experiences with his famous guests of yesteryear. Faded Hollywood photos decorate the open-air lobby walls, while nearby pathways wind through a hilltop jungle of palm, hibiscus, and spreading mangoes. The rooms, several with private, ocean-view balconies, perch on a cliffside that plummets into foaming breakers hundreds of feet below. Soft evening guitar music in an open-air sunset-view restaurant and a luxurious clifftop pool and patio complete the lovely picture. The 40 rooms, in standard, superior, and junior suite grades, run about $70, $82, and $93 d low season, respectively; and $82, $100, and $112 high season; add about $30 for an extra person. The hotel also rents **Casa Redonda,** a luxurious cliffside view house, Acapulco home-away-from-home of Johnny Weissmuller *(Tarzan),* where he died in 1984. All with parking, some a/c; credit cards are accepted. Adolfo says, show your copy of *Moon Handbooks Pacific Mexico* and get a 10 percent discount.

Costera Hotels

With few exceptions, these hostelries line both sides of the busy beach boulevard, Costera Miguel Alemán. Hotels are either right on or just a short walk from the beach. By location, moving easterly from the Papagayo amusement park, first comes the economy **Hotel del Valle,** G. Gomez Espinosa 150, Acapulco, Guerrero 39670, tel. 744/485-8336 or 744/485-8388, which shares its fortunate location with much more luxurious neighbors. Two motel-style tiers of plain but clean rooms border a small but inviting pool patio. On a side street away from the noisy boulevard, the del Valle is a tranquil winter headquarters for retirees and youthful budget travelers. The 20 rooms rent for about $35 s or d low season, $50 high, with hot water; add about $10 for a more deluxe a/c-equipped room. For more information, visit the website www.travelbymexico.com/guer/hoteldelvalle.

Around the corner, high-rise hotels occupy the Costera beachfront. After the towering Paraiso Las Glorias comes the more appropriately sized **Hotel Maris,** Av. Costera M. Alemán 59, Acapulco, Guerrero 39670, tel. 744/485-8440, fax

744/485-8492, where guests get spacious rooms with private view balconies for surprisingly reasonable rates. Lobby-level amenities include a small pool above the beach club with bar and restaurant (you may have to ask someone to turn down the TV volume). Street parking only, however. Rates for the 85 rooms run about $70 d low season, $110 high; with a/c, TV, and phones.

The renovated, long-time **Auto-Hotel Ritz,** welcomes guests, a block from the beach, at the corner of Costera M. Alemán and Wilfrido Massieu, Acapulco, Guerrero 39670, tel. 744/486-2081, toll-free Mex. tel. 800/715-4054, fax 744/484-0984, email panorami@aca-novenet.com.mx. The downstairs, with its chandeliered but dowdy lobby, invitingly tropical pool and patio, with spectacular old fan palms, remains as ever. The rooms (get an upstairs one for more privacy) however, are much improved: light and clean, with big double beds, marble baths, and airy, private patio-view balconies. Rates run a reasonable $50 d low season, $90 high, with a/c, cable TV, and parking.

Two blocks farther east, the low-rise former Howard Johnson affiliate has returned to being simply the **Hotel Maralisa,** Alemania s/n, Acapulco, Guerrero 39670, tel. 744/485-6677, fax 744/485-9228, maralisa@aca-novenet.com.mx. It nestles among its towering beachside condo neighbors. The Maralisa is a luxuriously simple retreat, where guests, after their fill of sunning beside the palm-lined pool patio, can step down onto the sand for a jog or stroll along the beach. Later, they might enjoy a light meal in the hotel's beachside café and go out for dancing in nearby resort hotels. Several of the Maralisa's 90 comfortable rooms, tastefully decorated in whites and warm pastels, have private balconies. Standard rooms rent for about $60 d low season, $153 high. Up to two kids under 12 stay free; with a/c, cable TV, phones, and parking; credit cards are accepted. (At this writing, some parts of the common areas and some rooms need repairs, such as the badly leaking toilet that I pointed out to the bellman who showed me around.) Check your room to see if everything works, before moving in.

A few blocks farther east, past McDonald's, the petite, three-story **Hotel Monaco,** Av. Costera Miguel Alemán 137, Acapulco, Guerrero 39670, tel./fax 744/485-6467, 744/485-6415, or 744/485-6518, stands beside the boulevard, on the beach side. Step inside and you discover a tropical miniretreat from the Costera noise and hustle. Past the small lobby, a big, round blue pool, decorated with shade umbrellas and edged by palms and leafy greenery invites relaxation. (The patio's attractiveness, however, leads to its drawback: For peace and quiet, spend your time here on the beach during the weekends, when families love to frolic in the pool. Weekdays by the pool are usually more tranquil.) Upstairs, the rooms are plain but clean, with the basics: hot showers and two double beds. Tariffs run about $46 d low season, $59 high, with a/c, phone, TV, and parking; it's close to everything, just a block from the beach.

Several blocks farther east the low-rise **Hotel Sands,** Costera Miguel Alemán 178, P.O. Box 256, Acapulco, Guerrero 39670, tel. 744/484-2261, 744/484-2262, 744/484-2263, or 744/484-2264, toll-free Mex. tel. 800/710-9800, fax 744/484-1053, sands@sands.com.mx, www.sands.com.mx, contrasts sharply with the monumental Hotel Costa Club on the beach side of the boulevard. In addition to a pool, patio, and restaurant next to the main 1960s-modern building, the deceivingly spacious grounds encompass a shady green park in the rear that leads to an attractive hidden cluster of garden cabanas. Of the main building rooms, the uppers are best; many have been redecorated with light, comfortable furnishings. Cabana guests, on the other hand, enjoy tasteful browns, tile decor, and big windows looking out into a leafy garden. Cabanas 1–8 are the most secluded. The 59 rooms and 34 cabanas run about $47 d low season, $55 high, holidays such as Christmas and Easter even higher. Low-season discounts weeksdays and for longer stays may be available, if you ask. All with a/c, cable TV, and phones. Parking and use of squash courts are included; credit cards are accepted.

A mile farther west, the super-popular luxury **Hotel Fiesta Americana Condesa,** Av. Costera M. Alemán 1220, Acapulco, Guerrero 39690, tel. 744/484-2828, or toll-free U.S./Can. tel. 800/FIESTA-1 (800/343-7821), fax 744/484-

1828, res1faca@posadas.com, presides atop its rocky shoreline perch smack in the middle of new Acapulco. Boulevard traffic roars nonstop past the front door and nightclubs rock all night nearby. By day, ranks of middle-class American and Canadian vacationers sun on the hotel's spacious pool deck and downstairs at its *palapa*-shaded beach club. Resort facilities include multiple restaurants and bars, nightly live music, shops, auto rental, golf nearby, and all aquatic sports. Rooms, most with private bay-view balconies, are furnished in luscious pastels, rattan, and designer lamps. Rooms rent from about $200 d low season, $250 high, with a/c, cable TV, phones, parking, and full wheelchair access; credit cards are accepted. Low-season promotions or discounts may be available.

In exclusive isolation several blocks uphill, guests at the **Hotel Villa Vera and Racquet Club** enjoy what seems like their own Acapulco country club, at Lomas del Mar 35, P.O. Box 3964, Acapulco, Guerrero 39690, tel. 744/484-0333, 744/484-0334, or toll-free Mex. tel. 800/710-9300, fax 744/484-7479, villavera@mexicoboutiquehotels.com.

The Villa Vera still basks in its glory days, when Lana Turner stayed for weeks, Elvis Presley swam up to the world's first swim-up bar, and Elizabeth Taylor married movie magnate Mike Todd in one of its villas.

Overlooking the entire city and bay, the hotel's luxuriously spacious villas and deluxe rooms and bungalows nestle in a manicured garden above an elegant hillside pool and terrace restaurant. The lodgings, which vary from one-room doubles to suites and villas, are decorated in creams, pastels, and earth tones and tastefully appointed with handicrafts and one-of-a-kind wall art. No children under 18 are admitted, however. Rates for the 48 rooms and suites run about $200 d low season, $220 d high for all superior grade rooms; $220 and $240, respectively, for suites; villas around $1,000. All with a/c, cable TV, phones, parking, clay tennis courts, gourmet restaurant, massage, and sauna; credit cards are accepted. You may also reserve through Boutique Hotels of Mexico's reservation numbers: toll-free U.S. tel. 877/278-8018 or Can. tel. 866/818-8342. Get

there, from the Costera, east of the Hotel Fiesta Americana, via the street that separates the Pizza Hut and the golf course, continuing uphill at each fork. The Villa Vera gate will appear on the left after about a quarter mile.

Those who want tranquility in the middle of Acapulco will most likely find it at the recently restored beachfront **Hotel Elcano,** which is two blocks removed—and whose rooms also face away—from the Costera traffic hubbub, at Av. Costera Miguel Alemán 75, Acapulco, Guerrero 39690, tel./fax 744/435-1500 or 744/484/2230, elcano@hotel-elcano.com.mx. The hotel was named after Ferdinand Magellan's navigator, Sebastián Elcano (who was actually the one who first circumnavigated the globe; Magellan died en route but got the credit).

Hotel Elcano is austerely luxurious, hued in shades of nautical blue, from the breezy, gracefully columned lobby and the spacious turquoise beachside pool to the 180 immaculate, marble-tiled view rooms. Unlike some of Acapulco's beachfront hostelries, the Elcano has plenty of space for guests to enjoy its load of extras, which include two restaurants, three bars, poolside hot tub, beach club, kiddie pool, gym, nine-hole golf course three blocks away, and video games center. Rooms, all with private ocean-view balconies, rent for a very reasonable $105 d low season, $200 high. Be sure to ask for possible promotional packages, or midweek or weekly rates. Reserve through toll-free U.S. tel. 800/917-4901 or Can. tel. 877/260-1765. For more information, visit the website www.hotel-elcano.com.mx.

Moving a few blocks farther east along the Costera, folks who want a low-season bargain-priced view room a block from the beach can find it at the **Casa Inn,** Costera M. Alemán 2310, Acapulco, Guerrero 39860, tel. 744/435-2000 or 744/435-2037, reserva@acabtu.com.mx. The youngish, mostly single clientele also like the lively late-night bar and the big pool deck where they can rest and recover during the day. The 279 light and comfortable rooms come with a/c, TV, views, and phones. Rooms, most with kitchenettes, rent, for one through four people, for about $65 low season, $150 high; parking is available, and credit cards are accepted.

Two blocks away rises the 20-story tower of the **Hyatt Regency Acapulco,** Costera M. Alemán 1, Acapulco, Guerrero 39860, tel. 744/469-1234, or toll-free Mex. tel. 800/091-2300 or U.S./Can. tel. 800/223-1234, or fax 744/484-3087. Its lavish facilities include spacious gardens, blue lagoon swimming pool, a Tarzan jungle waterfall, a squadron of personal beach *palapas,* restaurants, bars, frequent live music, shops, all aquatic sports, tennis, and golf nearby. The 690 rooms, all with private view balconies, are large and luxurious. Standard rooms rent from about $210 d low season, $360 high, with a/c, cable TV, phones, parking, and full wheelchair access; credit cards are accepted. (Low-season promotional prices, however, can range as low as $125. When reserving, don't forget to ask for a package or discount.)

Out-of-Town Hotels

The sleepy Pie de la Cuesta downscale resort village on placid Coyuca Lagoon (about six miles by the oceanfront Highway 200 northwest from the Acapulco *zócalo*) has many budget and moderately priced beachside lodgings. Drive, taxi (about $10), or ride a Pie de la Cuesta–marked bus from Av. Escudero in front of Sanborn's and Woolworth's near the *zócalo.* (For more details, see the end of the Ixtapa-Zihuatanejo and South to Acapulco Chapter.)

Past the southeast end of town along the airport road, the showplace **Hotel Fairmont Acapulco Princess** provides an abundance of resort facilities (including an entire 18-hole golf course), spreading from luscious beachfront garden grounds at Playa Revolcadero, P.O. Box 1351, Acapulco, Guerrero 39300, tel. 744/469-1000 or toll-free U.S./Can. tel. 800/866-5577, fax 744/469-1016, aca.reservations@fairmont.com. Although the hotel centers on a pair of hulking neopyramids (1,019-room total), the impression from the rooms themselves is of super-luxury; from the garden it is of Eden-like jungle tranquility—meandering pools, gurgling cascades, strutting flamingos, swaying palms—which guests seem to soak up with no trouble at all. Rooms rent from about $200 d low season, $400 high, including breakfast and dinner high season; the hotel has all facilities, all sports, and full wheelchair access; credit cards are accepted.

Alternatively, consider the **Vidafel Mayan Palace** about a mile farther along the beach from the Fairmont Acapulco Princess. Here, in a palace like the Mayan kings never had, you can have an 18-hole golf course, 12 clay tennis courts, a km-long swimming pool (no kidding), five bars, three restaurants, fountains, waterfalls, and an entire blue lagoon, all overlooking a gorgeous, breezy beach. Hotel rates run from about $350 d, high season, for a luxurious and spacious marble and pastel room with everything. Ask for a discount or promotional package. For information and reservations, contact Vidafel Mayan Palace, Av. Costera del las Palmas, Fracc. Playa Diamante, Acapulco, Guerrero 39300, tel./fax 744/469-0201, toll-free U.S./Can. tel. 800/VIDAFEL (800/843-2335) or 800/996-2926.

A few miles farther southeast (for directions, see Beaches Southeast of Town, under Sights) find the **Villas San Vicente,** a miniheaven for lovers of peace and quiet. Plenty of space, sweeping green lawns, swaying palms, and a long gorgeous strand, where seekers of tranquility and solitude can have it all: afternoons all alone, reading by the pool, long walks on the beach, savoring the tropical breeze, and watching the sun go down. Guests in the five spacious, super deluxe minivillas enjoy two bedrooms, with king-sized beds, and two baths, designer living-dining room, completely equipped kitchen, hot tub, a/c, and a small private pool. The two smaller units are more modest but still comfortable studios, with bath, kitchenette, and a/c, set at the upper edge of the property, a bit farther from the beach. All residents share a lusciously inviting main pool and patio, with bar, tennis courts, and parking, all on about 10 palm-shaded beachfront acres. High season (Jan. 3 through Easter) rentals run about $120 for the studios, upward from $220 to about $300 for the minivillas, depending on location and amenities. Low-season rates are about 30 percent less. Reservations (mandatory high season, strongly recommended low) are available by contacting the Villas' Acapulco office, Casas y Villas Real Estate, Centro Comercial Flamboyant, 180 Costera Miguel Alemán, Acapulco, Guerrero 39300, tel. 744/484-

7600, 744/484-2500, or 744/466-2040, fax 744/484-8500, casas@casasyvillas.com.mx, www.casasyvillas.com.mx. You may also contact the Villas San Vicente directly, tel. 744/462-0149 or 744/462-0120.

Trailer Parks and Camping

Although condos and hotels have crowded out virtually all of Acapulco's in-town trailer parks, good prospects exist nearby. The best are the **Acapulco Trailer Park** and the **KOA** campground, right on the beach in Pie de la Cuesta resort village, six miles by the coast highway northwest of the Acapulco *zócalo.* (For details, see the Pie de la Cuesta section at the end of the Ixtapa-Zihuatanejo and South to Acapulco Chapter.)

And although development and urbanization have likewise squeezed out in-town **camping,** possibilities exist in the trailer parks in Pie de La Cuesta and on Playa Larga near Barra Vieja. (See Beaches Southeast of Town.)

FOOD

Breakfast and Snacks near the Zócalo

Eat well for under $3 at **Lonchería Chatita,** Av. Azueta, corner of Hidalgo, open daily 8 A.M.–10 P.M., where a friendly female kitchen squad serves mounds of wholesome, local-style specialties. On a typical day, these may include savory *chiles rellenos,* rich *puerco mole de Uruapan, pozole* (savory hominy soup), or potato pancakes.

Something fancier is available at **Flor Es Acapulco** (formerly Restaurant La Parroquia) on the upstairs balcony, overlooking the *zócalo,* good for a snack or a light lunch as you soak in the scene below.

For something creamy and cool, go to **Bing** ice cream, open daily 9 A.M.–11 P.M., one block from the *zócalo* toward the steamship dock.

Continue another block to **Sanborn's,** *malecón* corner of Escudero, open daily 7:30 A.M.–11 P.M., where you can escape the heat and enjoy home-style ham and eggs, hamburgers, roast beef, and apple pie, although prices are fairly high.

Woolworth's, one block from the Costera,

Divers sell freshly caught oysters, clams, mussels, octopuses, and fish right on the Acapulco beaches.

behind Sanborn's, also offers air-conditioned ambience and similar fare at more reasonable prices.

Finally, for dessert, head back over to the other side of the *zócalo* to **La Espiga de Acapulco** bakery, for a tasty tart or piece of cake. On Juárez, tel. 744/482-2699, a block west of the *zócalo,* open daily 7 A.M.–10 P.M.

Costera Snacks and Breakfast

Snack food concentrates in Acapulco, as in many places, around **McDonald's,** with at least two branches, the original one, at the corner of Esclavo and Av. Costera M. Alemán, a few blocks east of the landmark Qualton Club; and also farther east, on the Costera, east of the Diana fountain and traffic circle. Here, you have it all, from breakfast Egg McMuffins to Chicken McNuggets and the Big Mac, priced about a third higher than back home. Open daily 8 A.M.–11 P.M.

For an interesting contrast, visit **Taco Tumbra** across the adjacent street from the original McDonald's. Here, piquant aromas of barbecued chicken, pork, and beef and strains of Latin music fill the air. For a treat, order three of the delectable tacos along with a refreshing fruit juice (*jugo*) or fruit-flavored *agua*. Open Sun.–Thurs. 6:30 P.M.–2 A.M., Fri.–Sat. 6:30 P.M.–4 A.M.

About two blocks east, **La Vaquita** (Little Cow), corner Costera M. Alemán and Sandoval, despite its soaring modern canopy, takes pride in its country Mexican cooking, served with a flourish that makes even a bowl of *pozole* seem like a party. If you're hankering for something a bit out of the ordinary, try the house specialty, nopales *en molcajete* (mohl-kah-HAY-tay)—a stone bowl draped with succulent cooked nopales (cactus leaves) and filled with big green onions and savory stewed beef, pork, or chicken. Enough for two. Open daily about 9 A.M.–midnight.

Sanborn's (formerly Denny's), tel. 744/485-5360, next door provides a blessedly cool, refined, and thoroughly modern Mexican refuge from the street. Here, around the clock daily, you can sample an international menu of either North American favorites (eggs, pancakes, bacon, and bottomless coffee) or hearty Mexican specialties. Sanborn's also offers a rack of American magazines, such as *Time, Glamour,* and *National Geographic,* and an ATM machine.

100% Natural, open daily 7 A.M.–11 P.M., tel. 744/485-3982, in competition directly across the Costera from Sanborn's, offers appropriately contrasting fare: many veggie and fruit drinks (try the Conga—made of papaya, guava, watermelon, pineapple, lime, and spinach), several egg breakfasts, breads, sandwiches, tacos, and enchiladas. You can also find 100% Natural branches at at least two more locations: mid-Costera, next door to Carlos'n Charlie's, tel. 744/484-6447, across from Hotel Presidente; and, on the east side, next to Baby O disco, tel. 744/484-8440.

Two miles farther along the Costera, at Hotel Calinda, **Sanborn's** central Costera branch, tel. 744/481-2426, offers the same Sanborn's refined atmosphere, good food, and a big book and gift store, open daily 6:30–1 A.M.

Zócalo and Peninsula de las Playas Restaurants

Even though Acapulco has seemingly zillions of restaurants, only a fraction may suit your expectations. Local restaurants come and go like the Acapulco breeze, though a handful of solid longtime eateries continue, depending on a steady flow of repeat customers.

For plain good eating and homey sidewalk atmosphere morning and night, try outdoor **Café Los Amigos,** Calle La Paz, a few steps off the *zócalo.* Shady umbrellas beneath a spreading green tree and many familiar favorites, from tuna salad and chili to waffles, T-bone steak, and breaded shrimp, attract a friendly club of Acapulco Canadian and American longtimers. Open daily 8:30 A.M.–10 P.M. Budget–moderate.

Meanwhile, on the *zócalo*'s opposite, east side, **La Rebanadata** (Big Slice) Pizza and Italian Restaurant profits from the abundant *zócalo* foot traffic. Here, you can choose between cool inside seating and umbrella-shaded outdoor tables. Select from several styles of pizza (veggie to seafood), four salad choices, many pastas, and more. Open daily except Tues. 11–3 A.M., tel. 744/482-5555. Moderate.

La Gran Torta, at La Paz 6, one block west from the *zócalo,* tel. 744/483-8476, is an old-town headquarters for hearty local-style food at local-style prices. Specialties here are *tortas* (hearty sandwiches), often of *pierna* (roast pork), chorizo (spicy sausage), or *pollo* (chicken) with tomato and avocado stuffed in a *bolillo* bun. Additional favorites include hearty *pozole* Thurs. and Friday. Open daily 8 A.M.–11 P.M. Budget.

Good, reasonably priced seafood restaurants are unexpectedly hard to come by in Acapulco. An important exception is the lineup of local-style seafood eateries along Av. Azueta three blocks west from the *zócalo.* Situated right where the boats come in, they get the freshest morsels first. Local longtimers swear by the excellence of seafood served at **El Amigo Miguel,** at the corner of Juárez and Azueta, where continuous patronage assures daily fresh shrimp, prawns, half a dozen kinds of fish, and lobster (big, $14, smaller, $10). Open daily 10 A.M.–9:30 P.M. Moderate. (Doing nearly as good a job is very worthy **Mariscos Nachos,** across the street, open about the same hours.)

If you prefer something a bit fancier, head a block farther from the *zócalo* to tourist favorite **Mariscos Pipos,** at 3 Almirante Breton, tel. 744/482-2237. The freshest of everything, cooked and served to please. Open daily around noon–9 P.M. Moderate–expensive.

A few steps away, on Costera M. Alemán 322, corner of Almirante Breton, seekers of home-style Mexican cooking need go no farther than **Tamales Licha,** tel. 744/482-2021. Here, appetizing south-of-the-border specialties—succulent tamales, savory *pozole,* crunchy tostadas, and tangy enchiladas—reign supreme. Portions are generous, ambience is relaxed, and hygiene standards are impeccable. Open nightly 6–11 P.M. Budget.

Many visitors' Acapulco vacations wouldn't be complete without a dinner at the luxuriously scenic clifftop *palapa* restaurant at the **Hotel Los Flamingos,** Av. López Mateos s/n, tel. 744/482-0690, about a mile uphill, west from Playa Caleta. Here all the ingredients for a memorable evening—attentive service, tasty seafood, chicken, and meat entrées, airy sunset view, and soft strumming of guitars—come together. Open daily 8 A.M.–10:30 P.M.; credit cards are accepted. Moderate. Coat not necessary.

Costera Restaurants

At **VIPs,** on the Costera, a block from Papagayo Amusement Park, tel. 744/486-8574, you can glimpse the Mexico of the future. Here, Mexican middle-class families flock to a south-of-the-border-style Denny's that beats Denny's at its own game. Inside, the air is as fresh as a spring breeze; the windows, water glasses, and utensils shine like silver; the food is tasty and reasonably priced; and the staff is both amiable and professional. Open Sun.–Thurs. 7 A.M.–midnight, Fri.–Sat. 7–2 A.M.; credit cards are accepted. Moderate. (Also, visit VIPs' newer Costera locations, beach side, near the Hotel Calinda, and east side, across the boulevard from the Hyatt Regency.)

One of Acapulco's most atmospheric and palate-pleasing Italian restaurants is **Dino's,** nearby on the Costera a block west of the Fiesta Americana Condesa, on Costera M. Alemán next to Hotel Tortuga, tel. 744/484-0037. Guests can choose to sit on a bay-view terrace in front or an intimate fountain patio in back. From the menu, select among antipastos, salads, meats, and many seafood and meat pastas smothered in sauces, made with a flourish right at the table. Open daily 6–11:30 P.M.; credit cards are accepted. Moderate–expensive.

No tour of Acapulco restaurants would be complete without a stop at **Carlos'n Charlie's,** which, like all of the late Carlos Anderson's worldwide chain, specializes in the zany. It's on the Costera, across from and a block east of the Hotel Fiesta Americana Condesa, tel. 744/484-0039. The fun begins with the screwy decor, continues via the good-natured, tongue-in-cheek antics of the staff, and climaxes with the food and drink, which is organized on the menu by categories, such as "Slurp," "Munch," "Peep," "Moo," and "Zurts," and is very tasty. Open daily 6 A.M.–midnight; credit cards are accepted. Moderate–expensive.

Another successful culinary experiment is the Acapulco branch of the worldwide **Suntory** Japanese restaurant chain, across from the Oceanic 2000 building, east end of the Costera, tel. 744/484-8088. Although a Japanese restaurant in Mexico is as difficult to create as a Mexican restaurant in Japan, Suntory, the giant beer, whiskey, and wine manufacturer, carries it off with aplomb. From the outside, the clean-lined wooden structure appears authentically classic Japanese, seemingly lifted right out of 18th-century Kyoto. The impression continues in the cool interior, where patrons enjoy a picture-perfect tropical Zen garden, complete with moss, a stony brook, sago palm, and feathery festoons of bamboo. Finally comes the food, from a host of choices—vegetables, rice, fish, and meat—which chefs (who, although Mexican, soon begin to look Japanese) individually prepare for you on the grill built into your table. Open daily 2–11 P.M.; credit cards are accepted. Moderate–expensive.

The Acapulco bent for restaurant fantasy continues right across the street, at **El Embarcadero,** tel. 744/484-8787. Inside, you enter a dim, Disneyesque world. A jungle waterfall cascades behind you while a rickety bridge leads you over a misty lagoon, where at any moment, you fear that a crocodile or a pirate is going to grab you. If you cross over safely your reward will be a cool salad bar and a choice of several intriguing specialties, such as Siamese chicken, Blackbeard's shrimp, or alligator steak. Credit cards are accepted. Open 7 P.M.–midnight.

Splurge Restaurants

Acapulco visitors and well-to-do residents enjoy a number of fashionable, top-of-the-line restaurants, renowned for their super-scenic locations, fine cuisine, or both. Here's a sampling of the worthy, west to east:

Long-time favorite **Coyuca 22** is both the name and the address of the restaurant so exclusive and popular it manages to close half the year. The setting is a spacious hilltop garden, where tables spread down an open-air bay- and city-view terrace. Arrive early (around 5:30 P.M. winter, 7 P.M. summer) to enjoy the sunset sky lighting up and painting the city ever-deepening colors, ending in a deep rose as finally the myriad lights shimmer and stars twinkle overhead. After that, the food (specialties, such as prime rib and lobster tails) and wines seem like dessert. Find it on Calle Coyuca (a side street off Blv. López Mateos on the Peninsula Las Playas), no. 22. Open daily 7–10:30 P.M. Nov. 1–April 30; credit cards are accepted. Reservations are required, tel. 744/482-3468 or 744/483-5030. Dress is elegant resortwear. Expensive; entrées alone run about $30.

Another super-romantic cocktail-dinner spot is the showplace **El Campanario,** commanding a second-to-none view of all of Acapulco. Here, owners have converted a former mansion into a regal bar and restaurant, leading through a princely, arched stone hall to airy vista terraces and a luxuriously inviting pool and patio outside. House specialties are red snapper Azteca, with *cuitlacoche* sauce, rolled filet of beef with spinach, and Chambertine chicken in mushroom sauce. Open daily 7 P.M.–midnight, closed May–Dec. Call tel. 744/484-8830 for reservations. Expensive.

Restaurant El Faro (The Lighthouse), of Hotel Elcano, has raised Acapulco to new heights of culinary fantasy, at least equal to that of the its rotating beacon high above the Costera. The cool subdued interior is reminiscent of a 1940s Hollywood supper club, tinted in suave greens and blues. The numerous nautical accents climax in an overhead stained glass submarine mural. The total impression is as if you and your fellow diners are inhabitants of a grand aquarium, visible only to the poor exterior denizens through the street-level porthole windows.

The cuisine is no less than you'd expect: mostly seafood, some exotic, such as *koktoxas* of grouper (fish cheeks), or more recognizable, such as cod a la Vasque, or grilled shrimp with vegetables and wild rice, sauteed in sesame oil. Meat lovers, neverthless, will do quite well, with entrées such as lusciously tender rib eye steak, or lamb ribs in their own juice, marinated in oils of wild grass, apple puree, and shallots. Open daily noon–11 P.M., high season reservations recommended, tel. 744/435-3100. Expensive.

The east-end bayview Las Brisas district has acquired an exclusive sprinkling of stylish restaurants. Among them, *the* place to be seen is **Kookaburra's,** where, among the beautiful people, you can gaze out on yet another view of Acapulco. In the cool of the evening, from afar, the heat, fumes, and congestion of the Costera give way to a curtain of twinkling lights, like a galaxy, sliced by the curving ebony line of the bay. The food (for example, start with crab cakes, continue with roast duck with mandarin sauce, finish with almond cake) only embellishes the effect. Open daily 6 P.M.–midnight. Reservations, tel. 744/446-6020 or 744/446-6039, are mandatory. Expensive.

Nearby, at **Casanova** Italian restaurant, at 5236 Carretera Escenica Las Brisas, you can enjoy either a cool inside section or the same starry, panoramic view outside, while sampling from a long list of tasty salads, pastas, meats, chicken, and seafood specialties. The house especially recommends its super-fresh shrimp fettuccine. Open daily 7 P.M.–midnight; reservations mandatory, closed low season, tel. 744/446-6237, 744/446-6238, or 744/446-6239. Expensive.

ENTERTAINMENT AND EVENTS

Strolling and Sidewalk Cafés
The old *zócalo* is the best place for strolling and people-watching. Bookstalls, vendors, band concerts, and, on weekend nights especially, pitchpenny games, mimes, and clowns are constant sources of entertainment. When you're tired of walking, take a seat at a sidewalk café, such as La Flor de Acapulco or Café Los Amigos, and let the scene pass *you* by for a change.

Movies
The best cinemas are the Costera multiplexes. As you move eastward, past Papagayo Park, first comes **Cineapolis,** in the shopping plaza next to VIPs restaurant, corner of the Costera and Wilfrido Massieu.

Next comes **Cinema 5,** admission $3, on the third floor of the Plaza Bahía shopping center, next to the Hotel Costa Club, tel. 744/485-5124. Screenings include first-run American drama and comedy.

Finally, in the east-end Oceanic 2000 plaza, you'll get about the same at the newest *cine* in town, tel. 744/481-0646, across from Baby O disco.

Tourist Shows
The **Mexican Fiesta,** Acapulco's dance performance extravaganza, goes on two, three, or four days a week, depending on the season, at the plaza-stage, behind the sprawling Centro Cultural de Convenciones convention center just east of the golf course. The all-Mexico sombrero and whirling-skirt folkloric dance show is often highlighted by a replica performance of the wheeling Papantla flyers. Tickets can include the show with open bar only ($25), or open bar and buffet ($42); kids get the buffet for half price. The food is customarily served around 7 P.M., followed by the performance at 8:15. Book your tickets through a travel or tour agent, or call Mexican Fiesta box office directly, tel. 744/484-3218.

Sunsets
West-side hills block Acapulco Bay's sunset horizon. Sunset connoisseurs remedy the problem

People gather late every afternoon at the Sinfonia del Sol sunset amphitheater near La Quebrada.

by gathering at ocean-view points on the westside Peninsula de las Playas, such as the **Sinfonia del Sol** sunset amphitheater (see Playa Angosta), La Quebrada, Playa Angosta, and the cliffside restaurant and gazebo/bar of the **Hotel Flamingos** (see Accommodations) before sunset.

Far east-side beach locations around the Hotel Hyatt Regency and hilltop viewpoints, such as restaurant-bar **El Campanario** and the east-end Las Brisas Scenic Highway (Carretera Escenica) restaurants (see Splurge Restaurants) also provide unobstructed sunset-viewing horizons.

Bay Cruise Parties
One popular way to enjoy the sunset and a party at the same time is via a cruise aboard the steel excursion ship *Bonanza.* It leaves from its bayside dock on the Costera half a mile (toward the Peninsula de las Playas) from the *zócalo.* Although cruise schedules vary seasonally, offerings can include midday (11 A.M.–2 P.M.), sunset (4:30–7 P.M.), and moonlight (10:30 P.M.–1 A.M.)

cruises. Tickets are available from hotels, travel agents, or at the dock, tel. 744/483-1803. Tickets run about $17 per person, kids 1.4 meters (about 4 feet 9 inches) tall and under go for half price.

Bullfights

Bullfights are staged every Sunday at 5:30 P.M. seasonally, usually Jan.–March, at the arena (here called a *frontón)* near Playa Caletilla. Avoid congestion and parking hassles by taking a taxi. Get tickets (about $25) through a travel agent or the ticket office, tel. 744/483-9561.

Jai-Alai, Bingo, and Offtrack Betting

About $10 gains you entrance to Acapulco's big jai-alai *frontón,* an indoor stadium—look for the Bingo sign—on the Costera, east end, across from the Hyatt Regency, open Tues.–Sun. 9 P.M.–1 A.M. Here, it's hard not to ooh and aah at the skill of players competing in the ancient Basque game of jai-alai. With a long, narrow, curved basket tied to one arm, players fling a hard rubber ball, at lethal speeds, to the far end of the court, where it rebounds like a pistol shot and must be returned by an opposing player. You can place wagers on your favorite player, or, downstairs, bet on horse races and other sports events taking place far away.

Dancing and Discoing

Several of the Costera hotels have live music for dancing at their lobby bars. As you move east along the Costera, the better possibilities are: the **Hotel Costa Club,** tel. 744/485-9050; the **Hotel Fiesta Americana Condesa,** tel. 744/484-2828; and the **Hyatt Regency,** tel. 744/469-1234. Call to verify times.

A number of restaurant/bars along the Costera have nightly dance music, both recorded and live. A pair of favorites of both longtime tourists and local people are the **Tropicana** (on beach side, across the Costera from Cine Hornos), tel. 744/485-3050, and the **Copa Cabana** (on beach side, near corner of Amal Espina), tel. 744/485-1051. Both have cocktails and live Latin (sometimes called "tropical") music for dancing till around 3 A.M. Call ahead to verify times.

A lively band also plays nightly during the high season (Fri., Sat., and Sun. 3–10 P.M., low season) at the restaurant/club **Paradise** (across from the Hotel Romano), on the Costera beachside entertainment strip west of the Hotel Fiesta Americana Condesa. Zany waiters, a lively and varied musical repertoire, and good-enough food all spell happy times at the Paradise, tel. 744/484-5988.

On the other hand, lovers of quieter music enjoy the **Escala** view piano bar, across the eastside highway from Hotel Las Brisas.

Discotheques usually monitor their entrances carefully and are consequently safe and pleasant places for a night's entertainment (provided you are either immune to the noise or bring earplugs). They open their doors around 10 P.M. and play relatively low-volume music and videos for starters until around 11 P.M., when fogs descend, lights flash, and the thumping begins, continuing sometimes till dawn. Admission runs about $7 to $15 or more for the tonier joints.

Acapulco's discos and dance hangouts concentrate in two major east-side spots. As you move east, between the Diana Circle and the Fiesta Americana Condesa, a solid lineup of clubs, hangouts, and discos occupies the Costera's beach side. During peak seasons, the dancing crowds spill onto the street. Stroll along and pick out the style and volume that you like.

Of the bunch, **Beach** disco is the loudest, brashest, and among the most popular. For the entrance fee of $5, the music and the lights go till dawn. Other neighboring discos, such as Mammy's, Baby Lobster, Blackbeard's, Crazy Lobster, and Beto Safari, while sometimes loud, are nevertheless subdued in comparison.

Another mile east, Planet Hollywood and Hard Rock Cafe, both of which actually serve food, signal the beginning of a second lineup on both sides of the street of about a dozen live-music or disco clubs. The energy they put out trying to outdo each other with brighter lights, louder music, and larger and flashier facades is exceeded only by the frequency at which they seem to go in and out of business. More or less permanently fixed are **Planet Hollywood,** with recorded music and videos, 10 P.M.–2 A.M., no cover, tel. 744/484-0717; **Hard Rock Cafe,** "Save the Planet," live music, 10:30 P.M.–2 A.M., no cover, tel. 744/484-0047; **Baby O** disco and concert hall, "There's only one Acapulco and only one Baby O," 10 P.M.–4 A.M., $12 cover, tel. 744/484-7474; and **Nina's** concert and night club, 10 P.M.–4 A.M., moderate cover, tel. 744/484-2828.

Reigning above all of these lesser centers of discomania is **Palladium,** visible everywhere around the bay as the pink neon glow on the east-side Las Brisas hill. Go there, if only to look, though call for a reservation beforehand, tel. 744/446-5490, or you might not be let in. Inside, the impression is of ultramodern fantasy—a giant spaceship window facing outward on a galactic star carpet—while the music explodes, propelling you, the dancing traveler, through inner space. A mere $35 cover (women $20) gets you through the door; inside, cocktails are around $10, while French champagne runs upward of $300 a bottle. Open Tues., Thurs. Fri. and Sat. low season, Mon.–Sat. high.

Child's Play

CICI (short for Centro Internacional de Convivencia Infantil) is the biggest of Acapulco's water parks. An aquatic paradise for families, CICI has acres of liquid games, where you can swish along a slippery toboggan run, plummet down a towering kamikaze slide, or loll in a gentle wave pool. Other pools contain performing whales, dolphins, and sea lions. Sea mammal performances occur at 12:30, 3:30, and 5:30 P.M. Patrons also enjoy a restaurant, a beach club, and much more. CICI is on the east end of the Costera between the golf course and the Hyatt Regency; open daily 10 A.M.–6 P.M., adult admission $6, kids $3, tel. 744/484-8210.

Mágico Mundo, tel. 744/483-1215, Acapulco's other water park, is on the opposite side of town at Playa Caleta. It includes an aquarium, museum, restaurant, water slides, cascades, and more; open daily 9 A.M.–5 P.M., admission $3 adult, $2 child.

SPORTS AND RECREATION
Walking and Jogging

The most interesting beach walking in Acapulco is along the two-mile stretch of beach between the Hotel Fiesta Americana Condesa and the rocky point at Parque Papagayo. Avoid the midday heat by starting early for breakfast along the Costera (a good choice is Sanborn's Restaurant, tel. 744/481-2426, at the Hotel Calinda) and walking west along the beach with the sun to your back. Besides the beach itself, you'll pass rocky outcroppings to climb on, tidepools to poke through, plenty of fruit vendors, and *palapas* to rest in from the sun. Bring a hat, shirt, and sunscreen and allow two or three hours. If you get tired, ride a taxi or bus back. You can do the reverse walk just as easily in the afternoon after about 3 P.M. from Playa Hamacas just past the steamship dock after lunch on the *zócalo* (try the Café Los Amigos).

Soft sand and steep slopes spoil most jogging prospects on Acapulco Bay beaches. However, the green open spaces surrounding the Centro Cultural de Convenciones, just east of the golf course, provide a good in-town substitute.

Tennis and Golf

Acapulco's tennis courts are all private and mostly at the hotels. Try the Costa Club, tel. 744/485-9050 ($6/hour days, $9 nights); Acapulco Park, tel. 744/485-5437, $5 an hour days, $10 nights, on the Costera near the Hotel Costa Club; Villa Vera, tel. 744/484-0333 (hard surface and clay courts, $9 by day only); Presidente, tel. 744/484-1700; and Hyatt Regency, tel. 744/484-1225. Lessons by in-house teaching pros customarily run $20–30 an hour.

One of the coziest places for tennis in town is **Alfredo's Tennis Club,** the home of the late former tennis champion Alfredo Millet. His family continues the tradition, renting two night-lit courts for $8 per hour during the day, $12 at night, including towel, refreshment, and use of the swimming pool. Lessons run about $5 extra per hour. At Av. Prado 29, tel. 744/484-0004 (call ahead of time); get there via Av. Deportes, next to the Pizza Hut. Go uphill one block, then left another to Alfredo's, at the corner of Prado.

The Acapulco **Campo de Golf** course, tel. 744/484-0781 or 744/484-0782, right on the mid-Costera, is open to the public on a first-come, first-served basis, daily 6:30 A.M.–5:30 P.M.

Exceptions are Wed. and Sat. after 1 P.M., when the course is limited to foursomes. Greens fee is about $40 for nine holes and $55 for 18 holes. Caddy costs $9, club rental $15.

Much more exclusive are the fairways at the **Club de Golf** of hotels Fairmont Acapulco Princess and Pierre Marques, tel. 744/469-1000, about five miles past the southeast edge of town. Here, the 18-hole greens fee runs $80.

The **Vidafel Mayan Palace,** farther east, past the Fairmont Acapulco Princess, also has a luxury beachfront golf course. For more information, call tel. 744/469-0201.

Swimming, Surfing, and Boogie Boarding

Acapulco Bay's tranquil (if not pristine) waters usually allow safe swimming from hotel-front beaches. The water is often too tranquil for surf sports, however. Strong waves off open-ocean Playa Revolcadero southeast of the city often give good rides. Be aware, the waves can be dangerous. The Fairmont Acapulco Princess on the beach provides lifeguards. Check with them before venturing in. Bring your own equipment; rentals may not be available.

Snorkeling and Scuba Diving

The best local snorkeling is off **Isla Roqueta.** Closest access point is by boat from the docks at Playa Caleta and Playa Tlacopanocha. Such trips usually run about $20 per person for two hours, equipment included. Snorkel trips can also be arranged through beachfront aquatics shops at hotels such as the Ritz, Hotel Costa Club, Hotel Fiesta Americana Condesa, the Hyatt Regency, and the scuba shops below.

Although local water clarity is often not ideal, especially during the summer-fall rainy season, Acapulco does have a few professional dive shops. Contact instructor José Vasquez's **Acapulco Scuba Center** near the Bonanza tour boat dock, about half a mile west, past the old-town *zócalo,* tel. 744/482-9474.

Another option, near the same old-town dockfront location, is the very professional, safety-conscious **Divers de Mexico,** tel. 744/482-1398 or 744/483-6020.

Sailing and Sailboarding

Close-in Acapulco Bay waters (except off of west-end Playa Icacos) are generally too congested with motorboats for tranquil sailing or sailboarding. Nevertheless, some beach concessionaires at the big hotels, such as the Hotel Costa Club and Hyatt Regency, do rent (or take people sailing in) simple sailboats from $15 per hour.

Outside of town, tranquil **Laguna Coyuca,** on the coast about 20 minutes' drive northwest of the *zócalo,* offers good sailboarding and sailing prospects (see Pie de la Cuesta in the Ixtapa-Zihuatanejo and South to Acapulco chapter).

Personal Watercraft Riding, Water-Skiing, and Parasailing

Power sports are very popular on Costera hotel beaches. Concessionaires—recognized by their lineup of beached minimotorboats—operate from most big hotel beaches, notably around the Qualton Club, Hotel Costa Club, Hotel Fiesta Americana Condesa, and the Hyatt Regency. Prices run about $60 per hour for personal watercraft, $50 per hour for water-skiing, and $20 for a 10-minute parasailing ride.

Sportfishing

Fishing boats line the *malecón* dockside across the boulevard from the *zócalo.* Activity centers on the dockside office of the 20-boat blue and white fleet of fishing boat cooperative **Sociedad Cooperativa Servicios Turístico,** whose dozens of licensed captains regularly take visitors for big-game fishing trips. Although some travel agents may book you individually during high season, the Sociedad Cooperativa Turísticas office, open daily 8 A.M.–6 P.M., tel. 744/482-1099 (managed by Captain Daniel Romero, home tel. 744/483-4822) rents only entire, captained boats, including equipment and bait.

Rental prices and catches depend on the season. Drop by the dock after 2 P.M. to see what the boats are bringing in. During good times, boats might average one big marlin or sailfish apiece. Best months for sailfish *(pez vela)* are said to be Nov., Dec., and Jan.; for marlin, Feb. and March.

Big 40-foot boats with five or six fishing lines rent from $250 per day. Smaller boats, with three or four lines and holding five or six passengers, rent from around $200. All of the Cooperativa boats are radio-equipped, with toilet, life preservers, tackle, bait, and ice. Customers usually supply their own food and drinks. Although the Cooperativa is generally competent, look over the boat and check its equipment before putting your money down.

You can also arrange fishing trips through a travel agent or your hotel lobby tour desk.

Sailfish and marlin are neither the only nor necessarily the most desirable fish in the sea. Competently captained *pangas* can typically haul in three or four large 15- or 20-pound excellent-eating *robalo* (snook), *huachinango* (snapper), or *atún* (tuna) in two hours just outside Acapulco Bay.

Such lighter boats are rentable from the cooperative for about $20 per hour or from individual fishermen on Playa Las Hamacas (past the steamship dock at the foot of Fort San Diego).

Marina and Boat Docking
A safe place to dock your boat is the 150-slip **Marina Acapulco** on the Peninsula de las Playas' sheltered inner shoreline, Av. Costera M. Alemán 215, Fracc. Las Playas, Acapulco, Guerrero 39300, tel. 744/483-7498, fax 744/483-7436. Boat launching (30-foot maximum) runs about $25 per day. The slip rate is around $.65 per foot per day, including 110/220-volt power ($.20 per kilowatt-hour extra), potable water, pumpout, toilets, showers, ice, restaurant, hotel, repair facilities, customs and immigrations paperwork, and access to the marina pool except weekends and holidays. Get there via the driveway past the suspension bridge over the Costera about a mile southeast of the *zócalo*.

SHOPPING
Market
Acapulco, despite its modern glitz, has a very colorful traditional market, which is fun for strolling through even without buying anything. It is open daily, dawn to dusk. Vendors arrive here with grand intentions: mounds of neonred tomatoes, buckets of nopales (cactus leaves), towers of toilet paper, and mountains of soap

bars. As you wander through the sunlight-dappled aisles, past big gaping fish, bulging rounds of cheese, and festoons of huaraches, don't miss **Piñatas Amanda,** one of the market's friendliest shops. You may even end up buying one of Amanda's charming paper Donald Ducks, Snow Whites, or Porky Pigs. The market is at the corner of Mendoza and Constituyentes, a quarter mile inland from Hornos Beach. Ride a Mercado-marked bus or take a taxi.

Supermarkets and Department Stores
In the *zócalo* area, **Woolworth's** is a good source of a little bit of everything at reasonable prices, on Escudero, corner of Morelos, behind Sanborn's; open daily 9:30 A.M.–8:30 P.M. Its lunch counter, furthermore, provides a welcome refuge from the midday heat.

Comercial Mexicana, with three Acapulco branches, is a big Mexican Kmart, which, besides the expected film, medicines, cosmetics, and housewares, also includes groceries and a bakery. Its locations are: on the Costera, at Cinco de Mayo, just east of the Fort San Diego; on Farallones, a couple of blocks uphill from the Costera's Diana Circle; and two miles farther, across from CICI water park. All open daily 9 A.M.–9 P.M.

If you can't find what you want at Comercial Mexicana, try the huge **Sam's Club,** just uphill from the Farallones Comercial Mexicana, and the giant **Wal-Mart,** at the far east end, across from the Hyatt Regency.

Photography
Acapulco visitors enjoy the services of a number of photo stores. On the Costera, several outlets have come and gone during the past few years. However, **Foto System Lab** (and Internet access), tel. 744/482-2112, seems to be fixed on the *zócalo*, supplying photofinishing, a few cameras and accessories, and several popular film varieties. Open daily 8 A.M.–10 P.M. on the corner of J. Carranza, right side as you enter the *zócalo* from the Costera.

Also near the *zócalo*, get your camera repaired, at experienced **Foto y Mechanica,** corner of Iglesia and Hidalgo, one block west of the *zócalo*.

On the east-side Costera, among the several photo stores, try **Foto Diamante,** open daily 8 A.M.–9 P.M., half a block west of McDonald's restaurant, for one-hour film developing and a fair stock of film, accessories, and point-and-shoot cameras.

Handicrafts

Despite much competition, asking prices for Acapulco handicrafts are relatively high. Bargaining, furthermore, seldom brings them down to size. **Sanborn's,** tel. 744/482-4095, two blocks from the *zócalo,* at Costera M. Alemán and Escudero, is open daily 8 A.M.–11 P.M., with bookstore and restaurant. Sanborn's all-Mexico selection includes, notably, black Oaxaca *barra* pottery, painted gourds from Uruapan, Guadalajara leather, Taxco silver jewelry, colorful plates from Puebla, and Tlaquepaque pottery and glass.

With Sanborn's prices in mind, head one block toward the *zócalo* to **Bonita** handicrafts store, where, in the basement of the big old Edificio Oviedo, glitters an eclectic fiesta of Mexican jewelry. Find it at I. de la Llave and Costera M. Alemán, local 1, tel. 744/482-0590 or 744/482-5240; open Mon.–Sat. 9 A.M.–7 P.M., Sun. (seasonally only) 9 A.M.–3 P.M. Never mind if the place is empty; cruise-line passengers regularly fill the aisles. Here you'll be able to see artisans adding to the acre of gleaming silver, gold, copper, brass, fine carving, and lacquerware around you. Don't forget to get your free margarita (or soft drink) before you leave.

Another bountiful handicrafts source near the *zócalo* is the artisans' market **Mercado de Parrazal.** From Sanborn's, head away from the Costera a few short blocks to Vasquez de León and turn right one block. There, a big plaza of semipermanent stalls offers a galaxy of Mexican handicrafts: Tonalá and Tlaquepaque papier-mâché, brass, and pottery animals; Bustamante-replica eggs, masks, and humanoids; Oaxaca wooden animals and black pottery; Guerrero masks; and Taxco jewelry. Sharp bargaining is necessary, however, to cut the excessive asking prices down to size.

For largely inexpensive, but still attractive, native-made handicrafts, go to the large indigenous **mercado de artesanías** warren of stalls, on the mid-Costera, just east of the Diana Circle, inland side.

Local artist Blanca Silviera has built a thriving business fashioning *alebrijes* (ahl-BREE-hays), fanciful painted animals. Stop by her handicrafts shop, **Alebrijes,** local 13, main floor, in the shopping Plaza Bahía, just west of the Hotel Costa Club. Open daily 10 A.M.–10 P.M.

INFORMATION
Tourist Information Office

An easily accessible local tourist information office is the *modulo* in front of the Convention Center, two blocks east of the golf course, tel. 744/484-4416 or 744/484-4583. Here, workers staff a small crafts shop, money exchange office, daily 9 A.M.–9 P.M.

Publications

The best new-book sources in town are **Sanborn's** three Acapulco branches: east to west, on the Costera, tel. 744/484-2035, open daily 7:30–1 A.M., ground floor of the east-side Oceanic 2000 shopping plaza, beach side of the Costera, a few blocks from the east end. Alternatively, try Sanborn's mid-Costera branch, tel. 744/482-2426, at the Hotel Calinda; or its *zócalo* branch, tel. 744/482-4095, open daily 7 A.M.–11 P.M., on the Costera across from the steamship dock, which stocks a similar, but smaller assortment.

English-language international newspapers, such as the Mexico City *News,* the *Los Angeles Times,* and *USA Today,* are often available in the large hotel bookshops, especially the Hotel Costa Club, Fiesta Americana Condesa, and the Hyatt Regency. In old town, newsstands around the *zócalo* regularly sell the *News* from Mexico City.

Pick up the commercial but handy and widely available American Express–sponsored tourist booklet *Acapulco Passport* free at a hotel, store, or travel agency.

Acapulco's former expatriate and tourist English-language newspaper *Acapulco Heat* has gone completely electronic, as the website www.acabtu.com.mx. It provides many useful links to mostly midscale hotels, restaurants, community events and organizations, travel activities, and entertainment.

Public Library

The small, friendly Acapulco *biblioteca* is near the *zócalo* adjacent to the cathedral, at Madero 5, corner of Quebrada, tel. 744/482-0388. Its collection, used mostly by college and high school students in the airy reading room, is nearly all in Spanish. Open Mon.–Fri. 9 A.M.–9 P.M., Sat. 9 A.M.–2 P.M.

Language Instruction

Get Spanish language instruction at the reputable private **Universidad Americana** on the Costera, approximately across from the Hotel Costa Club. For more information, contact coordinator Elba Molina, at the university at Costera Miguel Alemán 1756, Fracc. Magellanes, Acapulco 39670, tel. 744/486-5618, ext. 122, or 744/486-5619, ext. 122, uamerica@aca.uamericana.mx, www.uaa.edu.mx.

Service Club

The **Friends of Acapulco** charitable club holds fund-raising fiestas and fashion shows to support the Acapulco Children's home and other local good works. For information, write P.O. Box C-54, Acapulco, Guerrero 39300.

SERVICES

Money Exchange

In the *zócalo* neighborhood, long-hours **Banco Internacional** is the best bet, tel. 744/483-5722, open Mon.–Sat. 8 A.M.–7 P.M., at no. 8 Jesús Carranza, the one-block side street, tucked near the *zócalo*'s northeast corner. Alternatively, go to **Bancomer,** fronting the Costera, tel. 744/484-8055, to change U.S. cash or traveler's checks only, Mon.–Fri. 9 A.M.–4 P.M., Sat. 10 A.M.–2 P.M. Although the lines at **Banamex,** tel. 744/483-6425, nearby, two blocks from the *zócalo* next to Sanborn's, are usually longer, it exchanges major currencies Mon.–Fri. 9 A.M.–4 P.M. You can avoid the lines by using the bank **ATM**

machines, which are routinely connected with international networks.

On the new side of town, also change money at **Banco Internacional** across from McDonald's, open Mon.–Sat. 8 A.M.–7 P.M., tel. 744/485-5309; or at **Bancomer,** a few blocks west of the Glorieta Diana (Diana Circle), tel. 744/484-7245, open Mon.–Fri. 9 A.M.–4 P.M., Sat. 9 A.M.–2 P.M. for U.S. and Canadian currency and traveler's checks.

After hours on the Costera, the **Consultorio International,** tel. 744/484-3108, in Galería Picuda shopping center, across the street and a block west from the Hotel Fiesta Americana Condesa, exchanges currency and traveler's checks Mon.–Sat. 9 A.M.–7 P.M., Sun. 9 A.M.–3 P.M.

American Express Office

The Acapulco American Express branch, at Costera M. Alemán 1628, tel. 744/469-1121, 744/469-1122, 744/469-1123, or 744/469-1124, west end, across from McDonald's, cashes American Express traveler's checks at near-bank rates and provides member financial services and travel agency services. It's open Mon.–Fri. 10 A.M.–7 P.M., Sat. 10 A.M.–2 P.M., although check-cashing hours may be shorter.

Communications

The Acapulco main *correo* (post office) is in the Palacio Federal across the Costera from the steamer dock three blocks from the *zócalo*. It provides Mexpost fast, secure mail and philatelic services, Mon.–Sat. 8 A.M.–8 P.M. A branch **post and telegraph office** at the Estrella de Oro bus terminal, Cuauhtémoc and Massieu, is open Mon.–Fri. 9 A.M.–8 P.M., Sat. 9 A.M.–noon.

Telecomunicaciones, tel. 744/482-2622 or 744/482-2621, next to the main post office, provides money order, telegram, telex, and fax services, Mon.–Fri. 8 A.M.–8 P.M. and Sat.–Sun. 9 A.M.–noon.

In mid-Costera, go to the small branch post, tel. 744/484-8029, and Telecom, tel. 744/484-6976, offices at the Centro de Convenciones (Convention Center), both open Mon.–Fri. 9 A.M.–3 P.M.

For lowest **telephone** rates, use the widely available Ladatel cards in the many public street telephones. First dial 001 for long distance to the United States and Canada and 01 for Mexico. Otherwise, near the *zócalo,* you can call **larga distancia** daily 8 A.M.–10 P.M. from either the small office on J. Carranza at Calle de la Llave, or on the *zócalo*'s other side, next to Restaurant Los Amigos, Mon.–Fri. 9 A.M.–9 P.M., Sat. and Sun. 9 A.M.–2 P.M. and 4–9 P.M.

Beware of certain private "To Call Long Distance to the U.S.A. Collect and Credit Card" telephones installed prominently in airports, tourist hotels, and shops. Tariffs on these phones often run as high as $10 per minute (with a three-minute minimum), for a total of $30, whether you talk three minutes or not. Always ask the operator for the rate, and if it's too high, take your business elsewhere.

Health, Police, and Emergencies

If you get sick, ask your hotel to call a doctor for you or contact the **Hospital Magellanes,** one of Acapulco's most respected private hospitals, for both office calls or round-the-clock emergencies. Facilities include a lab, 24-hour pharmacy, and an emergency room with many specialists on call, at W. Massieu 2, corner of Colón, one block from the Costera and the Hotel Qualton Club; tel. 744/485-6544 or 744/485-6597, ext. 119, for the pharmacy.

A group of American-trained **IAMAT** (International Association for Medical Assistance to Travelers) **physicians** offers medical consultations in English. Contact them at the medical department, Hotel Fairmont Acapulco Princess, tel. 744/469-1000, ext. 1309.

For routine medications near the *zócalo,* go to one of many pharmacies, such as at **Sanborn's,** corner of Escudero and the Costera, tel. 744/482-6167, or the big **Farmacia Discuento** (discount pharmacy), tel. 744/482-0804, open daily 8 A.M.–10 P.M., at Escudero and Carranza, across the street from Woolworth's.

For police emergencies, contact one of the many **tourist police** (on the Costera, in safari pith helmets), tel. 744/485-0650 or 744/486/8220, or call the officers at the municipal police Papagayo station, tel. 744/485-

0490, at the end of Av. Camino Sonora, on the inland side of Papagayo Park.

In case of fire, call the **bomberos,** tel. 744/484-4122, on Av. Farallón, behind Comercial Mexicana, two blocks off the Costera from the Glorieta Diana.

Immigration and Customs

If you lose your tourist card go to **Migración,** at the airport (sufficiently early on your day of departure), or on the Costera, across the traffic circle from Comercial Mexicana, same side of the Costera, tel. 744/484-9022, open Mon.–Fri. 9 A.M.–1 P.M. Bring proof of your identity and some proof (such as your stamped passport, airline ticket, or a copy of your lost tourist card) of your arrival date in Mexico. If you try to leave Mexico without your tourist card, you may face trouble and a fine. Also report to Migración if you arrive in Acapulco by yacht.

The **Aduana** (Customs) office, tel. 744/466-9005, on the Costera, *zócalo* area, at the dock, across from Sanborn's, is open Mon.–Fri. 8 A.M.–3 P.M. If you have to temporarily leave your car in Mexico, check to see what paperwork, if any, must be completed.

Consulates

Acapulco has several consular agents and officers. The offices of the U.S. consular officer, Alexander Richards, tel. 744/481-1699, 744/484-0300, or 744/481-0100, fax 744/484-0300, Mon.–Fri. 10 A.M.–2 P.M., consular@prodigy.net.mx., are in the Hotel Continental Plaza. He's a busy man and asks that you kindly have your problem written down, together with a specific request for information or action. In emergencies only, contact him at tel. 744/431-0094.

The **Canadian consul**, Diane McLean de Huerta, tel. 744/484-1305, fax 744/484-1306 or 744/481-1349, holds office hours Mon.–Fri. 9 A.M.–5 P.M., at the Centro Comercial Marbella, suite 23. After hours, in an emergency, call toll-free Mex. tel. 800/706-2900.

For the **British consul,** Lorraine Bajas, call tel. 744/484-1735. Contact the **German consul,** Mario Wichtendahl, at Antone de Alamino 26, tel. 744/484-1860. The **Netherlands consul,** Ángel Díaz, can be reached by dialing tel. 744/486-6179.

For additional information and assistance, the consulates maintain a joint **Consular Corps** office, open Mon.–Fri. 9 A.M.–2 P.M., in the Centro de Convenciones (Convention Center) just east of the golf course, tel. 744/481-2533.

Laundry

Near the *zócalo,* get your laundry done at **Lavandería Laradin** open Mon.–Sat. 8 A.M.–10 P.M., at the corner of Iglesias and La Paz, one block west of the *zócalo.*

GETTING THERE AND AWAY

By Air

Several airlines connect the **Acapulco airport** (code-designated ACA, officially the Juan N. Álvarez International Airport) with U.S. and Mexican destinations.

Aeroméxico flights connect directly with Houston via Mexico City, Monterrey, Tijuana and Guadalajara. For reservations, contact Aeroméxico at tel. 744/485-1625 or 744/485-1600. For flight information, call the airport at tel. 744/466-9296 or 744/466-9109.

Mexicana Airlines flights connect five times daily with Mexico City. For reservations, call tel. 744/486-7586 or 744/486-7587, or toll-free Mex. tel. 800/502-2000; for flight information, call the airport at tel. 744/466-9136 or 744/466-9138.

America West Airlines flights connect with Phoenix; for reservations and information, call a local travel agent, such as American Express, tel. 744/469-1124 or toll-free U.S. tel. 800/235-9292.

Continental Airlines flights connect with Houston. For reservations, call a travel agent or toll-free Mex. tel. 800/900-5000; for flight information, call tel. 744/466-9063.

American Airlines flights connect with Dallas during the winter season. For reservations, call a travel agent, or toll-free Mex. tel. 800/904-6000; for flight information, call the airport at tel. 744/466-9227.

Aviacsa Airlines flights connect with Guadalajara, Mexico City, and Cuernavaca. For reserva-

tions, call tel. 744/486-0002 or 744/486/5630; for flight information, call the airport, at tel. 744/466-9013.

Delta Air Lines Aéromexico affiliate charter flights connect with Los Angeles, Portland, and Dallas during the winter season. For reservations, call a travel agent or Delta at toll-free Mex. tel. 800/902-2100.

Canadian **World of Vacations** charter flights connect with Winnipeg and Toronto during the winter-spring season. For reservations, call a travel agent, such as American Express, tel. 744/469-1124, or the local Canadian agent, tel. 744/446-5716.

Air Arrival and Departure

After the usually quick immigration and customs checks, Acapulco arrivees enjoy airport car rentals, efficient transportation for the 15-mile trip to town, post box *(buzon),* and ATMs.

Local car rental agents often available for arriving flights include Hertz, tel. 744/485-8947 or 744/485-6889; Avis, tel. 744/466-9190 or 744/466-0075; Alamo, tel. 744/466-9444 or 744/484-3305; Budget, tel. 744/481-2433; Quick, tel. 744/486-3420 or 744/486-2197; and SAAD jeep rentals, tel. 744/484-3445, 744/484-5325, or 744/466-9179. You can ensure availability and often save money by bargaining for a reservation with agencies via their national toll-free numbers (see chart "Car Rental Agencies" in the On the Road chapter).

Tickets for **ground transport** to town are sold by agents near the terminal exit. Options include collective GMC Suburban station wagon (about $8), that deposits passengers at individual hotels. *Taxis especiales* run about $11 to $22, depending on distance. GMC Suburbans can be hired *"especial"* as private taxis for $35–45 for up to seven passengers.

On your departure day, save money by sharing a taxi with fellow departees. Don't get into the taxi until you settle the fare. Having already arrived, you know what the airport ride should cost. If the driver insists on greed, hail another taxi.

Simplify your departure by saving $17 or its peso equivalent for your international (or $12 national) departure tax, if your ticket doesn't already cover it. If you lost your tourist permit (which immigration stamped upon your arrival) either go to Migración, tel. tel. 744/484-9022 (see Services) before your departure date, or arrive early enough at the airport to iron out the problem with airport Migración officials, tel. 744/446-9025, before departure. Bring some proof of your date of arrival, either a stamped passport, airline ticket copy, or a copy of your lost tourist permit.

The Acapulco air terminal building has a number of shops upstairs for last-minute handicrafts purchases, a *buzón* (mailbox), stamp vending machine, long-distance telephones (be sure to ask the operator for the price before completing a call), and a restaurant.

By Bus

Major competitors Estrella Blanca and Estrella de Oro operate three separate long-distance *centrales de autobús* (central bus terminals), one (Estrella Blanca (the Ejido) station on the west side) and two (both Estrella Blanca and Estrella de Oro) stations on the east side of town.

Estrella Blanca, tel. 744/469-2028, 744/469-2029, or 744/469-2030, coordinates the service of its subsidiary lines Elite, Flecha Roja, Autotransportes Cuauhtémoc, Turistar, Futura, and Gacela at two separate terminals. Credit cards are accepted. Most first- or luxury-class departures use the big west-side **Ejido** terminal at Av. Ejido 47. The airy station is so clean you could sleep on the polished onyx floor and not get dirty; bring an air mattress and blanket. Other conveniences include left-luggage lockers, food stores across the street, a deluxe and midscale hotel booking agency, and Sendatel 24-hour *larga distancia* and fax office open daily 6 A.M.–10 P.M.

Also from the Ejido station, scores of Estrella Blanca *salidas locales* (local departures) connect with destinations in three directions: northern interior, Costa Grande (northwest), and Costa Chica (southeast) coastal destinations. Most connections are first-class Elite, Turistar, and Futura. Specific northern interior connections include Mexico City (dozens daily, some via Taxco), Toluca, Morelia via Chilpancingo and Altamirano (six daily), and Guadalajara (three daily).

Many first-class (about 10 per day) and sec-ond-class (hourly) departures connect northwest with Costa Grande destinations of Zihuatanejo and Lázaro Cárdenas. Southeast Costa Chica connections with Puerto Escondido, some continuing to Huatulco and Salina Cruz, include four first-class daily (one via Ometepec) and several second-class connections per day.

Also from the Av. Ejido Estrella Blanca terminal, one or two daily departures connect with the U.S. border (Mexicali and Tijuana) via the entire Pacific coast route, through Zihuatanejo, Manzanillo, Puerto Vallarta, and Mazatlán. Other departures connect with the U.S. border at Ciudad Juárez, via San Luis Potosí, Zacatecas, Torreón, and Chihuahua.

Many additional first- and luxury-class buses depart from Estrella Blanca's separate west-side big **Papagayo** terminal, on Av. Cuauhtémoc, tel. 744/469-2028 or 744/469-2029, about five blocks west of the Estrella de Oro Terminal. Facilities and services include an a/c waiting room, left-luggage service, fax (744/485-8331) service, a snack bar, and hotel reservations. From the Papagayo terminal, luxury-class and first-class buses connect with northeast Mexico and the U.S. border, via Querétaro, San Luis Potosí, Monterrey, and Nuevo Laredo. Other departures connect northwest, with Guadalajara, León, Celaya, and Irapuato; and north with Puebla and Mexico City bus stations Norte and Sur; and northwest, with Zihuatanejo.

The busy, modern **Estrella de Oro** bus terminal on the east side of town, at Cuauhtémoc and Massieu, tel. 744/485-8758, 744/485-8705, or 744/485-9360, provides connections with the Mexico City corridor (Chilpancingo, Iguala, Taxco, Cuernavaca, Mexico City) and northwest Costa Grande destinations via Zihuatanejo with Lázaro Cárdenas. Services include left-luggage lockers, but no food except sweets, chips, and drinks. Correo (post) and telecomunicaciones (telephone, fax, and money orders) offices, open Mon.–Sat. 8 A.M.–9 P.M., are on the outside upstairs walkway, west end.

Estrella de Oro departures include dozens of first- and luxury-class with Mexico City and intermediate points. Several connect directly through Taxco. Four departures connect daily

MEXICO CITY DRIVING RESTRICTIONS

To reduce smog and traffic gridlock, authorities have limited which cars can drive on which days in Mexico City, depending upon the last digit of their license plates. If you violate these rules, you risk getting an expensive ticket. On Monday, no vehicle may be driven with final digits 5 or 6; Tuesday, 7 or 8; Wednesday, 3 or 4; Thursday, 1 or 2; Friday, 9 or 0. Weekends, all vehicles may be driven.

with Costa the Grande, three with Zihuatanejo, one only with Lázaro Cárdenas. Estrella de Oro offers no Costa Chica (Puerto Escondido) connections southeast.

By Car or RV

Good highways connect Acapulco north with Mexico City, northwest with the Costa Grande and Michoacán, and southeast with the Costa Chica and Oaxaca.

The Mexico City Highway 95 *cuota* (toll) superhighway would make the connection via Chilpancingo easy (83 miles, 133 km, about two hours) if it weren't for the Acapulco congestion. (Go by the toll tunnel.) The uncluttered extension (125 miles, 201 km) to Cuernavaca via Iguala is a breeze in 2.5 hours. For Taxco, leave the superhighway at Iguala

and follow the winding but scenic old Highway 95 cutoff 22 miles (35 km) northwest. From Cuernavaca, the over-the-mountain leg to Mexico City (53 miles, 85 km) would be simple except for possible Mexico City gridlock, which might lengthen it to two hours. Better allow a minimum of around 5.5 driving hours for the entire 261-mile (420-km) Acapulco-Mexico City trip.

The Costa Grande section of Highway 200 northwest toward Zihuatanejo is generally uncluttered and smooth (except for occasional bumps and potholes). Allow about four hours for the 150-mile (242-km) trip.

The same is true for the Costa Chica stretch of Highway 200 southeast to Pinotepa Nacional (157 miles, 253 km) and Puerto Escondido (247 miles, 398 km total). Allow about four driving hours to Pinotepa, 6.5 hours total to Puerto Escondido.

Acapulco's most congested ingress-egress bottleneck used to be the over-the-hill leg of Highway 95 from the middle of town. Although this route has speeded up by an expesive (about $6) one-mile toll tunnel, the scenery is much prettier if you drive east along the Costera past Hotel Las Brisas as if you were heading to the airport. At the big cloverleaf intersection downhill, near Puerto Marques, head north. When you reach Highway 200, head right for the Costa Chica, or left for Highway 95 and northern points.

Taxco

As Acapulco thrives on what's new, Taxco (pop. 150,000) luxuriates in what's old. Nestling beneath forest-crowned mountains and decorated with monuments of its silver-rich past, Taxco now enjoys an equally rich flood of visitors who stop en route to or from Acapulco. They come to enjoy its fiestas and clear, pine-scented air and to stroll the cobbled hillside lanes and bargain for world-renowned silver jewelry.

And despite the acclaim, Taxco preserves its diminutive colonial charm *because* of its visitors, who come to enjoy what Taxco offers. They stay in venerable, family-owned lodgings, walk to the colorful little *zócalo,* where they admire the famous baroque cathedral, and wander among the awning-festooned market lanes just downhill.

HISTORY

The traditional hieroglyph representing Taxco shows athletes in a court competing in a game of *tlatchtli* (still locally played) with a solid, natural rubber *(hule)* ball. "Tlachco," the Náhuatl name representing the place that had become a small Aztec garrison settlement by the eve of the conquest, literally translates as "Place of the Ball Game." The Spanish, more interested in local minerals than in linguistic details, shifted the name to Taxco.

Colonization

In 1524, Hernán Cortés, looking for tin to alloy with copper to make bronze cannon, heard that people around Taxco were using bits of metal for money. Prospectors hurried out, and within a few years they struck rich silver veins in Tetelcingo, now known as Taxco Viejo (Old Taxco), seven miles downhill from present-day Taxco. The Spanish crown appropriated the mines and worked them with generations of native forced labor.

Eighteenth-century enlightenment came to Taxco in the person of José Borda, who, arriving from Spain in 1716, modernized the mine franchise his brother had been operating. José improved conditions and began paying the miners,

thereby increasing productivity and profits. In contrast to past operators, Borda returned the proceeds to Taxco, building the monuments that still grace the town. His fortune built streets, bridges, fountains, arches, and his masterpiece, the church of Santa Prisca, which included a special chapel for the miners, who before had not been allowed to enter the church.

Independence and Modern Times

The 1810–1821 War of Independence and the subsequent civil strife, within a generation, reduced the mines to but a memory. They were nearly forgotten when William Spratling, an American artist and architect, moved to Taxco in

© BRUCE WHIPPERMAN

The Santa Prisca Church's ornate baroque scrollwork is sometimes called "Plateresque" (silver-like) because it resembles traditional European silver plate designs.

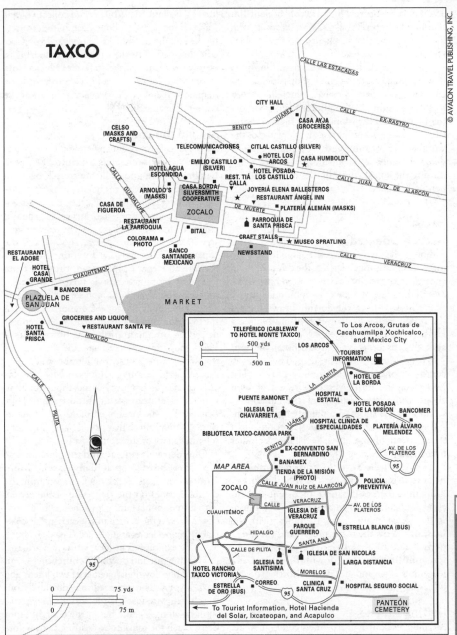

TAXCO

CELSO (MASKS AND CRAFTS)

CITY HALL

CASA AYJA (GROCERIES)

CALLE LAS ESTACADAS

BENITO · JUAREZ · CALLE · EX-RASTRO

TELECOMUNICACIONES

CITLAL CASTILLO (SILVER)

HOTEL LOS ARCOS

CASA HUMBOLDT

EMILIO CASTILLO (SILVER)

HOTEL AGUA ESCONDIDA

HOTEL POSADA LOS CASTILLO

REST. TIA CALLA

CALLE JUAN RUIZ DE ALARCON

ARNOLDO'S (MASKS)

CASA BORDA/ SILVERSMITH COOPERATIVE

JOYERIA ELENA BALLESTEROS

RESTAURANT ÁNGEL INN

CASA DE FIGUEROA

ZOCALO

DE MUERTE

PLATERÍA ALEMÁN (MASKS)

RESTAURANT LA PARROQUIA

PARROQUIA DE SANTA PRISCA

COLORAMA PHOTO

BITAL

MUSEO SPRATLING

RESTAURANT EL ADOBE

BANCO SANTANDER MEXICANO

CRAFT STALLS

NEWSSTAND

CALLE VERACRUZ

HOTEL CASA GRANDE

CUAUHTEMOC

BANCOMER

PLAZUELA DE SAN JUAN

MARKET

GROCERIES AND LIQUOR

HOTEL SANTA PRISCA

RESTAURANT SANTA FE

HIDALGO

CALLE DE PILITA

MOON

95

TELEFÉRICO (CABLEWAY TO HOTEL MONTE TAXCO)

To Los Arcos, Grutas de Cacahuamilpa Xochicalco, and Mexico City

0   500 yds
0   500 m

LOS ARCOS

TOURIST INFORMATION

PUENTE RAMONET

LA GARITA

HOTEL DE LA BORDA

IGLESIA DE CHAVARRIETA

HOSPITAL ESTATAL

HOTEL POSADA DE LA MISIÓN

BANCOMER

JUÁREZ

HOSPITAL CLINICA DE ESPECIALIDADES

PLATERÍA ÁLVARO MELENDEZ

BIBLIOTECA TAXCO-CANOGA PARK

BENITO

EX-CONVENTO SAN BERNARDINO

AV. DE LOS PLATEROS

95

MAP AREA

BANAMEX

TIENDA DE LA MISIÓN (PHOTO)

POLICIA PREVENTIVA

ZOCALO

CALLE JUAN RUÍZ DE ALARCÓN

CUAUHTÉMOC

CALLE

VERACRUZ

AV. DE LOS PLATEROS

IGLESIA DE VERACRUZ

HIDALGO

PARQUE GUERRERO

SANTA ANA

ESTRELLA BLANCA (BUS)

CALLE DE PILITA

IGLESIA DE SAN NICOLAS

HOTEL RANCHO TAXCO VICTORIA

IGLESIA DE SANTISIMA

LARGA DISTANCIA

MORELOS

ESTRELLA DE ORO (BUS)

CORREO

CLINICA SANTA CRUZ

HOSPITAL SEGURO SOCIAL

95

PANTEÓN CEMETERY

To Tourist Information, Hotel Hacienda del Solar, Ixcateopan, and Acapulco

0   75 yds
0   75 m

1929 and began reviving Taxco's ancient but moribund silversmithing tradition. Working with local artisans, Spratling opened the first cooperative shop, Las Delicias.

Spurred by the trickle of tourists along the new Acapulco highway, more shops opened, increasing the demand for silver, which in turn led to the reopening of the mines. Soon silver demand outpaced the supply. Silver began streaming in from other parts of Mexico to the workbenches of thousands of artisans in hundreds of family- and cooperatively owned shops dotting the still-quaint hillsides of a new, prosperous Taxco.

SIGHTS

Getting Oriented

Although the present city, elev. 5,850 feet (1,780 meters), spreads much farther, the center of town encompasses the city's original seven hills, wrinkles in the slope of a towering mountain.

For most visitors, the downhill town limit is the *carretera,* the local stretch of old National Highway 95, now named Av. de los Plateros, after the Taxco *plateros* (silversmiths) who put Taxco on Mexico's tourism map. The highway contours along the hillside from **Los Arcos** (The Arches) on the north, Mexico City, end of town about two miles, passing the Calle Pilita intersection on the south, Acapulco, edge of town. Along the *carretera,* immediately accessible to a steady stream of tour buses, lie the town's plusher hotels and many silver shops.

The rest of the town is fortunately insulated from tour buses by its narrow winding streets. From the *carretera,* the most important of them climb and converge, like bent spokes of a wheel, to the *zócalo* (main plaza). Beginning with the most northerly, the main streets (and the directions they run) are La Garita (uphill), Alarcón (downhill), Veracruz (downhill), Santa Ana (downhill), Salubridad (uphill), Morelos (downhill), and Pilita (downhill).

Getting Around

Although walking is Taxco's most common mode of transport, taxis go anywhere within the city

limits for about $2. White *combi* collective vans (fare about $.30) follow designated routes, marked on the windshields. Simply tell your specific destination to the driver. For side trips to nearby towns and villages, a fleet of **Flecha Roja** second-class local buses and *colectivo* vans leave frequently from their *carretera* terminal near the corner of Veracruz.

Around the Zócalo

All roads in Taxco begin and end on the *zócalo* at **Santa Prisca church.** French architect D. Diego Durán designed and built the church between 1751 and 1758 with money from the fortune of silver king Don José Borda. The facade, decorated with saints on pedestals, arches, and spiraled columns, follows the baroque churrigueresque style (after Jose Churriguera, 1665–1725, the "Spanish Michelangelo"). Interior furnishings include an elegant pipe organ, brought from Germany by muleback (via boat to Veracruz, thence overland) in 1751, and several gilded side altars. The riot of interior elaboration climaxes in the towering gold-leaf main altar, which seems to drip with ornamentation in tribute to Santa Prisca, the Virgin of Guadalupe, and the Virgin of the Rosary, who piously preside above all.

Dreamy Bible-story paintings by Miguel Cabrera decorate a chamber behind the main altar, while in a room to the right, portraits of Pope Benedict IV, who sanctioned all this, and Manuel Borda, Santa Prisca's first priest, hang amongst a solemn gallery of subsequent padres.

Outside, landmarks around the plaza include the **Casa Borda,** open daily except Mon. 10 A.M.–8 P.M., visible (as you face away from the church facade) on the right side of the *zócalo.* This former Borda family town house, built concurrently with the church in typical baroque colonial style, now serves as the Taxco Casa de Cultura, featuring exhibitions by local artists and artisans.

Heading out and down the church steps, you can continue downhill in either of two interesting ways. If you walk left immediately downhill from the church, you reach the lane Calle Los Arcos, running alongside and below the church. From there, reach the **market** by heading right before the quaint archway over the street, down the winding staircase-lane, where you'll soon be in a warren of awning-covered stalls.

If, however, you head right from the church steps, another immediate right leads you beside the church along legendary **Calle de Muerte** (Street of Death), so named because of the former cemetery where the workers who died constructing the church were buried. (Note the skeleton on the church-front corner facing Calle de Muerte.)

Continuing downhill, you'll find **Museo Guillermo Spratling,** fronting the little plaza behind the church. On the main and upper floors, the National Institute of Archaeology displays intriguing carvings and ceramics (including unusual phallic examples), such as a ball-game ring, animal masks, and a priestly statuette with knife in one hand, human heart in the other. Basement-floor displays interestingly detail local history from the Aztecs through William Spratling. The museum is open seasonally Tues.–Sat. 9 A.M.–6 P.M., Sun. 9 A.M.–3 P.M., although hours may vary seasonally, tel. 762/622-1660.

Back outside, one block down Alarcón (the downhill extension of Calle de Muerte), stands the **Casa Humboldt,** after the celebrated geographer (who is said to have stayed only one night, however). Now the state maintains it as the Museum of Viceregal (read colonial) Art. Displays feature a permanent collection of historical artifacts, including the Manila galleon, colonial technology, and colonial religious sculpture and painting. Open Tues.–Sat. 10 A.M.–5 P.M., Sun. 10 A.M.–4 P.M., although winter hours may be shorter, tel. 762/622-5501.

Nearby, the **Museo Platería,** 4 Alarcón, third floor, next door to the Hotel Posada, illustrates a history of Taxco silvercraft and displays outstanding pieces by local artisans. Open daily 10 A.M.–6 P.M. (Alternately, you may enter the museum through the *zócalo*-front shopping patio de Las Artesanías, next to the Casa Borda.)

Other In-Town Sights

A short ride, coupled with a walk circling back to the *zócalo,* provides the basis for an interesting half-day exploration. Taxi or ride a *combi* to the Hotel Posada de la Misión, where the **Cuauhtémoc Mural** glitters on a wall near the pool. Exe-

cuted by renowned muralist Juan O'Gorman with a riot of pre-Columbian symbols—yellow sun, pearly rabbit-in-the-moon, snarling jaguar, writhing serpents, fluttering eagle—the mural glorifies Cuauhtémoc, the last Aztec emperor. Cuauhtémoc, unlike his uncle Moctezuma, tenaciously resisted the conquest, but was captured and later executed by Cortés in 1525. His remains were discovered not long ago in Ixcateopan, about 24 miles away by local bus or car. (See Excursions.)

Continue your walk a few hundred yards along the *carretera* (Mexico City direction) from the Hotel Posada de la Misión. There, a driveway leading right just before the gas station heads to the Hotel Borda grounds. Turn left on the road just after the gate and you'll come to an antique brick smelter chimney and cable-hung derrick. These mark an inactive **mineshaft** descending to the mine-tunnel honeycomb thousands of feet beneath the town. The mines are still being worked from another entrance, but for mostly lead rather than silver. You can see the present-day works from the hilltop of the Hotel Hacienda del Solar on the south edge of town.

Now, return to the *carretera,* cross over and stroll the **Calle la Garita** about a mile back to the *zócalo.* Of special interest, besides a number of crafts stores and stalls, are the **Iglesia de Chavarrieta,** the **Biblioteca Taxco-Canoga Park** (library, with many English-language novels and reference books, open Mon.–Fri. 10 A.M.–7 P.M., Sat. 10 A.M.–1 P.M.), and the **ex-Convento San Bernardino.**

Farther on, a block before the *zócalo,* pause to decipher the colored stone mosaic of the **Taxco Hieroglyph,** which decorates the pavement in front of the Palacio Municipal (City Hall). Inside, climb the stairs for a balcony-front view of the hieroglyph and the wall mural for a graphic review of Mexican history. See the main actors, from left to right: stolid Benito Juárez ("Respect for the rights of all is peace"); elderly General Porfirio Díaz gives away church and communal land to foreigners; banderilla-laden Emiliano Zapata declares his Plan de Ayala; President Lázaro Cárdenas in overalls expropriates foreign oil

companies; and Aldolfo López Mateos declares
free school textbooks; while Juárez, Kennedy,
Kissinger, de Gaulle, and Nehru look on.

Cableway (Teleférico) to Hotel Monte Taxco

On the north side of town, where the *carretera*
passes beneath Los Arcos, a cableway above the
highway lifts passengers to soaring vistas of the
town on one side and ponderous, pine-stud-
ded mesas on the other. Open daily
7:30 A.M.–7:30 P.M.; round-trip tickets about
$4, kids half price; return by taxi if you miss the
last car. The ride ends at the Hotel Monte
Taxco, where you can make a day of it golf-
ing, horseback riding, playing tennis, eating
lunch, and sunning on the panoramic-view
pool deck.

Cristo del Monte

Above the opposite, west, side of town, about
two miles uphill from the *zócalo*, stands the
colossal new stone statue of Jesus, where folks
enjoy an airy panoramic town view framed by
lush, green looming mountains. Get there on
foot (if you relish a 1,500-foot climb, wear a
hat and carry water) or by taxi (about $2.50),
colectivo (to Casahuates village), or car, west
from the *zócalo*, via Calle Cuauhtémoc, past
the Hotel Victoria. After about two miles (three
km); fork right at the Huixteco sign and continue past Casahuates village about about 200
yards, where a dirt driveway leads right to the
Cristo del Monte park.

In-Town Vistas

You needn't go as far afield as the Hotel Monte
Taxco or the Cristo del Monte to get a good
view of the city streets and houses carpeting
the mountainside. Vistas depend not only on
vantage point but time of day, since the best
viewing sunshine (which frees you from squinting) should come generally from *behind*. Consequently, spots along the highway (more or
less east of town), such as the patios of the
Hotel Posada de la Misión and the *mirador*
atop the Hotel Borda, provide good morning
views, while afternoon views are best from

The Cristo del Monte offers a panoramic view of the town.

points west of town, such as the restaurant balcony or the hilltop of the Hotel Rancho Taxco
Victoria.

EXCURSIONS

The monumental duo of the Grutas de Cacahuamilpa caves and the ruins of ancient Xochicalco makes for a fascinating day trip. Start early;
the Grutas are 15 miles (25 km) north (Mexico
City direction) of town and Xochicalco is 25
miles (40 km) farther.

Grutas de Cacahuamilpa

They're well worth the effort. The Grutas de Cacahuamilpa (kah-kah-ooah-MEEL-pah) are one
of the world's great cavern complexes. Forests of
stalagmites and stalactites, in myriad shapes—
Pluto the Pup, the Holy Family, a desert caravan,
asparagus stalks, cauliflower heads—festoon a series of gigantic limestone chambers. The finale is a

grand, 30-story hall that meanders for half a mile, like a fairyland in stone. The caves are open daily; hourly three-mile, two-hour walking tours in Spanish are included in the $5 admission and begin at 10 A.M. A few gift shops sell souvenirs; snack bars supply food.

Getting There: *Combi* collective vans leave hourly for the caves, beginning at 8:30 A.M., from just north of the Estrella Blanca bus station on the *carretera*. Watch for "Grutas" written on the windshields; expect to pay about $4 for a one-way fare. By car, get to the caves via Highway 95 north from Taxco; after 10 miles (16 km) from the northside Pemex station, fork left onto Highway 55 toward Toluca. Continue five more miles (eight km) and turn right at the signed Grutas de Cacahuamilpa junction. After a few hundred yards, turn right again into the entrance driveway.

Xochicalco

Xochicalco (soh-shee-KAHL-koh), an hour farther north, although little publicized, is a foun-tainhead of Mesoamerican legend. The archeological zone, officially designated as a United Nations World Heritage site, spreads over a half dozen terraced pyramid hilltops above a natural lake-valley, which at one time sustained a large population. Xochicalco flowered during the late classic period around A.D. 800, partly filling the vacuum left by the decline of Teotihuacán, the previously dominant Mesoamerican classic city-state. Some archaeologists speculate that Xochicalco at its apex was the great center of learning, known in legend as Tamanchoan, where astronomer-priests derived and maintained calendars and where the Quetzalcoatl legend was born.

Exploring the Site: Walk about 100 yards directly west, uphill, from the parking lot, where the **Pyramid of Quetzalcoatl** (The Plumed Serpent) rises on the hilltop. Vermilion paint remnants hint at its original appearance, which was perhaps as brilliant as a giant birthday cake. In bas-relief around the entire base a serpent writhes, intertwined with personages, probably

TLATCHTLI: THE BALL GAME

Basketball fever is probably a mild affliction compared to the enthusiasm pre-Columbian crowds felt for *tlatchtli*, the ball game that was played throughout Mesoamerica and is still played in some places. Contemporary accounts and latter-day scholarship have led to a partial picture of *tlatchtli* as it was played centuries ago. Although details varied locally, the game centered around a hard, natural rubber ball, which players batted back and forth across a center dividing line with leg-, arm-, and torso-blows.

Play and scoring was vaguely similar to tennis. Opponents, either individuals or small teams, tried to smash the ball past their opponents into scoring niches at the opposite ends of an I-shaped, sunken court. Players also could garner points by forcing their opponents to make wild shots that bounced beyond the court's retaining walls.

Courts were often equipped with a pair of stone rings fixed above opposing ends of the center dividing line. One scoring variation awarded immediate victory to the team who could manage to bat the *tlatchtli* through the ring.

As in tennis, players became very adept at smashing the ball at high speed. Unlike in tennis, the ball was solid and perhaps as heavy as two or three baseballs. Although protected by helmets and leather, players were usually bloodied, often injured, and sometimes even killed from opponents' punishing *tlatchtli*-inflicted blows. Matches were sometimes decided like a boxing match, with victory going to the opponent left standing on the court.

As with everything in Mesoamerica, tradition and ritual ruled *tlatchtli*. Master teachers subjected initiates to rigorous training, prescribed ritual, and discipline not unlike the ascetic life of a medieval monastic brotherhood.

Potential rewards were enormous, however. Stakes varied in proportion to a contest's ritual significance and the rank of the players and their patrons. Champion players could win fortunes in gold, feathers, or precious stones. Exceptional games could result in riches and honor for the winner, and death for the loser, whose heart, ripped from his chest on the centerline stone, became food for the gods.

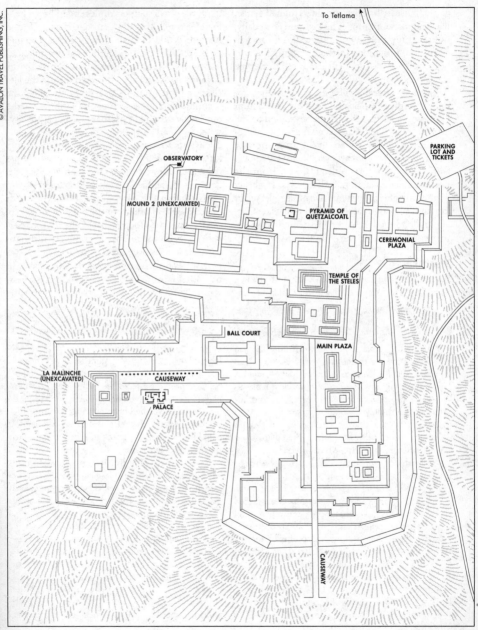

To Tetlama

PARKING LOT AND TICKETS

OBSERVATORY

MOUND 2 (UNEXCAVATED)

PYRAMID OF QUETZALCOATL

CEREMONIAL PLAZA

TEMPLE OF THE STELES

BALL COURT

MAIN PLAZA

LA MALINCHE (UNEXCAVATED)

CAUSEWAY

PALACE

CAUSEWAY

© AVALON TRAVEL PUBLISHING, INC.

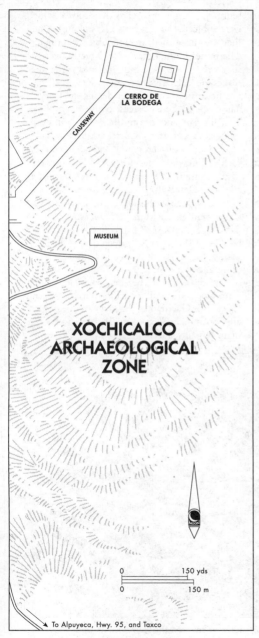

CERRO DE
LA BODEGA

CAUSEWAY

MUSEUM

XOCHICALCO ARCHAEOLOGICAL ZONE

0   150 yds

0   150 m

MOON

▲ To Alpuyeca, Hwy. 95, and Taxco

representing chiefs or great priests. Above these are warriors, identified by their helmets and *atlatl,* or lance-throwers.

Most notable, however, is one of Mesoamerica's most remarkable bas-reliefs, to the left of the staircase. It shows the 11th week sign, *ozomatli* (monkey), being pulled by a hand (via a rope) to join with the fifth week sign, *calli* (house). Latter-day scholars generally interpret this as describing a calendar correction that resulted from a grand conclave of chiefs and sages from all over Mesoamerica, probably at this very spot.

About 150 feet south rises the **Temple of the Steles,** so named for three large stone tablets found beneath the floor. They narrate the events of the Quetzalcoatl legend, wherein Quetzalcoatl (discoverer of corn and the calendar) was transformed into the morning star (the planet Venus); he continues to rule the heavens as the brightest star and the Lord of Time.

About 100 yards farther south, the **Main Plaza** was accessible to the common people via roads from below. This is in contrast to the sacrosanct **Ceremonial Plaza** nearby. A faintly visible causeway once connected the yet-to-be explored La Malinche pyramid, 200 yards to the southwest, with the Ceremonial Plaza.

That causeway passed the **Ball Court,** which is strikingly similar to ball courts as far away as Toltec Tula in the north and Mayan Copan in Honduras, far to the south. On the opposite side of the causeway from the Ball Court lies the **Palace,** a complex marked by many rooms with luxury features such as toilet drainage, fireplaces, and steam baths.

On the opposite side of the complex is the **Observatory,** a room hollowed into the hill and stuccoed and fitted with a viewing shaft for timing the sun and star transits essential for an accurate calendar.

Getting There: Get to Xochicalco by either tour (for example, Misión Tours, at the Hotel Posada de la Misión, tel. 762/622-1125 or 762/622-0065), or car. Get there by continuing past the Grutas de Cacahuamilpa driveway entrance (see directions above), northeast via Highway 160 toward Alpuyeca. After 25 miles (40

ACAPULCO/TAXCO

km) from the caves, a signed road heads left uphill to the Xochicalco ruins, which are open daily 10 A.M.–5 P.M. Admission runs about $4, Sunday and holidays free. Since caretakers shoo all visitors out by 5 P.M., arrive early enough to allow a couple of hours to explore the ruins. Bring food, drinks, a hat, and comfortable walking shoes.

Ixcateopan

The picturesque little furniture-making town of Ixcateopan (eeks-kah-tay-OH-pan—Land of Cotton) has become famous for the remains of the last Aztec emperor, Cuauhtémoc, which archaeologists discovered there on September 26, 1949.

Exploring Ixcateopan: The renown has been beneficial. The town streets and plaza are smartly cobbled with the local white marble, and houses and shops are neatly painted and whitewashed. At the center of all this stands Cuauhtémoc's resting place, the venerable **Iglesia de Santa María de la Asunción** church, beside the town plaza. Inside, Jairo Rodríguez, son of the codiscoverer of Cuauhtémoc's remains and lineal descendant of Cuauhtémoc himself, devotes his life to maintaining the sanctuary and its small adjoining mu-seum. Cuauhtémoc's relics themselves, which were subjected to rigorous investigation when they were unearthed, are undoubtedly authentic. The bones lie in a glass case directly over the spot where they were buried beneath the altar stones more than four centuries ago.

The **museum** next door details the story of Cuauhtémoc's heroic defense of the Aztec capital, Tenochtitlán, and his capture, torture, and subsequent execution by Cortés on February 28, 1525. Copies of pictograms, known as codices, such as the codex Vatican-Ríos (1528), displayed in the museum, represent Cuauhtémoc (literally, The Descending Eagle) with an inverted, stylized eagle above his head. The sanctuary and museum hours are Mon.–Sat. 9 A.M.–3 P.M. and 4–5 P.M., Sun. 9 A.M.–3 P.M. Jairo sells an excellent booklet ($3) in Spanish, which details the fascinating story of the discovery and authentication of his ancestor's remains.

Outside the church, be sure to take a look about three blocks downhill past the church, on main street Calle Guerrero, at the town **archaeological site,** open daily Wed.–Sun. 10 A.M.–5 P.M. The main remains, called the "Temple of Cotton,"

At Ixcateopan's archaeological site, investigators have uncovered the foundations of a ceremonial temple known as the "Temple of Cotton."

© BRUCE WHIPPERMAN

echoing the name Ixcateopan, reveal a ceremonial complex, including a pair of pedestals, royal rooms, and a former spring leading through what appear to have been wash basins (presumably for the cotton the high priests may have ritually processed there).

Farther afield, you might be able to find a guide to show you the limestone caves, **Grutas de San Miguel,** near neighboring San Miguel village (about an hour by high-clearance jeep, SUV, or truck); off the highway back to Taxco, fork right at the dirt road, at some houses, about seven miles from Ixcateopan.

Festivals: Customarily sleepy Ixcateopan wakes up for three annual fiestas. The fun kicks off in February, when folks celebrate their indigenous roots, with a weeklong party of daily flower processions, indigenous dances, fireworks, all climaxing around the Feb. 23 birthday of Cuauhtémoc.

The customary arrival of the governor of Guerrero, the Acapulco Symphony, and maybe even the president of Mexico, on Sept. 26, the discovery date of Cuautémoc's remains, culminates another week of celebrating.

Finally, townsfolk bring in the New Year in grand style with a combined Christmas-carnival-New Year celebration of their patron Santo Niño de Atocha.

Accommodation and Food: Besides its historic interest, Ixacateopan and its environs—the rustic old church and garden, the tranquil plaza, the surrounding lush oak-forested hills—invite lingering. Moreover, the amiable, frankly curious townsfolk—who are definitely not overwhelmed by tourists—are ready for visitors. They operate some pretty fair plaza-front country **restaurants** and a homey local hotel, the **Hotel Hernández,** on the main street, at Calle V. Guerrero 14, Ixcateopan, Guerrero, tel. 736/366-2368, a block past the plaza, across the street from the church. The heirs of late founder Sara Hernández offer eight clean rooms, around a tranquil inner patio, furnished with attractive, locally crafted wood furniture and homespun bedspreads. Rooms go for about $12 s, $16 d, with private hot-water shower baths.

Getting There: Get to Ixcateopan via *colectivo* van, labeled Ixcateopan. Catch it in front of the Estrella Blanca bus station in Taxco, or at any point on the *carretera* before the south-side, signed, turnoff road to Ixcateopan. Expect to pay about $2 per person, one-way. Drivers, follow the signed fork, west (turn right if traveling south) from the *carretera,* past the Pemex *gasolinera* about a mile south of town. Mark your odometer. Continue about an hour along the very scenic (a pair of waterfalls, good for picnicking and splashing, at mile 4.5, Km 7.2, and Mile 11, Km 17.7), sometimes potholed, paved road for 23 miles (37 km) to the town plaza.

ACCOMMODATIONS

Taxco's inexpensive and moderately priced hotels cluster in the colorful *zócalo* neighborhood, while the deluxe lodgings are scattered mostly along the *carretera.* The dry, temperate local climate relegates air-conditioning, ceiling fans, and central heating to frills offered only in the most expensive hotels. All of the hotel recommendations below have hot water and private baths, however.

Taxco's only *zócalo*-front hostelry, the **Hotel Agua Escondida,** stands on the diagonally opposite corner from the church, Calle Guillermo Spratling 4, Taxco, Guerrero 40200, tel. 762/622-0726 or 762/622-1166, fax 762/622-1306, hotelaguaesc@prodigy.net.mx. A multilevel maze of hidden patios, rooftop sundecks, and dazzling city views, the Agua Escondida has dozens of clean, comfortable rooms. The name, which translates as "Hidden Water," must refer to its big swimming pool, which is tucked away in a far rooftop corner. Rooms vary; if you have the choice, look at several. Try to avoid the oft-noisy streetfront rooms. If you don't mind climbing, some of the upper-floor rooms have airy, penthouse views. The 76 rooms run about $33 s, $44 d, $51 t, with limited parking; credit cards are accepted. For more information, visit the website www.aguaescondida.com.

On Alarcón just downhill behind the Agua Escondida, a pair of former colonial mansions, now popular hotels, face each other across the street. The **Hotel Los Arcos,** J. Ruiz de Alarcón 4, Taxco, Guerrero 40200, tel. 762/622-1836, fax

762/622-7982, losarcoshotel@hotmail.com, is the more inviting of the two. Its 24 rooms rise in three vine-draped tiers around an inviting inner patio, replete with reminders of old Mexico. The rooms, with thoughtfully selected handmade polished wooden furniture, tile floors, rustic wall art, and immaculate hand-painted cobalt-on-white tile bathrooms, complete the lovely picture. Rooms rent for about $25 s, $35 d.

The **Hotel Posada,** J. R. Alarcón 7, Taxco, Guerrero 40200, tel./fax 762/622-1396, across the street, is small and intimate, with plants, carved wood, paintings, and sculptures gracing every wall and corner. Rooms, in neocolonial decor, are clean and comfortable. The owners also run a nearby silver boutique, whose displays decorate the downstairs lobby. The 14 rooms rent for about $30 s, $35 d, $40 t; credit cards are accepted.

Heading past the opposite side of the plaza, follow Cuauhtémoc to the Plazuela de San Juan and the adjacent **Hotel Santa Prisca,** Cena Obscura 1, P.O. Box 42, Taxco, Guerrero 40200, tel. 762/622-0080 or 762/622-0980, fax 762/622-2938. This tranquil, dignified old hostelry was built around a fragrant garden of orange trees; its off-lobby dining room shines with graceful details, such as beveled glass, a fireplace, blue-white stoneware, and ivy-hung portals. Its tile-decorated rooms, in two tiers around the garden just outside, are clean and comfortable. Standard rooms go for about $29 s, $43 d; larger superior-grade rooms, $46 s or d, all with private baths, parking, and credit cards accepted.

Continue along the hill another two blocks past Plazuela de San Juan to the **Posada Lucy** on the left, at Carlos J. Nibbi 8, Taxco, Guerrero, 40200, tel./fax 762/622-1780. Here, owners offer 32 rooms in a rambling complex, fortuitously isolated below and away from street noise. Airy patios with chairs and tables invite quiet relaxation. Inside, rooms are simply but attractively decorated with color-coordinated curtains, bedspreads, and handmade wooden furniture. Prices run a reasonable $20 s or d in one bed; $40 for two to four people in two double beds.

A short block farther uphill, **Hotel Rancho Taxco Victoria,** Carlos J. Nibbi 5 and 7, Taxco, Guerrero 40200, tel. 762/622-0210 or 762/622-

0004, fax 762/622-0010, rambles, in a picturesque state of decay, along its view hillside. Built sometime back in the 1930s, the hotel usually slumbers on weekdays, reviving on weekends and holidays. (Actually, it's two hotels in one—the Victoria uphill and the Rancho Taxco, neglected and returning to the earth across the road, downhill.) The better-maintained Victoria, however, is brimming with rustic, old-world extras—hand-hewn furniture, whitewashed stucco walls, riots of bougainvillea, a spreading view garden—plus a big pool and a relaxed restaurant and bar where guests enjoy the best afternoon vista in town. Some of the spacious, comfortable rooms have luxurious view balconies. If you prefer peace and quiet, ask for one of the rooms away from the road, numbers 22–28, off the upper *terraza mirador* view patio, where, summer nights, you can enjoy the singing of the tree frogs and watch the lightning flicker in the clouds far away. Standard-grade rooms run about $58 s or d holidays and festivals, $40 s or d the rest of the time. Deluxe junior suites cost more, with parking; credit cards are accepted.

From a distance, the **Hotel Borda,** off the *carretera* downhill, appears to be the luxury hotel it once was, Cerro de Pedregal, P.O. Box 483, Taxco, Guerrero 40200, tel. 762/622-0225, fax 762/622-0617. Unenthusiastic management, however, has detracted from the hotel's magnificent assets—grand vistas, spacious garden, and luxurious blue pool and patio. Check to see if your room is clean and in working order before you move in. The 110 rooms rent for about $82 s or d, with restaurant, bar, and parking; credit cards are accepted. (*Note:* The Hotel Borda may be headed for improvement. New owners, who also own the spiffy Hotel Posada de la Misión, may soon renovate it.)

The **Hotel Posada de la Misión** decorates a hillside nearby, Cerro de la Misión 32, Taxco, Guerrero 40200, tel. 762/622-0063 or 762/622-0533, fax 762/622-2198. Its guests, many on group tours, enjoy cool, quiet patios, green gardens, plant-lined corridors, a sunny pool and patio, a view restaurant, and parking. Many of the luxurious rooms have panoramic city views; some have fireplaces. All rooms have color TV and phones.

Standard rooms rent for about $150 d, $200 including dinner and breakfast, Christmas-New Year's prices are higher; credit cards are accepted. It's just off the *carretera*, uphill side, 200 yards south of the Pemex gas station. Reserve by email at hpmreserva@posadamision.com; for more information, visit website www.posadamision.com.

The luxuriously exclusive **Hotel Hacienda del Solar**, P.O. Box 96, Taxco, Guerrero 40200, tel./fax 762/622-0857, hdadelsolar@prodigy.net.mx, spreads over a tranquil hilltop garden on the southern edge of town. Guests in many of the 22 airy and spacious rooms enjoy private patios, fireplaces, and panoramic valley and mountain views. Rooms, in deluxe and junior suite versions, vary individually but are all artfully furnished with appointments including handwoven rugs, colorful tile, paintings, and folk art. The standard rooms share a spacious living area near the lovely view pool and patio; deluxe and junior suite rooms have huge beds and deep tile bathtubs. Other amenities include a view restaurant, the Ventana (Window) de Taxco, and a cocktail lounge. Rooms for two go for about $120 deluxe, and $150 junior suite.

Vacationers who require plenty of activity and resort amenities stay at the **Hotel Monte Taxco**, Lomas de Taxco, Taxco, Guerrero 40200, tel. 762/622-1300 or 762/622-1301, fax 762/622-1428, atop a towering mesa accessible by either a steep road or cableway *(teleférico)* from the highway just north of town. On weekends, the hotel is often packed with well-heeled Mexico City families, whose kids play organized games while their parents enjoy the panoramic poolside view or play golf and tennis. The 156 deluxe rooms, many with view balconies, rent from about $130 s or d, with a/c, phones, and TV; facilities include restaurants, shops, a piano bar, disco, weekend live music, parking, a gym, pool, sauna, and spa. The adjacent country club offers a nine-hole golf course, tennis courts, and horseback riding; credit cards are accepted. For more information visit website www.montetaxco.com.

If you'd like to stay atop Monte Taxco, a more economical alternative to the hotel would be to rent one of the colonial-style apartments of the **Country Club Monte Taxco**, tel./fax 762/622-5609, adjacent to the golf course, 100 yards outside the Hotel Monte Taxco front door. For about $110, you get a deluxe, two-bedroom mountain-view apartment with kitchen, use of the country club's pool, and access to the golf course, tennis courts, horseback riding, mountain trails, and the Hotel Monte Taxco's facilities next door. For more information visit website www.montetaxco.com.

FOOD
Stalls and Snacks

The numerous *fondas* (foodstalls) atop the *artesanías* (ar-tay-sah-NEE-ahs) handicrafts section of the market are Taxco's prime source of wholesome country-style food. The quality of their fare is a matter of honor for the proprietors, since among their local patrons word of a little bad food goes a long way. It's very hard to go wrong, moreover, if your selections are steaming hot and made fresh before your own eyes (in contrast, by the way, to most restaurant and hotel fare).

You can choose from a potpourri that might include steaming bowls of *menudo* or *pozole*, or maybe plates of pork or chicken *mole*, or *molcajetes* (big stone bowls) filled with steaming meat and broth and draped with hot nopal cactus leaves.

Stalls offering other variations appear evenings on the *zócalo*. One family sells tacos and *pozole*, while another, which labels itself La Poblana, sometimes arrives in a truck and offers french-fried bananas, *churros*, and potato chips fried on the spot until about 10:30 P.M., next to the church.

Restaurants

Although its restaurants are not what draws Taxco's visitors, Taxco nevertheless offers some recommendable dining options. Of the *zócalo* restaurant choices, the upstairs **La Parroquia**, tel. 762/622-3096, a half block from the church steps, ranks among the best; open 9 A.M.–11 P.M.; credit cards are accepted. The front balcony tables are ideal perches for watching the people parade below while enjoying a good breakfast, lunch, or dinner. Moderate.

Another good bet on the *zócalo* is **Pizza Pazza**, at the corner, right-hand side of the cathedral, upstairs, tel. 762/622-5500. Although the menu offers a little bit of everything, the specialty is good pizza, in about 15 varieties. Extras include relaxed ambience, professional service, checkered tablecloths, and airy, plaza-view balcony tables. If the TV bothers you, the staff won't mind turning it down to low volume, if asked. Open daily noon–midnight. Moderate.

At least recommendable for its refined old-world ambience, the restaurant **Del Ángel Inn** adds an airy view and good food to the reasons for going there. Inside, rustic old-adobe walls, regal stone columns, and baroque statuary enhance the pleasing effect. As for food, choose from a very recognizable, tasty menu of appetizers, soups, salads, pasta, Mexican specialties, meats, and more. Find it at Calle de Muerte (now Celso Muñoz) 4, 2nd floor, a few steps downhill from the Santa Prisca churchfront, left side. Open daily 7 A.M.–10 P.M., tel. 762/622-5525. Moderate–expensive.

A block from the *zócalo*, along Calle Cuauhtémoc overlooking Plazuela de San Juan, try Mexican-style **Restaurant El Adobe,** Plazuela de San Juan 13, tel. 762/622-1416, for breakfast or a lunch break. For breakfast, you can enjoy juice, eggs, and hotcakes; for lunch, hamburgers, tacos, enchiladas, or, for dinner, steak Adobe-style and shrimp brochette. Open daily 8 A.M.–11 P.M. Budget–moderate.

Of the restaurant options, best for old-Mexico ambience is the local favorite **Restaurant Santa Fe,** tel. 762/622-1170, on the left a few doors downhill from Plazuela San Juan. Tasty, professionally prepared and served country fare keeps a battalion of faithful patrons happy. Although the long a la carte menu varies from *pozole* and soup to chicken and fish, the main event is the daily four-course *comida* of soup (try *crema de zanahoria*), spaghetti, main dish (try *chiles rellenos*) and dessert, about $5. Good for breakfast, too; open daily 8 A.M.–10 P.M. Budget–moderate.

Uphill a block past the Plazuela San Juan, you're likely to enjoy the **Hotel Rancho Victoria** restaurant, especially for lunch and dinner, where, although the food is quite good, the main attraction is the best afternoon view in town. From the *zócalo*, walk west along Cuauhtémoc; continue two blocks past Plazuela de San Juan. Open daily 7:30 A.M.–8 P.M.; credit cards are accepted. Moderate.

A classy spot where you can enjoy the view, a swim, and lunch after seeing the Cuauhtémoc Mural is the adjacent **Restaurant El Mural,** at the Hotel Posada La Misión on the *carretera;* open daily for breakfast 7–9:30 A.M., lunch 1–3:30 P.M., and dinner 7–11 P.M. If the place is packed with tour groups, have a drink, enjoy the mural, and go somewhere else. Expensive.

For good food in an elegant view setting, go to **Restaurant La Ventana de Taxco,** tel. 762/622-0587, at the Hotel Hacienda del Solar two blocks off the highway, south end of town. Open daily for breakfast 8:30–10:30 A.M., lunch 1–4:30 P.M., and dinner 7:30–10:30 P.M., when the whole town appears like a shimmering galaxy through the windows; reservations are recommended. The mostly Italian specialties include salads, lasagna, scallopini, saltimbocca, grilled red snapper, shrimp brochette, and wines. Expensive.

ENTERTAINMENT AND EVENTS

Taxco people mostly entertain each other. Such spontaneous diversions are most likely around the *zócalo,* which often seems like an impromptu festival of typical Mexican scenes. Around the outside stand the monuments of the colonial past, while on the sidewalks sit the native people who come in from the hills to sell their onions, tamales, and pottery. Kids run between them, their parents and grandparents watching, while young men and women flirt, blush, giggle, and jostle one another until late in the evening.

Three restaurant/bars on the side adjacent to the church provide good perches for viewing the hubbub. Visitors can either join the locals at **Bar Berta,** on the church corner, or take a balcony seat and enjoy the bouncy music with the mostly tourist crowd at **Bar Paco** next door. For more tranquility, head upstairs to **Restaurant La Parroquia** a few steps farther on.

Later, or another day, continue your Taxco party via the jazzy recorded music pouring out of the speakers at the restaurant/bar **Concha Nos-**

tra, upstairs at Hotel Casa Grande, at Plazuela de San Juan.

For more music, the **Hotel Monte Taxco,** tel. 762/622-1300 or 762/622-1301, offers a piano bar and discotheque and a trio weekends and seasonally. At the **Hotel Posada de la Misión,** tel. 762/622-0063 or 762/622-0533, patrons enjoy a roving trio for lunch and a piano bar nightly. Programs may vary; call to confirm.

Festivals

An abundance of local fiestas provide the excuses for folks to celebrate, starting on January 17 and 18 with the **Festival of Santa Prisca.** On the initial day, kids and adults bring their pet animals for blessing at the church. At dawn the next day, pilgrims arrive at the *zócalo* for *mañanitas* (dawn Mass) in honor of the saint, then head for folk dancing inside the church.

During the year Taxco's many neighborhood churches celebrate their saints' days (such as Chavarrieta, March 4; Veracruz, the four weeks before Easter; San Bernardino, May 20; Santísima Trinidad, June 13; Santa Ana, July 26; Asunción, Aug. 15; San Nicolas, Sept. 10; San Miguel, Sept. 19; San Francisco, Oct. 4; and Guadalupe, Dec. 12) with food, fireworks, music, and dancing.

Religious fiestas climax during Semana Santa (Easter week), when, on the Thursday and Good Friday before Easter, cloaked penitents proceed through the city, carrying gilded images and bearing crowns of thorns.

On the Monday after the Nov. 2 Día de los Muertos (Day of the Dead), Taxco people head to pine-shaded **Parque Huixteco** (PAR-kay weesh-TAY-koh) atop the Cerro Huixteco behind town to celebrate their unique **Fiesta de los Jumiles.** In a ritual whose roots are lost in pre-Columbian legend, people collect and feast on *jumiles* (small crickets)—raw or roasted—along with music and plenty of beer and fixings. Since so many people go, transportation is easy. Drive or ride a *colectivo* (Huixteco on windshield) along the west-side road (westward extension of Cuauhté-moc from the *zócalo*) uphill about two miles. Fork right at the Huixteco sign. Continue for several miles to the mountainop Parque Huixteco.

SPORTS AND RECREATION

Stay in shape as local folks do, by walking Taxco's winding, picturesque side streets and uphill lanes. And, since all roads return to the *zócalo*, getting lost is rarely a problem.

For more formal sports, the **Monte Taxco Country Club** has horses ready for riding ($10/hour), three good tennis courts ($10/hour), and a nine-hole golf course available for use by nonguests for $25 per person. Contact the country club sports desk, in the little house about 50 yards away from the Hotel Monte Taxco's front entrance. Informal *sendas* (hiking paths; ask directions from the horse-rental attendant) branch from the horse paths to the surrounding luscious pine- and cedar-forested mesa country. Take sturdy shoes, water, and a hat.

SHOPPING
Market

Taxco's big market day is Sunday, when the town is loaded with people from outlying villages selling produce and live pigs, chickens, and ducks. The market is just downhill from Los Arcos, the lane that runs below the right side of the *zócalo* church (as you face that church). From the lane, head right before the arch and down the staircase. Soon you'll be descending through a warren of market stalls. Pass the small Baptist church on Sunday and hear the congregation singing like angels floating above the market. Don't miss the spice stall, **Yerbería Castillo,** piled with the intriguing wild remedies collected by owner Elvira Castillo and her son Teodoro.

Farther on you'll pass mostly scruffy meat stalls but also some clean juice stands, such as **Liquados Memo,** open daily 7 A.M.–6 P.M., where you can rest with a delicious fresh *zanahoria* (carrot), *toronja* (grapefruit), or *sandía* (watermelon) juice.

Before leaving the market, be sure to ask for *jumiles* (hoo-MEE-lays), live crickets that sell in bags for about a penny apiece, ready for folks to pop them into their mouths.

If *jumiles* don't suit your taste, you may want to drop in for lunch at one of the *fondas* above the market's *artesanías* (handicrafts) section.

Handicrafts

The submarket **Mercado de Artesanías** (watch for the white sign above the market staircase) offers items for mostly local consumption, such as economical belts, huaraches, wallets, and inexpensive silver chains, necklaces, and earrings.

As you head out for tonier shops, don't miss the common but colorful handicrafts, such as the host of charming ceramic cats, turtles, doves, fish, and other figurines that local folks sell very cheaply. Find them everywhere, in the market, on street corners, and, especially in front of the Museo Spratling. If you buy, bargain—but not too hard, for the people are poor and have often traveled far.

Masks are the prime attraction at **Arnoldo,** Palma 1, tel. 762/622-1272, upstairs, across the uphill lane next to Hotel Agua Escondida, where the friendly proprietors, Arnoldo Jacobo and his son Raoul, are more than willing and able to explain every detail about their fascinating array of merchandise. Hundreds of masks from all over Guerrero—stone and wood, antique and new—line the walls like a museum. All of the many motifs, varying from black men puffing cigarettes and blue-eyed sea goddesses to inscrutable Aztec gods in onyx and grotesque lizard-humanoids, are priced to sell. Open Mon.–Sat. 9 A.M.–8:30 P.M., Sun. 10 A.M.–5:30 P.M.

Other shops nearby have similar offerings. Arnoldo's neighbor, **Celso,** at 4 Palma, just uphill, tel. 762/622-2848, is open Mon.–Tues. and Thurs.–Sat. 10 A.M.–2 P.M. and 4–8 P.M., and Sun. 10 A.M.–4 P.M., but closed Tuesday.

For a good general Mexico handicrafts selection—Puebla Talavera ceramics, Tonalá papier-mâché, metalwork, pewter—take a look inside the shop, confusingly named "Plaza San Juan," on the Plazuela San Juan, west side, beneath Restaurant Adobe, tel. 762/622-1683. Find it open Mon.–Sat. 10 A.M.–8 P.M., Sun. 10 A.M.–3 P.M.

> *Be sure not to miss what must be Mexico's most elegantly extravagant silver shop, the Joyería Elena Ballesteros, a virtual cathedral of silver, with dining-room tables loaded with enough plate for a maharaja's banquet, 10-pound $50,000 crucifixes, and a solid silver organ.*

Silver Shops

Among the many good silver shops that cluster around the *zócalo* and downhill on the highway, one of the most venerable is the family-owned shop of **Emilio Castillo** adjacent to the lobby of the Hotel Posada, downhill from the *zócalo,* to the right of the Hotel Agua Escondida. Run by a branch of the industrious and prolific Castillo family, the shop offers all in-house work, specializing in porcelain and silver, at reasonable prices. Here, unlike at many shops, you can bargain a bit. At J. R. Alarcón 7, tel. 762/622-3471, open Mon.–Fri. 9 A.M.–7 P.M.; Sat. 9 A.M.–6 P.M., Sun. 9 A.M.–4 P.M.; credit cards are accepted.

Step into the shop across the street and enjoy the offering of another of the Castillo clan, Citlal Castillo, personable owner of Hotel Los Arcos just downhill. Here, she displays many examples of her elegant designs, in addition to a small gallery of large colonial-era paintings. Open Mon.–Sat. 10 A.M.–8 P.M.

One of the more interesting silver shops, if only for a look around, is **Luna Collection,** in the *zócalo*-front complex, Patio de las Artesanías, next to the Casa Borda, tel. 762/622-6447. They say, with a smile, that the Grutas de Cacahuamilpa were modeled after their shop. Inside, plaster stalagmites hang above small mountains of fine silver jewelry. Open daily 9 A.M.–8 P.M.; credit cards are accepted.

While you're on the *zócalo,* be sure to step into the **Casa Borda** and admire the silver offering of the 60-member silversmithing cooperative, Soc. De Producción José de la Borda. Find them there Mon.–Sat. 9 A.M.–2 P.M. and 4–7 P.M.

For a very fitting silver-shopping finale, be sure not to miss what must be Mexico's most elegantly extravagant silver shop, the **Joyería Elena Ballesteros.** More than just a labor of love, hers is a virtual cathedral of silver, beginning with the simply exquisite, moving to dining-room tables loaded with enough plate for a maharaja's banquet, to gleaming, 10-pound $50,000 crucifixes, a solid silver organ, and a huge gold tree of life. At Calle de la Muerte 4, tel. 762/622-3767, fax 762/622-3907, silver@ballesteros.com. For more information visit website www.ballesteros.com.

Photo and Grocery Stores

The small **Colorama** photo shop, at 7 Cuauhté-moc, offers a modest stock of merchandise, such as batteries, point-and-shoot cameras, popular print film (100–1600 ASA) and slide film. Open Mon.–Sat. 10 A.M.–8 P.M., tel. 762/622-3394.

Better-stocked **Tienda la Misión,** formerly on Cuauhtémoc, now at Benito Juárez 215, a few blocks past the City Hall, next to Banamex, tel. 762/622-0116, offers some cameras and accessories, and Kodak film, including Tri-X Pan, Plus-X, and Ektachrome. It also does Xerox photocopying, including enlargement and reduction. Open Mon.–Sat. 10 A.M.–8 P.M., Sun. 10 A.M.–2 P.M.

A grocery store nearby, **Casa Ayja,** at Benito Juárez 7, tel. 762/622-0364, a rarity in silver-rich Taxco, three blocks down Juárez from the *zócalo,* stocks a bit of everything, including wine, cheese, and milk on its clean, well-organized shelves and aisles. Open Mon.–Sat. 9 A.M.–10 P.M., Sun. 10 A.M.–7 P.M. If it's closed, go to the similarly attractive **Super La Gloria,** open daily, on Hidalgo, a block downhill from Plazuela de San Juan.

INFORMATION AND SERVICES

Tourist Information Offices, Guide, and Travel Agent

Taxco has a pair of **tourist information offices,** both beside the highway at opposite ends of town, open daily approximately 9 A.M.–8 P.M. The knowledgeable and English-speaking officers readily answer questions and furnish whatever maps and literature they may have. The north office, tel. 762/622-0798, is next to the north-end Pemex gas station; the south office is about a quarter mile south of the south-end Pemex station.

Personable, veteran Mexico guide **Benito Flores Batalla,** tel./fax 762/622-0542, who staffs the north-side tourist information office, offers his services as a guide. For starters, he offers a 3.5-hour city tour for $30, without car; $60 with car supplied. Longer trips might include the Grutas de Cachuamilpa, Xochicalco, and Ixcateopan. (See Excursions.)

One of the most reliable travel agents in town is **Turismo Misión,** at the Hotel Posada de la Misión, tel. 762/622-1125 or 762/622-0063, on the *carretera.*

Publications

English-language books and newspapers are hard to find in Taxco. Nevertheless, the bookstore **Agente de Publicaciones Raoul Domínguez,** tel. 762/622-0794, has used English-language paperbacks. It's open daily 9 A.M.–2 P.M. and 4:30–8 P.M. on the Los Arcos lane adjacent to and below the church. If it doesn't have what you want, try **Casa Domínguez** newsstand, tel. 762/622-0133, at Los Arcos 7, a few doors downhill, open Mon.–Sat. 10:30 A.M.–2:30 P.M. and 4–7:30 P.M., Sun. 10 A.M.–2:30 P.M.

The scarcity of English reading matter makes the collection at the small library **Biblioteca Taxco-Canoga Park** even more precious. Browse its several shelves of English-language novels, nonfiction, magazines, and reference books Mon.–Fri. 9 A.M.–1 P.M. and 3–7 P.M., Sat. 9 A.M.–1 P.M. Most of the collection was donated by volunteers from Taxco's sister city, Canoga Park, California. The library is a five-minute walk downhill from the city hall on the alley off Juárez, on the right, half a block after Banamex.

Money Exchange

Banks near the *zócalo* and their ATMs are Taxco's cheapest source of pesos. The good longest-hours option is Banco Internacional (Bital), open Mon.–Sat. 8 A.M.–7 P.M., to the right of the church, tel. 762/622-7300 or 762/622-7506. Alternatively, a few doors along Cuauhtémoc from the *zócalo,* try **Banco Santander Mexicano,** tel. 762/622-3536 or 762/622-3270, open Mon.–Fri. 9 A.M.–4 P.M., or **Bancomer,** tel. 762/622-0287 or 762/622-02-88, open Mon.–Fri. 9 A.M.–5 P.M., a few doors farther along Cuauhtémoc.

Communications

The town center *correo* is in the Presidencia

Embedded in the street in front of the Palacio Municipal is the traditional Taxco Hieroglyph.

© BRUCE WHIPPERMAN

Municipal (post office), on Juárez, downhill, east from the *zócalo,* open Mon.–Fri. 8 A.M.–5 P.M., Sat. 9 A.M.–1 P.M. The highway branch downhill is half a block north (Mexico City direction) of the Estrella de Oro bus station, open Mon.–Fri. 8 A.M.–3 P.M. **Telecomunicaciones,** off the *zócalo,* behind the Casa Borda downhill, tel. 762/622-4885, fax 762/622-0001, offers telex, money order, and public fax services; open Mon.–Fri. 9 A.M.–3 P.M., Sat. 9 A.M.–noon.

Public street telephones all over the town center allow cheap, easy **long-distance** direct dialing with widely available Ladatel telephone cards. Get them everywhere, especially at pharmacies and liquor and grocery stores.

Internet access is available at **Plaza de Computación,** in the town market, 200 feet down the steps below the right (west) side of the church. Open Mon.–Sat. 9 A.M.–9 P.M., Sun. 9 A.M.–3 P.M. If Plaza de Computación is closed, go to the hole-

in-the-wall Internet store on Cuauhtémoc, half a block west of the *zócalo.* Open daily, 11 A.M.–11 P.M.

Health and Police

Taxco has a pair of respected private hospitals, both on the *carretera.* The **Clínica de Especialidades,** 33 Av. de los Plateros, tel. 762/622-1111 or 762/622-4500, has a 24-hour emergency room, X-rays, a laboratory, a 24-hour pharmacy, and many specialists on call. The **Clínica Santa Cruz,** tel. 762/622-3012, offers similar services, also on Carretera Plateros, at the corner of Morelos, across from the government Seguro Social hospital.

For routine medicines and remedies, go to one of the several good local pharmacies, such as **Farmacia Similares,** on Hidalgo, one block downhill from Plazuela San Juan, tel. 762/627-2214, open Mon.–Sat. 8 A.M.–9 P.M., Sun. 8 A.M.–8 P.M. Alternatively, go to the good 24-hour pharmacy at the Clínica de Especialidades, on the *carretera.*

For police emergencies, contact the ***policía,*** either on duty on the *zócalo;* at the city hall, two blocks downhill, at Juárez 6, tel. 762/622-0007; or at the substation on the side street Calle Fundaciones, one block below the *carretera* near the corner of Alarcón.

GETTING THERE AND AWAY
By Car or RV

National Highway 95 provides the main connection south with Acapulco in a total of about 167 miles (269 km) of easy driving via Iguala, accessible to and from Taxco via the winding, 22-mile (36-km) old Highway 95 cutoff. From there, sail south via the *cuota* (toll) *autopista.* Allow about four hours' driving time for the entire Taxco-Acapulco trip, either direction.

Highway 95 also connects Taxco north via Cuernavaca with Mexico City, a total of about 106 miles (170 km). The new leg of the Taxco-Mexico City toll *autopista* splits off from old Highway 95 about two miles north of town. For those in a hurry, it cuts about half an hour off the driving time. Otherwise, follow the scenic curving old Highway 95 about 20 miles (32 km) to its intersection with Highway 95 *cuota* (toll) super-highway. Congestion around Mexico City may lengthen the driving time to about three hours in either direction.

Note: Authorities limit driving your car in Mexico City according to the last digit of your license plate. (See the special topic "Mexico City Driving Restrictions.")

Highway 55 (junction at Cacahuamilpa) gives Michoacán- and Jalisco-bound drivers the desirable option of avoiding Mexico City by connecting Taxco directly with Toluca (and thence the fast east-west toll expressway 90 D, five hours to Guadalajara). The two-lane Highway 55 is paved and in good condition for its entire 74 miles (119 km). Fortunately, a faster, safer toll (cuota) **autopista** along the northern half of Highway 55 shortens the Taxco-Toluca driving time by at least an hour over the old winding, nontoll highway. Northbound, figure about 2.5

hours driving time to Toluca; southbound, allow about two hours.

By Bus

Competing lines **Estrella Blanca,** tel. 762/622-0131, and **Estrella de Oro,** tel. 762/622-0648, operate separate stations on the downhill *carretera* a few blocks apart. Both offer several luxury- and first-class connections north with Mexico City via Cuernavaca and south with Acapulco via Iguala and Chilpancingo.

Additionally, Estrella Blanca offers connections with Puebla, and the very useful option for northwest-bound travelers of bypassing Mexico City via the super-scenic Highway 55 route via Ixtapan del Sal (an interesting spa town) to Toluca. There, you can connect via Pátzcuaro, Michoacán, and Guadalajara, Jalisco, to the palmy Pacific Mexico beach destinations of Playa Azul, Manzanillo, Puerto Vallarta, San Blas, and Mazatlán.

The Costa Chica and Inland to Oaxaca

In reality, the Costa Chica, the "Little Coast," which includes the state of Guerrero south of Acapulco and the adjoining coast of Oaxaca, isn't so little after all. Highway 200, heading out of the Acapulco hubbub, requires 300 miles to traverse the scattered groves, forests, fields, and villages to the Costa Chica's southern bulge, where the coastline curves, like the belly of a dolphin, to its most southerly point near Puerto Ángel.

In the main resorts of the Costa Chica—Puerto Escondido, Puerto Ángel, and Bahías de Huatulco—the beaches face south, toward the Mar del Sur, the Pacific Ocean. On the other hand, if travelers head inland, they go north, over the verdant, jungle-clad Sierra Madre del Sur and into the Valley of Oaxaca, the native heartland of southern Mexico.

To about a million Oaxacan native peoples, Spanish is a foreign language. Many of them—

Fishing boats await the tide at Puerto Ángel's popular Playa Panteón.

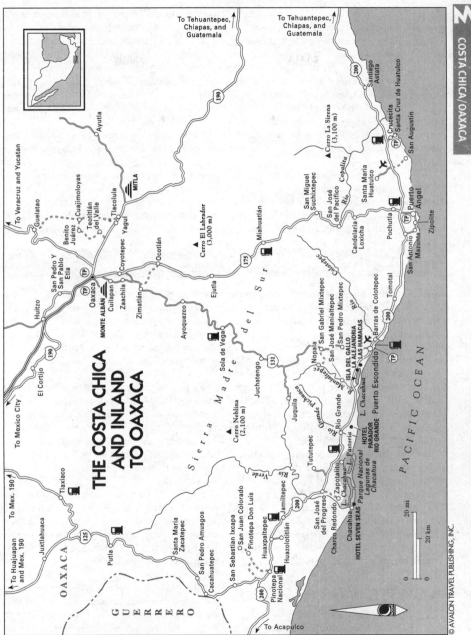

THE COSTA CHICA
AND INLAND
TO OAXACA

COSTA CHICA/OAXACA

Zapotecs, Mixtecs, and a score of smaller groups—live in remote mountain villages, subsisting as they always have on corn and beans, without telephones, sewers, schools, or roads. Those who live near towns often speak the Spanish they have learned by coming to market. In the Costa Chica town markets you will brush shoulders with them—mostly Mixtecs, Amusgos, and Chatinos—men sometimes in pure-white cottons and women in colorful embroidered *huipiles* over wrapped handwoven skirts.

Besides the native people, you will often see African Mexicans—*morenos,* brown ones—known as *costeños* because their isolated settlements are near the coast. Descendants of African slaves imported hundreds of years ago, the *costeños* subsist on the produce from their village gardens and the fish they catch.

Costa Chica *indígenas* and *costeños* have a reputation for being unfriendly and suspicious. If true in the past (although it's certainly less so in the present), they have had good reason to be suspicious of outsiders, who in their view have been trying to take away their land, gods, and lives for 400 years.

Communication is nevertheless possible. Your arrival, for the residents of a little mountain or shoreline end-of-road village, might be the event of the day. People are going to wonder why you came. Smile and say hello. Buy a soda at the store or *palapa*. If kids gather around, don't be shy. Draw a picture in your notebook. If a child offers to do likewise, you've succeeded.

Along the Road to Puerto Escondido

If driving from Acapulco, mark your odometer at the traffic circle where Highways 95 and 200 intersect over the hill from Acapulco. If, on the other hand, you bypass that congested point via the Acapulco airport road, set your odometer to zero at the east-side interchange near Puerto Marquez where the airport highway continues along the overpass—but where you exit to the right, and follow the Highway 200 Pinotepa Nacional sign. Mileages and kilometer markers along the road are sometimes the only locators of turnoffs to hidden villages and little beaches.

Fill up with gas before starting out in Acapulco. After that, Magna (unleaded) is available at Cruz Grande (56 miles, 91 km), Pinotepa Nacional (157 miles, 253 km), Puerto Escondido (247 miles, 398 km), and near Puerto Ángel (291 miles, 469 km).

If you're going by bus, ride one of the several daily first-class or second-class buses from the Estrella Blanca (Av. Ejido) terminal in Acapulco.

PLAYA VENTURA

Three miles east of the small town of Copala, 77 miles (123 km) from Acapulco, a roadside sign points toward Playa Ventura. Four miles down a paved road, which a truck-bus from Copala traverses regularly, you arrive pavement's-end at Ventura village. From there, a mile-long golden-sand beach arcs gently east. Past a lighthouse, the beach leads to a point, topped by a stack of granite rocks, known locally as Casa de Piedra (House of Stone).

Playa Ventura can provide nearly everything for a restful day or week in the sun. Several good tent camping or RV (maneuverable medium rigs, vans, or campers) spots sprinkle the inviting, outcropping-dotted shoreline. Shady *palapas* set up by former campers stand ready for rehabilitation and reuse by new arrivals.

Surf fishing (with net-caught bait fish) is fine from the beach, while *pangas* go out for deep-sea catches. Good surfing breaks angle in from the points, and, during the rainy season, the behind-the-beach lagoon is good for fishing, shrimping, and wildlife viewing. (Bring your kayak or inflatable raft.)

The palm-lined beach stretches southeast for miles. Past the picturesque Casa de Piedra outcropping, an intimate *palapa-* and *panga-*lined sandy cove curves invitingly to yet another palmy point, Pico del Monte. Past that

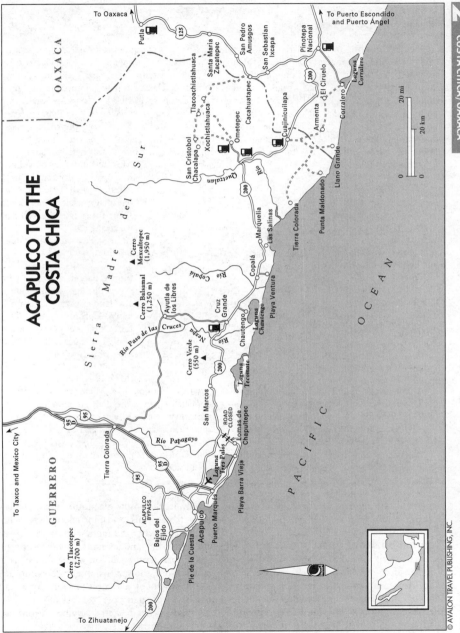

ACAPULCO TO THE
COSTA CHICA

To Oaxaca

To Puerto Escondido
and Puerto Ángel

OAXACA

Putla

125

Tlacoachistlahuaca

Santa María
Zacatepec

San Pedro
Amusgos

San Sebastián
Ixcapa

Pinotepa
Nacional

San Cristóbal
Chacalapa

Xochistlahuaca

Cacahuatepec

Cuajinicuilapa

El Ciruelo

Laguna
Corralero

Ometepec

Armenta

Corralero

San Marcos

Sierra   Madre   del   Sur

Cerro
Mexcaltepec
(1,950 m)

Cerro Balsamal
(1,250 m)

Ayutla de
los Libres

Río Copalá

Río Paso de las Cruces

Cerro Verde
(550 m)

Río Nexpa

200

Cruz
Grande

Llano Grande

Río Quetzalan

Copalá

Chautengo

Laguna
Chautengo

Playa Ventura

Tierra Colorada

Punta Maldonado

Las Salinas

Marquelia

Laguna
Tecomate

Chacahua

Lomas de
Chapultepec

ROAD
CLOSED

Río Papagayo

Tierra Colorada

95
D

95

95
D

GUERRERO

Cerro Tlacotepec
(2,700 m)

To Taxco and Mexico City

To Zihuatanejo

200

ACAPULCO
BYPASS

Bajos del
Ejido

Acapulco

Pie de la Cuesta

Puerto Marqués

Playa Barra Vieja

Laguna
Tres Palos

PACIFIC

OCEAN

20 mi

20 km

0

0

© AVALON TRAVEL PUBLISHING, INC.

THE MIXTECS

Sometime during the 1980s, the Mixtecs regained their preconquest population of about 350,000. Of that total, around one-third speak only their own language. Their villages and communal fields spread over tens of thousands of square miles of remote mountain valleys north, west, and southwest of Oaxaca. Their homeland, the Mixteca, is divided into three distinct regions: Mixteca Alta, Mixteca Baja, and the Mixteca Costera.

The **Mixteca Alta** centers in the mountains about 100 road miles due west of Oaxaca city, in the high, cool, roof of Oaxaca, centering on the market towns of Tlaxiaco and Juxtlahuaca.

Mixteca Baja communities, such as San Miguel Tequistepec, Tonalá, and Juxtlajuaca, dot the dry northwestern Oaxaca mountains and valleys, centering roughly on Huajuapan de León on Highway 190.

In the **Costera,** important Mixtec communities exist in or near Pinotepa Nacional, Huaxpaltepec, and Jamiltepec, all along Highway 200 in southwestern Oaxaca.

The Aztec-origin name Mixtecos (People of the Clouds) was translated directly from the Mixtecs' name for their own homeland: Aunyuma (Land of the Clouds). The Mixtecs' name for themselves, however, is Nyu-u Sabi (People of the Rain).

When the conquistadores arrived in Oaxaca, the Mixtecs were under the thumb of the Aztecs, who, after a long, bitter struggle, had wrested control of Oaxaca from combined Mixtec-Zapotec armies in 1486. The Mixtecs naturally resented the Aztecs, whose domination was transferred to the Spanish during the colonial period, and, in turn, to the mestizos during modern times. The Mixtecs still defer to the town Mexicans, but they don't like it. Consequently, many rural Mixtecs, with little state or national consciousness, have scant interest in becoming Mexicanized.

In isolated Mixtec communities, traditions still rule. Village elders hold final authority, parents arrange marriages through go-betweens, and land is owned communally. Catholic saints are thinly disguised incarnations of old gods such as Tabayukí, ruler of nature, or the capricious and powerful *tono* spirits that lurk everywhere.

In many communities, Mixtec women exercise considerable personal freedom. At home and in villages, they often still work bare-breasted. And while their men get drunk and carry on during festivals, women dance and often do a bit of their own carousing. Whom they do it with is their own business.

---

lies still another, even more pristine, cove and beach.

Accommodations and Food

Besides the village stores, food is available at a number of *loncherías* and beach *palapa* restaurants. Accommodations are available at a sprinkling of family *posadas,* the foremost of which is the **Restaurant and Ramada Pérez.** If anyone dispels the rumor that *costeño* folks are un-

friendly, it's the hospitable mother-son-daughter team of Inés, Luis, and Hortencia Pérez, who have put together the modest beginnings of a little resort. Inés and her family invite visitors to park RVs in their small lot, where they offer a friendly word, showers, a homemade swimming pool, kiddie pool, and a bit of shade for a reasonable $8 per party per day. For tenters, they rent spaces beneath their shady beachfront *ramada* for the same price.

SAN MARCOS, OMETEPEC, AND CUAJINICULAPA

A few larger towns along the road can provide a number of essential services. Thirty-six miles (58 km) east of Acapulco, San Marcos (pop. 10,000) has a bank (Banamex, tel. 745/453-0036, open Mon.–Fri. 9 A.M.–3 P.M., with 24-hour ATM), Seguro Social health center, pharmacies (El Pastillero, tel. 745/453-0527), a doctor (Mauricio Ibarra), a motel (Le Carma, tel. 745/453-0037, with 25 rooms around a petite pool and patio, for $19 d) and post and *telecomunicaciones* (long-distance telephone, money orders, and fax, tel. 745/453-0130) offices. Find the pharmacy, bank, doctor, and more on the town *jardín,* on main street Hidalgo, about .3 mile (.5 km) north of the highway.

Ometepec (pop. 15,000), a couple of hours' drive farther east, is accessible via a 10-mile paved road, which branches off Highway 200 at a well-marked intersection 110 miles (175 km) east of Acapulco. Besides being an important service center, Ometepec (elev. 2,000 feet) enjoys a cooler climate, drawing crowds of native peoples, notably Amusgos, from outlying villages to its big morning market. Many local buses follow dirt and gravel roads from Ometepec to more remote centers, such as **Xochistlahuaca** (so-chees-tlah-hoo-AH-kah, pop. 3,000), the Amusgo town about 30 miles northeast. Not far off the Xochistlahuaca road you can visit **Cochoapa,** the partially excavated archaeological site where a number of very ancient Olmec-style stelae and sculptures have been unearthed. Ask around for a local guide.

In Ometepec itself, banks (Banamex, tel. 741/412-0880 or 741/412-1354); a private hospital (De la Amistad, tel. 741/412-0985); public Seguro Social clinic (tel. 741/412-0392); a pharmacy (Farmacia Hernández); basic hotels (such as the Montero Mayren, tel. 741/412-0100, $14 s, $25 d, with fans and a/c); *telecomunicaciones* (tel. 741/412-0386, open Mon.–Fri. 9 A.M.–3 P.M., Sat. 9 A.M.–12:30 P.M.); and post office (open Mon.–Fri. 9 A.M.–3 P.M.) provide essential services.

Back on Highway 200, Cuajinicuilapa (kwah-hee-nee-kwee-LAH-pah, pop. 10,000), 125 miles (199 km) from Acapulco, has a Centro de Salud, a pharmacy (Santa Isabel, tel. 741/414-0017, open Mon.–Sat. 7 A.M.–2 P.M., 4–8 P.M. and Sun. 7 A.M.–2 P.M.); hotels (Marin, comfortable and attractively decorated, a few doors east of the town plaza, tel. 741/414-0021, $16 d with fan, $23 d with a/c); and the more basic Alejim, tel. 741/414-0310, $17 d with fan, $23 d with a/c); and post office (open Mon.–Fri. 8 A.M.–3 P.M.); and *telecomunicaciones* (tel. 741/414-0337, open Mon.–Fri. 9 A.M.–3 P.M. and Sat.–Sun. 9 A.M.–noon).

Cuajinicuilapa is a major market town for the scattering of *costeño* communities, such as San Nicolas (pop. 5,000, eight miles south), along the beach road (at Km 201) to Punta Maldonado, the local fishing port.

In Cuajinicuilapa, make it a priority to stop at the singularly unique **Museo de las Culturas Afromestizos,** open daily except Mon. 10 A.M.–2 P.M., 5–7 P.M., with many excellent displays, plus a library, and dance, theater, and handicrafts workshops.

PINOTEPA NACIONAL

Pinotepa Nacional (pop. about 50,000; 157 miles, 253 km, east of Acapulco; 90 miles, 145 km, west of Puerto Escondido) and its neighboring communities comprise the hub of an important coastal indigenous region. Mixtec, Amusgo, Chatino, and other peoples stream into town for markets and fiestas in their traditional dress, ready to combine business with pleasure. They sell their produce and crafts—pottery, masks, handmade clothes—at the market, then later get tipsy, flirt, and dance.

The Name

So many people asked the meaning of their city's name that the town fathers wrote the explanation on a wall next to Highway 200 on the west side of town. Pinotepa comes from the Aztec-language words *pinolli* (crumbling) and *tepetl* (mountain); thus "Crumbling Mountain." The second part of the name came about because, during colonial times, the town was called Pinotepa Real (Royal). This wouldn't do after independence, so the name became Pinotepa Nacional, reflecting the national consciousness that emerged during the 1810–1821 struggle for independence.

The Mixtecs, the dominant regional group, disagree with all this, however. To them, Pinotepa has always been Ñií Yo-oko (Little Place). Only within the town limits do the Mexicans (mestizos), who own most of the town businesses, outnumber the Mixtecs. The farther from town you get, the more likely you are to hear people conversing in the Mixtec language, a complex tongue that uses a number of subtle tones to make meanings clear.

Getting Oriented

On Pinotepa's west (Acapulco) side, Highway 200 splits into the town's two major arteries, which rejoin on the east (Puerto Escondido) side. The north, west-bound branch is called Aguirre Palancares; the south, west-bound branch, the more bustling of the two branches, passes between the town-center plaza and church and is called Av. Porfirio Díaz on the west side and Av. Benito Juárez on the east. The main north-south street, Av. Pérez Gasga, runs past both the church front and the *presidencia municipal* (city hall), which faces east, toward the town plaza.

Market

Highway 200 passes a block north of the main town market, by the big, fenced-in secondary school, on the west side, about a mile west of the central plaza. Despite the Pinotepa market's oft-exotic goods—snakes, iguanas, wild mountain fruits, forest herbs, and spices—its people, nearly entirely Mixtec, are its main attraction, especially on the big Wednesday and Sunday market days. Men wear pure-white loose cottons, topped by woven palm-leaf hats. Women wrap themselves in their lovely striped purple, violet, red, and navy blue *pozahuanco* saronglike, horizontally striped skirts. Many women carry a polished tan *jicara* gourd bowl atop their heads, which, although it's not supposed to, looks like a whimsical hat. Older women (and younger ones with babies at their breasts) go bare-breasted with only their white *huipil* draped over their chests as a concession to

POZAHUANCOS

To a coastal Mixtec woman her *pozahuanco* is a lifetime investment symbolizing her maturity and social status, something that she expects to pass on to her daughters. Heirloom *pozahuancos* are wraparound, horizontally striped skirts of hand-spun thread. Women dye the thread by hand, always including a pair of necessary colors: a light purple *(morada)*, from secretions of tidepool-harvested snails, *Purpura patula pansa*, and silk, dyed scarlet red with cochineal, a dye extracted from the beetle *Dactylopius coccus*, cultivated in the Valley of Oaxaca. Increasingly, women are weaving *pozahuancos* with synthetic thread, which has a slippery feel compared to the hand-spun cotton. Consider yourself lucky if you can get a traditionally made *pozahuanco* for as little as $100. If someone offers you a lookalike for $20, you know it's an imitation.

mestizo custom. Others wear an easily removable *mandil*, a light cotton apron-halter above their *pozahuanco*. A few women can ordinarily be found selling beautiful handmade *pozahuancos*. (Alternatively, Artemio López Clavel, in his market shop, local 35, sells *pozahuancos*, both machine- and genuine hand-made.)

Festivals

Although the Pinotepa market days are big, they don't compare to the week before Easter (Semana Santa). People get ready for the finale with processions, carrying the dead Christ through town to the church each of the seven Fridays before Easter. The climax comes on Good Friday (Viernes Santa), when a platoon of young Mixtec men paint their bodies white to portray Jews, and while intoning ancient Mixtec chants shoot arrows at Christ on the cross. On Saturday, the people mournfully take the Savior down from the cross and bury him, and on Sunday gleefully celebrate his resurrection with a riot of fireworks, food, and folk dancing.

Although not as spectacular as Semana Santa, there's plenty of merrymaking, food, dancing,

Along the Road to Puerto Escondido 531

and processions around the Pinotepa *zócalo* church on July 25, the day of Pinotepa's patron, Santiago (St. James).

Accommodations

The motel-style **Hotel Carmona,** Av. Porfirio Díaz 127, Pinotepa Nacional, Oaxaca 71600, tel. 954/543-2322, fax 954/543-2164, about three blocks west of the plaza, offers three stories of clean, not fancy but comfortable rooms, a big backyard garden with pool and sundeck. For festival dates, make reservations. The 50 rooms run about $16 s, $22 d, $28 t, fan only, $24, $33, and $40 for a/c.

If the Carmona is full, check the two high-profile newer hotels, Pepe's and Las Gaviotas, beside the highway on the west side of town. Of the two, **Pepe's,** at Carretera Pinotepa Nacional-Acapulco Km 1, Pinotepa Nacional, Oaxaca 71600, tel. 954/543-4347, fax 954/543-3602, is the much better choice. It offers 35 spacious, semideluxe rooms for a reasonable $12 s, $15 d fan only, $20 and $26 with a/c; with good TV, hot water, restaurant, and parking. Rooms at emergency-only **Hotel Las Gaviotas,** tel. 954/543-2838, fax 954/54320-56, rent for $14 d with fan, $18 with a/c.

Third choice goes to clean **Hotel Marisa,** downtown on the highway, Av. Juárez 134, north side of the street, tel. 954/543-2101, 954/543-2022, or 954/543-3190, $10 d, $13 t with fan, $16 s or d, $20 t with a/c; all with parking.

Campers enjoy a tranquil spot (best during the dry late fall-winter-spring season) on the **Río Arena** about two miles east of Pinotepa. Eastbound, turn left just after the big river bridge. Continue a few hundred yards, past a pumphouse on the left, to a track that forks down to the riverbank. Notice the waterfall cascading down the rocky cliff across the river. You will sometimes find neighbors—in RVs or tents and sand collectors, poor but friendly—set up on the riverside beneath the abandoned Restaurant La Roca (now just a rock-wall ruin), a few hundred yards up the smooth stream, excellent for kayaking (if you have some way of returning back upstream.)

Food

For a light lunch or supper, try the very clean, family-run **Burger Bonny,** at the southeast corner of the main plaza, open daily 11 A.M.–10 P.M. Besides six varieties of good hamburgers, Burger Bonny offers *tortas,* tacos, french fries, hot dogs, microwave popcorn, fruit juices, and *refrescos,* at very reasonable prices.

Also worthy is traditional-style **Fonda Toñita,** a block north of the church-front, at the corner of Aguirre Palancares. Local folks flock here for the hearty afternoon *comida* (pick the entrée, and you get rice and tortillas thrown in free); it's also good for breakfast. Open Mon.–Sat. 7 A.M.–9 P.M.

Third restaurant choice goes to restaurant **Tacos Orientales,** with 15 styles of tacos, from fish to carnitas, three for $2.50. Find it on Pérez Gasga, half a block north of the churchfront, open daily 6–11 P.M.

On the other hand, consider *marisquería* **Peñitas** next door, which specializes in fresh seafood however you like it: fried, baked, breaded, *al mojo,* and more. Open daily 8 A.M.–midnight.

For a quick and convenient on-the-road breakfast, lunch, or dinner, stop by the restaurant of high-profile **Pepe's Hotel** west of town, open daily 8 A.M.–10 P.M.

Shopping and Services

Visit the market on Wednesday and Sunday. For film and film-processing, step to the **photo shop** on the south side of the plaza.

Exchange money over the counter or use the ATM at all Pinotepa banks. Try **Bancomer,** open Mon.–Fri. 8:30 A.M.–4 P.M., corner of Díaz and Progreso, two blocks west of the plaza, tel. 954/543-3022 or 954/543-3190; or **Banamex,** across the street, open Mon.–Fri. 9 A.M.–4 P.M. Alternatively, try the long-hours (open Mon.–Fri. approximately 8 A.M.–7 P.M., Sat. 8 A.M.–3 P.M.) **Banco Internacional,** tel. 954/543-3949 or 954/543-3969, also on Av. Progreso, but across Porfirio Díaz and uphill a block from Bancomer.

The *correo* (post office), tel. 954/543-2264, is open Mon.–Fri. 8 A.M.–7 P.M., by the Estrella Blanca bus station, about two blocks west and across the street from Bancomer. The *telecomunicaciones* office (money orders, public telephone, and fax) is one block north of the plaza church, on Av. Pérez Gasga, open Mon.–Fri. 8 A.M.–7:30 P.M., Sat.–Sun. 9 A.M.–noon. *Larga distancia* Lada Central telephone and fax office, on the plaza, south side, is open longer, evening hours.

For a doctor, go to the **Clínica Rodriguez** at 503 Aguirre Palancares, tel. 954/543-2330, one block north, two blocks west of the central plaza church-front. Get routine medications at one of several town pharmacies, such as the 24-hour **Super Farmacia,** on Díaz, a block west of the central plaza church-front.

Getting There and Away

By **car or RV,** Highway 200 connects west to Acapulco (160 miles, 258 km) in an easy 4.5 hours' driving time. The 89-mile (143-km) connection to Puerto Escondido can be done safely in about 2.5 hours. Additionally, the 239-mile (385-km) Highway 125-Highway 190 route connects Pinotepa Nacional to Oaxaca, via Putla de Guerrero and Tlaxiaco (136 miles, 219 km). Although winding most of the way and potholed at times, the road is generally uncongested. It's safely driveable in a passenger car with caution, from Pinotepa to Oaxaca (follow the toll *autopista* near Oaxaca) in about eight hours (under dry conditions) at the wheel, and seven hours in the reverse, downhill, direction from Oaxaca.

Several long-distance **bus** lines connect Pinotepa Nacional with destinations north, northwest, east, and west. **Estrella Blanca,** via subsidiaries Elite, Gacela, and Flecha Roja, tel. 954/543-3194, offers several daily first- and second-class *salidas de paso* (buses passing through) departures west to Acapulco, Zihuatanejo, Lázaro Cárdenas, and Mexico City; and east to Puerto Escondido, Pochutla (Puerto Ángel), Bahías de Huatulco, and Salina Cruz, from its station on Porfirio Díaz about three blocks west of the *zócalo.*

Smaller, mostly second-class lines **Fletes y Pasajes, Estrella del Valle,** and **Oaxaca Pacífico** operate out of a pair of small stations one block north of the central plaza church-front, on side street Aguirre Palancares. Fletes y Pasajes, tel. 954/543-2163, connects daily with

Oaxaca via Putla, Tlaxiaco, and Nochixtlán, by Highways 125 and 190. Estrella del Valle and Oaxaca Pacífico buses, tel. 954/543-2697, also connect with Oaxaca, but in the opposite direction: first east, through Puerto Escondido to Pochutla (Puerto Ángel), then continuing north over the Sierra to Oaxaca via Highway 175.

First-class **Cristóbal Colón** also operates out of a small station on the same street, about one block farther west. A few daily departures connect, via Highways 175 and 190, northeast, via Putla and Tlaxiaco, with Oaxaca (by the fast *autopista* via Nochixtlán), and northwest, with Mexico City (via Puebla). Other departures connect east, with Puerto Escondido.

EXCURSIONS NORTH OF PINOTEPA

The local patronal festival year begins early, on January 20, at **Pinotepa Don Luis** (pop. 5,000), about 15 miles, by back roads, northeast of Pinotepa Nacional, with the uniquely Mixtec festival of San Sebastián. Village bands blare, fireworks pop and hiss, and penitents crawl, until the finale, when dancers whirl the local favorite dance, Las Chilenas.

Yet another exciting time around Pinotepa Nacional is during **Carnaval,** when nearby communities put on big extravaganzas. Pinotepa Don Luis, sometimes known as Pinotepa Chica (Little Pinotepa), is famous for wooden masks the people make for their big Carnaval festival. The celebration usually climaxes on the Sunday before Ash Wednesday, when everyone seems to be in costume and a corps of performers gyrates in the traditional dances: Paloma (Dove), Tigre (Jaguar), Culebra (Snake), and Tejón (Badger).

Pinotepa Don Luis bubbles over again with excitement during Semana Santa, when the faithful carry fruit- and flower-decorated trees to the church on Good Friday, explode Judas effigies on Saturday, and celebrate by dancing most of Easter Sunday.

San Juan Colorado, a few miles north of Pinotepa Don Luis, usually appears as just another dusty little town until Carnaval, when its festival rivals that of its neighbors. Subsequently, on November 29, droves of Mixtec people come into town to honor their patron, San Andres. After the serious part at the church, they celebrate with a cast of favorite dancing characters such as Malinche, Jaguar, Turtle, and Charros (Cowboys).

Amusgo Country

Cacahuatepec (pop. about 5,000; on Highway 125 about 25 miles north of Pinotepa Nacional) and its neighboring community **San Pedro Amusgos** are important centers of the Amusgo people. Approximately 20,000 Amusgos live in a roughly 30-mile-square region straddling the Guerrero-Oaxaca state border. Their homeland includes, besides Cacahuatepec and San Pedro Amusgos, Xochistlahuaca, Zacoalpán, and Tlacoachistlahuaca on the Guerrero side.

The Amusgo language is linguistically related to Mixtec, although it's unintelligible to Mixtec speakers. Before the conquest, the Amusgos were subject to the numerically superior Mixtec kingdoms until the Amusgos were conquered by the Aztecs in 1457, and later by the Spanish.

Now, most Amusgos live as subsistence farmers, supplementing their diet with occasional fowl or small game. Amusgos are best known to the outside world for the lovely animal-, plant-, and human-motif *huipiles,* which Amusgo women always seem to be hand-embroidering on their doorsteps.

Although Cacahuatepec enjoys a big market each Sunday, that doesn't diminish the importance of its big Easter weekend festival, the day of Todos Santos (All Saints' Day), Nov. 1, and Day of the Dead, Nov. 2, when, at the cemetery, people welcome their ancestors' return to rejoin the family.

San Pedro Amusgos celebrations are among the most popular regional fiestas. On June 29, the day of San Pedro, people participate in religious processions, and costumed participants dressed as Moors and Christians, bulls, jaguars, and mules dance before crowds of men in traditional whites and women in beautiful heirloom *huipiles.* Later, on the first Sunday of October, folks crowd into town to enjoy the traditional processions, dances, and sweet treats of the fiesta of the Virgen de la Rosario (Virgin of the Rosary).

Even if you miss the festivals, San Pedro Amusgos is worth a visit to buy *huipiles* alone. Three or four shops sell them along the main street through town. Look for the sign of **Trajes Regionales Elia,** the little store run by Elia Guzmán, tel. 954/582-8697. Besides dozens of beautiful embroidered garments, she stocks a few Amusgo books and offers friendly words of advice and local information.

EXCURSIONS EAST OF PINOTEPA

For 30 or 40 miles east of Pinotepa Nacional, where road kilometer markers begin at zero again near the central plaza, Highway 200 stretches through the coastal Mixtec heartland, intriguing to explore, especially during festival times. The population of **San Andres Huaxpáltepec** (oo-wash-PAHL-tay-payk), about 10 miles east of Pinotepa, sometimes swells from about 4,000 to 20,000 or more during the three or four days before the day of Jesus the Nazarene, on the fourth Friday of Lent (or in other words, the fourth Friday after Ash Wednesday). The entire town spreads into a warren of shady stalls, offering everything from TVs to stone metates. (Purchase of a corn-grinding metate, which, including *mano* stone roller, sells for about $25, is as important to a Mixtec family as a refrigerator is to an American. Mixtec husband and wife usually examine several of the concave stones, deliberating the pros and cons of each before deciding.)

The Huaxpaltepec Nazarene fair is typical of the larger Oaxaca country expositions. Even the highway becomes a lineup of stalls; whole native clans camp under the trees, and mules, cows, and horses wait patiently around the edges of a grassy trading lot as men discuss prices. (The fun begins when a sale is made, and the new owner tries to rope and harness his bargain steed.)

Even sex is customarily for sale within a quarter of very tightly woven no-see-through grass houses, patrolled by armed guards. Walking through, you may notice that, instead of the usual women, one of the houses offers men, dressed in low-cut gowns, lipstick, and high-heeled shoes.

Huazolotitlán

At nearby Santa María Huazolotitlán (pop. 3,000) several resident woodcarvers craft excellent **masks.** Local favorites are jaguars, lions, rabbits, bulls, and human faces. Given a photograph (or a sitting), one of them might even carve your likeness for a reasonable fee. (Figure perhaps $40–60.) Near the town plaza, ask for José Luna, Lázaro Gómez, or the master Idineo Gómez, all of whom are related and live in *barrio* Ñií Yucagua.

Textiles are also locally important. Look for the colorfully embroidered animal and floral motif *huipiles, manteles,* and *servilletas* (native smocks, tablecloths, and napkins). You might also be able to bargain for a genuine heirloom *pozahuanco* (handwoven wrap-around skirt) for a reasonable price.

Besides all the handicrafts, Huazolotitlán people celebrate the important local **Fiesta de la Virgen de la Asunción** around Aug. 13–16. The celebrations customarily climax with a number of favorite traditional dances, in which you can see why masks are locally important, especially in the dance of the Tiger and the Turtle. The finale comes a day later, celebrated with the ritual dance of the Chareos, dedicated to the Virgin.

Get to Huazolotitlán (ooah-shoh-loh-teet-LAN) in about two miles along the paved road that forks south uphill from Highway 200 in Huaxpaltepec. Drive, or hitchhike (with caution), ride the local bus, or hire a taxi for about $3.

Santiago Jamiltepec

About 18 miles (at Km 30) east of Pinotepa Nacional is the hilltop town of Santiago Jamiltepec (hah-meel-teh-PAYK, for short). Two-thirds of its 20,000 inhabitants are Mixtec. A grieving Mixtec king named the town in memory of his infant son, Jamilly, who was carried off by an eagle from this very hilltop.

The market, while busy most any day, is biggest and most colorful on Thursday. The town's main fixed-date festivals are celebrated on September 1, January 1, and February 15. In addition, Jamiltepec celebrates its famous pre-Easter (week following Domingo de Ramos, or Palm Sunday) festival, featuring neighborhood candlelight processions accompanied by 18th-century music. Hundreds of the faithful bear elaborate wreaths and palm decorations to the foot of their church altars.

Jamiltepec is well worth a stop if only to visit the handicrafts shops **Yu-uku Cha-kuaa** (Hill of Darkness) of Santiago de la Cruz Velasco. Personable Santiago runs both his home shop and a better stocked one at the Jamiltepec plaza market, because the government cluster of shops (Centro Artesanal de la Costa, on the highway) was closed down, victim of a dispute over control. The local Mixtec artisans wanted to manage their own handicrafts sales, while the regional branch of the INI (Instituto Nacional Indigenista) preferred to manage instead. The Mixtecs stuck together and refused to bring their handicrafts, closing the government operation.

Some of their crafts—masks, *huipiles,* carvings, hats—occupy the shelves and racks in Santiago's shop. Find it in the market, signed Artesanía Yu-uku Cha-kuaa, by the north entrance (ask for Santiago by name). He stays open until about 4 P.M. If you don't want to miss him, write Santiago a letter at his shop, Av. Principal, esquina Fco. Madero, Barrio Grande, Sec. 5, Jamiltepec, Oaxaca 71700.

LAGUNAS DE CHACAHUA NATIONAL PARK AND VICINITY

The Lagunas de Chacahua National Park spreads for about 20 miles of open-ocean beach shoreline and islet-studded jungly lagoons midway between Pinotepa Nacional and Puerto Escondido. Tens of thousands of birds typical of a host of Mexican species fish the waters and nest in the mangroves of the two main lagoons, Laguna Pastoría on the east side and Laguna Chacahua on the west.

The fish and wildlife of the lagoons, overfished and overhunted during recent years by local people, are now recovering. Commercial fishing is now strictly licensed. A platoon of

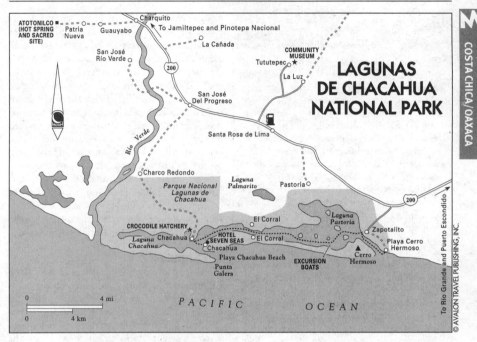

Marines patrols access roads, shorelines, and the waters themselves, making sure catches are within legal limits. Crocodiles were hunted out during the 1970s, but the government is restoring them with a hatchery on Laguna Chacahua.

For most visitors, mainly Mexican families on Sunday outings, access is by boat, except for one rugged road. From east-side Zapotalito village, the local fishing cooperative offers full-and half-day boat excursions to the beaches, Playa Hermosa on the east side and Playa Chacahua on the west.

Exploring Lagunas de Chacahua

Zapotalito, on the eastern shore of Laguna Pastoría, is the sole easy access point to the Lagunas de Chacahua. Get there from the Zapotalito turnoff at Km 82, 51 miles from Pinotepa and 41 miles from Puerto Escondido. (Local buses run from Río Grande all the way to Zapotalito on the lagoon, while second-class buses from Puerto Escondido and Pinotepa Nacional will drop you on the highway.)

From the Zapotalito landings, the fishing co-operative, Sociedad Cooperativa Turística Escondida, enjoys a monopoly for transporting visitors on the lagoons. The boatmen used to make their livings fishing; now they mostly ferry tourists. Having specialized in fishing, they are generally neither wildlife-sensitive nor wildlife-knowledgeable. Canopied powerboats, seating about 10, make long, full-day trips for about $70 per boat. Cheaper (about $30) half-day excursions take visitors to nearby **Playa Cerro Hermosa** at the mouth of Laguna Pastoría for a couple of hours' beach play and snorkeling—if you bring your own snorkeling gear. On the other hand, you can save yourself $30 and drive, taxi, or walk the approximately two miles along the shoreline road from Zapotalito to Playa Cerro Hermosa. Here you'll find a lovely open-ocean beach good for surf-fishing and beach sports, camping, a wildlife-rich lagoon mangrove wetland, and several *palapa* restaurants.

The full-day destination, Playa Chacahua, about 14 miles distant, unfortunately seems to necessitate a fast trip across the lagoon. It's difficult to get

LAGUNAS DE CHACAHUA ALTERNATIVES

Few roads penetrate the thick tropical deciduous forest surrounding the lagoons. Well-prepared adventurers can try to thumb a ride or drive a rugged high-clearance vehicle (dry season only) along the very rough 18-mile forest track to Chacahua village from San José del Progreso, which is on Highway 200, 36 miles (58 km) from Pinotepa Nacional. Before setting out, check with local residents or storekeepers about safety and road conditions.

If you have a boat or kayak, you can try launching your own excursion on Laguna Pastoría. The Cooperativa members, being both poor and protective of their interests, may ask you for a "launching fee," whether they're entitled to it or not.

Some of the islands in Laguna Pastoría are high and forested and might be bug-free enough during the dry Nov.–Feb. months for a relaxing few days of wilderness camping, kayaking, and wildlife-viewing. Another alternative is to pay a boatman to drop you at your choice of islands and pick you up at a specified later time. Take everything, especially drinking water and insect repellent.

them to slow down. They roar across broad Laguna Pastoría, scattering flocks of birds ahead of them. They wind among the islands, with names such as Escorpión (Scorpion), Venados (Deer), or Pinuelas (Little Pines), sometimes slowing for viewing multitudes of nesting pelicans, herons, and cormorants. They pick up speed again in the narrow jungle channel between the lagoons, roaring past idyllic, somnolent El Corral village, and break into open water again on Laguna Chacahua.

The **crocodile hatchery** is at Chacahua village on the west side of the lagoon, home to about two dozen local *costeño* families, a shabby hotel, and a pair of lagoonside *palapa* restaurants. Past the rickety crocodile caretaker's quarters are a few enclosures housing about 100 crocodiles segregated according to size, from hatchlings to six-foot-long toothy green adults.

The tour climaxes at the west half of Chacahua

village across the estuary. Here, palms line the placid lagoon, shading the **Hotel Siete Mares** (Seven Seas) bamboo tourist cabanas. The hotel, a quiet, rustic tropical retreat, offers a small restaurant, showers and toilets, a few cabins (rent negotiable from about $12, depending upon season), and a beautiful beach a short walk away.

Playa Chacahua is lovely *because* of its isolation. The unlittered golden-white sand, washed by gently rolling waves, seems perfect for all beach activities. You can snorkel off the rocks nearby, fish in the breakers, and surf the intermediate breaks that angle in on the west side. A few *palapas* provide food and drinks, and, for beachcombers, wildlife viewers, and backpackers (who bring their own water), the breezy, jungle-backed beach spreads for 10 miles both ways.

Río Grande

Río Grande (pop. 15,000), five miles east of the Lagunas de Chacahua-Zapotalito access road, is a transportation, supply, and service point for the region. Right on the highway are *abarroterías* (groceries), pharmacies and doctors, and a *larga distancia* telephone in an office-booth on the right (south) side, at the west edge of town.

The downscale **Hotel Río,** Av. Puebla, Río Grande, Oaxaca 71830, tel. 954/582-6033, is the big white building off the highway's north side, at the west end of town. It offers 22 plain but clean rooms on two floors, encircling a spacious parking courtyard. The rooms rent for about $6 s, $12 d, with fans, toilets, but tepid (not hot) water.

The friendly, family-run **Restaurant Río Grande,** across the street from the hotel, provides good cheer and hearty meals daily 7 A.M.–10 P.M.

On the east edge of town, the once inviting but now somewhat neglected **Hotel Paraíso Río Grande,** Carretera 200, Río Grande, Oaxaca 71830, tel. 954/582-6196, offers a big swimming pool (if it's in working order) and a kiddie pool in a spreading, grassy patio, plus large brick-and-tile rooms with either fans or a/c. The 20 rooms (check for mildew) rent for about $12 s, $17 d, $18 t with fan and TV, and $14 s, 23 d, $25 t with a/c and TV.

The hotel's soaring, classically vaulted ceilings and elegant brick arches flow from the expertise of its friendly and articulate architect builder. His life project has been to first build, and now extend, the hotel, using unreinforced brick and concrete only, not unlike ancient Roman buildings, but with the addition of innovative new designs. (If the hotel's pool wasn't functioning, stop instead for a swim and a picnic a few miles west, at **Balneario Las Delicias** water park, with shaded tables and snack bar, at Km 102.)

LAGUNA MANIALTEPEC

Sylvan, mangrove-fringed Laguna Manialtepec, about 10 miles west of Puerto Escondido, is a repository for a trove of Pacific Mexico wildlife. Unlike Lagunas de Chacahua, Laguna Manialtepec is relatively deep and fresh most of the year, except occasionally during the rainy season when its main source, the Río Manialtepec, breaks through its sandbar and the lagoon becomes a tidal estuary. Consequently lacking a continuous supply of ocean fry for sustained fishing, Laguna Manialtepec has been left to local people, a few Sunday visitors, and its wildlife.

Laguna Manialtepec abounds with birds. Of the hundreds of species frequenting the lagoon,

40 or 50 are often spotted in a morning outing. Among the more common are the olivaceous cormorant and its relative, the *anhinga;* and herons, including the tricolored, green-backed, little blue, and the black-crowned night heron. Other common species include ibis, parrots, egrets, and ducks, such as the Muscovy and the black-bellied whistling duck. Among the most spectacular are the huge great blue herons, while the most entertaining are the northern *jacanas,* or lily walkers, who scoot across lily pads as if they were the kitchen floor.

Lagoon tours are best arranged through travel agencies in Puerto Escondido. Although most of these advertise so-called "ecotours," a genuine one is **Hidden Voyages Ecotours,** led by Canadian ornithologist Michael Malone and arranged through the very competent travel agency Viajes Dimar, Av. Pérez Gasga 906, P.O. Box 22, Puerto Escondido, Oaxaca 71980, tel./fax 954/582-0734 or 954/582-0737.

Las Hamacas, La Alejandria, and Isla El Gallo

Laguna Manialtepec is ripe for kayaking, boating, and camping along its shoreline. Bring plenty of repellent, however. Alternatively, RV and tent

LAGUNA MANIALTEPEC

campers can settle in for a few days in one of a handful of shady restaurant compounds along the shore.

The most developed of these is Las Hamacas, tel. 954/588-7831, at the lake's eastern end, near the Km 126 marker, about 10 miles (16 km) west of Puerto Escondido. Friendly owner-manager Fernando Abascal López, of Santander, Spain (he's lived in Mexico since 1979) says he's "almost Mexican." A firm believer in ecologically appropriate land stewardship, Fernando is working to develop his environmentally friendly version of paradise. He's gotten off to a good start, with a minifarm of ducks, goats, sheep, cattle and rabbits, a lakeshore *palapa* restaurant, and kayaks, non-gasoline sailboats, a sturdy modern house with three comfortable rooms (about $25 d, whole house $75, with kitchen) and space for camping and RV parking for rent. A swimming pool, catamaran sailboat, and rustic cabanas are next, Fernando says.

One kilometer farther west is the sleepy little family-run pocket Eden of **La Alejandria,** which nestles along its 100 yards of lakefront, shaded by palms and great spreading trees. It's so idyllic that the *Tarzan* TV series picked La Alejandria for its setting, adding a rustic lake tree house (now destroyed by hurricanes) to the already gorgeous scene. Embellishing all this is a homey restaurant/bar, screened-in from bugs, decorated with animal trophies, and reminiscent of an old-time East African safari lodge.

La Alejandria rents about six palm-shaded RV spaces with electricity and water (be prepared with your own long extension and hose) for about $10. Camping spaces also go for the same price. (Although La Alexandria also offers four shady cabanas, with private toilets, they've been allowed to become too mildewed for healthy habitation. However, it might be worth taking a look. Managers may have cleaned them up by the time you read this.)

Another kilometer west of La Alejandria is lakefront restaurant and dock **Isla El Gallo,** perfect for a day on the lagoon. Stop for lunch at the restaurant, then follow up on more local options, such as snoozing in a hammock, volleyball, swimming, or bird-watching along the mangrove-decorated shoreline, launching your own canoe or boat, or hiring one of El Gallo's boatmen to take you on a lagoon excursion from the dock.

Puerto Escondido

Decorated by intimate coves, sandy beaches, and washed by jade-tinted surf, Puerto Escondido enjoys its well-deserved popularity. Despite construction of a jet airport in the 1980s, Puerto Escondido remains a place where everything is within walking distance, no high-rise blocks anyone's sunset view, and moderately priced accommodations and good food remain the rule.

Puerto Escondido (Hidden Port) got its name from the rocky Punta Escondida, which shelters its intimate half-moon cove, which perhaps would have remained hidden if local farmers had not discovered that coffee thrives beneath the cool forest canopy of the lush seaward slopes of the Sierra Madre del Sur. They began bringing their precious beans for shipment when the port of Escondido was established in 1928.

When the coast highway was pushed through during the 1970s, Puerto Escondido's then-dwindling coffee trade was replaced by a growing trickle of vacationers, attracted by the splendid isolation, low prices, and high waves. With some of the best surfing breaks in North America, a permanent surfing colony soon got established. This led to more nonsurfing visitors, who, by the 1990s, were arriving in droves to enjoy the comfort and food of a string of small hotels and restaurants lining Puerto Escondido's still-beautiful but no longer hidden cove.

AROUND TOWN
Getting Oriented
Puerto Escondido (pop. 35,000) seems like two small towns separated by Highway 200, which runs along the bluff above the beach. The upper town is where most of the local

© BRUCE WHIPPERMAN

mended nets, ready to use on Puerto Escondido's main beach

folks live and go about their business, while in the town below the highway, most of the restaurants, hotels, and shops spread along a single, touristy, beachfront street mall, **Av. Pérez Gasga.**

Avenida Pérez Gasga runs east-west, mainly as a pedestrian mall, where motor traffic is allowed only before noon. Afternoons, stop signs go up, blocking cars at either end.

Beyond the west-end stop sign, Pérez Gasga leaves the beach, winding uphill to the highway, where it enters the upper town at the *crucero*, Puerto Escondido's only signaled intersection. From there, Pérez Gasga continues into the upper town as Av. Oaxaca, National Highway 131.

Getting Around

In town, walk or take a taxi, which should run no more than $2 to anywhere. For longer excursions, such as to Lagunas Manialtepec and Chacahua (westbound), and as far as Pochutla (near Puerto Ángel) eastbound, ride one of the very frequent *urbano* minibuses that stop at the *crucero*, or rent a car from Budget, tel. 954/582-0312 or 954/582-0315, budget33@hotmail.com, or Alamo, tel. 954/582-3003, alamoescondido@hotmail.com.

BEACHES AND ACTIVITIES

Puerto Escondido's bayfront begins at the sheltered rocky cove beneath the wave-washed lighthouse point, Punta Escondida. The shoreline continues easterly along Playa Principal, the main beach, curving southward at Playa Marineros, and finally straightening into long, open-ocean Playa Zicatela. The sand and surf change drastically, from narrow sand and calm ripples at Playa Principal to a wide beach pounded by gigantic rollers at Zicatela.

Playa Principal

The best place to appreciate Puerto Escondido is not from the cluttered Pérez Gasga mall, but from one of the shady restaurants that front Playa Principal, the main beach. It's here that Mexican families love to frolic on Sunday and holidays and sun-starved winter vacationers doze in their chairs and hammocks beneath the palms. The sheltered west side is very popular with local people who arrive afternoons with nets and haul in small troves of silvery fish. The water is great for wading and swimming, clear enough for casual snorkeling, but generally too calm for anything else in the cove. However, a few hundred yards east around the bay the waves are generally fine for bodysurfing and boogie boarding, with a minimum of undertow. Although not a particularly windy location, sailboarders do occasionally bring their own equipment and practice their art here. Fishing is fine off the rocks or by small boat, easily launched from the beach. Shells, generally scarce on Playa Principal, are more common on less-crowded Playa Zicatela.

Playa Marinero

As the beach curves toward the south, it increasingly faces the open ocean. Playa Marinero begins about 100 yards from the "Marineros," the east-side rocky outcroppings in front of the Hotel Santa Fe. The rocks' jutting forms are supposed to resemble visages of grizzled old sailors. Here the waves can be rough. Swimmers beware: appearances can be deceiving. Intermediate surfers practice here, as do daring boogie boarders and bodysurfers.

Turn around and gaze inland at the giant Mexican flag, waving in the breeze on the hill above the east-side beach. At dawn every rainless day soldiers of the 54th infantry battalion raise the colossal banner, which measures about 82 by 59

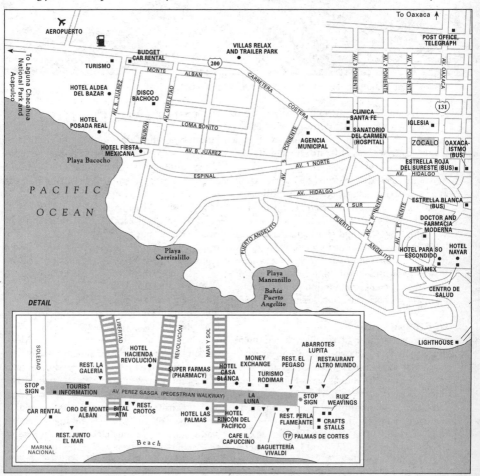

feet (18 by 25 meters) and is so heavy that it takes 25 of them to do it.

Playa Zicatela

Past the Marinero rocks you enter the hallowed ground of surfing, Playa Zicatela. The wide beach, of fine golden-white sand, stretches south for miles to a distant cliff and point. The powerful Pacific swells arrive unimpeded, crashing to the sand with awesome, thunderous power. Both surfers and nonsurfers congregate year-round, waiting for the renowned Escondido "pipeline," where grand waves curl into whirling liquid tunnels, which expert surfers skim through like trains in a subway. At such times, the spectators on the beach outnumber the surfers by as much as 10 or 20 to one. Don't try surfing or swimming at Zicatela unless you're expert at both.

West-Side Beaches: Playas Manzanillo, Carrizalillo, and Bachoco

About a mile west of town, the picture-postcard little blue bays of Bahía Puerto Angelito and Bahía Carrizalillo nestle beneath the seacliff. Their sheltered gold-and-coral sands are perfect

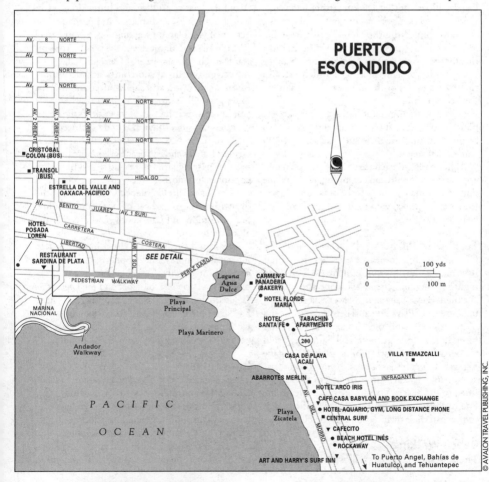

PUERTO ESCONDIDO

for tranquil picnicking, sunbathing, and swimming. Here, snorkeling and scuba diving are tops, among shoals of bright fish grazing and darting among the close-in coral shelves and submerged rocky outcroppings. Get there by launch from Playa Principal or by taxi. On foot (take a sun hat and water) follow the street that heads west from Pérez Gasga, uphill across from the Hotel Nayar. Continue to the second street on the left, Av. 1 Poniente, turn left and go a long block to Av. 5 Sur. Turn right and continue straight ahead for about a mile to Bahía Puerto Angelito. Follow the trail down the cliff. Bahía Carrizalillo is another 1.5 km farther west.

Playa Bachoco, yet another mile farther west, down the bluff from the Hotel Posada Real, is a long, scenic strip of breeze-swept sand, with thunderous waves and correspondingly menacing undertow. Swimming is much safer in the inviting pool of the adjacent Hotel Posada Real beach club.

If you're strong, experienced, and can get past the breaking waves, snorkeling is said to be good around the little surf-dashed islet 100 yards offshore.

Although Playa Bachoco's rock-sheltered nooks appear inviting for beach camping, local people don't recommend it because of occasional *rateros* (thugs and drunks) who roam Puerto Escondido beaches at night.

Trouble in Paradise

Occasional knifepoint robberies and muggings have marred the once-peaceful Puerto Escondido nighttime beach scene. Walk alone and you invite trouble, especially along Playa Bachoco and the unlit stretch of Playa Principal between the east end of Pérez Gasga and the Hotel Santa Fe. If you have dinner alone at the Hotel Santa Fe, avoid the beach by returning by taxi or walking along the highway to Pérez Gasga back to your hotel.

Fortunately, such problems seem to be confined to the beach. Visitors are quite safe on the Puerto Escondido streets themselves, often more so than on their own city streets back home.

Beach Walking

The *andador* concrete walkway, which circles the lighthouse point, provides a pleasant, breezy afternoon (or sunset) diversion. From the west stop sign, follow the street that heads toward the lighthouse. Soon, on the left, stairs head left down on to the beach cove, where, in front of the Capitania del Puerto building, the *andador* heads left along the rocks. It continues, above the spectacularly splashing surf, for about half a mile. Return by the same route, or loop back through side streets to Pérez Gasga.

For a longer walk, you can stroll as far out of town along on Playa Zicatela as you want, in outings ranging from an hour to a whole day. Avoid the heat of midday, and bring along a sun hat, shirt, drinks, and snacks (and perhaps sunglasses) if you plan on walking more than a mile past the last restaurant down the beach. Your rewards will be the acrobatics of surfers challenging the waves, swarms of shorebirds, and occasional finds of driftwood and shells. After about three miles you will reach a cliff and a sea arch, which you can scamper through at low tide to the beach on the other side, **Playa Barra de Colotepec.**

Playa Barra de Colotepec's surf is as thunderous as Zicatela's and the beach even more pristine, being a nesting site for sea turtles. The beach continues for another mile to the jungle-fringed lagoon of the Río Colotepec where, during the dry winter season, a host of birds and wildlife, both common and rare, paddle and preen in the clear, fresh water.

You could break this eight-mile round-trip into a pair of more leisurely options: Hike A could cover Zicatela only. On Hike B you could explore Playa Barra de Colotepec and the Laguna de Colotepec by driving, taxiing, or busing straight to La Barra, the beach village just west of the Río Colotepec. Access is via the signed side road just before (west of) the Río Colotepec bridge.

Boat Tours

Travel agencies and the local boat cooperative, **Sociedad Cooperativa Punta Escondida,** offer trips for parties of several passengers to beautiful local bays, including Carrizalillo and Puerto Angelito, plus Manzanillo, Puesta del Sol, and Coral. The minimum one-hour trip takes you to a number of sandy little coves east of town, including

Carrizalillo (Little Reeds), Manzanillo (Little Apple), Puerto Angelito, Coral, and Puesto del Sol (Sunset). Take drinks, hats, sunscreen, and perhaps sunglasses, and don't go unless your boat has a sunroof. Trips can be extended (about $15 per additional hour) to your heart's content of beach picnicking, snoozing, and snorkeling.

EXCURSIONS

Whether you go escorted or independently, outings away from the Puerto Escondido resort can reveal rewarding glimpses of flora and fauna, local cultures, and idyllic beaches seemingly half a world removed from the Pérez Gasga tourist hubbub.

Farthest afield, to the west of Puerto Escondido, are the festivals, markets, and handicrafts of Mixtec towns and villages around Jamiltepec and Pinotepa Nacional and the crystalline beaches and wildlife-rich mangrove reaches of the Lagunas de Chacahua National Park. To the east lie the hidden beaches of **Mazunte, Zipolite,** and the picture-book **Bay of Puerto Ángel,** with their turtle museum, au naturel sunbathing on Playa Zipolite, and very accessible off-beach snorkeling at Puerto Ángel. A bit farther beckon the nine breezy Bays of Huatulco, ripe for swimming, scuba diving, wildlife-viewing, biking, and river rafting.

Closer at hand, especially for wildlife lovers and beachgoers, are the jungly lagoons and pristine strands of the **Laguna de Manialtepec** and the nearby hot springs and Chatino sacred site of Atotonilco.

(For details of all of the above out-of-town sights, refer to the relevant sections of this chapter.)

Atotonilco Hot Springs

Also on the west side, the Aguas Termales Atotonilco hot springs, a Chatino sacred site, provides an interesting focus for a day's outing. The jumping-off point is the village of San José Manialtepec, about half an hour by bus or car west of Puerto Escondido.

At the village, you should hire someone to show you the way, up the semiwild canyon of the Río Manialtepec. The trail winds along cornfields, beneath forest canopies, and past Chatino

native villages. Finally you arrive at the hot spring, where a clear bathtub-sized rock basin bubbles with very hot (bearable for the brave), clear, sulfur-smelling water.

Get there by driving or busing to the Highway 200 turnoff for San José Manialtepec, around Km 116, just east of the Río Manialtepec bridge. Village stables provide horses and guides to the hot springs. It's a very easy two-mile walk, except in times of high water on the river, which the trail crosses several times.

Tours

Puerto Escondido agencies conduct outings to all of the above and more. Among the very best are the **Hidden Voyages Ecotours** of the Canadian husband-wife team of Michael Malone and Joan Walker. Working through the competent Viajes Dimar travel agency, Av. Pérez Gasga 906, P.O. Box 22, Puerto Escondido, Oaxaca 71980, tel./fax 954/582-0734 or 954/582-0737, ornithologist Michael and artist/ecologist Joan lead unusually informative beach, lagoon, and mountain tours seasonally, mid-December through Easter. In addition, they also offer a sunset lagoon wildlife and beach excursion, plus a two-day trip to Nopala, center of Chatino native culture, including Costoche and La Perla coffee plantations in the cool Sierra Madre del Sur mountain forest. Their trips ordinarily run $55 per day, per person.

Other Dimar tours include a full-day jaunt east to the turtle museum at Playa Mazunte, continuing to Playa Zipolite, where you can stop for lunch and an afternoon of snorkeling around Puerto Ángel. Evenings during the dark of the moon, trips can include night snorkeling when algae coat everthing underwater with an eerie bioluminiscent glow. The cost runs about $30 per person. Additionally, they offer an all-day hiking, picnic, and swimming excursion at a luxuriously cool mountain river and cascade in the sylvan Sierra Madre foothill jungle above Pochutla for about $40 per person, $80 two days, one night (minimum four people).

Alternatively, try one of the tours guided by tour guide **Ana Marquez,** aided by her daughter, also Ana, natives of Puerto Escondido. Her itineraries cover the coast, from the renowned blowhole at Huatulco's Maguey Bay to the crocodile nursery at Chacahua National Park. Contact her at home at Futuro Mzna 7 no. 214, Fracc. Costa Chica, Puerto Escondido, Oaxaca 71984, tel. 954/582-2001, or at her Tigre Azul cyber café, tel. 954/582-2954 or 954/582-2855, beach-side, near the west end stop sign, or email ana@anasecotours.com. For more information, visit her website www.anasecotours.com.

Personable Gina Machorro, of Puerto Escondido *turismo*, who often staffs the booth at the west-end Pérez Gasga stop sign, also leads tours. Contact her at tel. 954/582-0276 or email ginainpuerto@yahoo.com.

ACCOMMODATIONS
Hotels and Bungalows
The successful hotels in Puerto Escondido are appropriate to the town itself: small, reasonably priced, and near the water. They dot the beachfront from Playa Zicatela around the bay and continue up Av. Pérez Gasga to the highway. Most are either on the beach or within a stone's throw of it, which makes sense, because it seems a shame to come all the way to Puerto Escondido and not stay where you can soak up all the scenery.

Downhill along Pérez Gasga from the *crucero* is the **Hotel Paraíso Escondido** on a short side street to the left, Calle Union 1, Puerto Escondido, Oaxaca 71980, tel. 954/582-0444. A tranquil colonial-chic refuge, the hotel abounds in unique artistic touches—Mixtec stone glyphs, tiny corner chapels, stained glass, and old-world antiques—blended into the lobby, corridors, and patios. The two levels of rooms nestle around a lovely view pool and restaurant patio. The rooms themselves are large, with view balconies and designer tile bathrooms, wrought-iron fixtures, and handcrafted wooden furniture. Very popular with North American and German winter vacationers; get reservations in early. The 24 rooms rent for about $50 s, $58 d low season, $75 and $85 high, with a/c, pool, kiddie pool, and parking, but *no* credit cards are accepted.

Just downhill is the 1950s-genre **Hotel Nayar,** Pérez Gasga 407, Puerto Escondido, Oaxaca 71980, tel. 954/582-0113, fax 954/582-0319, hotelnayar@prodigy.net.mx, spreading from its inviting pool patio past the reception to a viewpoint restaurant. Its spacious, spartan but comfortable air-conditioned rooms have private balconies, many with sea views. Improved management has recently cleaned up this nicely situated hotel. The Nayar's 40 rooms run about $24

PUERTO ESCONDIDO ACCOMMODATIONS BY PRICE

Accommodations (telephone area code 954, postal code 71980) are listed in increasing order of approximate high-season, double-room rates.

Rockaway, Av. del Morro, tel. 582-0668 or 582-2420, $30

Hotel Las Palmas, Pérez Gasga s/n, tel. 582-0230, fax 582-0303, $30

Hotel Rincón del Pacífico, Pérez Gasga 900, tel. 582-0056 or 582-0193, fax 582-0101, rconpaci@prodigy.net.mx, $30

Casas de Playa Acali, Av. del Morro (P.O. Box 11), tel. 582-0754 or 582-0278, $32

Hotel Loren, Pérez Gasga 507, tel. 582-0057, fax 582-0591, $35

Hotel Nayar, Pérez Gasga 407, tel. 582-0113, fax 582-0319, hotelnayar@prodigy.net.mx, $36

Hotel Casa Blanca, Pérez Gasga 905, tel. 582-0168, fax 582-0737, $36

Beach Hotel Inés, Av. del Morro, P.O. Box 5844, tel. 582-0792, fax 582-2344, pedrovoss@yahoo.com, $43

Hotel Flor de María, Primera Entrada a Marinero, tel. 582-0536, fax 582-2617, pajope@hotmail.com, $50

Hotel Arco Iris, Av. del Morro, Colonia Marinero, tel./fax 582-1494 or 582-0432, arcoiris@hotelarcoiris.com.mx, $53

Hotel Paraíso Escondido, Calle Union 1, tel. 582-0444, $85

Hotel Santa Fe, Av. del Morro, P.O. Box 5896, tel. 582-0170 or 582-0266, fax 582-0260, info@hotelsantafe.com.mx, $90 s, $27 d, $32 t, low season, $31, $36, $42 high, add $8 for a/c. For more information, visit the website www.oaxaca-mio.com/hotelnayar.htm.

The popular **Hotel Loren,** Av. Pérez Gasga 507, Puerto Escondido, Oaxaca 71980, tel. 954/582-0057, fax 954/582-0591, downhill half a block farther, is as good as it first appears, from its leafy pool patio and its private balcony view rooms to its rooftop sundeck. Intelligent clerks staff the desk while *camaristas* scrub the rooms spotless every day. (They also may spray with DDT; tell them "no DDT" if you'd prefer they didn't.) The rooms spread through two three-story buildings; the front building rooms have better views. Reserve a *cuarto con vista* if you want a view room. Reservations are often necessary, especially in the winter. The 24 basic but comfortable fan-only rooms rent for about $20 s or d, $30 t low season; $35 s or d, $40 t high, with parking, fans, and some a/c (add $10); credit cards are accepted.

Right on the beach amid the tourist-mall hullabaloo is the longtime favorite, **Hotel Las Palmas,** Av. Pérez Gasga s/n, Puerto Escondido, Oaxaca 71980, tel. 954/582-0230, fax 954/582-0303. Its main plus is the palmy, vine-strewn patio where you can sit for breakfast every morning, enjoy the breeze, and watch the boats, the birds, and families frolicking in the billows. The big drawback, besides sleepy management and no pool, is lack of privacy. Exterior walkways pass the room windows, which anyone can see through. Closing the curtains unfortunately makes the (fan-only) rooms very dark and hot. This doesn't seem to bother the legions of return customers, however, since they spend little time in their rooms anyway. Tariffs for the 40 smallish rooms run about $17 s, $21 d, $24 t low season; $25 s, $30 d, $35 t high, with phones and restaurant, but no parking; credit cards are accepted.

The **Hotel Rincón del Pacífico,** next door to the Hotel Las Palmas, offers about the same, at Av. Pérez Gasga 900, Puerto Escondido, Oaxaca 71980, tel. 954/582-0056 or 954/582-0193, fax 954/582-0101, rconpaci@prodigy.net.mx. The two tiers of clean, comfortable rooms enfold a shady patio that looks out onto the lively beachfront. As at the Hotel Las Palmas above, a stay in one of the glass-front rooms sometimes feels like life in a fishbowl. This is nevertheless a very popular hotel. Reserve early. Rates for the 28 rooms run, year-round, about $24 s, $30 d, $36t, with fan only; $40, $50, and $60 with a/c. Ask for a discount. Four suites with TV and a/c rent for about $70 s or d; with a restaurant, but no parking nor pool; credit cards are accepted (but not American Express).

Although it's not right on the beach like its neighbors across the street, the rooms of the **Hotel Casa Blanca,** Av. Pérez Gasga 905, Puerto Escondido, Oaxaca 71980, tel. 954/582-0168, fax 954/582-0737, are larger, cooler, and much more private. Some rooms even have private balconies, fine for people-watching on the street below. Guests report noise is not a problem since cars and trucks are banned on Gasga noon–7 A.M. Other amenities include hot water, a shelf of used paperback books, and, beyond the graceful arches that border the lobby, a petite, inviting pool and patio. The 21 clean, comfortable rooms rent for about $26 s, $36 d, $38 t year-round, with fans; discounts are customarily available Sept. and Oct. Visa and MasterCard accepted, but there's no parking.

It's easy to miss the **Hotel Flor de María,** tucked on a quiet side street, off east-side Playa Marinero, at Primera Entrada Playa Marinero, Colonia Marinero, Puerto Escondido, Oax. 71980, tel. 954/582-0536, fax 954/582-2617, pajope@hotmail.com. That would be a pity, for the Flor de María is an attractive, reasonably priced hotel. Rooms rise in two stories around a tranquil, leafy interior patio. At rooftop, a breezy sundeck-bar, with a small but inviting pool and a hammock-hung *palapa* overlooks a beach-and-bay vista. The approximately dozen immaculate deluxe rooms are simply but thoughtfully decorated, each with two double beds with pretty violet covers and modern-standard hot-water shower baths. Additionally, the hotel offers a pair of similarly inviting but more spacious second-floor ocean-view suites. Accommodations rent, low season, from about $30 d standard, $45 d with ocean view, suites $50; high season $45, $50 and $55, with fans. For more information, visit the website www.mexonline.com/flordemaria.htm.

Puerto Escondido's classiest hostelry is the newish **Hotel Santa Fe,** Av. del Morro, Playa Marinero, Puerto Escondido, P.O. Box 96, Puerto Escondido, Oaxaca 71980, tel. 954/582-0170 or 954/582-0266, fax 954/582-0260, email info@hotelsantafe.com.mx. Built in graceful neo-colonial style, with curving staircases, palm-shaded pool patios, and flower-decorated walkways, the Santa Fe achieves an ambience both intimate and luxuriously private. Its restaurant is outstanding. The rooms are spacious, comfortable, and thoughtfully appointed with handpainted tile, rustic wood furniture, and regional handicrafts. Moreover, the big new room tier that owners added lately has enhanced the hotel's ambience, with an airy, elevated pool patio connecting the new tier with the original section. The 50 rooms rent, high season, for about $75 s, $90 d, $100 t; about 10 kitchenette suites go for around $85 s, $100 d, 110 t; low season, $55 s, $60 d, suites about $75 d. All accommodations have a/c, phones, and parking; credit cards are accepted. For more information, visit the website www.hotelsantafe.com.mx.

A few hundred yards south along the beach is the **Casas de Playa Acali,** Av. del Morro, P.O. Box 11, Puerto Escondido 71980, tel. 954/582-0278 or 954/582-0754, a small colony of rustic cabanas, clustered around a blue pool in a banana, palm, and mango minijungle. The cabanas themselves, like a vision out of a romantic South Seas tale, are built with walls made of sticks (non-see-through) and sturdy plank floors, raised above ground level. Units are clean and equipped with fans, mosquito nets, and good bathrooms. Rentals run about $18 s, $20d, $25 t low season; $30, $32, $38 high, with fan, hot water shower, small refrigerator, and parking. Additionally, the hotel offers a few rustic sunset-view bungalows perched on its bamboo- and mango-decorated hillside. Rentals cost about $30 low season, $40 high, for one to four, with kitchens, and beach-view hammock-hung front porches. Credit cards are accepted. For more information, look for Playas Acali, on the website www.puertoconnection.com.

Farther south on Av. del Morro, which runs along Playa Zicatela, rises the three-story **Hotel**

Arco Iris, Av. del Morro s/n, Colonia Marinero, Puerto Escondido, Oaxaca 71980, tel./fax 954/582-1494, fax 954/582-0432, arcoiris@hotel-arcoiris.com.mx. A flowery, shady green garden surrounds the hotel, leading to an attractive pool and patio. For those who love sunsets, sand, and waves (and don't mind their sometimes insistent pounding), one of the spacious, simply furnished top-floor view rooms might be just the ticket. The Arco Iris's proximity to the famous Puerto Escondido "pipeline" draws both surfers and surf-watchers to the third-floor restaurant La Galera, which seems equally ideal for wave-watching at breakfast and sky-watching at sunset. Low-season (May–June, Sept.–Nov. 15) asking rates for the 26 rooms run a reasonable $45 s or d; suites with kitchen, about $60 s or d (add about 15 percent high season); ask for a discount under any conditions. For more information, visit the website oaxaca-mio.com/arcoiris.htm.

Next comes **Beach Hotel Inés,** Av. del Morro, P.O. Box 44, Playa Zicatela, Puerto Escondido, Oaxaca 71980, tel. 954/582-0792, fax 954/582-2344, pedrovoss@yahoo.com, the life project of German expatriate Peter Voss and his daughter, Inés. Their 35 units occupy the palmy periphery of a lush, pool-café-garden layout, which climaxes with an attractive, stuccoed, two-story complex of rooms at the back side. At the poolside tables, longtime repeat guests linger for coffee and conversation after late-morning breakfasts, stroll the beach in the afternoon, and return for a balmy sunset happy hour. Other days they sunbathe au naturel or relax in the petite but luxurious health club, which provides massage and hot tub. Most of the rentals are hotel-style rooms, in deluxe and super-deluxe grades, with clean, light interiors, comfortable furnishings, and well-maintained bathrooms. Additionally, they rent six downscale second floor (popular with surfers) shared-bath cabanas, and a pair of bungalows with outdoor kitchens, sleeping four to six. Deluxe rooms go for about $30 s or d low season, $43 high; super-deluxe, about $50 low season, $80 high; cabanas, about $20 d; and bungalows, about $30 low, $40 high, all with discounts negotiable for long-term rentals. For more information, visit the website www.hotel-ines.com.

Farther along Playa Zicatela is the very tidy **Rockaway,** Av. del Morro, Playa Zicatela, Puerto Escondido, Oaxaca 71980, tel. 954/582-0668, fax 954/582-2420, a fenced-in cluster of about 15 clean, concrete-floored bamboo-and-thatch cabanas. Spacious and fan-equipped, they sleep about four and have private showers and toilets, mosquito nets, and shady, hammock-hung front porches. An inviting, leafy pool patio occupies the center, while the manager's cabana, offering water-sport rentals and supplies, stands to one side. Cabana rentals run, low season, about $10 s, $15 d, $25 per cabana for up to four; $20, $30 and $40 high season. Weekly or monthly discounts are negotiable, with parking and adjacent pizzeria.

Apartments and Long-Term Rentals

If you're planning on a stay of two weeks or more, you may be able to save money and yet have all the comforts of home in an apartment rental. First look over the classifieds in the *El Sol de la Costa* English-Spanish newspaper. Also check with local realtors, such as Vicki Cole, of Zicatela Properties, tel. 954/582-2495, email zicatela_properties@yahoo.com. Vicki also provides help—real estate matters, immigration papers, residency—for newcomers.

Alternatively, for rentals, you might also contact Nolan Van Way, of PEP Realty, tel. 954/582-0085, nvpep@yahoo.com.

Trailer Park and Camping

Occasional muggings and robberies on the beach have eliminated virtually all camping on Puerto Escondido beaches (with the possible exception of Easter week, when such large crowds flock into town that they spill onto the beaches).

Development and other uses have swallowed up Puerto Escondido's former recommendable trailer parks. A few trailer-camping parks (that I haven't recommended in the past because of on-beach security problems) are still functioning, however. I looked them over and found one that appears recommendable. It's the **Parque Trayler Palmas de Cortés,** tel. 954/582-3663, right on the beach, at the east end of Pérez Gasga, behind (beach side) of the Perla Flameante Restaurant. It's pretty enough, with about 40 smallish (up to about 20 feet) spaces in a palmy, fenced-in compound. Rates run about $10 for two people, with all hookups and showers. Camping costs $4 per person.

FOOD

Breakfast and Snacks

Mornings you can enjoy breakfast with the baked offerings of **Panadería Carmen** along Playa Marinero, on the little street that heads toward Playa Marinero from Highway 200, just past the bridge. It's a small homey shop with a few tables for savoring the goodies. Besides baking, co-owner Carmen Arizmendi's love is swimming. Afternoons, you might see her swimming in the bay, beyond the waves. Open Mon.–Sat. 7 A.M.–3 P.M.

Now, Carmen's devotees can have a second spot to enjoy her pastries: **Cafecito Zicatela,** right on Zicatela beach (next to Bungalows Acuario). Here, you can savor a cappuccino and one of her goodies as you watch the surfers conquering the waves.

Carmen has aquired some competition, **Baguettería Vivaldi,** the labor of love of friendly Jenny Sinnhuber, who, besides lots of homemade bread, serves a wide selection of delicious breakfasts and sandwiches for lunch. Find her shop, in the middle of beachfront Av. Pérez Gasga, across the street from the Hotel Casa Blanca; open daily 7:30 A.M.–10 P.M.

Nearby, right in the middle of the Av. Pérez Gasga bustle, **Café Capuchino** attracts a following of tourists and local folks who enjoy good desserts and coffee with their conversation. Furthermore, the best homesickness remedy in town is the apple pie, a slice of which enables you to endure a minimum of one more hard week on the local beaches. Open daily 8 A.M.–11 P.M.

Also fun for breakfast are the shady, scenic beach-view Restaurant Junto del Mar and Restaurant Crotos. (See Restaurants.)

Restaurants

Most of Puerto Escondido's reliable restaurants line Av. Pérez Gasga. Just inside the west end stop sign, on the inland side of Pérez Gasga, **Restaurant**

La Galería usually has customers even when most other local eateries are empty. The reason is the excellent Italian fare—crusty, hot pizzas, rich pastas and lasagna, bountiful salads, and satisfying soups—which the European-expatriate owner puts out for her batallion of loyal customers. Open daily 8 A.M.–midnight. Moderate.

Across the street, the local rage is the excellent, airy **Restaurant Junto del Mar** (By the Ocean), which offers class-act breakfasts—rich coffee, fresh fruit, hotcakes, eggs—and many delectable lunch and dinner options. Specialties include shrimp-stuffed fillets, octopus cooked with garlic, and lobster and shrimp brochettes. Mornings are brightened by the always-changing beach scene; evenings, the setting turns romantic, with soft candlelight and strumming guitars. Open daily 8 A.M.–11 P.M., tel./fax 954/582-1272. Credit cards are accepted. Moderate.

A block farther east, breakfast patrons at beachfront **Restaurant Crotos** sit at shady view tables, enjoying the fascinating morning beachside scene. Later, at lunch and dinner, back beneath the luxuriously breezy, palm-fringed *palapa,* the house specialties—jumbo shrimp, broiled lobster, and super-fresh pompano, attractively presented, competently served, and delicious—seem like an added bonus. Open daily 8 A.M.–11 P.M. Moderate.

Near the east end of the Pérez Gasga mall, the **Restaurant Perla Flameante** offers good food, incense, new-age jazz, and a beach view from beneath a big, cool *palapa.* The friendly, conscientious staff take pride that they make everything in-house, from the mayonnaise to the potato chips that come with the big fish burger. Seafood fillets rule the menu. The varieties, such as *sierra,* tuna, yellowtail, and mahimahi, are exceeded only by the number of styles—Cajun, teriyaki, wine and herbs, pepper-mustard, butter and garlic, orange—in which they are served. Open daily 7 A.M.–11 P.M.; credit cards are accepted. Moderate.

Devotees of authentic Italian food find paradise at **Restaurant Altro Mundo,** just half a block outside of the east-end stop sign. Here, white tablecloths and wine glasses set the stage. Start off, perhaps, with *crema* Altro Mundo, continue with an *insalata mista,* share a plate of lasagna *di cala-*

mari, and climax with fettuccine *flameante* and *filete di dorado.* Open for dinner only, daily 6 P.M.–midnight, tel. 954/582-1455. Moderate.

German owners have recently launched **El Pegaso,** tel. 954/582-0800, a worthy addition to the Puerto Escondido gastronomical roster, east end of the Pérez Gasga mall. Strictly European-international dishes fill the menu. For starters, go with French *frite aubergin* (stir-fried eggplant), continue with Italian *insalata Gorgonzola,* and top it off with German bratwurst with potatoes, onion, and bacon. Open daily, except Wed., 3 P.M.–11 P.M. Moderate–expensive.

If you have dinner at the restaurant of the **Hotel Santa Fe,** on Av. del Morro, east side of the bay, tel. 954/582-0170, you may never go anywhere else. Savory food, impeccably served beneath a luxurious *palapa* and accompanied by softly strumming guitars, brings travelers from all over the world. Although everything on the menu is good, the restaurant is proudest of its Mexican favorites, such as rich tortilla soup, bountiful plates of *chiles rellenos,* and succulent snapper, Veracruz style. Open daily 7:30 A.M.–11 P.M. Moderate–expensive.

Farther south along Zicatela beach, **Restaurant Cafecito** (formerly Bruno's) is headquarters for a loyal platoon of local surfers and Canadian and American residents. Breakfasts, hamburgers, and fresh seafood plates are bountiful, tasty, and won't cost you a bundle. Open daily, about 8 A.M.–10 P.M. Budget–moderate.

Back up on Highway 200, at the corner of Av. 1 Poniente, one block west of the Pérez Gasga crossing, is **Restaurant Candiles,** where the mission is Oaxacan traditional cuisine, professionally prepared and artfully presented. The day begins with breakfast at 8 A.M., with a long menu of goodies, such as hot cakes and veggie omelette, to *chilaquiles* Candiles and *picaditas.* Come back for lunch or dinner and be treated to, for example, *sopesitos* (thick, small tortillas), garnished with black beans, salsa, cheese and guacamole, followed by one of very best tortilla soups (called, in this case *sopa* Mixteca), made in Pacific Mexico. Open daily except Mon. 8 A.M.–11 P.M., tel. 954/582-0361. Moderate.

ENTERTAINMENT AND EVENTS

Sunsets and Happy Hours

Many bars have sunset happy hours, but not all of them have good sunset views. Since the Oaxaca coast faces south (and the sun sets in the west), bars along west-facing Zicatela Beach, such as the Hotel Santa Fe, Hotel Arco Iris, Restaurant Cafecito's, and Art and Harry's, are the only ones that can offer unobstructed sunset horizons.

If, on the other hand, you prefer solitude, stroll the bayfront *andador* walkway to near the lighthouse. Start on the Playa Principal (main beach), west side, past the Capitán del Puerto office. There, from breezy perches above the waves, you'll enjoy an equally panoramic sunset.

Strolling Pérez Gasga

Strolling the Pérez Gasga mall is Puerto Escondido's prime after-dinner entertainment. By around 9 P.M., however, people get weary of walking and, since there are few benches, begin sitting on the curb and sipping bottles of beer near the west-end stop sign. Unfortunately, city officials frown on such apparently dissolute behavior and occasionally have a few of the curb-sitters arrested. Meanwhile, people hope that some amiable compromise will be reached.

The main attraction of curb-sitting is watching other people sitting on the curb, while listening to the music blasting nightly from the tiny open-air bars of **Bar Fly, Tubo,** and **Wipe Out,** 50 feet away. The music is so loud little can be gained except hearing impairment by actually taking a seat in the bars themselves.

Those who prefer to gyrate to the beat go to some of the town's discos. On Pérez Gasga, try **Los Tres Diablos** (The Three Devils), across from the Hotel Las Palmas. Alternatively, try the old standby, **Disco Bachoco** on Av. Gueletao, in the west-side Bachoco suburb.

Festivals

Puerto Escondido pumps up with a series of fiestas during the low-season (but excellent for vacationing) month of November. Scheduled "Fiestas de Noviembre" events invariably include surfing and usually sportfishing, cooking, and beauty contests, and notably, the dance festival, **Fiesta Costeño,** when a flock of troupes—from Pochutla, Pinotepa Nacional, Jamiltepec, Tehuantepec, and more—perform regional folk dances.

Visitors who hanker for the old-fashioned color of a traditional fiesta, make sure you arrive in Puerto Escondido before December 18, when seemingly the whole town takes part in the fiesta of the **Virgen de Soledad.** Besides being the patron saint of the state of Oaxaca, the Virgen de Soledad is also protectress of fishermen. To honor her, the whole town accompanies the Virgin by boat out to the bay's far reach, and then returns with her to the church plaza for dancing, fireworks, and bullfights.

If you can't be in Puerto Escondido in time to honor the Virgin in December, perhaps you may be able to take a day trip one hour west of Puerto Escondido to enjoy a fiesta at one of the small towns around Pinotepa Nacional, to celebrate Carnaval, with parades, fireworks and lots of crazy street dancing, on the weekend before Ash Wednesday, the beginning of Lent. (See Festivals in the Pinotepa Nacional section.)

SPORTS AND RECREATION

Walking, Jogging, and Horseback Riding

Playa Zicatela is Puerto Escondido's most interesting walking course. Early mornings, before the heat and crowds, are good for jogging along the level section of Av. Pérez Gasga. Avenida del Morro, which parallels Playa Zicatela, is good for jogging anytime it isn't too hot. (For more walking details, see Beach Walking under Beaches and Activities.)

Ease your hiking by riding horseback along Zicatela beach. Rentals are available on the beach in front of Hotel Santa Fe.

Gym and Tennis

The **Acuario Gym** on Playa Zicatela at the Hotel Acuario has a roomful of standard exercise equipment. Single visits run about $3, one-month passes $30.

One of the only night-lit tennis courts in town available for public rental ($10/hour, daytime only) is at the **Hotel Posada Real.** Call the hotel at tel. 954/582-0133 for a reservation.

Surfing, Snorkeling, and Scuba Diving

Although surfing is de rigueur for the skilled in Puerto Escondido, beginners often learn by bodysurfing and boogie boarding first. Boogie boards and surfboards are for sale and rent ($7/day) at a number of shops along Pérez Gasga, such as **100 Hamacas** (next to Hotel Rincón del Pacífico) or **Central Surf** next door (and at Hotel Acuario on Playa Zicatela), open high season daily 9 A.M.–2 P.M. and 4–7 P.M. **Rockaway,** also on Playa Zicatela, rents surfboards ($7/day) and boogie boards ($7/day) and sells related supplies.

Beginners practice on the gentler billows of **Playa Principal** and adjacent **Playa Marinero** while advanced surfers go for the powerful waves of **Playa Zicatela,** which regularly slam foolhardy inexperienced surfers onto the sand with backbreaking force.

Clear blue-green waters, coral reefs, and swarms of multicolored fish make for good local snorkeling and diving, especially in little **Puerto Angelito** and **Carrizalillo** bays just west of town. A number of Av. Pérez Gasga stores sell serviceable amateur-grade snorkeling equipment.

A professional dive shop, **Aventura Submarina,** has recently gained a foothold in Puerto Escondido. It's run by friendly veteran PADI instructor Jorge Pérez Bravo, at Pérez Gasga 601 A, a few doors inside the west-end stop sign, tel. 954/582-2353, cellular tel. 044-954/588-1682, asubmarina@ptoescondido.com.mx. Introductory lesson, including one offshore dive, runs about $60, including equipment. For certified (bring your certificate) open water divers, a one-tank night dive costs about $45, a two-tank day dive, about $60.

Alternately, a number of divers operate out of Huatulco, a 1.5-hour drive east. Contact the very professional **Buceos Triton** shop in Santa Cruz de Huatulco, tel./fax 954/587-0844, or **Hurricane Divers,** tel. 954/587-1107. (For more details, see the Bays of Huatulco section.)

Sportfishing

Puerto Escondido's offshore waters abound with fish. Launches go out mornings from Playa Principal and routinely return with an assortment including big tuna, mackerel, snapper, sea bass, and snook. The sheltered west side of the beach is calm enough to easily launch a mobile boat with the help of usually willing beach hands.

The local **Sociedad Cooperativa Nueva Punta Escondida,** which parks its boats right on Playa Principal, regularly takes fishing parties of three or four out for about $20 an hour, including bait and tackle. Check with boatmen right on the beach. Additionally, travel agencies, such as Viajes Dimar, Av. Pérez Gasga 905, tel. 954/582-0734 or 954/582-0237, arrange such trips at about the same prices.

SHOPPING
Market and Handicrafts

As in most Mexican towns, the place to begin your Puerto Escondido shopping is the local **Mercado,** on Av. 10 Norte one long block west of the electric station on upper Av. Oaxaca. Although produce occupies most of the space, a number of stalls at the south end offer authentic handicrafts. These might include Guerrero painted pottery animals; San Bártolo Coyotepec black pottery; masks from Guerrero and Oaxaca with jaguar, devil, and scary human-animal motifs; the endearing multicolored pottery animals from Iguala and Zitlala in Guerrero; and beautiful crocheted *huipiles* from San Pedro Amusgos.

Back downhill on Av. Pérez Gasga, the prices increase along with the selection. Perhaps the most fruitful time and place for handicraft shopping is during the cooler evenings, within the illuminated cluster of crafts stalls just beyond the Gasga east stop sign.

One shop at that spot, the **Ruiz** textile stand, with genuine handmade rugs and serapes from Teotitlán del Valle near Oaxaca city, stands out. Fine-quality rugs are the most tightly woven— typically about 20 strands per centimeter (50 per inch).

Oaxaca's venerable jewelry tradition is well represented at the very professional **Oro de Monte Albán,** on Pérez Gasga, ocean side, inside the west-end stop sign. Here are authentic museum-grade replicas of the celebrated Mixtec-style trove discovered in Monte Albán's tomb 7. Find it open Mon.–Sat. 10 A.M.–2 P.M. and 6:30–10:30 P.M., closed Sun. low season, tel. 954/582-0530.

The Uribe silversmithing family well represents Taxco tradition at its **Platería Ixtlán,** open Mon.–Sat. 10 A.M.–10 P.M., tel. 954/582-1672, a few doors east. Choose from a host of fetching floral, animal, and abstract designs, in silver and turquoise, garnet, jade, and other semiprecious stones.

For unique women's resortwear, look for **Bamboleo,** tel. 954/582-0993, a gem among the T-shirt clutter, on the beach side, toward the Pérez Gasga east end, open high season 10 A.M.–10 P.M. (low season hours shorter.) Here, find a colorful selection of skirts and tops, locally crafted from lovely Mexican cottons woven in Puebla and plenty of fetching *huipiles* from San Pedro Amuzgos.

La Luna shop, across Gasga from the Hotel Casa Blanca, also displays an attractive selection, with a riot of bright silk scarves, and cool batik resort shirts, skirts, and pants, made in Bali. Open daily 10 A.M.–9 P.M., tel. 954/582-0929.

Groceries

Abarrotes Lupita, a fairly well-stocked small grocery, offers meats, milk, ice, and vegetables. In addition, it stocks a few English-language publications, such as the *News* of Mexico City and magazines such as *Time, Life,* and *Newsweek,* on the inland side of Gasga, outside of the east-end stop sign. Open daily 10 A.M.–11 P.M.

Out on Playa Zicatela, where stores are not nearly so common, the friendly **Abarrotes Merlin,** tel. 954/582-1130, offers a small grocery selection; open daily 9 A.M.–10 P.M.

Photography

Foto Express Figueroa, tel. 954/582-0526, on Gasga next to Viajes Dimar, offers fast photofinishing services, Kodak color print and slide film,

and a moderate stock of accessories, including point-and-shoot cameras. Open daily 9 A.M.–9 P.M.

For a better camera selection, visit **Foto Discuento,** west end of the Pérez Gasga mall, tel. 954/582-0354, open Mon.–Sat. 9 A.M.–9 P.M., Sun. 9 A.M.–4 P.M.

INFORMATION

Tourist Information Office, Guides, and Language Instruction

Most months of the year, Oaxaca tourism staffs a small **information booth** on Pérez Gasga, just inside the west-end stop sign. Otherwise, you can consult the friendly, well-informed *oficina de turismo,* staff, tel./fax 954/582-0175, ginainpuerto@yahoo.com, who distribute a map of Oaxaca. It's open Mon.–Fri. 9 A.M.–3 P.M. and 6–8 P.M., just off Highway 200, in the little office on the beach side of the highway, a couple of blocks east of the airport Pemex gas station.

Personable **Gina Machorro,** who usually staffs the Pérez Gasga information booth, also gives a walking tour of Puerto Escondido and other excursions. Contact her at tel. 954/582-0276 or email ginainpuerto@yahoo.com.

Alternatively, try one of the tours led by guide **Ana Marquez,** aided by her daughter, her daughter, also Ana. Her itineraries cover the coast, from the renowned blowhole at Huatulco's Maguey Bay to the crocodile nursery at Chacahua National Park. Contact her at home at Futuro Mzna 7, no. 214, Fracc. Costa Chica, Puerto Escondido, Oaxaca 71984, tel. 954/582-2001, or at her Tigre Azul cyber café, tel. 954/582-2954 or 954/582-2855, beach-side, near the west end stop sign, or email ana@anasecotours.com. For more information, visit her website www.anasecotours.com.

At least two teachers offer **Spanish lessons:** Sheila Clarke, tel. 954/582-0276, and Yolanda Park, tel. 954/582-0837.

Community Organizations and Projects

One of the major ongoing projects the local ecological organization, **Eco Escondido,** is the recycling plant at the Hotel Acuario on Playa Zicatela, directed by community leaders Alejandro Villanueva and Hector Marshelli. For more information, contact Gina Machorro, tel. 954/582-0276, or email ginainpuerto@yahoo.com. Or, if you want to pitch in, drop by the hotel, about a quarter of a mile south of east end of the Pérez Gasca mall.

Another nearby ecoproject is the **turtle sanctuary** at Playa Escobilla, about 20 miles (30 km) east of Puerto Escondido. There, a cadre of SE-MARNAT (Secretariat of Marine Natural Resources) professionals and volunteers is rescuing, hatching, and returning tens of thousands of baby turtles to the sea annually.

A community organization, the **International Friends of Puerto Escondido** (IFOPE), welcomes Puerto Escondido newcomers with information and assistance, a lending library, and educational and social events. For information on monthly meetings, call tel. 954/582-1900, or email ifope@hotmail.com.

Publications

One of the few outlets of any English-language newspaper is the **Abarrotes Lupita,** tel. 954/582-0872, on Pérez Gasga, just outside the east-end stop sign. The *News* from Mexico City usually arrives around 3:30 P.M. Prepay to assure yourself a copy. Sometimes there may be a few copies of popular magazines, such as *Time, Newsweek,* and *People.*

English-language books are available at at least two spots in Puerto Escondido: the **Book Exchange,** at the Café Casa Babylon, next to the Hotel Acuario on Playa Zicatela, and **Acuario Books,** tel. 954/582-0127, on Pérez Gasga, west-end, uphill, across from the Hotel Nayar.

The local English-Spanish tourist newspaper, *El Sol de la Costa,* provides a load of useful information, including community events listings, emergency numbers, apartment rental listings, and many service advertisements. Pick up a free copy in one of its many advertiser-businesses along the Pérez Gasga mall. If you can't find a copy contact editor Warren Sharpe, tel. 954/582-2230, elsol@escondido.com.mx.

SERVICES

Money Exchange

Banamex, at Pérez Gasga 314, with ATM, uphill from the Hotel Nayar, tel. 954/582-0626, changes U.S. and Canadian cash and traveler's checks Mon.–Fri. 9 A.M.–4 P.M., Sat. 10 A.M.–2 P.M. You can also use the Banco Internacional 24-hour ATM, around the midpoint of the Pérez Gasga mall, next to the Hotel Las Palmas.

After bank hours, the small *casa de cambio* (money exchange) office on Pérez Gasga, next to the Hotel Casa Blanca, tel. 954/582-1928, also exchanges cash and traveler's checks Mon.–Fri. 9 A.M.–9 P.M., Sat.–Sun. 9 A.M.–8 P.M. Another *casa de cambio* offers similar services, on Playa Zicatela, next to Hotel Acuario, tel. 954/582-0592, open daily 9 A.M.–7 P.M.

Communications

The *correo* and *telégrafo* are side by side on Av. 7 Norte, corner Av. Oaxaca, seven blocks into town from the *crucero.* The post office, tel. 954/582-0959, is open Mon.–Fri. 8 A.M.–4 P.M., Sat. 9 A.M.–1 P.M.; the *telégrafo,* which has public fax (tel. 954/582-0232), is open Mon.–Fri. 9 A.M.–7:30 P.M., Sat. 9 A.M.–noon (Mon.–Fri. 9 A.M.–1 P.M. and 3–5 P.M. for money orders).

For local and long-distance **telephone,** buy a Ladatel public telephone card at one of many Pérez Gasga stores and use it in street telephones. First dial 001 for calls to the United States and Canada, and 01 for long-distance calls within Mexico.

More conveniently situated on Pérez Gasga, west end, a *larga distancia* offers both telephone and fax service, daily 8 A.M.-10:30 P.M., tel./fax 954/582-0448, across Gasga and east from Restaurant La Galería. On Playa Zicatela, use the public long-distance telephone at the desk of the Hotel Acuario.

Beware certain prominently situated "Call Home with Your Credit Card" telephones. Tariffs on these phones can run $10 or more per minute, with a three-minute minimum, costing $30 whether you talk three minutes or not. Ask the operator for the rate; if it's too high, take your business elsewhere.

Internet access, daily until around 9 P.M., is available at cyber café **Tigre Azul**, run by guide Ana Marquez and her daughter Ana, beach-side, about a block inside the west-end Pérez Gasga stop sign.

Alternatively, across from the Banco Internacional ATM in the middle of the Gasga mall, **Coffee Net** offers Internet connection, fax, and long-distance telephone, daily, tel. 954/582-0797; or on Playa Zicatela, Internet connection is also available at **Hotel Acuario,** daily 8 A.M.–8:30 P.M.

Health, Police, and Emergencies

For medical emergencies, go to the 24-hour **Hospital Santa Fe,** tel. 954/582-0541, which has an internist, pediatrician, gynecologist, and a dental surgeon on call. For more routine consultations, office hours are Mon.–Fri. 9 A.M.–2 P.M. and 4–8 P.M., Sat. 9 A.M.–2 P.M. Find the hospital three blocks west of the *crucero,* uphill from the highway on Calle 3 Poniente between Calles 2 and 3 Norte.

Alternatively, go next door, to the **Sanatorio del Carmen,** tel. 954/582-1876 or 954/582-0174, with a number of female doctors on call.

You could also consult with English-speaking general practitioner **Dr. Francisco Serrano,** above the highway, at Calle 1 Norte 205, two blocks west of the main street, across Calle 1 Norte from Bancomer.

Another option is the 24-hour government health clinic, **Centro de Salud,** on Av. Pérez Gasga, just uphill from the Hotel Loren.

Get over-the-counter remedies and prescriptions at either of the two good tourist-zone pharmacies: the 24-hour **Farmacia La Moderna,** of Dr. José Luis Esparzar, tel. 954/582-0698 or 954/582-2780, on Gasga a block below the *crucero,* or **Super Farmas,** tel. 954/582-0112, on the Pérez Gasga mall, across from Hotel Las Palmas, open 8 A.M.–2 P.M. and 5–10 P.M.

For police or fire emergencies, call the **municipal police,** tel. 954/582-0498, or go to the headquarters in the Agencia Municipal on Highway 200, about four blocks west of the Pérez Gasga *crucero.*

Meditation and Massage

Healing is the mission of partners Patricia Heuze and Alejandro Villanuevo, who operate **Villa Temazcalli** meditation and massage center, west end of town, on Av. Infragante, two blocks uphill from the highway. Facilities include rustic hot baths, an indigenous-style *temazcal* hot room, and massage room in an invitingly tranquil tropical garden setting. Prices run about $20 each for massage and the hot tub, and about $15 for one, $20 for two, and $25 for three, for the *temazcal.* For information and appointments, call tel. 954/582-1023, or email masaje@temazcalli.com; for more information, visit the website www.temazcalli.com.

Travel Agent and Car Rental

One of the most respected travel agents in town is **Viajes Dimar,** at the middle of the tourist mall, at Av. Pérez Gasga 906, P.O. Box 22, Puerto Escondido, Oaxaca 71980, tel./fax 954/582-0734 or 954/582-0237.

Rent a car at **Budget Rent a Car** on Calle Juárez, beach side of Highway 200, in the Bachoco suburb, by the airport, tel. 954/582-0312.

Laundry

Get your laundry done Mon.–Sat. 8 A.M.–8 P.M., Sun. 8 A.M.–5 P.M., at the **Lavamático del Centro,** two doors downhill from Banamex, on Pérez Gasga, about two blocks uphill, from the west-end stop sign.

GETTING THERE AND AWAY

By Air

The small jetport, officially the **Aeropuerto Puerto Escondido** (code-designated PXM), is just off the highway a mile west of town. The terminal, only a plain waiting room with check-in desks, has no services save a small snack bar. Out in front, *colectivo* vans to hotels in town run $2 per person. Arrivees with a minimum of luggage, however, can walk a block to the highway and flag down one of the many eastbound local minibuses, which all stop at the main town highway crossing. Arrive with a hotel in mind (better yet a hotel reservation in hand), unless you prefer letting your taxi driver choose one, where he will probably collect a commission for depositing you there.

Although **car rental agents** may not routinely meet flights, they will meet you if you have a reservation. Call Budget, tel. 954/582-0312 or 954/582-0315, budget33@hotmail.com, or Alamo, tel. 954/582-3003, email alamoescondido@hotmail.com.

Be prepared to pay the $12 international **departure tax** or its Mexican peso equivalent, if your ticket doesn't already include it. If you lose your tourist card, avoid trouble or a fine by taking your passport and some proof of your arrival date (such as a stamped passport, a copy of your lost tourist card, or an air ticket) to **Migración** at the airport, tel. 954/582-3369, for help *before* your day of departure.

A few regularly scheduled flights connect Puerto Escondido with other Mexican destinations.

Aerocaribe Airlines flights connect daily with Mexico City, Oaxaca, and Huatulco. For reservations or flight information, call tel. 954/582-2024 or 954/582-2023.

If the above flights cannot take you where you want to go, try **Aerovega,** the dependable local air-taxi service, tel. 954/582-0151 (or in Oaxaca city, tel. 951/515-4982) or Viajes Dimar, on Gasga, tel. 954/582-0734 or 954/582-0737, for information and reservations.

Alternatively, charter airline **Aerotucan** also runs Oaxaca-Puerto Escondido flights, depending upon passenger demand. Call the airline, at tel. 954/582-1725, or travel agent Viajes Dimar, on Gasga, tel. 954/582-0734 or 954/582-0737, for information and reservations.

Puerto Escondido is also accessible via the Puerto Ángel-Huatulco airport, one hour away by road. (See the Bays of Huatulco and Vicinity section.)

By Car or RV

National Highway 200, although sometimes winding, is generally smooth and uncongested between Puerto Escondido and Pinotepa Nacional (89 miles, 143 km, 2.5 hours) to the west. From there, continue another 160 miles (258 km, 4.5 hours) to Acapulco. Fill up at Puerto Escondido before you leave, although gasoline is available at several points along the routes.

Traffic sails between Puerto Escondido and Puerto Ángel, 44 miles (71 km) apart, in an easy hour. Actually, Pochutla is immediately on the highway; Puerto Ángel is six miles downhill from the junction, or alternatively accessible via the very scenic paved shortcut, at San Antonio village, Km 198. Santa Cruz de Huatulco is an easy 22 miles (35 km) farther east.

To or from Oaxaca, all paved but sometimes roughly potholed National Highway 131 connects directly north, along main street Av. Oaxaca, via its winding but spectacular 158-mile (254-km) route over the pine-clad Sierra Madre del Sur. The route, which rises 9,000 feet through Chatino foothill and mountain country, can be chilly in the winter and has few services along the lonely 100-mile middle stretch between San Gabriel Mixtepec and Sola de Vega. Take water and blankets, and be prepared for emergencies. Allow about nine hours at the wheel from Puerto Escondido, eight hours the other way, from Oaxaca. Fill up with gasoline at the airport Pemex stations on either end before heading out. Unleaded gasoline is consistently available only at the Sola de Vega Pemex *gasolinera* en route.

By Bus

Several long-distance bus lines serve Puerto Escondido; some offer first-class service. **Estrella Blanca** subsidiary lines (luxury and first-class Elite and Futura and others), from the station on Av. Oaxaca just uphill from the *crucero,* tel. 954/582-0427, travel the Highway 200 Acapulco-Isthmus route. More than two dozen daily *salidas de paso* come through en route both ways between Acapulco and Pochutla and Huatulco (Crucecita) and Salina Cruz. Other additional buses pass through, connecting with either Ixtapa-Zihuatanejo or Mexico City via Acapulco.

Cristóbal Colón, the other major first-class bus line, maintains a station on Av. 1 Norte between Av. 2 Oriente and Av. 1 Oriente, about three blocks uphill, one block east from the Pérez Gasga highway crossing, tel. 954/582-1073. It serves the Oaxaca east coast, beginning in Puerto

Escondido, connecting all the way to San Cristóbal las Casas in Chiapas and Tapachula, at the Guatemala border. Intermediate destinations include Pochutla, Huatulco (Crucecita), and Sallina Cruz. At Pochutla, passengers can transfer to Cristobal Colón Oaxaca-bound buses. One of these continues, via Puebla, to Mexico City.

Cooperating lines **Autobúses Estrella del Valle** and **Autotransportes Oaxaca Pacífico** on Hidalgo, corner of 3 Oriente, tel. 954/582-0050, provide both first- and second-class connections east with Pochutla, Bahías de Huatulco

(Crucecita). Also, both first- and second-class buses connect with Oaxaca, via both Highway 175 through Pochutla and Highway 131 directly from Puerto Escondido.

Other minor mostly second-class bus lines offer departures from the gravel lot at Calle 10 Norte and Highway 131 main street, Av. Oaxaca. From there and also at a small storefront station on Hidalgo between 1 Oriente and 2 Oriente, **Autobúses Estrella Roja del Sureste** and **Transol** buses, tel. 954/582-0603, connect (via pilgimage town Juquila) along Highway 131 with Oaxaca.

Puerto Ángel and Vicinity

During his three presidencies, Oaxaca-born Benito Juárez shaped many dreams into reality. One such dream was to better the lot of his native brethren in the isolated south of Oaxaca by developing a port for shipping the lumber and coffee they could harvest in the lush Pacific-slope jungles of the Sierra Madre del Sur. The small bay of Puerto Ángel, directly south of the state capital, was chosen, and by 1870 it had become Oaxaca's busiest port.

Unfortunately, Benito Juárez died two years later. New priorities and Puerto Ángel's isolation soon wilted Juárez's plan, and Puerto Ángel lapsed into a generations-long slumber.

In the 1960s, Puerto Ángel was still a sleepy little spot connected by a single frail link—a tortuous cross-Sierra dirt road—to the rest of the country. Adventure travelers saw it at the far south of the map and dreamed of a South Seas paradise. They came and were not disappointed. Although that first tourist trickle has grown steadily, it's only enough to support the sprinkling of modest lodgings and restaurants that now dot the beaches and hillsides around Puerto Ángel's tranquil little blue bay.

BEACHES AND SIGHTS
Getting Oriented
Puerto Ángel is at the southern terminus of Highway 175 from Oaxaca, about six miles (nine km) downhill from its intersection with Highway

200. It's a small place, where nearly everything is within walking distance along the beach, which a rocky bayfront hill divides into two parts: Playa Principal, the main town beach, and sheltered west-side Playa Panteón, the tourist favorite. A scenic boulder-decorated shoreline *andador* (watch out for gaps and holes in the concrete) connects the two beaches.

A paved road winds west from Puerto Ángel along the coastline a couple of miles to Playa Zipolite, lined by a colony of hammock-and-bamboo beachfront cabanas, popular with an international cadre of budget-minded seekers of heaven on earth. Continuing west, the road passes the former turtle-processing village beaches of Playa San Agustinillo and Playa Mazunte. From there it goes on another four miles, joining with Highway 200 (and thence Puerto Escondido) at San Antonio village at Km 198.

The major local service and transportation center is **Pochutla** (pop. 35,000), a mile north along Highway 175 from its Highway 200 junction.

Getting Around
Local *colectivos* ferry passengers frequently between Pochutla and Puerto Ángel (fare, about $.50) from about 7 A.M. until 8 P.M., stopping at the Highway 200 intersection. Some buses continue to Zipolite and Mazunte after stopping on Boulevard Uribe, Puerto Ángel's main bayfront street. Also from Boulevard Uribe, a local shuttle bus connects frequently with Zipolite, San

Agustinillo, Mazunte, and back about every half hour during daylight hours, stopping everywhere en route. Taxis also routinely make runs between Puerto Ángel and either Zipolite or Pochutla for about $5.

You can also get around by boat. Captains routinely take parties of up to eight for sightseeing, snorkeling, and picnicking to a number of nearby beaches. Bargain at the Puerto Ángel pier (rate should run about $15/hour), or contact the local travel agent, **Agencia de Viajes Gambusino,** tel. 958/584-3080 or 958/584-3038.

Playas Principal, Panteón, and Estacahuite

Playa Principal's 400 yards of wide golden sand decorate most of Puerto Ángel's bayfront. Waves can be strong near the pier, where they often surge vigorously onto the beach and recede with some undertow. Swimming is more tranquil at the sheltered west end toward Playa Panteón. The clear waters are good for casual snorkeling around the rocks, on both sides of the bay.

Sheltered Playa Panteón (Cemetery Beach)

is Puerto Ángel's sunning beach, lined with squadrons of beach chairs and umbrellas in front of beachside restaurants. **Playa Oso** (Bear Beach) is a little dab of sand beside a rugged seastack of rock beyond Playa Panteón, fun to swim to from Playa Panteón.

Playa Estacahuite, just outside the opposite (east) side of the bay, is actually two beaches in one: a pair of luscious coral-sand nooks teeming with fish grazing the living reef just offshore. (Don't put your hands in crevices; a moray eel may mistake your finger for a fish and bite.) A pair of *palapa* restaurants perched picturesquely above the beaches provides food and drinks. Get there in less than a mile by taxi or on foot via the dirt road that forks right off the highway, about 400 yards uphill from beachfront Boulevard Uribe.

Playa Zipolite

Playa Zipolite is a wide, mile-long strand of yellow-white sand enfolded by headlands and backed by palm groves. It stretches from the intimate little cove and beach of **Playa del Amor**

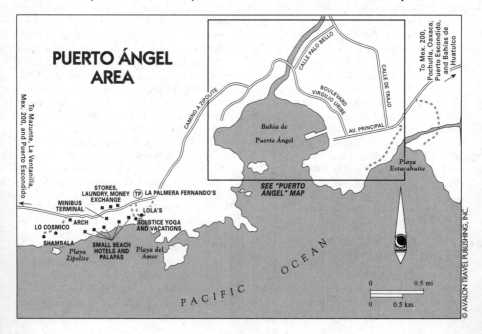

PUERTO ÁNGEL AREA

To Mazunte, La Ventanilla, Mex. 200, and Puerto Escondido

CAMINO A ZIPOLITE

CALLE PALO BELLO

BOULEVARD VIRGILIO URIBE

CALLE DE TRAJO

AV. PRINCIPAL

To Mex. 200, Pochutla, Oaxaca, Puerto Escondido, and Bahías de Huatulco

Bahía de Puerto Ángel

SEE "PUERTO ÁNGEL" MAP

Playa Estacahuite

MINIBUS TERMINAL

STORES, LAUNDRY, MONEY EXCHANGE

TP

LA PALMERA FERNANDO'S

LOLA'S

LO COSMICO

ARCH

SOLSTICE YOGA AND VACATIONS

SHAMBALA

Playa Zipolite

SMALL BEACH HOTELS AND PALAPAS

Playa del Amor

PACIFIC OCEAN

0   0.5 mi

0   0.5 km

© AVALON TRAVEL PUBLISHING, INC.

tucked on its east side to towering seacliffs rising behind the new-age Shambala retreat on the west end. The Playa Zipolite surf, although usually tranquil in the mornings (but always with significant undertow), can turn thunderous by the afternoon, especially when offshore storms magnify both the swells and the undertow. Experienced surfers love these times, when everyone but experts should stay out.

Good surfing notwithstanding, Zipolite's renown stems from its status as one of the very few nude beaches in Mexico. Bathing au naturel, practiced nearly entirely by visitors and a few local young men, is tolerated only grudgingly by local people, many of whose livelihoods depend on the nudists. If you're discreet and take off your clothes at the more isolated west end (behind the big rock), no one will appear to mind (and women will avoid voyeuristic attentions of Mexican boys and men).

Visitors' nude sunbathing habits may have something to do with the gruffness of some local people. Many of them probably prefer their former occupations in turtle fishing rather than serving tourists, who often seem to be in short supply compared to the battalion of beachfront *palapas* competing for their business.

Most Zipolite visitors stay in the palm-shaded east-end trailer park or in one of the score of hammock-equipped stick-and-thatch beachfront cabana hotels. Often with fans and outside cold-water showers and privies, cabanas rent for $10–15 double per night, depending upon amenities. Although many are indifferently managed, some, such as Lola's, Lo Cósmico, and Shambala (see Zipolite Accommodations), are unique.

Playas San Agustinillo and Mazunte

About a mile west of Zipolite, a wide, mile-long, yellow-sand beach curves past the village of San Agustinillo. On the open ocean but partly protected by offshore rocks, its surf is much like that of Zipolite, varying from gentle to rough, depending mostly upon wind and offshore swells. Small village groceries and beachside *palapa* restaurants supply food and drinks to the occasional Zipolite overflow and

local families on weekends and holidays. Fishing is excellent, either in the surf, from nearby rocks, by rented *panga,* or your own boat launched from the beach. Beach camping is customary, especially at the rustic, hammock-hung roadside *ramadas,* **Palapa Lucy, Palapa Kaly,** and **Palapa Sol Mar** at the east (Zipolite) end of the beach.

Remnants of the local turtle industry can be found at the rusting former processing factories on Playa San Agustinillo (west end) and Playa Mazunte two miles farther west.

The half-mile-long, yellow-sand Mazunte Beach, like San Agustinillo, is semisheltered and varies from tranquil to rough. Fishing is likewise good, beach camping is customary (as a courtesy, ask nearby business owners if it's okay), and local stores and seafood *palapa* restaurants sell basic supplies and food.

Mazunte people have also been renovating their houses and building cabanas to accommodate an increasing number of visitors. Some have even begun to advertise on the Internet. Signs along the road and at the beach advertise their homespun lodgings and restaurants, such as Posada Aketzalli, across from the turtle museum, Cabañas La Huerta (shady orchard, or *huerta*), Posada Lolo, Casa de Huéspedes Los Arcos, and Restaurant La Dolce Vita (good lasagna).

Turtle Museum and Cosmetics Factory and Store

The former turtle processing plant at Mazunte lives on as a turtle museum, including aquarium, study center, and turtle hatchery. Here, you can peruse displays illustrating the ongoing turtle research and conservation program and see members of most of Mexico's turtle species paddling in tanks overlooking the beach where their ancestors once swarmed. The center, on the main road, east end of village, is open Wed.–Sat. 10 A.M.–4:30 P.M., Sun. 10 A.M.–2:30 P.M. For more information contact the Centro Mexicano de la Tortuga, P.O. Box 16, Puerto Ángel, Oaxaca 70902, tel. 958/584-3603.

About half a mile farther west along the main road through Mazunte village, stop by the store and works of the **Fábrica Ecología de**

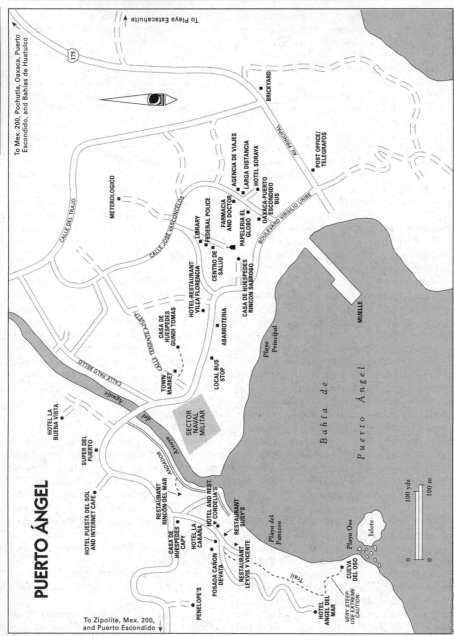

PUERTO ÁNGEL

To Mex. 200, Pochutla, Oaxaca, Puerto Escondido, and Bahías de Huatulco

To Playa Estacahuite

To Zipolite, Mex. 200, and Puerto Escondido

BRICKYARD

POST OFFICE/ TELEGRAFOS

AGENCIA DE VIAJES

LARGA DISTANCIA

HOTEL SORAYA

Oaxaca-Puerto Escondido BUS

FARMACIA AND DOCTOR

PAPELERIA EL GLOBO

FEDERAL POLICE

LIBRARY

CENTRO DE SALUD

HOTEL-RESTAURANT VILLA FLORENCIA

CASA DE HUESPEDES RINCON SABROSO

METEROLOGICO

CASA DE HUESPEDES GUNDI TOMAS

TOWN MARKET

ABARROTERIA

LOCAL BUS STOP

SECTOR NAVAL MILITAR

HOTEL LA BUENA VISTA

SUPER DEL PUERTO

HOTEL PUESTA DEL SOL AND INTERNET CAFE

RESTAURANT RINCÓN DEL MAR

HOTEL AND REST. CORDELIA'S

HOTEL LA CABAÑA

RESTAURANT SUSY'S

CASA DE HUESPEDES CAPY

POSADA CAÑON DEVATA

RESTAURANT LEYVIS Y VICENTE

PENELOPE'S

HOTEL ANGEL DEL MAR

VERY STEEP-USE EXTREME CAUTION

CUEVA DEL OSO

Playa Oso

Islote

Playa del Panteon

Trail

Playa Principal

MUELLE

Bahía de Puerto Ángel

BOULEVARD VIRGILIO URIBE

AV. PRINCIPAL

CALLE DEL TRAJO

CALLE JOSE VASCONCELOS

CALLE TENIENTE AZUETA

CALLE PALO BELLO

Arroyo

100 yds

100 m

© AVALON TRAVEL PUBLISHING, INC.

Cosméticos Naturales de Mazunte. Initially funded mostly by the Body Shop Foundation, spearheaded by the local chapter of ecology corps **Ec Solar** and supported by an international government-university consortium, local workers make and sell all-natural shampoo, skin cream, hair conditioner, and more. Staff are working hard to assure that the effort catches on, so that locally grown products, such as coconut, corn, and avocado oils and natural aromatics will form the basis for a thriving cottage cosmetics industry.

Playa La Ventanilla

Continue about a mile and a half west along the main road over the low hill west of Mazunte and turn left at the signed dirt road to pristine wildlife haven Playa and Laguna La Ventanilla. Now protected by local residents, swarms of birds, including pelicans, cormorants, and herons, nest there, and a population of wild *cocodrilos* and *lagartos* is making a comeback in a bushy mangrove wetland. Boatmen headquartered at the *palapa* beach village at road's end guide visitors on a two-hour ecotour ($4 per adult, kids half price), which includes a stop for refreshment at a little midlagoon island. The boatmen are known for their wildlife-sensitivity and allow no motor vehicles within 100 yards of their communally owned lagoon-sanctuary.

The Playa La Ventanilla community has also taken responsibility for protecting the turtles that arrive on their beach against poachers. During both February and June through October, hundreds of sea turtles come ashore to lay eggs. If necessary, community volunteers help the exhausted turtles up the steep beach, where they lay their eggs. Volunteers then gather the eggs and rebury them in a secure spot. After the hatchlings emerge about a month and a half later, volunteers nurture them for about three months and release them safely back into the ocean.

Moreover, the La Ventanilla *ejido* invites visitors to stay in its rough-and-ready, rustic but sturdy, concrete-floored cabanas with beds. (Bring your own mosquito net.)

ACCOMMODATIONS

Puerto Ángel Hotels and Guesthouses

Although only the newest of Puerto Ángel's 20-odd lodgings is directly on the beach, most of them are within a stone's throw of it. The successful lodgings have given their legion of savvy repeat customers what they want: clean, basic, tepid-water accommodations in tranquil, television-free settings where Puerto Ángel's natural isolation and tropical charm set the tone for long, restful holidays.

As you move west around the bay from the pier, first comes the 1960s motel-style **Hotel Soraya**, perched on the bluff above Playa Principal, Priv. José Vasconcelos 2A, Puerto Ángel, Oaxaca 70902, tel./fax 958/584-3009. Well managed by personable owner Hortencia Tanus, the hotel includes a restaurant with an airy bay view, fine for bright morning breakfasts and sunset-glow dinners. Outside, two tiers of spartan but light and comfortable rooms enclose a parking patio. Although some rooms have a/c, the fan-only ones are generally better. Rent on the upper tier for more privacy. The 32 rooms rent for about $35 s or d, and $40 t high season, ask for a discount low season.

At the splendidly isolated **Casa de Huéspedes Rincón Sabroso**, Puerto Ángel, Oaxaca 70902, tel. 958/584-3095, atop the adjacent bay-vista hill, guests enjoy lodgings that open onto a hammock-hung view breezeway adorned by luscious tropical greenery. Inside, rooms are very clean (but dark), with white walls, tile floors, shiny bathrooms, and natural wood furnishings. Guests have the additional option of good food and each other's company in an airy café, perched above a heavenly bay and sunset panorama. Rates for the eight rooms run about $14 s, $16 d, $19 t low season, about $18, $22, and $24 high, with fans. Owners have added a pair of more private, deluxe rooms (nos. 9 and 10), with hot water, for about $20 d low season, $30 high.

Travelers who enjoy being right in the middle of the Puerto Ángel beachfront street scene choose the worthy **Hotel Villa Florencia,** Blv. Virgilio Uribe s/n, Puerto Ángel, Oaxaca 70902, tel./fax 958/584-3044, villaserenaoax@hotmail.com. Here, in the shady interior lobby-patio, past the excellent streetfront restaurant, tranquility reigns as soft classic songs and instrumental music play in the background, while guests read and relax on comfortable chairs and couches. Upstairs, the approximately 15 rooms, with bath, are immaculate and thoughtfully decorated with local art and handicrafts. Rates run about $25 s, $35 d, $40 t year-round, add $3 for a/c.

Equally exceptional nearby is **Casa de Huéspedes Gundi y Tomás,** the life project of friendly German expatriate Gundi López, address simply Puerto Ángel, Oaxaca 70902, tel. 958/584-3068, gundtoma@hotmail.com. Her homey, rustic-aesthetic complex rambles up a leafy hillside to a breezy bay-view *palapa* where patrons relax, socialize, and enjoy food and drink from Gundi's kitchen. Just above that, guests enjoy a double row of several clean, simply furnished (although dark) rooms, shaded by a shared hammock-hung view porch. Besides all this, Gundi is happy to volunteer information about local sights and activities and arrange excursions for her guests. Rooms with shared showers and toilets cost about $14 d low season, $17 high; larger rooms with private shower and toilet run about $17 d low season, $20 high, all with fans. Get there by walking uphill along the little alley adjacent to the town market and just opposite the beachfront naval compound.

Another Puerto Ángel gem is **Hotel La Buena Vista,** P.O. Box 48, Puerto Ángel, Oaxaca 70902, tel./fax 958/584-3104, adriang@prodigy.net.mx, tucked on the hillside that rises just west of the Arroyo del Aguaje. The hotel's four tiers stairstep artfully up the jungly slope. First- and second-level rooms open to shady hammock-hung view porches. On the third level, a luxuriously airy restaurant *palapa* opens to a picture-perfect bay vista. The climax is a pair of large onyx-tile-floored fourth-floor rooms that share an entire private view patio with hammocks. Above that, owners have added a luxurious view pool-patio for guest enjoyment.

All rooms are immaculate, light, and simply but tastefully furnished, with spotless bathrooms. Low-season rates for the approximately 20 rooms run about $30 s, $33 d for standard, $35 s or d for deluxe room with private balcony, and $45 d for the top-floor deluxe room with double-sized onyx bathtub; high season, the same go for about $38, $40, and $46, all with fans, an excellent restaurant, and hot water in the deluxe rooms. For more information, visit the website www.labuenavista.com.

Heading around the curve of the bay to the Playa Panteón neighborhood, you'll find one of Puerto Ángel's old standby budget lodgings, **Casa de Huéspedes Capy,** Playa Panteón, P.O. Box 44, Puerto Ángel, Oaxaca 70902, tel./fax 958/58430-02, hotel_capy@hotmail.com, sitting on the bay-view hillside by the road fork to Zipolite. Rooms, in two tiers with views toward Playa Panteón, are basic but clean with fans and cool-water private baths. Good family management is the Capy's strong suit. This shows in the shady view restaurant, Arcely, where good food in a friendly atmosphere encourages guests to linger, reading or talking, for hours. The family also watch the community TV at night; if it bothers you, ask them to turn it down. The 10 rooms rent for about $10 s, $15 d low season, $12 and $16 high. Rooms with two beds go for $18 d, $19 t low season, $19 and $20 high.

Downhill, new **Hotel Cordelia,** Puerto Ángel's first beachfront lodging, stands right on Playa Panteón, Puerto Escondido, Oaxaca 70902, tel. 958/584-3109, azul_profundomx@hotmail.com. The Cordelia's seven rooms, most with bay views, are sparely but pleasingly decorated with rustic whitewashed walls, attractive native floor tiles, natural wood furniture, and artful tile touches in the modern-standard baths. No phone, no TV, just the murmur of the gentle Playa Panteón surf to lull you to sleep. Rooms rent for about $25 s or d, $50 t or q low season, $30 and $60 high. With fans and good restaurant downstairs.

This trip I was happy to discover that the family-operated Puerto Ángel gem, **Posada Cañon Devata,** P.O. Box 10, Puerto Ángel, Oaxaca 70902, tel./fax 958/584-3137, has reopened. Owner and artist Mateo López and his son Dashan have resumed management after a two-year hiatus. During the 1980s Mateo and his former spouse, Susana, restored their deforested canyon to health, artfully placing about a dozen charmingly petite, art-decorated guest cabanas along leafy hillside paths. Low-season rentals run about $30 s, $35 d, $45 and $50 high. With fans and good macrobiotic restaurant.

Atop the hill via the adjacent steep road, the **Hotel Ángel del Mar,** Puerto Ángel, Oaxaca 70902, tel. 958/584-3008, fax 958/584-3014, offers 42 rooms at about $20 s, $30 d low season, $35 and $48 high. Credit cards are accepted (but you'll get a discount if you pay cash). Guests enjoy a big, open-air dining room, swimming pool, and large light rooms with private balconies looking down upon a panoramic bay vista. Mornings, guests can enjoy sunrise over the bay and evening sunsets over the ocean. Revitalized management has recently brightened the place up with new paint everywhere and new bedspreads and lampshades to go with the venerable polished wood furniture in the rooms. For more information, visit the website www.hotel_angel_del_mar.com.

Not far away, about 100 yards uphill past the road fork to Zipolite (watch for the sign at the hilltop driveway on the left), consider the guesthouse **Penelope's** (of Homeric legend). With only a few rooms but benefiting from a breezy, quiet hilltop setting, owner Patricia enjoys sharing her home with guests, taking special pleasure in serving her uniquely delicious margarita cocktails. Rooms come comfortably furnished with hot water showers, and porches with hammocks and fans. Rentals run about $15 s, $15–32 d. Add about $4 per person for breakfast, $7 for dinner. Reserve at P.O. Box 49, Puerto Ángel, Oaxaca 70902, tel. 958/584-3073.

Vacationers hankering for splendid isolation can have it at **Bahía de la Luna,** on the coast about three small bays east of Puerto Ángel, at P.O. Box 90, Pochutla, Oaxaca 70900, tel./fax 958/584-6186, email bahia-de-la-lu@usa.net. Here, owner Ivan Wastchenko shares his paradise with visitors. His approximately 15 rustic-chic adobe, palm-thatched cabanas cluster on a lovely isolated crescent of golden sand. No phones, TV, or traffic; simply sun, sea, sand, and catch-of-the-day home-cooked seafood. Cabanas,

thoughtfully and comfortably furnished, rent for about $40 s, $45 d low season, $50 and $55 including three meals, with fans, but room-temperature water. Ivan also offers a beachfront house, sleeping five, with kitchen, for $180 low season, $200 high. For more information, visit the website www.totalmedia.qc.ca/bahiadelaluna.

Get there by the rugged jeep road, signed Bahía de la Luna, which forks east about four miles uphill from Puerto Ángel. Not far after the highway, follow the first fork right, along a ridge, then steeply (and ruggedly) downhill to the picture-perfect cove and beach.

Zipolite Accommodations

Zipolite's line of rustic (bring your own towel and soap) lodgings starts at **Lola's,** tel. 958/584-3201 or 958/58432-03, on the east end of the beach, Playa Zipolite, Puerto Ángel, Oaxaca 70902. The friendly owner continues her decades-long good management (although her equally personable daughter now does most of the day-to-day work) of her thatch-shaded restaurant and beach cabanas. For customers who hanker for a bit better lodging, Lola has broken new ground with Zipolite's first permanent units, eight new rooms with private baths (but only room-temperature water) and ceiling fans. The best are two front, top-floor units overlooking the gorgeous beach and sunset vista. The scene at Lola's resembles a miniresort, with the restaurant right on the beach, where guests enjoy late breakfasts, stroll out for swims, read thick novels, and kick back and enjoy convivial conversation with mostly North American and European fellow vacationers. Although past hurricanes wiped out the rustic wood cabanas, they've been rebuilt with modern-standard stucco units that rent for about $15 s, $20 d, $25 t year-round, with fan and private shower baths.

Alternatively, consider **Solstice Yoga and Vacations,** next door, west, from Lola's, at Playa Zipolite, P.O. Box 18, Puerto Ángel, Oaxaca 70902, fax 958/584-3070. Friendly European expatriate owners Brigette Longueville and Guy Hamaekers have built an inviting, authentically rustic minicolony of two-story cabanas on the gorgeous Zipolite beachfront. Accommodations

Lo Cósmico *palapas*, right on Playa Zipolite, feature hammocks or comfortable beds, fans, and private baths.

are in Robinson Crusoe–, South Sea Islands–open style in all natural wood, with ladders leading to upstairs sleeping-lounging areas, with serape-draped beds, hung with gauzy mosquito nets. Guests are about evenly divided between beach vacationers and yoga devotees, who attend sessions in the in-house studio.

Accommodations rent for about $20 d low season, $30 high, for the one smaller unit, and about $25 low, $35 high for the three larger units; $5 per extra person, with private bathroom with toilet and tepid-water shower baths and breakfast included. Dormitory accommodations are also available, for $8 per person low season, $10 high. Brigette and Guy offer Hatha yoga classes, for $5 per 1.5 hours. For more information, visit the website www.solstice-mexico.com.

The **Lo Cósmico** cabanas nestle on a cactus-decorated rocky knoll at the opposite, west, end of the beach, Playa Zipolite, P.O. Box 36, Pochutla, Oaxaca 70900, email locosmico@hotmail.com. White spheres perched on their thatched roof peaks lend a mystical Hindu-Buddhist accent to the cabanas' already picturesque appearance. In the restaurant atop the knoll, you're likely to find Regula and Antonio Nadurille, Lo Cósmico's European-Mexican owners. Regula manages the restaurant, specializing in a dozen varieties of tasty crêpes, while Antonio supervises the hotel. Their hillside and beach-level cabanas are clean, candle-lit, and equipped with hammocks and concrete floors, for about $12–17 d, with outside showers and toilets. Recently, Antonio has built a number of sturdy, rock-walled, hurricane-proof designer rooms on his view hillside. Figure about $20 d for these, including private baths. For more information, visit the website www.locosmico.com.

Shambala, on the adjacent forested hillside, is as it sounds—a tranquil Buddhist-style retreat, at Puerto Ángel, P.O. Box 68, Pochutla, Oaxaca, 70900, fax 958/584-3151 or 958/584-3152. Shambala's driving force is the friendly owner/community leader Gloria Esperanza Johnson, who arrived in Zipolite by accident in 1970 and decided to stay, eventually adopting Mexican citizenship. She built the Shambala from the ground up, gradually adding on until there were about five primitive "monk's cells" and about 10 small handcrafted rustic cabanas, an excellent macrobiotic panoramic vista restaurant, and a spiritual center.

Shambala is a quiet, alcohol-free haven for lovers of reading, sunbathing, hiking, yoga, and meditation. It sits atop an enviable few acres at the edge of a sylvan hinterland. Adjacent cactus-studded cliffs plummet spectacularly to surf-splashed rocks below, while trails fan out through lush tropical deciduous forest. The very simple candle-lit thatched concrete-floored cabanas with hammocks rent for about $7 per person (hammock space only, including hammock, $3). Toilets and showers are shared. Work exchange for room and board is negotiable. Gloria also welcomes lovers of the outdoors to camp (about $3 per person, per day) in Shambala's get-away-from-it-all jungle "El Encanto" retreat, in a pristine mountain river valley about an hour away by car or local bus. For more information and directions, ask Gloria or her staff assistants.

Get to both Shambala and Lo Cósmico by turning from the main road onto the dirt driveway just west of the arch at Zipolite's west end. Bear right at the first fork, then left at the next for Lo Cósmico, right for Shambala.

Posada Rancho Cerro Largo

Outstandingly innovative Posada Rancho Cerro Largo is the creation of ecoactivist Mario Corella, descendant of a longtime Hermosillo, Sonora, hotel family. After knocking around in the hospitality trade for several years, Mario decided to create his own version of utopia. Mario says that he wanted to "be in contact with nature and live among the community with as little impact as possible. I would welcome guests as friends, to share the dinner table with me and the hotel staff."

He's done it, with a reception-restaurant and several rustically charming tile-floored, wood-and-adobe cabanas, furnished with hand-loomed bedspreads and opening to hammock-hung ocean-view verandas. The entire complex nestles in a cactus-dotted leafy hillside forest, linked by a path that meanders, between panoramic ocean viewpoints, to a gorgeously isolated, wave-washed sandy beach below. Rates run a reasonable $60 s, $70 d, add $18 per person for breakfast and dinner. For reservations (mandatory in winter, highly recommended anytime), write the Posada Rancho Cerro Largo, P.O. Box 121, Pochutla, Oaxaca 70900, or fax 958/584-3063, or email ranchocerrolargomx@yahoo.com. Look for the signed driveway on the Puerto Ángel-Mazunte road, four miles (6.4 km) from the Puerto Ángel bus stop.

Trailer Parks and Camping

The homey **Trailer Park La Palmera Fernando's** and café has about 20 parking (big rigs possible) or camping spaces beneath a shady, tufted grove by the road at the east end of Playa Zipolite. Reserve by writing friendly owner Fernando Torres, at Carretera Playa Zipolite-Puerto Ángel, Oaxaca 70902. A spirit of camaraderie often blooms among the tents and assorted RVs of travelers from as far away as Miami, Medicine Hat, and Murmansk. About $8 for small RV, $12 large, $20 very large, gets you a space for two people, including electricity; shared dump station, shower, and toilets. Tent spaces cost $6 for two people.

One of Zipolite's best tenting spots is on the beach below Shambala (with fine food from neighboring Restaurant Alquimista or Shambala's restaurant uphill). The friendly owner, Gloria Johnson, will probably allow you to use Shambala's showers and toilets for a small fee. Ask at the Shambala office, tel./fax 958/584-3151 or 958/584-3152, for permission to camp.

FOOD

For a country place, Puerto Ángel has surprisingly good food, starting with the **Hotel Villa Florencia,** right on the main beachfront street. Lulu, the wife of the late Italian-born owner/chef, carries on his tradition, specializing in antipasti, salads, and meat and seafood pastas. Like any good country Italian restaurant, service is crisp and presentations are attractive. The modest wine list has, in the past, included some good old-country imports, and the pastas al dente and cappuccino are among the best on the coast. Open daily 8 A.M.–11 P.M. Moderate. (If you're in need of lodging, ask at the hotel desk in back to see some of clean, comfortable rooms.)

The unpretentiously elegant view *palapa* restaurant at the **Hotel La Buena Vista,** tel. 958/584-3104, is the best spot in town for a leisurely, intimate dinner. Here, the prodigious effort that owner/managers Lourdes and Carrie Díaz have invested in their kitchen and staff comes together beautifully. The servers, fetchingly attired in colorful Oaxaca *huipiles,* glide gracefully between kitchen and tables with a bounty of crisp salads, savory soups, tender pastas, and fresh broiled fish and meats. It's open 7:30–11 A.M. for breakfast, closed afternoons, then open for supper 6–10 P.M. Moderate.

Four or five *palapa* restaurants line Playa Panteón. Here, the charming beach scene is an extra added to the already good food, especially at **Restaurant Cordelia** (on far left as you approach the beach). Although seafood is the best choice in general, Cordelia offers an inviting list of good salads, pastas, meats, and poultry to boot. Open daily 8 A.M.–10 P.M. low season, 8 A.M.–midnight high.

If you appreciate vegetables, don't miss the open-air restaurant of the **Hotel Cañon Devata,** tel./fax 958/584-3137, tucked in the canyon uphill from Playa Panteón. Here, hearty macrobiotic vegetarian fare is the theme. During the low season the restaurant is open for breakfast only, daily 7 A.M.–2 P.M. High season, it's open for breakfast, lunch, and dinner daily 7 A.M.–9 P.M. Moderate.

For a spectacular view with late lunch or early dinner (or even just a drink), go to the family-run **Restaurant Rincón del Mar** that clings to the west-side headland overlooking the bay. (Follow the *andador* toward the beach from the beachfront Av. Uribe bridge, just west of the naval compound. At the restaurant sign, follow the stairway up the rocky headland.) The star of the show (aided by a husband-daughter team) is the wife Mari, who crafts a short but tasty menu of soups, salads, pastas, seafood, and meats. Open daily 4–10 P.M.

Zipolite also has some good eating places. For hearty macrobiotic-style fare and a breezy beach view, go to the restaurant at **Shambala** on the Playa Zipolite west-end headland above the beach. Personable owner Gloria Johnson runs a very tidy kitchen, which serves good breakfasts, soups, salads, and sandwiches. Open daily 8 A.M.–8 P.M. No alcohol. Budget–moderate.

Regula, the European co-owner of **Lo Cósmico** on the knoll just east of Shambala, cooks from a similar macrobiotic-style menu, although she specializes in several variations of crêpes, including egg, meat, cheese, and vegetable. Open daily, high season, from around 8 A.M. to about 7 P.M. Shorter hours and closed Monday during the low season.

Right on the Shambala–Lo Cósmico beachfront, a regiment of satisfied patrons of **Restaurant Alquimista** choose from a seeming mile-long menu of appetizers (hummus, guacamole), soups (onion, cream of carrot), salads (Greek, romaine), *tortas* (egg, ham, cheese), fish (10 styles of fillet), pastas (*al burro,* cream, Bolognese), hamburgers (fish, beef, chicken) and much, much more. Open daily, 4–10 P.M. low season; noon–midnight high season.

For homey elegance, continue past Zipolite to the view restaurant at **Posada Rancho Cerro Largo.** Here, friendly ecoactivist owner Mario Corella invites guests to share a meal with him and the hotel staff. Don't show up unannounced; fax 958/584-3063, or email ranchocerrolargomx@yahoo.com a few days ahead of time and ask for a reservation. (For access directions, see Posada Rancho Cerro Largo under Accommodations.)

ENTERTAINMENT AND EVENTS

Puerto Ángel's entertainments are mostly spontaneous. If anything exciting is going to happen, it will most likely be on the beachfront Boulevard Uribe, where people tend to congregate during the late afternoon and evenings. A small crowd may accumulate in the adjacent restaurant Villa Florencia for coffee, talk, or something from the bar.

The town's major scheduled event is the big

Fiesta de San Miguel Arcángel on October 1 and 2. Then the *mascaritas* (masked children) dancers romp, carnival games and rides light up the streetfront, and a regatta of fishing boats parades around the bay.

Sunsets

Sunset-watchers get their best chance from the unobstructed hilltop perch of the Hotel Ángel del Mar, or Lola's, on the beach in Zipolite, where the bar and restaurant at each place can provide something to enliven the occasion even if clouds happen to block the view.

Hotel Ángel del Mar sometimes provides music for dancing during the highest seasons, most likely between Christmas and New Year and the week before Easter.

For additional diversions, head west to Puerto Escondido or east to Bahías de Huatulco, each about an hour by car, for more and livelier entertainments.

SPORTS AND RECREATION

Jogging

Potholed streets, rocky roads, and lack of grass sharply curtail Puerto Ángel jogging prospects. The highway, however, which runs gradually uphill from near the pier, does provide a continuous, more or less smooth surface. Confine your jogging to early morning or late afternoon, and take water along.

Swimming and Surfing

Swimming provides better local exercise opportunities, especially in the sheltered waters off of Playa Panteón. Bodysurfing, boogie boarding, and surfing can be rewarding, depending on wind and swells, off Playa Zipolite. Be super-careful of undertow, which is always a threat, even on calm days at Zipolite. If you're inexperienced, don't go out alone. Novice and even experienced swimmers sometimes drown at Zipolite. If you get caught in a current pulling you out to sea, don't panic. Experts advise that you simply float and paddle parallel to the beach 100 yards or so, to a spot where the offshore current is not so severe (or may even push you back

toward the beach). Alcohol and surf, moreover, don't mix. On rough days, unless you're an expert, forget it. Bring your own board; few, if any, rentals are available.

Sailing and Sailboarding

If you have your own carryable boat or sailboarding gear, sheltered **Playa Panteón** would be a good place to put it into the water, although the neighboring headland may decrease the available wind. Calm mornings at **Playas Zipolite, San Agustinillo,** or **Mazunte** (see under Beaches and Sights), or afternoons, with more wind but rougher waves, might also be fruitful.

Snorkeling and Scuba Diving

Rocky shoals at the edges of Puerto Ángel Bay, especially just off **Playa Panteón,** are fine for casual snorkeling. **Playa Estacahuite,** on the open ocean just beyond the bay's east headland, is even better. Best bring your own equipment. If you don't, you can rent a snorkel and mask from restaurants Cordelia or Leyvis y Vicente, on Playa Panteón, for about $3 an hour.

Puerto Ángel now has a **professional scuba diving shop,** run by the owner-builder of Hotel Cordelia, at Playa Panteón, tel. 958/584-3109, azul_profundomx@hotmail.com.

Alternatively, beginners can contact the well-equipped and certified dive instructors of **Buceos Triton** dive shop, tel./fax 958/587-0844, or **Hurricane Divers,** tel. 958/587-1107, email hurricane divers@hotmail.com, both at the Santa Cruz de Huatulco marina. (For more details, see Swimming, Snorkeling, and Scuba Diving in the Bays of Huatulco section.)

Fishing

The bayfront pier is the best place to bargain for a boat and captain to take you and your friends out on a fishing excursion. Prices depend on season, but you can figure on paying about $20 an hour for a boat for four or five people with bait and two or three good rods and reels. During a three-hour outing a few miles offshore, a competently captained boat will typically bring in three or four big, good-eating *robalo* (snook), *huachinango* (snapper), *atún* (tuna), or pompano. If you're uncertain about what's biting, go down to the dock around 2 or 3 P.M. in the afternoon and see what the boats are bringing in.

Vicente, of Leyvis y Vicente restaurant on Playa Panteón, takes out fishing parties of up to six people for around $20 an hour, bait and tackle included. You can also arrange fishing trips through the **Gambusino Travel Agency,** tel. 958/584-3038, fax 958/584-3070, open Mon.–Sat. 9 A.M.–2 P.M. and 4–8 P.M., in the office across the street from the doctor and pharmacy on Av. Teniente Vasconcelos, just uphill from Uribe.

SHOPPING

Market

The biggest local market is the Monday *tianguis,* which spreads along the Pochutla main street, Highway 175, about seven miles from Puerto Ángel, one mile inland from the Highway 200 junction. It's mostly a place for looking rather than buying, as throngs of vendors from the hills line the sidewalks, even crowding into the streets, to sell their piles of onions, mangoes, forest herbs, carrots, cilantro, and jicama.

On other days, vendors confine their displays to the permanent Mercado 5 de Octubre, east side of the main street, between Calles 1 and 2 Sur.

Groceries

The best-stocked Puerto Ángel local store is the **Super Del Puerto** at the west end of beachfront street Uribe, uphill past the arroyo bridge. Also, a few little-bit-of-everything stores in Zipolite and on Uribe in the middle of Puerto Ángel sell cheese, milk, bread, some vegetables, and other essentials.

Handicrafts

For fine custom-made hammocks, visit local craftsman **Gabino Silva** at his country shop, off a jungly stretch of the road between Zipolite and San Agustín. He also rents a cabana. Watch for the sign labeled Hamacas and Cabaña on the beach side of the road, 4.2 miles (6.7 km) from the Puerto Ángel bus stop.

A handful of handicrafts have arrived in Puerto Ángel, at new **La Primavera** beachware store, on Vasconcelos, directly uphill from the pier, open daily daily 9 A.M.–10 P.M., TEL. 958/584-3251.

A few stores sell some unique handicrafts in Pochutla. **Foto Garcia**, on main street Lázaro Cárdenas 76, west side, offers many whimsical coconut carvings by a local craftsman. It's open Mon.–Sat. 8 a.m.–2 P.M. and 4–8 P.M., tel. 958/584-0735.

Additionally, the Pochutla *larga distancia,* **Caseta Cybeltel,** open daily 7 A.M.–10 P.M., between Calles 1 and 2 Norte (across the street from the Hotel Izola) offers a varied collection of mostly Guatemalan hand-embroidered purses, *huipiles,* shirts, vests, and 1960s-style tie-dyed apparel.

INFORMATION AND SERVICES

Money Exchange

The only regular local money exchange in Puerto Ángel is the **Gambusino Travel Agency,** on Vasconcelos, the street that runs from the Puerto Ángel pier uphill. Otherwise, go to **Banco Internacional** (Bital) on the Pochutla main street, Lázaro Cárdenas, tel. 958/584-0698, open Mon.–Fri. 8 A.M.–7 P.M., Sat. 8 A.M.–3 P.M. Alternatively, try **Bancomer,** corner of Lázaro Cárdenas and Av. 3A Norte, tel. 958/584-0259, open Mon.–Fri. 8 A.M.–5 P.M., Sat. 9 A.M.–1 P.M. Another option is **Bancrecer,** next door to Bancomer, tel. 958/584-0763, open Mon.–Fri. 9 A.M.–5 P.M., Sat. 10 A.M.–2 P.M. Call to confirm money-changing hours.

Communications and Travel Agent

The Puerto Ángel *correo* and *telecomunicaciones* stand side by side at the Agencia Municipal at the foot of Highway 175. Both are open Mon.–Fri. 9 A.M.–3 P.M.

The Puerto Ángel *larga distancia* telephone, fax office, and **Gela net** Internet access is on Calle José Vasconcelos, just uphill from main street Uribe, tel. 958/584-3046 or 958/584-3054, fax 958/584-3070, shenalo@hotmail.com. Hours are daily 7 A.M.–10 P.M.

Internet access is also available at **Hotel Puesta del Sol and Cyber Café,** about half a block west of the Blv. Uribe bridge, or **Caseta Cybeltel,** in Pochutla, main street, across from the Hotel Izola. Caseta Cybeltel also maintains a *lista de email,* of mail messages, like *lista de correo.*

Puerto Ángel's travel agent, friendly Mati Velasco (who also runs the *larga distancia* and Internet access) of **Agencia de Viajes Gambusino,** tel. 958/584-3080 or 958/584-3038, arranges tours and fishing trips and sells reserved air and bus tickets at her small office on Vasconcelos next door, uphill from the *larga distancia.*

Health and Police

Puerto Ángel's friendly and respected private doctor, **Dr. Constancio Aparicio Juárez,** holds consultation hours Mon.–Sat. 7 A.M.–2 P.M. and 5–9 P.M. and also runs the **pharmacy,** tel. 958/584-3058, on Av. Vasconcelos, across from the *larga distancia.* For serious illness requiring diagnostic specialists, Dr. Juárez recommends you go to the government Hospital Regional in Pochutla, tel. 958/584-0204, or the Seguro Social in Crucecita (Bays of Huatulco), tel. 958/587-0124 or 958/587-0264.

Another option is to go to the small government **Centro del Salud** health clinic, which concentrates on preventative rather than diagnostic medicine, on the hill behind the church. Go up Vasconcelos a long curving block, go left at the first corner, and continue another block to the health center.

For **police emergencies,** contact the federal police *(preventiva),* at the *agencia municipal,* tel. 958/584-3207, end of Blv. Uribe, or call the *policía preventiva,* at the Presidencia Municipal, in Pochutla, on the town plaza, one block east of the main north-south town thoroughfare, tel. 958/584-0273.

Ecological Project

Ecological activism has spread to Mazunte, where the **Asociación de Comuneros de Mazunte** has picked up the green banner. Led by its earnest activist-president Ermilo López Bustamante, the association is building an ecologically correct time-share development and encouraging waste composting and water and forest conservation. Partly as a result of their efforts, cutting trees around Zipolite, San Agustín, and Mazunte has become a definite community no-no. Consequently, the tropical deciduous forest zone between Zipolite and Mazunte is rapidly becoming a luxuriantly healthy ecopreserve. A good place to contact Bustamante might be through the turtle museum, where he's well known.

GETTING THERE AND AWAY
By Air

Scheduled flights to Mexican destinations connect daily with airports at **Huatulco,** 19 miles (30 km) east, or **Puerto Escondido,** 44 miles (71 km) west, by road from Puerto Ángel.

By Car or RV

Good roads connect Puerto Ángel to the west with Puerto Escondido and Acapulco, north with Oaxaca, and east with the Bahías de Huatulco and the Isthmus of Tehuantepec.

Highway 200 connects westward with Puerto Escondido in an easy 44 miles (71 km), continuing to Pinotepa Nacional (135 miles, 217 km, three hours) and Acapulco in a total of seven hours (291 miles, 469 km) of driving. In the opposite direction Bahías de Huatulco (actually Crucecita town) is a quick three-quarters of an hour, or 22 miles (35 km). The continuation to Salina Cruz stretches another 92 miles (148 km), or around 2.5 additional hours of driving time.

North to Oaxaca, paved but narrow and winding National Highway 175 connects 148 miles (238 km) over the Sierra Madre del Sur from its junction with Highway 200 at Pochutla. The road climbs to around 9,000 feet through cool (chilly in winter) pine forests and hardscrabble Chatino and Zapotec native villages. Fill up with gas in Pochutla. Unleaded gasoline is available at the Pochutla Pemex stations, both on through-town Highway 175: about 300 yards toward town from Highway 200, and on the north, uphill, edge of town. Carry water and blankets, and be prepared for emergencies. The first gas station is at Miahuatlán, 90 miles north. Allow about seven driving hours from Puerto Ángel to Oaxaca, about six in the opposite direction.

By Bus

One long-distance bus line, second-class **Estrella del Valle,** connects Puerto Ángel directly to Oaxaca and Pochutla, where many long-distance connections may be made. Buses depart from the main-street corner of Uribe and Vasconcelos. The Pochutla-bound buses depart hourly during daylight hours, the Oaxaca bus once, nightly, at 10 P.M. The adjacent Papelería El Globo serves as the information and ticket office.

In Pochutla, from three separate stations, many other long-distance buses connect with points west, east, and north. The stations cluster less than a mile north from the Highway 200 junction along Av. Lázaro Cárdenas, the Highway 175 main street into Pochutla.

As you enter the Pochutla business district, first you'll see first-class **Cristóbal Colón** station on the left (at L. Cárdenas 84, tel. 958/584-0274). Several departures per day connect east with Crucecita. Some continue east, connecting with Salina Cruz and Tehuantepec, continuing to Chiapas destinations of Tuxtla Gutiérrez San Cristóbal and Tapachula, at the Guatemala border. A few buses connect north with Oaxaca via the long, relatively level, Isthmus route, via Salina Cruz and Tehuantepec. During the dry season, buses also connect with the trans-Sierra but shorter Highway 175. One bus connects daily with Puebla and Mexico City. A few buses also connect daily west with Puerto Escondido.

Next, a few doors farther north, at L. Cárdenas 94, tel. 958/584-0380, **Estrella Blanca** subsidiary-line buses (such as first-class Elite, luxury-class Turistar, Flecha Roja, and Autotransportes Cuauhtémoc) connect west daily with Puerto Escondido, continuing to Acapulco and Lázaro Cárdenas in Michoacán, there continuing along the entire Pacific Mexico coast, all the way to the U.S. border. They also connect east (many per day) with Bahías de Huatulco destinations of Crucecita and Santa Cruz de Huatulco and Salina Cruz on the Isthmus. A few "plus" (say "ploos") luxury-class buses connect daily, all the way to Mexico City.

About a block farther, across the main street, **Autobúses Estrella del Valle, Autobúses Oaxaca Pacífico,** and **Fletes y Pasajes,** (tel. 958/584-0138 or 958/584-0349) operate out of their joint central bus station *central de autobus.* Frequent second-class and some first-class service is offered, connecting west with Puerto Escondido and Pinotepa Nacional; north with Oaxaca and Mexico City; and east with Huatulco, Salina Cruz, and the Chiapas border.

Bays of Huatulco and Vicinity

The nine azure Bahías de Huatulco decorate a couple of dozen miles of acacia-plumed rocky coastline east of Puerto Ángel. Between the bays, the ocean joins in battle with jutting, rocky headlands, while in their inner reaches the ocean calms, caressing diminutive crescents of coral sand. Inland, a thick hardwood forest seems to stretch in a continuous carpet to the Sierra.

Ecologists shivered when they heard that these bays were going to be developed. Fonatur, the government tourism development agency, says it has a plan, however. Relatively few (but all upscale) hotels will occupy the beaches; other development will be confined to a few inland centers. The remaining 70 percent of the land will be kept as pristine ecological zones and study areas.

Although this story sounds sadly familiar, Fonatur, which developed Ixtapa and Cancún, seems to have learned from its experience. Up-to-date sewage treatment was installed *ahead of time;* logging and homesteading were halted; and soldiers patrol the beaches, stopping turtle poachers. If all goes according to the plan, the nine Bahías de Huatulco and their 100,000-acre forest hinterland will be both a tourist and ecological paradise, in addition to employing thousands of local people, when complete in 2020. If this Huatulco dream ends as well as it has started, Mexico should take pride while the rest of the world should take heed.

HISTORY

Long before Columbus, the Huatulco area was well-known to the Aztecs and their predecessors. The name itself, from Aztec words meaning "Land where a Tree (or Wood) Is Worshipped," reflects one of Mexico's most intriguing legends—of the Holy Cross of Huatulco.

When the Spanish arrived on the Huatulco coast, the local native people showed them a huge cross they worshipped at the edge of the sea. A contemporary chronicler, Ignacio Burgoa, conjectured the cross had been left by an ancient saint—maybe even the Apostle Thomas—15 centuries earlier. The cross remained as the Spanish colonized the area and established headquarters and a port, which they named San Agustín, at the westernmost of the Bays of Huatulco.

Spanish ports and their treasure-laden galleons from Asia attracted foreign corsairs—Francis Drake in 1579 and Thomas Cavendish in 1587. Cavendish arrived at the bay now called Bahía Santa Cruz, where he saw the cross the natives were worshipping. Believing it was the work of the devil, Cavendish and his men tried to chop, saw, and burn it down. Failing at all of these, Cavendish looped his ship's mooring ropes around the cross and with sails unfurled tried using the force of the wind to pull it down. Frustrated, he finally sailed away, leaving the cross of Huatulco still standing beside the shore.

By 1600, a steady trail of pilgrims were chipping pieces from the cross; so much so that in 1612, Bishop Juan de Cervantes had to rescue it. He brought the cross to Oaxaca, where he made four smaller two-foot crosses of it. He sent one specimen each to church authorities in Mexico City, Rome, and Santa María de Huatulco, head town of the Huatulco *municipio.* Cervantes kept the fourth copy in the cathedral in Oaxaca, where it has remained, venerated and visible in a side chapel, to the present day.

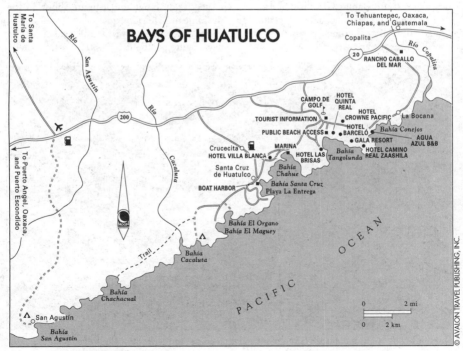

BAYS OF HUATULCO

SIGHTS

Getting Oriented

With no road to the outside world, the Bahías de Huatulco remained virtually uninhabited and undeveloped until 1982, about the time that coastal Highway 200 was pushed through. A few years later, Huatulco's planned initial kernel of infrastructure was complete, centering on the brand-new residential service town, Crucecita (pop. 10,000), and nearby Santa Cruz de Huatulco boat harbor and hotel village on Bahía Santa Cruz.

The Bays of Huatulco decorate the coastline both east and west of Santa Cruz. To the east, a paved road links Bahías Chahue, Tangolunda, and Conejos. To the west lie Bahías El Organo, El Maguey, and Cacaluta. Of the latter three, only Bahía Maguey is accessible by paved road. El Organo and Cacaluta are accessible only with the help of a guide; the former on foot or by horseback, the latter by truck or SUV. Isolated farther west are Bahías Chachacual and San Agustín, with no road from Santa Cruz (although a good dirt road runs to San Agustín from Highway 200 near the airport).

Besides Bahía Santa Cruz, the only other bays that have been extensively developed are Chahue, a mile east, and Tangolunda, four miles east. Chahue now has a marina and a sprinkling of small-to-medium-sized, medium-priced hotels. Tangolunda has a green and lovely golf course, small restaurant/shopping complex, and six resort hotels (Las Brisas, Quinta Real, Crown Pacific, Barceló, Club Gala Resort, and Zaashila) that have all been fully operational since the mid-1990s. (For more details, see Exploring the Bays of Huatulco.)

Getting Around

Frequent public **minibuses** connect Crucecita and Bahías Santa Cruz, Chahue, and Tangolunda. Taxis make the same trips for about $2 by day, $3 at night. No public transportation is available to the other bays. Taxi drivers are willing to drive you for a picnic to west-side bay El Maguey, or Playa Entrega (an isolated beach on Santa Cruz Bay), for about $5 one way, from Crucecita or Tangolunda; figure about $4 for the same to Bahía Conejos.

For an extended day trip to all road-accessible bays, figure on about $20–30 for a taxi, about

Santa Cruz de Huatulco harbor is the place to catch a boat to the Bays of Huatulco.

$50 for a rental car. Call Alamo in Santa Cruz (at Hotel Castillo), tel. 958/587-0135 or 958/581-9074; or Budget in Crucecita at Octillo and Jazmín, tel. 958/587-0010, fax 958/587-0019.

Another option is to go by boat. The local boat cooperative (Sociedad Cooperativa Turístico Tangolunda) runs a daily excursion—around 10:30 A.M., $20 per person, kids 5–9 half price—to all nine bays, including open bar, bilingual guide, and snacks; snorkeling is $5 extra. Reserve directly through its dock office, tel. 958/587-0081, or through a travel agent such as Paraíso Huatulco, tel. 958/581-0055, at the Hotel Barceló, ext. 784 or Servicios Turísticos del Sur, at the Hotel Castillo, tel./fax 958/587-1211; or Paraíso Huatulco, at the Hotel Flamboyan in Crucecita, tel. 958/587-0181, fax 958/587-0190.

The same cooperative also rents entire boats for up to 10 people. Drop-off runs to the nearest beach are about $10 per boat round-trip; to the more remote, around $20–30.

Local travel agents offer other tour options: several hours of sunning, swimming, picnicking, and snorkeling at a couple of Bahías de Huatulco beaches runs around $20 per person. Tours to Puerto Ángel, Puerto Escondido, and wildlife-rich lagoons go for $30–50 per person. For reservations, call Paraíso Huatulco, at the Hotel Barceló, tel. 958/581-0055, ext. 784; Servicios Turísticos del Sur, at the Hotel Castillo, tel./fax 958/587-1211; or Paraíso Huatulco, in Crucecita, tel. 958/587-0181, fax 958/587-0190.

Another option is to hire your own guide. An inexpensive way to do this is to hire an English-speaking taxi driver to take you wherever you want to go for several hours, up to a whole day, for $30–50, depending on the season.

Professional guides are another good option. (See Guide in the Information section.)

Crucecita and Santa Cruz de Huatulco

Despite its newness, Crucecita (Little Cross, pop. 10,000) resembles a traditional Mexican town, with life revolving around a central plaza and market nearby. Crucecita is where the people who work in the Huatulco hotels, businesses, and government offices live. Although pleasant enough for a walk around the square and a meal

in a restaurant, it's nothing special—mostly a place whose modest hotels and restaurants accommodate business travelers and weekenders who can't afford the plush hotels near the beach.

While in Crucecita, be sure to step into the church on the plaza's west side to admire the heavenly **ceiling mural** of Mexico's patron, the Virgin of Guadalupe. The mural, the largest of Guadalupe in Mexico, is the work of local artists José Ángel del Signo and Marco Antonio Contreras, whose for-sale art is on display locally. Besides the heavenly Virgin overhead, the muralists have decorated the space above the altar with the miraculous story of Don Diego and the Virgin of Guadalupe.

The four deluxe hotels and the few travel-oriented businesses of Santa Cruz de Huatulco (on Bahía Santa Cruz about two miles from Crucecita) cluster near the boat harbor. Fishing and tour boats come and go, vacationers sun themselves on the tranquil yellow-sand Playa Santa Cruz (beyond the restaurants adjacent to the boat harbor), while T-shirt and fruit vendors and boatmen hang around the quay watching for prospective customers. After the sun goes down, not much usually happens in Santa Cruz. Tourist quit the beach for their hotels and workers return to their homes in Crucecita, leaving the harbor and streets empty and dark.

Exploring the Bays of Huatulco

Isolation has left the Huatulco waters blue and unpolluted, the beaches white and clean. Generally, the bays are all similar: tropical deciduous (green July–Jan.) forested rocky headlands enclosing yellow-white coral sand crescents. The water is clear and good for snorkeling, scuba diving, sailing, kayaking, and sailboarding during the often-calm weather. Beaches, however, are typically steep, causing waves to break quickly near the sand, unsuitable for bodysurfing, boogie boarding, or surfing.

Your preparations depend on which bays you plan to explore. For the four developed and partially developed bays: Santa Cruz, Chahue, Tangolunda, Maguey, and San Agustín, you'll need nothing more than transportation, a hat, and sunscreen. Restaurants and stores can supply everything else.

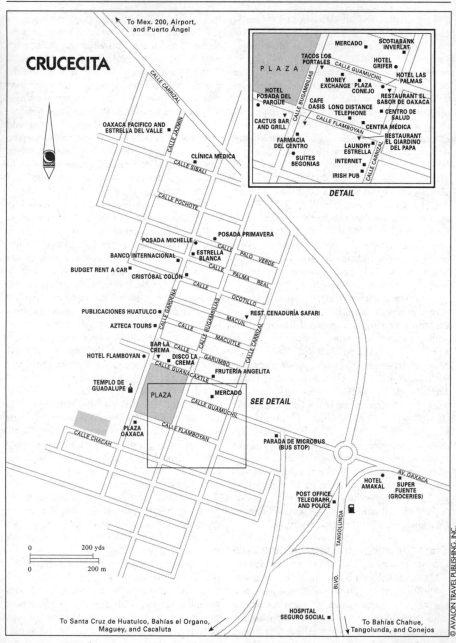

COSTA CHICA/OAXACA

To Mex. 200, Airport,
and Puerto Ángel

CRUCECITA

CALLE CARRIZAL

CALLE JAZMÍN

OAXACA PACIFICO AND
ESTRELLA DEL VALLE

CLÍNICA MÉDICA

CALLE SIBALI

CALLE POCHOTE

POSADA PRIMAVERA

POSADA MICHELLE

ESTRELLA
BLANCA

BANCO INTERNACIONAL

CALLE PALO VERDE

BUDGET RENT A CAR

CALLE PALMA   REAL

CRISTÓBAL COLÓN

CALLE

OCOTILLO

CALLE GARDENIA

PUBLICACIONES HUATULCO

REST. CENADURÍA SAFARI

MACUIL

CALLE BUGAMBILIAS

AZTECA TOURS

CALLE

MACUITLE

CALLE CARRIZAL

BAR LA
CREMA

CALLE

CALLE GARUMBO

HOTEL FLAMBOYAN

DISCO LA
CREMA

FRUTERÍA ANGELITA

CALLE GUANACAXTLE

TEMPLO DE
GUADALUPE

PLAZA

MERCADO

CALLE GUAMUCHIL

SEE DETAIL

PLAZA
OAXACA

CALLE CHACAH

CALLE FLAMBOYAN

PARADA DE MICROBUS
(BUS STOP)

AV. OAXACA

HOTEL
AMAKAL

SUPER
FUENTE
(GROCERIES)

POST OFFICE,
TELEGRAPH,
AND POLICE

TANGOLUNDA

BLVD.

0   200 yds
0   200 m

HOSPITAL
SEGURO SOCIAL

To Santa Cruz de Huatulco, Bahías el Organo,
Maguey, and Cacaluta

To Bahías Chahue,
Tangolunda, and Conejos

DETAIL

P L A Z A

MERCADO

SCOTIABANK
INVERLAT

TACOS LOS
PORTALES

HOTEL
GRIFER

CALLE GUAMUCHIL

HOTEL LAS
PALMAS

CALLE BUGAMBILIAS

MONEY
EXCHANGE

PLAZA
CONEJO

HOTEL
POSADA DEL
PARQUE

CAFE
OASIS

LONG DISTANCE
TELEPHONE

RESTAURANT EL
SABOR DE OAXACA

CENTRO DE
SALUD

CACTUS BAR
AND GRILL

CALLE FLAMBOYAN

CENTRA MÉDICA

FARMACIA
DEL CENTRO

LAUNDRY
ESTRELLA

RESTAURANT
EL GIARDINO
DEL PAPA

SUITES
BEGONIAS

INTERNET

CALLE CARRIZAL

IRISH PUB

By contrast, the four undeveloped Huatulco bays of El Organo, Cacaluta, Chacual, and Conejos have neither restaurants, stores, drinking water, nor much shade, since they're so pristine coconut palms haven't even gotten around to sprouting there. When exploring, bring food, drinks, hats, sunscreen, and mosquito repellent.

East Side

Bahía Chahue, about a mile from both Crucecita and Santa Cruz, is wide and blue, with a steep yellow dune behind the beach, stretching to the marina jetty at the east end. Chahue is uncrowded even on weekends and holidays and nearly empty the rest of the time.

About four miles farther east is the breezy and broad **Bahía Tangolunda.** Although hotels front much of the beach, a signed Playa Pública public access road borders the western edge of the golf course (turn right just past the creek bridge). Except for its east end, the Tangolunda beach is steep and the waves break quickly right at the sand. *Palapa* restaurants at the public beach serve food and drinks; or, if you prefer, stroll a quarter mile for refreshments at the luxurious poolside beach clubs of the Barceló and Club Gala Resort.

Over the headland about two miles farther east, **Punta Arena** (Sand Point), a forested thumb of land, juts out into wide **Bahía Conejos.** Three separate steep beaches spread along the inner shoreline. The main entrance road arrives at high-duned Playa Punta Arena. Playa Tejoncito (Little Wild Pig) is beyond the rocks far to the right; Playa Conejos (Rabbits) is to the left on the other side of Punta Arena. A few palm-frond *ramadas* for shade and a saltwater flush toilet lavatory occupy the Playa Punta Arena dune. Trees behind the dunes provide a few shady spots for RV or tent campers. (Playa Conejos is becoming a rapidly-developing residential zone. By the time you read this, most of the accessible wild dunes and beach may be occupied by houses.)

Beyond **La Bocana,** near the mouth of the Río Copalita, less than a mile farther on, a long, broad beach with oft-powerful surfing rollers (novices beware) stretches for at least a mile east. Beach *palapas* serve drinks and very fresh seafood.

A lagoon above the beach (bring your kayak) appears ripe for wildlife viewing.

After La Bocana, the road bends inland, paralleling the **Río Copalita wildlife sanctuary,** perfect for adventurous exploring. Several operators guide visitors on river ecotours: José Aussenac, owner of Posada Michelle, tel. 958/587-0535, organizes and guides outdoor adventure-tours. Options include bird- and animal-watching walks along riverine forest trails, kayaking river rapids, rafting, and mud baths at a riverside ranch.

West Side

Bahía Santa Cruz has a pair of beaches, **Playa Entrega,** and the most visited, **Playa Santa Cruz,** past the shops and restaurants, to the right (facing the ocean) of the boat harbor. During high season and weekends, kids play and tourists improve their tans at Playa Santa Cruz.

Playa Entrega is a hidden little dab of sand slipped onto the west side of Bahía Santa Cruz. It is the infamous spot where, on January 20, 1831, Vicente Guerrero, president and independence hero, was brought ashore in custody of arch-villain Francisco Picaluga and sent to be murdered in Oaxaca a few months later.

Quarter-mile-long Playa Entrega is the ideal Sunday beach, with calm, clear water and clean yellow sand. Swimming, kayaking, and often snorkeling, sailing, and sailboarding possibilities are excellent. A number of shoreline restaurants, notably, **Restaurant Arrecife,** tel. 958/587-0524, provide fresh seafood plates and drinks daily, until around 8 P.M.

Get there via the main street, Boulevard Santa Cruz, which passes the Santa Cruz boat harbor. Continue west, bearing left, at the Y intersection at the Hotel Binneguenda (mark your odometer) on the right. After a few hundred yards, the road bends left and winds uphill, past panoramic viewpoints of Bahía Santa Cruz. Follow the signs and you'll soon be at Playa Entrega.

If, instead of curving left to La Entrega, you follow the highway that continues straight ahead at the same spot, you'll be headed for the Bahías El Maguey, El Organo, Cacaluta and Chachacual. The roads to the latter three of these four bays have only been partly completed in recent years. Until authorities get around to finishing them, land access to the Bays of El Organo, Cacaluta, and remote Chachacual will be achievable only by experienced drivers in off-road vehicles who know the myriad dirt tracks that wind through the tropical deciduous forest west of Santa Cruz. If in doubt, rent a jeep and a guide, or take a boat tour.

Bahía El Organo is closest. About half a mile along the highway, look (inquire locally if you can't find it) for a rough dirt track angling sharply left. The beach is isolated, intimate, and enfolded by rocky shoals on both sides. Some trees behind the dune provide shade.

Continuing straight ahead, the paved highway forks again (about 1.3 miles from the hotel). Continue straight ahead downhill to El Maguey, or fork right to Cacaluta. The sandy crescent of **Bahía El Maguey** is bordered by tidepools tucked beneath forested headlands. Facing a protected fjordlike channel, the Maguey beach is usually calm, nearly waveless and fine for swimming, snorkeling, diving, and sailing. It would be a snap to launch a kayak or a rubber boat here for fishing in the bay. Beach access is on foot, via a downhill staircase, only. A clutter of permanent seafood *palapas* line the beach. Most days, especially weekends and holidays, picnickers arrive and banana towboats and *aguamotos* (minimotorboats) buzz the beach and bay.

At this writing, the paved road that forks right toward **Bahía Cacaluta** ends about .7 mile (1.1 km) past the fork, at an unsigned sandy but firm jeep track that bumps ahead, winding past several likewise unmarked forks (bring a guide or try to get directions from a local) another mile and bear left to Bahía Cacaluta. There, the bay spreads along a mile-long, heart-shaped beach, beckoningly close to a cactus-studded offshore islet. Swimmers beware, for waves break powerfully, surging upward and receding with strong undertow. Many shells—limpets and purple- and brown-daubed clams—speckle the beach. Surf fishing prospects, either from the beach itself or from rocks on either end, appear excellent.

Bahía Chachacual, past the Río Cacaluta about four miles farther west, is a sand-edged

azure nook accessible only with a guide, via forest tracks.

Bahía San Agustín, by contrast, is well known and easily reachable by Pochutla-bound bus, then by the good dirt road just across the highway (one-way taxi from the highway runs about $10, *colectivo* van $1.30) from the fork to Santa María Huatulco (at Km 236, a mile west of the airport). After about seven miles along a firm track, accessible by all but the bulkiest RVs, bear right to the modest village of *palapas* at the bay's sheltered west end. From there, the beach stretches eastward along a mile of forest-backed dune. Besides good swimming, sailing, sailboarding, shell-collecting, and fishing prospects, San Agustín has a number of behind-the-dune spots (follow the left fork shortly before the road's end) for possible RV and tent camping. Beachside *palapas* can, at least, supply seafood and drinks and maybe some water and basic groceries.

ACCOMMODATIONS

In Huatulco, as in other resorts, hotels on the beach are the most expensive. Crucecita's hotels are cheapest, Tangolunda's are most expensive, and the Santa Cruz hotels fall in between. All Huatulco lodgings have private baths with hot water.

Crucecita Accommodations

Most of the Crucecita lodgings are near the central plaza. The **Hotel Grifer,** at Guamuchil and Carrizal, a block east of the plaza, would be nothing special in most Mexican resorts, but in hotel-poor Huatulco, it is often full; reserve by writing the hotel, at P.O. Box 159, Crucecita, Oaxaca 70980, tel./fax 958/587-0048. Three stories of nondescript modern rooms enclose a TV-dominated atrium; a passable street-level restaurant is convenient for breakfast. The 16 rooms rent, low season, for about $30 s or d, $35 t, $40 and $5 high, with a/c and TV; no credit cards. Prices even higher Christmas and Easter holidays.

Across Guamuchil, half a block back toward the plaza, the **Hotel Las Palmas,** Calle Guamuchil 206, Crucecita, Oaxaca 70980, tel. 958/587-0060, fax 958/587-0057, offers small, plain but clean a/c rooms on the two floors above its good street-level restaurant. The eight rooms rent for about $25 s or d low season, $40 high; credit cards are accepted. For more information, visit the website www.hotel.baysofhuatulco.com.mx.

The **Hotel Suites Begonias,** at the southeast plaza corner, offers a more deluxe, family-run alternative, Bugambilias 503, Crucecita, Oaxaca 70980, tel./fax 958/587-1390. The rooms, although clean and comfortable, have motel-style walkways passing their windows, decreasing privacy. Rates for the 13 rooms run about $30 s or d, $35 t, with fan and TV; credit cards are accepted.

Half a block away, you might consider taking one of the attractive rooms on the very top floor of the **Hotel Posada del Parque,** Flamboyan 306, Crucecita, Oaxaca 70980, tel./fax 958/587-0219, on the south side of the plaza. Although not especially large, the top-floor rooms have high rustic beamed ceilings, nice views, and surround a cheery inner balcony-atrium. An airy sidewalk café downstairs serves breakfast, lunch, and dinner. All 14 rooms rent for about $20 s or d low season with fan, $25 with a/c; $50 high season with fan, $55 with a/c. All with TV; credit cards are accepted.

About three blocks east of the Crucecita plaza hubbub, the **Hotel Amakal** offers semideluxe, modern-standard rooms at reasonable prices. A stairway from the small, spartan lobby leads upstairs to about a dozen clean, light, white-tile-floored, tastefully decorated rooms with modern-standard baths. Rates are $32 s or d low season with fan, $51 high; $40 d low season with a/c, $66 high. Credit cards are accepted. Street parking only. Reserve in writing at Av. Oaxaca 1, Crucecita, Bahías de Huatulco, Oaxaca 70980, or by phone, tel. 958/587-1500, fax 958/587-1515. For more information, visit the website www.hotelamakal.com.

A pair of simple but attractive *posadas* near the bus stations on Gardenia, four blocks north of the plaza, offer other options. The **Hotel Posada Michelle,** Gardenia 8, Crucecita, Oaxaca 70980, tel./fax 958/587-0535, run by friendly ecotour guide José Aussenac, has about a dozen smallish but clean and comfortable rooms with big beds, baths, and good satellite TV. Some of the rooms are airy and light; others, although dark because of

their half-mirrored windows (for privacy), do have white walls and open to a light, breezy, second-story walkway that leads to a pleasant, hammock-hung, shady view porch. Rates, for a/c rooms, run about $30 d low season, $60 high; rooms with fans only cost $20 low season, and $35 high.

Posada Primavera, just around the corner, at Palo Verde 5, Crucecita, Oaxaca 70980, tel./fax 958/587-1167 and 958/587-0630, offers six simply furnished but clean, light, high-ceilinged upstairs rooms with bath. Windows look out onto the palmy, bougainvillea-adorned surrounding neighborhood. Rates are about $16 s or d low season, $27 high, with fans.

Santa Cruz Hotels

Three blocks from the beach in Santa Cruz, first choice goes to the **Hotel Meigas Binneguenda,** Blv. Santa Cruz 201, Santa Cruz de Huatulco, Oaxaca 70900, tel. 958/587-0077, fax 958/587-0284, binniguenda@huatulco.net.mx. Neocolonial arches, pastel stucco walls, and copper and ceramics handicrafts decorate the interiors, while in the adjacent leafy patio guests sun themselves around the elaborate cascade pool. In the restaurant, the customers seem as well fed and satisfied as the waiters are well trained and attentive. Upstairs, the colonial/modern-decor rooms are spacious, comfortable, and equipped with phones, TV, and a/c. Rates for the 75 rooms run about $60 s or d low season, $80 high, with parking, and credit cards are accepted. Bargain for a discount, especially during times of low occupancy.

Three blocks east, the **Hotel Castillo Huatulco,** Blv. Santa Cruz 303, Santa Cruz de Huatulco 70980, tel. 958/587-0135 or 958/587-0144, toll-free Mex. tel. 800/903-4900, fax 958/587-0131, east along the street three blocks, offers a recommendable alternative. Its 106 rooms, although deluxe and comfortable, are crowded into a smaller space than the Binneguenda's 75. They are nevertheless popular with families on weekends and holidays but nearly empty during quieter seasons. Low-season asking rates run about $100 s or d, $120 high. Ask for a discount, especially during times of low occupancy. Phones, TV, a/c, pool, and parking; credit cards are accepted.

For reservations telephone or email reservaciones@hotelcastillohuatulco.com.

Smaller, renovated **Hotel Marlin,** two blocks from the beach, at Paseo Mitla 107, Santa Cruz de Huatulco, Oaxaca 70989, tel. 958/587-0055, fax 958/587-0546, hmarlin@prodigy.net.mex, is only two blocks from the beach. From street level, the small lobby leads to an appealingly intimate coral-hued inner pool patio and restaurant, enfolded by three stories of rooms. Upstairs, the three dozen rooms are thoughtfully decorated with coral bedspreads, floor-length drapes, attractive, rustic tile floors, and deluxe 1990s-standard bathrooms. Rates run $75 s or d low season, $120 high, with a/c, cable TV, phones. Ask for a discount. One possible drawback (or advantage) to all this is the hotel's popular (Thursday, Friday, and Saturday low season, nightly high) adjoining discotheque, which the management swears cannot be heard in the rooms, even at full volume.

Tangolunda Luxury Resorts

Five luxury resort hotels spread along the Tangolunda shoreline. The Las Brisas dominates the sheltered western side-bay, with four stacklike towers that make the place appear as a big ocean liner. The smaller Hotel Barceló and Club Gala Resort stand side by side on the bay's inner recess next to the golf course. The Hotel Zaashila spreads gracefully to its east-end cove, while the gleaming white Crown Pacific stair-steps up the hillside, away from the beach.

The emphasis of all five resorts is on facilities, such as multiple pools, bars, and restaurants, full wheelchair access, live music, discos, shows, and sports such as tennis, golf, sailing, kayaking, sailboarding, snorkeling, diving, and swimming. Other amenities may include shops, baby-sitting, children's clubs, and arts and crafts instruction.

The **Barceló Huatulco** is a generic (but worthy) member of the worldwide Spanish chain, Paseo Benito Juárez, Bahía Tangolunda, Oaxaca 70989, tel. 958/581-0055, 958/581-0005, or 958/581-0039, fax 958/581-0103. Rooms are comfortable, deluxe, and decorated in soothing pastels, with private bay-view balconies, phones, cable TV, and a/c. Room-only rates for its 360 rooms and suites begin at about $110 d low sea-

son, $180 high. All-inclusive (all lodging, food, drinks, and in-house entertainment included) runs about $100 per person low season, 200 high. For more information, visit the Barceló website www.barcelo.com.

If the **Hotel Zaashila Resort,** Bahía de Tangolunda, Huatulco, Oaxaca 70989, tel. 958/581-0460, toll-free U.S./Can. tel. 800/7CAMINO (800/722-6466), fax 958/581-0461, caminozaarsv @prodigy.net.mx, hasn't yet gotten an architectural award, it should soon. Builders have succeeded in creating a modern luxury hotel that has an intimate feel. This begins right at the reception, a plush round *palapa,* where arriving guests are graciously invited to sit in soft chairs while being attended to by personable clerks, who are also seated, behind rustic, designer desks. Outside, you walk to your room through manicured tropical gardens, replete with gurgling fountains, splashing brooks, and cascading, green lawn terraces. If the Zaashila has a drawback, it's in some of the 120 rooms, which, although luxurious and comfortable, are entirely tile-floored and could use more color and warmth. However, the arrangement of separate units, nested like a giant child's building blocks, resembles a space-age Hopi Native pueblo, each unit uniquely perched among the whole, affording much privacy and light, especially in upper-floor units. Outside, a few steps downhill, past the big, meandering blue pool, comes the superb beachfront: acres of luscious, billow-washed yellow sand, intimately enclosed between wave-sculpted rocks on one side and a jungly headland on the other. Low-season rentals begin at about $200, or about $230 if you must have your own little private pool. Corresponding high-season rates are around $350 and $400, with access to water sports, tennis, golf, three restaurants, and nightly live music.

Of the five Tangolunda beach-level hotels, the **Crown Pacific** has the largest rooms. Perhaps this is meant to compensate for the drawback that it's not actually on the beach: guests must either walk or shuttle a couple of blocks to the beach club. The biggest plus of the Crown Pacific is the price, which, low season, runs only about $80 per person, double occupancy, including all meals, drinks, sports, kid's miniclub, and in-house entertainment. No fans—all rooms are air-conditioned. During high season, the same costs about $100 per person. Reserve directly at Crown Pacific, Boulevard Benito Juárez 8, Bahía Tangolunda, Bahías de Huatulco, Oaxaca 70989, tel. 958/581-0044 or fax 958/581-0221, boyce@boyce.com.mx.

At this writing, the **Hotel Las Brisas,** formerly Club Med, has been bought recently by the Mexican Las Brisas hotel chain and is closed for renovations. Judging from the fine deluxe amenities and good management of existing Las Brisas hotels, in Acapulco, Ixtapa, Puerto Vallarta, and Los Cabos, and given its lovely location, we can probably expect the same excellence for the Las Brisas Huatulco. If the past is any guide, all-inclusive rates will probably run, low season, about $100 per day, per adult, children 6–11 half price, about $200 high season. For room only, expect to pay about $150 d low season, $250 high. For reservations and information, dial toll-free Mex. tel. 800/227-4727 or U.S./Can. tel. 866/226-3161. For more information, visit the website www.brisas.com.mx.

The **Club Gala Resort,** originally built and operated by the competent Mexican Club Maeva chain, is among Mexico's classiest all-inclusive resorts. The beach setting is gorgeous, the tile floors in the halls and rooms shine, and bright bedspeads, immaculate bathrooms and private ocean-view balconies grace the accommodations. All-inclusive rates run about $100 per person, low season, $140 high; kids, five years or under, go free, while kids 6–12 are half price. You may reserve directly at Club Gala Resort Huatulco, galareserv@huatulco.net.mx, P.O. Box 227, Bahías de Huatulco, Oaxaca 70989, tel. 958/581-0000 or toll-free U.S./Can. tel. 800/888-4252, fax 958/581-0220. For more information, visit the website www.galaresorts.com.

Playa Conejo Bed-and-Breakfast
A personable North American couple, Richard and Brooke Gazer, have built six elegantly lovely and comfortable guestrooms into their home overlooking Playa Conejos. The luxuriously private accommodations stair-step down from the main house to an airy ocean-vista garden pool

patio. High-season rates are $95, $105, and $117 s or d; $77, $89, and $99 low, including breakfast. For Christmas, add 20 percent to the high-season rates; with fans, nonsmoking adults only, and a short downhill walk to a private, intimate beach. For more information, call tel. 958/581-0265, email guarei@hotmail.com, or visit the website www.aguaazullavilla.com.

Camping
Authorities permit camping and RV parking at some the Bahías de Huatulco: RV parking at a marina-front lot in Chahue runs about $11 per family per day; RV parking or tenting at Bahía Cacaluta costs about the same. Other Huatulco public camping areas may be available. For more information, call tel. 958/587-0808 or 958/587-0446, or contact the tourist information office (see Information) in the Tangolunda hotel zone, on the far inland side, west edge of the hotel-shopping complex, tel. 958/581-0176, open high season Mon.–Fri. 9 A.M.–5 P.M., Sat. 9 A.M.–2 P.M.

The soldiers who guard the beaches against turtle poachers and squatters also make camping much more secure. They usually welcome a kind word and maybe a cool drink as a break from their lonely and tedious vigil.

FOOD
Aside from the Tangolunda hotels, most of the good Huatulco eateries are near the Crucecita plaza.

Breakfast and Snacks
For inexpensive homestyle cooking, try the *fondas* at the Crucecita Mercado (Market), between Guamuchil and Guanacastle, half a block off the plaza.

The Mercado stalls are good for fresh fruit during daylight hours, as is the **Frutería Angelita,** open daily 7 A.M.–9 P.M., just across Guanacastle.

Also nearby, the **Panadería San Alejandro,** at the southeast plaza corner of Flamboyan and Bugambilias, tel. 958/587-0317, open 6 A.M.–10 P.M., offers mounds of scrumptious baked goodies.

The crowds will lead you to Crucecita's best-bet snack shop, **Los Portales Taco and Grill,** corner of

Guamuchil and Bugambilias, right on the plaza, tel. 958/587-0070. Breakfasts, a dozen styles of tacos, Texas chili (or, as in Mexico, *frijoles charros*—cowboy beans), and barbecued ribs are the specialties. Beer is less than $1. Open daily 6–2 A.M.

For a relaxing drink or a sandwich in Santa Cruz, go to the **Café Huatulco,** tel. 958/587-1228, cafeplumahua@huatulco.net.mx, at the bandstand in the shady Santa Cruz town plaza, a block west of the marina embarcadero. The friendly husband-wife team's mission is to promote the already well-deserved popularity of Huatulco's mountain-grown coffee, which they grind fresh daily for their good cappuccinos and café lattes. Open daily 8 A.M.–10 P.M. For more information on Huatulco coffee and the mountain *fincas cafeteleras* where it's grown, contact personable owner Roberto Garcia, at the café, or via cellular tel. 044-958/589-4113.

Restaurants

The refined sidewalk atmosphere of **Café Oasis** has made it Crucecita's plaza-front restaurant of choice. Beneath cooling ceiling fans, customers watch the passing plaza scene while enjoying a full bar and a professionally prepared and served menu of breakfast, good espresso, fruit, salads, hamburgers, Mexican and international specialties, and much more. At the southeast plaza corner (Bugambilias and Flamboyan), open daily 8 A.M.–midnight, tel. 958/587-0045.

Nearly as successful is **Restaurante Sabor de Oaxaca,** on the bottom floor of the Hotel Las Palmas on Guamuchil, half a block from the plaza, tel. 958/587-0060. Wall art, folk crafts, and quiet conversation set the tone, while tasty country specialties fill the tables. Try the Oaxacan-style tamales, or *botanas Oaxaqueños*—cheese, sausage, pork, beef, and guacamole snacks. Open daily 8 A.M.–11 P.M.

Lovers of fine Italian cuisine can't miss enjoying a meal at Crucecita's class-act restaurant, **El Giardino del Papa** (The Pope's Garden), brainchild of owner Rossana Pandolfini, of Amalfitano, and chef Mario Saggese of Salerno. Mario, who was once the pope's bodyguard, immigrated to Mexico to follow his passion for cooking. Rossana asked Mario to come to Huatulco be-

cause she craved pasta al dente the way it's "supposed to be" in the old country. Although Mario's suggestions include *calamari criollo, scampi al brandy, insalata* Mediterrenea, and spaghetti a la Mario, whatever you get will be tasty. Call for reservations, tel. 958/587-4763, especially during the winter. Find the restaurant one block west of the plaza's southwest corner, at Flamboyan 204, open daily 2 P.M.–midnight. Expensive.

ENTERTAINMENT
Hangouts and Dancing

Huatulco entertainments center on the Crucecita plaza. Although the hubbub cools down weekdays and low seasons (and hot clubs seem to change as often as the Huatulco breeze), many spots heat up significantly during the high winter season.

The **Cactus Bar and Grill,** tel. 958/587-0648, on the Flamboyan side of the plaza, sometimes livens up with videos and music. On the other hand, you can get swept up nightly by the seasonal salsa and Latin rock repertoire of the band at the **Sports Bar Iguana,** (or the La Selva Restaurant next door) both adjacent to Tacos Los Portales, Bugambilias side of the plaza. Open about 11 A.M.–2 A.M., in season.

You need only follow your ears to the source at **Mr. Don** bar, at the diagonally opposite plaza corner of Gardenia and Guanacastle, upstairs. Live Latin rock is featured nightly in season and on weekends, 8–2 A.M.

A growing platoon of visitors and expatriates go to **Café Dublin,** a little bit of Ireland in Huatulco. Good imported beer, Irish coffee, spaghetti and meat balls, hamburgers, satellite TV, and good fellowship keeps the customers happy. In a cozy upstairs room, patrons settle in for the evening, socializing, enjoying recorded music, and watching videos. Find Café Dublin open daily noon until after midnight low season, 6–2 A.M. high season, on Calle Carrizal, a block east, half a block south, of the Crucecita plaza's southeast corner.

In Santa Cruz, lights flash, fogs descend, and customers gyrate to the boom-boom at **Magic Circus** disco in the Marlin Hotel on Calle Mitla, two blocks behind Banamex off the main boulevard. Admission (from around 10 P.M.) runs about $10. Call tel. 958/587-0055 to confirm.

Nearby, continue your party at **Dexkite** disco, which offers continuous recorded reggae, salsa, and Latin rock from about 9:30 P.M. At the Marina Hotel and Resort, in Santa Cruz, Calle Tehuantepec 112; call for confirmation, tel. 958/587-0971.

Sunset Cruise, Live Music, and Tourist Shows

Lovers of quieter diversions might enjoy going on a wine and soft-music sunset cruise on the sailboat *Luna Azul,* tel. 958/587-0945.

The **Club Gala Resort** in Tangolunda is one of the most reliable sources of hotel nightlife. Live music often plays before dinner (about 6–8 P.M.) in the lobby bar, and "Gala Night" tourist buffet and shows rev up at least weekly year-round. Contact a travel agent or call the hotel direct at tel. 958/581-0400 for details and reservations (about $55 per person, including everything). Other hotels, such as the Crown Pacific, Barceló ("Caribe Tropical" buffet and show), and Zaashila, may also offer similar entertainment in season.

SPORTS AND RECREATION
Walking, Jogging, Tennis, and Golf

Huatulco's open spaces and smooth roads and sidewalks afford plenty of walking and jogging opportunities. One of the most serene spots is along the Tangolunda Golf Course mornings or evenings. Also, an interesting sea-view forest trail takes off from Bahía Conejos.

If you're planning on playing lots of tennis, stay at one of the Tangolunda luxury resorts. Otherwise, the Barceló, tel. 958/581-0055 or 958/581-0005, and the Tangolunda Golf Course, tel. 958/581-0037, fax 958/581-0059, rent tennis courts for about $10/hour. Call for rental information and reservations.

The breezy green **Tangolunda Golf Course,** tel. 958/581-0037, fax 958/581-0059, designed by the late architect Mario Chegnan Danto, stretches for 6,851 yards down Tangolunda Valley to the

bay. The course starts from a low building complex (watch for bridge entrance) off the Highway 200-Tangolunda highway across from the sanitary plant. Greens fee runs about $60, cart $32, club rental $13, caddy $15. The tennis courts, maintained by the same government corporation that owns the golf course, are next to the clubhouse on the knoll at the east side of the golf course.

The new luxury **Xquenda** ("soul" in Zapotec) spa and athletic club, in Chahue, west side, on the Santa Cruz-Tangolunda road, offers tennis, paddle tennis, lap swimming pool, and a number of spa services, such as massage, facials, *temazcal* ceremonial hot room, and more. Open daily 7 A.M.–8 P.M., tel. 958/583-4448 or 958/583-4449. For more information, visit the website www.huatulcospa.com.

Horseback Riding

Rancho Caballo del Mar on the road (east past Tangolunda) to Copalita, about a mile south of Highway 200, guides horseback trips along the ocean-view forest trail that stretches from its corral to the ecopreserve zone by the Río Copalita. The four-mile tour, which costs about $25 per person at the ranch (more if through an agent), returns via Bocana shoreline vista point for lunch. For more information and reservations (not usually necessary), taxi to the ranch, or contact a travel agent.

Adventurers can also walk the same four-mile round-trip in a leisurely three hours. Take a hat, water, and a bathing suit, and start early (around 8 A.M.) or late (around 3 P.M.) to avoid the midday heat.

Adventure Tours

For offroad adventuring, contact **Pancho Willy's 4x4 Adventures,** at Colorín 608 in Crucecita, tel. 958/587-1930, panchowillys@hotmail.com. It offers a sturdy Mercedes truck tour, along jungle roads, through rivers, and past waterfalls. Along the way, you get a chance to hike, climb, rappel, splash in a forest waterfall, and enjoy a barbecue at a mountain coffee farm.

You might also check out **Transportadora Turistica Bahía Chahue,** tel. 958/587-0589, ttchahue@hotmail.com, at Flamboyan 308, south side of the Crucecita plaza, which offers similar adventures.

By all means please resist the urge to go on a widely advertised rip-roaring "jungle tour" by four-wheel *moto* all-terrain vehicle (ATV) motorscooter. The vehicles are noisy, hazardous to the rider, polluting to the environment, destructive to forest trails, and frightening to animals. It would be healthier for both you and the Huatulco ecosystem to ask the provider to guide you along the same trip by much less intrusive mountain bike, or, even better, on foot.

Río Copalita Ecotouring and Rafting

José Aussenac, owner of Posada Michelle, organizes and guides outdoor adventure tours in the east-side Río Copalita wildlife sanctuary. Options include bird- and animal-watching walks along riverine forest trails, kayaking river rapids, and mud baths at a riverside ranch. Call him, tel. 958/587-0535, for more information and reservations.

Also highly recommended are the services of white-water rafting outfitter-guide **Aventuras Piraguas,** tel. 958/587-1333, piraguas@huatulco.net.mx. Its trips, mostly on the Río Copalita, go during the high-water Oct.–March months only.

Upland Jungle Ecotouring and Coffee Farms

Local tour operators guide hiking and birdwatching tours to waterfalls, springs, archaeological zones, pilgrimage and sacred sites, and coffee farms in the jungly foothill hinterland north of Huatulco. One of the most experienced and environmentally sensitive operators is **Turismo Conejo** in Crucecita, at Plaza Conejo, on Guamuchil, half a block east of the town plaza, tel. 958/587-0009, fax 958/587-0054, tonino@caramail.com. Turismo Conejo offers a range of options, from one-day walks along the Copalita River (ruins, bird-watching by canoe, mudbath) and jungle jeep safaris and lunch at La Gloria coffee plantation to jungle overnights (waterfalls, rock hieroglyphic paintings) to complete five-day excursions from Oaxaca city, including all

of the above. Other agents may also offer similar tours; contact your hotel tour desk.

Swimming, Snorkeling, and Scuba Diving

Swimming is ideal in the calm corners of the Bahías de Huatulco. Especially good swimming beaches are at **Playa Entrega** in Bahía Santa Cruz and **Bahía El Maguey.**

Generally clear water makes for rewarding snorkeling off the rocky shoals of all of the Bays of Huatulco. Local currents and conditions, however, can be hazardous. Novice snorkelers should go on trips accompanied by strong, experienced swimmers or professional guides. Bring your own equipment; gear purchased locally will be expensive at best and unusable at worst.

Huatulco scuba divers enjoy the services of well-equipped and professional **Hurricane Divers** scuba shop, tel. 958/587-1107, hurricane-divers@hotmail.com., in the small complex between the Santa Cruz main beach and boat harbor. It starts novices out with a pool minicourse, followed by a three-hour ($60) resort dive in a nearby bay. Snorkelers go for about $30, with good equipment furnished. Hurricane Divers' open-water certification course takes about five days and runs about $380, complete. The shorter 12-meter certificate course runs about $220. With your certificate, you are qualified for the advanced (one-tank, $43; two-tank, $68) dives. After that, you may be ready for more advanced trips, which might include local shipwrecks, night dives, and marine flora, fauna, and ecology tours. Open Mon.–Sat. 9 A.M.–7 P.M.

Buceos Triton dive shop, tel./fax 958/587-0844, in the same complex, run by friendly certified PADI instructor Enrique La Clette, offers similar services. La Clette, a marine biologist by training, has had extensive training in France, the United States, and Mexico City.

Fishing and Boat Launching

The local boat cooperative **Sociedad Servicios Turísticos Bahía Tangolunda** takes visitors out for fishing excursions from the Santa Cruz boat quay. For a launch with two lines and bait, figure on paying about $40 minimum for a three-hour excursion. For big-game fishing, rent a big 40-foot boat, with lines for several people, for about $400. More reasonable prices might be obtained by asking around among the fishermen at the Santa Cruz boat harbor or the village at San Agustín.

On the other hand, you can leave the negotiations up to a travel agent, who will arrange a fishing trip for you and your friends. You can stop afterward at a beachside *palapa*, which will cook up a feast with your catch. Save money by bringing your own tackle. Rates for an approximately three-hour trip for three run about $60 if you supply your own tackle, $120 if you don't. Contact the agent at your hotel travel desk, or an outside agent, such as **Paraíso Huatulco** in the Hotel Flamboyan, on the Crucecita plaza, tel. 958/587-0181, fax 958/587-0190, or **Turismo Conejo,** also in Crucecita, tel. 958/587-0009.

Huatulco's best **boat-launching site** is at easily reachable Bahía Chahue marina, with about 40 slips and an excellent heavy-duty boat ramp. From the east-west beachfront boulevard, follow the sign "remolques" (trailers) to the big parking lot and ramp.

SHOPPING
Market and Handicrafts

Crucecita has a small traditional market (officially the Mercado 3 de Mayo) east of the plaza, between Guanacastle and Guamuchil. Although produce, meats, and clothing occupy most of the stalls, a few offer Oaxaca handicrafts. Items include black *barra* pottery, hand-crocheted Mixtec and Amusgo *huipiles,* wool weavings from Teotitlán del Valle, and whimsical duck-motif wooden bowls carved by an older, but sharp-bargaining, local gentleman.

In Santa Cruz, just west of the boat harbor, a warren of dozens of stalls offer nearly everything, from T-shirts and Taxco silver, to carved wooden fish and laquerware.

Steep rents and lack of business force many local silver, leather, art, and other handicrafts shops to hibernate until tourists arrive in December. The few healthy shops with good selections cluster either around the Crucecita plaza, the Santa Cruz boat quay, or in the Punta Tan-

golunda shopping complex adjacent to the Barceló (or shops in the hotel itself).

In Crucecita, one of the most reliable crafts stores is **Plata de Taxco,** open daily, 9 A.M.–9 P.M., tel. 958/587-0818 (next to Hotel Suites Begonias, a few doors south of the plaza's southwest corner). Here you can select from an all-Mexican assortment—shiny *barro negro* (black pottery) from the Valley of Oaxaca, pottery moon and sun faces from Tonalá, Jalisco, Talavera ware from Puebla, crazy wooden animals *(alebrijes)* from Arrazola, near Oaxaca, and lots of glistening silver jewelry from Taxco.

Supermarket, Laundry, and Photography

The supermarket **La Fuente** in Crucecita on east-side Av. Oaxaca offers a large stock of groceries, an ice machine, and a little bit of everything else, a block east of the Pemex station, tel. 958/587-0222. Open daily 8 A.M.–10 P.M.

Take your washing to the **Lavandería Estrella,** tel. 958/587-0585, open Mon.–Sat. 8 A.M.–9 P.M. Find it a block east of the Crucecita plaza, on Flamboyan, corner of Carrizal.

For film and quick develop-and-print, go to **Foto Conejo,** tel. 958/587-0054, just off the Crucecita plaza, across Guamuchil from the market. Besides a photo-portfolio of the Bays of Huatulco, the friendly owner stocks supplies, point-and-shoot cameras, and Kodak, Fuji, and Konica slide and print film. Open daily 9 A.M.–8 P.M.

INFORMATION
Tourist Information Office

The Huatulco office of the Oaxaca Secretary of Tourism is in the Tangolunda hotel zone, inland side, west edge of the hotel-shopping complex., tel./fax 958/581-0176, open high season, Mon.–Fri. 9 A.M.–5 P.M., Sat. 9 A.M.–2 P.M.

Guide

Savvy local folks recommend the services of ecologically sensitive guide **Mario Cobos,** tel. 958/587-1883. Although Mario's first love is bird-watching, he also offers fishing excursions and backcountry ecotours. His fee begins at $50 per day, for one or two people, with your wheels. Jeep rental (figure a minimum of about $50) is extra. (See also Sports and Recreation.)

Publications

The **bookshop** at the Barceló, tel. 958/581-0055, in Tangolunda stocks English-language paperback novels, Mexico art and guidebooks, newspapers such as *USA Today,* and many magazines.

In Crucecita, the small **Publicaciones Huatulco** newsstand sells the English-language *News* of Mexico City (which arrives around noon), at the corner of Gardenia and Macuil, three blocks north of the plaza; open daily 6 A.M.–9 P.M. Reserve your copy by paying in advance.

Pick up a copy of *Huatulco Magazine,* the handy commercial tourist booklet, at your hotel or a store or travel agent, or at the magazine office, tel. 958/587-0342, at Cerrada de Tlacolula no. 3, in Santa Cruz.

Ecology Association

Local ecologists and community leaders monitor Huatulco's development through their **Asociación Pro Desarrollo Sociocultural y Ecologíos de Bahías de Huatulco.** Members, such as marine biologist Enrique La Clette and his associates, are working earnestly to assure the government's plan—that 70 percent of Huatulco will remain undeveloped—continues in force as development proceeds. One of their initial victories was to dissuade the then-Club Med from dumping its raw sewage into Tangolunda Bay. Enrique, who is friendly and fluent in English, enjoys talking to fellow nature lovers. Drop into his dive shop, Buceos Triton, in Santa Cruz de Huatulco, in the complex between the boat harbor and the beach, tel./fax 958/587-0844.

SERVICES

Money Exchange

For cash, you may either use the **ATMs** at all of Huatulco's banks, or go inside. In Crucecita, try the **Banamex** ATM, on Carrizal, just north of the Hotel Grifer, or **Banco Inverlat** and ATM, a few doors north. Alternatively, use the **Bancomer** ATM, on the Crucecita plaza, southwest corner.

Other banks are in Santa Cruz. **Banamex,** on the main street Av. Santa Cruz, corner of Pochutla, tel. 958/587-0322, exchanges both U.S. and Canadian traveler's checks Mon.–Fri. 9 A.M.–4 P.M., Sat. 10 A.M.–2 P.M. **Bancomer,** across Pochutla, tel. 958/587-0003, does about the same thing Mon.–Fri. 8:30 A.M.–4 P.M. and Sat. 10 A.M.–2 P.M. Call to check money-changing hours.

After bank hours, go to the hole-in-the-wall **Money Exchange** booth on Guamuchil, near the corner, at the east side of the Crucecita plaza, tel. 958/587-1309, open Mon.–Sat. 7 A.M.–9 P.M.

Communications

The Huatulco *correo* and *telecomunicaciones* stand side by side, across from the Pemex gas station on east-side Blv. Tangolunda. The **post office,** tel. 958/587-0551, is open Mon.–Fri. 8 A.M.–3 P.M. only. **Telecom,** tel. 958/587-0894, is open Mon.–Fri. 8 A.M.–7 P.M. and Sat.–Sun. 9 A.M.–2 P.M.

For **telephone,** buy a Ladatel telephone card and use it at public telephones, or go to one of the *larga distancia* businesses on Carrizal, near the Hotel Grifer, such as **Caseta Telefónica Gemenis,** tel. 958/587-0735 or 958/587-0736, open daily 8 A.M.–9:30 P.M.

Internet connection is available at **Cuijosnet** store, at Carrizal 504, between Flamboyan and Chaca, next to the Irish pub. Find it open daily 10 A.M.–10 P.M., tel. 958/587-1569.

Health and Police

Among the better of Huatulco private clinics is **Clínica Médico,** with 24-hour emergency service, tel. 958/587-0600 or 958/587-0687. Find it at 403 Sabali, corner of Gardenia, about eight blocks north of the Crucecita plaza.

For an English-speaking, U.S.-trained doctor, go to IAMAT (International Association for Medical Assistance to Tourists) member and general practitioner **Dr. Andrés González Ayvar,** tel. 958/587-0687, cellular tel. 044-958/587-6065. His regular consultation hours are Mon.–Sat. 11 A.M.–1 P.M. and 6–9 P.M.

Alternatively, go to the 24-hour government

Centro de Salud clinic, tel. 958/587-1421, on Carrizal, a block east of the Crucecita plaza, or the big **Seguro Social** hospital, tel. 958/587-1182, 958/587-1183, or 958/587-1185 in Crucecita, on the boulevard to Tangolunda, a quarter mile south of the Pemex gas station.

For routine medications, Crucecita has many pharmacies, such as **Farmacia del Centro,** plaza corner of Flamboyan and Bugambilias, tel. 958/587-0232, open Mon.–Sat. 8 A.M.–10 P.M., Sun. 9 A.M.–2 P.M. and 5–10 P.M., at street level, below the Hotel Begonias.

For police emergencies, call the Crucecita *policía,* tel. 958/587-0210, in the Agencia Municipal behind the post office, across the Tangolunda boulevard from the Pemex *gasolinera.*

Immigration and Customs

Both Migración and the Aduana are at the Huatulco airport. If you lose your tourist permit, try to avoid trouble or a fine at departure by presenting Migración with proof of your date of arrival— stamped passport, an airline ticket, or preferably a copy of your lost tourist permit—a day (or at least three hours) before your scheduled departure.

GETTING THERE AND AWAY

By Air

The **Huatulco airport** (officially the Aeropuerto Internacional Bahías de Huatulco, code-designated HUX) is just off Highway 200, eight miles (13 km) west of Crucecita and 19 miles (31 km) east of Puerto Ángel. The terminal is small, with only check-in booths, a few snack bars, and handicrafts and trinket shops (but, fortunately, with an ATM for arrival cash.)

A few reliable carriers connect with U.S. and Mexican destinations:

American Airlines connects with Dallas, during the winter-spring high season. For reservations, call a travel agent, such as Paraíso Huatulco, tel. 958/587-0181, fax 958/587-0190.

Mexicana Airlines flights connect daily with Mexico City. For reservations, call Mexicana's office on Plaza Chahue shopping center, tel. 958/587-0223 or 958/587-0243, or toll-free Mex. tel. 800/502-2000.

Aerocaribe connects with Oaxaca and Puerto Escondido. For reservations, call a travel agent.

United Airlines, American Airlines, Canada 3000 and **Canadian Air Transat** offer seasonal, mostly winter **charter-flight** connections with U.S. and Canadian destinations. For reservations, call a travel agent.

Huatulco **air arrival** is usually simple. Since the terminal has no hotel booking agency or money-exchange counter (although there is an ATM), come with a hotel reservation and sufficient pesos to last until you can get to the bank in Santa Cruz or Crucecita. After the typically quick immigrations and customs checks, arrivees have a choice of efficient ground transportation to town. Agents sell tickets for collective GMC Suburbans to Crucecita or Santa Cruz or Tangolunda (about $8). A private *taxi especial* outside the airport gate only, for three, possibly four passengers, runs about $12. Prices to Puerto Ángel are double or triple these.

Mobile travelers on a budget can roll their suitcase the couple of blocks from the terminal to Highway 200 and catch one of the frequent public **minibuses** (about $1–2) headed either way to Crucecita (east, left) or the Pochutla (Puerto Ángel) junction (west, right).

Car rental agents are usually on duty for flight arrivals. If they're not, make a reservation and they will meet your flight: Budget in Crucecita, tel. 958/587-0010, fax 958/587-0019; or Alamo in Santa Cruz, at the Hotel Castillo, tel. 958/587-0135. During the winter especially, make reservations in the United States and Canada before departure.

By Car or RV

Paved highways connect Huatulco east with the Isthmus of Tehuantepec, west with Puerto Ángel and Puerto Escondido, and north with Oaxaca.

Highway 200, the east-west route, runs an easy 100 miles (161 km) to Tehuantepec, where it connects with Highway 190. From there, it continues northwest to Oaxaca or east to Chiapas and the Guatemala border. In the opposite direction, the Highway 200 route is equally smooth, connecting with Pochutla (Puerto Ángel), 22 miles (35 km) west, and Puerto Escondido, 66 miles (106 km), continuing to Acapulco in a long 322 miles (519 km). Allow about three hours to Tehuantepec, 1.5 hours to Puerto Escondido, and to Acapulco, a full nine hours' driving time, either direction.

Highway 175, the cross-Sierra connection north with the city of Oaxaca, although paved, is narrow, winding, and oft-potholed, with few services in the 80-mile high Sierra stretch between its junction with Highway 200 at Pochutla (22 miles west of Crucecita) and Miahuatlán in the Valley of Oaxaca. The road climbs to 9,000 feet into pine-tufted, winter-chilly Chatino and Zapotec country. Be prepared for emergencies. Allow eight hours northbound, seven hours southbound, for the entire 175-mile (282-km) Huatulco-Oaxaca trip.

By Bus
Four main long-distance bus lines connect Huatulco with destinations east, west, and north.

They depart from three small separate terminals in Crucecita, several blocks north of the plaza.

Many daily **Cristóbal Colón** first-class buses, terminal on Gardenia, corner of Ocotillo, four blocks north of the plaza, tel. 958/587-0261, connect west with Pochutla (Puerto Ángel) and Puerto Escondido. Buses also connect east with the Salina Cruz and Tehuantepec on the Isthmus, continuing either east to San Cristóbal de las Casas and Tapachula in Chiapas, or northwest to Mexico City via Oaxaca and Puebla.

One block farther north, corner of Palma Real, a few **Estrella Blanca** buses, tel. 958/587-0103, connect west with Pinotepa Nacional and Acapulco via Pochutla and Puerto Escondido, and east with Salina Cruz.

A few second- and first-class **Estrella del Valle** and **Autobúses Oaxaca Pacífico** buses connect daily with Oaxaca via Pochutla, from Jazmin, corner Sabali, nine blocks north of the plaza, tel. 958/587-0193.

Oaxaca City

The Valley of Oaxaca is really three valleys, which diverge, like the thumb, index finger, and middle finger of a hand, from a single strategic point. Aztec conquerors called that hilltop spot Huaxyacac (oo-AHSH-yah-kahk, Point of the Guaje) for the forest of pod-bearing trees that still carpets its slopes. The Spanish, who founded the city at the foot of the hill, shifted that name to the more-pronounceable Oaxaca (wah-HAH-kah).

The people of the Valley of Oaxaca, walled in by mountains from the rest of Mexico, both benefit and suffer from their long isolation. They are poor but proud inheritors of rich traditions that live on despite 300 years of Spanish occupation.

A large proportion of Oaxacans are pure native Mexicans who speak one of dozens of native languages and dialects. Significant numbers speak little or no Spanish at all. Even in the valley around Oaxaca city itself they make up a sizable fraction of the people. Far out in the country, they *are* the people. Mostly speaking dialects of Zapotec or Mixtec, they harvest their corn for tortillas and their maguey for *pulque* and *aguardiente* (fire

water). They spin their wool, hoe their vegetables, then go to market and sit beside their piles of blankets and mounds of onions, wondering if their luck is going to change.

HISTORY
Before Columbus
Evidence of human prehistory litters the riverbottoms and hillsides of the Valley of Oaxaca. Cave remains near the ancient city-state of Mitla tell of hunters who lived there as long as 8,000 years ago. Several thousand years later, their descendants, heavily influenced by the mysterious Olmecs of the Gulf coast, were carving gods and glyphs on stone monuments in the Valley of Oaxaca. Around 600 B.C., people speaking a Zapotec mother tongue, similarly influenced by the Olmecs, founded Monte Albán on a mountaintop above the present city of Oaxaca.

Monte Albán ruled the Valley of Oaxaca for more than a millennium, climaxing as a sophisticated metropolis of perhaps 40,000, controlling a large and populous area of southern Mexico and enjoying diplomatic and trade relations with distant kingdoms. But, for reasons unknown, Monte Albán had declined to a shadow of its former glory by A.D. 1000.

Mixtec-speaking people filled the vacuum. They took over Monte Albán, using it mostly as a burial ground. Their chiefs divided up the Valley of Oaxaca and ruled from separate feudalistic city-states, such as Mitla, Yagul, Mazatlán, and Zaachila, for hundreds of years.

The Mixtecs in turn gave way to the Aztecs, whose invading warriors crossed the mountains and threatened Oaxaca during the A.D. 1440s. In A.D. 1456 the Aztecs established a garrison on the hill of Huaxyacac (now called Cerro del Fortín), overlooking the present city of Oaxaca, ruling their restive Zapotec and Mixtec subjects for only two generations. On November 21, 1521, conquistador Francisco de Orozco and his soldiers replaced them on the hill of Huaxyacac, scarcely four months after the Spanish tide had flooded the Aztecs' Valley of Mexico homeland.

Conquest and Colonization

Spanish settlers began arriving soon after the conquistadores. At the foot of the hill of Huaxyacac, they laid out their town, which they christened Antequera after the old Spanish Roman city. Soon, however, the settlers came into conflict with Cortés, whom the king had named marquis of the Valley of Oaxaca, and whose entire valley domain surrounded the town. Townspeople had to petition the queen of Spain for land on which to grow vegetables: they were granted a one-league square in 1532.

For hundreds of years, Cortés's descendants reigned, the church grew fat, the colonists prospered, and the natives toiled—in cane and corn, in cattle pastures and silk mulberry groves.

Independence, Reform, and the Porfirian Era

In contrast to its neighbors in the state of Guerrero, conservative Oaxaca was a grudging player in the 1810–1821 War of Independence. But, as the subsequent republican tide swept the country, local fervor produced a new state constitution,

including a state legislature and governmental departments, as well as public instruction and an Institute of Arts and Sciences.

By the 1850s, times had changed. Oaxacans were leading a new national struggle. Benito Juárez, a pure Zapotec native Mexican, was rallying liberal forces in the civil War of the Reforms against the oligarchy that had replaced colonial rule. Born in Guelatao, north of the valley, Juárez at age 12 was an orphan sheepherder. A Catholic priest, struck by the boy's intelligence, brought him to the city as a servant and taught him Spanish in preparation for the priesthood.

Instead, Benito became a lawyer. He hung out his shingle in Oaxaca, first as a defender of the poor, then state legislator, governor, chief justice, and finally the president of Mexico. In his honor, the city's official name was again changed—to Oaxaca de Juárez—in 1872.

In 1861, after winning the three-year civil war, Juárez's Reformista forces had their victory snatched away. France, taking advantage of the United States's preoccupation with its own civil war, invaded Mexico and installed an Austrian Hapsburg prince as Emperor Maximilian of Mexico.

It took Juárez five years to prevail against Maximilian and his conservative Mexican backers. Although Maximilian and Juárez paradoxically shared many of the same liberal ideas, Juárez had Maximilian executed after his defeat and capture in 1867. Juárez bathed Mexico in enlightenment as he promulgated his "Laws of the Reform" (which remain essentially in force). Although the country rewarded him with reelection, he died of exhaustion in 1871.

Another Oaxacan of native Mexican descent, General Porfirio Díaz, vowed to carry Juárez's banner. Díaz, the hero who defeated the French in the battle of Puebla on Cinco de Mayo (May 5) of 1862, was elected president in 1876. "No Reelección" was his campaign cry. He subsequently ruled Mexico for 34 years.

Under Díaz's "Order and Progress," Mexico, and to a lesser degree, Oaxaca, was modernized at great human cost. As railroads, factories, and mines mushroomed, property ownership increasingly became concentrated among rich Mexicans and

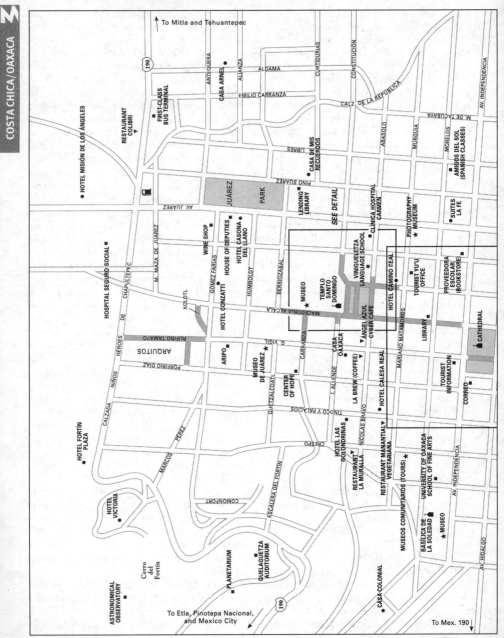

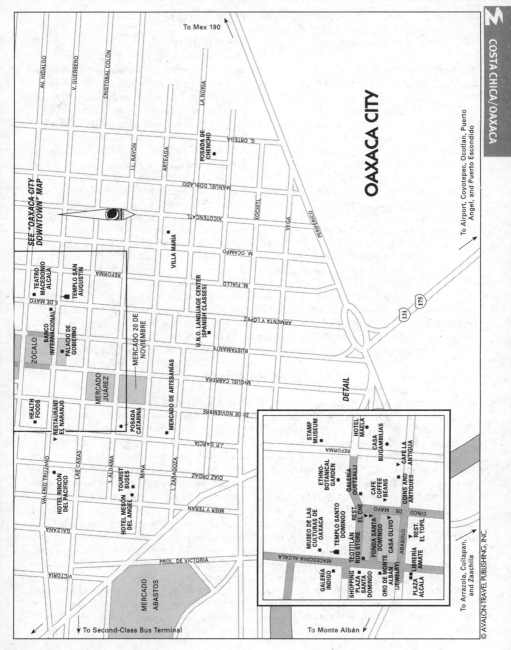

OAXACA CITY

To Mex 190

To Airport, Coyotepec, Ocotlan, Puerto Angel, and Puerto Escondido

DETAIL

To Arrazola, Cuilapan, and Zaachila

To Second-Class Bus Terminal

To Monte Albán

© AVALON TRAVEL PUBLISHING, INC.

SEE "OAXACA CITY DOWNTOWN" MAP

Main map labels:
- AV. HIDALGO
- V. GUERRERO
- CRISTÓBAL COLÓN
- LA NORIA
- ARTEAGA
- G. ORTEGA
- POSADA DE CHENCHO
- MANUEL DOBLADO
- XICOTÉNCATL
- XOCHITL
- VEGA
- M. OCAMPO
- M. FIALLO
- I.L. RAYON
- VILLA MARÍA
- REFORMA
- TEATRO MACEDONIO ALCALÁ
- TEMPLO SAN AGUSTÍN
- 5 DE MAYO
- U.N.O. LANGUAGE CENTER (SPANISH CLASSES)
- ARMENTA Y LÓPEZ
- BANCO INTERNACIONAL
- PALACIO DE GOBIERNO
- ZÓCALO
- MERCADO 20 DE NOVIEMBRE
- BUSTAMANTE
- PERIFÉRICO
- 131
- 175
- MIGUEL CABRERA
- MERCADO JUÁREZ
- HEALTH FOODS
- RESTAURANT EL NARANJO
- POSADA CATARINA
- MERCADO DE ARTESANÍAS
- J.P. GARCÍA
- 20 DE NOVIEMBRE
- VALERIO TRUJANO
- HOTEL RINCÓN DEL PACÍFICO
- GALEANA
- LAS CASAS
- I. ALDAMA
- TOURIST BUSES
- MINA
- DÍAZ ORDAZ
- I. ZARAGOZA
- HOTEL MESÓN DEL ÁNGEL
- MIER Y TERÁN
- PROL. DE VICTORIA
- VICTORIA
- MERCADO ABASTOS

Detail map labels:
- STAMP MUSEUM
- HOTEL MAELA
- ETHNO-BOTANICAL GARDEN
- REFORMA
- CASA BUGAMBILIAS
- GALERIA QUETZALLI
- CAFE COFFEE BEANS
- CAFE LA ANTIGUA
- MUSEO DE LAS CULTURAS DE OAXACA
- TEMPLO SANTO DOMINGO
- REST. EL CHE
- COINS AND ANTIQUES
- 5 DE MAYO
- CINCO
- TEOTITLÁN RUG STORE
- FONDA SANTA DOMINGO
- CASA OLIVO
- REST. EL TOPIL
- GALERIA INDIGO
- SHOPPING PLAZA SANTA DOMINGO
- ORO DE MONTE ALBÁN (JEWELRY)
- ABASOLO
- PLAZA ALCALÁ
- LIBRERIA AMATE
- MACEDONIA ALCALÁ

their foreign friends. Smashed protest marches, murdered opposition leaders, and rigged elections returned Díaz to office time and again.

Modern Oaxaca

But Díaz couldn't last forever. The revolution that ousted him in 1911 has, in theory, never ceased. The PRI, the Institutional Revolutionary Party, presided over a uniquely imperfect Mexican form of democracy. Under three generations of PRI rule, the lives of native Oaxacans improved gradually. Although native families now go to government health centers and more of their children attend government rural schools, the price for doing so is to become less *indígena* and more Mexican.

Times in the Valley of Oaxaca nevertheless seem to be getting gradually better. In the late 1980s, UNESCO recognized Oaxaca as one of several world sites belonging to the "Cultural Patrimony of Mankind." The government took notice and began preparing Oaxaca for an influx of visitors. Museums were built, monuments refurbished, and the venerable buildings restored. Burgeoning tourism during the 1990s has visibly improved the economic well-being of many Oaxaca families.

Increased international and national awareness seems to have contributed to other improvements. Some longstanding grievances are being recognized. In 1995, moderate PRI governor Diodoro Carrasco Altamirano pushed through an unprecedented "Usos y Costumbres" law, which legalized Oaxacan native rights to their indigenous language and their traditional, town-meeting form of government.

Nevertheless, by developed-world standards, most Oaxaca city families remain very poor, and the political system is far from perfect. Now, however, the December 1, 2000, inauguration of opposition President Vicente Fox has excited new hope in the minds and hearts of Oaxacans: they hope and pray that grievances stemming from bad former governments—police bruality, corruption, and political assassination—will diminish and finally become things of the past.

CITY SIGHTS

Getting Oriented

The streets of Oaxaca (pop. 350,000, elev. 5,110 feet, 1,778 meters) still run along the same simple north-south grid the city fathers laid out in 1529. If you stand at the center of the old *zócalo* and look out toward the *catedral* across the Av. Hidalgo, you will be looking north. Diagonally left, to the northwest, you'll see the smaller plaza, **Alameda de León,** and directly beyond, in the distance, the historic hill of Huaxyacac, now called **Cerro del Fortín.**

Along the base of that hill, the Pan American Highway (National Highway 190) runs generally east-west through the northern suburbs. Turn around and you'll see the porticoed facade of the **Palacio de Gobierno,** where Oaxaca's governor tends to the state's business. Half a mile behind that (although you can't see it from the *zócalo*) the *periférico* (peripheral) boulevard loops around the town's south end. There it passes the yawning but oft-dry wash of the **Río Atoyac** and the sprawling **Mercado Abastos** market and second-class bus terminal on the southwest. Finally, if you find a clear vantage point you'll see the hill of **Monte Albán** looming 1,000 feet (450 meters) above the southwest horizon.

A Walk Around Town

The venerable restored downtown buildings and the streets, some converted to traffic-free malls, make a delightful strolling ground for discovering traditional Mexico at its best. The *zócalo* itself sometimes seems to be a place of slow, leisurely motion, perfect for sitting at one of many sidewalk cafés and watching the world glide by.

Step to the *zócalo*'s south side and give the guards at the front door of the **Palacio de Gobierno** a cheery *"buenos días"* or *"buenas tardes"* and step under the entrance arch. Straight ahead, across the courtyard, you'll see the main mural, by Arturo Bustos, completed during the 1980s. It depicts the struggles of Oaxaca's independence, reform, and revolutionary heroes. In the center is Oaxaca's favorite son and Mexico's revered *presidente,* Benito Juárez, and his wife, Margarita

Maza. Below them is Juárez's *reformista* cabinet (notice the young, restive, General Porfirio Díaz with the sword on the right), which struggled through two bloody wars, finally emerging, with Juárez, triumphant in 1867.

Head to the *zócalo's* opposite, north side, for a look at the present **cathedral**. It replaced the 1550 original, demolished by an earthquake in 1696. Finished in 1733, with appropriately burly twin bell towers, the present cathedral is distinguished by its Greek marble main altar, where a polished Italian bronze Virgin of the Assump-

tion is being drawn upward to the cloud-tipped heavenly domain of the Holy Spirit (the dove) and God (the sunburst). Flanking opposite sides of the altar, notice the glass images of noble, bearded St. Peter and St. Paul.

Of considerable historical interest is the **Santa Cruz de Huatulco** (Holy Cross of Huatulco), enshrined in a chapel at the middle, south (right) side of the nave. The cross, about two feet high, is one of four made in 1612 by Oaxaca bishop Juan Cervantes from the original mysterious cross worshipped by the natives on the southern Oaxaca

© AVALON TRAVEL PUBLISHING, INC.

© BRUCE WHIPPERMAN

Angel Gabriel mounts a column on a narrow lane in the picturesque Los Arguitos neighborhood, about ten blocks north of the Oaxaca cathedral.

coast long before the conquest. (See the Bays of Huatulco section.) An explanation, in Spanish, gives three versions of the story of the cross, which, the natives reported to the conqueror Pedro Alvarado in 1522, was erected long before by a strange, white-robed holy man, who soon departed and never returned. Bishop Cervantes sent the three other copies to authorities at Santa María Huatulco town, Mexico City, and Rome.

Continue behind the cathedral north along the tranquil **Andador de Macedonio Alcalá** pedestrian mall, named after the composer of the Oaxacan hymn "Dios Nunca Muere" (God Never Dies). Paved with Oaxaca green stone in 1985 and freed of auto traffic, the mall connects the *zócalo* with a number of distinguished Oaxaca monuments.

Among them is the **Teatro Alcalá,** at 900 Independencia, tel. 951/516-2969 (from the back of the cathedral head right one block along Inde-

pendencia to the corner of Independencia and 5 de Mayo). Christened by a 1909 opening performance of *Aida,* the Alcalá houses a treasury of Romantic-era art. Above the foyer, a sumptuous marble staircase rises to a bas-relief medallion allegorizing the triumph of art. Also take a look around the theater's gallery of paintings of Miguel Cabrera (1695–1768), a native Zapotec who rose to become New Spain's renowned baroque painter.

Continuing north along the Alcalá street mall, you soon pass the so-called **Casa de Cortés,** now the **Museo de Arte Contemporaneo de Oaxaca,** Macedonio Alcalá 202, tel. 951/514-2818 or 951/514-2228, open daily except Tues. 10:30 A.M.–8 P.M. Past the bookstore (mostly Spanish but some English-language history, art, and guidebooks), exhibitions feature works of local and nationally known modern artists. Although named popularly for Hernán Cortés, the building is at least 100 years too new for Cortés to have lived there. The coat of arms on the facade above the door reveals it to have been the 17th-century home of a different Oaxaca family.

Continue uphill and, at Murguia, detour right again, to the **Ex-convento de Santa Catalina,** the second-oldest women's convent in New Spain, founded in 1576. Although the quarters of the first initiates were spare, the convent grew into a sprawling chapel and cloister complex decorated by fountains and flower-strewn gardens. Juárez's reforms drove the sisters out in 1862; the building has since served as city hall, school, and movie theater. Now, it stands beautifully restored as the Hotel Camino Real. Note the native-motif original murals that the renovation revealed on interior walls.

Return to the Alcalá street mall and continue another block uphill to Oaxaca's pride, the **Centro Cultural de Santo Domingo,** which contains two main parts, side by side: the **Museum of the Cultures of Oaxaca** and the **Church and Ex-convent of Santo Domingo,** both behind the broad Plaza Santo Domingo maguey garden and pedestrian square.

Inside, Santo Domingo church (open daily 7 A.M.–1 P.M. and 5–8 P.M.), glows with a wealth of art. Above the antechamber spreads the entire genealogical tree of Santo Domingo de Guzmán, starting with Mother Mary and weaving through a score of noblemen and women to the saint himself over the front door.

Continuing inside, the soaring, Sistine Chapel–like nave glitters with saints, cherubs, and Bible-story paintings. The altar climaxes in a host of cherished symbols—the Last Supper, sheaves of grain, loaves and fishes, Jesus and Peter on the Sea of Galilee—in a riot of gold leaf.

Continue next door, to the museum, open daily except Mon. 10 A.M.–7:30 P.M., tel. 951/516-2991, which occupies the completely restored convent section of the Santo Domingo church. Exhibitions begin on the bottom floor in rooms adjacent to the massive convent cloister, restored in 1998 to all of its original austere glory. A downstairs highlight is the long-neglected but now safely preserved **Library of Francisco Burgoa,** which you can walk right through and examine some of the more important works on display. The collection, 23,000 titles in all, includes its earliest work, a 1484 commentary on the works of Aristotle by Juan Versor.

A Museo sign points you upstairs, via a glitteringly restored, towering domed chamber, adorned overhead with the Dominican founding fathers, presided over by Santo Domingo de Guzmán himself.

It's hard not to be impressed by the seeming miles of meticulously prepared displays, divided into about a dozen long rooms covering respective historical periods. One room exhibits priceless Monte Albán–era artifacts, including one of the most important of the original so-called *danzantes,* with the typically mutilated sex organs. The highlight comes in the Tesoros of Tomb 7 room, where the entire gilded trove discovered at Monte Albán Tomb 7 is on display. Besides a small mountain of gold and turquoise ornaments, notice the small but masterfully executed golden head of Ecéchatl, god of the wind, made eerie by the omission of facial skin over the jaw, to produce a nightmarishly skeletal piece of jewelry.

The museum has recently established an **ethnobotanical garden** in its big backyard. Staff customarily conduct both English and Spanish tours, Tues.–Sat. 10–11 A.M. and 5–6 P.M. Inquire at the museum front desk, tel. 951/516-2991, for schedule and access details.

Back outside, step across Alcalá, a few doors uphill, into the rust-colored old building, now tastefully restored as the museum of the **Instituto de Artes Gráficos de Oaxaca,** tel. 951/516-6980. Inside, displays exhibit mostly contemporary etchings, wood-block prints, and paintings by artists of both national and international renown. Exhibits change approximately monthly; open daily except Tues. 9:30 A.M.–8 P.M.

Head west one block (along the Plazuela Carmen mall, off Alcalá across from the museum) to 609 Garcia Vigil and the **Casa de Juárez** museum, tel. 951/516-1860. The modest but beautifully restored house was the home of Juárez's benefactor, priest and bookbinder Father Antonio Salanueva. Rooms decorated with homey mid-19th-century furnishings realistically illustrate the life and times of a man as revered in Mexico as is his contemporary, Abraham Lincoln, north of the border. Open daily except Mon. 10 A.M.–6 P.M.

Sights West and South of the Zócalo

The **Museo Arte Prehispánico de Rufino Tamayo,** 503 Morelos, tel. 951/516-4750, two blocks west and north of the *zócalo,* exhibits the brilliant pre-Columbian artifact collection of celebrated artist Rufino Tamayo (1899–1991). Displays include hosts of animal motifs—Colima dogs, parrots, ducks, snakes—whimsically crafted into polychrome vases, bowls, and urns. Open Mon. and Wed.–Sat. 10 A.M.–2 P.M. and 4–7 P.M., Sun. 10 A.M.–3 P.M.

Continue three blocks west, past the University of Oaxaca School of Fine Arts and the airy Plaza of Dances, to the baroque **Basílica de Nuestra Señora de la Soledad.** Inside, the Virgin of Solitude, the patron of Oaxaca, stands atop the altar with her five-pound solid gold crown, encrusted with 600 diamonds.

Step into the **Museo de la Soledad,** at the downhill side of the church, rear end. A multitude of objects of adornment—shells, paintings, jewelry—crowd cabinets, shelves, and aisles of musty rooms. Large stained-glass panels tell of the images of Jesus and the Virgin that arrived miraculously in 1620, eventually becoming Oaxaca's patron symbols. Open daily 10 A.M.–2 P.M. and 4–6 P.M., tel. 951/516-5076.

Return to the vicinity of the *zócalo* and the traditional **Juárez Market,** which occupies the one-block square that begins just one block southwest of the *zócalo*. Stroll around for fun and perhaps a bargain in the honeycomb of traditional leather, textile, and clothing stalls.

ACCOMMODATIONS

Oaxaca offers a wide range of good hotels. Air-conditioning is not particularly necessary in temperate Oaxaca, although hot-water showers (furnished by all lodgings listed below) feel especially comfy during cool winter mornings and evenings. The less expensive hotels, which generally do not accept credit cards, are mostly near the colorful, traffic-free *zócalo*. With one exception, Oaxaca's plush, resort-style hostelries dot the northern edge of town. During holidays and festivals (Easter week, July, August, late Oct.–early Nov., Dec. 15–Jan. 4) many Oaxaca hotels raise their prices 20–30 percent above the tariffs listed below. You can book a number of the following hotels via the Internet: visit the website www.oaxaca4less.com.

Hotels near the Zócalo

Along with an enviable *zócalo* location, the **Hotel Señorial,** Portal de Flores 6, Oaxaca, Oaxaca 68000, tel. 951/516-3933, fax 951/516-3668, provides clean rooms, efficient management, a reliable restaurant, and an inviting (but unheated) swimming pool and patio. The hotel's only drawback is that a number of its interior rooms have louvered (nonsoundproof) communal air shaft windows and hallway transoms. This, especially during high fiesta seasons, results in noise that can't be shut out. Light sleepers should bring earplugs, especially on weekends and holidays, when the popular Señorial will be brimming with guests. The 107 rooms rent for about $60 s or d, with TV, limited wheelchair access, phones, parking, and credit cards are accepted.

A number of good budget to moderately priced hotels cluster beside or behind the Hotel Señorial, within a block or two of the *zócalo*.

Moving generally clockwise around the *zócalo*, first comes the petite **Hotel Las Rosas,** Trujano 112, Oaxaca, Oaxaca 68000, tel./fax 951/514-2217, behind the Señorial and half a block from the *zócalo*. Climb a flight of stairs to the small lobby, relatively tranquil by virtue of its second-floor location. Beyond that, a double tier of rooms surrounds a homey inner patio. Adjacent to the lobby is a cheery sitting room with big, beautiful tropical aquarium, and a TV, usually kept at subdued volume. In the back, guests enjoy an airy terrace for sunning and relaxing. The rooms themselves, although plainly furnished, are clean and tiled (except some bathrooms, which could use an extra scrubbing). Prices, moreover, at about $30 s, $37 d, $47 t, while not the bargain they once were, are relatively reasonable for such a well-situated hotel. No credit cards, parking, or wheelchair access.

Hotel Rivera del Ángel, at Mina 518, Oaxaca, Oaxaca 68000, tel. 951/516-6666, fax 951/514-5405, offers several advantages. Downstairs, an airy, shiny, but busy lobby and restaurant area offers nothing special, but through the lobby windows, feast your eyes on the inviting big blue pool and sunny central patio. Upstairs, you'll find the rooms semideluxe, clean, spacious, and comfortable, many with private terraces overlooking the pool patio. The hotel's main drawback, besides the sleazy (street prostitutes, low-life bars, and drunks at night) neighborhood, is street noise, from buses along Mina. Ask for a *tranquilo* off-street room. Asking rates run a reasonable $39 s, $53 d, low season, $60 and $65 high, with TV, fans, phones, restaurant, parking, travel agency, and tour buses to Mitla and Monte Albán. Credit cards not accepted. If you can't bargain for a better rate, especially during times of low occupancy, take your business elsewhere.

Return to the immediate *zócalo* vicinity, to the newly renovated **Hostal Santa Rosa,** a block from the *zócalo*'s southwest corner, at Trujano 201, Oaxaca, Oaxaca 68000, tel./fax 951/514-6714 or 951/514-6715. The streetside lobby leads past an airy restaurant to the rooms, recessed along a meandering inner passageway and courtyard. Inside, the rooms are very clean, comfortably furnished, and decorated in pastels. Rents, although raised,

OAXACA ACCOMMODATIONS BY PRICE

Accommodations (area code 951, postal code 68000 unless otherwise noted) are listed in increasing order of approximate double-room rates. Prices may be much higher during holidays and festivals, especially July, Christmas, Easter, and Day of the Dead (Oct. 28–Nov. 4).

Hotels

Hotel Las Rosas, Trujano 112, tel./fax 514-2217, $37

Hotel Las Golondrinas, at Tinoco y Palacios 411, tel. 514-3298, tel./fax 514-2126, lasgolon@prodigy.net.mx, $40

Hostal Santa Rosa, Trujano 201, tel. 514-6714 or 514-6715, $42

Hotel Monte Albán, Alameda de León 1, tel. 516-2777, fax 516-3265, hotelmontealban@prodigy.net.mx, $45

Hotel Gala, Bustamante 103, tel. 514-2251 or 514-1305, fax 516-3660, galaoax@prodigy.net.mx, $55

Hotel Señorial, Portal de Flores 6, tel. 516-3933, fax 516-3668, $60

Hotel Rivera del Ángel, Mina 518, tel. 516-6666, fax 514-5405, $65

Hotel Misión de Los Angeles, Calz. Porfirio Díaz 102, Oaxaca, Oaxaca, 68050, tel. 515-1500, fax 515-1680, hmision@prodigy.net.mx, $83

Hotel Fortín Plaza, Av. Venus 118, Colonia Estrella, Oaxaca 68040, tel. 515-7777, fax 515-1328, hfortin@prodigy.net.mx, $94

Hotel Marqués del Valle, Portal Clavería, P.O. Box 13 or P.O. Box 35, tel. 514-0688 or 516-3474, fax 516-9961, hmarques@prodigy.net.mx, $100

Hotel Victoria, Km 545, Carretera Panamericana, Oaxaca 68070, tel. 515-2633, fax 515-2411, ventas@hotelvictoriaoax.com.mx, $160

Camino Real, Calle 5 de Mayo 300, tel. 516-0611, 800/7-CAMINO (800/722-6466), fax 516-0732, www.caminoreal.com, $250

Apartments and Bed-and-Breakfasts

Casa Arnel, Aldama 404, Colonia Jalatlaco, 68080, tel./fax 515-2856, casa.arnel@spersaoaxaca.com, $27

Villa María, Arteaga 410 A, tel. 516-5056, fax 514-2562, $45, $350–600/month

Casa Colonial, Calle Miguel Negrete 105, tel./fax 516-5280, 800/758-1697, colonial@spersaoaxaca.com.mx, $95

continue to be reasonable, usually at $35 s, $42 d, except during festivals and holidays, when they might rise as much as 40 percent. With TV, phones, parking, limited wheelchair access, and an in-house travel-tour agency included, but no credit cards accepted. For more information, visit the website www.mitla@prodigy.net.mx.

Head two blocks north, one one block east to the southwest corner of leafy Alameda de León square in front of the cathedral and the very popular **Hotel Monte Albán,** Alameda de León 1, Oaxaca, Oaxaca 68000, tel. 951/516-2777 or 951/516-2330, fax 951/516-3265. The hotel centers on a big patio/restaurant that hosts folkdance shows nightly 8:30–10 P.M. During the first evening this could be understandably exciting, but after a week you might feel as if you were living in a three-ring circus. The 20 rooms, which surround the patio in two tiers, are gen-

uinely colonial, with soaring beamed ceilings and big bedsteads. For such a nicely situated hotel, rates run a relatively reasonable $30 s, $45 d, and $53 t; credit cards accepted. Reserve by email at hotelmontealban@prodigy.net.mx.

For a fancier option, go to the long-time standby **Hotel Marqués del Valle** on the north side of the *zócalo,* Portal Clavería, P.O. Boxes 13 and 35, Oaxaca, Oaxaca 68000, tel. 951/514-0688 or 951/516-3474, fax 951/516-9961. Guests enjoy a restored lobby, with bright chandeliers, mirrors, and shiny dark wood paneling. Upstairs, however, massive wrought-iron fixtures cast gloomy nighttime shadows through the soaring, balconied central atrium. The 96 rooms, nevertheless, retain their original 1940s polish, with handcrafted cedar furniture and marble-finished baths. Deluxe rooms have TV, carpets, and some balconies looking out on to the *zócalo.*

Standard rooms rent for a sharply increased (ask for a discount) $81 s, $100 d, $122 t, with restaurant/bar, limited wheelchair access, and credit cards accepted. Reserve by telephone or email hmarques@prodigy.net.mx.

The 1980s-vintage **Hotel Gala,** Bustamante 103, Oaxaca, Oaxaca 68000, tel. 951/514-2251 or 951/514-1305, fax 951/516-3660, just a few doors south of the *zócalo*'s southeast corner, is for those who want comfortable, modern-standard deluxe accommodations at relatively moderate prices. Rooms, although tastefully decorated and carpeted, are small. Get one of the quieter ones away from the street. The 36 rooms rent for a refreshingly moderate $41 s, $55 d, and $71 t; credit cards are accepted. With phones, TV, fans, and a restaurant, but parking is not included. Reserve either by phone or email galaoax@prodigy.net.mx. For more information, visit the website www.gala.com.mx.

Oaxaca's classiest hotel, the **Camino Real,** Calle 5 de Mayo 300, Oaxaca, Oaxaca 68000, tel. 951/516-0611, or toll-free U.S./Can. tel. 800/7-CAMINO (800/722-6466), fax 951/516-0732, occupies the lovingly restored ex-convent of Santa Catalina, four blocks north, one block east of the *zócalo*. Flowery secluded courtyards, massive arched portals, soaring beamed ceilings, a big blue pool, and impeccable bar and restaurant service combine to create a refined but relaxed old-world atmosphere. Rooms are large, luxurious, and exquisitely decorated with antiques and folk crafts and furnished with modern-standard conveniences. If street noise is likely to bother you, get a room away from bustling Calles Abasolo and 5 de Mayo. Rates run about $215 s, $250 d; with phones and TV, parking not included; credit cards accepted.

Although a six-block walk (four north, two west) away from the *zócalo*, **Hotel Las Golondrinas,** at Tinoco y Palacios 411, Oaxaca, Oaxaca 68000, tel. 951/514-3298 or tel./fax 951/514-2126, lasgolon@prodigy.net.mx, is nearly always full. Step inside and you'll immediately see why. Rooms enfold an intimate garden, lovingly decorated with festoons of hothouse verdure. Leafy bananas, bright bougainvillea, and platoons of potted plants line pathways, which meander past an intimate fountain patio in one corner and lead to an upstairs panoramic vista sundeck on the other. The care also shows in the rooms, which are immaculate and adorned with spartan-chic pastel earth-toned curtains and bedspreads and natural wood furniture. Guests additionally enjoy use of laundry facilities, a TV sitting room, a shelf of paperback books, and a breakfast restaurant 8–10 A.M. All this for only about $31 s, $40 d, and $47 t. In addition to the 27 regular rooms, two honeymoon suites rent for about $50.

North-Side Luxury Hotels

Three upscale suburban hostelries dot the north side of Highway 190. The resort **Hotel Victoria,** Km 545, Carretera Panamericana, Oaxaca, Oaxaca 68070, tel. 951/515-2633, fax 951/515-2411, choicest of the three, spreads over a lush hillside garden of panoramic vistas and luxurious resort ambience. The 1950s-style lobby extends from an upstairs view bar downhill past a terrace restaurant to a flame tree and jacaranda-decorated pool patio. As for rooms, the best ones are in the newer view wing detached from the lobby building. There, the all-renovated junior suites are spacious, comfortable, and luxuriously appointed, with deluxe tile and marble bathrooms and private view balconies (in the upper-floor units). The 150 rooms, villas, and junior suites rent for a hefty $160, $200, and $250 d, respectively; with TV, phones, a/c, tennis court, Tues.–Sat. live music, handicrafts shop, parking and wheelchair access; credit cards accepted. Reserve by telephone or email ventas@hotelvictoriaoax.com.mx; for more information, visit the website www.hotelvictoriaoax.com.mx.

The **Hotel Fortín Plaza,** Av. Venus 118, Colonia Estrella, Oaxaca, Oaxaca 68040, tel. 951/515-7777, fax 951/515-1328, hfortin@prodigy.net.mx, next to the highway two blocks downhill, is hard to miss, especially at night. Its yellow-lit six-story profile tops everything else in town. The hotel offers the usual modern facilities—restaurant/bar, pool, live Tues.–Sat. music, disco, and parking—in a compact, attractively designed layout. Upstairs, guests enjoy deluxe, clean, and comfortable rooms with private view balconies (whose tranquility is reduced, however, by considerable highway noise; ask for a more *tranquilo* mountain-view room). Room rates run about $82 s and $94 d, with phones, TV, wheelchair access, and parking; credit cards accepted. Discounts are sometimes negotiable.

Hotel Misión de Los Angeles, Calz. Porfirio Díaz 102, Oaxaca, Oaxaca 68050, tel. 951/515-1500, fax 951/515-1680, hmision@prodigy.net.mx, half a mile farther east (on the prolongation of Juárez), rambles like a hacienda through a spreading oak- and acacia-dotted garden-park. After a rough few days on the sightseeing circuit, it's an ideal place to kick back beside the big pool or enjoy a set or two of tennis. The rooms and suites are spacious and comfortable, decorated in tans and pastels with big garden-view windows or private balconies. Upper rooms are quieter and more private. Rooms locations vary from choice to ho-hum, however. Look at the options before moving in. The 162 rooms and suites rent from about $83 d for standard, $130 d for junior suite; with phones, parking, disco, and restaurant; credit cards accepted.

Apartments and Bed-and-Breakfasts

The recent influx of Oaxaca visitors has generated a host of bed-and-breakfast and long-term rentals. Many Oaxacans now offer either lodging in their homes, or apartment and house rentals. Look over the classified sections of the English-language newspaper, *Oaxaca Times,* which customarily lists many such rentals. Get your free copy at hotels, shops, or the federal-state tourist information office, north side of the *zócalo,* corner of Independencia and Hidalgo. Failing those, contact the newspaper office at 307 Alcalá, tel. 951/516-3443, fax 951/516-3265, info@oaxacatimes.com, www.oaxacatimes.com.

If you want to reserve your rental early, visit websites that advertise rentals, such as www.oaxaca4less.com and www.oaxaca.com.mx. Also, if you're planning a monthlong or more stay in Oaxaca, you would very likely profit by buying a copy of *Moon Handbooks Oaxaca,* which offers a wealth of detail of all of Oaxaca. This includes a host of city hotels and several good apartment

and bed-and-breakfast rentals scattered all over downtown Oaxaca.

Beginning on the far northeast side of downtown, about a mile from the *zócalo,* find **Casa Arnel,** Aldama 404, Colonia Jalatlaco, Oaxaca, Oaxaca 68080. Casa Arnel stands at the far edge of downtown, so removed from the urban bustle that it feels as if it's embedded in another era. Across Casa Arnel's stone-cobbled street the ancient village church, San Matias Jalatlaco, abides in repose within a shady neighborhood plaza. Casa Arnel (enter on the right-hand side street) guests enjoy about 20 rooms around a jungly garden, blooming with birdcalls, flowers, and big, leafy plants. Additional amenities include a broad roof deck, with umbrellas, a curiously "monumental" library, tables, and chairs for sunning and relaxing. Old-style rooms, all with bath, are clean but bare-bulb plain. A new crop of renovated rooms are more attractive, with new bedspreads, curtains, and shiny furniture and fixtures. Prices, however, are reasonable: old-style rooms $22 s, $27 d; new-style $30 s, $35 d; breakfast extra; a few shared-bath rooms rent for a rock-bottom $10 s, $20d, all with (sometimes) restaurant, travel agency, and just three blocks from big, shady El Llano park with good restaurants and services. Bargain for a cheaper long-term rate. Reserve via tel./fax 951/515-2856, or email casaarnel@spersaoaxaca.com.mx; for more information visit the website www.casaarnel.com.mx.

On the south side of downtown, you'll find the more modest but attractive **Villa María,** at Arteaga 410 A, tel. 951/516-5056, fax 951/514-2562. Villa María is the labor of love of a trilingual (English, French, Spanish) owner-manager so welcoming that you immediately feel at home. Step inside her domain and you'll see the other reason for Villa María's popularity: about 15 apartments surrounding an inviting, plant-adorned inner patio, where stairways rise to rooftop view sundecks furnished with comfortable chairs and shady umbrellas. The immaculate, thoughtfully decorated all one-bedroom housekeeping apartments, with themes such as "Mixteco," are completely furnished, including dishes, silverware, and maid service. Apartments vary in cost from $45 to $65 d per night, $350–600 per month, depending on location, size, and amenities.

On the west edge of downtown, about 10 blocks due west of the *zócalo,* stands **Casa Colonial,** at Calle Miguel Negrete 105, tel./fax 951/516-5280. Personable owners Jane and Thornton Robisson, who seem to know everyone in town, call their domain the "posada with no sign," because they don't advertise and accept only guests with reservations. Upon arrival, you immediately see why Casa Colonial is such a favorite among savvy visitors. Low-rise rooms and apartments enfold a spacious, gracefully lovely inner garden. Rooms vary from high-ceilinged antique-decorated Victorians to smaller, one-person garden-side units. Besides all the leisurely tropical ambience, guests enjoy the use of a spacious, refined but homey living room with a fine library and Internet connection. Room prices vary, according to size and elegance, from $50 s to about $95 d. Monthly guests welcomed at a discount, April through October. In the United States and Canada, reserve through the toll-free tel. 800/758-1697, or email colonial@spersaoaxaca.com.mx. You can also reserve through Casa Colonial directly by the above tel./fax, or email (which you can find via the website www.mexonline.com/colonial.htm.)

Trailer Parks and Camping

Oaxaca has at least two trailer-camping parks. First choice goes to the long-time, now tired **Oaxaca Trailer Park,** at the far northeast side of town, 900 Av. Violetas, Oaxaca, Oaxaca 68000, tel. 951/515-2796. The 100 all-hookup spaces include showers, toilets, laundromat, and a fence. Spaces rent for about $12 per night, with discounts for extended stays. Pets okay. Get there by turning left at Violetas (marked, one block before the turn, by the baseball stadium), from Highway 190, several blocks east of the first-class bus terminal. Continue uphill six long blocks to the trailer park on the left.

Second choice goes to a newish trailer park atop a panoramic valley-view hilltop in foothill village San Felipe del Agua village, about three miles (five km) north of downtown. Here, the American expatriate owner offers all hookups in a large country lot, with lots of room for big rigs and tent space. A small clubhouse with kitchenette, shower, and toilet is also available for resident use. He asks about $5 per party for camping, $12 for RVs, including water, electricity, and drainage. For more information and reservations, write P.O. Box 252, Oaxaca, Oaxaca 68000, or call tel. 951/520-0947. (This spot appears ideal for hikers and backpackers, at the jumping-off point for hiking trails, past waterfalls and meadows, en route to the summit of towering, pine-tufted Cerro San Felipe, elevation in excess of 10,000 feet or 3,000 meters. The trailer park manager, who also rents horses, might, for a reasonable fee, also serve as a guide.)

Get there by bus, taxi or driving to San Felipe del Agua village. By bus, ride San Felipe-marked Choferes del Sur bus, from the corner of Independencia and Reforma, two blocks east of the *zócalo,* thence following Pino Suárez uphill, past El Llano park. Get off at the San Felipe del Agua village plaza (see the old church on the right) and follow drivers' directions below.

For drivers, the jumping-off point for San Felipe del Agua is Av. Netzahualcoyotl (nay-tzah-oo-wahl-coh-YOH-tuhl), which heads uphill at the big green San Felipe sign from its intersection with Highway 190 (Av. Niños Héroes), one block east of the Pemex station. Continue about two-thirds of a mile (one km), bear left at the hotel sign, then right one block and left one long block, and right again. You'll be on your way uphill, heading along Calz. San Felipe, which parallels the old stone aqueduct (on your left). In a few miles the road becomes San Felipe village's Calle Hidalgo. Just before the San Felipe plaza, at the restaurant on the right, turn left (west) on to Calle Iturbide, then right again at the first street, Morelos, then another quick left on to the "Prologation of Iturbide." Another long block or two downhill, at the arroyo bottom, turn right on to Chigolera; continue, winding uphill .4 mile (.6 km) to the trailer park sign and gate on left.

On your way into town, from the north, RVers might check to see if the old **Rosa Isabel Trailer Park,** Km 539, Carretera Nacional, Colonia Loma del Pueblo, Oaxaca, Oaxaca 68000, tel. 951/512-7210 or 951/516-0770, mimimonroy@hotmail.com, is open. The owner, Elia Hernandez, tel. 951/515-3143, assured me that she was going to keep it running and rent RV spaces with all hookups for about $10. (Find it by looking along the right side of Highway 190, heading southeast, into town, about a half mile past the big Hotel Villas Del Sol sign.)

FOOD

Snacks, Stalls, and Coffeehouses

During fiestas, snack stalls along Hidalgo at the cathedral-front Alameda de León square abound in local delicacies. Choices include *tlayudas,* giant crisp tortillas loaded with avocado, tomato, onions, and cheese, and *empanadas de amarillo,* huge tacos stuffed with cheese and red salsa. For dessert, have a *buñuelo,* a crunchy, honey-soaked wheat tortilla.

At nonfiesta times, you can still fill up on the sizzling fare of taco, *torta,* hamburger, and hot dog (eat 'em only when they are served hot) stands that set up in the same vicinity.

For very economical, wholesome local-style fare, go to the acre of foodstalls inside the **Mercado 20 de Noviembre,** two blocks south of the *zócalo*'s southwest corner. Here, adventurous eaters will be in heaven among a wealth of succulent *chiles rellenos;* piquant *moles* (moh-LAYS); fat, banana leaf–wrapped tamales Oaxaqueños; and savory *sopas* and *guisados* (soups and stews). Insist, however, that your selection is served hot.

The airy, tranquil interior patio of **Hostería Alcalá** at Alcalá 307, open daily 8:30 A.M.–11 P.M., is ideal for a relaxing refreshment or lunch break from sightseeing along Alcalá mall.

For coffee and dessert, you have a number of additional downtown choices, notably **Coffee Beans,** at Cinco de Mayo 400, five blocks north of the *zócalo;* or nearby **Restaurant La Antigua** a block east, at Reforma 401, just uphill from Abasolo.

For baked goods by themselves, a trio of good carry-out bakeries stand within a stone's throw of the *zócalo.* First, try the sweet offerings of **Tartamiel Pastelería Frances** on Trujano, half a block west from the Del Jardín café *zócalo* corner, open Mon.–Sat. 7 A.M.–8 P.M., Sun.

11:30 A.M.–7 P.M. Continue clockwise, north of the *zócalo* a block, to **Panadería Bamby,** at the northwest corner of G. Vigil and Morelos, open Mon.–Sat. 6 A.M.–9 P.M. Finally, stop by the **Pastelería La Vasconia,** a block east of the *zócalo,* at Independencia 907, between Cinco de Mayo and Reforma, open daily 7 A.M.–9 P.M.

Cafés and Restaurants Around the Zócalo

Oaxaca visitors enjoy many good eateries right on or near the *zócalo.* In fact, you could spend your entire Oaxaca time enjoying the fare of the several *zócalo*-front sidewalk cafés. Of the seven cafés, five offer recommendable food and service. As you move counterclockwise from the northwest corner, they are: Primavera, La Cafetería, Del Jardín, Terranova, and Amarantos. First place overall goes to the pricier upper-class **Terranova,** at the southeast corner, for its professionally prepared and served lunch and dinner entrées. For the best breakfasts, however, go to **Primavera,** at the diagonally opposite corner. **La Cafetería** and **Del Jardín** (with loud marimba music most

The traffic-free Oaxaca plaza, lined with half a dozen good sidewalk cafés, is one of the most pleasant in all of Mexico.

nights) rate generally good for food (notably Del Jardín's tummy-warming apple strudel) but their service can be spotty. While service at **Amarantos** is usually good, its food is only fair. They all are open long hours, about 8 A.M.–midnight, and serve from very recognizable menus.

The one drawback of *zócalo*-level eating is the persistent flow of vendors, which can be unnerving. If, however, you refuse (or bargain for) their offerings gently and with humor, you might begin to accept and enjoy them as part of the entire colorful scene. (If they really get to you, take an inside table, or retreat to the one restaurant that shoos them away, the Terranova.)

Serious-eating longtimers return to **El Asador Vasco** restaurant, tel. 951/514-4755, on the second-floor balcony above the Restaurant Jardín, Portal Flores 10A. The menu specializes in hearty Basque-style country cooking: salty, spicy, and served in the decor of a medieval Iberian manor house. Favorites include fondues (bean, sausage, and mushroom), garlic soup, salads, veal tongue, oysters in hot sauce, and the *carnes asadas* (roast meats) house specialties. Open daily 1–11 P.M. Expensive; expect to pay about $20 per person.

Longtimers swear by the Oaxacan specialties at **Casa de la Abuela**, at the *zócalo*'s northwest corner, above the Primavera café. Here, you can enjoy tasty, professionally prepared regional dishes and airy *zócalo* vistas from the balcony. Open daily 1–9 P.M. Call tel. 951/516-3544 for reservations and a good view table. Moderate.

For a tasty regional-style meal or snack, try **La Casita** around the corner, upstairs, on Hidalgo, at the plaza Alameda de León, Hidalgo 612, tel. 951/516-2917. You can order either a hearty *comida corrida* multicourse lunch or one of the tasty "mystery" offerings, such as tortilla, "cat," or "nothing" soup. Open daily 8 A.M.–10 P.M. Moderate.

For many loyal local upper-class patrons, **Restaurant Catedral,** two blocks north of the *zócalo,* at García Vigil 105, corner of Morelos, tel. 951/516-3285, serves as a tranquil refuge from the street hubbub. Here, the refined ambience—music playing softly in the background, tables set around an airy, intimate fountain patio crowned by the blue Oaxaca sky above—is half the show. The finale is the very correct service

and quality food for breakfast, lunch, or supper. The Aguilar family owners are especially proud of their *moles* (MOH-lays), sauces that flavor their house specialties. These include fillets, both meat and fish, and regional dishes such as banana leaf–wrapped tamales Oaxaqueños. It's open daily 8 A.M.–midnight. Moderate–expensive.

Back on Hidalgo, just past the *zócalo*'s northeast corner, the spotless little *fonda* **El Mesón** specializes in a lunch buffet, at Hidalgo 805, tel. 951/516-2729. For about $3, you can select your fill of fresh fruit, salads, chili beans, and several entrées, including roast beef and pork, chicken, *moles,* tacos, tamales, and enchiladas. Open daily 8 A.M.–11:30 P.M. Budget.

More good eating, in a genteel but relaxed atmosphere, awaits you at the very popular **Restaurant El Sagrario,** around the corner behind the church at 120 Valdivieso, tel. 951/514-0303 or 951/514-0303. Here, mostly local, youngish upper-class customers enjoy either a club/bar atmosphere (lower level), pizza parlor booths (middle level), or restaurant tables (upper level). At the restaurant level during the evening, you can best take in the whole scene around you—chattering, upbeat crowd, live guitar, flute, or jazz melodies, elegantly restored colonial details. Then, finally, comes the food: beginning, perhaps, with an appetizer, continuing with a soup or salad, then an international or regional specialty, which you top off with a light dessert and a savory espresso coffee. Open daily 8 A.M.–midnight. Music volume goes up later in the evening. Credit cards are accepted. Moderate–expensive.

On the other hand, a legion of American, Canadian, and European budget travelers swear by the no-nonsense **Restaurant Quickly,** half a block farther from the *zócalo,* at 100 Alcalá, tel. 951/514-7076, on the Alcalá pedestrian mall. Once you taste the giant hamburgers, chocolate milk shakes, or pancakes (or veggies, if you prefer), you'll understand why. Open daily 8 A.M.–11 P.M. Budget.

Cafés and Restaurants North of the Zócalo

Devotees of light, vegetarian-style cuisine get what they're hungering for at **La Manantial Veg-**

etariana, tel. 951/514-5602, at Tinoco y Palacios 303 (west side of street, just above Matamoros, two blocks west and three blocks north of the *zócalo*). The tranquil patio ambience sets the tone for the specialty, a set lunch *comida*. Typically it might offer soup (onion or cream of zucchini), salad (mixed greens or tomato cucumber), stew (mushroom or soya steak), bread, fruit drink, dessert, and coffee or tea. About $4 until 7 P.M., $5 after that. (When they have no customers, the employees are in the habit of playing the radio loudly. However, if you ask, they'll gladly turn it off.) Open daily 9 A.M.–9:30 P.M. (*Note:* La Manantial Vegetariana has done so well that you have a second branch to try out, in the Plaza Santo Domingo commercial, diagonally southwest, across Alcalá, from the Santo Domingo church.)

Although **Restaurant La Muralla** (The Wall), tel. 951/516-2268, is a seven-block walk or taxi ride (four north, three west) from the *zócalo* to the corner of N. Bravo and Crespo, your effort will be amply rewarded. Enter the door and immediately it appears as if you've been transported to a foreign realm, perhaps somewhere in the country outside Xian or Guangzhou. Besides the standard but tastily prepared dishes (such as wonton soup, chicken chow mein, and barbecued spareribs), you will be entertained by the occupants of a big, midroom tropical aquarium. Open daily 1–8 P.M.; Visa accepted. Moderate.

Restaurants South of the Zócalo

Only a few good sit-down restaurants sprinkle the south *zócalo* neighborhoods. A trio of them, well-known for Oaxacan cuisine, shouldn't be missed.

Local folks strongly recommend the no-nonsense, country-style (but refined) **La Flor de Oaxaca,** at Armenta y López 311, a block east, half a block south from the *zócalo*'s southeast corner, tel. 951/516-5522. Here, along with spotless linen and very correct service, you'll get the customary bottomless plate of warm corn tortillas to go with your entrée. The *mole*-smothered regional specialties come mostly in four styles, *con tasajo* (with a thin broiled steak), *con pollo* (chicken), *con cesina* (roast pork), or *sola* (without meat). Besides those, you can choose

from an extensive menu of equally flavorful items such as tamales Oaxaqueños (wrapped in banana leaves), pork chops, several soups, spaghetti, and much more. Vegetable lovers get started off right with the crisp *ensalada mixta* (sliced tomato, cucumber, onions, avocado, and lettuce with vinegar and oil dressing). Open Mon.–Sat. 7:30 A.M.–10 P.M., Sun. 7:30 A.M.–3 P.M. Credit cards accepted. Moderate.

If, however, you hanker for some nouveau variations on the Oaxaca regional theme, head to **Restaurant El Naranjo** (The Orange Tree), at Trujano 203, two blocks west of the *zócalo*'s southwest corner. Here, the quiet, genteel patio atmosphere sets the tone, and the long, inviting menu tempts the palate. Choose among soups, salads, and Oaxaca's seven *moles,* one for each day of the week. Use them to flavor any one of a host of stuffed *chiles,* tamales, stewed chicken, roast pork, and much, much more. Open Mon.–Sat. 1–10 P.M., tel. 951/514-1878. Moderate–expensive.

For yet another treat, try **Restaurant Los Ángeles** in the Hotel Parador San Agustín, at Armenta y López 215, tel. 951/516-2022, one block east and half a block south of the *zócalo*'s southeast corner. Here, again, the specialty is nouveau food with a Oaxacan twist. If possible, dine with a party of three or four so you can taste as many of the delicacies as possible: squash flower, stuffed with cheese with mild *chile* sauce; lettuce festival salad, with white cheese, red bell pepper, avocado, and sesame; cream of broccoli soup; and *raviolis de* Cuitlacoche. Open daily, high season, 7 A.M.–11 P.M.; breakfast 7–11 A.M. only low season. Moderate–expensive.

ENTERTAINMENT AND EVENTS
Around the Zócalo

The Oaxaca *zócalo,* years ago relieved of traffic, is ideal ground for spontaneous diversions. A concert or performance seems to be going on nearly every evening. When it isn't, you can run like a kid over the plaza, bouncing an eight-foot-long *aeroglobo* into the air. (Get them from vendors in front of the cathedral.) If you're in a sitting mood, watch the world go by from a *zócalo* sidewalk café. Later, take in the folk-dance performance at the Hotel Monte Albán on the adjacent Plaza Alameda de León, nightly 8:30 A.M.–10 P.M., about $5. After that, return to a *zócalo* café and enjoy the musicians who entertain most every evening until midnight.

Fiestas

There seems to be a festival somewhere in the Valley of Oaxaca every week of the year. Oaxaca's wide ethnic diversity explains much of the celebrating. Each group celebrates its own traditions. Sixteen languages, in dozens of dialects, are spoken within the state. Authorities recognize around 500 distinct regional costumes.

All of this ethnic ferment focuses in the city during the July **Lunes del Cerro** festival. Known in preconquest times as the Guelaguetza (gay-lah-GAY-tzah, or Offering), tribes reunited for rituals and dancing in honor of Centeotl, the god of corn. The ceremonies, which climaxed with the sacrifice of a virgin who had been fed hallucinogenic mushrooms, were changed to tamer mixed Christian-native rites by the Catholic Church. Lilies replaced marigolds, the flower of death, and saints sat in for the native gods.

Now, for the weeks around the two Mondays following July 16, the Virgin of Carmen day, Oaxaca is awash with native Mexicans in costume from all seven traditional regions of Oaxaca. The festivities, which include a crafts and agricultural fair, climax with dances and ceremonies at the Guelaguetza open-air auditorium on the Cerro del Fortín hill northwest of the city. Entrance to the Guelaguetza dances runs about $30; bring a hat and sunglasses. Make hotel reservations months ahead of time. For more information, contact the downtown tourist information office, north edge of the *zócalo,* corner of Indpendencia and Alcalá, tel./fax 951/516-0123, info@oaxaca.gob.mx.

Note: If the first Monday after July 16 happens to fall on July 18, the anniversary of Benito

> *There seems to be a festival somewhere in the Valley of Oaxaca every week of the year. Oaxaca's wide ethnic diversity explains much of the celebrating. Each group celebrates its own traditions. Authorities recognize around 500 distinct regional costumes.*

Juárez's death, the first Lunes del Cerro shifts to the next succeeding Monday, July 25.

On the Sunday before the first Lunes del Cerro, Oaxacans celebrate their history and culture at the Plaza de Danzas adjacent to the Virgen de la Soledad church. Events customarily include a big sound, light, and dance show and depictions in tableaux of Oaxacan history, including the story of Donaji, Oaxaca's beloved princess-heroine.

Besides the usual national holidays, Oaxacans celebrate a number of other locally important fiestas. The first day of spring, March 20, kicks off the **Flower Games** (Juegos Florales). Festivities go on for 10 days, including crowning of a festival queen at the Teatro de Alcalá, poetry contests, and performances by renowned artists and the National Symphony.

On the second Monday in October, residents of Santa María del Tule venerate their ancient tree in the **Lunes del Tule** festival. Locals in costume celebrate with rites, folk dances, and feats of horsemanship beneath the boughs of their beloved great cypress.

Oaxacans venerate their patron, the **Virgin of Solitude** (Soledad), Dec. 16–18. Festivities, which center on the Virgin's basilica (on Independencia six blocks west of the *zócalo*), include fireworks, dancing, food, and street processions of the faithful bearing the Virgin's gold-crowned image decked out in her fine silks and satins.

For the **Festival of the Radishes** (*Fiesta de los Rábanos)* on December 23, celebrants fill the Oaxaca *zócalo,* admiring displays of plants, flowers, and figures crafted of giant, bulging radishes. Ceremonies and prizes honor the most innovative designs. Foodstalls nearby serve traditional delicacies, including *buñuelos* (honey-soaked fried tortillas), plates of which are traditionally thrown into the air before the evening is over.

Oaxaca people culminate their Posada week on **Nochebuena** (Christmas Eve) with candle-lit processions from their parishes, accompanied by music, fireworks, and floats. They converge on the *zócalo* in time for a midnight cathedral Mass.

Folkloric Dance Shows

If you miss the Lunes del Cerro festival, some towns and villages stage smaller Guelaguetza celebrations at other times. So do a number of hotels, the most reliable of which occurs nightly at 8:30 P.M. at the Hotel Monte Albán, on Plaza de León, tel. 951/516-2777, adjacent to the *zócalo*. At other hotels, days may change, so call ahead to confirm: Hotel Camino Real, tel. 951/516-0611, Friday, show with dinner, $30, not including drinks; Restaurant Casa de Cantera, Murguia 102, at 8:30 P.M., $10 per person, varied schedule, tel. 951/514-7585.

Films, Theater, Music, Dance, and Art Exhibits

Many Oaxaca institutions, such as the **Museo de Arte Contemporáneo de Oaxaca,** the **Teatro Macedonio Alcalá,** the **Instituto de Artes Gráficos de Oaxaca,** the **Cinema El Pochote** (on García Vigil, near the corner of Humboldt, one block west and about three blocks north from the Santo Domingo churchfront plaza) and others sponsor many first-rate cultural events. See the excellent monthly calendars of events in the English-language newspaper *Oaxaca Times* for details.

Nightlife

When lacking an official fiesta, you can create your own at a number of nightspots around town.

The big hotels are most reliable for live dance music and discotheques. Call to confirm programs: Camino Real, tel. 951/516-0611; Fortín Plaza, tel. 951/515-7777; and the Victoria, tel. 951/515-2633.

Besides many of the sidewalk cafés around the *zócalo,* a number of restaurants also offer live music seasonally. Try the El Sagrario, tel. 951/514-0303, evenings, beginning at about 9 P.M., and the Hotel Marques del Valle, tel. 951/516-3474, restaurant on the *zócalo.*

Perhaps the most popular in-town nightspot is **Candela,** which jumps with hot salsa and African-Latin rhythms, usually Thurs.–Sat., from about 10 P.M., at Murguia 413, corner of Pino Suárez, tel. 951/514-2010.

© BRUCE WHIPPERMAN

Folkloric dancers from all regions of Oaxaca perform in the July Guelaguetza celebration.

SPORTS AND RECREATION

Jogging, Walking, and Horseback Riding

For jogging, try the public **Ciudad Deportiva** (Sports City) fields on the west side of Highway 190 about two miles north of the town center. Closer in, you might also jog around the big **Juárez Park** (El Llano), on Av. Juárez, three blocks east and about 10 blocks north of the *zócalo*.

For an invigorating in-town walk, climb the **Cerro del Fortín** hill. Your reward will most likely be a breezy city, valley, and mountain view. The key to getting there through the maze of city streets is to head to the **Escalera del Fortín** (staircase), which will lead you conveniently to the instep of the hill. For example, from the northeast *zócalo* corner walk north along the Alcalá mall. After five blocks, in front of the Santo Domingo church turn left onto Allende, continue four blocks to Crespo, and turn right. After three blocks, you'll see the staircase on the left. Continue uphill, past the Guelaguetza open-air auditorium, to the road (Nicolas Copernicus) heading north to the **Planetarium.** After that, enjoying the panorama, you can keep walking along the hilltop for at least another mile. Take a hat and water. The round-trip from the *zócalo* is a minimum of two miles; the hilltop rises only a few hundred feet. Allow at least a couple of hours.

Sierra Madre Horse Trails offers horseback tours (around $11/hour) in the wooded, panoramic-view foothills above San Felipe del Agua village north of town. For more information and reservations (at least one day in advance), call tel. 951/520-0947. Get there by the directions to the associated trailer park. (See Trailer Parks and Camping under Accommodations.)

Swimming and Tennis

Swimmers do their thing at multipool **Balneario La Bamba,** about 2.5 miles (four km) south of town along Highway 175 before the airport, on the left side, just past the big green Experimental sign over the highway. The pools are open daily except Mon. 10 A.M.–5 P.M.; entrance is about $3 for adults, kids $2. Serious lap swimmers should choose days and hours to avoid crowds, Sunday afternoon being the most crowded.

For tennis, stay at either the **Hotel Victoria** or the **Misión de los Ángeles,** which have courts. Otherwise, call the **Club de Tenis Brenamiel,** next to the Hotel Villas del Sol, Km 539.5 on Highway 190, about three miles north of the center of town, tel. 951/512-6811, and reserve a court for about $6 an hour.

SHOPPING

The city of Oaxaca is renowned as a handicrafts shopper's paradise. Prices are moderate, quality is high, and sources—in both large traditional markets and many dozens of private stores and galleries—are manifold. In the city, however, vendors do not ordinarily make the merchandise they sell. They buy wholesale from family shops in town, the surrounding valley, and remote localities all over the state of Oaxaca. If your time is severely limited, buy from the good in-town sources, many of which are listed below. (If, on the other hand, you have the time to benefit—both because of lower prices and person-to-person contact with the artisans-by going to the villages, consult the Around the Valley of Oaxaca section for sources of local village handicrafts.)

Traditional Markets

The original town market, **Mercado Juárez,** covers the entire square block just one block south and one block west of the *zócalo*. Many dozens of stalls offer everything; cotton and wool items—such as dresses, *huipiles,* woven blankets, and serapes—are among the best buys. Despite the overwhelming festoons of merchandise, bargains are there for those willing to search them out.

Before diving into the Juárez market's cavernous interior, first orient yourself by looking over the lineup of stalls on the market's west side, along the block of 20 de Noviembre, between Las Casas and Trujano. Here, you'll be able to select from a reasonably priced representative assortment—black and green pottery, tinware, *huipiles,* leather goods, *alebrijes* (fanciful wooden animals), pewter, cutlery, filigree jewelry—of much that Oaxaca offers.

After your Juárez market tour, walk a block west, to J. P. Garcia, and 3.5 blocks south, between Mina and Zaragoza, for a look inside the **Mercado de Artesanías** handicrafts market. Here, you'll find more of the same—tons of textiles—*huipiles, camisas* (shirts), *blusas* (blouses), and *tapetes* (carpets)—plus *alfarería* (pottery), *alebrijes,* and some for-tourist masks.

Private Handicrafts Shops

Although pricier, the private shops generally offer the choicest merchandise. Here you can select from the very best: *huipiles* from San Pedro de Amusgos and Yalalag; richly embroidered "wedding" dresses from San Antonino de Castillo; rugs and hangings from Teotitlán del Valle; pottery—black from San Bártolo Coyotepec and green from Atzompa; carved *alebrijes* animals from Arrazola; whimsical figurines by the Aguilar sisters of Ocotlán; mescal from Tlacolula; and masks from Huazolotitlán.

Most of the best individual shops lie scattered along three streets–5 de Mayo, Macedonio Alcalá, and Garcia Vigil, which run uphill, north of the *zócalo.*

A good place to get prices and selection in perspective is the crafts shop in the federal tourist information center, at 607 Independencia, off the *zócalo,* diagonally north of the cathedral, tel. 951/516-0123. It's open Mon.–Sat. 9 A.M.–8 P.M.

Next, head north along the Alcalá mall; two blocks north of Independencia, you'll arrive at a Oaxaca favorite, the **Palacio de las Gemas,** corner of Morelos and Alcalá, tel. 951/514-4603. Although specializing in semiprecious stones and jewelry, it has much more, including a host of charming handpainted tinware Christmas decorations, Guerrero masks, and pre-Columbian reproductions in onyx and turquoise. Open Mon.–Sat. 10:30 A.M.–3 P.M. and 5:30–9 P.M.

Head a block east to Cinco de Mayo, turn left (north) half a block to the big house on the right, no. 204, headquarters of MARO, **Mujeres Artesanas de las Regiones de Oaxaca** (Craftswomen of the Regions of Oaxaca). Here a remarkable all-Oaxaca grass-roots movement of women artisans has gotten the government to stake them to a building, where they sell their goods and demonstrate their manufacturing techniques. The artisans are virtually pure native Mexicans from all parts of Oaxaca, and their offerings reflect their unique effort. Hosts of gorgeous handicrafts—wooden masks, toys, carvings; cotton *traje* native clothing, such as *huipiles, pozahuancos, quechquémitles;* wool serapes, rugs, and hangings; woven palm hats, mats, and baskets; fine steel knives, swords, and machetes; tinplate mirrors, candlesticks, and ornaments; leather saddles, briefcases, wallets, and belts—fill the shelves of several rooms. It's open daily 9 A.M.–8 P.M., at 204 Cinco de Mayo, Oaxaca, Oaxaca 68000, tel./fax 951/516-0670. Don't miss it; better still, do a major part of your Oaxaca shopping at this store.

Walk a block west along Murguia back to Alcalá and step into **La Mano Mágico** on the west side, just below the corner of Murguia, at Alcalá 203, tel./fax 951/516-4275. The shop offers both a colorful exposition of crafts from all over Mexico and a patio workshop, where artisans work, dyeing wool and weaving examples of the lovely, museum-quality rugs and serapes that adorn the walls. Open Mon.–Sat. 10:30 A.M.–3 P.M. and 4–7:30 P.M.

Across the street, step into **Cuchillos Alcalá,** at no. 206, and view the best—knives, swords, scissors—and more, from the venerable Oaxaca family Martínez cutlery tradition. Open Mon.–Sat. 10 A.M.–2:30 P.M. and 3:30–8 P.M., tel. 951/514-7943.

Continue uphill on Alcalá, a block farther north, to the **Plaza Alcalá** complex, southwest corner of N. Bravo, which has both a tranquil courtyard restaurant and some good shops. Outstanding among them is the excellent **Librería Amate** bookstore, tel. 951/516-6960, on the lower level. Its extensive and expertly selected offering of English-language books about Mexico includes guides, literature, ethnography, archaeology, history, cookbooks, maps, postcards, and much more. Upstairs, Libros Amate's brother shop, **Corazón del Pueblo** (Heart of the People), accomplishes the same with a fine, eclectic collection of Mexican handicrafts. At Alcalá 307, tel. 951/516-6960; open Mon.–Sat. 10:30 A.M.–2:30 P.M. and 3:30–7:30 P.M.

Half a block farther uphill, be sure to look inside **Oro de Monte Albán** jewelry store, at Alcalá 403, just downhill half a block from the Santo Domingo church front. This extraordinary family-run enterprise carries on Oaxaca's venerable goldsmithing tradition as the sole licensed manufacturer of replicas from the renowned treasure trove of Monte Albán tomb 7. Besides the luscious, museum-quality reproductions, Oro de Monte Albán offers a fine assortment of its own silver and gold earrings, charm bracelets, necklaces, brooches, and much more. Open Mon.–Sat. 10 A.M.–8 P.M., Sun. noon–8 P.M., tel. 951/514-3183.

Rewards await shoppers who are willing to walk a few long blocks farther uphill, to the state-run **ARIPO** (Artesanías y Industrias Populares de Oaxaca) at 809 Garcia Vigil, tel. 951/514-4030 or 951/514-0861. There, you can pick from a broad, authentic, and very traditional selection of masks, *huipiles*, wedding dresses, carved animals, ceramics, tinware, and much more. Prices vary: cheap on some items and high on others. Open Mon.–Sat. 9 A.M.–7 P.M., Sun. 11 A.M.–4 P.M.

Fine Arts Galleries

The tourist boom has stimulated a Oaxaca fine arts revival. Several downtown galleries bloom with the sculpture and paintings of masters, such as Rufino Tamayo, Rudolfo Morales, Francisco Toledo, and a host of up-and-coming local artists. Besides La Mano Mágico, listed above, a number of galleries stand out. Foremost among them is **Arte de Oaxaca,** the gallery of the Rudolfo Morales Foundation, at Murguia 105, between Alcalá and 5 de Mayo, open Mon.–Fri. 10 A.M.–2 P.M. and 5–8 P.M., Sat. 10 A.M.–2 P.M., tel. 951/514-2324 or 951/514-0910.

Also outstanding is **Galería Quetzalli,** local outlet for celebrated artist Francisco Toledo, opposite the south wall-flank of Santo Domingo church, at Constitución 104, between Reforma and 5 de Mayo, open Mon.–Sat. 10 A.M.–2 P.M. and 5–8 P.M., tel. 951/514-2606, fax 951/514-9407. Also well worth visiting is **Galería Arte Mexicano** in the Santo Domingo shopping complex, southwest corner of Alcalá and Allende, across Alcalá from the Santo Domingo church.

It's open Mon.–Sat. 10 A.M.–2 P.M. and 4–8 P.M., Sun. 11 A.M.–5 P.M., tel. 951/514-3815.

Groceries and Natural Food

For fruits and vegetables, the cheapest and freshest are in the Juárez and 20 de Noviembre markets, which take up the two square blocks immediately southwest of the *zócalo.*

For simpler, straightforward grocery shopping, stop by **Abarrotes Lonja** on the *zócalo* next to the Hotel Señorial; open daily 8 A.M.–9:30 P.M.

Local natural food devotees get their heart's content of teas—arnica, anise, manzanilla—and ginseng, organic grains, granola, and soy burgers at **Tienda Naturista Trigo Verde,** two blocks west of the *zócalo,* at J. P. Garcia 207, tel. 951/516-2369. Open Mon.–Sat. 8:30 A.M.–9 P.M., Sun. 9 A.M.–6 P.M.

Camera and Photo

Downtown has some good photo shops, most on 20 de Noviembre, a block west of the *zócalo.* Best of all is **Oaxakolor,** at 20 de Noviembre 108, tel. 951/516-3487, perhaps the best-stocked photo store in Oaxaca. It carries dozens of cameras–35 mm point-and-shoot, SLRs, professional medium format—as well as an abundance of film, including popular and professional color, slides, sheet, black and white, and a host of accessories. Open Mon.–Sat. 9 A.M.–8:30 P.M.

More ordinary, but still well-stocked, is **Foto Figueroa** at Hidalgo 516, corner 20 de Noviembre, tel. 951/516-3766. With plenty of Kodak film and accessories, it also offers quick develop-and-print. Open Mon.–Sat. 9 A.M.–8 P.M.

Express Kolor, half a block farther down at 20 de Noviembre 225, tel. 951/516-1492, is better stocked, with scores of point-and-shoot cameras and many Minolta, Vivitar, and Olympus accessories. It also stocks Konica, Fuji, Kodak, and Agfa films in color and black and white, both roll and sheet. Open Mon.–Sat. 9 A.M.–8 P.M.

Sporting Goods

A modest sporting goods and clothing selection is available at **Deportes Ziga,** on the southwest corner of Alcalá and Matamoros, next to La

Mano Mágico handicrafts shop. Open Mon.–Sat. 9 A.M.–3 P.M. and 4–9 P.M., Sun. 11 A.M.–2 P.M., tel. 951/514-1463.

INFORMATION
Tourist Information Office
The city, state, and federal governments maintain a good information office, which includes a handicrafts shop, at the zócalo's north edge, at 607 Independencia, corner G. Vigil, tel./fax 951/516-0123, info@oaxaca.gob.mx, open daily 8 A.M.–8 P.M.

Publications
One of Mexico's richest sources of new English-language books about Mexico is the **Librería Amate** bookstore on the ground floor of Plaza Alcalá, Alcalá 307, four blocks north of the zócalo, tel. 951/516-6960; open Mon.–Sat. 10 A.M.–2:30 P.M. and 3:30–7 P.M.

Another good source is bookstore **Librería Universitaria,** at Guerrero 104, half a block east of the zócalo, tel. 951/516-4243. It has English paperbacks, both used and new, a number of indigenous language dictionaries, and guides, cookbooks, art, and history books. Open Mon.–Sat. 9:30 A.M.–2 P.M. and 4–8 P.M.

The daily English-language News of Mexico City is usually available late mornings at stands near the southwest corner of the zócalo. If not, try the small news shop near the same corner at Trujano 106A, open daily 8 A.M.–9:30 P.M.

Pick up a copy of the informative tourist newspaper, the **Oaxaca Times,** at your hotel, the tourist information office, or at the publisher, the Instituto de Comunicación y Cultura, tel. 951/516-3443, email info@oaxacatimes.com, at 307 Alcalá, 2nd floor. The newspaper prints cultural and historical features, tourist hints, and a list of local events. For more information, visit the website www.oaxacatimes.com.

Libraries
The city *biblioteca* (public library), in a lovingly restored ex-convent, is worth a visit, if only for its graceful, cloistered Renaissance interiors and patios. At the corner of Morelos and Alcalá, two blocks north of the zócalo, tel. 951/516-5681. Open Mon.–Sat. 9 A.M.–8:30 P.M.

Visitors starving for a good read will find satisfaction by borrowing (or buying upstairs) at least one of the thousands of volumes at the **Oaxaca Lending Library,** at 519 Pino Suárez, open Mon.–Fri. 10 A.M.–1 P.M. and 4–7 P.M., Sat. 10 A.M.–1 P.M.

SERVICES
Money Exchange
Several banks, all with ATMs, dot the downtown area. The long-hours Banco Internacional, tel. 951/516-5010 or 951/512-9753, is a block east of the zócalo's southeast corner, at the intersection of Guerrero and Armenta y López, open Mon.–Sat. 8 A.M.–7 P.M. The most convenient downtown branch is **Banamex,** open Mon.–Fri. 9 A.M.–4 P.M., Sat. 10 A.M.–24 P.M. on one-block Valdivieso, behind the cathedral. A second branch serves customers just one block due east of the zócalo, at Hidalgo and Cinco de Mayo, tel. 951/516-5900, money exchange hours Mon.–Fri. 9 A.M.–4 P.M., Sat. 10 A.M.–2 P.M. If it's too crowded, go to **Banco Serfin** on the Independencia corner just north of the cathedral, open Mon.–Fri. 9 A.M.–4 P.M., Sat. 10 A.M.–2 P.M.; (U.S., Canadian, Japanese, and many European currencies and traveler's checks), tel. 951/516-1100; or Serfin's neighbor, **Banco Santander Mexicano,** just northwest of the cathedral, at Independencia 605, tel. 951/516-2526, open Mon.–Fri. 9 A.M.–4 P.M., Sat. 10 A.M.–2 P.M.

After bank hours, go to **Casa de Cambio Internacional de Divisas,** tel. 951/516-3399, on the Alcalá street mall just north of the zócalo, behind the cathedral. Although it may pay about a percent less than banks, it changes many major currencies and traveler's checks. Open Mon.–Sat. 8:30 A.M.–7:30 P.M., Sun. 9 A.M.–5 P.M.

Communications
The Oaxaca *correo* (post office), tel. 951/516-2661, is across from the cathedral at the corner of the Alameda de León square and Independencia. Open Mon.–Fri. 8 A.M.–7 P.M., Sat. 9 A.M.–1 P.M.

Telecomunicaciones, tel. 951/516-4902, at the next corner of Independencia and 20 Noviembre, offers money orders, telephone, and public fax. Hours are Mon.–Fri. 8 A.M.–7:30 P.M., Sat. 9 A.M.–4 P.M., Sun. 9 A.M.–noon.

For long-distance and local **telephone service,** buy a Ladatel phone card (widely available in stores; look for the yellow Ladatel sign) and use it in public street telephones. Lacking that, take advantage of the efficient **Computel** long-distance phone and public fax office on Independencia, across from the Plaza Alameda de León, tel. 951/514-8084, open 7 A.M.–10 P.M.

Connect to the **Internet** at any one of a number of downtown spots. For example, try the warren of small stalls and telephone booths, at Alacalá 100, behind the cathedral, a block north of the *zócalo;* open daily 7 A.M.–11 P.M., tel. 951/516-6510; alternatively, go to **Desvan,** on the *zócalo's* east side, open daily 9:30 A.M.–10 P.M.; or walk three blocks west to **Comunitel,** at 20 de Noviembre 208, open daily 7 A.M.–10 P.M.

Health, Police, and Emergencies

If you get sick, ask your hotel desk to recommend a doctor. Otherwise, go to **Clínica Hospital Carmen,** staffed by English-speaking IAMAT Doctors Horacio Tenorio S. and Germán Tenorio V., at Abasolo 215, tel./fax 951/516-0027.

For routine medicines and drugs, go to one of many pharmacies, such as the **Farmacias Ahorro,** tel. 951/516-8001, on Cinco de Mayo, near the northeast corner of Murguia, two blocks north, and one block east of the cathedral, open daily 7 A.M.–11 P.M. After hours, call Farmacia Ahorro's 24-hour free delivery service, tel. 951/515-5000.

For police emergencies, call the emergency number, tel. 066, or have a taxi take you to the **Dirección de Seguridad,** at Aldama 108, just north of the *zócalo.* For fire, call the *bomberos,* tel. 951/516-2231.

Consulates and Immigration

The **U.S. Consul,** tel./fax 951/514-3054, holds hours Mon.–Fri. 10 A.M.–3 P.M. at Plaza Santo Domingo, Alcalá 407, across from the Santo Domingo church. The **Canadian Consul** does the same for Canadian citizens Mon.–Fri. 11 A.M.–2 P.M., at 700 Pino Suárez, local 11B, tel. 951/513-3777, fax 951/515-2147. In an emergency, call the Canadian Embassy in Mexico City, toll-free Mex. tel. 800/706-2900.

Other consuls customarily available in Oaxaca are the **French,** at Vicente Guerrero 105, tel. 951/514-1900; **Italian,** Alcalá 400, tel. 951/516-5058; and **Spanish,** Porfirio Díaz 340, tel. 951/515-3525. For more information, look for consulate contact numbers in the *Oaxaca Times* or the telephone directory Yellow Pages, under *Embajadas, Legaciones, y Consulados,* or call the U.S. or Canadian Consuls above for information.

If you lose your tourist permit, make arrangements with **Migración** at least several hours before your scheduled departure from Mexico. Take proof of arrival date in Mexico—stamped passport, airline ticket, or copy of lost permit—to the airport Migración, tel. 951/511-5733.

Travel Agencies and Tour Services

Although the former local American Express agency, travel agent **Viajes Mexico Istmo y Caribe** (MICSA) behind the cathedral, at Valdivieso 2, tel. 951/516-2700, no longer handles American Express business, it's still a worthy, experienced general travel agency.

Among the other reliable downtown travel agents is **Oaxaca Tours,** at Alcalá 417 upstairs (four blocks uphill from the plaza), tel./fax 951/516-1005. Although Oaxaca Tours mostly arranges Oaxaca city and valley destinations, it can arrange farther-ranging excursions, through the Mixteca regions, the mountains north of Oaxaca, and the southern coast Huatulco-Puerto Escondido region.

Another reliable tour agent is longtime **Viajes Turísticos Mitla,** branch office at Hóstal Santa Rosa, Trujano 201 (a block west of the plaza's southwest corner), tel. 951/514-7800 or 951/514-7806. It offers tours, usually around the Valley of Oaxaca, including guide and transportation, for small or medium sized-groups. Its main office is at the Hotel Rivera del Ángel, at F. J. Mina 518 (two blocks south, three blocks west of the plaza), tel. 951/514-7806, 951/516-6175, or 951/514-3152. It also provides economical bus-only tourist transportation to Oaxaca Valley sights. For more information and reservations, contact the bus departure ticket desk at the Hotel Rivera del Ángel, tel. 951/514-3161.

More athletic travelers might enjoy the services of **Mountain Bike Tours** at J. P. Garcia 509, east side, between Mina and Aldama, a few blocks west and south of the plaza, tel. 951/514-3144, which both rents bikes and conducts guided bike tours into the nearby countryside.

For even more extensive backcountry adventure bicycling, hiking, and camping in the mountains north of Oaxaca city, contact **Expediciones Sierra Norte,** at 201 M. Bravo, tel. 951/8271, fax 951/516-7745, sierranorte@oaxaca.com.

A Oaxaca regiment of private individual guides also offer tours. Among the most highly recommended is English-fluent **Juan Montes Lara,** backed up by his wife, Karin Schutte. Besides cultural sensitivity and extensive local knowledge, they can also provide comfortable transportation in a GMC Suburban wagon. Contact them at their home, at Prol. de Eucaliptos 303, Colonia Reforma, Oaxaca, Oaxaca 68050, tel. 951/513-0126.

Former clients volunteer rave reviews of the tours given by English-speaking expatriate **Susan McGlynn,** who can be reached by email at labrujita_oax@yahoo.com.

For more guide recommendations, go to the government tourist information office, north side of the *zócalo,* at Independencia 607, corner of G. Vigil. tel. 951/516-0123, becarioax@oaxaca.gob.mx.

Language Instruction and Courses

A long list of satisfied clients attests to the competence of the **Becari Language School,** N. Bravo 210, tel./fax 951/514-6076, becarioax@prodigy.net.mx, www.mexonline.com/becari.htm. Offerings include small-group Spanish instruction, as well as cooking and dancing classes. If you desire, the school can arrange homestays with local families. Its modest midtown facility includes, besides classrooms, a social area for sitting and getting to know other students.

Similarly recommended is the **Vinigulaza Lan-**guage and Tradition (Vinigulaza Idioma y Tradición) school, associated with the local English-language Cambridge Academy, at Abasolo 209 (about two blocks east, four blocks north, of the plaza), tel. 951/514-6426, vinigu@prodigy.net.mx, www.vinigulaza.com. The star of the show is the friendly and hospitable director Catherine Kumar. Offerings include informative (and even fun) small-group Spanish instruction. Schedules are flexible, and prices, at around $45 for 10 hours per week, are very reasonable. Social activities often include no-host dinners at local restaurants and a small on-site café where students can enjoy tea, coffee, and conversation.

Also highly recommended is the language instruction of Oaxaca **Instituto Cultural de Oaxaca,** at the north-side corner of Niños Héroes (Highway 190), and Juárez. For more information, email incuoax@prodigy.net.mx or visit the website www.instculturaloax.com.mx.

GETTING THERE AND AWAY
By Air

The **Oaxaca Airport** (code-designated OAX) has several daily flights that connect with Mexico City and other Mexican destinations. Many of the Mexico City flights allow same-day connections between Oaxaca and many U.S. gateways.

Mexicana Airlines flights connect a number of times daily with Mexico City. For reservations or flight information, call tel. 951/516-8414 or 951/514-7253.

Aeroméxico flights connect several times daily with Mexico City. For reservations, call tel. 951/516-3765 or 951/516-1066; for flight information, call tel. 951/511-5055.

Mexicana Airlines affiliate **Aerocaribe** flights connect daily with Huatulco and Puerto Escondido; and also daily with Cancún, via Tuxtla Gutiérrez, Villahermosa, and Mérida. For reservations, call tel. 951/516-0266 or 951/516-0229; for flight information, call tel. 951/511-5247.

Aviacsa airlines connects once daily with Mexico City and once daily with Tijuana via Mexico City. For information and reservations, call tel. 951/514-5123.

The Oaxaca airport provides a modicum of

services, such as a good upstairs view restaurant, several shops, international newsstand, car rentals, a helpful tourist information office (that will call hotels for you free), open daily 7 A.M.–8 P.M., tel. 951/511-5040, a bank, open Mon.–Sat. 8 A.M. A.M.–7 P.M., tel. 951/503-3188, and an ATM.

Arrival transportation for the six-mile trip into town is easy. Fixed-fare collective taxi tickets run about $2 per person for downtown ($5 to north-side Hotels Misión de los Angeles, Fortín Plaza, and Victoria). For the same trip, a *taxi especial* (private taxi) ticket runs about $10 for four people; larger GMC Suburbans, $19 for up to eight people. No public buses run between the airport and town.

Car rental agents operating at the Oaxaca Airport are Budget, tel./fax 951/511-5252 or 951/516-4445; Hertz, tel. 951/516-2434, fax 951/516-0009, hertz_oax@hotmail.com; and Alamo, tel./fax 951/514-8534, fax 951/514-8686.

On **departure,** save taxi money by getting your *colectivo* airport transportation ticket ahead of time, at Transportacion Terrestres on the west side of Plaza Alameda de León, across from the cathedral, tel. 951/514-4350, open daily 9 A.M.–2 P.M. and 5–8 P.M.

Furthermore, keep enough dollars or pesos for your $12 international departure tax (which may be collected in Mexico City) if your air ticket doesn't already cover it. If you lose your tourist permit, make arrangements with **Migración** several hours before departure from Mexico. Take proof of arrival date in Mexico, such as stamped passport, airline ticket, or copy of lost permit, to airport Migración, tel. 951/511-5733.

By Car or RV

Paved (but mostly long, winding, and sometimes potholed) roads connect Oaxaca city with all regions of Oaxaca and neighboring states.

South to the coast via the southern Sierra, narrow National Highway 175 connects along 148 winding, sometimes potholed, miles (238 km) over the del Sur with its junction with Highway 200 at Pochutla (thence six miles to Puerto Ángel). The road climbs to more than 9,000 feet through winter-chilly pine forests and indige-

nous Chatino and Zapotec villages. Fill up with gas at the last-chance Pemex in Mihuatlán heading south and at Pochutla (north edge of town) heading north; carry water and blankets and be prepared for emergencies. Under dry, daylight conditions, count on about seven hours at the wheel, south from Oaxaca to Puerto Ángel, about eight hours in the opposite direction.

About the same is true for the paved National Highway 131 route south from Oaxaca, which splits off of Highway 175 two miles (three km) south of San Bártolo Coyotepec. On your way out of town, fill up with gasoline at the airport Pemex. Continue, via Zimatlán and Sola de Vega (fill again with Magna here), over the pine-clad Pacific crest, a total of 158 miles (254 km) to Puerto Escondido. Under dry, daylight conditions, allow about seven hours southbound, about eight hours in the opposite direction. Unleaded gasoline is regularly available, midroute, at the Sola de Vega Pemex only.

The 229-mile (368-km) Highway 190-Highway 125 route connects Oaxaca southwest with coastal Pinotepa Nacional, via the Mixtec country destinations of Yanhuitlán, Teposcolula, and Tlaxiaco. Although winding most of the way, the generally uncongested road is safely driveable (subject to some potholes however) from Oaxaca in about eight driving hours if you use the *cuota* (toll) Highway 190 *autopista* northwest of Oaxaca city. Add an hour for the 5,000-foot climb in the opposite direction.

The 350-mile (564-km) winding Highway 190-160 from Oaxaca to Cuernavaca and Mexico City via Huajuapan de León requires a very long day, or better, two, for safety. Under the best of conditions, the Mexico City-Oaxaca driving time runs 11 hours either way. Take it easy and stop overnight en route. (Make sure you arrive in Mexico City on a day when your car is permitted to drive. (See the special topic "Mexico City Driving Restrictions" in the Acapulco and Inland to Taxco chapter.)

Alternatively, you can cut your the Mexico City-Oaxaca driving time significantly via the Mexico City-Puebla-Oaxaca *autopista,* combined 150 D-131 D, which, southbound, takes off from the southeast end of Mexico City's Calz.

General Ignacio Zaragoza. Northbound, follow the signs on Highway 190 a few miles north of Oaxaca. Allow about six hours driving time at a steady 60 mph (about 100 kph). Tolls, which are worth the increased speed and safety, run about $30 for a car, much more for a big RV.

By Bus

Luxury and First Class: Cristóbal Colón (CC) and Autobuses del Oriente (ADO), Oaxaca's major luxury- and first-class carriers, operate out of the modern terminal on Highway 190, Calz. Héroes de Chapultepec 1036, at Carranza, on the north side of town. All bus lines accept credit cards and operate using the reservations-information line, toll-free Mex. tel. 800/702-8000. Here passengers enjoy a squad of public telephones out in front, snack stands, luggage lockers, and cool, refined Restaurant Colibri, across the street.

Cristóbal Colón (CC) offers service to most major points in Oaxaca. Buses connect northwest with Mixteca destinations of Nochixtlán, Tamazulapan, and Huajapan de León, continuing to Puebla and Mexico City. Westerly, they connect with the Mixteca Alta, via Teposcolula, Tlaxiaco, Juxtlahuaca, Putla de Guerrero, and Pinotepa Nacional on the coast. Southerly, they connect (often via the surer, but long, Isthmus route) with Puerto Escondido, Pochutla, Puerto Ángel, and Huatulco; southeasterly, with Tehuantepec, Chiapas, and Guatemala; and northerly, with Villahermosa.

Moreover, Cristóbal Colón, operating through its agency, **Ticket Bus,** sells tickets for all first-class bus lines at both the 1036 Héroes de Chapultepec station and a convenient downtown outlet, at 20 de Noviembre 204A, toll-free Mex. tel. 800/702-8000, a block west of the zócalo.

Autobúses del Oriente, (ADO), offers limited Oaxaca connections, mostly along the Highway 190 corridor, connecting northwest with Mexico City (Tapo and Norte stations), via Nochixtlán and Huajapan de León, and southeast, with Tehuantepec and Salina Cruz, and northeast to the U.S. border, at Reynosa. Other departures connect northwest with Veracruz, Coatzacoalcos, Villahermosa, Palenque, and Mérida.

Regional **Cuenca** buses connect with Northern Oaxaca points along Highway 175, including Ixtlán de Juárez, Valle Nacional, and Tuxtapec, continuing all the way to Veracruz.

Sur departures connect with Mexico City Tapo station, along old Highways 190 and 160, via Huajuapan de León, Izucar de Matamoros, Puebla, and Cuatla, Morelos.

Autobúses Unidos (AU) departures connect with Mexico City along the fast *autopista* expressway, via Nochixtlán, Coixtlahuaca, and Puebla; or along the old Highway 131 via Cuicatlán, Teotitlán del Camino, Tehuacán, and Puebla.

Second Class: A swarm of long-distance second-class buses runs from the ***camionera central segunda clase*** southwest of downtown, just north of the Abastos market. It's best to get there early by taxi, or by walking due west about eight blocks from the *zócalo,* to the west end of Calle Las Casas. Cross the *periférico* (peripheral boulevard) straight across the railroad tracks; keep walking the same direction, along the four-lane street for two more blocks, where you'll see the terminal gate on the right. Inside, you'll find an orderly array of snack stalls, a cafeteria, luggage lockers, a long-distance telephone and fax, and a squad of *taquillas* (ticket booths).

Auto Transportes Oaxaca-Pacífico, tel. 951/516-2908, and **Autobúses Estrella del Valle,** tel. 951/516-5429, travel the Highway 175 north-south route between Oaxaca and Pochutla-Puerto Ángel. Both lines continue, connecting along east-west coastal Highway 200 with Bahías de Huatulco, Puerto Escondido, and Pinotepa Nacional.

Estrella Roja del Sureste second-class and first-class buses, tel. 951/516-0694, connect along Highway 131 north-south via Sola de Vega and Juquila, directly with Puerto Escondido. From there, you can make coastal connections with Pochutla-Puerto Ángel, Bahías de Huatulco, and Pinotepa Nacional.

Fletes y Pasajes, tel. 951/516-2270, offers very broad second-class and some first-class service, connecting with nearly everywhere in Oaxaca. Three separate booths sell tickets: westerly, with Mixteca destinations of Nochistlán,

Tamazulapan, Huajuapan, and Tlaxiaco, connecting all the way, via Highway 125, with Pinotepa Nacional on the coast; northerly, via Teotitlán del Camino and Mazateca destinations around Huatla de Jiménez; easterly, with Mitla and Mixe destinations of Ayutla, Zacatepec, and Juquila Mixes; and southeasterly, with Isthmus destinations of Tehuantepec, Juchitán, and Salina Cruz.

Several other semilocal lines connect mostly with Oaxaca Valley points. **Choferes del Sur** connects with northwest Oaxaca Valley, from San Felipe del Agua north of the city to Etla

northwest. **Autobúses de Oaxaca** (no booth, pay on the bus) connects south with Cuilapan and Zaachila. **Sociedad Cooperativa Valle del Norte** connects west with Teotitlán del Valle and Tlacolula. Finally, if you want a bone-jangling (but scenic) backroads adventure, ride **Flecha de Zempoatepetl** northeast to remote Zapotec mountain native market towns of Villa Alta and Yalalag, via Tlacolula and Cuajimoloyas.

By Train

Privatization has ended all of Mexico's train passenger service. Fly, drive, or ride the bus instead.

Around the Valley of Oaxaca

Oaxaca offers a load of interest—archaeological sites, crafts villages, ecoadventures, weekly markets, venerable Dominican missionary churches—outside the city. Valley market towns each have a market day, when local color is at a maximum and prices are at a minimum. Among the choices, starting on the east side, are: **Teotitlán del Valle,** half an hour east, Saturday; **Tlacolula,** one hour east, Sunday; **Ocotlán,** half an hour south, Friday; **Zaachila,** half an hour southwest, Thursday; **Zimatlán,** one hour southwest, Wednesday; and **Etla,** half an hour northwest, Wednesday.

These market visits can be conveniently combined with stops at handicrafts villages, ruins (notably Mitla, on the east side, and Monte Albán, west), and other sights along the way.

Getting Around the Valley of Oaxaca

Droves of second-class buses from the Abastos terminal run everywhere in the Valley of Oaxaca. Those with plenty of time could spend a week or month exploring the valley this way. (For destination details, consult the Second Class section, under By Bus in the Oaxaca City section.)

For those on a limited time budget, it's best to rent a car, ride a tourist bus, or see a travel agent for a tour. For car rentals, call **Budget,** tel. 951/511-5252 or 951/516-4445; **Hertz,** tel. 951/516-2434, fax 951/516-0009; or **Alamo,** tel. 951/514-8534, fax 951/514-8686.

For **tourist buses,** ride one of the many leaving daily from the **Hotel Rivera del Ángel,** at F. J. Mina 518 (two blocks south, three blocks west of the plaza), bus desk tel. 951/516-6175, 951/514-3152, or 951/514-7806. The Hotel Señorial (on the *zócalo*, tel. 951/516-3933) and other hotels also have such tour arrangements. See your desk clerk.)

An excellent alternative is to go with the well-organized **Community Museums of Oaxaca** (Museos Comunitarios de Oaxaca), headquartered at Crespo 103, tel. 951/516-5562, muscoax@prodigy.net.mx. This office acts as agent for 14 local community museums, including five important spots in the Valley of Oaxaca (Teotitlán del Valle, Santa Ana del Valle, San Pablo Huixtepec, San José Mogote, and Santiago Suchilquitongo). The museums offer guided tours of their localities, including ruins, lakes, springs, mountain summits, and artisans' shops, including lunch with a local family, from $15 per person. The headquarters furnishes an English-speaking guide to the museum, via your car or taxi or public bus.

Village Accommodations: Tourist Yu'u

Several Oaxaca Valley communities invite visitors to stay in their **community tourist lodging: "Yu'u"** in Zapotec (say "You"). The Yu'u are locally managed and generally well-maintained modern-standard kitchenette bungalows, typically sleeping four, with private hot water shower bath and toilet. Yu'u are situated, mostly on the east side of the Valley of Oaxaca, at (as you move eastward) San Sebastián Abasolo, Santa Cruz Papalutla, Teotitlán del Valle, San Marcos Tlapazola, San Bártolo Quialana, Santa Ana del Valle, Tlacolula, and Hierve El Agua. For more information, stop by the city Tourist Yu'u office, at Murguia 206 (up the driveway, in the back), tel. 951/514-2155. If you fail to make contact with the Yu'u office, try Oaxaca government tourism, at tel./fax 951/516-0123, or email info@oaxaca.gob.mx.

EAST SIDE: EL TULE AND TEOTITLÁN DEL VALLE

Enough attractions lie along this route for weeks of exploring. For example, you could visit El Tule and the Teotitlán market on Saturday, continuing for an overnight at Mitla. Next morning, explore the Mitla ruins for a couple of hours, then return, stopping at the hilltop Yagul ruins and the Sunday market at Tlacolula. In either direction going or coming from the city, you could pause for an hour's exploration of the Dainzu and Lambityeco roadside archaeological sites. One more day would allow more time to venture past Mitla, to the remarkable

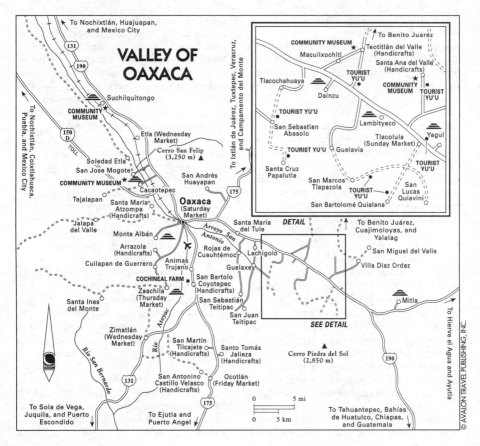

mountainside springs and mineral deposits at Hierve de Agua.

El Tule is a gargantuan Mexican cypress *(ahue-huete)*, probably the most massive tree in Latin America. Townsfolk celebrated their beloved El Tule's 1,000th birthday in October 2002.

Its gnarled, house-sized trunk divides into a forest of elephantine limbs that rise to festoons of bushy branches reaching 15 stories overhead. The small town of Santa María del Tule, nine miles (14 km) east of the city on Highway 190, seems built around the tree. A crafts market, a church, and the town plaza, where residents celebrate their El Tule with a fiesta on October 7, all surround the beloved living giant.

Dainzu and Lambityeco Archaeological Sites

Among the Valley of Oaxaca's dozen-odd buried cities, Dainzu and Lambityeco, both beside the highway, are the most accessible. Dainzu comes first, on the right about six miles (nine km) east of El Tule.

Dainzu (in Zapotec, Hill of the Organ Cactus), open daily 10 A.M.–5 P.M., spreads over an approximate half-mile square, consisting of a partly restored ceremonial center surrounded by clusters of unexcavated mounds. Beyond that, on the west side, a stream runs through fields, which, at Dainzu's apex (around A.D. 300) supported a town of about 1,000 inhabitants.

The major excavation, at the foot of the hill about 100 yards south of the parking lot, reveals more than 30 bas-reliefs of ball players draped with leather head, arm, and torso protectors. Downhill, to the west, lies the partly reconstructed complex of courtyards, platforms, and stairways. The northernmost of these was excavated to reveal a tomb, with a carved door supporting a jaguar head on the lintel and arms—note the claws—extending down along the stone doorjambs. The jaguar's face, with a pair of curious vampire teeth and curly nostrils, appears so batlike that some investigators have speculated that it may represent a composite jaguar-bat god.

A couple of hundred yards diagonally southwest you'll find the ball court, running east-west,

in the characteristic capital "I" shape, with a pair of "scoring" niches at each end and flanked by a pair of stair-step stone-block grandstand-like "seats." Actually, archaeologists know that these were not seats, because the blocks were once stuccoed over, forming a pair of smooth inclined planes that flanked the central playing area.

Lambityeco, open daily 10 A.M.–5 P.M., six miles (10 km) farther, is on the right, a few miles past the Teotitlán del Valle side road. The excavated part, only about 100 yards square, is a small but significant part of Yegui (Small Hill, in Zapotec), a large buried town of 200 mounds, covering about half a square mile.

Salt-making appears to have been the main occupation of Yegui people during the town's heyday, around A.D. 700. The name Lambityeco probably derives from the Arabic-Spanish *alam-bique,* the equivalent of English "alembic," or distillation or evaporation apparatus. This would explain the intriguing presence of the more than 200 local mounds. It's tempting to speculate that they are the remains of *cujetes,* raised leaching beds, still used in Mexico for concentrating brine, which workers subsequently evaporate into salt. (See the Cuyutlán section in the South to Zihuatanejo and Inland to Pátzcuaro chapter.)

In the present small restored zone, archaeologists have uncovered, besides the remains of the Valley of Oaxaca's earliest known *temazcal* (ritual-therapeutic hot room), a number of fascinating ceramic sculptures. Next to the parking lot, a platform, mound 195, rises above ground level. If, after entering through the gate, you climb up its partially restored slope and look down into the excavated hollow in the adjacent east courtyard, you'll see stucco friezes of a pair of regal, lifelike faces, one male and one female, presumably of the personages who were found buried in the regal grave (tomb 6) below. Experts believe this to be the case, because the man was depicted with the symbol of his right to rule—a human femur bone, presumably taken, as was the custom, from the grave of his chieftain father.

Mound 190, sheltered beneath the adjacent large corrugated roof about 50 yards to the south, contains a restored platform decorated by pair of remarkably lifelike, nearly identical divine stucco masks. These are believed to be of Zapotec rain god Cocijo (see the water flowing from the mouths). Notice also the rays, probably lightning, representing power, in one hand, and flowers, for fertility, in the other.

Teotitlán del Valle, Tlacolula, and Yagul Archaeological Zone

Teotitlán del Valle, nine miles east of El Tule, at the foot of the Sierra, means "Place of the Gods" in Náhuatl; before that it was known as Xa Quire, or "Foot of the Mountain," by the Zapotecs who settled it around A.D. 1000. Dominican missionaries introduced the first sheep, whose wool, combined with local traditional skills, results in the fine serapes, carpets, and blankets that seem to fill every shop in town.

Nearly every house is a minifactory where people card, spin, and dye wool, often using traditionally cultivated cochineal, and hand-gathered natural indigo and moss dyes. Every step of wool preparation is laborious; pure water is even a chore—families typically spend two days a week collecting it from mountain springs. The weaving, on traditional hand looms, is the fun part.

In Teotitlán you have many choices. First, visit the weaving shops. Don't miss the shop of friendly master weaver **Isaac Vasquez** (Hidalgo 30, tel. 951/514-4122, open daily 10 A.M.–6 P.M.) and others, such as the **Cooperativa Mujeres Tejedoras** (Women Weavers Cooperative), at Hidalgo 37, half a block east of main ingress street, Juárez. Later, you can select from the hosts of fine offerings at the market itself, by the church, end of Hidalgo.

The best weaving is generally the densest, typically packing in about 45 strands per inch (18 strands per centimeter); ordinary weaving has about half that. Please don't bargain too hard. Even the highest prices typically bring the weavers less than a dollar an hour for their labor.

While you're at the Teotitlán market, stop by the local museum, called, in Zapotec, the **Balaa Xtee Guech Gulal** (House of the Old Town), open daily except Mon. 10 A.M.–6 P.M., in the brick building at the plaza end of Hidalgo. Ask for a copy of its excellent English-language brochure (*folleto,* say foh-YAY-toh). Exhibits detail the Teotitlán weaving tradition, archaeological artifacts, and traditions surrounding the traditional Zapotec marriage ceremony.

For **food,** sample Teotitlán's best, at the charmingly traditional **Tlamanalli** restaurant. The menu of made-to-order Zapotec specialties—such as *sopa de calabaza* (squash soup) and *guisado de pollo* (chicken stew)—is limited but highly recommended by Oaxaca city chefs. Open daily 1–4 P.M., longer hours when more people stop by.

The Zapotecs who founded Tlacolula (24 miles, 38 km, from Oaxaca) around A.D. 1250 called it Guichiibaa (Town of Heaven). Besides its big Sunday market, its 1523 chapel, **Capilla del Señor de Tlacolula** (with a headless St. Paul), and its adjacent 1531 church, Tlacolula is famous for mescal liquor. Get a good free sample at friendly **Pensamiento** shop, Juárez 9, as you head toward the market. Besides a selection of local handicrafts, Pensamiento offers mescal in 24 flavors, 17 for women and seven for men.

The Yagul (Zapotec for Old Tree) ruined city stands regally on its volcanic hilltop, 28 miles (45 km) east of Oaxaca city. Although only six miles from Mitla and sharing architectural details, such as Mitla's famous *greca* fretwork, the size and complexity of Yagul's buildings suggests that Yagul was an independent city-state. Local folks call the present ruin the Pueblo Viejo and remember it as the forerunner of the present town of Tlacolula. Archaeological evidence, which indicates that Yagul was occupied for about 1,000 years, until at least around A.D. 1100 or 1200, bears them out.

One of Yagul's major claims to fame is its **Palace of Six Patios,** actually three nearly identical but separate complexes of two patios each. In each patio, rooms surround a central courtyard. The northerly patio of each complex is more private, and probably was the residence, while the other, more open, patio served administrative functions.

South of the palace sprawls Yagul's huge **ball court,** the second largest in Mesoamerica, shaped in the characteristic Oaxaca "I" configuration. Southeast of the ball court is Patio 4, of four mounds, surrounding a courtyard. A boulder sculpted in the form of a frog lies at the base of the east mound. At the courtyard's center, a tomb

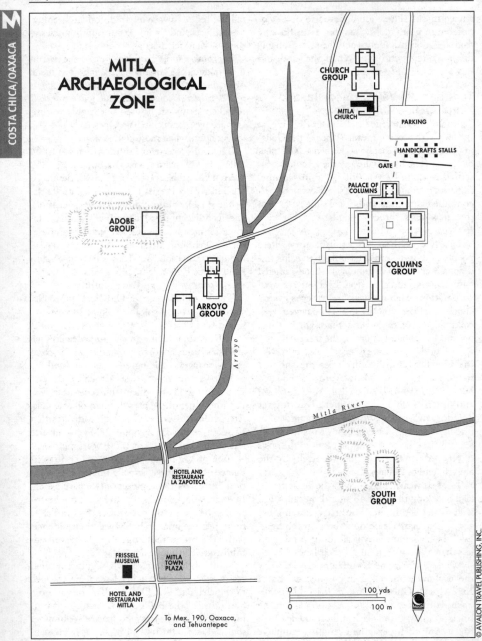

MITLA
ARCHAEOLOGICAL
ZONE

CHURCH
GROUP

MITLA
CHURCH

PARKING

HANDICRAFTS STALLS

GATE

PALACE OF
COLUMNS

ADOBE
GROUP

COLUMNS
GROUP

ARROYO
GROUP

Arroyo

Mitla River

SOUTH
GROUP

HOTEL AND
RESTAURANT
LA ZAPOTECA

FRISSELL
MUSEUM

MITLA
TOWN
PLAZA

HOTEL AND
RESTAURANT
MITLA

To Mex. 190, Oaxaca,
and Tehuantepec

0   100 yds
0   100 m

MooN

© AVALON TRAVEL PUBLISHING, INC.

was excavated; descend and explore its three *greca*-style fretwork-decorated chambers.

If it's not too hot, gather your energy and climb to the hilltop **citadel** above the parking lot for a fine view of the ruin and the entire Valley of Oaxaca. The name for this prominence probably was accurately descriptive, for Yagul's defenders long ago added rock walls to enhance the hilltop's security.

The airy *palapa* **Restaurant Centeotl,** tel. 951/516-6186, on the Yagul archaeological zone entrance road is worth a stop all by itself. Here, you can quickly double your Mexican food vocabulary by sampling such regional delights as *coloradito* (savory red *mole* chicken or beef stew), *verde de espinazo* (similar ingredients, but stewed in green *mole*), *sopa de guias* (corn and squash soup), and *estofado* (tasty *chile*-tomato-pork soup). Open daily 11 A.M.–7 P.M.

Besides its gastronomical significance, Centeotl (sayn-tay-OH-tl) is an earnest cultural-ecological endeavor of the friendly owner, who articulately explains his purpose in prose and verse. Ask for his pamphlet, or *folleto* (foh-YAY-toh), about Centeotl.

As you leave, take a look at the pre-Columbian ball game ring mounted by the restaurant entrance. Although the ring is interesting all by itself, the cannonball-sized stone sphere perched atop the ring doubles the intrigue, since (if it's authentic, as the owner claims) a stone ball is in variance with general archaeological opinion that the pre-Columbian ball game was played with a rubber, rather than a rock ball. (Pity the pre-Columbian ball players who had to bat such a hard, heavy missile around with their arms, shoulders, and torsos).

MITLA

The ruins at Mitla, open daily 10 A.M.–5 P.M., about 31 miles (50 km) from Oaxaca city, are a "must" for Valley of Oaxaca sightseers. Mitla (Liobaa in Zapotec, the Place of the Dead) flowered late, reaching a population of perhaps 10,000 during its apex around A.D. 1350. It remained occupied and in use for generations after the conquest.

During Mitla's heyday, several feudalistic, fortified city-states vied for power in the Valley of Oaxaca. Concurrently, Mixtec-speaking people arrived from the north, perhaps under pressure from Aztecs and others in central Mexico. Evidence suggests that these Mixtec groups, in interacting with the resident Zapotecs, created the unique architectural styles of late cities such as Yagul and Mitla. Archaeologists believe, for example, that the striking *greca* (Greek-like) frets that honeycomb Mitla facades result from the Mixtec influence.

Exploring the Site

In a real sense, Mitla lives on. The ruins coincide with the present town of San Pablo Villa de Mitla, whose main church actually occupies the northernmost of five main groups of monumental ruins. Virtually anywhere archaeologists dig within the town they hit remains of the myriad ancient dwellings, plazas, and tombs that connected the still-visible landmarks.

Get there by forking left from main Oaxaca Highway 190 onto Highway 176. Continue about two miles to the Mitla town entrance, on the left. Head straight through town, cross a bridge, and, after about a mile, arrive at the site. Of the five ruins clusters, the best preserved is the fenced-in Columns Group. Its exploration requires about an hour. The others—the Arroyo and Adobe groups beyond an arroyo, and the South Group across the Mitla River—are rubbly, unreconstructed mounds. The North Group has suffered from past use by the local parish. Evidence indicates the Adobe and South groups were ceremonial compounds, while the Arroyo, North, and Columns groups were palaces.

The public entrance to the **Columns Group** leads from the parking lot, past a tourist market and through the gate (open daily 9 A.M.–5 P.M., admission $2). Inside, two large patios, joined at one corner, are each surrounded on three sides by elaborate apartments. A shrine occupies the center of the first patio. Just north of this stands the **Palace of Columns,** the most important of Mitla's buildings. It sits atop a staircase, inaccurately reconstructed in 1901.

Inside, a file of six massive monolithic columns supported the roof. A narrow "escape" passage exits out the right rear side to a large patio enclosed by a continuous narrow room. The purely decorative *greca* facades, which required around 100,000 cut stones for the entire complex, embellish the walls. Remnants of the original red and white stucco that lustrously embellished the entire complex hide in niches and corners.

Walk south to the second patio, which has a similar layout. Here, the main palace occupies the east side, where a passage descends to a tomb beneath the front staircase. Both this and another tomb beneath the building at the north side of the patio are intact, preserving their original crucifix shapes. (The guard, although he is not supposed to, may try to collect a tip for letting you descend.) No one knows who and what were buried in these tombs, which were open and empty at the time of the conquest.

The second tomb is similar, except that it contains a stone pillar called the **Column of Life;** by embracing it, legend says, you will learn how many years you have left.

The Church Group (notice the church domes) on the far side of the Palace of Columns is worth a visit. Builders used the original temple stones to erect the church here. On its north side is a patio leading to another interior patio surrounded by another *greca* fret-embellished palace.

Museum, Accommodations, and Food

The University of the Americas (Mexico City) houses an exceptionally fine Oaxaca artifact collection at the **Frissell Museum,** just west of (left as you enter) the Mitla town plaza. Displays include a host of finely preserved ceramic figurines, yet-to-be-deciphered Zapotec glyphs, and a Zapotec marriage certificate in stone. Open daily 9 A.M.–5 P.M. For food, a restaurant in the museum serves regional dishes 9 A.M.–4:30 P.M. or so, or, alternatively, go to the homey **Hotel and Restaurant Mitla** across the street from the museum.

A few blocks back toward the ruins, just before the Mitla River bridge, **Hotel La Zapoteca,** 5 de Febrero 12, Mitla, Oaxaca 70430, offers both a

good restaurant and clean, reasonably priced lodgings, fine for an overnight. The 20 rooms with bath rent for about $18 s, $22 d, $26 t with hot water and parking.

Get to Mitla by Fletes and Pasajes second-class bus from the second-class bus central bus station, *camionera central segunda clase* southwest of downtown Oaxaca.

Hierve de Agua Mineral Springs

Although the name of this place translates as "boiling" water, the springs that seep from the side of the limestone mountain less than an hour's drive east of Mitla are not hot. Instead, they are loaded with minerals. These minerals, over time, have built up into rock-hard deposits, forming great algae-painted slabs in level spots and, on steep slopes, accumulating into what appear to be grand frozen waterfalls.

© BRUCE WHIPPERMAN

Although from a distance it resembles a waterfall, Hierve de Agua's main formation is actually limestone deposited by lime-rich seepage from a hillside spring.

Get there by driving or riding a bus east out of Mitla along Highway 179, the road that branches east from Highway 190, two miles before the town of Mitla. After another approximately 11 miles (18 km), follow the gravel road that branches right another five miles (eight km), through San Lorenzo village to Hierve de Agua.

Although the road's end may be crowded on weekends and holidays, you'll probably have the place nearly to yourself on weekdays. A tourist Yu'u (lodging, in Zapotec) offers six newish housekeeping bungalows with baths for about $11 d, $38 for housekeeping cabin for up to six, with pool, and a lineup of snack and curio stalls surrounds the cliffside parking lot. Reserve through the Yu'u office in Oaxaca city, at Murguia 206 (up the driveway, in the back), tel. 951/514-2155.

Part of the appeal of Hierve de Agua is the panoramic, sun-dappled mountain and valley vista. On a clear day on the eastern horizon rises **Zempoateptl**, the grand holy mountain range of the Mixe people.

A trail leads downhill to the main spring, which bubbles from the mountain and trickles into a huge basin that the operators have dammed as a swimming pool. Bring your bathing suit.

From the pool, agile walkers can hike farther down the hill, following deposits, curiously accumulated in the shape of limestone minidikes that trace the mineral water's downhill path. Soon you'll glimpse the towering limestone formation, like a giant petrified waterfall, appearing to ooze from the cliff on the right.

SOUTH SIDE: SAN BÁRTOLO COYOTEPEC AND OCOTLÁN DE MORELOS

These crafts towns make a nice pair to visit on Ocotlán's Friday market day. **Coyotepec** (Hill of the Coyote) on Highway 175, 14 miles (23 km) south of Oaxaca, is famous for its pottery and its August 24 festival, when masked villagers, costumed half-man, half-woman in tiaras, blond wigs, tin crowns, and velvet cloaks, dance in honor of their patron, San Bártolo.

Their pottery, the renowned black *barra* sold

all over Mexico, is available at a number of cottage factory-shops (watch for signs) off the highway on both the east and west sides of the highway. Especially prominent is the sign directing passersby to the pottery Mercado on the west side (right, traveling south), and the shops along east-side Juárez Street.

Doña Rosa, who died in 1980, pioneered the technique of crafting lovely, big, round jars without a potter's wheel. With the local clay, Doña Rosa's descendants and neighbor families regularly turn out acres of glistening black plates, pots, bowls, trees of life, and fetching animals for very reasonable prices (figure on $25 for a pearly three-gallon vase, and perhaps $2 for a cute little black rabbit).

Ocotlán (Place of Pines), 26 miles, 42 km south of Oaxaca, has the equally interesting trio of shops run by the Aguilar sisters, Irene, Guillerma, and Josefina. Watch for the signs at the edge of town on the right as you arrive from Oaxaca. Their creations include a host of fanciful figures in clay: vendors with big ripe strawberries, green and red cactus, goats in skirts, and bikini-clad blondes.

About a quarter mile farther north, by the town plaza, your main Ocotlán attraction (unless you're lucky enough to arrive during the May 18 fiesta) will be the big Friday market. Since markets are best in the morning, make Ocotlán your *first* Friday stop.

SOUTHWEST SIDE: ARRAZOLA, CUILAPAN, AND ZAACHILA

This excursion is best on Thursday, when you can begin fresh in the morning at the big weekly market and ruins in Zaachila, then reverse your path back to the ex-convent Santiago Aposto near Cuilapan. On the final reverse leg, stop to see the *alebrijes* (fanciful animals) being crafted in Arrazola village.

Get there by tour bus or by car heading toward Monte Albán (look for the big road sign) southwest over the Atoyac River from the *periférico* at the south edge of town. Just after crossing the bridge, fork left (south) from the Monte Albán road onto the Zaachila road.

Your destination is the Zaachila town plaza-market about 10 miles south of Oaxaca. Like Mitla, **Zaachila** overlies the ruins of its ancient namesake city, which rose to prominence after the decline of Monte Albán. Although excavations have uncovered many Mixtec-style remains, historical records nevertheless list a number of Zapotec kings who ruled Zaachila as a virtual Zapotec capital. On the eve of the conquest, it was a Mixtec noble minority who dominated the Zapotec-speaking inhabitants, whose leaders the Mixtec warriors had sent fleeing for their lives to Tehuantepec.

The big forested hill that rises north of the plaza market is topped by a large, mostly unexplored pyramid. Several unexcavated mounds and courtyards dot the hill's north and south flanks. The site parking lot and entrance gate are adjacent to the colonial church just north of the plaza.

In 1962, archaeologist Roberto Gallegos (guarded by soldiers against hostile villagers) uncovered a pair of unopened tombs beneath the summit of the Zaachila pyramid. They yielded a trove of polychrome pottery, gold jewelry (including a ring still on a left hand), and jade fan handles. Tomb 1, which is open for public inspection, descends via a steep staircase to an entrance decorated with a pair of ornamental cat heads. On the antechamber walls a few steps farther on are depictions of owls and a pair of personages (perhaps former occupants) inscribed respectively with name-dates (month-week) 5 Flower and 9 Flower. Do not miss the bas-reliefs on the tomb's back wall (take a flashlight), which depict a man whose torso is covered with a turtle shell and another whose head is emerging from a serpent.

The narrow tomb staircase is negotiable by only a few people at a time and often requires an hour for a tour bus crowd to inspect it. Rather than wasting your market time standing in line, go downhill, stroll around the market, and return when the line is smaller. If driving, arrive early, around 9 A.M. on Thursday, to avoid tour bus crowds.

Cuilapan de Guerrero, a few miles back north toward Oaxaca, is known for its elaborate unfinished ex-convent of Saint James, or Santiago (visible from the highway), where President Guerrero was executed in 1831. Although the project was started in 1535, the basilica and associated monastery's costs began to balloon. In 1550, King Philip demanded humility and moderation of the builders, whose work was finally ended by a 1570 court ruling. The extravagances—soaring, roofless basilica, magnificent baptismal font, splendid Gothic cloister, and elaborate frescoes—remain as national treasures.

Arrazola, a few miles farther north, is the source of the intricately painted *alebrijes* (ah-lay-BREE-hays), fanciful wooden creatures that have been turning up in shops all over Mexico and foreign countries during recent years. To get there turn west (left) onto Highway 145 a few miles north of Cuilapan, or 3.2 miles (5.1 km) miles south of the Atoyac River Bridge. Pass through San Javier village and continue from the turnoff, a total of three miles (five km), to just before the Arrazola town plaza. Turn right onto E. Zapata, then turn left after one block, at Independencia. After one more block, you will be at Calle Obregón, where everyone seems to be making *alebrijes*.

Although every family along the street crafts its own variations, **Pepe Santiago** and his Santa's workshop of craftspeople appear to have the edge. Inside the Santiago compound (on the right, just below the hilltop), men saw and carve away, while a cadre of young women painstakingly add riots of painted brocade to whimsical dragons, gargoyles, armadillos, giraffes, rabbits, and everything in between.

WEST SIDE: MONTE ALBÁN AND ETLA

Monte Albán is among Mesoamerica's most regal and spectacular ruined cities. The original name is lost in antiquity. "Monte Albán" was probably coined by a local Spaniard because of its resemblance to a similarly named Italian hill town.

Monte Albán's people cultivated corn, beans, squash, *chiles,* and fruits on the hillsides and adjacent valleys, occasionally feasting on meat from deer, small game, and perhaps (as did other ancient Mexicans) domesticated dogs. Tribute from surrounding communities directly enriched Monte Albán's ruling classes, and, by extension, its artisans and farmers.

Monte Albán reigned for at least 1,200 years, between 500 B.C. and A.D. 750, as the capital of the Zapotecs and the dominant force between Teotihuacán in the Valley of Mexico and the Maya empires of the south.

Archaeologists have organized the Valley of Oaxaca's history from 500 B.C. to the conquest in five periods, known as Monte Albán I through V. Over those centuries, the hilltop city was repeatedly reconstructed, with new walls, plazas, and staircases, which, like peels of an onion, now overlie earlier construction.

Remains from Monte Albán Period I (500 B.C.-A.D. 0) reveal an already advanced culture, with gods, permanent temples, a priesthood, writing, numerals, and a calendar. Sharply contrasting house styles indicate a differentiated, multilayered society. Monte Albán I ruins abound in graceful polychrome ceramics of uniquely Zapotec style.

Concurrent Olmec influences have also been found, notably in the buildings known as the **Danzantes** (Dancers), decorated with bas-reliefs similar to those unearthed along the Veracruz and Tabasco coasts.

Monte Albán II people (A.D. 0–300), by contrast, came under heavy influence from Chiapas and Guatemala in the south. They built strange, ship-shaped buildings, such as Monte Albán's Building J, and left unique remains of their religion, such as the striking jade bat-god now on display in the Anthropology Museum in Mexico City.

Monte Albán reached its apex during Period III (A.D. 300–800), attaining a population of perhaps 40,000 in an urban zone of about three square miles, which spread along hilltops (including the El Gallo and Atzompa archaeological sites) west of the present city of Oaxaca.

Vigorous Period III leaders rebuilt the main hilltop complex as we see it today. Heavily influenced by the grand Teotihuacán styles, the buildings were finished with handsome sloping staircases, corniced walls, monumental carvings,

ball courts, and hieroglyph-inscribed stelae depicting gods, kings, and heroic scenes of battle.

By A.D. 750 few foreign influences were continuing to enrich Monte Albán's uniquely Zapotec pottery styles. Quality declined until they seemed like mere factory copies. Concurrently, the Zapotec pantheon expanded to a horde of gods, as if mere numbers could protect the increasingly isolated Valley of Oaxaca from the outside world.

In A.D. 800, Monte Albán, mysteriously cut off from the rest of Mesoamerica, was declining in population and power. By A.D. 1000, the city was nearly abandoned. The reasons—whether drought, disease, or revolt—and the consequent loss of the necessarily imported water, wood, salt, and food supplies, remain an enigma.

During Periods IV and V, Mixtec peoples from the north invaded the Valley of Oaxaca. They warred with valley Zapotecs and, despite their relatively small numbers, became a ruling class in a number of valley city-states. The blend of Mixtec and Zapotec art and architecture sometimes led to new forms, especially visible at the west-valley sites of Yagul and Mitla.

Monte Albán, meanwhile, although abandoned, was not forgotten. It became both a refuge and a venerated burial place. In times of siege, local people retreated within the walls of a fortress built around Monte Albán's South Platform. At other times, Mixtec nobles opened tombs and reused them as burial vaults right down until the eve of the conquest.

Exploring Monte Albán

Visitors to Monte Albán enjoy a panoramic view of green mountains rising above the checkerboard of the Valley of Oaxaca. Monte Albán is fun for a picnic; alternatively, it is an auspicious place to perch atop a pyramid above the grand Main Plaza, etched by lengthening afternoon shadows, and contemplate the ages.

As you enter past the visitors' center, north is on your right, marked by the grand **North Platform,** topped by clusters of temples. The **Ball Court** will soon appear below on your left. Twenty-foot-high walkways circumscribe the sunken "I"-shaped playing field. To ensure true

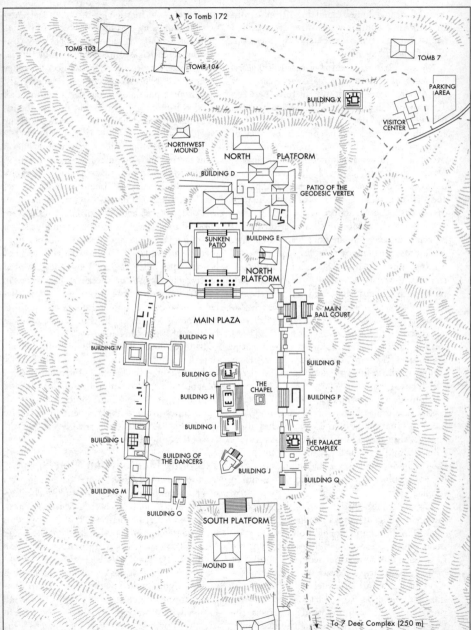

To Tomb 172

TOMB 103

TOMB 104

TOMB 7

BUILDING X

PARKING AREA

VISITOR CENTER

NORTHWEST MOUND

NORTH   PLATFORM

BUILDING D

PATIO OF THE GEODESIC VERTEX

BUILDING E

SUNKEN PATIO

NORTH PLATFORM

MAIN BALL COURT

MAIN PLAZA

BUILDING N

BUILDING IV

BUILDING II

BUILDING G

THE CHAPEL

BUILDING P

BUILDING H

BUILDING I

BUILDING L

THE PALACE COMPLEX

BUILDING OF THE DANCERS

BUILDING J

BUILDING Q

BUILDING M

BUILDING O

SOUTH PLATFORM

MOUND III

To 7 Deer Complex (250 m)

To Tomb 72   To Oaxaca

SMALL BALL COURT

TOMB 105

MONTE ALBÁN
ARCHAEOLOGICAL
ZONE

0   100 yds

0   100 m

bounces, builders spread smooth stucco over all surfaces, including the slopes on opposite sides (which, contrary to appearances, did not seat spectators). This, like all Oaxacan ball courts, had no stone ring (for supposed goals), but rather four mysterious niches at the court's opposite "I"-end corners.

The **Main Plaza,** 1,000 feet long and exactly two-thirds that wide, is aligned along a precise north-south axis. Probably serving as a market and civic-ceremonial ground, the monumentally harmonious Main Plaza was the Zapotec "navel" of the world.

Monte Albán's oldest construction, of the **Danzantes** (surmounted by newer Building L, on the west side of the plaza between Buildings M and IV), dates from Period I. Its walls are graced with a host of personages, known commonly as the *danzantes* (dancers) from their oft-contorted postures—probably chiefs vanquished by Monte Albán's armies. Their headdresses, earplugs, bracelets, and necklaces mark them among the nobility, while glyphs around their heads identify each individual.

Building J (circa A.D. 0), one of the most remarkable in Mesoamerica, stands nearby in mid-plaza at the foot of the South Platform. Speculation has raged since excavators unearthed its arrow-shaped base generations ago. It is not surprising that Alfonso Caso, Monte Albán's principal excavator, theorized it was an astronomical observatory. In the mind's eye, it seems like some fantastic ocean (or space?) vessel, being navigated to some mysteriously singular southwest destination by a ghostly crew oblivious of its worldly, earthbound brother monuments.

The **South Platform,** especially during the late afternoon, affords Monte Albán's best vantage point. Starting on the right-hand, palace complex side, **Building II** has a peculiar tunnel on its near side, covertly used by priests for privacy or perhaps some kind of magical effect. To the south stands Building P, an undistinguished multiroom palace.

The South Platform itself is only marginally explored. Looters have riddled the mounds on its top side. Its bottom four corners were embellished by fine bas-reliefs, two of which had their engraving intentionally buried from view. You can admire the fine sculpture and yet-undeciphered Zapotec hieroglyphs on one of them, along with others, at the South Platform's plaza-edge west side.

Still atop the South Platform, turn southward, where you can see the 7 Deer complex, a few hundred yards away, labeled for the name-date inscribed on its great lintel.

Turning northward again, look just beyond Building J to Buildings G, H, and I at plaza center, erected mostly to cover a rocky mound impossible to remove without the then-unavailable dynamite. Between these buildings and the palace complex on the right stands the small chapel where the remarkable bat-god jade sculpture was found.

On Monte Albán's northern periphery stand a number of tombs which, when excavated, yielded a trove of artifacts, now mostly housed in museums. Walking west from the Northern Platform's northeast base corner, you will pass Mound X on the right. A few hundred yards farther comes the **Tomb 104** mound, presided over by an elaborate ceramic urn representing Cojico, the Zapotec god of rain. Just north of this is **Tomb 172,** with the skeletons and offerings left intact.

Heading back along the northernmost of the two paths from Tomb 104, you will arrive at **Tomb 7** a few hundred feet behind the visitors' center. Here, around A.D. 1450, Mixtec nobles removed the original 8th-century contents and reused the tomb, burying a deceased dignitary and two servants for the netherworld. Along with the bodies they left a fabulous treasure in gold, silver, jade, alabaster, and turquoise, now visible in Oaxaca at the regional Museum of the Cultures of Oaxaca.

A few hundred feet toward town on the opposite side of the road from the parking lot is a trail, leading past a small ball court to the Cerro de Plumaje (Hill of Plumage), site of **Tomb 105.** A magnificent entrance door lintel, reminiscent of those at Mitla, welcomes you inside. Past the patio, descend to the mural-decorated tomb antechamber. Inside the cruciform tomb itself, four figures walk in pairs toward a great glyph, flanked by a god and goddess, identified by their name-dates.

Monte Albán is open daily from 10 A.M., closing promptly at 5 P.M.

Visitors' Center

The Monte Albán Visitors' Center has an excellent museum, café, information counter, and good store, with many books—guides, histories, art, folklore—on Mesoamerica. One of the most useful archaeological guides is Ignacio Bernal's *Official Guide of the Oaxaca Valley,* which includes Monte Albán, Cuilapan, Zaachila, Dainzu, Lambityeco, Yagul, and Mitla. Also covering the same territory, but in more depth, is *Oaxaca, the Archeological Record,* by archaeologist Marcus Winter.

Getting There

Get to Monte Albán by driving yourself (follow the big Monte Albán sign on the *periférico,* south end of Cabrera) over the Río Atoyac bridge; bear

© BRUCE WHIPPERMAN

The Etla market, held on Wednesdays, is just about the most colorful (but least touristed) of all the Oaxaca Valley weekly markets.

right after the bridge and continue about four miles (six km), bearing uphill, to the summit. Alternatively, go by very economical **tourist bus** departing from downtown Hotel Rivera del Ángel, at Mina 518, two blocks south, three blocks west of the *zócalo*. (Bus desk tel. 951/516-6175, 951/514-3152, or 951/514-7806.) Several buses leave for Monte Albán daily.

A third, more difficult, but slightly cheaper option is to ride a Monte Albán–bound bus, from the second-class bus terminal, about 10 blocks west of the *zócalo,* near the Abastos market. (See By Bus, in the Oaxaca City Getting There and Away section.)

Etla

The untouristed, very colorful Wednesday market at Villa de Etla, northwest of Oaxaca, could be visited either separately or in coordination with a visit to Monte Albán. Although Etla's market invariably has stalls overflowing with

its famous white cheese, vendors offer much other old-fashioned merchandise. (How would you like, for example, some fresh sheepskins, burro packframes, green Atzompa pottery, or red Oaxaca tamales?)

Preferably visit the market in the forenoon and Monte Albán in the midafternoon. Arrive at Monte Albán by 2:30 P.M. to allow enough leisure to tour the ruins before they close at 5 P.M.

Getting There: By car, head north along Highway 190 about nine miles (15 km) from the city center and turn left at the big green Etla sign, just before the Pemex station. The Etla market is in a handsome stone building, about half a mile from the highway, on the right, where the street ends at the railroad station.

By bus, ride one of the many Etla-marked Choferes del Sur buses from the Abastos second-class terminal, or a tour bus from the hotel Rivera del Angel (see Getting There in the Monte Albán section).

Resources

Glossary

Many of the following words have a social-historical meaning; others you will not find in the usual English-Spanish dictionary.

abarrotería—grocery store
alcalde—mayor or municipal judge
alfarería—pottery
alfarero, alfarera—potter
andando—walkway or strolling path
antojitos—native Mexican snacks, such as tamales, *chiles rellenos,* tacos, and enchiladas
artesanías—handicrafts, as distinguished from *artesano, or artesana,* a person who makes handicrafts
audiencia—one of the royal executive-judicial panels sent to rule Mexico during the 16th century
ayuntamiento—either the town council or the building where it meets
bienes raíces—literally "good roots," but popularly, real estate
birria—goat, pork, or lamb stew, in spiced tomato broth, especially typical of Jalisco
boleto—ticket, boarding pass
cabecera—head town of a municipal district, or headquarters in general
cabrón—literally a cuckold, but more commonly, bastard, rat, or S.O.B.; sometimes used affectionately
cacique—chief or boss
calandria—early 1800s-style horse-drawn carriage, common in Guadalajara
camionera—bus station
campesino—country person; farm worker
canasta—basket of woven reeds, with handle
casa de huéspedes—guesthouse, usually operated in a family home
caballero—literally, "horseman," but popularly, gentleman
caudillo—dictator or political chief
charro, charra—gentleman cowboy or cowgirl
chingar—literally, "to rape," but also the universal Spanish "f" word, the equivalent of

"screw" in English
churrigueresque—Spanish baroque architectural style incorporated into many Mexican colonial churches, named after José Churriguera (1665–1725)
científicos—literally, scientists, but applied to President Porfirio Díaz's technocratic advisers
cofradía—Catholic fraternal service association, either male or female, mainly in charge of financing and organizing religious festivals
colectivo—a shared public taxi or minibus that picks up and deposits passengers along a designated route
colegio—preparatory school or junior college
colonia—suburban subdivision/satellite of a larger city
Conasupo—government store that sells basic foods at subsidized prices
correo—post office
criollo—person of all-Spanish descent born in the New World
cuadra—Huichol yarn painting, usually rectangular
Cuaresma—Lent
curandero(a)—indigenous medicine man or woman
damas—ladies, as in "ladies room"
Domingo de Ramos—Palm Sunday
ejido—a constitutional, government-sponsored form of community, with shared land ownership and cooperative decision making
encomienda—colonial award of tribute from a designated indigenous district
estación de ferrocarril—railroad station
farmacia—pharmacy or drugstore
finca—farm
fonda—foodstall or small restaurant, often in a traditional market complex
fraccionamiento—city sector or subdivision
fuero—the former right of clergy to be tried in separate ecclesiastical courts
gachupín—"one who wear spurs"; a derogatory term for a Spanish-born colonial

gasolinera—gasoline station

gente de razón—"people of reason"; whites and mestizos in colonial Mexico

gringo—once-derogatory but now commonly used term for North American whites

grito—impassioned cry, as in Hidalgo's Grito de Dolores

hacienda—large landed estate; also the government treasury

hidalgo—nobleman; called honorifically by "Don" or "Doña"

indígena—indigenous or aboriginal inhabitant of all-native descent who speaks his or her native tongue. Commonly, but incorrectly, an Indian *(indio)*

jardín—garden

jejenes—"no-see-um" biting gnats, especially around San Blas, Nayarit

judiciales—the federal or state "judicial" or investigative police, best known to motorists for their highway checkpoint inspections

jugería—stall or small restaurant providing a large array of squeezed vegetable and fruit *jugos* (juices)

juzgado—the "hoosegow," or jail

larga distancia—long-distance telephone service, or the *caseta* (booth) where it's provided

licenciado—academic degree (abbrev. Lic.) approximately equivalent to a bachelor's degree

lonchería—small lunch counter, usually serving juices, sandwiches, and *antojitos* (Mexican snacks)

machismo; macho—exaggerated sense of maleness; person who holds such a sense of himself

mestizo—person of mixed native-European descent

mescal—alcoholic beverage distilled from the fermented hearts of maguey (century plant)

milpa—native farm plot, usually of corn, squash and beans

mordida—slang for bribe; literally "little bite"

palapa—thatched-roof structure, often open and shading a restaurant

panga—outboard launch *(lancha)*

papier-mâché—the craft of glued, multilayered paper sculpture, especially in Tonalá,

Jalisco, where creations resemble fine pottery or lacquerware

Pemex—acronym for Petróleos Mexicanos, the national oil corporation

peninsulares—the Spanish-born ruling colonial elite

peón—a poor wage-earner, usually a country native

petate—a mat, traditionally woven of palm leaf

piñata—papier-mâché decoration, usually in animal or human form, filled with treats and broken open during a fiesta

plan—political manifesto, usually by a leader or group consolidating or seeking power

Porfiriana—the 34-year (1876–1910) ruling period of President-dictator Porfirio Díaz

pozole—stew, of hominy in broth, usually topped by shredded pork, cabbage, and diced onion

preventiva—municipal police

presidencia municipal—the headquarters, like a U.S. city or county hall, of a Mexican *municipio,* countylike local governmental unit

pronunciamiento—declaration of rebellion by an insurgent leader

puta—whore, bitch, or slut

pueblo—town or people

quinta—a villa or country house

quinto—the royal "one-fifth" tax on treasure and precious metals

retorno—cul-de-sac

rurales—former federal country police force created to fight *bandidos*

Semana Santa—pre-Easter holy week

taxi especial—private taxi, as distinguished from *taxi colectivo,* or collective taxi

telégrafo—telegraph office, lately converting to high-tech *telecomunicaciones,* or *telecom,* offering telegraph, telephone, and public fax services

tenate—soft, pliable basket, without handle, woven of palm leaf

vaquero—cowboy

vecinidad—neighborhood

vinchuca—"kissing" or "assassin" bug

yanqui—Yankee

zócalo—town plaza or central square

Glossary

Abbreviations

Av.—*avenida* (avenue)

Blv.—*bulevar* (boulevard)

Calz.—*calzada* (thoroughfare, main road)

Fco.—Francisco (proper name, as in "Fco. Villa")

Fracc.—*Fraccionamiento* (subdivision)

Nte.—*norte* (north)

Ote.—*oriente* (east)

Pte.—*poniente* (west)

s/n—*sin número* (no street number)

Spanish Phrasebook

Your Mexico adventure will be more fun if you use a little Spanish. Mexican folks, although they may smile at your funny accent, will appreciate your halting efforts to break the ice and transform yourself from a foreigner to a potential friend.

Spanish commonly uses 30 letters—the familiar English 26, plus four straightforward additions: ch, ll, ñ, and rr, which are explained in "Consonants," below.

Pronunciation

Once you learn them, Spanish pronunciation rules—in contrast to English—don't change. Spanish vowels generally sound softer than in English. (Note: The capitalized syllables below receive stronger accents.)

Vowels

a — like ah, as in "hah": *agua* AH-gooah (water), *pan* PAHN (bread), and *casa* CAH-sah (house)

e — like ay, as in "may:" *mesa* MAY-sah (table), *tela* TAY-lah (cloth), and *de* DAY (of, from)

i — like ee, as in "need": *diez* dee-AYZ (ten), *comida* ko-MEE-dah (meal), and *fin* FEEN (end)

o — like oh, as in "go": *peso* PAY-soh (weight), *ocho* OH-choh (eight), and *poco* POH-koh (a bit)

u — like oo, as in "cool": *uno* OO-noh (one), *cuarto* KOOAHR-toh (room), and *usted* oos-TAYD (you); when it follows a "q" the **u** is silent; when it follows an "h" or has an umlaut, it's pronounced like "w"

Consonants

b, d, f, k, l, m, n, p, q, s, t, v, w, x, y, z, and **ch** — pronounced almost as in English; **h** occurs, but is silent—not pronounced at all.

c — like k as in "keep": *cuarto* KOOAR-toh (room), Tepic tay-PEEK (capital of Nayarit state); when it precedes "e" or "i," pronounce

c like s, as in "sit": *cerveza* sayr-VAY-sah (beer), *encima* ayn-SEE-mah (atop).

g — like g as in "gift" when it precedes "a," "o," "u," or a consonant: *gato* GAH-toh (cat), *hago* AH-goh (I do, make); otherwise, pronounce **g** like h as in "hat": *giro* HEE-roh (money order), *gente* HAYN-tay (people)

j — like h, as in "has": *Jueves* HOOAY-vays (Thursday), *mejor* may-HOR (better)

ll — like y, as in "yes": *toalla* toh-AH-yah (towel), *ellos* AY-yohs (they, them)

ñ — like ny, as in "canyon": *año* AH-nyo (year), *señor* SAY-nyor (Mr., sir)

r — is lightly trilled, with tongue at the roof of your mouth like a very light English d, as in "ready": *pero* PAY-doh (but), *tres* TDAYS (three), *cuatro* KOOAH-tdoh (four).

rr — like a Spanish r, but with much more emphasis and trill. Let your tongue flap. Practice with *burro* (donkey), *carretera* (highway), and Carrillo (proper name), then really let go with *ferrocarril* (railroad).

Note: The single small but common exception to all of the above is the pronunciation of Spanish **y** when it's being used as the Spanish word for "and," as in "Ron y Kathy." In such case, pronounce it like the English ee, as in "keep": Ron "ee" Kathy (Ron and Kathy).

Accent

The rule for accent, the relative stress given to syllables within a given word, is straightforward. If a word ends in a vowel, an n, or an s, accent the next-to-last syllable; if not, accent the last syllable.

Pronounce *gracias* GRAH-seeahs (thank you), *orden* OHR-dayn (order), and *carretera* kah-ray-TAY-rah (highway) with stress on the next-to-last syllable.

Otherwise, accent the last syllable: *venir* vay-NEER (to come), *ferrocarril* fay-roh-cah-REEL (railroad), and *edad* ay-DAHD (age).

Exceptions to the accent rule are always marked with an accent sign: (á, é, í, ó, or ú), such as *teléfono* tay-LAY-foh-noh (telephone), *jabón* hah-BON (soap), and *rápido* RAH-pee-doh (rapid).

Basic and Courteous Expressions

Most Spanish-speaking people consider formalities important. Whenever approaching anyone for information or some other reason, do not forget the appropriate salutation—good morning, good evening, etc. Standing alone, the greeting *hola* (hello) can sound brusque.

Hello. — *Hola.*
Good morning. — *Buenos días.*
Good afternoon. — *Buenas tardes.*
Good evening. — *Buenas noches.*
How are you? — *¿Cómo está usted?*
Very well, thank you. — *Muy bien, gracias.*
Okay; good. — *Bien.*
Not okay; bad. — *Mal* or *feo.*
So-so. — *Más o menos.*
And you? — *¿Y usted?*
Thank you. — *Gracias.*
Thank you very much. — *Muchas gracias.*
You're very kind. — *Muy amable.*
You're welcome. — *De nada.*
Goodbye. — *Adios.*
See you later. — *Hasta luego.*
please — *por favor*
yes — *sí*
no — *no*
I don't know. — *No sé.*
Just a moment, please. — *Momentito, por favor.*
Excuse me, please (when you're trying to get attention). — *Disculpe* or *Con permiso.*
Excuse me (when you've made a boo-boo). — *Lo siento.*
Pleased to meet you. — *Mucho gusto.*
How do you say . . . in Spanish? — *¿Cómo se dice . . . en español?*
What is your name? — *¿Cómo se llama usted?*
Do you speak English? — *¿Habla usted inglés?*
Is English spoken here? (Does anyone here speak English?) — *¿Se habla español?*
I don't speak Spanish well. — *No hablo bien el español.*
I don't understand. — *No entiendo.*
How do you say . . . in Spanish? — *¿Cómo se dice . . . en español?*
My name is . . . — *Me llamo . . .*
Would you like . . . — *¿Quisiera usted . . .*
Let's go to . . . — *Vamos a . . .*

Terms of Address

When in doubt, use the formal *usted* (you) as a form of address.

I — *yo*
you (formal) — *usted*
you (familiar) — *tu*
he/him — *él*
she/her — *ella*
we/us — *nosotros*
you (plural) — *ustedes*
they/them — *ellos* (all males or mixed gender); *ellas* (all females)
Mr., sir — *señor*
Mrs., madam — *señora*
miss, young lady — *señorita*
wife — *esposa*
husband — *esposo*
friend — *amigo* (male); *amiga* (female)
sweetheart — *novio* (male); *novia* (female)
son; daughter — *hijo; hija*
brother; sister — *hermano; hermana*
father; mother — *padre; madre*
grandfather; grandmother — *abuelo; abuela*

Transportation

Where is . . . ? — *¿Dónde está . . . ?*
How far is it to . . . ? — *¿A cuánto está . . . ?*
from . . . to . . . — *de . . . a . . .*
How many blocks? — *¿Cuántas cuadras?*
Where (Which) is the way to . . . ? — *¿Dónde está el camino a . . . ?*
the bus station — *la terminal de autobuses*
the bus stop — *la parada de autobuses*
Where is this bus going? — *¿Adónde va este autobús?*
the taxi stand — *la parada de taxis*

the train station — *la estación de ferrocarril*
the boat — *el barco*
the airport — *el aeropuerto*
I'd like a ticket to . . . — *Quisiera un boleto a . . .*
first (second) class — *primera (segunda) clase*
roundtrip — *ida y vuelta*
reservation — *reservación*
baggage — *equipaje*
Stop here, please. — *Pare aquí, por favor.*
the entrance — *la entrada*
the exit — *la salida*
the ticket office — *la oficina de boletos*
(very) near; far — *(muy) cerca; lejos*
to; toward — *a*
by; through — *por*
from — *de*
the right — *la derecha*
the left — *la izquierda*
straight ahead — *derecho; directo*
in front — *en frente*
beside — *al lado*
behind — *atrás*
the corner — *la esquina*
the stoplight — *la semáforo*
a turn — *una vuelta*
right here — *aquí*
somewhere around here — *por acá*
right there — *allí*
somewhere around there — *por allá*
street; boulevard — *calle; bulevar*
highway — *carretera*
bridge; toll — *puente; cuota*
address — *dirección*
north; south — *norte; sur*
east; west — *oriente (este); poniente (oeste)*

Accommodations

hotel — *hotel*
Is there a room? — *¿Hay cuarto?*
May I (may we) see it? — *¿Puedo (podemos) verlo?*
What is the rate? — *¿Cuál es el precio?*
Is that your best rate? — *¿Es su mejor precio?*
Is there something cheaper? — *¿Hay algo más económico?*
a single room — *un cuarto sencillo*
a double room — *un cuarto doble*

double bed — *cama matrimonial*
twin beds — *camas gemelas*
with private bath — *con baño*
hot water — *agua caliente*
shower — *ducha*
towels — *toallas*
soap — *jabón*
toilet paper — *papel higiénico*
blanket — *frazada; manta*
sheets — *sábanas*
air-conditioned—*aire acondicionado*
fan — *abanico; ventilador*
key — *llave*
manager — *gerente*

Food

I'm hungry — *Tengo hambre.*
I'm thirsty. — *Tengo sed.*
menu — *lista; menú*
order — *orden*
glass — *vaso*
fork — *tenedor*
knife — *cuchillo*
spoon — *cuchara*
napkin — *servilleta*
soft drink — *refresco*
coffee — *café*
tea — *té*
drinking water — *agua pura; agua potable*
bottled carbonated water — *agua mineral*
bottled uncarbonated water — *agua sin gas*
beer — *cerveza*
wine — *vino*
milk — *leche*
juice — *jugo*
cream — *crema*
sugar — *azúcar*
cheese — *queso*
snack — *antojo; botana*
breakfast — *desayuno*
lunch — *almuerzo*
daily lunch special — *comida corrida* (or *el menú del día* depending on region)
dinner — *comida* (often eaten in late afternoon); *cena* (a late-night snack)
the check — *la cuenta*

eggs — *huevos*
bread — *pan*
salad — *ensalada*
fruit — *fruta*
mango — *mango*
watermelon — *sandía*
papaya — *papaya*
banana — *plátano*
apple — *manzana*
orange — *naranja*
lime — *limón*
fish — *pescado*
shellfish — *mariscos*
shrimp — *camarones*
meat (without) — *(sin) carne*
chicken — *pollo*
pork — *puerco*
beef; steak — *res; bistec*
bacon; ham — *tocino; jamón*
fried — *frito*
roasted — *asada*
barbecue; barbecued — *barbacoa; al carbón*

Shopping

money — *dinero*
money-exchange bureau — *casa de cambio*
I would like to exchange traveler's checks. — *Quisiera cambiar cheques de viajero.*
What is the exchange rate? — *¿Cuál es el tipo de cambio?*
How much is the commission? — *¿Cuánto cuesta la comisión?*
Do you accept credit cards? — *¿Aceptan tarjetas de crédito?*
money order — *giro*
How much does it cost? — *¿Cuánto cuesta?*
What is your final price? — *¿Cuál es su último precio?*
expensive —*caro*
cheap — *barato; económico*
more — *más*
less — *menos*
a little — *un poco*
too much — *demasiado*

Health

Help me please. — Ayúdeme por favor.
I am ill. — *Estoy enfermo.*
Call a doctor. — *Llame un doctor.*
Take me to . . . — *Lléveme a . . .*
hospital — *hospital; sanatorio*
drugstore — *farmacia*
pain — *dolor*
fever — *fiebre*
headache — *dolor de cabeza*
stomach ache — *dolor de estómago*
burn — *quemadura*
cramp — *calambre*
nausea — *náusea*
vomiting — *vomitar*
medicine — *medicina*
antibiotic — *antibiótico*
pill; tablet — *pastilla*
aspirin — *aspirina*
ointment; cream — *pomada; crema*
bandage — *venda*
cotton — *algodón*
sanitary napkins — use brand name, e.g., Kotex
birth control pills — *pastillas anticonceptivas*
contraceptive foam — *espuma anticonceptiva*
condoms — *preservativos; condones*
toothbrush — *cepilla dental*
dental floss — *hilo dental*
toothpaste — *crema dental*
dentist — *dentista*
toothache — *dolor de muelas*

Post Office and Communications

long-distance telephone — *teléfono larga distancia*
I would like to call . . . — *Quisiera llamar a . . .*
collect — *por cobrar*
station to station — *a quien contesta*
person to person — *persona a persona*
credit card — *tarjeta de crédito*
post office — *correo*
general delivery — *lista de correo*
letter — *carta*

stamp — *estampilla, timbre*
postcard — *tarjeta*
aerogram — *aerograma*
air mail — *correo aereo*
registered — *registrado*
money order — *giro*
package; box — *paquete; caja*
string; tape — *cuerda; cinta*

At the Border

border — *frontera*
customs — *aduana*
immigration — *migración*
tourist card — *tarjeta de turista*
inspection — *inspección; revisión*
passport — *pasaporte*
profession — *profesión*
marital status — *estado civil*
single — *soltero*
married; divorced — *casado; divorciado*
widowed — *viudado*
insurance — *seguros*
title — *título*
driver's license — *licencia de manejar*

At the Gas Station

gas station — *gasolinera*
gasoline — *gasolina*
unleaded — *sin plomo*
full, please — *lleno, por favor*
tire — *llanta*
tire repair shop — *vulcanizadora*
air — *aire*
water — *agua*
oil (change) — *aceite (cambio)*
grease — *grasa*
My . . . doesn't work. — *Mi . . . no sirve.*
battery — *batería*
radiator — *radiador*
alternator — *alternador*
generator — *generador*
tow truck — *grúa*
repair shop — *taller mecánico*
tune-up — *afinación*
auto parts store — *refaccionería*

Verbs

Verbs are the key to getting along in Spanish. They employ mostly predictable forms and come in three classes, which end in *ar, er,* and *ir,* respectively:

to buy — *comprar*
I buy, you (he, she, it) buys — *compro, compra*
we buy, you (they) buy — *compramos, compran*

to eat — *comer*
I eat, you (he, she, it) eats — *como, come*
we eat, you (they) eat — *comemos, comen*
to climb — *subir*
I climb, you (he, she, it) climbs — *subo, sube*
we climb, you (they) climb — *subimos, suben*

Got the idea? Here are more (with irregularities marked in **bold**).

to do or make — *hacer*
I do or make, you (he she, it) does or makes — ***hago,*** *hace*
we do or make, you (they) do or make — *hacemos, hacen*

to go — *ir*
I go, you (he, she, it) goes — ***voy, va***
we go, you (they) go — ***vamos, van***

to go (walk) — *andar*
to love — *amar*
to work — *trabajar*
to want — *desear, querer*
to need — *necesitar*
to read — *leer*
to write — *escribir*
to repair — *reparar*
to stop — *parar*
to get off (the bus) — *bajar*
to arrive — *llegar*
to stay (remain) — *quedar*
to stay (lodge) — *hospedar*
to leave — *salir* (regular except for ***salgo,*** I leave)
to look at — *mirar*
to look for — *buscar*

to give — *dar* (regular except for ***doy,*** I give)
to carry — *llevar*
to have — *tener* (irregular but important: ***tengo,
tiene,*** *tenemos,* ***tienen***)
to come — *venir* (similarly irregular: ***vengo,
viene,*** *venimos,* ***vienen***)

Spanish has two forms of "to be." Use *estar* when speaking of location or a temporary state of being: "I am at home." *"**Estoy** en casa."* "I'm sick." *"**Estoy** enfermo."* Use *ser* for a permanent state of being: "I am a doctor." *"**Soy** doctora."*

Estar is regular except for ***estoy,*** I am. *Ser* is very irregular:

to be — *ser*
I am, you (he, she, it) is — ***soy, es***
we are, you (they) are — ***somos, son***

Numbers

zero — *cero*
one — *uno*
two — *dos*
three — *tres*
four — *cuatro*
five — *cinco*
six — *seis*
seven — *siete*
eight — *ocho*
nine — *nueve*
10 — *diez*
11 — *once*
12 — *doce*
13 — *trece*
14 — *catorce*
15 — *quince*
16 — *dieciseis*
17 — *diecisiete*
18 — *dieciocho*
19 — *diecinueve*
20 — *veinte*
21 — *veinte y uno* or *veintiuno*
30 — *treinta*
40 — *cuarenta*

50 — *cincuenta*
60 — *sesenta*
70 — *setenta*
80 — *ochenta*
90 — *noventa*
100 — *ciento*
101 — *ciento y uno* or *cientiuno*
200 — *doscientos*
500 — *quinientos*
1,000 — *mil*
10,000 — *diez mil*
100,000 — *cien mil*
1,000,000 — *millón*
one half — *medio*
one third — *un tercio*
one fourth — *un cuarto*

Time

What time is it? — *¿Qué hora es?*
It's one o'clock. — *Es la una.*
It's three in the afternoon. — *Son las tres de la
tarde.*
It's 4 A.M. — *Son las cuatro de la mañana.*
six-thirty — *seis y media*
a quarter till eleven — *un cuarto para las once*
a quarter past five — *las cinco y cuarto*
an hour — *una hora*

Days and Months

Monday — *lunes*
Tuesday — *martes*
Wednesday — *miércoles*
Thursday — *jueves*
Friday — *viernes*
Saturday — *sábado*
Sunday — *domingo*
today — *hoy*
tomorrow — *mañana*
yesterday — *ayer*
January — *enero*
February — *febrero*
March — *marzo*
April — *abril*
May — *mayo*

June — *junio*
July — *julio*
August — *agosto*
September — *septiembre*
October — *octubre*
November — *noviembre*

December — *diciembre*
a week — *una semana*
a month — *un mes*
after — *después*
before — *antes*

Suggested Reading

Some of these books are informative, others are entertaining, and all of them will increase your understanding of Mexico. Some are easier to find in Mexico than at home, and vice versa. Take a few along on your trip. If you find others that are especially noteworthy, let us know. Happy reading.

History

Calderón de la Barca, Fanny. *Life in Mexico, with New Material from the Author's Journals.* New York: Doubleday, 1966. Edited by H. T. and M. H. Fisher. An update of the brilliant, humorous, and celebrated original 1913 book by the Scottish wife of the Spanish ambassador to Mexico.

Casasola, Gustavo. *Seis Siglos de Historia Gráfica de Mexico (Six Centuries of Mexican Graphic History).* Mexico City: Editorial Gustavo Casasola, 1978. Six fascinating volumes of Mexican history in pictures, from 1325 to the present.

Collis, Maurice. *Cortés and Montezuma.* New York: New Directions Publishing Corp., 1999. A reprint of a 1954 classic piece of well-researched storytelling. Collis traces Cortés's conquest of Mexico through the defeat of his chief opponent, Aztec Emperor Montezuma (also called Moctezuma). He uses contemporary eyewitnesses—notably Bernal Díaz de Castillo—to revivify one of history's greatest dramas.

Cortés, Hernán. *Letters From Mexico.* Translated by Anthony Pagden. New Haven: Yale University Press, 1986. Cortés's five long letters to his king, in which he describes contemporary Mexico in fascinating detail, including, notably, the remarkably sophisticated life of the Aztecs at the time of the conquest.

Díaz del Castillo, Bernal. *The True Story of the Conquest of Mexico.* Translated by Albert Idell. Garden City: Doubleday, 1956. A soldier's still-fresh tale of the conquest from the Spanish viewpoint.

Garfias, Luis. *The Mexican Revolution.* Mexico City: Panorama Editorial, 1985. A concise Mexican version of the 1910–1917 Mexican revolution, the crucible of present-day Mexico.

Gugliotta, Bobette. *Women of Mexico.* Encino, CA: Floricanto Press, 1989. Lively legends, tales and biographies of remarkable Mexican women, from Zapotec princesses to Independence heroines.

León-Portilla, Miguel. *The Broken Spears: The Aztec Account of the Conquest of Mexico.* New York: Beacon Press, 1962. Provides an interesting contrast to Díaz del Castillo's account.

Meyer, Michael, and William Sherman. *The Course of Mexican History.* New York: Oxford University Press, 1991. An insightful, 700-plus-page college textbook in paperback. A bargain, especially if you can get it used.

Novas, Himlice. *Everything You Need to Know About Latino History.* New York: Plume Books (Penguin Group), 1994. Chicanos, Latin rhythm, La Raza, the Treaty of Guadalupe Hidalgo, and much more, interpreted from an authoritative Latino point of view.

Reed, John. *Insurgent Mexico.* New York: International Publisher's Co., 1994. Republication of 1914 original. Fast-moving, but not unbiased, description of the 1910 Mexican revolution by the journalist famed for his reporting of the subsequent 1917 Russian revolution.

Reed, memorialized by the Soviets, was resurrected in the 1981 film biography *Reds.*

Ridley, Jasper. *Maximilian and Juárez.* New York: Ticknor and Fields, 1999. This authoritative historical biography breathes new life into one of Mexico's great ironic tragedies, a drama that pitted the native Zapotec "Lincoln of Mexico" against the dreamy, idealistic Archduke Maximilian of Austria-Hungary. Despite their common liberal ideas, they were drawn into a bloody no-quarter struggle that set the Old World against the New, ending in Maximilian's execution, insanity of his wife, and the emergence of the United States as a power to be reckoned with in world affairs.

Ruíz, Ramon Eduardo. *Triumphs and Tragedy: A History of the Mexican People.* New York: W.W. Norton, Inc., 1992. A pithy, anecdote-filled history of Mexico from an authoritative Mexican-American perspective.

Simpson, Lesley Bird. *Many Mexicos.* Berkeley: The University of California Press, 1962. A much-reprinted, fascinating broad-brush version of Mexican history.

Unique Guidebooks, Tip Books, and Newsletters

American Automobile Association. *Mexico TravelBook.* Heathrow, FL: 1995. Published by the American Automobile Association, offices at 1000 AAA Dr., Heathrow, FL 32746-5063. Short sweet summaries of major Mexican tourist destinations and sights. Also includes information on fiestas, accommodations, restaurants, and a wealth of information relevant to car travel in Mexico. Available in bookstores, or free to AAA members at affiliate offices.

Burton, Tony. *Western Mexico, A Traveller's Treasury.* Guadalajara: Editorial Agata (Juan Manuel 316, Guadalajara 44100). A well-researched and lovingly written and illustrated guide to dozens of fascinating places to visit, both well-known and out of the way, in Michoacán, Jalisco, and Nayarit.

Church, Mike, and Terry Church. *Traveler's Guide to Mexican Camping.* Kirkland, WA: Rolling Homes Press, P.O. Box 2099, Kirkland, WA 98083-2099. This is an unusually thorough guide to trailer parks all over Mexico, with much coverage of the Pacific Coast in general and the Puerto Vallarta region in particular. Detailed maps guide you accurately to each trailer park cited, and clear descriptions tell you what to expect. The book also provides very helpful information on car travel in Mexico, including details of insurance, border crossing, highway safety, car repairs, and much more.

Franz, Carl. *The People's Guide to Mexico.* Emeryville, CA: Avalon Travel Publishing, 2002. An entertaining and insightful A to Z general guide to the joys and pitfalls of independent economy travel in Mexico, , including many pithy details on camping and auto and RV travel.

Freedman, Jacqueline, and Susan Gerstein. *Traveling Like Everybody Else.* Brooklyn, NY: Lambda Publishing, Inc. Your disability needn't keep you at home. This book was out of print at press time, but libraries may have copies.

Graham, Scott. *Handle with Care.* Chicago: The Noble Press, 1991. Should you accept a meal from a family who lives in a grass house? This insightful guide answers this and hundreds of other tough questions for people who want to travel responsibly in the third world.

Howells, John, and Don Merwin. *Choose Mexico.* Oakland, CA: Gateway Books (distributed by Publishers Group West, Berkeley, CA). A pair of experienced Mexico residents provide a wealth of astute counsel about the important questions—health, finance, home ownership, work, driving, legalities—of long-term travel, residence, and retirement in Mexico. Includes specific sections on Puerto Vallarta, Guadalajara, and Lake Chapala.

Jeffries, Nan. *Adventuring with Children.* San Francisco: Foghorn Press, 1992. This unusually detailed book starts where most travel-with-children books end. It contains, besides a wealth of information and practical strategies for general travel with children, specific chapters on how you can adventure—trek, kayak, river-raft, camp, bicycle, and much more—successfully with the kids in tow.

Mader, Ron. *Adventures in Nature Mexico.* Santa Fe, NM: John Muir Publications, 1998. Internationally acknowledged expert on eco-travel in Latin America details dozens of environmentally sensitive adventure tours in Mexico. Destinations range widely, from scuba diving off Cozumel and exploring lost Mayan cities to jeeping through the Copper Canyon to rescuing turtle eggs on Oaxaca beaches.

Pint, John, and Susy Pint. *Outdoors in Western Mexico.* Guadalajara: Editorial Agata. These plucky adventurers lead their readers in a year's worth of weekend explorations to off-the-beaten track corners of Jalisco and Nayarit. Replete with pithy details of wildlife, access, history and more, in locations as diverse as Tequila Volcano and Bosque de Primavera wilderness to Cristero rebellion guerrilla caves at Cascada El Salto near Tapalpa and the jungly depths of the Grand Canyon of the Río Santiago in Guadalajara's backyard.

Rogers, Steve, and Tina Rosa. *The Shopper's Guide to Mexico.* Santa Fe, NM: John Muir Publications. A hard-to-find but well-written guide to shopping in Mexico, with emphasis on handicrafts. Contains inventory details and locations of out-of-the-ordinary shops in towns and cities all over Mexico, including much on the Pacific centers, especially Puerto Vallarta, greater Guadalajara,

Mazatlán, Pátzcuaro, and Oaxaca.

Sanborn's *Recreational Guide to Mexico.* Sanborn's Insurance, P.O. Box 310, McAllen, TX 78502, tel. 800/222-0158. A compilation of hunting sites and lodges mostly from "Mexico Mike" Nelson's travels for Sanborn's during the 1990s. The latest edition, although still useful, is in many places out of date and/or ambiguous.

Simmonds, David, ed. *The Mexico File.* La Jolla, CA: Simmonds Publications, 5580 La Jolla Blvd., #306, La Jolla, CA 92037. A monthly newsletter that, besides featuring pithy stories by Mexico travelers and news updates, offers an opportunity-packed classified section of Mexico vacations rentals, publications, services, and much more. Subscribe ($39/year) by writing or dialing tel./fax 858/456-4419 or 800/563-9345 (voice mail), or logging on to the website www.mexicofile.com.

Stillman, Alan Eric. *Kwikpoint.* Alexandria, VA: GAIA Communications, P.O. Box 238, Alexandria, VA 22313-0238, www.kwikpoint.com. Eight dollars by cash or check gets you a super handy, durable color foldout of pictures to point to when you need something in a foreign country. The pictures, such as a frying pan with fire under it (for "fried"), a compass (for "Which direction?"), a red lobster, and a cauliflower, are imaginative and unmistakable, anywhere between Puerto Vallarta and Pakistan or San Blas and Santander.

Weisbroth, Ericka, and Eric Ellman. *Bicycling Mexico.* New York: Hunter, 1990. These intrepid adventurers describe bike trips from Puerto Vallarta to Acapulco, coastal and highland Oaxaca, and highland Jalisco and Michoacán.

Werner, David. *Where There Is No Doctor.* Palo Alto, CA: Hesperian Foundation (P.O. Box 1692, Palo Alto, CA 94302). How to keep well in the backcountry.

Fiction

Bowen, David, and Juan A. Ascencio. *Pyramids of Glass.* San Antonio: Corona Publishing Co., 1994. Two dozen-odd stories that lead the reader along a monthlong journey through the bedrooms, the barracks, the cafés, and streets of present-day Mexico.

Doerr, Harriet. *Consider This, Señor.* New York: Harcourt Brace, 1993. Four expatriates tough it out in a Mexican small town, adapting to the excesses—blazing sun, driving rain, vast, untrammeled landscapes—meanwhile interacting with the local folks while the local folks observe them, with a mixture of fascination and tolerance.

Fuentes, Carlos. *Where the Air Is Clear.* New York: Farrar, Straus and Giroux, 1971. The seminal work of Mexico's celebrated novelist.

Fuentes, Carlos. *The Years with Laura Díaz.* New York: Farrar, Straus, and Giroux, 2000. A panorama of Mexico from Independence to the 21st century, through the eyes of one woman, Laura Díaz, and her great-grandson, the author. As one reviewer said, that she ". . . as a Mexican woman, would like to celebrate Carlos Fuentes; it is worthy of applause that a man who has seen, observed, analyzed and criticized the great occurrences of the century now has a woman, Laura Díaz, speak for him." Translated by Alfred MacAdam.

Jennings, Gary. *Aztec.* New York: Atheneum, 1980. Beautifully researched and written monumental tale of lust, compassion, love, and death in preconquest Mexico.

Peters, Daniel. *The Luck of Huemac.* New York: Random House, 1981. An Aztec noble family's tale—of war, famine, sorcery, heroism, treachery, love, and finally disaster and death—in the Valley of Mexico.

Porter, Katherine Ann. *The Collected Stories.* New York: Delacorte, 1970.

Rulfo, Juan. *The Burning Plain.* Austin: University of Texas Press, 1967. Stories of people torn between the old and new in Mexico.

Rulfo, Juan. *Pedro Paramo.* Rulfo's acknowledged masterpiece, published last in 1980, established his renown. The author, thinly disguised as the protagonist, Juan Preciado, fulfills his mother's dying request by returning to his shadowy Jalisco hometown, Comala, in search of this father. Although Preciado discovers that his father, Pedro Páramo (whose surname that implies "wasteland"), is long dead, Preciado's search resurrects his father's restless spirit, which recounts its horrific life tale of massacre, rape, and incest.

Traven, B. *The Treasure of the Sierra Madre.* New York: Hill and Wang, 1967. Campesinos, *federales,* gringos, and *indígenas* all figure in this modern morality tale set in Mexico's rugged outback. The most famous of the mysterious author's many novels of oppression and justice set in Mexico's jungles.

Villaseñor, Victor. *Rain of Gold.* New York: Delta Books (Bantam, Doubleday, and Dell), 1991. The moving, best-selling epic of the author's family's gritty travails. From humble rural beginnings in the Copper Canyon, they flee revolution and certain death, struggling through parched northern deserts to sprawling border refugee camps. From there they migrate to relative safety and an eventual modicum of happiness in Southern California.

People and Culture

Berrin, Kathleen. *The Art of the Huichol Indians.* Lovely, large photographs and text by a symposium of experts provide a good interpretive introduction to Huichol art and culture.

Castillo, Ana. *Goddess of the Americas.* New York, Riverhead Books, 1996. Here, a noted author has selected from the works of seven interpreters about Mesoameriacan female deities; and whose visions range as far and wide as Sex Goddess, the Broken-Hearted, the Subversive, and the Warrior Queen.

Lewis, Oscar. *Children of Sanchez.* New York: Random House, 1961. Poverty and strength in the Mexican underclass, sympathetically described and interpreted by renowned sociologist Lewis.

Medina, Sylvia López. *Cantora.* New York: Ballantine Books, 1992. Fascinated by the stories of her grandmother, aunt, and mother, the author seeks her own center by discovering a past that she thought she wanted to forget.

Meyerhoff, Barbara. *Peyote Hunt: The Sacred Journey of the Huichol Indians.* Ithaca: Cornell University Press, 1974. A description and interpretation of the Huichol's religious use of mind-bending natural hallucinogens.

Palmer, Colin A. *Slaves of the White God.* Cambridge: Harvard University Press. A scholarly study of why and how Spanish authorities imported African slaves into America and how they were used afterward. Replete with poignant details, taken from Spanish and Mexican archives, describing how the Africans struggled from bondage to eventual freedom.

Riding, Alan. *Distant Neighbors: A Portrait of the Mexicans.* New York: Random House Vintage Books. Rare insights into Mexico and Mexicans.

Toor, Frances. *A Treasury of Mexican Folkways.* New York: Crown Books, 1947, reprinted by Bonanza, 1985. An illustrated encyclopedia of vanishing Mexicana—costumes, religion, fiestas, burial practices, customs, legends—compiled during the celebrated author's 35 years' residence in Mexico.

Wauchope, Robert, ed. *Handbook of Middle American Indians.* Vols. 7 and 8. Austin: University of Texas Press, 1969. Authoritative surveys of important native-speaking groups in northern and central (vol. 8) and southern (vol. 7) Mexico.

Flora and Fauna

Goodson, Gar. *Fishes of the Pacific Coast.* Stanford, CA: Stanford University Press, 1988. More than 500 beautifully detailed color drawings highlight this pocket version of all you ever wanted to know about the ocean's fishes (including common Spanish names) from Alaska to Peru.

Howell, Steve N. G., and Sophie Webb. *A Guide to the Birds of Mexico and Northern America.* Oxford: Oxford University Press, 1995. All the serious birder needs to know about Mexico's rich species treasury. Includes authoritative habitat maps and 70 excellent color plates that detail the male and females of around 1,500 species. (For a more portable version of the above, check out Steve Howell's *Bird-Finding Guide to Mexico.*)

Howell, Steve N. G. *Bird-Finding Guide to Mexico.* Ithaca, NY: Cornell University Press, 1999. A unique guide for folks who really want to see birds in Mexico. Unlike other bird books, the author presents a unique and authoritative site guide, with dozens of clear maps and lists of birds seen at sites all over Mexico. Pacific sites include Mazatlán, San Blas, Puerto Vallarta, El Tuito, Manzanillo, Oaxaca, and many more. Use this book along with Howell and Webb's *A Guide to the Birds of Mexico and North America.*

Leopold, Starker. *Wildlife of Mexico.* Berkeley: University of California Press. Classic, illustrated layperson's survey of common Mexican mammals and birds.

Mason, Jr., Charles T., and Patricia B. Mason. *Handbook of Mexican Roadside Flora.* Tucson:

University of Arizona Press, 1987. Authoritative identification guide, with line illustrations, of all the plants you're likely to see in the Puerto Vallarta region.

Morris, Percy A. *A Field Guide to Pacific Coast Shells.* Boston: Houghton Mifflin. The complete beachcomber's Pacific shell guide.

Novick, Rosalind, and Lan Sing Wu. *Where to Find Birds in San Blas, Nayarit.* Order through the authors at 178 Myrtle Ct., Arcata, CA 95521, tel. 707/822-0790.

Pesman, M. Walter. *Meet Flora Mexicana.* Delightful anecdotes and illustrations of hundreds of common Mexican plants. Published around 1960, now out of print.

Peterson, Roger Tory, and Edward L. Chalif. *Field Guide to Mexican Birds.* Boston: Houghton Mifflin. With hundreds of Peterson's crisp color drawings, this is a must for serious birders and vacationers interested in the life that teems in the Puerto Vallarta region's beaches, jungles, lakes, and lagoons.

Wright, N. Pelham. *A Guide to Mexican Mammals and Reptiles.* Mexico City: Minutiae Mexicana, 1989. Pocket-edition lore, history, descriptions, and pictures of commonly seen Mexican animals.

Art, Architecture, and Crafts

Baird, Joseph. *The Churches of Mexico.* Berkeley: University of California Press. Mexican colonial architecture and art, illustrated and interpreted.

Cordrey, Donald, and Dorothy Cordrey. *Mexican Indian Costumes.* Austin: University of Texas Press, 1968. A lovingly photographed, written, and illustrated classic on Mexican Indians and their dress, emphasizing textiles.

Covarrubias, Miguel. *Indian Art of Mexico and Central America.* New York: Knopf, 1957. A timeless work by the renowned interpreter of *indígena* art and design.

Martínez Penaloza, Porfirio. *Popular Arts of Mexico.* Mexico City: Editorial Panorama, 1981. An excellent, authoritative, pocket-sized exposition of Mexican art.

Morrill, Penny C. and Carol A. Berk. *Mexican Silver.* Atglen, PA (4880 Lower Valley Road, zip 19310): Shiffer Publishing Co. Lovingly written and photographed exposition of the Mexican silvercraft of Taxco, Guerrero, revitalized through the initiative of Frederick Davis and William Spratling in the 1920s and 1930s. Color photos of many beautiful, museum-quality pieces supplement the text, which describes the history and work of a score of silversmithing families who developed the Taxco craft under Spratling's leadership. Greatly adds to the traveler's appreciation of the beautiful Taxco silvercrafts so widely available in many Puerto Vallarta and Guadalajara (Tlaquepaque) shops.

Sayer, Chloë. *Arts and Crafts of Mexico.* San Francisco: Chronicle Books, 1990. All you ever wanted to know about your favorite Mexican crafts, from papier-mâché to pottery and toys and Taxco silver. Beautifully illustrated by traditional etchings and David Lavender's crisp black-and-white and color photographs.

Internet Resources

Travel in General

www.travel.state.gov
The U.S. State Department information website. Lots of subheadings and links of varying completeness. Many links furnish plenty of solid information, especially consular advice, such as travel advisories or reaching U.S. citizens arrested overseas. Didn't seem to contain many specifics on Mexico, however.

www.orbitz.com
www.travelocity.com
www.expedia.com
Major sites for airline and hotel bookings.

www.travelinsure.com
www.worldtravelcenter.com
Good for travel insurance and other services.

Specialty Travel

www.elderhostel.org
Site of Boston-based Elderhostel, Inc., with a huge catalog of ongoing study tours, including three or four in the Guadalajara region.

www.miusa.org
Site of Mobility International, with a number of services for the disabled, including many connections in Mexico.

Home Exchange

www.homexchange.com
www.intervacus.com
www.homelink.org
Sites for temporarily trading your home with someone else in dozens of places in the world, including dozens of spots in Pacific Mexico.

Mexico in General

www.visitmexico.com
The official website of the public-private Mexico Tourism Board; a good general site for official information, such as entry requirements. It has lots of summarily informative subheadings, not unlike an abbreviated guidebook. If you can't find what you want here, call its toll-free information number tel. 800/4-MEXICO (800/463-9426).

www.thenewsmexico.com
Keep up on Mexico news and much more with daily updated excerpts from Mexico's best English-language newspaper, comparable to or better than most U.S. dailies. Much syndicated information, including columns, feature articles, weather forecast for many Mexican cities, classified, exhange rates. Search back issues for 30 days.

www.ticketbus.com.mx
A good Spanish-language work-in-progress that furnishes schedules and sells tickets for major southeastern (Mexico City, Puebla, Veracruz, Oaxaca, Tabasco, Campeche, Chiapas, Yucatán, Quintana Roo) bus lines: Cristóbal Colón, ADO (Autobuses del Oriente), UNO (Lineas Unidos) and associated small carriers. Perhaps by the time you read this other major lines will have joined in.

www.mexconnect.com
An extensive Mexico site, with dozens upon dozens of subheadings and links, especially helpful for folks thinking of traveling, working, living, or retiring in Mexico.

www.choice1.com
An excellent site for picking a vacation rental house, condo, or villa, with information and reservations links to individual owners. Prices vary from moderate to luxurious. Coverage includes Pacific Mexico, from Mazatlán to Oaxaca, especially Puerto Vallarta and the neighboring coast (Bucerías, Sayulita, San Francisco), plus Guadalajara, Lake Chapala,

Manzanillo, Troncones, Zihuatanejo, Acapulco, Taxco, Oaxaca, Puerto Escondido, and Huatulco.

www.go2mexico.com
An aspiring commercial site that covers the Pacific Mexico destinations of Mazatlán, Puerto Vallarta, Ixtapa-Zihuatanejo, Acapulco, Huatulco, Oaxaca, Guadalajara, and Manzanillo (including current weather reports.) However, a number of destinations are very incomplete at this writing. A work in progress, potentially good if completed.

www.mexicodesconocido.com.mx
The site of the excellent magazine *Mexico Desconocido (Undiscovered Mexico)*, which mostly features stories of unusual and off-the-beaten-path destinations.

www.planeta.com
Life project of Latin America's dean of ecotourism, Ron Mader, who furnishes a comprehensive clearinghouse of everything ecologically correct, from rescuing turtle eggs in Jalisco to preserving cloud forests in Peru. Contains dozens of subheadings compentently linked for maximum speed. For example, check out the Mexico travel directory for ecojourneys, maps, information networks, parks, regional guides, and a mountain more.

Destinations
Mazatlán
www.mazatlan.com.mx
Commercial site in English with a good hotel section, with links to more than a dozen high-end hotels. Much of the other information, such as restaurants, for example, is limited to summaries or lists only. A fair site, overall.

Puerto Vallarta
puertovallarta.net
Wow! All you need to prepare for your Puerto Vallarta trip. Contains a wealth of details in dozens of competently linked subheadings, such as hotels (some with guest evaluations), both humble and grand, with links to car rentals, tours, news, real estate, vacation rentals, restaurants, and much more.

virtualvallarta.com
The website of *Vallarta Lifestyles* magazine furnishes a wealth of links to upscale art galleries, restaurants, condo, house, and villa sales and rentals, hotels, and travel services.

Guadalajara
www.guadalajarareporter.com
Site of the English-language Guadalajara newspaper, articles, calendar of events, and local news.

www.rr-mexico.com
Information on tours, counseling, and resettlement services in the Guadalajara area. Maintained by the friendly and very professional team of Sandy Brown and Mark Kunce, owners-operators of R and R in Mexico.

Ixtapa-Zihuatanejo
www.zihuatanejo.net
A top-notch, very complete, and well-maintained commercial site, listing nearly everywhere to stay (with reservation and email links) and dine and everything to do and much more in Zihuatanejo, Ixtapa, Troncones, and Barra de Potosí. In English or Spanish. Excellent.

www.zihuatanejo-rentals.com
The site of savvy local resident Leigh Roth, who lists (with gorgeous photos and descriptions) several high-end (and a few moderately priced) condo, apartment, and villa rental options, most near the plumy La Madera ands La Ropa beaches. She also includes pithy sections on restaurants, shopping, activities, personal anecdotes ("Who's Been to Huatla de Jiménez?"), and stories.

www.ixtapa-zihuatanejo.com
The official site of the Ixtapa-Zihuatanejo

government tourism bureaus, with listings (but sparse details) of many hotels, villas, bungalows, restaurants (by food category), tours, sports, and more. At this writing, however, a number of links lead to dead ends. Although it was not generally possible to book hotel reservations directly, hotel email and websites were listed in a number of cases.

Acapulco and Taxco
www.acapulco.org
The website of the Acapulco Convention and Visitor's Bureau broadly covers the ground—from sightseeing and shopping to hotels and transportation. The information is neutral, however, without much detail and generally lacking links for booking hotel reservations.

www.acabtu.com.mx
The website of the former tourist newspaper *Acapulco Heat,* which now has gone electronic. It provides many useful links to mostly midscale hotels, and restaurants, community events and organizations, travel activities, and entertainments.

www.hotelestaxco.com
Provides details of the hotels of the mountain silver town, north of Acapulco.

Oaxaca
www.oaxaca.gob.mx/sedetur
Website of the Oaxaca Secretary of Tourism.

Good Tourist Guide section with archaeological sites, recipes, churches, museums, festivals, myths and legends, recipes, murals, handicrafts, and more. Features an excellent updated calendar of cultural events and a number of other useful sections, such as investing in Oaxaca, and ecotourism. Mostly Spanish only, however, at this writing.

www.oaxaca.com
Commercial community guide to Oaxaca city with loads of noncommercial information. It has links to a long list of Mexico websites and much, much more. Its good Oaxaca Tourist Guide section might be especially useful for planning a Oaxaca trip. Hotels, however, are thinly covered with neutral lists only, with few or no photos or reservations links.

www.oaxacamagazzine.net
A useful, but brief work in progress, with email links to about a dozen top hotels. Also provides email links to some restaurants, auto rentals, and travel agents.

www.baysofhuatulco.com.mx
Restaurants, hotels, general information, events, real estate, tour operators, and water and land sports. A work in progress with lots of hotels with prices. The hotel association subsite is functioning well. Only in Spanish at this writing, however. Good.

Index

Index

Beaches

M

Index

Museums

Index

Acknowledgments

I thank the dozens of kind, unnamed Mexican people, such as the boy who stood on the road warning trucks away as I changed a tire, the men who pulled my car from the edge of a cliff one night atop a mountain in Oaxaca, and the staff who patiently answered my endless queries at many *turismo* offices. They all deserve credit for this book.

In Mazatlán, my special thanks go to Luis Chavez and Augustín Arellano, who taught me much of Mexico.

In Manzanillo, thanks to Bart Varelman of Hotel La Posada, Susan Dearing and Carlos Cuellar of Underworld Scuba, and to the late Alfred Hasler and and his tireless mechanics at SIMPSA Engineering who kept my car running.

My special thanks also go to ecoornithologist Michael Malone in Puerto Escondido for helping me appreciate Pacific Mexico's wildlife treasury, and to his excellent partners in agency Turismo Rodemar.

Thanks to Bill Dalton, Moon Handbooks' founder and former publisher, for undertaking this project with me, and to present Avalon Travel Publishing publisher Bill Newlin for continuing it to the present. Thanks, furthermore, to everyone else at ATP for their super-fine editing, graphics, and layout work. Also thanks to my original editors Mark Morris (who coined the name "Pacific Mexico"), Beth Rhudy, Pauli Galin, and Deana Corbitt Shields for their ton of work, kind encouragement, and hundreds of suggestions that saved my manuscript.

I owe a load of thanks to Susan Hall and other members of the Bay Area Travel Club, where I first met Bill Dalton; and to Gordon Barbery, another club member, who encouraged me to join the Bay Area Travel Writers, where the idea for this book was born.

To others I owe a unique debt for their continuous generosity. In Puerto Vallarta, thanks to Nancy Adams, who made my work so much more pleasant by gracefully allowing me to set up shop in a corner of her lovely Café Sierra. I also owe much to Gary Thompson, of Galería Pacífico, who introduced me to both Puerto Vallarta art and his many gracious friends and associates. For their helpful kindness, I also specially thank John and Nancy Erickson, Kathy von Rohr, Diana Turn, María Elena Zermeño, and Victoria Pratt.

In my hometown, thanks to the understanding workers at my office-away-from-home, the Espresso Roma, where espresso maestro Miguel's luscious lattes became essential to the writing of this book.

Thanks also to my friends Akemi Nagafuji and Anne Shapiro, who opened my eyes to the world.

This book could not have been written if not for Halcea Valdes, my friend and business partner, to whom I am grateful for managing without me while I was on the road for nine months in Pacific Mexico.

Finally, a heap of credit is due to my wife, Linda, who kept the home fires burning while I was away, came and nursed me when I got sick in Oaxaca, and was patient about everything I had to neglect back home while finishing this book.

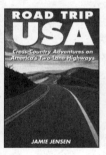

U.S. ~ Metric Conversion

1 inch	=	2.54 centimeters (cm)
1 foot	=	.304 meters (m)
1 yard	=	0.914 meters
1 mile	=	1.6093 kilometers (km)
1 km	=	.6214 miles
1 fathom	=	1.8288 m
1 chain	=	20.1168 m
1 furlong	=	201.168 m
1 acre	=	.4047 hectares
1 sq km	=	100 hectares
1 sq mile	=	2.59 square km
1 ounce	=	28.35 grams
1 pound	=	.4536 kilograms
1 short ton	=	.90718 metric ton
1 short ton	=	2000 pounds
1 long ton	=	1.016 metric tons
1 long ton	=	2240 pounds
1 metric ton	=	1000 kilograms
1 quart	=	.94635 liters
1 US gallon	=	3.7854 liters
1 Imperial gallon	=	4.5459 liters
1 nautical mile	=	1.852 km

To compute Celsius temperatures, subtract 32 from Fahrenheit and divide by 1.8. To go the other way, multiply Celsius by 1.8 and add 32.

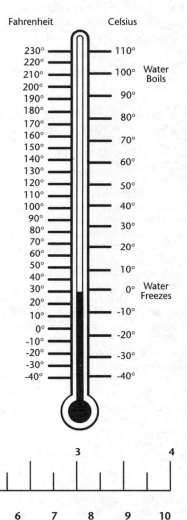

TOCAR

Keeping Current

Although we strive to produce the most up-to-date guidebook humanly possible, change is unavoidable. Between the time this book goes to print and the moment you read it, a handful of the businesses noted in these pages will undoubtedly change prices, move, or even close their doors forever. Other worthy attractions will open for the first time. If you have a favorite gem you'd like to see included in the next edition, or see anything that needs updating, clarification, or correction, please drop us a line. Send your comments via email to atpfeedback@avalonpub.com, or use the address below.

Moon Handbooks Pacific Mexico
Avalon Travel Publishing
1400 65th Street, Suite 250
Emeryville, CA 94608, USA
www.moon.com

Editor: Kathryn Ettinger
Series Manager: Kevin McLain
Copy Editor: Karen Gaynor Bleske
Graphics Coordinator: Justin Marler
Production Coordinator: Justin Marler
Cover Designer: Kari Gim
Interior Designers: Amber Pirker, Alvaro Villanueva, Kelly Pendragon
Map Editor: Olivia Solís
Cartographers: Mike Morgenfeld, Naomi Adler Dancis, Suzanne Service, Kat Kalamaras, Olivia Solís
Proofreader: Candace English
Indexer: Deana Shields

ISBN: 1-56691-503-1
ISSN: 1533-418X

Printing History
1st Edition—1993
6th Edition—November 2003
5 4 3 2 1

Text © 2003 by Bruce Whipperman.
Maps © 2003 by Avalon Travel Publishing, Inc.
All rights reserved.

Avalon Travel Publishing is a division of Avalon Publishing Group, Inc.

Some photos and illustrations are used by permission and are the property of the original copyright owners.
Front cover photo: © Steven McBride
Table of Contents photos: ©Bruce Whipperman

Printed in the United States by Malloy